Professional Perl Programming

Peter Wainwright

with

Aldo Calpini
Arthur Corliss
Simon Cozens
Juan Julián Merelo Guervós
Chris Nandor
Aalhad Saraf

Professional Perl Programming

Published by Wrox Press Ltd,
Arden House, 1102 Warwick Road, Acocks Green,
Birmingham, B27 6BH, UK

02-19-02

Printed in the United States
ISBN 1-861004-49-4

Trademark Acknowledgements

Wrox has endeavored to provide trademark information about all the companies and products mentioned in this book by the appropriate use of capitals. However, Wrox cannot guarantee the accuracy of this information.

Credits

Author
Peter Wainwright

Contributing Authors
Aldo Calpini
Arthur Corliss
Simon Cozens
Juan Julián Merelo Guervós
Chris Nandor
Aalhad Saraf

Technical Architect
Louay Fatoohi

Technical Editors
Mankee Cheng
David Mercer
Andrew Polshaw
Dan Robotham

Additional Editorial
Mohammed Rfaquat

Category Managers
Viv Emery
Paul Cooper

Author Agents
Julia Gilbert
Velimir Ilic

Project Administrator
Nicola Phillips

Indexers
Alessandro Ansa
Adrian Axinte
Bill Johncocks

Technical Reviewers
Simon Cozens
Carl Culvett
David Fannin
Iain Georgeson
Terry Gliedt
Jim Harle
Chris Lightfoot
Mark Mamone
Neil Matthews
Bill Moss
Nathan Neulinger
Gavin Smyth
Rick Stones
Paul Warren
Andrew Yourtchenko
Philips Yuson

Production Manager
Simon Hardware

Production Project Coordinator
Mark Burdett

Illustrations
Shabnam Hussain

Cover
Shelley Frazier

Proof Readers
Chris Smith
Keith Westmoreland
Diana Skeldon

About the Authors

Peter Wainwright

Peter Wainwright is a freelance developer and software consultant. He got his first taste of programming on a BBC Micro and gained most of his early programming experience writing applications in C on Solaris. He then discovered Linux, shortly followed by Perl and Apache, and has been happily programming there ever since.

Outside of the software industry, he is a partner of Space Future Consulting, an international space tourism consultancy firm. He spends much of his free time maintaining the non-profit Space Future website at www.spacefuture.com and writes the occasional article on space tourism. He is also an advisor to the board of one or two companies engaged in space tourism and vehicle development. If you have $50m to spare, he would like to have a word with you.

As well as being the primary author of *Professional Perl Programming*, he is the author of *Professional Apache (ISBN: 1861003021)*, also published by Wrox Press, as well as a contributing author to *Beginning Perl (ISBN: 1861003145)*. Formerly based in London, he recently moved from England to the Upper West Side of New York to be with his new wife, a professional editor, whom he met through a mutual interest in space tourism and low-rent apartments.

Aldo Calpini

Aldo Calpini is well known in the Perl community for his many important Win32 modules. His active participation on several mailing lists has helped the Perl language grow in the Win32 community. He began programming twenty years ago and still enjoys hacking every kind of computer he can put his hands on. He works today as lead programmer in an Italian Internet startup company.

Arthur Corliss

Arthur Corliss has been programming since buying his first home computer a Timex Sinclair 1000 with a whopping 2K of RAM (which he still has). Having worked his way through several languages, Perl has become his most frequent language of choice at his latest venture, Gallant Technologies, Inc., a software development company. On his own time he continues the madness by working on the Curses::Widgets and Curses::Forms modules, which he authored and is available on CPAN.

Simon Cozens

Simon Cozens is an Open Source programmer and author; he writes for the Perl Journal, www.perl.com, and other sites, and is the author of Wrox Press' *Beginning Perl (ISBN: 1861003145)*. He is a member of the Perl development team, and his hobbies include reading, typography and the Greek language and culture.

Juan Julián Merelo Guervós

Juan Julián Merelo Guervós was born in Ubeda, Jaén, Spain, the 10th of March of 1965. Juan received a degree in Theoretical Physics by the University of Granada in 1989, and a PhD in Physics in 1994. He has been hacking PERL since 1993 or 1994, and is the author of a widely popular (and pioneer) web tutorial of PERL in Spanish (available from http://www.granavenida.com/perl). Currently Juan is an associate professor at Granada University, in Spain. He is married and has three wonderful daughters, two of whom are fraternal twins, born in 1998 and 1999. He can be reached at jmerelo@geneura.ugr.es, and his homepage (which is, so far, in Spanish) is at http://geneura.ugr.es/~jmerelo

Chris Nandor

Chris Nandor, pudge@pobox.com, is a programmer for OSDN, working on theSlashdot code. He co-authored the book *MacPerl: Power and Ease (ISBN: 1881957322)* from Prime Time Freeware, writes the Perl News column for the Perl Journal, and runs the web sites http://use.perl.org/ and http://news.perl.org/. Chris lives in Massachusetts with his three dogs, two cats, and one wonderful and supportive wife, Jennifer.

I'd like to dedicate this book to my wife, my parents, and my in-laws who've all given me encouragement & put up with me during deadlines.

Aalhad Saraf

Aalhad Saraf is in the Systems Software Group in IBM Labs. He has been with Linux since 1995. Perl, C, and C++ are his favorite tools. Has a Bachelors degree in Electronics Engineering from the University of Pune, a Post Graduate Diploma awarded by the national resource center of the 'Center for Development of Advanced Computing' (a scientific society of the Ministry of IT, Govt. of India). He worked on microcontrollers/embedded systems and hand-held computing devices in Syslab Automation and on an interactive gaming server for DishnetDSL – one of India's leading ISPs. He also teaches Perl, Software Engineering and Quality systems during his spare time. He Takes his table tennis seriously, fiddles around with a guitar, juggles tennis balls and is an omnivore when it comes to reading. He likes networks. He dreams of traveling through space sitting in a packet; playing with the civilization of Data, providing the subjects – bytes, with new worlds and increasingly better means of transport. Aalhad is 22 years old and aspires to get a Ph.D. in Computer Science some day.

Table of Contents

Introduction   1

Chapter 1: Introduction   7

Introduction   **7**
    Key Features   8
    Supported Platforms   9
    Perl History and Versions   10
    Essential Information   10

Building and Installing Perl   **12**
    Installing Pre-built Perl Distributions   12
        Installing Perl on UNIX   13
        Installing Perl on Windows   13
        Installing Perl on Macintosh   14
    Building Perl from Source   14
        Building a Threaded Perl Interpreter   17
        Differences for Windows and Macintosh   17
        Other Platforms   17
    Building and Installing Modules   18
    Installing Modules with the 'CPAN' Module   18
        Starting and Configuring CPAN   19
        Installing Modules   20
        Listing and Searching CPAN   21
        Reading Module Documentation Without Installing   23
        Reloading CPAN   23
        Configuring CPAN Options   24
        Installing Modules by Hand   24

Running Perl   **27**
    Starting Perl Applications   27
        Perl on UNIX   28
        Perl on Windows   28
        Perl on Macintosh   29
    The Command Line   29
    Command Line Syntax   30
        Supplying Arguments to Perl Scripts   30
        Using Perl as a Generic Command Line Utility   31
    The Perl Environment   32
        General Environment Variables Used by Perl   32
        Perl Specific Environment Variables   32

Summary   **33**

Table of Contents

Chapter 2: Basic Concepts   35

Values and Variables   35

Whitespace   36

Data Types   36

Special Variables   39

Interpolation   39

Context   40
- Scalar and List Context   41
- Void Context   42

Operators   42

Blocks   43

Control Constructs   43

Loop Modifiers   45

Subroutines   46

Functions   47

Scoping   47

Chapter 3: Scalars   51

Value Conversion and Caching   51

Numbers   52
- Integers   53
  - Integer Range and Big Integers   53
  - Converting Integers into Floating-Point Numbers   54
  - Converting Integers into Strings   54
  - Handling Different Number Bases   55
- Floating-Point Numbers   56
  - Converting Floats into Integers   58
  - Converting Floats into Strings   58
- The 'use integer' Pragma   60
- Mathematical Functions   61

Strings   62
- Quotes and Quoting   62
- 'Here' Documents   65
- Bareword Strings and Version Numbers   67
- Converting Strings into Numbers   68
- Converting Strings into Lists and Hashes   69
- Functions For Manipulating Strings   71
  - Print   71
  - Line Terminator Termination   72
  - Characters and Character Codes   73
  - Length and Position   73
  - Substrings and Vectors   74
  - Upper and Lower Case   75
  - Interpolation   75
  - Pattern Matching and Transliteration   75
  - Password Encryption   76
  - Low Level String Conversions   76
- String Formatting   80

Summary   84

Chapter 4: Operators   87

Operators Versus Functions   87

Operator Types and Categories   88
Assignment   89
Arithmetic   89
Shift   91
String and List   91
Logical   93
Bitwise   94
Combination Assignment   97
Increment and Decrement   98
Comparison   99
Regular Expression Binding   101
Comma and Relationship   101
Reference and Dereference   102
The Arrow   102
Range   103
Ternary   105

Precedence and Associativity   106
Precedence and Parentheses   107

Disabling Functions and Operators   110

Overriding Operators   113

Summary   114

Chapter 5: Beyond Scalars – More Data Types   117

Lists and Arrays   117
Manipulating Arrays   119
Modifying the Contents of an Array   119
Counting an Array   121
Adding Elements to an Array   122
Resizing and Truncating an Array   123
Removing Elements from an Array   123
Removing All Elements from an Array   125
Sorting and Reversing Lists and Arrays   125
Changing the Starting Index Value   127
Converting Lists and Arrays into Scalars   127
Taking References   127
Converting Lists into Formatted Strings   127

Hashes   129
Manipulating Hashes   131
Adding and Modifying Hash Values   131
Removing Hash Keys and Values   132
Converting Lists and Arrays into Hashes   132
Reversing Hashes   133
Accessing and Iterating Over Hashes   134
Converting Hashes into Scalars   137
Converting Hashes into Arrays   138
The Special Hash '%ENV'   138
Configuring Programs via '%ENV'   140
Handling Tainted Input from '%ENV'   140
'Env.pm'   141

Table of Contents

References   **142**

Hard References   142
    Creating References   143
    Comparing References   144
    Dereferencing   145
    Working with References   146
    Passing References to Subroutines   147
    Finding the Type of a Reference   148

Complex Data Structures   **151**

The Problem with Nesting – My Lists Went Flat!   151
Lists of Lists and Multidimensional Arrays   151
Hashes of Hashes and Other Animals   153
Adding to and Modifying Complex Data Structures   154
Creating Complex Data Structures Programmatically   155
Traversing Complex Data Structures   158

Typeglobs   **161**

Defining Typeglobs   161
Manipulating Typeglobs   162
Accessing Typeglobs   163

The Undefined Value   **164**

Tests of Existence   166
Using the Undefined Value   167
Using 'undef' as a Function   168

Constants   **169**

Declaring Scalar Constants with the 'constant' Pragma   169
Declaring List and Hash Constants   171
Constant References   171
Listing and Checking for the Existence of Constants   172

Summary   **172**

Chapter 6: Structure, Flow, and Control   **175**

Expressions, Statements, and Blocks   **175**

Declarations   176
Expressions and Simple Statements   176
Blocks and Compound Statements   177
    Blocks in Perl Statements   178
    Naked Blocks   178
    Defining the Main Program as a Block   179
    Blocks as Loops   180
    The 'do' Block   181
    Special Blocks   182

Conditional Statements   **183**

What Is Truth?   184
'if', 'else', and 'elsif'   185
'unless'   187
Writing Conditions with Logical Operators   188
The Ternary Operator   189
Switches and Multi-Branched Conditions   192
Returning Values from Multi-Branched Conditions   194

Loops and Looping   **195**

  Writing C-style Loops with 'for'   195
  Writing Better Loops with 'foreach'   197
    Using 'foreach' with Multi-Branched Conditions   198
    Variable Aliasing in 'foreach' Loops   199
  Conditional Loops – 'while', 'until', and 'do'   200
    Variable Aliasing with 'while'   201
    Looping over Lists and Arrays with 'while'   201
    Looping on Self-Modifying Arrays   202
    Looping over Hashes with 'while'   203
    'do...while' and 'do...until'   203
  Controlling Loop Execution   204
    The 'continue' Clause   206
    Controlling Nested Loops   207
    The Trouble with 'do'   208
  The 'goto' Statement   209
  'maps' and 'greps'   210
    'map'   211
    'grep'   211

Summary   **213**

Chapter 7: Subroutines   **215**

Declaring and Calling Subroutines   **216**

  Anonymous Subroutines and Subroutine References   217
  Strict Subroutines and the 'use strict subs' Pragma   219
  Predeclaring Subroutines   219
    Overriding Built-in Functions   220
  The Subroutine Stack   221
    Recursion   223
  Checking for Subroutines and Defining Subroutines On the Fly   226

Passing Parameters   **228**

  Passing Lists and Hashes   229
  Converting Scalar Subroutines into List Processors   231
  Passing '@_' Directly into Subroutines   232
  Named Parameters   233

Prototypes   **236**

  Defining the Number of Parameters and Their Scope   237
  Prototyping Code References   239
  Subroutines as Scalar Operators   239
  Requiring Variables Rather than Values   240
  Optional Parameters   241
  Disabling Prototypes   242

Returning Values from Subroutines   **243**

  Returning the Undefined Value   244
  Determining and Responding to the Calling Context   246
    Handling Void Context   247
    Handling Context: an Example   247
  Closures   248
  Assignable Subroutines   250

Attribute Lists   **251**
   Defining Attributes on Subroutines   251
   Accessing Attributes   252
   Special Attributes   252
   Package Attributes   253

Summary   **254**

Chapter 8: Scope and Visibility   **257**

Package Variables   **257**
   Defining Package Variables   258
   Using 'strict' Variables   259
   Declaring Global Package Variables   260
   Declaring Global Package Variables with 'use vars'   260
   Lexically Declaring Global Package Variables with 'our'   261
   Automatic Localization in Perl   262
   Localizing Package Variables with 'local'   262

Lexical Variables   **264**
   Declaring Lexical Variables   265
   Preserving Lexical Variables Outside Their Scope   266

The Symbol Table   **267**
   The 'main' Package   267
   Typeglobs and the 'main' Package   268
   The Symbol Table Hierarchy   269
   Manipulating the Symbol Table Directly   270
   Accessing the Symbol Table   271

Summary   **273**

Chapter 9: Using Modules   **275**

Modules and Packages   **276**

Loading Code Using 'do', 'require', and 'use'   **277**
   'import' Lists   278
   Suppressing Default Imports   279
   Disabling Features with 'no'   279
   Testing for Module Versions and the Version of Perl   279

Pragmatic Modules   **280**
   How Pragmatic Modules Work   280
   Scope of Pragmatic Modules   281

The Special Hash '%INC'   **282**

The Special Array '@INC'   **283**
   Modifying '@INC' directly   283
   Modifying @INC with the 'lib' Pragma   284

Locating Libraries Relative to the Script   **285**

Checking for the Availability of a Module   **286**

Finding Out What Modules are Installed   **286**

Postponing Module Loading Until Use   **290**

Summary   **292**

Chapter 10: Inside Modules and Packages | 295

'BEGIN' blocks, 'END' blocks and Other Animals | 296
'BEGIN' Blocks | 297
'END' Blocks | 299
'CHECK' and 'INIT' | 299

Manipulating Packages | 300
Removing a Package | 302
Forbidding Package Variables | 303

Finding a Package Name Programmatically | 303

Autoloading | 304
Autoloading Subroutines | 305
Using an 'AUTOLOAD' Subroutine as a Substitute | 305
Defining Subroutines On the Fly | 308
Self-Defining Instead of Autoloading Subroutines | 309
Autoloading Modules | 310
Using the 'AutoLoader' Module | 311
Using the 'SelfLoader' Module | 314

Importing and Exporting | 316
The 'import' Mechanism | 316
Exporting | 319
Setting Flags with Exports | 321
When to Export, When not to Export | 321
The 'Exporter' Module | 322

Creating Installable Modules | 330
Well-Written Modules | 330
Creating a Working Directory | 331
Building an Installable Package | 332
Adding a Test Script | 334
Uploading Modules to CPAN | 334

Summary | 335

Chapter 11: Regular Expressions | 337

String Interpolation | 337
Perl's Interpolation Syntax | 337
Interpolating Metacharacters and Character Codes | 338
Common Special Characters | 339
Special Effects | 339
Interpolating Variables | 340
Interpolating Code | 341
Interpolative Context | 342
Interpolation in Regular Expressions | 342
Interpolating Text Inside String Variables | 343
Protecting Strings Against Interpolation | 344

Regular Expressions | 345
Where Regular Expressions Occur | 346
Matching and Substitution | 346
The 'split' Function | 347
Pre-compiled Regular Expressions | 348

Table of Contents

Regular Expression Delimiters	349
Elements of Regular Expressions	350
More Advanced Patterns	352
Matching Arbitrary Characters and Character Classes	352
Repetition and Grouping	354
Matching Sequential and Overlapping Terms	361
Pattern Match Modifiers	362
Regular Expressions versus Wildcards	363
Metacharacters	365
Character Class Metacharacters	365
Zero-Width Metacharacters	368
Extracting Matched Text	369
Special Variables	369
Parentheses and Numbered Variables	371
Backreferences	374
Extracting Lines with the Range Operator	376
Matching More than Once	378
Regular Expressions and Loops	378
Nested Regular Expression Loops	380
Position	382
Matching In and Across Multiple Lines	384
Counting the Total Number of Matches	386
Overlapping Matches and Zero-Width Patterns	386
Extended Patterns	389
Documenting Regular Expressions	389
Writing Efficient Regular Expressions	391
Making Regular Expressions More Specific	391
'study'	393
Avoiding Recompilation with the Empty Pattern	394
Avoiding Recompilation with the 'once-only' Modifier	394
Generating Regular Expressions with 'eval'	395
Predefining Search Patterns with 'qr'	397
Checking the Validity of Regular Expressions	399
Regular Expressions, Tainted Variables, and Debugging	401
Untainting Tainted Variables	401
Maintaining Taintedness in Regular Expressions	401
Understanding and Debugging the Regular Expression Engine	402
Substitution	407
Substituting Matched Text and Interpolation	407
Evaluating the Replacement String	408
Interpolating and Evaluating the Replacement String	409
Transliteration	409
Transliteration Modifiers	411
Summary	**412**
Chapter 12: Input and Output with Filehandles	**415**
IO and Filehandles	**416**
The Filehandle Data Type	**416**
Standard Filehandles	**416**

Creating Filehandles — **417**
Creating Filehandles with 'open' — 417
Opening Files for Reading, Writing, and Updating — 418
Opening Arbitrary Filenames — 419
Opening Standard Input and Standard Output — 419
Creating Filehandles with 'IO::File' — 420
The Data Filehandle — 422
Other Filehandles — 423

Referring to Filehandles — **424**

Reading from Filehandles — **426**
The Readline Operator — 426
Redefining the Line Separator — 426
Aliasing Readline in 'while' Loops — 427
Counting Line Numbers — 427
Readline and the '@ARGV' Array — 428
Finer Control Over Reading — 428
Detecting the End-of-File — 429
Reading a Single Character — 430

Writing to Filehandles — **430**
Buffering and Autoflush Mode — 432
Alternatives to 'print' — 432

Handling Binary and Text Files — **433**
The 'binmode' Function — 433
The 'open' Pragma — 434

Random Access — **434**
'seek' to a Specific Place within a File — 434
Clearing the End-of-File Condition with 'seek' — 435
Writing at the End-of-File — 436
Finding the Current Position — 437
Object-Oriented Random Access — 437

Truncating and Resizing Files — **437**

File Locking — **439**
Establishing File Locks — 440
File Locking Issues and Caveats — 442

Changing the Default Output Filehandle — **442**
Using Special Variables to Configure Other Filehandles — 443
Automatically Restoring the Default Filehandle — 443
Using Default Variables vs, 'IO::Handle' Methods — 444

Duplicating and Aliasing Filehandles — **444**

Redirecting Filehandles — **445**

Caching Many Filehandles — **446**

'IO::Handle' Methods and Special Variables — **448**

Table of Contents

System Level IO   **452**

Opening Filehandles at the System Level   453

    Open Mode Flags   453

    Non-blocking IO   454

    The Permissions Mask   455

    Using 'sysopen' via 'IO::File'   456

Unbuffered Reading   456

Unbuffered Writing   457

System-Level File Positioning   458

'fcntl' and 'ioctl'   459

    Setting Filehandle Attributes with 'fcntl'   459

    Controlling Devices with 'ioctl'   462

POSIX IO   462

    POSIX Filehandle Routines   463

    POSIX File Descriptor Routines   463

    Moving between POSIX and Standard IO   464

Summary   **465**

Chapter 13: Manipulating Files and Directories   **467**

Files and Filenames   **467**

Getting User and Group Information   468

    User Information   468

    Group Information   473

The Unary File Test Operators   475

    Link Transparency and Testing for Links   477

    Testing Binary and Text Files   477

    Reusing the Results of a Prior 'stat' or 'lstat'   478

    Using 'stat' Objects   479

    Access Control Lists, the Superuser, and the 'filestat' Pragma   480

    Automating Multiple File Tests   482

Interrogating Files   484

Changing File Attributes   485

    File Ownership   485

    File Permissions   487

The 'Fcntl' Module   488

Linking, Unlinking, and Renaming Files   490

    Linking Files   491

    Unlinking Files   491

    Renaming Files   492

    Symbolic Links   492

Copying and Moving Files   493

    System Level Copies and Platform Portability   495

Comparing Files   496

Finding Files   497

Deciphering File Paths   501

Filename Globbing   503

'glob' Syntax   504

    UNIX Style File Globbing   505

    DOS-Style File Globbing   507

Temporary Files   508

    Creating a Temporary Filehandle   508

    Temporary Filenames via the POSIX module   509

    Using 'File::Temp'   511

Manipulating Directories   **513**

  Reading Directories   513

    Directory Positions   514

    Directory Handle Objects   515

    Directories as Tied Hashes   515

    Finding the Name of a Directory or File from its Handle   516

  Creating and Destroying Directories   517

    Creating Single Directories   517

    Creating Multiple Directories   518

    Destroying Single Directories   519

    Destroying Multiple Directories   520

  Moving Around Directories   520

Summary   **523**

Chapter 14: Command-Line and Shell Interaction   **525**

Parsing-Command Line Arguments   **525**

  Command-Line Conventions   526

  The '@ARGV' Array   527

    Passing Arguments to Perl Itself   528

    Setting Variables from '@ARGV'   528

    Reading Files from '@ARGV'   529

    '@ARGV' and Standard Input   531

  Simple Command-Line Processing with 'Getopt::Std'   532

    Basic Processing with 'getopt'   532

    Slightly Smarter Processing with 'getopts'   534

  More Complex Command-line Processing with 'Getopt::Long'   535

    Simple Argument Processing   535

    Option Prefixes   537

    Defining Option Values   538

    Abbreviations   541

    Aliases   541

    Handling Option Values   542

    Documenting Options   544

    Bundling Options   544

    Case Sensitivity   546

    Handling Unrecognized Option and Value Arguments 547

    'POSIX' Mode   549

    Summary of Configuration Options   549

Shells, Shell Commands, and Perl   **551**

  Creating a Simple Perl Shell   551

  Writing a More Useful Shell   552

  Integrating the Shell into Perl   555

  Emulating UNIX Commands on Windows   557

Summary   **559**

Table of Contents

Chapter 15: Terminal Input and Output   **561**

  Talking to Terminals   **561**
    Determining if a Script is Interactive   562

  Reading from the Keyboard   **563**
    Simple Input   563
    Controlling Terminal Input with 'Term::ReadKey'   564
      Read Modes   564
      Reading a Single Character   566
    Reading Complete Lines   568
      Passwords and Invisible Input   569
      Finding and Setting the Screen Size   569
      Serial Connections and Terminal Speed   571
      Line Ending Translation   571
      Getting and Setting Control Characters   572
    Advanced Line Input with 'Term::ReadLine'   574
    Creating a Terminal Object   575
      Supported Features   577
      Setting the Prompt Style and Supplying Default Input   578
      Command-Line History   579
    Word Completion   580

  Writing to the Screen   **581**
    Terminal Capabilities   581
      Creating a Termcap Object   582
      Clearing the Screen, Moving the Cursor, and Other Tricks   584
    Writing in Colors   584

  Higher-Level Terminal Modules   **588**
    'Term::Screen'   588
    The Curses Library   590
      A Simple Curses Application   591
      Curses Windows   593
      Third-Party Extensions to Curses   594

  Programming the Terminal Directly via 'POSIX'   **594**

  Summary   **597**

Chapter 16: Warnings and Errors   **599**

  Enabling Warnings   **599**

  Enabling Diagnostics   **600**

  Generating Warnings and Errors   **602**

  Intercepting Warnings and Errors   **603**

  Deciphering Error Results from System Calls   **604**
    Error Numbers and Names   604
    Setting the Error Number   605
    Errors from Evaluated Code   605
    Extended Error Messages   606
    'Errno' and The 'POSIX' Module   607
    Checking the Exit Status of Subprocesses and External Commands   607

Making Non-Fatal Errors Fatal   **608**

Returning Warnings and Errors in Context with 'Carp'   **609**

Error Logs and System Logs   **611**

Advanced Warnings   **612**

Summary   **615**

Chapter 17: Debugging   **617**

Pragmatic Debugging Support   **617**

Applications that Debug Themselves   **618**
A Simple Debugging System   619
A Better Debugging System   619
Creating Debug Logs   621
Adding Calling Context to Debug Messages   621

The Perl Debugger   **622**
Starting the Debugger   622
Entering Commands   623
Simple Debugging Commands – Single Stepping   624
Running Arbitrary Code   625
Multiline Commands   625
Debugging Commands   626
Configuring the Debugger   636
Interactively   636
Through the Environment   636
The '.perldb' Script   637
Debugger Configuration Options   638
Tracing and Terminals   641
Entering the Debugger Programmatically   642
Using Debugger Hooks   643

Debugging and Informational Modules   **645**
The 'Dumpvalue' Module   645
The 'Safe' Module   649
Creating Compartments   649
Sharing Variables and Subroutines   649
Operator Masks   650
The 'Safe' Module in Use   651

Debugging the Perl Interpreter   **652**

Automated Testing   **653**
Writing a Test Script   653
Automating Tests   655

Profiling   **656**
Profiling Perl Applications   657
Generating Profile Reports   657
Collecting Timing Information Directly   661
Testing for Performance   663
'timeit'   665
'timethis'   666
'timethese'   667
'cmpthese'   667
'countit'   668

Summary   **669**

Table of Contents

Chapter 18: Text Processing and Document Generation   **671**

Text Processing   **672**
Expanding and Contracting Tabs with 'Text::Tabs'   672
Calculating Abbreviations with 'Text::Abbrev'   673
Parsing Words and Phrases with 'Text::ParseWords'   675
    Parsing Space-Separated Text   676
    Parsing Arbitrarily Delimited Text   677
    Batch Parsing Multiple Lines   678
    Parsing a Single Line Only   679
Formatting Paragraphs with 'Text::Wrap'   679
    Formatting Single Paragraphs   679
    Customized Wrapping   680
    Formatting Whole Documents   681
    Formatting on the Command Line   681
Matching Similar Sounding Words with 'Text::Soundex'   682
    Tokenizing Single Words   682
    Tokenizing Lists of Words and E-Mail Addresses   683
    The 'Soundex' Algorithm   684
    Handling Untokenizable Words   684
Other Text Processing Modules   684

Documenting Perl   **684**
Comments   685
plain old documentation   685
    pod Paragraphs   685
    Using pod with 'DATA' or 'END' tokens   690
    Interior Sequences   691
Pod Tools and Utilities   691
    Translator Tools   691
    Retrieval Tools   692
    pod Verification   692
Programming pod   694
    Using Pod Parsers   695
    Writing a pod Parser   695
    Locating pods   698

Reports – The 'r' in Perl   **699**
Formats and the Format Datatype   699
    Formats and Filehandles   701
    Assigning Formats to Standard Output   702
    Determining and Assigning Formats to Other Filehandles   703
Format Structure   704
    Picture Lines and Placeholders   704
    Data Lines   707
    Suppressing Redundant Lines   708
    Autorepeating Pattern Lines   709
Page Control   709
    Creating Footers   711
Combining Reports and Regular Output   712
    Mixing 'write' and 'print'   712
    Generating Report Text with 'formline'   714

Summary   **715**

Chapter 19: Object-Oriented Perl — 717

Introducing Objects — 718
Object Concepts — 718
  Classes — 718
  Objects — 718
  Inheritance, Multiple Inheritance, and Abstraction — 719
  Public and Private Methods and Data — 720
  Polymorphism — 720
  Overloading — 720
  Adaptabilty (also called Casting or Conversion) — 721

Programming with Objects — 721
Creating Objects — 721
Using Objects — 722
  Accessing Properties — 722
  Calling Class Methods — 723
  Calling Object Methods — 724
  Nesting Method Calls — 724
Determining what an Object Is — 724
Determining Inherited Characteristics — 725
  Determining an Object's Ancestry — 725
  Determining an Object's Capabilities — 725
  Determining an Object's Version — 726

Writing Object Classes — 727
Constructors — 727
  Choosing a Different Underlying Data Type — 729
  Methods — 732
  Object Data — 736
  Class Data — 740
Debugging Object Classes — 747

Inheritance and Subclassing — 753
Inheriting from a Parent Class — 754
  Overriding and Calling Overridden Methods — 754
  Overriding and Calling Overridden Constructors — 755
Writing Inheritable Classes — 756
  More on Class Data through Objects — 756
  Exports — 759
Private Methods — 760
Extending and Redefining Objects — 761
  Extending a Parent Class — 761
  Constructing Subclasses On the Fly — 762
Multiple Inheritance — 764
  Writing Classes for Multiple Inheritance — 765
  Drawbacks with Multiple Inheritance — 767
A 'UNIVERSAL' Constuctor — 768
  Is-a Versus Has-a — 770

Autoloading Methods — 773

Keeping Data Private — 777
Private Class Data — 778
Private Object Data — 778

Table of Contents

Destroying Objects   **782**
Destructors and Inheritance   783
Destructors and Multiple Inheritance   784

Overloading Operators   **785**
Basic Overloading   785
Determining the Operand Order and Operator Name   786
Overloading Comparisons   787
Overloading Conversion Operations   788
    Overloading String Conversion   788
    Overloading Numeric Conversion   790
Falling Back to Unoverloaded Operations   791
Overloading and Inheritance   793
Autogenerated Operations   793
Overloadable Operations   795

Automating Object Class Development   **795**

Ties and Tied Objects   **799**
Using Tied Objects   800
    Handling Errors from 'tie'   800
    Accessing Nested References   801
    Testing a Variable for 'tied'ness   801
    'Untie'ing Objects   802
Writing Tied Objects   802
Standard Tie Object Classes   803
Tied Object Methods   803
An Example Tied Hash Class   807
An Example Class Using 'Tie::StdHash'   809

Summary   **811**

Chapter 20: Inside Perl   **815**

Analyzing the Perl Binary – 'Config.pm'   **815**
'perl -V'   816
How It Works   817
    Platform   817
    Compiler   817
    Linker and Libraries   818
    Dynamic Linking   818

Under the Hood   **818**
Around the Source Tree   818
Building Perl   821
    'metaconfig' Rather than 'autoconf'?   821

How Perl Works   **822**
Parsing   822
Compiling   824
Interpreting   826

Internal Variable Types   **827**
PVs   828
IVs   828
NVs   829
Arrays and Hashes   830
Examining Raw Datatypes with 'Devel::Peek'   830

The Perl Compiler   **833**
   The 'O' Module   834
   The 'B' Module   834
   The 'B::' Family of Modules   836
     'B::Terse'   836
     'B::Debug'   837
     'B::Deparse'   839
     'B::C'   840
     'B::CC'   841
     'B::Bytecode'   842
     'B::Disassembler'   843
     'B::Lint'   843
     'B::Showlex'   845
     'B::Xref'   845
     'B::Fathom'   848
     'B::Graph'   848
     'B::JVM::Jasmin'   849
   Writing a Perl Compiler Backend   850

Summary   **853**

Chapter 21: Integrating Perl with Other Programming Languages   **855**

Using C from Perl   **856**
   An Overview of XS   857
   'h2xs', or Where to Start   857
     Converting C Header Files   858
     Starting from Scratch   860
   The XS File   860
     Declaring the 'MODULE' and 'PACKAGE'   861
   XS Functions   862
     Putting the 'CODE' in   862
     Complex Output, 'PPCODE' and the Stack   863
     Complex Input, Default Values and Variable Input Lists   865
   The 'TYPEMAP'   867
   The 'Makefile'   870

Dynamic Linking   **871**
   Using the 'FFI' Module   872
   Using the 'C::DynaLib' Module   874
   Using the 'Win32::API' module   875

Using Perl from C   **875**
   First Steps   875
     Building a Program (The Hard Way)   876
     Building a Program (The Easy Way)   877
   Implementing the Perl Interpreter   877
   Embedding Perl Code   880
   Getting Perl Values   881
   Using Perl Subroutines   882
   Working with Perl Internals   884
   Using Modules   886

The Java-Perl Lingo   **888**

Perl and COM   **889**
PerlCOM   889
'PerlCtrl'   890

Miscellaneous Languages   **891**
The Filter Module   892

Summary   **893**

Chapter 22: Creating and Managing Processes   **895**

Signals   **895**
Signal Handling   898
    The 'die' and 'warn' Handlers   900
    Writing Signal Handlers   900
    Avoid Complex Handlers   901
    Flexibly Installing Signal Handlers   903
Sending Signals   905
Alarms   906
    A Simple Use of Alarms   906
    Using Alarms to Abort Hung Operations   907

Starting New Processes   **908**
Replacing the Current Process with Another   909
Process IDs   909
Process, Groups and Daemons   909

Handling Children and Returning Exit Codes   **911**
Waiting for an Only Child   912
Getting the Exit Status   912
Handling Multiple Child Processes   913
POSIX Flags and Functions   914

Communicating Between Processes   **916**
Very Simple Solutions   916
Pipes   917
Opening and Running External Processes   919
Bi-directional Pipes   920
Avoiding Shells with the Forked Open   922
Bi-directional Pipes to External Processes   923
    Handling Bi-directional Communications   925

Sharing Data Between Processes   **926**
IPC::SysV   927
Messages Queues   928
Semaphores   931
Shared Memory Segments   935

Threads   **937**
Checking for Thread Support   938
Creating Threads   938
Identifying Threads   939
Thread-specific Data   940
Thread Management   940
Variable Locks   942
Condition Variables, Semaphores, and Queues   943
    Condition Variables   943
    Semaphores   947
    Queues   950
Thread Safety and Locked Code   953

Summary   **954**

Chapter 23: Networking with Perl 957

An Introduction to Networks 957
Protocol Layers 957
Frames, Packets, and Encapsulation 959
The Internet Protocol 960
UDP & TCP 964
ICMP 965
Other Protocols 966
Presentation/Application Layers 966
Anonymous, Broadcast, and Loopback Addresses 966

Networking with Perl 967
Sockets 967
'Socket.pm' 967
'IO::Socket.pm' 976
TCP INET Examples 979
UDP INET Examples 986
UNIX Sockets 989

Multiplexed Servers 992
Polling Servers 993
The 'select' Function 993
The' IO::Select' Module 995
A Simple Polling Server 996
A Simple Forking Server 998
A Simple Threaded Server 999

Getting Network Information 1000
System Network Files 1001
Hosts 1003
Networks 1007
Network Services 1009
Network Protocols 1011
Determining the Local Hostname 1012

Summary 1013

Chapter 24: Writing Portable Perl 1015

Maybe We Shouldn't Bother? 1016

Newlines 1016

Files and File Systems 1018
Portable File Handling with 'File::Spec' 1020

Endianness and Number Width 1023

System Interaction 1024

Inter-Process Communication (IPC) 1025

External Subroutines (XS) 1025

Modules 1026

Time and Date   **1026**

Character Sets and Character Encoding   **1027**

Internationalization   **1028**

System Resources   **1028**

Security   **1028**

Style   **1028**

Platforms   **1031**
UNIX   1032
DOS and Derivatives   1033
Mac OS   1033
Other Perls   1035

Function Implementations   **1035**

Summary   **1041**

Chapter 25: Unicode   **1043**

Whom Does It Affect?   **1044**

What Are the Solutions?   **1044**

Characters and Unicode 101   **1044**

Data in Perl   **1046**

Unicode and Regular Expressions   **1047**
Writing Our Own Character Property   1049

Bi-directional Scripts   **1050**
Rendering bidi   1051
What the bidi Algorithm Does   1053
Perl and bidi   1053

Perl, I18n and Unicode   **1055**
Installing Unicode Fonts   1055
Installing a Unicode Editor   1055
Creating the HTML Template   1056
Processing the Resource Files   1057
Running the Script   1058
The Output Files   1058

Work in Progress   **1059**

Summary   **1060**

Chapter 26: Locale and Internationalization   1063

Why Go Locale?   1064
Delving Deeper into Local Culture   1067

It's About Time: Time Zones   1077

Looks Like a Foreign Language   1080

Conjugating in Portuguese   1082

The 'Lingua::*' Modules   1084
Spelling and Stemming   1086

Writing Multilingual Web Pages   1089

Creating our own Local Perl module   1094

Summary   1096

Appendix A: Command Line Options   1099

Appendix B: Special Variables   1103

Appendix C: Function Reference   1113

Appendix D: Regular Expressions   1141

Appendix E: Standard Pragmatic Modules   1149

Appendix F: Standard Functional Modules   1153

Appendix G: Perl Resources   1163

Appendix H: Support, Errata, and p2p.wrox.com   1167

Index   1173

Introduction

Flexible, portable, versatile, and freely available, Perl has grown from a simple replacement for shell scripts to a powerful all purpose language with object oriented support and an enthusiastic following. This very popular, feature rich language is gaining even more popularity as it acquires more features with every new release. One particularly powerful feature of Perl is its implementation of libraries with modules, which has made it a genuinely extensible language.

With its clarity, logical structure, and practical approach, **Professional Perl Programming** is the ideal guide and companion into the world of Perl programming.

Who Is This Book For?

The breadth and depth of this book make it immensely useful for both the newcomer to Perl and the experienced Perl programmer. The former will find in this book a comprehensive tutorial, which starts its coverage from the basics of the language and requires no previous knowledge of Perl whatsoever. It provides a thorough understanding of the language in its many aspects, from shell scripting to object orientation. However, the tutorial contains enough details that even experienced Perl programmers will find worth dipping into.

This book was written by experienced programmers, each of them drawing on their respective personal experience with Perl to provide their own expertise and insight. The tone of the book is therefore of professional developers sharing their hard earned knowledge. Following in the Wrox tradition, this book goes beyond merely reprising the original (and free) documentation supplied with the language and applies a pragmatic, example based approach to every subject that it covers.

Whether Perl is an old acquaintance or a new frontier, any Perl developer will find plenty to discover in **Professional Perl Programming**.

What's Covered in This Book?

Here is a quick introduction to the contents of this book.

We start off **Chapter 1** with a general introduction to Perl. We look at installing Perl from both binary and source distributions on UNIX, Windows, and Macintosh systems. We also cover installing Perl modules and third party libraries, and finish with an overview of Perl's command line options and environment variables.

Before delving into the details of Perl, **Chapter 2** lays the groundwork with a brief introduction to some of the basic concepts of the language: data types, special variables, operators, expressions, and others. This allows newcomers to Perl to become familiar with these concepts before we investigate them in more detail.

In **Chapter 3**, we examine the first and most basic of Perl's data types: scalars. We look at the three main types of scalars – integers, floating-point numbers, and strings – and how to convert between them. Next, we examine functions that can be used for manipulating strings. Finally, we talk about low-level functions for string conversions.

To use scalars requires operators. **Chapter 4** introduces and reviews the use of all Perl's operators and looks at the related concepts of precedence and associativity, and how they apply in Perl. For the more advanced reader, we also see how to disable and override operators.

Chapter 5 introduces more of Perl's data types, principally arrays, hashes, and typeglobs. It also introduces two special classes of scalar: references and the undefined value. We see how to manipulate these data types, and use them to create complex data structures such as multidimensional arrays and hashes of hashes. Finally, the chapter covers constants, including how to declare scalar, list, and hash constants.

Chapter 6 builds on the previous chapters to look at Perl's programming structures, starting with expressions and statements, moving on to conditional statements, and finishing with a look at loops and looping constructs.

Subroutines are reusable blocks of code that make scripts easier to maintain and adapt. **Chapter 7** demonstrates how we declare and pass parameters to subroutines. It also looks at how we use prototypes to specify what parameters a subroutine may take, and how subroutines return values. The chapter rounds off with a more advanced discussion of subroutine attributes, and how they may be used to modify subroutine behavior.

The twin concepts of scope and visibility are essential for understanding how variables and code interact. Perl's scoping rules can seem complex because it supports both 'package scope' (also called 'dynamic scope') and 'lexical scope'. Both are explained and contrasted in detail in **Chapter 8**. This chapter also introduces the symbol table and the related concept of namespaces.

Perl implements libraries with modules, a powerful feature of the language that allows it to be genuinely extensible. **Chapter 9** illustrates the different ways in which modules can be used, and explains pragmatic modules that change the behavior of the Perl compiler. We also cover the special variables @INC and %INC, and how they relate to module usage. In addition, we show how to check for the presence and availability of modules, as well as some techniques to delay the loading and compilation of modules unless and until they are actually used.

Having looked at modules from the outside, **Chapter 10** now looks at them from the inside – from the perspective of implementing them. We first tackle basic module construction, and the special blocks BEGIN, END, and friends. We then introduce autoloading, and discuss various autoloading techniques and strategies, including on the fly subroutine definition. Next, the subject of importing and exporting subroutines between different packages is examined in detail. In the last section, we cover how to create installable module packages using the h2xs tool.

Perl's regular expression engine, one of the features most often cited as a reason for using the language, is the subject of **Chapter 11**. We start with interpolation, which shares some of the same concepts and can be used to great effect both on its own and in combination with regular expressions. After covering interpolation, the chapter provides a complete tutorial on regular expressions, discussing the definition and construction of regular expressions patterns as well as their evaluation, from basic concepts to advanced techniques.

Chapter 12 introduces us to another distinct data type, filehandles. We learn several ways to create filehandles and also learn how to read and write to them. Locking files, random access, and the default output filehandle are discussed. Next, we learn about handling filehandles at the system level, something that allows us a greater degree of control over them, at the cost of greater responsibility.

Following filehandles, **Chapter 13** covers filenames, including file permissions and ownership. We cover the unary file test operator, and learn how to change file attributes, and perform operations on files through the filing system. Next, we have a look at Perl's glob operator, and the creation and manipulation of temporary files. The last part of the chapter concentrates on directories and looks at reading, creating, and destroying directories.

Chapter 14 is about the parsing and handling of command line arguments. We look in detail at the special array @ARGV, which contains the arguments passed to a Perl program when it is started. Next, the chapter examines the command line processing modules Getopt::Std and Getopt::Long. The second part of the chapter demonstrates how to create simple Perl shells and how to integrate the underlying shell into our Perl scripts.

The next chapter discusses programming terminal input and output. We show different ways of writing to terminals, including using the Term::ReadKey and Term::ReadLine modules. The chapter then addresses how to write to the screen and introduces high-level terminal modules. Finally, **Chapter 15** shows us the low-level interface to the terminal provided by the POSIX::Termios module.

In **Chapter 16**, we introduce warnings and errors, including the generation of warnings, finding out about errors, and dealing with them both. We learn how to interpret error results from system calls. At times, we need to make nonfatal errors fatal, and the Fatal module shows us how to do that. This chapter also covers the Carp module, and logging errors using both the underlying system and Perl functions.

Debugging is discussed in **Chapter 17**. The chapter shows in detail how to use Perl's debugger and covers a number of debugging modules that are part of the Perl standard library. The chapter then shows how to automate testing, before moving on to explain profiling – the process of collecting timing statistics for an application.

Chapter 18 is divided into three major sections, the first of which examines various modules that Perl provides for processing text. Modules covered in this section include Text::ParseWords, for parsing words and phrases, and Text::Wrap, for formatting paragraphs. The second section covers Perl's Plain Old Documentation (POD). The last section shows how to generate formatted text using special layout definitions called formats.

Object oriented programming is the subject of **Chapter 19**. The chapter starts with a general introduction to object concepts before delving into discussing programming with Perl objects. We are shown how to write object classes and are given a detailed look at inheritance and subclassing. The chapter covers keeping data private, destroying objects, and operator overloading. The last section discusses a special feature of Perl: ties and tied objects.

Chapter 20 stops looking at Perl from the surface and takes us inside the Perl interpreter. We examine how Perl is built, the `Config.pm` module, the internal data types used by Perl, and the Perl compiler. In the latter section, we look into the workings of the O module and the B:: family of modules.

In **Chapter 21**, we look at integrating Perl with other languages. We first see how to use C from Perl, looking in detail at the XS interface. Next, we learn how to access code in a dynamic library, be it a UNIX shared object or a Windows DLL. We then look at using Perl from C. Finally, we look at the Java-Perl Lingo (JPL), and using Perl in a COM environment.

Chapter 22 tackles the subject of creating and managing processes, starting with an introduction to signals and signal handling. Next, we show how to manipulate and communicate between processes, as well as how to share data. We finish with a look at a more recent feature of Perl: threads.

Chapter 23 treats us to an introduction of networking concepts before moving on to discuss sockets and basic network programming. We read about TCP and UDP networking, as well as UNIX Domain sockets. Socket configuration options are also covered, as well as multiplexed servers, polling, forking, and implementing a threaded server. In the last section, we see how to get information about network hosts, networks, protocols, and services.

Perl is a highly portable language. It runs on all major, and most minor, operating systems. But while most Perl code is portable, we still need to be aware of the differences between platforms and the pitfalls that can trap us. **Chapter 24** highlights the issues that we need to keep in mind if we are to write truly portable Perl code.

Chapter 25 looks at Perl's support for Unicode. The chapter starts with an introduction to basic Unicode concepts before talking about Perl's Unicode support for regular expressions. Next, we see how bidirectional text is rendered. The chapter finishes by demonstrating how to put Perl's support for Unicode into action.

Having explored Unicode in the previous chapter, it is natural to follow up with a chapter on locale and internationalization. **Chapter 26** explains Perl's support for locales and how to use it. The chapter then looks at a number of language related modules, and writing multilingual web pages.

The book finishes with a number of appendices of useful reference material, including Perl's command line options, special variables, functions, and standard library modules.

What You Need to Use This Book

Perl is available for many platforms, but it is most widely supported on UNIX (notably Linux and BSD) and Microsoft Windows 9x, 2000, and NT. Some sections of the book contain platform specific examples and will not apply to both UNIX and Windows. All examples use Perl 5.6, and while any version of Perl from 5.003 onwards can be used, a Perl 5.6 installation is preferable. At various points throughout the book we will need to install Perl modules, all of which are available from CPAN.

Although not required, some knowledge of UNIX/Linux may be helpful when dealing with certain topics.

Source Code

We have tried to provide example programs and code snippets that best illustrate the concepts discussed in the text. The complete source code from the book is available for download from:

http://www.wrox.com

This code is available under the terms of the GNU Public License. We suggest you get hold of a copy to save yourself a lot of typing, although almost all the code you need is listed in the book.

Conventions

To help you get the most from the text, we have used a number of conventions throughout the book. We have used several different fonts in the text of this book:

❑   Filenames, function names, and words that may be used in code or typed into a configuration file are shown in a monospaced font: `use warnings` or `Config.pm`.

❑   URLs are written like this: http://www.cpan.org

Asides to the current discussion are indented and italicized:

This style is used for asides.

Commands typed at the command line are shown with a > prompt:

```
> perl myscript.pl
  this is my output
```

Commands that must be executed with superuser privileges are shown with a # prompt:

 # make install

When we list the contents of complete scripts or want to highlight something important in a piece of code, we use the following convention:

```
#!/usr/bin/perl
# petunias.pl
use warnings;
use strict;
print "Oh no, not again\n";
```

Snippets of code that should be used as parts of other examples will be typed like this:

```
if (-f $file && -T $file) {
    ...
}
```

1

Introduction

In this introductory chapter, we cover a little of the background of Perl and what makes it popular. We also cover installing Perl and building it from source – a recommended step, if feasible, for those with the confidence in their systems. For those who already have Perl installed, these sections can be skipped, though if we want to use features such as **threading** it may be to our advantage to build Perl from source even if we do have a binary installation already in place.

We also cover installing third-party modules and introduce the **Comprehensive Perl Archive Network** (**CPAN**), the first, and frequently only, port of call for all Perl extensions and add-ons. It has mirrors all over the world, and there is also a CPAN module that provides a simple but powerful way to use it. We also cover some of the options for installing packages containing C code on non-UNIX ports of Perl, notably **ActivePerl**'s PPM package tool.

Finally, we look at the various ways of running Perl, and setting up the operating system to recognize Perl scripts as Perl scripts. We also take a look at the Perl command line together with special environment variables, and examine one way to create stand-alone Perl applications that can run without the benefit of a Perl installation.

Introduction

Perl is a tremendously adaptable language that combines an extremely versatile syntax with a powerful range of features. Originally inspired by UNIX text processing tools like sed and awk, and shell scripting languages, Perl is a synthesis of features that provides a scripting environment which is vastly more powerful than the original tools and traditional shell scripts, while also being easier to learn and faster to develop in.

Perl's versatility is one of its greatest strengths, but it can also be a liability if used incorrectly. Unlike languages that have a strong sense of what is the right way or the wrong way to do things, Perl is adaptable enough to adopt almost any approach – 'There's More than One Way to Do It', as the Perl motto goes. This lets Perl adapt to the programming style of the programmer, and not the other way around. In the eyes of Perl programmers, this is a good thing; in the eyes of advocates of some other languages, it isn't. Perl's anti-motto really ought to be 'Just Because You Can Do It, Doesn't Mean You Should.'; Perl does not impose good programming practices, so it is also easy to write badly constructed and hard-to-read code through sloppy programming.

Perl is a very practically-minded language, and takes a no-frills approach to almost everything including things like object-oriented programming, which are pivotal to the entire ethos of other programming languages. This is again, both a boon and a potential pitfall. Perl is also the language of a thousand handy shortcuts, many of which are intuitive, and others become indispensable once they are known. We have tried to cover as many as we can during the course of this book.

Key Features

Perl has many features that contribute to its popularity. Some of them are obvious to anyone who is familiar with Perl – its easy learning curve, powerful text manipulation features, and cross-platform availability.

Ironically, experienced programmers sometimes have a harder time than newcomers; Perl makes some things so easy it is necessary to do a double-take and start from scratch rather than attempting to use familiar coding styles from other languages. This is especially true of the regular expression engine.

Others are hidden strengths – its open source credentials and licensing, independence from commercial interferences, and active online communities. Here are a few items for those who are less familiar with Perl to ponder upon:

❑ Perl has a relatively simple and intuitive syntax that makes it extremely quick to learn and lends itself to very rapid prototyping, especially compared to languages that involve an explicit compilation step. This is one reason it is popular as a scripting language – it can be faster to code a Perl tool to do a job than to find and learn how to use an existing one.

❑ Perl is a cross-platform language, supported on almost every operating system of sufficient complexity that has ever existed. This means that, with a few caveats, a Perl program written on one platform, Linux say, will usually run on another, Windows say, with little or no modification. Better still, Perl's standard library contains considerable support for handling different platforms in such a way that Perl applications frequently need little or no additional effort to handle multiple platforms.

❑ Perl's versatility allows programmers to learn the language and adapt it to their own particular styles. Conversely, of course, if their styles aren't very good, Perl won't straighten them out.

❑ Perl contains a very powerful suite of features for the manipulation of text. A key feature is the regular expression engine, which when properly used, is capable of almost any kind of textual transformation we can conceive, and text manipulation is one reason for Perl's popularity both as a command line tool and a web programming language.

❑ Perl's standard library comes with comprehensive support for database access and web programming. In addition, CPAN and ActiveState distribute modules for Linux and Windows respectively, which provide many powerful extensions to the standard library including very comprehensive XML support, graphical user interfaces, and several flavors of embedded Perl scripting. Perl can also be integrated into several different web servers.

❑ Perl supports references (at least, from version 5) but doesn't directly support addressable pointers. This is one of the biggest problems with C programming. References allow the easy construction of complex data structures, but without the dangers inherent in pointer arithmetic. As an adjunct to this, like most reference-based languages (Java is another) Perl has a garbage collector that counts references and removes data when it is no longer required.

❑ Perl has a flexible object-oriented programming syntax, which is both powerful and at the same time extremely simple. Its simplicity comes at the price of not implementing some of the more advanced object-oriented concepts available in other languages, but it is capable of a lot more than it is often given credit for.

❑ Perl is not commercially oriented. This is an important point and not one to overlook. Perl has no commercial agenda, and does not have features added to boost anyone's market position at the expense of the language itself. This gives it a major advantage over commercial scripting languages like Visual Basic which, while popular, are not developed by the communities that use them.

❑ Perl is an open source project, developed by the community of programmers who use it. Its license allows it to be used and copied freely, under the terms of the Artistic or GNU Public Licenses, whichever suits our needs better. This means that it cannot be commercially coerced, and also allows it to benefit from the input of thousands of programmers around the world. Despite that, commercial support is available from several companies both on UNIX and Windows for those that require it.

❑ Finally, Perl is not just a programming language but also a thriving online community. One of the most obvious signs of this is the CPAN (headquartered at http://www.cpan.org, but use a mirror) and its comprehensive repository of Perl programming libraries and modules. Another is the Perl Mongers, a network of regional Perl clubs and societies – see http://www.pm.org for a list of locations.

Supported Platforms

Perl is supported on many platforms, and ports exist to more or less every operating system that still has life in it (and a few that don't). The most commonly used of these are:

❑ **UNIX**: More or less every UNIX or UNIX-like operating system ever created, notably AIX, IRIX, HP/UX, BSD, Linux, Solaris, and Tru64

❑ **MS Windows**: DOS, Windows 3.1, 95, 98, NT and 2000, and the Cygwin UNIX-to-Windows compatibility environment

❑ **Other Desktop OSs**: Apple Macintosh (68k and PPC, both pre and post MacOS X), Acorn Risc OS, Amiga, BeOS, OS/2, and many others

❑ **Mainframes**: AS/400, OS390, VMS and OpenVMS, Stratus (VOS), and Tandem

❑ **PDAs**: EPOC (Psion/Symbian), but not PalmOS or Windows CE at time of writing, although porting efforts are being made for both platforms

Binary versions of Perl for all of these operating systems and many others are available from the Ports page on CPAN at: http://www.cpan.org/ports/index.html.

Perl also builds from source on many of these platforms. This is generally preferable since binary distributions tend to lag behind the source code in version number (the delay depends a lot on the platform – UNIX is near instantaneous). For UNIX-like platforms, building from source should not be a problem, and may even be educational. Other platforms that should be able to compile Perl directly from source include DOS, OS/2, BeOS, EPOC, VMS, and Windows; see later in the chapter for details.

In addition, when building from source, Perl is able to take advantage of additional facilities on the platform if they are available, and to extend its support to new data types like 64 bit integers and extended floating-point numbers where possible. It also allows the possibility of including support for threads and other features that are frequently not enabled by default in binary distributions. Also, if we are on a UNIX-like platform, we can, try out a development version of Perl.

Perl History and Versions

Perl, the **P**ractical **E**xtraction and **R**eport **L**anguage, is an evolving language, continuously being updated to support new features. Despite this, it is still an easy language to learn and has not lost its basic simplicity, regardless of evolving from a simple scripting tool into a fully-fledged object-oriented application development language.

Perl evolved hand-and-glove with the Internet, and gained rapid popularity in its early days as a language for writing quick utility scripts. This was thanks in part to its powerful text handling features and familiarity to programmers used to the sed and awk tools by which Perl was partly inspired. It also gained popularity as a language for writing server-side CGI scripts for web servers, again because of its text handling abilities and also because of its rapid prototyping. This culminated in version 4 of Perl.

Release 5 took Perl to a new level by introducing object-oriented programming features. Perl's object orientation is a very back-to-basics approach. Like the language itself, it applies itself to actually getting the job done rather than overly worrying about ideology, but nonetheless, turns out to be very capable. The ability to support objects, derived principally from the introduction of hard references to the language. Up until this point, Perl only had symbolic references, which are now deprecated (and indeed disallowed with the strict module). It was in version 5 that Perl became more than just a language for writing short utility scripts and became a language in which serious applications could be developed.

Version 5.005 introduced initial support for threaded programming, albeit only inside the interpreter itself. This gave Windows, and other platforms that did not support child processes, an emulation of the UNIX fork system call, thus greatly improving Perl's support on those platforms.

In version 5.6, the current stable version, Perl revised its version numbering system to be more in line with version numbers elsewhere. In particular, it adopted the Linux system of numbering stable and development releases with even and odd release numbers. The first stable version of Perl to use this is version 5.6; the development version is version 5.7. Version 5.6 introduced a number of important improvements, the main one being full support for Unicode character sets – not only can Perl 5.6 handle multi-byte characters, it can even handle code written using them. From version 5.6, experimental support for threads in user-level programming is provided too, but only if built from source and requested at that time. In this book we will be using Perl 5.6 in our examples, though we will point out incompatibilities and alternatives for earlier versions as we go.

In the future is Perl 6, a complete and fully object-oriented re-implementation of Perl from the ground up. The exact details have just been finalized at the time of writing, so the eventual release of Perl 6 is some way off. In the meantime, updates to 5.6 will continue, and more experimental features will make their way into 5.7.

Essential Information

Perl comes with a lot of documentation as standard, including a complete set of manual pages that can be accessed with the perldoc program, if we already have Perl installed. For an index of available pages, use the command line:

> **perldoc perl**

This should return a list of the (many) standard Perl manual pages available as part of every Perl installation. The `perldoc` command can also return information on specific Perl modules; for example, to pick two popular Perl modules named CGI and DBI, which we shall meet later:

> **perldoc CGI**

> **perldoc DBI**

Type **perldoc perldoc** for information on using `perldoc` itself, and **perldoc -h** for a brief summary of options. Key options and command variants are:

> **perldoc -f funcname   # look up a function in the perlfunc page**
> **perldoc -m module   # display source code file**
> **perldoc -q pattern   # search the perlfaq documentation**
> **perldoc -r pattern   # search the entire Perl installation**
> **perldoc -i [options]   # do a case insensitive lookup or search**

For example:

> **perldoc -f split**
> **perldoc -m CGI**
> **perldoc -q '(mailladdress)'**
> **perldoc -i cgi**

A complete set of manual pages for Perl in HTML, PDF, Postscript, and plain text formats are available from CPAN's documentation page at: http://www.cpan.org/doc/index.html, or from http://www.perldoc.com. Users of ActivePerl can also use ActivePerl Online Documentation (or similarly named) from the Start Menu in order to obtain the Windows version.

These are direct conversions of the manual pages supplied with Perl, but may be the wrong version (in either direction) for a local Perl installation. We can generate our own specific versions with the conversion tools `pod2html`, `pod2man`, `pod2latex`, or `pod2text`, for example:

> **pod2html --in=/usr/lib/perl5/5.6.0/CGI.pm --out=./CGI.pm.html**

To generate an entire HTML tree from our own installation, which includes all the HTML documents available from CPAN and additional documents for every module installed on our platform we can use `pod2html` in a recursive mode.

Also available from http://www.cpan.org/doc/index.html is the current version of the Perl FAQ, and some other useful essays that go beyond the basic Perl documentation.

There are many useful web sites for Perl programmers, of which http://www.cpan.org is probably the most important. A list of useful URLs for Perl resources is given in Appendix G.

Building and Installing Perl

Perl is released in two different versions, the **stable** version, also known as the **maintenance** version, and a development version. Both versions update in small ways from time to time, and occasionally take a big leap. The last such big leap was from Perl version 5.005 to Perl 5.6.0, which revised the version numbering system at the same time; the new development release, as mentioned earlier, became Perl 5.7.0. This does not mean Perl 5.7 is better than Perl 5.6, it just means it is more experimental. Some development releases are more stable than others, but only officially stable releases are recommended for production environments. The new numbering scheme means that the latest stable version will always have an even second digit – incremental updates will be in the 5.6.X series, the next major release will be 5.8.

Getting the most current maintenance release is almost always a good idea; reasons not to do this are because the platform on which we want to install Perl does not have an up-to-date binary release, and it is not possible to directly build Perl from source. New maintenance versions of both stable and development releases increment the last digit; depending on what is in them, we may or may not need to care about upgrading Perl immediately.

Before fetching and installing a Perl distribution it is worth taking time to consider whether a binary distribution is suitable or whether it would be worth building from source. Source distributions include the following advantages:

❑   They can be built to take advantage of the underlying hardware; for example, Pentium+ class processor instructions. Binary distributions are frequently 'dumbed down' in terms of processor capabilities in order to be more widely installable.

❑   Enhanced and experimental features such as extended precision integers, floating point numbers, and user-level threads can be included into the Perl interpreter.

❑   Support for additional packages like the GNU DBM (GDBM) and Berkley DB (DB) libraries can be built if they are present on the system when Perl is built.

Disadvantages of source distributions are that they take longer to carry out and require a compiler and supporting tools for the build process. They are also not immediately portable to all the platforms on which Perl can run (which is an alarmingly large number), while binary distributions have already solved the installation issues for their target platform. Having said this, the source is quite capable of being built on the bulk of platforms that we are likely to be using.

Installing Pre-built Perl Distributions

Perl is available from many web sites and FTP servers. Two places to look for it are http://www.perl.org and http://www.cpan.org, both of which carry the latest releases and links to all the distributions, free and commercial, for all platforms on which Perl is known to work. Note that it is generally a very good idea to pick a local mirror before downloading from CPAN, for reasons of both speed and good neighborliness. FTP access to both sites and their mirrors is supported, of course. The main CPAN site automatically tries to redirect browsers to a local site.

Binary distributions are available from a number of places, most notably CPAN's binary ports page at http://www.cpan.org/ports/index.html, which contains links to a large number of binary ports and incidental notes on availability. Some platforms lag behind the current source code release by a few version points – if this is important, consider building from source instead.

Many platforms can take advantage of pre-built packages that will install onto a system using the standard installation tools. Linux, for example, has both .deb and RPM packages, both of which are commonly available from the web sites of the respective distributions (Debian and distributions based on Debian for .deb packages, and Red Hat with various other distributions, including SuSe using RPM also). Additionally, RPMs can for be found at ftp.rpmfind.net and can be searched for using the rpmfind utility. Solaris packages can be installed with the pkgadd facility, and so on.

In general, packages keep up to date with the current Perl release, but check first and make a note of any changes that may mean getting a more up-to-date release.

Installing Perl on UNIX

Installing a binary distribution of Perl is trivial – we just need to unpack it into the place we want it to live; to install it into a system-wide place like /usr/local or /usr/lib we will need to be **superuser**, of course, which is usually denoted by the prompt # on the command line. The latest version of the standard package in both RPM and Debian formats can be tracked down at http://www.activestate.com. After retrieving the correct package, the following command lines for .rpm and .deb files will place them in the relevant location and install Perl for us:

 # rpm -i ActivePerl-5.6.0.620-i686-linux-thread-multi.rpm

 # dpkg -i ActivePerl-5.6.0.620-i686-linux-thread-multi.deb

In addition, if we wish to run Perl and attendant scripts like perldoc from the command line, we need to either place them in a standard place for executables that is on the system path or, if system administration states that installing Perl off /usr is not possible, then it isn't necessary to install Perl into an official place. We can install it in our own home directory perfectly well too.

Installing Perl on Windows

There are three main ports of Perl to Windows; the **native** port, the **ActiveState** port, and the **Cygwin** port. The native port can be built straight from the source, which is the preferred alternative; a straight binary port is available from the ports page for those who really can't build from source and can't (or won't) use one of the available alternative binary ports.

The ActiveState port, ActivePerl, is available from http://www.activestate.com. If we are using Windows 9x, we will need the Microsoft Windows Installer (Windows 2000 and ME have this as standard). It is available from the Windows Download page at ActiveState's web site: http://www.activestate.com/Products/ActivePerl/Download.html. Select the appropriate Installer and install it first. We can then download the binary distribution from the Windows Download page or FTP it from ftp://ftp.activestate.com/ActivePerl/Windows/5.6.

In addition, there is a Cygwin port for the Cygwin UNIX compatibility library available from http://sourceware.cygnus.com/cygwin (actually a part of Red Hat now). The Cygwin Port has the advantage of supporting (and indeed coming supplied with) many of the GNU utilities, including gcc, gzip, make, and tar, which the CPAN module CPAN.pm prefers to use.

Note that Cygwin is a supported build option in the Perl source distribution (see the file README.cygwin in the top directory of the unpacked source), but if required, a port of Perl 5.6 for Cygwin V1.1 is available from http://cygutils.netpedia.net, which may be unpacked and installed with tar (which comes with Cygwin), just as with UNIX binary ports.

Installing Perl on Macintosh

The Macintosh port of Perl, also known as **MacPerl** comes in several different forms, divided into two stand-alone versions and either a binary or source distribution based around the Macintosh Programmers Workbench (MPW). At the time of writing, the current version of MacPerl is based on Perl 5.004. Either version works on any version of MacOS from 7 through 9. All of the files needed, can be found at a mirror of http://www.cpan.org/ports/mac. Additional information is available at the MacPerl homepage at: http://www.macperl.org/.

All versions of MacPerl require the core binary `Mac_Perl_520r4_appl.bin` (for version 5.004). To get the stand-alone application with all the trimmings (libraries and documentation), install `Mac_Perl_520r4_bigappl.bin`.

To get the stand-alone application only, install `Mac_Perl_520r4_appl_only.bin`. 68k-based Macintoshes with dynamic library loading may instead use `Mac_Perl_520r4_appl_cfm68K.bin`. For the version based on the MPW, first make sure that the MPW is actually installed. Then add: `Mac_Perl_520r4_tool.bin` and `Mac_Perl_520r4_bigtool.bin`.

To use the MPW to build MacPerl, use `Mac_Perl_520r4_tool.bin` and `Mac_Perl_520r4_src.bin`.

MacOS X ships with Perl preinstalled, so installing it is not a problem. In addition, since MacOS X is UNIX-based underneath, most of the details for managing UNIX installations apply to it also, including **shebang** lines for script identification (`#!\usr\bin\perl`).

Building Perl from Source

Building Perl from source is not actually necessary for most platforms, so this section can be skipped by those who would prefer not to experiment with compilers or are simply impatient to get on to actually writing Perl code. This is a brief introduction and rundown of building Perl for those who are curious (or have no choice) about building Perl from source, or want to do more than the standard binary installations allow, such as enabling support for threads. We highlight the main points for a UNIX installation; the general technique is either identical or easily adapted for the other platforms supported by the source code distribution.

Source distributions are available from a number of places, most notably CPAN's Perl Source code page at http://www.cpan.org/src/index.html. The current production release is always available as the files `stable.tar.gz` (for systems with `gzip`, typically UNIX) and `stable.zip` (for systems with `zip` and `unzip` utilities, typically Windows, Macintosh, and many desktop operating systems). Development releases are available as `devel.tar.gz` and `devel.zip`. In both cases, the actual version number is not reflected in the filename; it is in the archive inside, which unpacks under the directory `perl-<version>` (for example `perl-5.6.0`).

System administrators, who are concerned with the accounting of the files they install, can still use a package installation and build from source. This gives us the advantage of having Perl installed as an accountable package, while at the same time taking advantage of the benefits of compiling it from source. Rather than installing a binary RPM for example, we can acquire the source RPM or SRPM (use `--sources` as an argument to `rpmfind` to locate one) and use **>rpm --rebuild perl.srpm** to build a new binary package we can then install.

Building Perl is mostly just a matter of unpacking the source archive (stable or development version) and choosing how to configure the build process. Before moving on to configuring the installation, we need to extract the archive. For example, assuming we have the **gzipped** source on a UNIX system, we use the following command lines:

> **> gunzip -c stable.tar.gz | tar -xvf -**
> **> cd perl-5.6.0**

If we have the GNU version of `tar` we can also do the unpacking in one step with:

> **> tar -xzvf stable.tar.gz**

Perl builds easiest on UNIX platforms; the majority of these can use the supplied `Configure` script to set up and compile Perl with the features and installation locations they want. Other platforms supported by the source bundle are documented in one of the `README` files available in the top-level directory of the source tree. For instance, instructions and additional details for building Perl on Windows are contained in the `README.win32` document. If the platform we want to build on has an associated `README` file, we can build and install Perl on it, but there may be more involved than simply running `Configure`.

The `Configure` script sets up the source distribution for compilation on the chosen platform. It has two modes of operation. The first is an interactive step-by-step question and answer session that asks us how we want to build the interpreter, where we want to install it and the libraries that come with it. At any stage, where a reasonable default can be assumed, the script does so. We usually change just the options we care about and accept the defaults for the rest. At its simplest we can use `Configure` this way by entering:

> **> ./Configure**

The second mode of operation skips the question and answer session and assumes the defaults for all questions. Without qualification this will build a standard Perl that installs into the default place (`/usr/lib/perl5` on most systems) when we subsequently carry out the installation. To run `Configure` in this way we use the `-d` option, for 'default':

> **> ./Configure -d**

In either mode, if we want to have `Configure` automatically start the compilation process after finishing the initial set-up, we can specify the `-e` option. To stop `Configure` being concerned about the less important issues of how and why it is making its decisions, we can also specify `-s`, for 'silent'. These are both good options to specify together, with `-d` to configure and build Perl with minimal fuss:

> **> ./Configure -des**

Both modes also allow us to specify configuration options on the command line. In the interactive mode, this changes the default option presented to us when `Configure` asks us the appropriate question; we can then change our minds again if we want to. In the non-interactive mode this is the only chance we get to determine how the resulting Perl is built.

There are potentially many options that can be specified; the question and answer session describes most of the ones that it sets so it is worth running through it once just to see what is set by which question. Possibly the most likely option to specify is the `prefix` option, which determines where Perl is installed after it is built and presets the values of many other options. Configuration options are set with the `-D` flag, so to tell Perl to install itself in `/usr/local/perl5_6_0` rather than the default location we would use:

> **./Configure -des -Dprefix=/usr/local/perl5_6_0**

This example uses the non-interactive mode of `Configure` to install Perl under the `/usr/local` directory. We might do this, for example, if we already have a Perl installation and we do not want to disturb it.

Another option to combine with `prefix` to ensure we don't upset an existing installation is the `installusrbinperl` option. By default this is enabled, and causes the installation stage to copy `perl` and a few supporting scripts into the default place for system executables. Unless we change it, this default is `/usr/bin`. To disable an option we use `-U`, so to set up Perl to install elsewhere and leave the existing installation untouched, we would use:

> **./Configure -des -Dprefix=/usr/local/perl5_6_0 -Uinstallusrbinperl**

A complete list of `Configure`'s options can also be viewed by using the `-h` or `--help` option on the command line:

> **./Configure --help**

If we have been through the configuration process at least once before, there will be a `config.sh` file present. In the interactive mode, `Configure` will ask if we want to use it, and then preset itself with defaults from the previous run. This file contains all the names of the options that we can supply on the command line too, so it can be handy for finding out how to set options. Note that if we are rebuilding Perl with different options, we should additionally execute a `make distclean` before we configure and build Perl a second time:

> **make distclean**
> **./Configure**

Once configuration is complete, we actually build and install Perl by typing:

> **su**
Password:
make install

This will build and install Perl according to the choices we made at the configuration stage. If we are overwriting an existing installation and prudently want to test the new build before we wreck anything, we can build Perl without installing it, test it, and then install it only if we are happy:

> **make**
> **make test**
> **su**
Password:
make install

At the end of the build process a file called `myconfig` is generated and this contains complete details of the configuration used to build Perl. This is handy for checking what was actually used to build Perl; a similar output can be generated from Perl itself with the `-V` option:

> **perl -V**

Building a Threaded Perl Interpreter

One specific reason for building Perl from the source distribution rather than installing a precompiled binary is to enable support for **threads**. Threads are a powerful way to write multi-tasking applications without the overheads of multiple processes, and are fundamental to languages such as Java. In Perl, threads are still experimental, so they are not built by default.

The interactive question and answer session that Configure provides asks two questions about threads; firstly Build a threading Perl?, and secondly, Use interpreter-based threads? The answers to these questions are y and n respectively. Unfortunately though, this will not result in a working threaded Perl interpreter; we must also select thread support on the command line with the usethreads and use5005threads options. Here is how we would do that before entering an interactive question and answer session:

> ./Configure -des -Dusethreads -Duse5005threads

Or, to build a threaded version of Perl non-interactively, and in a different location as described above:

> ./Configure -des -Dusethreads -Duse5005threads -Dprefix=/usr/local/perl5_6_0
-Uinstallusrbinperl

Either way, we will now have a correctly working **threaded Perl**. If all has gone well we should have a Thread module in the standard library. We can check that it is there by executing (in the above example):

> /usr/local/perl5_6_0/bin/perldoc Thread

See the end of Chapter 22 for a description of threads and why we might want to use them, and also the threaded network server example in Chapter 23.

Differences for Windows and Macintosh

Building Perl from source on Windows is broadly similar to building it on UNIX with the primary difference being the choice of compiler and make utility used. Running >perldoc perlwin32 provides some reasonably detailed information on the options available. For those without a Perl to use to run perldoc the pages are also available on the Web – see earlier in the chapter for some URLs to gain more information.

To build Perl for Macintosh first requires installing the base packages and then compiling the source code with the **M**acintosh **P**rogrammer's **W**orkbench (**MPW**). Refer to the above section titled '*Installing Perl on Macintosh*' for details on which files to get and install.

Other Platforms

Other than generic UNIX Windows support and, several other platforms are supported by the source distribution. Each of these has a README file located in the top of the tree that provides information to get Perl built and installed on that platform. Here is a short summary of them:

README.amiga	Amiga
README.beos	BeOS
README.cygwin	Windows port using Cygwin
README.dos	DOS port using djgpp
README.epoc	Symbian/Psion EPOC
README.hpux	HP/UX
README.hurd	GNU Hurd

README.machten	Power MachTen
README.mint	Atari ST
README.mpeix	HP 3000 MPE
README.os2	OS/2
README.os390	OS 390
README.plan9	Plan 9
README.posix-bc	BS2000 OSD V3.1A Posix
README.qnx	QNX4
README.vmesa	VM/ESA 3.20
README.vms	VMS
README.vos	VOS (Stratus)
README.win32	Windows 9x/NT

Note that Windows has more than one option, depending on whether we want to use the native win32 port, the Cygwin support libraries, or the DOS version (which requires the djgpp compiler, a DOS port of gcc is available from http://www.midpec.com/djgpp/). Other ports on this list are more or less functional – don't necessarily expect them to work completely, especially very old, very new, or very obscure platforms.

Building Perl from source on other platforms may or may not be possible, depending on the platform. See the ports page on CPAN for availability and instructions if available.

Building and Installing Modules

Perl comes with a very feature-rich and comprehensive standard library. However, many more modules are available from CPAN, so it would be nice to be able to install them too. The easiest way to download and install modules on most platforms is the CPAN module. Many module packages also include C code, however. In these cases the CPAN module requires a C compiler and make tool, which can limit its ability to function on non-UNIX platforms. Users of the popular ActivePerl distribution are well provided for here; ActivePerl supplies it own package management tool PPM, which is strongly inspired by the CPAN module and allows us to download and install precompiled Windows versions of CPAN modules, avoiding the need for a compiler.

We can also download and install module packages manually by, downloading a package file from CPAN or (preferably) one of its mirrors using either HTTP or FTP. To get to the modules, either FTP to the CPAN mirror of your choice or point a web browser to: http://www.cpan.org/modules/. This, or the local mirrored equivalent, contains links that list the modules in the archive by author, category, name, or archive time. We can also make use of http://search.cpan.org/ to search for modules in various different ways.

Installing Modules with the 'CPAN' Module

The CPAN module provides a Perl-based interface to the CPAN archive for UNIX platforms, and possibly others. We can use the module to scan CPAN for new packages, check for updates on existing packages, and install new ones, including dependent modules and module bundles. With the optional CPAN::WAIT module (available from CPAN, naturally) also installed, we can carry out full text searches using the **CPAN Wide Area Information Server** (a.k.a. WAIS) database.

The CPAN module takes a little while to set up, because it needs to be told about the availability of certain system resources and also the nearest CPAN mirrors to use. This is almost always effort well spent, however, since it allows us to search, examine, build, and install modules all from the same command line prompt.

Starting and Configuring CPAN

To start the CPAN module from the command-line, use:

 # perl -MCPAN -e shell

This runs Perl, loads the CPAN module into memory and runs the shell subroutine, which provides an interactive interface. Note that if we have Perl installed in a privileged place we will need to be superuser to actually install anything, though we can still perform queries. If CPAN has never been configured before it will run through a set of questions to get itself up and running. Like Perl's build configuration a lot of these are self-evident, and others are computed by default. However, the module needs to fetch several resources including a current list of CPAN mirrors during the installation process so it is very helpful (though not absolutely necessary) to have an active Internet connection during the configuration process.

UNIX systems will generally have no trouble here, but non-UNIX systems will need to make sure that they have acceptable versions of at least some of the following command-line utilities:

- ❑ A copy of gzip
- ❑ A tar program
- ❑ A zip/unzip program (WinZip, infozip, etc)
- ❑ A make program (for example, dmake or nmake for Windows)
- ❑ A copy of the open source **lynx** browser (this is only necessary if Net::FTP is not installed yet)
- ❑ A non-interactive FTP command line client (such as ncftpget, freely available and installed on many Linux and other UNIX-like platforms)

The configuration process will also ask about FTP and HTTP proxies, and then fetch a list of mirrors from which we should pick two or three in the local area. This is the only part of the configuration that needs considered user input; select three or so numbers from the list for the appropriate area and all should be well. Note that any option can be changed after the initial configuration with the o command from within the interactive shell. (The process will also ask about a WAIT server. This is an optional feature that looks for the CPAN searchable WAIS database and enables the search commands listed under **Other CPAN commands**. The default server offered works fine.)

The CPAN module supports command line editing and history, if supplied by the Term::ReadLine module. This, and the Term::ReadKey module, can of course be installed with the CPAN module once it is in place.

Once we have the CPAN module configured, we should have a cpan> prompt at which we can enter a variety of commands. Typing h or ? will generate a helpful list of available commands. If we have Term::ReadLine and Term::ReadKey installed and the **GNU readline library** available (see Chapter 15 for more on all of these) the prompt should be highlighted and underlined, otherwise we can install them ourselves:

cpan> **install Term::ReadKey**
...

cpan> **install Term::ReadLine**
...

Installing these modules significantly improves the CPAN shell by adding better interactivity and command line history. Alternatively, we can install the CPAN bundle, which contains all the modules that CPAN can make use of, with:

cpan> **install Bundle::CPAN**

...

Either way, the CPAN module will go off and try to fetch the module or modules we requested. If we do not have an up-to-date copy of the Net::FTP or LWP modules (for FTP or HTTP transfers respectively) installed then it will try to use the lynx browser to fetch it. If we don't have any of these installed, we will have to use an FTP client to fetch and install at least one of them manually. We should use reload cpan after executing any of the above commands to update the running CPAN shell.

Installing Modules

The CPAN module provides four commands related to installation. The main one, and in practice the one we tend to use the most often, is install. This takes a bundle, distribution, or module name (it is not practical to install an author, although it would be an intriguing concept) and determines the appropriate distribution file or files to fetch, build, and install. This means we can install modules without needing to worry about which actual distribution file they belong in. For example, we can say:

cpan> **install Apache::Registry**

Installation is a multi-step process:

❑ The currently installed version (if any) is compared with that available from CPAN. If the installation is up-to-date and we are not doing a force (see below) then the installation terminates.

❑ The distribution file (named explicitly, by bundle, or inferred from the module requested) is fetched from the first configured CPAN mirror and unpacked.

❑ Next, the module is built using **perl Makefile.PL** followed by **make**.

❑ Next, the module is tested using **make test**. For most distributions this executes a test suite implemented using the Test and Test::Harness modules. If this stage fails, the module installation aborts with an error, unless we used the force modifier, which is explained shortly.

❑ Finally, if the distribution passed the test stage, it is installed into Perl's library.

We can, if we choose, also carry out these stages individually, but this is usually only done if there is a problem with the automatic installation.

Installing Modules in Stages

Instead of using the install command to fetch, build, test, and install a module in one go, we can use the get, make, and test commands to perform individual steps, and then finish with install. This can be occasionally useful for examining the outcome of each stage before proceeding to the next; generally useful if the automated install process fails for some reason.

In fact, each command implies the ones before, so if we use make for a module that has not been fetched, get is used to fetch its distribution first. We don't actually need to issue get, make, or test commands, since install implies all of them – or as many of them as still remain to be done.

Forcing Installation

If an installation fails in the `test` phase, or CPAN thinks that a module or distribution is already installed and up-to-date, it will decline to do so a second time. We can override this with `force`, for example:

cpan> **force install Term::ReadLine**

It is perfectly fine to do this, but we should be aware that the distribution might not function entirely correctly (or in more extreme cases, function at all). Some test failures may involve features that are not applicable to a particular site or operating system. Read the output of the test phase carefully before deciding whether to use `force`.

Examining the Contents of a Distribution

It is rare that we would actually want to examine the contents of an unpacked distribution directly, but if we want to we can do so with the `look` command. This opens a system shell in the root directory of the unpacked distribution where we can list files:

cpan> **get CGI**
...

cpan> **look CGI**
> **ls**
...

We can also execute `make` commands here directly if we need to (for example `>make install UNINST=1` to install a new module removing any older installed versions at the same time). However, `look` does not perform any kind of remote access; if we look for something that we don't have installed then it will need to be fetched and downloaded first.

Cleaning Up

Once a package has been installed we can clean up the files generated during the build process with `clean`. This takes a bundle, module, or distribution as an argument and issues a `make clean` on the unpacked sources cached by the CPAN module. Clearly this makes sense only if the package has actually been installed recently. For example:

cpan> **clean Net::FTP**

Cleaning up is useful if we are very short of disk space, otherwise we can usually skip it as the CPAN module automatically clears out the oldest build sources. This occurs whenever the total exceeds the cache size specified when we configured it at the module start up.

Listing and Searching CPAN

CPAN categorizes its archive in four different ways: by author, by bundle, by distribution, and by module:

❑ **Author**: These are the authors of the distributions available on CPAN, listed by code and full name.

❑ **Bundle**: Groups of module distributions that are commonly installed together are collected together into special distributions called **bundles**, which simply list a set of related distributions. Installing a bundle saves time and effort by avoiding the need to install a collection of modules one by one. Note that bundles do not contain any source code themselves; they are just a list of other distributions to install. All bundles are given names starting with `Bundle::` to distinguish them from 'real' packages.

❑ **Distribution**: The actual distribution files for Perl packages, including the directory prefixes for the author whose distribution it is.

❑ **Module**: As well as a list of distributions, CPAN keeps track of all the modules provided by those distributions. Since we can install distributions by naming a module inside them, we rarely need to actually type in a distribution name.

To search CPAN and list records, the CPAN module provides the a, b, d, and m commands for specific categories, or the i command, which returns information on all of these categories. On its own, the i command will return a complete list of every record on CPAN:

cpan> **i**

This is of course takes time and produces a very long and unwieldy list, even though the information is fetched from the mirror and stored locally. More usefully, we can narrow down the result by supplying a literal string or a regular expression. The literal string must match exactly:

cpan> **i CGI**

A regular expression (covered in Chapter 11) can be more specific as well as more flexible. To search for anything with 'CGI' in it (case insensitively, incidentally):

cpan> **i /CGI/**

To search for anything that begins with 'CGI', 'cgi', 'Cgi', and so on use:

cpan> **i /^CGI/**

To search for anything in the CGI module hierarchy:

cpan> **i /^CGI::/**

Alternatively, we can use the a, b, d, or m commands to search for specific authors, bundles, distributions or modules. These work identically to the i command but only return information for the specified category. For example, to list all modules containing XML but not distributions:

cpan> **m /XML/**

To find information for a particular author:

cpan> **a DOUGM**

To find all authors called Bob:

cpan> **a /^Bob/**

To find distributions with a version number of 1.x:

cpan> **d /-1.\d/**

Finally, to list all available bundles:

cpan> **b**

Listing Out-of-date Modules

We can find out which modules and distributions have been updated on CPAN compared to our locally installed copies with the r command:

```
cpan> r
Package namespace      Installed      Latest     in CPAN file
Apache::Session        1.51           1.53       J/JB/JBAKER/Apache-Session-1.53.tar.gz
CGI                    2.68           2.74       L/LD/LDS/CGI.pm-2.74.tar.gz
DBD::CSV               0.1023         0.1024     J/JW/JWIED/DBD-CSV-0.1024.tar.gz
DB_File                1.72           1.73       P/PM/PMQS/DB_File-1.73.tar.gz
Date::Manip            5.37           5 39       S/SB/SBECK/DateManip-5.39.tar.gz
Devel::Symdump         2.00           2.01       A/AN/ANDK/Devel-Symdump-2.01.tar.gz
```

Since this command requires that the entire contents of the locally installed Perl library are examined for version numbers and compared to the current versions available on CPAN, it takes a short while to execute. We can narrow down the list we want to check for by supplying a string or regular expression. For example to check for all out-of-date XML modules, the following works:

```
cpan> r /XML/
```

This regular expression simply matches any module with 'XML' in the title. If we only want to know about XML modules in the XML hierarchy, we can specify a more explicit expression by anchoring it at the front:

```
cpan> r /^XML::/
```

Listing Uninstalled Modules

In a similar manner to the r command, we can also list all currently uninstalled modules with u. Not surprisingly, this generates a rather large list of modules, so it is more useful with a regular expression. For example, to find all uninstalled modules in the 'XML' family:

```
cpan> u /^XML::/
```

Reading Module Documentation Without Installing

If we want to find out more about a module before installing it, since there are often multiple modules available for some tasks, we can use the readme command. This will look for the readme file within the distribution and, if present, fetch and display it to us without installing the module:

```
cpan> readme Apache::Session
```

Reloading CPAN

We can reload both the index information and the CPAN module itself with the reload command, should either be out of date (it is possible, though perhaps not likely, to have a permanent CPAN shell active on a server; updating the index from time to time would then be useful). To reload the index, use:

```
cpan> reload index
```

To reload the CPAN and associated modules, use `reload cpan`. For example, to upgrade CPAN itself we can use:

```
cpan> install Bundle::CPAN
cpan> reload cpan
```

The module will even prompt us to do this if our version of the CPAN module has been superseded.

Configuring CPAN Options

The o command configures CPAN options, and allows us to change any choice that we made during the original set-up. To list all current configurations use:

```
cpan> o conf
```

To view a specific option, name the option. For example, to find the size of the build cache for unpacked distribution sources:

```
cpan> o conf build_cache
build_cache   10
```

To set an option, name the option and the new value. For example, to increase the build cache to 20 megabytes:

```
cpan> o conf build_cache 20
```

We can also set debugging options for various parts of the CPAN module. For general usage we would not normally want to do this, but a list of debugging options can be generated with:

```
cpan> o debug
```

We have now mentioned in brief all of the most important CPAN commands.

Installing Modules by Hand

If we can't make use of the CPAN module then we can still install modules by hand. The process is essentially the same for every platform; the principal difference being the tools required on each platform to perform the unpacking, building and installation of the module.

Installing Modules on UNIX

UNIX systems can install module packages downloaded directly from a CPAN mirror. The package filename generally resembles `Some-Module-1.23.tar.gz`, that is, a **gzipped tarball**. To install it we first unpack it:

```
> gunzip -c (or gzip -dc ) Some-Module-1.23.tar.gz | tar xvf -
```

If we have the GNU version of tar (any Linux or BSD based system should have this), we can perform both steps in one go with:

```
> tar -zxvf Some-Module-1.23.tar.gz
```

The advantage of either approach is, of course, that we avoid uncompressing the distribution, which can be handy if we're short on disk space.

Having unpacked the module, we go into the source directory (which should have the same name, minus the `tar.gz` suffix) and generate the `Makefile` from the supplied `Makefile.PL` file:

> **cd Some-Module-1.23**
> **perl Makefile.PL**

Finally we install and test the module, using `make`:

> **make**
> **make test**
> **su**
Password:
make install

If we want to keep the original source directory but clean out all the additional files created by the building and installation process we can use the standard:

> **make clean**

If we change our minds and still have the source to hand we can also (sometimes) uninstall the package again using:

make uninstall

Installing Modules on Windows

The ActiveState port of Perl comes with a utility called PPM, which can install pre-built CPAN modules archived into ppd files. It works in a very similar way to the CPAN module that inspired it and by default connects to the archive at http://www.activestate.com/PPMPackages/5.6/.

Say we wish to install a package named `Math::Matrix`, which is not installed by default. We simply have to issue the command line at the prompt:

> **ppm install Math::Matrix**

As if by magic, and in a similar fashion to the CPAN module for UNIX, the package is retrieved and installed automatically ready for your use and abuse.

The PPM facility is a very capable tool and one of the most attractive reasons to use ActivePerl; more information and a list of alternative mirrors is available in the PPM FAQ document at: http://velocity.activestate.com/docs/ActivePerl/faq/ActivePerl-faq2.html. An excellent resource for an up-to-date list of modules available for use with PPM is http://www.activestate.com/ppmpackages/5.6/. This is maintained by ActiveState so it will be reliable and of great use.

We continue with installing modules by hand, since that is the topic of the conversation. The native port of Perl for Windows is essentially similar to the UNIX method, only with different decompression software. The `.zip` package files can be decompressed using `WinZip`, `infozip`, or any other ZIP-compatible decompression tool. `WinZip` can also handle UNIX-style gzipped and tarred files of the kind supplied by CPAN.

Once the package is uncompressed and extracted we can install it with a make tool (such as dmake) in the usual way. For example, assuming dmake:

```
> dmake
> dmake test
> dmake install
> dmake clean
```

This of course relies on a functional C compiler being available if the module happens to contain C code too. For pure Perl modules, this isn't a problem.

If we don't have a make equivalent and we don't have any C code to deal with, we can sometimes get away with simply copying the files that were unpacked into an appropriate part of the standard library tree, for instance the \site\lib branch. Some modules use a module called AutoSplit on installation to carve up the module source. Another module, AutoLoad then loads and compiles pieces of the module on demand. Since we are unable to make use of the standard installation process here we may also need to perform a split ourselves before the module is completely installed. If a module file uses the AutoLoad module, we will need to run the following from the top of Perl's installation to finish the installation:

```
> perl -MAutoSplit -e "autosplit site\lib\ to \module.pm site\lib\auto"
```

(The AutoLoad and AutoSplit modules are covered in more detail in Chapter 10.)

Installing Modules on Macintosh

Precompiled binary versions of some packages for MacOS created by Chris Nandor are also available from http://www.cpan.org/authors/id/CNANDOR/. As usual, we use a mirror of http://www.cpan.org if possible. Also available from this page is cpan-mac, a package of utilities that makes it possible to use the CPAN module with MacPerl. However, this will not build modules that contain C code.

Macintosh systems can unpack source package files with Stuffit or one of its many similarly inclined cousins to get the unpacked source. If the package requires building C source then things get tricky – a copy of the Macintosh Programmers Workbench (MPW) is required, plus a certain amount of dexterity. The MacPerl homepage http://www.macperl.org/ offers some advice and links that may help with this, as well as installing MacPerl itself.

If the package does not contain C code then we can install it by manually moving the package files to the Perl library, generally under the site_perl folder, replicating the directory structure of the package as we go. Note that the line endings of the source files need to be Apple format – LF/CR, rather than CR/LF or just LF. The decompression should handle this automatically, but it might not.

As with Windows, we may also need to manually split the module to complete its installation. This will be the case if the module file uses the AutoLoad module. Since there is no command line on a Macintosh we will need to create and run the following to finish the installation:

```
#!perl use warnings;
use AutoSplit;
autosplit "${MACPERL}site_perl:Path:To:Module.pm",
    "${MACPERL}site_perl:auto";
```

Installing Modules on Other Platforms

The CPAN web site contains some instructions for installing modules on several platforms on the Installing CPAN Modules page at http://www.cpan.org/modules/INSTALL.html. Some of this information is also available from >perldoc perlmodinstall, both sources with varying degrees of concurrency.

Running Perl

Having retrieved, compiled if necessary, and installed Perl, we now need to consider how to get the actual programs and Perl scripts running. The core of Perl is the **Perl interpreter**; the engine that actually interprets, compiles, and runs Perl scripts. Perl is not a traditional interpreted language like shell scripts; instead the interpreter compiles it from the original human readable version into a condensed internal format generically known as **bytecode**. This bytecode is then executed by the interpreter. All Perl programs therefore go through two phases; **a compile phase** where the syntax is checked and the source code, including any modules used, is converted into bytecode, and **a run-time phase**, where the bytecode is processed into machine instructions and executed.

Perl tries hard to be platform independent, but every platform has its own way of doing things, including its own way of running Perl. The first item on the agenda is usually to teach the operating system how to recognize a Perl script as a Perl script. UNIX-like platforms have it easiest, possibly because the whole system is geared towards scripts since much of the boot-up sequence is controlled through scripting. Windows, Macintosh, and other platforms on the other hand can be set up to handle Perl too, in their own particular ways.

The interpreter supports several command line options that affect its behavior in both the compile and run-time phases. These include obvious and essential features like enabling warnings or extracting configuration information, and less obvious but very useful features like implicit loops and automated input parsing that allow us to use Perl as a generic Swiss-army knife command line tool. Since we don't always want to specify command line options directly, Perl allows us to set them, as well as some of Perl's other default values, through environment variables. In the case of Windows, we can instead or additionally, set some values via the registry too.

Sometimes it isn't convenient to install Perl just to run a Perl script. Up until recently there wasn't a choice; all scripts need the Perl interpreter to run them, therefore they need to have it, plus any library modules that they need, installed. However, Perl 5.6 comes with an experimental compiler utility called perlcc that attempts to generate a stand-alone Perl application. We take a look at this in Chapter 20.

Starting Perl Applications

In order for a Perl script to run it must be given to the Perl interpreter to execute. Depending on the platform there are various different ways this can happen. The simplest way, which works on all platforms that have a shell or equivalent command line mechanism, is to run Perl directly, and supply the script name as an argument:

> **perl myscript.pl**

This presumes, of course, that the Perl interpreter perl, perl.exe, etc. is somewhere on the path defined for the shell. We can also supply command line switches to Perl when we run it directly. For example, to enable warnings:

> **perl -w myscript.pl**

However, we usually want to run a Perl application directly, that is to type:

> **myscript.pl**

For this to work, the shell has to know that `myscript.pl` is a Perl script, find and execute the Perl interpreter, and feed the program to it. Since Perl tries to be helpful, it will actually tell us the best way to start up an application this way if we ask it using the `-V` option:

> **perl -V:startperl**

If the platform supports a form of implicit indication which allows a script to indicate that it is a Perl script and not some other form of executable, this will produce the information required, adjusted for the location that Perl is installed in. For example, on a UNIX system we get something like:

> **startperl='#!/usr/bin/perl';**

This indicates that `#!/usr/bin/perl` can be added to the start of any script to enable it to start up using Perl automatically.

Perl on UNIX

UNIX systems have it easiest when it comes to setting up scripts to run with Perl automatically, largely due to its close and long term relationship with shells.

When the operating system comes to execute a Perl script, it doesn't know it is actually a Perl script to start with. However, when it sees that the first line starts with `#!` (shebang), it executes the remainder of the line and passes the name of the script to it as an argument, for example:

```
#!/usr/bin/perl
... rest of script ...
```

In this case the command happens to run the Perl interpreter. So, to start a script up directly on UNIX systems we need to add this line, (possibly embellished with additional command line options) to the start of a Perl script and make the script file executable.

The shebang line technique is a standard on most UNIX platforms and should work unless we are using a particularly obscure and/or old platform. Shells on other platforms don't understand the significance of a first line beginning `#!` and so we have to adopt other approaches.

Perl on Windows

MS Windows 9x and Windows NT 4.0 and above can make use of file extension associations stored in the registry to associate the `.pl` extension with the Perl interpreter. When you install the ActiveState distribution of Perl, it does this automatically, as long as the script isn't run from a DOS window. Otherwise, we need to follow these next instructions. Select Settings | Control Panel | Folder Options from the Start menu and click on the File Types tab. From here click on the New Type button and a new dialog will appear. Click on the New Icon button and type in the location. Now fill in the relevant boxes appropriately, using the `.pl` extension. When we click the New button to create a new action, we have the option to give the action a name and specify the path of the Perl interpreter, in this case.

Alternatively, we can simply convert a Perl script into a batch file. We can do this by using the supplied executable pl2bat. This makes the script stand-alone, but leaves the original file untouched also. It also changes the script name, so $0 (the batch file variable that refers to the name of itself) will be different inside scripts. Alternatively, if the script has no extension, we can copy the supplied batch file, runperl.bat, to another batch file with the same name as the Perl script. This achieves exactly the same result as it uses the $0 variable to call the Perl script via the Perl interpreter.

There is also a commercial package called perl2exe, which will convert the Perl script into a stand-alone executable, which may be appropriate for your needs.

Perl on Macintosh

Running Perl programs on Macintoshes with MacOS versions 7 to 9 is simple – each script just needs to have the appropriate creator and type attributes set and the operating system will automatically recognize it as a Perl script and invoke the interpreter. Running Perl from the command line is also simple, or rather, impossible since there is no command line. MacOS X is based on a BSD kernel, so we can run any Perl script using UNIX methodologies like shebang lines. With MacPerl there is also the ability to save scripts as **applets** which can be executed by the usual double-click or even just packaged up into a fully self-contained executable file. This is all done in the Save of the MacPerl editor. Direct integration with editors is also possible, for example using BBEdit. For more information on all issues concerning MacPerl consult the web site www.macperl.com.

The Command Line

Whether we invoke Perl directly or implicitly, we can supply it with a number of command line options. We do not always have to supply command line options explicitly. For systems that support shebang lines, we can add them to the end of the command contained in the first line:

```
#!/usr/bin/perl -wT
...
```

Alternatively, for systems that don't support shebang lines, we can set an environment variable. Perl examines several of these when it starts up and configures itself according to their contents. For command line options the special environment variable is PERL5OPT. This variable may contain command line options, exactly as if they were appearing on a real command line. Here is how we can use it to cause Perl to enable warnings (-w), and taint mode (-T), and load the strict module for strict syntax checks:

```
rem Windows
set PERL5OPT = wMstrict
```

```
# Unix - csh-like
setenv PERL5OPT "-Mstrict -wT"
```

```
# Unix - Bourne shell-like
export PERL5OPT="-Mstrict -wT"
```

We can set PERL5OPT in a shell startup script or batch file (.profile or similar for UNIX shells, AUTOEXEC.BAT for Windows 9X, or alternatively the registry for Windows in general). With the PERL5OPT environment variable under MS Windows, we cannot specify more than two command line options. Hence in this example, the -T switch is omitted.

Command Line Syntax

Perl's command line syntax is simple enough, but has a few wrinkles that are worth exploring. All of the following examples are assuming a UNIX system, however most will run on MS Windows (as some of the UNIX features were passed on to the DOS and Windows OS) and many will also be relevant to MacOS, of which the later versions have a UNIX core. The simplest use is to run a script with no arguments:

> **perl myscript.pl**

Perl expects to see a script name at some point on the command line, otherwise it executes whatever input it receives. We can also therefore say:

> **perl < myscript.pl**

Command line options, if we choose to specify them, go before the script. This command switches on warnings, taint mode (useful for CGI scripts and covered in Chapter 17), and includes the strict module:

> **perl -w -T -Mstrict myscript.pl**

Some command line options take an argument. For example, -e takes a string of code to evaluate, enclosed in quotes. Some options (-e included) allow a space after them. Others, like -m and -M do not – if we try to do so Perl will return an error message:

No space is allowed after -M

Command line options that take no argument (or may optionally take no argument) may be grouped together, so -w and -T can be grouped into either -wT or -Tw. We can also add one command with an argument, such as -M, if it is the last in the group. For example:

> **perl -TwMstrict myscript.pl**

Supplying Arguments to Perl Scripts

If we run a script directly, we can pass arguments to it that can be read inside the program (by examining the special array variable @ARGV):

> **myscript.pl -testing -1 -2 -3**

If we run a script via the Perl interpreter explicitly, however, we cannot just add options to the end of the command line, because Perl will absorb them in its own command line processing. However, if we add the special sequence - - to Perl's command line, it will stop processing at that point and any further arguments will be passed to the script instead:

> **perl -TwMstrict myscript.pl -- -testing -1 -2 -3**

If the script's arguments do not look like options (that is, are not prefixed with a minus) this is not a problem and we can say:

> **perl -TwMstrict myscript.pl testing 1 2 3**

We will discuss and expand on the special variable @ARGV and sequence -- later on in Chapter 14.

Using Perl as a Generic Command Line Utility

Perl can be surprisingly powerful on its own even without involving an actual program. By using a little imagination we can make Perl do a lot with just a few of its command line options.

In particular, the -e, -n, -p, and -l options allow us to perform fairly powerful functions with a single command. The -e option allows us to execute code directly, rather than specifying a program file, so we don't need to actually write a program, save it to a file, and then execute it. The -n and -p options put an implicit while loop that reads from standard input around the code we specify. The -l option (among other things) strips off the terminator from each line read, then configures print to put it back afterwards.

By combining these options together creatively we can produce any manner of quick one-line text processing commands using Perl. Say we wanted to add line numbers to the start of every line of a program. We could write a program to do that, but we could also just type:

> **perl -ne 'print "$.: $_"' < in.pl > out.txt**

The same command in MS Windows would be:

> **perl -ne "print ""$.: $_ """ <in.pl >out.txt**

The special variable $. holds the line number, and $_ the contents of the line just read from the input (both variables are described in more detail in Chapters 4, and 2 respectively, and in Appendix B). The option -n puts the whole thing in a loop, and the rest is redirection. If for some reason we wanted the line numbers on the end, we could enter this command for the Bourne shell in UNIX:

> **perl -nle 'print "$_ [$.]"' < in.pl > out.txt**

Here -l strips the original line ending, but redefines Perl's output formatting so that the print puts it back. Of course these are just simple examples, but throw in a regular expression, or a module loaded by the -m or -M flags and we can do some surprising things. For example, this command pulls a web page from a remote server and prints it out using the LWP::Simple module:

> **perl -MLWP::Simple -e 'getprint "http://www.myserver.com/img.gif"'**

Other options we can use in these kinds of super-simple scripts are -a and -F, which enable and configure autosplit mode. This, among other things, allows us to tell Perl to automatically break down lines into individual words. -i edits a file in-place, so that transformations we perform on what we read from it are actually enacted on the file itself.

Finally, we can use the Perl debugger as a generic Perl shell by passing -d and -e with a trivial but valid piece of Perl code such as 1, and possibly -w to enable warnings:

> **perl -dwe1**

See Chapter 17 for more on the debugger and the features available from this 'shell'.

A full listing of Perl's command line options can be found in Appendix A.

The Perl Environment

All environment variables present in the shell that executes Perl are made available inside Perl scripts in the special hash variable %ENV. In addition, Perl pays special attention to several environment variables and adjusts its configuration according to their contents.

Windows machines may (but are not required to) specify environment information in the registry, under either of:

```
HKEY_CURRENT_USER\Software\Perl
```

Or:

```
HKEY_LOCAL_MACHINE\Software\Perl
```

In the case of duplicate entries, the local machine settings are overridden by the current user settings. Entries are of type REG_SZ or REG_EXPAND_SZ and may include any of the standard Perl environment variables (that is, any variable starting PERL) as described below. We can also specify additional path information to the library include path @INC, in both generic and version specific forms (we use version 5.6.0 here for example purposes) by setting some or all of the entries below:

lib	standard library path extension
sitelib	site library path extension
vendorlib	vendor library path extension
lib-5.6.0	version-specific standard library path extension
sitelib-5.6.0	version-specific site library path extension
vendorlib-5.6.0	version-specific vendor library path extension

General Environment Variables Used by Perl

There are three general environment variables that are used by Perl, which we consider here. The first of these is PATH. This is actually the standard shell search path that Perl uses to locate external commands when executed from Perl scripts. Sensible programs often set this variable internally and do not rely on the supplied value. It is also used by the -S command line option that causes Perl to search for the specified script using the path.

The other two variables are HOME and LOGDIR. If the chdir function is used in Perl without an argument then Perl checks the value of HOME and changes to that directory if set. If HOME is not set, Perl checks LOGDIR as a last resort. If neither is set, chdir does nothing.

Perl Specific Environment Variables

Here we take a brief look at Perl specific environment variables.

The variable PERL5LIB, previously known as PERLLIB, defines the library search path which consists of a list of directories that Perl searches in when the do, require, or use statements are used. The value of this variable becomes @INC inside the program. The old name for this variable, PERLLIB, is only used if PERL5LIB is not set. We can also modify the default value of @INC, defined when Perl was built, using the -I flag.

The environment variable PERL5OPT, as its name may suggest, may contain a list of the command line options, in the same format as they would be if supplied directly.

The variable PERL5DB specifies the command used to load the debugger when the -d option is used. By default this is set to be the code fragment:

```
BEGIN {require 'perl5db.pl'}
```

If we have created our own modified debugger, we can set this variable to have Perl use it by default.

Finally, the last of the most commonly used Perl environment variables is Windows-specific and basically invokes an alternative shell. We use this variable to specify the name of a different command line interpreter, for example when executing external commands with backticks or the qx operator. The default is:

```
command.com /c    (Windows)
cmd.exe /x/c      (Windows NT)
```

Note that in general it is desirable to avoid starting an external shell, and we devote some time in Chapter 14 to the why and how of avoiding shells.

Less commonly used, and generally only of interest to those involved in developing or debugging Perl itself, are the PERL_DESTRUCT_LEVEL and PERL_DEBUG_MSTATS variables, both of which are advanced options. If the Perl interpreter supports the -D flag, PERL_DESTRUCT_LEVEL controls the behavior of Perl's garbage collector for the destruction of references. If Perl was built to use the malloc library that comes supplied with it (perl -V:d_malloc), PERL_DEBUG_MSTATS enables an additional memory statistics debugging mode for the -D flag (which must also be available). If set to a False value, statistics are dumped after the program completes. If set to a True value, statistics are also dumped after the compilation stage and before the execution stage.

Plenty of Perl modules have their own special environment variables that they look out for. For example, to pick a module that is close to the core of Perl, the Perl debugger examines the PERL5DB_OPTS environment variable for configuration information.

Certain Perl features are also sensitive to certain locale environment variables if the use locale directive is specified. See Chapter 26 : Locale and Internationalization towards the latter part of the book for more extensive details.

Summary

In this introductory chapter we have covered the following:

- ❑ A short background of Perl and reasons for its popularity
- ❑ Obtaining and installing Perl on various platforms
- ❑ Some of the many ways in which Perl can be configured and set up to run on various operating systems

Basic Concepts

In this chapter we will give a brief introduction to a number of Perl concepts and definitions, which we will look into in much more detail in the coming chapters. This brief introduction, however, should allow us to use those concepts and definitions before we explore them in depth in their respective chapters.

Values and Variables

All programming languages need a way to manage the data that they manipulate. Data is held as **values**, which are referred to by **variables**. A value is simply any piece of data that can be used in operations or passed to functions within a program. The following are all values:

```
6
3.1415926
"Hello World"
```

These examples, however, are anonymous values, which means they are not associated with any label or identifier. As they are we cannot manipulate them; in order to do this we need variables.

Variables are labels (also known as identifiers) that take and store a value. Once stored, the value can be accessed, manipulated, and processed by referring to the label. In order to identify what kind of value a variable is holding, Perl requires the data type of the variable to be indicated by prefixing it with a punctuation symbol. This is different from languages like C, which use variable declarations. For instance, scalar variables, which we will talk about in a moment, are prefixed with a $, as shown in the following examples (note that the semicolon is not part of the name but a special Perl symbol that indicates the end of a statement):

```
$number;
$name;
```

The label that follows the leading symbol can consist of any mixture of alphanumeric characters and the underscore character, up to a total of 251 characters. However, a variable name cannot start with a number. The following are legal variable names:

```
$A_Scalar_Variable;
$scalarNo8;
$_private_scalar;
```

These variable names are not legal:

```
$8bit_characters;    # leading '8' not legal
$cash_in_£;    # pound symbol not legal
$long-var;    # - not legal
```

Note that the # tells Perl that everything that comes after it to the end of the line is just a comment. Comments are pieces of text that have no effect on the program at either compile or run time. They are provided to describe what the program is doing at that point and to allow the programmer to make notes. Comments are discarded by the Perl run-time interpreter.

Perl has a number of keywords that have special meanings to the language, such as print, which is self-explanatory. Using the names of keywords in variable names can be a source of confusion and should be avoided. $print, for instance, is not a good choice for a scalar name.

Assigning values to variables is done with the equals sign. To assign values to our scalar variables we can write:

```
$number = 6;
$name = "Dave Mercer";
```

Whitespace

In the above examples, we surrounded the assignment with space characters. We don't really need to do that, but it is considered good practice. Perl is very forgiving when it comes to the use of whitespace, that is tabs, spaces, and new lines. We can make the most of this to improve the readability of our code.

However, the use of whitespace in Perl is not without restrictions. Basically, whitespace cannot be used in places where it can confuse Perl. For instance, we cannot use whitespace in file names, so the following file name is not legal:

```
$sca lar;    # ERROR: we may use $scalar or $sca_lar instead.
```

Note that comments are considered white space from the perspective of the code stream.

Data Types

Perl is commonly described as defining three basic data types: **scalars**, **arrays**, and **hashes**. Between them, these three cover most of the kinds of data that a Perl program will manipulate. However, this is not the whole story. Perl also understands the concept of **filehandles, typeglobs** (an amalgam of all the other types) and the **undefined value**, all of which are fundamental to the language. In addition, while **references** and **objects** are both technically types of scalar value, the manner in which Perl treats them means that they can be considered separately.

Scalars are solitary values, such as a number, a string of text or a reference. Unlike more strongly typed languages like C, Perl makes no distinction between numbers and strings and provides no mechanism to define the 'type' of a scalar. Instead Perl freely and automatically converts between different scalar types when they are used, as we shall, in Chapter 3. So, the following are legal declarations of scalar variables:

```
$scalar = 9;
$scalar = 9.5;
$scalar = "I am a scalar";
```

Note from the last example that strings in Perl start and end with some sort of quotation mark. We will read more about scalars in Chapter 3.

The second data type is the **array**. An array is an ordered list of values. Names of arrays are prefixed with the @ symbol. These are examples of arrays:

```
@first_array =   (1, 2, 3, 4);
@second_array =  ('one', '2', 'three', '4', '5');
```

Being **ordered** lists of values, the following arrays are not the same:

```
@array1 =  (1, 2, 3, 4);
@array2 =  (1, 2, 4, 3);
```

Hashes, on the other hand, are lists of pairs of values. Each pair consists of one **key**, associated with one **value**. A hash variable is declared by prefixing it with %. This is an example of a hash:

```
                 key        value
%hash = (Mouse, 'Jerry', Cat, 'Tom', Dog, 'Spike');
```

So, Mouse is a key whose value is Jerry, Tom is the value for the key Cat and Dog is the key of the value Spike. Since hash keys can only be strings, we can omit the quotes around them because Perl will treat them as constant strings.

Perl provides us with the => operator to use with hashes as an alternative to the comma that separates a key from its value, so we can write the above hash as follows:

```
%hash = (Mouse => 'Jerry', Cat => 'Tom', Dog => 'Spike');
```

It is also notable that, unlike elements in array lists, the key-value pairs in a hash are not ordered. So, while we can say that the 'first' element in @array1 is 1, we cannot talk about the 'first' key-value pair of a hash.

Scalars, arrays, and hashes are the main data types of Perl. But, as mentioned earlier, there are other types of data, so let's start with references.

References are not strictly a separate data type. A reference is a value that points to another value, which may be a scalar, array, hash, and so on. So a reference is a pointer that is used to refer indirectly to a value stored somewhere else.

We create a reference for an existing variable by putting a backslash in front of it, as in the following examples:

```
$scalarref = \$scalar;
$arrayref = \@array;
$hashref = \%hash;
```

handwritten annotation: \ creates ref #

Note that whether referencing a scalar, an array, or a hash, we always end up with a scalar, which is obvious from prefixing the names of the references with the dollar sign. Arrays, hashes, and references are investigated in detail in Chapter 5.

The **undefined value**, which is also not strictly a data type, represents a lack of value or data type. It is 'undefined' because it is neither a scalar, list, hash, nor any other data type. We can assign the undefined value to a variable explicitly using the undef function, or implicitly by simply declaring it but not initializing it with a value.

```
$a = undef;
$a;
```

The undefined value is more useful than it at first might seem. One of its primary uses is to indicate situations when no value can legally be returned from a function.

The **typeglob** is a strange beast unique to Perl. It is a kind of super-value, an amalgam of exactly one of each of the other primary data types: scalar, array, hash, filehandle. In addition a typeglob can hold a code reference that is a pointer to a piece of Perl code, for example a subroutine. It can also hold a format, which is a template that can be used with the write function to generate formatted and paginated output. The typeglob is not a single reference to something, rather it has six slots that can contain six different references all at once, hence it is prefixed distinctly with a *. Thus, the typeglob *name contains the values of $name, @name, and %name and other values as well.

Typeglobs are most often used for their ability to hold file and directory handles, since these are sometimes difficult to manipulate otherwise.

The other Perl data type is **filehandle**. A filehandle represents a channel for input and/or output within a Perl program, for instance an open file or a network connection. Unlike the previous data types, filehandles are not prefixed with a special character. One way to create a filehandle is to use the open function as follows:

```
open FILEHANDLE, $filename;
```

This example opens a filehandle called FILEHANDLE to the file called filename, so we can now manipulate this file using its handle.

Finally, we come to **objects**. An object in Perl is a reference that has been marked to be in a particular Perl package. So, it is a specialized type of reference, which is in turn a specialized form of scalar. Objects, therefore, are really scalars. Perl also enables objects to be treated as scalars for the purposes of operations like addition and concatenation. There are two mechanisms for doing this: using Perl's tie function to tie the object underneath a normal-seeming scalar variable, and overloading Perl's operators so the object can be treated like a scalar in some contexts.

We will read more about the undefined value, typeglobs and filehandles in Chapters 5 and 12 respectively.

Special Variables

Perl provides a number of 'special' variables, which are always available from inside any Perl script. For instance, $_ is a variable that many functions read from and write to if no other variable is available, and the hash %ENV contains key-value pairs of the environment variable. Special variables cover such diverse areas as input and output, regular expressions, file handles, system configuration, and errors.

To see a special variable in action, simply issue the following command, which prints the paths to Perl libraries (Windows users need to replace the single quotes with double quotes, and escape the double quotes surrounding the \n):

> **perl -e 'foreach (@INC){print $_, "\n"}'**
/usr/local/lib/perl5/5.6.0/i686-linux-thread-multi
/usr/local/lib/perl5/5.6.0
/usr/local/lib/perl5/site_perl/5.6.0/i686-linux-thread-multi
/usr/local/lib/perl5/site_perl/5.6.0
/usr/local/lib/perl5/site_perl
.
>

The following example prints the value of the environment variable PATH using the special variable %ENV (note the syntax for extracting the value of a key in a hash; hashes are explored in detail in Chapter 5):

> **perl -e 'print $ENV{PATH}'**
/usr/local/bin:/bin:/usr/bin:/usr/X11R6/bin:/home/mankeec/bin>

Some special variables like %ENV and @ARGV, which stores the supplied command line arguments, are reasonably self explanatory. However, the majority of Perl's special variable names are composed of punctuation. In theory most of these are mnemonic so their nature can be determined, but since there are over fifty of them and only so much meaningful punctuation to go around the mnemonic hints are a little stretched. However, there is the English module, which provides a longer, descriptive name for each special variable. For example, $_ is also $ARG, and $. becomes $INPUT_LINE_NUMBER.

For a list of all Perl's special variables and their English names see Appendix B.

Interpolation

When placing a variable inside a double-quoted string, Perl replaces that variable with its value. We call this **variable interpolation**. For instance, the print statement in the following example prints the value the variable $Friday, which is sunny, rather than the word that constitutes the variable name, which is $Friday:

```
#!/usr/bin/perl
# interpolate1.pl
use warnings;

$Friday = "sunny";
print "It is $Friday \n";
```

39

> **perl interpolate1.pl**
It is sunny

However, if we wanted to get the characters $Friday, we can prevent interpolation by prefixing the variable name with a backslash:

```perl
#!/usr/bin/perl
# interpolate2.pl
use warnings;

$Friday = "sunny";
print "It is \$Friday \n";
```

Now if we run this we get It is \$Friday preceded by a warning that the scalar $Friday was used only once. For the moment don't worry about this warning; we will discuss it in Chapter 16.

Alternatively, we could use non-interpolating quotes to prevent the variable from being interpolated. In that case our print statement will look like this:

```perl
print 'It is $Friday \n';
```

The output we get from this is:

It is $Friday \n>

You'll notice that Perl has printed out the \n. The reason for this is that, in addition to variables, Perl has a number of special combinations of characters that have special meanings, and as a result they are interpolated to their meanings when placed inside double quotes. The \n in the above example is one such case which means 'a new line'. If we wanted to print the \n then we have to escape it with a backslash. Perl supports the standard conventions for special characters like tabs and newlines first established by C. All of these are converted into the appropriate characters when they are seen by Perl in a double quoted string. For example, for tabs and returns we use \t and \r.

Interpolating an array variable will cause each element to be converted into text and placed into the resulting string.

There is a lot more to interpolation than this, however, and it is in fact a more complex and versatile part of Perl than many people realise. Accordingly we devote a good chunk of Chapter 11 to covering the subject of interpolation in depth, including inserting character codes, interpolating source code, and interpolating text more than once.

Context

An important concept in Perl is the idea of context. This is the context in which a Perl variable or section of Perl code is evaluated, and indicates the type of value that is wanted in a given situation.

Perl has three different contexts, scalar, list, and void. Which one applies depends on the way in which the value is being used (as opposed to what it actually is). In **scalar context**, a single scalar value is required. In **list context**, a list of values (zero or more) is required.

Finally, when no value of any kind is required, we call this **void context**.

Scalar and List Context

Most of the time we will be dealing with scalar and list context. The most obvious example of context is when we assign to a variable. The data type of the variable, be it scalar, array, or hash defines the context. The following shows a scalar value being used in a scalar context:

```
$variable = "One value";
```

Similarly, this example shows a list value (defined by the enclosing parentheses) in list context:

```
@variable = ('a', 'list', 'of', 'strings');
```

If we assign a list to a scalar, we cause it to be evaluated in scalar context. Since a scalar cannot store a list, only the last value is recorded:

```
$variable = ('a', 'list', 'of', 'strings');
print $variable;   # returns 'strings'
```

Arrays are slightly different; using one in scalar context counts and returns the number of elements instead:

```
$count = @variable;   # returns 4 for @variable above.
```

Just as we can assign a list in a scalar context, we can assign a scalar value in a list context:

```
@array = "One value";
```

In this case the scalar value One value is converted into a list with exactly one value in it, and assigned to the variable @array. So the above is exactly equivalent, but not as clearly expressed, as using parentheses to explicitly define the value as a list:

```
@array = ("One value");
```

Hash variables are assigned in list context too, with each pair of values being assigned as the key and value of a hash element:

```
%permissions = (read => 4, write => 2, execute => 1);
```

Assigning a scalar value defines a hash with one key paired with an undefined value, as in the following example:

```
#!/usr/bin/perl
# novalue.pl
use warnings;

%hash = "One value";
print "$hash{'One value'}\n"
```

Since we have warnings switched on (something that we should always do), when we run this script, Perl will complain of Odd number of elements in hash assignment at novalue.pl line 4.

Void Context

More rarely encountered is the void context. Generally, we only come across this in statements that perform an action of their own, such as a `print` statement:

```
print "Out of Context Problem";
```

Although it is almost always ignored, `print` actually returns a value to indicate success or failure. So this is actually an example of a scalar value in a void context. It is even more common to encounter the void context unintentionally. If we accidentally write a Perl program with a value in it, but forget to assign it or use it, when we run it, we get a warning from Perl (but only if we have warnings switched on):

```
#!/usr/bin/perl
# void.pl
use warnings;

"Out of Context Problem";    #oops, forgot the 'print'
```

> **perl void.pl**
Useless use of a constant in void context ...

A `print` statement does not produce this error because it does something useful – printing. A warning like this indicates a value or variable that is not being used in any way and is usually a sign that there is a problem in the code.

Perl provides a special built-in function called `wantarray` for subroutines to determine what kind of context the subroutine was called in – scalar, list, or void. Subroutines are introduced later in this chapter and explored in detail in Chapter 7.

Operators

The most basic of the tools that Perl uses to manipulate values and variables are operators. There are two main groups of operators to be used with the two main types of data (numbers and strings). The assignment symbol that we have been using to assign values to variables is one such operator.

Numerical operators include those that enable us to perform operations like addition, subtraction, multiplication, division, and raising powers as shown in the following examples:

```
$scalar = 4 + 5;    # $scalar is equal to 9.
$scalar = 4 ** 5;   # $scalar is equal to 1024.
$scalar = 4 * 5;    # $scalar is equal to 20.
```

While operators such as + and * act on two operands, other numerical operators are unary, requiring only one operand, such as the ++ and -- operators that are used to increment and decrement their operands:

```
$scalar = 20 / 4;   # $scalar is equal to 5.
$scalar ++;   # $scalar is now 6.
```

Similarly, using string operators we can do things such as concatenating strings. The Perl operator for concatenation is the dot character, as in the following example:

```
print "P" . "e" . "r" . "l"; # prints 'Perl'.
```

We will read more on operators in Chapter 4.

Blocks

A block in Perl is a unit that consists of several statements and/or smaller blocks. We define blocks by enclosing their contents in curly braces, as in the following example:

```
#!/usr/bin/perl
# block.pl
use warnings;

{
    print "This is a first level block. \n";
    {
        print "   This is a second level block. \n";
    }
}
```

Note that we do not need to end blocks with a semicolon. We will look in detail at blocks in Chapter 6.

Control Constructs

Perl provides us with a number of constructs, which we can use to control how our program behaves under a given condition. These control constructs make use of the concept of blocks. One such tool is the if statement, which allows us to execute the statements inside a block *if* a particular condition is met, as demonstrated in this example:

```
#!/usr/bin/perl
# if1.pl
use warnings;

$input=<>;
if ($input >= 5 ) {
    print "The input number is equal to or greater than 5 \n";
}
```

We use the operator >= to test whether our input was 5 or greater. If so, the block containing the print statement is executed. Otherwise, the program doesn't execute the block.

Note that we have used what is known as the **diamond operator** <> in our example above. This operator allows us to read a line at a time from the standard input (this is usually the keyboard, though it could be a file). This is why the construction <> is also known as the **readline operator**.

We can create a more flexible version of if by combining it with else, as shown in the new version of our previous example:

```perl
#!/usr/bin/perl
# ifelse.pl
use warnings;

$input=<>;
if ($input >= 5 ) {
    print "The input number is equal to or greater than 5 \n";
} else {
    print "The input number is less than  5 \n";
}
```

Another very useful looping tool is the foreach statement. This control statement loops through a list, executing a block for each value of that list:

```perl
#!/usr/bin/perl
# foreach1.pl
use warnings;

@array = ("one", "two", "three", "four");
foreach $iterator (@array) {
    print "The value of the iterator is now $iterator \n";
}
```

> **perl foreach.pl**
The value of the iterator is now one
The value of the iterator is now two
The value of the iterator is now three
The value of the iterator is now four

Earlier we mentioned the special variable $_ and we said that many functions read from this variable and write to it in the absence of any other variable. So, let's see how we can modify our above example to use $_:

```perl
#!/usr/bin/perl
# foreach2.pl
use warnings;

@array = ("one", "two", "three", "four");
foreach (@array) {
    print "The value of the iterator is now $_ \n";
}
```

Having not stated explicitly our iterator, Perl has used $_ as the iterator, something that we can test by printing $_.

Control constructs and loops are explored in depth in Chapter 6.

Loop Modifiers

At times we need to change the course of execution of a loop from within the loop. There are three loop modifiers that we can use to alter the flow of execution of a loop.

The first loop modifier is next, which corresponds to continue in the C language. next starts the next iteration of the loop, stopping the processing of any code in the loop in the current iteration. Consider for example this modification to the first of our two previous foreach examples:

```
#!/usr/bin/perl
# next.pl
use warnings;

@array = ("one", "two", "three", "four");
foreach $iterator (@array) {
    if ($iterator eq "three") {
    next;
    }
    print "The value of the iterator is now $iterator \n";
}
```

The if statement tests if the value of $iterator is equal to three using the string comparison operator eq which stands for 'equals to'. When the condition is met, next is executed, causing the program to abandon the rest of the code inside the foreach loop, that is the print function, and starting the next iteration with the fourth element of @array, four. Therefore, running this program would produce this:

> **perl next.pl**
The value of the iterator is now one
The value of the iterator is now two
The value of the iterator is now four

Perl also provides us with an equivalent for the break statement in C. The effect of last is simply to exit the loop. Let's modify the above example to use last:

```
#!/usr/bin/perl
# last.pl
use warnings;

@array = ("one", "two", "three", "four");
foreach $iterator (@array) {
    if ($iterator eq "three") {
    last;
    }
    print "The value of the iterator is now $iterator \n";
}
```

> **perl last.pl**
The value of the iterator is now one
The value of the iterator is now two

45

Finally, redo restarts the loop block without evaluating the conditional again. Without redo, the following example would print Hello 1 and exit because of the presence of last:

```
$n = 1; { print "Hello $n \n";
last if (++$n > 3); redo; }
```

However, this is the output that we get as a result for the presence of redo:

Hello 1
Hello 2
Hello 3

Loop modifiers are explained in detail in Chapter 6.

Subroutines

A subroutine is a section of code, which we place inside our main script and can call upon to perform a particular task. Subroutines are particularly good to use for repeated tasks, because we don't need to repeat the same piece of code every now and then in our program. Because of their effectively independent nature, they can be copied across to other programs, making them reusable. Subroutines allow us to write well-structured, useable and maintainable scripts.

Intuitively, subroutines are declared with the keyword sub followed by the subroutine name, and then a block. This is an example:

```
sub my_sub {
print "Hi \n";
}
```

The subroutine called my_sub does nothing other than printing the word Hi. However, its presence inside our program won't automatically cause it to execute, unless we call upon it. We do that by simply using its name:

```
my_sub;
```

Subroutines are usually passed parameters to perform some tasks with and then return a result. For example, this subroutine calculates the factorial of the number passed to it and then returns the result to the main program:

```
#!/usr/bin/perl
# factorial.pl
use warnings;

# read the value of the number $input from the standard input
$input=<>;

# call the subroutine with $input as its argument
factorial($input);
```

```
# The subroutine
sub factorial {
$step=1;
$result=1;
    while ($step <= $input) {
    $result=$result*$step;
    $step++;    # this is equivalent to '$step = $step + 1';
    }
# if $input is zero then $result is also zero
if ($input == 0) {
$result = 0;
}
return $result;
}

print "The result is $result \n";
```

Note that we have used the while loop to test the value of $step and see whether it is less than or equal to the $input, and if it is then the product of the multiplication is updated using the current value of $step. The value of $step is then incremented, and the loop is repeated. Once $step becomes greater than $input, the program exits the while loop and executes the return function. The if test is carried out to make sure that $result is equal to zero when $input is zero.

For more on subroutines see Chapter 7.

Functions

Functions are very similar to subroutines. However, this term is usually used in Perl to refer to built-in tools that we can call on to perform certain tasks. We have already come across some functions, such as the undef function, which assigns the undefined values to variables. The previous example used the function return to return a value from the subroutine.

Perl has a large number of functions to handle various tasks. We will use many of those functions throughout the book. For a comprehensive list of all functions see Appendix C.

Scoping

Any variable created in a Perl program is global by default. **Global variables** can be seen and manipulated from anywhere in the program. For instance, the hash %hash in the novalue.pl program (from earlier) is a global variable. However, there are situations where we would like to localize our variables. Suppose we have a scalar called $input that we would like to use in several places in our program to store input from the user. If we do this while $input is a global variable then we will lose its previous value whenever we get new input from the user, unless of course we have saved the previous input in another variable.

The need to localize the scope of a variable becomes more apparent when we deal with subroutines, which are sections of code that we use from time to time for a particular task before returning to our main program. Perl has a solution for this – **lexical variables**.

Lexical variables exist only inside the block in which they are declared and all other blocks inside that main block. A variable is declared as lexical with the keyword my. Let's have a look at an example:

```perl
#!/usr/bin/perl
# scope1.pl
use warnings;

$scalar = "global";
$Second_Global = "Another Global";
print "Outside the block, \$scalar is a $scalar variable \n";
{
        my $scalar = "lexical";
        my $other_scalar = "I am also lexical";
        print "Inside the block, \$scalar\ is a $scalar variable \n";
}
print "Outside the block, \$scalar is that same $scalar variable \n";
print "\$Second_Global is $Second_Global \n";
```

> **perl scope1.pl**
Outside the block, $scalar is a global variable
Inside the block, $scalar is a lexical variable
$Second_Global is Another Global
Outside the block, $scalar is that same global variable

In the above example, the lexical variable $scalar that occurs inside the block is completely different from the global variable, which was declared in the main program, and carries the same name. If we add a print statement to our above program, outside the block, that prints out the value of the lexical variable $other_scalar, Perl will give us the complaint Name "main::other_scalar" used only once, because that variable wasn't declared in the main program. On the other hand, because $Second_Global is a global variable it can be seen inside the block.

Perl also provides the strict module that we can use to force ourselves to declare all our variables before using them. If we use the strict model in our above program we will have to declare the global variable $scalar with the keyword our, just like using my for lexical variables. So, with strict turned on, this is how our example looks now:

```perl
#!/usr/bin/perl
# scope1.pl
use warnings;
use strict;

our $scalar = "global";
print "Outside the block, \$scalar is a $scalar variable \n";
{
        my $scalar = "lexical";
        my $other_scalar = "I am also lexical";
        print "Inside the block, \$scalar\ is a $scalar variable \n";
}
print "Outside the block, \$scalar is that same $scalar variable \n";
```

It is always good practice to enable strict and warnings in our programs, something that we will adhere to in the examples of the book. It is also better to avoid using global variables, because it can lead to conflicts and confusion if we inadvertently change the value of a global variable from within one of our blocks.

For more on scoping, see Chapter 8.

3

Scalars

In this chapter, we start our exploration of Perl data types with one of the main data types: scalars.

Scalar values may be subdivided into three primary groups: **numbers**, which in turn may be integer or floating-point values, **strings**, and **references**, which are pointers to values stored elsewhere. Of these three, the first two are what we might call 'normal' scalar values. References are sufficiently different in the way they work as to be considered almost a different data type. Perl's objects are references in disguise, so they can also be considered different. When we talk about scalars, therefore, we usually, but not always, mean numbers or strings. We will talk about references in Chapter 5.

In this chapter we take a detailed look at numbers and strings, and see how Perl handles them. We will also cover the various operators we use in order to manipulate numbers and strings.

Value Conversion and Caching

Perl does not make a strong distinction between numbers and strings. In fact, it allows a scalar variable to store its value as an integer, a floating-point number, and a string simultaneously. When a scalar variable is first assigned only one representation is known. When the scalar is used with an operator that expects a different representation, Perl automatically performs the conversion behind the scenes, and then caches the result inside the scalar. The original value is not altered, so the variable now has two representations of the same value. If the same conversion is needed again, Perl can retrieve the previously cached conversion instead of doing it all over again.

The same automatic conversion also happens to values that are not being accessed via a variable. However, in this case, Perl cannot cache the result of a conversion because there is no variable in which to store it.

To illustrate how Perl handles conversions, consider the assignment of an integer value to a scalar variable:

```
$number = 3141;
```

This stores an integer value inside the variable. The scalar is now combined into a string by concatenating it with another string using the dot operator:

```
$text = $number.' is a thousand PIs';
```

This causes Perl to convert the scalar into a string, since concatenation only works between strings, not numbers. The converted string representation is *cached* inside the scalar alongside the integer representation. So, if the scalar is requested as a string a second time, Perl does not need to redo the conversion, it just retrieves the string representation.

The same principle works for floating-point numbers too. Here we divide the same scalar by 1000, which requires that it be converted to a floating-point number:

```
$new_number = $number/1000;
```

So, our scalar variable has three different representations of its value stored internally. If the variable is reassigned, then one of the representations is updated and the other two are marked as no longer valid:

```
$number = "Number Six";
```

In this case, the previous integer and floating-point number values of $number are now invalid.

All this behind-the-scenes shuffling may seem convoluted, but it allows Perl to optimize the retrieval and processing of scalar values in our programs, thereby allowing them to run faster. It also allows us to write simpler and more legible programs, because we do not have to worry about converting the type of a scalar in order to meet the expectations of the language.

Numbers

As we stated earlier, numbers fall into one of two categories, integer, or floating-point. In addition, both types of number can be represented as a numerical string, which is converted to the appropriate format when used.

As well as handling integers in base 10, or decimal, numbers may be expressed and displayed in binary, octal, and hexadecimal formats, all of which Perl handles transparently. Conversely, displaying numbers in a different base requires converting them into a string with the correct representation, so this is actually a special case of an integer to string conversion.

In many cases, calculations will produce floating-point results, even if the numbers are integers; for example division by another integer that does not divide evenly. Additionally, the range of floating-point numbers exceeds that of integers, so Perl sometimes returns a floating-point number if the result of a calculation exceeds the range in which Perl can store integers internally, as determined by the underlying platform.

Integers

Integers are one of the two types of numerical value that Perl deals with. When written explicitly, integers are usually expressed as decimal (base 10) integers but can be specified in several different formats:

Number	Format
123	regular decimal integer
0b1101	binary integer
0127	octal integer
0xabcd	hexadecimal integer
12_345	underscore annotated integer
0xca_fe_ba_be	underscore annotated hexadecimal integer

It is also possible to specify an integer value as a string. When used in an integer context the string value is translated into an integer before it is used:

```
"123"   # regular decimal integer expressed as a string
```

The underscore notation is permitted in integers in order to allow them to be written more legibly. Ordinarily we would use commas for this:

```
10,023
```

However, in Perl, the comma is used as a list separator, so this would represent the value 10 followed by the value 23. In order to make up for this, Perl allows underscores to be used instead:

```
10_023
```

Underscores are not required to occur at regular intervals, nor are they restricted to decimal numbers. As the hexadecimal example above illustrates, they can also be used to separate out the individual bytes in a 32 bit hexadecimal integer. It is legal to put an underscore anywhere in an integer except at the start:

```
1_2_3   # ok
123_    # trailing underscore also ok
_123    # leading underscore makes '_123' an identifier - not a number!
```

Integer Range and Big Integers

When Perl stores an integer value as an integer (as opposed to a numerical string), the maximum size of the integer value is limited by the maximum size of integers on the underlying platform. On a 32-bit architecture this means integers can range from:

```
0 to 4294967295 (unsigned)
-2147483648 to 2147483647 (signed)
```

Perl can take advantage of 64-bit integers on platforms that support them, but only if it has been built to support them.

If an integer calculation falls outside the range that integers can support then Perl automatically converts the result to a floating-point format. An example of such a calculation is:

```
print "2 to the power of 100:1 against and falling: ", 2**100;
```

This results in a number larger than integers can handle, so Perl produces a floating-point result and prints the message:

2 to the power of 100:1 against and falling: 1.26765060022823e+30

Because the accuracy of the floating-point number is limited by the number of significant digits it can hold (which is determined by the capabilities of the underlying platform), this result is actually only an approximation of the value 2**100. While it is perfectly possible to *store* a large integer in a floating-point number or a string (which has no limitations on the number of digits and so can store an integer of any length accurately), we cannot necessarily *use* that number in a numerical calculation without losing some of the precision. Perl must convert the string into an integer or, if that is not possible due to range limitations, a floating-point number in order to perform the calculation. Because floating-point numbers cannot always represent integers perfectly, this results in calculations that can be imprecise.

Fortunately Perl provides a solution to this dilemma. To avoid conversion of large integers into floating-point numbers we can make use of the Math::BigInt package, which comes as part of the standard Perl library; basic use of packages will be described more fully in Chapter 9. Math::BigInt works by storing integers in a string format and applying specialized computational codes to manipulate them. In this way it can handle arbitrarily large numbers, albeit much more slowly than conventional integer arithmetic.

Converting Integers into Floating-Point Numbers

To convert an integer into a floating-point number is straightforward. No special function or operation is required; we can just multiply (or divide) it by 1:

```
$float = 1 * $integer;
```

Multiplication is a floating-point operation, so this gives both scalars a floating-point representation internally. We can prove this by using Dump from the Devel::Peek (which is covered in Chapter 20) module if we really want to, although if we print out $float we still get '1' and nothing appears to have happened. The reason for this is that it is the most efficient way to display '1', even if it is a floating-point value. However this conversion is almost always unnecessary. If we just want to use the number in a floating-point calculation, Perl will do the conversion automatically.

Converting Integers into Strings

Just as with floating-point numbers we do not usually have to convert integers into strings since Perl will do it for us as and when required. However, if we want to impose different formatting requirements, this automatic conversion may not be enough.

For instance, one reason for converting a number into a string explicitly is to pad it with leading spaces or zeros (to align columns in a table, or print out a uniform date format). This is a task for sprintf, a generic string formatter inspired by (though not actually based on) the C function of the same name, and which we cover in detail under 'String Formatting', in the strings section later in the chapter. It works using special tokens or 'placeholders' to describe how various values, including numbers, should be rendered textually.

Formatting of integer values is carried out by the %..d and %0..d placeholders. Here .. is a numeric value that describes the desired width of the resulting text, such as %4d for a width of 4 characters. The 0, if present, tells sprintf to pad the number with leading zeros rather than spaces:

```
printf '%d/%d/%d', 2000, 7, 4;      # displays "2000/7/4"
printf '%d/%2d/%2d', 2000, 7, 4;    # displays "2000/ 7/ 4"
printf '%d/%02d/%02d', 2000, 7, 4;  # displays "2000/07/04"
```

Other characters can be added to the placeholder to handle other cases. For instance, if the number is negative, a minus sign is automatically prefixed, which will cause a column of mixed signs to be misaligned. However, if a space or + is added to the start of the placeholder definition, positive numbers will be padded, with a space or + respectively:

```
printf '% 2d', $number;    # pad with leading space if positive
printf '%+2d', $number;    # prefix a '+' sign if positive
```

Handling Different Number Bases

As well as base 10 integers, Perl allows numbers to be expressed in octal (base 8), hexadecimal (base 16) and binary. To express a number in octal, prefix it with a leading zero, for example:

```
0123    # 123 octal (83 decimal)
```

Similarly we can express numbers in hexadecimal using a prefix of 0x:

```
0x123    # 123 hexadecimal (291 decimal)
```

Finally, from Perl 5.6 onwards, we can express numbers in binary with a prefix of 0b:

```
0b1010011    # 1010011 binary (83 decimal)
```

Converting a number into a string that contains the binary, octal, or hexadecimal representation of that number can be achieved with Perl's sprintf function. As mentioned above, sprintf takes a format string containing a list of one or more placeholders, and a list of scalars to fill those placeholders. The type of placeholder defines the conversion that each scalar must undergo to be converted into a string.

Numbers are converted into decimal strings when used in a string context, which is equivalent to using the %d placeholder:

```
$number = 6;
$text = sprintf '%d', $number;    # convert number to integer string
```

We would rarely (if ever) want to do this, however, because Perl automatic conversions will do the job for us when we use the scalar in a string context. In this example the scalar variables $text and $number are effectively set to the same value, but with different internal representations. From the perspective of the programmer, however, they are identical.

To convert into a different base, we just use a different placeholder, %b, %o, %x, or %X:

```
$bintext = sprintf '%b', $number;    # convert to binary string (5.6.0+ only)
$octtext = sprintf '%o', $number;    # convert into octal string
$hextext = sprintf '%x', $number;    # convert into lower case hexadecimal
$hextext = sprintf '%X', $number;    # convert into upper case hexadecimal
```

Note that `sprintf` (and its relative `printf`) do not prefix their conversions with the appropriate number base prefix (0, 0x, or 0b) and so do not produce strings that convert back using the same base as they were created with. In order to fix that problem we have to add the base prefix ourselves:

```
$bintext = sprintf '0b%b', 83;   # produces '0b1010011'
$octtext = sprintf '0%o', 83;    # produces '0123'
$hextext = sprintf '0x%bx', 83;   # produces '0x53'
```

The `%b` placeholder is only available from Perl version 5.6.0 onwards. Versions of Perl prior to this do not have a simple way to generate binary numbers and have to resort to somewhat unwieldy expressions using the pack and unpack functions. This is covered in more detail in the section entitled 'Pack and Unpack' later.

```
$bintext = unpack("B32", pack("N", $number));
```

This handles 32-bit values. If we know that the number is smaller, that is, it will fit into a `short` integer, we can get away with fewer bits:

```
$smallbintext = unpack("B16", pack("n", $number));
```

Unfortunately for small values this is still likely to leave a lot of leading zeros, since unpack has no idea what the most significant bit actually is, and so it just ploughs through all 16 or 32 bits regardless. The number '3' would be converted into:

```
'0000000000000011'   # '3' as a 16-bit binary string
```

We can remove those leading zeros using the string functions `substring` and `index`:

```
#hunt for and return string from the first '1' onwards

$smallbintext = substring($smallbintext, index($smallbintext, '1'));
```

Though this works, it is certainly not as elegant (or as fast) as using `sprintf`; upgrading Perl may be a better idea than using this work-around.

Floating-Point Numbers

Perl allows floating-point numbers to be written in one of two forms, either fixed point, where the decimal point is fixed in the number to indicate where the fractional part starts, or scientific, consisting of a mantissa with the actual number value, and an exponent representing the power of 10 that the mantissa is multiplied by:

```
123.45   # fixed point
-1.2345e2   # scientific, lowercase, negative
+1.2345E2   # scientific, uppercase, explicitly positive
```

Likewise, fractions can be expressed either in fixed-point notation or as a negative exponent:

```
0.000034   # fixed point
-3.4e-4   # scientific, lowercase, negative
+3.4E-4   # scientific, uppercase, explicitly positive
```

Floating-point numbers can be expressed over a very large range:

```
1e100    # a 'googol' or 1 x 10(100)
3.141    # 3.141 x 10(0)
1.6e-22  # 0.00000000000000000000000016
```

A googol is actually the correct mathematical term for this number (1e100), believe it or not. Likewise, a 'googolplex' is 10 to the power of a googol, or 10(10)(100), which is hard for both humans and programming languages to handle.

Floating-point numbers are used to store what in mathematical terms are called real numbers, the set of all possible values. The accuracy of floating-point numbers is limited, so they cannot represent all real numbers. However, they are capable of a wider range of values than integers, both in terms of accuracy and in terms of scale.

In general integers are represented internally as four-byte binary numbers, with the highest bit reserved for the sign. Floating points by contrast are usually held in eight bytes, with 11 bits reserved for the exponent, leaving 53 for the mantissa. This allows floating-point numbers to express a much larger range of values, though not every possible value in that range.

The above example of 1e100 is mathematically an integer, but it is one that Perl's integer representation is unable to handle, since one hundred consecutive zeros is considerably beyond the maximum value of 4294967295 that integers can manage on most platforms. For a floating-point number however it is trivial, since an exponent of 100 coupled to a mantissa of '1' represents the value perfectly.

The standard C library of the underlying platform on which Perl is running determines the range of floating-point numbers. On most platforms floating-point numbers are handled and stored as 'doubles', double accuracy 8-byte (64-bit) values, though the actual calculations performed by the hardware may use more bits. Of these 64 bits, eleven are reserved for the exponent, which can range from two to the power of -1024 to +1024, which equates to a range of around ten to the power of -308 to +308. The remaining 53 are assigned to the mantissa, so floating-point numbers can represent values up to fifty three binary places long. That equates to fifteen or sixteen decimal places, depending on the exact value.

However, just because a value is within the range of floating numbers does not mean that can represent it accurately. Unforeseen complications can arise when using floating-point numbers to perform calculations. This comes about because while Perl understands and displays floating-point numbers in decimal (base 10), it stores them internally in binary (base 2). Fractional numbers expressed in one base cannot always be accurately expressed in another, even if their representation seems very simple. This can lead to slight differences between answer that Perl calculates and the one we might expect.

To give an example, consider the floating-point number 0.9. This is easy to express in decimal, but in binary this works out to:

0.111001101101101101101101101101101101101101110....

That is, a recurring number. This is because floating-point numbers may hold a finite number of 53 binary digits; we cannot accurately represent this number in the mantissa alone. As it happens, 0.9 can be accurately represented as 9e-1: a mantissa of '9' with an exponent of '-1', but this is not always the case. Consequently calculations involving floating-point values, and especially comparisons to integers and other floating-point numbers, do not always behave as we expect.

Converting Floats into Integers

The quickest and simplest way to convert floating-point numbers into integers is to use the `int` function. This strips off the fractional part of the floating-point number and returns the integer part:

```
$int = int($float);
```

However, `int` is not very intelligent about how it calculates the integer part. First, it truncates the fractional part of a floating-point number and so only rounds down, which may not be what we want. Second, it does not take into account the problems of precision, which can affect the result of floating-point calculations. For example, the following calculation produces different results if we return the answer as an integer, even though the resulting calculation ought to result in a round number:

```
$number = 4.05/0.05;
print "$number \n";    # returns 81, correct
print int($number);    # returns 80, incorrect!
```

Similarly, a comparison operator (see Chapter 4) will tell us that `$number` is not really equal to 81:

```
$number = 4.05/0.05;
# if $number is not equal to 81 then execute the print statement
# in the block
if ($number != 81) {
    print "\$number is not equal to 81 \n";
}
```

The reason for this is that `$number` does not actually have the value 81 but a floating-point value that is very slightly less than 81. When we display it, the conversion to string format handles the slight discrepancy for us and we see the result we expect.

To round the above to the nearest integer rather than the next highest or next lowest, we can add 0.5 to our value and then round it down:

```
print int($number+0.5);    # returns 81, correct
```

We can also use the `floor` and `ceil` functions of the standard C library through the `POSIX` module. `floor` works exactly like `int` (and with the same rounding problems) rounding to the next lowest integer, whereas `ceil` rounds to the next highest integer. The difference is that the values returned from these functions are floating-point values, not integers. That is, though they appear the same to us, the internal representation is different.

Converting Floats into Strings

As mentioned earlier, Perl automatically converts floating-point numbers into strings when they are used in a string context, for example:

```
print "The answer is $floatnum";
```

The number is converted into string format according to the values of the mantissa and exponent. If the number can be represented as an integer, Perl converts it before printing:

```
$floatnum = 4.3e12;    # The answer is 4300000000000
```

Alternatively, if the number is a fraction that can be expressed as a fixed decimal (that is, purely in terms of a mantissa without an exponent), Perl converts it into that format:

```
$floatnum = 4.3e-3;    # The answer is 0.0043
```

Otherwise it is converted into the 'standard' mantissa+exponent form:

```
$floatnum = 4.3e99;    # The answer is 4.3e99
```

Sometimes we might want to alter the format of the generated text, to force consistency across a range of values or to present a floating-point value in a different format. The sprintf and printf functions can do this for us, and provide several placeholder formats designed for floating-point output:

```
printf '%e', $floatnum;    # force conversion to fixed decimal format
printf '%f', $floatnum;    # force conversion to mantissa/exponent format
printf '%g', $floatnum;    # use fixed if accurately possible, otherwise
```

Perl's default conversion of floating-point numbers is therefore equivalent to:

```
$floatstr = sprintf '%g', $floatnum;
```

A field width can be inserted into the format string to indicate the desired width of the resulting number text. Additionally, a decimal point and second number can be used to indicate the width of the fractional part. We can use this to force a consistent display of all our numbers:

```
printf '%6.3f', 3.14159;    # display a minimum width of 6 with 3
                            # decimal places; produces ' 3.142'
```

The width, 6, in the above example, includes the decimal point and the leading minus sign if the number happens to be negative. This is fine if we only expect our numbers to range from 99.999 to -9.999, but printf will exceed this width if the whole part of the number exceeds the width remaining (two characters) after the decimal point and three fractional digits have taken their share. Allowing a sufficient width for all possible values is therefore important if sprintf and printf are to work as we want them to.

Just as with integers, we can prefix the format with a space or + to have positive numbers format to the same width as negative ones:

```
printf '% 7.3f', 3,14159;    # pad with leading space if positive,
                             # produces '  3.142'
printf '%+7.3f', 3.14159;    # prefix a '+' sign if positive,
                             # produces ' +3.142'
printf '%07.3f', 3.14159;    # prefix with leading zeros,
                             # produces '003.142'
printf '% 07.3f', 3.14159;   # pad with a leading space, then leading zeros,
                             # produces ' 03.142'
printf '%+07.3f', 3.14159;   # pad with a leading +, then leading zeros,
                             # produces '+03.142'
```

The 'use integer' Pragma

We discussed earlier how Perl automatically converts between integers, strings, and floating-point numbers as and when it needs to. However, we might specifically want an integer, either because we want a result in round numbers or simply for speed. One way to restrict the result of a calculation to integers is to use the int function, as shown in 'Converting Floats into Integers' earlier.

This still requires Perl to do the calculation with floating-point numbers, since it does not know any different. If the underlying hardware does not support floating-point operations (rare, but still possible in embedded systems) this can result in unnecessarily slow calculations when much faster integer calculations could be used. To remedy this situation and allow Perl to intelligently use integers where possible, we can encourage integer calculations with the use integer pragma:

```
use integer;
$integer_result = $nominator / $divisor;
```

While use integer is in effect, all calculations that would normally produce floating-point results but are capable of working with integers will operate interpreting their operands as integers. This applies even to simple assignments:

```
use integer;
$PI = 3.1415926;   # sets $PI to '3'
print $PI;   # prints '3.1415926'
print $PI + 5;   # prints '8'
```

We can switch off integer-only arithmetic again by writing a no integer, which cancels out the effect of a previous use integer. This allows us to write sections (or blocks) of code that are integer only, but leave the rest of the program using floating-point numbers as usual, or vice versa. For example:

```
sub integersub {
   use integer;
   ...integer only code...
   {
   no integer;
    floating-point in this block
   }
   ...more integer only code...
}
```

Using use integer can have some unexpected side-effects. While it is in effect Perl passes integer calculations to the underlying system (which means the standard C library for the platform on which Perl was built) rather than doing them itself. That might not always produce exactly the same result as Perl would, for example:

```
print -13 % 7;   # produces '1'

use integer;
print -13 % 7;   # produces '-6'
```

The reason for this behavior is that Perl and the standard C library have slightly different perspectives on how the modulus of a negative number is calculated. The fact that, by its nature, a modulus calculation cannot produce a floating-point result does not alter the fact that use integer affects its operation.

Even with use integer enabled, Perl will still produce a floating-point number if an integer result makes no sense or if the result would otherwise be out of range. For example:

```
use integer;
print sqrt(2);   # produces 1.4142135623731
print 2 ** 100;  # produces 1.26765060022823e+030
```

use integer has one final effect that is not immediately obvious: It disables Perl's automatic interpretation of bitwise operations as unsigned, so results that set the highest bit (that is, the 32nd bit in a 32 bit architecture) will be interpreted by Perl as signed rather than unsigned values:

```
print ~0, ' ',-1 << 0;   # produces '4294967295 4294967295'

use integer;
print ~0, ' ',-1 << 0;   # produces '-1 -1'
```

This can be useful behavior if we want it, but is a potential trap for the unwary.

Mathematical Functions

Perl provides a number of mathematical functions for managing numbers. We look in this section at some of the most commonly used.

The abs function returns the absolute (unsigned) value of a number:

```
print abs(-6.3);   # absolute value, produces 6.3
```

Perl provides three functions for computing powers and logarithms, in addition to the ** exponentiation operator. They are:

```
print sqrt(6.3);   # square root, produces 2.50998007960223
print exp(6.3);    # raise 'e' to the power of, produces 544.571910125929
print log(6.3);    # natural (base 'e') logarithm, produces 1.84054963339749
```

Perl's support for logarithms only extends to base (e) natural logarithms. To work in other bases, we divide the natural log of the number by the natural log of the base, that is:

```
$n=2;
$base = 10;
print log($n) / log($base);    # calculate and print log(10)2
```

For the specific case of base 10 logarithms, the standard C library defines a base 10 logarithm function that we can use via the POSIX module as log10:

```
use POSIX qw(log10);
print log10($n);   # calculate and print log(10)2
```

Perl provides three built-in trigonometric functions: sin, cos, and atan2 for the sine, cosine and arctangent of an angle, respectively. Perl does not provide built-in inverse functions for these three, nor does it provide the standard tan function, because these can all be worked out easily (ignoring issues of ranges, domains, and result quadrants):

```
atan2($n, sqrt(1 - $n ** 2))    # asin (inverse sine)
atan2(sqrt(1 - $n ** 2), $n)    # acos (inverse cosine)
sin($n) / cos($n)   # tan
```

We can easily define subroutines to provide these calculations, but to save us the trouble of writing our own trigonometric functions Perl provides a full set of basic trigonometric functions in the `Math::Trig` module, as well as utility subroutines for converting between degrees and radians and between radial and Cartesian coordinates.

Strings

Perl provides comprehensive support for strings, including interpolation, regular expression processing, and even a selection of ways to specify them. Arguably, string processing is Perl's single biggest strength, and accordingly much of this book is concerned with it in one way or another, notably Chapter 18.

In version 5.6 Perl gained the ability to handle Unicode characters not only in scalar variables and literally specified text, but also throughout, even including variable and subroutine names. We cover this in Chapter 25, along with other internationalization issues in Chapter 26.

Quotes and Quoting

Literal strings can be written in a variety of different quoting styles, each of which treats the text of the string in a different way. The result (with one exception) is always string data. They are:

Quote type	Operator	Result
single quotes	q	literal string
double quotes	qq	interpolated string
n/a	qr	regular expressions string
n/a	qw	list of words
backticks (``` `` ```)	qx	execute external program

As the table shows, Perl provides two syntaxes for most kinds of strings. The ordinary punctuated kind uses quotes, but we can also use a quoting operator to perform the same function:

```
'Literal Text'    # is equivalent to  q(Literal Text)
"$interpolated @text"    # is equivalent to  qq($interpolated @text)
`./external -command`    # is equivalent to  qx(./external -command)
```

One of the advantages of the quoting operators is that they allow us to place quote marks inside a string that would otherwise cause syntax difficulties. Accordingly, the delimiters of the quoting operators can be almost anything, so we have the greatest chance of being able to pick a pair of characters that do not occur in the string:

```
$text = q/a string with 'quotes' is 'ok' inside q/;
```

Perl accepts both paired and single delimiters. If a delimiter has a logical opposite, such as (and), <
and >, [and], or { and }, the opposing delimiter is used for the other end, otherwise the same
delimiter is expected again:

```
$text = qq{ "$interpolated" ($text) 'and quotes too' };
```

Other than their more flexible syntax, the quoting operators have the same results as their quote
counterparts. Two quote operators, qw and qr, do not have quote equivalents, but these operators are
more specialized.

The single quoted string treats all of its text as literal characters; no processing, interpolation, or escaping
is performed. The quoting operator for literal text is q, so the following are equivalent:

```
'This is literal text'

q/This is literal text/
```

Or with any other delimiter we choose, as noted above.

The quoting operator for interpolation is qq, so the above can also be written as:

```
qq/There are $count matches in a $thing./;
```

Note that only the outer quotes are significant when determining whether a string is interpolated or not,
quotes within the text are just punctuation.

The qr operator is a recent addition to Perl just prior to version 5.005 that prepares regular expressions
for use ahead of time. It takes a regular expression pattern, and produces a ready-to-go regular
expression that can be used anywhere a regular expression operator can:

```
# directly
$text =~ /pattern/;

# via 'qr':
$re = qr/pattern/;
$text =~ $re;
```

The qr operator also interpolates its argument in exactly the same way that double quoted strings and
the qq operator do. Do not despair if this seems rather abstract at the moment, we will learn more about
this in Chapter 11, where qr is covered in more detail.

Quoting a string with backticks, `, causes Perl to treat the enclosed text as a command to be run
externally. The output of the command (if any) is captured by Perl and returned to us. For example:

```
#!/usr/bin/perl
# external.pl
use strict;
use warnings;

my $files = `ls /home`;    # use something like `dir c:` for DOS/Windows
print $files;
```

> perl external.pl
AndrewP
DanR
DaveM
MankeeC

Interpolation is carried out on the string before it is executed, and then passed to a temporary shell if any shell-significant characters like spaces or quotes are present in the resulting string. The equivalent quoting operator is qx:

```
my $files = qx(ls /home);   # use something like qx(dir c:) for DOS/Windows
```

There are serious security issues regarding the use of backticks however. This is partly because they rely on environment variables like $PATH, which is represented in Perl as $ENV{'PATH'}, that we may not be able to trust, and partly because a temporary shell can interpret characters in a potentially damaging way.

The qw operator takes a whitespace separated string and turns it into a list of values. In this respect it is unlike the other quoting operators on which all return string values. Its purpose is to allow us to specify long lists of words without the need for multiple quotes and commas that defining a list of strings normally requires:

```
# the quotey way
@array = ('a', 'lot', 'of', 'quotes', 'is', 'not', 'very', 'legible');

# much more legible using 'qw'
@array = qw(a lot of quotes is not very legible);
```

Both these statements produce the same list of single word string values as their result, but the second is by far the more legible. The drawback to qw is that it will not interpolate variables or handle quotes, so we cannot include spaces within words. In its favor, though, qw also accepts tabs and newlines, so we can also say:

```
@array = qw(
a lot
of quotes
is not
very legible
);
```

Note that with qw we need to avoid commas, which can be a hard habit to break. If we accidentally use commas, Perl will warn against it, since commas are just another character to qw and so comma separated words would result in a single string; words, commas, and all:

```
@oops = qw(a, comma, separated, list, of, words);
```

If we try to do this Perl will warn us (assuming we have warnings enabled) with:

Possible attempt to separate words with commas at ...

If we actually want to use commas, we can, but in order to silence Perl we will need to turn off warnings temporarily with no warnings and turn them back on again afterward (the new warning system brought in for Perl 5.6 also allows us to turn off specific warnings, so we could do that too. See Chapter 16 for more details).

'Here' Documents

As we have just seen, the usual way to define literal text in source code is with quotes, or the equivalent quoting operators q and qq. Here documents are an additional and alternative way that is particularly well suited to multiple line blocks of text like document templates. Here documents are interpolated, and so make a convenient alternative to both concatenating multiple lines together and Perl formats, which also provide a document template processing feature, but in an entirely different way.

To create a here document we use a << followed immediately by an end token, a bareword or quoted string that is used to mark the end of the block. The block itself starts from the next line and absorbs all text, including the newlines, until Perl sees the end token. Normal Perl syntax parsing is disabled while the document is defined, and continues only after the end token is seen:

```
$string = <<_END_OF_TEXT_;
Some text
Split onto multiple lines
Is clearly defined
_END_OF_TEXT_
```

This is exactly equivalent to, but easier on the eye than:

```
$string = "Some text \n".
"Split onto multiple lines \n".
"Is clearly defined \n";
```

The << and token define where the document is used, and tells Perl that it is about to start on the next line. There must be no space between the << and the token, otherwise Perl will complain. The token may be an unquoted bareword, like the above example, or a quoted string, in which case it can contain spaces, as in the example below:

```
# the end token may contain spaces if it is quoted
print <<"print to here";
This is
some text
print to here
```

If used, the type of quote determines whether or not the body of the document is interpolated or not. If single quotes are used, no interpolation takes place:

```
# this does not interpolate
print <<'_END_OF_TEXT_'
This %is @not %interpolated
_END_OF_TEXT_
```

Note that in all examples the here document is used within a statement, which is terminated by a semicolon, as normal. It is not true to say that the <<TOKEN absorbs all text following it; it is a perfectly ordinary string value from the point of view of the statement around it. Only from the next line does Perl switch into document definition mode:

```
# a foreach loop on one line
foreach (split "\n", <<LINES) { print "Got $_ \n"; }
Line 1
Line 2
Line 3
LINES
```

Alternatively, we can define a here document within a statement if the statement spans more than one line; the rest of the lines fall after the end token:

```perl
#!/usr/bin/perl
# heredoc.pl
use warnings;
use strict;

# a foreach loop split across the 'here' document
foreach (split "\n", <<LINES) {
Line 1
Line 2
Line 3
LINES
    print "Got: $_ \n";
}
```

Since here documents are interpolated (unless we use single quotes to define the end token at the top, as noted above) they make a very convenient way to create templates for documents. Here is an example being used to generate an email message with a standard set of headers:

```perl
#!/usr/bin/perl
# formate.pl
use warnings;
use strict;

print format_email('me@myself.net', 'you@yourself.org', "Wishing you were here",
                   "...instead of me!", "Regards, Me");

# subroutines will be explained fully in Chapter 7
sub format_email {
my ($me, $to_addr, $subject, $body_of_message, $signature) = @_;

return <<_EMAIL_;
To: $to_addr
From: $me;
Subject: $subject

$body_of_message
--
$signature
_EMAIL_
}
```

The choice of end token is arbitrary; it can be anything, including a Perl keyword. For clarity's sake however a clearly defined token, preferably in capitals and possibly with surrounding underscores, is a good idea. The end token must also appear at the start of the line; if it is indented with anything, Perl will not recognise it. Likewise, any indentation within the here document will remain in the document. This can present a stylistic problem since it breaks formatting in things like subroutines:

```perl
sub return_a_here_document {
return <<DOCUMENT;
This document definition cannot be indented
if we want to avoid indenting
the resulting document too
DOCUMENT
}
```

If we do not mind indenting the document then we can indent the end token by defining it with the indent to start with:

```
sub return_a_here_document {
return <<'              DOCUMENT';
This document is indented, but the
end token is also indented, so it parses OK
          DOCUMENT
}
```

Although it uses the same symbol, the here document $\ll$ has nothing whatsoever to do with the shift right operator. Rather, it is a unary operator with a rather unusual operand. It can be seen as a distant relative of the DATA filehandle, which reads data placed after the __END__ or __DATA__ tokens in source files, and which we discuss in Chapter 12.

Bareword Strings and Version Numbers

The use strict pragma forces us to declare variables properly, forbids symbolic references, and does not allow us to leave strings unquoted, because of the possible confusion with subroutines. Without strict subs we can in fact quite legally say:

```
# 'use strict subs' won't allow us to do this
$word = unquoted;
```

instead of the more correct:

```
$word = "unquoted";
```

This is a fairly obvious example where we really ought to be using quotes, but it is easy to get into the habit of omitting quotes in things like hash keys:

```
$value = $hash{animal}{small}{furry}{cat};
```

The problem with this, apart from the fact we cannot include spaces, is that if at a future point, we write a subroutine called unquoted then our string assignment suddenly becomes a subroutine call. This is one of the many reasons we should always use strict in Perl programs.

However, there are a few places where bareword strings are allowed. The first, and most obvious, is the qw operator, which we covered earlier:

```
qw(startword bareword anotherbareword endword);
```

A second place where barewords are allowed is on the left-hand side of the relationship (or digraph) operator. This is just a clever form of comma that knows it is being used to define hash keys and values. Since a hash key can only be a string, the left-hand side of a => must be a string:

```
%hash = (bareword => "still need quotes on this side");
```

Finally, Perl supports a very special kind of string called a version string, which in fact must be unquoted to be treated as such. The format of a version string must resemble a version number, and can only be made of digits, points, and an optional v prefix:

```
$VERSION = 1.2.34;
```

If the version number has only one, (or no) points in it then we must use the v prefix to ensure that Perl does not interpret it as a regular integer or floating-point number:

```
$float = 5.6    # oops, that is a floating-point number
$version = v5.6    # now it is a version string
```

The special variable $^V ($PERL_VERSION) also returns a string of this kind, unlike the older $], which returns a floating-point number for compatibility with older Perl versions (for example, 5.003). The objective is to allow version numbers to be easily compared without straying into the dangerous world of floating-point comparisons, as in this example that tests the version of Perl itself, and aborts with an error message if it is too old:

```
# 'require 5.6.0' is another way to do this:
die "Your Perl is too old! Get a new one! \n" if $^V lt v5.6.0;
```

The characters in a version string are actually directly constructed from the digits, so a 1 becomes the character Control-A, or ASCII 1. 5.6.0 is therefore equivalent to the interpolated string "\05\06\00" or the expression chr(5).chr(6).chr(0). This is not a very printable string, but it is still a string, so we must be sure to use the string comparison operators like lt (less than) and ge (greater or equal to) rather than their numeric equivalents < and >=.

Converting Strings into Numbers

As we have seen, Perl automatically converts strings into an integer or floating-point form when the context demands it, for instance if we perform a numeric operation. This provides us with a simple way to convert a string into a number when we actually want a number, for example in a print statement, which is happy with any kind of scalar. All we have to do is perform a numeric operation on the string that doesn't change its value, multiplying or dividing by 1 for example. Of all the no-op numeric operations, adding zero is probably the simplest:

```
# define a numeric string
$scalar = '123.4e5';

# evaluate it in original string context
print $scalar;    # produces '123.4e5'

# evaluate it in numeric context
print $scalar + 0;    # produces '12340000'
```

Perl will evaluate the string as a floating-point number unless we constrain it by either using the int function or the use integer pragma:

```
# evaluate as an integer
print int($scalar);
```

If the string does not look like a number then Perl will do the best job it can, while warning us that the string is not completely convertible, and some information is being lost:

```
print "123.4e5abc" + 0   #   produces '12340000' and a warning
```

Converting Strings into Lists and Hashes

To transform a string into a list basically consists of dividing it up into pieces. For this purpose Perl provides the `split` function, which takes two arguments, a pattern to split on, and a string to perform the splitting on. For example, this splits a comma separated sequence of values in a string into a list of those values:

```
$csv = "one, two, three, four, five, six";
@list = split ',' , $csv;
```

Although it is commonly used to split up strings by simple delimiters like commas, the first argument to `split` is in fact a regular expression, and is able to use the regular expression syntax of arbitrary delimiters:

```
@list = split /, /, $csv;
```

This also means that we can be more creative about how we define the delimiter. For instance, to divide up a string with commas and arbitrary quantities of whitespace we can replace the comma with a pattern that absorbs whitespace on either side:

```
@list = split /\s*, \s*/, $csv;
```

This does not deal with any leading or trailing whitespace on the first and last items (and in particular any trailing newline) but it is effective none the less. However, if we want to split on a character that is significant in regular expressions, we have to escape it. The `//` style syntax helps remind us of this, but it is easy to forget that a pipe symbol, (`|`), will not split up a pipe-separated string:

```
$pipesv = "one | two | three | four | five | six";
print split('|', $pipesv);   # prints one | two | three | four | five | six
```

This will actually return the string as a list of single characters, including the pipes, because `|` defines alternatives in Perl. There is nothing either side of the pipe, so we are actually asking to match on nothing or nothing, both of which are zero-width patterns (they successfully match no characters). Perl treats zero-width matches as a special case in multiple matches, incrementing the position one character despite having matched no characters. As a result we get a stream of single characters. This is better than an infinite loop, which is what would occur if Perl didn't treat zero-width matches specially, but it's not what we intended either. Here is how we should have done it:

```
print split('\|', $pipesv);   # prints one two three four five six
```

A use for alternation is this `split` statement, which parses hash definitions in a string into a real hash:

```
$hashdef = "Mouse=>Jerry, Cat=>Tom, Dog=>Spike";
%hash = split /, |=>/, $hashdef;
```

Because it uses a regular expression, `split` is capable of lots of other interesting tricks, including returning the delimiter if we use parentheses. If we do not actually want to include the delimiters in the returned list we need to suppress it with the extended `(?:...)` pattern:

```
# return (part of) delimiters
@list = split /\s*(, |=>)\s*/, $hashdef;
# @list contains 'Mouse', '=>', 'Jerry', ',' , 'Cat', ...

# suppress return of delimiters, handle whitespace, assign resulting
# list to hash
%hash = split /\s*(?:, |=>)\s*/, $hashdef;
```

Both examples use more complex forms of regular expression such as \s to match whitespace, which we have not fully covered yet; see Chapter 11 for more details on how they work. The last example also illustrates how to define the contents of a hash variable from a list of values, which we will cover in detail when we come to hashes later.

If split is passed a third numeric parameter, then it only splits that number of times, preserving any remaining text as the last returned value:

```
my $configline = "equation=y = x ** 2 + c";
# split on first = only
my ($key, $value) = split (/=/, $configline, 2);
print "$key is '$value'";   # produces "equation is 'y = x ** 2 + c'"
```

split also has a special one and no-argument mode. With only one argument, it splits the default argument $_, which makes it useful in loops like the while loop that read lines from standard input (or files supplied on the command line), like the short program below:

```
#!/usr/bin/perl
# readconfig.pl
use warnings;
use strict;

my %config;

# read lines from files specified on command line or (if none)
# standard input
while (<>) {
    my ($key, $value) = split /=/;   # split on $_
    $config{$key} = $value if $key and $value;
}

print "Configured: ", join(', ', keys %config), "\n";
```

We can invoke this program with a command like:

> **readconfig.pl configfile**

Supplied with a configfile containing:

```
first = one
second = two
```

This produces:

Configured: first, second

If no arguments are supplied at all, `split` splits the default argument on whitespace characters, after skipping any leading whitespace. The following short program counts words in the specified files or what is passed on standard input using the '<>' readline operator covered in Chapter 6:

```perl
#!/usr/bin/perl
# split.pl
use warnings;
use strict;

my @words;

# read lines from files specified on command line or (if none)
# standard input
while (<>) {
    # split lines into words and store
    push @words, split;
}

print "Found ", scalar(@words), " words in input \n";
```

`split` and other aspects of regular expressions that can be applied to `split` are covered in more detail in Chapter 11 'Regular Expressions'.

Functions For Manipulating Strings

Perl provides us with a set of operators that we can use for manipulating strings. We will explore those operators in Chapter 4. In this section, we will look into a number of functions for handling strings.

Print

The ubiquitous `print` statement is not technically a string function, since it takes a list of arbitrary scalar values and sends them to the currently selected filehandle. We have already seen `print` in many of the examples so far; the general form is one of the following:

```perl
print @list;
print FILEHANDLE @list;
```

The output of `print` is affected by several of Perl's special variables:

Variable	Action
`$,`	The output field separator determines what `print` places between values, by default `''` (nothing). Set to `','` to print comma separated values.
`$\`	The output record separator determines what `print` places at the end of its output after the last value, by default `''` (nothing). Set to `'\n'` to print out automatic linefeeds.
`$#`	The output format for all printed numbers (integer and floating-point), in terms of a `sprintf` style placeholder. The default value is something similar to `%.6g`. To print everything to two fixed decimal places (handy for currency, for example) change to `%.2f`, but note that use of `$#` is now deprecated in Perl.
`$|`	The `autoflush` flag determines if line or block buffering should be used. If `0`, it is block, if `1`, it is line.

Although not directly related to `print`, it is worth noting that interpolated arrays and hashes use `$"` as a separator, rather than `$,` (a space by default). See Appendix B for more on these and other special variables.

Beware of leaving off the parentheses of `print` if the first argument (after the filehandle, if present) is enclosed in parentheses, since this will cause `print` to use the first argument as an argument list, ignoring the rest of the statement.

Line Terminator Termination

The `chop` and `chomp` functions both remove the last character from a string. This apparently esoteric feature is actually very handy for removing line terminators. `chop` is not selective, it will chop off the last character irrespective of what it is or whether it looks like a line terminator or not, returning it to us in case we want to use it for something:

```
chop $input_string;
```

The string passed to `chop` must be an assignable one, such as a scalar variable, or (more bizarrely) the return value of `substr` used on a scalar variable, since `chop` does not return the truncated string but the character that was removed. If no string is supplied, `chop` uses the default argument `$_`:

```
while (<>) {
    chop;
    print "$_ \n";
}
```

Note that if we want to get the string without the terminator, but also leave it intact we can use `substr` instead of chop. This is less efficient because it makes a copy of the line, but it preserves the original:

```
while (<>) {
    my $string = substr $_, 0, -1;
    print $string;
}
```

`chomp` is the user-friendly version of `chop`; it only removes the last character if it is the line terminator, as defined by the input record separator special variable `'$/'` (default `"\n"`), but is otherwise identical:

```
chomp $might_end_in_a_linefeed_but_might_not;
```

Both `chop` and `chomp` will work on lists of strings as well as single ones:

```
# remove all trailing newlines from input, if present
@lines = <>;
chomp(@lines);
```

Giving either `chop` or `chomp` a non-string variable will convert it into a string. In the case of `chomp` this will do nothing else; `chop` will return the last digit of a number and turn it into a string missing the last digit.

Characters and Character Codes

The ord function produces the integer character code for the specified letter. If passed a string of more than one character it will return the code for the first one. ord will also handle multi-byte characters and return a Unicode character code:

```
print ord('A');   # returns 65
```

The inverse of ord is chr, which converts a character code into a character:

```
print chr(65);   # returns 'A'
```

chr will happily handle Unicode character codes as well as single-byte ASCII character for codes (though the results of displaying it are dependent on the character set in effect: code 65 is usually, but not necessarily, 'A'). See Chapter 25 for more information on Unicode.

Note that these examples will only produce this output if ASCII is the default character set – In Japan the output would be different.

Length and Position

The length function simply returns the length of the supplied string:

```
$length = length($string);
```

If the argument to length is not a string it is converted into one, so we can find out how wide a number will be if printed before actually doing so:

```
$pi = atan2(1, 0) * 2;   # a numeric value
$length_as_string = length($pi);   # length as string
```

The index and rindex functions look for a specified substring within the body of a string. They do not have any of the power or flexibility of a regular expression, but by the same token, they are considerably quicker. They return the position of the first character of the matched substring if found, or -1 (technically one less than the index start $ [) otherwise:

```
$string = "This is a string in which looked for text may be found";
print index $string, "looked for";   # produces '26'
```

We may also supply an additional position, in which case index and rindex will start from that position:

```
print index $string, "look for", 30;   # not found, produces -1
```

index looks forward and rindex looks backward, but otherwise they are identical. Note that unlike arrays, we cannot specify a negative number to specify a starting point relative to the end of the string, nice though that would be.

While we are on the subject of positions, the pos function actually has nothing whatsoever to do with functions like index and rindex. It is a regular expression function for returning the position of successful matches.

Substrings and Vectors

The very versatile `substr` extracts a substring from a supplied string in very much the same way that `splice` returns parts of arrays, and indeed the two functions are modeled to resemble each other. It takes between two and four arguments – a string to work on, an offset to start from, a length, and an optional replacement:

```
# return characters from position 3 to 7 from $string
print substr "1234567890", 3, 4;   # produces 4567
```

String positions start from 0, like arrays (and are also controlled by the special variable $ [). If the length is omitted, `substr` returns characters up to the end of the string:

```
print substr "1234567890", 3;   # produces 4567890
```

Both the offset and the length can be negative, in which case they are both taken relative to the end of the string:

```
print substr "1234567890", -7, 2;    # produces 45
print substr "1234567890", -7;   # produces 4567890
print substr "1234567890", -7, -2;    # produces 45678
```

We can also supply a replacement string, either by specifying the new string as the fourth argument, or more interestingly assigning to the `substr`. In both cases the new string may be longer or shorter (including empty, if we just want to remove text) and the string will adjust to fit. However, for either to work we must supply an assignable value like a variable or a subroutine or function that returns an assignable value (like `substr` itself, in fact). Consider the following two examples:

```
$string = "1234567890";
print substr($string, 3, 4, "abc");
# produces '4567'
# $string becomes '123abc890'

$string = "1234567890";
print substr($string, 3, 4) = "abc";
# produces 'abc8'
# $string becomes '123abc890'
```

The difference between the two variants is in the value they return. The replacement string version causes `substr` to return the original substring before it was modified. The assignment on the other hand returns the substring after the substitution has taken place. This will only be the same as the replacement text if it is the same length as the text it is replacing; in the above example the replacement text is one character shorter, so the return value includes the next unreplaced character in the string, which happens to be 8.

Attempting to return a substring that extends past the end of the string will result in `substr` returning as many characters as it can. If the start is past the end of the string then `substr` returns an empty string. Note also that we cannot extend a string by assigning to a `substr` beyond the string end (this might be expected since we can do something similar to arrays, but it is not the case.)

Upper and Lower Case

Perl provides no less than four different functions just for manipulating the case of strings. uc and lc convert all character in a string into upper and lower case (all characters that have a case, that is) and return the result:

```
print uc('upper');   # produces 'UPPER'
print lc('LOWER');   # produces 'lower'
```

ucfirst and lcfirst are the limited edition equivalents, they only operate on the first letter:

```
print ucfirst('daniel');   # produces 'Daniel';
print lcfirst('Polish');   # produces 'polish';
```

If we are interpolating a string we can also use the special sequences \U...\E and \L...\E within the string to produce the same effect as uc and lc for the characters placed between them. See Chapter 11 for more details. And talking of interpolation...

Interpolation

The quotemeta function processes a string to make it safe in interpolative contexts. That is, it inserts backslash characters before any non-alphanumeric characters, including $, @, %, existing backslashes, commas, spaces, and all punctuation except the underscore (which is considered an honorary numeric because it can be used as a separator in numbers). We also cover quotemeta in Chapter 11.

Pattern Matching and Transliteration

Perl's regular expression engine is one of its most powerful features, allowing almost any kind of text matching and substitution on strings of any size. It supplies two main functions, the m// match and s/// substitution functions, plus the pos function and a large handful of special variables. For example, to determine if one string appears inside another ignoring case:

```
$matched = $matchtext =~ /some text/i;
```

Or to replace all instances of the word green with yellow:

```
$text = "red green blue";
$text =~ s/\bgreen\b/yellow/g;
print $text;   # produces 'red yellow blue'
```

Closely associated but not actually related to the match and substitution functions is the transliteration operator tr///, also known as y///. It transforms strings by replacing characters from a search list with the character in the corresponding position in the replacement list. For example, to uppercase the letters a to f (perhaps for hexadecimal strings) we could write:

```
$hexstring =~ tr/a-f/A-F/;
```

Entire books have been written on pattern matching and regular expressions, and accordingly we devote Chapter 11 to it.

Password Encryption

The crypt function performs a one-way transform of the string passed; it is identical to (and implemented using) the C library crypt on UNIX systems. crypt is not always available, in which case attempting to use it will provoke a fatal error from Perl. Otherwise, it takes two arguments: the text to be encrypted and a salt, which is a two character string made of random characters in the range 0..9, a..z, A..Z, '/', or '.'. Here is how we can generate a suitable encrypted password in Perl:

```
@characters = (0..9, 'a'..'z' ,'A'..'Z', '.', '/');
$encrypted = crypt($password, @characters[rand 64, rand 64]);
```

Since we do not generally want to use the salt for anything other than creating the password we instead supply the encrypted text itself as the salt for testing an entered password (which works because the first two characters are in fact the salt):

```
# check password
die "Wrong!" unless crypt($entered, $encrypted) eq $encrypted;
```

Note that for actually entering passwords it is generally a good idea to not echo to the screen, see Chapter 15 for some ways to achieve this.

crypt is not suitable for encrypting large blocks of text, it is a one-way function that cannot be reversed, and so is strictly only useful for generating passwords. Use one of the cryptography modules from CPAN like Crypt::TripleDES or Crypt::IDEA for more heavyweight and reversible cryptography.

Low Level String Conversions

Perl provides three functions that perform string conversions at a low level. The pack and unpack functions convert between strings and arbitrary machine-level values, like a low-level version of sprintf. The vec function allows us to treat strings as if they were long binary values, obviating the need to convert to or from actual integer values.

'Pack' and 'Unpack'

The pack and unpack functions convert between strings and lists of values: The pack function takes a format or template string and a list of values, returning a string that contains a compact form of those values. unpack takes the same format string and undoes the pack, extracting the original values.

pack is reminiscent of sprintf. They both take a format string and a list of values, generating an output string as a result. The difference is that sprintf is concerned with converting values into legible strings, whereas pack is concerned with producing byte-by-byte translations of values. Whereas sprintf would turn an integer into a textual version of that same integer, for example, pack will turn it into a series of characters whose binary values go up to make up the integer:

```
$string = pack 'i', $integer;
```

Or, using real numbers:

```
print pack 'i', 1819436368;   # produces the string 'Perl'
```

To pack multiple integers we can put more 'i's, or use a repeat count:

```
$string = pack 'i4', @integers[0..3];
```

To pack as many as the list supplies, we use * for a repeat count:

```
$string = pack 'i*', @integers;
```

We can combine multiple template characters into one template. The following packs four integers, a null character (given by x), and a string truncated to ten bytes with a null character as a terminator (given by Z):

```
$string = pack 'i4xZ10', @integers[0..3], "abcdefghijklmonop";
```

We can also add spaces for clarity:

```
$string = pack 'i4 x Z10', @integers[0..3], "abcdefghijklmonop";
```

To unpack this list again we would use something like:

```
($int1, $int2, $int3, $int4, $str) = unpack 'i4xZ10', $string;
```

pack and unpack can simulate several of Perl's other functions. For example, the c template character packs and unpacks a single character to and from a character code, in exactly the same way that ord and chr do:

```
$chr = pack 'c', $ord;
$ord = unpack 'c', $chr;
```

The advantage is of course that with pack and unpack we can process a whole string at once:

```
@ords = unpack 'c*', $string;
```

Similarly, here is how we can use x (which skips over or ignores, for unpack) and a (read as-is) to extract a substring somewhat in the manner of substr:

```
$substr = unpack "x$position a$length", $string;
```

pack supports a bewildering number of template characters, each with its own properties, and a number of modifiers that alter the size or order in which they work. Here is a brief list; note that several only make sense with an additional count supplied along with the template character:

Character	Properties
a	Arbitrary (presumed string) data, null padded if too short
A	Arbitrary (presumed string) data, space padded if too short
Z	Null terminated string
b	Bit string, ascending order (as used by vec)
B	Bit string, descending order
h	Hex string, byte order low-high
H	Hex string, byte order high-low
c	Signed character (8-bit) value
C	Unsigned character (8-bit) value
s	Signed short (16-bit) value
S	Unsigned short (16-bit) value
i	Signed integer value (length dependent on C)
I	Unsigned integer value (length dependent on C)
l	Signed long (32-bit) value
L	Unsigned long (32 bit) value
q	Signed quad/long long (64-bit) value
Q	Unsigned quad/long long (64-bit) value
n	Unsigned short, big-endian (network) order
N	Unsigned long, big-endian (network) order
v	Unsigned short, little-endian (VAX) order
V	Unsigned long, little-endian (VAX) order
f	Single precision floating-point number
d	Double precision floating-point number
p	Pointer to null terminated string
P	Pointer to fixed length string
u	Unencoded string
U	Unicode character (works regardless of use utf8)
w	BER (base 128) compressed integer
x	Null/ignore byte
X	Backup a byte
@	Fill to absolute position with null characters

One of the most important uses of pack and unpack is for generating and expanding argument lists and structures for C library routines, which expect to see values packed together in a format that the compiled C code will understand. See Chapter 24 for more on this aspect.

Vector Strings

Perl also provides the vec function, which allows us to treat a string as if it were a long binary value rather than a sequence of characters. vec treats the whole string as a sequence of bits, with each character holding eight. It therefore allows us to handle arbitrarily long bit masks and binary values without the constraints of integer size or assumption of byte order.

In operation, vec is somewhat like the substr function, only at the bit level. substr addresses a string by character position and length and returns substrings, optionally allowing us to replace the substring through assignment to a string. vec addresses a string by element position and length and returns bits as an integer, optionally allowing us to replace the bits through assignment to an integer. It takes three arguments: a string to work with, an offset, and a length, exactly as with substr, only now the length is in terms of bits and the offset is in multiples of the length. For example, to extract the tenth to twelfth bits of a bitstring with vec we would write:

```
$twobitflag = vec($bitstr, 5, 2);    # 5th 2-bit element is bits 10 to 12
```

The use of the word string with vec is a little stretched; in reality we are working with a stream of bytes in a consistent and platform-independent order (unlike an integer whose bytes may vary in order according to the processor architecture). Each byte contains eight bits, with the first character being bits 0-7, the second being 8-15, and so on, so this extracts the 2nd to 4th bits of the second byte in the string. Of course the point of vec is that we do not care about the characters, only the bits inside them.

vec provides a very efficient way to store values with constrained limits. For example, to store one thousand values that may range between 0 and 9 using a conventional array of integers would take up 4 x 1000 bytes (assuming a four byte integer), and 1000 characters if printed out to a string for storage. With vec we can fit the values 0 to 9 into 4 bits, fitting 2 to a character and taking up 500 bytes in memory, and saved as a string. Unfortunately, the length must be a power of two, so we cannot pack values into 3 bits if we only had to store values from 0 to 7.

```
# a function to extract 4-bit values from a 'vec' string
sub get_value {
   # return flag at offset, 4 bits
   return vec $_[0], $_[1], 4;
}

# get flag 20 from the bitstring
$value = get_value ($bitstr, 20);
```

It does not matter if we access an undefined part of the string, vec will simply return 0, so we need not worry if we access a value that the string does not extend to. Indeed, we can start with a completely empty string and fill it up using vec. Perl will automatically extend the string as and when we need it.

Assigning to a vec sets the bits from the integer value, rather like a supercharged version of chr. For example, here is how we can define the string Perl from a 32-bit integer value:

```
# assign a string by character code
$str = chr(0x50). chr(0x65). chr(0x72). chr(0x6c);    # $str = "Perl";

# the same thing more efficiently with a 32-bit value and 'vec'
vec ($str, 0, 32) = 0x50_65_72_6c;

# extract a character as 8 bits:
print vec ($str, 2, 8);    # produces 114 which is the ASCII value of 'r'
```

Using this, here is the counterpart to the get_value subroutine for setting flags:

```
# a function to set 4-bit values into a 'vec' string
sub set_value {
    # set flag at offset, 4 bits
    vec $_[0], $_[1], 4;
}

# set flag 43 in the bitstring
$value = set_value ($bitstr, 43, $value);
```

String Formatting

We have already seen some examples of the printf and sprintf functions when we discussed converting numbers into different string representations. However, these functions are far more versatile than this, so here we will run through all the possibilities that these two functions afford us. The two functions are identical except that sprintf returns a string while printf combines sprintf with print and takes an optional first argument of a filehandle. It returns the result of the print, so for generating strings we want sprintf.

sprintf takes a format string, which can contain any mixture of value placeholders and literal text. Technically this means that they are not string functions per se, since they operate on lists, but describing them as list functions does not really make sense either (well, no more than it would for join, so we'll cover them here).

For each placeholder of the form %... in the format, one value is taken from the following list and converted to conform to the textual requirement defined by the placeholder. For example:

```
# use the 'localtime' function to read the year, month and day
($year, $month, $day) = (localtime) [5, 4, 3];
$year += 1900;
$date = sprintf '%4u/%02u/%02u',  $year, $month, $day;
```

This defines a format string with three unsigned decimal integers (specified by the %u placeholder). All other characters are literal characters, and may also be interpolated if the string is double-quoted. The first is a minimum of four characters wide padded with spaces. The other two have a minimum width of two characters, padded with leading zeros.

The %u format interprets the supplied value into an unsigned integer and converts it into a string format, constrained by whatever additional requirements are imposed. In addition, the following groups of placeholders are accepted:

Below are the character and string placeholders:

Placeholder	Description
%c	a character (from an integer character code value)
%s	a string
%%	a percent sign

Next we look at integer and number base placeholders:

Placeholder	Description
%d	Signed decimal integer
%I	(Archaic) alias for %d
%u	Unsigned decimal integer
%o	Unsigned octal integer
%x	Unsigned hexadecimal integer, lowercase a..f
%X	Unsigned hexadecimal integer, uppercase A..F
%b	Unsigned binary integer

In addition, all these characters can be prefixed with 'l' to denote a long (32-bit) value, or h to denote a short (16-bit) value, for example:

```
%ld    long signed decimal
%hb    short binary
```

If neither is specified, Perl uses whichever size is more natural for int according to how it was built and the underlying C library (if 64-bit integers are supported, %d will denote 64 bit integers, for example). The %D, %U, and %O are archaic aliases for %ld, %lu, and %lo. sprintf supports them but their use is not encouraged.

Extra long (64-bit) integers may be handled by prefixing the placeholder letter with either ll (long long), L (big long), or q (quad):

```
%lld    64-bit signed integer
%qo     64-bit octal number.
```

This is dependent on Perl supporting 64-bit integers, of course.

These are the placeholders for floating-point numbers:

Placeholder	Description
%e	Scientific notation floating-point number, lowercase e
%E	Scientific notation floating-point number, uppercase E
%f	Fixed decimal floating-point number
%F	(Archaic) alias for %f
%g	'Best' choice between %e and %f
%G	'Best' choice between %E and %f

By their nature, floating-point values are always double precision in Perl, so there is no l prefix. However, quadruple to store precision (long double) floating-point values can be handled with the ll or L prefixes:

%llE   long double scientific notation, uppercase E
%Lf   long double fixed decimal

As with 64-bit integers, this is dependent on Perl actually supporting long double values.

Other placeholders are as below:

Placeholder	Description
%p	pointer value (memory address of value)
%n	writes length of current output string into next variable

The %p placeholder is not often used in Perl, since messing with memory addresses is not something Perl encourages, though it can occasionally be useful for debugging references. The %n placeholder is unusual in that it assigns the length of the string generated so far, to the next item in the list (which must therefore be a variable).

As the above lists show, much of the functionality of sprintf is related to expressing integers and floating-point numbers in string format. We covered many of its uses in this respect earlier in the chapter. In brief, however, placeholders may have additional constraints to determine the representation of a number or string placed by adding modifiers between the % and the type character:

Modifier	Action
n	A number, the minimum field width
*	Take the width for this placeholder from the next value in the list
.m	Precision. This has a different meaning depending on whether the value is string, integer or floating-point:
	string - the maximum width
	integer - the minimum width
	float - digits after the decimal place
.*	Take the precision for this placeholder from the next value in the list
n.m	Combined width and precision
.	Take the width and precision for this placeholder from the next two values in the list

If a string or character placeholder has a width, then strings shorter than the width are padded to the left with spaces (zeroes if 0 is used). Conversely, if a precision is specified and the string is longer, then it is truncated on the right. Specifying both as the same number gives a string of a guaranteed width irrespective of the value, for example %8.8s.

A floating-point number uses the width and precision in the normal numerical sense. The width defines the width of the field as a whole, and the precision defines how much of it is used for decimal places. Note that the width includes the decimal point, the exponent, and the e or E. For example, %+13.3e.

The precision and width are the same for integers except that a leading '.' will pad the number with leading zeros in the same way in which 0 (below) does. If the integer is wider than the placeholder then it not truncated. For example, %.4d.

If asterisks are used for either width or precision then the next value in the list is used to define it, removing it from the list for consideration as a placeholder value:

```
$a = sprintf "%*.*f", $float, $width, $precision;
```

Note that negative numbers for either will cause an additional implicit -, see below.

The table below shows the effects of characters on the formatting of strings:

Character	Action
space	Pad values to the left with spaces (right-justify)
0	Pad values to the left with zeros
-	Pad values to the right with spaces (left-justify)

Justification is used with a placeholder width to determine how unfilled places are handled when the value is too short. A space, which is the default, pads to the left with spaces, while 0 pads to the left with zeroes, shifting sign or base prefixes to the extreme left if specified. '-' pads with spaces to the right (even if 0 is also specified). For example:

%04d	pad to four digits with 0
% 8s	pad to eight characters with spaces
%8s	the same
%-8s	pad to the right to eight characters with spaces

Using the prefixes below, we can format numbers in different ways:

Prefix	Action
+	represent positive numbers with a leading +
#	prefix non-decimal based integers with 0, 0x, or 0b if they have a non-zero value

Either of these prefixes can be enabled (even on strings, though there is not much point in doing that) by placing them after the % and before anything else. Note that + is for signed integers and that # is for other number bases, all of which treat signed numbers as if they were very large unsigned values with their top bit set. This means that they are exclusive, in theory at least. Note that both of them are counted in the width of the field, so for a 16 bit binary number plus prefix, allow for 18 characters. For example:

```
%+4d        give number a sign even if positive
%+04d       signed and padded with zeros
%#018hb     16-bit padded and prefixed short binary integer
```

Finally we look briefly at vectors and versions:

The v flag specifies that the supplied value is converted into a version number string of character codes separated by points, in the format defined by the placeholder (d for decimal, b for binary, and so on). A different separator may be used if a * is used before the v to import it. Note that specifying the separator directly will not work, as v does not conform to the usual rules for placeholders. For example:

```
printf "v%vd", $^V;         # print Perl's version

printf "%v08b", 'aeiou';    # print letters as 8 bit binary digits
                            # separated by points

printf "%*v8o", '-', 'aeiou';  # print letters as octal numbers
                               # separated by minus signs
```

Summary

In this chapter, we have talked about scalar numbers and strings, and their relationships to functions and modifiers. We were introduced to integers and floating-point numbers, and took a brief look at the use integer pragma. The different types of quotes and quoting operators were discussed, and we learned how to use a here document. We also saw what mathematical functions Perl provides, and also how extend these using the Math::Trig module. After seeing how to manipulate strings, we went on to look at low-level string conversions like pack and unpack, all of which has given us the foundation, for number and string manipulation, which we will need throughout the rest of the book.

4

Operators

Operators are the basic tools that allow us to manipulate variables and values to produces new ones. Operators and values go together to make expressions, which in turn can be integrated into larger expressions by using more operators. Subroutines and functions can also become involved; we will get to that subject in a moment.

All operators are characterized by requiring one or two (and in one case, three) expressions to work on, then returning a value as their result. With the exception of the eponymous **ternary** operator, operators are either **unary**, taking a single value and producing a new value from it, or **binary**, combining two expressions to produce a new value. An example of an unary operator is the logical not operator !, which logically inverts the value supplied to it; an example of a binary operator is +, which (of course) adds its two values together to produce a value that is the sum. +, along with -, can also be unary, and indicate a positive or negative sign, so they are also examples of operators with more than one mode of use.

The values that operators work on are **operands**. The value on the left of a binary operator is therefore the left operand and the value on the right is the right operand. These values may, in turn, be simple scalar or list values or expressions involving further operations. The order in which operators in the same expression are evaluated is determined by the rules of precedence, which are built into Perl.

Operators Versus Functions

Perl has operators, like +, and it also has **functions**, like print. The distinction is apparently simple, operators have an algebraic look and operate on operands. Functions take arguments, have names rather than symbols, and use parentheses to group their arguments together. Besides, operators are documented in the perlop manual page, and functions are in the perlfunc manual page. Simple.

Unfortunately, it is not actually that simple. Things like ! and + are clearly operators because they are simply fundamental to the language. Additionally, in its binary form, + takes an operand on each side, something a function never does. So these cases are unambiguous. Conversely, functions like print are clearly functions because their main purpose is to do something other than return a value (it comes as a surprise to many that print returns a value at all, in fact). However, there are plenty of less clear examples.

Many functions are called operators because they look like operators, the **file test** operators, also known as the -X operators, are one example. The readline operator <> is another. The -X operators are examples of a **named unary operator**, operators that have names rather than symbols and take single operand on their right. They resemble unary operators like not, which also has a name and takes a single operand on its right. So, the distinction between operators and functions is more vague than we might at first think. They also appear in *both* the perlop and perlfunc manual pages, just to keep things nicely ambiguous.

An alternative way to look at functions is to say that they are all either named unary operators (taking a single argument) or named list operators (taking a list of arguments). How we describe them then becomes a case of how we use them: if we use parentheses, they are functions, and if we do not, they are (or at least, resemble) operators:

```
print -e($filename);   # file test '-e', functional style
print -e $filename;    # file test '-e', operator style
```

This is a useful idea because we can declare subroutines so that they also do not need parentheses, so they can be used as named list operators. With prototypes we can even implement subroutines that resemble named unary operators. It does not help that subroutines are also called functions at the same time that functions are being called operators. In this book we generally try to call a subroutine a subroutine, reserving 'function' for Perl's own built-in functions.

In this section we are only going to talk about operators in the conventional sense of the term – basic operations that form the core essential abilities of the Perl language. + is essential, the readline operator,< >, is merely very useful.

Operator Types and Categories

Perl supplies around seventy operators in total, ranging from basic arithmetic operators, to reference creation and file testing. In order to cover them in a reasonable manner we have divided them up into fourteen categories. Some are expansive; there are fifteen different assignment operators, while others contain a single unique operator. These categories are arbitrary, however, and there are plenty of other ways they might be subdivided.

We have already seen a number of operators in action. We introduced them very briefly in Chapter 2, and then used some of them when we discussed working with integers, floating-point numbers, and strings in Chapter 3. As a result, we are to some extent treading the same ground twice. However, here we are looking at the subject from the point of view of the operators, rather than the values they operate on.

Assignment

The assignment operator, which we introduced in Chapter 2, simply assigns the value of the expression on its right side to the variable (technically, `lvalue`) on its left:

```
$variable = "value";
```

The value returned from this operation is the value of the right-hand side, which is why this is an operation at all. As a result it can be used in other expressions, as in:

```
$c = $b = $a = 'This is the value of a, b and c';
```

The left-hand side of an assignment is usually a scalar variable, but it need not be. Any `lvalue` is acceptable. Two obvious examples are assigning to an array element or a hash key:

```
@array[$index] = 42;
$hash{'key'} = "value";
```

A less obvious example is an array slice, which we can assign a list to (more on arrays in Chapter 5):

```
@array = (1, 2, 3, 4, 5);
@array[1..3] = (7, 8, 9);
print "@array";    # produces 1 7 8 9 5
```

Assigning a list longer than the slice will cause the remaining values to be ignored, while assigning a shorter list will result in undefined values.

Some Perl functions also return `lvalues`, the most common of which is `substr`, which we saw in Chapter 3.

Although subroutines cannot ordinarily provide assignable values, Perl 5.6 contains an experimental feature that allows us to define subroutines, that can be assigned to, just like `substr`.

The precedence of assignment operators is low, as it should be so that all the expressions on its right will be evaluated before the assignment. The comma and relationship operators, as well as the `not`, `and`, `or`, and `xor` operators which we will see later in the chapter, have lower precedence, however, so that statements like the following do what they appear to do:

```
@array = ($a = 1, $b = 2, $c = 3);    # assigns (1, 2, 3) to @array
```

Related to the assignment operator are the **combination assignment operators**, which we will investigate later in this chapter.

Arithmetic

Perl provides the standard set of mathematics operators for manipulating integers and floating-point numbers:

```
6 + 2    # addition, produces 8
6.3 - 2.8    # subtraction, produces 3.5
6*2    # multiplication, produces 12
6.3 * 2.8    # multiplication, produces 17.64
6 % 2    # modulus, produces 0
6.3 ** 2.8    # exponentiation, produces 173.04280186355
```

Multiplication and division have slightly higher precedence than addition and subtraction, so the following produces 13, the sum of 4 and 9, rather than 21.

```
$result = 2*2 + 3*3;    # produces 2*2 plus 3*3 = 4 + 9 = 13
$result = (2*2) + (3*3);   # the same thing, explicitly
```

To force the precedence of the addition higher we need to use parentheses:

```
$result = 2 * (2 + 3) * 3;   # produces 2 * 5 * 3 = 30
```

Other than this, all arithmetic operators have left associativity, which means they evaluate their left-hand side before their right. Multiplication and division have the same precedence, so associativity is used to work out which order to evaluate them in, from left to right. Therefore the following produces 7.5, not 0.3:

```
$result = 2 * 3 / 4 * 5;   # produces 2 * 3, /4, *5 = 7.5
$result = ((2 * 3) / 4) * 5;   # the same thing, explicitly
```

To force the precedence of the final multiplication so it happens before the division we again need to use parentheses:

```
$result = (2 * 3) / (4 * 5);   # produces 6 / 20 = 0.3
```

The modulus operator is a complement to the division operator. It divides the left operand by the right, but returns only the remainder:

```
print 4 % 2;   # produces 0, 2 divides evenly into 4
print 5 % 2;   # produces 1, 5 divided by 2 leaves a remainder of 1
```

% also works on negative numbers, but varies slightly depending on whether the use integer pragma is in effect or not. With it, modulus produces the same result that positive numbers would have:

```
print -13 % 7;   # produces 1

use integer;
print -13 % 7;   # produces -6, same as -(13 % 7)
```

Both results are correct, but from different perspectives, -13 divides by 7 with a remainder of 1 (it is short of -14 by -1), or a remainder of -6 (it is -6 more than -7).

The exponentiation operator is also binary, with a higher precedence than all the other arithmetic operators. It raises the numeric value given as its left operand by the power of the right. Both left and right operands can be floating point, in which case the result is also floating point (possibly converted to an integer for display purposes):

```
print 4 ** 0.5;   # produces 2
```

Both + and - also have a unary form, where they have no left-hand side. Typically these appear in assignments:

```
$negative = -3;
```

The unary minus has plenty of uses in this context. The unary plus, on the other hand, has no relevance at all except to stop parentheses being interpreted as part of a function:

```
print ("Hello"), " World";   # prints "Hello", returns " World"
print +("Hello"), " World";  # prints "Hello World";
```

This particular example is rather obvious, but in cases where parentheses are actually necessary for the first expression in a `print` statement this can be a useful trick, and is an alternative to enclosing the whole argument list in parentheses.

Shift

The `<<` and `>>` shift operators manipulate integer values as binary numbers, shifting their bits one to the left and one to the right respectively. In integer terms this multiplies or divides the value by 2, losing the remainder:

```
print 2 << 1;    # produces 4
print 2 << 3;    # produces 16
print 42 >> 2;   # produces 10
```

The result of `>>` and `<<` is treated as unsigned, even if the topmost bit of the resulting value is set, so the following produce large positive values:

```
print -1 >> 1;   # produces 2147483647 (on a 32 bit platform)
print -1 << 0;   # produces 4294967295 (on a 32 bit platform)
```

If the `use integer` pragma has been used then Perl uses signed integer arithmetic and negative values behave more reasonably, rather than being treated as bit-patterns:

```
use integer;
print -1 << 1;   # produces -2
print -1 >> 1;   # produces -1
```

The reason for the slightly odd looking second result is that -1 is actually all ones in binary, so shifting it right 1 bit makes all bits except the topmost bit 1, and then the effect of `use integer` resets the top bit to 1 again.

Note that the shift operators have nothing to do with here documents, which also use `<<` to assign all the text up to a specified token to the given string variable or operation.

String and List

Perl provides the concatenation operator, `'.'` ,and the repetition operator `x` for string variables. `x` is usually used for strings, but can also replicate lists.

The concatenation operator takes two strings and joins them, returning the result:

```
$good_egg = "Humpty" . "Dumpty";   # produces "HumptyDumpty"
```

This is how Perl performs string addition. Adding strings with + actually converts both operands to integers (which in the above case would be 0 and 0) and then adds them, returning an integer result. If the strings happen to contain numeric values then this may be what we want, otherwise we probably meant to use '.'.

The repetition x operator works on both strings and lists. If the left operand is a string, it is multiplied by the number given by the right operand:

```
print "abc" x 3;    # produces 'abcabcabc'
```

A common application of x is for generating padding for formatted text, like this example, which calculates $padding in terms of tabs (presumed 8 characters wide) and spaces:

```
$width = 43;    # the padding width in characters
$padding = "\t" x ($width/8) . " " x ($width%8);
print $padding;
```

If the left operand is a list (enclosed in parentheses) then the values are replicated:

```
@array = (1, 2, 3) x 3;    # @array contains (1, 2, 3, 1, 2, 3, 1, 2, 3)
```

This is also a good way to produce a large list of identical values:

```
@columns = (1) x 80;    # produce an 80 element array of 1's
```

Note that if the left operand is an array then it is taken in scalar context and the number of elements is repeated:

```
@array1 = (1, 2, 3);
@array2 = @array1 x 3;    # @array2 contains (3, 3, 3)
```

However, if the array is enclosed in parentheses, we get the desired result:

```
@array2 = (@array1) x 3;    # @array2 contains (1, 2, 3, 1, 2, 3, 1, 2, 3)
```

Correspondingly, if the right-hand side is a list or array then it multiplies the left operand by the number of elements it contains:

```
print "string" x (1, 2, 3);    # produces "stringstringstring"
```

Finally, giving x a numeric value as its left operand causes it to be converted into a string for the replication:

```
print 3 x 3;    # produces 333
```

In addition to the '.' and x operators, most other operators will work on strings, though many will convert them into integer or floating-point values before operating on them.

Logical

The logical operators perform Boolean operations, returning 1 on success and 0 on failure. For instance, this is a Boolean and operation:

```
$true = $a && $b;
```

This returns 1 (True) if both $a and $b are True. The meaning of true and false in this context is quite flexible, and we discuss it in more detail in the next chapter. For now though, it is enough to say that Perl generally does the 'right thing' with its operands, so strings like 0 and " " are False and others are True, while arrays and hashes are True if they have one or more elements and False if they have none. Numeric values are True if they have a value, positive or negative, and False if they are zero.

Perl has two sets of logical operators, one appearing as conventional logic symbols and the other appearing as named operations. These two sets are identical in operation, but have different precedence:

&&	AND	Return True if operands are both True
||	OR	Return True if either operand is True
xor		Return True if only one operand is True
!	NOT	(Unary) Return True of operand is False

The ! operator has a much higher precedence than even && and ||, so that expressions to the right of a ! almost always mean what they say:

```
!$value1 + !$value2;   # adds result of !$value1 to !$value2
!($value1 + !$value2);   # negates result of $value1 + !$value2
```

Conversely, the not, and, or, and xor operators have the lowest precedence of all Perl's operators, with not being the highest of the four. This allows us to use them in expressions without adding extra parentheses:

```
# ERROR: evaluates 'Done && exit', which exits before the 'print'
# is executed
print "Done && exit";

# correct - prints "Done", then exits
print "Done" and exit;
```

All the logical operators (excepting the unary not/!) are efficient in that they always evaluate the left-hand operand first. If they can determine their final result purely from the left operand then the right is not even evaluated. For instance, if the left operand of an or is True then the result must be True. Similarly, if the left operand of an and is False then the result must be False.

The efficiency of a Boolean expression can be dramatically different depending on how we express it:

```
# the subroutine is always called
expensive_subroutine_call(@args) || $variable;

# the subroutine is called only if '$variable' is false
$variable || expensive_subroutine_call(@args);
```

The practical upshot of this is that it pays to write logic so that quickly evaluating expressions are on the left, and slower ones on the right. The countering problem is that sometimes we want the right side to be evaluated. For example, the following two statements operate quite differently:

```
# $tests will only be decremented if '$variable' is false.
do_test() if $variable || $tests--;

# $tests will always be (post-)decremented
do_test() if $tests-- || $variable;
```

Bitwise

The **bitwise operators**, or **bitwise logical operators**, bear a strong resemblance to their Boolean counterparts, even down to a similarity in their appearance:

&	Bitwise AND
|	Bitwise OR
^	Bitwise Exclusive or (XOR)
~	Bitwise NOT

The distinction between the two is that Boolean logic operators deal with their operands as whole values and return a 1 or 0. Bitwise operators on the other hand treat their operands as binary values and perform a logical operation between the corresponding bits of each value. The result of the operation is a new value composed of all the individual bit comparisons. To demonstrate the effect of these we can run the following short program:

```perl
#!/usr/bin/perl
# bitwise.pl
use warnings;
use strict;

my $a = 3;
my $b = 6;
my $r;

printf "$a = %03b \n", $a;
printf "$b = %03b \n", $b;

$r = $a & $b;   printf "$a & $b = %03b = %d\n", $r, $r;
$r = $a | $b;   printf "$a | $b = %03b = %d\n", $r, $r;
$r = $a ^ $b;   printf "$a ^ $b = %03b = %d\n", $r, $r;
$r = ~$a;    printf "~$a   = %03b = %d\n", $r, $r;
```

> **perl bitwise.pl**
```
3 = 011
6 = 110
3 & 6 = 010 = 2
3 | 6 = 111 = 7
3 ^ 6 = 101 = 5
~3 = 11111111111111111111111111111100 = -4
```

The bitwise operators can be used on any numeric value, but they are most often used for bitmasks and other values where individual bits have meanings. While we can certainly perform bitwise operations on ordinary decimal values, it does not make much sense from a legibility point of view. For instance, the following statement does the same as the one above, but it is less than clear how the result is achieved:

```
$bits = 11 & 6;    # produces 2
```

As a more practical example, the mode flag of the sysopen function is composed of a series of flags each of which sets a different bit. The Fcntl and POSIX modules give us symbolic names for these values so we often write things like:

```
$mode = O_RDWR | O_CREAT | O_TRUNC;
```

What this actually does is combine three different values using a bitwise OR to create a mode value of the three bits. We can also apply bitwise logic to permissions masks similar to that used by sysopen, chmod, and umask:

```
# set owner-write in umask
umask (umask |002);
```

This statement gets the current value of umask, bitwise ORs it with 002 (we could have just said 2 but permissions are traditionally octal) and then sets it back again – in this case the intent is to ensure that files are created without other-write permission. We don't know or care whether the bit was already set, but this makes sure that it is now.

The unary NOT operator deserves a special mention. It returns a value with all the bits of the expression supplied inverted (up to the word size of the underlying platform). That means that on a 32-bit system, ~0 produces a value with 32 on bits. On a 64-bit system, ~0 produces a value with 64 on bits. This can cause problems if we are manipulating bitmasks, since a 32 bit mask can suddenly grow to 64 bits if we invert it. For that reason, masking off any possible higher bits with & is a good idea:

```
# constrain an inverted bitmask to 16 bits
$inverted = ~$mask & (2 ** 16 - 1);
```

Note that the space before the ~ prevents =~ from being seen by Perl as a regular expression binding operator.

The result of all bitwise operations including the unary bitwise NOT is treated as unsigned by perl, so printing ~0 will typically produce a large positive integer:

```
print ~ 0;    # produces 4294967295 (or 2 ** 32 - 1) on a 32 bit OS.
```

This is usually an academic point since we are usually working with bitmasks and not actual integer values when we use bitwise operators. However, if the use integer pragma is in effect, results are treated as signed, which means that if the uppermost bit is set then numbers will come out as negative two's-complement values:

```
use integer;
print ~3;    # produces -4
```

See Chapter 3 for more on the use integer pragma.

A feature of the bitwise operators that is generally overlooked is the fact that they can also work on strings. In this context they are known as **'bitwise string operators'**. In this mode they perform a character-by-character comparison, generating a new string as their output. Each character comparison takes the numeric ASCII value for the character and performs an ordinary bitwise operation on it, returning a new character as the result.

This has some interesting applications. For example, to turn an uppercase letter into an lowercase letter we can bitwise OR it with a space, because the ASCII value for a space happens to be the difference in the ASCII value between capital and lower case letters:

```
print 'A' | ' ';    # produces 'a'
```

Examining this in terms of binary numbers show why and how this works:

```
'A' = 10000001
' ' = 01000000
'a' = 11000001
```

The inverse of ' ', bitwise, is an underscore, which has the Boolean value '10111111', so ANDing characters with underscores will uppercase them:

```
print 'upper' & '_____';    # produces 'UPPER'
```

Similarly, bitwise ORing number strings produces a completely different result from bitwise ORing them as numbers:

```
print 123 | 456;    # produces '507'
print '123' | '456';    # produces '577'
```

The digit 0 happens to have none of the bits that the other numbers use set, so ORing any digit with 0 produces that digit:

```
print '2000' | '0030';    # produces '2030'
```

Note that padding is important here:

```
print '2000' | '30';    # produces '3000'
```

If one string is shorter than the others, then implicit zero bits (or NULL characters, depending on our point of view) are added to make the string equal length, unless the operation is &, in which case the longer string is truncated to the shorter to avoid extra NULL characters appearing at the end of the resulting string.

Of course in a lot of cases it is simpler to use uc, lc, or simply add the values numerically. However, as an example that is hard to achieve quickly any other way, here is a neat trick for turning any text into alternating upper and lower case characters:

```
# translate every odd character to lower case
$text |= " \0" x (length ($text) / 2 + 1);

# translate every even character to upper case
$text &= "\377_" x (length($text / 2 + 1);
```

And here's a way to invert the case of all characters (that have a case):

```
$text ^= ' ' x length $text;
```

Of course both these examples presume normal alphanumeric characters and punctuation and a standard Latin-1 character set, so this kind of behavior is not advisable when dealing with other character sets and Unicode. Even with Latin-1, control characters will get turned into something completely different, such as \n, which becomes an asterisk.

Primarily, the bitwise string operators are designed to work on vec format strings (as manipulated by the vec function), where the actual characters in the string are not important, only the bits that make them up. See the 'Vector Strings' section from Chapter 3 for more on the vec function.

Combination Assignment

Perl also supports C-style combination assignment operators, where the variable on the right of the assignment is also treated as the value on the right-hand side of the attached operator. The general syntax for such operators is this:

```
$variable <operator>= $value;
```

For example:

```
$variable += 2;
```

Is a quicker way to write:

```
$variable = $variable + 2;
```

There are fifteen combination assignment operators in all, each of which is an assignment combined with the relevant binary operation:

Arithmetic	String	Shift	Logical	Bitwise
+=	x=	<<=	||=	|=
-=	.=	>>=	&&=	&=
*=	N\A	N\A	N\A	^=
/=	N\A	N\A	N\A	N\A
**=	N\A	N\A	N\A	N\A
%=	N\A	N\A	N\A	N\A

For illustration, this is how each of the arithmetic combination assignment operators changes the value of $variable from 10:

```
print $variable += 2;    # prints '12'
print $variable -= 2;    # prints '8'
print $variable *= 2;    # prints '20'
print $variable /= 2;    # prints '5'
print $variable **= 2;   # prints '100'
print $variable %= 2;    # prints '0'
```

This is also an example on concatenating one string onto another using the `. =` operator:

```perl
#!/usr/bin/perl
# concat.pl
use warnings;
use strict;

my $First = "One ";
my $First_Addition = "Two ";
my $Second_Addition = "Three";
my $string = $First;

print "The string is now: $string \n";
$string.= $First_Addition;
print "The string is now: $string \n";
$string.= $Second_Addition;
print "The string is now: $string \n";
```

> **perl concat.pl**
The string is now: One
The string is now: One Two
The string is now: One Two Three

Beware of using combination assignments in other expressions. Without parentheses, they have lower precedence than the expression around them, causing unintended results:

```perl
$a = $b + $c += 2;    # syntax error, cannot assign to '$b + $c'
```

Because + has higher precedence than += this is equivalent to:

```perl
$a = ($b + $c) += 2;    # the reason for the error becomes clear
```

What we really meant to say was this:

```perl
$a = $b + ($c += 2);    # correct, increments $c then adds it to $b
```

The regular expression binding operator looks a little like an assignment operator, BUT it isn't. =~ is a binding operator, and ~= is a bitwise not assignment.

Increment and Decrement

The ++ and -- operators are unary operators, which increment and decrement their operands respectively. Since the operand is modified, it must be a scalar variable. For instance, to increment the variable $number by one we can write:

```perl
$number ++;
```

The unary operators can be placed on either the left or right side of their operand, with subtly differing results. The effect on the variable is the same, but the value seen by expressions is different depending on whether the variable is modified before it is used, or used before it is modified. To illustrate, consider these examples in which we assume that $number starts with the value 6 each time we execute a new line of code:

```
print ++$number;   # preincrement variable, $number becomes 7, produces 7
print $number++;   # postincrement variable, $number becomes 7, produces 6
print --$number;   # predecrement variable, $number becomes 5, produces 5
print $number--;   # postdecrement variable, $number becomes 5, produces 6
```

Because of these alternate behaviors, ++ and -- are called **pre-increment** and **pre-decrement** operators when placed before the operand. Surprisingly enough, they are called **post-increment** and **post-decrement** operators when placed after them. Since these operators modify the original value they only work on variables, not values (and attempting to make them do so will provoke an error).

Somewhat surprisingly, Perl also allows the increment and decrement operators for floating point variables, incrementing or decrementing the variable by 1 as appropriate. Whether or not the operation has any effect depends on whether the number's exponent allows its significant digits to resolve a difference of 1. Adding or subtracting 1 from a value like 2.8e33 will have no effect:

```
$number = 6.3;
print ++$number; # preincrement variable, $number becomes 7.3, produces 7.3
print $number++; # postincrement variable, $number becomes 8.3, produces 7.3

$number = 2.8e33;
print ++$number;   # no effect, $number remains 2.8e33
```

Interestingly, Perl will also allow us to increment (but not decrement) strings too, by increasing the string to the next 'logical' value. For example:

```
$antenna_unit = "AE35";
print ++ $antenna_unit;   # produces 'AE36'


# turn a benefit in a language into a hairstyle
$language = "Perk";
print ++ $language;   # produces 'Perl'
print ++ $language;   # produces 'Perm'

# make a dated TV series (a bit) more current
$serial = "Space1999";
print ++ $serial;   # produce 'Space2000'
```

Only strings that are exclusively made up of alphanumeric characters (a-z, A-Z, and 0-9) can be incremented.

Comparison

The comparison operators are binary, returning a value based on a comparison of the expression on their left and the expression on their right. For example, the equality operator, ==, returns True (1) if its operands are numerically equal, and False (' ') otherwise:

```
$a == $b;
```

There are two complimentary sets of operators. The numeric comparison operators appear in conventional algebraic format and treat both operands as numeric, forcing them into numeric values if necessary:

```
print 1 < 2;   # produces 1
print "a" < "b";   # produces 0, since "a" and "b" both evaluate
                   # as 0 numerically, and 0 is not less than 0.
```

Note that if we have warnings enabled attempting to compare strings with a numeric comparison operator will cause Perl to emit a warning:

Argument "a" isn't numeric in numeric lt (<) at ...
Argument "b" isn't numeric in numeric lt (<) at ...

The string comparison operators, appear as simple mnemonic names, and are distinct from the numerical comparison operators in that they perform alphanumerical comparisons on a character-by-character basis. So, 2 is less than 12 numerically, but it is greater in a string comparison because the character 2 (as opposed to the number) is greater than the character 1. They are also dependent on locale, so the meaning of 'greater than' and 'less than' is defined by the character set in use (see the discussion on locale in Chapter 26).

```
print 2 > 12;   # numeric, produces 0
print 2 gt 12;   # string, produces 1 because the string "2" is
                 # greater than "12"
```

Unlike the counter example above, comparing numbers with a string comparison operator does not produce an error.

There are seven comparison operations in all, each with a numeric and string operator. Of these, the first six are standard Boolean tests that return True if the comparison succeeds and an empty value (' ' in string context, 0 numerically) otherwise. The seventh is the compare operator, which is slightly different:

Numeric	String	Operation
!=	ne	Return True if operands are not equal
>	gt	Return True if left operand is greater than right
==	eq	Return True if operands are equal
>=	ge	Return True if left operand is greater or equal to right
<	le	Return True if left operand is less than right
<=	lt	Return True if left operand is less than or equal to right
<=>	cmp	Return -1 if left operand is less than right, 0 if they are equal, and +1 if left operand is greater than right

The cmp and <=> operators are different from the other comparison operators because they do not return a Boolean result. Rather, they return one of three results depending on whether the left operand is less than, equal to, or greater than the right. Using this operator we can write efficient code like:

```
SWITCH: foreach ($a <=> $b) {
    $_ == -1 and do {print "Less"; last;};
    $_ == +1 and do {print "More"; last;};
    print "Equal";
}
```

To do the same thing with ordinary if...else statements would take at least two statements. The <=> and cmp operators are frequently used in sort subroutines, and indeed the default sort operation uses cmp internally.

> *The string comparison functions actually compare strings according to the value of the localization variable LC_COLLATE, including the implicit cmp of the sort function. See Chapter 26 'Locale and Internationalization' for more details.*

None of the comparison operators work in a list context, so attempting to do a comparison such as @a1 == @a2 will compare the two arrays in scalar context; that is, the number of elements in @a1 will be compared to the number of elements in @a2. This might actually be what we intend, but it looks confusing. $#a1 == $#a2 would probably be a better way to express the same thing in this case.

Regular Expression Binding

The regular expression binding operators =~ and !~ apply the regular expression function on their right to the scalar value on their left:

```
# look for 'pattern' in $match text
print "Found" if $match_text =~ /pattern/;

# perform substitution
print "Found and Replaced" if $match_text =~ s/pattern/logrus/;
```

The value returned from =~ is the return value of the regular expression function. Tis is – 1 if the match succeeded but no parentheses are present inside the expression, and a list of the match subpatterns (the values of $1, $2 ..., see Chapter 11 'Regular Expressions') if parentheses are used. It returns undef if the match failed. In scalar context this is converted to a count of the parentheses, which is a True value for the purposes of conditional expressions.

The !~ operator performs a logical negation of the returned value for conditional expressions, that is 1 for failure and ' ' for success in both scalar and list contexts.

look for 'pattern' in $match text, print message if absent
print "Not found" if $match_text !~ /pattern/;

Comma and Relationship

We use the **comma operator** all the time, usually without noticing it. In a list context it simply returns its left and right-hand side as parts of the list:

```
@array = (1, 2, 3, 4);   # construct a list with commas
mysubroutine(1, 2, 3, 4);   # send a list of values to 'mysubroutine'.
```

In a scalar context, the list operator returns the value of the right-hand side, ignoring whatever result is returned by the left:

```
return 1, 2, 3, 4;    # returns the value '4';
```

The **relationship** or **digraph operator** is a 'smart' comma. It has the same meaning as the comma operator but is intended for use in defining key-value pairs for hash variables. It also allows barewords for the keys:

```
# define a hash from a list, but more legibly
%hash = ('Tom'=>'Cat', 'Jerry'=>'Mouse', 'Spike'=>'Dog');

# define a hash from a list with barewords
%hash = (Tom=>'Cat', Jerry=>'Mouse', Spike=>'Dog');
```

We will return to both of these operators when we come to lists, arrays and hashes in Chapter 5.

Reference and Dereference

The reference constructor \ is a unary operator that creates and returns a reference for the variable, value, or subroutine that follows it. Alterations to the value pointed to by the reference change the original value:

```
$number = 42;
$numberref = \$number;
$$numberref = 6;
print $number;    # displays '6'
```

To dereference a reference (that is, access the underlying value) we can prefix the reference, a scalar, by the variable type of whatever the reference points to. In the above example we have a reference to a scalar, so we use $$ to access the underlying scalar. Since this sometimes has precedence problems when used in conjunction with indices or hash keys, we can also explicitly dereference with curly braces (See Chapter 5 for more details of this and other aspects of references):

```
$number = $$numberref;
$number = ${$numberref};
```

Alternatively, and often more legibly, we can use the **arrow operator**.

The Arrow

The dereference or arrow operator, ->, has two meanings, depending on the nature of its left-hand side. The first occurs when the left-hand side is an array or hash reference, or something that produces one, such as a subroutine.

```
# look up a hash key
$value = $hashref -> {$key};

# take a slice of an array
@slice = $arrayref -> [7..11];

# get first element of subroutine returning array reference:
$result = sub_that_returns_an_arrayref() -> [0];
```

The arrow operator is also implicitly used whenever we stack indices or hash keys together when we use multidimensional arrays (arrays of arrays) or hashes of hashes. That is:

```
$element = $pixel3d [$x] [$y] [$z];
```

Is actually shorthand for:

```
$element = $pixel3d [$x] -> [$y] -> [$z];
```

Which is, in turn, shorthand for:

```
$yz_array = $pixel3d [$x];
$z_array = $yz_array -> [$y];
$element = $z_array -> [$z];
```

This is because an array or hash can only contain scalars, so an array of arrays is really an array of array references. Perl is smart enough to know what we mean when we access a variable with stacked indices or hash keys though, so in this case we do not need the arrow operator, though it is still quite legal to put it in if we want.

The other application of the arrow operator is an object-oriented one. It occurs when the left-hand side is either a blessed object or a package name, in which case the right-hand side is a method name (a subroutine in the package), a subroutine reference, or a scalar variable containing a method name:

```
# call a class method
My::Package::Name -> class_method(@args);

# call an object method
$my_object -> method(@args);

# call an object method via a scalar variable (symbolic reference)
my $method_name = 'method';
$my_object -> $method_name(@args);
```

Interestingly, when a method is called via a scalar variable in this way, it is exempt from the usual restrictions on symbolic references that use strict refs normally imposes. The logic behind this is that by using the arrow operator we are being sufficiently precise about what we are trying to do for the symbolic reference to be safe – it can only be an object method.

Note that the arrow operator -> has nothing to do with the relationship (a.k.a. digraph) operator =>, which is just a slightly smarter comma for use in defining key-value pairs. Confusing the two can be a plentiful source of syntax errors, so be sure to use the right one in the right place.

Range

The range operator is one of the most poorly understood of Perl's operators. It has two modes of operation, depending on whether it is used in a scalar or list context. The list context is the most well known and is often used to generate sequences of numbers, as in:

```
foreach (1..10) {
   print "$_\n";   # print 1 to 10
}
```

In a list context, the range operator returns a list, starting with its left operand and incrementing it until it reaches the value on the right. So 1..10 returns the list (1, 2, 3, 4, 5, 6, 7, 8, 9, 10). The increment is done in the same manner as the increment operator, so strings also increment:

```
print "A".."E"   # returns ABCDE
```

If the left-hand side is equal to the right then a single element list containing that value is returned. If it is greater, an empty list is returned. To generate a reverse list therefore we need to use the reverse function on the result:

```
print reverse "A".."E"   # returns EDCBA
```

The use of the range operator in scalar context is less well understood, and consequently is rarely used. Its most common use is with numeric operands, which as a convenience, Perl compares to the input line number (or 'sequence number') special variable $.. More generally, the range operator is a bistable flip-flop, which alternates between returning 0 and 1 depending on the Boolean tests provided as its left and right arguments.

To begin with, it returns 0 until the left-hand side becomes True. Once the left-hand side becomes True it returns 1 until the right-hand side becomes True. When that happens, it starts returning 0 again until the left-hand side becomes True, and so on until input runs out. If the left or right-hand sides are literal numeric values then they are tested for equality against $., the sequence number. For example, this loop prints out the first ten lines of input:

```
while (<>) {
    1..10 and print;
}
```

If the left or right-hand operands are not literal numerics then they are simply used as Boolean tests, and their value is used to switch the range operator to the other state. Consequently using scalar variables or expressions will not work:

```
# ERROR: this does not work
$start = 1;
$end = 10;
while (<>) {
    $start .. $end and print;
}
```

What happens here is that both the left and right operands always return True, so the range operator returns True for every line, flip-flopping to False and back to True each time. So this is just a hard way to print every line of input.

What will work (usefully) are tests that involve either the sequence number $. or the current line, contained in $_. To make the above example work we have to involve $. explicitly, as in this repaired (and complete) example:

```
#!/usr/bin/perl
# range.pl
use warnings;
use strict;

my $start = 2;
my $end = 4;

while (<>) {
    ($. == $start)..($. == $end) and print "$.: $_";
}
```

Unfortunately the logic gets a little complex, and in this case we'd be better off with an `if` statement. Another class of solutions uses the range operator with regular expressions, which return Boolean results if the associated string matches. Without an explicitly bound string, the default argument $_ is used, so we can create very effective and impressively terse code like the next example. This code attempts to collect the header and body of an email message or an HTTP response, both of which separate the header from the body with an empty line, into different variables:

```
$header = "";
$body = "";
while (<>) {
    1 .. /^$/ and $header. = $_;
    /^$/ .. eof() and $body. = $_;
    exit if eof;   # ensure we only pass through one file
}
```

When used with expressions that test $_, we can also make use of a variant of the range operator expressed as three dots rather than two:

```
(/^BEGIN/) ... (/END$/)
```

The three-dot form of the range operator is identical in all respects except that it will not flip state twice on the same line. That is, the above range will alternate from False to True whenever BEGIN starts a line, and from true to false whenever END finishes a line, but if a line both starts with BEGIN and finishes with END then only one of the two transitions will occur. If the operator was False to start with then the BEGIN sets it to True and the END is ignored. If the operator was already True then the END is seen and the operator resets to False.

For a more advanced example of how the range operator can be used with regular expressions, see 'Extracting Lines with the Range Operator' in the discussion on regular expressions in Chapter 11.

Ternary

The ternary operator, `? :`, is an `if` statement that returns an expression. It takes three expressions, and returns the second or third as its result, depending on whether the first is True or False respectively. The logic is essentially:

```
if <expr1> then return <expr2> else return <expr3>:
```

For example:

```
$a ? $b : $c;   # return $b if $a is true, otherwise return $c

# print 'word' or 'words' as appropriate ($#array is 0 for one element)
print scalar(@words), " word", ($#words?'s':''), "\n";
```

The precedence of the ternary operator is low, just above that of assignment operators and the comma, so in general, expressions do not need parentheses. Conversely, however, the whole operator often does need to be parenthesized to stop precedence swallowing up terms to the right if it is followed by operators with higher precedence:

```
# result is $c + $d if $a is false
$result = $a ? $b : $c + $d;

# result is $b + $d or $c + $d
$result = ($a ? $b : $c) + $d;
```

Precedence and Associativity

We have already briefly discussed precedence and associativity earlier in the chapter, but they certainly warrant a closer look, so we will discuss them in more detail here. We also provide a table of all the operators and their precedence at the end of this section.

Arithmetic operators have a relatively high precedence, with multiplication having higher precedence than addition. The assignment operators like = have a very low precedence, so that they are only evaluated when both their operands (in particular, the rest of the statement to the right) has returned a result.

Associativity comes in to play when operators have the same precedence, as + and - do. It determines which operand is evaluated first. All the arithmetic operations and so on have left associativity, so it's given they will always evaluate their left before they evaluate their right. For example, multiplication * and division / have the same precedence, so they are evaluated left to right:

```
1 / 2 * 3 = (1 / 2)*3 = 1.5
```

If the association was to the right, the result would be:

```
1/(2 * 3) = 1/6 = 0.1666...
```

When Perl sees a statement, it works through all the operators contained within, working out their order of evaluation based on their precedence and associativity. As a more complete example, here is a sample of the kind of logic that Perl uses to determine how to process it. The parentheses are not actually added to the statement, but they show how Perl treats the statement internally. First, the actual statement as written:

```
$result = 3 + $var * mysub(@args);
```

The = operator has the lowest precedence, since the expressions on either side must obviously be evaluated before the = can be processed. In the compilation phase Perl parses the expression starting from the lowest precedence operator, =, with the largest expressions and divides the surrounding expressions into smaller, higher precedence expressions until all that is left is terms, which can be evaluated directly:

```
($result) = ((3) + (($var) * (mysub(@args))))
```

In the run-time phase, Perl evaluates expressions in order of highest precedence, starting from the terms and evaluating the result of each operation once the results of the higher precedence operations are known. A 'term' is simply any indivisible quantity, like a variable name, literal value, or a subroutine call with its arguments in parentheses. These have the highest precedence of all, since their evaluation is unambiguous, indivisible, and independent of the rest of the expression.

We don't often think of = as being an operator, but it returns a value, just like any other operator. In the case of =, the return value is the value of the assignment. Also like other binary operators, both sides must be evaluated first. The left-hand side must be assignable, but need not be a variable. Functions like substr can also appear on the left of =, and need to be evaluated before = overwrites (in the case of substr) the substring that it returns.

Having established the concepts of precedence and associativity, here is a complete table of all of Perl's basic operators in order of precedence (highest to lowest) and their associativity:

Associativity	Operators
Left	terms, list operators
Left	->
None	++ --
Right	**
Right	! ~ \, unary +, unary -
Left	=~ !~
Left	* / % x
Left	+ - .
Left	<< >>
None	Named unary operators (for example, -X)
None	< > <= >= lt gt le ge
None	== != <=> eq ne cmp
Left	&
Left	| ^
Left	&&
Left	||
None	.. ...
Right	?:
Right	= += -= *= /= %= .= etc.
Left	, =>
None	List operators (to the right)
Right	not
Left	and
Left	or xor

Precedence and Parentheses

Parentheses alter the order of evaluation in an expression, overriding the order of precedence that would ordinarily control which operation gets evaluated first, then in the following expression the + is evaluated before the *:

```
4 * (9 + 16)
```

It is sometimes helpful to think of parentheses as a 'precedence operator'. They automatically push their contents to the top of the precedence rankings by making their contents appear as a term to the surrounding expression. Within the parentheses, operators continue to have the same precedence as usual, so the 9 and 16 have higher precedence than the + because they are terms.

We can nest parentheses to any depth we like, entirely overriding the rules of precedence and associativity if we wish:

```
(3 - ((4 + 5)*6))
```

Parentheses are also used to construct list values. Whether as part of a subroutine or function argument list, or as a simple list value, they still have the same effect of overriding precedence.

Functions and subroutines may be used with or without parentheses. With parentheses they are simply terms from the point of view of the rest of the statement, since they are by nature, indivisible. The parentheses explicitly define the arguments to the function or subroutine.

Without parentheses the behavior of functions and subroutines changes – they become operators. Some functions take fixed numbers of arguments, or just one (in which case they are named unary operators). Others, like push, and all subroutines that are declared without prototypes, are named list operators.

List operators have high precedence to their left but low precedence to their right. The upshot of this is that anything to the right of a list operator is evaluated before the list operator is, but the list operator itself is evaluated before anything to the left. Put another way, list operators tend to group as much as possible to their right, and appear as terms to their left. In other words:

```
$result - $value + listop $value + $value, $value;
```

Is always evaluated as if it were:

```
$result = $value + (listop ($value + $value, $value));
```

This behavior makes sense when we recall that functions and subroutines only process arguments to their right. In particular, the comma operator has a higher precedence than list operators. Note however that even on their right side, list operators have a higher precedence than the named logical operators not, and, or, and xor, so we can say things like the following without requiring parentheses:

```
open FILEHANDLE, $filename or die "Failed to open $filename: $!";
```

Beware using the algebraic form of logical operators with list operators, however. In the above example, replacing or with || would cause the open to attempt to open the result of $filename || die ..., which would return the value of $filename in accordance with the shortcut rules of the logical operators, but which would swallow the die so that it was never called.

Functions that take only one argument also change their behavior with regard to precedence when used as operators. With parentheses they are functions and therefore have term precedence. As operators, they have a lower precedence than the arithmetic operators but higher than most others, so that the following does what it looks like it does:

```
$name1 = "myfile";
$name2 = ".txt";
if (-f $name1. $name2) {
    print "The concatenation occurred before -f acted.";
}
```

Assuming we have a file in our directory called myfile.txt then the concatenated variables make up the filename, which -f then acts on returning 1 because our file is present. The if statement then executes as per usual.

Using functions and subroutines without parentheses can sometimes make them more legible (and sometimes not). However, we can get into trouble if they swallow more expression that we actually intended:

```
print "Bye! \n", exit if $quitting;
```

The problem with this statement is that the exit has higher precedence than the print, because print as a list operator gives higher precedence to its right-hand side. So the exit is evaluated first and the Bye! is never seen. We can fix this in two different ways, both using parentheses:

```
# turn 'print' into a function, making the arguments explicit
print("Bye! \n"), exit if $quitting;

# make the 'print' statement a term in its own right
(print "Bye! \n"), exit if $quitting;
```

As we noted earlier, if the next thing after a function or subroutine name is an open parentheses then the contents of the parentheses are used as the arguments and nothing more is absorbed into the argument list. This is the function-like mode of operation, as opposed to the list-operator-like mode of operation, and is why the first example above produces the result we want. However, this can also trip us up:

```
# displays sum, returns string
print ($value1 + $value2), " is the sum of $value1 and $value2 \n";
```

This statement tries to group an addition within parentheses to make it stand out from the rest of the statement. However, it is the first thing after the print statement so the laws of parentheses dictate that it is the only argument to print. So we get the sum printed out. The comma operator then discards the result of the print and returns the string is the sum of... into void context, which discards it also.

To make this statement work correctly we have to disambiguate the parentheses so that they are used to group only, rather than define an argument list. There are two ways to do this, either use more parentheses around the whole argument list, or use operators:

```
# add parentheses
print (($value1 + $value2), "is the sum of $value1 and $value2 \n");

# disambiguate by adding zero
print 0 + ($value1 + $value2), "is the sum of $value1 and $value2\n";

# disambiguate with unary plus
print + ($value1 + $value2), "is the sum of $value1 and $value2 \n";
```

The last two examples work by simply preventing a parenthesis from being the first thing Perl sees after the print. The unary plus is a little friendlier to the eye (and this is in fact the only use for a unary plus). Of course in this case we can simply drop the parentheses since + has higher precedence than the comma anyway:

```
print $value1 + $value2, "is the sum of $value1 and $value2 \n";
```

Or, if we want to keep the parentheses, we can just rewrite the print statement into an equivalent but less problematic form:

```
print "The sum of $value1 and $value 2 is ",($value1 + $value2);
```

This final solution is probably the best of all, so the moral of this story is that it pays to think about how we express list arguments to functions and subroutines, especially for functions like print where we can rearrange arguments with a little imagination.

Disabling Functions and Operators

Occasionally we might want to prevent certain operators or functions from being used. One possible reason for doing this is for scripts run by untrusted users such as CGI scripts on a web server.

We can achieve this with the use ops and no ops pragmas, which allow us to selectively enable or disable Perl's operators (including all Perl's built-in functions). The typical use of the ops pragma is from the command line. For example, to disable the system function we can use:

> **perl -M-ops=system myprogram.pl**

The ops pragma controls how Perl compiles code by altering the state of an internal bitmask of opcodes. As a result, it is not generally useful inside a script, but if it is then it must be in a BEGIN block in order to have any effect on code:

```
BEGIN {
    no ops qw(system backtick exec fork);
}
```

An opcode is not the same thing as an operator, though there is a strong correlation. In this example system, exec, and fork are directly comparable, but the backtick opcode relates to backticks and the qx quoting operator. Opcodes are what Perl actually uses to perform operations, and the operators and functions we use are mapped onto opcodes – sometimes directly and sometimes conditionally, depending on how the operator or function is used.

The ops pragma is an interface to the Opcode module, which provides a direct interface to Perl's opcodes, and thereby to its operators and functions. It defines several functions for manipulating sets of opcodes, which the ops pragma uses to enable and disable opcodes, and it also defines a number of import tags that collect opcodes into categories. These can be used to switch collections of opcodes on or off. For example, to restrict Perl to a default set of safe opcodes we can use the :default tag:

> **perl –M-ops=:default myprogram.pl**

Similarly, to disable the open, sysopen, and close functions (as well as binmode and umask) we can switch off the :filesys_open tag:

> **perl -M-ops=:filesys_open myprogram.pl**

We can also disable the system, backtick, exec, and fork keywords with the :subprocess tag:

> **perl -M-ops=:subprocess myprogram.pl**

Or, programmatically:

```
BEGIN { no ops qw(:subprocess); }
```

A reasonably complete list of tags defined by Opcode is below, but bear in mind that the Opcode module is still under development and that the functions and operators controlled by these categories are subject to change.

Tags	Category
:base_core	Core Perl operators and functions, including arithmetic and comparison operators, increment and decrement, and basic string and array manipulation.
:base_mem	Core Perl operators and functions that allocate memory, including the anonymous array and hash constructors, the range operator, and the concatenation operator. In theory disabling these can prevent many kinds of memory hogs.
:base_loop	Looping functions such as while and for, grep and map, and the loop control statements next, last, redo, and continue. In theory disabling these prevents many kinds of CPU throttling.
:base_io	Filehandle functions such as readline, getc, eof, seek, print, and readdir. Disabling these functions is probably not a useful thing to do. Disabling open and sysopen is a different matter, but they are not in this category.
:base_orig	Miscellaneous functions including tie and untie, bless, the archaic dbmopen and dbmclose, localtime and gmtime, and various socket and network related functions.
:base_math	The floating-point mathematical functions sin, cos, atan2, exp, log, and sqrt, plus the random functions rand and srand.
:base_thread	The threaded programming functions lock and threadsv.
:default	All of the above :base_ tags; a reasonably default set of Perl operators
:filesys_read	Low-level file functions such as stat, lstat and fileno.
:sys_db	Perl's functions for interrogating hosts, networks, protocols, services, users, and groups, such as getpwent. Note that the actual names of the opcodes differ from the functions that map to them.
:browse	All of the above tags, a slightly extended version of :default that also inludes :filesys_read and :sys_db.
:filesys_open	open, sysopen, close, binmode, and umask.
:filesys_write	File modification functions like link and unlike, rename, mkdir, and rmdir, chmod, chown, and fcntl.

Table continued on following page

Tags	Category
:subprocess	Functions that start subprocesses like fork, system, the backtick operator (opcode backtick), and the glob operator. This is the set of opcodes that trigger errors in 'taint' mode, and a particularly useful set of opcodes to disable in security-conscious situations like CGI scripts.
:ownprocess	Functions that control the current process, such as exec, exit, and kill.
:others	Miscellaneous opcodes, mostly to do with IPC, such as msgctl and shmget.
:dangerous	Also miscellaneous, but more dangerous, opcodes. Currently this contains syscall, dump, and chroot.
:still_to_be_decided	Anything left over from the above categories. As we mentioned at the start, the Opcode module is under development, so the precise opcodes controlled by each tag are subject to change.

Many operators have more than one opcode, depending on the types of value that they can operate on. The addition operator + maps to the add and I_add opcodes, which perform floating-point and integer addition respectively. Fortunately we can use the dump function to generate a table of opcodes and descriptions. For example, to generate a complete (and very long) list of all opcodes and descriptions:

> **perl -MOpcode -e 'Opcode::opdump'**

This generates a table starting with:

```
     null  null operation
     stub  stub
   scalar  scalar
 pushmark  pushmark
wantarray  wantarray
    const  constant item
     gvsv  scalar variable
       gv  glob value
    gelem  glob elem
    padsv  private variable
    padav  private array
    padhv  private hash
   padany  private value
    ....
```

Alternatively, to search for opcodes by description we can pass in a string (actually, a regular expression). Any opcode whose description contains that string will be output. For example, to find the opcodes for all the logical operators:

> **perl -MOpcode=opdump -e 'opdump("logical")'**

This produces:

```
        and  logical and (&&)
         or  logical or (||)
        xor  logical xor
  andassign  logical and assignment (&&=)
   orassign  logical or assignment (||=)
```

Since the argument to opdump is a regular expression we can also get a list of all logical operators, bitwise, and Boolean with:

> **perl -MOpcode=opdump -e 'opdump("bit|logic")'**

So, if we wanted to disable logical assignments, we now know that the andassign and orassign opcodes are the ones we need to switch off. Note that the description always contains the operator, or function names, for those opcodes that map directly to operators and functions.

The Opcode module also contains a number of other functions for manipulating opcode sets and masks. Since these are unlikely to be of interest except to programmers working directly with the opcode tables, we will ignore them here. For more information see **>perldoc Opcode**.

Overriding Operators

As well as disabling operators we can also override them with the overload pragma. This is an object-oriented technique called **overloading**, where additional meanings are layered over an operator. The overloaded meanings come into effect whenever an object that defines an overloaded operator is used as an operand of that operator. For example, consider a module that implements an object class called MyObject that starts with the following lines:

```
package MyObject;

use overload '+' => &myadd, '-' => &mysub;
...
```

Normally we cannot add or subtract objects because they are just references, and Perl does not allow us to perform arithmetic on references. However, if we try to perform an addition or subtraction involving objects of type MyObject then the myadd and mysub methods in the MyObject package are called instead of Perl simply returning an error. This forms the basis of operator overloading for objects.

Since this involves concepts we have not yet introduced, in particular object-oriented programming, we cover it only briefly here. For more information see Chapter 19.

Summary

In this chapter, we compared and contrasted functions and operators. We then took an in-depth look into the different types of operators, including:

- ❏ Assignment
- ❏ Arithmetic
- ❏ Shift
- ❏ String and List
- ❏ Logical
- ❏ Bitwise
- ❏ Increment and Decrement
- ❏ Comparison
- ❏ Comma and Relationship
- ❏ Reference
- ❏ Arrow
- ❏ Range
- ❏ Ternary

We then covered precedence and associativity, and looked at the effect of parentheses on precedence. Finally, we took a brief look at overriding operators, and, as an example, saw how it could define syntaxes for object-oriented programming.

5

Beyond Scalars - More Data Types

Having introduced scalars in Chapter 3, we consider in this chapter the other data types except filehandles, which we examine in Chapter 12. References, which we cover here, can be seen as scalars. However, they are sufficiently different to warrant being considered more extensively.

This chapter will cover arrays, hashes, references, and typeglobs. We will also look at the more complex data that can be created by mixing data types. Later in the chapter, we show how we can define scalar, list, and hash constants, as well as checking for their existence, and finally we discuss the undefined value.

Lists and Arrays

A **list** is a compound value that may hold any number of scalar values (including none at all). Each value, or element, in the list is ordered and indexed; it is always in the same place, and we can refer to it by its position in the list. In Perl, lists are written out using parentheses and the comma operator:

```
(1, 2, 3, 4, 5, 6)
```

A list is simply a sequence of scalar values; we can copy it about, store it in arrays, and index it, but we can't alter its contents; it is immutable. To change it, we need to store the list in a variable. This variable is called an **array**.

An array provides dynamic storage for a list, and so can be grown, shrunk, and manipulated by altering its values. In Perl, we often use the terms array and list interchangeably, but the difference can be important. The most obvious example of an array is a named array variable, which is prefixed with an at-sign @ in the same way that scalar variables are prefixed with a $:

```
# define a six element array from a six element list
@array = (1, 2, 3, 4, 5, 6);
```

The **array variable** is a handle that we can use to access the values inside it, also known as array **elements**. Each element has an index number that corresponds to its position in the list. The index starts at **zero**, so the index number of an element is always one less than its place in the list. To access it, we supply the index number after the array in square brackets:

```
@array = (1, 2, 3, 4, 5, 6);
# print the value of the fifth element (index 4, counting from 0)
print "The fifth element is $array[4] \n";
```

We can also place an index on the end of a list, for example:

```
print "The fifth element is ", (1, 2, 3, 4, 5, 6)[4];   # produces 5
```

Of course, there isn't much point in writing down a list and then only using one value from it, but we can use the same approach with lists returned by functions like `localtime`, where we only want some of the values that the list contains:

```
$year = (localtime)[5];
```

For the curious, the parentheses around `localtime` prevent the `[5]` from being interpreted as an anonymous array and passed to `localtime` as an argument.

The values of an array are scalars (though these may include references), so the correct way to refer to an element is with a $ prefix, not an @ sign. It is the type of the returned value that is important to Perl, not where it was found:

```
print "The first element is $array[0] \n";
```

If we specify a negative index, Perl rather smartly counts from the end of the array:

```
print "The last element is $array[-1] \n";
```

We can also extract a list from an array by specifying a range of indices or a list of index numbers, also known as a **slice**:

```
print "The third to fifth elements: @array[2..4] \n";
```

Or, using negative numbers and a list:

```
print "The first two and last two elements: @array[0, 1, -2, -1] \n";
```

We can also retrieve the same index multiple times:

```
# replace array with first three elements, in triplicate
@array = @array[0..2, 0..2, 0..2];

# pick two elements at random:
@random = @array[rand scalar(@array), rand scalar(@array)];
```

Arrays can only contain scalars, but scalars can be numbers, strings, or references to other values like more arrays, which is exactly how Perl implements multidimensional arrays. They can also contain the undefined value, which is and isn't a scalar, depending on how we look at it.

The standard way of defining lists is with the comma operator, which concatenates scalars together to produce list values. We tend to take the comma for granted because it is so obvious, but it is in fact performing an important function. However, defining arrays of strings can get a little awkward:

```
@strings = ('one', 'two', 'three', 'four', 'five');
```

That's a lot of quotes and commas; an open invitation for typographic errors. A better way to define a list like this is with the list quoting operator qw, which we covered earlier in Chapter 3. Here's the same list defined more legibly with qw:

```
@strings = qw(one two three four five);
```

Or, defined with tabs and newlines:

```
@strings = qw(
    one
    two
    three
    four
    five
);
```

As well as assigning lists to array variables we can also assign them to scalars, by creating an assignable list of them:

```
($one, $two, $three) = (1, 2, 3);   # $one is now 1, $two 2 and $three 3
```

This is a very common sight inside subroutines, where we will often see things like:

```
($arg1, $arg2, @listarg) = @_;
```

Manipulating Arrays

Arrays are flexible creatures. We can modify them, extend them, truncate them and extract elements from them in many different ways. We can add or remove elements from an array at both ends, and even in the middle.

Modifying the Contents of an Array

Changing the value of an element is simple; we just assign a new value to the appropriate index of the array:

```
$array[4] = "The Fifth Element";
```

We are not limited to changing a single element at a time, however. We can assign to more than one element at once using a list or range in just the same way that we can read multiple elements. Since this is a selection of several elements we use the @ prefix, since we are manipulating an array value:

```
@array[3..5, 7, -1] = ("4th", "5th", "6th", "8th", "Last");
```

We can even copy parts of an array to itself, including overlapping slices:

```
@array = (1, 2, 3, 4, 5, 6);
@array[2..4] = @array[0..2];
print "@array \n"; @array = (1, 2, 1, 2, 3, 6);
```

We might expect that if we supply a different number of elements to the number we are replacing then we could change the number of elements in the array, replacing one element with three, for example. However, this is not the case. If we supply too many elements, then the later ones are simply ignored. If we supply too few, then the elements left without values are filled with the undefined value. There is a logic to this, however, as the following example shows:

```
# assign first three elements to @array_a, and the rest to @array_b
@array_a[0..2], @array_b = @array;
```

There is, however, a function that does replace parts of arrays with variable length lists. Appropriately enough it is called splice, and takes an array, a starting index, a number of elements and a replacement list as its arguments:

```
splice @array, $from, $quantity, @replacement;
```

As a practical example, to replace element three of a six-element list with three new elements (creating an eight element list), we would write something like:

```
#!/usr/bin/perl
# splice1.pl
use warnings;
use strict;

my @array = ('a', 'b', 'c', 'd', 'e', 'f');
# replace third element with three new elements
my $removed = splice @array, 2, 1, (1, 2, 3);

print "@array \n";    # produces 'a b 1 2 3 d e f'
print "$removed \n";  # produces 'c'
```

This starts splicing from element 3 (index 2), removes one element, and replaces it with the list of three elements. The removed value is returned from splice and stored in $removed. If we were removing more than one element we would supply a list instead:

```
#!/usr/bin/perl
# splice2.pl
use warnings;
use strict;

my @array = ('a', 'b', 'c', 'd', 'e', 'f');
# replace three elements with a different three
my @removed = splice @array, 2, 3, (1, 2, 3);

print "@array\n";     # produces 'a b 1 2 3 f'
print "@removed\n";   # produces 'c d e'
```

If we only want to remove elements without adding new ones we just leave out the replacement list, shrinking the array:

```perl
#!/usr/bin/perl
# splice3.pl
use warnings;
use strict;

my @array = ('a', 'b', 'c', 'd', 'e', 'f');
# remove elements 2, 3 and 4
my @removed = splice @array, 2, 3;

print "@array\n";    # produces 'a b f'
print "@removed\n";   # produces 'c d e'
```

Leaving out the length as well removes everything from the specified index to the end of the list. We can also specify a negative number as an index, just as we can for accessing arrays, so combining these two facts we can do operations like this:

```perl
#!/usr/bin/perl
# splice4.pl
use warnings;
use strict;

my @array = ('a', 'b', 'c', 'd', 'e', 'f');
# remove last three elements
my @last_3_elements = splice @array, -3;

print "@array\n";    # produces 'a b c'
print "@last_3_elements\n";   # produces 'd e f'
```

splice is a very versatile function and forms the basis for several other, simpler array functions like pop and push. We'll be seeing it a few more times before we are done with arrays.

Counting an Array

If we take an array or list and treat it as a scalar, Perl will return the number of elements (including undefined ones, if any) in the array. Treating an array as a scalar can happen in many contexts. For example a scalar assignment like this:

```perl
$count = @array;
```

This is a common cause of errors in Perl, since it is easy to accidentally assign an array in scalar rather than list context. While we're on the subject, remember that assigning a list in scalar context assigns the last value in the list rather than counts it:

```perl
$last_element = (1, 2, 3);   # last_element becomes 3
```

If we really mean to count an array we are better off using the scalar function, even when it isn't necessary, just to make it clear what we are doing:

```perl
$count = scalar(@array);
```

We can also find the index of the last element of the array using the special prefix $#. As indices start at zero, the highest index is one less than the number of elements in the list:

```perl
$highest = $#array;
```

This is useful for looping over ranges and iterating over arrays by index rather than by element, as this foreach loop demonstrates:

```perl
#!/usr/bin/perl
# byindex.pl
use warnings;
use strict;

my @array = ("First", "Second");
foreach (0..$#array) {
    print "Element number $_ contains $array[$_] \n";
}
```

> **perl byindex.pl**
Element number 0 contains First
Element number 1 contains Second

Loops will be discussed in Chapter 6.

Adding Elements to an Array

Extending an array is also simple – we just assign to an element that doesn't exist:

```perl
#!/usr/bin/perl
# add.pl
use warnings;
use strict;

my @array = ('a', 'b', 'c', 'd', 'e', 'f');
print "@array \n";    # produces 'a b 1 2 3 d e f'
$array[6] = "g";
print "@array \n";    # produces 'a b 1 2 3 d e f g'
```

We aren't limited to just adding directly to the end of the array. Any missing elements in the array between the current highest index and the new value are automatically added and assigned undefined values. For instance, adding $array[10] = "k"; to the end of the above example would cause Perl to create all of the elements with indices 7 to 9 (albeit without assigning storage to them) as well as assign the value k to the element with index 10.

To assign to the next element we could find the number of elements and then assign to that number (since the highest existing element is one less than the number of elements, due to the fact that indices start at zero). We find the number of elements by finding the scalar value of the array:

```perl
$array[scalar(@array)] = "This extends the array by one element";
```

However, it is much simpler to use the push function, which does the same thing without the arithmetic:

```perl
push @array, "This extends the array by one element more simply";
```

We can feed as many values as we like to push, including more scalars, arrays, lists and hashes. All of them will be added in turn to the end of the array passed as the first argument. Alternatively we can add elements to the start of the array using unshift:

```
unshift @array, "This becomes the zeroth element";
```

With unshift the original indices of the existing elements are increased by the number of new elements added, so the element at index five moves to index 6, and so on.

push and unshift are actually just special cases of the splice function. Here are their equivalents using splice:

```
# These are equivalent
push @array, @more;
splice @array, @array, 0, @more;


# These are equivalent
unshift @array, @more;
splice @array, 0, 0, @more;
```

Passing in @array twice to splice might seem a bizarre way to push values onto the end of it, but the second argument is constrained to be scalar by splice, so it is actually another way of saying scalar(@array), the number of elements in the array and one more than the current highest index, as we saw earlier.

Resizing and Truncating an Array

Interestingly, assigning to $#array actually changes the size of the array in memory. This allows us both to extend an array without assigning to a higher element and also to truncate an array that is larger than it needs to be, allowing Perl to return memory to the operating system:

```
$#array = 999;    # extend @array to 1000 elements


$#array = 3;    # remove @elements 4+ from array
```

Truncating an array destroys all elements above the new index, so the last example above is a more efficient way to do the following:

```
@array = @array[0..3];
```

This assignment also truncates the array, but by reading out values and then reassigning them. Altering the value of $#array avoids the copy.

Removing Elements from an Array

The counterparts of push and unshift are pop and shift, which remove elements from the array at the end and beginning, respectively:

```
#!/usr/bin/perl
# remove.pl
use warnings;
use strict;
```

```
my @array = (1, 2, 3, 4, 5, 6);
push @array, '7';    # add '7' to the end
print "@array\n";    # array is now (1, 2, 3, 4, 5, 6, 7)

my $last = pop @array;   # retrieve '7' and return array to six elements
print "$last\n";    # print 7

unshift @array, -1, 0;
print "@array\n";    #  array is now (-1, 0, 1, 2, 3, 4, 5, 6)
shift @array;   # remove the first element of the array
shift @array;   # remove the first element of the array
print "@array\n";    #  array is now again (1, 2, 3, 4, 5, 6)
```

While the push and unshift functions will add any number of new elements to the array, their counterparts are strictly scalar in operation, they only remove one element at a time. If we want to remove several at once we can use the splice function. In fact, pop and shift are directly equivalent to specific cases of splice:

```
# These are equivalent
pop @array;
splice(@array, -1);

# These are equivalent
shift @array;
splice(@array, 0, 1);
```

From this we can deduce that the pop function actually performs an operation very similar to this:

```
# read last element and then truncate array by one - that's a 'pop'
$last_element = $array[$#array--]
```

Extending this principle, here is how we can do a multiple pop operation:

```
@last_20_elements = $array[-20..-1];
$#array-=20;
```

Both undef and delete will remove the value from an array element, replacing it with the undefined value, but neither will actually remove the element itself, and higher elements will not slide down one place. This would seem to be a shame, since delete removes a hash key just fine. Hashes, however, are not ordered and indexed like arrays.

To truly remove elements from an array, we can use the splice function, omitting a replacement list:

```
@removed = splice(@array, $start, $quantity);
```

For example, to remove elements 2 to 5 (four elements in total) from an array we would use:

```
@removed = splice(@array, 2, 4);
```

Of course if we don't want to keep the removed elements we don't have to assign them to anything.

As a slightly more creative example, here is how we can move elements from the end of the list to the beginning, using a splice and an unshift.

```
unshift @array, splice(@array, -3, 3);
```

Or, in the reverse direction:

```
push @array, splice(@array, 0, 3);
```

The main problem with `splice` is not getting carried away with it.

Removing All Elements from an Array

To destroy an array completely we can undefine it using the `undef` function. This is a different operation from undefining just part of an array as we saw previously:

```
undef @array;    # destroy @array
```

This is equivalent to assigning an empty list to the array, but more direct:

```
@array = ();
```

It follows that assigning a new list to the array also destroys the existing contents. We can use that to our advantage if we want to remove lines from the start of an array without removing all of them:

```
@array = @array[-100..-1];    # truncate @array to its last one hundred lines
```

This is simply another way of saying:

```
splice(@array, 0, $#array-100);
```

Sorting and Reversing Lists and Arrays

Perl supplies two additional functions for generating differently ordered sequences of elements from an array or list. The `reverse` function simply returns a list in reverse order:

```
# reverse the elements of an array
@array = reverse @array;

# reverse elements of a list
@ymd = reverse((localtime)[3..5]);    # return in year/month/day order
```

This is handy for all kinds of things, especially for reversing the result of an array slice made using a range. `reverse` allows us to make up for the fact that ranges can only be given in low to high order.

The `sort` function allows us to perform arbitrary sorts on a list of values. With only a list as its argument it performs a standard alphabetical sort:

```
@words = ('here', 'are', 'some', 'words');
@alphabetical = sort @words;
print "@words";    # produces 'are here some words'
```

`Sort` is much more versatile than this, however. By supplying a code or subroutine reference we can sort the list in any way we like. `sort` automatically defines the global variables $a and $b for bespoke sorting algorithms, so we can specify our own sort:

```
@alphabetical = sort { $a cmp $b} @words;
```

This is actually the default sort algorithm that Perl uses when we specify no sort algorithm of our own. In order to be a correct and proper algorithm, the sort code must return -1 if $a is less than $b (however we define that), 0 if they are equal, and 1 if $a is greater than $b. This is exactly what cmp does for strings, and <=> does for numbers.

We should take care never to alter $a or $b either, since they are aliases for the real values being sorted. At best this can produce an inconsistent result, at worst it may cause the sort to lose values or fail to return. The best sorts are the simple ones, here are some more sort algorithms:

```
@ignoring_case = sort {lc($a) cmp lc($b)} @words;
@reversed = sort {$b cmp $a} @words;
@numerically = sort {$a <=> $b} @numbers;
@alphanumeric = sort {int($a) <=> int($b) or $a cmp $b} @mixed;
```

The last example above is worth a moment to explain. It first compares $a and $b as integers, forcing them into numeric values with int. If the result of that comparison is non-zero then at least one of the values has a numeric value. If however the result is zero, which will be the case if $a and $b are both non-numeric strings, the second comparison is used to compare the values as strings. Consequently this algorithm sorts numbers and strings that start numerically and all other strings alphabetically, even if they are mixed into the same list. Parentheses are not required because or has a very low precedence.

We can also use a named subroutine to sort with. For example, we can create a subroutine named reversed that allows us to invent a sort reversed syntax:

```
sub reversed {$b cmp $a};
@reversed = sort reversed @words;
```

Similarly, a subroutine called numerically that also handles floating point:

```
# force interpretation of $a and $b as floating point numbers
sub numerically {$a*1.0 <=> $b*1.0 or $a cmp $b};

@number_order = sort numerically @words;
```

Note however that both functions must be defined in the same package as they are used in order to work, since the variables $a and $b are actually package variables. Similarly, we should never declare $a and $b with my since these will hide the global variables. Alternatively we can define a prototype, which provokes sort into behaving differently:

```
sub backwards ($$) {$_[0] cmp $_[1]};
```

The prototype requires that two scalars are passed to the sort routine. Perl sees this and passes the values to be compared though the special variable @_ instead of via $a and $b. This will allow the sort subroutine to live in any package, for example a fictional 'Order' package containing a selection of sort algorithms:

```
use Order;
@reversed = sort Order::reversed @words;
```

We'll see how to create such a package in Chapter 10.

Changing the Starting Index Value

Perl allows us to change the starting index value from 0 to something else. For example, to have our lists and arrays index from 1 (as Pascal would) instead of 0, we would write:

```
$[=1;
@array = (11, 12, 13, 14, 15, 16);
print $array[3];   # produces 13 (not 14)
```

The scope of $ [is limited to the file that it is specified in, so subroutines and object methods called in other files will not be affected by the altered value of $ [more on scoping in Chapter 8. Even so, messing with this special variable is dangerous and discouraged. As a rule of thumb, do not do it.

Converting Lists and Arrays into Scalars

Since lists and arrays contain compound values, they have no direct scalar representation – that's the point of a compound value. Other than counting an array by assigning it in scalar context, there are two ways that we can get a scalar representation of a list or array. First, we can create a reference to the values in the list or, in the case of an array, generate a direct reference. Second, we can convert the values into a string format. Depending on our requirements, this string may or may not be capable of being transformed back into the original values again.

Taking References

An array is a defined area of storage for list values, so we can generate a reference to it with the backslash operator:

```
$arrayref = \@array;
```

This produces a reference through which the original array can be accessed and manipulated. Alternatively, we can make a copy of an array and assign that to a reference by using the array reference constructor (also known as the anonymous array constructor) [...]:

```
$copyofarray = [@array];
```

Both methods give us a reference to an anonymous array that we can assign to, delete from, and modify. The distinction between the two is important, because one will produce a reference that points to the original array, and so can be used to pass it to subroutines for manipulations on the original data, whereas the other will create a copy that can be modified separately.

Converting Lists into Formatted Strings

The final way to turn an array into a scalar is via the join and pack functions. join creates a string from the contents of the array, optionally separated by a separator string:

```
# join values into comma-separated-value string
$string = join ',', @array;

# concatenate values together
$string = join '', @array;
```

join is the counterpart to split, which we covered under 'Strings' earlier in Chapter 3. Unlike split however, it takes a simple string as its separator argument, not a regular expression, since the separator is a literal output value rather than an input pattern.

The sprintf function takes a format string and a list of values, and returns a string created from the values in the list rendered according to the specified format. Like any function that accepts list arguments, sprintf does not care if we supply them one by one or all together in an array:

```
# get current date and time into array
@date = (localtime)[5, 4, 3, 2, 1, 0];    # Y, M, D, h, m, s
$date[0]+=1900;    # fix year

# generate time string using sprintf
$date = sprintf "%4d/%02d/%02d %2d:%02d:%02d", @date;
```

This example produces date and time strings from localtime. It uses indices to extract the values it wants from localtime in the correct order for sprintf, so that each individual format within the format string lines up and controls the corresponding value. sprintf then applies each format in turn to each value in the date array to produce its string result.

The pack function also converts list values into strings using a format string, but in this case the format string describes the types of the supplied arguments at a much lower level, and the resulting string is really just a sequence of bytes in a known order, rather than a string in the conventional sense. For example, the C format packs integers into a character representation, much the same way that chr does:

```
$char = pack 'C', $code;    # $char = 'A' if $code = 65
```

This only uses a single value, however. For lists containing the same data type we can either repeat the pattern, for example, CCCC for four characters, or add a repeat count – C4 for four characters, or C* for as many elements as the list provides. Extending this example to a list or array, this is one way we might convert a list of character codes into a string:

```
@codes = (80, 101, 114, 108);
$word = pack 'C*', @codes;
print $word;    # produces 'Perl'
```

Similarly, to collect the first letters of a list of strings we can use the a format. Unlike the C format, a extracts multiple characters from a list item. The repeat count therefore has a different meaning; a4 would extract four characters from the first item in the list, ignoring the other elements. To get the first letter of each element we need to use aaaa instead. In the next example we use the x operator to generate a string of a's the right length for the supplied list.

```
@words = ('Practical', 'extraction', 'reporting', 'language');
$first_letters = pack 'a'x@words, @words;
print $first_letters;    # guess...
```

The examples above not withstanding, the string returned by pack is usually not suitable for printing. The N format will pack 'long' integer values into a four-byte string, each 'character' of the string being 8 bits of the 32 bit integer. The string that results from these four characters is unlikely to produce something that prints out well, but can be stored in a file and retrieved very conveniently:

```
$stored_integers = pack('N' x @integers), @integers;
```

This string will contain four bytes for every integer in the list. If the integers are large and so is the list, this is a lot more efficient than something like `join`, which would create textual versions of the integers (so `100000` takes seven characters) and would need to add another character to separate each value from its neighbors too.

Hashes

Hashes, also known as associative arrays, are Perl's other compound data type. While lists and arrays are ordered and accessed by index, hashes are ordered and indexed by a **descriptive key**. There is no 'first' or 'last' element in a hash like there is in an array (the hash does have an internal order, but it reflects how Perl stores the contents of the hash for efficient access, and cannot be controlled by us).

Hashes are defined in terms of keys and values, or **key-value pairs** to use an alternative expression. They are stored differently from arrays internally, in order to allow for more rapid lookups by name, so there is no 'value' version of a hash in the same way that a list is a 'value' version of an array. Instead, lists can be used to define either arrays or hashes, depending on how we use them.

The following list of key-value pairs illustrates a potential hash, but at this point it is still just a list:

```
('Mouse', 'Jerry', 'Cat', 'Tom', 'Dog', 'Spike')
```

Since hashes consist of paired values, Perl provides the `=>` operator as an alternative to the comma. This helps differentiate the keys and values and makes it clear to anyone reading our source code that we are actually talking about hash data and not just a list. Hash values can be any scalar, just like array elements, but hash keys can only be strings, so the `=>` operator also allows us to omit the quotes by treating its left-hand side as a constant string. The above list would thus be better written as:

```
(Mouse => 'Jerry', Cat => 'Tom', Dog => 'Spike')
```

At the moment we only have a list, even if it is made out to show the key-value pairs. To turn it into a hash we need to assign it to a hash variable. Hashes, like lists and scalars, have their own special prefix, in this case the `%` symbol (it is not a hash character because hash is used for different symbols in different countries, and in any case was already in common use by shells for comments). So, to create a hash from the above we would write:

```
%hash = (Mouse => 'Jerry', Cat => 'Tom', Dog => 'Spike');
```

When this assignment is made, Perl takes the keys and values supplied in the list and stores them in an internal format that is optimized for retrieving the values by key. To achieve this, Perl requires that the keys of a hash be string values, which is why when we use `=>` we can omit quotes, even with `strict vars` in operation. This doesn't stop us using a variable to store the key name, as Perl will evaluate it in string context, but it does mean that we must use quotes if we want to use spaces or other characters meaningful to Perl such as literal $, @, or % characters:

```
# using variables to supply hash keys
($mouse, $cat, $dog)=>('Souris', 'Chat', 'Chien');
%hash = ($mouse => 'Jerry', $cat => 'Tom', $dog => 'Spike');

# using quotes to use non-trivial strings as keys (with and without
# interpolation)
%hash =('Exg Rate' => 1.656, '%age commission' => 2, "The $mouse" => 'Jerry');
```

This restriction on keys also means that if we try to use a non-string value as a key we will get unexpected results. In particular, if we try to use a reference as a key it will be converted into a string, which cannot be converted back into the original reference. Therefore, we cannot store pairs of references as keys and values unless we use a symbolic reference as the key (see 'References' later in the chapter for more on this subject).

Alternatively we can use the qw operator and separate the keys and values with whitespace. A sensible layout for a hash might be:

```
%hash = qw(
    Mouse    Jerry
    Cat      Tom
    Dog      Spike
);
```

Note how this is very similar to creating an array. In fact the assignment is identical, but the type of the variable means that the list data is stored differently from an array. We can now access elements of the hash, which we do by providing a key after the hash in curly brackets:

```
print "The mouse is ", $hash{'Mouse'};
```

This is similar in concept to how we index an array, but note that if we are using strict variables (courtesy of use strict) we ought to use quotes now; it is only the => operator that lets us get away with omitting the quotes when strict vars are in effect. Note that just like an array, a hash can only store scalars as its values, so the prefix for the returned result is $, not %, just as it is for array elements.

We can also specify multiple keys to extract multiple values:

```
@catandmouse = @hash{'Cat', 'Mouse'};
```

This will return the list (Tom, Jerry) into the array @catandmouse. Once again, note that the returned value is a list so we use the @ prefix.

We can even specify a range, but this is only useful if the keys are incremental strings, which typically does not happen too often; we would probably be better off using a list if our keys are that predictable. For example, if we had keys with names AA, AB ... BY, BZ inclusive (and possibly others) then we could use:

```
@aabz_values = @hash{'AA'..'BZ'};
```

We cannot access the first or last elements of a hash, since hashes have no concept of first or last. We can however return a list of keys with the keys function, which returns a list of the keys in the hash:

```
@keys = keys %hash;
```

The order of the keys returned is random (or rather, it is determined by how Perl chooses to store the hash internally), so we would normally sort the keys into a more helpful order if we wanted to display them. To sort lexically we can just say sort keys %hash like this:

```
print "The keys are:";
print join(',', sort keys %hash);
```

We can also use the keys as a list and feed it to a `foreach` loop:

```
# dump out contents of a hash
foreach (sort keys %hash) {
    print "$_ => $hash{$_} \n";
}
```

Manipulating Hashes

We can manipulate hashes in all the same ways that we can manipulate arrays, with the odd twist due to their associative nature. Accessing hashes is a little more interesting than accessing arrays however. Depending on what we want to do with them we can use the keys and values functions, sort them in various different ways, or use the each iterator if we want to loop over them.

Adding and Modifying Hash Values

We can manipulate the values in a hash through their keys. For example, to change the value of the key Cat, we could use:

```
$hash{'Cat'} = 'Sylvester';
```

If the key exists already in the hash then its value is overwritten. Otherwise it is added as a new key:

```
$hash{'Bird'} = 'Tweety';
```

Assigning an array (or another hash) produces a count of the elements, as we have seen in the past, but we can assign multiple keys and values at once by specifying multiple keys and assigning a list, much in the same way that we can extract a list from a hash:

```
@hash{'Cat', 'Mouse'} = ('Sylvester', 'Speedy Gonzales');
```

Or, a possibly clearer example using arrays throughout:

```
@hash{@keys} = @values;
```

We can even use ranges to generate multiple keys at once, for example this assignment which creates key-value pairs from A=>1 to Z=>26.

```
@lettercodes{'A'..'Z'} = 1..26;
```

Keys and values are added to the hash one by one, in the order that they are supplied, so our previous example of:

```
@hash{'Cat', 'Mouse'} = ('Sylvester', 'Speedy Gonzales');
```

Is equivalent to:

```
$hash{'Cat'} = 'Sylvester';
$hash{'Mouse'} = 'Speedy Gonzales';
```

This can be an important point to keep in mind, since it allows us to overwrite the values associated with hash keys, both deliberately and accidentally. For example, this code snippet defines a default set of keys and values and then selectively overrides them with a second set of keys and values, held in a second input hash. Any key in the second hash with the same name as one in the first overwrites the key in the resulting hash. Any keys not defined in the second hash keep their default values:

```perl
#!/usr/bin/perl
# hash.pl
use warnings;
use strict;

# define a default set of hash keys and values
my %default_animals = (Cat => 'Tom', Mouse => 'Jerry');

# get another set of keys and values
my %input_animals = (Cat => 'Ginger', Mouse => 'Jerry');

# combining keys and values of supplied hash with those in default hash overrides
# default
my %animals = (%default_animals, %input_animals);
print "$animals{Cat}\n"; # prints 'Ginger'
```

Removing Hash Keys and Values

Removing elements from a hash is easier, but less flexible, than removing them from a list. Lists are ordered, so we can play a lot of games with them using the splice function among other things. Hashes do not have an order (or at least, not one that is meaningful to us), so we are limited to using undef and delete to remove individual elements.

The undef function removes the value of a hash key, but leaves the key intact in the hash:

```perl
undef $hash{'Bird'};   # 'Bird' still exists as a key
```

The delete function removes the key and value entirely from the hash:

```perl
delete $hash{'Bird'};   # 'Bird' removed
```

This distinction can be important, particularly because there is no way to tell the difference between a hash key that doesn't exist and a hash key that happens to have an undefined value as its value simply by looking at the result of accessing it:

```perl
print $hash{'Bird'};   # produces 'Use of uninitialized value in print ...'
```

It is for this reason that Perl provides two functions for testing hash keys, defined and exists.

Converting Lists and Arrays into Hashes

In contrast with scalars, converting a list or array into a hash is extremely simple; we just assign it:

```perl
%hash = @array;
```

What actually happens here is that the values extracted from the array are assigned to the hash in pairs, with even elements (starting at index 0) as the keys and odd elements (starting at index 1) as their values. If the array contains an odd number of elements then the last key to be assigned to the hash will end up with an undefined value as its value. If we have warnings enabled (as we should), Perl warn against this with:

Odd number of elements in hash assignment ...

Reversing Hashes

One special trick that is worth mentioning while we are on the subject of hashes is how to reverse the keys and values, so that the values become the keys and vice versa. This at first might seem to be a hard, or at least a non-trivial task involving code like the following:

```perl
#!/usr/bin/perl
# reverse.pl
use warnings;
use strict;

my %hash = ('Key1' => 'Value1', 'Key2' => 'Value2');

print "$hash{Key1}\n";   # print 'Value1'
foreach (keys %hash) {
    # invert key-value pair
    $hash{$hash{$_}} = $_;

    # remove original key
    delete $hash{$_};
}
print "$hash{Value1}\n";   # print 'Key1'
```

Reversing, or **transposing** as it is also known, offers plenty of problems. For a start, if the values are references then turning them into keys will convert them into strings, which cannot be converted back into references. Also, if two keys have the same value, we end up with only one of them making it into the reversed hash, since we cannot have two identical keys. Worse, if a key and value are the same this code wipes out the key-value pair from the hash entirely.

We can't fix the problem with duplicate keys, that is just in the nature of hashes, but we can reverse the keys and values much more simply than the code above, and without endangering identical key-value pairs, by converting the hash into a list, reversing the list, and then assigning it back to the hash again:

```perl
%hash = reverse %hash;
```

We have to look closely to see the list in this example. It is returned by the %hash because reverse is a function that gives its argument(s) a list context. There is no such thing as hash context in Perl, for the same reason that there is no such thing as a hash value, as we noted at the start of this discussion. The reverse then reverses the list, which also happens to reverse the orientation of the keys and values, and then the reversed list is assigned back to the hash.

If more than one key has the same value then this trick will preserve the first one to be found. Since this is entirely random (because we cannot sort the list) we cannot determine which key will be preserved as a value in the new hash. If we want to handle that we will have to either process the hash the slow way, find a way to eliminate duplicates first, or use a different storage strategy. For simple hashes without duplicates though, this is a very simple way to achieve the desired end.

Accessing and Iterating Over Hashes

The simplest, or at least the most common, way of iterating across a hash is to use the `keys` function to return a list of the keys. This list is actually a copy of the hash keys, so we cannot alter the key names through this list. However, it provides a very simple way to iterate across a hash. We will use `foreach` loops in this section, which are explained in detail in Chapter 6.

```perl
#!/usr/bin/perl
# iterate.pl
use warnings;
use strict;

my %hash = ('Key1' => 'Value1', 'Key2' => 'Value2');
# dump of hash
foreach (keys %hash) {
    print "$_ => $hash{$_} \n";
}
```

If we want a list for output we probably want to sort it too:

```perl
# sorted dump of hash
foreach (sort keys %hash) {
    print "$_ => $hash{$_} \n";
}
```

We can also access the values directly through the `value` function:

```perl
@values = values %hash;
```

This provides a convenient way to process a hash when we do not care about the keys, with the caveat that we cannot easily find the keys if we need them; since hashes are one way, there is no 'look up key by value' syntax:

```perl
# print list of sorted values
foreach (sort values %hash) {
    print "Got: $_ \n";
}
```

This returns a copy of the values in the hash, so we cannot alter the values this way. If we want a list of values that we can assign to, we can do so with a loop like this:

```perl
# increment all hash values by one
foreach (@hash {keys %hash} ) {
    $_++;
}
```

This example makes use of **aliasing**, where the default argument variable $_ becomes a direct alias for, rather than a copy of, the value that it refers to. Aliasing occurs only when the values being iterated over come from a variable, as they do in the example above, but not in the one before it. See Chapter 6 for more on aliasing in loops and subroutines.

The catch with `foreach` is that it pulls all of the keys (or values) out of the hash at one time, and then works through them. This is inefficient in terms of memory usage, especially if the hash is large. An alternative approach is offered by the `each` function, which returns the next key-value pair each time it is used, and is ideal for use in `while` loops:

```
while (($key, $value) = each %hash) {
    print "$key => $value \n";
    $hash{$key}++;
}
```

The order of the key-value pairs produces by `each` is the same as that produced by `keys` and `values`, in other words it follows an internal logic that is all Perl's, and nothing of ours, so it isn't convenient for producing sorted output. `each` actually works by moving an internal index pointer through the hash, so that each subsequent call to `each` returns the next key-value pair. We cannot access this pointer externally, however (and even if we could we cannot use it). The index is reset after we reach the last key, and also if we use `keys` to return the whole list.

Sorting and Indexing

If we want to generate an ordered list of hash keys and values we can do so with the `sort` function. A simple alphabetical list of keys can be produced with `sort keys %hash` as we saw earlier. However, `sort` is a versatile function and we can play all kinds of tricks with it. One not so clever trick is simply to sort the values directly, as we saw earlier:

```
# print list of sorted values
foreach (sort values %hash) {
    print "Got $_ \n";
}
```

The catch with this is that we can't easily get back to the keys if we want to. The solution to this problem is to give `sort` a subroutine that accesses the values via the keys:

```
# sort a hash by values
foreach (sort { $hash{$a} cmp $hash{$b} } keys %hash) {
    print "$hash{$_} <= $_ \n";
}
```

This is important if we want to change the values in the hash, since `values` just returns a copy of the hash values, which we cannot assign to.

Creative uses of `sort` gives us other possibilities too. For instance, we can create a hash with an index by replacing the values with references to two-element arrays or hashes containing an index value and the original value. This is an example of a complex data structure, which we cover in more detail in Chapter 6, so we'll just give a simple example of defining and then sorting such a hash:

```
#!/usr/bin/perl
# indexhash.pl
use warnings;
use strict;
```

```
# create a hash with integrated index
my %hash = (
    Mouse => {Index => 0, Value => 'Jerry'},
    Cat   => {Index => 1, Value => 'Tom'},
    Dog   => {Index => 2, Value => 'Spike'}
);

# sort a hash by integrated index
foreach (sort {$hash{$a} {'Index'} cmp $hash{$b}{'Index'}} keys %hash) {
    print "$hash{$_} {'Value'} <= $_ \n";
}
```

The only catch with this is that we will need to keep track of the index numbers ourselves, since unlike an array we don't get it done for us automatically.

Named Arguments

Perl does not have an official mechanism for passing named arguments to subroutines, but hashes allow us to do exactly this if we write our subroutines to use them:

```
animate(Cat => 'Tom', Mouse => 'Jerry');

sub animate {
    my %animals = @_;

    # rest of subroutine...
}
```

Some existing modules in the Perl library allow this and also adapt between ordinary or named arguments by prefixing the key names with a minus sign. Here is a quick example of how we can do it ourselves:

```
#!/usr/bin/perl
# arguments.pl
use warnings;
use strict;

# list form takes mouse, cat, dog as arguments, fixed order.
animate('Jerry', 'Tom', 'Spike');

# hash form takes animals in any order using '-' prefix to identify type,
# also allows other animal types
animate(-Cat => 'Sylvester', -Bird => 'Tweety', -Mouse => 'Speedy Gonzales');

# and the subroutine...
sub animate {
    my %animals;

    # check first element of @_ for leading minus...
    if ($_[0]!~/^-/) {
        # it's a regular argument list, use fixed order
        @animals{'-Mouse', '-Cat', '-Dog'} = @_;
    } else {
        # it's named argument list, just assign it.
        %animals = @_;
    }
}
```

```
      # rest of subroutine...
      foreach (keys %animals) {
         print "$_ => $animals{$_} \n";
      }
}
```

See Chapter 7 for more on this theme, as well as some improved examples that check arguments more closely.

Converting Hashes into Scalars

Evaluating a hash in scalar context returns 0 (False) if the hash is empty. If it contains data, we get a string of the form N/M that describes in approximate terms how efficiently Perl has been able to store the keys and values in the hash. Loosely speaking, the numbers are a ratio and can be read as a fraction, the higher the first relative to the second, the more efficient the storage of the hash:

```
#!/usr/bin/perl
# convert.pl
use warnings;
use strict;

my %hash = (one => 1, two => 2, three => 3, four => 4, five => 5);

# check the hash has data
if (%hash) {
    # find out how well the hash is being stored
    print scalar(%hash);   # produces '4/8'
}
```

While this is interesting if we are concerned with how well Perl is storing our hash data, it is unlikely to be of much use otherwise. We might have expected to get a count of the elements in the hash, or possibly the keys, but we can't count a hash in the same way that we can an array, simply by referring to it in scalar context. To count a hash we can use either keys or values and evaluate the result in scalar context. For example:

```
# count the keys of a hash
$elements = scalar(keys %hash);
```

If we really wanted to know the number of elements we would only need to multiply this result by 2.

Alternatively, we can create a reference to the hash with the backslash operator:

```
$hashref = \%hash;
```

Dereferencing a hash reference is very much like dereferencing an array reference, only with a key instead of an index:

```
$dog = $hash -> {'Dog'};
```

Alternatively we can dereference the entire hash with a '%' prefix:

```
%hash == %$hashreference;
```

We can also create a hash reference with the { . . . } constructor, which creates a brand new anonymous hash with the same contents as the old one. This is different from, and produces a different result to, the array reference constructor [. . .] because the reference points to an anonymous hash, which is therefore organized and stored like one:

```
$hashref = {Mouse => 'Jerry', Cat => 'Tom', Dog => 'Spike'};
```

Since the contents of the constructor are just a list, we can also create a hash reference to an anonymous hash with the contents of an array, and vice versa:

```
$hashref = {@array};
$arrayref = [%hash];
```

Both constructors take lists as their arguments, but organize them into different kinds of anonymous compound value.

Converting Hashes into Arrays

Converting a hash into a list or array is very simple, we just assign it:

```
@array = %hash;
```

This retrieves all the keys and values from the hash in pairs, the order of which is determined by the internal structure of the hash. Alternatively we can extract the hash as two lists, one of keys, and one of values:

```
@keys = keys %hash;
@values = values %hash;
```

This gives us two arrays with corresponding indices, so we can look up the value by the index of the key (and vice versa, something we cannot do with a hash).

A final option that is sometimes worth considering is turning the hash into an array of arrays or array of hashes, in order to create an index but preserve the key-value pairs in a single variable. Here is one way to do that:

```
my @array;
foreach (keys %hash) {
    push @array, {$_ => $hash{$_}};
}
```

This creates an array of hashes, each hash with precisely one key-value pair in it. Of course there are other, and arguably better, ways to create indexed hashes, one of which we covered earlier in this section. Again, it's a matter of preference, depending on whether we want to be able to look up the index and value by key, or the key and value by index.

The Special Hash '%ENV'

The special variable %ENV is one main source of information available to a Perl program when it starts. This hash, defined by Perl automatically, contains key-value pairs of the script's environment. This is, for example, the primary mechanism for transmitting details of a client request from a web server to a CGI script run by that server. We can dump out the contents of the environment with a short script, which we write here as a command line:

> perl -we 'foreach (sort keys %ENV) { print "$_ => $ENV{$_}\n"}'

In an xterm window running on a Linux X-Window System desktop, this produces something like:

```
DISPLAY => :0.0
ENV => /home/gurgeh/.bashrc
HISTFILESIZE => 1000
HOME => /home/gurgeh
HOSTDISPLAY => localhost.localdomain:0.0
HOSTNAME => localhost.localdomain
HOSTTYPE => i386
LOGNAME => gurgeh
MAIL => /var/spool/mail/gurgeh
OSTYPE => Linux
PATH => /usr/local/bin:/bin:/usr/bin:/usr/X11R6/bin:.
SHELL => /bin/bash
SHLVL => 6
TERM => xterm
TZ => Ikroh/Chiark_Orbital
USER => gurgeh
WINDOWID => 62914563
```

In a Windows DOS or NT shell, we would instead type:

> perl -e "foreach (sort keys %ENV) { print qq($_ => $ENV{$_}\n); }"

Which would produce something like:

```
ALLUSERSPROFILE => C:\Documents and Settings\All Users
APPDATA => C:\Documents and Settings\Ken Wronkiewicz\Application Data
CLASSPATH => C:\WINNT\System32\QTJava.zip
COMMONPROGRAMFILES => C:\Program Files\Common Files
COMPUTERNAME => WIREMONSTER2
COMSPEC => C:\WINNT\system32\cmd.exe
DIRCMD => /a
HOMEDRIVE => C:
HOMEPATH => \
INCLUDE => C:\Program Files\Microsoft Visual Studio\VC98\atl\include;C:\Program
Files\Microsoft Visual Studio\VC98\mfc\include;C:\Program Files\
Microsoft Visual Studio\VC98\include
LIB => C:\Program Files\Microsoft Visual Studio\VC98\mfc\lib;C:\Program Files\
Microsoft Visual Studio\VC98\lib
LOGONSERVER => \\WIREMONSTER2
MSDEVDIR => C:\Program Files\Microsoft Visual Studio\Common\MSDev98
NUMBER_OF_PROCESSORS => 1
OS => Windows_NT
OS2LIBPATH => C:\WINNT\system32\os2\dll;
...
```

The exact contents of %ENV can vary wildly depending on the underlying platform, the operating system, and the chosen shell and user preferences. However, we can usually expect $ENV{PATH} to be defined, and (on a UNIX system at least), HOME, USER, TERM, SHELL, and OSTYPE (though this is often better deduced by looking at the special variable $^O (or $OSNAME with use English)).

Configuring Programs via '%ENV'

One major reason for examining %ENV is to allow users to create local definitions for our own environment variables. This provides a simple and easy way to configure a script without having to go to the trouble of looking for and reading a configuration file. This sort of configuration is common on UNIX systems. For example, to provide a program with a default location for locating scripts but allow that default to be overridden if the environment variable MY_SCRIPTDIR is set, we might write:

```
$default_scriptdir = "/usr/local/myapp/scripts";
$scriptdir = $ENV{MY_SCRIPTDIR}?$ENV{MY_SCRIPTDIR}:$default_scriptdir;
```

More creatively, we can scan for any environment variable with a specific prefix, say MY_, and create a configuration hash based on it:

```
foreach (keys %ENV) {
    # regular expressions are covered in Chapter 11
    /^MY_(.*)/ and $conf{$1} = $ENV{$_};
}
```

This is an ideal mechanism for establishing defaults, too, if we iterate over a list of keys in a default hash:

```
%defaults = {
    SCRIPTDIR => '/usr/local/myapp/scripts',
    # other defaults...
}

foreach (keys %defaults) {
    $conf{$1} = (defined $ENV{"MY_$1"})?$ENV{"MY_$1"}:$defaults{$1};
}
```

We can modify, add to or remove (with undef) any of the entries in %ENV just as we can with any other hash. %ENV is not a copy of the script's environment, it actually is the script's environment. This means that any changes we make to %ENV change the environment for any child processes that are started after the change, for example with fork (see Chapter 22 for more on processes). It is not possible to change the environment of the parent, and therefore Perl scripts cannot return information back to the parent via the environment (Windows platforms emulate fork since they don't have a real one, but the same rules apply).

Handling Tainted Input from '%ENV'

Taint mode is a security feature that marks data retrieved from an external source as potentially dangerous. If we attempt to use tainted data in an unsafe operation, which primarily means any attempt to run or communicate with an external process, Perl will raise a fatal security error. The main use of tainting is in CGI and other server-side applications that may be executed by unknown and unauthenticated third parties. We mention it here because one of the primary sources of input for CGI scripts is the environment, as we noted earlier.

Taint mode is enabled with the -T option, and is automatically switched on if the real and effective user Ids are different, which is typical on UNIX-based web servers. The concept of real and effective user Ids doesn't apply to non-UNIX platforms, so there the -T option needs to be supplied or specified in Perl's startup configuration (via PERL5OPT, for example – see Chapter 14).

All the values in the %ENV hash fall into the category of insecure input, so attempting to use them in a potentially insecure operation will cause a fatal error. To prevent this we must either avoid using %ENV, place operations into the safe block, or untaint the values explicitly. Regular expressions can be used to untaint data, though this should be used with extreme caution. To untaint DOCUMENT_ROOT for instance, a variable we might expect to trust since it is set by the web server and should not change, we could use:

```
$ENV{DOCUMENT_ROOT} =~ /(.*)/ and $docroot = $1;
```

Of course, sometimes we might want to avoid untainting data simply because we used a regular expression on it. To avoid this we can use the re pragmatic module described in the discussion on regular expressions in Chapter 11.

'Env.pm'

Perl provides one module, Env.pm that simplifies the handling of the %ENV hash by allowing us to import environment variables into our program as scalar or array variables. In its simplest form of usage, we can use it to pull in several environment variables as scalars:

```
# import environment variables via Env.pm
use Env qw(PATH HOME TERM);

# environment variables now available as scalars:
print $PATH, $HOME, $TERM;
```

Note that it does not matter if the environment variable exists yet. As soon as it is defined, either by the imported name or the %ENV hash, the new value will be reflected in both places.

We can also read and write environment variables in arrays if we prefix the variable name with @:

```
use Env qw(@PATH);   # access path via array
$first_dir = $PATH[0];   # find name of first directory in path
unshift @PATH, $scriptdir;   # add a new directory to start of path
```

The separator used by the Env module for splitting environment variables is the value of $Config::Config{'path_sep'}, which by default is set to a colon. This is the standard separator for most multiple-value environment variables (and path information variables in particular) on UNIX. We can change it to handle other kinds of variable, for example, comma separated values:

```
use Env qw(@PATH);
$Config::Config {'path_sep'} = ',';
use Env qw(@MY_CSV_VAR);
```

Note, however, that all variables are stored as scalar strings in the %ENV hash underneath whatever labels we give them. That means that any alteration to an array variable causes the module to rebuild and then re-split the variable to regenerate the array. That will cause problems if we changed the separator in the meantime.

Interestingly, we can access the same variable in both scalar and array form by importing both names:

```
#!/usr/bin/perl
# config.pl
use warnings;
use strict;

use Env qw($PATH @PATH);

$sep = $Config::Config{'path sep'};
# add current directory if not already present
unless ($PATH =~ /(^|$sep)\.($sep|$)/) {
    push @PATH, '.';
}
```

Since both variables access the same underlying environment variable, a change to one of these (or the underlying $ENV{PATH}) will change the other too.

The Env module is a good example of a **simple tied object class**. Each imported variable is actually an object in disguise that simply accesses the environment variable of the same name. We discuss ties and tied objects in detail in Chapter 19.

References

Rather than referring to a variable directly, Perl lets us refer to it by a reference – a pointer to the real value stored somewhere else. There are two kinds of reference in Perl: **hard references**, which are immutable values, and **symbolic references**, which are strings that name the variable they point to.

Of the two, hard references are by far the most common, and are the basis for complex data structures like arrays of arrays. Internally they are memory pointers, and we can access the value that they point to by following or dereferencing the reference. Perl provides a flexible syntax for doing this, involving the backslash and arrow operators.

Conversely, symbolic references are actually banned by use strict (more accurately, use strict refs) because they are a common source of bugs due to their malleable nature and resistance to compile-time error checking – by changing the contents of the string we change the thing that it points to. It is also possible to accidentally create a symbolic reference when we didn't mean to, especially if we fail to turn on warnings as well. Having made these points, symbolic references can be useful in the right places, so long as we are careful.

Hard References

Hard references, usually just called references, are not really a data type, they are just a kind of scalar value, but a different and specialized one compared to the other value types like integer, floating-point or string. They differ from these because they are a pointer to another value, and are not malleable – unlike C, we cannot perform operations to change the value of a reference to make it point to something else. We can assign a new reference to a scalar variable, but that is all. Worldly programmers generally consider this a good thing.

Creating References

To create a reference for an existing value or variable we use the backslash operator. This will convert any value or data type, be it scalar, array, hash, subroutine, and so forth, and create a scalar reference that points to it:

```
# references to values
$numberref = \42;
$messageref = \"Don't Drink The Wine!\n";
@listofrefs = \(1, 4, 9, 16, 25);

# references to variables
$scalarref = \$number;
$arrayref = \@array;
$hashref = \%hash;
$globref = \*typeglob;    # typeglobs are introduced later in the chapter

# reference to anonymous subroutine
$subref = \sub { return "This is an anonymous subroutine" };

# reference to named subroutine
$namedsubref = \&mysubroutine;
```

If we pass a list to the backslash operator, it returns a second list of references, each one pointing to an element of the original list:

```
@reflist = \(1, 2, 3);
```

This is identical to, but shorter than:

```
@reflist = (\1, \2, \3);
```

References have implicit knowledge of the type of thing that they are pointing to, so an array reference is always an array reference, and we can demonstrate this by attempting to print a reference. For example, this is what we might get if we attempted to print $scalarref:

SCALAR(0x8141f78)

A common mistake in Perl is to try to use the backslash operator to create a reference to an existing list, but as we showed above, this is not what backslash does. In order to create an array reference from a list, we must first place the list into an array. This causes Perl to allocate an array structure for the values, which we can then create a reference for – the original list is not stored as an array, so it cannot be referenced. This is essentially what the [...] construct does.

The [...] and {...} constructors also create a reference to an array or hash. These differ from the backslash operator in that they create a copy of their contents and return a reference to it, not a reference to the original.

```
$samearrayref = \@array;
$copyarrayref = [@array];
$samehashref = \%hash;
$copyhashref = {%hash};
```

The [..] and'{..} constructors are not strictly operators and have the precedence of terms (like variable names, subroutines and so on) which is the highest precedence of all. The contents of the constructors are always evaluated before they are used in other expressions.

The hash reference constructor constructs a hash, which requires key-value pairs, and so spots things like odd numbers of elements. We can't create hash references with the backslash operator either – we have to pass it a hash variable. That is why we have the { ... } constructor.

Confusing constructors with lists is a very common Perl error, especially as Perl is quite happy for us to do the following:

```
# this does not do what it might appear to
@array = [1, 2, 3, 4];
```

What this probably meant to do was assign @array a list of four elements. What it actually does is assign @array one element containing a reference to an anonymous array of four elements, that is it is actually the same as:

```
@inner_array = (1, 2, 3, 4);
@array = \@inner_array;
```

When arrays and hashes do not appear to contain the values that they should, this is one of the first things to check. The error 'Reference found where even-sized list expected ...' is a clue that this may be happening during a hash definition, but for arrays we are on our own.

Perl sometimes creates references automatically, in order to satisfy assignments to complex data structures. This saves what would otherwise be a lot of monotonous construction work on our part. For instance, the following statements create several hash references and automatically chain them together to form a composite structure, a process known immemorially as **autovivification**:

```
my %hash;
$hash{'name'}{'address'}{'street'}{'number'} = 88;
```

Comparing References

References to the same underlying value are equal, but only if they point to the same actual value:

```
#!/usr/bin/perl
# ref1.pl
use warnings;
use strict;

my $text = "This is a value";

my $ref1 = \$text;
my $ref2 = \$text;

print $ref1 == $ref2    # produces '1'

$$ref1 = 'New value';
print $$ref2;    # produces 'New value'
```

Pointing to two values that happen to be equal will not result in equal references:

```
#!/usr/bin/perl
# ref2.pl
use warnings;
use strict;

my $text1 = "This is a value";
my $text2 = "This is a value";

my $ref1 = \$text1;
my $ref2 = \$text2;

print $ref1 == $ref2;   # produces ''

$$ref1 = 'New value';
print $$ref2;   # produces 'New value'
```

Dereferencing

A reference is only useful if we can access the underlying value, a process called **dereferencing**. We can extract the value and assign it to a variable, or we can simply work through the reference, a little like keyhole surgery.

Dereferencing is dependent on the type of the reference, we can only get a scalar from a scalar reference, and we can only get an array from an array reference. However, since all references, regardless of type, are scalars, Perl cannot perform compile-time syntax checks to ascertain whether a reference is being dereferenced with the correct type. This compels us to take a little care when using references, since incorrectly using a reference may only show up as a run-time error.

Dereferencing any reference can be done by prefixing the reference with the symbol appropriate for the underlying data type; the previous comparison example includes four scalar dereferences using $$. As a more complete example, here is how we can copy out the value pointed to by a scalar, array, hash, and typeglob reference into a new variable:

```
$value = $$ref;
@array = @$arrayref;
%hash = %$hashref;
*glob = *$globref;
```

Similarly, we can call a code reference like this:

```
&$coderef(@args);
```

We cannot dereference with impunity – attempting to access an array or hash reference as a scalar produces a syntax error:

Not a SCALAR reference ...

Similarly, while a statement like @a=21 will create an array with one element (the value 21), and might conceivably be what we intended, Perl is skeptical that we would ever want to create such an array by dereferencing, and so produces a run-time error if we say:

```
@a = @$scalarref;
```

If we want to use the values held by a reference from a hash as an array, we have to recreate the reference (or generate a new one), because hashes are not organized in the same way as arrays. So the values must be extracted and stored in the other format:

```
$ref = {a=>1, b=>2, c=>3};
print %$ref;   # produces a1b2c3 (dependent on internal ordering of hash)
print @$ref;   # run-time error 'Not an ARRAY reference ...'

$ref = [ %$ref ];   # convert '$ref' from hash to array reference

print %$ref;   # run-time error 'Can't coerce array into hash ...'
print @$ref;   # produces a1b2c3 (dependent on order of hash)
```

Working with References

Instead of just pulling out the value from a reference and assigning it to something else, we can work directly through the reference. For example, to access a scalar value in an array or hash value we would use:

```
$element_2 = $$arrayref[1];
$hashvalue = $$hashref{'key_name'};
```

If we mentally replace the $arrayref and $hashref with array and hash we can see that these are really just conventional array and hash accesses, just being done through a reference (the keyhole). Similarly, we can get an array slice via a reference:

```
@slice = @$arrayref[6..9];
```

This works well when we are accessing a scalar containing an array reference, but it can cause problems if we try to access an array containing array references. For example, consider the following nested array:

```
@array = (1, [2, 3, 4], 5);
```

This array contains an array reference as its second element (note that if we had not used an array reference constructor and just used parentheses we would have ended up with a plain old five element array). We might try to access that array with:

```
@subarray = @$array[1];
```

Unfortunately this gives us an array with an array reference as its only element, not the three elements 2, 3, 4. This is because prefixes bind more closely than indices, and so the '@' is applied before the '[1]'. The above is therefore actually equivalent to:

```
@subarray = ($$array[1]);
```

This explains why we get a single array reference as the only element of @subarray. In order to get the index to happen first we need to use curly braces to apply the dereferencing operation to the array element instead of to the array:

```
@subarray = @{$array[1]};
```

This more explicit dereferencing syntax also has its scalar, hash, code, and typeglob counterparts, for example:

```
%subhash = %{$hashofhashes{$hashkey}};
```

An alternative technique for dereferencing is the arrow or dereference operator. This is often more legible than the double prefix syntax:

```
$element_2 = $arrayref->[1];
$hashvalue = $hashref -> {'key_name'};
```

Multidimensional arrays and hashes can omit the arrow, since Perl is smart enough to translate adjacent indices or hash keys into an implicit dereference. The following are therefore equivalent, but the first is easier to read:

```
$value = $threedeepreference[9]{'four'}[1];
$value = $threedeepreference[9] -> {'four'} -> [1];
```

This only applies to the second and subsequent indices or hash keys, however. If we are accessing a reference we still need to use the first arrow so Perl knows that we are going via a reference and not accessing an element or hash value directly.

Passing References to Subroutines

One of the major advantages of hard references is that they allow us to package up a compound value like an array or hash into a scalar. This allows us to create complex data structures and to pass arrays and hashes into subroutines keeping them intact.

As we observed earlier, if we combine lists directly then they merge together. This is handy if we want to create a combined list, but problematic if we want to pass, say, a couple of arrays to a subroutine, since inside the subroutine we will be unable to tell one from the other:

```
mysub (@array1, @array2);

sub mysub {
   my @combinedarray = @_;

   foreach (@combinedarray) {
      ...
   }
}
```

References solve this problem by replacing the arrays with array references:

```
mysub (\@array1, \@array2);

sub mysub {
   my ($arrayref1, $arrayref2) = @_;

   foreach (@$arrayref1) {
      ...
   }
   foreach (@$arrayref2) {
      ...
   }
}
```

Not only does this solve the problem, but it is also more efficient if the arrays happen to be large ones, we pass two scalars, and not an indefinite number of values.

However, see the section on 'typeglobs' for an alternative, and also subroutine 'Prototypes' in Chapter 7 for two alternative approaches to passing arrays and hashes without using references. Each has its merits and drawbacks.

Finding the Type of a Reference

Perl cannot perform syntax checks to ensure that references are being dereferenced with the correct prefix because the content of a scalar variable is defined at run time, and can change during the lifetime of a program. Consequently it is occasionally useful to be able to check the type of a reference before we access it. Fortunately we can find out the type of a reference with the `ref` function. This is analogous to a 'type of' function, but only for references. Since non-references are implicitly typed by their syntax of prefixes, this is all we actually need in Perl.

`ref` takes a single reference as an argument, or uses `$_` if no argument is supplied. It returns a string containing the reference type, or `undef` if the argument is not a reference:

```
$ref = \[1, 2, 3];
print "The reference type of $ref is '", ref($ref),"' \n";
```

When executed, these lines produce a message of the form:

The reference type of ARRAY(0x8250290) is 'ARRAY'

The string representation of a reference is the reference type followed by the memory address it points to. While useful for debugging, we cannot convert this back into a reference again, so it is rarely useful otherwise. Conversely, `ref` returns a string description of the reference type, which is more useful as well as being easier to use.

The values returned for references are strings containing the name of the reference. These are the same names produced when we print a reference, for example SCALAR, and include:

SCALAR	A scalar reference
ARRAY	An array reference
HASH	A hash reference
CODE	A reference to an anonymous subroutine
GLOB	A reference to a typeglob
IO (or IO::Handle)	A Filehandle reference
REF	A reference to another reference
LVALUE	A reference to an assignable value that isn't a SCALAR, ARRAY or HASH (such as, the return value from substr)

In general the first three reference types on this list are by far the most commonly encountered; see 'Complex Data Structures' for an example that uses `ref` to recursively explore an arbitrarily complex structure of scalars, arrays, and hashes.

Finding the Type of a Blessed Reference

Blessed references are a very specific and important subclass of hard references, being the primary mechanism by which Perl implements objects and object-oriented programming. They are created by using the `bless` function on a hard reference to assign a package name to it, converting it from an ordinary reference into an object of the class defined by the package.

The `ref` function will return the name of the blessed class when called on an object, rather than the type of the underlying reference. In general this is what we want, because the point of objects is that we treat them as opaque values that hide the details of their implementation from us. In the rare cases that we do want to know the underlying reference type (perhaps because we want to dump out the object's state or save it to a file on disk) we can use the `reftype` function from the `attributes` module:

```perl
#!/usr/bin/perl
# reftype.pl
use warnings;
use strict;

use attributes qw(reftype);

die "Usage: $0 <object module> ...\n" unless @ARGV;

foreach (@ARGV) {
    my $filename = $_;
    $filename =~ s|::|/|g;
    require "$filename.pm";
    my $obj = new $_;

    print "Object class ", ref($obj), " uses underlying data type ", reftype($obj),
    "\n";
}
```

We can use this script like this:

> **perl reftype.pl CGI**
Object class CGI uses underlying data type HASH

Note that the `attributes` module does a lot more than provide the `reftype` subroutine, much of which is rather esoteric for the average Perl application. We cover it in a little more detail at the end of Chapter 7.

Symbolic References

Symbolic references, as opposed to hard references, are simply descriptions of variables represented as text. For instance, the symbolic reference for the variable `@array` is the string '@array'. Here is an example of a symbolic reference in action:

```perl
#!/usr/bin/perl
# symbolic_ref.pl
use warnings;
use strict;
no strict 'refs';
```

```
our @array = (1, 2, 3);    # only package variables allowed
my $symref = 'array';
my $total = $#$symref;
$total++;
print "$symref has $total elements \n";
foreach (@$symref) {
    print "Got: $_ \n";
}
```

The notation for symbolic references is exactly the same as it is for hard references – in both cases we say things like `@$arrayref` to dereference the reference. The distinction is that in the case of a hard reference the scalar variable contains an immutable pointer, whereas in the case of a symbolic reference it contains an all-too-mutable string.

Symbolic references can only refer to global variables, or to be more technical, variables that exist in the symbol table, though they themselves can be lexical. We cannot therefore refer to variables that have been declared lexically (with my), only those declared with our, use vars or defined explicitly with `@main::array` and so on. This is a significant caveat and a common gotcha for programmers who forget. If the symbolic reference is unqualified, it is presumed to be a reference to a variable in the current package (most likely main, since we have not introduced packages yet), otherwise it refers to the variable in the named package:

```
my $symbolrefinotherpackage = 'My::Other::Package::variable';
```

Unlike hard references, symbolic references do not have a type; they are just strings after all. We can therefore dereference any variable whose name matches the reference by prefixing it with the relevant symbol:

```
my $symref = "Package::variable";

my $scalar = $$symref;
my @array = @$symref;
my %hash = %$symref;
print "And call a subroutine, returning ", &$symref(@args);
```

Since symbolic references are mutable, they are banned by the strict module by default:

```
use strict;    # strict 'vars', 'subs' and 'refs'
```

To enable symbolic references we therefore have to make special dispensation:

```
no strict 'refs';
```

Since this is not in general an advisable idea (we should generally use the strict pragma unless we are writing 'throwaway' code) it is best to do this inside a subroutine or other lexically limited scope, where the range of permissibility of symbolic references is clearly defined.

The reason for restricting the use of symbolic references is that it is very easy to accidentally create a symbolic reference where we did not mean to, especially if we don't have warnings enabled (which we should never do globally anyway, but might do temporarily inside a subroutine). However, a few places do allow symbolic references as special cases, such as functions that take filehandles as arguments (like print).

Complex Data Structures

Combining lists and hashes with references allows us to create arbitrarily complex data structures such as lists of lists, hashes of hashes, and lists of hashes of lists of lists and so on. However, Perl lacks the ability to explicitly declare things like multidimensional arrays, because lists and hashes can only contain scalar values.

The Problem with Nesting – My Lists Went Flat!

One consequence of not being able to declare multidimensional arrays explicitly is that nesting lists does not work the way we might expect it to. A seemingly obvious way to store one list in another would be to write:

```
@inner = (3, 4);
@outer = (1, 2, @inner, 5, 6);
```

We would then like to be able to access the inner list by writing $outer[2] and then access its elements with something like $outer[2][1]. Unfortunately this does not work because the above example does not produce a list containing another list. Instead the lists are 'flattened', the inner list being converted into its elements and integrated into the outer list. The above example actually results in this:

```
@outer = (1, 2, 3, 4, 5, 6);
```

While this is a perfectly acceptable way to merge lists together, it does not produce the nested data structure that we actually intended. The heart of the problem is that Perl does not allow lists and hashes to store other lists or hashes as values directly. Instead we must store a reference (which is a scalar value) to the hash or list we want to nest.

We can fix the flattening problem above using either of the modified examples below, the first using square brackets to construct a reference and the second using a backslash to get the reference to the original array:

```
@outer = (1, 2, [@inner], 5, 6);    # using square brackets
@outer = (1, 2, \@inner, 5, 6);     # using a backslash
```

Note that the second example avoids duplicating the inner array by taking a direct reference but assumes we only do this once. In a loop this would cause duplicated references, which we probably did not intend. For more on this issue, see 'Creating Complex Data Structures Programmatically'.

Now we know how to construct complex data structures we can go on to create more complex animals like lists of lists and hashes of hashes.

Lists of Lists and Multidimensional Arrays

The way to create a list of lists is to create a list of list references, either with the square bracket [...] notation, or using the backslash operator. Defining a list of lists is actually quite simple. The following example shows a list of lists defined using square brackets:

```
@array = (
    ["One", "Two", "Three"],
    ["Red", "Yellow", "Blue"],
    ["Left", "Middle", "Right"],
);
```

The important point to note about this is that the outer array contains a list of references – one for each inner list. The result is, in effect, a two-dimensional array which we can access using two sets of indices:

```
print $array[0][2];   # displays third element of first row - 'Three'
print $array[2][1];   # displays second element of third row - 'Middle'
```

This is actually a piece of Perl shorthand, in deference to languages like C where real multidimensional arrays can be defined and accessed using multiple indices. In Perl an index is just a count into an array, so the value of $array[0] is in fact a reference, which we should not be able to tack a '[2]' onto. In other words we would expect to have to write:

```
print $array[0] -> [2];
```

This does indeed work, because this is exactly what happens internally. Perl is clever enough to automatically spot multiple indices and do the additional dereferencing without having to be told explicitly.

We can retrieve an individual array row by using one index, which will give us a scalar array reference, as we just observed:

```
$second_row = $array[1];
```

We can dereference this reference to get an array:

```
@second_row = @{$array[1]};
```

There is an important difference between using $second_row and @second_row, however. $second_row is a reference to the second row of the original multidimensional array, so if we modify the array that $second_row points to we are actually affecting the original array:

```
print $array[1][1];   # prints 'Yellow'
$second_row [1] = "Green";
print $array[1][1];   # prints 'Green'
```

By contrast, @second_row contains a copy of the second row (because the assignment is actually a straight array copy), so modifying it does not affect @array. This distinction can be very important when working with complex data structures since we can affect values we did not mean to, or conversely, not modify the contents of arrays that we meant to.

Instead of defining a straight list of lists we can also define a reference to a list of lists, in which case we just have to modify the outer array definition by replacing the parentheses with square brackets and changing the variable type to a scalar, like so:

```
$arrayref = [
    ["One", "Two", "Three"],
    ["Red", "Yellow", "Blue"],
    ["Left", "Middle", "Right"],
];
```

Accessing the elements of this array can be done either by dereferencing the outer array reference $arrayref, or by using the dereferencing operator '->' to access the underlying array, which is somewhat clearer to read:

```
print $$arrayref[0][2];
print $arrayref->[0][2];    # using -> is clearer
```

Accessing a row is similar to before, but with an extra layer of dereferencing. Either of the following will do the trick, though again the second is clearer:

```
$second_row = $$array[1];
$second_row = $array->[1];
```

Hashes of Hashes and Other Animals

Creating a hash of hashes is similar to creating a list of lists, differing only in our use of syntax. Here is an example of a three-deep nested hash of hashes:

```
%identities = (
    JohnSmith => {
        Name => {First=>"John", Last=>"Smith"},
        Phone => {Home=>"123 4567890", Work=>undef},
        Address => {Street => "13 Acacia Avenue",
        City => "Arcadia City",
        Country => "El Dorado",
    }
},
    AlanSmithee => {
        Name => {First=>"Alan", Last=>"Smithee"},
        Phone => {Work=>"not applicable"},
    }
);
```

Accessing this structure is similar too, and again Perl allows us to omit the dereferencing operator for consecutive hash keys:

```
$alans_first_name = $identities{'AlanSmithee'}{'Name'}{'First'};
```

Since nesting data structures is just a case of storing references, we can also create lists of hashes, hashes of lists, and anything in between:

```
#!/usr/bin/perl
# lists.pl
use warnings;
use strict;

my (@list_of_hashes, %hash_of_lists, %mixed_bag, $my_object);
my @my_list = (1, 2, 3, 4, 5);

@list_of_hashes = (
    {Monday=>1, Tuesday=>2, Wednesday=>3, Thrusday=>4, Friday=>5},
    {Red=>0xff0000, Green=>0x00ff00, Blue=>0x0000ff},
);
```

```
print "Tuesday is the $list_of_hashes[0]{Tuesday}nd day of the week.", "\n";

%hash_of_lists = (
   List_1 => [1, 2, 3],
   List_2 => ["Red", "Yellow", "Blue"],
);

print "The second element of List_1 is: $hash_of_lists{List_1}[1]", "\n";

%mixed_bag = (
   Scalar1 => 3,
   Scalar2 => "Hello World",
   List1 => [1, 2, 3],
   Hash1 => { A => 'Horses', C => 'Miles' },
   List2 => ['Eenie','Meenie',
   ['Meenie1','Meenie2'],
    'Mini', 'Mo'],
   Scalar3 => $my_object,
   Hash2 => { Time => [ gmtime ],
   Date => scalar(gmtime),
   },
List3 => @my_list[0..2],
);

print "Eenie Meenie Mini $mixed_bag{List2}[4]";
```

Adding to and Modifying Complex Data Structures

Manipulating nested data structures is essentially no different from manipulating simple ones, we just have to be sure to modify the correct thing in the right way. For example, to add a new row to our two-dimensional array we can either define the row explicitly, or use the push function to add it. In either case we have to be sure to add a reference, not the list itself, or we will end up adding the list contents to the outer array instead.

```
# Right - adds a reference
$array[2] = \@third_row;   # backslash operator creates reference to array
push @array, ["Up", "Level", "Down"];   # explicit reference
push @array, \( "Large", "Medium", "Small" );   # backslashed reference


# ERROR: this is probably not what we want
$array[2] = (8, 9, 10);   # $array[2] becomes 10, the 8 and 9 are discarded
push @array, @third_row;   # contents of @third_row added to @array
```

In the first wrong example we will get a warning from Perl about the useless use of a constant in void context. The second example, which is perfectly legal Perl, will not generate any warnings. This is consequently one of the commonest sources of bugs when manipulating complex data structures. The way to avoid it is to be extremely clear and consistent about the structure of the data, and to avoid complicated mixtures of scalars, lists, and hashes unless their use is transparent and obvious.

Modifying the contents of nested lists and hashes is likewise simple. We have already seen how to replace a row in a list of lists, but we can also replace individual elements and array slices:

```
# Right
$array[2][1] = 9;    # replace an individual element
$array[2][12] = 42;    # grow the list by adding an element

@{$array[2]} = (8, 9, 10);    # replace all the elements
@{$array[2]}[1..2] = (9, 10);    # replace elements 2 and 3, keeping 1


# ERROR: Wrong
$array[2][1..2] = (9, 10);    # cannot take a slice of a list reference
```

The essential point to remember is that this is no different from manipulating simple lists and hashes, so long as we remember that we are really working through references. Perl allows a shorthand for indices when accessing elements but this doesn't extend to array slices or more complex manipulations, so we need to handle the reference ourselves in these cases.

Creating Complex Data Structures Programmatically

Explicitly writing the code to define a complex structure is one way to achieve our goal, but we might also want to generate things like lists of lists programmatically. This is actually straightforward, but a couple of nasty traps lurk for the unwary Perl programmer. Here is a loop that appears to create a list of lists, but actually constructs a list of integers:

```
#!/usr/bin/perl
# complex1.pl
use warnings;
use strict;

my (@outer, @inner);
foreach my $element (1..3) {
    @inner = ("one", "two");
    $outer[$element] = @inner;
}
print '@outer is ', "@outer \n";
```

> **perl complex1.pl**
Use of uninitialized value in join at test.pl line 11.
@outer is 2 2 2

Although this might appear correct, we are in fact assigning a list in a scalar context. All that actually happens is that a count of the two elements in each of the three instances of the @inner array that the foreach loop reads is assigned to an element of the @outer array. This is why @outer consists of three 2 rather than three @inner arrays each of which has the two elements one and two.

The following variant is also defective – it suffers from list flattening, so the contents of all the inner arrays will be merged into the outer array:

```
#ERROR: list flattening
#!/usr/bin/perl
# complex2.pl
use warnings;
use strict;
```

155

```
my (@outer, @inner);
foreach my $element (1..3) {
    @inner = ("one", "two");
    push @outer, @inner;
}
print '@outer is ', "@outer \n";
```

> **perl complex2.pl**
@outer is one two one two one two

The correct thing to do is to assign references, not lists. The following loop does the task we actually wanted. Note the additional square brackets:

```
#!/usr/bin/perl
# complex3.pl
use warnings;
use strict;

my (@outer, @inner);
foreach my $element (1..3) {
    @inner = ("one", "two");
    push @outer, [@inner];   # push reference to copy of @inner
}
print '@outer is ', "@outer \n";
```

> **perl complex3.pl**
@outer is ARRAY(0x176f0d0) ARRAY(0x176505c) ARRAY(0x17650bc)

Note that @outer consists of three different arrays despite the fact that @inner didn't change. The reason for this is that each of the three instances of @inner has a different address which we used to create @outer.

We have already referred to the important distinction between creating a reference with square brackets and using the backslash operator to take a reference to the list. In the above code, the brackets make a copy of the contents of @inner and return a reference to the copy, which is pushed onto the end of @outer. By contrast, a backslash returns a reference to the original list, so the following apparently equivalent code would not work:

```
#!/usr/bin/perl
# complex4.pl
use warnings;
use strict;

my (@outer, @inner);
foreach my $element (1..3) {
    @inner = ("one", "two");
    push @outer, \@inner;   # push reference to @inner
}
print '@outer is ', "@outer \n";
```

> **perl complex4.pl**
@outer is ARRAY(0x1765188) ARRAY(0x1765188) ARRAY(0x1765188)

156

What actually happens is that the @outer array is filled with the same reference to the @inner array three times. Each time the @inner array is filled with a new double of elements, but the elements of @outer all point to the same list, the current contents of @inner. At the end of the loop all the elements of @outer are identical and only two different elements are actually stored in total.

Another way to approach this task avoiding the pitfalls of accidentally creating duplicate references, or counting lists we meant to assign as references, is to use references explicitly. This makes it much harder to make a mistake, and also saves a list copy:

```perl
#!/usr/bin/perl
# complex5.pl
use warnings;
use strict;

my (@outer, $inner_ref);
foreach my $element (1..3) {
    $inner_ref = ["one", "two"];
    push @outer, $inner_ref;    # push scalar reference
}
print '@outer is ', "@outer \n";
```

> **perl complex5.pl**
@outer is ARRAY(0x176f0ac) ARRAY(0x1765044) ARRAY(0x17650a4)

Rather than redefining a list, this time we redefine a list reference, so we are guaranteed not to accidentally assign the same reference more than once. Finally, another way to ensure that we don't assign the same array is to create a new array each time by declaring @inner inside the loop:

```perl
#!/usr/bin/perl
# complex6.pl
use warnings;
use strict;

my @outer;
foreach my $element (1..3) {
    my @inner = ("one", "two");
    push @outer, \@inner;    # push reference to @inner
}
print '@outer is ', "@outer \n";
```

> **perl complex6.pl**
@outer is ARRAY(0x17651b8) ARRAY(0x176f0d0) ARRAY(0x1765074)

Here @inner is declared each time around the loop, and remains in scope for that iteration only. At the start of each new iteration, the old definition of @inner is discarded and replaced by a new one (note that while the elements of @inner don't change, their addresses change). As with the explicit reference example this is also more efficient than using square brackets since no additional array copy takes place. However, it is more prone to bugs if we omit warnings since there is nothing programmatically wrong with assigning the same reference multiple times, even if it wasn't what we actually intended.

Although we have only discussed lists of lists in this section, exactly the same principles also apply to any other kind of complex data structure such as hashes of hashes or hybrid structures; just substitute braces { } for square brackets and percent signs for @ signs where appropriate.

Traversing Complex Data Structures

Iterating over simple data structures is easy, as we saw when we covered arrays and hashes earlier. Traversing more complex structures is also simple if they are **homogenous** (that is, each level of nesting contains the same type of reference and we don't have other data types like scalars or undefined values lurking). Here's a simple loop that iterates over a list of lists:

```perl
#!/usr/bin/perl
# simple1.pl
use warnings;
use strict;

my @outer = (['a1', 'a2', 'a3'], ['b1', 'b2', 'b3'], ['c1', 'c2', 'c3']);

foreach my $outer_el (@outer) {
   foreach (@{$outer_el}) {
      print "$_\n";
   }
   print "\n";
}
```

And here's one that iterates over a hash of hashes:

```perl
#!/usr/bin/perl
# simple2.pl
use warnings;
use strict;

my %outer = (A=> {a1=>1, a2=>2, a3=>3}, B=> {b1=>4, b2=>5, b3=>6},
             C=> {c1=>7,c2=>8, c3=>9});

foreach my $outer_key (keys %outer) {
   print "$outer_key => \n";
   foreach (keys %{$outer{$outer_key}} ) {
      print"\t$_ => $outer{$outer_key} {$_} \n";
   }
   print "\n";
}
```

Finally, here is another list-of-lists loop that also prints out the indices and catches undefined rows:

```perl
#!/usr/bin/perl
# simple3.pl
use warnings;
use strict;

my @outer;
@outer[1, 2, 5] = (['First', 'Row'], ['Second', 'Row'], ['Last', 'Row']);

for my $outer_elc (0..$#outer) {
   if ($outer [$outer_elc] ) {
      my $inner_elcs = $#{ $outer[$outer_elc] };
      print "$outer_elc : ", $inner_elcs+1," elements \n";
      for my $inner_elc (0..$inner_elcs) {
         print "\t$inner_elc : $outer[$outer_elc] [$inner_elc] \n";
      }
   } else {
      print "Row $outer_elc undefined\n";
   }
}
```

Traversing other structures is just a matter of extending these examples in the relevant direction. Things become more complex however if our structures contain a mixture of different data types. In most cases when we have structures like this it is because different parts of the structure have different purposes, and we would therefore not normally want to traverse the whole structure. It can be useful for debugging purposes though; so in order to handle structures that could contain any kind of data we can resort to the `ref` function. The following recursive subroutine will print out nested scalars (which includes objects), lists, and hashes to any level of depth, using `ref` to determine what to do at each stage:

```perl
#!/usr/bin/perl
# print_struct.pl
use warnings;
use strict;

my $mixed = ['scalar', ['a', 'list', ['of', 'many'], 'values'], {And=>{'A
Hash'=>'Of Hashes'}}, \'scalar ref'];

print_structure($mixed);

sub print_structure {
    my ($data, $depth) = @_;

    $depth=0 unless defined $depth;    # for initial call

    foreach (ref $data) {
        /^$/ and print($data,"\n"), next;
        /^SCALAR/ and print('-> ', $$data, "\n"), next;
        /^HASH/ and do {
        print "\n";
        foreach my $key (keys %{$data}) {
            print "\t" x$depth, "$key => ";
            print_structure ($data->{$key}, $depth+1);
        }
        next;
    };

    /^ARRAY/ and do {
        print "\n";
        for my $elc (0..$#{$data}) {
            print "\t" x$depth, "[$elc] : ";
            print_structure ($data->[$elc], $depth+1);
        }
        next;
    };
    # it is something else - an object, filehandle or typeglob
    print "?$data?";
    }
}
```

If all we are interested in is debugging data structures, then we can have the Perl debugger do it for us, as this short example demonstrates (there is much more on the Perl debugger in Chapter 17):

> **perl -d -e 1;**
Default die handler restored.

Loading DB routines from perl5db.pl version 1.07
Editor support available.

Enter h or 'h h' for help, or 'man perldebug' for more help.

```
main::(-e:1):   1
DB<1> $hashref={a=>1,b=>2,h=>{c=>3,d=>4},e=>[6,7,8]}

DB<2> x $hashref
0  HASH(0x82502dc)
   'a' => 1
   'b' => 2
   'e' => ARRAY(0x8250330)
      0  6
      1  7
      2  8
   'h' => HASH(0x80f6a1c)
      'c' => 3
      'd' => 4
DB<3>
```

Here we have just used the debugger as a kind of shell, created a hash containing an array and another hash, and used the 'x' command of the Perl debugger to print it out in a nice legible way for us.

Several Perl modules perform similar functions. Notably, the Data::Dumper module generates a string containing a formatted Perl declaration that, when executed, constructs the passed data structure:

```perl
#!/usr/bin/perl
# datadumper.pl
use warnings;
use strict;

use Data::Dumper;

my $hashref = {a=>1, b=>2, h=>{c=>3, d=>4}, e=>[6, 7, 8]};

print Dumper($hashref);
```

> perl datadumper.pl
```
$VAR1 = {
   'e' => [
      6,
      7,
      8,
   ],
   h' => {
      c' => 3,
      d' => 4
   },
   'a' => 1,
   'b' => 2
};
```

Note that the output of Data::Dumper is actually Perl code. We can also configure it in a variety of ways, most notably by setting the value of $Data::Dumper::Indent (which ranges from 0 to 4, each producing an increasing level of formatting, with 2 being the default) to control the style of output.

Finally, if we want to store complex data structures in a file then we will also want to look at modules like `Data::Dumper`, `FreezeThaw`, and `Storable`, and possibly also the `MLDBM` module.

Typeglobs

The **typeglob** is a composite data type that contains one instance of each other data types. It is an amalgam (or in Perl-speak, glob) of all Perl's data types, from which it gets its name. It is a sort of 'super reference' whose value is not a single reference to something but six slots that can contain six different references, all at once:

```
scalar      - a reference to a scalar
array       - a reference to an array
hash        - a reference to a hash
code        - a code reference to a subroutine
handle      - a file or directory handle
format      - a format definition
```

Typeglobs programming is a little obscure and rather lower level than many programmers are entirely happy with. It is actually quite possible (and even recommended) to avoid typeglobs in everyday Perl programming, and there are now few reasons to use typeglobs in Perl programs. In ancient days, before references were invented, typeglobs were the only way to pass arguments into subroutines by reference (so they could be assigned to) instead of by value.

The other common use of typeglobs was to pass filehandles around, since filehandles have no specific syntax of their own and so cannot be passed directly. The `IO::Handle`, `IO::File`, and `IO::Dir` modules have largely replaced typeglobs for dealing with filehandles, but since the `IO::` family of modules is comparatively bulky, typeglobs are still a popular choice for dealing with filehandles (see Chapter 12 for more on filehandles).

Defining Typeglobs

Typeglobs are defined using an asterisk prefix, in exactly the same way as scalars are prefixed with a $, or arrays with an @. To create a typeglob we need only assign a value to it. The most obvious example is assigning a typeglob from another typeglob:

```
*glob = *anotherglob;
```

This copies all the six references (which need not all be defined) held in `anotherglob` to the typeglob `glob`. For example:

```
$message = "some text";
*missive = *message;
print $missive;    # produce 'some text';
```

Alternatively we can assign references individually:

```
*glob = \$scalar;
```

This creates a new typeglob containing a defined scalar reference, and an undefined value for the other five. We can access this new scalar value with:

```
print $glob;    # access typeglob scalar reference
```

Assigning a scalar reference to a typeglob creates a new variable called $glob that contains the same value as the original scalar.

Interestingly, we can then fill other slots of the typeglob without affecting the ones currently defined (unless of course we overwrite one). Perl treats glob assignments intelligently, and only overwrites the part of the glob that corresponds to the reference being assigned to it, a property unique among Perl's data types. The following statement fills the array reference slot, but leaves the scalar reference slot alone:

```
*glob = \@array;
```

By filling in the array slot we create a variable called @glob which points to the same values as the original @array; changing either variable will cause the other to see the same changes. The same applies to our earlier $glob variable. Changing the value of $glob also changes the value of $scalar, and vice versa. This is called variable aliasing, and we can use it to great effect in several ways on variables, subroutines, and filehandles.

The upshot of this is that we rarely need to access a typeglob's slots directly, since we can simply access the relevant variable (the exception is of course filehandles, which do not have their own syntax for direct access), but we can play some interesting tricks by assigning to typeglobs.

Manipulating Typeglobs

We have already seen how we can create aliases for scalars and arrays (the same applies to hashes too, of course):

```
*glob = \$scalar;    # create $glob as alias for $scalar
*glob = \@array;     # create @glob as alias for @array
*glob = \%hash;      # create %glob as alias for %hash
```

If we assign the typeglob to a new name, we copy all three references. For example, the following statement invents the variables $glob2, @glob2, and %glob2, all of which point to the same underlying values as the originals:

```
*glob2 = *glob;
```

So far we have considered only the three standard variable types, but typeglobs also contain a **code reference slot**, which is how Perl defines subroutine names. A roundabout way to define a named subroutine is to assign a code reference to a typeglob:

```
*subglob = sub {return "An anonymous subroutine?"};
```

Or:

```
*subglob = \&mysubroutine;
```

Both of these assignments cause a subroutine called `subglob` to spring into existence. The first demonstrates that the only difference between a named and an anonymous subroutine (see Chapter 7 for more on subroutines) is a typeglob entry. The second creates an alias for the subroutine `mysubroutine`, so we can now call `mysubroutine` or `subglob` with equal effect:

```
# these two statements are identical
print mysubroutine(@args);
print subglob(@args);
```

Both typeglobs contain the same code reference, so the two names are simply two different ways to refer to the same thing.

Accessing Typeglobs

If we want to access the different parts of a typeglob we can do so by casting it into the appropriate form. For example:

```
# assign a new key to %glob
${*glob}{'key'} = $value;
```

The same approach works for `${*glob}`, `@{*glob}`, and `&{*glob}`, which access the scalar, array, and subroutine parts of the typeglob respectively. However, we cannot do the same for filehandles or reports, since they do not have a prefix.

A recent addition to Perl is the ability to access the different parts of a typeglob directly. This uses a notation similar to hashes, but with a typeglob rather than a scalar prefix. There are five slots in a typeglob, which can be accessed (reports being the exception), each with its own specific key that returns the appropriate reference, or `undef` if the slot is not defined:

```
$scalarref = *glob{SCALAR};
$arrayref = *glob{ARRAY};
$hashref = *glob{HASH};
$subref = *glob{CODE};
$fhref = *glob{IO};
```

We can also generate a reference to the typeglob itself with:

```
$globref = *glob{GLOB};
```

Much of the time we do not need to access the contents of a typeglob this way. Scalar, array, hash, and code references are all more easily accessed directly. Perl's file handling functions are also smart, in that they can spot a typeglob and extract the filehandle from it automatically:

```
print STDOUT "This goes to standard output";

print *STDOUT "The same thing, only indirectly";
```

This is actually another form of selective access, much the same as when we assign a reference to a typeglob. When we say `*STDOUT`, `print` looks for the filehandle reference, ignoring the other references that come with it. Indeed, we can also pass a reference to a filehandle to all Perl's file-handling functions for exactly this reason.

Assigning a typeglob to anything other than another typeglob causes it to be interpreted like a reference. That is, the name of the typeglob, complete with package specifier and asterisk prefix is written into the scalar:

```
$globname = *glob;
print $globname;   # produces '*main::glob'
```

This is basically just a way to create a symbolic reference to a typeglob, which is getting dangerously abstract and obscure, and is exactly the sort of thing that use strict was implemented to prevent:

```
*$globname = *anotherglob;   # aliases '*anotherglob' to '*glob'
```

However it does have one use, which comes about from the fact that we can refer to filehandles via typeglobs, coupled with the fact that Perl's file-handling functions accept the name of a filehandle (in a string) as a substitute for the filehandle itself.

We can take a reference to a typeglob in the usual manner, and then access it via the reference:

```
$globref = \*glob;

$scalarref = $globref->{SCALAR};
```

Since a glob reference is very much like any other reference, a scalar, we can store it in an array element, a hash value or even another glob:

```
*parentglob = $globref;
```

The Undefined Value

The undefined value is a curious entity, being neither a scalar, list, hash, nor any other data type, which is essentially the point. Although it isn't strictly speaking a datatype, it can be helpful to think of it as a special datatype with only one possible value (NULL). It isn't any of the other data types, and so cannot be confused for them. We can assign an undefined value to a scalar variable, or anywhere else a literal value may live, so the undefined value can also be considered a special case of a scalar value. Conveniently, it evaluates to an empty string (or zero, numerically), which is a False value, so we can ignore its special properties in Boolean tests if we wish, or check for it and handle it specially if we need to. This dual nature makes the undefined value particularly useful.

The concept of a 'value that is not a value' is common to many languages. In Perl, the undef function returns an undefined value, performing the same role as NULL does in C – it also undefines variable arguments passed to it, freeing the memory used to store their values. If we declare a variable without initializing it, it automatically takes on the undefined value too. Perl also provides the defined function that tests for the undefined value and allows us to distinguish it from an empty string or numeric zero:

```
$a = undef;   # assign undefined value to $a
$b;   # assign undefined value to $b implicitly
$a = 1;   # define $a
print defined($a)   # produces '1'
undef $a   # undefine $a
print defined ($a)   # produces '0'
```

The undefined value is returned by many of Perl's built-in functions to indicate an error or an operation that did not complete. Since many operations cannot legally return any other value for failure, undef becomes a useful way to indicate failure because it is not a real value. We can distinguish between undef and zero with the defined function, as the following example demonstrates. The main code passes a filename to a subroutine called get_results and handles three different possible outcomes, one 'success' and two different kinds of 'failure':

```perl
#!/usr/bin/perl
# undef.pl
use warnings;
use strict;

# get a filename
my $file = $ARGV[0] or die "Usage $0 <result file> \n";

# process and return result
my $result = get_results($file);

# test result
if ($result) {
    print "Result of computation on '$file' is $result \n";
} elsif (defined $result) {
    print "No results found in file \n";
} else {
    print "Error - could not open file: $! \n";
}

# and the subroutine...
sub get_results {
    # return 'undef' to indicate error
    open RESULTS, $_[0] or return undef;

    # compute result (simple sum)
    my $file_result = 0;
    while (<RESULTS>) {
        $file_result += $_;
    }

    # return result, 0 if file empty
    return $file_result;
}
```

The get_results subroutine uses undef to distinguish between two different but equally possible kinds of non-result. It is designed to read results from a file and performs a calculation on them (for simplicity, we've just used a simple sum), returning the result. It is possible that there are no results, so the calculation returns zero, but this isn't actually an error, just a lack of result. If the results file is missing, however, that is an error. By passing back undef rather than zero for an error we can distinguish between these two possible results of calling the subroutine and act accordingly. If we did not care about the reason for the non-result we could simplify our code to:

```perl
if ($result) {
    print "Result of computation on '$file' is $result \n";
} else {
    print "No results \n";
}
```

Without an argument to undefine, undef is very much like a value that happens to be undefined. We can treat it almost as a number with no value. However, it is always distinct from a scalar because it returns false when given to the defined function. Having said that, the undefined value does have some things in common with a scalar, it is a single value (in a manner of speaking) and we can even take a reference to it, just like a scalar or list:

```perl
my $undefref = \undef;
print defined($$undefref);    # produces '0'
```

Tests of Existence

The defined function tests a value to see if it is undefined, or has a real value. The number 0 and the empty string are both empty values, and test False in many conditions, but they are defined values unlike undef. The defined function allows us to tell the difference:

```perl
print "It is defined!" if defined $scalar;
```

defined comes up short when we use it on hashes, however, since it cannot tell the difference between a non-existent key and a key with an undefined value, as noted above. All it does is convert undef to an empty value (' ' or 0, depending on the context) and everything else to one. In order to test for the existence of a hash key we instead use the exists function:

```perl
%hash = ('A Key' => 'A Value', 'Another Key' => 'Another Value');
print "It exists!" if exists $hash{'A Key'};
```

Or, in a fuller example that tests for definition as well:

```perl
#!/usr/bin/perl
# exists.pl
use strict;
use warnings;

my %hash = ('Key1' => 'Value1', 'Key2' => 'Value2');
my $key = 'Key1';

# the first if tests for the presence of the key 'Key1'
# the second if checks whether the key 'Key1' is defined
if (exists $hash{$key}) {
    if (defined $hash{$key}) {
        print "$key exists and is defined as $hash{$key} \n";
    } else {
        print "$key exists but is not defined \n";
    }
} else {
    print "$key does not exist\n";
}
```

In a sense, defined is the counterpart of undef and exists is the counterpart of delete (at least for hashes). For arrays, delete and undef are actually the same thing, and exists tests for array elements that have never been assigned to. exists is not applicable to scalar values; use defined for them.

Using the Undefined Value

If we do not define a variable before using it Perl will emit a warning, if warnings are enabled:

```
my $a;
print "The value is $a \n";    # produces 'Use of uninitialized value ...'
```

If warnings are not enabled, undef simply evaluates to an empty string. A loop like the following will also work correctly, even if we do not predeclare the count variable beforehand, because on the first iteration the undefined variable will be evaluated as 0:

```
#!/usr/bin/perl
# no_warnings.pl;
# warnings not enabled...

while ($a<100) {
    print $a++, "\n";
}
```

Disabling warnings globally is not good programming, but if we know what we are doing we can disable them locally to avoid warnings when we know we may be using undefined values. In this case we should really declare the loop variable, but for illustrative purposes we could use a warnings pragma, or a localized copy of $^W to disable warnings temporarily like this:

```
# warnings enabled here ...
{
    no warnings;    # use 'local $^W = 0' for Perl < 5.6
    while ($a < 100) {
        print $a++, "\n";
    }
}
# ... and here
```

Perl is smart enough to let some uses of the undefined value pass, if they seem to be sensible ones. For example, if we try to increment the value of an undefined key in a hash variable, Perl will automatically define the key and assign it a value without complaining about it. This allows us to write counting hashes that contain keys only for items that were actually found, as this letter counting program illustrates:

```
#!/usr/bin/perl
# frequency.pl
use warnings;
use strict;

sub frequency {
    my $text = join('', @_);
    my %letters;
    foreach (split //, $text) {
        $letters{$_}++;
    }
    return %letters;
}
```

```
my $text = "the quick brown fox jumps over the lazy dog";

my %count = frequency($text);

print "'$text' contains: \n";
foreach (sort keys %count) {
    print "\t", $count{$_}, " '$_", ($count{$_} == 1)? "'": "'s", "\n";
}
```

This will create a hash of letter keys with the frequency of each letter's occurrence as their values. (The split statement uses an empty pattern, which we cover in Chapter 11, which is an efficient way of returning characters one at a time.)

The trick to this program lies in the line $letters{$_}++. To start with, there are no keys in the hash, so the first occurrence of any letter causes a new key and value to be entered into the hash. Perl allows this, even though the increment implies an existing value. If a letter does not appear at all, there won't even be a key in the hash for it, eliminating redundant entries.

Using 'undef' as a Function

Although we often use undef as if it were a value by assigning it or returning it from subroutines, it is in fact a function that returns the undefined value (for which there is no written equivalent). When used on variables, undef undefines them, destroying the value. The variable remains intact, but now returns undef when it is accessed. For example:

```
undef $scalar;
```

This is essentially the same as:

```
$scalar = undef;
```

If undef is used on an array or a hash variable, it destroys the entire contents of the variable, turning it into an empty array or hash. The following two statements are therefore equivalent:

```
undef @array;
@array = ();
```

Undefining an array element, a slice of an array, or a hash key, undefines the value, but not the array element or hash key, which continues to exist:

```
undef $hash{'key'};    # undefine value of key 'key'
my $value = $hash{'key'};    # $value is now 'undef'
```

Similarly:

```
my @array = (1, 2, 3, 4, 5);    # define a five element array
@array[1..3] = undef;    # @array contains (1, undef, undef, undef, 5)
```

To really remove the element or hash key, we use the delete function:

```
my @array = (1, 2, 3, 4, 5);    # define a five element array
delete @array[1..3];    # no more second, third, and fourth elements
```

Constants

A constant is a value that remains unchanged throughout the lifetime of a program. By defining **named constants** and then using them rather than the values we can avoid retyping, and potentially mistyping, the value, and additionally it makes our code more legible. A good example of a constant is the value of pi, 3.14159265358979.... Clearly it would be preferable to just type PI in our programs than reel out a string of digits each time. A second reason for using a constant is that we can, if we wish, change it. By defining it in one place and then using the definition in every other place in our code we can easily alter the value throughout the application from a single definition.

One simple but not very satisfactory way to define a constant is with a scalar variable. By convention, constants use fully capitalized names, for example:

```
# define constant '$PI'
$PI = 3.1415926;

# use it
$deg = 36;
print "$deg degrees is ", $PI*($deg/180), " radians";
```

However, this constant is constant in typography only. It is still a regular scalar variable and can be reassigned. A more reliable way to define a scalar constant is by assigning a value, by reference, to a typeglob. Here is how we could define the constant $PI using this approach:

```
# define constant
*PI = \3.1415926;
```

This causes Perl to create the variable $PI, since the assigned reference is to a scalar, but because the reference is to a literal value rather than a variable it cannot be redefined and so the scalar 'variable' $PI is read-only, a true constant. Attempting to assign a new value to it will provoke an error message from Perl:

```
# A more rational, if inaccurate, value of PI
$PI = 3;   # produces 'Modification of a read-only value attempted ...'
```

However, this still does not reinforce the fact that PI is supposed to be constant, because it looks like a regular scalar variable, even if we are prevented from altering it. What we would ideally like is constants that look constant, without any variable prefix character, which is what the constant pragma provides us with.

Declaring Scalar Constants with the 'constant' Pragma

The constant pragma allows us to define scalar constants that both look and behave like constants. Like any module, we use it through a use statement, providing the name and value of the constant we wish to define. To define a value for PI we could write:

```
use constant PI => 3.1415926;
```

This notation is an immediate improvement over using a scalar variable or a typeglob since it legibly declares to the reader, as well as to Perl, that we are defining a constant. The use of => is optional, we could equally have used a comma. In this context, however, it makes sense since we are defining an association. It also allows us to omit the quotes we would otherwise need if use strict is in effect, which is elegant since the result of this statement is to define a constant PI which we can use like this:

```
print "$deg degrees is ", PI*($deg/180);
```

This is an immediate improvement over the first example, since PI is clearly a constant, not a variable like $PI. It also cannot be assigned to, since it is no longer a scalar variable. (For the curious, it is actually a subroutine, defined on the fly by the module that takes no arguments and returns the value we supplied. This makes a surprisingly effective constant even though it is not actually a built-in feature of the language.)

Constants are a good place to perform one-off calculations too. The definition of pi above is adequate for most purposes, but it is not the best that we can do. We saw earlier that we can calculate pi easily using the expression 4*atan2(1, 1). We can use this expression to define our constant PI:

```
use constant PI => 4 * atan2(1, 1);
```

Although this is more work than just defining the value explicitly, Perl only evaluates it once, and we end up with the best possible value of pi that can be handled on any architecture that we run the program on without needing to rewrite the code.

Calculating constants is also useful for clarity and avoiding errors, it is easier to get the expression above correct because it is shorter to type and errors are more obvious. Detecting one wrong digit in a fifteen digit floating-point number is not so simple. Similarly, computed values such as the number of seconds in a year look better like this:

```
use constant SECONDS_IN_YEAR => 60 * 60 * 24 * 365;
```

than this:

```
use constant SECONDS_IN_YEAR => 31536000;
```

Conventionally constants are defined in entirely upper case, to enable them to be easily distinguished from functions that happen to take no arguments. This is not an enforced rule, but it is often a good idea to improve the legibility of our code.

Expressions used to define constants are evaluated in a list context. That means that if we want the scalar result of a calculation we need to say so explicitly. For example, the gmtime function returns a list of date values in list context, but a nicely formatted string containing the current date in a scalar context. To get the nicely formatted string we need to use scalar to force gmtime into a scalar context:

```
use constant START_TIME => scalar(gmtime);
```

As a final note on scalar constants, we can also define a constant to be undefined:

```
use constant TERMINATION_DATE => undef;
use constant OVERRIDE_LIST => ();
```

Both of these statements create constants that evaluate to undef in a scalar context and () in a list context.

Declaring List and Hash Constants

Unlike the typeglob definition of constants, which only works for literal values and hence only defines scalar constants, the `constant` pragma also allows us to define constant arrays and constant hashes. Both of these work in essentially the same way as a scalar constant, with the values to be made constant passed to the module and a subroutine that is defined behind the scenes to implement the resulting constant. Here is how we can define a constant list of weekdays that we can use to retrieve the day names by index:

```
use constant WEEKDAYS=>('Monday', 'Tuesday', 'Wednesday', 'Thursday', 'Friday');
```

Accessing the individual elements of a constant array can be tricky though, because the constant returns a list of values to us, not an array. Due to this, we cannot simply use an index to retrieve an element:

```
print "The third day is", WEEKDAYS[2];    #ERROR: syntax error
```

To solve this problem we only need to add parentheses to make the returned list indexable:

```
print "The third day is, (WEEKDAYS)[2];    # works ok
```

A similar technique can be used to create hash constants, though the values are stored and returned as a list, so they cannot be accessed through a key without first being transferred into a real hash:

```
use constant WEEKABBR => (Monday=>'Mon', Tuesday=>'Tue', Wednesday=>'Wed',
Thu=>'Thursday', Fri=>'Friday');

%abbr = WEEKABBR;
$day = 'Wednesday';
print "The abbreviation for $day is ", $abbr{$day};
```

This limitation means constant hashes are better defined via a reference, which can hold a real hash as its value, rather than a simple list of keys and values that happen to resemble a hash.

Constant References

Since references are scalars, we can also define constant references. As a simple example, the array above could also have been declared as:

```
use constant WEEKDAYS=>[ 'Monday', 'Tuesday', 'Wednesday', 'Thursday', 'Friday'];
```

Since the constant is a reference to an array we must dereference it to access the elements, which is marginally more attractive (and certainly more legible) than adding parentheses:

```
print "The third day is ", WEEKDAYS->[2];
```

However, all that is being defined here is a constant reference; we cannot assign a new value to WEEKDAYS, but we can still alter the values in the array through the existing reference. The list is not truly constant, though it still looks like a constant:

```
WEEKDAYS->[0]='Lundi';    #this is perfectly legal
```

Depending on our programming goals this might actually be a good thing, allowing us to secretly customize the value of a constant inside a package while presenting it as an unchanging and unmodifiable value to the outside world. However, this kind of behavior should be exercised with caution.

Listing and Checking for the Existence of Constants

To check for the existence of a constant we can make use of the declared hash in the constant package to see if the constant exists or not:

```
unless (exists $constant::declared{'MY_CONSTANT'}) {
    use constant MY_CONSTANT => "My value";
}
```

We can also dump out a list of all the currently declared constants by iterating over the keys of the hash:

```
foreach (keys %constant::declared) {
    print "Constant $_ is defined as '$constant::declared{$_}'";
}
```

Summary

We began this chapter by looking at lists and arrays. Specifically, we saw how to:

- ❏ Manipulate arrays
- ❏ Modify the contents of an array
- ❏ Count an array
- ❏ Add elements to an array
- ❏ Resize arrays
- ❏ Remove elements from an array
- ❏ Sort lists and arrays
- ❏ Change the starting index of an array

We then took a similar look at hashes, and also saw how to convert them into scalars and arrays. From there we discussed references, and learned how to:

- ❏ Create a reference
- ❏ Compare references
- ❏ Dereference
- ❏ Pass references to subroutines
- ❏ Find the type of a reference

Next we went over complex data structures, and mentioned problems inherent with nesting. As well as this, we learned how to construct hashes of hashes, arrays of hashes, and so on. From there we learned how to create complex data structures programmatically, and saw how to 'navigate' them.

We covered typeglobs and saw how to define and manipulate them. We looked at the undefined value, and, among other things, explored its use as a function.

Then we examined constants and put the `constant` pragma to use. Finally, we saw how to declare constant lists, hashes, and references, and how to detect constants.

6

Structure, Flow, and Control

In this chapter we look at Perl's control structures, starting with the basic syntax of the language, expressions and statements. We will then build these into more complex structures such as **compound statements** (also known as **blocks**) and **conditional statements**.

We will consider Perl's conditional statements, and then move on to read about **loops** in Perl. We will look at the various statements that we can use to create loops and how to use them in particular with lists, arrays, and hashes. We will also look into the modifiers provided by Perl to change the behavior of loops.

Expressions, Statements, and Blocks

A Perl program consists of a mixture of statements, declarations, and comments. **Statements** are executed by the Perl interpreter at run time. **Declarations**, on the other hand, are directives that affect the way that the program is compiled. Therefore, a declaration's effect ends after compilation, whereas a statement will affect the program each time that section of code is run. Subroutine and format declarations are the two most obvious types of declaration; use and my statements are also, arguably, declarations too.

Statements are made up of expressions, and can combined together into a block or compound statement. An expression is any piece of Perl code that produces a value when it is evaluated. For example, the number '3' is an expression because it produces 3 when evaluated. Operators combine expressions to form larger expressions. For example, '3+6' is an expression that produces the number 9.

Expressions are intended to return a value that is used in a larger expression or a statement. Conversely, a statement is executed because it has some useful effect such as printing text, assigning a value to a variable, and so on. However, the distinction between statements and expressions is rather narrow – most statements are really expressions whose values are not used.

Blocks are combinations of statements, created and defined by curly braces. A block has its own scope, so variables declared inside a block only last so long as the block is being executed. More technically, blocks create a new stack frame, and variables allocated within it last only so long as that frame exists.

Declarations

Declarations are statements that take effect at compile time, rather than at run time. The most common examples of declarations are modules that are included into our application source code with use. Another example is declaring a subroutine before it is defined (subroutines are covered in Chapter 7). For example, the following are all declarations:

```perl
sub mysubroutine ($);   # declare a subroutine with one scalar argument

my $scalar;   # declare a lexical variable (at compile-time)

# define a format for STDOUT
format =
@<<<< = @>>>>

$key, $value

use warnings;   # use pragmatic module

use strict;   # use pragmatic module

use CGI qw (:standard);   # use CGI module

BEGIN {
    print "This is a compile-time statement";
}
```

However, the idea that declarations happen at compile-time and statements happen at run time is not quite as clear-cut as this. A use declaration is really a require and import statement (see Chapter 9) wrapped inside a BEGIN block so that they execute at compile time. So, arguably, use is not a declaration, but a mechanism to execute code during the compile phase. Whether a BEGIN block is a declaration or not is a moot point, but it happens at the compile phase, so it is certainly not a regular block. The BEGIN block will be covered in more detail in Chapter 10.

Expressions and Simple Statements

An expression is anything in Perl that returns a value (be it scalar, list, or undefined), from a literal number to a complex expression involving multiple operators, functions and subroutine calls. That value can then be used in larger expressions or form part of a statement.

Statements differ from expressions in that they must be separated from each other by semicolons, although at the end of a block (where there is no following statement) it is optional but recommended. The chief distinction between a statement and an expression is that either a statement does not return a value (for example, an if statement), or if it does, it is ignored (for example, a print statement).

Constructs such as if, foreach, and while aside, the majority of statements are expressions whose return value is discarded – in Perl terminology, they exist in a void context. Having said that, blocks and subroutines will return the value of the last expression evaluated in them, so it is not necessarily true that an expression is in a void context just because it is not assigned to something explicitly.

For example, the statement $b = $a is also an expression, which returns the value of the assignment ($a). We can see this in action by considering the following two statements:

```
$b = $a;    # $b = $a is a statement
$c = $b = $a;    # $b = $a is now an expression
```

Another way of looking at this is that a statement is an expression that is executed because it performs an action, rather than for its return value. For instance, consider the following `print` statement:

```
print "Hello World";
```

This is a statement by virtue of the fact that the return value from `print` is not used. However `print` actually returns a True value if it succeeds and a False value if the filehandle to which it is printing is invalid. We rarely bother to check for this, but if we wanted to we could turn this statement into an expression by writing:

```
$success = print "Hello World";
```

Now we have a `print` expression whose value is used in an assignment statement. Of course a `print` statement like this is unlikely to fail because it prints to STDOUT (the standard output), which is why the return value from `print` is rarely checked. However it does illustrate that any statement is also an expression even if we do not always think of it in those terms.

Blocks and Compound Statements

The block is a Perl construct that allows several statements (which in turn may be simple statements or further blocks) to be logically grouped together into a compound statement and executed as a unit. Blocks are defined by enclosing the statements within in curly braces; the general form of a block is therefore:

```
{ STATEMENT; STATEMENT; ... ; STATEMENT }
```

This is the most common form of block. However, blocks can also be defined by the limits of the source file. A simple Perl script is a block that starts at the top of the file and ends at the bottom (or a __DATA__ or __END__ token, if one is present in the file; see Chapter 12 for more on __END__). Likewise, an included file that has been read in using `require` also defines a block.

The definition of a block is important because in addition to grouping statements together logically, a block also defines a new scope in which variables can be declared and used. Here are two short programs, one of which executes the other via `require`. Both files define their own scope, and in addition the explicit block in the second program `child.pl` defines a third. Here is the parent process:

```
#!/usr/bin/perl
# parent.pl
use warnings;
use strict;

my $text = "This is the parent";
require 'child.pl';
print "$text \n";    # produces "This is the parent"
```

...and here is the child process:

```perl
#!/usr/bin/perl
# child.pl
use warnings;
use strict;

my $text = "This is the child";
{
    my $text = "This is block scoped";
    print "$text \n";   # produces "This is block scoped";
}
print "$text \n";    # produces "This is the child";
```

Variables that are defined within a particular scope only exist so long as that block is being executed, and are not seen or usable by the wider scope outside the block. This has a lot of significant implications, as we will see.

Blocks in Perl Statements

Almost all of Perl's control structures (such as `if` statements, `for` and `while` loops, and subroutine declarations) can accept a block in their definitions, and many require it. For example, the `if` statement requires a block to define the Boolean test that follows its condition; a simple statement will not do and will cause Perl to generate a syntax error:

```perl
if (EXPRESSION) { STATEMENT; STATEMENT; ... STATEMENT }
```

Or put more simply:

```perl
if (EXPRESSION) BLOCK
```

Note that a block is not the equivalent of a statement. As we just saw blocks are accepted in places where simple statements are not. Also, blocks do not require a terminating semicolon, unlike the statements inside them. Be aware that if the return value of a block is used, the statement requires a trailing semicolon, as we shall see later.

Naked Blocks

Although it is their most common application, blocks do not have to belong to a larger statement. They can exist entirely on their own, purely for the purposes of defining a scope. The following example shows a block in which several scalar variables are defined using `my`. The variables exist for the lifetime of the block's execution and then cease to exist.

```perl
#!/usr/bin/perl
# time.pl
use warnings;

# a bare block definition
{
    # define six scalars in new block scope:
    my ($sec, $min, $hour, $day, $month, $year) = localtime();
    # variables exist and can be used inside block
    print "The time is: $hour: $min. $sec \n";
    $month++;
    $year += 1900;
    print "The date is: $year/ $month/ $day \n";
    # end of block - variable definitions cease to exist
}

# produces 'uninitialized value' warning - $sec does not exist here
print "$sec seconds \n";
```

The ouput from this is:

Name "main::sec" used only once: possible typo at d.pl line 18.
The time is: 2: 30. 5
The date is: 2000/ 12/ 15
Use of uninitialized value in concatenation (.) at d.pl line 18.
 seconds

Note that adding use strict would turn the above warning into a compile-time syntax error as strictness requires declaring all variables.

If we take reference to bare blocks, they can also be used to define anonymous subroutines, a subject we will cover in Chapter 7.

Defining the Main Program as a Block

An interesting use of blocks is to put the main program code into a block within the source file. This helps to distinguish the actual program from any declarations or initialization code (in the shape of use statements and so forth) that may occur previously. It also allows us to restrict variables needed by the main program to the scope of the main program only, rather than turning them into global variables, which should be avoided. Consider the following simple but illustrative program:

```perl
#!/usr/bin/perl
# blockmain.pl

# declarations first
use strict;
use warnings;

# initialization code, global scope

my $global_variable = "All the World can see Me";
use constant MY_GLOBAL_CONSTANT => "Global Constant";

# here is the main program code

MAIN: {
    # variable defined in the main program scope, but not global
    my $main_variable = "Not visible outside main block";
    print_variables ($main_variable);
}

# no-one here but us subroutines...

sub print_variables {
    print $global_variable, "\n", MY_GLOBAL_CONSTANT, "\n";
    # print $main_variable, "\n";   #error!
    print $_[0], "\n";   # passed from main block, ok now
}
```

We have used a label MAIN: to prefix the start of the main program block to make it stand out. The use of the label MAIN: is entirely arbitrary – we could as easily have said MY_PROGRAM_STARTS_NOW:. However, MAIN: is friendlier to those coming from a C programming background where a main function is required. Of course, we could also create a real main subroutine, and we need to make sure that we call it.

179

The issue of scoping variables so they are invisible from subroutines is not a minor one. If we had failed to enable `warnings` and `strict` mode, and if we had uncommented the second line of `print_variables`, Perl would have happily accepted the undefined variable `$main_variable` and printed out a blank line. By placing otherwise global variables inside the scope of a `main` block we prevent them from being accidentally referred to inside subroutines, which should not be able to see them.

Blocks as Loops

Bare blocks can sometimes be treated as loops, which are discussed in detail later in the chapter. A block that is not syntactically required (for example, by an `if` statement) or is part of a loop statement can be treated as a loop that executes only once and then exits. This means that loop control statements like `next`, `last`, and `redo` will work in a block. Since blocks are one-shot loops, `next` and `last` are effectively the same. However, `redo` will re-execute the block.

In short, these three loops all do the same thing, one with a `while`, one with a `foreach`, and one with a bare block and a `redo`:

```perl
#!/usr/bin/perl
# while.pl
use warnings;
use strict;

my $n = 0;

print "With a while loop:\n";
while (++$n < 4) {print "Hello $n \n";}

print "With a foreach loop:\n";
foreach my $n (1..3) { print "Hello $n \n"; }

print "With a bare block and redo: \n";
$n = 1; { print "Hello $n \n";
last if (++$n > 3); redo; }
```

The block of an `if` statement is required syntactically and `if` is not a loop statement, so the `redo` statement here will not work:

```perl
#!/usr/bin/perl
# badblockloop.pl
use warnings;
use strict;

if (defined(my $line = <>)) {
    last if $line =~/quit/;
    print "You entered: $line";
    $line = <>;
    redo;
}
print "Bye! \n";
```

The fact that `redo`, `next`, and `last` do not work in `if` blocks is actually a blessing. Otherwise it would be hard, albeit not impossible, to break out of a loop conditionally. Instead we get a syntax error:

Can't "redo" outside a loop block at ./badblockloop.pl line 10, <> line 2.

However we can nest blocks inside each other, so by adding an extra bare block we can fix the above program so that it will work:

```perl
#!/usr/bin/perl
# blockloop.pl
use warnings;
use strict;

if (defined(my $line = <>)) { {    # <- note the extra block
    last if $line =~/quit/;
    print "You entered: $line";
    $line = <>;
    redo;
} }
print "Bye! \n";
```

Using blocks as loops is an interesting approach to solving problems, but they are not always the simplest or easiest to understand. The above script could more easily be fixed simply by replacing the if with a while. This makes more sense and does not require an extra block because while is a looping statement:

```perl
#!/usr/bin/perl
# blockwhile.pl
use warnings;
use strict;

while (my $line = <>) {
    last if $line =~/quit/;
    print "You entered: $line";
}
print "Bye! \n";
```

We cover loops in more detail later in the chapter.

The 'do' Block

Blocks do not normally return a value; they are compound statements, not expressions. They also provide a void context, which applies to the last statement in the block. This causes its value to be discarded just as those of all the statements before it are. However, the do keyword allows blocks to return their values as if they were expressions, the value being derived from the last statement:

```perl
@words = do {
    @text = ("is", "he", "last");
    sort @text;
};
```

In this example, a list generated by the sort function.

We could make this more explicit by adding a return beforehand just as we do for subroutines, but it is not actually necessary. Moreover, return is not necessary in subroutines either, and for the same reason.

Note that the result of prefixing do to a block is to turn it into an expression. That means that when it is used in a statement, the statement still needs to be terminated by a semicolon, which in this case goes after the block. This may look as if the block needs to be terminated, but this is not the case. In truth it is the statement containing the block that needs terminating. Omitting the final semicolon from statements like the above is a common mistake because in any other context a block does not require a following semicolon.

There is another, syntactic, reason for needing a do to return the value of a block. Without the requirement of a do Perl would have a hard time telling apart a bare block with one statement and a list of statements from a hash definition:

```
$c = do { $a = 3, $b = 6 };    # a block, $c = 6

{ $a = 3; $b = 6 }    # has a semicolon, therefore a block

# a hash definition, $c = {3 => 6}, which we can test with 'print keys %{$c}'
$c = { $a = 3, $b = 6 };
```

Regarding the use of blocks as loops, do blocks are not considered loops by Perl, because the block is syntactically required by the do. Loop control statements will therefore not work inside a do block. However, a do block can be suffixed with a loop condition such as while or until, in which case it is transformed into loop:

```
do { chomp($line = <>); $input. = $line } until $line =~/^stop/;
```

The block is executed before the condition is tested, so in this example the word stop will be added to the end of $line before the loop terminates.

Special Blocks

Perl provides four kinds of special blocks which differ from each other in the stage of their execution during the life of the application.

BEGIN blocks are executed during the compilation phase as they are encountered by the interpreter, so their contents are compiled and run before the rest of the source code is even compiled. We can define multiple BEGIN blocks, which are executed in the order the interpreter encounters them.

END blocks are the inverse of BEGIN blocks, they are executed by the interpreter after the application exits and before the exit of the interpreter itself. They are useful for 'clean-up' duties such as closing database connections, resetting terminal properties, or deleting temporary files. We can also define multiple END blocks, in which case they are executed in reverse order of definition.

There is also the much less used CHECK and INIT blocks that are executed just after the compile phase and just before the run phase respectively.

The following is a short script that shows both BEGIN and END blocks in action:

```perl
#!/usr/bin/perl
# begend.pl
use warnings;
use strict;

END {
    print "Exiting... \n";
}

print "Running... \n";

BEGIN {
    print "Compiling... \n";
    }
```

> **perl begend.pl**
Compiling...
Running...
Exiting...

As the output shows, the BEGIN block was executed first despite the fact that it is the last piece of the program. The END block, on other hand, which in fact occurs first in the program, is executed last. The print statement is executed after the BEGIN block but before the END block.

This brief introduction is to allow us to use the BEGIN and END blocks before we look at the four special blocks in detail in Chapter 10.

Conditional Statements

Conditional statements execute the body of the statement (sometimes known as a branch or branch of execution) only if a given Boolean condition is met. The condition is expressed in the form of an expression whose value is used to determine the course of execution.

Perl's primary mechanism for conditional execution is the if statement and its related keywords, unless, else, and elsif. However, Perl being as flexible as it is, there are other ways we can write conditions. For instance, the use of Perl's logical operators && and ||, without using if or unless.

Multiple-branch conditions are implemented in other languages using special multiple-branch conditional statements like switch or case. Perl has no such equivalent, because it does not need one. As we will see, there are already plenty of ways to write a multiple-branch condition in Perl.

However, before embarking on a detailed look at these functions it is worth talking a brief diversion to discuss the nature of truth in Perl.

What Is Truth?

Perl has a very broad-minded view of the meaning of true and false – in general, anything that has a 'non-zero' value is True. Anything else is False. By 'non-zero' we mean that the value is in some sense 'set'. Even 0 is information of a sort, especially compared to undef.

There are a few special cases. The string 0 is considered False even though it has a value, as a convenience to calculations that are performed in string context. The undefined value also evaluates to false for the purposes of conditions. However, a string of spaces is True, as is the string 00. The following examples illustrate various forms of truth and falsehood:

Value	True/False
1	True
-1	True
"abc"	True
0	False
"0"	False
""	False
" "	True
"00"	True
"0E0"	True (this is returned by some Perl libraries)
"0 but true"	True (ditto)
()	False (empty list)
undef	False

To distinguish between the undefined value and other values that evaluate to False, we can use the defined function; for instance:

```
if (defined $var) {
    print "$var is defined";
}
```

The ability to handle undef as distinct from true and false is very useful. For example, it allows functions and subroutines that return a Boolean result to indicate an 'error' by returning undef. If we want to handle the error we can do so by checking for undef. If we do not care or need to know we can just check for truth instead:

```
if (defined($var) && $var) {
    print "true \n";
}
```

'if', 'else', and 'elsif'

As we have already seen, basic conditions can be written using an `if` statement. The basic form of an `if` statement is (note that the trailing semi-colon is not required):

```
if (EXPRESSION) BLOCK
```

Here EXPRESSION is any Perl expression, and BLOCK is a compound statement, one or more Perl statements enclosed by curly braces. BLOCK is executed only if EXPRESSION is True. For instance, in the above example, the block that contains `print "true \n"` would be executed only if the expression `(defined($var) && $var)` evaluates to True, that is, only if `$var` is defined *and* True.

We can invert the syntax of an `if` statement and put the BLOCK first. In this case we can both omit the parentheses of the condition and also replace the block with a bare statement or list of statements. The following forms of `if` statement are all legal in Perl:

```
BLOCK if EXPRESSION;
STATEMENT if EXPRESSION;
STATEMENT, STATEMENT ... if EXPRESSION;
```

For example:

```
print "Equal" if $a eq $b;

print (STDERR "Illegal Value"), return "Error" if $not_valid;

close FILE, print ("Done"), exit if $no_more_lines;

return if $a ne $b;
```

The use of the comma operator here deserves a little attention. In a list context (that is, when placed between parentheses), the comma operator generates lists. However, that is not how it is being used here. In this context it simply returns the right-hand side, discarding the left, so it becomes a handy way to combine several statements into one, and relies on the fact that most statements are also expressions.

The inverted syntax is more suitable for some conditions than others. As Perl's motto has it, there is more than one way to do it, so long as the program remains legible. In the above examples, only the last `return` statement is really suited to this style; the others would probably be better off as normal `if` statements.

Beware declaring a variable in an inverted conditional statement, since the variable will only exist if the condition succeeds. This can lead to unexpected syntax errors if we have warnings enabled and unexpected bugs otherwise:

```
use warnings;

$arg = $ARGV[1] if $#ARGV;
if ($arg eq "help" ) {    # $arg may not be declared
print "Usage: \n";
...
}
...
```

185

We would be unlikely to leave $arg undefined if we had written a conventional if statement because the declaration would be inside the block, making it obvious that the scope of the variable is limited. However, the inverted syntax can fool us into thinking that it is a declaration with wider scope.

If, then, and else conditions are implemented with the else keyword:

```
if (EXPRESSION) BLOCK else BLOCK
```

For example:

```
# first 'if else' tests whether $var is defined
if (defined $var) {
# if $var is defined, the second 'if else' tests whether $var is true
    if ($var) {
        print "true \n";
    } else {
        print "false \n";
    }
} else {
    print "undefined \n";
}
```

However, it is not legal (and not elegant even if it were) to invert an if statement and then add an else clause:

```
# ERROR!
return if $not_valid else { print "ok" };
```

If we have multiple mutually exclusive conditions then we can chain them together using the elsif keyword, which may occur more than once and may or may not be followed by an else:

```
if (EXPRESSION) BLOCK elsif (EXPRESSION) BLOCK elsif...
if (EXPRESSION) BLOCK elsif (EXPRESSION) BLOCK else BLOCK
```

For example, to compare strings using just if and else we might write:

```
if ($a eq $b) {
    print "Equal";
} else {
    if ($a gt $b) {
        print "Greater";
    } else {
        print "Less";
    }
}
```

The equivalent code written using elsif is simpler to understand, is shorter, and avoids a second level of nesting:

```
if ($a eq $b) {
    print "Equal";
} elsif ($a gt $b) {
    print "Greater";
} else {
    print "Less";
}
```

Note that the `else if` construct, while legal in other languages such as C is not legal in Perl and will cause a syntax error. In Perl, use `elsif` instead. Also note that if $a is less than $b most of the time then we would be better off rewriting this statement to test $a `lt` $b first, then $a `gt` $b or $a `eq` $b second. It pays to work out the most likely eventuality and then make that the fastest route through our code.

If the conditions are all testing the same expression with different values then there are more efficient ways to do this, however. See 'Switches and Multi-Branched Conditions' later in the chapter for some examples.

The `if`, `unless`, and `elsif` keywords all permit a variable to be declared in their conditions. For example:

```
if (my @lines = <HANDLE>) {    # test if there is a filehandle called HANDLE
   ...do something to file contents...
} else {
   "Nothing to process \n";
}
```

The scope of variables declared in this fashion is limited to that of the immediately following block, so here `@lines` can be used in the `if` clause but not the `else` clause or after the end of the statement.

'unless'

If we replace the `if` in an `if` statement with `unless`, the condition is inverted. This is handy for testing a condition, which we want to act on if it evaluates to False, such as trapping error conditions:

```
# unless file filename is successfully opened then return a failure message
unless (open FILE, $filename) {
   return "Failed to open $filename: $!";
}
```

We can also invert the syntax of an `unless` statement, just as we can with `if`:

```
return "Failed to open $filename: $!" unless (open FILE, $filename);
```

This is exactly the same as inverting the condition inside the parentheses but reads a little better than using an `if` and `not`:

```
if (not open FILE, $filename) {
   return "Failed to open $filename: $!";
}
```

It is perfectly legal, though possibly a little confusing, to combine `unless` with an `else` or `elsif` as in the following:

```
unless (open FILE, $filename) {
   return "Failed to open $filename: $!";
} else {
   @lines = <FILE>;
foreach (0..$#lines)  {
   print "This is a line \n"
   }
   close FILE;
}
```

In this case it is probably better to write an `if`...`not` expression or to invert the clauses, since `unless`...`else` is not a natural English construct.

Writing Conditions with Logical Operators

Perl's logical operators automatically execute a short-cut to avoid doing unnecessary work whenever possible (see Chapter 4). Take the following example:

```
$result = try_first () or try_second () or try_third ();
```

If `try_first` returns a True value then clearly Perl has no need to even call the `try_second` or `try_third` functions, since their results will not be used; `$result` takes only one value and that would be the value returned by `try_first`. So Perl takes a shortcut and does not call them at all.

We can use this feature to write conditional statements using logical operators instead of `if` and `unless`. For example, a very common construct to exit a program on a fatal error uses the `die` function which, upon failure, prints out an error message and finishes the program:

```
open (FILE, $filename) or die "Cannot open file: $!";
```

This is equivalent to, but more direct than, the more conventional:

```
unless (open FILE, $filename) {
    die "Cannot open file: $!";
}
```

We can also provide a list of statements (separated by commas) or a `do` block for the condition to execute on success. Here is an example that supplies a list:

```
open (FILE, $filename) or print (LOG "$filename failed: $!"), die "Cannot open
file:$!";
```

Not every programmer likes using commas to separate statements, so we can instead use a `do` block. This also avoids the need to use parentheses to delineate the arguments to `print`:

```
open (FILE, $filename) or do {
    print LOG "$filename failed: $!";
    die "Cannot open file: $!";
};
```

When writing conditions with logical operators it is good practice to use the low precedence `and`, `or`, and `not` operators instead of the higher priority `&&`, `||`, and `!`. This prevents precedence from changing the meaning of our condition. If we were to change the previous example to:

```
open (FILE, $filename) || print (LOG "$filename failed: $1"), die "Cannot open
file:$!";
```

Perl's precedence rules would cause it to interpret this as a list containing a condition and a `die` statement:

```
(open (FILE, $filename) || print (LOG "$filename failed: $1")), die "Cannot open
file:$!";
```

As a result this statement will cause the program to die with a "Cannot open file" message regardless of whether the open failed or succeeded.

Using a do block avoids all these problems and also makes the code easier to comprehend. Either a || or an or will work fine in this re-written example:

```
open (FILE, $filename) || do {
   print LOG "$filename failed: $1";
   die "Cannot open file:$!";
};
```

Whether this is better than the original if form is questionable, but it does serve to emphasize the condition in cases where the condition is actually the point of the exercise. In this case the open is the most significant thing happening in this statement, so writing the condition in this way helps to emphasize and draw attention to it.

The drawback of these kinds of conditions is that they do not lend themselves easily to else type clauses. The following is legal, but is tending towards illegibility:

```
open (FILE, $filename), $text = <FILE> or die "Cannot open file: $!";
```

It would also fail with a closed filehandle error if we used || instead of or since that has higher precedence than the comma and would test the result of $text = <FILE> and not the open.

The Ternary Operator

The ternary ?: operator is a variant of the standard if style conditional statement that works as an expression and returns a value that can be assigned or used in other expressions. It works identically to the ternary operator in C, from which it is derived. The operator evaluates the first expression; if that expression is True, it returns the value of the second expression, and if the first expression was False then the operator returns the value of the third expression. This is what it looks like:

```
expression1 ? expression2 : expression3
```

The ternary operator is very convenient when the purpose of a test is to return one of two values rather than follow one of two paths of execution. For example, the following code snippet adds a plural s conditionally, using a conventional if...else condition:

```
#!/usr/bin/perl
# plural_if.pl
use warnings;
use strict;

my @words = split ('\s+', <>);   # read some text and split on whitespace

my $count = scalar (@words);

print "There ";
if ($count == 1) {
   print "is";
```

```
    } else {
       print "are";
    }
    print " $count word";

    unless ($count == 1) {
       print "s";
    }

    print " in the text \n";
```

Note that in this program we are making a numeric comparison, so we use ==. If we were doing a string comparison we would use eq. A common mistakes in both C and Perl programming is to use = (assigment) instead of == (numeric equality). Another common mistake is to use == where eq was meant, or vice versa.

Running this program and entering some text produces messages like:

There are 0 words in the text
There is 1 word in the text
There are 4 words in the text

The same code rewritten using the ternary operator is considerably simpler:

```
#!/usr/bin/perl
# plural_ternary.pl
use warnings;
use strict;

my @words = split ('\s+', <>);   # read some text and split on whitespace
my $words = scalar (@words);

print "There ", ($words == 1)?"is":"are"," $words word", ($words == 1)?"":"s","
in the text \n";
```

We can also nest ternary operators, though doing this more than once can produce code that is hard to read. The following example uses two ternary operators to compute a value based on a string comparison using cmp, which can return -1, 0, or 1:

```
#!/usr/bin/perl
# comparison.pl
use warnings;
use strict;

my @words = split ('\s+',<>);
die "Enter two words \n" unless scalar(@words) == 2;

my $result = $words[0] cmp $words[1];
print "The first word is ", $result ? $result > 0?"greater than":"less
than":"equal to "," the second \n";
```

This program checks that we have entered exactly two words, and if so prints out one of the following thee messages:

The first word is less than the second
The first word is greater than the second
The first word is equal to the second

Note that the nested ternary operators know which ? and : belongs where, but it does not make for legible code. To improve upon this, the last line is probably better written with parentheses:

```
print "The first word is ", $result ? ($result > 0 ? "greater than" : "less than")
: "equal to", " the second \n";
```

This makes it much simpler to see which expression belongs to which condition.

Be careful when combining the ternary operator into larger expressions. The precedence of operators can sometimes cause Perl to group the parts of an expression in ways we did not intend, as in the following example:

```
#!/usr/bin/perl
# plural_message.pl
use warnings;
use strict;

my @words = split ('\s+', <>);
my $words = scalar (@words);
my $message = "There ". ($words == 1) ? "is" : "are". " $words word". ($words ==
1)?"" :                  "s". " in the text \n";

print $message;
```

This appears to do much the same as the previous example, except it stores the resulting message in an intermediate variable before printing it. But (unlike the comma operator) the precedence of the concatenation operator '.' is greater than that of the ternary '?' or ':', so the meaning of the statement is entirely changed. Using explicit parentheses, the first expression is equivalent to:

```
"There ", (($words == 1)? "is" : "are"), " $words word", (($words == 1)?"" : "s"),
" in the text \n";
```

But with the concatenation operator what we actually get is:

```
("There ". ($words == 1))? "is" : ("are". " $words word", ($words == 1)?"" : "s".
" in the text \n");
```

The expression ("There ". ($words == 1)) always evaluates to a True value, so the result of running this program will always be to print the word is regardless of the input we give it.

One final trick that we can perform with the ternary operator is to use it with expressions that return an lvalue (that is, an assignable value). An example of such an expression is the substr function:

```
#!/usr/bin/perl
# fix.pl
use warnings;
use strict;
```

```
my $word = "mit";
my $fix = "re";
my $before = int(<>);    # no warnings in case we enter no numeric text

($before ? substr($word, 0, 0): substr ($word, length($word), 0)) = $fix;
print $word, "\n";
```

In this program the contents of $fix are either prefixed or postfixed to the contents of the variable $word. The ternary operator evaluates to either the beginning or the end of the value in $word as returned from substr. This value is then assigned the value of $fix, modifying the contents of $word, which is then printed out.

The result of this program is either the word remit, if we enter any kind of True value (such as 1), or mitre if we enter either nothing or a string that evaluates to False (such as '0', or a non-numeric value).

Switches and Multi-Branched Conditions

A **switch** is a conditional statement that contains multiple branches of execution. It can be thought of as rotary switch with several different positions. One simple but crude way to implement a switch is with an if...elsif...else statement, as we saw earlier:

```
if ($value == 1) {
   print "First Place";
} elsif ($value == 2) {
   print "Second Place";
} elsif ($value == 3) {
   print "Third Place";
} else {
   print "Try Again";
}
```

The problem with this kind of structure is that after a few conditions it becomes hard to understand. Perl does not have a multiple-branch conditional statement like C or Java, but we do not need one to produce the same effect. Here are two ways of writing the same set of conditions in a block:

```
SWITCH: {
    if ($value == 1)    { print "First Place" };
    if ($value == 2)    { print "Second Place" };
    if ($value == 3)    { print "Third Place" };
    if ($value > 3)     { print "Try Again" };
}

SWITCH: {
    $value == 1 and print "First Place";
    $value == 2 and print "Second Place";
    $value == 3 and print "Third Place";
    $value > 3 and print "Try Again";
}
```

Here the block does not actually do anything useful except to allow us to group the conditions together for clarity. The SWITCH: label that prefixes the block likewise has no function except to indicate that the block contains a multiple-branch condition.

Unfortunately both of these examples are less efficient than the original example because all conditions are tested even if an earlier one matches. As we saw earlier, bare blocks can be treated as loops, so we can use `last` statements to break out of the condition when we have found the correct match. This also allows us to drop the condition on the last condition:

```
SWITCH: {
    $value == 1 and print ("First Place"), last;
    $value == 2 and print ("Second Place"), last;
    $value == 3 and print ("Third Place"), last;
    print "Try Again";   # default case
}
```

We can also make use of the label to make our `last` statements more explicit:

```
SWITCH: {
    $value == 1 and print ("First Place"), last SWITCH;
    $value == 2 and print ("Second Place"), last SWITCH;
    $value == 3 and print ("Third Place"), last SWITCH;
    print "Try Again";   # default case
}
```

In this case the meaning of `last` is clear enough, but the label can be very useful in longer clauses, particularly if we have loops or further blocks inside them.

If the cases we want to execute have only one or two statements, and are similar, it is fine just to write them as a comma-separated list, as in this example. If the cases are more complex, however, this rapidly becomes illegible. A better solution in this case might be to use do blocks:

```
SWITCH: {
    $value == 1 and do {
        print "First Place";
        last;
    };

    $value == 2 and do {
        print "Second Place";
        last;
    };

    $value == 3 and do {
        print "Third Place";
        last;
    };

    print "Try Again";
}
```

Note that a do block does not count as a loop, so the `last` statements still apply to the switch block that encloses them. This is fortunate otherwise we would have to say `last SWITCH` to ensure that the right block is referred to. Of course, we can choose to use the label anyway for clarity, as noted above.

If we are testing the value of a string rather than an integer we can reproduce the above techniques but just replace the conditions with string equality tests:

```
SWITCH: {
    $value eq "1" and print ("First Place"), last;
    $value eq "2" and print ("Second Place"), last;
    $value eq "3" and print ("Third Place"), last;
    print "Try Again";
}
```

Having said this, if our strings are numeric we can do a numeric comparison if needs be. In this example $value eq "1" and $value == 1 have precisely the same result, thanks to Perl's automatic string number conversion. Of course, this only holds so long as we don't go past '9'.

We can also use regular expression matching:

```
SWITCH: {
    $value =~/^1$/ and print("First Place"), last;
    $value =~/^2$/ and print("Second Place"), last;
    $value =~/^3$/ and print("Third Place"), last;
    print "Try Again";
}
```

This might not seem much of an improvement, but regular expressions have the useful feature that if they are not associated with a value then they use the contents of the special variable $_ that Perl provides internally. As we mentioned earlier, it is the 'default variable' that functions read or write from if no alternative variable is given. We will see in 'Using 'foreach' with Multi-Branched Conditions' how to use this with foreach to rewrite our switch.

Returning Values from Multi-Branched Conditions

Simple if and unless statements do not return a value, but this is not a problem since we can write a conditional expression using the ternary operator. For multiple-branch conditions we have to be more inventive, but again Perl provides several ways for us to achieve this goal. One way to go about it is with logical operators using a do block:

```
print do {
    $value == 1 && "First Place" ||
    $value == 2 && "Second Place" ||
    $value == 3 && "Third Place" ||
    "Try again"
}, "\n";
```

If this approach does not suit our purposes we can always resort to a subroutine and use return to return the value to us:

```
sub placing {
    $_[0] == 1 and return "First Place";
    $_[0] == 2 and return "Second Place";
    $_[0] == 3 and return "Third Place";
    return "Try Again";}

print placing ($value), "\n";
```

Or, using the ternary operator:

```
sub placing {
    return $_[0] == 1? "First place" :
    $_[0] == 2? "Second place" :
    $_[0] == 3? "Third place" :
    "Try Again";
}
```

Finally, there is another solution involving using `foreach`, which we will also consider in 'Using 'foreach' With Multi-Branched Conditions'.

Loops and Looping

A loop is a block of code that is executed repeatedly, according to the criteria of the loop's controlling conditions. Perl provides two kinds of loop:

❑   Iterating loops, provided by `for` and `foreach`

❑   Conditional loops, provided by `while` and `until`.

The distinction between the two types is in the way the controlling conditions are defined.

The `for` and `foreach` loops iterate over a list of values given either explicitly or generated by a function or subroutine. The sense of the loop is 'for each of these values, do something'. Each value in turn is fed to the body of the loop for consideration. When the list of values runs out, the loop ends.

The `while` and `until` loops, on the other hand, test a condition each time around the loop. The sense of the loop is 'while this condition is satisfied, keep doing something'. If the condition succeeds, the loop body is executed once more. If it fails, the loop ends. There is no list of values and no new value for each iteration, unless it is generated in the loop body itself.

Both kinds of loop can be controlled using statements like `next`, `last`, and `redo`. These statements allow the normal flow of execution in the body of a loop to be restarted or terminated, which is why they are also known as loop modifiers. We have already talked about loop modifiers briefly in Chapter 2, but will learn more about them later in this chapter.

Since Perl is such a versatile language there are also ways to create loop-like effects without actually writing a loop. Perl provides functions such as `map` and `grep`, while not technically loops, can often be used to produce the same effect as a loop but more efficiently. In particular, if the object of a loop is to process a list of values and convert them into another list of values, `map` may be a more effective solution than an iterative `foreach` loop.

Writing C-style Loops with 'for'

The `for` and `foreach` keywords are actually synonyms, but in practice differ in how they are used. The `for` loop imitates the structure of the `for` loop in C and is most frequently used by those migrating from a C background. Here's how a `for` loop can be used to count from 9 to 0:

```
for ($n = 9; $n >= 0; $n--) {
    print $n;
}
```

Any C programmer will recognize this syntax as being identical to C, with the minor exception of the dollar sign of Perl's scalar data type syntax. Similarly, to count from 0 to 9 we could write:

```
for ($n = 0; $n < 10; $n++) {
    print $n, "\n";
    sleep 1;
}
print "Liftoff! \n";
```

The parenthesized part of the for loop contains three statements, an initialization statement, a condition, and a continuation statement. These are usually (but not always) used to set up and check a loop variable, $n in the first example above. The initialization statement (here '$n=0') is executed before the loop starts. Just before each iteration of the loop the condition $n<10 is tested, and if true the loop is executed. If False, the loop finishes. After each completion of the loop body, the continuation statement $n++ is executed. When $n reaches 10, the condition fails and the loop exits without executing the loop body, making 9 the last value of $n to be printed and giving $n the value 10 after the loop has finished.

In the above example we end up with the scalar variable $n still available, even though it is only used inside the loop. It would be better to declare the variable so that it only exists where it is needed. Perl allows the programmer to declare the loop variable inside the for statement. A variable declared this way has its scope limited to the body of the for loop, so it exists only within the loop statement:

```
for (my $n = 0; $n < 10; $n ++) {
    print $n,' is ', ($n % 2)? 'odd' : 'even';
}
```

In this example we declare $n lexically with my, so it exists only within the for statement itself. See Chapter 8 for more on variable scope and the my statement.

As an aside, the for loop can happily exist with nothing supplied for the first or last statement in the parentheses, though the semicolons are still required to distinguish from a Perl-style foreach loop, since for and foreach are synonyms. The following is thus a funny looping while loop:

```
for (; eof (FILE) ;) {
    print <FILE>;
}
```

While we are on the subject, the optional continue block is the same construct as the last statement of the for loop, just with a different syntax. Here is the equivalent of the earlier for loop written using while:

```
$n = 0;
while ($n < 10) {
    print $n, ' is ', ($n % 2)? 'odd': 'even';
} continue {
    $n ++;
}
```

We'll cover while loops in their own right in more detail a little later in the chapter.

Writing Better Loops with 'foreach'

The `for` loop is familiar to C programmers but for Perl programmers it is often unnecessarily complicated. For instance, one of the most common uses of a `for` loop in C is to iterate over the contents of an array using a loop variable to index the array (in this case, $n):

```
$n;
for ($n = 0; $n < $#array; $n ++) {
    print $array [$n], "\n";
}
```

However, we do not need to use an index variable and index into the array each time, we can just iterate directly over the contents of the array, using `foreach`:

```
$element;
foreach $element (@array) {
    print $element, "\n";
}
```

Even better, `foreach` allows us to declare the loop variable in the loop. This saves a line because no separate declaration is needed. More importantly, it restricts the scope of the variable to the loop, just as with the `for` loop above. This means that if the variable did not exist beforehand, neither will it after:

```
foreach my $element (@array) {
    print $element,"\n";
}
# $element does not exist here
```

If the loop variable already happens to exist, Perl localizes the variable when it is used as a loop variable, equivalent to using the `local` keyword. When the loop finishes the old value of the variable is re-established:

```
#!/usr/bin/perl
# befaft.pl
use warnings;
use strict;

$var = 42;
print "Before: $var \n";
foreach $var (1..5) {
    print "Inside: $var \n";
}
print "After: $var \n";    # prints '42', not '5'
```

This localization means that we cannot accidentally overwrite an existing variable, but it also means we cannot return the last value used in a `foreach` loop as we would be able to in C. In order to do that we would need to declare another variable outside the loop and assign the value of the loop variable to it each time or (if we know when the loop will exit) on the last iteration. If we need to do so this we may be better off using a `while` loop, or a `map`.

Although in practice, `for` is usually used for the C style and `foreach` for the Perl style, the two keywords are actually synonyms, and both may be used in either of the C and Perl syntaxes. The convention of using each in its allotted place is not enforced by Perl, but is generally considered good practice anyway.

If we really want to index an array by element number we can still do that with `foreach`. A `foreach` loop needs a list of values, and we want to iterate from 0 to the highest element in the array, so we need to generate a list from 0 to the highest element index and supply that to the `foreach` loop. We can achieve that easily using the range operator and the `$#array` notation to retrieve the highest index:

```
foreach $element (0..$#array) {
    print "Element $element is @array[$element] \n";
}
```

Using a range is easier to read but in versions of Perl prior to 5.005 is less efficient than using a loop variable in a `for` (or `while`) loop, for the simple reason that the range operator creates a list of all the values between the two ranges. For a range of 0 to one hundred million this involves the creation of a list containing one hundred million integers, which requires at least four hundred million bytes of storage. Of course it is unlikely that we are handling an array with one hundred million values in the first place. However, the principle holds true, so be wary of creating large temporary arrays we should can avoid them. From Perl 5.005 onwards the range operator has been optimized to return values iteratively (rather like `each`) in `foreach` loops, so it is now much faster than a loop variable. This can be considered a reason to upgrade as much as a programming point, of course.

If no loop variable is supplied, Perl uses the default variable `$_` to hold the current loop value:

```
foreach (@array) {
    print "$_ \n";
}
```

This is very convenient, especially with functions that default to using `$_` if no argument is supplied, like the regular expression operators:

```
foreach (@array) {
    /match_text/ and print "$_ contains a match! \n";
}
```

A final, somewhat unusual form of the `for`/`foreach` loop inverts the loop to place the body before the `for`. This is the same syntax as the inverted `if`, but applied to a loop instead. For example:

```
/match_text/ and print ("$_ contains a match! \n") foreach @array;
```

This syntax can be convenient for short loop bodies, but it is not really suitable if the `foreach` becomes obscured. The above example is borderline legible, for example, and a `map` or the former version would probably be better.

Using 'foreach' with Multi-Branched Conditions

We have already mentioned that, when used with switches and multi-branched conditions, regular expressions have the particularly useful feature of using `$_` when they are not associated with a value. By combining this with a `foreach` loop, we can remove the test variable altogether. Without a defined loop variable `foreach` assigns each value that it is given in turn to `$_` inside the block that follows it, so we can rewrite this SWITCH statement:

```
SWITCH: {
    $value =~/^1$/ and print("First Place"), last;
    $value =~/^2$/ and print("Second Place"), last;
    $value =~/^3$/ and print("Third Place"), last;
    print "Try Again";
}
```

like this:

```
foreach ($value) {
    /^1$/ and print ("First Place"), last;
    /^2$/ and print ("Second Place"), last;
    /^3$/ and print ("Third Place"), last;
    print "Try Again";
}
```

We have also seen how to return a value from multi-branched conditions using a do block, subroutine or the ternary operator. However, foreach also comes in very handy here when used with logical operators:

```
foreach ($value) {
    $message =
    /^1$/ && "First Place" ||
    /^2$/ && "Second Place" ||
    /^3$/ && "Third Place" ||
    "Try Again";
    print "$message \n";
}
```

Here we use a foreach to alias $value to $_, then test with regular expressions. Since $value is a scalar, not a list, the loop only executes once, but the aliasing still takes place. The short-cut behavior of logical operators will ensure that the first matching expression will return the string attached to the && operator. Note that if we were writing more complex cases, parentheses would be in order; for this simple example we don't need them.

This approach works only so long as the resulting values are all True. In this case we are returning one of the strings First Place...Try Again, which are all True, so there is no problem. For more complex situations when zero, an undefined value, or an empty string, all of which evaluate to False, is desired this will not work. Instead we can make use of the ternary operator to produce a similar effect:

```
foreach ($value) {
    $message =
    /^1$/? "First Place":
    /^2$/? "Second Place":
    /^3$/? "Third Place":
    "Try Again";
    print "$message \n";
}
```

The regular expressions in this example are testing against $_, which is aliased from $value by the foreach.

Variable Aliasing in 'foreach' Loops

If we are iterating over a real array (as opposed to a list of values) then the loop variable is not a copy but a direct alias for the corresponding array element. If we change the value of the loop variable then we also change the corresponding array element. This can be a source of problems in Perl programs if we don't take this into account, but it can also be very useful. This example uses aliasing to convert a list of strings into a consistent capitalized form:

```
#!/usr/bin/perl
# capitalize.pl
use warnings;
use strict;

my @array = ("onE", "two", "THREE", "fOUR", "FiVe");
foreach (@array) {
    # lc turns the word into lowercase, ucfirst then capitalizes the first letter
    $_ = ucfirst lc;   # lc uses $_ by default with no argument
}
print join(',', @array);
```

Sometimes we might want to avoid the aliasing feature and instead modify a copy of the original array. The simplest way to do that is to copy the original array before we start:

```
foreach (@tmparray = @array) {
    $_ =~tr/a-z/A-Z/;
    print;
}
```

The assignment to a local lexically scoped variable creates a temporary array, which can be modified without affecting the original array. It is also disposed of at the end of the loop.

Conditional Loops – 'while', 'until', and 'do'

Unlike the foreach loop, which iterates over a list of values, the while and until loops do not use a loop variable. Instead they test a condition and continue to execute the loop for so long as the condition holds. Here is an example of counting from 1 to 10 using a while loop rather than a for or foreach loop:

```
#!/usr/bin/perl
# count10.pl
use warnings;
use strict;

# count from 1 to 10 (note the post-increment in the condition)
my $n = 0;
while ($n++ < 10) {
    print $n, "\n";
}
```

The while and until loops are well suited to tasks where we want to repeat an action continuously until a condition that we can have no advance knowledge of occurs, such as reaching the end of a file. The following example shows a while loop being used to read the contents of a file line by line. When the end of the file is reached the readline operator returns False and the loop terminates:

```
$filename=<>;
open FILE, $filename;
while ($line = <FILE>) {
    print $line;
    }
close FILE;
```

If we replace `while` with `until`; the meaning of the condition is reversed, in the same way that `unless` reverses the condition of an `if` statement. This make more sense when the nature of the question asked by the Boolean test implies that we are looking for a 'no' answer. The `eof` function is a good example, it returns True when there is no more data:

```
$filename=<>;
open FILEHANDLE, $filename;
until (eof(FILEHANDLE)) {
    $line = <FILEHANDLE>;
    print $line;
}
```

Variable Aliasing with 'while'

`While` loops do not alias their conditions the way that a `foreach` loop does its controlling list, because there is no loop variable to alias with. However, a few Perl functions will alias their values to `$_` if placed in the condition of a `while` loop. One of them is the readline operator. This means we can write a loop to read the lines of a file one by one without a loop variable:

```
$filename=<>;
open FH, $filename;
while (<FH>) {
    print "$.: $_";
}
```

Or more tersely:

```
print "$.: $_" while <FH>;
```

Looping over Lists and Arrays with 'while'

We can loop over the contents of an array with `while` if we don't mind destroying the array as we do it:

```
while ($element = shift @array) {
    print $element, "\n";
}
# @array is empty here
```

On the face of it this construct does not appear to have any advantage over a more intuitive `foreach` loop. In addition, it destroys the array in the process of iterating through it, since the removed elements are discarded. However, it does have some advantages.

One simple advantage is if the elements of `@array` are very large memory-consuming values (like image data), removing them from the array as soon as we have finished with them allows Perl to release memory.

There are also computational advantages. Assume we have a list of unique strings and we want to discard every entry before a particular 'start' entry. This is easy to achieve with a `while` loop because we discard each non-matching string as we test it:

```
#!/usr/bin/perl
# startexp.pl
use warnings;
use strict;
```

```
# define a selection of strings one of which is 'start'
my @lines = ("this", "that", "the other", "start", "the data", "we want");

# discard lines until we see the 'start' marker
while (my $line = shift @lines) {
    last if $line eq 'start';
}

# print out the remaining elements using interpolation ($")
print "@lines";
```

Looping on Self-Modifying Arrays

We can use array functions like push, pop, shift, and unshift to modify the array even while we are processing it. This lets us create some interesting variations on a standard loop that are otherwise hard to achieve.

As an example, the following program oscillates indefinitely between two values. It works by shifting elements off an array one by one and adding them to the other end after subtracting each value from the highest value in the range, plus 1:

```
#!/usr/bin/perl
# oscillator.pl
use warnings;
use strict;

my $max = 20;
my @array = (1..$max-1);

while (my $element = shift @array) {
    push (@array, $max - $element);
    sleep 1;   # delay the print for one second to see the output
    print '*' x $element, "\n";   # multiply single '*' to get a bar of '*'s
}
```

A slight variation of this program produces a loop that counts from one to a maximum value, then back to one again, and terminates. The principal difference is that the array ranges from one to $max not one to $max-1:

```
#!/usr/bin/perl
# upanddown.pl
use warnings;
use strict;

my $max = 6;
my @array = (1..$max);

while (my $element = shift @array) {
    push (@array,$max - $element);
    print $element, " : ", join(",", @array), "\n";
}
```

Why should such a trivial difference cause the loop to terminate? This program produces the following output, which shows us why it terminates after passing through the array only twice:

```
1 : 2,3,4,5,6,5
2 : 3,4,5,6,5,4
3 : 4,5,6,5,4,3
4 : 5,6,5,4,3,2
5 : 6,5,4,3,2,1
6 : 5,4,3,2,1,0
5 : 4,3,2,1,0,1
4 : 3,2,1,0,1,2
3 : 2,1,0,1,2,3
2 : 1,0,1,2,3,4
1 : 0,1,2,3,4,5
```

We can see from this what is actually going on. The values of the array are each replaced with a value one lower. Since the first array element contained 1, this is reduced to zero. When it comes around for the second time the result of the shift is a False value, because 0 is False, so the loop terminates.

These particular examples are chosen for simplicity, and could also be implemented using simpler loops. For example, using an increment variable that oscillates between +1 and -1 at each end of the number range. While we have only used an ordered list for clarity, the oscillator will work even if the array does not contain ordered numbers.

Looping over Hashes with 'while'

We can iterate over a hash with while instead of foreach using the each function, which in a list context returns the next key-value pair in the hash, in the same order that keys and values return the keys and values, respectively. When there are no more key-value pairs, each returns undef, making it suitable for use in the condition of a while loop:

```
while (($key, $value) = each(%hash)) {
    print "$key => $value\n";
}
```

Using foreach and keys, or while and each for this kind of task is mostly a matter of personal preference. However, foreach is generally more flexible as it allows sorting keys and aliasing with $_, neither of which are possible in a while/each loop. However while avoids extracting the entire key list at the start of the loop, and is preferable if we intend to quit the loop once a condition is met. This is particularly true if the hash happens to be tied to something that is resource-heavy (in comparison to in-memory hash) like a DBM database.

Note that a foreach loop is a much safer option if we want to alter the contents of the array or hash we are iterating over. In particular, the internal iterator that each uses can get confused if the hash is modified during the course of the loop.

'do...while' and 'do...until'

One problem with while and until loops is that they test the condition first and only execute the loop body if the test succeeds. This means that if the test fails on the first pass, the loop body is never executed. Sometimes, however, we want to ensure that the body is executed at least once. Fortunately we can invert while and until loops by appending them to a do block to produce a do...while or do...until loop:

```
do {
    $input = <>;
    print "You typed: $input \n";
} while ($input !~ /^quit/);
```

Or, alternatively:

```
do {
    $input = <>;
    print "You typed: $input \n";
} until $input =~ /^quit/;
```

Note that parentheses around the condition are optional in an inverted while or until loop, just as they are in an inverted if.

Interestingly, this inverted loop structure applies to all the looping statements, even foreach:

```
# this works, but is confusing - don't do it.
do {
    print;
} foreach (@array);
```

However there is little point in doing this for foreach, first because it will not work except using $_, second because the loop body does not execute first as it needs the loop value to proceed, and third because it's just plain confusing. We mention it only because Perl allows it, and it is conceivably possible that we may encounter it in code.

Note that in the inverted form we cannot declare a variable in the conditional expression. We also cannot use loop control statements to control the loop's execution as these are not permitted in a do block – see 'The Trouble with do' later in the chapter.

Controlling Loop Execution

Ordinarily a loop will execute according to its controlling criteria. Frequently, however, we want to alter the normal flow of execution from within the loop body itself, depending on conditions that arise as the loop body is executed. Perl provides three statements for this, collectively known as **loop modifiers**: next, which advances to the next iteration (retesting the loop condition), last, which immediately exits the loop, and redo, which restarts the current iteration (without retesting the loop condition).

The next statement forces the loop immediately on to the next iteration, skipping any remaining code in the loop body, but executing the continue block if it is present. It is most often used when all the tasks necessary for a given iteration have been completed or the loop variable value for the current iteration is not applicable.

The following code snippet reads configuration parameters from the user, consisting of lines of name = value pairs. It uses next to skip past empty lines, comments (lines beginning with a #), and lines without an equals sign:

```
#!/usr/bin/perl
# config.pl
use warnings;
use strict;
```

```
my %config = ();
while (<>) {
    chomp;    #strip linefeed

    next if /^\s*$/;    #skip to the next iteration on empty lines
    next if /^\s*\#/;   #skip to the next iteration on comments
    my ($param, $value) = split("=", $_, 2);   #split on first '='
    unless ($value) {
        print ("No value for parameter '$_' \n");
        next;
    }

    $config{$param} = $value;
}

foreach (sort keys %config) {
    print "$_ => $config{$_} \n";
}
```

The last statement forces a loop to exit immediately, as if the loop had naturally reached its last iteration. A last is most often used when the task for which the loop was written has been completed, such as searching for a given value in an array, once found, no further processing is necessary:

```
#!/usr/bin/perl
# last.pl
use warnings;
use strict;

my @array = ("One", "Two", "Three", undef, "Five", "Six");

# copy array up to the first undefined element
my @newarray = ();
foreach my $element (@array) {
    last unless defined ($element);
    push @newarray, $element;
}

foreach (@newarray) {
    print $_." \n";   # prints One, Two, Three
}
```

The redo statement forces the loop to execute the current iteration. At first sight this appears similar to next. The distinction is that with redo the loop condition is not retested, and the continue block, if present, is not executed. In the case of a foreach loop, this means that the loop variable retains the value of the current loop rather than advances to the next. In the case of a while or until loop the code in the conditional clause is not re-executed, and any functions in it are not called. A redo is most often used when more than one iteration may be needed before the main body of a loop can be executed, for example reading files with multiple-line statements:

```
#!/usr/bin/perl
# backslash.pl
use warnings;
use strict;
```

```
my @lines = ();
while (<>) {
    chomp;
    if (s/\\$//) {     # check for and remove a trailing backslash character
        my $line = <>;
        $_ .= $line, redo;    # goes to the 'chomp' above
    }
    push @lines, $_;
}

foreach (0..$#lines) {
    print "$_ : $lines[$_] \n";
}
```

In this example the while statement reads a line and aliases it to $_. The chomp removes the trailing newline, and the remainder of the line is checked for a trailing backslash. If one is found, another line is read and appended to $_.

Inside the if statement, the redo is called to pass execution back up to the chomp statement. Since redo does not re-execute the while statement the value of $_ is not overridden and the chomp is performed on the value of $_ that was assigned inside the if statement. This process continues so long as we continue to enter lines ending with a backslash.

All of the loop control statements next, last, and redo can be used in any kind of loop (for, foreach, while, until). Exceptions to this are the do...while and do...until loops. This is because loops built around do blocks do not behave quite the way we expect, as we will see shortly.

The 'continue' Clause

All of Perl's loops can accept an additional continue clause. Code placed into the block of a continue clause is executed after the main body of the loop. Ordinarily this has no different effect from just adding the code to the end of the main loop, unless the loop body contains a next statement, in which case the continue block is executed before returning to the top of the loop. This makes a continue block a suitable place to increment a loop variable:

```
$n = 0;

while ($n < 10) {
    next if ($n % 2);
    print $n, "\n";

} continue {
    # 'next' comes here
    $n++;
}

# 'last' comes here
```

Note, however, that a last statement will not execute the continue block before exiting the loop. Similarly, redo will not execute the continue block because it re-executes the loop body on the same iteration, rather than continuing to the next.

There are few, if any, instances where a continue block is actually necessary, since most loops with a continue clause can be easily rewritten to avoid one.

The continue clause is actually an explicit way to write the third part of a for loop, which deals with next, last, and redo in the same way as the while...continue loop above:

```
for ($n = 0; $n < 10; $n++) {
    next if ($n % 2);
    print $n, "\n";
}
```

This example is exactly equivalent in both execution and semantics to the while loop above, with the single exception that the scope of $n is limited to the body of the loop itself. If we placed enclosing braces before the my $n = 0; and after the continue block, the two examples would be effectively identical, except that the for loop is a lot shorter and simpler to read.

Controlling Nested Loops

So far we have just seen how to use loop control statements to affect the execution of the current loop. However, the next, last, and redo statements all accept an optional loop label as an argument. This allows us to jump to the start or end of an outer loop, so long as that loop has a name. To give a loop a name we just prefix it with a label:

```
@lines = ();
LINE: foreach (<>) {
    chomp;
    next LINE if /^$/;    # skip blank lines
    push @lines, $_;
}
```

Even in a simple loop this allows us to write slightly more legible code in places. Since the label indicates the purpose of the loop and of the control statements inside it, next LINE literally means 'do the next line'. However, if we have two nested loops, labeling the outer loop allows us to jump to the next iteration of the outer loop using next:

```
OUTER: foreach my $outer (@array) {
    INNER: foreach my $inner (@{$outer}) {
        next OUTER unless defined $inner;
    }
    # 'last' or 'last INNER' would come here
}
```

This is very similar to using a last statement, except that it will jump to the top of the outer loop rather than the end of the inner loop. If the outer loop contains more code after the inner loop, next will avoid it while last will execute it.

Similarly, we can use last to exit both loops simultaneously. This is a much more efficient way to exit nested loops than exiting each loop individually:

```
LINE: foreach my $line (<>) {
    chomp;
    ITEM: foreach (split /, /, $line) {
        last LINE if /^_END_/;    # abort both loops on token
        next LINE if /^_NEXT_/;   # skip remaining items on token
        next ITEM if /^\s*$/;     # skip empty columns
```

```
            # process item
            print "Got: $_ \n";
        }
    }
}
```

Labeling the inner loop is optional. The outer loop does need to be labeled, allowing loop control statements to apply themselves to the outer loop and not to the inner loop. However, if we use labels for some loop control statements it is generally more legible to use them for all of the loop control statements.

Perl allows labels to be defined multiple times. When a label is used, the label definition that is closest in scope is taken to be the target. For loop control statements, the first matching loop label in the stack of loops surrounding the statement is used. In general we do not expect to be giving two loops the same name if one is inside the other, so it is always clear which label a loop control statement is referring to. Reusing labels is also handy for switch style conditional statements, and any other constructs where we want to make the purpose of the construct clear.

Intriguingly, we can jump to a loop label of an outer loop even if there is a subroutine call in the way. This is not really a good idea, and Perl will warn us if we do it inadvertently:

Exiting subroutine via next at ...

> Although we would not expect to do this normally, it is possible to mistype the name of a label, especially if we copy and paste carelessly.

The Trouble with 'do'

The fact that loop modifiers do not work in do...while, or do...until loops may seem strange. The reason for this is slightly obscure, but comes about because unlike a normal while or until loop, the while and until conditions in a do...while or do...until loop are considered modifiers that modify the behavior of the do block immediately before them. The do block is not considered to be a loop, so loop control statements do not work in them.

It is possible, though not terribly elegant, to get a next statement to work in a do...while loop through the addition of an extra bare block inside the do block, as in this example:

```
#!/usr/bin/perl
# even1.pl
use warnings;
use strict;

# print out even numbers with a do...while loop
my $n = 0;
do { {
    next if ($n % 2);
    print $n, "\n";
} } while ($n++ < 10);
```

Unfortunately while this works for next, it does not work for last, because both next and last operate within the bounds of the inner block. All last does in this case is take us to the end of the inner block, where the while condition is still in effect. In order to get last to work we have to invert the blocks and put the do block inside the bare block. Unfortunately, this will now cause next to do the same as last. It will take us to the next iteration of the outer bare block, which, as it only executes once, exits the loop. The only way to have both working is to use a label for an outer block and an inner block:

```perl
#!/usr/bin/perl
# even2.pl
use warnings;
use strict;

# print out even numbers with a do...while loop
my $n = 0;
DO_LOOP: { do { {
    next if ($n % 2);
    print $n, "\n";
    # ...do other stuff
    last DO_LOOP if $n == 10;
} } while (++$n) }
```

This is extremely ugly code. The better solution at this point is to find a way to rephrase this code as a normal while, until, or foreach loop and avoid the whole problem:

```perl
$n = 0;
while (++$n <= 10) {
    next if ($n % 2);
    print $n, "\n";

    # do other stuff
}
```

The 'goto' Statement

The goto statement has two basic modes of operation. The simpler and more standard use allows execution to jump to an arbitrary labeled point in the code, just as in C and many other languages.

```perl
($lines, $empty, $comment, $code) = (0, 0, 0, 0);

while (<>) {
    /^$/ and $empty++, goto CONTINUE;
    /^#/ and $comment++, goto CONTINUE;
    $code++, goto CONTINUE;

CONTINUE:
    $lines++;
}
```

There are few, if any, reasons to use a goto with a label. In this case, we would be better off replacing goto with next statements and putting the continue code into a continue block:

```perl
while (<>) {
    /^$/ and $empty++, next;
    /^#/ and $comment++, next;
    $code++;

} continue {
    $lines++;
}
```

A goto statement can also take an expression as its argument. The result of the expression should be a label that execution can jump to. This gives us another, albeit rather ugly, way to write a compound switch statement:

```
$selection = int (4*rand);    # $selection is a random integer

@selections = ("ZERO", "ONE", "TWO", "THREE");
goto $selections[$selection];

{
    ZERO:
    print "None";
    next;
    ONE:
    print "One";
    next;
    TWO:
    print "Two";
    next;
    THREE:
    print "Three";
    next;
}

print "...done \n";
```

Again, there are better ways to write compound statements. We covered these earlier, so we should not have to resort to goto here.

The second, and more interesting use of goto, is used to call subroutines. When used in this context the new subroutine entirely replaces the current one, so that on return from the second subroutine execution is returned to the caller of the first subroutine. The primary use of this form is in autoloaded functions, which will be covered later in this chapter, and also in Chapter 10.

It can also be used for so called **tau-recursion**. This is where a recursive subroutine can call itself repeatedly without causing Perl to create an ever-growing stack of subroutine calls. A subroutine that calls itself ten thousand times can return directly to the original caller instead of returning a value through ten thousand intermediate subroutine calls. We will cover this in Chapter 7.

'maps' and 'greps'

The map and grep functions are list-processing functions that convert one list into another. If the goal of a foreach or while loop is to generate a new list, we might be able to do the job better using map or grep. The syntax of map (and grep) takes one of two equivalent forms:

```
map EXPRESSION, LIST    grep EXPRESSION, LIST
map BLOCK LIST          grep BLOCK LIST
```

In each case the EXPRESSION or BLOCK is executed for each value of LIST, and the results returned as a new list. This is not dissimilar to the way that foreach works, except that map returns a value that can be immediately used in a larger expression or statement.

The purpose of map is to convert the elements of a list one by one, and produce a new list as a result. The expression or block performs the conversion, so map is conceptually related to a foreach loop. Similarly, the purpose of grep is to return a list containing a subset of the original list. The expression or block is evaluated to a True or False value to see if the element is eligible for inclusion, so grep is conceptually related to a while loop. Both functions perform aliasing to $_ in the same way that foreach does.

'map'

To illustrate how map works in practice, let's take an example. Assume that we have a list of integers representing ASCII values, and we want to turn it into a list of character strings. We can do that with a foreach loop like this:

```
@numbers = (80, 101, 114, 108);
@characters;

foreach (@numbers) {
    push @characters, chr $_;
}

print @characters;
```

With map we can do it like this:

```
@numbers = (80, 101, 114, 108);
@characters = map (chr $_, @numbers);
```

Or, equivalently:

```
@characters = map {chr $_} @numbers;
```

Even better, we can turn the result into a string and print it in one go, because map returns the resulting list, unlike the foreach loop:

```
print join ('-', map {chr $_} @numbers);    # displays 'P-e-r-l'
```

As we can see, map is closely related to foreach, and operates in a similar way, especially with regards to aliasing. Unlike foreach however, map cannot choose its own loop variable and must use $_ within the block or expression. It also cannot make use of loop control variables in the same way that a do block cannot.

The choice between foreach and map mainly boils down to the purpose of the loop. If the purpose of the loop is to generate a new list, and we intend to immediately use that list in a larger expression, we should use map. If the loop has effects other than building the list, or needs to use loop control statements, we are better off using foreach.

'grep'

The grep function gets its name from the UNIX grep command, which scans text files and returns lines from them that match a given regular expression search pattern. The Perl grep function is similar in concept in that it returns a list containing a subset of the original list, though it does not directly have anything to do with regular expressions.

The syntax of grep is identical to map, but while the expression or block in a map statement is used to convert each value in a list, the corresponding expression or block in a grep statement is evaluated as a condition to determine if the value should be included in the new list.

For example, the following while loop calculates the lines starting with numbers, and then builds up a list of the lines input:

```
@numerics = ();
while (<>) {
    push @numerics, $_ if /^\d+/;
}
print "@numerics\n";
```

The same thing is much shorter with map, but involves a conditional operation:

```
@numerics = map {/^\d + /?$_:()} <>;
```

This works because () returns nothing and so adds nothing to the list being built by map. This is essentially what grep does automatically, so we can simplify the above to just:

```
@numerics = grep {/^\d + /} <>;
```

Here we have used a regular expression as the condition, in keeping with the spirit of the UNIX grep command, which works on a similar basis. However, since grep accepts any expression or block to test the condition, we can use any kind of condition we like.

Note that because grep tests each value that it is supplied with, rather than manipulating it like map, does not mean that it has to leave the values untouched. Since grep aliases $_ to the values of the original list, we can alter the resulting list by assigning to $_, so long as we are prepared to accept that this also alters the original list. This is fine if we intend to discard the original list, but bad practice otherwise, it leads to confusing and hard-to-understand code.

The following example uses grep and assigns to $_ to produce a modified version of the elements that match. First it strips the leading numbers with a substitution, then assigns $_ to give the remaining string a prefix:

```
@numerics = grep {

    if (s/\d+//) {
        $_ = "Got: $_";
    }
}
<>;
```

Due to the fact that the result of the assignment is the value assigned, which in this case is a string that starts with Got:, the whole block evaluates to a true value if the initial substitution succeeds, and an undefined value otherwise.

As with map, there is a limit to how far this kind of approach should be pushed. Once the complexity reaches a certain point it becomes more practical and certainly more legible to use a foreach or while loop instead.

Summary

We started this chapter by exploring the basic structures of Perl. We covered statements, declarations, expression, and blocks. We looked in particular at the facilities provided by blocks.

We covered Perl's conditional statements, if, else, elsif, and unless. We also looked in detail at how to create loops with for and foreach, and how to create conditional loops with while, until, do, do...while and do...until.

The chapter also covered how to control the execution of loops with the modifiers next, last, redo, and continue. Finally, the chapter covered the goto statement as well as map and grep.

7

Subroutines

Subroutines are autonomous blocks of code that function like miniature programs and can be executed from anywhere within a program. Because they are autonomous, calling them more than once will also reuse them.

There are two types of subroutine, **named** and **anonymous**. Most subroutines are of the 'named' persuasion. Anonymous subroutines do not have a name by which they can be called, but are stored and accessed through a code reference. Since a code reference is a scalar value, it can be passed as a parameter to other subroutines.

The use of subroutines is syntactically the same as the use of Perl's own built-in functions. We can use them in a traditional function-oriented syntax (with parentheses), or treat them as named list operators. Indeed, we can override and replace the built-in functions with our own definitions provided as subroutines through the use of the use subs pragma.

Subroutines differ from ordinary bare blocks in that they can be passed a list of parameters to process. This list appears inside subroutines as the special variable @_, from which the list of passed parameters (also known as arguments) can be extracted.

Because the passed parameters take the form of a list, any subroutine can automatically read in an arbitrary number of values, but conversely the same flattening problem that affects lists that are placed inside other lists also affects the parameters fed to subroutines.

The flexibility of the parameter passing mechanism can also cause problems if we want to actually define the type and quantity of parameters that a subroutine will accept. Perl allows us to define this with an optional prototype, which, if present, allows Perl to do compile-time syntax checking on how our subroutines are called.

Subroutines, like bare blocks, may return either a scalar or a list value to the calling context. This allows them to be used in expressions just as any other Perl value is. The way this value is used depends on the context in which the subroutine is called.

Declaring and Calling Subroutines

Subroutines are declared with the sub keyword. When Perl encounters sub in a program it stops executing statements directly, and instead creates a subroutine definition that can then be used elsewhere. The simplest form of subroutine definition is the explicit named subroutine:

```
sub mysubroutine {
    print "Hello subroutine! \n";
}
```

We can call this subroutine from Perl with:

```
# call a subroutine anywhere
mysubroutine ();
```

In this case we are calling the subroutine without passing any values to it, so the parentheses are empty. To pass in values we supply a list to the subroutine. Note how the subroutine parentheses resemble a list constructor:

```
# call a subroutine with parameters
mysubroutine ("testing", 1, 2, 3);
```

Of course just because we are passing values into the subroutine does not mean that the subroutine will use them. In this case the subroutine entirely ignores anything we pass to it. We'll cover passing values in more detail shortly.

In Perl it does not matter if we define the subroutine before or after it is used. It is not necessary to predeclare subroutines. When Perl encounters a subroutine call it does not recognize, it searches all the source files that have been included in the program for a suitable definition, and then executes it. However, defining or predeclaring the subroutine first allows us to omit the parentheses and use the subroutine as if it were a list operator:

```
# call a previously defined subroutine without parentheses
mysubroutine;
mysubroutine "testing", 1, 2, 3;
```

> Note that calling subroutines without parentheses alters the precedence rules that control how their arguments are evaluated, which can cause problems, especially if we try to use a parenthesized expression as the first argument. If in doubt, use parentheses.

We can also use the old-style & code prefix to call a subroutine. In modern versions of Perl (that is, anything from Perl 5 onwards) this is strictly optional, but older Perl programs may contain statements like:

```
# call a Perl subroutine using the old syntax
&mysubroutine;
&mysubroutine();
```

The ampersand has the property of causing Perl to ignore any previous definitions or declarations for the purposes of syntax, so parentheses are mandatory if we wish to pass in parameters. It also has the effect of ignoring the prototype of a subroutine, if one has been defined. Without parentheses, the ampersand also has the unusual property of providing the subroutine with the same @_ array that the calling subroutine received, rather than creating a new one. In general, the ampersand is optional and, in these modern and enlightened times, it is usually omitted for simple subroutine calls.

Anonymous Subroutines and Subroutine References

Less common than named subroutines, but just as valid, are anonymous subroutines. As their name suggests, anonymous subroutines do not have a name. Instead they are used as expressions, which return a code reference to the subroutine definition. We can store the reference in a scalar variable (or as an element of a list or a hash value) and then refer to it through the scalar:

```
my $subref = sub {print "Hello anonymous subroutine";};
```

In order to call this subroutine we use the ampersand prefix. This instructs Perl to call the subroutine whose reference this is, and return the result of the call:

```
# call an anonymous subroutine
&$subref;
&$subref ("a parameter");
```

This is one of the few places that an ampersand is still used. However, even here it is not required; we can also say:

```
$subref->();
$subref->("a parameter");
```

These two variants are nearly, but not quite, identical. Firstly, &$subref; passes the current @_ array (if any) directly into the called subroutine, as we briefly mentioned earlier. Secondly, the ampersand disables any prototypes we might have defined for the subroutine. The second pair of calls retains the prototype in place. (We cover both of these points later in the chapter.)

We can generate a subroutine reference from a named subroutine using the backslash operator:

```
my $subref = \&mysubroutine;
```

This is more useful than one might think, because we can pass a subroutine reference into another subroutine as a parameter. The following simple example demonstrates a subroutine taking a subroutine reference and a list of values, and returning a new list generated from calling the subroutine on each value of the passed list in turn:

```
#!/usr/bin/perl
# callsub.pl
use warnings;
use strict;

sub do_list {
    my ($subref, @in) = @_;
    my @out;
    map {push @out, &$subref ($_)} @in;
    return @out;
}
```

```
sub add_one {
    return $_[0] + 1;
}

$, = ",";
print do_list (\&add_one, 1, 2, 3);    # prints 2, 3, 4
```

Some Perl functions (notably sort), also accept an anonymous subroutine reference as an argument. We do not supply an ampersand in this case because sort wants the code reference, not the result of calling it. Here is a sort program that demonstrates the different ways we can supply sort with a subroutine. The anonymous subroutine appearing last will not work with Perl 5.005:

```
#!/usr/bin/perl
# sortsub.pl
use warnings;
use strict;

# a list to sort
my @list = (3, 4, 2, 5, 6, 9, 1);

# directly with a block
print sort {$a cmp $b} @list;

# with a named subroutine
sub sortsub {
    return $a cmp $b;
}
print sort sortsub @list;

# with an anonymous subroutine
my $sortsubref = sub {return $a cmp $b;};
print sort $sortsubref @list;
```

Of course, since we can get a code reference for an existing subroutine we could also have said:

```
$sortsubref = \&sortsub;
```

The advantage of using the anonymous subroutine is that we can change the subroutine that sort uses elsewhere in the program, for example:

```
# define anonymous subroutines for different sort types:
$numericsort = sub {$a <=> $b};
$stringsort = sub {$a cmp $b };
$reversenumericsort = sub {$b <=> $a};

# now select a sort method
$sortsubref = $numericsort;
```

The disadvantage of this technique is that unless we take care to write and express our code clearly, it can be very confusing to work out what is going on, since without running the code it may not always be possible to tell which subroutine is being executed where. We can use print $subref to print out the address of the anonymous subroutine, but this is not nearly as nice to read as a subroutine name.

It is also possible to turn an anonymous subroutine into a named one, by assigning it to a typeglob. This works by manipulating the symbol table to invent a named code reference that Perl thereafter sees as a subroutine definition. This leads to the possibility of determining the actual code supported by a subroutine name at run time, which is handy for implementing things like state machines. This will be covered more fully in 'Manipulating the Symbol Table Directly' in Chapter 8.

Strict Subroutines and the 'use strict subs' Pragma

The `strict` pragma has three components, `refs`, `vars`, and `subs`. The `subs` component affects how Perl interprets unqualified (that is, not quoted or otherwise identified by the syntax) words or 'barewords' when it encounters them in the code.

Without strict subroutines in effect, Perl will allow a bareword and will interpret it as if it were in single quotes:

```
$a = bareword;
print $a;    # prints "bareword";
```

The problem with this code is that we might later add a subroutine called `bareword`, at which point the above code suddenly turns into a function call. Indeed, if we have `warnings` enabled, we will get a warning to that effect:

Unquoted string "bareword" may clash with future reserved word at ...

Strict subroutines is intended to prevent us from using barewords in a context where they are ambiguous and could be confused with subroutines. To enable them, use one of the following:

```
use strict;    # enables strict refs, vars, and subs
use strict subs;    # enables strict subs only
```

Now any attempt to use a bareword will cause Perl to generate a fatal error:

Bareword "bareword" not allowed while "strict subs" in use at ...

Ironically, the second example contains the illegal bareword `subs`. It works because at the point Perl parses the pragma it is not yet in effect. Immediately afterwards, barewords are not permitted, so to switch off strict subs again we would have to use either quotes or a quoting operator like qw:

```
no strict 'subs';
no strict q(subs);
no strict qw(subs);
```

Predeclaring Subroutines

Perl allows subroutines to be called in two alternative syntaxes: functions with parentheses or list operators. This allows subroutines to be used as if they were one of Perl's built-in list operator functions such as `print` or `read` (neither of which require parentheses).

This syntax is only valid if Perl has already either seen the subroutine definition or a declaration of the subroutine. The following subroutine call is not legal, because the subroutine has not yet been defined:

```
debug "This is a debug message";    # ERROR: no parentheses
#...rest of program...

sub debug {
   print STDERR @_, "\n";
}
```

The intention here is to create a special debug statement, which works just like the print statement, but prints to standard error rather than standard out, and automatically adds a linefeed. Because we want it to work like print in all other respects we would prefer to omit the brackets if we choose to, since print allows us to do that.

```
# predeclare subroutine 'debug'
sub debug;

debug "This is a debug message";    # no error
#...rest of program...

sub debug {
   print STDERR @_, "\n";
}
```

Subroutines are also predeclared if we import them from another package (see Chapter 10 for more on packages), as in:

```
use mypackage qw(mysubroutine);
```

It is worth noting here that even if a package automatically exports a subroutine when it is used, that does not predeclare the subroutine itself. In order for the subroutine to be predeclared, we must name it in the use statement. Keeping this in mind, we might prefer just to stick to parentheses.

Overriding Built-in Functions

Another way to predeclare subroutines is with the use subs pragma. This not only predeclares the subroutine, but also allows us to override Perl's existing built-in functions and replace them with our own. We can access the original built-in function with the CORE:: prefix. For example, here is a replacement version of the srand function, which issues a warning if we use srand in a version of Perl of 5.004 or greater without arguments (see Appendix C for more on the srand function):

```
#!/usr/bin/perl
# srandcall.pl
use warnings;
use strict;
use subs qw(srand);

sub srand {
   if ($] >= 5.004 and not @_) {
      warn "Unqualified call to srand redundant in Perl $]";
   } else {
      # call the real srand via the CORE package
      CORE::srand @_;
   }
}
```

Now if we use `srand` without an argument and the version of Perl is 5.004 or greater, we get a warning. If we supply an argument we are assumed to know what we are doing and are supplying a suitably random value.

Subroutines like this are generally useful in more than one program, so we might want to put this definition into a separate module and use it whenever we want to override the default `srand`:

```perl
#!/usr/bin/perl
# mysrand.pm

package mysrand;

use strict;

use vars qw(@ISA @EXPORT @EXPORT_OK);
use Exporter;

@ISA = qw(Exporter);
@EXPORT = qw(mysrand);
@EXPORT_OK = qw(srand);

sub mysrand {
    if ($] >= 5.004 and not @_) {
        warn "Unqualified call to srand redundant in Perl $]";

    } else {
    # call the real srand via the CORE package
    CORE::srand @_;
    }
}

use subs qw(srand);
sub srand {&mysrand;};    # pass @_ directly to mysrand
```

This module, which we would keep in a file called `mysrand.pm` to match the package name, exports the function `mysrand` automatically, and the overriding `srand` function only if we ask for it.

```perl
use mysrand;    # import 'mysrand'
use mysrand qw(mysrand);    # import and predeclare mysrand;
use mysrand qw(srand);    # override 'srand'
```

We'll talk about packages, modules, and exporting subroutines in Chapter 10.

The Subroutine Stack

Whenever Perl calls a subroutine, it pushes the details of the subroutine call onto an internal stack. This holds the context of each subroutine, including the parameters that were passed to it in the form of the `@_` array, ready to be restored when the call to the next subroutine returns. The number of subroutine calls that the program is currently in is known as the 'depth' of the stack. Calling subroutines are higher in the stack, and called subroutines are lower.

This might seem academic, and to a large extent it is, but Perl allows us to access the calling stack ourselves with the `caller` function. At any given point we are at the 'bottom' of the stack, and can look 'up' to see the contexts stored on the stack by our caller, its caller, and so on, all the way back to the top of the program. This can be handy for all kinds of reasons, but most especially for debugging.

In a purely scalar context, `caller` returns the name of the package from which the subroutine was called, and `undef` if there was no caller. Note that this does not require that the call came from inside another subroutine – it could just as easily be from the main program. In a list context, `caller` returns the package name, the source file, the line number from which we were called, and the name of the subroutine that was called (that is, us). This allows us to write error traps in subroutines like:

```
sub mysub {
    ($pkg, $file, $line) = caller;
    die "Called with no parameters at $file line $line" unless @_;
}
```

If we pass a numeric argument to `caller`, it looks back up the stack the requested number of levels, and returns a longer list of information. This level can of course be '0', so to get everything that Perl knows about the circumstances surrounding the call to our subroutine we can write:

```
@caller_info = caller 0;   # or caller(0), if we prefer
```

This returns a whole slew of items into the list, which may or may not be defined depending on the circumstances. They are, in order:

- ❏ `package`: the package of the caller
- ❏ `filename`: the source file of the caller
- ❏ `line`: the line number in the source file
- ❏ `subroutine`: the subroutine that was called (that is, us). If we execute code inside an `eval` statement then this is set to `eval`
- ❏ `hasargs`: this is `true` if parameters were passed (`@_` was defined)
- ❏ `wantarray`: the value of `wantarray` inside the caller, see 'Returning Values from subroutines' later in the chapter
- ❏ `evaltext`: the text inside the `eval` that caused the subroutine to be called, if the subroutine was called by `eval`
- ❏ `is_require`: true if a `require` or `use` caused the `eval`
- ❏ `hints`: compilation details, internal use only
- ❏ `bitmask`: compilation details, internal use only

In practice, only the first four items: package, filename, line, and subroutine are of any use to us, which is why they are the only ones returned when we use caller with no arguments. Unfortunately we do not get the name of the calling subroutine this way, so we have to extract that from further up the stack:

```
# get the name of the calling subroutine, if there was one
$callingsub = (caller 1)[3];
```

Or, more legibly:

```
($pkg, $file, $line, $callingsub) = caller 1;
```

Armed with this information, we can create more informative error messages that report errors with respect to the caller. For example:

```
# die with a better error message

sub mysub {
    ($pkg, $file, $line) = caller;
    die "Called from ", (caller(1)) [3], " with no parameters at $file line $line
\n" unless    @_;
    ...
}
```

If debugging is our primary interest, a better solution than all the above is to use the `Carp` module. The `Carp` module and other debugging aids are covered in Chapter 17.

One final point about the calling stack: if we try to access the stack above the immediate caller we may not always get the right information back. This is because Perl can optimize the stack under some circumstances, removing intermediate levels. The result of this is that `caller` is not always as consistent as we might expect, so a little caution should be applied to its use.

Recursion

Recursion happens when a subroutine calls itself, either directly, or indirectly, via another subroutine (also known as mutual recursion). For example, consider this subroutine that calculates the Fibonacci sequence up to a specified number of terms:

```
#!/usr/bin/perl
# fib1.pl
use warnings;
use strict;

sub fibonacci1 {
    my ($count, $aref) = @_;

    unless ($aref) {
        # first call - initialize
        $aref = [1, 1];
        $count -= scalar(@{$aref});
    }

    $aref = [1,1] unless $aref;
    if ($count--) {
        my $next = $aref->[-1] + $aref->[-2];
        push @{$aref}, $next;
        return fibonacci1($count, $aref);
    } else {
        return wantarray?@{$aref}: $aref->[-1];
    }
}

# calculate 10th element of standard Fibonacci sequence
print scalar(fibonacci1(10)), "\n";

# calculate 10th element beyond sequence starting 2, 4
print scalar(fibonacci1(10, [2, 4])), "\n";

# return first ten elements of standard Fibonacci sequence
my @sequence = fibonacci1(10);
print "Sequence: @sequence \n";
```

Each time the subroutine is entered, it calculates one term, decrements the counter by one and calls itself to calculate the next term. The subroutine takes two arguments, the counter, and a reference to the list of terms being calculated. (As a convenience, if we don't pass in a reference the subroutine initializes itself with the start of the standard Fibonacci sequence, 1, 1.) We pass in a reference to avoid copying the list repeatedly, which is wasteful. When the counter reaches zero, the subroutine exits without calling itself again, and returns either the whole list or the last term, depending on how it was called.

This is an example of forward recursion, where we start at the beginning of the task and work our way towards the end. Elements are calculated one by one as we continue with our recursion. An alternative way of doing the same job is to use reverse recursion, which starts by trying to calculate the last term first:

```perl
#!/usr/bin/perl
# fib2.pl
use warnings;
use strict;

sub fibonacci2 {
    my ($count, $internal) = @_;

    if ($count <= 2) {
        # we know the answer already
        return $internal?[1,1]: 1;
    } else {
        # call ourselves to determine previous two elements
        my $result = fibonacci2($count -1, 'internal');
        # now we can calculate our element
        my $next = $result->[-1] + $result->[-2];

        if ($internal) {
            push @{$result}, $next;
            return $result;
        } else {
            return $next;
        }
    }
}

foreach (1..20) {
    print "Element $_ is ", fibonacci2($_), "\n";
}
```

This time the subroutine starts by trying to work out the last term, starting at the end, and reversing back towards the beginning until we can determine the answer without a further call. If the requested term is the first or second, it just returns the result, otherwise, it needs to work out the terms prior to the one we have been asked for, which it does by calling itself for the previous terms. In this model, we descend rapidly to the bottom of the recursion stack until we get the answer '[1,1]'. We then calculate each new term as we return back up.

Reverse recursion is not as obvious as forward recursion, but can be a much more powerful tool, especially in algorithms where we do not know in advance exactly how the initial known results will be found. Problems like the Queen's Dilemma (placing eight queens on a chessboard such that no Queen can take another) are more easily solved with reverse recursion, for example.

Both approaches suffer from the problem that Perl generates a potentially large call stack. If we try to calculate a sufficiently large sequence then Perl will run out of room to store this stack and will fail with an error message:

Deep recursion on subroutine "main::fibonacci2" at ...

Some languages support 'tail' recursion, an optimization of forward recursive subroutines where no code exists after the recursive subroutine call. Because there is no more work to do at the intermediate levels of the subroutine stack, they can be removed. This allows the final call to the recursed subroutine call to directly return to the original caller. Since no stack is maintained, no room is needed to store it.

Perl's interpreter is not yet smart enough to figure out this optimization automatically, but we can code it explicitly using a goto statement. The fibonacci1 subroutine we showed first is a recursive subroutine that fits the criteria for 'tau' recursion, as it returns. Here is a modified version, fibonacci3 that uses goto to avoid creating a stack of recursed subroutine calls. Note that the goto statement and the line immediately before it are the only difference between this subroutine and fibonacci1:

```
#!/usr/bin/perl
# fib3.pl
use warnings;
use strict;

sub fibonacci3 {
    my ($count, $aref) = @_;

    unless ($aref) {
    # first call - initialize
    $aref = [1,1];
    $count -= scalar(@{$aref});
    }

    if ($count--) {
        my $next = $aref->[-1] + $aref->[-2];
        push @{$aref}, $next;
        @_ = ($count, $aref);
        goto &fibonacci3;
    } else {
        return wantarray?@{$aref}:$aref->[-1];
    }
}
# calculate 1000th element of standard Fibonacci sequence
print scalar(fibonacci3(1000)), "\n";
```

The goto statement jumps directly to another subroutine without actually calling it (which creates a new stack frame). The automatic creation of a localized @_ does not therefore happen. Instead, the context of the current subroutine call is used, including the current @_. In order to 'pass' arguments we therefore have to predefine @_ before we call goto. Examining the code above, we can see that although it would sacrifice legibility, we could also replace $count with $_[0] to set up @_ correctly without redefining it.

Recursion is a nice programming trick, but it is easy to get carried away with it. Any calculation that uses recursion can also be written using ordinary iteration too, so use recursion only when it presents the most elegant solution to a programming problem.

Checking for Subroutines and Defining Subroutines On the Fly

We can check for the existence of a subroutine before we call it using Perl's `defined` function:

```
if (defined &capitalize) {
    capitalize(@countries);
}
```

This is more useful than it might seem. For instance, when using a library that may or may not support a particular subroutine (depending on the installed version) we can safeguard against a possible exit from our program by checking that the library has the function before we try to call it.

If we are writing object-oriented Perl, we can use the special object method `can` (supplied by the UNIVERSAL object – that's a subject for Chapter 19 though), in order to do the same thing in a more object-oriented style:

```
$bean->jump('left') if $bean->can('jump');
```

We are not limited to just testing for the existence of subroutines. We can also substitute for them and even define them on-the-fly by defining an AUTOLOAD subroutine. If an AUTOLOAD subroutine exists in the same package as a non-existent subroutine, Perl will call it, rather than exiting with an error. The name of the missing subroutine, complete with package name, is placed in the special package variable $AUTOLOAD, and the arguments passed to the subroutine are instead passed to AUTOLOAD. As a trivial example, the following AUTOLOAD subroutine just returns the missing subroutine name as a string:

```
sub AUTOLOAD {
    our $AUTOLOAD;    # or 'use vars' for Perl < 5.6
    return $AUTOLOAD;
}
```

Because $AUTOLOAD is a package variable which we have not declared, we need to gain access to it with the `our` directive if `use strict` is in effect (Perl versions before 5.6 need to have `use vars` instead). The example above allows us to write strange looking statements like this:

```
$, = " ";
print "", Hello, Autoloading, World;
```

This is identical in effect to:

```
print "main::Hello", "main::Autoloading", "main::World";
```

In other words, this AUTOLOAD subroutine interprets unqualified barewords as strings. A slightly more useful example of the same technique is shown by this HTML tag generator, which automatically creates matching start and end tags, with any supplied parameters sandwiched in between. Note the regular expression to strip off the package prefix:

```
sub AUTOLOAD {
    our ($AUTOLOAD);    # again, 'use vars' if Perl < 5.6
    $AUTOLOAD =~ s/^.*:://;    # strip the package name
    return "<$AUTOLOAD> \n". join("\n",@_). "</$AUTOLOAD> \n";
}
```

We can now write an HTML page programmatically using functions that we haven't actually defined, in a similar (and much shorter, albeit less sophisticated) way to the CGI module. Here is an example HTML document created using the above autoloader subroutine in a single line of code:

```
print html(head(title("Autoloaded HTML")), body(h1("Hi There")));
```

While functional, this example has a few deficiencies. For a start, we can invent any tag we like, including mis-spelled ones. Another problem is that it does not learn from the past; each time we call a non-existent subroutine, Perl looks for it, fails to find it, then calls AUTOLOAD. It would be more elegant to define the subroutine so that next time it is called, Perl finds it. The chances are that if we use it once, we'll use it again. To do that, we just need to create a suitable anonymous subroutine and assign it to a typeglob with the same name as the missing function, which inserts the new subroutine into the symbol table for us. Here is a modified version that does this for us:

```
sub AUTOLOAD {
    our ($AUTOLOAD);
    no strict 'refs';
    my $tag = $AUTOLOAD;
    $tag =~s/.*:://;
    *$AUTOLOAD = sub {
        "<$tag> \n". join("\n", @_). "</$tag> \n";
    };

    &$AUTOLOAD;    # we can use a 'goto' here too -- see below
}
```

Now, whenever a tag is asked for, a subroutine for that tag is defined. The next time the same tag is asked for, the newly defined subroutine catches the call and handles it.

Aside from the anonymous subroutine definition, the other interesting point about this autoloading subroutine is the call to the new subroutine at the end.

Since AUTOLOAD has to define the subroutine the first time it is called, it has to call it as well. We make use of the &subname; syntax to pass the contents of @_ directly to the new subroutine. However, $AUTOLOAD is a symbolic reference, so we use no strict refs at the top of the subroutine.

AUTOLOAD subroutines that define subroutines are one place where using goto does make sense. We can replace the last line of this subroutine with:

```
goto &$AUTOLOAD;
```

Why is this useful? Because it removes the AUTOLOAD subroutine itself from the calling stack, so caller will not see the AUTOLOAD subroutine, but rather the original caller. So goto is consequently a common sight in AUTOLOAD subroutines that define subroutines on-the-fly.

Autoloading is quite handy in functional programming, but much more useful in modules and packages. Accordingly we cover it in more depth in Chapter 10.

Passing Parameters

Basic Perl subroutines do not have any formal way of defining their arguments. We say 'basic' because we can optionally define a prototype that allows us to define the types of the arguments passed, if not their names inside the subroutine. However, ignoring prototypes for the moment, we may pass any number of parameters to a subroutine:

```
mysubroutine ("parameter1", "parameter2", 3, 4, @listparameter);
```

It is helpful to think of the parentheses as a conventional list definition being passed to mysubroutine as a single list parameter – remove mysubroutine from the above statement and what we are left with is a list. This is not far from the truth, if we recall that declaring a subroutine prior to using it allows us to use it as if it were a built-in list operator. Consequently, arrays and hashes passed as arguments to subroutines are flattened into one list internally, just as they are when combined into a larger list.

The parameters that are passed into a subroutine appear inside the subroutine as a list contained in the special variable @_. This variable is made local to each subroutine, just as $_ is inside nested foreach loops. The definition of @_ is thus unique to each subroutine, despite the fact that @_ is a package variable.

One simple and common way to extract parameters passed to a subroutine is simply to assign @_ to a list of scalar variables, like so:

```
sub volume {
    ($height, $width, $length) = @_;
    return $height * $width * $length;
}
```

This gives us named scalar variables we can write code for more legibly, and also takes care of any aliasing problems that might otherwise occur (as we will see in a moment). Alternatively, we can use shift to pull values off the array one by one:

```
sub volume {
    $height = shift;
    $width = shift;
    $length = shift;
    return $height * $width * $length;
}
```

This differs from the previous example in that it actually modifies @_, removing passed parameters from the front of the list. After all the shifts have been processed @_ may be empty or it may contain further passed parameters. We can use that to our advantage to write subroutines that only use some parameters and pass the rest on. For example, here is a speculative object method that is a wrapper for the volume function:

```
sub volume {
    my $self = shift;    #remove the object passed as the first parameter
    return Functions::volume(@_);   #pass remaining parameters on
}
```

If it's brevity we are after, we can avoid assigning the contents of @_ to anything, and simply use the values of @_ directly. This version of volume is not as clear as the first, but makes up for it by being only one line long. As a result the workings of the subroutine are still fairly obvious:

```
sub volume {
    return $_[0] * $_[1] * $_[2];
}
```

The @_ array is a local array defined when the subroutine is first entered. However, while the array is local, the values of @_ are aliases for the original parameters that were passed in to the subroutine. This means that, if the parameter was a variable, modifying the values in the @_ array modifies the original variable as well. Used unwisely this can be an excellent way to create hard-to-understand and difficult-to-maintain code, but if the purpose of a subroutine is to manipulate a list of values in a consistent and generic way, it can be surprisingly useful. Here is an example of such a subroutine that emulates the chomp function:

```
#strip the line separator '$/' from the end of each passed string:
sub mychomp {
    foreach (@_) {
        s|$/$||;
    }
}
```

This also happens to be a good demonstration of aliasing. The subroutine actually aliases twice over; once to alias the variables $string and @lines in the @_ array inside the subroutine, and again in the foreach loop that aliases the loop variable $_ to the values in the @_ array one by one.

We can call this subroutine in the same way as the real chomp:

```
mychomp $string;
mychomp @lines;
```

Modifying the passed arguments implies that they are modifiable in the first place. Passing a literal value rather than a variable will produce a syntax error. For example:

```
mychomp "you can't touch this \n";
```

This produces:

Modification of a read-only value attempted at ...

When we come to discuss prototypes we will see how we can define subroutines that can be checked for correct usage at compile time. This means we can create a subroutine like mychomp that will produce a syntax error if used on a literal variable at compile time, just like the real chomp.

Passing Lists and Hashes

We mentioned earlier, when we started on the subject of passed arguments, that passing lists and hashes directly into a subroutine causes list flattening to occur, just as it does with ordinary list definitions. Consequently, if we want to pass an array or hash to a subroutine, and keep it intact and separate from the other arguments, we need to take additional steps. Consider the following snippet of code:

```
$message = "Testing";
@count = (1, 2, 3);
testing ($message, @count);   # calls 'testing' -- see below
```

The array @count is flattened with $message in the @_ array created as a result of this subroutine, so as far as the subroutine is concerned the following call is actually identical:

```
testing ("Testing", 1, 2, 3);
```

In many cases this is exactly what we need. To read the subroutine parameters we can just extract the first scalar variable as the message and put everything else into the count:

```
sub testing {
    ($message, @count) = @_;
    ...
}
```

Or, using shift:

```
sub testing {
    $message = shift;
    # now we can use @_ directly in place of @count
    ...
}
```

The same principle works for hashes, which as far as the subroutine is concerned are just more values. It is up to the subroutine to pick up the contents of @_ and convert them back into a hash:

```
sub testing {
    ($message, %count) = @_;
    print "@_";
}

testing ("Magpies", 1 => "for sorrow", 2 => "for joy", 3 => "for health", 4 =>
"for wealth", 5 => "for sickness", 6 => "for death");
```

However, this only works because the last parameter we extract inside the subroutine absorbs all the remaining passed parameters. If we were to write the subroutine to pass the list first and then the scalar afterwards, all the parameters are absorbed into the list and the scalar is left undefined:

```
sub testing {
    (@count, $message) = @_;   # ERROR
    print "@_";
}

testing(1, 2, 3, "Testing");
# results in @count = (1, 2, 3, "Testing") and $message = undef
```

If we can define all our subroutines like this we won't have anything to worry about, but if we want to pass more than one list we still have a problem.

If we attempt to pass both lists as-is, then extract them inside the subroutine, we end up with both lists in the first and the second left undefined:

```
sub testing {
    my (@messages, @count) = @_; # wrong!
    print "@_";
}
```

```
@msgs = ("Testing", "Testing");
@count = (1, 2, 3);
testing(@msgs, @count);
# results in @messages = ("Testing", "Testing", "Testing", 1, 2, 3) and
# @count = ();
```

The correct way to pass lists and hashes, and keep them intact and separate, is to pass references. Since a reference is a scalar, it is not flattened like the original value and so our data remains intact in the form that we originally supplied it:

```
testing (["Testing", "Testing"], [1, 2, 3]);   # with two lists
testing (\@messages, \@count);   # with two array variables
testing ($aref1, $aref2);   # with two list references
```

Inside the subroutine we then extract the two list references into scalar variables and dereference them using either @{$aref} or $aref->[index] to access the list values:

```
sub testing {
    ($messages, $count) = @_;
    # print the testing messages
        foreach (@ {$messages}) {
        print "$_ ... ";
    }
    print "\n";
    # print the count;
    foreach (@ {$count}) {
        print "$_! \n";
    }
}
```

Another benefit of this technique is efficiency; it is better to pass two scalar variables (the references) than it is to pass the original lists. The lists may contain values that are large both in size and number. Since Perl must store a local copy of the @_ array for every new subroutine call in the calling stack, passing references instead of large lists can save Perl a lot of time and memory.

Converting Scalar Subroutines into List Processors

Consider this subroutine, which capitalizes the first letter of the string that it is passed:

```
sub capitalize {
    $_[0] = ucfirst(lc $_[0]);
    print "$_[0]";
}
```

```
$country = "england";
capitalize($country);   # produces 'England'
```

Simple enough, but it only works on one string at a time. However, just because we wrote this subroutine to work as a scalar operator does not alter the fact that in reality it is working on a list. We have just limited it to handle a list with one value. With only a little extra effort we can turn this subroutine into something that works on scalars and lists alike:

```
sub capitalize {
    foreach (@_) {
        $_ = ucfirst lc;    # lc uses $_ if argument is omitted
        print "$_[0]";
    }
}
```

Or more efficiently, with map:

```
sub capitalize {
    map {$_ = ucfirst lc} @_;
    print "$_[0]";
}
```

This version works identically for calls like the above that pass only one parameter, but also happily works on arrays too:

```
sub capitalize {
    map {$_ = ucfirst lc} @_;
    print "@_[0, 1, 2]";
}
```

```
@countries = ("england", "scotland", "wales");
capitalize (@countries);    # produces ("England", "Scotland", "Wales")
```

Passing '@_' Directly into Subroutines

We said earlier that the @_ array is distinct to each subroutine and masks any previous definition. That is almost true – there is one exception provided, for reasons of efficiency, to the Perl programmers dedicated to optimizing their code. Normally @_ is defined locally, on entry to each subroutine. So, if we pass in no parameters at all we get an empty array. However, if we call a subroutine using the & prefix and do not pass parameters or use braces then the subroutine inherits the @_ array of the calling subroutine directly:

```
&mysubroutine;    # inherit @_ from parent
```

The problem with this technique is that it is rather arcane, and not obvious to the reader of our code. Therefore, if we use it, a comment to the effect that this is what we are doing (such as the one above) is highly recommended.

As far as the subroutine is concerned this is no different to passing the @_ array as a parameter:

```
mysubroutine(@_);
```

Although, this may seem equivalent, in the second case the @_ array is copied each time the call is made. If @_ contains a large number of values, or many calls are made (for instance in a recursive subroutine) then this is potentially expensive. The &mysubroutine; notation passes the @_ array directly, without making a copy, and so avoids the unnecessary work. Whether this is worth the trouble or not is of course another matter. If @_ only contains a few elements, it is probably better to live with the very minor inefficiency of copying the array and use the explicit version.

Note that the aliasing of the values in the @_ array to the original variables (if the parameter was a variable) happens in either case, so it is not necessary to resort to this practice if all we want to do is modify the variables that were passed to us.

Named Parameters

Unlike other languages such as C or Java, Perl does not have any way to define formal parameter names for subroutines. The closest it gets is prototypes combined with retrieving parameters as lexical variables, as in:

```
sub surname {
    my ($scalar1, $scalar2, @listarg) = @_;
    ...
}
```

However, we can implement named parameters using a hash. This provides an elegant way to pass in parameters without having to define them formally. The trick is to assign the @_ array to a hash variable. This converts the passed list into key-value pairs:

```
sub volume {
    my %param = @_;
    return $param{'height'} * $param{'width'} * $param{'length'};
}
```

The disadvantage of this approach is that we have to name all the parameters that we pass. It is also slower, since hashes are inherently slower than arrays in use. The advantage is that we can add more parameters without forcing the caller to supply parameters that are not needed. Of course, it also falls upon us to actually check the arguments passed and complain if the caller sends us arguments that we do not use.

We can call this subroutine using the => operator to make it clear that we are passing named parameters:

```
volume (height => 1, width => 4, length => 9);
```

We can also write the subroutine so that it accepts both named parameters and a simple list. One common technique borrowed from UNIX command line switches is to prefix named arguments with a minus, to distinguish them from unnamed arguments. To determine how the subroutine has been called, we just check the first character of the first parameter to see if it is a minus:

```
sub volume {
    my %param;
```

```perl
        if ($_[0]=~/^-/) { # if the first argument starts '-', assume named
                           # arguments
    while (@_) {
        my ($key, $value)=(shift, shift);
        # check all names are legal ones
        die "Invalid name '$key'"
        if $key!~/^-(height|width|length|color|density)$/;
            $key =~ s/^-//;    #remove leading minus
            $param{$key} = $value;
            }

        } else {
            # no '-' on first argument - assume list arguments
            $param{'height'} = shift;
            $param{'width'} = shift;
            $param{'length'} = shift;
        }

        foreach ('height', 'width', 'length') {
            unless (defined $param{$_}) {
            warn "Undefined $_, assuming 1";
            $param{$_} = 1;
        }
    }
    }
    return $param{'height'} * $param{'width'} * $param{'length'};
}
```

In this version of the volume subroutine we handle both simple and named parameters. For named parameters we have also taken advantage of the fact that we know the names of the parameters to report a handy informative warning if any of them are undefined.

Named parameters allow us to create a common set of parameters and then add or override parameters. This makes use of the fact that if we define a hash key twice, the second definition overrides the first:

```perl
# define some default parameters
%default = (-height => 1, -width => 4, -length => 9);

# use default
print volume(%default);

# override default
print volume(%default, -length => 16);
print volume(%default, -width => 6, -length => 10);
# specify additional parameters
print volume(%default, -color => "red", -density => "13.4");
```

Before leaving the subject of named parameters, it is worth briefly mentioning the Alias module, available from CPAN. Alias provides the subroutines alias and attr, which generates aliases from a list of key-value pairs. Both subroutines use typeglobs to do the job.

The alias subroutine takes a list of key-value pairs as its argument, and is therefore suited to subroutines. The type of variable defined by the alias is determined by the type of value it is aliased to; a string creates a scalar, a list creates an array. Here is yet another volume subroutine that uses alias:

```perl
#!/usr/bin/perl
# volalias.pl
use warnings;
use strict;

no strict 'vars';
use Alias;

# subroutine using 'alias'
sub volume {
    alias @_;
    return $height * $width * $length;
}

# a call to the subroutine
print volume(height => 1, length => 9, color => 'red', width => 4);

# aliased variables visible here
print " = $height x $width x $length \n";
```

However, `alias` suffers from three serious deficiencies. The first is that it is not compatible with `strict vars`; if we want strict variables we will have to declare all the aliased variables with `use vars` or (preferably) `our`. Another is that `alias` creates global aliases that persist outside the subroutine, which is not conducive to good programming. The third is that if we only use the variable once we'll get a warning from Perl about it. The script above does not do that because of the last line. Comment out that line, and all three variables will generate used only once warnings.

`attr` takes a reference to a hash and creates aliases based on the keys and values in it. `attr $hashref` is similar to `alias %{$hashref}`, but localizes the aliases that it creates. It is ideal to use with object methods for objects based around hashes since each object attribute becomes a variable (hence the name):

```perl
#!/usr/bin/perl
# attr.pl
use warnings;
use strict;

{
    package Testing;
    use Alias;
    no strict 'vars';    # to avoid declaring vars

    sub new {
        return bless {
            count => [3, 2, 1],
            message => 'Liftoff!',
        }, shift;
    }

    sub change {
        # define @count and $message locally
        attr(shift);
        # this relies on 'shift' being a hash reference
        @count = (1, 2, 3);
        $message = 'Testing, Testing';
    }
}
```

```
my $object = new Testing;
print "Before: ", $object->{'message'}, "\n";
$object->change;
print "After : ", $object->{'message'}, "\n";
print $Testing::message, "\n";   # warning - 'attr' vars do not persist
close Testing::count;
```

We can also define 'constants' with the `const` subroutine. This is actually just an alias for `alias` (it's even defined using `alias` inside the module, and must be imported explicitly:

```
# const.pl
use Alias qw(const);   # add 'alias' and/or 'attr' too, if needed

const MESSAGE => 'Testing';
print $MESSAGE, "\n";
```

Attempting to modify the value of a constant produces an error:

```
# ERROR: produce 'Modification of a read-only value attempted at ...'
$MESSAGE = 'Liftoff!';
```

The `Alias` module also provides several customization features, mainly for the `attr` subroutine, which allows us to control what gets aliased and how. Refer to 'perldoc Alias' for a rundown and some more examples.

Prototypes

The subroutines we have considered so far exert no control over what arguments are passed to them; they simply try to make sense of what is passed inside the subroutine. For many subroutines this is fine, and in some cases allows us to create subroutines that can be called in a variety of different ways. For example, we can test the first argument to see if it is a reference or not, and alter our behavior accordingly. However, we are not enforcing a calling convention, so we will only discover our subroutines are being called incorrectly when we actually execute the call, and then only if we have written the subroutine to check its arguments thoroughly. Since some subroutine calls may not occur except under very specific circumstances, this makes testing and eliminating bugs very difficult.

Fortunately there is a way to define compile-time restrictions on the use of subroutines through the use of prototype definitions. Although entirely optional, by specifying the types of the expected parameters, prototypes can eliminate a lot of the problems involved in ensuring that subroutines are called correctly. This allows us to specify what parameters a subroutine takes (scalars, lists/hashes, or code references), and whether a parameter can be either a simple literal value, or whether it must be an actual variable. Good use of prototypes early in the development process can be invaluable.

A prototype definition is a parenthesized list of characters mirroring the Perl variable type syntax (that is, $, @, %, and so on). It is placed after the `sub` keyword and subroutine name but before anything else, be it a subroutine definition, declaration, or anonymous subroutine:

```
sub mysub (PROTOTYPE);   # subroutine declaration
sub mysub (PROTOTYPE) {...}   # subroutine definition
$subref = sub (PROTOTYPE) {...}   # anonymous subroutine
```

Defining the Number of Parameters and Their Scope

Prototypes allow us to explicitly define how many arguments a subroutine expects to receive. This is something that for efficiency reasons we would clearly prefer to check at compile time. We do not have to wait until the subroutine call is used to find out that it is faulty, and passing the wrong number of parameters is an obvious candidate for a bug.

To illustrate, consider the `volume` subroutine that we defined in various different forms earlier. With the exception of the named argument example, the subroutine expects three scalar parameters. Using prototypes we can enforce this by adding `($$$)`, meaning three mandatory scalar arguments, to the subroutine definition:

```
sub volume ($$$) {
    # ... as before ...
}
```

With this prototype in place, `volume` can only be called with three scalar arguments. They can be literals or variables, but there must be three of them, and they must be scalar. Hence, this is legal:

```
print volume(1, 4, 9), "\n";   # displays 1 * 4 * 9 == 36
```

This, however, is not. Even though it provides the right number of values, it doesn't supply them in a way that fits the prototype:

```
@size = (1, 4, 9);
print volume(@size), "\n";
```

Instead, we get the error:

Not enough arguments for main::volume at ... near @size

So far, so good. However, due to Perl's concept of context, prototypes do not enforce things quite as strictly as this might imply. The prototype does not actually enforce a data type – it *attempts* to force it. What the first `$` in the prototype actually does is force `@size` to be interpreted in scalar context and not as a list, in other words, it is exactly as if we had written:

```
print volume(scalar @size), "\n";
```

Having turned the three element array into a scalar '3', the prototype goes on to interpret the second argument as a scalar also. It then finds there isn't one, and produces an error. The fact that we passed an array is not relevant, since an array can be converted to a scalar. However, by passing just one array, we omitted two mandatory arguments, which is important. To illustrate this, the following actually works just fine, the array not withstanding:

```
print volume(@size, 4, 9);   # displays 3 * 4 * 9 == 108
```

We have not supplied three scalars, but we have supplied three values that can be interpreted as scalars, and that's what counts to Perl.

We can also use @ and % in prototype definitions, and it is sometimes helpful to consider subroutines without prototypes as having a default prototype of (@); that is:

```
sub mysubroutine (@) {...}
```

Just like unprototyped subroutines, the single @ prototype will absorb all values, flattening any lists or hashes it finds. It follows from this that a prototype of (@,@) is just as invalid as it was before. However, if we want to enforce an array variable, as opposed to a mere list, that's a different story, as we will see shortly.

A @ or % prototype matches all parameters in the argument list from the point it is defined to the end of the list. Indeed, % and @ are actually identical in meaning to Perl, since passing a hash turns it into a list. Recall that there is no such thing as 'hash context'. It cannot check that passed parameters came from a hash due to flattening, nor that the remaining parameters divide evenly into pairs because that is a run-time issue. However, this does not mean they are of no use. It means that the only useful place for either prototype character is at the end of the prototype. As an example, here is a subroutine, which joins array elements incorporating a prefix and suffix. It takes a minimum of three parameters, but has no maximum because of the @ prototype:

```
#!/usr/bin/perl
# join.pl
use warnings;

sub wrapjoin ($$$@) {
    my ($join, $left, $right, @strings) = @_;
    foreach (@strings) {
        $_ = $left. $_. $right;
        }
    return join $join, @strings;
}

print wrapjoin("\n", "[","]", "One", "Two", "Three");
```

Without the @ we could only pass three arguments. If we added more $ characters we could allow more, but then we would be forced to supply that many arguments. The @ allows an arbitrary number, so long as we also supply three scalars to satisfy the initial $$$.

Lists can validly be empty, so the prototype does not ensure that we actually get passed something to join. We could attempt to fix that by requiring a fourth scalar, like this:

```
sub wrapjoin ($$$$@) {
    ($join, $left, $right, @strings) = @_;
}
```

However, a little thought reveals a flaw in this design. A literal list of strings works fine, but if the caller supplies an actual array variable for the fourth argument it gets converted to a scalar. In effect, we have introduced a new bug by adding the prototype.

The moral here is that prototypes can be tricky and can even introduce bugs. They are not a universal band-aid for fixing subroutine calling problems. If we want to detect and flag an error for an empty list, prototypes cannot help us – we will have to write the subroutine to handle it explicitly at run time.

Prototyping Code References

Other than $, @ (and the synonymous %), we can supply one other basic prototype character: &. This tells Perl that the parameter to be supplied is a code reference to an anonymous subroutine. This is not as far-fetched as it might seem; the sort function accepts such an argument, for example.

Here is how we could prototype the do_list subroutine we introduced when we covered anonymous subroutines earlier:

```
sub do_list (&@) {
   my ($subref, @in) = @_;
   my @out;
   foreach (@in) {
      push @out, &$subref ($_);
   }
   return @out;
}
```

The prototype requires that the first argument be a code reference, since the subroutine cannot perform any useful function on its own. Either a subroutine reference or an explicit block will satisfy the prototype; for example:

```
@words = ("ehT", "terceS", "egasseM");
do_list {print reverse($_[0] =~/./g), "\n"} @words;
```

Note how this syntax is similar to the syntax of Perl's built-in sort, map, and grep functions.

Subroutines as Scalar Operators

We mentioned previously that subroutines can be thought of as user-defined list operators, and used much in the same way as built-in functions (that also work as list operators) like print, chomp, and so on. However, not all of Perl's functions are list operators. Some, such as abs, only work on scalars, and interpret their argument in a scalar context (or simply refuse to execute) if we try to supply a list.

Defining subroutines with a prototype of ($) effectively converts them from being list operators to scalar operators. Returning to our capitalize example, if we decided that, instead of allowing it to work on lists, we want to force it to only work on scalars, we would write it like this:

```
sub capitalize ($) {
   $_[0] = ucfirst (lc $_[0]);
}
```

However, there is a sting in the tail. Before the prototype was added this subroutine would accept a list and capitalize the string in the first element, coincidentally returning it at the same time. Another programmer might be using it in the following way, without our knowledge:

```
capitalize (@list);
```

While adding the prototype prevents multiple strings being passed in a list, an array variable still fits the prototype, as we saw earlier. Suddenly, the previously functional capitalize turns the passed array into a scalar number:

```
@countries = ("england", "scotland", "wales");
capitalize (@countries);
```

239

The result of this is that the number '3' is passed into `capitalize`. Since this is not a variable, it causes a syntax error when we try to assign to `$_[0]`. If we chose to return a result rather than modifying the passed argument, then the code would all be perfectly valid, but badly bugged. However, a program that is used to print 'England' might start printing '3' instead. This is more than a little confusing, and not intuitively easy to track down.

The key problem here is not that we are passing an array instead of a scalar, but that we are checking for a scalar value rather than a scalar variable, which is what we actually require. In the next section we will see how to do that.

Requiring Variables Rather than Values

So far we have seen how to enforce a specific number of arguments and their scope, if not their data type. We can also use prototypes to require that an actual variable be passed. This is invaluable when we want to implement a subroutine that modifies its passed parameters, such as the `capitalize` example just above.

To require a variable, we again use a $, @, and % character to specify the type, but now we prefix it with a backslash. This does not, as it might suggest, mean that the subroutine requires a reference to a scalar, array, or hash variable. Instead, it causes Perl to require a variable instead of merely a value. It also causes Perl to automatically pass the variable as a reference:

```perl
#!/usr/bin/perl
# varproto.pl
use warnings;
use strict;

sub capitalize (\$) {
    ${$_[0]} = ucfirst (lc ${$_[0]});
}

my $country = "england";
capitalize $country;
print $country, "\n";
# capitalize "scotland";   # ERROR: compile-time syntax error!
```

If we tried to call `capitalize` with a literal string value, we would get the error:

Type of arg 1 to main::capitalize must be scalar (not constant item) at ..., near ""england";"

The fact that Perl automatically passes variables as references is very important, because it provides a new way to avoid the problem of list flattening. In other words, prototypes allow us to pass arrays and hashes to a subroutine as-is, without resorting to references in the subroutine call.

A push is an example of a built-in function that works by taking an array as its first argument. We do not need to treat that variable specially to avoid flattening, and we can replicate that syntax in our own code by defining a prototype of (\@@). The following subroutine uses the list-processing version of `capitalize` to produce a capitalizing push subroutine. First it removes the array variable using `shift`, then capitalizes the rest of the arguments and adds them to the variable with push. Perl, being versatile, lets us do the whole thing in one line:

```perl
sub pushcapitalize (\@@) {
    push @{shift}, capitalize(@_);
}
```

We can use this subroutine just like we use the `push` function

```
pushcapitalize @countries, "england";
pushcapitalize @countries, "scotland", "wales";
pushcapitalize @countries, @places;   # no flattening here!
```

Note that we omitted the parentheses, which requires that the subroutine be either already defined or predeclared.

Hash variables are requested using \%, which unlike % does have a different meaning to its array counterpart \@. Here is an example that flips a hash variable around so that the keys become values and the values become keys. If two keys have the same value one of them will be lost in the transition, but for the sake of simplicity we'll ignore that here:

```
sub flip (\%) {
    @hash = %{$_[0]};
    %{$_[0]} = reverse @hash;
}
```

This subroutine makes use of the fact that a hash is essentially just a list with an even number of values, and a little extra cleverness allows quick key access. So, to flip the hash we turn it into a list and reverse it. This also reverses each key-value pair with respect to each other; we then turn it back into a hash again.

Although Perl will automatically pass variables as references when a variable prototype is in effect, it will allow an explicit reference if we dereference it first. The two following calls are both valid uses of the above subroutines:

For the `pushcapitalize` subroutine:

```
pushcapitalize @{$countries_ref}, "england";
```

And for the `flip` subroutine:

```
flip %{$hash_ref};
```

Before we finish with variable prototypes it is worth mentioning, just for completeness, that \& also has a meaning subtly different from &. It requires that the passed code reference be a reference to an actual subroutine, that is, a code reference defined using $coderef = sub {...} or $coderef = \&mysubroutine. A reference to an in line bare block (such as in mysub {...} @list) will not be accepted. Another way to look at \ is that it requires that the argument actually starts with the character it precedes: \& therefore means that the argument must start &, not {.

Optional Parameters

A prototype such as ($$$@) allows us to define a subroutine with three required parameters and any number of optional ones, but it is something of an all-or-nothing solution. It does not allow us to define a subroutine that is intended to take at least three, and no more than four, parameters. Instead we use a semicolon, to separate the mandatory parameters from the optional ones.

The following subroutine, which calculates mass, is a variation on the `volume` subroutine from earlier. It takes the same three dimensions and a fourth optional parameter of the density. If the density is not supplied it is assumed to be 1.

```perl
sub mass ($$$;$) {
    return volume(@_) * (defined($_[3])? $_[3] : 1);
}
```

We might be tempted to use &volume to pass the local version of @_ to it directly. However, using & suppresses the prototype, so instead we pass @_ explicitly. Since mass has its own prototype we could arguably get away with it, but overriding the design of our subroutines for minor increases in efficiency is rarely a good idea.

Using a semicolon does not preclude the use of @ to gobble up any extra parameters. We can for instance define a prototype of ($$$;$@), which means three mandatory scalar parameters, followed by an optional scalar followed by an optional list. That differs from ($$$;@) in that we don't have to pass a fourth argument, but if we do it must be scalar.

We can also define optional variables. A prototype of ($$$;\$) requires three mandatory scalar parameters and an optional fourth scalar variable. For instance, we can extend the `volume` subroutine to place the result in a variable passed as the fourth argument, if one is supplied:

```perl
sub volume ($$$;\$) {
    $volume = $_[0] * $_[1] * $_[2];
    ${$_[3]} = $volume if defined $_[3];
}
```

And here is how we could call it:

```perl
volume(1, 4, 9, $result);   # $result ends up holding 36
```

Disabling Prototypes

All aspects of a subroutine's prototype are disabled if we call it using the old-style prefix &. This can occasionally be useful, but is also a potential minefield of confusion. To illustrate, assume that we had redefined our capitalize subroutine to only accept a single scalar variable:

```perl
sub capitalize (\$) {
    $_[0] = ucfirst (lc $_[0]);
}
```

Another programmer who had been calling the unprototyped version with a list to capitalize the first string now encounters a syntax error.

```perl
capitalize (@countries);   # ERROR: not a scalar variable
```

One way they could fix this is to pass in just the first element. However, they can also override the prototype and continue as before by prefixing their subroutine call with an ampersand:

```perl
capitalize ($countries[0]);   # pass only the first element
&capitalize @countries;   # disable the prototype
```

Naturally this kind of behavior is somewhat dangerous, so it is not encouraged; that's the whole point of a prototype. However, the fact that an ampersand disregards a prototype means that we cannot generate a code reference for a subroutine and still enforce the prototype:

```
$subref = \&mysubroutine;    # prototype not active in $subref
```

This can be a real problem. For instance, the sort function behaves differently if it is given a prototyped sort function (with a prototype of ($$)), passing the values to be compared rather than setting the global variables $a and $b. However, defining a named subroutine with a prototype and then passing a reference to it to sort doesn't work. The only way to retain a prototype on a subroutine reference is to define it as an anonymous subroutine in the first place:

```
# capitalize as a anonymous subroutine
$capitalize_sub = sub (\$) {
   $_[0] = ucfirst (lc $_[0]);
};
```

And using reverse:

```
# an anonymous 'sort' subroutine - use as 'sort $in_reverse @list'
$in_reverse = sub ($$) {
   return $_[1] <=> $_[0];
}
```

Returning Values from Subroutines

Subroutines can return values in one of two ways, either implicitly, by reaching the end of their block, or explicitly, through the use of the return statement.

If no explicit return statement is given, then the return value of a subroutine is the value of the last statement executed (the same as for ordinary bare blocks). For example, the string 'implicit return value' is returned by the following simple subroutine because it is the last (and in this case, only) statement in the subroutine:

```
sub implicit_return {
   my $string = "implicit return value";
}
```

Or even just:

```
sub implicit_return {
   "implicit return value";
}
```

To explicitly define the return value we use the return statement; return takes an expression as its argument, and returns its value to the caller:

```
sub explicit_return {
   return "explicit return value";
}
```

It follows from this that it is never actually necessary to use `return` when passing back a value from the last statement in the subroutine. However, it is good practice, to indicate that we know what we are doing and are aware of what the return value is. If a subroutine does not have an explicit `return`, the implication is that it does not return a value of use.

There is nothing to stop us putting several `return` statements into the same subroutine. Whichever `return` statement is encountered first will cause the subroutine to exit with the value of the supplied expression, aborting the rest of the subroutine. The following simple subroutine illustrates this:

```
sub list_files {
    $path = shift;
    return "" unless defined $path;   # return an empty string if no path
    return join(', ', glob "$path/ * ");   # return comma separated string
}
```

Here we have used two `return` statements. The first returns the undefined value if we fail to supply a pathname for the subroutine to look at. The second is only reached if a defined (but not necessarily valid or existent) path is supplied. We could call this subroutine with code that looks like this:

```
if (my $files = list_files ("/path/to/files")) {
    print "Found $files \n";
}
```

Multiple `return` statements are a convenient way to return values from a subroutine as soon as the correct value has been computed, but for large subroutines they should be used with caution. Many programming problems stem from over-complex subroutines that have more than one `return` in them, causing a crucial piece of code to be skipped in some cases and not others. This is often a sign that the subroutine is too large to be easily maintained and should be split into smaller functional blocks. Otherwise, it is better to funnel the execution of the subroutine to just one `return` statement at the end, or otherwise make it very clear in the source where all the exits are.

The `list_files` subroutine above works, but it is a little clumsy. It does not allow us to distinguish between an undefined path and a path on which no files were found. It also returns the files found as a string rather than a list, which would have been more useful. The first of these we can fix by using the undefined value to indicate an error. The second we can fix by returning a list, or more cunningly, by detecting the calling context and returning a scalar or list value as appropriate. We will cover each of these in turn.

Returning the Undefined Value

Although it might seem a strange idea, it is quite common for subroutines and many of Perl's built-in functions to return the undefined value `undef` instead of a real (that is, defined) value.

The advantage of `undef` is that it evaluates to 'False' in conditions, but is distinct from a simple zero because it returns False when given as an argument to `defined`. This makes it ideal for use in subroutines that want to distinguish a failed call from one that just happens to return no results. This modified version of `list_files` uses `undef` to flag the caller when no path is specified:

```
#!/usr/bin/perl
# findfiles.pl
use warnings;
use strict;
```

```
   my $files = list_files ($ARGV[0]);

   if (defined $files) {
      if ($files) {
         print "Found: $files \n";
      } else {
         print "No files found \n";
      }
   } else {
      print "No path specified\n";
   }

   sub list_files {
      my $path = shift;

      return undef unless defined $path;   # return an empty list if no path
      return join(',', glob "$path/*");    # return comma separated string
   }
```

If no path is supplied, the subroutine returns undef, which evaluates to False in the if statement. If the path was supplied but no files were found, the subroutine returns an empty string which would evaluate to False on its own but is still defined and so tests True in the if statement. We then test the value of $files with the ternary operator and print out an appropriate message if the string happens to be empty. Note that in this particular application checking @ARGV first would be the correct way to handle a lack of input, but we are concerned with the subroutine here, which cannot know how, where, or why it is being called.

undef works well in a scalar context, but is not so good for lists. While it is perfectly possible to assign undef to an array variable, it is confusing because what we end up with is an array of one value, which is undefined. If we naively tried to convert our subroutine to return a list instead of a scalar string we might write:

```
sub list_files {
   my $path = shift;

   return undef unless defined $path;   # return undef if no path
   return glob "$path/*";   # return a list of files
}
```

Unfortunately if we try to call this function in a list context, and do not specify a defined path, we end up with anomalous behavior:

```
foreach (list_files $ARGV[0]) {
   print "Found: $_\n";   # $_ == undef if path was not defined
}
```

If the path is undefined this will execute the loop once, print 'Found: ' and generate an uninitialized value warning. The reason for this is that undef is not a list value, so when evaluated in the list context of the foreach loop, it is converted into a list containing one value, which happens to be undefined. As a result, when the subroutine is called with an undefined path the loop executes once, with the value of the loop variable $_ being undefined.

In order for the loop to behave the way we intended, and not execute even once when no results are found, we need to return an empty list. Here's another version of list_files that does this:

```perl
sub list_files {
    my $path = shift;
    return () unless defined $path;   # return empty list if no path
    return glob "$path/*";   # return list of files.
}
```

This fixes the problem we had when returning undef, but at the cost of losing the ability to distinguish between an undefined path and a path that happens to contain no files. What we would really like to do is return either undef or the empty list depending on whether a scalar or list result is required. The wantarray function provides exactly this information, and we cover it next.

Determining and Responding to the Calling Context

Sometimes it is useful to know what the calling context is, so we can return different values based on the caller's requirements. The return statement already knows this implicitly, and makes use of the context to save time, returning a count of a returned list if the subroutine is called in a scalar context. This is more efficient than returning all the values in the list and then counting them – passing back one scalar is simpler when that is all the calling context actually requires.

Perl allows subroutines to directly access this information with the wantarray function. Using wantarray allows us to intelligently return different values based on what the caller wants. For example, we can return a list either as a reference or a list of values, depending on the way in which we were called:

```perl
return wantarray? @files: \@files;
```

We can also use wantarray to return undef or an empty list depending on context, avoiding the problems of assigning undef to an array variable as we discussed above:

```perl
return wantarray? (): undef;
```

Modifying our original subroutine to incorporate both these changes gives us the following improved version of list_files that handles both scalar and list context:

```perl
sub list_files {
    my $path = shift;

    return wantarray? ():undef unless defined $path;
    my @files = glob "$path/ *";
    return wantarray? @files: \@files;
}
```

This is an example of Perl's reference counting mechanism in action; @files may go out of scope, but the reference returned in scalar context preserves the values it holds.

We can now call `list_files` with two different results. In list context we get either a list of files, or an empty list if either no files were found, or the path is undefined. This allows the return value to be used in a `foreach` loop. If we want to distinguish between a defined path with no files and an undefined path we call `list_files` in scalar context. In return, we get a reference to a list of files, a reference to an empty list if no files were found, or the undefined value if the path was undefined. By additionally testing for the undefined value with `defined`, we can now distinguish all three cases:

```perl
# list context
@files = list_files ($ARGV[0]);
die "No path defined or no files found" unless @files;
print "Found: @files \n";


# scalar context
$files = list_files($ARGV[0]);
die "No path defined! \n" unless defined $files;
die "No files found! \n" unless $files;
print "Found: @{$files} \n";
```

One final note about `wantarray`: If we want to find the number of files rather than retrieve a list, then we can no longer call the subroutine in scalar context to achieve it. Instead, we need to call the subroutine in list context and then convert it into a scalar explicitly:

```perl
$count = $#{list_files $ARGV[0]}+1;
```

This is much clearer, because it states that we really do mean to use the result in a scalar context. Otherwise, it could easily be a bug that we have overlooked. However, be very careful not to use `scalar` here. We often use `scalar` to count arrays, but `scalar` forces its argument into a scalar context. `$#` requires that its argument is a list, and then counts it.

Handling Void Context

So far we have considered list and scalar contexts. If the subroutine is called in a void context that is undefined. We can use this fact to save time computing a return value, or even to produce an error:

```perl
sub list_files {
    die "Function called in void context" unless defined wantarray;
    ...
}
```

Handling Context: an Example

Putting all the above together, here is a final version of `list_files` that handles both scalar, list, and void contexts, along with a sample program to test it out in each of the three contexts:

```perl
#!/usr/bin/perl
# listfile.pl
use warnings;
use strict;

sub list_files {
    die "Function called in void context" unless defined wantarray;
    my $path = shift;

    return wantarray?():undef unless defined $path;
    chomp $path;   # remove trailing linefeed, if present
```

```
        $path.='/*' unless $path =~/\*/;    # add wildcard if missing
        my @files = glob $path;
        return wantarray?@files:\@files;
    }

print "Enter Path: ";
my $path = <>;

# call subroutine in list context
print "Get files as list:\n";
my @files = list_files($path);
foreach (sort @files) {
    print "\t$_\n";
}

# call subroutine in scalar context
print "Get files as scalar:\n";
my $files = list_files($path);
foreach (sort @{$files}) {
    print "\t$_ \n";
}

# to get a count we must now do so explicitly with $#...
# note that 'scalar would not work, it forces scalar context.
my $count = $#{list_files($path)}+1;
print "Count: $count files\n";

# call subroutine void context - generates an error
list_files($path);
```

The name wantarray *is something of a misnomer, since there is no such thing as 'array context'.*
A better name for it would have been wantlist.

Closures

Closures are subroutines that operate on variables created in the context in which they were defined, rather than passed in or created locally. This means that they manipulate variables outside their own definition, but within their scope. Here is a simple example of a closure at work:

```
$count = 0;
sub count {return ++ $count;}
print count, count, count;    # print 123
```

Here the subroutine count uses the variable $count. But the variable is defined outside of the subroutine, and so is defined for as long as the program runs. Nothing particularly remarkable so far, all we are doing is defining a global variable. However, what makes closures useful is that they can be used to implement a form of memory in subroutines where the variable is global inside the subroutine, but is invisible outside. Consider the following example:

```
{
$count = 0;
    sub count {return ++ $count;}
}
print count, count, count;    # still print 123
```

What makes this interesting is that the variable $count is no longer directly accessible by the time we get to the print statement. Ordinarily it would have ceased to exist at the end of the block in which it is defined because it is lexical, and therefore bounded by the block's scope. However, it is referred to in the subroutine count, which is by nature a global definition. Consequently, Perl still has a reference to the variable and so it persists. The only place the reference exists is in the subroutine count, so we have effectively created a persistent and private variable inside count.

Closures get more interesting when we create them in an anonymous subroutine. If we replace the block with a subroutine definition and count with an anonymous subroutine, we end up with this:

```
sub make_counter ($) {
    $count = shift;
    return sub {return $count++;}
}
```

The outer subroutine make_counter accepts one scalar variable and uses it to initialize the counter variable. We then create an anonymous subroutine that refers to the variable (thus preserving it) and returns the code reference of the anonymous subroutine. We can now use make_counter to create and use any number of persistent counters, each using its own secret counter variable:

```
$tick1 = make_counter(0);    #counts from zero
$tick2 = make_counter(100);   #counts from 100

$, = ",";
print &$tick1, &$tick2, &$tick1, &$tick2;   # displays 0, 100, 1, 101
```

Just because the subroutine is anonymous does not mean that it cannot accept parameters – we just access the @_ array as normal. Here is a variation of make_counter that allows us to reset the counter variable by passing a number to the anonymous subroutine:

```
#!/usr/bin/perl
# closure.pl
use warnings;
use strict;

sub make_counter ($) {
    my $count = @_?shift:0;

    return sub {
        $count = $_[0] if @_;
        return $count++;
    }
}

my $counter = make_counter(0);
foreach (1..10) {
    print &$counter, "\n";
}
print "\n";   # displays 0, 1, 2, 3, 4, 5, 6, 7, 8, 9

$counter -> (1000);   #reset the counter
foreach (1..3) {
    print &$counter, "\n";
}
print "\n";   # displays 1000, 1001, 1002
```

Closures also provide a way to define objects so that their properties cannot be accessed from anywhere other than the object's own methods. The trick is to define the object's underlying data in terms of an anonymous subroutine that has access to an otherwise inaccessible hash, in the same way that the variable $count is hidden here. We will take a look at doing this in Chapter 19, along with tied objects, which would allow us to disguise a counter like the one above as a read-only scalar variable that increments each time we access it.

Assignable Subroutines

Some of Perl's built-in functions allow us to assign to them as well as use them in expressions. In programming parlance, the result of the function is an lvalue, or a value that can appear on the left-hand side of an assignment. The most common and obvious lvalues are variables, which we assign to all the time:

```
$scalar_value = "value";
```

Some Perl functions can also be assigned to in this way, for example the substr function:

```
$mystring = "this is some text";
substr ($mystring, 0, 7) = "Replaced";
print $mystring;    # produces "Replaced some text";
```

The substr function returns part of a string. If the string happens to be held in a variable then this returned string segment is an lvalue, and can be assigned to. Perl does not even require that the new text be the same length, as the above example illustrates. It would be wonderful to be able to do this kind of thing in our own subroutines.

In fact, Perl does allow us to this, albeit only experimentally at the moment. Assignable subroutines make use of subroutine attributes (an experimental feature of Perl in version 5.6). Since attributes are likely to evolve, or possibly even disappear entirely, this technique is not guaranteed to work and should be avoided for production code. However, for the moment, to make a subroutine assignable we can use the special attribute lvalue, as this simple assignable subroutine script demonstrates:

```
#!/usr/bin/perl
# assignable.pl
use warnings;
use strict;

my $scalar = "Original String";

sub assignablesub : lvalue {
    $scalar;
}

print $scalar, "\n";
assignablesub = "Replacement String";
print $scalar, "\n";
```

In order for an assignable subroutine to function correctly, it must return a variable. In addition, it must not use return, because with an assignable subroutine data can pass in as well as out. Currently (as of Perl 5.6) only scalar values may be used as assignable return values. This includes an array element or hash value, however. Future versions of Perl are expected to lift this restriction.

Attributes do not preclude prototypes. If we want to specify a prototype, we can do so after the subroutine, before any attributes. The following example shows a prototyped assignable subroutine that provides an example of assigning to an array via the returned lvalue.

```
my @array = (1, 2, 3);

sub set_element (\@$) : lvalue {
    @{$_[0]} [$_[1]];   # return element of passed array
    # @{$_[0]} is the array
    # [$_[1]] is the $_[1]th element of that array
}

set_element (@array, 2) = 5;
```

In itself this is not a particularly useful example, of course, but it may lead to some interesting possibilities.

Attribute Lists

Attributes are a largely experimental feature, still under development, and only present from Perl version 5.6 onwards, so accordingly we have left them to the end of the chapter. The use of attributes in production code is not recommended, but being aware of them is not a bad idea, since they will ultimately mature into an official part of the language.

In brief, attributes are pieces of information associated with either variables or subroutines that can be set to modify their behavior in specific ways. The primary users of attributes are subroutines. Perl recognizes and understands three special attributes, lvalue, locked, and method, which alter the way in which the Perl interpreter executes subroutines. It is more than likely other special attributes will appear as Perl evolves. We have already seen lvalue in this chapter, and cover locked and method in brief below.

Currently, we cannot define our own attributes on either variables or subroutines, only those defined and understood by Perl. However, an experimental package attribute mechanism, which associates user-defined attributes with packages, is under development. All variables and subroutines that reside in the package automatically have the package attributes associated with them.

Attributes can be placed on both subroutines and lexical variables. The basic form of a variable attribute list is one or more variables declared with my followed by a semicolon and the attribute list. However, there are no variable attributes currently understood by Perl.

Defining Attributes on Subroutines

The basic form of a subroutine attribute list is a standard subroutine definition (or declaration), followed by a colon and the attributes to be defined. Attributes are separated by whitespace, and optionally a colon, these are then followed by the body of the subroutine or (in the case of a declaration) a semicolon:

```
sub mysubroutine : attr1 : attr2 {   # standard subroutine
    ... body of subroutine ...
}
sub mysubroutine : attr1 attr2;   # subroutine declaration
```

```
my $subref = sub : attr1 : attr2 {    # anonymous subroutine
    ... body of subroutine ...
}
sub mysubroutine (\@$$;$) : attr;    # declaration with prototype
sub mysubroutine attr (parameters);    # attribute with parameters
```

At the time of writing, the attributes lvalue, locked, and method are the only attributes that can be set. None of these use a parameter list as shown in the last example, but the syntax accepts the possibility in anticipation of future applications.

Accessing Attributes

Attribute definitions are actually handled by the attributes pragmatic module, which implements the modified syntax for variables and subroutines that allows them to be defined. The attributes module also supplies subroutines to access these attributes, which we can use by importing them from the attributes module:

```
use attributes qw(get reftype);    # import 'get' and 'reftype' subroutines
```

The get subroutine takes a variable, or subroutine reference, and returns a list of attributes defined on that reference. If there are none, then the list is empty. For example:

```
sub mysubroutine : locked method {
    ...
}

my @attrlist = get \&mysubroutine;    # contains ('locked', 'method')
```

The reftype subroutine also takes a reference to a variable or subroutine. It returns the underlying reference type; HASH for a hash variable, CODE for a subroutine reference, and so on. Blessed references return the underlying data type, which makes reftype a potentially useful subroutine as a replacement for ref, even if we are not using attributes.

Special Attributes

Perl currently defines three attributes with special meanings – locked, method, and lvalue. Of all the aspects of attributes discussed so far, these are the most immediately useful.

The lvalue attribute allows subroutines to return assignable values, rather like the substr function does when used on a variable, as we discussed earlier in the chapter.

The locked attribute is useful in threaded programming, when more than one thread of execution can call the same subroutine simultaneously. In many cases, such subroutines need to complete one call before the next can proceed, such as writing complex information to a file or the screen, or handing a database transaction. In order to stop simultaneous calls from treading on each other's toes, we can lock the subroutine so that only one thread can execute it at any time:

```
sub oneatatimeplease : locked {
    # only one thread can execute this subroutine at a time.
}
```

The method attribute is used in object classes to indicate that a locked subroutine should lock on a per-object basis. It modifies the effect of the locked attribute to apply itself to the first argument of the subroutine. In an object method this is the blessed reference representing the object. As a result, the method block only calls if the object being passed is already busy in that method; other objects of the same class proceed unhindered:

```
sub objectmethodlock : locked : method {
    my $self = shift;
    # only one thread can execute this method on the same object
    # but different threads can execute it on different objects
}
```

Whether or not it is used with locked, method also prevents Perl from confusing it with a built-in function of the same name. We can therefore create a method called print and be sure that it will only be used when an object-oriented call to print is made. Only if the subroutine is called as an object method will Perl call it instead of the built-in function.

We cover the locked and method attributes in a little more detail when we discuss threaded programming in Perl in Chapter 22.

Package Attributes

Package attributes are an experimental feature implemented in the attributes module. We will do no more than take a brief look at what they are supposed to do here, because the mechanism and syntax of how they are defined and used is likely to change at some point.

The idea of package attributes is that we can implement our own attributes that work on a package-wide basis. To implement them, we write specially named subroutines within the package that will be called by the get subroutine mentioned above. Each different type may (or may not) have a distinct set of attributes associated with it, so a scalar variable has different attributes from an array, but all scalar variables in the package share the same set of attributes. This is very similar in concept to the way that tied variables work.

Attributes are stored and returned according to the package implementation. A given attribute data type is implemented by writing FETCH_X_ATTRIBUTES and MODIFY_X_ATTRIBUTES subroutines, where X is the data type – either SCALAR, ARRAY, or HASH. The package may implement the details of storage and retrieval any way it likes, just as with tied variables. To retrieve attributes on subroutines, we define FETCH_CODE_ATTRIBUTES, and to allow them to be set as well, we define MODIFY_CODE_ATTRIBUTES.

FETCH subroutines are called by get whenever we use it on a reference of the correct type in the same package. They are passed a single argument, which is a reference to the entity being queried. They return a list of the attributes defined for that entity.

MODIFY subroutines are called during the import stage of compilation. They take a package name and a reference as their first two arguments, followed by a list of attributes to define. They return a list of unrecognized attributes, which may be empty.

The current design also allows for packages that inherit attributes from a parent package by calling SUPER::FETCH_X_ATTRIBUTES and SUPER::MODIFY_X_ATTRIBUTES. The intent is that a child FETCH or MODIFY subroutine should first call its parent, and then deal with any attributes returned. In the case of FETCH, it adds its own attributes to the list and returns it. In the case of MODIFY, it deals with the list of unrecognized attributes passed back from the parent.

Summary

In this chapter we saw how to declare and call subroutines. Specifically we looked at anonymous subroutines, subroutine references, and the `use strict subs` pragma. Next we looked at predeclaring subroutines, and learned how to override built-in functions. After this, we learned about the internal stack, which Perl uses to hold details of subroutines, and saw an example of a recursive subroutine.

Several issues concerning the passing of parameters were covered, including:

❑ Passing lists and hashes.

❑ Converting scalar subroutines into list processors

❑ Passing @_ directly into subroutines

❑ Named parameters

Prototypes were discussed in-depth, and the topics covered included the following:

❑ Defining the number of parameters

❑ Prototyping code references

❑ Subroutines as scalar operators

❑ Optional parameters

❑ Disabling prototypes

Following this, we looked at how to return values from subroutines, and saw how to return the undefined value, and determine and respond to the calling context. Finally, we covered attribute lists, and looked at defining attributes on subroutines, accessing attributes, special attributes, and package attributes.

8

Scope and Visibility

We touched on the concept of scope briefly in Chapter 2 and mentioned it in following chapters several times without going into the full details. While it is true that a programmer can often just ensure that all their scripts start with `use strict` and all their variables are declared with my without worrying about scope too much, a better understanding of the subject can unlock many useful features.

The scope of a variable is simply the range of places in code from which the variable can be accessed. However, there are two fundamentally different types of variable scope in Perl, **package scope** (also called dynamic scope) and **lexical scope**. These work in fundamentally different ways, and are frequently the source of much confusion among Perl programmers. One useful rule-of-thumb for understanding the distinction between the two is that package variables have a scope that is determined at run time from the current contents of the symbol table (for details on the symbol table, see the section entitled *'The Symbol Table'* later in the chapter), whereas lexical variables have a scope that is determined at compile time from the structure of the source code itself. Another rule-of-thumb is to avoid using package/dynamic scope unless we actually need it.

Package Variables

A package is simply a namespace in which declarations of variables and subroutines are placed, confining their scope to that particular package. A great deal of the time we can avoid defining package variables at all by simply declaring all our variables as lexical variables. This lets us define local variables in the way they are normally understood in other languages. However, we often use package variables without being aware of it, for example, the variables $_, @_, %ENV, and @ARGS are all package variables in the main package.

Defining Package Variables

Packages are defined by the package keyword. In and of itself, a package declaration does nothing, but it states that all further declarations of subroutines or package variables will be placed into the package named by the declaration, until further notice. The notice in this case is either the end of the file, or less commonly, but perfectly legally, another package declaration. The package keyword takes one argument; a list of namespaces separated by double colons. For example:

```
package My::Package;
```

Package variables have the scope of the package in which they were declared. A package variable can be accessed from other packages by specifying the full package name, in the same way that we can refer to any file on a hard disk from the current directory by starting at the root directory and writing out the full path of the file. For example:

```
package My::Package;

$package_variable = "implicitly in 'My::Package'";
$My::Package::another_variable = "explicitly declared in 'My::Package'";
$Another::Package::variable = "explicitly declared in 'Another::Package'";
```

The effect of a package declaration is to cause all unqualified package variables and (more significantly) subroutines that follow it to be located in the namespace that it defines. We don't have to use a package declaration though; we can define all our variables and subroutines with an explicit package name, as we showed in the above example. It just makes writing code a bit simpler if we do.

Package variables are defined simply by using them, as in the above example. No extra syntax or qualifier is needed. Unfortunately this makes them very easy to define accidentally by misspelling the name of another variable. Perl prevents us from making this mistake with the use strict vars pragma, covered later.

A package is not the same as a module, however, and certainly not the same as a file. In simple terms, a package defines a namespace in which variable names are defined. This namespace is contained by a table known as the **symbol table**. Whenever a new variable or subroutine is defined, a new entry is added to the table for that package. The same variable name in a different package is not confused with it because the namespaces of the two variables are different and they are defined in different symbol tables (albeit all contained in the same master symbol table).

Package scope is not the same as file scope. Even though a package is most often defined in a single file (a module), Perl allows packages to be spread across many files. This is uncommon, but is one approach we can take if we want to split up subroutines or methods in a package into separate functional files. We define one main module with the same name as the package, translated into a pathname, and use or require all the other supporting modules from it:

```
package My::Module;

require My::Module::Input;
require My::Module::Output;
require My::Module::Process;
```

The modules `Input.pm`, `Output.pm`, and `Process.pm` in this scheme would all contain a first line of `package My::Module;`, rather than a package that reflects the actual name of the file. This allows them to add additional subroutine definitions to the `My::Module` namespace directly, without the need to use the `Exporter` module to export all the names explicitly. There is no requirement for a module to have the same package name as its filename suggests, it is just the usual case.

It follows from this that package variables must be global variables. In practice, what we usually think of as global variables are package variables that are accessed from within their own package, where the package prefix is not required. For instance, the variable `$package_variable` is global within the package `MyPackage`. This does not alter the fact that we can access it from anywhere in our code so long as the contents of `MyPackage` have been compiled and executed by the interpreter.

New package variables can be created by executing code, and existing variables given local temporary values. Both of these events modify the contents of the symbol table as the program progresses. As a result, package scope is ultimately determined at run time and is dependent on the structure of the data in the symbol tables. This differs from lexical variables, whose scope is determined at compile time when the source code is parsed.

All subroutines and package variables must have a package, in the same way that all files in a filing system must have a directory, even if it is the root. In Perl, the 'root' namespace is `main`, so any subroutine or package variable we define without an explicit package name or prior package declaration is part of the main package. In effect, the top of every source file is prefixed by an implicit:

```
package main;
```

Perl's special variables, as well as the filehandles `STDIN`, `STDOUT`, and `STDERR`, are exempt from the normal rules of package scope visibility. All of these variables are automatically used in the main package, wherever they are used, irrespective of the package declaration that may be in effect. There is therefore only one `@_` array, only one default argument `$_`, and only one `%ARGV` or `@INC`. However, these variables have a special status in Perl because they are provided directly by the language; for our own variable declarations and subroutines, the normal rules of packages and namespaces apply.

Using 'strict' Variables

Since it is easy to accidentally define a new global variable without meaning to, Perl provides the `strict` module. With either of `use strict` or `use strict vars`, a compile time syntax check is enabled that requires variables to either be declared lexically or be declared explicitly as package variables. This is generally a good idea, because without this check it is very easy to introduce hard-to-spot bugs, either by forgetting to define a variable before using it, creating a new variable instead of accessing an existing one, or accessing a global variable when we actually meant to create and use a local copy.

With strict variables in effect, Perl will no longer allow us to define a variable simply by assigning to it. For instance:

```perl
#!/usr/bin/perl
# package.pl
use warnings;
use strict;

package MyPackage;

$package_variable = "This variable is in 'MyPackage';    # ERROR
```

If we attempt to run this code fragment Perl will complain with an error:

Global symbol "$package_variable" requires explicit package name at ...

Usually the simplest fix for this problem is to prefix the variable with my, turning the variable into a file-scoped lexical variable. However, if we actually want to define a global package variable, we now need to say so explicitly.

Declaring Global Package Variables

The traditional meaning of 'global' variable is a variable that can be seen from anywhere – it has global visibility. In Perl the distinction between package and lexical variables means that there are two different kinds of global variable, 'package-global' and 'file-global'.

In essence, a package variable is a global variable within the package in which it is defined, as we discussed above. Any code in the same package can access the variable directly without qualifying it with a package prefix, except when the variable has been hidden by another variable with the same name (defined in a lower scope). A lexical variable is a global variable if it is defined at the file level (that is, not between braces), in which case it is a global variable within the file in which it is defined. Only package variables are truly global, because they can always be accessed by referring to them via their full package-prefixed name.

The simplest way to define a package variable is to write it out in full, including the package name, for example:

```
$MyPackage::package_variable = "explicitly defined with package";
```

However this can be inconvenient to type each time we want to define a new package variable, and also causes a lot of editing if we happen to change the name of the package. We can avoid having to write the package name by using either use vars or our. These both define package variables in the current package, but work in slightly different ways.

Declaring Global Package Variables with 'use vars'

To define a package variable with use vars we pass the list of variables we want to declare as a list, for example with qw:

```
use vars qw($package_variable $another_var @package_array);
```

This defines the named variables in the symbol table for the current package, and therefore the variables are directly visible anywhere the package is defined, and can be accessed from anywhere by specifying the full variable name including the package.

Variables declared with use vars are plugged into the symbol table for the current package at compile time, because use takes effect at compile time.

As they are simply added to the symbol table, package variables know nothing about lexical scope. Consequently, the following script defines the variable $package_variable and makes it immediately visible anywhere within the package, despite the fact the use is in a subroutine:

```
#!/usr/bin/perl
# globpack.pl
use warnings;
use strict;

sub define_global {
    use vars qw($package_variable);
    $package_variable = "defined in subroutine";
}

print $package_variable;   # visible here but not yet defined
define_global;
print $package_variable;   # visible here and now defined
```

What we probably intended to do here was create a local package variable with our, which was introduced into Perl 5.6 for precisely this sort of occasion.

Lexically Declaring Global Package Variables with 'our'

The our keyword is a replacement for use vars. It allows us to defined lexically scoped package variables in the same manner as my does. This can be a little tricky to understand, since the whole point of lexical and package scope is that they work in different ways.

To explain, our works like use vars in that it adds a new entry to the symbol table for the current package. However, unlike use vars it does this at compile time, not run time. This means that the variable can be accessed without a package prefix from any package, but only so long as its lexical scope exists. This means that a package variable, declared with our at the top of the file, is global throughout the file even if it contains more than one package, just as we would normally expect a global variable to be. It exists in the symbol table under the package in which it was defined, but other packages may still access it without a prefix, so long as they are in its lexical scope. Or, to put it another way, our makes package variables 'work right' from the point of view of what we normally expect of global variables.

Another way to look at our is to think of it as causing Perl to rewrite accesses to the variable in other packages (in the same file) to include the package prefix before it compiles the code. For instance, we might create a Perl script containing the following four lines:

```
package MyPackage;
our $scalar = "value";    # defines $MyPackage::scalar

package AnotherPackage;
print $scalar;
```

When Perl parses this, it sees the lexically scoped variable $scalar and invisibly rewrites all other references to it in the same file to include the package, that is, $MyPackage::scalar.

Using our also causes variables to disappear at the end of their lexical scope. Used inside a subroutine, our hides the value of the global variable in the same way that local does (see below), but it does so at compile time. The new value is therefore not visible from called subroutines; they see the original global value. The variable is also not required to exist, unlike local, which under strict vars will only localize a variable that exists already. our differs from use vars in that a variable declared with use vars has package scope even when declared inside a subroutine. With our the variable is removed when the subroutine exits.

our behaves exactly like my in every respect except that it adds an entry to the symbol table and removes it afterwards (more correctly, it tells Perl to define the symbol in advance, since it happens at compile time). Like my, the added entry is not visible from subroutine calls since it is lexically scoped. See the 'Declaring Lexical Variables' section for more details on how my works.

Automatic Localization in Perl

Perl automatically localizes some variables for us. The most obvious example is the @_ array in subroutines. Each time a subroutine is called a fresh local copy of @_ is created, temporarily hiding the existing one until the end of the subroutine. When the subroutine call returns, the old @_ reappears. This allows chains of subroutines to call each other, each with its own local @_, without overwriting the @_ of the caller.

Other instances of automatically localized variables include loop variables, including $_ if we do not specify one explicitly. Although the loop variable might (and with strict variables in effect, must) exist, when it is used for a loop, the existing variable is localized and hidden for the duration of the loop:

```perl
#!/usr/bin/perl
# autolocal.pl
use warnings;
use strict;

my $var = 42;
my $last;
print "Before: $var \n";
foreach $var (1..5) {
    print "Inside: $var \n";   # print "Inside: 1", "Inside: 2" ...
    $last = $var;
}

print "After: $var \n";   # prints '42'
print $last;
```

It follows from this that we cannot find the last value of a foreach loop variable if we exit the loop on the last statement without first assigning it to something with a scope outside the loop, like we have done for $last in the example above.

Localizing Package Variables with 'local'

Package variables can be temporarily localized inside subroutines and other blocks with the local keyword. This hides an existing variable by masking it with a temporary value that exists for as long as the local statement is in lexical scope. As a statement, local takes either a single variable name or a list enclosed in parentheses, and optionally an assignment to one or more values:

```perl
local $hero;
local ($zip, @boing, %yatatata);
local @list = (1, 2, 3, 4);
local ($red, $blue, $green, $yellow) = ("red", "blue", "green");
```

local does not, as its name suggests, create a local variable; that is the job of my. The local keyword only operates on an existing variable, which can be either a global, or a variable defined in the calling context. Most of the time we want to create a local variable we really should be using my instead.

> *Having said this, a lot of Perl code uses* local *to create variables by avoiding the* strict *module. This works, but is not sound programming now that* our *exists.*

Localized variables are visible inside subroutine calls, just as the variable they are masking would be if they had not been defined. They are global from the perspective of the subroutines in the call-chain below their scope, so they are not visible outside the subroutine call. This is because localization happens at run time, and persists for the scope of the local statement. In this respect they differ from lexical variables, which are also limited by the enclosing scope but which are not visible in called subroutines.

The following demonstration script illustrates how local works, and also the differences and similarities between my, our, and use vars:

```perl
#!/usr/bin/perl
# scope-our.pl
use warnings;
use strict;

package MyPackage;

my $my_var = "my-var";    # file-global lexical variable
our $our_var = "our-var";    # global to be localized with 'our'
our $local_var = "global-var";    # global to be localized with 'local'
use vars qw($use_var);    # define 'MyPackage::use_var' which exists
                          # only in this package
$use_var = "use-var";

### ERROR: the global variable is not declared
# $package_variable = "eek";

package AnotherPackage;

print "Outside, my_var is '$my_var' \n";    # display 'my-var'
print "Outside, our_var is '$our_var' \n";    # display 'our-var'
print "Outside, local_var is '$local_var' \n";    # display 'global-var'

### ERROR: $use_var doesn't exist in this package
# print "Outside, use_var is '$use_var' \n";

sub mysub {
    my $my_var = "my_in_mysub";
    our $our_var = "our_in_mysub";
    local $local_var = "local_in_mysub";

    ### ERROR: global $use_var does not exist in this package
    # local $use_var = "local_use_in_mysub";

    print "In mysub, my_var is '$my_var'\n";    # display 'my_in_mysub'
    print "In mysub, our_var is '$our_var'\n";    # display 'our_in_mysub'
    print "In mysub, local_var is '$local_var'\n"; # display 'local_in_mysub'
    mysub2();
}
```

```
sub mysub2 {
    print "In mysub2, my_var is '$my_var' \n";    # display 'my-var'
    print "In mysub2, our_var is '$our_var' \n";   # display 'our-var'
    print "In mysub2, local_var is '$local_var' \n";   # display 'local_in_mysub'
}

mysub;

print "Again outside, my_var is '$my_var' \n";    # display 'my-var'
print "Again outside, our_var is '$our_var' \n";   # display 'our-var'
print "Again outside, local_var is '$local_var' \n"; # display 'global-var'
```

Although it is not common, there are a few places where only local will do what we want. One is where we want to create a local version of one of Perl's built-in variables. For example, if we want to temporarily alter the output separator in a subroutine, we would do it with local like this:

```
sub printwith {
    ($separator, @stuff) = @_;
    local $, = $separator;    # create temporary $,
    print @stuff;
}
```

This is also the correct approach for variables such as @ARGV and %ENV. The special variables defined automatically by Perl are all package variables, so creating a lexical version with my would certainly work from the point of view of our own code, but would be totally ignored by built-in functions like print. To get the desired effect we need to use local to create a temporary version of the global variable that will be seen by the subroutines and built-in functions we call.

Another use for local is for creating local versions of filehandles. For example, this subroutine replaces STDOUT with a different filehandle, MY_HANDLE, presumed to be opened and visible before the subroutine will be called. Because we have used local, both the print statement below and any print statements called from this subroutine will go to MY_HANDLE. In case MY_HANDLE is not a legal filehandle, we check the result of print and die on a failure:

```
sub print_to_me {
    local *STDOUT = *MY_HANDLE;
    die unless print @_;
    a_sub_that_calls_print ();
}
```

If we had used our, only the print in the same subroutine would use the new filehandle. At the end of the subroutine the local definition of STDOUT vanishes. The use of local here is safe since STDOUT always exists.

Lexical Variables

Lexical variables have the scope of the file, block, or eval statement in which they were defined. Their scope is determined at compile time, determined by the structure of the source code, and their visibility is limited by the syntax that surrounds them.

Unlike package variables, a lexical variable is not added to the symbol table, and so cannot be accessed through it. It cannot be accessed from anywhere outside its lexical scope, even by subroutines that are called within the scope of the variable. When the end of the variable's scope is reached, it simply ceases to exist.

Although Perl now allows us to declare package variables lexically with our, in this section we are concerned with my. While our also declares variables lexically, it declares variables whose visibility is greater than their lexical scope. They can be seen anywhere in the chain of subroutine calls beneath the scope of the declaration, so while their scope is lexical, their visibility is not.

Declaring Lexical Variables

The following is a short summary of all the different ways in which we can declare lexical variables with my, most of which should already be familiar:

```
my $scalar;    # simple lexical scalar
my $assignedscalar = "value";   # assigned scalar
my @list = (1, 2, 3, 4);   # assigned lexical array
my ($red, $blue, $green);   # list of scalars
my ($left, $right, $center) = (1, 2, 0);   # assigned list of scalars
my ($param1, $param2) = @_;   # inside subroutines
```

All these statements create lexical variables that exist for the lifetime of their enclosing scope and are only visible inside it. If placed at the top of a file, the scope of the variable is the file. If defined inside an eval statement, the scope is that of the evaluated code. If placed in a block or subroutine (or indeed inside curly braces of any kind), the scope of the variable is from the opening brace to the closing one:

```perl
#!/usr/bin/perl
# scope-my.pl
use warnings;
use strict;

my $file_scope = "visible anywhere in the file";
print $file_scope, "\n";

sub topsub {
    my $top_scope = "visible in 'topsub'";
    if (rand > 0.5) {
        my $if_scope = "visible inside 'if'";
        # $file_scope, $top_scope, $if_scope ok here
        print "$file_scope, $top_scope, $if_scope \n";
    }

    bottomsub();
    # $file_scope, $top_scope ok here
    print "$file_scope, $top_scope\n";
}

sub bottomsub {
    my $bottom_scope = "visible in 'bottomsub'";
    # $file_scope, $bottom_scope ok here
    print "$file_scope, $bottom_scope \n";
}

topsub();

# only $file_scope ok here
print $file_scope, "\n";
```

In the above script, we define three lexical variables, each of which is visible only within the enclosing curly braces. Both subroutines can see $file_scope because it has the scope of the file in which the subroutines are defined. Likewise, the body of the if statement can see both $file_scope and $top_scope. However, $if_scope ceases to exist as soon as the if statement ends and so is not visible elsewhere in topsub. Similarly, $top_scope only exists for the duration of topsub and $bottom_scope only exists for the duration of bottomsub. Once the subroutines exit, the variables and whatever content they contain cease to exist.

Preserving Lexical Variables Outside Their Scope

Normally a lexically defined variable (either my or our) ceases to exist when its scope ends. However, that is not always the case. In the earlier example it happens to be true because there are no references to the variables other than the one created by the scope itself. Once that ends, the variable is unreferenced and so is consumed by Perl's garbage collector. The variable $file_scope appears to be persistent only because it drops out of scope at the end of the script, where issues of scope and persistence become academic.

However, if we take a reference to a lexically scoped variable and pass that reference back to a higher scope, the reference keeps the variable alive for as long as the reference exists. In other words, so long as something, somewhere, is pointing to the variable (or to be more precise, the memory which holds the value of the variable), it will persist even if its scope ends. The following short script illustrates the point:

```perl
#!/usr/bin/perl
# persist.pl
use warnings;
use strict;

sub definelexical {
    my $lexvar = "the original value";
    return \$lexvar;   # return reference to variable
}

sub printlexicalref {
    my $lexvar = ${$_[0]};   # dereference the reference
    print "The variable still contains $lexvar \n";
}

my $ref = definelexical();
printlexicalref($ref);
```

In the subroutine definelexical, the scope of the variable $lexvar ends once the subroutine ends. Since we return a reference to the variable, and because that reference is assigned to the variable $ref, the variable remains in existence, even though it can no longer be accessed as $lexvar. We pass this reference to a second subroutine, printlexicalref, which defines a second, $lexvar, as the value to which the passed reference points to. It is important to realize that the two $lexvar variables are entirely different, each existing only in its own scope, but both pointing to the same underlying scalar. When executed, this script will print out: The variable still contains the original value.

> *In this particular example there is little point in returning a reference. Passing the string as a value is simpler and would work just as well. However, complex data structures can also be preserved by returning a reference to them, rather than making a copy as would happen if we returned them as a value.*

The fact that a lexical variable exists so long as a reference to it exists can be extended to include 'references to references' and 'references to references to references'. So long as the 'top' reference is stored somewhere, the lexical variable can be hidden at the bottom of a long chain of references, each one being kept alive by the one above. This is in essence how lexical array of arrays and hashes of hashes work. The component arrays and hashes are kept alive by having their reference stored in the parent array or hash.

The Symbol Table

We have seen that package variables are entered into the symbol table for the package in which they are defined, but can be accessed from anywhere by their fully qualified name. This works because the symbol tables of packages are jointly held in a master symbol table, with the main:: package at the top and all other symbol tables arranged hierarchically below. Although for most practical purposes we can ignore the symbol table most of the time and simply let it do its job, a little understanding of its workings can be informative and even occasionally useful.

Perl, being Perl, implements its symbol table in a manner that we can easily comprehend with a basic knowledge of data types; it is really a hash of typeglobs. In fact, the symbol table is the origin of typeglobs and the reason for their existence. This close relationship between typeglobs and the symbol table means that we can examine and manipulate the symbol table through the use of typeglobs.

Whenever we create a global (declared with our or use vars but not my) variable in Perl we cause a typeglob to be entered into the symbol table and a reference for the data type we just defined to be placed into the typeglob.

The Perl symbol table is an example of a hash containing globs. Each key is the name of the typeglob, and therefore the name of the scalar, array, hash, subroutine, filehandle, and report associated with that typeglob. The value is a typeglob containing the references, or a hash reference to another symbol table, which is how Perl's hierarchical symbol table is implemented.

Let's take the following example:

```
our $variable = "This is a global variable";
```

What we are actually doing here is creating a typeglob called variable in the main package, and filling its scalar reference slot with a reference to the string This is a global variable. The name of the typeglob is stored as a key in the symbol table, which is essentially just a hash, with the typeglob itself as the value, and the scalar reference in the typeglob defines the existence and value of $variable. Whenever we refer to a global variable, Perl looks up the relevant typeglob in the symbol table and then looks for the appropriate reference, depending on what kind of variable we asked for.

The only thing other than a typeglob that can exist in a symbol table is another symbol table. This is the basis of Perl's package hierarchy, and the reason we can access a variable in one package from another. Regardless of which package our code is in, we can always access a package variable by traversing the symbol table tree from the top.

The 'main' Package

The default package is main, the root of the symbol table hierarchy, so any package variable declared without an explicit package prefix or preceding package declaration automatically becomes part of the 'main package':

```
our $scalar;    # defines $main::scalar
```

Since main is the root table for all other symbol tables, the following statements are all equivalent:

```
package MyPackage;
our $scalar;

package main::MyPackage;
our $scalar;

our $MyPackage::scalar;
our $main::MyPackage::scalar
```

Strangely, since every package must have main as its root, the main package is defined as an entry in its own symbol table. The following is also quite legal and equivalent to the above, if somewhat bizarre:

```
our $main::main::main::main::main::main::main::MyPackage::scalar;
```

This is more a point of detail than a useful fact, of course, but if we write a script to traverse the symbol table then this is a special case we need to look out for.

In general we do not need to use the main package unless we want to define a package variable explicitly without placing it into its own package. This is a rare thing to do, so most of the time we can ignore the main package. It does however allow us to make sense of error messages like: Name "main::a" used only once: possible typo at ....

Typeglobs and the 'main' Package

All global variables are really package variables in the main package, so the following two assignments are the same:

```
*subglob = \&mysubroutine;
*main::subglob = \&main::mysubroutine;
```

We can of course alias to a different package too. This is actually how Perl's import mechanism works underneath the surface when we say use module and get subroutines that we can call without qualification in our own programs:

```
# import 'subroutine' into our namespace
*main::subroutine = \&My::Module::subroutine;
```

Be wary of assigning things other than references or other typeglobs, however. For example, assigning a string does have an interesting but not entirely expected effect. We might suppose the following statement creates a variable called $hello with the value world:

```
*hello = "world";
```

However, if we try to print $hello we find that it does not exist. If we print out *hello we find that it has become aliases instead:

```
print *hello;   # produce '*main::world'
```

In other words, the string has been taken as a symbolic reference to a typeglob name, and the statement is actually equivalent to:

```
*hello = *world;
```

This can be very useful, especially since the string can be a scalar variable:

```
*hello = $name_to_alias_to;
```

However, it is also a potential source of confusion, especially as it is easily done by forgetting to include a backslash to create a reference. Assigning other things to typeglobs has less useful effects. An array or hash for example will be assigned in scalar context and alias the typeglob to a typeglob whose name is a number:

```
@array = (1, 2, 3);
*hello = @array;
print *hello;   # produces 'main::3' since @array has three elements
```

This is unlikely to be what we wanted, and we probably meant to say *hello = \@array in this case. Assigning a subroutine aliases the typeglob to the value returned by the subroutine. If that's a string, it's useful, otherwise it probably isn't:

```
*hello = subroutine_that_returns_name_to_alias_to(@args);
```

The bottom line is that typeglobs can be used for all kinds of interesting effects.

The Symbol Table Hierarchy

Whenever we define a new package variable in a new package, we cause Perl to create symbol tables to hold the variable. In Perl syntax, package names are separate by double colons :: in much the same way that directories are separated by / or \, and domain names by a dot. For the same reason the colons define a location in a hierarchical naming system.

For example, if we declare a package with three package elements we create three symbol tables, each containing an entry to the one below:

```
package World::Country::City;
our $variable = "value";
```

This creates a chain of symbol tables. The World symbol table created as an entry of main contains no actual variables. However, it does contain an entry for the Country symbol table, which therefore has the fully qualified name World::Country. In turn Country contains an entry for a symbol table called City. City does not contain any symbol table entries, but it does contain an entry for a typeglob called *variable which contains a scalar reference to the value value. When all put together as a whole, this gives us the package variable:

```
$main::World::Country::City::variable;
```

Since `main` is always the root of the symbol table tree we never need to specify it explicitly, so we can also just say:

```
$World::Country::City::variable;
```

This is the fully qualified name of the package variable. The fact that we can omit the package names when we are actually in the `World::Country::City` package is a convenience extended to us by Perl. There is no actual variable called `$variable`, unless we declare it lexically. Even if we were in the main package the true name of the variable would be `$main::variable`.

Manipulating the Symbol Table Directly

We can edit the symbol table directly by creating and manipulating typeglobs, since the symbol table entries are actually typeglobs. This allows us to do some interesting things, particularly in conjunction with `local`.

For example, we can alias a global variable with a local name, so that altering the local variable also affects the global:

```perl
#!/usr/bin/perl
# changeglobal.pl
use warnings;
use strict;

our $global = 'before';

sub changeglobal {
    local *local = *global;
    our $local = 'after';
}

print "$global \n";
changeglobal;
print "$global \n";
```

The assignment to `$global` creates a typeglob in the symbol table, `*global`, with its scalar reference pointing to the string `before`. In the subroutine we make a local copy of this typeglob, which contains all the same references to its different subtypes as the original typeglob. The only defined reference is the scalar one, so the assignment to `*local` creates the local variable `$local`. Since we are using `strict` we declare it with `our`, but the variable already exists so `our` just keeps the `strict` module happy about us using it. Since `*local` contains the same references as `*global`, `$local` is an alias for `$global` and altering it also alters the global variable.

Typeglob assignment works for any of the possible types that a typeglob can contain, including filehandles and code references. So we can create an alias to a filehandle this way too:

```perl
local *OUT = *STDOUT;
print OUT "this goes to standard output";
```

We can create an alias for a previously defined subroutine with a similar approach. This lets us do things like choose from a selection of subroutines in:

```perl
# choose a subroutine to call and alias it to a local name
local *aliassub = $debug? *mydebugsub: *mysubroutine;

# call the chosen subroutine via its alias
aliassub("Testing", 1, 2, 3);
```

270

This even works if `aliassub` already exists as a function, because `local` creates a local version of the name that temporarily replaces the original.

All this works because package typeglobs are actually entries in the symbol table itself. Everything else is held in a typeglob of the same name. Once we know how it all works it is relatively easy to see how Perl does the same thing itself. For example, when we define a named subroutine we are really causing Perl to create a code reference, then assign it to a typeglob of that name in the symbol table. To prove it, here is a roundabout way to define a subroutine:

```perl
#!/usr/bin/perl
# anonsub.pl
use warnings;
use strict;

our $anonsub = sub {print "Hello World"};

*namedsub = \&{$anonsub};
namedsub();
```

Here we have done the same job as defining a named subroutine, but in explicit steps. First creating a code reference, then assigning that code reference to a typeglob. The subroutine is defined in code rather than as a declaration, but the net effect is the same.

Accessing the Symbol Table

Interestingly, the symbol table itself can be accessed in Perl by referring to the name of the package with a trailing `::`. Since symbol tables are hashes, and the hashes are stored in a typeglob with the same name, the hash that defines the `main` symbol table can be accessed with `%{*main::}`, or simply `%{*::}`, as this short script demonstrates:

```perl
#!/usr/bin/perl
# dumpmain.pl
use warnings;
use strict;

foreach my $name (sort keys %{*::}) {
    next if $name eq 'main';
    print "Symbol '$name' => \n";

# extract the glob reference
my $globref = ${*::} {$name};

# define local package variables through alias
local *entry = *{$globref};
# make sure we can access them in 'strict' mode
our ($entry, @entry, %entry);

# extract scalar, array, and hash via alias
print "\tScalar: $entry \n" if defined $entry;
print "\tArray : [@entry] \n" if @entry;
print "\tHash  : {", join(" ", (%entry)), "} \n" if %entry;

# check for subroutine and handle via glob
print "\tSub '$name' defined \n" if *entry{CODE};
    print "\tHandle '$name' (", fileno(*entry), ") defined \n"
    if *entry{IO};
}
```

The `Dumpvalue` module provides a more convenient interface to the symbol table and forms a core part of the Perl debugger. It does essentially the same thing as the example above, but more thoroughly and with a more elegant output. The following script builds a hierarchy of symbol tables and variables and then uses the `Dumpvalue` module to print them out:

```perl
#!/usr/bin/perl
# dumpval.pl
use warnings;
use strict;

use Dumpvalue;

# first define some variables
{
    # no warnings to suppress 'usage' messages
    no warnings;

    package World::Climate;
    our $weather = "Variable";

    package World::Country::Climate;
    our %weather = (
        England => 'Cloudy'
    );

    package World::Country::Currency;
    our %currency = (
        England => 'Sterling',
        France => 'Franc',
        Germany => 'Mark',
        USA => 'US Dollar',
    );

    package World::Country::City;
    our @cities = ('London', 'Paris', 'Bremen', 'Phoenix');

    package World::Country::City::Climate;
    our %cities = (
        London => 'Foggy and Cold',
        Paris => 'Warm and Breezy',
        Bremen => 'Intermittent Showers',
        Phoenix => 'Horrifyingly Sunny',
    );

    package World::Country::City::Sights;
    our %sights = (
        London => ('Tower of London','British Museum'),
        Paris => ('Eiffel Tower','The Louvre'),
        Bremen => ('Town Hall','Becks Brewery'),
        Phoenix => ('Arcosanti'),
    );
}

my $dumper = new Dumpvalue (globPrint => 1);
$dumper->dumpValue(\*World::);
```

Summary

This chapter began with a discussion of package variables. The topics covered include:

- ❑ Defining package variables
- ❑ Using 'strict' variables
- ❑ Declaring global package variables
- ❑ Declaring global package variables with `use vars`
- ❑ Lexically declaring global package variables with `our`
- ❑ Automatic localization in Perl
- ❑ Localizing package variables with `local`

We then talked briefly about lexical variables before working through the following aspects of the symbol table:

- ❑ The `main` package
- ❑ Typeglobs and the `main` package
- ❑ The symbol table hierarchy
- ❑ Manipulating the symbol table directly
- ❑ Accessing the symbol table

9

Using Modules

Modules are the basic unit of reusable code in Perl, the equivalent of libraries in other languages. Perl's standard library is almost entirely made up of modules. When we talk about Perl libraries we usually mean modules and older library files that are included as part of the standard Perl library – the collection of files that comes as standard with Perl. The words 'module' and 'library' are frequently used interchangeably, but they are not equivalent because not all libraries are modules. The exception is the term 'standard Perl library', which we use to refer to the entire assembly of supporting modules that ship as standard with Perl.

A library is simply a file supplied either by the standard Perl library or another package that contains routines that we can use in our own programs. Older Perl libraries were simple collections of routines collected together into a file, generally with a .pl extension. The do and require functions can be used to load this kind of library into our own programs, making the routines and variables they define available in our own code.

Modern Perl libraries are defined as modules and included into our programs with the use directive, which requires that the module name ends in .pm. The use keyword provides additional complexity over do and require, the most notable difference being that the inclusion happens at compile time rather than run time.

Modules come in two distinct flavors, functional and pragmatic. Functional modules are generally just called modules or library modules. They provide functionality in the form of routines and variables that can be used from within our own code. They are what we usually think of as libraries. Conversely, pragmatic modules implement pragmas that modify the behavior of Perl at compile time, adding to or constraining Perl's syntax to permit additional constructs or limit existing ones. The use directive is always used to load them. The strict, vars, and warnings modules are all examples of pragmatic modules that we frequently use in Perl scripts. Some pragmatic modules also provide routines and variables that can be used at run time, but most do not.

In this chapter we will examine the different ways of using modules in our scripts. In Chapter 10 we will look inside modules, that is, examine them from the perspective of how they work as opposed to how to use them.

Modules and Packages

A package declaration is the naming of a new namespace in which further declarations of variables and subroutines are placed. A module is simply a library file that defines subroutines and variables in a given namespace, courtesy of a package declaration. The link between package name and module file would therefore appear to be a strong one, but this is not necessarily true. The module that is loaded corresponds to the named package, but this does not imply that the module actually defines anything in that package. As an example, many of Perl's pragmatic modules are purely concerned with compile time semantics and do not contribute anything new to the symbol table.

In fact, a module doesn't have to include a package declaration, but it usually does. By including a package definition we are able to use many different modules without worrying about clashes between similarly named definitions – namespace collisions, as the technical jargon has it.

Since a module file usually only contains declarations of subroutines and variables, rather than code that actually does something, executing it has no visible effect. However, subroutines and package variables are added to the symbol table, under the namespace defined by the package declaration. Most of the time that will be the same package that the use statement asked for, but it isn't actually required. In some cases we might use a different package, or define symbols in more than one package at the same time.

Whatever else it does, in order for a module to be loaded successfully by either require or use, it must return a True value. Unless the module actually contains a return statement outside a subroutine definition, this must be the last statement in the file. Since a typical module contains mainly subroutine definitions (which don't return anything), we usually need to add an explicit return value to let Perl know that the module is happy. We can also add code for initialization that does do something actively, and have that return a conditional value. This means we can, for example, programmatically have a module fail compilation if, say, an essential resource like a configuration file that it needs is missing.

Most modules do not have any initialization code to return a value, so in general we satisfy Perl by simply appending a 1 to the end of the module file. As the last statement in the file, this is returned to the use or require that triggered the loading of the module file. Taking all this together, the general form of a module file is simply:

```
package My::Module;

... use other modules ...
... declare global variables ...
... define subroutines ...

1;
```

This module would be called Module.pm, placed in a directory called My, which in turn can be located in a variety of places. The My Directory can be situated under any of the paths in @INC, in our own personal location, or in Perl modules that we can use by adding it to @INC or using the lib module, as we shall see shortly.

Loading Code Using 'do', 'require', and 'use'

Perl provides three mechanisms of increasing usefulness for incorporating code (including modules), in other files into our own programs. These are the do, require, and use statements. Any code that is loaded by any of these statements is recorded in the special hash %INC (more on this later on).

The simplest is do, which simply executes the contents of an external file by reading it and then evaling the contents. If that file happens to contain subroutine declarations, then those declarations are evaluated and become part of our program:

```
do '/home/perl/loadme.pl';
```

A more sophisticated version of do is the require statement. If the filename is defined within quotes it looks for it as-is, otherwise it appends a .pm extension and translates instances of :: into a directory separator:

```
# include the old-style (and obsolete) getopts library
require 'getopts.pl';

# include the modern and trendy Getopt::Std library
# (i.e. PATH/Getopt/Std.pm)
require Getopt::Std;
```

This first checks that the file has not already been loaded by looking in the %INC hash. Next it searches for those files in the paths contained in the special array @INC, which we will examine later in the chapter.

More sophisticated still is the use statement. This does exactly the same as require, but evaluates the included file at compile time, rather than at run time as require does. This allows modules to perform any necessary initializations and to modify the symbol table with subroutine declarations before the main body of the code is compiled. This in turn allows syntax checks to recognize valid symbols defined by the module and flag errors on non-existent ones. For example, this is how we can include the Getopt::Std module at compile time:

```
# include Getopt::Std at compile time
use Getopt::Std;
```

Like require, use takes a bare unquoted module name as a parameter, appending a .pm to it and translating instances of :: or the archaic ` into directory separators. Unlike require, use does not permit any filename to be specified with quotes and will flag a syntax error if we attempt to do so. Only true library modules may be included via use.

The traditional way to cause code to be executed at compile time is with a BEGIN block, so this is (almost) equivalent to:

```
BEGIN {
    require Getopt::Std;
}
```

However, use also attempts to call the subroutine `import` in the module being included. This provides the module with the opportunity to define symbols in our namespace, making it simpler to access its features without prefixing them with the module's package name. `use Module` is therefore actually equivalent to:

```
BEGIN {
    require Module;
    Module->import;    # or 'import Module'
}
```

This one simple additional step is the foundation of Perl's entire `import` mechanism. There is no more additional complexity or built-in support for handling modules or importing variables and subroutine names. It is all based around a simple function call that happens at compile time.

'import' Lists

As we just discussed above, the major advantage that `use` has over `require` is the concept of importing. While it is true that we can import directly by simply calling `import` ourselves, it is simpler and more convenient with `use`.

If we execute a `use` statement with just a module name as an argument we cause the `import` subroutine within the module to be called with no argument. This produces a default response from the module. This may be to do nothing at all, or to import a default set of symbols (subroutines, definitions, and variables) for our use. Object-oriented modules tend not to import anything, since they expect us to use them by calling methods.

Function-oriented modules often do import symbols by default, and optionally may import further symbols if we request them in an import list. An import list is a list of items specified after the module name. It can be specified as a comma separated list within parentheses, or as a space-separated list within a qw operator. If we only need to supply one item we can also supply it directly as a string:

```
# importing a list of symbols with a comma separated list:
use Module ('sub1', 'sub2', '$scalar', '@list', ':tagname');

# it is more legible to use 'qw':
use Module qw(sub1 sub2 $scalar @list :tagname);

# a single symbol can be specified as a simple string:
use Module 'sub1';
```

Symbols can either be subroutine names, variables, or sometimes tags, prefixed by a `:`, if the module in question supports them. These are a feature of the `Exporter` module, which is the source of many modules' import mechanisms. We discuss it from the module developer's point of view in Chapter 10.

We cannot import any symbol or tag into our code – the module must define it to be able to export it. A few modules like the `CGI` module have generic importing functions that handle anything we pass to them. However, most do not, and we will generate a syntax error if we attempt to export symbols from the module that it does not supply.

Suppressing Default Imports

Sometimes we want to be able to use a module without importing anything from it. To do that we can specify an empty import list, which is subtly different from supplying no import list at all:

```
use Module;    # import default symbols
use Module();   # suppress all imports
```

When used in this way, use is exactly equivalent to a require, except that it takes place at compilation time; that is:

```
BEGIN {require Module;}
```

Note that we cannot suppress the default import list and then import a specific symbol – any import will trigger the default (unless of course the module in question is written to allow special cases to do this). Remember that the entire import mechanism revolves around a subroutine called import in the module being loaded.

Disabling Features with 'no'

no, which is the opposite of the use directive, attempts to unimport features imported by use. This concept is entirely module-dependent. In reality it is simply a call to the module's unimport subroutine. Different modules support this in different ways, including not supporting it at all. For modules that do support no, we can unimport a list of symbols with:

```
no Module qw(symbol1 symbol2 :tagname);
```

This is equivalent to:

```
BEGIN {
    require Module;
    unimport('symbol1', 'symbol2', ':tagname');
}
```

Unlike use, a no statement needs the subroutine unimport to exist. A fatal error is generated if this is not present.

Whether or not no actually removes the relevant symbols from our namespace, or undoes whatever initialization was performed by use depends entirely on the module. It also depends on what its unimport subroutine actually does. Note that even though it supposedly turns off features, no still requires the module. In general this happens after the module has been used, so the require has no effect as the module will already be present in %INC.

Testing for Module Versions and the Version of Perl

Quite separately from their usual usage, both the require and use directives support an alternative syntax taking a numeric value as the first or only argument. When specified on its own, this value is compared to the version of Perl itself. It causes execution to halt if the comparison reveals that the version of Perl being used is less than that stated by the program. For instance, to require that only Perl version 5.6.0 or higher is used to run a script we can write any of the following:

```
require 5.6.0;
use 5.6.0;
require v5.6.0;
```

Older versions of Perl used a version resembling a floating-point number. This is also supported, for compatibility with older versions of Perl:

```
require 5.001;    # require Perl 5.001 or higher
require 5.005_03;   # require Perl 5.005 patch level 3 or higher
```

Note that for patch levels (the final part of the version number), the leading zero is important. The underscore is just a way of separating the main version from the patch and is a standard part of Perl's numeric syntax; 5.005_03 is the same as 5.00503, but more legible.

A version number may also be specified after a module name (and before the import list, if any is present), in which case it is compared to the version defined for the module. For example, to require CGI.pm version 2.36 or higher we can write:

```
use CGI 2.36 qw(:standard);
```

If the version of CGI.pm is less than 2.36 this will cause a compile time error and abort the program. Note that there is no comma between the module name, the version, or the import list.

Like the import mechanism, this is not built-in functionality but simply calls a subroutine called VERSION to extract a numeric value. Usually this subroutine is supplied by the UNIVERSAL module, from which all packages inherit, which in turn returns the value of the variable $<package name>::VERSION. This is how most modules define their version number.

Pragmatic Modules

Pragmatic modules alter the behavior of the Perl compiler to expand or constrict the syntax of the Perl language itself. Unlike functional modules they take effect at compile time, rather than run time. One pragma that should be familiar to us by now is the strict pragma.

It is conventional for pragmatic modules to be defined using all lower case letters, unlike functional modules, which conventionally use a capitalized or uppercased name.

It sometimes comes as a surprise to programmers new to Perl that all pragmas are defined in terms of modules, all of which can be found in the standard Perl library. The strict pragma is implemented by strict.pm, for example. Although it is not necessary to understand exactly how this comes about, a short diversion into the workings of pragmatic modules can be educational.

How Pragmatic Modules Work

Many of these modules work their magic by working closely with special variables such as $^H, which provides a bitmask of compiler 'hints' to the Perl compiler, or $^W, which controls warnings. A quick examination of the strict module (the documentation for which is much longer than the actual code), illustrates how three different flags within $^H are tied to the use strict pragma:

```
package strict;
$strict::VERSION = "1.01";

my %bitmask = (
refs => 0x00000002,
subs => 0x00000200,
vars => 0x00000400
);
```

```
sub bits {
    my $bits = 0;
    foreach my $s (@_){ $bits |= $bitmask{$s} || 0; };
    $bits;
}

sub import {
    shift;
    $^H |= bits(@_ ? @_ : qw(refs subs vars));
}

sub unimport {
    shift;
    $^H &=~ bits(@_ ? @_ : qw(refs subs vars));
}
1;
```

The strict module is particularly simple, which is why we have used it here. The entirety of the code in strict.pm is shown above. Of course it is not necessary to understand how this module actually works, but it does provide an insight into how pragmatic modules, in general, do what they do.

Scope of Pragmatic Modules

Most pragmatic modules have lexical scope, since they control the manner in which Perl compiles code – this is by nature a lexical process. For example, this short program illustrates how strict references can be disabled within a subroutine to allow symbolic references:

```
#!/usr/bin/perl
# pragmascope.pl
use warnings;
use strict;

# a subroutine to be called by name
sub my_sub {
    print @_;
}

# a subroutine to call other subroutines by name
sub call_a_sub {
    # allow symbolic references inside this subroutine only
    no strict 'refs';

    my $sub = shift;
    # call subroutine by name - a symbolic reference
    &$sub(@_);
}

# all strict rules in effect here
call_a_sub('my_sub', "Hello pragmatic world \n");
```

> **perl pragmascope.pl**
Hello pragmatic world

The exceptions are those pragmas that predeclare symbols, variables, and subroutines in preparation for the run time phase, or modify the values of special variables, which generally have a file-wide scope.

The Special Hash '%INC'

As mentioned earlier, any file or module that the do, require, and use statements load is recorded in the special hash %INC, which we can then examine to see what is loaded in memory. The keys of %INC are the names of the modules requested, converted to a pathname so that :: becomes something like / or \ instead. The values are the names of the actual files that were loaded as a result, including the path where they were found. Loading a new module updates the contents of this hash as shown in the following example:

```perl
#!/usr/bin/perl
# INC.pl
use strict;

print "\%INC contains: \n";
foreach (keys %INC) {
print "  $INC{$_}\n";
}


require File::Copy;
do '/home/perl/include.pl';

print "\n\%INC now contains: \n";
foreach (keys %INC) {
print "  $INC{$_}\n";
}
```

> **perl INC.pl**
%INC contains:
 /usr/local/lib/perl5/5.6.0/strict.pm

%INC now contains:
 /usr/local/lib/perl5/5.6.0/Exporter.pm
 /usr/local/lib/perl5/5.6.0/Carp.pm
 /home/perl/include.pl
 /usr/local/lib/perl5/5.6.0/strict.pm
 /usr/local/lib/perl5/5.6.0/File/Copy.pm

Note that %INC contains Exporter.pm and Carp.pm although we have not loaded them *explicitly* in our example. The reason for this is that the former is required and the latter is used by Copy.pm, itself required in the example. For instance, the IO module is a convenience module that loads all the members of the IO:: family. Each of these loads further modules. The result is that no less than twenty nine modules are loaded as a consequence of issuing the simple directive use IO.

It should also be noted that that we did not specify in our example the full path to the modules. use and require, as well as modules like ExtUtils::Installed (more on this later in the chapter), look for their modules in the paths specified by the special array @INC.

The Special Array '@INC'

This built-in array is calculated when Perl is built and is provided automatically to all programs. To find the contents of @INC we can run a one-line Perl script like the following for a Linux terminal:

> **perl –e 'foreach (@INC) { print "$_\n";}'**

On a Linux Perl 5.6 installation, we get the following listing of the pathnames that are tried by default for locating modules:

/usr/local/lib/perl5/5.6.0/i686-linux-thread
/usr/local/lib/perl5/5.6.0
/usr/local/lib/perl5/site_perl/5.6.0/i686-linux-thread
/usr/local/lib/perl5/site_perl/5.6.0
/usr/local/lib/perl5/site_perl
.

Equivalently for Windows the Perl script is:

> **perl -e "foreach (@INC) { print \"$_\n\";}"**
C:/perl/ActivePerl/lib
C:/perl/ActivePerl/site/lib
.

When we issue a require or use to load a module Perl searches this list of directories for a file with the corresponding name, translating any instances of :: (or the archaic `) into directory separators. The first file that matches is loaded, so the order of the directories in @INC is significant.

It is not uncommon to want to change the contents of @INC, to include additional directories into the search path or (less commonly) to remove existing directories. We have two basic approaches to doing this – we can either modify the value of @INC directly, or use the use lib pragma to handle it for us.

Modifying '@INC' directly

One way of modifying @INC is by using the command line option -I, which takes a directory as an argument and adds it to the start of @INC:

> **perl -I/home/httpd/perl/lib -e 'print join"\n",@INC'**

/home/httpd/perl/lib
/usr/local/lib/perl5/5.6.0/i686-linux-thread
/usr/local/lib/perl5/5.6.0
/usr/local/lib/perl5/site_perl/5.6.0/i686-linux-thread
/usr/local/lib/perl5/site_perl/5.6.0
/usr/local/lib/perl5/site_perl

We can also modify @INC programmatically, which allows us to add directories to the end of @INC rather than the beginning and also remove directories if we so desire.

Since @INC is an array, all of the standard array manipulation functions will work on it:

```
# add directory to end of @INC
push @INC, "/home/httpd/perl/lib";

# add current directory to start of @INC using the 'getcwd'
# function of the 'Cwd' module
use Cwd;
unshift @INC, getcwd();
```

However, since the use directive causes modules to be loaded at compile time rather than run time, modifying @INC this way will not work for used modules, only required ones. To modify @INC so that it takes effect at compile time we must enclose it in a BEGIN block:

```
# add directory to start of @INC at compile time
BEGIN {
    unshift @INC, '/home/httpd/perl/lib';
}

use MyModule;   # a module in 'home/httpd/perl/lib'...
...
```

Modifying @INC with the 'lib' Pragma

Since BEGIN blocks are a little clunky, we can instead use the lib pragma to add entries to @INC in a friendlier manner. As well as managing the contents of @INC more intelligently, this module provides both a more legible syntax and a degree of error checking over what we try to add. The use lib pragma takes one or more library paths and integrates them into @INC. This is how we could add the directory /home/httpd/perl/lib using the lib pragma:

```
use lib '/home/httpd/perl/lib';
```

This is almost but not quite the same as using an unshift statement inside a BEGIN block, as in the example above. The difference is that if an architecture-dependent directory exists under the named path and it contains an auto directory, then this directory is assumed to contain architecture -pecific modules and is also added, ahead of the path named in the pragma. In the case of the Linux system used as an example earlier, this would attempt to add the directories:

```
/home/httpd/perl/lib/i386-linux/auto
/home/httpd/perl/lib
```

Note that the first directory is only added if it exists, but the actual path passed to lib is added regardless of whether it exists or not. If it does exist, however, it must be a directory; attempting to add a file to @INC will produce an error from the lib pragma.

We can also remove paths from @INC with the no directive:

```
no lib 'home/httpd/perl/lib';
```

This removes the named library path or paths, and also removes any corresponding auto directories.

The `lib` pragma has two other useful properties that make it a superior solution to a BEGIN block. First, if we attempt to add the same path twice, the second instance is removed. Since paths are added to the front of @INC this effectively allows us to bump a path to the front:

```
# search for modules in site_perl directory first
use lib '/usr/lib/perl5/site_perl';
```

Second, we can restore the original value of @INC as built in to Perl with the statement:

```
@INC = @lib::ORIG_INC;
```

Locating Libraries Relative to the Script

A common application of adding a library to @INC is to add a directory whose path is related to that of the script being run. For instance, the script might be in /home/httpd/perl/bin/myscript and the library modules that support it in /home/httpd/perl/lib. It is undesirable to have to hard-code this information into the script however, since then we cannot relocate or install it in a different directory.

One way to solve this problem is to use the getcwd function from Cwd.pm to determine the current directory and calculate the location of the library directory from it. However, we do not need to, because Perl provides the FindBin module for exactly this purpose.

FindBin calculates paths based on the current working directory and generates six variables containing path information, each of which we can either import into our own code or access directly from the module. They are:

Variable	Path information
$Bin	The path to the directory from which the script was run
$Dir	An alias for $Bin
$Script	The name of the script
$RealBin	The real path to the directory from which the script was run, with all symbolic links resolved
$RealDir	An alias for $RealBin
$RealScript	The real name of the script, with all symbolic links resolved.

Using FindBin we can add a relative library directory by retrieving the $Bin/$Dir or $RealBin/$RealDir variables and feeding them, suitably modified, to a use lib pragma:

```
use FindBin qw($RealDir);   # or $Bin, $Dir, or $RealBin ...
use lib "$RealDir/../lib";
```

Using the FindBin module has significant advantages over trying to do the same thing ourselves with getcwd and its relatives. It handles various special cases for Windows and VMS systems, and it deals with the possibility that the script name was passed to Perl on the command line rather than triggering Perl via a #! header (of course it's shorter too). Be careful using FindBin with CGI scripts, however, since we cannot always be sure what directory we start in when the script is executed. Basing the paths we feed to use lib on the CGI environment is a much better idea.

Checking for the Availability of a Module

One way to check if a given module is available is to look in the %INC hash to see if the module is present. We can avoid fatal errors by checking for each module and using it only if already loaded. In the following example, if Module1 is available, then we use it, otherwise we use Module2 if loaded:

```
if ($INC{'Module1'}) {
# use some functions from Module1
} elsif ($INC{'Module2'}) {
# use some functions from Module2
}
```

However, the simplest way would be to try to load it using require. Since this ordinarily produces a fatal error, we use an eval to protect the program from errors:

```
warn "GD module not available" unless eval {require GD; 1};
```

In the event that the GD module, which is a Perl interface to the libgd graphics library, is not available, eval returns undef and the warning is emitted. If it does exist, the 1 at the end of the eval is returned, suppressing the warning. This gives us a way of optionally loading modules if they are present but continuing without them otherwise, so we can enable optional functionality if they are present. In this case, we can generate graphical output if GD is present, or resort to text otherwise. The special variable $@ holds the syntax error message that is generated by the last eval function.

Note that a serious problem arises with the above approach if we replace require with use. The reason is that eval is a run time function whereas use is executed at compile time. So, use GD would be executed before anything else, generating a fatal error if the GD module was not available. To solve this problem we simply enclose the whole thing in a BEGIN block, making sure that the whole block is executed at compile time:

```
BEGIN {
    foreach ('GD', 'CGI', 'Apache::Session') {
        warn "$_ not available" unless eval "use $_; 1";
    }
}
```

Finding Out What Modules are Installed

We can find out which library module packages are installed using the ExtUtils::Installed module. This works not by scanning @INC for files ending in .pm, but by analyzing the .packlist files left by module distributions during the installation process. Not unsurprisingly, this may take the module a few moments to complete, especially on a large and heavily extended system.

Scanning .packlist files allows the ExtUtils::Installed module to produce more detailed information, for example, the list of files that should be present for a given module package. Conversely, this means that it does not deal with modules that are not installed but are simply pointed to by a modified @INC array. This is one good reason to create properly installable modules, which we discuss later in the chapter.

The resulting list is of installed module packages, not modules, and the standard Perl library is collected under the name `Perl`, so on a vanilla Perl installation we may expect to see only `Perl` returned from this module.

To use the module we first create an `ExtUtils::Installed` object with the new method:

```
use ExtUtils::Installed;
$inst = ExtUtils::Installed->new();
```

On a UNIX-based system this creates an installation object that contains the details of all the `.packlist` files on the system, as determined by the contents of `@INC`. If we have modules present in a directory outside the normal directories contained in `@INC`, then we can include it by modifying `@INC` before we create the installation object, as shown earlier.

Once the installation object is created, we can list all available modules in alphabetical order with the `modules` method. For example, this very short script simply lists all installed modules:

```
# list all installed modules;
print join "\n", $inst->modules();
```

On a vanilla Perl installation this will produce just Perl, or possibly Perl plus one or two other modules in vendor-supplied installations. A more established Perl installation with many packages installed might produce something like this:

```
Apache::DBI
Apache::Session
Archive::Tar
CGI
CPAN
CPAN::WAIT
Compress::Zlib
Curses
DBI::FAQ
Date::Manip
Devel::Leak
Devel::Symdump
Digest::MD5
...
```

Note that for reasons known only to ActiveState, ActivePerl 5.6 will not run this, even though it worked on ActivePerl 5.005, an earlier version.

The `ExtUtils::Installed` module does far more than simply list installed module packages, however. It provides the basics of library package management by providing us with the ability to list the files and directories that each module distribution created when it was installed, and to verify that list against what is currently present. In addition to new and `modules`, which we saw in action earlier, `ExtUtils::Installed` provides the following six other methods:

Method	Description

directories	Returns a list of installed directories for the module. For example:
	
	`@dirs = $inst->directories($module);`
	
	A second optional parameter of prog, doc, or all (the default) may be given to restrict the returned list to directories containing code, manual pages, or both:
	
	`directories(module, 'prog'|'doc'|'all');`
	
	Further parameters are taken to be a list of directories within which all returned directories must lie:
	
	`directories(module, 'prog'|'doc'|'all', @dirs);`
	
	For instance, this lists installed directories contained by @locations:
	
	`@dirs = $inst->directories($module, 'prog', @locations);`

directory_tree	Returns a list of installed directories for the module, in the same way as directories, but also including any intermediate directories between the actual installed directories and the directories given as the third and greater parameters:
	
	`directory_tree(module, 'prog'|'doc'|'all', @dirs);`
	
	For instance, the following example lists installed directories and parents under /usr:
	
	`@dist = $inst->directories($module, 'all', '/usr');`

files	Returns a list of installed files for the module, for example:
	
	`@files = $inst->files($module);`
	
	A second optional parameter of prog, doc, or all may be given to restrict the returned list to files containing code, documentation, or both:
	
	`files (module, 'prog'|'doc'|'all')`
	
	Further parameters are taken to be a list of directories within which all returned files must lie:
	
	`files(module, 'prog'|'doc'|'all', @dirs)`
	
	This is how we list the installed files contained by @dirs:
	
	`@files = $inst->files($module, 'prog', @dirs);`

packlist	Returns an ExtUtils::Packlist object containing the raw details of the .packlist file for the given module: `packlist(module);` See the ExtUtils::Packlist documentation for more information.

Method	Description

validate	Checks the list of files and directories installed against those currently present, returning a list of all files and directories missing. If nothing is missing, an empty list is returned:
	
	`validate(module);`
	
	For instance,
	
	`$valid = $inst->validate($module)?0:1;`

version	Returns the version number of the module, or undef if the module does not supply one. The CPAN module uses this when the r command is used to determine which modules need updating, for example. `version(module);`

The ability to distinguish files types is a feature of the extended .packlist format in any recent version of Perl. Note that not every installed module yet provides a packing list that supplies this extra information, so many modules group all their installed files and directories under prog (the assumed default), and nothing under doc. To get a more accurate and reliable split between program and documentation files, we can use additional paths such as /usr/lib/perl5/man as the third and greater parameters.

As a more complete example of how we can use the features of ExtUtils::Installed, here is a short script to run on UNIX that lists every installed module distribution, the files that it contains, and the version of the package, complete with a verification check:

```perl
#!/usr/bin/perl
# installedfiles.pl
use warnings;
use strict;

use ExtUtils::Installed;

my $inst = new ExtUtils::Installed;

foreach my $package ($inst->modules) {
    my $valid = $inst->validate($package)?"Failed":"OK";
    my $version = $inst->version($package);
    $version = 'UNDEFINED' unless defined $version;

    print "\n\n--- $package v$version [$valid] ---\n\n";
    if (my @source = $inst->files($package, 'prog')) {
        print "\t", join "\n\t", @source;
    }
    if (my @docs = $inst->files($package, 'doc')) {
        print "\n\n\t", join "\n\t", @docs;
    }
}
```

Postponing Module Loading Until Use

Modules can be very large, frequently because they themselves use other large modules. It can, therefore, be convenient to postpone loading them until they are actually needed. This allows a program to start faster, and it also allows us to avoid loading a module at all if none of its features are actually used.

We can achieve this objective with the `autouse` pragmatic module, which we can use in place of a conventional use statement to delay loading the module. To use it we need to specify the name of the module, followed by a `=>` (since that is more legible than a comma) and a list of functions:

```
use autouse 'Module' => qw(sub1 sub2 Module::sub3);
```

This will predeclare the named functions, in the current package if not qualified with a package name, and trigger the loading of the module when any of the named functions are called:

```
sub1("This causes the module to be loaded");
```

We can also supply a prototype for the subroutine declaration, as in:

```
use autouse 'Module' => 'sub3($$@)';
```

However, there is no way for this prototype to be checked against the real subroutine since it has not been loaded, so if it is wrong we will not find out until we attempt to run the program.

There are two important caveats to bear in mind when using the `autouse` pragma. First, the module will only be loaded when one of the functions named on the `autouse` line is seen. Attempting to call another function in the module, even if it is explicitly called with a package name, will cause a run time error unless the module has already been loaded. For instance, this does not delay loading the `Getopt::Long` module:

```
use autouse 'Getopt::Long';
# ERROR: ''Getopt::Long' is not loaded, so 'GetOptions' is unavailable
GetOptions(option =>\$verbose);
```

But this does:

```
use autouse 'Getopt::Long' => 'GetOptions';
# OK, 'GetOptions' triggers load of 'Getopt::Long'
GetOptions(option =>\$verbose);
```

For this reason `autouse` works particularly well with object-oriented modules. We need only list class methods and constructors to ensure that the module is loaded at the right time.

Second, `autouse` only works for modules that use the default `import` method provided by the `Exporter` module (see Chapter 10). Modules that provide their own `import` method such as the `CGI` module cannot be used this way. Any module that defines an export tag like `:tagname` falls into this category. Such modules frequently provide their own specialized loading techniques instead, `CGI.pm` being one good example.

A significant problem when using autouse is that initialization of modules that have been autoused does not take place until run time; BEGIN blocks are not executed, nor are symbols imported. This can cause significant problems, as well as hiding syntax errors that would otherwise be found at compile time. For this reason it is smart to include modules directly for development and testing purposes, and to only use autouse in the production version (though we must still test that, we can eliminate autouse as a cause of problems in the debugging phase). Alternatively, use a debug flag to switch between the two:

```
if ($debug) {
    use 'Getopt::Long';
    ...other modules...
} else {
    use autouse 'Getopt::Long' => 'GetOptions';
    ...other modules...
}
```

If a module is already present when an autouse declaration is seen, it is translated directly into the equivalent use statement. For example:

```
use Module;
use autouse 'Module' => qw(sub1 sub2);
```

Is the same as:

```
use Module qw(sub1 sub2);
```

This means that it does no harm to attempt to autouse a module that is already loaded (something that might commonly happen inside a module, which has no idea what is already loaded), but conversely the autouse provides no benefit.

The autouse module is an attempt to provide load-on-demand based on the requirements of the user. The AUTOLOAD subroutine, and the AutoLoader and Selfloader modules also provide us with the ability to load modules and parts of modules on demand, but as part of the module's design. See Chapter 10 for more details.

Summary

Over the course of this chapter we examined what Perl modules are. Throughout the chapter we have covered the following:

- ❑ Loading code into our scripts, using the do, require and use statements, and the differences between them

- ❑ Manipulating the importing of subroutines definitions and variables from modules

- ❑ Pragmatic modules, how they work and their scope

- ❑ The special variables %INC and @INC and how to manipulate them

- ❑ Checking for the availability of modules

- ❑ Finding out which modules are installed

- ❑ Postponing module loading until use

10

Inside Modules and Packages

We have already seen how modules work from the user's perspective through the do, require, and use statements. In this chapter we take a look at modules from the perspective of implementing them ourselves.

Perl provides a number of special features that can be used in any Perl code but which are particularly useful for packages. The BEGIN, END, INIT, and (from Perl 5.6) CHECK blocks allow a module to define initialization and cleanup code to be automatically executed at key points during the lifetime of the module. They allow us to utilize features such as write packages (class constructors and destructors in object-oriented terms).

The Autoload subroutines permit a package to react to unknown subroutine calls and stand in for them. This allows us to:

❑ Emulate the existence of a subroutine without actually defining it.

❑ Define it on the fly at the moment it is used.

❑ Delay the compilation of a subroutine until it is needed

None of these features are restricted to packages, but it is in packages that they come into their own.

In order for modules to be easily reusable, they need to be well behaved. That means not defining variables and subroutines outside their own package unless explicitly asked to do so. It also means not allowing external definitions to be made unless the design of the module permits it. Exporting definitions from one package into another allows them to be used directly, without prefixing the name of the original package, but it also runs the risk of a namespace collision, so both the module and the application need to be able to cooperate, to control what happens. They can do this through the import mechanism, which defines the interface between the module and the application that uses it.

At the application end, we specify our requirements with the use or require statements, with which we can pass a list of symbols (often, but not necessarily, subroutine names). Conversely, at the module end, we define an import subroutine to control how we respond to import (or, from our point of view, export) requests. The Exporter module provides one such import subroutine that handles most common cases for us. Either way, the interface defined through the import mechanism abstracts the actual module code, making it easier to reuse the module, and minimizing the chances of an application breaking if we made changes to the module.

'BEGIN' blocks, 'END' blocks and Other Animals

Perl defines four different kinds of special block that are executed at different points during the compile or run phases. The most useful of these is BEGIN, which allows us to compile and execute code placed in a file before the main compilation phase is entered. At the other end of the application's life, the END block is called just as the program exits. We can also define CHECK (from Perl 5.6 on) and INIT blocks, though these are considerably less common.

All four blocks look and behave like subroutines, only without the leading sub. Like signal handlers, they are never called directly by code (in the case of BEGIN it isn't even possible), but directly by Perl whenever it passes from one state to another. The distinction between the block types is simply that each is executed at a different transition. The precise order is:

```
BEGIN
(compile phase)
CHECK
INIT
(run phase)
END
```

Here is a short program that demonstrates all four blocks in use, and also shows how they relate to the main code and a __DIE__ signal handler:

```
#!/usr/bin/perl
# blocks.pl
use warnings;
use strict;

$SIG{__DIE__} = sub {
    print "Et tu Brute?\n";
};

print "It's alive!\n";
die "Sudden death!\n";

BEGIN {
    print "BEGIN\n";
}

END {
    print "END\n";
}

INIT {
    print "INIT\n"
}

CHECK {
    print "CHECK\n"
}
```

When run, this program prints out:

```
BEGIN
CHECK
INIT
It's alive!
Et tu Brute?
Sudden death!
END
```

Note that in Perl versions before 5.6, CHECK blocks are ignored entirely, so we would not see the CHECK line. Apart from this, the program would run perfectly. Of course if the CHECK block needs to perform vital functions we may have a problem, so CHECK blocks are best used for checks that are better made after compilation but which can also be made, less efficiently perhaps, at run time too.

We can define multiple instances of each block; each one is executed in order, with BEGIN and INIT blocks executing in the order in which they are defined (top to bottom) and CHECK and END blocks executed in reverse order of definition (bottom to top). The logic for END and CHECK blocks executing in reverse is clearer once their purpose is understood. BEGIN blocks allow modules to initialize themselves, and may be potentially dependent upon the initialization of prior modules. Therefore, when the program exits, END blocks are executed in the reverse order to allow dependent modules to free their resources before earlier modules free the resources on which they rely. As an example, consider a network connection to a remote application – we might open a connection and 'start' a new session in the BEGIN blocks of different modules. When the application ends, we need to stop the session then close the connection – the reverse order. This will be done by the END blocks automatically. The new CHECK block has a similar symmetry with BEGIN, but around the compilation phase only, not the whole lifetime of the application.

Additional blocks read in by do, use, or require are simply added to the respective list at the time they are defined. Then, if we have a BEGIN and END block and we require a module that also has a BEGIN and END block, our BEGIN block is executed first, followed by the module's BEGIN block. At the end of the script, the module's END block is called first, then ours. If we include a module with use rather than require, however, the order of BEGIN blocks is determined by the order of the use relative to our BEGIN block and any other use statements. This is because use creates a BEGIN block of it's own, as we have already seen.

'BEGIN' Blocks

If we need to perform initialization within a module before it is used, we can place code inside the source file to perform whatever tasks we need to do, for example loading a configuration file:

```
package My::Module;

return initialize();

sub initialize {
...
}

... other sub and var declarations ...
```

This module doesn't need a 1 at the end because its success or failure is returned explicitly. However, the problem with this is that our initialization only takes place once the module starts to execute; we can't set anything up to be present before we define critical subroutines. Fortunately there is a solution. We can make use of a BEGIN block to force execution of a module's initialization code before the rest of it compiles. This is essential, for example, if we want to be able to export subroutine names so that their use can be recognized as valid subroutine calls during Perl's compile time syntax checking.

As an example of the kind of thing we can do with a BEGIN block, here is a module that computes a list of variables to export at compile time, and exports them before the code that uses the module compiles. For simplicity we have used a local hash to store the variable definitions, and kept it to scalars, but it is easily extensible:

```perl
# My/SymbolExporter.pm

package My::SymbolExporter;

use strict;

BEGIN {
    use vars '@SYMBOLS';
    # temporary local configuration - we could read from a file too
    my %conf = (
        e => 'mc2',
        time => 'money',
        party => 'a good time',
    );

    sub initialize {
        no strict 'refs';
        foreach (keys %conf) {
            # define variable with typeglob
            *{__PACKAGE__.'::'.$_} = \$conf{$_};

            # add variable (with leading '$') to export list
            push @SYMBOLS, "\$$_";
        }
        return 1;
    }

    return undef unless initialize;
}

use Exporter;
our @ISA = qw(Exporter);
our @EXPORT = ('@SYMBOLS',@SYMBOLS);
```

Ordinarily we'd use the Exporter module, or an import method to deal with this sort of problem, but these are really just extensions to the basic BEGIN block. Just to prove it works, here is a script that uses this module and prints out the variables it defines:

```perl
#!/usr/bin/perl
# symbolexportertest.pl
use warnings;
use strict;

use My::SymbolExporter;

print "Defined: @SYMBOLS\n\n";
```

```
print "e = $e\n";
print "time = $time\n";
print "party = '$party'\n";
```

This example also shows how we can use the __PACKAGE__ token to represent the current package, something we'll return to later when we come to writing import methods. Another use of BEGIN blocks is to pre-configure a module before we use it. For example, the AnyDBM_File module allows us to reconfigure its @ISA array by writing something like the following:

```
BEGIN {
    @AnyDBM_File::ISA = qw(GDBM_File SDBM_File);
}

use AnyDBM_File;
```

Inside the module, the code simply checks to see if the variable is defined before supplying a default definition:

```
our @ISA = qw(NDBM_File DB_File GDBM_File SDBM_File ODBM_File) unless @ISA;
```

It is vital that we put our definition in a BEGIN block so that it is executed and takes effect before the use statement is processed. Without this, the implicit BEGIN block of the use statement would cause the module to be loaded before our definition is established; the BEGIN block ensures that we prevail, as long as we place it before the use statement.

'END' Blocks

The opposite of BEGIN blocks are END blocks. These are called just as Perl is about to exit (even after a __DIE__ handler), and allow a module to perform closing duties like cleaning up temporary files or shutting down network connections cleanly:

```
END {
    unlink $tempfile;
    shutdown $socket, 2;
}
```

The value that the program is going to exit with is already set in the special variable $? when the END blocks are processed by Perl, so we can modify it at this point if we choose. To make sure it is passed back to the caller, if required, we also need to preserve it if an external program is called during the course of the block. END blocks are also not caught if we terminate on a signal, and (obviously) not if we use exec to replace the application with a new one.

'CHECK' and 'INIT'

The CHECK and INIT blocks are considerably rarer than BEGIN and END, but are occasionally useful. The CHECK blocks execute in reverse order just after the compilation phase ends and correspond to the END blocks, which run at the end of the run phase. Their purpose is to perform any kind of checking of the compiled source that might be required before proceeding with the run phase. Note, however, that unlike INIT, CHECK is new to Perl 5.6.

```
# Perl > = 5.6.0 for CHECK blocks
use 5.6.0;

# check that conditional compilation found at least one implementation
CHECK {
    die "No platform recognized" unless
    defined &unixsub or
    defined &win32sub or
    defined &macsub or
    defined &os2sub;
}
```

This block will be called as soon as Perl has finished compiling all the main code (and after all BEGIN blocks have been executed), so it is the ideal point to check for the existence of required entities before progressing to the execution stage. By placing the code in a CHECK block rather than in the module's main source we give it a chance to object before other modules, which may be used before it, get a chance to run.

The INIT blocks execute just before the run phase and just after the compile phase – CHECK blocks are also included if any are defined. They execute in order of definition and correspond to BEGIN blocks, which run just before the compile phase. Their purpose is to initialize variables and data structures before the main run phase starts:

```
# establish a package variable for all modules
INIT {
    $My::Module::start_time = time;
}
```

Both blocks types have little effect over simply placing code at the top of a file when only one of either type exists. However, if several modules define their own CHECK and INIT blocks, Perl will queue them up and run through them all before commencing execution of the main application code.

Manipulating Packages

The package directive changes the default namespace for variables and subroutine declarations, but we are still free to define our own fully qualified definitions if we choose. For instance, rather than creating a module file containing:

```
package My::Module;

sub mysub {
    return "Eep!\n";
}

1;
```

We could, with equal effect (but losing some maintainability), declare the subroutine to be in the package explicitly:

```
sub My::Module::mysub {
    return "Eep!\n";
}

1;
```

It isn't very likely that we would do this in reality – if we copied the subroutine to a different source file we would need to rename it. It has possibilities if we are generating subroutines on the fly, a subject we will cover in more detail later in the chapter, but otherwise, a `package` declaration is far more convenient. The same goes for `our` and `use vars` declarations, which are simply shorthand that uses the package declaration to omit the full variable name.

We sometimes want to handle package names programmatically. One simple way to get the name of the current package is the `__PACKAGE__` token, which we return to later. Otherwise, the `Symbol` module provides subroutines for creating and manipulating variable names with respect to packages without dealing with the package name directly, notably the `gensym` and `qualify` subroutines.

The `gensym` subroutine generates and returns a reference to a fully anonymous typeglob – that is, a typeglob that does not have an entry anywhere in any symbol table. We can use the anonymous typeglob as we like, for example as a filehandle (though `IO::Handle` does this better in these more enlightened days, and, as a point of fact, uses `gensym` underneath). It takes no arguments and just returns the reference:

```
use Symbol;

my $globref = gensym;
open ($globref, $filename);
...
```

More useful is the `qualify` subroutine, which provides a quick and convenient way to generate fully qualified names (and therefore symbolic references) for variables from unqualified ones. It operates on strings only, and with one argument generates a name in the current package. For example:

```
#!/usr/bin/perl
# symbol1.pl
use warnings;

use Symbol;

my $fqname = qualify('scalar');
$$fqname = "Hello World\n";
print $scalar;    # produces 'Hello World'
```

Since this is a simple script without a package declaration, the variable created here is actually called `$main::scalar`. If we supply a package name as a second argument to `qualify`, it places the variable into that package instead.

```
#!/usr/bin/perl
# symbol2.pl
use warnings;

use Symbol;

my $fqname = qualify('scalar','My::Module');
$$fqname = "Hello World\n";
print $My::Module::scalar;
```

In both cases, qualify will only modify the name of the variable passed to it if it is not already qualified. It will correctly qualify special variables and the standard filehandles like STDIN into the main package, since these variables always exist in main, wherever they are used. This makes it a safer and simpler way than trying to make sure our symbolic references are correct and in order when we are assembling them from strings.

Unfortunately qualify is not very useful if we have strict references enabled via use strict, since these are symbolic references. Instead, we can use qualify_to_ref, which takes a symbolic name and turns it into a reference for us, using the same rules as qualify to determine the package name:

```perl
#!/usr/bin/perl
# symbol3.pl
use warnings;
use strict;

use Symbol;

my $fqref = qualify_to_ref('scalar','My::Module');
$$fqref =\"Hello World\n";
print $My::Module::scalar;
```

All three of these examples work but produce a warning from Perl that the variable main::scalar (or My::Module::scalar) is only used once, which is true. Perl doesn't see that we defined the variable name through a reference, so it (correctly) points out that we appear to have used a variable we haven't defined. The correct thing to do would be to declare the variable so we can use it without complaint, as this modified example, complete with embedded package, illustrates:

```perl
#!/usr/bin/perl
# symbol4.pl
use warnings;
use strict;

use Symbol;

my $fqref = qualify_to_ref('scalar','My::Module');
$$fqref =\"Hello World\n";
print My::Module::get_scalar();

package My::Module;

our $scalar;   # provide access to scalar defined above

sub get_scalar {
   return $scalar;
}
```

Removing a Package

It is very rare that we would want to remove a package during the course of a program's execution, but if we want to we can by removing all traces of the package's namespace from the symbol table hierarchy. For example, to delete the My::Module package we could write:

```perl
my $table = *{'My::Module::'}{'HASH'};
undef %$table;
my $parent = *{'My::'}{'HASH'};
my $success = delete $parent->{'Module::'};
```

This is more than a little hairy, but basically boils down to deleting the entries of the symbol table for `My::Module` and removing the `Module` namespace entry from the `My` namespace. We delete the hash explicitly because we store the result of the `delete` in a variable, and thus the symbol table too. This is because Perl cannot reuse the memory allocated by it, or the references contained in it, while something still holds a reference to it. Deleting the actual table means that `delete` returns an empty hash on success, which is still good for a Boolean test but avoids trailing a complete and unrecycled symbol table along with it.

Fortunately the `Symbol` module provides a `delete_package` function that does much the same thing but hides the gory details. It also allows us more freedom as to how we specify the package name (we don't need the trailing colons, for instance, and it works on any package). To use it we need to import it specifically, since it is not imported by default:

```
use Symbol qw(delete_package);

...

print "Deleted!\n" if delete_package('My::Module');
```

The return value from `delete_package` is undefined if the delete failed, or a reference is made to the (now empty) namespace.

If we wanted to create a package that we could remove programmatically, we could do so by combining `delete_package` with an `unimport` subroutine; see 'Importing and Exporting' later in the chapter for an example.

Forbidding Package Variables

It is often good programming practice to make variables lexical rather than package variables wherever possible. This is because the more restrictive scope of variables makes them harder to misuse. The `use strict` pragma enforces the use of `my`, `our`, or `use vars` for unqualified variable names so we must be explicit about what kind of variable we are defining.

However, if we want to prevent the use of unqualified package symbols at all, we can do so by using a `package` declaration with no namespace:

```
package;   # no package here
```

The effect of this statement is to forbid the use of any package symbol that is not fully qualified, since there is no local package name to prefix to unqualified names. This affects not only regular variables but filehandles and subroutines as well, so we have to refer to `STDIN` as `main::STDIN`, for example.

Finding a Package Name Programmatically

It can be occasionally useful for a subroutine to know the name of the package in which it is defined. Since this is a compile time issue (remembering that package declarations are lexical even though they affect run time scope) we can simply copy the package name from the top of the module (or whichever package declaration the subroutine falls under if we have more than one).

However, this is prone to failure if we happen to change the name of the package at any point. This is a more serious problem than it might at first appear because it will not necessarily lead to a syntax error. For instance, if we are declaring a variable or subroutine in a lower package this operation will still succeed, since we are simply declaring something in a different package, but the package name will no longer reflect the name of the parent package.

To avoid this kind of problem we should avoid ever naming the package explicitly except in the package declaration itself. Within the code, we can instead use the special bareword token __PACKAGE__ thus:

```
sub self_aware_sub {
    print "I am in the ",__PACKAGE__," package.\n";
}
```

As a more expressive but less functional example, the following series of package declarations shows how the value produced by __PACKAGE__ changes if more than one package is present in a given file:

```
package My::Module;
print __PACKAGE__,"\n";
package My::Module::Heavy;
print __PACKAGE__,"\n";
package My::Module::Light;
print __PACKAGE__,"\n";
package A::Completely::Different::Package;
print __PACKAGE__,"\n";
```

When Perl loads and compiles a file containing this token the interpreter first scans and substitutes the real package name for any instances of __PACKAGE__ it finds, before proceeding to the compilation stage. This avoids any potential breakages if the package name should change.

Autoloading

Normally when we try to call a non-existent subroutine (or method, since in Perl they are the same thing) Perl generates a syntax error, if possible at compile time. However, by defining an autoload subroutine, we can intercept non-existent calls and deal with them in our own way at run time, if we wish.

Autoloading is a very powerful aspect of Perl, and conversely one that is also prone to abuse. However, when used wisely it provides us with some very handy techniques, such as the ability to write one subroutine to handle many different cases and masquerade it as many subroutines that handle a specific case. We can also, with deft usage of the eval and sub keywords, generate subroutines on the fly, as they are needed. This is a great technique for allowing a module to be powerful and flexible but at the same time minimizing the amount of memory that it takes up with code.

Perl provides several modules in the standard library that take advantage of autoloading to make library modules more memory-efficient by delaying the compilation of subroutines until the moment they are required. This allows modules to both take up less memory and also load much faster. The compromise is that calling a subroutine not yet compiled will incur a speed penalty at that point, as well as sidestepping the compile time syntax check, so errors will not be caught until it is called. The AutoSplit module carves up a module file into separate subroutines, which the AutoLoader module can read and compile at the moment each routine is required; it is typically used during the installation of installable packages, but we can use it independently if we wish to. The SelfLoader module provides a similar solution, but allows us to store code as text inside the module file, compiling it at the time it is needed; this is simpler for code that we don't want to install before we can use it.

Autoloading Subroutines

To use autoloading we only need to define a subroutine called AUTOLOAD. This will automatically intercept all calls to non-existent subroutines in the package in which it is defined, receiving the same arguments as the original (non-existent) subroutine would have. The name of the subroutine that was not found is placed by Perl in the special variable Packagename::$AUTOLOAD. Here's a short example that intercepts non-existent calls and prints out their names and arguments:

```perl
#!/usr/bin/perl
# autoload.pl
use warnings;
use strict;

sub AUTOLOAD {
    our $AUTOLOAD;    # "use vars '$AUTOLOAD'" for Perl < 5.6
    $" = ',';
    print "You called '$AUTOLOAD(@_)'\n";
}

fee('fie','foe','fum');
testing(1,2,3);
```

When run, this script should produce:

You called 'main::fee(fie,foe,fum)'
You called 'main::testing(1,2,3)'

We use our to get a version of the $AUTOLOAD variable (Perl prior to version 5.6 needs to use use vars instead) that doesn't involve a package prefix. Since only the AUTOLOAD subroutine needs to know the value of $AUTOLOAD, we place the our declaration inside the subroutine to define a temporary alias.

Using an AUTOLOAD subroutine has one significant disadvantage – it thwarts Perl's ability to check for legal subroutine calls at compile time. Since an AUTOLOAD subroutine accepts any otherwise invalid subroutine call at run time, it is not possible for Perl to tell the difference between a call intended for the autoloader, and a misnamed though perfectly ordinary subroutine call. Defining a prototype for the autoloader can help if the calls it is intended to intercept have a similar calling convention, but this is only a partial solution.

We can use AUTOLOAD subroutines in a variety of ways that break down into one of two general approaches: use the AUTOLOAD subroutine as a substitute for a collection of subroutines, or use the AUTOLOAD subroutine to define missing subroutines on the fly.

Using an 'AUTOLOAD' Subroutine as a Substitute

The first and simplest use of the autoloader is simply to stand in for another subroutine or collection of similar subroutines. We can define the interface to a module in terms of these other calls, but actually implement them in the AUTOLOAD subroutine. The disadvantage of this is that it takes Perl slightly longer to carry out the redirection to the autoloader subroutine (although conversely the compile time is also slower, possibly relevant if the code forms part of a command line tool or utility script). The advantage is that we can replace potentially hundreds of subroutine definitions with just one. Here is a simple example that performs just a few simple statistical calculations, but illustrates the technique:

```perl
#!/usr/bin/perl
# autostat.pl
use warnings;
use strict;

use Carp;

sub AUTOLOAD {
    our $AUTOLOAD;

    my $result;
    SWITCH: foreach ($AUTOLOAD) {
        /sum/ and do {
            $result = 0;
            map { $result+= $_ } @_;
            last;
        };
        /average/ and do {
            $result = 0;
            map { $result+= $_ } @_;
            $result/=scalar(@_);
            last;
        };
        /biggest/ and do {
            $result = shift;
            map { $result = ($_ > $result)?$_:$result } @_;
            last;
        };
        /smallest/ and do {
            $result = shift;
            map { $result = ($_ < $result)?$_:$result } @_;
            last;
        }
    }
    croak "Undefined subroutine $AUTOLOAD called" unless defined $result;
    return $result;
}

my @values = (1,4,9,16,25,36);

print "Sum: ",sum(@values),"\n";
print "Average: ",average(@values),"\n";
print "Biggest: ",biggest(@values),"\n";
print "Smallest: ",smallest(@values),"\n";
print "Oddest: ",oddest(@values),"\n";
```

This AUTOLOAD subroutine supports four different statistical operations and masquerades under four different names. If we call any of these names then the autoloader performs the requested calculation and returns the result. If we call any other name, it croaks and exits. We use croak from the Carp module because we want to return an error for the place from which the AUTOLOAD subroutine was called (since that is where the error really is).

This script also illustrates the problem with autoloading – errors in subroutine names are not caught until run time. With real subroutines, the call to oddest would be caught at compile time. With this script, it isn't caught until the autoloader is actually called and sees that it isn't a name that it recognizes.

The above example demonstrates the general principle of substituting for a collection of other subroutines, but it doesn't really provide any benefit; it would be as easy to define the subroutines individually, since each one requires its own special case anyway. However, we can be more creative with how we name subroutines. For example, we can use an autoloader to recognize and support the prefix print_ for each operation. Here is a modified version of the previous example that handles both the original four operations and four new variants that print out the result as well:

```perl
#!/usr/bin/perl
# printstat.pl
use warnings;
use strict;

use Carp;

sub AUTOLOAD {
    our $AUTOLOAD;

    my $subname;
    $AUTOLOAD =~/([^:]+)$/ and $subname = $1;

    my $print;
    $subname =~s/^print_// and $print = 1;

    my $result;
    SWITCH: foreach ($subname) {
        /^sum$/ and do {
            $result = 0;
            map { $result+= $_ } @_;
            last;
        };
        /^average$/ and do {
            $result = 0;
            map { $result+= $_ } @_;
            $result/= scalar(@_);
            last;
        };
        /^biggest$/ and do {
            $result = shift;
            map { $result = ($_>$result)?$_:$result } @_;
            last;
        };
        /^smallest$/ and do {
            $result = shift;
            map { $result = ($_<$result)?$_:$result } @_;
            last;
        }
    }
    croak "Undefined subroutine $subname called" unless defined $result;
    print ucfirst($subname),": $result\n" if $print;
    return $result;
}

my @values = (1,4,9,16,25,36);

print_sum(@values);
print_average(@values);
print_biggest(@values);
print_smallest(@values);
```

The subroutine name actually passed in the $AUTOLOAD variable contains the package prefix, main::
as well. In the previous example we didn't check from the start of the name, so it did not matter. In this
case we strip it off so that we can in turn detect and remove the print_ prefix. We take advantage of
the fact that we are left with just the subroutine name to anchor them at the start and end for a little
extra efficiency – the first example worked only because we didn't use anchors and none of our
subroutine names contained another. If we wanted to be even more inventive we could remove the
trailing $ anchors and use the suffix of the subroutine name to further adapt each function if we chose.

Defining Subroutines On the Fly

Using an autoload subroutine as a substitute for defining real subroutines can have significant
advantages in terms of reducing code size – the example above replaces eight definitions with just one,
and the benefits increase the more permutations we add. However, implementing functionality via the
autoloader also incurs a performance loss. Perl must check for the original definition, find that it is not
there, check for the autoloader, find that it is there, preset the $AUTOLOAD variable and finally call the
autoloader. If the function being implemented is complex and time consuming this is not a problem, but
for simple operations we expect to call often we can sometimes do better by actually defining a new
subroutine so that future calls are passed to it and not the autoloader.

As an example of this approach, here is a simple autoloader that defines subroutines to return HTML
syntax, much in the way that the CGI module can if asked nicely enough. It isn't nearly as feature-rich
as that module, but it serves for demonstration purposes (and is a lot smaller too):

```perl
#!/usr/bin/perl
# autofly.pl
use warnings;
use strict;

sub AUTOLOAD {
    our $AUTOLOAD;

    my $tag;
    $AUTOLOAD =~ /([^:]+)$/ and $tag = $1;

    SWITCH: foreach ($tag) {
        /^start_(.*)/ and do {
            eval "sub $tag { return \"<$1>\@_\" }";
            last;
        };
        /^end_(.*)/ and do {
            eval "sub $tag { return \"</$1>\" }";
            last;
        };
        eval "sub $tag { return \"<$tag>\@_</$tag>\" }";
    }
    no strict 'refs';
    &$tag;
}

# generate a quick HTML document
print html(
    head(title('Autoloading Demo')),
    body(ul(
        start_li('First'),
        start_li('Second'),
        start_li('Third'),
    ))
);
```

This autoloader supports automatic tag completion, as well as generating the start and end of tags if start_ or end_ is prefixed to the subroutine name. It works by defining a subroutine to generate the new tag, then calling it. The first time start_li is called, the autoloader generates a new subroutine called start_li, then calls it. The second time start_li is called the subroutine already exists, so Perl calls it directly and the autoloader is not involved.

A little deftness with interpolation is required for the subroutines to be defined correctly. We want the tag name itself interpolated, both as the subroutine name and inside the returned string, but we want interpolation of the passed arguments delayed until the subroutine is actually called. To achieve that we put double quotes around the returned string but escape both them and @_ so that they are not interpreted when the subroutine is defined – instead they become active when it is actually called.

Self-Defining Instead of Autoloading Subroutines

A variation on the theme of delaying the definition of subroutines and methods when they are first called, is to retrieve their definition from somewhere else and compile it when they are first called. For instance, we may have a large and complex module with many features, of which we may only actually use some. In order to avoid compiling all the subroutines redundantly, we can put aside compiling them until they are called. If they are never called, we never need to define them.

The essence of this approach is to define a subroutine as a stub only. This doesn't contain much code, so it is quick to compile and does not occupy much memory. When the stub is actually called, it defines and replaces itself with the real subroutine. Here is a short program that shows one way to do this:

```perl
#!/usr/bin/perl
# autodefine.pl
use warnings;
use strict;

sub my_subroutine {
    print "Defining sub...\n";

    # uncomment next line and remove 'no warnings' for Perl < 5.6
    # local $^W = 0;
    eval 'no warnings; sub my_subroutine { print "Autodefined!\n"; }';

    &my_subroutine;
}

my_subroutine;
my_subroutine;
```

Running this program produces:

Defining sub...
Autodefined!
Autodefined!

A variant of this approach would be to store all the subroutine definitions in a different file, or after a __DATA__ token, and read the subroutine code from there. Alternatively, we can create a typeglob alias to an evaluated anonymous subroutine, with equal effect to the above:

```perl
#!/usr/bin/perl
# globdefine.pl
use warnings;
use strict;

sub my_subroutine {
    print "Defining sub...\n";
    no warnings;
    # remove above and add the following for Perl < 5.6
    # local $^W = 0;

    *my_subroutine = eval {
        sub {
            print "Autodefined!\n";
        }
    };

    &my_subroutine;
}

my_subroutine;
my_subroutine;
```

In both cases we suppress the redefinition warning by switching off warnings locally with no warnings, or by locally clearing $^W. In this case we know we want to redefine the subroutine, so we don't need Perl telling us about it.

The drawback of this approach compared to defining an AUTOLOAD subroutine is that we need to define a stub for each subroutine we want to delay the compilation of. The advantage is that because a stub is present we don't lose the ability to syntax-check subroutine names at compile time. This is particularly useful if we are also providing prototypes for our subroutines since they clearly cannot be checked at compile time if they are only created at run time. Note however that the contents of the subroutines are only checked at run time; an unavoidable compromise if we wish to avoid parsing them until we use them.

Autoloading Modules

The Perl standard library provides two modules that implement the strategy of delayed loading of subroutines in two different ways. The more complex one is the AutoLoader module, which loads in additional files containing subroutine definitions generated previously by the AutoSplit module using an AUTOLOAD subroutine. This implies that the module is split into separate pieces prior to being used, that is, at installation time.

The SelfLoader module operates along broadly similar lines, but keeps all the subroutines to be loaded later inside the source file. The advantage of this is that we do not need to remember to use the AutoSplit module, so it will always work and does not require that the module be reprocessed each time it changes. Conversely, however, we must load all the source code into memory in an uncompiled form so that it can be compiled on demand.

Before we discuss these two approaches in more detail it is worth mentioning another approach – the autouse pragma. While not as powerful as either of the two approaches mentioned here it has the advantage of being considerably simpler to use. Rather than being used within the module to be handled, it modifies the use statement of the code that uses the module – see Chapter 9 for details on this matter.

Using the 'AutoLoader' Module

The `AutoLoader` module allows us to split out individual subroutines into separate files and then load them on demand. It works in conjunction with the `AutoSplit` module, which parses a module source file to generate the separate files, each containing one individual subroutine. It is not terribly convenient during development because the process of splitting the module must be repeated each time the source is changed, but when it comes to creating installable packages (which we cover later in the chapter) it is highly effective. Indeed, the build files generated by the `h2xs` utility, which we will encounter later in this chapter and in Chapter 21, automatically invokes the `AutoSplit` module for us, so that this step is taken care of when we create our own installable packages.

In order to use the `AutoLoader` module, we place the subroutines we want to delay the loading of after an __END__ token. To put it another way, we put an __END__ token somewhere in the module source between the subroutines we always want compiled and the subroutines we want to load later, conditionally. This may require a little reorganization of the source, of course.

We then add a `use` statement to include the `AutoLoader` module and import its `AUTOLOAD` subroutine, which does the work of retrieving the subroutines that were split out. Note that importing the subroutine is important – the `AutoLoader` will not work without it:

```
use AutoLoader qw(AUTOLOAD);
```

The __END__ token causes the Perl interpreter to stop reading the file at this point, so it never sees the subroutines placed after it. To make them available again, we use the `AutoSplit` module to carve out the subroutines after the __END__ token into separate files placed in an `auto` directory relative to the module file. This often takes place in installation scripts and typically takes the form of a one line Perl program. For example, to autosplit a module from the directory in which it is placed:

> **perl -MAutoSplit -e 'autosplit "My/AutoModule.pm","./auto"'**

Again there are slight modifications required for the Windows version of this one line program:

> **perl -MAutoSplit -e "autosplit\"My/AutoModule.pm\",\"./auto\""**

This takes a module called `My::AutoModule` contained in a file called `AutoModule.pm` in a directory called `My` in the current directory and splits it into parts inside an `auto` directory (which is created at the time if it doesn't exist). Inside are the directories `My/AutoModule`, inside which we find an index file `autosplit.ix` and one file for each subroutine split out of the module, named for the subroutine followed by `.al` (for autoload).

As an example of how the AutoLoader is used, take this simple module file that implements a package called `My::AutoModule`:

```
# My/AutoModule.pm

package My::AutoModule;

use strict;
use Exporter;
use AutoLoader qw(AUTOLOAD);

our @ISA = qw(Exporter);
our @EXPORT = qw(zero one two three);
```

```
sub one {
   print "This is always compiled\n";
}

__END__

sub two {
   print "This is sub two\n";
}

sub three {
   print "This is sub three\n";
}

1;
```

The file, which in this case is named AutoModule.pm, and contained in a directory called My, to match the package name, has three subroutines. The first, one, is a regular subroutine – it is always compiled. The other two, two and three, are actually just text at the end of the file – the __END__ ensures that Perl never sees them, and never even reads them in. Note that the only changes from a normal module are the use AutoLoader line and the __END__ token. The trailing 1 is not actually needed any longer, but we retain it in case we ever convert the module back into an unsplit one.

However, when we run autosplit over the file, it creates three files autosplit.ix, two.al, and three.al, all in the auto/My/AutoModule directory. Since we specified . as the installation directory, this new directory is immediately adjacent to the original AutoModule.pm file. If we had wanted to split a module that was installed into the Perl standard library tree we would have used a different path here, according to the position of the file we wanted to split.

The autosplit.ix file contains the essential information about the subroutines that have been split out:

```
# Index created by AutoSplit for My/AutoModule.pm
#    (file acts as timestamp)
package My::AutoModule;
sub two  ;
sub three  ;
1;
```

Close inspection of this file reveals that it is in fact a snippet of Perl code that pre-declares two subroutines, the two that were split out, in the package My::AutoModule. When the module is used in an application, the line use AutoLoader causes the AutoLoader module to be read in and initialized for that module. This has the effect of loading this index file, and thus declaring the subroutines.

The point of this file may seem obscure, since the AUTOLOAD subroutine will seek the split out files regardless, but it carries out the important function of allowing us to declare prototypes for subroutines and have them active within the application even before the subroutine is called – without this the prototype would not be seen until the subroutine is called, which is clearly far too late. It also allows us to call subroutines without parentheses, in the list operator style, as we discussed in Chapter 9. Here is a short test script that calls the subroutines defined by this module:

```
#!/usr/bin/perl
# automoduletest.pl
use warnings;
use strict;
```

```
use lib '.';
use My::AutoModule;

one;
two;
three;
```

The .al files contain the subroutines that were split out – here is one of them, for illustrative purposes. Note that due to varying locations, slightly different scripts used, and so on we may have small variations in the actual contents of the .al files obtained. This provides a rough idea of what can be expected:

```
# NOTE: Derived from My/AutoModule.pm.
# Changes made here will be lost when autosplit again.
# See AutoSplit.pm.
package My::AutoModule;

#line 18 "My/AutoModule.pm (autosplit into ./auto/My/AutoModule/two.al)"
sub two {
    print "This is sub two\n";
}

# end of My::AutoModule::two
1;
```

The AutoSplit module is smart enough to check that the AutoLoader module is actually used by a file before it attempts to split it. We can disable this check (if we insist) as well as determine whether old subroutine .al files are removed if they no longer exist and check to see if the module has actually changed before splitting it again (this is the reason for the (file acts as timestamp) comment in the autosplit.ix file). This is achieved by adding one or more of three optional Boolean arguments to the autosplit subroutine:

> **perl -MAutoSplit -e 'autosplit "My/AutoModule.pm","./auto", $keep, $check, $changed'**

Or for Windows it is:

> **perl -MAutoSplit -e "autosplit\"My/AutoModule.pm\",\"./auto\", $keep, $check, $changed"**

If any of these Boolean arguments is True then the following actions occur:

- ❏ keep – deletes any .al files for subroutines that no longer exist in the module (ones that do still exist are overwritten anyway). The default is 0, so .al files are automatically preserved.

- ❏ check – causes the autosplit subroutine to verify that the file it is about to split actually contains a use AutoLoader directive before proceeding. The default is 1.

- ❏ changed – suppresses the split if the timestamp of the original file is not newer than the timestamp of the autosplit.ix file in the directory into which the split files are going to be placed. The default is 1.

For example, the explicit version of the two-argument call above would be:

> **perl -MAutoSplit -e 'autosplit "My/AutoModule.pm","./auto", 0, 1, 1'**

Again the equivalent for Windows is:

> **perl -MAutoSplit -e "autosplit\"My/AutoModule.pm\",\"./auto\", 0, 1, 1"**

Be aware that lexical variables declared globally (that is, declared with my in the file but outside a subroutine) are not visible to autoloaded subroutines because they are stored in separate files and therefore do not have the same lexical scope. However, variables declared with our (or use vars) are fine.

We are not obliged to use the AutoLoader's AUTOLOAD subroutine directly, but we need to use it if we want to load in split files. If we already have an AUTOLOAD subroutine and we want to use AutoLoader too, we must not import the AUTOLOADER subroutine from AutoLoader but instead call it from our own AUTOLOAD subroutine:

```
use AutoLoader;

sub AUTOLOAD {
... handle our own special cases ...

    # pass up to AutoLoader
    $AutoLoader::AUTOLOAD = $AUTOLOAD;
    goto &AutoLoader::AUTOLOAD;
}
```

Note the goto – this is needed so that the call stack reflects the correct package names in the right place, or more specifically, doesn't include our own AUTOLOAD subroutine in the stack which will otherwise confuse the AutoLoader's AUTOLOAD subroutine. Of course if we have our own AUTOLOAD subroutine we might not need the AutoLoader at all – multiple autoloading strategies in the same module or application is probably getting a little over-complex.

Using the 'SelfLoader' Module

The SelfLoader module is very similar in use to the AutoLoader module, but avoids the need to split the module into files as a separate step. To use it, we use the SelfLoader module and place the subroutines we want to delay the loading of after a __DATA__ token. Here is a module called My::SelfModule that is modified from the My::AutoModule module given earlier to use SelfLoader instead:

```
# My/SelfModule.pm

package My::SelfModule;

use strict;
use Exporter;
use SelfLoader;

our @ISA = qw(Exporter);
our @EXPORT = qw(zero one two three);

sub one {
    print "This is always compiled\n";
}

__DATA__

sub two {
    print "This is sub two\n";
}
sub three {
    print "This is sub three\n";
}

1;
```

This module is identical to the `AutoLoader` version except for the two alterations. We replace `use AutoLoader qw(AUTOLOAD)` with `use SelfLoader` and `__END__` with `__DATA__`. If we also want to place actual data in the module file we can do so as long as we make sure to read it before loading the `SelfLoader` module, i.e. in a `BEGIN` block prior to the `use SelfStubber` statement.

The `SelfLoader` module exports its `AUTOLOAD` subroutine by default however, so if we want to define our own and call `SelfLoader` from it, we need to specify an explicit empty list:

```
use SelfLoader ();

sub AUTOLOAD {
    # ... handle cases to be processed here

    # pass up to SelfLoader
    $SelfLoader::AUTOLOAD = $AUTOLOAD;
    goto &SelfLoader::AUTOLOAD;
}
```

To test this module we can use a script similar to the one we used for `My::AutoModule`, except that we need to use `My::SelfModule` instead. We also need to add parentheses to the subroutine calls because `SelfLoader` does not provide declarations (as we discover if we try to run it). To solve this problem we can make use of the `Devel::SelfStubber` module to generate the declaration stubs we need to add:

> **perl -MDevel::SelfStubber -e 'Devel::SelfStubber->stub("My::SelfModule",".")'**

As ever here is the Windows version for your use and abuse:

> **perl -MDevel::SelfStubber -e "Devel::SelfStubber->stub (\"My::SelfModule\",\".\")"**

This generates the following declarations for our example module, which we can add to the module to solve the problem:

sub My::SelfModule::two ;
sub My::SelfModule::three ;

We can also regenerate the entire module, stubs included, if we first set the variable `$Devel::SelfStubber::JUST_STUBS = 0`. This gets a little unwieldy for a command line, but is possible:

> **perl -MDevel::SelfStubber -e '$Devel::SelfStubber::JUST_STUBS = 0; Devel::SelfStubber->stub("My::SelfModule",".")' > My/SelfModule-stubbed.pm**

For Windows it is:

> **perl -MDevel::SelfStubber -e "$Devel::SelfStubber::JUST_STUBS = 0; Devel::SelfStubber->stub (\"My::SelfModule\",\".\")" > My/SelfModule-stubbed.pm**

This generates a new module, `SelfModule-stubbed.pm`, which we have named differently just for safety; it is still `My::SelfModule` inside. If all looks well, we can move or copy `SelfModule-stubbed.pm` over `Selfmodule.pm`. Note that running this command more than once can generate extra sets of stubs, which may cause problems, or at least confusion, and may even end up with an empty file if we forget to put the `__DATA__` token in. For this reason it is not advisable to attempt to replace a file with a stubbed version in one step.

Importing and Exporting

We have already looked at how to import symbols from one package into our own using the `use` and `require` statements. In this section we look at importing and exporting from the other side of the fence – from the perspective of the module.

The term 'importing' is used for the process of taking symbols from another package and adding them to our own. From the perspective of the module being imported from, it is 'exporting', of course. Either way, the process consists of taking a symbol visible in the namespace of one package and making it visible, without qualification, in another. For instance, even if we can see it we would rather not refer to a variable called:

```
$My::Package::With::A::Long::Name::scalar
```

It would be much better if we could refer to this variable simply as `$scalar` in our own code. From Chapter 5, we know that we can do this explicitly using typeglobs to create aliases, since that is one of the things we can do with them:

```
my *scalar =\$My::Package::With::A::Long::Name::scalar;
```

Likewise, to create an alias for a subroutine:

```
my *localsub =\&My::Package::With::A::Long::Name::packagesub;
```

This is a simple case of symbol table manipulation, and isn't all that tricky once we understand it. However, it is clumsy, since we have to create an alias for every variable or subroutine we want to use without the prefix. It is also prone to problems in later life, since we are defining the interface between this package and our own code in our own code, and not in the package. This is very bad – if the package is updated, there is a high chance our code will break.

Good programming practice suggests that all packages should have a well-defined interface and that all code that uses it should use that interface. The package, not the user of the package, should dictate what the interface is. Therefore, we need a way to ask the package to create appropriate aliases for us; this is the import mechanism that the `use` and `no` statements (but not `require`) do automatically.

If our requirements for importing subroutines and variables from our module into other packages are simple, we can for the most part ignore the technicalities of Perl's import mechanism, and use the `Exporter` module to define our interface. For the majority of packages, the `Exporter` can handle all the necessary details. If we just want to export a few subroutines, we can skip part of the next section of this chapter and head straight to the section titled 'The Exporter Module'. However, the import mechanism isn't actually all that hard to understand (because it isn't all that complex) and a basic understanding of it can help with implementing more complex modules with more involved export requirements. It is also applicable to simpler import mechanisms that, rather than actually exporting symbols, allow us to configure a package using the import list as initialization data. This is a perfectly legal use for the list supplied to `use` or `require`, as well as being a very useful one.

The 'import' Mechanism

Perl's mechanism for importing symbols is simple, elegant, and shockingly ad hoc, all at the same time. In a nutshell, we call a subroutine called `import` in the package that we want to import symbols from.

The import stage is a secondary stage beyond actually reading and compiling a module file, so it is not handled by the require directive; instead, it is a separate explicit step:

```
require My::Module;    # load in the module
My::Module->import;    # call the 'import' subroutine
```

Perl allows us to invert the package and subroutine names (a syntax trick mostly aimed at object-oriented programming), so we can also say:

```
import My::Module;
```

This fools many programmers into thinking that import is actually a Perl keyword, since it looks exactly like require, but in fact it is only a subroutine. This becomes clearer when it becomes apparent that we can pass import a list of arguments describing the symbols we want to import. For example, a typical import statement looks like this:

```
import My::Module qw(subone subtwo $scalar);
```

This appears to be a core Perl feature for importing symbols, but in fact all it does is call the subroutine import in the package My::Module and pass the arguments subone, subtwo, and $scalar to it.

The name of the import subroutine is not entirely a matter of convention. The use directive binds up a require and a call to import inside a BEGIN block. Then use My::Module is therefore (almost) equivalent to:

```
BEGIN {
    require My::Module;
    import My::Module;
}
```

Note that the import has no parentheses; any arguments passed to use therefore get automatically passed through to the import subroutine as the @_ array, without being copied, as covered in Chapter 9. If there is no import subroutine, however, use will not complain; a more correct import statement would be:

```
import My::Module if My::Module->can('import');
# 'can' is a universal method (see Chapter 19)
```

Similarly, the no directive calls a function called unimport. The sense of no is to be the opposite of use, but this is a matter purely of convention and implementation, since the unimport subroutine is just another subroutine. In this case though, Perl will issue an error message if there is no unimport method defined by the module. The no My::Module code is (roughly, with the same proviso as above) equivalent to:

```
BEGIN {
    require My::Module;
    unimport My::Module;
}
```

It may seem strange that no incorporates a require within it, but there is no actual requirement that we use a module before we no parts of it. Having said that, the module may not work correctly if the import subroutine is not called initially. If use has already pulled in the module, the require inside no will see that the module is already in %INC, and so won't load it again. This means that in most cases no is just a way of calling unimport in the module package at compile time.

In the same way that aliasing can be done with typeglobs, removing aliases can be done by editing an entry out of the symbol table. Here is an example that does just that, using the delete_package subroutine of the Symbol module that we introduced previously:

```
# Uninstallable.pm

package Uninstallable;

use Symbol qw(delete_package);

$message = "I'm here\n";

sub unimport {
    delete_package(__PACKAGE__);
}

1;
```

This module, which for the purposes of testing we shall call Uninstallable.pm, defines one variable simply so we can prove whether or not it is present by testing it, as this short test script does:

```
#!/usr/bin/perl
# uninstall.pl
use strict;

print "Now you see me: ";
use Uninstallable;
print $Uninstallable::message;

print "Now you don't!\n";
no Uninstallable;
print $Uninstallable::message;
```

As interesting as this is, it is rare (though not impossible) that we would actually want to delete a package programmatically. Where they are implemented, most unimport subroutines simply clear flags that an import sets. Many of Perl's pragmatic modules like strict and warnings work this way, for example, and are actually very small modules in themselves.

The use and no directives incorporate one extra trick: If we pass them an explicit empty parameter list, they don't call the import function at all. This means that we can suppress a module's default import if we only want to use some of its features. Take the CGI module as an example:

```
use CGI;    # parse environment, set up variables
use CGI qw(:standard);   # import a specific set of features
use CGI ();    # just load CGI, don't parse anything.
```

Suppressing the default `import` by passing an empty list is more useful than it might seem. The CGI module in the above examples does rather a lot more than simply importing a few symbols by default; it examines the environment and generates a default CGI object for functional programming, as well as automatically generating a number of methods. If we just want to use the CGI module's HTML generation features, we don't need all that, so we can stop the module initializing itself by explicitly passing nothing to it.

Exporting

Having examined the import mechanism from the side of the importer, we can take a look at how modules handle import requests. From the module's perspective of course, this is exporting. As we mentioned earlier, most modules make use of the Exporter module covered a little later in the chapter to do the work for them, but we are not compelled to. Here is a simple exporting subroutine that illustrates how a module can implement a simple `import` subroutine:

```
# default import
sub import {
    my $caller = caller(1);    # get calling package
    *{"$caller\:\:mysub"} =\&mysub;
    *{"$caller\:\:scalar"} =\$scalar;
    *{"$caller\:\:hash"} =\%hash;
}
```

The principal technique is that we find the caller's package by inspecting the subroutine stack with `caller`. It so happens that when called in a scalar context, `caller` returns just the package name, so `caller(1)` returns the package of the caller – in other words, the place from which the use was issued. Once we know this, we simply use it to define typeglobs in the calling package filled with references to the variables we want to export.

This import subroutine doesn't pay any attention to the arguments passed to it (the first one of which is the package name). Here is a more versatile import subroutine that exports any subroutine requested, if it exists:

```
# export if defined
sub import {
    my $caller = caller(1);    # get calling package
    my $package = shift;   # remove package from arguments
    no strict refs;   # we need symbolic references for this

    foreach (@_) {
        if (defined &{"$package\:\:$_"}) {
            *{"$caller\:\:$_"} =\&{"$package\:\:$_"}
        } else {
            die "Unable to export $_ from $package\n";
        }
    }
}
```

The use of the variable `$package` here is strictly optional, since in this example the package passed in is the package we are in anyway – we could as easily have said `\&{$_}` to generate the reference. However, it is good practice to use the package name if there is any possibility that we might be inherited from by another package – by using the passed package name, our `import` will also serve for any packages that inherit from it (via @ISA). This is exactly how the Exporter module works, and we'll cover it in more detail shortly.

The above example only works for subroutines, so it only constructs subroutine references. A more versatile version would examine (and remove if appropriate) the first character of the symbol and construct a scalar, array, hash, code, or typeglob reference accordingly. Here is an example that does that, though we have removed the check for whether the symbol actually exists for brevity:

```perl
# export arbitrary
sub import {
    my $caller = caller(1);    # get calling package
    my $package = shift;    # remove package from arguments
    no strict refs;    # we need symbolic references for this

    foreach (@_) {
        my $prefix;
        s/^([&%$@*])// and $prefix = $1;

        $prefix eq '$' and *{"$caller\:\:$_"} =\${"$package\:\:$_"}, last;
        $prefix eq '%' and *{"$caller\:\:$_"} =\%{"$package\:\:$_"}, last;
        $prefix eq '@' and *{"$caller\:\:$_"} =\@{"$package\:\:$_"}, last;
        $prefix eq '*' and *{"$caller\:\:$_"} =*{"$package\:\:$_"}, last;
        *{"$caller\:\:$_"} =\&{"$package\:\:$_"}, last;
    }
}
```

It is up to the import subroutine whether or not to carry out additional default imports when an explicit list is passed. In general the answer is no but it is usual to define a special symbol like :DEFAULT that imports all the default symbols explicitly. This allows the module user maximum flexibility in what to allow into their namespace:

```perl
sub import {
    my $package = shift;

    # if an empty import list, use defaults
    return _default_import() unless @_;

    foreach (@_) {
        /:DEFAULT/ and _default_import(), last;
        _export_if_present($package,$_);
    }
}

sub _default_import {
    # ... as above ...
}

sub _export_if_present {
    my ($package,$symbol) = @_;
    my $prefix;
    $symbol = s/^([&%$@*])// and $prefix = $1;

    if ($prefix and $prefix ne '&') {
        SWITCH: foreach ($prefix) {
            m'$' and do {
                if (defined ${"$package\:\:$_"}) {
                    *{"$caller\:\:$_"}=\${"$package\:\:$_"};
                    return;
                }
            };
```

```
              m'@' and do {
                  # ... ditto for arrays ...
              };
              m'%' and do {
                  # ... ditto for hashes ...
              };
              m'*' and do {
                  # ... ditto for typeglobs ...
              };
          }
      } elsif (defined &{"$package\:\:$_"}) {
          *{"$caller\:\:$_"}=\&{"$package\:\:$_"}
      } else {
          die "Unable to export $_ from $package\n";
      }
  }
}
```

As a final example, and an indication of what else we can do with import lists, here is an import subroutine that invents generators for HTML tags by defining a subroutine for any symbol passed to it that it doesn't recognize (The CGI module uses exactly this approach, though its HTML methods are a good deal more advanced):

```
sub import {
   my $package = shift;

   foreach (@_) {
       # for each passed symbol, generate a tag subroutine in the
       # caller's package.
       *{"$package\:\:$_"} = sub {
          "<$tag>\n".join("\n",@_)."</$tag>\n";
       };
   }
}
```

This is frequently a better way to handle automatic generation of subroutines than autoloading is, since it is more controlled and precise. Also we have to declare the subroutines we want to use at compile time (as use executes the import subroutine during this phase) where they can be subjected to syntax checking. With autoloading, we can only check at run time, and then only if we take extra steps to do so.

Setting Flags with Exports

Just because the use directive calls import in our package to import symbols, it does not mean that we actually have to import symbols of the same name, or even import symbols at all – we can use the import list to trigger any kind of behavior we like, for instance to enable or disable debugging, or to pass a list of initial keys and values to configure a package.

When to Export, When not to Export

Having shown how to export symbols, it is worth taking a moment to consider whether we should or not. The point of packages is to restrain the scope of variables by placing them into different namespaces; we can write application code in the main package free from worry about name clashes because modules place their variables and subroutines into their own packages. Importing symbols goes against this strategy, and uncontrolled importing of lots of symbols is always a bad idea, polluting the application code with unnecessary variables and subroutine definitions that consume memory at best and cause unexpected bugs at worst.

In general we should take time to consider:

❑   What should and should not be exported by default from a module (as little as possible)

❑   What should be allowed to be exported

❑   What should be denied export

Object-oriented modules should usually not export anything at all; the entire point of object orientation is to work through the objects themselves, not to bypass them by importing parts of the module class into our own code. Additionally, exporting symbols directly bypasses the inheritance mechanism, which makes code that uses the exported symbols hard to reuse and likely to break.

In summary, the export list of a module is far more than just a list of symbols that will/may be imported into another package; it is the functional interface to the module's features, and as such should be designed, not accreted. The Exporter module helps with this by allowing us to define lists of conditionally exported symbols.

The 'Exporter' Module

The Exporter module provides a generic import subroutine for modules to configure to their own particular tastes. It handles almost all the possible issues that a module needs to consider, and for many modules it is all they need – they do not actually need to define their own import subroutine.

Using the 'Exporter'

To use the Exporter, a module needs to do three things; use the Exporter, inherit from it, and define the symbols to export. Here is a very short module that demonstrates the basic technique, using fully qualified names for the package variables @ISA and @EXPORT:

```
# My/Module.pm

package My::Module;

use strict;

# use Exporter
use Exporter;

# inherit from it
@My::Module::ISA = qw(Exporter);

# define export symbols
@My::Module::EXPORT = qw(greet_planet);

sub greet_planet {
    return "Hello World\n";
}
```

The @ISA array is the basis of Perl's object inheritance mechanism – it tells the interpreter that we are a subclass of the Exporter class, and to refer to it for any methods we don't support. The only ones of importance here are the import and unimport methods, of course. We don't need to worry too much about the object-oriented nature of inheriting from Exporter, unless we want to define our own import subroutine and still use the Exporter, which we come on to later in the chapter. Otherwise, we can ignore the object nature of the Exporter and leave the subject of object-oriented programming to Chapter 19, where we cover it in full.

The @EXPORT array defines the actual symbols we want to export; when import is called on our module it passes that call up to the Exporter module, which provides its own generic import method. It in turn examines the definition of @EXPORT in our module, @My::Module::EXPORT and satisfies or denies the requested import list accordingly.

For completeness, here's a short script that uses the above module, assuming it is in a file named Module.pm in a directory called My in the same directory as the script:

```perl
#!/usr/bin/perl
# import.pl
use warnings;
use strict;

use lib '.';

use My::Module;

print greet_planet;
```

Importing from the 'Exporter'

One advantage of the Exporter module is that the import method it provides is well developed and handles many different situations for us. Even if we decide to provide our own import subroutine we may want to use Exporter too, just for the richness of the features it provides (and if we don't we probably ought to document it). For example, it accepts regular expressions as well as literal symbol names, which means that we can define a collection of symbols with similar prefixes and then allow them to be imported together rather than individually. Here is how we can import a collection of symbols all starting with prefix_ from a module that uses the Exporter module:

```perl
use My::Module qw(/^prefix_/);
```

The Exporter also understands negations, so we can import all symbols that do not match a given name or regular expression:

```perl
# import everything except the subroutine 'greet_planet'
use My::Module qw(!greet_planet);

# import anything not beginning with 'prefix_'
use My::Module qw(!/^prefix_/);
```

We can also collect symbols together into groups and then import the groups by prefixing the group name with a colon. Again, this isn't a core Perl feature, it is just something that the Exporter's import method does. For example:

```perl
use My::Module qw(:mygroup);
```

We'll see how to actually define a group for Exporter in a moment.

Default and Conditional Exports

The @EXPORT variable defines a list of default exports that will be imported into our code if we use the module with no arguments, that is:

```perl
use My::Module;
```

323

But not:

```
use My::Module ();
```

Nor:

```
use My::Module qw(symbola symbolb symbolc);
```

If we give an explicit list of symbols to import, even if it is an empty list, `Exporter` will export only those symbols. Otherwise, we get them all.

Since exporting symbols automatically is not actually all that desirable (the application didn't ask for them, so we shouldn't spray it with symbols), `Exporter` also allows us to define conditional exports in the @EXPORT_OK array. Any symbol in this array may be exported if named explicitly, but will not be exported by default:

... in `My::Module` (`Module.pm`) ...

```
# change sub to be exported only on request
@EXPORT_OK = qw(greet_planet);
```

... in application (`import.pl`) ...

```
# now we must import the sub explicitly
use My::Module qw(greet_planet);
```

The contents of the @EXPORT array are also checked when an explicit list is given, so any name or regular expression passed to `import` will be imported if it matches a name in either the @EXPORT or @EXPORT_OK list. However, any explicit list suppresses the exporting of the default list – which is the point, of course.

We can regain the default symbols if we use the special export tag `:DEFAULT`. For example, this statement imports all the default symbols, and additionally imports two more (presumably on the @EXPORT_OK list; they could also be in the @EXPORT list, but then they would be redundant as `:DEFAULT` would have imported them already).

```
use My::Module qw(:DEFAULT symbola symbolb);
```

Alternatively, we can import the default list but remove symbols from it:

```
use My::Module qw(:DEFAULT !symbola !symbolb);
```

Since this is a common case, we can also omit the `:DEFAULT` tag and simply put:

```
use My::Module qw(!symbola !symbolb);
```

If fact this is the same as the example of negation we gave earlier; in effect, an implicit `:DEFAULT` is placed at the front of the list if the first item in the list is negated.

As a working example of the different ways that import lists can be defined, here is a short demonstration module, called `TestExport.pm`, and a test script that we can use to import symbols from it in different ways. First the module, which exports two subroutines by default and two if asked:

```
# TestExport.pm

package TestExport;

use strict;
use Exporter;

our @ISA = qw(Exporter);
our @EXPORT = qw(sym1 sym2);
our @EXPORT_OK = qw(sym3 sym4);

sub sym1 {print "sym1\n";}
sub sym2 {print "sym2\n";}
sub sym3 {print "sym3\n";}
sub sym4 {print "sym4\n";}

1;
```

The following script contains a number of different use statements that import different symbols from the module, depending on their argument. To use it, uncomment one (and only one) use statement and the script will print out the subroutines that were imported as a result. It also demonstrates a simple way of scanning the symbol table and the use of %INC to check for a loaded module.

```
#!/usr/bin/perl
# testexport.pl
use warnings;
use strict;

# :DEFAULT import
#use TestExport;

# no imports
#use TestExport();

# just 'sym1'
#use TestExport qw(sym1);

# everything but 'sym1'
#use TestExport qw(!sym1);

# just 'sym3'
#use TestExport qw(sym3);

# everything but 'sym3'
#use TestExport qw(!sym3);

# implicit :DEFAULT
#use TestExport qw(!sym1 sym3);

# no implicit :DEFAULT
#use TestExport qw(sym3 !sym1);

unless (exists $INC{'TestExport.pm'}) {
    die "Uncomment a 'use' to see its effect\n";
}

foreach (keys %::) {
    print "Imported: $_\n" if /^sym/;
}
```

Note that in these examples we have concentrated on subroutines, since these are the symbols we most commonly export, though we are equally free to export variables too.

Export Lists

In addition to adding symbol names to @EXPORT and @EXPORT_OK we can define collections of symbols as values in the hash variable %EXPORT_TAGS. The key is a tag name that refers to the collection. For example:

```
our (@EXPORT @EXPORT_OK %EXPORT_TAGS);

$EXPORT_TAGS{'subs'} = [qw(mysub myothersub subthree yellowsub)];
$EXPORT_TAGS{'vars'} = [qw($scalar @array %hash)];
```

Or, more succinctly:

```
our %EXPORT_TAGS = (
    subs => ['mysub','myothersub,'subthree','yellowsub'],
    vars => [qw($scalar @array %hash)],
);
```

Note that in accordance with the principles of nested data structures, we need to assign a reference to an anonymous array to each tag name key – otherwise we just count the list.

However, defining a list and assigning it to a tag does not automatically add the names in the list to either @EXPORT or @EXPORT_OK; in order for the tag to be imported successfully, the names have to be in one or other of the arrays too. Fortunately, Exporter makes this simple for us by providing a pair of subroutines to add the symbols associated with a tag to either list automatically. To add a tag to the default export list:

```
Exporter::export_tags('subs');
```

To add a tag to the conditional export list:

```
Exporter::export_ok_tags('vars');
```

We can now import various permutations of tags and symbol names:

```
# import two tags
use My::Module qw(:subs :vars);

# import the default list excepting the items in ':subs'
use My::Module qw(:DEFAULT !:subs);

# import ':subs' excepting the subroutine 'myothersub'
use My::Module qw(:subs !myothersub);
```

To show tags in action, here is a modified example of the TestExport module we gave above, rewritten to use tags instead. We define the default and on-request export lists using the export_tags and export_ok_tags subroutines:

```
# TestTagExport.pm

package TestTagExport;

use strict;
use Exporter;

our @ISA = qw(Exporter);
our %EXPORT_TAGS = (
   onetwo => ['sym1','sym2'],
   threefour => ['sym3','sym4'],
   onetwothree => [qw(sym1 sym2 sym3)],
   all => [qw(sym1 sym2 sym3 sym4)],
);

Exporter::export_tags('onetwo');
Exporter::export_ok_tags('threefour');

sub sym1 {print "sym1\n";}
sub sym2 {print "sym2\n";}
sub sym3 {print "sym3\n";}
sub sym4 {print "sym4\n";}

1;
```

Here is a script that tests out the export properties of the new module, concentrating on tags rather than symbols, though all the tests that applied to the first module will work with the same effect with this one:

```
#!/usr/bin/perl
# testtagexport.pl
use warnings;
use strict;

# import tag
#use TestTagExport;

# import symbol plus tag
#use TestTagExport qw(:threefour sym2);

# import tag minus symbol
#use TestTagExport qw(:onetwothree !sym2);

# import one tag minus another
#use TestTagExport qw(:onetwothree !:DEFAULT);

unless (exists $INC{'TestTagExport.pm'}) {
   die "Uncomment a 'use' to see its effect\n";
}

foreach (keys %::) {
   print "Imported: $_\n" if /^sym/;
}
```

Versions

The use and require directives support a version number syntax in addition to their regular use in module loading. The Exporter module also allows us to handle this usage by defining a require_version method that is passed the package name (because it is a method), and the version number requested:

```
our $VERSION = "1.23";

sub require_version {
    my ($pkg,$requested_version) = @_;
    return $requested_version ge $VERSION;
}
```

If we do not supply a require_version method then a default definition provided by Exporter is used instead; this also tests the requested version against the value of $VERSION defined in the local package (if any is defined), but uses a numeric comparison. This works well for version number string comparison (containing at least two points or prefixed with a v). The version above works better if versions resemble ordinary floating-point numbers because it uses a numeric comparison – see version strings in Chapter 3 for more on this issue.

Handling Failed Exports

The Exporter module automatically causes an application to die if it attempts to import a symbol that is not legal. However, by defining another array, @EXPORT_FAIL, we can define a list of symbols to handle specially in the event that Exporter does not recognize them. For example, to handle cross-platform special cases we might define three different subroutines:

```
our (@EXPORT_FAIL);

@EXPORT_FAIL = qw(win32sub macsub unixsub);
```

In order to handle symbols named in the failure list, we need to define a subroutine, or rather a method, called export_fail. The input to this method is a list of the symbols that the Exporter did not recognize, and the return value should be any symbols that the module was unable to process:

```
sub export_fail {
    my $pkg = shift;

    my @fails;
    foreach (@_) {
        # test each symbol to see if we want to define it
        push @fails,$_ if supported($_);
    }

    # return list of failed exports (none if success)
    return @fails;
}

sub supported {
    my $symbol = shift;
    ... test for special cases ...
    return $ok_on_this_platform;
}
```

If we do not define an `export_fail` method then Exporter supplies its own, which returns all the symbols, causing them all to fail as if the `@EXPORT_FAIL` array was not defined at all. Note that we cannot have Exporter call `export_fail` for any unrecognized symbol, only those listed in the `@EXPORT_FAIL` array. However, if we wanted to handle situations like this ourselves we can always define our own `import` method, which we discuss next.

Using 'Exporter' with a Local 'import' Method

If we don't want to do any special handling ourselves then we can simply provide definitions for the `@EXPORT` or `@EXPORT_OK` arrays and have the Exporter module deal with everything for us. If, however, a module needs to do its own initialization we need to define our own `import` method. Since this will override the `import` method defined by Exporter, we will need to take the steps to call it explicitly if we still want to take advantage of it as well. Fortunately the Exporter module has been written with this in mind.

Assuming we're familiar with object-oriented programming, we might guess that calling `SUPER::import` from our own import subroutine would do the trick, since `SUPER::` is the named method in the parent package or packages, as covered in Chapter 19. The parent package is the Exporter module since it is in our `@ISA` array, so this calls Exporter's `@ISA` from our own. Unfortunately, although this works, this imports symbols to the wrong package, because Exporter's import method examines the package name of the caller to determine where to export symbols. Since that is the module, and not the user of the module, the export doesn't place anything in the package that issues the use statement. Instead, we use the `export_to_level` method, which traces back up the calling stack and supplies the correct package name to Exporter's `import` method. Here's how we can use it:

```
our @ISA = qw(Exporter);
our @EXPORT_OK = qw(mysub myothersub subthree yellowsub);

sub import {
   my $package = $_[0];
   do_our_own_thing(@_);
   $package->export_to_level(1, @_);
}
```

The first argument to `export_to_level` is a call-stack index (identical to that passed to the `caller` function). This is used to determine the package to export symbols to, thereby allowing `export_to_level` to be completely package-independent. Note that because the package information needs to be preserved intact, it is important that we do not remove the package name passed as the first argument, which is why we used `$_[0]` and not `shift` in the above example.

Debugging Exports

The Exporter module also has a special verbose mode we can use when we are debugging particularly complex import problems. To enable it, define the variable `$Exporter::Verbose` before using the module, and note that for this to be successful it needs to be in a BEGIN block:

```
BEGIN {
   $Exporter::Verbose = 1;
}
```

Note also that this will produce debug traces for all modules that use Exporter. Since a very large number of modules use Exporter, this may produce a lot of output. However, since BEGIN blocks (including the implicit ones in use statements) are executed in order, we can plant BEGIN blocks in between the use statements to restrain the reporting to just those modules we are interested in:

```
use Exporter;
use A::Module::Needed::First;

BEGIN {$Exporter::Verbose = 1;}
use My::Problematic::Exporting::Module;

BEGIN {$Exporter::Verbose = 0;}
use Another::Module;
```

Creating Installable Modules

An installable package is one that we can bundle up, take somewhere else, and then install by unpacking it and executing an installation script (obviously, the term 'package' in this section doesn't mean a Perl namespace which is created using the keyword package). A Perl module is best installed as part of an installable package.

If we want to make our scripts and modules easily portable between systems, it is far better to automate the process of installation than manually copy files into a library directory. In addition, if we want to distribute the module more widely, or upload it to CPAN for the enjoyment of all, we need to make sure that the module is well behaved and has all the right pieces in all the right places. Fortunately, the h2xs utility supplied with Perl automates a great deal of this process for us, allowing us to concentrate on the actual code.

Different platforms have different requirements for building installable packages. Most UNIX platforms will build any package created with h2xs without difficulty, but Windows systems will need a make tool like dmake installed, for instance. However, packages consisting purely of Perl (as opposed to a mixture of Perl and C) should be easily installed on most platforms given some minimal supporting tools. Chapter 24 covers installing packages on different systems and the tools required for different platforms.

Well-Written Modules

When we are writing modules for our own personal use, we can be fairly lax about how they are structured; a package declaration at the top and a 1 at the bottom are all we really need. However, a well-written and well-behaved module for general consumption should have some essential attributes.

Its own unique package name: In the case of modules designed for wider distribution this should not only be chosen wisely but also checked against other modules already available from CPAN to see if it fits well with existing nomenclature. For modules destined for CPAN, consult the module list document and the advice therein at: http://www.cpan.org/modules/00modlist.long.html.

A version number: All module files (that is, files ending in .pm) destined for distribution should have a version number defined inside them, either in the package variable $VERSION, or in a VERSION subroutine that returns a version number.

Strict mode: No Perl code should really be without the strict pragma. It must be said that there are several examples of modules in the Perl standard library that do not adhere to these standards. Mostly these are tried and tested modules from early in the development of the standard library that are known to work. For new modules, strict mode is a good idea.

Documentation: All subroutine calls, exported and exportable symbols, and configuration details should be written up and distributed along with the module, preferably in the form of Plain Old Documentation (pod) within the main module file (see Chapter 18 for more on pod documents). It is not necessary for every module to be documented if some modules are only support modules and not intended to be used directly, but all salient features should be there. To be properly structured, the pod document should contain at least the following sections:

- ❑ NAME: The package name and brief description
- ❑ SYNOPSIS: Code example of how the module is used
- ❑ DESCRIPTION: A description of what the module does
- ❑ EXPORT: What the module exports
- ❑ SEE ALSO: Any related modules or Perl documentation
- ❑ HISTORY: Optionally, a history of changes

Tools that are written to look for these sections, such as the podselect utility and the translators that are based on it, can use properly constructed documentation to extract information selectively. Additional optional sections include BUGS, CHANGES, AUTHOR, COPYRIGHT, and SUPPORTED PLATFORMS, some of which h2xs will also generate in particular circumstances.

Conveniently, the h2xs tool creates a basic module file with all of the above already defined and in place.

Creating a Working Directory

The first and main step to use h2xs to create an installable module is to create a working directory tree where the module source code will reside. This resembles a local library directory (and indeed we can use the module directly if we add it to @INC via Perl's -I option or the use lib pragma). In its most basic usage, h2xs creates a directory tree based on the package name we give it, and creates an initial module file with all the basic attributes in place. For example:

> h2xs -n Installable::Module

This creates a directory Installable inside which is a directory called Module within which is a file called Module.pm. In addition, h2xs also creates the following files:

File	Description
Makefile.PL	This is a Perl script that generates a makefile script for the module. The makefile is generated by simply running Perl on this file, for example: **> perl Makefile.PL** In turn, the makefile defines various targets, notably dist, which creates a distribution file and install, which carries out the building, testing, and installation of the module.
test.pl	A test script to test the module's functionality which is compatible with the Test::Harness module and which is executed (using Test::Harness) by the test makefile target. We can create our own tests using the Test module and add them to this script.

Table continued on following page

File	Description
Changes	A Changes file that documents the module's history. This file is suppressed by the -C option; see later.
MANIFEST	A list of the files in the distribution. By adding files to this list we can add them to the distribution that is created by the dist target.

The actual donkeywork of creating the makefile is done by a collection of modules in the ExtUtils family, the principal one being ExtUtils::MakeMaker. A single call to this module actually takes up the bulk of the Makefile.PL script:

```
use ExtUtils::MakeMaker;
# See lib/ExtUtils/MakeMaker.pm for details of how to influence
# the contents of the Makefile that is written.
WriteMakefile(
    'NAME' => 'Installable::Module',
    'VERSION_FROM' => 'Module.pm',    # finds $VERSION
    'PREREQ_PM' => {},    # e.g., Module::Name => 1.1
);
```

If we already have a module and we want to convert it into an installable one, the best option is probably to create a new module source file and then copy the existing source code from the old module file into it. This way we get the extra files correctly generated by h2xs for us.

Either way, once we have the directory set up and the appropriate files created within it we can create a functional and (preferably) fully documented module.

Building an Installable Package

To create an installable package file from our module source we only need to create the makefile and then use make dist (or nmake or dmake if that is what we have installed, for example, on a Windows system) to create the distribution file:

> **perl Makefile.PL**
> **make dist**

If we have added other modules to our source code, or additional files we want to include with the distribution, we add them to the MANIFEST file. At the start, this file contains just the files generated by h2xs, that is Changes, MANIFEST, Makefile.PL, Module.pm, and test.pl.

Assuming the make dist executes successfully we should end up with an archived installation file comprising the package name (with colons replaced by hyphens) and the version number. On a UNIX system, our example module gets turned into Installable-Module-0.01.tar.gz.

We can now take this package to another system and install it with (again on a UNIX system):

> **gunzip Installable-Module-0.01.tar.gz**
> **tar -xvf Installable-Module-0.01.tar**

Once the source is unpacked, we create the makefile and run the install target from it:

```
> cd Installable-Module-0.01
> perl Makefile.PL
> make
> su
Password:
# make install
```

Or, for the more cautious who prefer to test first:

```
> make
> make test
> su
Password:
# make install
```

This will install files into a directory called blib in the current directory. To use a module in this directory we can make use of the blib module to seek out a corresponding directory somewhere nearby and (if it finds one) add appropriate paths to @INC automatically. For example, if we have a script called moduleuser.pl that makes use of our module, we can have the use statement in the script find our locally installed version with:

```
> perl -Mblib moduleuser.pl
```

Or, if the blib directory is not local to the application:

```
> perl -Mblib=startdirectory moduleuser.pl
```

Alternatively, to install the package into the site_perl directory under Perl's main installation tree, use the install_site target:

```
> su
Password:
# make install_site
```

We can have install install the module into the site_perl directory automatically by adding the a definition for INSTALLDIRS to the key-value pairs of WriteMakefile:

```
use ExtUtils::MakeMaker;

WriteMakefile(
    'INSTALLDIRS' => 'site',
    'NAME' => 'Installable::Module',
    'VERSION_FROM' => 'Module.pm',    # finds $VERSION
    'PREREQ_PM' => {},    # e.g., Module::Name => 1.1
);
```

Note that on a platform with a decent privilege system we will need to have permission to actually install the file anywhere under the standard Perl library root. Once the installation is complete we should be able to see details of it by running perldoc perllocal.

Alternatively, to install a module into our own separate location we can supply a LIB parameter when we create the makefile. For example, to install modules into a master library directory lib/perl in our home directory on a UNIX system we could type:

> **cd Installable-Module-0.01**
> **perl Makefile.PL LIB=~/lib/perl**
> **su**
Password:
make install

The LIB parameter causes the Makefile.PL script to create a makefile that installs into that directory rather than the main or site installation locations. We could produce the same effect by setting both INSTALLSITELIB and INSTALLPRIVLIB to this same value in Makefile.PL, though it is unlikely that we would be creating an installable package that installed into a non-standard location. Hence LIB is a command line feature only.

Adding a Test Script

The makefile generated by ExtUtils::MakeMaker contains an impressively larger number of different make targets. Among them is the test target, which executes the test script test.pl generated by h2xs. To add a test stage to our package we only have to edit this file to add the tests we want to carry out.

Tests are carried out under the aegis of the Test::Harness module, which we will cover in Chapter 17, but which is particularly aimed at testing installable packages. The Test::Harness module expects a particular kind of output, which the pre-generated test.pl satisfies with a redundant automatically succeeding test. To create a useful test we need to replace this pre-generated script with one that actually carries out tests and produces an output that complies with what the Test::Harness module expects to see.

Once we have a real test script that carries out genuine tests in place, we can use it by invoking the test target, as we saw in the installation examples above:

> **make test**

By default the install target does not include test as a dependent target, so we do need to run it separately if we want to be sure the module works. The CPAN module automatically carries out the test stage before the install stage, however, so when we install modules using it we don't have to remember the test stage.

Uploading Modules to CPAN

Once a module has been successfully turned into a package (and preferably reinstalled, tested, and generally proven) it is potentially a candidate for CPAN. Uploading a module to CPAN allows it to be shared among other Perl programmers, commented on and improved, and made part of the library of Perl modules available to all within the Perl community.

This is just the functional stage of creating a module for general distribution, however. Packages cannot be uploaded to CPAN arbitrarily. First we need to get registered so we have an upload directory to upload things into. It also helps to discuss modules with other programmers and see what else is already available that might do a similar job. It definitely helps to choose a good package name and to discuss the choice first. Remember that Perl is a community as well as a language; for contributions to be accepted (and indeed, noticed at all) it helps to talk about them.

Information on registration and other aspects of contribution to CPAN are detailed on the Perl Authors Upload Server (PAUSE) page at http://www.cpan.org/modules/04pause.html (or our favorite local mirror). The modules list, which contains details of all the modules currently held by CPAN and its many mirrors, is at: http://www.cpan.org/modules/00modlist.long.html.

Summary

In this chapter, we explored the insides of modules and packages. We began by looking at blocks, specifically the BEGIN, END, CHECK, and INIT blocks. Following this we saw how to manipulate packages, and among other things we learned how to remove a package namespace from the symbol table hierarchy and how to find a package name programmatically.

The next main topic discussed was autoloading of subroutines and modules. From here we looked at importing and exporting, and covered the following areas:

- ❑ The import mechanism
- ❑ Setting flags with export
- ❑ When to export, and when not to export
- ❑ The Exporter module

Finally, we went through the process of creating installable module packages, and talked about the following:

- ❑ Well-written modules
- ❑ Creating a working directory
- ❑ Building an installable package
- ❑ Adding a test script
- ❑ Uploading modules to CPAN

11

Regular Expressions

Regular expressions are one of Perl's most powerful features, providing the abilities to match, substitute, and generally mangle text in almost any way we choose. To the uninitiated, they can look nonsensical, but we will talk you through them. In this chapter, we look in detail at how Perl handles regular expressions.

However, in order to understand Perl's handling of regular expressions we need to learn about its underlying mechanism of interpolation. This is the means by which Perl evaluates the contents of text and replaces marked areas with specified characters or the contents of variables. While this is not in the same league as regular expressions, there is more to interpolation than first meets the eye.

String Interpolation

The literary definition of **interpolation** is the process of inserting additional words or characters into a block of text (the mathematical definition is quite different but not pertinent here). In Perl, interpolation is just the process of substituting variables and special characters in strings. We have already seen quite a lot of interpolated strings, for instance, the answer to this tricky calculation:

```
$result = 6 * 7;
print "The answer is $result \n";
```

In this section we are going to take a closer look at what interpolation is and where it happens (and how to prevent it). We'll then look briefly at interpolation in combination with regular expressions before the full exposition.

Perl's Interpolation Syntax

When Perl encounters a string that can be interpolated, it scans it for three significant characters, $, @ and \. If any of these are present and not escaped (prefixed with a backslash) they trigger interpolation of the text immediately following. What actually happens depends on the character:

Character	Action
\	Interpolate a metacharacter or character code
$	Interpolate a scalar variable or evaluate an expression in scalar context
@	Interpolate an array variable or evaluate an expression in list context

If a string does not contain any of these then there is nothing to interpolate and Perl will use the string as it is. Furthermore, Perl first checks for strings that can be interpolated at compile-time, weeding out all those that are either already constant and do not require interpolation, or can be interpolated to a constant value. Consequently it does not matter much if we use double quotes for our constant strings or not; Perl will detect and optimize them before execution starts.

Interpolating Metacharacters and Character Codes

The backslash character \ allows us to insert characters into strings that would, otherwise, be problematic to type, not to mention display. The most obvious of these is \n, which we have used a great deal to produce a newline. Other common examples include \t for a tab character, \r for a return, and \e for escape. Here is a brief list of them:

Character	Description
\000..\377	An ASCII code in octal
\a	Alarm (ASCII 7)
\b	Backspace (ASCII 8)
\c<chr>	A control character (e.g. \cg is ctrl-g, ASCII 7, same as \a)
\e	Escape character (ASCII 27)
\E	End effect of \L, \Q, or \U.
\f	Form Feed (New Page) character (ASCII 12)
\l	Lowercase next character
\L	Lowercase all following characters to end of string or \E
\n	Newline character (ASCII 10 on UNIX, 13+10 on Windows, etc.)
\N{name}	A named character
\Q	Escape (backslash) all non-alphanumeric characters to end of string or \E
\r	Return character (usually ASCII 13)
\t	Tab character (ASCII 8)
\u	Uppercase next character
\U	Uppercase all following characters to end of string or \E
\x<code>	An ASCII code 00 to ff in hexadecimal
\x{<code>}	A UTF8 Unicode character code in hexadecimal
\\, \$, \@, \"	A literal backslash, dollar sign, at sign or double quote. The backslash disables the usual metacharacter meaning. These are actually just the specific cases of general escapes that are most likely to cause trouble as unescaped characters.

Some metacharacters are specific and generate a simple and consistent character. Others, like \0..\7, \c, \x, and \N, take values that produce characters based on the immediately following text. The \l and \u metacharacters lower the case of, or capitalize, the immediately following character, respectively. Finally, the \L, \Q, and \U metacharacters affect all characters after them until the string ends or a \E is encountered.

Common Special Characters

Metacharacters that produce direct codes like \e, \n, and \r simply evaluate to the appropriate character. We have used \n many times so far to produce a new line, for example.

However, it is not quite that simple. There is no standard definition of a 'new line'. Under UNIX, it is a linefeed (character 10), under Windows it is a carriage return followed by a linefeed (character 13 + character 10), on Macintosh systems it is reversed (a linefeed followed by a return). This can cause a lot of confusion when sending data between different systems. In practice, the values of \n and \r are defined by the underlying platform to 'do the right thing', but for networking applications we are sometimes better off specifying new lines explicitly using either an octal notation or control characters:

```
# Newlines on a Macintosh
print "This is a new line in octal \012\015";
print "This is a new line in control characters \cJ\cM";
```

Special Effects

Perl provides five metacharacters, \l, \u, \L, \Q, and \U, which affect the text following them. The lowercase characters affect the next character in the string, whereas the upper case versions affect all characters until they are switched off again with \E or reach the end of the string.

The \l and \u characters modify the case of the immediately following character, if it has a case to change. Note that the definition of lower and upper case is locale dependent and varies between character sets. If placed at the beginning of a string they are equivalent to the lcfirst and ucfirst functions:

```
print "\lPolish";  # produce 'polish'
print "\uperl";  # produce 'Perl'
```

The \L and \U characters by contrast are equivalent to the lower and upper functions, changing the case of all cased characters until an \E or the end of the string is encountered:

```
print "This is \Uupper\E case\n";  # produces UPPER
print "This is \LLOWER\E case\n";  # produces lower
```

We can also combine both types of metacharacter. Putting \l or \u inside a \L...\E or \U...\E would produce no useful effect, but we can immediately precede such a section to reverse the effect on the first character:

```
$surname = "rOBOTHAM";
print "\u\L$surname\E";  # produces 'Robotham'
```

This is equivalent to using print ucfirst(lower $surname) but avoids two function calls.

The \Q metacharacter is similar to \L and \U, and like them affects all following characters until stopped by \E or the end of the string. The \Q metacharacter escapes all non-alphanumeric characters in the string following it, and is equivalent to the quotemeta function. We discuss it in more detail in 'Protecting Strings Against Interpolation' later. Note that there is no \q metacharacter, since a single backslash performs this function on non-alphanumeric characters, and alphanumeric characters do not need escaping.

Interpolating Variables

Other than embedding otherwise hard-to-type characters into strings, the most common use of interpolation is to insert the values of variables, and in particular scalars. This is the familiar use of interpolation that we have seen so far:

```
$var = 'Hello World';
print "Greetings, $var \n";
```

There is no reason why we cannot chain several interpolated strings together, as in:

```
$var = 'Hello';
$message = "$var World";
$full_message = "$message \n";
print "Greetings, $full_message";    # print 'Greetings, Hello World'
```

Arrays interpolate similarly, but not quite in the way that we might expect. One of Perl's many 'smart' tweaks is that it notices arrays and automatically separates their values when interpolating them into a string. This is different from simply printing an array outside of interpolation where the values usually run together, as shown below:

```
@array = (1, 2, 3, 4);
$\ = "\n";

print @array;   # display '1234'
print "@array";   # display '1 2 3 4'
$, =',';   # change the output field separator
print @array;   # display '1, 2, 3, 4'
print "@array";   # still display '1 2 3 4'
$"=':';   # change the interpolated list separator
print "@array";   # display '1:2:3:4'
```

Whereas printing an array explicitly uses the output field separator $,, just as an explicit list of scalars does, arrays and lists evaluated in an interpolative context use the interpolated list separator $", which is by default set to a space (hence the result of the first interpolation above).

If we try to interpolate a variable name and immediately follow it with text, we run into a problem. Perl will think that the text is part of the variable name because it has no reason to assume otherwise. It will end the variable name at the first character that is not legal in variable names. For instance, the following does not work (or at least, does not do what we expect):

```
$var = "Hello ";
print "Greetings, $varWorld \n";    # try to interpolate $varWorld
```

We can fix this by splitting the string into two after $var, but this rather defeats the point of interpolation. We can instead keep the string together by placing the variable name within curly braces.

```
print "Greetings, ${var}World \n";   # interpolate $var
```

Note that although this looks reminiscent of dereferencing a scalar reference, it actually has nothing to do with it. However, a related trick allows us to embed code into interpolated strings; see the next section.

Variable interpolation works on any valid variable name, including punctuation. This includes array indices, hash keys, and even the maximum-array-index notation $#:

```
@ary = (1, 2, 3, 4);

print "$#ary";   # display 3 (number of elements)
print "$ary[2]";   # display 3 (the value of the third element)
```

Interpolating Code

Perl allows us to embed not just literal characters and variables but code too. How we embed code depends on whether we want the result to be a scalar or a list, that is, we must define the execution context for the code to run in. To embed and evaluate code in a scalar context we use the delimiters ${\ and }, that is, a dereference of a scalar reference. The additional reference constructors (backslash and square brackets) are what distinguish embedded code from an explicitly defined variable name. For example:

```
# print out the data from first 10 characters of scalar 'gmtime'
print "Today is ${\ substr(scalar(gmtime), 0, 10)} \n";
```

To embed and evaluate in list context we use @{ [and] }, that is, a dereference of an anonymous array reference. For example:

```
# print out the keys of a hash
print "Keys: @{[keys %hash]}";

# print out the time, hms
print "The time is @{[reverse((gmtime)[0..2])]} exactly \n";
```

Note that the interpolated list separator $" also affects lists generated through code, though the origin of the list is not important.

In order for code to embed properly it has to return a value. That means that we cannot use things like foreach loops to build lists, or execute an if statement. However, we can use versions of these constructs that do return an expression. In the case of a condition, the ternary condition?doiftrue?doiffalse operator will do just fine. In the case of a loop, the map or grep functions can do the same work as a foreach loop, but also return the value:

```
# subtract each array element from its maximum index
print "Mapping \@ary:@{[map{$_ = $#ary-$_}@ary]}\n";
```

Embedding code into strings is certainly possible, but before embarking, it is worth considering whether it is practical; for a start it is not naturally inclined to legibility. It also bypasses Perl's compile-time syntax checking, since the code is not evaluated until Perl tries to interpolate the string at run time. In this sense it is (slightly) similar to an `eval`, except that it is evaluated in the current context rather than defining its own.

Interpolative Context

Interpolation happens in a number of different places. The most obvious and common are double quotes and the double quote operator qq:

```
print "@ary";
print qq(@ary);
```

Backtick quoted strings also interpolate their contents, as does the qx operator which is their equivalent:

```
$files = `ls $directory`;   # Or 'dir' for a Windows system
$files = qx(ls $directory);
```

The qx operator can be prevented from interpolating if its delimiters are changed to a single quote. This is a mnemonic special case:

```
$ttytype = qx'echo $TERM';   # getting it from %ENV is simpler!
```

Note that `eval` statements will interpolate quotes inside the strings that they evaluate. This is not the same as simply giving `eval` a double-quoted string – that is just regular double-quoted interpolation, which is then passed to `eval`. What we mean is that double quotes inside string variables cause `eval` to interpolate the strings. We will see how useful that is in a moment.

While we are on the subject of quotes and quoting operators, the qw operator does not interpolate, and neither of course does q, which wouldn't be expected to since it is the equivalent of a single quote.

Interpolation in Regular Expressions

The final place where interpolation occurs is in regular expressions, and these are the focusing points of this chapter. In the following example, $pattern is given a single-quoted value, yet it is interpolated when used as a regular expression:

```
$input = <>;
# match any pair of alphanumeric characters separated by space
$pattern = '\w\s\w';
# $pattern is interpolated when treated as a regular expression
print "Yes, got a match \n" if $input =~ /$pattern/;
```

Since the variable value may change, interpolation happens each time the regular expression is evaluated, unless we use the /o flag. This can be an important time saver, since interpolation can be an involved process, but has its own caveats, as we shall see later in the chapter.

Interpolation does not just include regular expressions in match and substitution operations. It also includes functions like split, which (as many programmers forget and thereby end up being considerably confused) takes a regular expression as its first argument, and the qr operator.

Unfortunately the syntax of regular expressions collides with ordinary variable names as seen in an interpolated string. In particular, an array index looks like a regular expression character class (which is denoted by a pair of square brackets):

```
$match = /$var[$index]/;
```

This could either mean the value of $var followed by one of the characters $, i, n, d, e, or x, or it could mean the $index element of the array variable @var. To resolve this, Perl tries to 'do the right thing' by looking for @var, and if it finds it will try to return an element if $index looks at all reasonable (the number 3 would be reasonable, a string value would not). If there is no @var, or $index does not look like an index value, then Perl will look for $var and treat the contents of the square brackets as a character class instead. Clearly this is prone to breaking as the program evolves, so we are better off rewriting the expression to avoid this guesswork if possible.

Substitutions also carry out interpolation in the replacement text, but only on a successful match, so embedded code in the replacement text will only be executed if a match is found.

```
$text =~ s/($this|$that|$other)/$spare/;
```

Interpolating Text Inside String Variables

So far we have only looked at interpolation in literal strings. However, it is sometimes useful to cause Perl to interpolate over text in a string variable. Unfortunately the trick to doing this is not immediately obvious – if we interpolate the variable name we get the text that it contains as its value, but the text itself remains uninterpolated:

```
@array = (1, 2, 3, 4);
$text = '@array';   # note the single quotes!
print "$text";    # produce '@array'
```

In fact the solution is simple once we see it; use eval and supply the variable to be interpolated directly to it:

```
print eval $text;   # produce 1234
```

This is not actually interpolation, but it points the way toward it. This particular example works because the content of $text is a valid Perl expression, that is, we could replace $text with its contents, sans quotes, and the resulting statement would still be legal. We can see that no quotes (and therefore no interpolation) are involved because the output is 1234, not 1 2 3 4 as it would be if $" had taken effect.

To produce interpolation inside string variables we combine eval with double quotes inside the string, that is, around the string value:

```
$text = 'The array contains: @array';
print eval '"'.$text.'"';   # produce 'The array contains: 1 2 3 4'
print eval "\"$text\"";   # an alternative way to do the same thing
print eval qq("$text");   # and another
```

Adding literal double quotes to the string without causing a syntax error, disabling interpolation, or otherwise going wrong takes a little thought. Simply enclosing the whole string in single quotes stops the eval seeing double quotes as anything other than literal quote symbols. The correct way to interpolate is either to concatenate double quotes, as in the first example above, or use literal double quotes inside regular ones, as in the second and third examples.

Protecting Strings Against Interpolation

Sometimes we may want to protect part or all of a body of text against interpolation. The most obvious way to do that is to just use single quotes and combine variables into the string through concatenation:

```
$contents = '@array contains'. join(', ',@array). "\n";
```

It is easy to accidentally put characters that can be interpolated into a string. One common mistake is to forget the @ in e-mail addresses, for instance:

```
$email = "my@myself.com";
```

This can be a little inconvenient if we have a lot of at signs, dollar signs, or real backslashes (that are actually meant to be backslashes, not metacharacter prefixes). Instead we can use a backslash to escape the punctuation we want to keep. (This is not in fact confusing because only alphanumeric characters go together with backlashes to make metacharacters or ASCII codes):

```
print "\@array";   # produce '@array'
```

This is inconvenient, however, and prone to errors. It also does not take into account the fact that the text might have been generated dynamically. A better solution is to get Perl to do the job for us. One simple way of completely protecting a string is to pass it through a regular expression:

```
# escape all backlashes, at signs and dollar characters
$text = 'A $scalar, an @array and a \backslash';
$text =~ s/([\$\@\\])/\\$1/mg;
print $text;   # produce 'A \$scalar, an \@array, and a \\backslash'
```

Unfortunately this regular expression requires many backslashes to make sure the literal characters remain literal, since this makes it hard to read. Even in the character class we need extra backslashes because both $@ and @$ have meanings that can be interpolated. The \ in front of the @ symbol is the only one that is not actually required, but we have added it for consistency anyway. A better way to do the same thing is with Perl's built-in quotemeta function. This runs through a string using backslashes to escape all non-alphanumeric characters, so it also escapes quotes, punctuation and spaces. While this might not be important for interpolation, it makes strings safe for passing to shells with reasonable quoting rules (which is to say most UNIX shells, but not the various standard Windows shells). It also makes it safe to use user-inputted strings in a regular expression:

```
$text = '"$" denotes a scalar variable';
$text = quotemeta $text;
print $text;   # display '\"\$\"\ denotes\ a\ scalar\ variable'
print eval qq("$text");   # display '"$" denotes a scalar variable'
```

The quotemeta function uses $_ if no explicit variable is passed, making it possible to write loops like this:

```
foreach (@unescaped_lines) {
    print "Interpolating \"", quotemeta, "\" produces '$_' \n";
}
```

The quotemeta function can also be triggered in every part of a string by inserting the metacharacters \Q and \E around the text to be protected. This use of quotemeta is primarily intended for use in regular expressions. Although it also works on literal strings as well, the effects can be counter-intuitive, since the special interpolation characters, \, @, and $ will not be escaped – they are interpreted literally and the contents escaped instead:

```
$variable = "contains an @ character";
# produce 'This\ string\ contains\ an\ \@\ character'
print "\QThis string $variable\E";
```

In a regular expression this behavior becomes useful. It allows us to protect sensitive characters in interpolated variables used in the search pattern from being interpreted as regexp syntax, as this example illustrates:

```
$text = "That's double+ good";
$pattern = "double+";
print "Matched" if $text =~ /\Q$pattern/;   # return 'Matched'
$text = "That's double plus good";
print "Matched" if $text =~ /$pattern/;   # (incorrectly) return 'Matched'
print "Matched" if $text =~ /\Q$pattern/;   # do not match, return nothing.
$pattern = quotemeta($pattern);
print "Matched" if $text =~ /$pattern/;   # now pattern don't match,
                                          # returns nothing.
```

Without the \Q the pattern would match double (and doublee, and so on), which is not what we intended. As the last example shows, it is as easy to use quotemeta as it is to use \Q when we want to protect the entire string.

Regular Expressions

Regular expressions, now commonly abbreviated to **regexp**s, are a very powerful tool for finding and extracting patterns within text, and Perl just happens to be graced with a particularly powerful engine to process them. Regexps have a long history, and Perl's implementation was inspired a great deal by the regexp engine of the UNIX utility awk. A good understanding of how to use it is an invaluable skill for the practicing Perl programmer. Here is a simple example that uses . to match any character, just for illustration:

```
print "Matched!" if $matchtext =~ /b.ll/;
# match 'ball', 'bell', 'bill', 'boll', 'bull', ...
```

A regexp is, in simple terms, a search pattern applied to text in the hope of finding a match. The phrase 'search pattern' is however, laden with hidden details. Regexps may consist of a simple sequence of literal characters to be found in the text, or a much more complex set of criteria. These can possibly involve repetitions, alternative characters or words, and re-matching sequences of previously found text. The role of a regexp engine is to take a search pattern and apply it to the supplied text (or possibly apply the supplied text to it, depending on our point of view), exhausting all possibilities in an attempt to find a part of the text that satisfies the criteria of the search pattern.

Regexps may match more than once if we so choose, and we can write loops to handle each match or extract them all as strings into a list. We can control case sensitivity and the position from which subsequent match attempts start, and find multiple matches allowing or disallowing overlapping. We also have the choice to use variables to define part or all of the pattern, because Perl interpolates the search pattern before using it. This interpolation can be an expensive process, so we also have means to optimize it.

A key to writing regexps successfully is to understand how they are matched. Perl's regexp engine works on three basic principles in this order:

❏ **Eagerness**: it will try to match as soon as possible

❏ **Greediness**: it will try to match as much as possible

❏ **Relentlessness**: it will try every possible combination before giving up

Programmers new to regexps are often surprised when their patterns do not produce the desired effects. Regexps are not sensible and do not follow 'common sense' – they will always match the first set of criteria that satisfies the pattern, irrespective of whether or not a 'better' match might occur later. This is perfectly correct behavior, but to make use of regexps effectively we need to think carefully about what we want to achieve.

During the course of this chapter we will cover all the various aspects of regexps, from simple literal patterns to more complex ones. First we will take a brief look at how and where regexps are used.

Where Regular Expressions Occur

Regexps occur in a number of places within Perl. The most obvious are the match and substitution operators, and indeed the bulk of regexps are used this way. However, a fact sometimes overlooked is that the `split` function also uses a regexp.

Additionally, we can pre-compile regexps with the `qr` quoting operator. This operator does not actually trigger the regexp engine, but carries out the interpolation and compilation of a regexp so that it need not be repeated later. This allows us to prepare a potentially long and complex regxp ahead of time, and then refer to it through a variable, which can provide an advantage in terms of both speed and legibility.

Finally, the transliteration operators `tr` and `y` closely resemble the match and substitution operators, but in fact do not use regexps at all. However they do have some aspects in common other than syntax, which are also covered here.

Matching and Substitution

The match operator `m//` and substitution operator `s///` are the main interfaces to Perl's regexp engine. Both operators attempt to match supplied text to a pattern. Note that the preceding `m` can be dropped from `m//`. In the case below we are looking for the text 'proton':

```
# true if $atom contains the text 'proton'
if ($atom =~ /proton/) {
    ...
}

# replace first occurrence of 'proton' with 'neutron'
$atom =~ s/proton/neutron/;
```

The search text is **bound** to the regexp operator with the `=~` and `!~` operators and in the examples above we have used the former. The difference between the two is that `!~` logically negates the result, so it returns True for a failed match. For example, to check that $atom does not in fact contain a `proton`, we could write:

```
if ($atom !~ /proton/) {
    print "No protons here!";
}
```

This is more useful than it might seem, since it is very hard to test for non-matches within a regexp. This is due to the regexp engine's relentless checking of all possible matches before giving up. We will come back to this later as we progress.

It is important to realize that =~ is not a relative of the assignment operator = even though it might look a little like one. Novice Perl programmers in particular sometimes write ~= by mistake, thinking that it follows the same pattern as combined operators, like +=. It is also important not to place a space between the = and ~. This would mean an assignment and a bitwise NOT, legal Perl but not what we intended.

If neither binding operator is used, both the match and substitution operators default to using $_ as their input. This allows us to write very concise Perl scripts when used in combination with functions that set $_. For instance, this while loop uses a regexp to skip past lines that look like comments, that is, the first non-whitespace character is a #:

```
while (<>) {
    next if /^\s*#/;   # test $_ and reject comments
    print $_;
}
```

Similarly, this foreach loop applies the regular expressions to $_ in the absence of an explicit iterator:

```
foreach (@particles) {
    /proton/ and print ("A positive match \n"), last;
    /electron/ and print ("Negative influence \n"), last;
    /neutron/ and print ("Ambivalent \n"), last;
}
```

We can use regexps inside the blocks of map and grep in a similar way.

The m of the match operator is optional if forward slashes are used to encapsulate the pattern, so Perl programs are frequently sprinkled with sights like this:

```
# match $_ against pattern and execute block on success
/pattern/ and do { ... };

# a Perl-style multiple-if statement
foreach ($command) {
    /help/ and usage(), last;
    /run/ and execute($command), last;
    /exit/ and exit;
    print "Sorry, command '$command' unknown \n";
}
```

As an aside, both the match and substitution operators, as well as the split function and qr operator allow other delimiters to be used. We shall see this demonstrated under 'Regular Expression Delimiters'. A more detailed explanation of the binding operators =~ and !~ can be found later in this chapter.

The 'split' Function

Aside from the match and substitution operators, the split function also takes a regexp as its first argument. This isn't immediately obvious from many normal uses of split, as in:

```
# split text into pieces around commas
@values = split (',',$text);
```

The comma is used as a regexp, but as it only matches a single comma we do not notice this fact. We can replace the comma with a regexp that removes whitespace as well. This is done using the special **whitespace metacharacter** \s in combination with the * modifier, which matches on zero or more occurrences:

```
# split text into pieces around commas plus whitespace
@values = split('\s*,\s*',$text);

# the same statement written in a more regexp style
@values = split /\s*,\s*/,$text;
```

There are a few things wrong with this example though. For one it does not handle leading whitespace at the start of the string or trailing whitespace at the end. We could fix that with another regexp, but more on that later. As the above examples show, the first argument to split can be expressed in regexp syntax too.

The split function operates on $_ if it is given no value to work on:

```
@csv = split /,/;    # split $_ on commas
```

> *Note this does not handle quoted comma so use 'Text::CSV' for this purpose.*

If split is given no parameters at all, it splits on whitespace. To be strictly accurate, it splits on the special pattern ' ' (which is special only to split). It is equivalent to \s+ except that it does not return an initial empty value if the match text starts with whitespace:

```
# split $_ on whitespace, explicitly (leading whitespace returns an empty
# value)
@words = split /\s+/,$_;

# split $_ on whitespace, implicitly (leading whitespace does not return an
# empty value)
@words = split;

# The same as 'split' on its own
@words = split ' ';
```

If we actually want to split on single spaces, we supply split with a literal regexp instead. This is the one time when it makes a difference what the delimiters are:

```
# split on individual spaces
@words = split / /;
```

The split function does not use =~ or !~, which is largely the point. Its functionality can be easily replicated using a match regexp, but split reads a lot better and pairs up with the join keyword that performs the opposite function.

Pre-compiled Regular Expressions

The qr operator is a member of Perl's family of quoting operators. It takes a string and compiles it into a regexp, interpolating it as it goes unless a single quote is used as the delimiter. This is exactly the same way the match operator deals with it. For example, here is a particularly hairy piece of regexp, complete with some trailing modifiers, just for illustrative purposes:

```
# an arbitrary complex regexp, precompiled into $re
my $re = qr/^a.*?\b ([l|L]ong)\s+(and|&)\s+(?:$complex\spattern)/igsm;
```

Once compiled, we can use the regexp in our code without ever having to define it again:

```
# 'if' statement is much more legible...
if ($text =~ $re) { ... }
```

The qr operator has many more other advantages: it is more legible, it is not recompiled each time the regexp is used, and it is faster as a result. There are other things we can do with the qr operator in combination with other regexp features, as we will see.

Regular Expression Delimiters

All forms of regexp can use delimiters other than the forward slash, though the match operator must include them if any other delimiter is used:

```
$atom =~ /proton/;    # traditional match, no 'm'
$atom =~ m|proton|;   # match with pipes
$atom =~ m ?proton?;   # match with a space and question marks
$atom =~ s/proton/neutron/;   # traditional substitution
$atom =~ s|proton|neutron|;   # substitution with pipes
$atom =~ s'proton'neutron';   # substitution with single quotes
my @items = split m|\s+|,$text;   # split using pipes
my @items = split(',',$text);   # traditional split using quotes
```

This last example explains why we can supply something like , to split and have it work. The single quotes are really regexp delimiters and not a single quoted string. It just happens to look that way to the untutored eye. Single quotes also have an additional meaning, which we will come to in a moment.

Another reason for changing the delimiter is to avoid what is known as 'leaning-toothpick-syndrome', where real forward slashes are escaped with backslashes to avoid them being interpreted as the end of the pattern:

```
# match expression with forward slashes
if ($path =~ /\/usr\/local\/lib\/perl5/) { ... }

# same expression using pipes
if ($path =~ m|/usr/local/lib/perl5/|) { ... }
```

We can even use # as a delimiter, so long as we do not leave a space between the operator and the first delimiter:

```
$atom =~ s#proton#neutron#;   # substitution with '#' signs
$atom =~ s #proton#neutron#;   # ERROR: 's' followed by a comment
```

In fact, we can even use alphanumeric characters as delimiters, but since regexps such as msg$mmsg are pathologically unfriendly, it is not encouraged. That regular expression would be better written /sg$/msg.

The delimiter is not limited to single characters, however. Perl also allows paired characters like brackets and braces:

```
$atom =~ s{proton}{neutron};
```

All of the following character pairs can be used in this fashion:

```
()    []    {}    <>
```

Using a pair of characters provides another benefit when using the substitution operator; it allows the pattern and its replacement to be placed on separate lines:

```
$atom =~ s{proton}    # the pattern
          {neutron};  # the replacement
```

The only drawback to this style is that the braces might be mistaken for blocks of code, especially when the /e is involved. It is a good idea to make the delimiters stand out from the surrounding code as well.

It is not even necessary for the delimiters of the pattern to be the same as those of the replacement (though how comprehensible this might be is another matter):

```
$atom =~ s[proton]<neutron>;
```

If the delimiter is a single quote, then interpolation is not carried out on the pattern. This allows us to specify characters like dollar signs, at signs, and normal forward and back slashes without using backslashes to escape them from special interpretation:

```
$atom =~ m/$proton/;    # match contents of $proton
$atom =~ m'$proton';    # match '$proton'
```

If the delimiter is a question mark, a special one-shot optimization takes place inside the regexp engine:

```
?proton?    # match proton once only
```

This pattern will never match again, even if we call it a second time from inside a loop. It is useful when we only want to match something once, and will not match again unless `reset` is used without arguments. This resets all one-shot patterns in the same package scope:

```
reset;    # reset one-shot patterns in current package
```

The benefits of ? delimited regexps are dubious, however. Similar (though not as thorough) effects can be obtained more traditionally with the /o pattern match modifier detailed later, although the benefits aren't great, and it is even possible that this syntax may disappear completely one day.

Elements of Regular Expressions

Before getting into the details of regexp syntax, let's take a brief look at four of the most important elements of regexp syntax:

❑   Metacharacters
❑   Pattern match modifiers
❑   Anchors
❑   Extended Patterns

Once we have a preliminary idea of these four aspects of regexps we will be able to use them in other examples before we get to the nitty-gritty of exactly what they are and what features they provide.

The role of a regexp is to match within the text to which it is applied. The simplest regexps consist of nothing more than literal characters that must be present in the string for the match to succeed. Most of the regular expressions we have seen so far fall into this category. For example:

```
$match = $colors =~ /red/;   # literal pattern 'red'
```

Here the variable $match is set to 1 if the variable $colors contains the text red at any point, and is undefined otherwise. Although this pattern is perfectly functional, it has some major limitations. It cannot discriminate between finding a word and part of another word, for instance shred or irredeemable. One way to test for a specific word is to check for spaces around it. We could do that with an explicit space, or:

```
$match = $colors =~ / red /;   # match ' red '
```

A better way of doing this is using **metacharacters**. Perl provides several metacharacters for regexps that handle common cases, including \s, which matches any whitespace character, which includes spaces, tabs, and newlines. If we just want to pick out words, using \s is better than using a space as it matches more cases.

```
$match = $colors =~ /\sred\s/;   # match ' red ', '<tab>red\n' ...
```

However, neither is particularly effective, because they do not cater for cases such as the word occurring at the beginning or end of the text, or even punctuation like quotes, colons, and full stops. A better solution is to use another metacharacter, \b, which matches the boundary between words and the surrounding text:

```
$match = $colors =~ /\bred\b/;
```

The boundary, defined by \b, is where a word character (defined as alphanumeric plus underscore) falls adjacent to a non-word character or at either end of the string. As a result, it catches many more cases than previously. (It still does not manage hyphenated words, apostrophes, or quoted phrases, though – for that the Text::ParseWords module is a good choice, see Chapter 18 for more on processing text).

Finally, we might want to match the word red regardless of its case. To do that we can use one of the **pattern match modifiers**, which may be placed after the pattern of a regular expression. Other pattern match modifiers include /g for multiple matches and /x to allow documentation within a search pattern. In this case we want the /i modifier to turn off case sensitivity:

```
$match = $colors =~ /\bred\b/i;   # match 'red', 'RED', 'rEd' ...
```

We can also **anchor** a regular expression so that it matches only at the beginning or the end of the match text. To anchor at the beginning, we prefix the pattern with a caret:

```
$match = $colors =~ /^red/;   # match 'red' at the start of the string
```

Likewise, to anchor at the end, we use a dollar sign:

```
$match = $colors =~ /red$/;   # match 'red' at the end of the string
```

We can even use both together, which on a simple pattern like this is equivalent to using the eq comparison operator:

```
$match = $colors =~ /^red$/;   # match whole line to 'red'
$match = ($colors eq 'red');   # the same thing, with 'eq'
```

Perl also defines a whole range of so-called **extended patterns** that can be used to modify the nature of sub-patterns (parts of a pattern) within the main pattern. Two that are particularly useful are the **zero-width lookahead** assertion, which matches the text ahead without absorbing it, and the **clustering modifier**, which allows grouping without the other side effects of parentheses:

```
(?=zerowidth)   # match but do not touch!
(?:no|value|extracted|here)   # group terms but do not extract match
```

We will see more of all of those elements of regular expressions later in the chapter.

More Advanced Patterns

Literal patterns are all very well, but they are only the simplest form of regexps that Perl supports. In addition to matching literal characters, we have the ability to match any particular character, a range of characters, or between alternative sub-strings. Additionally we can define optional expressions that may or may not be present, or expressions that can match multiple times. Most crucially, we can extract the matched text in special variables and refer to it elsewhere, even inside the regexp.

Matching Arbitrary Characters and Character Classes

Regexps may use the period . to match any single character. This immediately gives us more flexibility than a simple literal pattern. For example, the following regular expression (which we saw at the start of the chapter) will match several different words:

```
$matchtext =~ /b.ll/;   # match 'ball', 'bell', 'bill', 'boll', 'bull'...
```

Unfortunately this is a little too flexible since it also matches bbll, and for that matter bsll bXll, b ll, and b?ll. What we really want to do is restrict the characters that will match to the lower case vowels only, which we can do with a character class.

A character class is a sequence of characters, enclosed within square brackets, that matches precisely one character in the match text. For example, to improve the previous example to match on a lower case vowel only, we could write:

```
$matchtext =~ /b[aeiou]ll/;
# only match 'ball', 'bell', 'bill', 'boll', or 'bull'
```

Similarly, to match a decimal digit we could write:

```
$hasadigit =~ /[0123456789]/;   # match 0 to 9
```

Since this is a very common thing to want to do, we can specify a range of characters by specifying the ends separated by a hyphen:

```
$hasdigit =~ /[0-9]/;    # also match 0 to 9 (as does the \d metacharacter)
```

> *As a brief aside, ranges are sensitive to the character set that is in use, as determined by the* use locale *pragma, covered in Chapter 26. However, most of the time we are using ASCII (or an ASCII-compatible character set like Latin-1), so it does not make too much difference.*

If we want to match the minus sign itself we can, but only if we place it at the beginning or end of the character class. This example matches any math character, and also illustrates that ranges can be combined with literal characters inside a character class:

```
$hasmath =~ /[0-9.+/*-]/;
```

Note that the period '.' character loses its special regexp meanings when inside a character class, as does * (meaning match zero or more times). Likewise, the ?, (,), {, and } characters all represent themselves inside a character class, and have no special meanings.

Several ranges can be combined together. Here are two regexps that match any alphanumeric character (according to Perl's definition this includes underscores) and a hexadecimal digit respectively:

```
$hasalphanum =~ /[a-zA-Z0-9_]/;
$hashexdigit =~ /[0-9a-fA-F]/;
```

Ranges are best used when they cover a simple and clearly obvious range of characters. Using unusual characters for the start or end of the range can lead to unexpected results, especially if we handle text that is expressed in a different character set.

Ranges like a-z, A-Z, and 0-9 are predictable because the range of characters they define is intuitively obvious. Ranges like a-z, ?-!, and é-ü are inadvisable since it is not immediately obvious what characters are in the set, and it is entirely possible that a different locale setting can alter the meaning of the range.

The sense of a character class can be inverted by prefixing it with a caret ^ symbol. This regexp matches anything that is not a digit:

```
$hasnondigit =~ /[^0-9]/;
```

Similar to the minus sign, if we want to actually match a caret then we can do, so long as we place it anywhere but at the start of the class:

```
$hasdigitorcaret =~ /[0-9^]/;
```

If we want to match a closing bracket we have to get a little more inventive. The backslash is allowed inside character classes and still escapes the character following it. To match a closing square bracket we need to escape it with backslash, as this example shows:

```
$hasbrackets =~ /[[\]]/;
```

Interestingly, we do not need to escape an opening square bracket (though we can anyway, for clarity's sake) since Perl already knows we are in a character class, and character classes do not nest. Anywhere else in a regexp where we want a literal opening square bracket, we need to escape the special meaning to avoid starting a character class we do not want.

Characters that are meaningful for interpolation also need to be escaped if the search pattern is delimited with anything other than single quotes. This applies to any part of a regexp, not just within a character class. However, since characters like . and * lose their special meaning inside character classes, programmers often forget that $ and @ symbols do not:

```
$bad_regexp =~ /[@$]/;    # ERROR: try to use '$]'
$empty_regexp =~ /[$@]/;   # use value of $@
```

We can match these characters by escaping them with a backslash, including the backslash itself:

```
$good_regexp =~ /[\$\@\\]/;   # matches $, @ or \
```

Strangely, the pattern [@] is actually valid, because Perl does not define @] as a variable and so correctly guesses that closing bracket is actually the end of the character class. Relying on this kind of behavior is, however, dangerous as we are bound to get tripped up by it sooner or later.

Here is a summary of the standard character class syntax and how different characters behave within it:

Syntax	Action
[	Begin a character class, unless escaped
n	Match character n
n-m	Match characters from n to m
-	At end of string, matches -, otherwise defines a range
. ? * ( ) { }	Match the literal characters ., ?, (,), { and }
^	At beginning of string, negates sense of class
$ @ \	Interpolate, unless escaped or pattern is single quoted
]	End character class, unless escaped

In addition to the standard syntax, we can also use character class metacharacters like \w or \d as shortcuts for common classes. These metacharacters can also be used inside character classes, as we will see shortly when we come to metacharacters. From Perl 5.6 onwards, regexps may also use POSIX and Unicode character class definitions; see Chapter 25 for full details.

Repetition and Grouping

Literal characters, and character classes, permit us to be as strict or relaxed as we like about what we can match to them, but they still only match a single character. In order to allow repeating matches we can use one of the three repetition modifiers:

?	match zero or one occurrences
*	match zero or more occurrences
+	match one or more occurrences

Each of these modifies the effect of the immediately preceding character or character class, in order to match a variable number of characters in the match text. For example, to match bell! or bells! we could use:

```
$ringing =~ /bells?!/;   # match 'bell!' or 'bells!'
```

Alternatively, if we use the * modifier we can match zero or more occurrences of a character:

```
$ringings =~ /bells*!/;   # match 'bell!', 'bells!', 'bellss!', etc.
```

Finally, if we use +, we require at least one match but will accept more:

```
$ringings =~ /bells+!/   # match 'bells!', 'bellss!', etc.
```

Repetition modifiers also work on character classes. For instance, here is one way to match any decimal number using a character class:

```
$hasnumber =~ /[0-9]+/   # match '1', '007', '1701', '2001', '90210', etc.
```

Repeating Sequences of Characters

We can use parentheses to define a string of characters, which allows us to match repeating terms rather than just single characters. For example, we can match either of the strings such or nonesuch by defining none as an optional term:

```
$such =~ /(none)?such/;   # match either 'such' or 'nonesuch'
```

We can even nest parentheses to allow optional strings within optional strings. This regular expression matches such, nonesuch, and none-such:

```
$such =~ /(none(-)?)?such/;   # match 'such', 'nonesuch' or 'none-such'
```

Note that in this case we could have omitted the nested parentheses since they are surrounding only one character.

Grouping Alternatives

We can also use parentheses to group terms in a way analogous to character classes. The syntax is simple and intuitive; we simply specify the different terms within parentheses separated by a pipe symbol:

```
$such =~ /(none|all)such/;   # match 'nonesuch' or 'allsuch'
```

We can nest grouped terms to produce various interesting effects, for example:

```
$such =~ /(no(ne|t as )|a(ny|ll))such/;
```

This regexp uses two inner groups nested inside the outer one, and matches nonesuch, not as such, anysuch, and allsuch. We could equally have written:

```
$such =~ /(none|not as |any|all)such/;
```

In theory, the first example is more efficient, since we have grouped similar terms by their common characters and only specified the differences. Perl's regexp engine is very good at optimizing things like this, and in reality both expressions will execute with more or less the same speed.

In fact, it is not always necessary to use parentheses around the alternatives. The following is a perfectly legal way to match sharrow, miz, or dloan:

```
$who =~ /sharrow|miz|dloan/;
```

This works because there is no ambiguity about the start of the first term or the end of the last – they are delimited by the pattern itself. Any regexp syntax like [ ], ( ), +, *, and so on will also define limits:

```
$who =~ /^(.*)sharrow|miz|dloan/;
```

If we want to specify literal text adjacent to a set of alternatives however, we need to use parentheses to make the beginning and end explicit. Since getting regexps right can be tricky at the best of times, many programmers include parentheses anyway, whether or not they are strictly necessary.

Specifying a Number of Repetitions

We can exercise a greater degree of control over the * and + modifiers by specifying a particular number or range of repetitions that we will allow. A single specified number of matches take the form of a number in curly braces:

```
$sheep =~ /ba{2}!/;    # match 'baa!'
```

To define a range we specify two numbers separated by a comma:

```
$sheep =~ /ba{2,4}!/    # match 'baa!', 'baaa!', or 'baaaa!'
```

We have included a trailing exclamation mark in this example, since without it anything can follow the search pattern, including more 'a's, so the above two examples would have been equivalent in their ability to succeed. If we were extracting the matched text with parentheses, that would be another matter of course.

As a special case, if we use a comma to define a range of repetitions but omit the second value, the regexp engine interprets this as 'no upper limit'. We can match a sheep with unlimited lung capacity with:

```
$sheep =~ /ba{2,}!/;    # match 'baa!', 'baaaaaaaaaaa!', etc...
```

From this it follows that the standard repetition modifiers are just shorthand for the following expanded versions:

?	equivalent to {0,1}
*	equivalent to {0,}
+	equivalent to {1,}

Note that using interpolation to specify a range with variables is perfectly acceptable as it is anywhere else in a search pattern. For example, we can supply a variable range at the point of execution by writing something like the following:

```
($min, $max) = (2, 4);
$sheep = "baaa!";
if ($sheep =~ /ba{$min,$max}!/) {    # equivalent to '/ba{2,4}!/'
    print "match \n";
}
```

Number repetitions are useful when we want to find a specific occurrence within the match text. Here's an example that uses a repetition count to find the fourth (and only the fourth) word in a colon-separated list:

```
$text = "one:two:three:four:five";
# extract the 4th field of colon separated data
$text =~ /(([^:]*):?){4}/;
print "Got: $2\n";   # print 'Got: four'
```

This regexp looks for zero-or-more non-colon characters, followed (optionally) by a colon, four times. The optional colon ensures that we will match the last field on the line, while the greediness of the pattern as a whole ensures that if a colon is present it will get matched. Parentheses are used here to group the non-colon characters and the colon into a single term for the repetition. They are also used to extract the part of the text we are interested in (not the colon).

Note that the match of each set of parentheses in a regular expression is placed in a **numbered variable**. In the above example, the numbered variable $1 represents the match of the *first* set of parentheses, that is (([^:]*):?). Printing $1, therefore, would output four:. We are interested in the text matched by the *second* (inner) set of parentheses [^:]*), so we print $2. We will be using numbered variables a couple of times in the next sections before looking at them in detail in 'Extracting Matched Text'.

Eagerness, Greediness, and Relentlessness

As we mentioned earlier, Perl's regexp engine has three main characteristics that define its behavior. While these rules always hold, they become more important once we start adding repetitions and groups to our regexps. Wherever a repetition or a group occurs in a search pattern, Perl will always try to match as much as it can from the current position in the match text.

It does this by grabbing as much text as possible and then working backwards until it finds a successful match. For instance, when given a regexp like baa+ and a match text of baaaaaaa, Perl will always ultimately find and return all the as in the match text, though depending on the circumstances it might take the engine more or less time to arrive at this final result.

However, regexps always match as soon as possible. This means that the left-most match satisfying the search pattern will always be found first, irrespective of the fact that a bigger match might occur later in the string:

```
$sheep = "baa baaaaaaaaaa";
$sheep =~ /baa+/;   # match first 'baa'
```

If we really want to find the longest match we will have to find all possible matches with the /g pattern match modifier and then pick out the longest. The /g modifier causes the regular expression engine to restart from where it left off last time, so by calling it repeatedly we extract each matching string in turn:

```
$sheep = "baa baaaaaaaaaa";
while ($sheep =~ /(baa+)/g) {
    $match = $1 if length($1) > length($match);
}
# print 'The loudest sheep said 'baaaaaaaaaa''
print "The loudest sheep said '$match' \n";
```

This can lead to unexpected results if we forget it. For example, the following regexp supposedly matches single-quoted text:

```
$text =~ /'.*'/;   # text contains a single quoted string
```

Unfortunately, although it does indeed do what it should, it does it rather too well. It takes no account of the possibility that there might be more than one pair of quotes in the match text (we will disregard the possibility of apostrophes just to keep things under control). For example, assume we set $text to a value like:

```
$text = "'So,' he said. 'What will you do?'";
```

The regexp /'.*'/ will match the first quote, grab as much as possible, match the last quote and everything in between – the entire string in other words. One way to fix this is to use a **non-greedy match**, which we'll cover in a moment. Another is to be more precise about what we actually want. In this case we do not want any intervening quotes, so our regexp would be better written as:

```
$text =~ /'[^']*'/;   # a better match between quotes
```

This says 'match a quote, zero or more characters that can be anything but a quote, and then another quote'. When fed the previous sample text, it will match 'So,' as we intended.

Writing regexps is full of traps like this. The regexp engine is not so much greedy as bloody-minded – it will always find a match any way it can, regardless of how apparently absurd that match might seem to us. In cases of disagreement, it is the engine that is right, and our search pattern that needs a rethink.

The zero-or-more quantifier, * is especially good at providing unexpected results. Although it causes whatever it is quantifying to match as many times as possible, it is still controlled by the 'as soon as possible' rule. It could be better expressed as 'once we have matched as soon as possible, match as much as possible at that point'. In the case of *, nothing at all may be the only match at the current position. To illustrate this, the following example attempts to replace spaces with dashes, again using the /g pattern match modifier to match all occurrences within the string:

```
$text =~ s/\s*/-/g;
```

If $text is given a value of something like 'journey into space!', we might expect to get the result:

journey-into-space!

However, \s* matches zero or more spaces. That condition is satisfied not only between the words, but between each letter too (no spaces there) and even at the start and end of the string. So what we actually get is:

-j-o-u-r-n-e-y-i-n-t-o-s-p-a-c-e-!-

This might have been what we wanted, but it's probably not. The solution in this case is simple, replace the * with a +. However, in bigger regexps problems like this can be a lot harder to spot.

Lean (Non-Greedy) Matches

Lean (or more conventionally, non-greedy) matches alter the operation of the regexp engine to match as little as possible instead of as much as possible. This can be invaluable in controlling the behavior of regexp, and also in improving its efficiency.

To make any repetition non-greedy, we suffix it with a question mark. For example, the following are all non-greedy quantifiers:

`(word)??`	Match zero or one occurrence
`(word)*?`	Match zero or more occurrences
`(word)+?`	Match one or more occurrence
`(word){1,3}?`	Match one to three occurrences
`(word){0,}?`	Match zero or more occurrences (same as *?)

Note that these all apparently have the same meanings as their greedy counterparts. In fact they do, but the difference comes in the way the regexp attempts to satisfy them. Following the rule of 'as soon as possible', a regexp will normally grab as much text as possible and try to match 'as much as possible'. The first successful match is returned. With a non-greedy quantifier, the regexp engine grabs one character at a time and tries to match 'as little as possible'.

For example, another way we could have solved the single-quote finder we gave earlier would have been to make the 'match any characters' pattern non-greedy:

```
$text =~ /'.*?'/   # non-greedy match between quotes.
```

Lean matches are not a universal remedy to cure all ills, however. For a start, they can be less efficient than their greedy counterparts. If the above text happened to contain a very long speech, a greedy match would find it far faster than a lean one, and the previous solution of /'[^']*'/ is actually far superior.

Additionally, making a match non-greedy does not alter the fact that a regexp will match as soon as possible. This means that a lean match is no more guaranteed to match the shortest possible string than a greedy match is to match the largest possible. For example, take the following, fortunately fictional, company and regexp:

```
$company = "Greely, Greely, and Spatsz";
$partners = $company =~ /Greely.*?Spatsz/;
```

On executing these statements, $partners contains the entire string. The reason for this is simple: While it is true that matching from the second Greely would produce a shorter match, the regexp engine doesn't see the second Greely – it sees the first, matches, and then matches the second Greely with .*?. To fix this problem we need to match repeatedly from each Greely and then take the shortest result. To do that we need to use a zero-width assertion; we will see how to do that, and give an example that solves the problem with the example above, at the end of 'Overlapping Matches and Zero-Width Patterns' later in the chapter.

Repetition and Anchors

We have already mentioned anchors, but a few examples of their use in combination with repetition bears discussion. For instance, a common task in Perl scripts is to strip off trailing whitespace from a piece of text. We can do that in a regexp by anchoring a repetition of whitespace (as defined by the \s metacharacter) to the end of the string using the $ anchor:

```
s/\s+$//;    # replace trailing whitespace with nothing
```

Similarly, if we are parsing some input text and want to skip over any line that is blank or contains only whitespace or whitespace plus a comment (which we will define as starting with a #), we can use a regexp like the one in the following short program:

```
#!/usr/bin/perl
# repanchor1.pl
use warnings;
use strict;

while (<>) {
    chomp;    # strip trailing linefeed from $_
    next if /^(\s*(#.*)?)?$/;    # skip blank lines and comments
    print "Got: $_ \n";
}
```

The regexp here is anchored at both ends. The () and ? state that the body of the regexp is optional. The regexp /^$/, which matches a completely blank line, will satisfy the regexp and trigger the next iteration of the loop.

If the line is not blank, we have to look inside the body. Here we can match zero or more occurrences of whitespace followed optionally by a # and any text at all, represented by .*. This will match a line containing only spaces, a line starting with zero or more spaces and then a comment starting with # but it will not match a line that starts with any other character.

This is not a very efficient regexp. The problem being that it is needlessly complex and slow since a comment line requires the regexp engine to read and match every letter of the comment in order to satisfy the .*. It only needs to do that because the regexp is anchored at the end, and the only reason for that is so we can match the case of an empty line with /^$/.

We can actually make the anchors themselves optional. Since anchors do not match characters, this may not be immediately obvious, but it works nonetheless. Here is a better version of the loop using an improved regexp:

```
#!/usr/bin/perl
# repanchor2.pl
use warnings;
use strict;
```

```
while (<>) {
    chomp;    # strip trailing linefeed from $_
    next if /^\s*($|#)/;    # skip blank lines and comments
    print "Got: $_ \n";
}
```

This regexp is only anchored at the beginning. It matches zero or more spaces, followed by either the end of the line or a hash. What comes after the hash, if there is one, we neither care nor check.

This loop behaves no differently from the earlier example, but because the regexp does not have to analyze the whole line to find a match, it returns much faster so this loop executes quicker.

Matching Sequential and Overlapping Terms

One task frequently required of regexps is to check for the presence of several tokens within the match text. This basically comes down to a case of logic; do we want all of the terms, or just one of them? If we only want to know if one of them is present we can use alternatives:

```
$text =~ /proton|neutron/;    # true if either proton or neutron present
```

This regexp is matched if $text contains either sort of particle, a classic or condition. If we want to test that both are present we have more of a problem; there is no and variant. Instead, we have to divide the problem into two halves:

1. Is there a proton, and if so is it followed by a neutron?

2. Is there a neutron, and if so is it followed by a proton?

Either of these conditions will satisfy our criteria, so all we need to do is express them as alternatives, as before. The search pattern that implements this logic is therefore:

```
$text =~ /(proton.*neutron|neutron.*proton)/;
```

Sometimes a single regexp is not the best solution to a problem like this. Although fine for just two terms, we'd have to extend this expression to six alternatives for three, containing things like proton.*neutron.*electron. Four does not even bear thinking about. The same thing can be achieved more easily with conventional Boolean logic:

```
$text =~ /proton/ && $text =~ /neutron/;
```

This is better, and certainly more scalable, but differs from the first example in that it will match overlapping terms, whereas the previous example does not. This is because the regexp starts all over again at the beginning of the match text in the second regexp. That is, it will match protoneutron.

If we want to allow matches to overlap inside a single regexp we have to get a little more clever and use zero-width lookahead assertions as provided by the (?=...) extended pattern. When Perl encounters one of these it checks the pattern inside the assertion as normal, but does not absorb any of the characters into the match text. This gives us the same 'start all over again' mechanics as the Boolean logic but within the same regexp.

Pattern Match Modifiers

Pattern match modifiers are flags that modify the way the regexp engine processes matches in matches, substitutions, and splits. We have already seen the /i and /g modifiers to match regardless of case and match more than once, respectively. The full set of pattern match modifiers are as follows:

Modifier	Description
/i	Case-insensitive: match regardless of case
/g	Global match: match as many times as possible
/m	Treat text as multiple lines: allow anchors to match before and after newline
/o	Compile once: interpolate and compile the search pattern only once
/s	Treat text as single line: allow newlines to match
/x	Expanded regular expression: allow documentation within search pattern

In fact the convention of describing modifiers as /x rather than x is just that, a convention, since the delimiters of the search pattern can easily be changed as we have already seen. In addition, any combination of modifiers can be applied at one time; they do not all need a forward slash (or whatever delimiter we are using):

```
$matched =~ /fullmonty/igmosx;   # the full monty!
```

In addition to this list, the substitution operator allows e and ee as modifiers, which cause Perl to treat the replacement text in a substitution as executable code. These are however not pattern match modifiers as they alter how the replacement text is handled. We will cover them in more detail when we discuss the **substitution** operator in more depth later in the chapter.

All of the pattern match modifiers can be placed at the end of the regexp. In addition, with the exception of /g, they can be placed within the search pattern to enable or disable one or more modifiers partway through the pattern. To switch modifiers on we use (?<flags>) and to switch them off we use (?-<flags>). By default no modifiers are active, and specifying them at the end of the pattern is equivalent to specifying them in line at the start:

```
$matched =~ /pattern/igm;    # with explicit modifiers
$matched =~ /(?igm)pattern/;   # with in-lined modifiers
```

Without enclosing parentheses, the effect of the inline modifier controls the entire pattern coming after them. For instance, the following matches the word pattern, regardless of the case of the letters ttern:

```
matched =~ /pa(?i)ttern/;   # 'ttern' is case insensitive
```

So, if we wanted to restrict the case insensitivity to the letters tt only, we can use this:

```
$matched =~ /pa(?i)tt(?-i)ern/;   # 'tt' is case insensitive
```

However, using parentheses is a neater way of doing it:

```
$matched =~ /pa((?i)tt)ern/;   # 'tt' is case insensitive
```

Since using parentheses to limit the effect of an inline modifier generates possibly unwanted backreferences, we can use the (?:...) extended pattern instead of parentheses to suppress them. Better still, we can combine it with the inline modifier into one extended pattern. Here is a better way of phrasing the last example, avoiding the backreference:

```
$matched =~ /pa(?i:tt)ern/;
```

The most commonly used in line modifier is the case insensitive i modifier. Here are two different ways of matching the same set of commands using in line modifiers. All the commands are case-insensitive except EXIT, which must be in capital letters:

```
if ($input =~ /(?i:help|start|stop|reload)|EXIT/) {...}
if ($input =~ /help|start|stop|reload|(?-i:EXIT)/i) {...}
```

In the first example we switch on case insensitivity for the first four commands, and switch it off again for the last (which side of the pipe symbol we place the parentheses is of course a matter of taste since the pipe is not affected). In the second example we switch on case-insensitivity for the whole regexp using a conventional /i flag, then switch it off for the last command.

Referring back to our earlier comment about the equivalence of a trailing modifier and an in line modifier at the start of a search pattern, we can see that these two examples are not only equivalent, but identical to the regexp engine. The difference is that the inline modifier can be interpolated into the search pattern, whereas the trailing modifier cannot:

```
# set flags to either 'i' or ''
$flags = ENV{'CASE_SENSITIVE'}?'':'i';
# interpolate into search pattern for match
if ($input =~ /(?$flags:help|start|stop|reload)|EXIT/) { ... }
```

If this approach seems particularly useful, consider using the qr quoting operator instead to precompile regexps, especially if the intent is to control the modifiers over the whole of the search pattern. We cover qr in detail later in the chapter.

Regular Expressions versus Wildcards

Regexps bear a passing resemblance to filename wildcards, which is often a source of confusion to those new to regexps but familiar with wildcards. Both use special characters like ? and * to represent variable elements of the text, but they do so in different ways. UNIX shell wildcards (which are more capable than those supported by any of the standard Windows shells) equate to regexps as follows:

❏   The wildcard ? is equivalent to the regexp .

❏   The wildcard * is equivalent to the regexp .*

❏   Character classes [...] are equivalent.

Converting from a regexp to a wildcard is not possible except in very simple cases. Conversely though, we can convert wildcards to regexps reasonably simply, by handling the four characters ?, *, [, and] as special cases and escaping all other punctuation. The following program does just that in the subroutine wild2re:

```perl
#!/usr/bin/perl
# wildre.pl
use warnings;
use strict;

$| = 1;    # enable autoflush for prompt display of prompt (sic)

print "Wildcard: ";
while (<>) {
    chomp;
    print "Regular Expression: ", wild2re($_), "\n";
    print "Wildcard: ";
}

sub wild2re {
    my $re = shift;
    $re =~ s/([^\w\s])/($1 eq '?')?'.'
    :($1 eq '*')?'.*'    :($1 eq '[' || $1 eq ']')?$1
    :"\\$1"/eg;
    return "^$re\$";    #anchor at both ends
}
```

And here is an example of it in use:

> **perl wildre.pl**
Wildcard: file[0-9]*.*
Regular expression: ^file[0-9].*\..*$

It should come as no surprise that the solution to converting wildcards into regexps involves regexps. In this case we have checked for any character that is neither a word character or a whitespace character, handled it specially if it is one of the four that we need to pay particular attention to, and escaped it with a backslash if it isn't. We have used parentheses to extract each matching character into the numbered variable $1, the g pattern match modifier to match every occurrence within the string, and the e flag to treat the substitution as Perl code, the result of which is used as the replacement text.

Before returning the regexp we also add anchors to both ends to prevent it from matching in the middle of a filename, since wildcards do not do that. Although we could rewrite the regexp to do so, it is more trouble than it is worth and would make the pattern needlessly complex. It is simpler to add them afterwards.

To illustrate that there are many solutions to any given problem in Perl, and regexps in particular, here is another version of the same regexp that also does the job we want:

```perl
$re =~ s/(.)/($1 eq '?')?'.'
            :($1 eq '*')?'.*'
            :($1 eq '[' || $1 eq ']')?$1
            :"\Q$1"/eg;
```

This alternative regexp extracts every character in turn, checks for the four special characters and then uses \Q to escape the character if it is not alphanumeric. This is not quite as efficient since it takes a little more effort to work through every character, and it also escapes spaces (though for a filename that would not usually be a problem).

Metacharacters

In addition to character class, repetition, and grouping, search patterns may also contain metacharacters that have a special meaning within the search pattern. We have seen several metacharacters in use already, in particular \s, which matches any whitespace character and \b, which matches a word boundary.

In fact there are two distinct groups of metacharacters. Some metacharacters, like \s and \b have special meaning in regexp. The rest have special meaning in interpolated strings. Since regexp search patterns are interpolated, however, both sets apply to regexps.

We can loosely subdivide regexp metacharacters because regexps contain two fundamentally different kinds of subpattern: patterns that have width and absorb characters when they match, and patterns that have no width and must simply be satisfied for the match to succeed. We call the first **character class metacharacters**. These provide shortcuts for character classes (for example, \s). The second category of regexp metacharacters are called **zero-width metacharacters**. These match conditions or transitions within the text (for example, \b).

Character Class Metacharacters

Several metacharacters are shortcuts for common character classes, matching a single character of the relevant class just as if the character class had been written directly. Most of the metacharacters in this category have an inverse metacharacter with the opposing case and meaning:

Metacharacter	Match Property
\d	Match any digit – equivalent to the character class [0..9].
\D	Match any non-digit – equivalent to the character class [^0-9].
\s	Match any whitespace character – equivalent to the character class [\t\r\n].
\S	Match any non-whitespace character – equivalent to the character class [^ \t\r\n] or [^\s].
\w	Match any 'word' or alphanumeric character, which is the set of all upper and lower case letters, the numbers 0..9 and the underscore character _, usually equivalent to the character class [a-zA-Z0-9_].
	The definition of 'word' is also affected by the locale if use locale has been used, so an é will also be considered a match for \w if we are working in French, but not if we are working in English.
\W	The inverse of \w, matches any 'non-word' character. Equivalent to the character class [^a-zA-Z0-9_] or [^\w].
[:class:]	POSIX character class, for example, [:alpha:] for alphanumeric characters.

Table continued on following page

Metacharacter	Match Property
\p	Match a property, for example, \p{IsAlpha} for alphanumeric characters.
\P	Match a non-property, for example, \P{IsUpper} for non-uppercase characters.
\X	Match a multi-byte Unicode character ('combining character sequence').
\C	Match a single octet, even if interpretation of multi-byte characters is enabled (with use utf8).

Character class metacharacters can be mixed with character classes, but only so long as we do not try to use them as the end of a range, since that doesn't make sense to Perl. The following is one way to match a hexadecimal digit:

```
$hexchar = qr/[\da-fA-F]/;   # matches a hexadecimal digit
$hexnum = qr/$hexchar+/;   # matches a hexadecimal number
```

The negated character class metacharacters have the opposite meaning to their positive counterparts:

```
$hasnonwordchar =~ /\W+/;   # match one or more non-word characters
$wordboundary =~ /\w\W/;   # match word followed by non-word characters
$nonwordornums =~ /[\W\d]/;   # match non-word or numeric characters
$letters =~ /[^\W\d_]/;   # match any letter character
```

The last two examples above illustrate some interesting possibilities for using negated character class metacharacters inside character classes. We get into trouble, however, if we try to use two negated character class metacharacters in the same character class:

```
$match_any =~ /[\W\S]/;   # match punctuation?
```

The intent of this regexp is to match anything that is not a word character or a whitespace character. Unfortunately for us, the regexp takes this literally. A word character is not a whitespace character, so it matches \S. Likewise, a space is not a word character so it matches \W. Since the character class allows either to satisfy it, this will match any character and is just a bad way of saying 'any character at all', that is, a dot.

What we really need to do to achieve the desired effect is to invert the class and use the positive versions:

```
$match_punctuation =~ /[^\w\s]/;   # ok now
```

This will now behave the way we originally intended.

The POSIX character classes (introduced in Perl 5.6) and 'property' metacharacters provide an extended set of character classes for us to use. If the utf8 pragma has been used, the property metacharacter \p follows the same definition as the POSIX equivalent. Otherwise it uses the underlying C library functions isalpha, isgraph, and so on. The following classes and metacharacters are available:

Description	POSIX Character Classes	Property Metacharacter
Alphabetical character	`[:alpha:]`	`\p{IsAlpha}`
Alphanumeric character	`[:alnum:]`	`\p{IsAlnum}`
ASCII character	`[:ascii:]`	`\p{IsASCII}` (equivalent to `[\x00-\x7f]`)
Control character	`[:cntrl:]`	`\p{IsCntrl}` (equivalent to `[\x00-\x20]`)
Numeric	`[:digit:]`	`\p{IsDigit}` (equivalent to `\d`)
Graphical character	`[:graph:]`	`\p{IsGraph}` (equivalent to `[[:alnum:][:punct:]]`)
Lower case character	`[:lower:]`	`\p{IsLower}`
Printable character	`[:print:]`	`\p{IsPrint}` (equivalent to `[[:alnum:][:punct:][:space:]]`)
Punctuation	`[:punct:]`	`\p{IsPunct}`
Whitespace	`[:space:]`	`\p{IsSpace}` (equivalent to `\s`)
Upper case character	`[:upper:]`	`\p{IsUpper}`
Word character	`[:word:]`	`\p{IsWord}` (equivalent to `\w`)
Hexadecimal digit	`[:xdigit:]`	`\p{IsXDigit}` (equivalent to `[/0-9a-fA-F/]`)

POSIX character classes may only appear inside a character class, but the properties can be used anywhere, just like any other metacharacter. For example, to check for a digit we can use any of:

```
/\d/
/\p{IsDigit}/
/[[:digit:]]/
```

The brackets of the POSIX class are part of the character class, so to use one we need two sets of brackets, as the last example above shows. We can also use properties inside character classes, as these three equivalent matches illustrate:

```
/[01\w\s89]/
/[0[:word:]18[:space:]9]/
/[\p{IsWord}0189\p{IsSpace}]/
```

We can negate both the class and the metacharacter to get the opposite sense. For the metacharacter we just use \P instead of \p. For example, to match anything but a numeric character:

```
/\P{IsDigit}/
```

For the class, we can add a caret after the first colon, but note this is a Perl extension and not part of the POSIX standard:

```
/[[:^IsDigit:]]/
```

These sequences are useful for two reasons. First, they provide a standard way of referring to character classes beyond the ones defined by Perl's own metacharacters. Second, they allow us to write regular expressions that are portable to other regular expression engines (that also comply with the POSIX specification). However, note that most of these classes are sensitive to the character set in use, the locale, and the utf8 pragma. \p{IsUpper} is not the same as [A-Z], which is only one very narrow definition of 'upper case', for example.

Zero-Width Metacharacters

Zero-width metacharacters match conditions within the match text, rather than actual characters. They are called zero-width because they do not consume any characters when they match.

The zero-width metacharacters can be subdivided again into those that deal with transitions, which consist of \b and \B, and those that are alter the behavior of anchors in the search pattern, which are \G, \A, \z, and \Z.

\b matches on a word boundary. This occurs whenever a word character, as matched by \w falls adjacent to a non-word character, as matched by \W, in either order. It is equivalent to (\w\W|\W\w) except that unlike this pattern, \b does not consume any characters from the match text.

The metacharacter \B matches on a non-word boundary. This occurs whenever two word characters or two non-word characters fall adjacent to each other. It is equivalent to (\w\w|\W\W) except that \B does not consume any characters from the match text.

\A and \z (lowercase z) are only significant if the /m pattern match modifier has been used. /m alters the meaning of the caret and dollar anchors so that they will match after and before (respectively) a newline character \n, usually in conjunction with the /g global match modifier. \A and \z retain the original meanings of the anchors and still match the start and end of the match text regardless of whether /m has been used or not. In other words, if we are not using /m, then \A and ^ are identical and the same is true of \Z and $.

The upper case \Z is a variation on \z. It matches at the end of the match text, before the newline if any is present. Otherwise it is the same as \z.

\G applies when we use a regular expression to produce multiple matches using the g pattern modifier. It re-anchors the regular expression at the end of the previous match, so that previously matched text takes no part in further matches. It behaves rather like a forwardly mobile \A.

The \G, \A, \z, and \Z metacharacters are all covered in more detail in 'Matching More than Once'.

None of the zero-width metacharacters can exist inside a character class, since they do not match a character. The metacharacter \b however can exist inside a character class. In this context it takes on its interpolative meaning and is interpreted by Perl as a backspace:

```
$text =~ /\b/;      # search for a word boundary in $text
$text =~ /[\b]/;    # search for a backspace in $text
$text =~ /\x08/;    # search for a backspace, expressed as a character code
```

It follows from this that if we want a literal backspace in a search pattern (however unlikely that might be), we need to put it in a character class to prevent it from being interpreted as a zero-width word boundary, or write it out as a character code.

Extracting Matched Text

Regexps become particularly useful when we use them to return the matched text. There are two principal mechanisms for extracting text. The first is through special variables provided by Perl's regexp engine, and the second by adding parentheses to the search pattern to extract selected areas. The special variables have the advantage of being automatically available, but they are limited to extracting only one value. Using them also incurs a performance cost on the regexp engine. Parentheses, by contrast, allow us to extract multiple values at the same time, which means we don't incur the same performance cost. The catch with parentheses is that they are also used to group terms within a pattern, as we have already seen – this can be either a double bonus or an unlooked-for side effect.

Having extracted values using parentheses, we can reuse the matched text in the search pattern itself. This allows us to perform matches on quotes, or locate repeating sequences of characters within the match text.

Finally, the range operator . . is very effective at extracting text from between two regexps. Before we leave the subject of extracting text, we will consider a few examples that show how effective this operator can be in combination with regexps.

Special Variables

Perl defines several special variables that correspond to the final state of a successfully matched regexp. The most obvious of these are the variables $&, $`, and $', which hold the matched text, *all* the text immediately before the match and *all* the text immediately after the match, respectively. These are always defined by default after any successful match and, with the use English pragma, can also be called by the names $MATCH, $PREMATCH, and $POSTMATCH. Let's look at an example:

```perl
#!/usr/bin/perl
# special.pl
use warnings;
use strict;

my $text = "One Two Three 456 Seven Eight 910 Eleven Twelve";
while ($text =~ /[0-9]+/g) {
    print " \$& = $& \n \$` = $` \n \$' = $' \n";
}
```

> **perl special.pl**
$& = 456
$` = One Two Three
$' = Seven Eight 910 Eleven Twelve
$& = 910
$` = One Two Three 456 Seven Eight
$' = Eleven Twelve

The simple regular expression in this example searches for matches of any combination of digits. The first match 456 gets assigned to $&. The value of $` is then all the text before the match, which is One Two Three . The rest of the string after the match,  Seven Eight 910 Eleven Twelve, is assigned to $'. When the second match is found, the values of all three variables change. $& is now 910, $` is One Two Three 456 Seven Eight , and $' is Eleven Twelve.

One problem with these variables is that they are inefficient because the regexp engine has to do extra work in order to keep track of them. When we said these variables are defined by default, it is not entirely true. They are, in fact, not defined until we use one of them, after which all of them become available for every regexp that we execute, and not just the ones that we use the variables for. For this reason parentheses are better in terms of clarity, since we can be more selective about what we extract (see next section). This is also true in terms of efficiency, since only regexps that use them will cause the regexp engine to do the extra work. For short and simple Perl applications, however, these variables are acceptable.

Having warned of the undesirability of using $&, $`, and $', the latter two variables are actually quite useful. This is especially true for $', since this represents all the text we have so far not matched (note that this does not mean it hasn't been looked at, just that the last successful match matched none of the characters in it). However, we can perform repeated matches in the same regexp, which only match on the text unmatched so far by using the /g metacharacter, as we did in the above example. See 'Matching More than Once' for details.

If we really want to use the values of $&, $` and $', without having Perl track them for every regexp, we can do so with the special array variables @- and @+. The zeroth elements of these arrays are set to the start and end positions of $& whenever a match occurs. They are not related directly to parentheses at all. This modified version of our previous example uses substr and the zeroth elements of @- and @+ to extract $&, $`, and $':

```
#!/usr/bin/perl
# substr.pl
use warnings;
use strict;

my $text = "One Two Three 456 Seven Eight 910 Eleven Twelve";
$text =~ /[0-9]+/;
while ($text =~ /[0-9]+/g) {
    my $prefix = substr($text,0,$-[0]);   # equals $`
    my $match = substr($text,$-[0],$+[0]-$-[0]);   # equals $&
    my $suffix = substr($text,$+[0]);   # equals $'
    print " \$match = $match \n \$prefix = $prefix \n \$suffix = $suffix \n";
}
```

> **perl substr.pl**
$match = 456
$prefix = One Two Three
$suffix = Seven Eight
$match = 910
$prefix = One Two Three 456 Seven Eight
$suffix = Eleven Twelve

This is certainly better than having Perl do the extractions for us, since we only extract the values we want when we require them – although it doesn't do anything for the legibility of our programs. It is also a lot of effort to go through to avoid using parentheses, which generally do the job more simply and as efficiently. For a few cases, however, this can be a useful trick to know.

Parentheses and Numbered Variables

Sometimes we are not so much interested in what the whole search pattern matches, rather what specific parts of the pattern match. For example, we might look for the general structure of a date or address within the text and want to extract the individual values, like the day and month or street and city when we make a successful match. Rather than extract the whole match with $&, we can extract only the parts of interest by placing parentheses around the parts of the pattern to be extracted. Using parentheses we can access the numbered variables $1, $2, $3 etc, which are defined on the completion of the match. Numbered variables are both more flexible and more efficient than using special variables.

Perl places the text that is matched by the regular expression in the first pair of parentheses into the variable $1, and the text matched by the regular expression in the second pair of parentheses into $2, and so on. **Numbered variables** are defined in order according to the position of the left-hand parentheses. Note that these variables start from $1, not $0. The latter is used to hold the name of the program, and has nothing to do with regexps. Let's consider this example:

```perl
#!/usr/bin/perl
# parentheses.pl
use warnings;
use strict;

my $text= "Testing";
if ($text =~ /((T|N)est(ing|er))/) {
    print " \$1 = $1 \n \$2 = $2 \n \$3 = $3 \n \$4 = $4 \n";
}
```

> **perl parentheses.pl**
Use of uninitialized value in concatenation (.) at test.pl line 6.
$1 = Testing
$2 = T
$3 = ing
$4 =

There are three pairs of parentheses in this example. The first one is that which surrounds the whole regular expression, hence $1 evaluates to the whole matched text, which is Testing. The match caused by the second pair of parentheses (T|N), which is T, is assigned to $2. The third pair of parentheses (ing|er) causes $3 to be assigned the value ing. Since we don't have more parentheses, $4 is undefined, hence the warning.

There is no limit to the number of parenthesized pairs that we can use (each of which will define another numbered variable). As shown in our example, we can even nest parentheses inside each other. The fact that $1 contains all the characters of $2 and $3, and more, does not make any difference; Perl will fill out the variables accordingly.

Even if the pattern within the parentheses is optional (it will successfully match nothing at all), Perl assigns a variable for the parentheses anyway:

```perl
$text =~ /^(non)?(.*)/;
# $1 = 'non' or undefined, $2 = all or rest of text
```

Sometimes we do not want to extract a match variable, we just want to use parentheses to define or group terms together. In practice it doesn't hurt too much if we extract a value we don't want to use, but it can be a problem if it alters the ordering of the extracted variables. The solution to this problem is to prevent Perl from spitting out a value by using the (?:...) notation. This works like regular parentheses for the purposes of defining and grouping terms, but does not give rise to a value:

```
#!/usr/bin/perl
# extended.pl
use warnings;
use strict;

my $text = "Testing";
if ($text =~ /((?:T|N)est(ing|er))/) {
    print " \$1 = $1 \n \$2 = $2 \n \$3 = $3 \n \$4 = $4 \n";
}
```

> **perl extended.pl**
Use of uninitialized value in concatenation (.) at extended.pl line 7.
Use of uninitialized value in concatenation (.) at extended.pl line 7.
$1 = Testing
$2 = ing
$3 =
$4 =

Note how the parenthesis containing the T|N are no longer associated with a numbered variable so $2 is shifted to (ing|er), hence its value is ing. Accordingly, the print statement is now trying to use two undefined variables, $3 and $4, hence the two warnings.

The special (?:...) syntax is one of many extended patterns that Perl regexps support, and possibly the most useful in day-to-day usage. We will cover the others later on in the chapter under 'Extended Patterns'.

We know from earlier examples that if we place a quantifier inside parentheses then all matches are returned concatenated. We have used this fact plenty of times in expressions like (.*). However, quantifiers cannot multiply parentheses. That means that if we place a quantifier outside rather than inside parentheses, the last match is placed in the corresponding numbered variable. We do not get extra numbered variables for each repetition. To illustrate this, let's consider this modified version of an example that we used earlier on:

```
#!/usr/bin/perl
# overwrite1.pl
use warnings;
use strict;

my $text = "one:two:three:four:five";
# match non-colon characters optionally followed by a colon, 3 times
if ($text =~ /(([^:]+):?){3}/) {
    print " \$1 = $1 \n \$2 = $2 \n";
}
```

> **perl overwrite1.pl**
$1 = three:
$2 = three

In this example, only one pair of $1 and $2 will exist after the regexp finishes. Each repeated match overwrites the values found by the previous match, so once the match is finished we only have three: and $three (the latter containing the word we want without the preceding colon).

If we actually want to extract all the repetitions rather than the last we will have to write out each repetition explicitly:

```perl
#!/usr/bin/perl
# overwrite2.pl
use warnings;
use strict;

my $text = "one:two:three:four:five";
# match non-colon characters optionally followed by a colon, 3 times
if ($text =~ /^(([^:]+):?)(([^:]+):?)(([^:]+):?)/) {
    print " \$2 = $2 \n \$4 = $4 \n \$6 = $6 \n";
}
```

> **perl overwrite2.pl**
$2 = one
$4 = two
$6 = three

Although this works, it is neither elegant nor particularly legible. A better alternative is to use the /g global pattern match modifier:

```perl
#!/usr/bin/perl
# repeat3.pl
use warnings;
use strict;

my $text = "one:two:three:four:five";
while ($text =~ /(([^:]+):?)/g) {
    print " \$1 = $1 \n \$2 = $2 \n";
}
```

> **perl overwrite3.pl**
$1 = one:
$2 = one
$1 = two:
$2 = two
$1 = three:
$2 = three
$1 = four:
$2 = four
$1 = five
$2 = five

An alternative, and sometimes simpler, approach to getting the value we want is to use the special variable $+ or $LAST_PAREN_MATCH. This is defined by the regexp engine as holding the value of whatever the last set of parentheses matched, or to put it another way, the same value as the highest numbered variable. Thus, in the extended.pl example, the value of $+ is ing, which is the value of $2 (the highest numbered variable). If we are only interested in what matched the last set of parentheses, $+ will return it for us, irrespective of how many parentheses might have occurred previously.

As we have already mentioned, whenever we use parentheses to extract values, Perl sets the start and end positions of each successful match in the special array variables @- and @+. Each pair of elements in these arrays corresponds to the start and end position of the corresponding numbered variable. So, $-[1] is the position at which $1 matched inside the text, and $+[1] is the position it finished.

One practical upshot of this is that we can find the number of parentheses that matched by counting the size of either array. We don't count the zeroth element for this since it corresponds to $& (not the parentheses), so the number of matches is equal to the index of the highest element:

```
$no_of_parens = $#-;    # count number of matching parentheses
```

Since parentheses are always extracted if they are present (even if they are conditional), this doesn't make a lot of difference for hard-coded patterns. However, for patterns that may vary and thus, may contain differing numbers of parentheses, this is a convenient way of handling an arbitrary number of returned numbered variables, without knowing in advance how many parentheses are present.

Purely for illustrative purposes, we could also extract the value of a numbered variable directly using substr. This is effectively what the regexp does for us when we use parentheses. Similarly, we can find the text that matched between one set of parentheses and the text. Here is how we can find the text between $1 and $2:

```
$between1and2 = substr($1,$-[2]-$+[1]);
```

Backreferences

The numbered variables $1 and onwards are defined after a successful match, but are not available within the regexp itself. That is, a regexp like this will not do what we expect unless the value of $1 just happens to have been set to the right quote character in a previous match:

```
$text =~ /('|")(.*?)$1/;    # do not match single or double quoted strings
```

The reason this does not work as expected is because interpolation attempts to supply the value of the variable $1 before the match proceeds, which clearly cannot define $1 until after it has started. The numbered variables are clearly not useful in this case.

In fact we can refer to an extracted value within the same regexp using a **backreference**, the number of the extracted parameter preceded by a backslash:

```
$text =~ /('|")(.*?)\1/;    # do match single or double quoted strings
```

Backreferences are so called because they refer back to an earlier part of the pattern. They give access to the same values as the numbered variables $1 ... , so for each numbered variable defined there is a corresponding backreference. Since they are prefixed by a backslash they are left alone by interpolation, which attaches no special significance to escaped numerals (to be specific, single digit escaped numerals). If we have more than nine backreferences, things can get sticky and they are handled by the regexp engine instead.

The point of backreferences is, of course, that they can be used in the pattern. In fact the values of the backreferences can change several times during the course of an attempted match as the regexp engine searches through different possibilities. Consider the quote-finding regexp we gave a moment ago. It will find one single quoted string or one double quoted string. Now assume we feed it the following text:

```
Today's quote is "This is the way to the future".
```

Following the 'as soon as possible' rule, the regexp finds the unmatched single quote in Today's and goes looking for a mate. At this point \1 contains a single quote. Eventually the engine runs out of places to look for another single quote, since there is only one (fortunately for us there is no apostrophe in 'today's quote'). It backtracks, drops the first single quote and goes looking for another one. Shortly afterwards it finds the double quote, defining the backreference \1 once again, this time as a double quote. Since there are two double quotes, the match succeeds and the backreference is assigned to the numbered variable $1.

It follows from this that backreferences are defined as and when the corresponding part of the pattern is matched. This means that we cannot use a backreference earlier than the part of the search pattern that gives it a value – it does not make logical sense:

```
$text =~ /\1(.*?)('|")/;   # ERROR: backreference before backreference
                           # definition!
```

Of course in this particular example the problem is obvious. In more complex regexps it is easier to make this kind of mistake, especially with a lot of backreferences involved.

Interestingly, a backreference can be placed inside parentheses, so long as they are not the parentheses that are meant to be defining it. Perl will happily use the value of an earlier backreference within a pattern that defines a later backreference (and numbered variable, if the match succeeds):

```
$text =~ /('|")([^\1]*)\1/;
print "Found quote:$1$2$1\n";
```

This is an example of quote matching that avoids using the lean .*? pattern and uses a character class to exclude precisely the character we don't want to find, as we covered earlier. In this case the character is whatever was found by the first part of the pattern and is now held in the backreference \1. As this example shows, there is nothing to stop us using a backreference more than once.

We mentioned, when we introduced the numbered variables, that Perl allows us to extract any number of substrings from the match text, one for each pair of parentheses that we use. This is not a problem for numbered variables, which Perl will happily define up to $100 if necessary.

Backreferences do have a problem, however, since the backreference \10 is ambiguous – it also represents a 'Form Feed' character. Perl resolves this conflict of syntax by using one of its 'common sense' rules: if a backreference is defined then its value is substituted at the position of the backreference in the pattern. If the backreference is not defined, Perl assumes that the backreference is not really a backreference but an ASCII octal character code, and so replaces it with the appropriate character. Since most regexp, at least most sensible ones, do not contain more than nine backreferences, this is fairly safe. Note that if we actually wanted to say 'backreference 1 followed by a zero' we could do it by using a character class of one character: \1[0].

Why this confusion in syntax? It comes about because Perl draws upon several sources for its features, and brought much of the syntax with them. The use of the backslash to define and escape metacharacters comes from shell scripting languages like csh, which in turn get it from the C programming language. The use of the backslash to define a backreference comes from the venerable UNIX utilities sed and awk, both of which are (loosely speaking) regexp engines with a command line. Perl combines the best features of all these tools, but as a result occasionally has to deal with the conflict of syntax this sometimes causes.

So what do we do if we have a lot of backreferences, and we actually do want to insert an ASCII code? In fact this is not a problem so long as we don't mind using something other than octal for the character code. The confusion with backreferences comes because both syntaxes use a backslash followed by digits. If we specify a character code in hexadecimal instead we can use the \x metacharacter, which, since x is not a number, is not mistaken for a backreference:

```
$text =~ /^(.)(.)(.)(.)(.)(.)(.)(.)(.)(.)\x08/;    # match 10 chrs followed
                                                   # by a backspace
```

Extracting Lines with the Range Operator

An interesting alternative to extracting text with a single regexp is to extract it using two simpler regexps and the range operator '..'. If the intent of a regexp is to read a potentially large body of text between two markers, using the range operator may provide a faster alternative.

The drawback is that the range operator works on lines, not within them, so we might have to do some trimming afterwards.

Consider the following single regexp that extracts the text between the two literal markers START and FINISH:

```
$text =~ /^START$(.*?)^FINISH$/msg;
```

The intent of this regexp is to extract the text between each START and FINISH in the body of the match text. We use:

❑   The /g pattern match modifier to extract all the matches

❑   The /s pattern match modifier to allow newlines to match the dot

❑   The /m pattern match modifier so the ^ and $ anchors will match newlines within the text (note that this can be combined with /s) and makes the extracted text pattern non-greedy

So, we match between each START and FINISH pair and not between the first START and the last FINISH.

Unfortunately if the text between the two markers is large, then this regular expression will take a long time to analyze and extract each pair. It would be considerably more convenient to match the very simple text START with one search pattern, FINISH with a second, and then to extract the text between the two matches. This is what the range operator allows us to do.

The following program is an example of the range operator in action. It attempts to retrieve records between START and FINISH markers and store the results into an array of matches. Any line inside a record gets added to the current match in progress. Any line outside gets silently dropped.

```
#!/usr/bin/perl
# range.pl
use warnings;
use strict;

my @records;    # list of found records
my $collect = "";    # collection variable for records
my $in = 0;    # flag to check if we've just completed a record
```

```
    while (<>) {
        print "Considering:$_";
        if (/^START/ ... /^FINISH/) {
            # range is true - we are inside a record
            print "In \n";
            # collect lines for record
            $collect .= $_;
            $in = 1;
        } else {
            # false - we are outside a record
            if (not $in) {
                # we were already outside
                print "Out \n";
            } else {
                # we have just left, found a collect
                print "In -> Out \n";
                # add collected lines to list
                push @records, $collect;
                # clear the collection variable
                $collect = "";
                # set flag to say we are out
                $in = 0;
            }
        }
    }

    foreach (0..$#records) {
        print "Record $_: \n$records[$_] \n";
    }
```

The range operator works on a line-by-line basis. Each side can either be a line number, or a regexp that must match the line to satisfy that side of the range. In operation, the range operator 'remembers' its current state, which is 'off' before the left-hand side becomes True, it then returns False and turns 'on' when the left-hand side is satisfied, in this case, when the line contains the text START. When the right hand side is satisfied, the range operator turns 'off' again. It is in effect a Boolean toggle switch that is first triggered on, and then triggered off.

This script works by keeping track of its own Boolean toggle $in so it knows whether the range operator has just finished a record or not. If it has, we store the results in @matches otherwise we do nothing. Although it works, it does have one flaw: if a START immediately follows a FINISH then the range operator toggles from 'on' to 'off', and back to 'on', with the result that immediately adjacent records get merged together. We have to ensure there is at least one line between records, though whether the line is empty or not we do not care.

Although it is a lot more verbose, this code can run a lot faster than the single regexp approach, not just because the regexp engine has a much simpler task, but also because we do not need to read all the text we want to match against before we start. Having said that, it is verbose and not always suited to tasks involving repeated matches. For simple tasks requiring only one match it shines, however.

One common task that web servers and web clients have to perform is separating the header from the body of an e-mail message or an HTTP response. Both these protocols use a completely blank line to indicate the end of the header and the start of the body. Here is a short program that uses the range operator to read the header and body into separate array variables:

```perl
#!/usr/bin/perl
# header.pl
use warnings;
use strict;

my (@head, @body);

while (<>) {
    if (1 .. /^$/) {
        push @head, $_;
    } else {
        push @body, $_;
        last;   # found start of body, quit loop
    }
}

push @body, <>;
print "Head: \n", join('', @head);
print "Body: \n", join('', @body);
```

Here we have used a 'while' loop to read the header, jumping out of it as soon as the header finishes. The range starts at 1, which corresponds to the first line of the file and therefore is immediately true, so we don't need any special toggle variable to check whether we are before or after the header. It ends at /^$/, which matches a completely empty line.

The range operator actually comes in two guises, '..' and '...'. The difference between them is that ... will not complete a range from start to finish on a single line; that is, if the left-hand side has just become True then the right-hand side is not tested even if it would also be True. In the examples we have used here, there is no difference since all our regexps have been anchored at the start and so cannot simultaneously match. However, in the event that we wanted to handle an e-mail body that had no head (that is, it starts with an empty line as the first line), we would need to choose between .. and ... depending on whether we wanted to recognize the first line as the end of the header or ignore it and look for a second empty line before ending the header and starting the body.

Matching More than Once

On many occasions we do not just want to find the first or best match available, but all of them. Unmodified, a regexp will only match the requested text once (if it can, that is). Modified by the global /g pattern match modifier, however, it will match as many times as it can.

The pattern match modifier /g turns a regexp into an iterative rather than a one-off function. In much the same way that the each operator, when called in list context returns the next key and value from a hash, a global regexp will match repeatedly. It will also set the numbered variables, backreferences from parenthesized expressions, and the special variables $&, $`, and $' if we are using them. In the case of regexps, next means the next best match according to the rules of the regexp engine.

Regular Expressions and Loops

When called in a scalar context, a global regexp will return True for each successful match, with the numbered variables and the special variables $&, $`, $', and $+ containing the values for each successful match. Likewise, numbered variables are set per match. When called in a straight scalar context (that is, not a while or until loop), only the first match is made and sets the variables on exit:

```
$text = "one two three";
$matched = $text =~ /\b(\w+)\b/g;   # match once...
print $1;   # print first word found which is 'one'
```

However, when called in a list context, all matches are returned as a list:

```
@matches = $text =~ /\b\w+\b/g;   # collect all words
```

This is a handy way to collect successful matches because it requires neither the use of $& nor parentheses plus a numbered variable, but it is only effective when we are only interested in the text the whole pattern matches. More conventionally, a global regexp is often combined with a foreach or while loop.

Both foreach and while loops (and for that matter, map and grep statements) can be used to handle the results of a global regexp. There are, however, important differences between them. The following short program contains one of each, both producing the same result:

```
#!/usr/bin/perl
# globalloop.pl
use warnings;
use strict;

my $text = "one, two, three, four";

# iterate over matches with foreach and $_
foreach ($text =~ /\b\w+\b/g) {
    print $_, "\n";
}

# iterate over matches with while and $1
while ($text =~ /\b(\w+)\b/g) {
    print $1, "\n";
}
```

Although identical in result, these two loops are different in the way that they execute. The foreach loop extracts all the matching values from the regexp before the loop starts, so the special variables $& and $1 have the values associated with the last successful match for every iteration of the loop. The foreach loop above is, in effect, no different from this more explicit loop:

```
@matches = $text =~ /\b\w+\b/g;
foreach (@matches) {
    print $_, "\n";
}
```

If we try to extract subpattern matches with parentheses in a foreach loop, then we will be in for a nasty shock. By contrast, the while loop extracts one match from the regexp each time around the loop. The values of the numbered variables are therefore correct for each match in turn, making it suitable for extracting subpattern matches.

Nested Regular Expression Loops

One pitfall that many programmers have fallen into with the /g flag is that there is only one set of the special and numbered variables $&, $1, and so on. When a second regexp is executed, the results overwrite those of the first, which can have disastrous consequences if we were relying on the initial values of the special variables to remain. The following example program illustrates the perils of trying to use variables like $& and $1 in a pair of nested foreach loops:

```
#!/usr/bin/perl
# nest1.pl
use warnings;
use strict;

my $text = "one, two, three, four";

# iterate over matches with foreach and $_
foreach ($text =~ /\b(\w+)\b/g) {
    print "outer: got: $_, matched: $&, extracted: $1 \n";
    foreach (/(\w)/g) {
        print "\tinner: got: $_, matched $&, extracted $1 \n";
    }
}
```

When run, this produces the following output:

```
> perl nest1.pl
outer: got: one, matched: four, extracted: four
        inner: got: o, matched e, extracted e
        inner: got: n, matched e, extracted e
        inner: got: e, matched e, extracted e
outer: got: two, matched: e, extracted: e
        inner: got: t, matched o, extracted o
        inner: got: w, matched o, extracted o
        inner: got: o, matched o, extracted o
outer: got: three, matched: o, extracted: o
        inner: got: t, matched e, extracted e
        inner: got: h, matched e, extracted e
        inner: got: r, matched e, extracted e
        inner: got: e, matched e, extracted e
        inner: got: e, matched e, extracted e
outer: got: four, matched: e, extracted: e
        inner: got: f, matched r, extracted r
        inner: got: o, matched r, extracted r
        inner: got: u, matched r, extracted r
        inner: got: r, matched r, extracted r
```

The value of $_ is as expected, because foreach loops localize the value of the loop variable (which in this case is $_) within the scope of the loop. Each time the inner loop is entered, the value of $_ in the outer loop is hidden by a local $_, and pops back into view each time the inner loop exits again. However, the values of $& and $1 slavishly hold the results of the last match (because these are foreach loops, see above) of whichever regexp executed most recently.

Similar problems occur when we use while loops. This program appears to do much the same as the example above, but aborts matching of the individual characters after the first character of each word:

```
#!/usr/bin/perl
# nest2.pl
use warnings;
use strict;

my $text = "one, two, three, four";

# iterate over matches with foreach and $_
while ($text =~ /\b(\w+)\b/g) {
    print "outer: matched: $&, extracted: $1 \n";
    while ($1 =~ /(\w)/g) {
        print "\tinner: matched $&, extracted $1 \n";
    }
}
```

When we run this program we do not get quite what we expected:

```
outer: matched: one, extracted: one
        inner: matched o, extracted o
outer: matched: two, extracted: two
        inner: matched t, extracted t
outer: matched: three, extracted: three
        inner: matched t, extracted t
outer: matched: four, extracted: four
        inner: matched f, extracted f
```

The problem here is that we are matching the inner regexp against $1, though it would not have made any difference if we had used $&. After the first match of the inner loop, $1 contains the character that matched. Unaware that its foundations have been shifted, the regexp advances past the first character, finds there are no more and promptly finishes. In order to make this program work we need to make a copy of the matched text and use that for the inner loop:

```
#!/usr/bin/perl
# nest3.pl
use warnings;
use strict;

my $text = "one, two, three, four";
# iterate over matches with foreach and $_
while ($text =~ /\b(\w+)\b/g) {
    print "outer: matched: $&, extracted: $1 \n";
    my $inner = $1;
    while ($inner =~ /(\w)/g) {
        print "\tinner: matched $&, extracted $1 \n";
    }
}
```

When we run this modified program we now get the result we were looking for:

```
outer: matched: one, extracted: one
        inner: matched o, extracted o
        inner: matched n, extracted n
        inner: matched e, extracted e
outer: matched: two, extracted: two
        inner: matched t, extracted t
        inner: matched w, extracted w
```

```
         inner: matched o, extracted o
 outer: matched: three, extracted: three
         inner: matched t, extracted t
         inner: matched h, extracted h
         inner: matched r, extracted r
         inner: matched e, extracted e
         inner: matched e, extracted e
 outer: matched: four, extracted: four
         inner: matched f, extracted f
         inner: matched o, extracted o
         inner: matched u, extracted u
         inner: matched r, extracted r
```

The moral of the story is, think carefully about what kind of loop we want to use and make sure we make copies of any part of the regexp state that we might want to make use of later. It also pays to test code thoroughly, consider empty strings, and expect failures as well as successful matches. It is important to remember that a library subroutine may contain a regexp we are unaware of, so controlling the use of regexps in our own code is not always adequate protection.

Position

Each time a match is made, the regexp engine updates its position within the match text. This is so that previously matched text is not taken into consideration for the next match, otherwise the next match would just be the first one again. This position can be extracted and, more dangerously, set with the pos function if the match text is held in a scalar variable:

```perl
#!/usr/bin/perl
# position.pl
use warnings;
use strict;

my $text = "one, two, three, four";

# display matches with their positions
while ($text =~ /\b(\w+)\b/g) {
    print "matched $1 at position ", pos($text), "\n";
    pos($text) = 0 if pos($text) > 15;
}
```

This program uses pos to both display and set back to zero the regexp engine's position. It loops indefinitely matching each word in turn:

```
> perl position.pl
matched one at position 3
matched two at position 8
matched three at position 15
matched four at position 21
matched one at position 3
matched two at position 8
...
```

The position returned by pos is the index of the character in the match text immediately beyond the text that matched, that is, the first character of the next match attempt. That is why the position of the first match is 3, not 0. To get the start position we can subtract the length of $& from the value returned by pos, or $1 if we have extracted the pattern in parentheses, as we have in this case.

Note that pos (and not reset) is the correct way to reset the position of a multi-line match. The reset on its own, with no arguments, resets one-shot regexps that are defined with ? as the delimiter. Although this does for one-shot regexps what pos($text) = 0 does for global regexps, there is no direct link or correlation between the two.

For the curious, the value returned by pos is the same as the value of the first element of the special array @+, which we covered earlier than the chapter.

Moving the Start Anchor to the Current Position

We have already mentioned the \A, \z, and \Z metacharacters and explained their significance as anchors in conjunction with the /m modifier. The \G metacharacter is another kind of anchor that moves to the current position at the end of each match in a global regexp. It only has significance in conjunction with /g since position is not kept at all in regexps that only match once.

At first sight, \G would appear to not be terribly useful. After all, a global regexp already advances through the match text without needing to be re-anchored each time. However, the advantage of the \G anchor is that it allows us to process the match text in much smaller bites than we would otherwise be able to do – this can simplify regexp in some cases.

As an example, consider the following substitution. It replaces leading spaces with an equivalent number of dashes (minus signs) over one or more lines:

```
$text =~ s/^(\s+)/'-' x length($1)/mge;
```

While this is perfectly fine, it is not as elegant as it could be. To get the right number of dashes, we have to extract the matched spaces and count them to generate a string of dashes of the same length, which means using the /e modifier to execute the replacement text as code.

With \G, we can rewrite this search pattern to match only one space at a time and re-anchor the search at the start of the remaining text:

```
$text =~ s/\G\s/-/mg;
```

Not only is this a great deal simpler to understand, it avoids that nasty executable code too.

Retaining Position between Regular Expressions

When matching text with a global regexp, the regexp engine automatically keeps track of where it is. However, when the regexp runs out of valid matches and fails, the position is reset and deleted. Trying to use pos to find the end of the last match after the regexp has ended will only produce an undefined result.

Sometimes, however, we might want to know where the regexp stopped so that we can feed the remaining match text to a different regexp. Fortunately, by using a variant of the /g modifier, /gc, we can tell the regexp engine to remember the position of the last match. In combination with \G this allows us to have one regexp pick up where a previous one left off.

To illustrate how this works, consider this sample text, and assume we know only the smallest details about it:

```
$text = 3 2 1 liftoff;
```

All we know is that we have a sequence of numbers followed by a message of some kind. We don't know how many numbers, and we do not want to try and match the whole text at one go because it might be large. We therefore write one regexp to find the numbers, using /gc to retain the position at the end of the last match, then a second using \G to pick up where we left off. Here is a sample program that does just that:

```perl
#!/usr/bin/perl
# liftoff.pl
use warnings;
use strict;

my $text = "3 2 1 liftoff";

# use /gc to remember position
while ($text =~ /(\d)/gc) {
    print "$1...\n";
}

# use \G to match rest of text
if ($text =~ /\G\s*(.+)$/) {
    print ucfirst($1), "!\n";
}
```

As with many solutions in Perl, there are other ways to do this. For instance we could also have copied the value of $' to $text between the two regexps to produce much the same effect without the use of /gc or the \G anchor. However, as we noted earlier, it is generally a good thing to avoid using variables like $' because of the performance loss this causes in all future pattern matches.

Matching In and Across Multiple Lines

The /s and /m modifiers both alter the way in which the regexp engine handles search patterns. The /s modifier causes the newline character, \n to match a dot, which it would not do otherwise. The /m modifier alters the meaning of the ^ and $ anchors so that they match either side of a newline, as well as at the start and end of the text overall.

Although neither modifier is tied to global regexps, they both have a lot of uses in combination with the /g modifier. In particular, the combination of /m and /g makes an effective way to re-anchor a search pattern at the start of each new line. This code snippet extracts configuration values from a string containing one key-value pair per line:

```perl
#!/usr/bin/perl
# mflag.pl
use warnings;
use strict;

# put <> into slurp mode
undef $/;
# read configuration file supplied on command line into string
my $configuration = <>;

my %config;
# read all configuration options from config string
while ($configuration =~ /^\s*(\w+)\s* = \s*(.+?)\s*$/mg) {
    $config{$1} = $2;
}

print "Got: $_ => '$config{$_}'\n" foreach (sort keys %config);
```

If we run this program on a file of lines like the following:

```
one = sorrow
two = joy
three = one too many
```

It produces:

> **perl mflag.pl mytextfile**
Got: one => 'sorrow'
Got: three => 'one too many'
Got: two => 'joy'

The regular expression says 'start, find me a word (optionally surrounded by whitespace) followed by an equals sign and some more text (also optionally surrounded by whitespace), end'.

With the /m modifier present, ^ and $ match at the start and end of each line in the string $configuration, so each line read from the file is checked in turn.

As a point of fact, the ^, $ and /m modifier in this code are redundant since a newline character cannot match any part of the regexp in this particular example. However, the /m modifier causes the expression to execute a lot faster, since the regexp engine first extracts a line and anchors it at each end before commencing the rest of the search. That means that a small part of the whole string is actually involved in each attempted match.

The \s modifier allows a newline to match a dot. This is mainly useful for matching multiple-line records in a document and extracting them in one go:

```perl
#!/usr/bin/perl
# sflag.pl
use warnings;
use strict;

undef $/;
my $database = <>;
my @records;

while ($database =~ /item:(.*?)(?=item:|$)/sg) {
    my $record = $1;
    $record =~ s/\n/ /g;
    push @records, $record;
}

print "Got: $_\n" foreach @records;
```

If we give this program a file of lines like the following:

```
item: this is item one
item: this is
the second item
item: and
a third item
```

It produces the following output:

> **perl sflag.pl mytextfile**
Got: this is item one
Got: this is the second item
Got: and a third item

The /s modifier allows the .*? to match multiple lines between each instance of item:. We have also used a zero-width lookahead extended pattern (the (?=...) syntax) to match the next occurrence of item:, so we can find the full extent of each record, without absorbing it into the match. This is important because we will need to start from it on the next iteration.

The /s and /m modifiers are not mutually exclusive. Although /s allows a newline to match a dot, it does not change the fact that it is a newline. The ^ and $ anchors will still match on either side of it. The database example above has a flaw in that it will match item: in the middle of a line, when we probably only wanted item: to be a record separator if it starts a line. We can fix that by using /m, /s, and /g together, as this replacement while loop does:

```
while ($database =~ /^item: (.*?)(?=(^item:|\z))/msg) {
    $record = $1;
    $record =~ s/\n/ /g;
    push @records, $record;
}
```

However, be aware that unlike a ^, a $ cannot be used as an anchor in the middle of a pattern, only at the end. In addition, to handle the last record we have had to provide \z as an alternative match as well, to match the end of the string. We cannot use $ in this case because /m has altered its meaning.

Counting the Total Number of Matches

Sometimes we do not actually want to return matches from a regexp but just determine how many there are. One obvious way to do this is to count matches using a while loop:

```
$count = 0;
while ($atom =~ /\bproton\b/g) {
    $count++;
}
```

Alternatively, if the cumulative size of all the matched text is not excessively large, we can take the scalar result of the regular expression in list context:

```
$count = scalar($atom =~ /\bproton\b/g);
```

Overlapping Matches and Zero-Width Patterns

The regexp engine ordinarily moves over matched text each time it succeeds, enabling us to find all matches in the match text without matching the same text twice. Unfortunately this makes it extremely difficult to find overlapping matches because as soon as the text has matched once, it will not be considered for any further matches. The following example illustrates an instance of when this can be a problem:

```
#!/usr/bin/perl
# vowels1.pl
use warnings;
use strict;

my $text = "beautiful creature";

# find adjacent vowels
while ($text =~ /([aeiou]{2})/g) {
    print "Found adjacent '$1' at position ", pos($text), "\n";
}
```

When run this finds the ea in beautiful and ea of creature, but not the au in beautiful. This is because by the time the regexp engine gets to the u, the a has already been matched and passed over:

> **perl vowels1.pl**
Found adjacent 'ea' at position 3
Found adjacent 'ea' at position 14

Fixing this problem would appear to be nearly impossible, but fortunately Perl allows us to cheat using a zero-width assertion. Zero-width assertions require the text to match, but do not cause the regexp engine to absorb the match by moving its position beyond it. The text matched by the assertion can be matched again on the next pass. The trick here is to turn the entire pattern into a zero-width assertion using the extended pattern (?=...).

In order to explain why zero-width assertions are useful, it's helpful to look at a simple example. The following program has been deliberately 'broken' by placing a zero-width assertion around the entire pattern (.):

```
#!/usr/bin/perl
# zerowidthloop.pl
use warnings;
use strict;

my $text = "proton";
while ($text =~ /(?=(.))/g) {
    print "[$1]";
}
```

We would expect this code to go into an infinite loop. The regexp contains no subpatterns that absorb characters, so the position should never move past the first character. Since the position never moves, each successive match ought start at the beginning of the string and match the same text again, and so on indefinitely. So this program ought to produce:

> **perl zerowidthloop.pl**
[p][p][p][p][p][p][p]...

However, Perl has a special optimization that deals with this case:

If the whole of a global regexp is zero-width, then a successful match will move the position one character forward from the start of the match.

As a result, the program actually produces:

> **perl zerowidthloop.pl**
[p][r][o][t][o][n]

The optimization is useful for avoiding infinite loops, but it has its own extra uses too. By rewriting our vowel program to use a zero-width assertion we can deal with overlapping matches correctly:

```perl
#!/usr/bin/perl
# vowels2.pl
use warnings;
use strict;

my $text = "beautiful creature";
# find adjacent vowels
while ($text =~ /(?=([aeiou]{2}))/g) {
    print "Found adjacent '$1' at position ", pos($text), "\n";
}
```

Now when we run the program we get the correct result:

> **perl vowels2.pl**
Found adjacent 'ea' at position 1
Found adjacent 'au' at position 2
Found adjacent 'ea' at position 12

It takes a little effort to understand this completely, but examining what has happened to the position is illuminating. In the first example, the position after the end of the first match was 3, indicating that the next match would start at the t of beautiful (remembering we are counting from zero). In the second example the position after the first match is 1, which points to the e of beautiful, because the zero-width assertion has matched but not absorbed the characters ea. This is the same position that Perl found the last match (because the b did not match the pattern at all). Perl notices that it is starting from the same place a second time and automatically moves the position by one.

It is important to realize that this 'special case' rule only applies to successful matches. The b of beautiful does not match the pattern at all, so it is moved over by the regexp engine following its 'as-soon-as-possible' rule. The zero-width assertion only comes into play when a match succeeds, or in other words, only after the first ea has been matched. This is why we do not get the first ea twice.

We can see that the rule comes into effect just before the beginning of each match because the position we get is correct for the start of the match just made. The position is not, as we might possibly expect, 'ready' for the next match.

As another example, here is a short program that follows on from our discussion of lean matches, and searches for the shortest match in the string Greely Greely & Spatsz:

```perl
#!/usr/bin/perl
# Greely.pl
use warnings;
use strict;

my $company = 'Greely Greely & Spatz';
my $match = $company;    #set to longest possible match

while ($company =~ /(Greely)(?=(.*?Spatz))/g) {
    my $got = $1.$2;     #assemble match from both parts
    $match = $got if length($got) < length($match);
}

print "Shortest possible match is '$match' \n";
```

Extended Patterns

Extended patterns are an extension to the syntax of regexps covered so far. They enable us to adjust the operation of the regexp engine within the search pattern. Each extended pattern causes the engine to behave in a different way, but only for the region over which it has control.

Extended patterns all have a syntax following the rule (?<character>pattern). The <character> determines the effect that the extended pattern has, and pattern is the pattern affected by it. We have already seen two extended patterns, the backreference suppressing cluster and the zero-width lookahead:

```
(?:these|terms|do|not|create|a|backreference)    # cluster pattern
(?=zerowidthpattern)    # zero width pattern
```

In addition to these two, Perl defines several other extended patterns to perform various tasks. Some of them are currently still classified as experimental as of Perl 5.6 (the current list and status of extended patterns can be found in the perlre manual page which you can see using the command **>perldoc perlre**), and all of them should be used with some care and a lot of forethought.

Documenting Regular Expressions

If regexps have a down side, other than their tendency to do avoid doing what we want given the slightest loophole, it is their confusing syntax. Most regexps of any size are hard to read. Take the following expression as an example, borrowed from earlier in the chapter:

```
# read a 'key = value' configuration from a configuration string
while ($configuration =~ /^\s*(\w+)\s*=\s*(.+?)\s*$/mg) {
    %config{$1} = $2;
}
```

Although we can work out what this regexp says, 'find me a word, optionally surrounded by whitespace, followed by an equals sign and some more text, also optionally surrounded by whitespace', it takes a certain amount of squinting to do so. Fortunately we can improve the legibility of this expression by using /x.

The /x pattern match modifier allows us to embellish our regexps with extra whitespace (which, significantly, includes newlines) and comments to improve its legibility and describe what it does. The x stands for **extended** and so regexps that have been written this way are often referred to as 'extended regexps'. This term is a little misleading, however, since /x does not add any new features to the regexp engine; it merely extends the syntax.

When /x is in effect, any whitespace character is assumed not to be part of the pattern:

```
print "hello" =~ /h e l l o/;   # no '/x', no match
print "hello" =~ /h e l l o/x;  # '/x' ignores spaces, produces '1'
print "h e l l o" =~ /h e l l o/x;  # '/x' ignores spaces, no match
```

We can also rewrite groups to place alternatives on different lines, just as we can with if statements:

```
$atom =~ {(
   proton
   | electron
   | neutron
)}x and print "Found a particle";
```

Similarly, a # is assumed to start a comment, unless it forms part of a character class:

```
while ($text =~ {
    (
        [aeiou]   # find a vowel
        {2}    # match it twice
        [#]    # then a hash/pound
    )
}/xg) {
    print "Found adjacent '$1' at position ", pos($text), "\n";
}
```

If we want to use literal whitespace or hashes inside an /x modified pattern we can either escape them to make them literal, or place them inside a character class as in the above example. We can escape spaces to make them literal, and of course tabs and newlines already have metacharacter representations:

```
$text =~ /
    (\ |\t)?   # start with optional space or tab
    space   # literal word
    \ +separated   # one or more spaces then a word
    \ +text   # one or more spaces then a word
    \n?   # optionally match newline
/x;
```

Unfortunately we cannot escape a hash directly, so we have to express it in octal (\43) or hexadecimal (\x23), or from Perl 5.6, a named Unicode character (\N{NUMBER SIGN}).

Using both whitespace and comments, we can rewrite our regexps to be much more legible. Admittedly the following may be overdoing it a little, but it serves to illustrate what /x allows us to do:

```
# read configuration from config string
while ($configuration =~ /

    ^     # anchor at start of line. Note '/m' is in effect

    # match config name
    \s*    # absorb leading whitespace, if any
    (\w+)   # return name, alphanumeric only
    \s*    # absorb any whitespace between name and =
        # must have an equals sign
    =    # match '='

    # match config value, avoiding surrounding whitespace
    \s*    # absorb any whitespace between = and value
    (.+?)   # return value
    # - note, non-greedy, \s* takes precedence
    \s*    # absorb whitespace between value and end of line
    $    # anchor at end of line

    /mg) {
    %config{$1} = $2;
}
```

Although not directly related to the /x modifier, it is worth noting that if we are using the /e modifier, then we can use whitespace and comments in the replacement part of a substitution. This is because the replacement is then evaluated as code, and follows Perl's normal syntax rules. We cover substitution and the /e modifier shortly.

Writing Efficient Regular Expressions

Writing a regexp that works is one thing. Writing one that works quickly is something else. For every fast regexp there is another that does the same job but runs like a snail. The regexp engine is already very good at determining the most efficient way to carry out a pattern match, but it can only optimize what we give it.

Writing a regexp so it can match faster is always a good idea. Writing it so it can fail faster is an even better idea – many regexps are good at matching quickly but can take a very long time to run through all the possibilities. In general, there are three ways we can make our regexps more efficient:

❑   Make the regexp more specific

❑   Avoid recompiling search patterns

❑   Use many simple expressions instead of one complex one

The last of these is actually one way to solve the second. Recompilation happens when a search pattern contains interpolated variables, and is a major cause of performance loss in regexps. Often this interpolation is not necessary. On other occasions it is necessary, but not every time. Eliminating vagueness and avoiding unnecessary interpolation are the two biggest areas of improvement that we can apply to any regular expression.

Making Regular Expressions More Specific

The more specific a regexp is, the fewer possibilities the engine will have to run though to find a match. There are two main ways to make regexps more specific. One is to eliminate subpatterns that are too vague, and the other is to anchor the expression, if possible, to limit the possible start and end points of any prospective match.

Eliminating Vague Subpatterns

Patterns such as .* are very flexible, but terrible in terms of speed, since they can match anything. Many regexp programmers reach for expressions like .* because they are quick and simple to use, and can be 'fixed' by making the rest of the search pattern more specific. Unfortunately this can cause Perl a lot of extra work. Consider the following two almost-equivalent regexps:

```
$text =~ /('|")(.*)\1/ and print $2;     # extract single or double
                                         # string quoted
$text =~ /('|")([^\1]*?)\1/ and print $2;   # ditto...
```

The second of these examples is superior to the first in several ways, it matches the first pair of quotes, not the first and last quotes in the entire text. Since the text might be long, we make the match non-greedy by adding a ? so the engine will look for the second quote forward from the first and not backtrack from the end. The first example by contrast will be greedy and match the whole text with .*, then backtrack to try to find a match for the backreference \1. As a result, the second example will usually find a single quoted section within a large body of text much faster than the first. The only time the first will win is if the match text contains a pair of quotes near the beginning and end of the overall text.

If we are only matching word characters, \w* is far better, since it can terminate part of a search earlier than would otherwise be the case. \w+ is even better if we actually require a match, since unlike \w*, it has to match something for the rest of the pattern to be considered at all. The trick is to have a very good understanding of the nature of the text we will be matching; the more information we can give the regexp engine, the better it will perform:

```
$text =~ /(.*) = (.*)/;    # bad
$text =~ /(\w*) = (\S*)/;    # better
$text =~ /^(\w+) = (\S+)/;    # even better
```

It is a common misconception that non-greedy matches are intrinsically more efficient than greedy ones. This is often the case, but only because of the nature of the text we wish to match. Take the following two examples:

```
$text =~ /^(.*)\\?/;    # greedy match
$text =~ /^(.*?)\\?/;    # non-greedy match
```

Both examples look for any text (.*) followed by an optional literal backslash (\\?), but they go about it in different ways. Consider the most likely scenario for this application – a series of lines that are optionally suffixed with a backslash to indicate continuation. The first grabs the whole match text and then looks for an optional backslash, starting from the end. The second grabs one character at a time and then looks to see if the next character is a backslash. If it isn't, the engine backtracks, matches another character to .*?, then checks again, and so on all the way to the end of the match text. In this case the first, greedy, match is clearly more efficient.

> *Using a $ anchor possibly prefixed by optional whitespace would be even more efficient, though we're trying to keep to examples simple here for clarity. The same problem is less easily fixed in more complex examples, but they're not as easy to analyze. We'll come to anchors in a moment.*

Another reason for using caution with the dot (.) match is that it is not matched by a newline \n, unless we use the /s modifier. It is easy to forget this when writing regexps, which leads us to trip up when the match text unexpectedly contains a newline. Writing a more specific pattern can often force us to consider possibilities such as this before they happen.

Anchors

Some regexps can be made faster by relatively simple modifications – adding anchors is one such example. If we want to look for the word omega in a string we could write:

```
$text =~ /omega/;
```

However, if we know that omega is only going to occur at the end of the string we can anchor it:

```
$text =~ /omega$/;
```

This is a vastly more efficient regexp. Not only will it run faster if omega is indeed present, it will run a lot faster if it is not. In the first case, the regexp engine must check for omega anywhere in the string. In the second case, the engine can check that the last letter in the string is an a. If it is not, it can fail immediately.

Anchors are a very effective way of speeding up matches. Even if we cannot anchor a search pattern directly, we can sometimes anchor it to something else with a little more thought. For instance, omega might not occur at the end of the line, but we happen to know that if it does not, it can only be followed by whitespace. That means we can anchor it using:

```
$text =~ /omega\s*$/;
```

This is not as fast as the previous example, but it is still faster than not anchoring it at all. If we can anchor at both ends then so much the better. Similarly, to check for alpha at or near the beginning of the line we can say:

```
$text =~ /^\s*alpha/;
```

'study'

Perl provides a built-in function called study, which attempts to make regexps more efficient by analyzing the match text (note, not the pattern) in advance. For some regexps this can provide a useful speed improvement. For others it is almost entirely useless.

The function works by examining the text and building lists of positions within the text for each character present (so, for example, the a list contains a list of positions for every a present in the text). When the text is matched, the regexp engine checks for literal characters in the search pattern and scans for them in the match text in order of rarity. If the pattern contains a literal q, and this is the rarest character in the match text that is also present in the pattern, the engine will start by looking for instances of q and then go on from there.

This studying is most effective when we expect to make a lot of different matches on the same piece of text, since it will benefit all of them. It is also most effective when matching a series of short literal strings in large bodies of text like large documents and whole books. For example:

```
undef $/;    # undefined record separator
$book = <>;   # slurp in large buckets of text
study $book;   # perform pre-match analysis of $book

# search for short literal strings
@matches = $book =~ /\b(sharrow|miz|dloan)\b/sig;
```

In this case, the least common characters are probably w and z, so they would be used as the starting point for determining likely matches by the engine.

In practice study is hard to use effectively. First, it is severely limited by the fact that only one string can be studied at once – if we study a second string then the first becomes 'unstudied' again. Second, it takes time for study to build its lists, which may take longer than the actual search. Lastly, its benefits in terms of speed are only effective when there are a reasonable number of literal characters in the pattern. The function has no beneficial effect for regexps like:

```
$text =~ /^\s*\w+[0-9]*/;   # no literal characters to look for!
```

Remember that when considering whether to use study or not, a good source of literal characters can often be found in interpolated variables, especially if they hold user input. It is the pattern after interpolation that determines whether studying the text is beneficial or not.

Avoiding Recompilation with the Empty Pattern

Normally, each time the regexp engine reconsiders a search pattern containing variables, it must re-interpolate and recompile it in case the variables have changed. This can slow down the engine considerably. However, if an empty pattern is supplied to the regexp engine, the engine will resort to a default of the last successfully matched pattern that was passed to it. This is one way to rematch a regexp without recompiling it:

```
if ($text =~ /$complex\b($interpolated)\b$pattern/) {
    do {
        print "Found '$1';
    } while ($text =~ //);   # reuse pattern without recompiling it
}
```

It is important to remember that the reused pattern is the last successful one. If the previous match failed, the empty pattern will instead cause the engine to reuse the pattern before it instead (presuming that that one was successful). If no successful patterns have been seen, the pattern defaults to being truly empty, which is unlikely to be what we want.

The moral of the story, with regards to using //, is therefore to make sure that the previously successful pattern is the one we want to use. The example above makes sure of this because the empty pattern is only reached inside the if statement that tests the success of the pattern we want to reuse.

It is entirely possible to generate an empty pattern either deliberately or accidentally through interpolation. For instance, if we have a pattern that is completely interpolated from variables, and none of them happen to be set, we can get some very strange results when the regexp engine appears to use the 'wrong' pattern.

As a final point about the empty pattern, note that it only applies to matches and substitutions – it has no special properties in split. Rather, splitting on an empty pattern falls under the rules of zero-width patterns (see earlier in the chapter under 'Overlapping Matches and Zero-Width Patterns' for details).

Avoiding Recompilation with the 'once-only' Modifier

The /o or 'once-only' pattern match modifier is an invaluable tool for speeding up regexps that interpolate variables to create the search pattern. By using this modifier, we can tell the engine that the variables cannot and will not change (or more accurately, that it can ignore them even if they have). If we do not expect the variables to change over the lifetime of the program, /o is an effective way to speed up a match:

```
while (/($search_pattern)/g) { ... }    # reinterpolates each time
while (/($search_pattern)/go) { ... }   # quicker - interpolates once
```

The /o modifier allows the regexp engine to cache the results of compiled regexps for reuse, so it is not just effective for global pattern matches like the above. It also has a beneficial effect on non-global regexps if they are used repeatedly:

```
# get something to search for
$search_string = shift @ARGV;

# once-only optimized pattern inside body of while loop
while (<>) {
    if (/$search_string/o) {
        print "Found '$1' at line $. \n";
    }
}
```

The problem with /o is that it prevents us changing the pattern of interpolation when we do want to. Another solution to the same problem uses the qr operator, which (in a sense) provides the same functionality as /o, but in a more flexible way. We will discuss it in more detail at the end of this section.

The /o modifier is also particularly effective when combined with eval to generate a regexp on the fly, but it is not the only way to avoid recompiling search patterns.

Generating Regular Expressions with 'eval'

The eval function is another excellent way of generating regexps on the fly without having to deal with interpolation. Rather than search for several terms at once we can generate regexps and then evaluate them.

Here is a simple program that accepts an arbitrary number of search terms (each specified with -t). It then scans whatever files we pass it (anything not prefixed with -t) for each of them:

```perl
#!/usr/bin/perl
# multisearch.pl
use warnings;
use strict;

use Getopt::Long;

my @terms;
GetOptions('term:s' => \@terms);

die "Usage $0 [-t term [-t term]] file ...\n" unless @terms;

# build regular expressions
my $regexp = "";
foreach (@terms) {
    $regexp .= 'print("$ARGV:$.('.$_.')$_\n") if /\b'.$_.'\b/o;'. "\n";
}

# dump out the loop body for interest
print "Searching with:\n$regexp";

# build loop
my $loop = 'while (<>) {chomp; '.$regexp.'}';

# evaluate loop
eval $loop;
```

The trick in this program comes in the assembling of the regexps. Each term supplied is built into its own regexp which is, in turn, built into the condition of an if statement. Although the terms are elements of the @terms array variable, the code constructed by the foreach loop uses their values as literal search patterns, so we can add the /o modifier to further improve the speed of the program.

Another aspect of this program that displays some cunning is the while loop that retrieves lines from the input. Since eval is an expensive call to make, we avoid calling it repeatedly for each line of the input by placing the while loop inside the eval, rather than the other way around. The <> readline operator does not care either way, and the result is a much faster search.

We can use this program to search for several different terms at the same time:

> **perl multisearch.pl -t one -t two search.txt**

In this case we are looking for instances of one and two. The code generated by the program and placed in $regexp in response to this command line is (as reported by the program):

```
print ("$ARGV:$. (one) $_\n") if /\bone\b/o;
print ("$ARGV:$. (two) $_\n") if /\btwo\b/o;
```

Note that the final \n on the end of the '$regexp.=...' line in the program is purely cosmetic so the above prints out nicely on separate lines. If we removed that code, we could remove the trailing \n as well. Now let us assume that search.txt contains the lines:

```
one two three
four
five
six
one seven eight
two nine
four three
six
nine five
zero one one
```

When run, we get the following:

```
search.txt:1(one)one two three
search.txt:1(two)one two three
search.txt:5(one)one seven eight
search.txt:6(two)two nine
search.txt:10(one)zero one one
```

Both one and two were found on the first line, so it appears for both of them. The one also appears on lines five and ten, while two additionally appears on line six. Whatever was on the other lines did not contain either term.

Another approach to assembling a regexp using eval, but avoiding the embedded loop, is to generate an anonymous subroutine instead (see Chapter 7 for more on anonymous subroutines). Here is a variant of the multisearch.pl program above that works this way:

```
#!/usr/bin/perl
# multifind.pl
use warnings;
use strict;

use Getopt::Long;

my @terms;
my $all = 0;    # find any term by default

GetOptions('term:s' => \@terms, 'all' => \$all);

die "Must specify search term" unless @terms;
```

```
# build regular expressions and logic
my @regexps = map {"/\\b$_\\b/o"} @terms;
my $logic = join $all?' && ':' || ',@regexps;

# dump out the logic for interest
print "Searching with: $logic \n";

# interpolate an anonymous sub to test logic
my $match = eval "sub {$logic;}";

# scan input
while (<>) {
    print "$ARGV:$.:$_" if &$match;
}
```

We can use this program to search for several different terms at the same time, printing out the lines if any. Here is an example of an any search:

> **perl multifind.pl -t one -t two search.txt**

In this case we are looking for instances of one or two, and printing out any line on which either is present. The anonymous subroutine generated by the program in response to this command line contains this logic (as reported by the program):

```
Searching with: /\bone\b/o || /\btwo\b/o
```

Using the same sample text as before, we get an output of:

```
search.txt:1:one two three
search.txt:5:one seven eight
search.txt:6:two nine
search.txt:10:zero one one
```

Alternatively, if we can use the --all option (here abbreviated to -a):

> **perl multifind.pl -t one -t two -a search.txt**

Now the logic is changed to:

```
Searching with: /\bone\b/o && /\btwo\b/o
```

And the resulting output is:

```
search.txt:1:one two three
```

This approach is basically similar to the first, but by placing the code we want to match in an anonymous subroutine, and then calling eval to create it, we avoid having to call eval repeatedly or embed a while loop inside the eval.

Predefining Search Patterns with 'qr'

The qr operator allows us to precompile regexps and then use them at a later date. This is handy for verifying the legality of a regexp as we saw earlier in the chapter, and it allows us to be selective about when we recompile a regexp as we saw above when we tackled the /o modifier.

The real value of qr is that it allows us to remove the uglier aspects of regexp syntax to another place where they don't interfere with the legibility of the program. While the /x modifier can help to make a regexp more comprehensible, it still gets in the way of understanding the surrounding code. With qr we can transplant the regexp entirely. We do not even need to use delimiters, although they are necessary if we want to use a modifier:

```
$re = qr/^a.*?pattern/;   # define a regexp

if ($re){   ...   }   # use regexp without delimiters
if (/$re/o) {   ...   }   # use regexp with delimiters and modifier
```

Like the match, substitute, and split functions, qr has the same rules regarding delimiters – anything within reason is allowed, and single quotes prevent the contents from being interpolated. See 'Regular Expression Delimiters' earlier in the chapter for more information.

Using Pattern Match Modifiers with 'qr'

One of the conveniences of qr is that it allows us to attach pattern match modifiers to a regexp, so we don't need to specify them later. That is, we can specify the modifier to qr and then use the regexp without modifiers:

```
$re = qr/^a.*?pattern/ism;
if ($re) {   ...   }   # use regexp with precompiled modifiers
```

If we print out the regexp, we can see what is actually happening. The pattern is embedded into an inline modifier that surrounds and entirely controls it:

```
print qr/^a.*?pattern/;   # produces '(?-xism:^a.*?pattern)'
print qr/^a.*?pattern/ism;   # produces '(?msi-x:^a.*?pattern)'
```

Notice that the inline modifier is thorough (excluding the /o and /g modifiers) – it switches on everything we ask for, and switches off anything we did not. This expression will work as we intended even when combined with other expressions and additional modifiers:

```
$re1 = /^a.*?pattern/ism;
$re2 = /form \s+ and \s+ void/x;

if (/^$re1$re2$/gm) {   ...   }   # combine two regular expressions
```

The /o modifier is not included in the 'thorough' inline modifier for a good reason. While it is legal, it does not do anything in qr. In a sense, qr does the same job as /o since interpolation of the pattern only happens once – at the time the regexp is defined. In fact we can use qr to solve interpolation problems in a similar but more flexible way to the /o modifier.

The /g modifier is not legal in a qr pattern at all, since it is not legal as an inline modifier – we cannot have some of a pattern global and some not. If we try to use /g with qr we get a Bareword found where operator expected syntax error, which can be a little confusing. If this error ever occurs when trying to use qr, check that the /g modifier is not present.

Using 'qr' as a Replacement for the 'once-only' Modifier

As we mentioned earlier when we covered the /o modifier, we can use the qr quoting operator to selectively recompile our regexp when we want to, without losing the benefits of once-only compilation the rest of the time:

```perl
#!/usr/bin/perl
# regb.pl
use strict;

undef $/;
my $text = <>;
my ($this,$that,$other) = ('red','green','blue');

my $pattern = qr/($this|$that)/;
while ($text =~ /$pattern/g) {
    if ($1 eq $this) {
        print "Found '$this' - rotating\n";
        ($this, $that, $other) = ($that,$other,$this);
        $pattern = qr/($this|$that)/;
    } else {
        print "Found '$that' - staying put\n";
    }
}
```

This code starts off by looking for red or green. The moment it sees red, it starts looking for green or blue. If it sees green, it starts looking for blue or red and so on in a cycle. By using qr to compile and recompile the pattern, we get the benefits of /o without the drawbacks.

Checking the Validity of Regular Expressions

If we are taking input from the user and using it as part or all of a regexp, it can be very hard to determine if the resulting search pattern is valid or not. Regexps being indeterminately complex means there is no way to easily check a pattern unless we limit the input to permit only a few elements of regexp syntax.

The simple way to test the validity of a pattern is to try to compile it and see if we get an error. In order to do that without causing the program to grind to a halt, we use an eval:

```perl
#!/usr/bin/perl
# checkre1.pl
use warnings;
use strict;

while (<>) {
    chomp;
    eval {qr/$_/;};
    print $@?"Error in '$_': $@\n": "'$_' is legal \n";
}
```

We can save the result of successful compilations if we adapt the above technique slightly. Here is a short program implementing a subroutine that tries to compile a pattern, returning the pattern for use on success, or an undefined value on failure:

```perl
#!/usr/bin/perl
# checkre2.pl
use warnings;
use strict;
```

```
while (<>) {
    chomp;
    if (my $re = compile_re($_)) {
        print "Pattern ok: $re \n";
    } else {
        print "Illegal pattern: $@ \n";
    }
}

sub compile_re {
    my $pattern = shift;

    my $re;    # local package variable
    eval {$re = qr/$pattern/;};

        return $re; #undef on error
}
```

We can run this script and feed it a selection of good and bad patterns as follows:

> **perl checkre2.pl**
plaintext
Pattern ok: (?-xism:plaintext)
^good[pat]e(r|n)
Pattern ok: (?-xism:^good[pat]e(r|n))
bad[pattern
Illegal pattern: /bad[pattern/: unmatched [ ] in regexp at ...

The catch with this compilation is that we do not provide for pattern match modifier flags after the pattern. However, it is still a useful technique. For the curious, the (?-xism....) construct place around our pattern by qr is an in line modifier; it's explained in 'Using Pattern Match Modifiers with qr' above.

If we want to allow user input into regexps without allowing users to enter regexp syntax, then we can use quotemeta to escape any potentially dangerous characters (or place \Q...\E around their input within the regexp):

```
#!/usr/bin/perl
# quote.pl
use warnings;
use strict;

$| = 1;

print "Enter a pattern: ";
my $pattern = <>;
chomp $pattern;

print "Enter some search text: ";
my $input = <>;

if ($input =~ /\Q$pattern\E/) {
    print "'$&' found! \n";
}
```

We can run this program and pass it any kind of pattern to search for, even one with regular expression characters:

> **perl quote.pl**
Enter a pattern: *ship
Enter some search text: *ship troopers
'*ship' found!

It is important to remember that \Q and \E take effect after variables have been interpolated, so the above does actually do what it suggests, and doesn't escape the dollar of $input. See the section on 'Protecting Strings Against Interpolation' above, for more on the quotemeta function and the metacharacters \Q and \E.

Regular Expressions, Tainted Variables, and Debugging

Perl supports the concept of **tainted** data, where information gleaned from an external source is considered insecure. This is primarily a feature designed for CGI scripts and other code that is run on a server due to the actions of a third party. There is no reason why it cannot be used to improve the security of any and all Perl scripts.

Each time a piece of tainted data is used in an expression, the result of that expression is also marked as tainted. If we try to do something potentially dangerous, like execute an external program, Perl will raise a security error and exit. The Taint mode is enabled with the -T command line option, and is automatically enabled if we run a Perl script under a different effective user ID.

Untainting Tainted Variables

Perl has the concept of security built into the language at a basic level. We can enable this security through the taint mode by using -T, for example:

```
#!/usr/bin/perl -T
use warnings;
#enable warnings and Taint mode
```

Taint mode tracks the input of data into our applications from any external source, be it standard input, the environment variables in %ENV, or command line arguments passed via @ARGV, and marks it as 'tainted'. We can untaint a tainted variable by extracting a substring from it. Although Perl is aware that the match text is tainted, it assumes that by running a regexp across it, we are taking adequate steps to ensure that any security issues are being dealt with, and so does not mark the extract text as tainted.

We can use this fact to untaint variables that we know to be secure. For example, to untaint the DOCUMENT_ROOT environment variable we could use:

```
$ENV{DOCUMENT_ROOT} =~ /^.*/ &&
$ENV{DOCUMENT_ROOT} = $1;
```

We can usually justify doing this, because if DOCUMENT_ROOT has been compromised then the web server is probably already in more trouble than our CGI script.

Maintaining Taintedness in Regular Expressions

The pragmatic re module allows us to control various aspects of the regexp engine. One mode, taint, disables the detaining feature of regexps:

```
use re 'taint';
$ENV{DOCUMENT_ROOT} =~ /^.*/ &&
$ENV{DOCUMENT_ROOT} = $1;
# document root is still tainted!
```

Like most pragmatic modules, we can switch off this feature with no:

```
no re 'taint';
```

This allows us to control which regexps can untaint data, and which cannot.

A related feature of the re module is the eval mode:

```
use re 'eval';
```

This permits the presence of the extended patterns (?{ code }) and (??{ code }) in regexps that also contain interpolated variables. This is otherwise a forbidden combination for security reasons (with or without taint mode).

Why is it so dangerous? Because interpolation happens before compilation, and the interpolated variables might therefore contain embedded code that is integrated into the pattern before it is executed. This means that any kind of user input that is used in the regexp could cause our program to execute arbitrary code. This is not a good thing for system security. If we really want to allow user input to regexps see the quotemeta function in 'Protecting Strings Against Interpolation' for ways to protect against problems like this.

Interpolated variables that contain patterns compiled with qr are not subject to this prohibition, even if the compiled regexp contains embedded code, so the eval mode is often unnecessary and should probably be avoided. If we really want to embed code, this is how we could do it (a little) more safely:

```
# allow embedded code patterns
use re 'eval';

# compile a pattern with embedded code
$re1 = qr/a pattern (?{print "that doesn't contain user input";})/;

# disable embedded code, enable taint mode
no re 'eval';
use re 'taint';

# allow user to enter regexp! We would probably want much stricter
# limits on what they can enter, in reality.
$re2 = qr/<>/;

# process combination of both regexps.
while ($text =~ /$re1$re2/g) {
    ...
}
```

Note that eval mode is not compatible with taint mode, since taint enforces a stricter level of security.

Understanding and Debugging the Regular Expression Engine

The re module also provides a debugging mode. We can enable it with:

```
use re 'debug'   # or use re qw(debug taint) etc...
```

When enabled, the regexp engine within Perl will produce a stream of diagnostic information about what it is doing, both at the compilation stage and the matching stage. For instance, here is a short program that uses debug mode to print out the processing of a moderately complex regular expression:

```perl
#!/usr/bin/perl
# debugre.pl
use warnings;
use strict;

use re 'debug';

my $matchtext = "helium contains two protons, two neutrons and two electrons";

my $re = qr/(\w+\s(?:proton|neutron)s?)/;

while ($matchtext =~ /$re/g) {
    print "Found $1 \n";
}
```

The regexp in this program attempts to find a word (\w+) followed by a space (\s) and either proton or neutron, optionally followed by an s (s?). The whole thing is extracted into $1 by parentheses. When run, this program outputs first a **compilation dialog** and then a **match dialog**. The compilation dialog looks something like this:

```
Compiling REx '(\w+\s+(?:proton|neutron)s?)'
size 22 first at 4
   1: OPEN1(3)
   3:   PLUS(5)
   4:    ALNUM(0)
   5:  PLUS(7)
   6:  SPACE(0)
   7:  BRANCH(11)
   8:    EXACT <proton>(16)
  11: BRANCH(15)
  12:    EXACT <neutron>(16)
  15:  TAIL(16)
  16:  CURLY {0,1}(20)
  18:    EXACT <s>(0)
  20: CLOSE1(22)
  22: END(0)
stclass 'ALNUM' plus minlen 8
```

This is the execution plan of a state machine, which is what the regexp engine creates from the patterns that we supply it. The state numbers, which are also the position of the relevant parts of the pattern in the pattern text, are the column on the left. The numbers in parentheses on the right are transitions to other states (or jumping points to other parts of the pattern text, which is the same thing) that take place in the right circumstances. For example, state 7 is a BRANCH with two possible successors, 8 and 11. The engine will first move to state 8, and if it succeeds, move on to 16. If state 8 fails, the engine returns to state 7 and takes the other branch to state 11.

Of course we do not need to understand this state machine in detail, but it can be useful for working out what a regexp actually says, as opposed to what we thought it said. Failing that, we can look at the match dialog to see how the pattern is processed against our match text.

The match dialog is a lot longer, so we won't reproduce it in full. However, from the start of the match text to the first match (two protons) it looks like this, with some additional explanatory comments:

```
Matching REx '(\w+\s+(?:proton|neutron)s?)' against 'helium contains two protons, two neutrons and
two electrons'
  Setting an EVAL scope, savestack=10
  0 <> <helium conta>   | 1:  OPEN1
  0 <> <helium conta>   | 3:  PLUS
                    ALNUM can match 6 times out of 32767...
```

Aha, the engine has found helium at position 0 in the match text, matching the \w+ that ends at position 3 in the pattern. Note that all of helium matches at once because \w+ is greedy.

```
  Setting an EVAL scope, savestack=10
  6 <elium> < contai>   | 5:   PLUS
                    SPACE can match 1 times out of 32767...
```

It is followed by a space at position 6, so that satisfies the \s that ends at position 5. So far, so good...

```
  Setting an EVAL scope, savestack=10
  7 <lium > <contain>   | 7:     BRANCH
  Setting an EVAL scope, savestack=10
  7 <lium > <contain>   | 8:     EXACT <proton>
                    failed...
```

Oops, the next character does not match the start of proton...

```
  7 <lium > <contain>   | 12:    EXACT <neutron>
                    failed...
```

And it does not match the start of neutron either...

```
                    failed...
```

So it does not match proton OR neutron...

```
                    failed...
```

As there are no other alternatives, the match for \s must be wrong, so backtrack...

```
  5 <heliu> <m conta>   | 5:   PLUS
                    SPACE can match 0 times out of 32767...
```

Now the greediness of \w+ counts against it. The engine tries to match \w+ against one less character, and then sees if that allows \s to match. Of course, it does not.

```
  Setting an EVAL scope, savestack=10
                    failed...
  4 <heli> <um conta>   | 5:   PLUS
                    SPACE can match 0 times out of 32767...
  Setting an EVAL scope, savestack=10
                    failed...
```

```
  3 <hel> <ium conta>   | 5:   PLUS
                SPACE can match 0 times out of 32767...
Setting an EVAL scope, savestack=10
                failed...
  2 <he> <lium conta>   | 5:   PLUS
                SPACE can match 0 times out of 32767...
Setting an EVAL scope, savestack=10
                failed...
  1 <h> <elium conta>   | 5:   PLUS
                SPACE can match 0 times out of 32767...
Setting an EVAL scope, savestack=10
                failed...
```

The engine backtracks all the way back down helium, matching \w+ against one less character each time and trying to match \s with the following character...

```
                failed...
```

Oops, run out of characters to backtrack. So the match to \w+ must also be incorrect. Look for somewhere else to match \w+

```
Setting an EVAL scope, savestack=10
  7 <lium > <contain>   | 1: OPEN1
  7 <lium > <contain>   | 3: PLUS
                ALNUM can match 8 times out of 32767...
```

The next place that fits \w+ is the word contains. The story for the next few messages is a repeat of the earlier failed match that started with helium, since contains is followed by a space but the space is not followed by proton or neutron...

```
Setting an EVAL scope, savestack=10
 15 <tains> < two pr>   | 5:   PLUS
                SPACE can match 1 times out of 32767...
Setting an EVAL scope, savestack=10
 16 <ains > <two pro>   | 7:     BRANCH
Setting an EVAL scope, savestack=10
 16 <ains > <two pro>   | 8:       EXACT <proton>
                        failed...
 16 <ains > <two pro>   | 12:      EXACT <neutron>
                        failed...
                        failed...
                        failed...
```

Again, we find that neutron does not match, so (proton|neutron) does not match, so the \s cannot match. Time to backtrack...

```
 14 <ntain> <s two p>   | 5:   PLUS
                SPACE can match 0 times out of 32767...
Setting an EVAL scope, savestack=10
                failed...
 13 <ontai> <ns two >   | 5:   PLUS
                SPACE can match 0 times out of 32767...
```

```
Setting an EVAL scope, savestack=10
                    failed...
12 <conta> <ins two>   | 5:   PLUS
                    SPACE can match 0 times out of 32767...
Setting an EVAL scope, savestack=10
                    failed...
11 < cont> <ains tw>   | 5:   PLUS
                    SPACE can match 0 times out of 32767...
Setting an EVAL scope, savestack=10
                    failed...
10 <m con> <tains t>   | 5:   PLUS
                    SPACE can match 0 times out of 32767...
Setting an EVAL scope, savestack=10
                    failed...
 9 <um co> <ntains >   | 5:   PLUS
                    SPACE can match 0 times out of 32767...
Setting an EVAL scope, savestack=10
                    failed...
 8 <ium c> <ontains>   | 5:   PLUS
                    SPACE can match 0 times out of 32767...  Setting an EVAL scope, savestack=10
                    failed...
```

We backtrack all the way to the start of contains trying to match \s and failing. Exactly as we did before with helium...

```
                    failed...
```

But there is no match. Ergo \w+ cannot match any part of contains either. The engine gives up and moves forward again looking for the next match for \w+...

```
Setting an EVAL scope, savestack=10
16 <ains > <two pro>   | 1: OPEN1
16 <ains > <two pro>   | 3: PLUS
                    ALNUM can match 3 times out of 32767...
```

The next word is two, matching the \w+...

```
Setting an EVAL scope, savestack=10
19 <s two> < proton>   | 5:   PLUS
                    SPACE can match 1 times out of 32767...
```

Which is followed by a space, matching the \s...

```
Setting an EVAL scope, savestack=10
20 < two > <protons>   | 7:    BRANCH
Setting an EVAL scope, savestack=10
20 < two > <protons>   | 8:     EXACT <proton>
```

Aha, this time the test for proton succeeds. We never test for neutron because proton is given first in the regexp.

```
26 <roton> <s, two >   | 16:    CURLY {0,1}
                    EXACT <s> can match 1 times out of 1...
```

The optional s also matches, so we grab it too. Note how the ? is internally expanded to {0,1}.

```
Setting an EVAL scope, savestack=10
27 <otons> <, two n>   | 20:       CLOSE1
27 <otons> <, two n>   | 22:       END
Match successful!
```

And now we have reached the end of the regexp (CLOSE1). Since there is no more pattern left, we must have matched. Hurrah! We leave the regexp and execute the body of the while loop:

```
Found two protons
```

Substitution

Just to prepare for the following section on the substitution operator, let us recap on what we looked at during the regexp introduction. Substitution is performed by the s (or s///) operator; its syntax is nearly identical to that of the match operator that we have used in most of the examples so far. The key difference is that substitution replaces matched text with a replacement string. For example, to replace all neutrons with protons we might use:

```
$atom =~ s/neutron/proton/g;
```

Substitutions permit all the same pattern match modifiers that matches do – like the /g global modifier in this example. Also, like matches, substitutions return the same values and set the same variables if we use parentheses. All these are aspects of the pattern match rather than the substitution, so they apply to matches, substitutions, and splits alike.

Substituting Matched Text and Interpolation

We are not limited to literal text in the replacement string. To begin with, we can substitute the matched text with part of itself. For instance, this (admittedly over-simplistic) regexp attempts to turn Perl-style comments into C-style ones:

```
$program =~ s|#(.*)$|/*$1*/|mg;
```

Notice that characters like * do not need to be escaped on the right-hand side of the substitution – it is not a pattern. Given a line like:

```
print "Hello World \n";   #standard greeting
```

It should produce:

```
print "Hello World \n";   /*standard greeting*/
```

Of course this does not take into account that # can occur in Perl programs in other ways, (for example, as a character class).

This example also illustrates another important aspect of the replacement string – it is interpolated. This means that all the interpolation metacharacters (but not, of course, the regexp metacharacters) can be used in it, and that variables can be interpolated into it. Interpolation of the replacement text happens each and every time a match occurs. This is fortunate because variables like $1, which can change between matches, would not work correctly.

The following pattern looks for literal periods that are followed by one or more spaces and replaces them with a full stop plus a linefeed:

```
$text =~ s/\.[ ]+/.\n/;    # put each sentence on a new line
```

As a brief note on this expression, we have looked for spaces rather than whitespace to avoid matching and replacing newlines with themselves, which is unnecessary. We have also used a character class to make the space stand out. While the square brackets are unnecessary, a space on its own in a regexp can be hard to spot.

A little-known fact about backreferences is that they also work on the right-hand side of a substitution. That is, instead of using $1 in the replacement string, we can use \1:

```
$program =~ s|#(.*)$|/*\1*/|mg;
```

The reason for this is that it is compatible with sed, one of the UNIX tools from which Perl evolved, and is present for backward compatibility to help people migrating from tools like sed and awk. However, it is not a good idea because \1 really ought to mean *Cntrl-A* outside of a pattern, and is not compatible with the /e flag for exactly that reason. In other words, don't use it, but be aware that it might pop up in old Perl scripts.

If we want to replace the matched text with part of itself followed by some numeric digits, then we have a slight problem. How do we distinguish the numbered variable from the following characters? For example, this regexp would like to replace Kilo suffixes with the appropriate number of zeros:

```
/\b(\d+)K\b/$1000/g;    # $1000 does not exist
```

In order to fix this problem we can make the numbered variable explicit by surrounding the numeral(s) that are part of it with curly braces:

```
/\b(\d+)K\b/${1}000/g;    # correct
```

Evaluating the Replacement String

In addition to substituting replacement text, interpolated or otherwise, we can actually determine the replacement text by evaluating Perl code at the time of the match. This is enabled through the use of the /e evaluation modifier. Note that we do not say 'pattern match modifier' because /e has no bearing on the pattern at all, only the replacement text.

To illustrate how /e works, here is an example of a program that uses a substitution and /e (in combination with /g) to replace numbers with qualitative descriptions:

```
#!/usr/bin/perl
# quality.pl
use warnings;
use strict;

my $text = "3 Stumps, 2 Bails, and 0 Vogons";

$text =~ s/\b(\d+)\b/$1 > 0?$1 > 1?$1 > 2? "Several":"A pair of":"One":"No"/ge;

print $text, "\n";
```

> **perl quality.pl**
Several Stumps, A pair of Bails, and No Vogons

The right-hand side of this substitution contains a perfectly normal (if slightly confusing) Perl expression. Admittedly, this regexp could stand being a little more legible. Since this is executable code we can format it how we like; we do not need the /x modifier to add whitespace and comments:

```
$text =~ s{\b(\d+)\b}
    {
$1 > 0?(
$1 > 1?($1 > 2?"Several":"A pair of"
):"One"     # $1 == 1
):"No"      # $1 == 0
    }ge;     # global, execute
```

The /e modifier is very similar in operation to eval and a single-quoted, that is, uninterpolated, string (do not confuse evaluating an expression with interpolating a string!). One advantage /e has over eval, however, is that Perl does perform a compile-time syntax check on the replacement string. Perl can do this because in this case it knows interpolation cannot alter the syntax of the right-hand side – so if it is legal at compile-time it will be legal at run time.

Interpolating and Evaluating the Replacement String

Having just said that /e evaluates but does not interpolate the right-hand side, we can add another e and have Perl interpolate the right-hand side too. The /ee modifier first interpolates the right-hand side, and then evaluates the result of the interpolation, much in the same way as eval deals with a double-quoted string.

As an example, the following substitution expands any scalar or array variable in the supplied match text (in the same way that interpolation does on literal text), but without processing any metacharacters that might also be present:

```
$text =~ s/ ([\$\@]\w+) /$1/gee;
```

The search pattern will match any standard Perl variable name like $scalar or @array. For each successful match, $1 is first interpolated, and replaced with text containing the name of the variable (say, $scalar). This is then evaluated to get the value of the variable, which is then used as the replacement string.

The drawback of /ee is that it is an expensive, and hence slow operation involving both an interpolation and an eval each time a match occurs. It also suffers from not being syntax checked at compile-time, since Perl does not know what the replacement text is going to be when it executes the substitution. It is therefore not an advisable solution for regexps that match often.

Transliteration

Transliteration is the process of replacing one letter with another. The synonymous transliteration operators tr and y are usually grouped with the regexp operators because of the similarity of their syntax to the substitution operator. Like the substitution operator, they can be used with any suitable delimiters, are associated with match text with =~, have search and replace criteria, and even accept modifiers.

However, syntax apart, transliteration really has nothing to do with regexps at all. The left-hand side of a transliteration is not a regexp but a list of characters to be transformed (that is, transliterated), and the right hand side is another list of characters that they are to be transformed into. Each character on the left-hand side is converted into the matching character on the right, determined by their respective positions in the left and right lists.

As a simple example, this transliteration converts the letter a into the letter z, the letter b into the letter y, and the letter c into the letter x:

```
$text =~ tr/abc/zyx/;
```

If the replacement list is longer than the search list then the trailing characters are ignored. If, however, it is shorter, Perl replicates the final character until the replacement list is long enough:

```
$text =~ tr/abcd/zy/;
```

This example replaces a with z and all of b, c, and d with y.

The return value from a transliteration is a count of the number of successful matches. Since transliteration is faster than a regexp for finding single characters, one way we could (for instance) count the number of vowels in a piece of text would be with a transliteration:

```
$vowel_count = $text =~ tr/aeiou/aeiou/;
```

Although the search list of a transliteration is not a regexp, it has a lot in common with character classes, and accepts both ranges and interpolation (but not, ironically, character class) metacharacters. Here is a transliteration that uses ranges to uppercase the letters a to f and z:

```
$text =~ tr/a-fz/A-FZ/;
```

In a similar vein, here is a transliteration that replaces tabs and newlines with spaces:

```
$text =~ tr/\t\n/ /;
```

Here is a transliteration that matches the entire range of characters except ASCII 255 and adds one to the ASCII value of each character:

```
$text = "HAL";
$text =~ tr/\x00-\xfe/\x01-\xff/;
# \x00 is a long way of saying \0 but it looks better here
print $text;    # produces 'IBM'
```

Finally, here is an implementation of ROT-13, which swaps the first half of the alphabet with the second:

```
$text =~ tr/a-nA-Nm-zM-Z/m-zM-Za-nA-N/;
```

Note that we cannot use a transliteration to say things like 'replace a tab with four spaces' – for that we need a substitution (or the Text::Tabs module). Transliteration can only replace a character with another character, never more.

Transliteration lists are compiled by Perl at compile-time, so neither the search or replace lists are interpolated. If we want to use lists determined at run-time, then we must use an `eval`:

```
eval "tr/$search/$replace/";
```

As with its regexp siblings, the transliteration operator will use $_ by default if no explicit match text is supplied:

```
tr/a-z/A-Z/;   # capitalize all lower case characters in $_
```

If the replacement list is empty, characters are transliterated into themselves without change. On its own this is not especially useful, but this behavior is altered by both the /d and /s modifiers.

Transliteration Modifiers

Standard transliterations support three modifiers (c, d, and s) that alter the nature of the transliteration.

The /c or **complement** modifier inverts the sense of the search list to include all characters except those listed (somewhat similar to the opening caret of a negated character class). For example, to replace all non-alphabetic characters or whitespace characters with question marks we could use:

```
$text =~ tr/a-zA-Z\t\n/?/c;
```

The /d or **delete** modifier removes any character in the search list (possibly inverted by /c) that is not transliterated. That is, if the search list is longer than the replacement list then the replacement list is not extended, and characters on the search list, for which there is no replacement, are deleted.

```
$text =~ tr/a-zA-Z/A-Z/d;   # uppercase a-z and delete existing A-Z
```

The /s or **squash** modifier removes duplicate characters in the resulting text if both characters were the product of transliteration. Existing duplicates, or duplicates that occur because only one character has been transliterated are left alone. Here is an example that flattens whitespace:

```
$text =~ tr/\t\n//s;
# translate any whitespace to literal space and remove resulting duplicates
```

Note that for this example to work we had to transliterate spaces to themselves in order for them to be considered for duplicate removal.

To remove existing duplicates we can transliterate them into themselves by specifying the /s modifier and an empty replacement list. This causes every character to be transliterated into itself, after which duplicates are removed:

```
$text =~ tr/a-zA-Z0-9/s/;   # remove duplicate alphanumeric characters
```

All three modifiers may be used in combination with each other. As an example, here is an improved duplicate character eliminator that works for any character at all:

```
$text =~ tr///cs;
```

This works by taking the complement of no characters at all (which is all characters), and translating them into themselves, removing duplicates. Beware however, of using a complemented nothing as a search list to mean 'all characters'. Although it does mean this, the width of the search list is still zero, so we only get the expected result if the replacement list is also empty.

Summary

In this chapter we have seen and explored one of Perl's richest features – regular expressions. Perl has the capacity to handle them in such a fashion that it is one of the strongest cases for using the programming language to manipulate text in a very amicable way. In short we have looked at:

❏ The ways in which Perl performs the task of string interpolation, which are open to use and abuse whenever they are implemented.

❏ Where regular expressions occur, leading to the kinds of patterns, both simple and complex, that can be created and used in scripts.

❏ How to write efficient regular expressions making sure that they are valid and free from bugs that would otherwise lead to Perl misinterpreting our intended matches.

12

Input and Output with Filehandles

Input and Output, or IO for short, is one of the most fundamental concepts in programming, and indeed in computing as a whole. In a very real sense, any application that does more than print out 'Hello World' is a mechanism for taking input, doing something with it, and producing output. Consequently, it is an important topic.

Basic IO is the foundation of many other topics – network programming, one of the most important (or at least, popular) subtopics, is covered in Chapter 23, as is inter-process communication (IPC) in Chapter 22. Text-based interactive input and output is also covered in Chapter 18. All of these topics, to some extent, extend the basic IO concepts covered in this chapter.

In order to read or write to any kind of data source, we need a way of communicating with it. Filehandles provide that facility, acting as one end of a channel along which data can pass in one or both directions. The other end of the channel is largely abstract, so aside from the details of how we create the filehandle, one filehandle is very much like another. This abstraction allows a lot of different IO programming tasks to be condensed down into one set of concepts.

Once we have a filehandle we can read from it and write to it. If the filehandle points to an actual file or another device that supports the concept of a position, we can also use random access to read or write to different parts of the file.

We can do more with filehandles than read or write, however. One important feature is file locking, restricting access to a file by other processes or programs while we are busy. This is often an important issue for CGI scripts, for example. Additionally, we can redirect data streams by replacing file handles, duplicate filehandles, and even redefine the default filehandle used by functions such as `print`. All of these issues will be covered in this chapter. In Chapter 13, we look more into manipulating files and directories.

IO and Filehandles

Filehandles are a connection between our program and an external data source. This source may be an actual file, or it may be something different, such as a serial device, network connection, or the keyboard. Since filehandles are abstract concepts, any of these wildly different forms of communication can be treated in very similar ways for the purposes of programming. The name 'filehandle' is something of a misnomer, only a small subclass of filehandles actually point to a file. However, the name is used generically, so standard output is a filehandle even though it normally writes to the screen.

A lot of documentation, particularly in the C world, makes reference to 'file descriptors', which are apparently numeric equivalents to filehandles. In fact, a file descriptor is at the heart of every filehandle, and represents the numeric value of a data stream within the operating system itself. Here we primarily talk about filehandles, since Perl allows us to ignore file descriptors most of the time. However, we will return to the subject of file descriptors where appropriate in the chapter.

The Filehandle Data Type

Filehandles in Perl are a distinct data type. They are unrelated to scalars, and have their own slot in the symbol table typeglobs, as we covered in Chapter 5. The reason for this differentiation is that underneath the opaque and impenetrable skin of a filehandle is a structured collection of information that describes the actual connection. By keeping this information private, the filehandle is able to conceal the physical aspects of the device that it is associated with. This allows it to make use of buffering to improve the efficiency of IO operations, storing up writes until there is enough to send, and reading larger chunks of data than we ask for. Further attempts to read can then be supplied from memory rather than by accessing the data source again. In the case of files this minimizes the number of disk accesses required, and for other filehandles it minimizes the number of interruptions that the system must undergo.

The fact that filehandles are a different data type from anything else in Perl can cause a lot of confusion, because filehandles are not scalar values despite the fact that they clearly represent a single value. This means that assigning a filehandle to a scalar does not work. By the same token, passing a filehandle into or out of a subroutine also doesn't work. Since there is no special prefix for filehandle variables, only a data type, the only way to pass filehandles around is to refer to them via their typeglob entry.

Standard Filehandles

Perl provides three standard filehandles to all Perl programs automatically, STDIN, STDOUT, and STDERR.

Standard input, or STDIN, represents the default input filehandle, and is usually connected to the keyboard. This is the filehandle that functions like getc and the readline operator use by default.

Standard output, or STDOUT, represents the default output filehandle, and is usually connected to the screen (technically, the console device). This is the filehandle that the print function uses by default. Both STDIN and STOUT are 'smart' and buffer their connections automatically (buffering whole blocks of data unless they are connected to an interactive device, in which case they only perform line buffering).

Standard error, or STDERR, is the default error output filehandle. Like STDOUT it is normally connected to the screen. Unlike STDOUT it is usually not buffered at all, which ensures that error messages are always written in a timely manner.

For many applications the standard filehandles are actually all we need, and indeed many of the examples in the book so far make implicit use of them without touching on the subject of IO at all. However, if we want to read or write to anything else we will need to create a filehandle to access it.

Creating Filehandles

There are two primary ways to create a filehandle in Perl. The first and most obvious is the open function, which attempts to open a file and create a filehandle to talk to it. The second is to use the IO:: modules (the IO::File module in particular), to create filehandles that can be more easily manipulated and passed to subroutines without messing around with typeglobs. The IO:: modules also provide an object-oriented interface, which is more suitable to an object-oriented programming style.

Creating Filehandles with 'open'

The open function takes a filename and creates a filehandle for it. Traditionally it takes two arguments, the filehandle to create and the filename, optionally prefixed by an open mode. Without any prefix, files are opened for reading only, as in these two examples:

```
open (MYHANDLE, "myfile");   # explicit filename
open MYHANDLE $filename;   # filename in variable
```

The filehandle MYHANDLE is a package variable that is defined by the call to open. Once open, we can read from the file. For example, reading with the readline operator:

```
while (<MYHANDLE>) {
    print "Got: $_";
}
```

For ordinary files, the return value from open is 1 on success and the undefined value on failure. The filehandle will be created in either case, but if the call to open fails, the filehandle will be unopened and unassigned. In the event that the open fails, the reason is stored in the special variable $! (or $ERRNO with use English) which produces a message in string context. Since failing to open a file is often a fatal problem for Perl scripts, open and die are often combined together:

```
open (MYHANDLE, $filename) or die "Can't open $filename: $!\n";
```

Even if we do not want to die, it is a good idea to check the return value of open; failing to check the return value from open can lead to all sorts of problems when we try to use the filehandle.

An open also has a one-argument form where only the filehandle is specified. In this case open will attempt to use the contents of the scalar variable with the same name for the filehandle and the filename. However, this only works for package variables, not lexical ones, so its usefulness is somewhat limited:

```
our $FILE = "myfile";
open $FILE or die "Failed to open: $! \n";
```

What actually happens, in the case of only one argument, open looks up the name of the typeglob containing the scalar variable, and places the new filehandle into its handle slot. It is a minor piece of symbol table manipulation, which is why the argument must be a package variable.

Opening Files for Reading, Writing, and Updating

Without a prefix of any kind open opens a file for reading only. In order to write to or change the contents of a file, we have to prefix the filename with an open mode – optionally separated from the filename by spaces. The 'read' mode prefix < is usually omitted because it is the default. To write or append to a file we use the > or >> modes respectively:

```
open MYHANDLE, ">$file";    # open file for writing
open MYHANDLE, "> $file";   # the same, with optional spacing added
open MYHANDLE, ">>$file";   # open file for appending
```

Both these modes open the file for writing only, but they differ in significant ways. > will create the file if it does not exist, but destroy its existing contents if it does. >> also creates the file if it does not exist, but it will append to the end of the file if it does.

open understands six modes in total; the three standard modes and three 'update' variations. The full list with explanations is given in the table below:

Mode	Symbol	Description
Read	<	Open the file for read access only, for example: `open FH, "<$file";` This is the default mode and so the < prefix is usually optional. The exception is if the first character of the filename is significant to open, see 'Opening Arbitrary Filenames' below. If the file does not exist then the open fails.
Write	>	Open the file for write access only, for example: `open FH, ">$file";` If the file does not exist then it is created and opened. If the file does exist then it is truncated and its existing contents are lost.
Append	>>	Open the file for write access only, for example: `open FH, ">>$file";` If the file does not exist then it is created. If the file does exist then it is opened and the existing contents are preserved. Any writes to the file will be appended to the end of the existing contents.
Read-Update	+<	Open the file for read and write access, for example: `open FH, "+<$file";` This is the standard way to open a file for both read and write access. If the file does not exist then the open fails. If the file does exist then its existing contents are preserved and both read and write will start from the beginning of the file. Note that this is the correct mode to use if we want to open a file and write over the existing contents. The +>> mode appears to do this job, but will generally append to the end of the file instead, irrespective of the file position.

Mode	Symbol	Description
Write-Update	+>	Open the file for read and write access, for example: `open FH, "+>$file";` As with +<, the file is opened for read and write access. If the file does not exist then it is created. If the file does exist then it is truncated and its existing contents are lost. Because of this, this mode is usually only used to create new files that will first be written to and later read from.
Append-Update	+>>	Open the file for read and write access, for example: `open FH, "+>>$file";` If the file does not exist then it is created. If the file does exist then both read and write commence from the end of the file. On most (but frustratingly not all) platforms reads may take place from anywhere in the file, presuming the file position is first moved with seek. Writes always append to the end of the file, moving the file position with them. For this reason this mode is not usually used for read-write access; +< is preferred.

Opening Arbitrary Filenames

Some files may legally have filenames that open has trouble with. For instance, a file could start with a mode sign such as >, which ordinarily opens a file for writing. Any of the punctuation symbols +, <, >, | and & have special significance to the open function. This causes problems with the traditional use of open to open a file for reading where the optional < prefix is omitted:

```
$file = ">file";   # tricky filename (starts with a prefix)
open MYHANDLE, $file;   # opens 'file' for writing, prefix in file is used
open MYHANDLE, "<$file";   # opens '>file' for reading
```

To resolve these cases, Perl also provides a three-argument version of open where the mode is supplied separately from the file name. This also allows us to protect leading or trailing spaces, should we be using a filename containing them:

```
$file = " file ";   # leading space
open MYHANDLE, "<$file";   # incorrect, opens 'file' (leading space stripped
                          # after interpolation)
open MYHANDLE, '<', $file;   # correct, opens ' file ' (no interpolation,
                          # space is preserved)
```

Another way to handle awkwardly named files is to use the system-level open function sysopen instead of open. This will be covered later in the chapter.

Opening Standard Input and Standard Output

An open treats certain filenames as special. If the filename passed to open is a single minus - or a minus prefixed with a < symbol then open will instead open standard input:

```
open MYSTDIN, '-';
```

At first glance this may not seem particularly useful, but it is in fact very handy. For a start, we can tell a program to either read from an explicit filename, or its standard input, by passing in either the filename or a minus:

```
$filename = get_filename();   # may return undef...
open FILE, $filename?$filename: '-';   # open standard input if no filename
```

Perl also makes use of this feature when processing the @ARGV array using the readline <> operator. It does this by placing a single minus into @ARGV if it is otherwise empty so that <> will read from standard input. See Chapter 14 for more details of using @ARGV in this way.

If the filename passed to open is >- then standard output is opened instead:

```
open MYSTDOUT, '>-';
```

Again, although not apparently useful this allows programs to pass in standard output as a filename to functions and subroutines that accept an arbitrary filename.

There is no equivalent way to open standard error in this fashion, at least portably, as it does not have a shorthand filename alias. If we want to explicitly open standard error we can do so, but only by opening platform-specific files (for example, /dev/stderr on some UNIX implementations) or duplicating or aliasing the existing filehandle, which we will cover later in 'Duplication and Aliasing Filehandles'. Note that if we really want to read and write to a file called -, which is rather dubious, we can use the three-argument version of open to do so:

```
open FILE, '+<', '-';   # open a file called '-'.
```

Creating Filehandles with 'IO::File'

To simplify the creation and use of filehandles, Perl comes with a set of library modules in the IO:: family that abstract much of the awkward aspects of filehandles. At the same time they also provide an object-oriented interface. The IO::Handle module provides basic filehandle support. Support for filehandles representing real files comes from the IO::File module.

If we plan to use several of the IO:: modules we can save some typing and use the generic IO module instead. This is simply a convenient umbrella module that pulls several of the IO:: modules all at once. So, we can say this:

```
use IO::Dir;
use IO::File;
use IO::Handle;
use IO::Pipe;
use IO::Seekable;
use IO::Socket;
```

Or, more tersely:

```
use IO;
```

Opening a file with IO::File is not dissimilar to opening it with open, but with a much more convenient interface. For example to open a file in write-only mode we can supply a single parameter:

```
use IO::File;    # or 'use IO';

$fh = new IO::File;    # create a filehandle object
$fh->open("> myfile") or die "Unable to open: $!";    # open a file
```

Or, more tersely:

```
# create and open new filehandle
use IO::File;
$fh = new IO::File("> myfile") or die "Unable to open: $!";
```

The filehandle returned from the IO::File new is a filehandle object that we can use anywhere a regular filehandle goes. In addition we can manipulate the filehandle with methods from the IO::File, IO::Handle, or IO::Seekable modules:

```
$fh->autoflush(1);
$fh->seek(0, SEEK_END);
$fh->print("Message...\n");
$fh->close();
$fh->open("> $anotherfile");
```

The new method also handles a two-argument form, in which case the second argument is the mode to open the file in:

```
$fh->open($anotherfile, ">");
```

The mode may be any of the modes acceptable to open. In addition, it will accept one of the equivalent C-style fopen modes, for which Perl's modes are synonyms. In both cases IO::File maps the call into an open and returns the filehandle created. Finally, the mode may be a combination of numeric flags, which together make up the mode. In this case IO::File translates the call into a sysopen, and as with sysopen, we may also supply a permissions mask. The standard open modes are all shorthand codes for their equivalent sysopen mode flags, as the following table illustrates:

'open' Mode	'fopen' mode	'sysopen' flags
<	r	O_RDONLY
>	w	O_WRONLY | O_CREAT | O_TRUNC
>>	a	O_WRONLY | O_APPEND | O_CREAT
+<	r+	O_RDWR
+>	w+	O_RDWR |O_CREAT | O_TRUNC
+>>	a+	O_RDWR |O_APPEND | O_CREAT

Examination of the sysopen flags is revealing. A base mode is always required, and must be one of O_RDONLY, O_WRONLY, or O_RDWR, which open a file for reading only, writing only (not supported on Windows) or both reading and writing, respectively.

421

To append to a file we add the O_APPEND flag. Clearly this needs a writable file so it only combines with O_WRONLY or O_RDWR. Similarly, O_CREAT will create the file if it does not exist, and O_TRUNC will truncate it if it does. By examining this table we can see why the standard open modes do what they do.

One of the benefits of IO::File is that it allows us to choose whichever method suits us at the time. However, if we want to specify file permissions too, then we must use the sysopen style and supply a numeric mode. We'll cover this and the other flags that can be supplied in a sysopen mode in 'System Level IO' later in the chapter.

The Data Filehandle

Perl defines a special pseudo-filehandle, DATA, which will read input data from within the source file. To create data within a source file we insert the special token __DATA__ on a line of its own. Everything below this token will not be parsed or compiled by Perl but will instead be made available as input to the DATA pseudo-filehandle, up to the end of the file or an __END__ token, if present.

> *We may sometimes see Perl programs use __END__ for this purpose. This may seem confusing since __END__ is supposed to stop Perl parsing, period. The reason for this is for backwards compatibility with the era before Perl 5, where __END__ officially had the role that __DATA__ now does. Consequently __END__ works like __DATA__ in the main source file, but not in other packages or in files included by do or require.*

Defining data within a source file can be very convenient. For example, we can define a default configuration file without actually creating or installing a separate file to hold it. It is also convenient for defining large data structures with complex syntax, or where the data is very unlikely to change. Here is an example of a program that stores planetary data in a table and reads it with the DATA filehandle:

```perl
#!/usr/bin/perl
# planets.pl
use warnings;
use strict;

my $columns = <DATA>;
chomp $columns;
my @columns = split /\s*, \s*/, $columns;
shift @columns;   # lose first name

my %table;

while (<DATA>) {
    next if /^#/;   # skip comments
    my @data = split /\s*, \s*/;
    my $name = shift @data;

    foreach (0..$#data) {
        print "$_ : $columns[$_] : $data[$_] \n";
        $table{$name}{$columns[$_]} = $data[$_];
    }
}

foreach (sort keys %table) {
    print "$_\n";
    foreach my $stat (sort keys %{$table{$_}}) {
        print "\t$stat = $table{$_}{$stat}\n";
    }
}
```

```
__DATA__
Body     , Radius , Mass      , Distance, Moons, Day         , Year
# The Sun
Sun      , 6.960e8, 1.989e30, 0         , n/a  , 25.36 days , n/a
# The Planets
Mercury , 2.420e6, 3.301e23, 5.791e10, 0       , 58.7 days  , 87.97 days
Venus   , 6.085e6, 4.869e24, 1.082e11, 0       , 243 days   , 224.7 days
Earth   , 6.378e6, 5.978e24, 1.496e11, 1       , 23.93 hours, 365.3 days
Mars    , 3.375e6, 6.420e23, 2.279e11, 2       , 24.6 hours , 687 days
Jupiter , 7.140e7, 1.899e27, 7.783e11, 13      , 9.9 hours  , 11.86 years
Saturn  , 6.040e7, 5.685e26, 1.427e12, 10      , 10.2 hours , 28.46 years
Uranus  , 2.360e7, 8.686e25, 2.869e12, 5       , 10.7 hours , 84.02 years
Neptune , 2.230e7, 1.025e26, 4.498e12, 2       , 15.8 hours , 164.8 years
Pluto   , 3.000e6, 5.000e23, 5.900e12, 1       , 6.3 days   , 248 years
# And the Moon, just for luck
Moon    , 1.738e6, 7.353e22, 1.496e11, n/a     , 27.32 days , 27.32 days

__END__
A comment - this is neither part of the program nor the data (but see below...)
```

If an __END__ token appears after the __DATA__ token then the data ends as soon as it encounters the __END__, otherwise it finishes at the end of the file. __DATA__ tokens are actually package scoped, so multiple __DATA__ tokens in different files but within the same package concatenate together in the order in which the package files are used or `required`. To access the data in a different package we can prefix the filehandle with the package name:

```
# access data in MyPackage
while (<MyPackage::DATA>) {
    ...
}
```

As mentioned earlier, the main source file treats __END__ differently, for compatibility reasons. Consequently if we use __END__ in the main package it works like a second __DATA__ and is ignored (since we have already seen one __DATA__). The planets program above is actually written to avoid us noticing that it does in fact read both the __END__ and the comment following it as data; the errant lines are eliminated because they do not contain any commas. If __END__ does not appear to be working correctly, this may be the reason.

Other Filehandles

Before moving on to reading and writing filehandles, it is worth mentioning the other kinds of filehandle that we can create in Perl. Three other functions in Perl return filehandles: pipe, socket, and socketpair. In the case of pipe and socketpair, they actually return two filehandles, which are used in different circumstances.

Pipes are simply a pair of filehandles wired back to back, one read-only and one write-only. We write into one end, and read from the other. Pipes are mainly used for communicating between different processes and external programs, and are consequently covered in detail in Chapter 22. The open function supports the creation of implicit pipes and the execution of external programs, and can also be made to carry out a fork and exec at the same time. These extended uses of the open function are also covered in Chapter 22.

The socket function is the equivalent of open for sockets. Sockets are the backbone of Perl's network programming support and accordingly take up the bulk of Chapter 23. Sockets have more than one mode of operation, but they can operate very much like regular filehandles for the purposes of reading and writing. The socketpair function creates the equivalent of a pipe using sockets, returning two sockets connected back to back. Unlike ordinary pipes, a pair of sockets created this way permits two-way communications.

The term 'filehandle' is thus rather more general than it might at first seem, since a handle need not refer to a file, or even a known hardware or network device. The elegance of filehandles is that once created we can for most intents and purposes ignore what they actually represent. This does not mean we do not have to deal with the special circumstances of a filehandle – a network socket has to deal with networking issues that do not apply to a text file. It does mean, however, that for simple reading and writing we can treat all filehandles as basically similar.

Referring to Filehandles

Referring to filehandles correctly is a large source of confusion in Perl. This confusion arises from two sources. First, there is no explicit syntax for filehandles. Second, what we think of as filehandles in Perl source code are actually symbolic references to typeglobs containing filehandles. Perl's syntax and the use strict module conspire to make this invisible to us, but the conspiracy is not perfect and so sometimes things do not work as we expect. Once we understand this, a lot of the mystery surrounding Perl's filehandles can be dispelled.

All Perl's built-in functions that take filehandles as arguments allow filehandles to be specified directly or indirectly. Directly just means writing the name of the filehandle, as in:

```
print MYHANDLE "Hello Filehandle \n";
```

The print statement knows that MYHANDLE is a filehandle because:

❑   It is the first parameter
❑   It is followed by a space
❑   It isn't a quoted string

Unfortunately if we try to copy this filehandle to a scalar variable we get an illegal bareword syntax error under use strict:

```
use strict;

$fh = MYHANDLE;    # ERROR: syntax error
```

This is perfectly understandable. We are not allowed barewords with use strict, and MYHANDLE is just a string without quotes in this statement. It may also be the name of a filehandle, but that does not mean it looks like a filehandle. Contrary to what the print statement above might imply, a bareword is not the syntax for a filehandle. It is actually a special case of a symbolic reference that is permitted by the strict module, precisely for the use of functions that take filehandles.

The point to bear in mind is that a filehandle's data type is different from that of a scalar, so we cannot simply store one inside the other, even though a filehandle is intuitively a 'single' value. We cannot actually refer to a filehandle at all, only to the typeglob within which it resides. However, since all Perl's file-handling functions accept typeglobs and references to typeglobs (both hard and symbolic) as filehandle arguments, we do not notice. In reality, a bareword filehandle is just a symbolic reference that we can omit the quotes from. Once we realize this, the confusion starts to lessen somewhat.

To store and pass filehandles, therefore, we need to take a reference to the typeglob of the same name. The reference can be a hard reference or a symbolic reference; either is acceptable to Perl's filehandle functions. Fortunately, treating typeglobs in scalar context generates a symbolic reference for the typeglob, so we can do this:

```
$fh = *MYHANDLE;    # $fh becomes '*main::MYHANDLE'
# symbolic reference OK as filehandle
print $fh "Hello Symbolic Reference to Filehandle \n";
```

Alternatively, we can create a hard reference to the typeglob and use that:

```
$fh = \*MYHANDLE;    # reference to typeglob
print $fh "Hello Reference to Typeglob \n";
```

The print statement is a little more fastidious than the other filehandle-based functions because its syntax is so flexible in other respects. It will accept a typeglob, filehandle reference, or string stored in a scalar variable. It will not accept the filehandle name as a literal string since that looks to print like a value to actually print out, not a filehandle. However, it will accept an expression, including a literal string, but only if it is inside a block:

```
print "STRING";    # a regular text string
print {'HANDLE'.$hno} "Text...\n"    # print 'Text...' to HANDLE1, etc
print {$err?STDERR:STDOUT} "Text...\n";    # STDOUT or STDERR
```

This requirement for a block to differentiate between a filehandle and a string is purely an artifact of the accepted syntax of the print statement. Other filehandle-based functions do not have to worry about this distinction between filehandles and text arguments, so they allow the use of strings and string expressions directly. To demonstrate, here are open and close (which we will cover in more detail shortly) taking a string expression and interpreting it as a filehandle:

```
open 'A'.'B'.'C', '>test.file';
print ABC "Yes, this actually works \n";
close "ABC";    # or even close uc('abc')
```

The relationship between typeglobs, filehandles, and symbolic references is an ancient and mysterious one. Since filehandles cannot be stored directly in scalars, typeglobs used to be the only way to pass filehandles into or out of subroutines:

```
# example of passing a filehandle to a subroutine
sub print_to_filehandle {
    $fh = shift;
    print $fh @_;
}

# pass filehandle as typeglob
print_to_filehandle(*STDOUT, "Hello Passed Filehandle \n");

# pass filehandle as scalar reference to typeglob
$fh = *STDOUT;
print_to_filehandle($fh, "Hello Again");
```

Closer observation of this code reveals that this is just another case of symbolic references. Whether or not we pass a filehandle directly to the subroutine or copy it into a scalar first, it is cast into a scalar by being passed as an argument. This is so that the typeglob is turned into a symbolic reference to itself, from which print extracts the filehandle. In other words we are passing a string, and not a typeglob.

It is largely on account of this kind of thing that the `IO::Handle` and `IO::File` modules were created. In these more enlightened times we can use the `IO::File` module to create filehandles that can be automatically passed around and manipulated without worrying about any of the issues discussed above:

```
use IO::File;

$fh = new IO::File(">$filename");
print $fh "Typeglobs and references begone! \n";
```

The drawback with the `IO::File` and `IO::Handle` modules is that they add a level of abstraction to file handling. This causes Perl to load in a collection of modules it does not otherwise need, and incurs a corresponding performance loss. For most applications, however, the advantages of the `IO::` family in simplifying filehandles more than make up for their disadvantages.

Reading from Filehandles

Once we have a filehandle, we can use it to read or write to a file, presuming that the filehandle is opened in the right direction and that (in the case of reading) there is something to read. We can also read a specific numbers of bytes, or retrieve them one by one if necessary.

The Readline Operator

The simplest way to read from a filehandle is to use the readline operator `<>`:

```
open MYHANDLE, "myfile" or die "Unable to open: $! \n";
$line = <MYHANDLE>;   # read a line
```

In a scalar context the readline operator reads one line at a time, returning its value. In a list context, however, it reads all the lines at once:

```
@lines = <MYHANDLE>;   # read entire file at one go
```

A line is defined by the input record separator (held in the special variable $/). By default this is set to the newline character \n, which takes account of any special translations for the specific platform. This makes it very convenient for reading text files with lines delimited by newlines, and is even platform-independent.

Redefining the Line Separator

However, we do not have to read lines. By redefining the input record separator $/ ($INPUT_RECORD_SEPARATOR or $RS with use English), we can read on any delimiter we choose, for example colons:

```
$/ = ':';
@lines = <MYHANDLE>;   # read file delimited by ':'
```

We can even undefine $/, or equivalently set it to an empty string. In this case, the readline operator works in slurp mode and reads an entire file into a single scalar string:

```
undef $/;
$file = <MYHANDLE>;   # read entire file as one scalar
```

This is particularly handy if we want to run a regular expression across the whole file. However, if we redefine $/ it is usually a good idea to restore it afterward to avoid unexpected problems elsewhere. A simple solution to that problem is to localize the value of $/ and redefine the local definition:

```
sub readfile {
    $file = shift;
    if (open FILE, $file) {
        # undefine $/ if called in a scalar context
        local $/ = undef unless wantarray;
        # return file contents as array or single scalar
        return <FILE>;
    }
    return undef;   # failed to open, check $! for the reason
}
```

If the input record separator is defined as a scalar reference to an integer value (which may include a reference to a scalar variable), the readline operator goes into a fixed record mode, reading exactly that many characters each time:

```
$record_size = 32;
$/ = \$record_size;   # or, equivalently, $/ = \32
while (<MYHANDLE>) {
    print "Got $_\n";
    # $_ contains 32 characters unless end of file intervenes
}
```

In this mode the readline operator is similar in nature to the read function, which we will discuss in a moment.

Aliasing Readline in 'while' Loops

When used in the conditional part of a while loop, the readline operator has the useful property of setting the default scalar variable $_. This is a special case for the while loop, which does not ordinarily set $_. We can use this fact to read a file line by line like this:

```
open MYHANDLE, "myfile" or die "Unable to open: $! \n";
while (<MYHANDLE>) {
    print "Read: $_\n";
}
```

Unlike a foreach loop, we cannot provide our own variable to be the loop variable; in this case it has to be $_. See the section on 'Conditional Loops' in Chapter 6 for more details.

Counting Line Numbers

The special variable $. contains the number of lines read from the most recently read filehandle. For example, to print out matches in a file in a grep-like manner we could use $. like this:

```
while (<MYHANDLE>) {
    /$searchpattern/ and print "$.: $_ \n";
}
```

Since $. is a package variable it persists even after the file has run out of lines, so we can consult it after we have finished reading:

```
@lines = <MYHANDLE>;
print "$. lines read \n";
```

Technically, $. is not the line count but the input record number, as its value is dependent on the input record separator $/, so it does not necessarily reflect the number of lines in the file as we might understand it. So, if $/ is undefined, $. will most likely be 1. The value of $. is reset when the filehandle is closed.

Readline and the '@ARGV' Array

If no filehandle is given to <>, it interprets the elements of the @ARGV array as filenames and attempts to open and read from them, (as discussed at the start of Chapter 14). In brief, this is how it is done:

```
# read one or more files and print them out, prefixed by filename and line
# number
print "$ARGV:$.:$_" while <>;
```

The name of the file currently being read is held in $ARGV, while the filehandle is stored as ARGV. If @ARGV is empty, <> defaults to standard input by supplying a - behind the scenes, which can also be seen in $ARGV. Conversely, if more than one file is present, each is read in turn, although $. is not reset between files. To fix this we can use eof and close, resetting $.:

```
while (<>) {
    print "$ARGV: $.: $_";
    close (ARGV) if eof;
}
```

See Chapter 14 for more details and examples of using the readline operator with command line arguments.

Finer Control Over Reading

The readline operator is best suited to reading files with known delimiters or fixed record lengths. For other applications we may be better off using the read function. This function takes a filehandle, a scalar variable, and a length as arguments, and attempts to read the number of bytes given by the length into the scalar variable.

```
read MYHANDLE, $text, 60;   # attempt to read 60 bytes into $text
```

The return value of read is either the number of bytes read (which may be less than length if the end of the file was reached), 0 if we are already at the end of the file, and undef if there was an error:

```
$text = <>;
open MYHANDLE, "$text";
$result = read MYHANDLE, $text, 60;   # attempt to read 60 bytes into $text
die "Failed to read: $!" unless defined $result;   # handle an error
print "read $result bytes: $text \n";   # print out the result
```

The current value of $text, if any, is overwritten and the scalar is shrunk to fit the result. If we want to partially or completely retain the existing contents of $text we can add an extra offset argument to the read statement. If present, this causes read to write text into the variable from the offset character (offset into the variable, that is, not the file). For example, to concatenate reads without having to use a temporary variable, we can supply the length of the current text as the offset, in order to have read place new text at the end of the string:

```
$text = <>;
open MYHANDLE, "$text";
$result;
while ($result = read MYHANDLE, $text, 60, length $text) {
    print "appended $result bytes \n"
}

if (not defined $result) {
    print "Error: $! \n";
} else {
    print "Done \n";
}
```

read and <> both deal with buffered input. The unbuffered system-level equivalent of read is sysread, which behaves in a very similar manner on unbuffered input. It is safe to mix read and <>, but not sysread as well. See 'System Level IO' later in the chapter for more information.

Detecting the End-of-File

If we attempt to read beyond the end of a file, we encounter the end-of-file condition. This is a flag set on the filehandle that indicates that no more data is available. Further attempts to read from the file will return with failure.

We can detect the end-of-file condition with the eof function that takes a filehandle as an argument, and returns True or False depending on whether the filehandle has encountered the end-of-file condition or not. For example:

```
$text = <>;
open MYHANDLE, "$text";
if (eof MYHANDLE) {
    print "No more to read \n";
} else {
    ...read some more...
}
```

Operators like the readline operator automatically detect the end-of-file condition and return False when they encounter it. So eof is not necessary for loops like this:

```
while (<>) {
    print "Got: $_\n";
}
```

The distinction between the end-of-file condition and the actual end of the file is often negligible, but it can be occasionally important. For instance, the file can grow if more data is written into it from another process, but this does not clear the end-of-file condition because our filehandle does not know about it. To clear the condition we can use seek to move the current position to itself, as documented in the next section:

```
seek MYHANDLE, 0, 1;
```

The end-of-file condition does not just apply to files, but to any filehandle that is open for input. In cases where the filehandle does not refer to an actual file, an end-of-file condition indicates simply that there is no more data to read at the moment. Because this condition may be temporary, the end-of-file condition is transient, and we can only detect it once. If we attempt to read from one of these filehandles after eof has returned True, or attempt to use eof twice on the same filehandle, then the end-of-file condition will be cleared and eof will return False. Similarly, an attempt to read will block until more data becomes available.

Reading a Single Character

Single characters can be read with the getc function. Like readline, it takes a filehandle as an argument but returns a single character:

```
$char = getc MYHANDLE;   # get a character from MYHANDLE
$char = getc;   # get a character from STDIN
```

Filehandles created by IO::File can use the object-oriented equivalent:

```
$fh->getc;
```

IO::File also supports an ungetc method, though this is only guaranteed to work for one character. It takes the ordinal (ASCII code) value of the character as its argument:

```
$fh->ungetc ord($char);   # push $char back onto $fh
```

If getc is not given a filehandle to read from it defaults to STDIN. However, since terminal buffering means that a typed character will not be sent until the return key is pressed, this alone is not enough to react to a single key press. In order to do this we need to control the behavior of the terminal, which we can do in a number of ways, such as using the Term::ReadKey module discussed in detail in Chapter 15.

Writing to Filehandles

Writing to filehandles is usually done via the print statement, which by default writes to standard output. In its simplest usage we usually call print with one or more things we wish to display. However, this is actually shorthand for printing to standard output, and the following two statements are (almost) identical:

```
print "Calling Major Tom";   # implicit print to STDOUT
print STDOUT "Calling Major Tom";   # explicit print to STDOUT
```

They are not quite identical since, in the first case, select can be used (and could have been used in advance) to change where print actually prints. In the second case, select will have no effect as the filehandle is given explicitly.

The print statement will also accept an expression for the filehandle, but due to the flexible nature of its syntax, it requires that a block be used to delimit the expression (other functions, such as eof, do not have this restriction):

```
print {$error?STDERR:STDOUT} "This -might- be an error \n";
```

Like other filehandle functions, print will accept a string if it is held in a scalar variable (or array element, hash value, etc.), but as this is considered a symbolic reference it will only be allowed if strict refs are not in effect. This is the rationale behind the one-argument open, which creates a filehandle with the same name as the file that it is associated with:

```
use strict;
no strict 'refs';

open ">$filename";    # one argument 'open', filename = handle
print $filename, "Ashes to Ashes";
close $filename;
```

Because the filehandle has the same name as the opened file, using the filename as an alias for the filehandle causes print to do a symbolic dereference and look up the filehandle through the typeglob with the same name. For this reason the filename must be stored in a package and not a lexical variable. To achieve the same effect with a lexical variable we must specify the filename for both handle and filename:

```
open $filename, ">$filename";   # two argument 'open', filename = handle
print $filename, "Dust to Dust";
close $filename;
```

The IO::File module also generates storable filehandles. It works by creating an object based on the fileglob containing the filehandle that it creates, and so avoids all the problems to do with symbolic references and other shenanigans encountered in the examples above:

```
$fh = new IO::File(">myfile");
print $fh "This is the content of the file";
close $fh;
```

The only catch with IO::File is that it exacts a performance penalty when we use it. In most cases this is acceptable, but for efficient file handling we might want to stick with basic filehandles instead. As a lightweight alternative, we can create our own filehandles using the gensym subroutine of the Symbol module. This creates a reference to an anonymous typeglob that can be freely passed between subroutines and methods in different packages:

```
#!/usr/bin/perl
#gensym.pl
use warnings;
use strict;

use Symbol;

my $fh = gensym;
open $fh, "> newfile.txt";
print $fh "some text";
close $fh;
```

gensym is the basis of the objects returned by IO::Handle and its inheritors like IO::File; see the gensym source code and the new method in IO::Handle for a perspective on how they actually co-operate to create object-oriented filehandles. (We can use > **perldoc -l System** and > **perldoc -l IO/Handle.pm** to locate the files, if perldoc is available).

Buffering and Autoflush Mode

Ordinarily, output to filehandles is buffered, either block-buffered if the output is to a non-interactive device like a flat file, or line-buffered if it is to an interactive device. The distinction between these is that in block buffering, output is saved until a maximum threshold, usually several kilobytes, is reached and then written out all at once. In line buffering, the filehandle buffers output until a newline character is written, at which point the whole line is sent to the output. Interactive devices like screens default to line buffering since that is more logical when communicating with a user.

> *Note that we are talking only about application-level buffering here, as provided by the filehandle. Operating systems also buffer IO at a lower level, which we have no direct control over, but can manipulate if we want to get our hands dirty. For the sake of simplicity we will overlook this for the purposes of this discussion.*

Block buffering is useful, but it can be confusing to other programs that are expecting to see the output in a timely manner, such as clients waiting to see the output of a CGI script. Fortunately the output can be switched from block buffering to line buffering even on filehandles that would normally block buffer by setting the autoflush flag. For the default output the special autoflush variable $| ($OUTPUT_AUTOFLUSH with use English) performs this duty:

```
$| = 1;   # set line buffering, 'autoflush' mode
print "Hello World \n";   # write a line
$| = 0;   # restore block buffering
```

Filehandles created with IO::File or IO::Handle can have their autoflush state altered with the autoflush method:

```
$fh->autoflush(1);   # set line buffering. 'autoflush' mode
print $fh "Hello World \n";   # write a line
$fh->autoflush(0);   # restore block buffering
```

If we have used IO::Handle then we can also use the autoflush method on any filehandle:

```
use IO::File;   # inherits from IO::Handle

# '$$' returns the process ID:
open TMP, "> /tmp/tmp_pid$$" or die "Open failed: $!";
TMP->autoflush(1);
```

It is important to remember that the autoflush flag does not disable buffering. To write to a file or device unbuffered we can use the system-level IO function syswrite. $| does not disable buffering, it merely allows block-buffered filehandles to be turned into line-buffered ones. For filehandles that are already connected to an interactive device such as a screen, the autoflush flag has no effect.

Alternatives to 'print'

As an alternative to print, we can also use the printf function, covered in Chapter 3, or the unbuffered system-level syswrite function, covered in Chapter 22. The enticingly named write function is not in fact a synonym for print, or the opposite of read, but rather it is connected to report generation, an entirely different concept.

Handling Binary and Text Files

Most modern and intelligently written operating systems do not make any distinction between 'binary' and 'text' files. Unfortunately, some operating systems do, Windows (in all its various versions and suffixes) and MacOS being two of them. In these cases we have to ensure that the underlying operating system knows what kind of file we are working with before we attempt to read or write it.

The problem lies in the definition of a 'line'. Under UNIX and many other operating systems, the end of a line is a single linefeed (newline or LF) character. On Windows, lines are terminated by a carriage return (return or CR) followed by a linefeed. On a Macintosh it is the other way around. See Chapter 15 for more.

Whenever we use \n to generate a new line, or read a file using the readline operator (which uses $/, by default set to \n), Perl, the underlying C libraries, and the operating system all band together to guess how to deal with line terminators. Between them, they convert between what Perl expects and what the underlying file format requires. By default, files are assumed to be textual, so a new line in Perl becomes a single linefeed, a linefeed plus return, or a return plus linefeed depending on the underlying platform. Similarly, when a file is read, combinations of linefeed plus return are invisibly compressed into a single linefeed so that the readline operator will work as expected. The chomp function, which strips line endings, also uses $/, so it will always work irrespective of what the line ending is (as long as it is set to \n, which it is by default).

The 'binmode' Function

The practical upshot of all this is that if we are working with text files we can let Perl deal with the complications of line endings for us. If we are working with a binary file (which has no lines and thus no line endings), on a platform that makes a distinction, then we need to tell Perl to prevent this automatic translation from taking place. The simplest way to do this is to use the binmode function with a filehandle:

```
binmode HANDLE;   # make HANDLE a binary filehandle
```

This sets both the input and output disciplines of HANDLE to be binary (or technically, raw, which is a related, but not identical, concept to raw terminal IO covered in Chapter 15). We can also do this explicitly by setting the discipline directly:

```
binmode HANDLE ':raw';   # make HANDLE a binary filehandle
```

Similarly, we can switch on line ending translation using the :crlf discipline, assuming the underlying platform cares:

```
binmode HANDLE ':crlf';   # make HANDLE a DOS text filehandle
```

In general, specifying the input and output disciplines is never necessary, but they provide a potential interface to setting other kinds of line discipline and in future will likely do so. The curious reader may turn to the section on terminal capabilities in Chapter 15, which contains more on the subject of line disciplines.

The 'open' Pragma

Perl also supplies a pragmatic module called open.pm, not to be confused with the open function. open performs a similar job to binmode but allows the disciplines for input and output to be set independently. However, whereas binmode is set on a per-filehandle basis, the open pragma sets a default for all file handles opened in its lexical scope.

For example, to set the input discipline to text and the output to binary we could use:

```
use open IN => ':crlf', OUT => ':raw';
```

This sets a default input discipline of :crlf and a default output discipline of :raw for all filehandles that are opened in the same lexical scope as the declaration.

Currently only :crlf and :raw are defined by the open module, but it is likely this will be extended to cover other kinds of line discipline along with binmode. See, once again Chapter 15 for more information on disciplines and terminal capabilities.

Random Access

If a filehandle refers to an actual file then we can use **random access methods** to move about within the file, thereby reading or writing to different parts of it selectively. To achieve this we make use of the **file pointer**, which is a position within the file that is associated with the filehandle. Using the built-in functions, seek and tell, we can set and retrieve the current position of the file pointer to allow reads or writes to take place at a specific point within the file.

'seek' to a Specific Place within a File

The seek function allows us to change the position of the file pointer associated with our filehandle, so that it points to a different part of the file. It takes three parameters: the filehandle to modify, the new position, and a relationship flag (also known as the whence flag). It will work with either a filehandle or an expression that evaluates to the name of the filehandle as a string.

The actual effect of seek depends on the value of the whence flag, which can be 0, 1, or 2:

Flag	Effect
seek FH, $pos, 0	Seek to the absolute position given by $pos. For example, seek FH, 0, 0 moves the pointer to the beginning of the file
seek FH, $pos, 1	Seek forward ($pos > 0) or backward ($pos < 0) by the number of bytes given by $pos from the current position. For example, seek FH, 60, 1 moves the file pointer forward 60 bytes. Note that seeking beyond the end of the file and then writing to the file extends it, but does not guarantee that the new extent is 'zeroed' out.
seek FH, $pos, 2	Seek relative to the end of the file. If $pos is negative, seek backwards $pos bytes from the end of the file. If it is zero, seek to the end of the file. If it is positive, attempt to seek forwards past the end of the file. For example, seek FH, -60, 2 moves the file pointer to a position sixty characters before the end of the file.

seek returns a true value if it succeeds, and 0 otherwise, for example, if we try to seek to before the beginning of the file. This will cause the file pointer to land at the end of the file, if the file is not open for writing. Alternatively, if it is open for writing, the file will be extended to satisfy the pointer, so an easy way to create a large file is to open it for writing and then move the pointer to a large value:

```
open (BIGFILE, "> bigfile");
seek BIGFILE, 100 * 1024 * 1024, 0;   # move the pointer to the  100MB point

syswrite BIGFILE, 'end';   # write to the file, thereby setting its size to
                           # 100MB (plus three characters)
close BIGFILE;
```

On some filing systems, particularly on UNIX platforms, this does not actually assign 100MB of disk space; it actually creates a sparse file that contains only the beginning and the end, a file with a hole in it, so to speak.

Since the meanings of the values 0, 1, and 2 are not particularly memorable we can use labels for them instead if we use the Fcntl module. This defines three constants, SEEK_SET, SEEK_CUR, and SEEK_END for 0, 1, and 2 respectively:

```
use Fcntl qw(:seek);    # get SEEK_ constants
seek MYHANDLE, $position, SEEK_SET;
seek MYHANDLE, $moveby, SEEK_CUR;
```

Note that seek is not the same as the sysseek function. The seek function works with buffered filehandles; sysseek works at the system level. Using both interchangeably is not a good idea. For more information on sysseek, see 'System Level IO' later in the chapter.

Clearing the End-of-File Condition with 'seek'

Using seek has the occasionally useful side effect of resetting the end-of-file condition on a filehandle (as read by eof), since by moving the file pointer we are explicitly overriding its position. This can be handy for monitoring the end of growing logfiles, among other applications. The end-of-file condition on non-position based filehandles is transient, so this is not an issue here, but for filehandles associated with files it is permanent since files are assumed not to grow. To clear it, we can use seek.

The simplest way to remove the end-of-file condition without actually moving the file pointer is to seek to the current position:

```
seek MYHANDLE, 0, 1;    # (possibly) reset eof.
```

This works because although we have moved the position to the end of the file we have not tried to read data there. It is the attempt to read rather than the position of the file pointer that causes the end-of-file condition to be raised.

After calling seek we can attempt to read the file again from the current position, and see if any new data has been written. If it has not, we will just raise the end-of-file condition once more. Here is a short loop that uses this technique and a sleep to periodically check for output, essentially similar in intent to the UNIX command tail -f:

```perl
for(;;) {
   # read lines while there are lines to read
   while (<LOGFILE>) {
      print "$.: $_";
   }

   # got an 'eof' - sleep, reset 'eof', then loop back and try again
   sleep(1);
   seek LOGFILE, 0, 1;
}
```

Writing at the End-of-File

When multiple programs or processes are all writing to the same file we cannot always guarantee that our file pointer is actually pointing at the end of the file. In order to make sure that anything we write goes at the end of the file we can seek to the end explicitly using SEEK_END and a distance of 0:

```perl
seek MYHANDLE, 0, SEEK_END;
```

If several processes have the same file open in an append mode, lines will not overlap each other, but the order in which they appear cannot be determined. If the file is not open in an append mode, even this cannot be guaranteed. In order to ensure that different processes do not overwrite each other we also need to use some form of file locking, for instance with flock. Here is a short logging program that uses this technique in combination with file locking to make absolutely sure that it is writing to the current end of the file:

```perl
#!/usr/bin/perl
#logging.pl
use warnings;
use strict;

use Fcntl qw(:seek :flock);

# open file for update, position is at current end of file
open LOGFILE, ">>/tmp/mylog" or die "Unable to open: $! \n";

# lock file for exclusive access
flock LOGFILE, LOCK_EX;

# now seek to end of file explicitly, in case it changed since the open
seek LOGFILE, 0, SEEK_END;

# write our log message
print LOGFILE "Log message...\n";

# remove lock and close file
flock LOGFILE, LOCK_UN;
close LOGFILE;
```

This program takes advantage of file locking to prevent any other program or process extending the file while it is still busy writing to it. So long as all processes that access the file cooperate with flock, all will be well. It also takes advantage of the fact that flock causes all buffered output on the filehandle to be flushed on both locking and unlocking operations. In this sample program the close would have done that for us anyway, but the principle still applies.

Finding the Current Position

The `tell` function is the counterpart to `seek`. It returns the current value of the file pointer. It takes one parameter (a filehandle), and returns the current position, in bytes, within the file:

```
$position = tell MYHANDLE;
```

Like `seek`, `tell` will work on either a filehandle or an expression that evaluates to the name of the filehandle as a string. If no filehandle is given, `tell` defaults to the last file opened:

```
open (MYHANDLE, "myfile") or die "could not open myfile: $!";
$line = <MYHANDLE>;
print "The first line was ", tell," characters long \n";
```

If the filehandle has no file pointer associated with it, which is the case with serial connections and sockets, the returned pointer value is -1 (rather than `undef` which we might have expected):

```
$position = tell MYHANDLE;
print "The file position is", $position >- 1?$position:" not applicable";
```

Object-Oriented Random Access

Programmers who are using filehandles generated by the `IO::File` module can make use of the object-oriented methods supplied by the `IO::Seekable` module for filehandles that can have their file positions modified. These methods are direct object-oriented replacements for the standard Perl functions:

```
$fh->seek($position, 0);   # seek to absolute position
$fh->seek($distance, SEEK_CUR);   # seek forward 'distance' bytes
$pos = $fh -> tell();   # find current position
```

Truncating and Resizing Files

To make a file longer we can use the `seek` function to move beyond the current end of the file, or simply append more data to it, so long as we have the file opened in a writable state. However, we cannot make a file shorter this way.

One simple, albeit destructive, way to make a file shorter is to simply write a new file over it, using an open mode that destroys the original contents of the file. If we want to retain part of the original file we can read it first, then close and reopen the file for writing. For example, this code snippet replaces a file of more than ten lines with the last ten lines in the file:

```
#!/usr/bin/perl
# lastten.pl
use warnings;
use strict;

print "Reading...";
```

```
open READ, "myfile" or die "Cannot open: $! \n";
my @lines = <READ>;
print "$. lines read \n";
close READ;

if ($#lines < 9) {
    exit;
}

print "Writing...";
open WRITE, "> myfile" or die "Cannot write: $! \n";
foreach (@lines[-10..-1]) {
    print WRITE $_;
}
print "done \n";
close WRITE;
```

This works fine, and could well be simpler if we want to modify the contents of the file while at the same time shortening it. However, if we just want to make a file shorter without otherwise altering its contents we can use `truncate`.

`truncate` is a very simple function. It takes a filehandle, or an expression giving the name or reference of a filehandle, which must be open for writing, and a length:

```
truncate FILE, 100;    # truncate file to first 100 bytes
```

Since opening a file for writing truncates it automatically to nothing, use the +< or read-update mode to truncate an existing file:

```
open FILE, '+< myfile';
truncate FILE, 100;
close FILE;
```

`truncate` works on bytes, not lines, so it is good for setting an exact length, but not so good for truncating to the first n lines of a file. Unfortunately, simply counting the lengths of the lines is not enough, since the newline character in Perl may in reality be two or more characters in the file; as we observed before, both Windows (all of them) and MacOS use two characters for the line ending. So the only reliable and simple way to truncate the file accurately is to read it up to the desired number of lines and then use `seek` to find out where the last line ended:

```
#!/usr/bin/perl
# truncate.pl
use warnings;
use strict;

die "Specify a file \n" unless @ARGV;
die "Specify a length \n" unless defined($ARGV[1]) and ($ARGV[1] >= 1);
my $file = $ARGV[0];
my $truncate_to = int($ARGV[1]);

print "Reading...";
open READ, "$file" or die "Cannot open: $! \n";
while (<READ>) {
    last if $. == $truncate_to;
}
```

```
my $size = tell READ;
print "$. lines read ($size bytes) \n";
exit if $. < $truncate_to;    # already shorter
close READ;

print "Truncating to $size bytes...";
open WRITE, "+< $file" or die "Cannot write: $! \n";
truncate WRITE, $size;
print "done \n";
close WRITE;
```

This program truncates the given file to the given number of lines. It only reads lines to move the file pointer, so it doesn't do anything with the returned lines. Once it has finished, it checks $. to determine if the file is actually long enough to need truncating. If it is, it finds the current position, which will be the character immediately after the end of the line terminator of the last line, reopens the file for modification, and truncates it.

Interestingly, truncate will extend a file if the new length is longer than the old, so a better name for truncate would have been setlength. The extended bytes, if any, are filled with zeros or null characters, which makes it a better solution to extending a file than seek if a complete and empty file is desirable. Note that truncate can fail with undef if the disk runs out of capacity or we reach a quota limit imposed by the operating system. That is not an issue for the example above since it is making the file shorter, so in that case we did not check (though to be really thorough we ought to anyway).

File Locking

In situations where more than one program or process may wish to write to the same file at the same time, we need to take care that different processes do not tread on each other's toes. For example, several clients may attempt execute a script simultaneously. CGI scripts are a common class of Perl program that fall into this category.

As an example of a Perl application that fails as a result of not using file locking, take this hit counter CGI script, designed to be used in a server-side include:

```
#!/usr/bin/perl -T
# badcounter.cgi
use warnings;
use strict;

# script assumes file exists, but may be empty
my $counter = "/home/httpd/data/counter/counter.dat";

open(FILE, "+< $counter") or die "Cannot access counter: $! \n";
my $visitors = <FILE>;
chomp $visitors;
seek FILE, 0, 0;
print FILE $visitors ?++ $visitors:1;
close(FILE);

print "Content-type: text/html\n\n";
print $visitors, "\n";
```

Without protection, the counter will only register one hit if the script is executed twice at the same time. Instance 1 adds one to the count, writes, and closes file. However, when instance 2 adds one to the count, it overwrites the value left by instance 1, and closes the file having updated it once. One way to test this is by writing a short script that calls this program over and over, and running a copy of the script from a different shell at the same time.

To avoid this problem we need to use **file locks**, so other processes will not attempt to work with a file while we are busy with it. With a lock in place, other processes that attempt to place their own locks on the file must wait (or block) until our process finishes its business and unlocks the file. By adhering to the file lock mechanism processes can avoid overwriting each other, preventing the kind of problems inherent in the above example.

Establishing File Locks

Perl provides file locking through the flock function. flock is modeled on but not necessarily implemented by the C flock system call; Perl uses whatever locking facilities are available and presents them to us through its own flock. flock takes a filehandle and an operation as arguments. The filehandle is the filehandle of the file we want to lock, and the operation is a numerical flag representing the type of lock that we want to establish. There are two basic lock operations, shared and exclusive, an unlock operation, and a 'non-blocking' flag that can be combined with the other three to allow a process to continue executing rather than wait for the lock to become available. Numerically, these are represented by the numbers 1, 2, 8, and 4 respectively, but for convenience sake we can import descriptive symbols from the Fcntl module:

```
use Fcntl ':flock';   # import LOCK_ symbols
```

The four flags are:

Flag	Number	Function
LOCK_SH	1	Establish a shared lock, also known as a read lock:
		`flock FH, 1;`
		`flock FH, LOCK_SH;`
		When LOCK_SH is in effect, other processes may also establish a shared lock, but may not establish an exclusive or write lock. This is the lock to use when we want to read a file while ensuring that its contents do not change.
LOCK_EX	2	Establish an exclusive lock, also known as a write lock:
		`flock FH, 2;`
		`flock FH, LOCK_EX;`
		When LOCK_EX is in effect no other process can establish a lock. This is the lock to use when we want to change the contents of a file and prevent other processes reading it while we do.

Flag	Number	Function
LOCK_UN	8	Unlock a previously established lock:

```
flock FH, 8;
flock FH, LOCK_UN;
```

This unlocks a lock that has been previously established. Since the process owns the lock that it is unlocking, this use never blocks.

Flag	Number	Function
LOCK_NB	4	Do not block when attempting to acquire a lock:

```
flock FH, 5;
flock FH, LOCK_SH|LOCK_NB;
flock FH, 6;
flock FH, LOCK_EX|LOCK_NB;
```

Normally an attempt to establish a shared or exclusive lock will block on the flock statement until whichever process is currently holding the lock releases it. By combining LOCK_NB with the lock operation we can have our program do something else while waiting:

```
until (flock FH, LOCK_EX|LOCK_NB) {
    print "Waiting for lock...\n";
    sleep 5;
    die "Handle no longer valid"
    unless defined(fileno *FH);
}
```

Note that to be safe we also check that the filehandle is still valid before trying to lock it again.

Using flock we can rewrite our counter script so that it functions correctly. All that we need to do is to add an exclusive lock (LOCK_EX) immediately after we open the file, and unlock it again (LOCK_UN) immediately before we close it:

```
#!/usr/bin/perl -T
# counter.cgi
use warnings;
use strict;

use Fcntl ':flock';

# script assumes file exists but may be empty
my $counter = "/home/httpd/data/counter/counter.dat";

open(FILE,"+< $counter") or die "Cannot access counter: $!\n";
flock(FILE, LOCK_EX);
my $visitors = <FILE>;
chomp $visitors;
seek FILE, 0, 0;
print FILE $visitors ?++ $visitors:1;
flock(FILE, LOCK_UN);
close(FILE);

print "Content-type: text/html\n\n";
print $visitors, "\n";
```

441

From Perl 5.004 `flock` flushes the output of any filehandle that it successfully locks or unlocks, to ensure that file writes are properly synchronized. In this case the `close` would have flushed remaining output anyway, however for larger applications this additional feature of `flock` is extremely convenient.

File Locking Issues and Caveats

One thing that is often overlooked is that locks established by `flock` are advisory only, another program is totally free to ignore the lock if it so chooses (by not checking for it). File locks are therefore a co-operative system, all participants have to observe locks for them to be effective. Many operating systems also support mandatory locking schemes, but these are largely platform-specific.

A potential problem with `flock` is that its exact behavior may vary depending on what file locking mechanisms are available on the underlying platform. Most platforms support a `flock` system call, so Perl's `flock` can map directly onto it. However, in the event that a true `flock` is not available Perl must resort to an emulation based on the less versatile `lockf` or, if that is not available, basic calls to `fcntl`. From Perl 5.005, Perl prefers `fcntl` due to the fact `lockf` requires files to be writable to lock them. `fcntl` also has an advantage over the `flock` system call in that it will work on network-mounted (for example, NFS) filesystems, which some implementations of `flock` do not. We may want to support this, in which case we should use `fcntl` rather than `flock` in Perl.

In addition, locks established with a `flock` emulation will not survive across duplicated filehandles, nor across a call to `fork`. However, on any serious modern platform this should not be a problem. Consult the `flock`, `fcntl`, or other file locking documentation of the operating system for details of how the platform supports file locking.

Changing the Default Output Filehandle

The default output filehandle is normally `STDOUT`, but we can change this by using the `select` function. This takes a single filehandle (which may not be derived from an expression) as an argument, and switches it for the current default:

```
select MYHANDLE;
print "Message to MYHANDLE \n";   # write to MYHANDLE;
```

With no arguments, `select` returns the current default output filehandle, which makes it useful for storing the existing output filehandle should we wish to restore it at a later date:

```
# save existing default output
$original_out = select;

# select a new default output and use it
select NEWOUT;
$| = 1;   # set autoflush on filehandle NEWOUT
print "write data to new default output";

# restore original default output
select $original_out;
```

Or, more tersely:

```
$original_out = select(NEWOUT);
$| = 1;
select $original_out;
```

Or, even more tersely, avoiding a temporary variable but edging into illegibility:

```
select( (select(NEWOUT), $| = 1)[0] );
```

This relies on the fact that the two statements `select(NEWOUT)` and `$|=1` generate a two element list. The outer `select` uses the first element (the original filehandle), to restore the default filehandle after both statements have executed. The `IO::Handle` module and its descendants package this into an object method, so if we have `IO::Handle` loaded we can also say:

```
NEWOUT->autoflush(1);
```

Note that the `select` function also has an entirely different four-argument form that is used to select between multiple inputs, and which has nothing whatsoever to do with its usage here.

Using Special Variables to Configure Other Filehandles

The special variables that are related to output all operate on a per-filehandle basis, each filehandle having its own set of output properties associated with it. The special variables bring out and make available the properties of whatever filehandle is currently selected; changing the value of a special variable affects that filehandle only. For instance, to switch on `autoflush` mode on a filehandle other than `STDOUT` we can use:

```
# enable autoflush on MYHANDLE
select MYHANDLE;
$| = 1;
# STDOUT is not affected
select STDOUT;
```

Similarly, we can set or read the values of the special variables `$.` (line number), `$/` (input record separator), `$\` (output record separator), `$,` (output field separator), and `$"` (interpolated output field separator) on a per-filehandle basis. The special format variables such as `$~` (format name) are also associated with individual filenames. See the section on reports (Chapter 18) for more information on these.

Automatically Restoring the Default Filehandle

As an alternative to using the `select` function directly, we can make use of the `SelectSaver` module. This provides an object-oriented interface to `select` that has the advantage of automatically resetting the default output filehandle to its original state when the `SelectSaver` object is destroyed. In other words, statements like `select STDOUT` become unnecessary after we have finished with another filehandle:

```
use SelectSaver;

...
```

```
# scope of SelectSaver defined by 'if' statement
if ($redirect) {
    my $saver = new SelectSaver(NEWOUT);
    $| = 1;
    print "Message to NEWOUT handle"
}
# $saver goes out of scope here, object destroyed
print "Message to original default output handle";
```

SelectSaver works by remembering what filehandle was currently selected when the object was created. When the variable $saver falls out of scope at the end of the block the object is destroyed, and as part of its clean up, restores the filehandle that was originally selected.

Using Default Variables vs, 'IO::Handle' Methods

If the intention is to modify the output properties of a filehandle rather than to make it the default output, a preferred approach is to use the IO::Handle methods inherited by filehandles generated by IO::File. These also allow the properties of filehandles to be modified, without the need to select them first:

```
# set autoflush on an IO::Handle based filehandle
$fh->autoflush(1);
```

The advantage of the IO::Handle approach is that it is simpler to read and less 'clunky', since selecting a filehandle just to modify its output properties is not very elegant. Conversely, IO::Handle is a potentially expensive module that defines a lot of methods and properties.

All the standard variables that relate to output can also be set on a filehandle directly this way. See the section on 'IO::Handle Methods and Special Variables' for a rundown.

Duplicating and Aliasing Filehandles

If we supply open with a mode containing an ampersand it will duplicate an existing filehandle. For example, to duplicate STDIN we could write:

```
open(NEWIN, "&STDIN") or die "Open failed: $! \n";
```

The mode of the new filehandle should be the same as that of the old, in this case read-only. Once duplicated, the new filehandle can be used in place of the old, and either handle may be used to read or write to the associated data stream. To duplicate a filehandle that is open in read-update mode we can use:

```
open(DUPLICATE, "+< &ORIGINAL");
```

This actually maps to the dup system call (or its nearest equivalent). Both filehandles, DUPLICATE and ORIGINAL, refer to the same file. However, each is independent of the other, with its own buffering and its own file position. This allows us to work at two different points within the same file simultaneously. To avoid potential conflicts we can use file locking via flock to prevent the filehandles from treading on each others toes; as well as preventing overwrite, flock also flushes all buffered output whenever a file is locked or unlocked. See 'Writing at the End-of-File' for an example.

Duplication works on file numbers as well as filehandles. If we happen to have the file number instead we can use that in place of the filehandle name. For instance, STDOUT and STDERR usually have the file numbers 1 and 2 (STDIN is 0), so the following is equivalent to the above presuming that no redirection has happened yet:

```
open(OLDOUT, "> &1");    # duplicate fileno 1 (STDOUT)
open(OLDERR, "> &2");    # duplicate fileno 2 (STDERR)
```

We can create an alias for a filehandle by using &= in place of & with the file number. We can find the file number of a filehandle using fileno, so to create a filehandle alias we would write something like:

```
open(ALIAS, "> &=".fileno (MYHANDLE));
```

If we happen to have only a file descriptor and we want to create a filehandle to manage it, we can also create one using this technique. Alternatively, if we are using IO::Handle or IO::File we can use the new_from_fd of IO::Handle:

```
$fh = IO::Handle->new_from_fd(fileno MYHANDLE);
```

We might want to do this is when we are inheriting filehandles from a previous process via exec; we cannot retrieve the filehandle, but we can access the file descriptor and create a new filehandle around it. Other instances include C library functions that generate and return file descriptors, such as the fdaccept call for sending file descriptors between processes (supported on some UNIX implementations).

Note that these special modes only work with the two argument form of open; they do not work with the mode separated from the filename, which is why we have concatenated the mode and file number in the open example above.

If we happen to have entirely lost the original standard input or standard output that we started out with we can attempt to reacquire them by opening the special file - (or >- for STDOUT). See 'Opening Standard Input and Standard Output' earlier in the chapter for details.

Redirecting Filehandles

To redefine the default output filehandle we can use select, but this only allows us to change the output filehandle from STDOUT to something else. It does not allow us to change the input filehandle from STDIN, or the error filehandle STDERR. Even if we select a different output filehandle, output will still go to the original STDOUT if it is explicitly given:

```
select NEWOUT;
print STDOUT "This still goes to standard output";
```

The solution to these problems is to replace the filehandles themselves. For instance, to temporarily redirect standard output and standard error to a log file, we first need to make copies of the current filehandles, which we can do with the & notation. Since both filehandles are write-only, the correct mode to use is > &:

```
open(OLDOUT, "> &STDOUT");
open(OLDERR, "> &STDERR");
```

Having duplicated the original filehandles we can now redirect them to the new file:

```
open(STDOUT, "> $logfile");
open(STDERR, "> $logfile");
```

Both filehandles will likely be block-buffered. At this point we can enable `autoflush` for both of them, to get line-buffering, using `select`:

```
select STDOUT;
$| = 1;
select STDERR;
$| = 1;
```

Finally, after we have finished printing to the log file we can restore the original STDOUT and STDERR by redirecting them back again:

```
close(STDOUT); open(STDOUT, "> &OLDOUT");
close(STDERR); open(STDERR, "> &OLDERR");
```

Note that it is important to close the filehandles before we redirect them. If we do not do this, data buffered on those filehandles may not get flushed unless (and until) the program terminates. If we are going to redirect back to the underlying file descriptors of the original STDOUT and STDERR later we do not need to worry.

In this example we have redirected the standard output and error filehandles, but any filehandle can be duplicated and/or redirected in this fashion. Here is an example of duplicating a filehandle that is open in read-update mode:

```
open(MYDUPLICATE, "+< &MYHANDLE");
```

It is important not to duplicate a filehandle with modes it does not have. Although Perl will let us duplicate a read-only filehandle into a write-only one, the results are unpredictable and unlikely to be what we want; buffering may give the impression that something is working when in fact it is not.

Redirecting the standard file handles is subtly different, in one way, from redirecting other filehandles. System file handles are only closed if the open succeeds, so in the event that the open fails, the original filehandle remains open and intact. This threshold that defines what a `system` filehandle is, is governed by the special variable `$^F` (or `$SYSTEM_FD_MAX` with `use English`). It contains the value of the highest system file number, usually 2 corresponding to STDERR. Attempts to open an existing file handle on a new file whose file number is higher than `$^F` will cause the file to be closed before the new one is opened. In the even the `open` fails, the original file remains closed.

Caching Many Filehandles

If we try to open very many filehandles all at the same time, we may run into an operating system limit. The `FileCache` module provides a solution to this problem by allowing filehandles to be cached. If we attempt to access a file, for which a filehandle already exists, the cached handle is used. If we attempt to access a file for which no filehandle exists, and we have reached our limit, a filehandle is closed to make room for the new filehandle.

FileCache works by supplying one method, cacheout, which takes the name of a file as a parameter. We never use a filehandle directly, but supply the name of the file instead. This short example illustrates the technique, caching two filehandles:

```perl
#!/usr/bin/perl
# cache.pl
use warnings;
use strict;
no strict 'refs';

use FileCache;

my $myfile = "/tmp/myfile.txt";
my $anotherfile = "/tmp/anotherfile.txt";

cacheout $myfile;
print $myfile "Message to my file \n";
cacheout $anotherfile;
print $anotherfile "Message to another file \n";
print $myfile "Second message to my file \n";

close $myfile;
close $anotherfile;
```

The module works by creating each filehandle with exactly the same name as the path of the file with which it is associated. This allows the scalar holding the filename to be used as a filehandle, and also allows FileCache to look up the filehandle in an internal hash, to see if it exists or not, when we request that the file be opened.

Files are opened in write mode (>) if they do not currently exist, or update mode (>>) if they do. Consequently this module is no use for handling multiple files in a read-write mode. However, it is a short and relatively simple module, so adapting it for caching other kinds of filehandle modes should be a reasonable proposition.

The maximum number of files that can be opened by the FileCache module is determined from the operating system (the /usr/include/sys/param.h header file on UNIX systems). In the event that the value in this file is wrong (which does happen) or that this file does not exist (as on a Windows or MacOS based system) we can override it by setting the value of $FileCache::cacheout_maxopen:

```perl
if ($FileCache::cacheout_maxopen <= 16) {
    $FileCache::cacheout_maxopen = 64;
}
```

If the FileCache module cannot determine a value for the maximum allowed open files at all, it defaults to 16. So, a value of 16 in $FileCache::cacheout_maxopen is usually a sign that the maximum number of open files needs to be established in some other way, and then be supplied to the FileCache module.

Note that just because we can set this value to allow the maximum number of open files possible, does not mean that we necessarily ought to, since filehandles consume valuable system resources. If we use this module we might want to take advantage of the caching mechanism to actually restrict the number of active filehandles:

```perl
$FileCache::cacheout_maxopen = 32 if $FileCache::cacheout_maxopen > 32;
```

447

'IO::Handle' Methods and Special Variables

IO::Handle is a generic filehandle module that provides an easier interface to filehandles than the standard Perl interface. It is the basis of the IO::File module, among others, and provides methods for using and configuring filehandles, which are loosely categorized into creation methods, built-in methods, configuration methods and utility methods.

The following **creation methods** create new IO::Handle objects:

Method	Action
new	Create a new IO::Handle object, for example:
	`$fh = new IO::Handle;`
	To create a filehandle and associate it with an open file, use IO::File's new instead.
new_from_fd	Create a new IO::Handle object and associate it with the given file descriptor. For example:
	`$fh = IO::Handle->new_from_fd(1);`
	`$fh = IO::Handle->new_from_fd(fileno MYHANDLE);`
	The file descriptor is the underlying file number that represents the raw connection to the file or device. It can be specified explicitly, for example, 0, 1 or 2 for STDIN, STDOUT, or STDERR, or derived from an existing filehandle via fileno. Note that this is the underlying functionality behind the open functions &= mode.

Each of these **built-in function methods** is a wrapper for the equivalent built-in function:

Method	Action
close	Close the file
eof	Test for end of file condition
fileno	Return file descriptor (file number) of filehandle
format_write	Write a format string (equivalent to write)
getc	Get a single character
read	Read a specific number of bytes
print	Print to the file
printf	Format a string and print to the file
stat	Return information about the file
sysread	System-level read
syswrite	System-level write
truncate	Truncate or extend the file

The **configuration methods** configure an aspect of the filehandle, and have a one-to-one correlation to one of Perl's special variables, which performs the equivalent function on the currently selected default output filehandle, as chosen by select. In each case the original value is returned. The methods and their related special variables fall into two groups: those that work on a per-filehandle basis, and those that are global in effect and apply to all filehandles.

The following special variables and IO::Handle methods are specified on a **per-filehandle** basis.

Method	Variable	Action

autoflush	$|	Sets the autoflush flag. Takes a Boolean parameter, for example:
		
		`$fh->autoflush(1);    # enable autoflush`
		`$fh->autoflush(0);    # disable autoflush`
		
		Or:
		
		`select $fh; $| = 1;`

format_page_number	$%	The current page number of the currently selected output channel.
format_lines_per_page	$=	The current page length (printable lines) of the currently selected output channel.
format_lines_left	$-	The number of lines left on the page of the currently selected output channel.
format_name	$~	The name of the current report format for the currently selected output channel.
format_top_name	$^	The name of the current top-of-page format for the currently selected output channel.

input_line_number	$.	The current line number. For example:
		
		`$lineno = $fh->input_line_number();`
		
		Or:
		
		`select $fh; $lineno = $.;`
		
		Note that although it is possible to set this value it should usually be treated as read-only.

The following special variables and IO::Handle methods are **global**, but can be set via the appropriate method:

Method	Variable	Action
format_line_break_ characters	$:	The current set of characters after which a string may be broken to fill continuation fields (starting with ^) in a format.
format_formfeed	$^L	Which formats output as a form feed.

Table continued on following page

Method	Variable	Action

format_field_ separator	$,	The string output between items in a print statement. By default, nothing. To print out comma-separated values, set to ,:
		
		`$old = $fh->output_field_separator(',');`
		
		Or:
		
		`$, = ',';`

output_record_ seperator	$\	The string placed output after the end of a print statement. By default, nothing. To print out lines automatically terminated by newlines, set to "\n":
		
		`$old = $fh->output_record_separator("\n");`
		
		Or:
		
		`$\ = "\n";`

input_record_ seperator	$/	The string used to separate lines for the readline operator. By default, it is \n. To read in a whole file at one go, set to nothing or undefine:
		
		`$old = $fh->input_record_separator('');`
		
		Or:
		
		`$/ = '';`
		`undef $/;`

Finally, these are the **utility methods**:

Method	Action

fdopen FILENO	Associate the filehandle with the given filehandle name, IO::Handle object or file descriptor, for example:
	
	`$fh->fdopen(1);`
	
	`$fh->fdopen(fileno STDOUT);`
	
	`$fh->fdopen($other_fh);`
	
	This is the underlying function behind the new_from_fd method.

opened	Returns True if the filehandle is currently open, False otherwise. For example:
	
	`if ($fh->opened) {`
	`    $line = $fh->getline;`
	`} else {`
	`    # cannot read...`
	`}`

Method	Action

getline	Return the next line from a file, for example:
	
	`$line = $fh->getline();`
	`while ($fh->getline) {`
	    `print "$_ \n";`
	`}`
	
	This is equivalent to the readline operator when called in a scalar context, even when called in a list context.

getlines	Return all available lines from a file, for example: `@lines = $fh->getlines();` This is equivalent to the readline operator when called in a list context. If called in a scalar or void context this method will croak with an error.
ungetc CHAR	Push a character back into the input buffer, for example: `$fh->ungetc(ord $char);` The character must be specified as an ASCII code, rather than a string. Only one character is guaranteed to be pushed back; attempting to push back more than one without an intermediate read may fail.

write BUF, LEN, OFFSET	Equivalent to the syswrite function, this writes a given number of characters to the filehandle, for example:
	
	`# write all of string to filehandle`
	`$fh->write $string;`
	`# write first 20 chars of string to filehandle`
	`$fh->write $string, 20;`
	`# write chars 20 to 40 of string to filehandle`
	`$fh->write $string, 20, 20;`
	
	See syswrite in 'System Level IO' for more information. Note that the built-in Perl write function is mapped to the format_write method, since this makes more logical sense.

error	Returns True if the filehandle has experienced any errors since it was opened, or the last called to clearerr.
clearerr	Clear the filehandle's error condition (including end-of-file), for example: `$fh->clearerr;`
sync	Synchronize in-memory state of all opened files with their states on disc and update all other filesystem changes. For example: `$fh->sync;` Note that this is a kernel-level function, which is not supported on all platforms. It does not work on a per-filesystem basis and does not flush buffered output at the filehandle level – use flush for that.

Table continued on following page

Method	Action
flush	Flush buffered output at the application level, for example: `$fh->flush;` This method will flush any data that has been buffered by either block or line buffering down to the operating system. It does not guarantee that the data is actually written, however; sync above does that.
printflush ARGS	Enable autoflush mode, print arguments to filehandle and then restore the original autoflush state, for example: `$fh->printflush("This works", "just", "like print");`

blocking 0|1	Set blocking or non-blocking mode on the filehandle, for example:
	
	 `$fh->blocking(0);   # enable non-blocking mode`
	 `$blocking = $fh->blocking();   # retrieve mode`
	
	 Returns the value of the previous setting, or the current setting if no flag is specified.

untaint 0|1	Set or unset untainting mode. For example: `$fh->untaint(1);   # trust data read from $fh` This method only has an effect when taint mode has been enabled (-T). Ordinarily when taint mode is enabled any data read from a filehandle is considered tainted and a potential security risk. Setting the untaint flag marks the filehandle as being a source of trusted data, so any data read from it is considered untainted. Note that this is a very trusting thing to do and should not be undertaken lightly. In particular, do not use this method just get a program to work.

System Level IO

Conventional input and output uses buffered filehandles that optimize file accesses by reducing the number of reads or writes that actually take place. The advantage of this is that file handling is a much more efficient process from the operating system's point of view, and for the most part is transparent to us. The disadvantage is that sometimes we want to read and write data with immediate effect, in which case buffering can get in the way.

Buffering is a feature of the standard input/output library, more conventionally known as the stdio library. To avoid buffering we need a way to bypass the stdio library and access filehandles directly. Fortunately, Perl allows us to do just this with the sys family of built-in functions sysread, syswrite, and sysseek.

Handling filehandles at the system level also allows us a greater degree of control over them; for instance, we can carry out things like non-blocking IO much more easily. Much of this control comes from the sysopen function.

> *The standard IO functions use buffered IO, and the system-level functions bypass these buffers. Mixing buffered and non-buffered functions in the same code is extremely dangerous and highly inadvisable, as inconsistent file positions and corrupted data can very easily be the result. As a general rule, use one set of functions or the other, never both, on the same filehandle.*

Opening Filehandles at the System Level

Opening files at the system level is handled by sysopen. This, like open, takes a filehandle name and a filename as an argument. Unlike open, sysopen does not take a mode string like > or +<, but a numeric mode made up of several mode flags whose values specify the desired attributes of the filehandle. The Fcntl module defines labels for these numeric flags, such as O_WRONLY for write-only access or O_CREAT to create the file if it does not exist. The mode cannot be combined with the filename as it is with open, instead it comes after the filename as an additional third parameter:

```
use Fcntl;   # import standard symbols
sysopen SYSHANDLE, $filename, O_WRONLY | O_CREAT;
```

The standard open modes can all be expressed in terms of a sysopen mode value; < is equivalent to O_RDONLY, and > is equivalent to O_WRONLY| O_CREAT| O_TRUNC. The following two statements are actually identical, but phrased differently:

```
# open a file write-only with 'open'
open HANDLE, "> $filename";

# open a file write-only with 'sysopen'
sysopen HANDLE, $filename, O_WRONLY|O_CREAT|O_TRUNC;
```

Note that sysopen does not create a different sort of filehandle from open. In particular, it does not create an unbuffered handle. Whether or not the filehandle is buffered or unbuffered depends on how we read and write with it. Functions like read, getc, and the readline operator work via the standard IO buffers, while functions like sysread and syswrite bypass them. sysopen itself has no opinion on the use of buffers or not – it merely provides a lower-level way to create filehandles.

> *For the curious coming from a C background: while it is true that sysopen uses the open system call to generate an unbuffered file descriptor, it then uses fdopen to create a filehandle from that file descriptor and returns this to Perl. So sysopen does create a filehandle, even though it does not use the fopen system call.*

For many applications we only need to supply three parameters to sysopen. (In fact, in many cases we can get away with two, because an open mode flag of 0 is usually equivalent to O_RDONLY. However it is dangerous to assume this, always use the Fcntl symbols.) We can also supply a fourth optional parameter describing the permissions of the file in cases where the file is created. We will come to that in a moment.

Open Mode Flags

sysopen allows us to specify all manner of flags in the open mode, some generically useful, others very specific, and a few more than a little obscure. The main point of using sysopen rather than open is to gain access to these flags directly, allowing us to create open modes other than the six standard combinations supported by open. Some are relevant only to particular kinds of file, such as terminal devices. The following tables show the flags that are combined to make up the various modes used by open.

Always specify one (and only one) of the **primary modes**:

O_RDONLY	Open file for reading only.
O_RDWR	Open file for reading and writing.
O_WRONLY	Open file for writing only (not supported on Windows).

These are **additional modes**:

O_APPEND	Open file for appending.
O_CREAT	Create file if it does not exist.
O_TRUNC	Truncate file on opening it (writing).

See the table in the 'Creating Filehandles with IO::File' section earlier in the chapter for a comparison of open and sysopen modes to see how these mode flags are combined to create the six modes of open. Some other useful flags we can *only* access with sysopen include the following:

Text and Binary files	O_BINARY	Use binary mode (no newline translation).
	O_TEXT	Use text mode (do newline translation).
Non-blocking IO	O_NONBLOCK	Enable non-blocking mode.
	O_NDELAY	Alias (usually) for O_NONBLOCK. Semantics may vary on platforms for filehandles that are associated with networking.
Additional Modes	O_EXCL	Create file only if it does not already exist (meaningful only with O_CREAT). If it does exist, fail rather than open it.

Non-blocking IO

One of the main reasons for using sysopen over open is for non-blocking IO. Normally when a read or write (including a system read or write performed by sysread or syswrite) is performed, the system will wait for the operation to complete. In the case of reading, Perl will wait for input to arrive and only return control to our application when it has something for us. Frequently, however, we do not want to wait because we want to do other things in the meantime, so we use sysopen and the O_NONBLOCK flag, (although it should be noted that the O_NONBLOCK flag is not recognized by Windows at present):

```
use Fcntl;

# open serial port read only, non-blocking
sysopen SERIAL, '/dev/ttyS0', O_RDONLY|O_NONBLOCK;

# attempt to read characters
my $key;
while (sysread SERIAL, $key, 1) {
    if (defined $key) {
        print "Got '$key' \n";
    } else {
        warn "No input available \n";
```

```
         # wait before trying again
         sleep(1);
      }
   }

   # close the port
   close SERIAL;
```

When non-blocking mode is enabled, it attempts to read from a filehandle. When no data is available it will raise the EAGAIN error in $!. We can get the symbol for EAGAIN from the POSIX module, so a better way to write the above example would have been:

```
use POSIX qw(EAGAIN);
use Fcntl;

# open serial port read only, non-blocking
sysopen SERIAL, '/dev/ttyS0', O_RDONLY|O_NONBLOCK;

# attempt to read characters
my $key;

while (sysread SERIAL, $key, 1) {
   if (defined ($key)) {
      print "Got '$key' \n"
   } else {
      if ($!==EAGAIN) {
         warn "No input available \n";

         # wait before trying again
         sleep(1);
      } else {
         warn "Error attempting to read: $! \n";
         last;
      }
   }
}

# close the port
close SERIAL;
```

In this case we have used sysread to read an individual character directly from the serial port. We could also have used read or even getc to do the same thing via the filehandle's buffers. This probably would have been better as the filehandle will read in several kilobytes of characters if it can, and then return them to us one by one. From our perspective there is no difference, but from the point of view of the serial port it makes a lot of difference.

The Permissions Mask

Since it works at a lower level than open, sysopen also allows us to specify a numeric permissions mask as a fourth argument to sysopen, either in the conventional octal format, or as a combination of flags defined by the :mode import label:

```
# permissions mode, as octal integer
open HANDLE, $filename, O_WRONLY|O_CREAT, 0644;
```

```
# permissions mode, as set of Fcntl flags:
open HANDLE, $filename, O_WRONLY|O_CREAT, S_IRUSR
|S_IWUSR
|S_IRGRP
|S_IROTH;
```

If the open creates the file (generally because O_CREAT is present in the open mode), its permissions are set according to the permissions mask, as modified by the umask value as discussed earlier in the chapter. Otherwise the permissions mask has no effect.

Using 'sysopen' via 'IO::File'

It is not actually necessary to use sysopen to make use of its features; the new method of IO::File automatically uses sysopen if we give it a numeric mode instead of a string:

```
# 'IO::File' open for read/write using 'open'
$fh = new IO::File ($filename, '+<');

# 'IO::File' open for read/write using 'sysopen'
$fh = new IO::File ($filename, O_RDWR);
```

Since new can automatically detect a numeric mode flag and pass it to sysopen instead of open, we can also pass in the permissions mask too:

```
# 'IO::File' open for read/write using 'sysopen' with permissions mask
$fh = new IO::File ($filename, O_RDWR, 0644);
```

The advantage of IO::File is, of course, that it makes filehandles much easier to manipulate and to pass in and out of subroutines. This makes it a good choice for programming regardless of whether we choose to use open or sysopen underneath.

Unbuffered Reading

Reading at the standard IO level is handled by Perl functions such as read and print. The unbuffered system-level equivalents are sysread and syswrite.

sysread looks suspiciously similar to read at first glance. Like read, it takes a filehandle to read from, a scalar variable to store the result in, a length giving the amount of data to read (or attempt to read), and an optional offset:

```
#!/usr/bin/perl
# sysread.pl
use warnings;
use strict;

use POSIX;

my $result;

die "Usage: $0 file \n" unless @ARGV;
sysopen HANDLE, $ARGV[0], O_RDONLY|O_NONBLOCK;
```

```
# read 20 chrs into $result
my $chrs = sysread HANDLE, $result, 20;
if ($chrs == 20) {
    # got all 20, try to read another 30 chrs into $result after the first 20
    $chrs += sysread HANDLE, $result, 30, 20;
    print "Got '$result' \n";
    if ($chrs < 50) {
        print "Data source exhausted after $chrs characters \n";
    } else {
        print "Read $chrs characters \n";
    }
} elsif ($chrs > 0) {
    print "Got '$result' \n";
    print "Data source exhausted after $chrs characters \n";
} else {
    print "No data! \n";
}
```

The return value from sysread is the number of characters successfully read. This may be less than the number requested if the data source runs out, and 0 if there is no data to read. However, note that if O_NONBLOCK is not set, then sysread will wait for more data to arrive rather than returning 0. If there is some data but not enough to satisfy the request then sysread will return when it exhausts the data source. As stated before, Windows does not recognize O_NONBLOCK, so this example will not work properly on that platform.

In fact, the above example is more of an example of how to use sysopen (to get a non-blocking filehandle) than it is of how to use sysread, as we could just as easily have used read in this example, and with the same effect. The difference between the two is that read would read as much data as possible in the first call, and the second call would only cause a read of the file if the first failed to retrieve 50 characters. The fact that it only returns 20 to us is irrelevant; buffering stores up the rest until we need them. Of course we might not want to buffer the data; we may want to share the filehandle between different processes instead. In cases like that, we would use sysread.

There is no system-level definition of the end-of-file condition, but we can do the equivalent by checking for a zero return from sysread instead.

Unbuffered Writing

The counterpart to sysread is syswrite, which writes data directly to the filehandle rather than into the filehandle's buffer. This is very useful in all kinds of applications, especially those that involve sending short bursts of information between different processes.

syswrite takes a filehandle, some data, a length, and an optional offset as parameters. It then writes data from the string to the filehandle up to the end of the text contained in the scalar, or the value supplied as the length, whichever is shorter. If an offset is supplied, syswrite starts writing data from that character position. For example, this code snippet writes out the contents of the scalar $data to HANDLE (presumably a serial or network connection) at a rate of five hundred characters per second:

```
$pos = 0; $span = 500; $length = length($data);
while ($pos <= $length) {
    syswrite HANDLE, $data, $span, $pos;
    $pos += $span;
    sleep 1;
}
```

Unlike `sysread`, the length is also an optional parameter. If omitted, the length of the supplied data is used instead, making `syswrite` a close analogue for an unbuffered print, only without the ability to accept a list of arguments. We can invent a `sysprint` that will work like print using `syswrite` though:

```
# an unbuffered print-a-like

sub sysprint {
    # check for a leading filehandle and remove it if present
    $fh = (defined fileno($_[0]))?shift:*STDOUT;
    # use $, to join arguments, just like print
    $joiner = $, ?$, :'';
    syswrite $fh, join($joiner, @_);
}

sysprint(*STDOUT, "This ", "works ", "like ", "print ", "(sort of) ", "\n");
```

See the section on pipes in Chapter 22 for another example where `sysread` and `syswrite` are useful to avoid deadlocks between communicating processes.

System-Level File Positioning

The system-level equivalent of the `seek` and `tell` functions is `sysseek`, which carries out both roles. Like `seek`, it takes a filehandle, a position, and a whence flag that is set to either 0, 1, or 2, or the `Fcntl` equivalent symbols SEEK_SET, SEEK_CUR, and SEEK_END:

```
# seek using whence numbers
sysseek HANDLE, 0, 0;    # rewind to start
sysseek HANDLE, 0, 2;    # seek to end of file
sysseek HANDLE, 20, 1;   # seek forward 20 characters


# seek using Fcntl symbols
use Fcntl qw(:seek);

sysseek HANDLE, 0, SEEK_SET;    # rewind to start
sysseek HANDLE, 0, SEEK_END;    # seek to end of file
sysseek HANDLE, 20, SEEK_CUR;   # seek forward 20 characters
```

The old file position is returned by `sysseek`. To find the current position using `sysseek` we can simply seek to it using a whence flag of SEEK_CUR and a position of zero:

```
use Fcntl qw(:seek);
$pos = sysseek HANDLE, 0, SEEK_CUR;
```

Apart from the difference caused by buffering, `sysseek` is identical in operation to `seek`. However, `tell` and `sysseek` can (and often do) return radically different values for the file position. This is because the position returned by `tell` is determined by the amount of data read by our application, whereas the position returned by `sysseek` is determined by the amount of data read by Perl, which includes the data buffered by the filehandle. We can calculate the amount of data currently buffered by taking the difference between the two values:

```
print "There are ", tell(HANDLE) - sysseek(HANDLE, 0, 1), " bytes in the buffer
\n";
```

Needless to say, mixing up system-level file positioning with standard IO file positioning is rarely a good idea, for precisely this reason. If we are using print and readline, we should be using seek and tell. If we are using sysread and syswrite, we should be using sysseek instead.

'fcntl' and 'ioctl'

No discussion of system-level IO would be entirely complete without a brief look at the fcntl and ioctl functions. These provide very low-level access to filehandles, retrieving and setting parameters that are often otherwise inaccessible to us. fcntl is more generic, and works across most kinds of filehandle. ioctl is targeted at special files, such as character and block devices, and is much more UNIX-specific.

Returned values, if any, are placed into a passed scalar variable; the return value is used to indicate success or failure only. Both functions return undef on failure and set the error in $!. Otherwise they either return a positive value (if the underlying system call returns one), or the special return value '0 but true', which returns 0 in a numeric context but tests true otherwise. To get the original underlying return value (which is -1 for failure, 0 or a positive value for success), we can write:

```
# calculate original numeric return value from system 'fcntl'
$result = int (fcntl(HANDLE, $action, $value) || -1);
```

Both functions will return a fatal error if used on a platform that does not support the underlying system calls. On Windows, they return 0, but do not actually do anything, although they are not fatal.

Setting Filehandle Attributes with 'fcntl'

The fcntl function (not to be confused with the Fcntl module) performs miscellaneous actions on a filehandle. It takes three parameters, a filehandle, an action to perform, and a value. For actions that retrieve information this value must be a scalar variable, into which fcntl places the results of the call. The names of the actions are defined, appropriately enough, in the Fcntl module. For example, we can use fcntl to set a filehandle into non-blocking mode after we have opened it:

```
use POSIX;
use Fcntl qw(:mode);

# get the current open mode flags
my $mode;
fcntl HANDLE, F_GETFL, $mode;

# add O_NONBLOCK and set
fcntl HANDLE, F_SETFL, $mode | O_NONBLOCK;
```

A reasonably complete list of actions (some platform-specific) supported by fcntl follows. Consult the system documentation for details of which actions fcntl supports on a particular platform; it may vary from the list below.

This action duplicates the underlying file descriptor:

F_DUPFD	Duplicate the file descriptor, returning the new descriptor. A low-level version of open's & mode.

The following actions get or set the close-on-exec flag. This flag determines whether the filehandle survives across an exec call. Normally STDIN, STDOUT, and STDERR survive and other filehandles are closed. The threshold for new filehandles can be set with the special variable $^F. The F_SETFD action allows the flag of an individual, and already extant, filehandle to be modified.

F_GETFD	Read the close-on-exec flag. File descriptors with this flag set are closed across a call to exec.
F_SETFD	Set the close-on-exec flag. For example, to preserve a filehandle across exec we would use: `fcntl HANDLE, F_SETFD, 0;`

The following actions get and set the mode flags of the filehandle, as specified by open modes like > or sysopen mode flags like O_RDONLY:

F_GETFL	Get the open mode flags, as set by open or sysopen. A combination of flags such as O_RDONLY, O_CREAT, O_APPEND, and so on.
F_SETFL	Set the open mode flags. Usually only the flags O_APPEND, O_ASYNC (Linux/BSD), and O_NONBLOCK can be set, others are unaffected. See above for an example.

The following actions, which handle discretionary file locking, are similar to but *not* the same as the flock system call (unless flock is implemented in terms of fcntl, which is sometimes the case). For most purposes, flock is a lot simpler and more portable, but may not work on network-mounted filesystems (for example, Via NFS). See the flock discussion earlier in the chapter for a more detailed comparison of the two approaches (and how Perl's own flock relates to them).

F_GETLK	Determine if a file is locked or not. The parameter needs to be a scalar variable, into which details of the lock are written. The l_type field is set to F_UNLCK if no lock is present.
F_SETLK	Set a lock, returning immediately with undef on failure. The parameter needs to be a packed flock structure containing the lock details. $! is set to the reason for the failure if the lock attempt fails.
F_SETLKW	Set a lock, waiting for the file to become available if necessary. Returns undef if interrupted.

The lock type can be one of F_RDLCK, F_WRLCK, or F_UNLCK, which have the obvious meanings. There is no nonblock flag as there is for flock because that function is handled by F_SETLK and F_SETLKW. However, the values passed and returned to these actions are packed lock structures (not simple values), so we need to use pack and unpack to create arguments that are suitable for fcntl when using these actions. Here is a short script that implements a generic locking subroutine, three specific lock subroutines that use it, and a quick demonstration of using them:

```
#!/usr/bin/perl
# fcntl.pl
use warnings;
use strict;

use Fcntl;
```

```
# generic lock subroutine
sub _do_lock {
    my ($locktype, $fh, $block) = @_;
    $block |= 0;    # don't block unless asked to

    # is this a blocking or non-blocking attempt
    my $op = $block?F_SETLKW:F_SETLK;

    # pack a structure suitable for this operation
    my $lock = pack('s s l l s', $locktype, 0, 0, 0, 0);

    # establish the chosen lock in the chosen way
    my $res = fcntl($fh, $op, $lock);
    seek($fh, 0, 0);
    return $res;
}

# specific lock types
sub read_lock {return _do_lock(F_RDLCK, @_);}
sub write_lock {return _do_lock(F_WRLCK, @_);}
sub undo_lock {return _do_lock(F_UNLCK, @_);}

# called like this:
open MYHANDLE, "+> myfile" or die "Failed to open: $! \n";

# block write lock
write_lock(*MYHANDLE, 1) or die "Failed to lock: $! \n";

print MYHANDLE "Only I can write here \n";
# undo (can't block anyway)
undo_lock(*MYHANDLE) or die "Failed to unlick: $! \n";
close MYHANDLE;
```

If (assuming the platform supports it) the O_ASYNC mode flag is specified in sysopen (or enabled using fcntl and F_SETLF), then signals are generated by open file descriptors whenever reading or writing becomes possible, which allows us to write synchronous IO routines that respond to events. These actions allow the target and type of signal generated to be configured:

F_GETOWN	Get the process id (or process group) that is receiving signals (SIGIO or SIGURG) on this file descriptor, if the O_ASYNC mode flag is enabled. By default the process id is that of the process that opened the filehandle, that is, us.
F_SETOWN	Set the process id (or process group) that will receive signals on this file descriptor, if O_ASYNC is enabled.
F_GETSIG	(Linux only) Get the signal type generated by filehandles with O_ASYNC enabled. The default of zero generates a SIGIO signal, as does a setting of SIGIO.
F_SETSIG	(Linux only) Set the signal type generated by filehandles with O_ASYNC enabled.

The POSIX module also defines symbols for the various signal names.

Controlling Devices with 'ioctl'

The ioctl function closely resembles fcntl, both in syntax and in operation. Like fcntl, it takes a filehandle, an action, and a value (which in the case of retrieval actions, must be a scalar variable). It also returns '0 but true' on success and undef on failure, setting $! to the reason if so. Also like fcntl, attempting to use ioctl on a platform that does not support it will cause a fatal error.

ioctl is an interface for controlling filehandles that are associated with devices, such as serial ports, terminals, CR-ROM drives, and so on. ioctl is a very low-level tool for analyzing and programming the device underlying a filehandle, and it is relatively rarely that we need to use it. Most of the useful ioctl actions are already encapsulated into more convenient modules or are, at the least, handled more elegantly by the POSIX module. However in a few cases it can be useful, so long as we realize that it is not very portable (many platforms do not support it) and that higher-level and more portable solutions are generally preferable.

The different actions supported by ioctl can be considerable (as well as highly platform-dependent) since different device categories may support their own particular family of ioctl actions – serial ports have one set, terminals have another, and so on. When Perl is built, it analyzes the underlying system and attempts to compile a list of constant-defining functions, each one corresponding to the equivalent C header file. The most common symbols are placed in sys/ioctl.ph. Other ioctl symbols may be defined in different header files – on a Linux system, CR-ROM ioctls are defined in the header file linux/cdrom.ph. Here's how we can eject a CD on a Linux box:

```
#!/usr/bin/perl
# ioctl.pl
use warnings;
use strict;

# require 'linux/cdrom.ph';

open CDROM, '/dev/cdrom';
ioctl CDROM, 0x5309, 1;   # the ioctl number for CDROMEJECT
# ioctl CDROM, &CDROMEJECT, 1;
close CDROM;
```

For a complete list of ioctl actions consult the system documentation for the device type in question – Linux defines ioctls in the manual page ioctl_list. Serial port definitions can also be found in the header files compiled by Perl, /usr/lib/perl5/5.6.0/<platform-type>/bits/ioctls.ph for the actions, ioctl_types.ph for flags such as TCIOM_RTS, and TCIOM_CD in a standard UNIX Perl 5.6 installation. Terminal definitions are covered by the POSIX routines POSIX::Termios and documented in the POSIX module manual page.

Note that many of the more common actions performed by ioctl are better handled elsewhere (by several of the standard Perl library modules covered in this chapter). In Chapter 15, the POSIX getattr and setattr routines and the POSIX::Termios module are covered.

POSIX IO

The POSIX module provides a direct interface to the standard C library upon which Perl is built, including all of the file-handling routines. Most of the time we never need to bother with these since Perl already supports most of them in its own file functions. However, on occasion, the POSIX calls can come in useful, so we will quickly detail what is available.

The POSIX module provides three main categories of routines that relate to file handling and IO. The first works on filehandles, and the majority of these are identical in every respect to the standard Perl file functions. The second works on file descriptors, and is the basis of the system-level IO functions. The third is specifically aimed at talking to terminals, and we discuss it further in Chapter 15.

Intuitively we might expect Perl's sys file functions to return and operate on file descriptors (not filehandles), since they are after all supposed to be 'system' level. In fact they do, by using fileno to determine the underlying file descriptor and then using the appropriate system-level POSIX call. So, even though we have a filehandle complete with buffers, we may never actually use them. The advantage of this approach is that we can use filehandles and still carry out unbuffered IO without ever having to worry about file descriptors unless we really want to.

POSIX Filehandle Routines

The POSIX module provides interfaces to the standard filehandle routines as a convenience to programmers migrating from backgrounds such as C, who are used to routines called fopen, flush, fstat, fgetpos, and so on. In actual fact all of these routines either map directly onto Perl's built-in functions (POSIX::getc simply calls CORE::getc for example), or methods in the IO::File (open goes to IO::File::open), IO::Handle (ungetc goes to IO::Handle::getc), or IO::Seekable modules (ftell goes to IO::Seekable::tell) modules.

In short, there is really no reason to use these functions, and we are almost certainly better off using Perl's built-in functions and the IO:: family of modules. However, for those who have a lot of experience with the POSIX library calls and are interested in a quick port with minimal fuss, the POSIX module does provide their equivalents in Perl.

POSIX File Descriptor Routines

The POSIX routines that operate on file descriptors are summarized below. Note that we can use fdopen to create a filehandle from a file descriptor that was created using open or creat. We can use fileno to get a file descriptor from a filehandle for use in these routines:

close fd	Close a file descriptor created by open or create.
creat fd, perm	Create a file with an open mode of O_WRONLY|O_CREAT|O_TRUNC. Takes a permissions mask as a second parameter. Shorthand for open.
fdopen fd	Create a filehandle from a file descriptor – equivalent to the open mode &=<fd>.
stat fd	Return 'stat' information for the file descriptor. The returned list of values is identical to that returned by Perl's stat.
dup fd	Duplicate an existing file descriptor, returning the number of the new file descriptor. Equivalent to the open mode &<fd>, except it returns a file descriptor.
dup2 oldfd, newfd	Make newfd a duplicate of oldfd, closing newfd first if it is currently open. No direct Perl equivalent.
open file, mode, perm	Open a file descriptor. Identical to sysopen except that it returns a file descriptor not a filehandle. sysopen can be simulated by following open with fdopen on the generated file descriptor.

Table continued on following page

Pipe	Create a pair of file descriptors connected to either end of a unidirectional pipe. Returns a list of two descriptors; the first is read-only, the second is write-only. Identical to Perl's `pipe` except that it returns file descriptors, not filehandles.
`read fd, $buf, length`	Read from a file descriptor. Identical to Perl's `sysread` except that it uses a file descriptor and not a filehandle.
`write fd, $buf, length`	Write to a file descriptor. Identical to Perl's `syswrite` except that it uses a file descriptor and not a filehandle.

Note that importing these functions into our own applications can cause problems, since many of them have the same name as a Perl counterpart that uses filehandles rather than file descriptors. For that reason, these routines are better called through their namespace prefix:

```
$fd = POSIX::open($path, O_RDWR|O_APPEND|O_EXCL, 0644);
@stat = POSIX::fstat $fd;
$fd2 = POSIX::dup $fd;
POSIX::close $fd;
```

Technically, the directory-handling functions such as `opendir` also deal in file descriptors rather than filehandles, since it makes no sense to buffer the data read from a directory. However Perl also handles this for us automatically, so we should never have to worry about it.

Moving between POSIX and Standard IO

Occasionally we might want to work with both a POSIX file descriptor and a filehandle for the same file. For example, we may want to make use of functions in the POSIX library or third party C libraries that expect file descriptors as arguments. This takes a lot of care and attention to pull off, because as we remarked when we started, mixing buffered and unbuffered operations can corrupt data and confuse the file position. However, if we really want to do this we can convert between filehandles and file descriptors.

Generating a filehandle from a file descriptor involves wrapping it in a `stdio` file structure containing a pair of buffers. In C this is done by the `fdopen` system call. In Perl we can do the same thing with the special `&=` open mode, which takes a file descriptor as an argument:

```
# wrap a file descriptor in a new filehandle
open HANDLE, "&= $descriptor";
```

Much the same thing happens implicitly when we duplicate a filehandle with `open`. The `&` mode is a shorthand for extracting the file descriptor of a filehandle and then creating a new filehandle structure around it:

```
# duplicate a filehandle the quick way
open NEWOUT, "& STDOUT";

# duplicate a filehandle the explicit way
$stout = fileno STDOUT;
open NEWOUT, "& $stout";
```

Note that there is a difference between & and &=. &= associates a new filehandle with an existing file descriptor. Closing any filehandle associated with that descriptor closes all of them. & creates a new file descriptor that is associated with the same file, but is nonetheless a different descriptor. The file descriptors and their associated filehandles share file positions, but can be closed independently of each other. See the section on open at the start of the chapter for more on these special modes.

Extracting the file descriptor from a file handle is trivial; we just use the fileno function:

```
$descriptor = fileno HANDLE;
```

We can also use fileno to find out if filehandles are duplicated, since they will have the same file descriptor:

```
if (fileno(HANDLE1) == fileno(HANDLE2)) {
   print "Handles are duplicated \n";
}
```

Summary

In this chapter we looked at using filehandles as a means of communication between our Perl programs and external data sources. We saw that Perl provides us with a rich suite of functions for manipulating filehandles. We examined various ways of creating, referring to, reading, and writing to filehandles. As well as this, we also investigated changing the default output filehandle, duplicating and aliasing filehandles, redirecting filehandles, and caching many filehandles.

We looked into the extra control that we gain when manipulating filehandles at the system level, including performing unbuffered reading and writing.

Finally, we examined the fcntl and ioctl functions, and the POSIX module, and discussed when we might need to use them and how to do that.

13

Manipulating Files and Directories

Files and Filenames

There are plenty of applications involving files that do not necessarily involve opening a filehandle. Obvious examples include copying, moving or renaming files, and interrogating files for their size, permissions or ownership. In this chapter we cover testing files for different properties such as their type (file, directory, and so on) and accessibility (can we read and/or write it?). We also delve deeper into file attributes with the stat and lstat functions, and take a look at file globbing, which is an interface to the wildcard file-naming features usually supplied by shells.

In addition to file globbing and interrogation, the Perl standard library supplies a toolkit of modules for copying, comparing, and processing files that are written to work portably and produce the correct results regardless of the underlying platform. Modules that fall into this group include File::Copy, File::Compare, and File::CheckTree.

We also take a look at creating and using temporary files, both privately and as a mechanism for sharing transient data between different programs. Having covered files, we then move to manipulating directories.

Let's start first by examining how Perl allows us to extract user and group information, which is useful for managing files.

Getting User and Group Information

Perl provides built-in support for handling user and group information on UNIX platforms through the `getpwent` and `getgrent` families of functions. This support is principally derived from the underlying C library functions of the same names, which are in turn dependent on the details of the implementation provided by the operating system. All UNIX platforms provide broadly the same features for user and group management in terms of user and group names and ids, but they vary slightly in what additional information they store. Perl makes a reasonable attempt to unify and handle all the variations, but the system documentation is the best source of information on what values these functions return.

UNIX platforms define user and group information in the `/etc/passwd` and `/etc/group` files, but this oversimplifies the actual process of looking up user and group information for two reasons. First, if a shadow password file is in use then the user information in `/etc/passwd` will not contain an encrypted password in the password field. Second, if alternative sources of user and group information are configured (such as NIS or NIS+), then requesting user or group information may additionally (or alternatively) initiate a network lookup to retrieve information from a remote server. On most UNIX platforms the order in which local and remote information sources are consulted is typically defined by the file `/etc/nsswitch.conf`.

Support for other security models and platforms is not provided through built-in functions, but is available through extension modules. Windows NT programmers, for example, can make use of the `Win32::AdminMisc` module to gain access to the Win32 Security API. Windows and other non-UNIX platforms do not support `getpwent` or `getgrent`, though the Cygwin port does provide a veneer of UNIX security that allows these functions to work on Windows platforms with limited functionality. Access Control Lists (ACLs) and other advanced security features are beyond the reach of the built-in functions even on UNIX platforms, but they can be handled via various modules available from CPAN – modules exist for most common security solutions.

User Information

UNIX platforms store local user information in the `/etc/passwd` file (though as noted above they may also retrieve information remotely). The format varies slightly, but typically has a structure like this:

```
fred:RGdmsaynFgP56:301:200:Fred A:/home/fred:/bin/bash
jim:Edkl1y7NMtO/M:302:200:Jim B:/home/jim:/bin/ksh
mysql:!!:120:120:MySQL server:/var/lib/mysql:/bin/csh
```

Each line follows the same format, and contains the following fields: name, password, user id, primary group id, comment/GECOS, home directory, and login shell. In this case we are not using a shadow password file, so the password field contains an encrypted password. The first two lines are for regular users, while the third defines an identity for a MySQL database server to run as. It doesn't want or need a password since it is not intended as a login user, so the password is disabled with `!!` (`*` is often also used for this purpose).

`getpwent` (pwent is short for 'password entry') retrieves one entry from the user information file at a time, starting from the first. In list context it returns no less than ten fields:

```
($name, $passwd, $uid, $gid, $quota, $comment, $gcos, $dir, $shell, $expire) =
getpwent;
```

Since the format and source of user information varies, not all these fields are always defined, and some of them have alternative meanings. A summary of each field and its possible meanings is given in the table opposite; consult the manual page for the `passwd` file (typically via **man 5 passwd**) for exact details of what fields are provided on a given platform.

Field Name	Number	Meaning
name	0	The login name of the user.
passwd	1	The encrypted password. Depending on the platform, the password may be encrypted using the standard UNIX crypt function, or the more secure MD5 hashing algorithm. If a shadow password file is in use, this field returns an asterisk. Additionally, disabled accounts often prefix passwords with ! to disable them.
uid	2	The user id of this user.
gid	3	The primary group of this user. Other groups can be found using the group functions detailed later.
quota	4	The disk space quota allotted to this user. Frequently unsupported. On some systems this may be a change or age field instead.
comment	5	A comment, usually the user's full name. On some systems this may be a class field instead. The comment field is often called the gcos field, but this is not technically accurate; this or the next item may therefore actually contain the comment.
gcos	6	Also known as GECOS, standing for 'General Electric Computer Operating System'. An extended comment containing a comma separated series of values – for example the user's name, location and work/home phone numbers. Frequently unimplemented, but see note on comment above.
dir	7	The home directory of the user, for example, /home/name.
shell	8	The preferred login shell of the user, for example, /usr/bin/bash.
expire	9	The expiry date of the user account. Frequently unsupported, often undefined.

In scalar context, getpwent returns just the name of the user, that is, the first field. To illustrate, we can generate a list of user names with a program like the following:

```
#!/usr/bin/perl
# listusers.pl
use warnings;
use strict;

my @users;
while (my $name = getpwent) {
    push @users, $name;
}
print "Users: @users \n";
```

Supporting getpwent are the setpwent and endpwent functions. The setpwent function resets the pointer for the next record returned by getpwent to the start of the password file. It is analogous to the rewinddir function in the same way that getpwent is analogous to both opendir and readdir combined. Since there only is one password file, it takes no arguments:

```
setpwent;
```

The endpwent function is analogous to closedir: It closes the internal file pointer created whenever we use getpwent (or getpwnam /getpwuid, detailed below). We cannot get access to this internal filehandle, but we can still free it if we are resource-conscious programmers. Additionally, if a network query was made then this will close the connection:

```
endpwent;
```

The getpwnam and getpwuid functions look up user names and user ids from each other. getpwnam takes a user name as an argument and returns the user id in scalar context or the full list of ten fields in a list context:

```
$uid = getpwnam($username);
@fields = getpwname($username);
```

Similarly, getpwuid takes a numeric user id and returns either the name or a list of fields, depending on context:

```
$username = getpwuid($uid);
@fields = getpwuid($uid);
```

Both functions also have the same effect as setpwent in that they reset the position of the pointer used by getpwent, so they cannot be combined with it in loops.

Since ten fields is rather a lot to manage, Perl provides the User::pwent module to provide an object-oriented interface to the pw functions. It is one of several modules that all behave similarly; others are User::grent (for group information), Net::hostent, Net::servent, Net::netent, Net::protoent (for network information) and Stat (for the stat and lstat functions).

User::pwent works by overloading the built-in getpwent, getpwnam, and getpwuid functions with object-oriented methods returning a pw object, complete with methods to extract the relevant fields. It also has the advantage of knowing what methods actually apply, which we can determine using the pw_has class method. Here is an object-oriented user information listing program, which uses getpwent to illustrate how the User::pwent module is used:

```perl
#!/usr/bin/perl
# listobjpw.pl
use warnings;
use strict;

use User::pwent qw(:DEFAULT pw_has);

print "Supported fields: ", scalar(pw_has), "\n";

while (my $user = getpwent) {
    print 'Name    : ', $user->name, "\n";
    print 'Password: ', $user->passwd, "\n";
    print 'User ID : ', $user->uid, "\n";
    print 'Group ID: ', $user->gid, "\n";

    # one of quota, change or age
    print 'Quota   : ', $user->quota, "\n" if pw_has('quota');
    print 'Change  : ', $user->change, "\n" if pw_has('change');
    print 'Age     : ', $user->age, "\n" if pw_has('age');
```

```perl
    # one of comment or class (also possibly gcos is comment)
    print 'Comment : ', $user->comment, "\n" if pw_has('comment');
    print 'Class   : ', $user->class, "\n" if pw_has('class');

    print 'Home Dir: ', $user->dir, "\n";
    print 'Shell   : ', $user->shell, "\n";

    # maybe gcos, maybe not
    print 'GECOS   : ',$user->gcos,"\n" if pw_has('gcos');

    # maybe expires, maybe not
    print 'Expire  : ', $user->expire, "\n" if pw_has('expire');

    # seperate records
    print "\n";
}
```

If called with no arguments, the pw_has class method returns a list of supported fields in list context, and a space-separated string suitable for printing in scalar context. Because we generally want to use it without prefixing User::pwent:: we specify it in the import list. However, to retain the default imports that override getpwent etc., we also need to specify the special :DEFAULT tag.

We can also import scalar variables for each field and avoid the method calls by adding the :FIELDS tag (which also implies :DEFAULT) to the import list. This generates a set of scalar variables with the same names as their method equivalents but prefixed with pw_. The equivalent of the above object-oriented script written using field variables is:

```perl
#!/usr/bin/perl
# listfldpw.pl
use warnings;
use strict;

use User::pwent qw(:FIELDS pw_has);

print "Supported fields: ", scalar(pw_has), "\n";

while (my $user = getpwent) {
    print 'Name     : ', $pw_name, "\n";
    print 'Password: ', $pw_passwd, "\n";
    print 'User ID : ', $pw_uid, "\n";
    print 'Group ID: ', $pw_gid, "\n";

    # one of quota, change or age
    print 'Quota   : ', $pw_quota, "\n" if pw_has('quota');
    print 'Change  : ', $pw_change, "\n" if pw_has('change');
    print 'Age     : ', $pw_age, "\n" if pw_has('age');

    # one of comment or class (also possibly gcos is comment)
    print 'Comment : ', $pw_comment, "\n" if pw_has('comment');
    print 'Class   : ', $pw_class, "\n" if pw_has('class');

    print 'Home Dir: ', $pw_dir, "\n";
    print 'Shell   : ', $pw_shell, "\n";

    # maybe gcos, maybe not
    print 'GECOS   : ', $pw_gecos, "\n" if pw_has('gecos');
```

```
        # maybe expires, maybe not
        print 'Expire  : ', $pw_expire, "\n" if pw_has('expire');

        # seperate records
        print "\n";
    }
```

We may selectively import variables if we want to use a subset, but since this overrides the default import we must also explicitly import the functions we want to override:

```
use User::grent qw($pw_name $pw_uid $pw_gid getpwnam);
```

To call the original getpwent, getpwnam, and getpwuid functions we can use the CORE:: prefix. Alternatively, we could suppress the overrides by passing an empty import list or an list containing neither :DEFAULT nor :FIELDS. As an example, here is another version of the above script that invents a new object method has for the Net::pwent package and then uses that and class method calls only, avoiding all imports:

```
#!/usr/bin/perl
# listcorpw.pl
use warnings;
use strict;

use User::pwent();

sub User::pwent::has {
my $self = shift;
    return User::pwent::pw_has(@_);
}

print "Supported fields: ", scalar(User::pwent::has), "\n";

while (my $user = User::pwent::getpwent) {
    print 'Name     : ', $user->name, "\n";
    print 'Password: ', $user->passwd, "\n";
    print 'User ID : ', $user->uid, "\n";
    print 'Group ID: ', $user->gid, "\n";
    # one of quota, change or age
    print 'Quota    : ', $user->quota, "\n" if $user->has('quota');
    print 'Change   : ', $user->change, "\n" if $user->has('change');
    print 'Age      : ', $user->age, "\n" if $user->has('age');

    # one of comment or class (also possibly gcos is comment)
    print 'Comment : ', $user->comment, "\n" if $user->has('comment');
    print 'Class    : ', $user->class, "\n" if $user->has('class');

    print 'Home Dir: ', $user->dir, "\n";
    print 'Shell    : ', $user->shell, "\n";

    # maybe gcos, maybe not
    print 'GECOS    : ', $user->gecos, "\n" if $user->has('gecos');

    # maybe expires, maybe not
    print 'Expire  : ', $user->expire, "\n" if $user->has('expire');
```

```
        # separate records
        print "\n";
}
```

As a convenience, the Net::pwent module also provides the getpw subroutine, which takes either a user name or a user id, returning a user object either way:

```
$user = getpw($user_name_or_id);
```

If the passed argument looks numeric, then getpwuid is called underneath to do the work; otherwise getpwnam is called.

Group Information

UNIX groups are a second tier of privileges between the user's own privileges and those of all users on the system. Files, for example, carry three sets of permissions for reading, writing, and execution – one for the file's owner, one for the file's owning group, and one for everyone else (see later in the chapter for more on this). All users belong to one primary group, and files they create are assigned to this group. This information is locally recorded in the /etc/passwd file and can be found locally or remotely with the getpwent, getpwnam, and getpwuid functions as described above. In addition, users may belong to any number of secondary groups. This information, along with the group ids (or 'gid's) and group names, is locally stored in the /etc/group file and can be extracted locally or remotely with the getgrent, getgrnam, and getgrgid functions.

The getgrent function reads one entry from the groups file each time it is called, starting with the first and returning the next entry in turn on each subsequent call. It returns four fields, the group name, a password (which is usually not defined), the group id, and the users who belong to that group:

```
#!/usr/bin/perl
# listgr.pl
use warnings;
use strict;

while (my ($name, $passwd, $gid, $members) = getgrent) {
        print "$gid: $name [$passwd] $members \n";
}
```

Alternatively, if we call getgrent in a scalar context, it returns just the group name:

```
#!/usr/bin/perl
# listgroups.pl
use warnings;
use strict;

my @groups;
while (my $name = getgrent) {
    push @groups, $name;
}
print "Groups: @groups \n";
```

As with `getpwent`, using `getgrent` causes Perl (or more accurately, the underlying C library) to open a filehandle (or open a connection to an NIS or NIS+ server) internally. Mirroring the supporting functions of `getpwent`, `setgrent` resets the pointer of the group filehandle to the start, and `endgrent` closes the file (and/or network connection) and frees the associated resources.

Perl provides the `User::grent` module as an object-oriented interface to the `getgrent`, `getgrnam`, and `getgrid` functions. It works very similarly to `User::pwent`, but provides fewer methods as it has fewer fields to manage. It also does not have to contend with the variations of field meanings that `User::pwent` does, and is consequently simpler to use. Here is an object-oriented group lister using `User::getgrent`:

```
#!/usr/bin/perl
# listbigr
use warnings;
use strict;

use User::grent;

while (my $group = getgrent) {
    print 'Name    : ', $group->name, "\n";
    print 'Password: ', $group->passwd, "\n";
    print 'Group ID: ', $group->gid, "\n";
    print 'Members : ', join(', ', @{$group->members}), "\n\n";
}
```

Like `User::pwent` (and indeed all similar modules like `Net::hostent`, etc.) we can import the `:FIELDS` tag to variables that automatically update whenever any of `getgrent`, `getgrnam`, or `getgrgid` are called. Here is the previous example reworked to use variables:

```
#!/usr/bin/perl
# listfldgr.pl
use warnings;
use strict;

use User::grent qw(:FIELDS);

while (my $group = getgrent) {
    print 'Name    : ', $gr_name, "\n";
    print 'Password: ', $gr_passwd, "\n";
    print 'Group ID: ', $gr_gid, "\n";
    print 'Members : ', join(', ', @{$group->members}), "\n\n";
}
```

We can also selectively import variables if we only want to use some of them:

```
use User::grent qw($gr_name $gr_gid);
```

In this case the overriding of `getgrent` etc. will not take place, so we would need to call `User::grent::getgrent` rather than just `getgrent`, or pass `getgrent` as a term in the import list. To avoid importing anything at all, just pass an empty import list.

The Unary File Test Operators

Perl provides a full complement of file test operators. They test filenames for various properties, for example, determining whether they are a file, directory, link, or other kind of file, determining who owns the them, and their access privileges. All of these file tests consist of a single minus followed by a letter, which determines the nature of the test, and either a filehandle or a string containing the file name. Here are a few examples:

```
-r $filename    # return true if file is readable by us

-w $filename    # return true if file is writable by us

-d DIRECTORY    # return true if DIRECTORY is opened to a directory

-t STDIN   # return true if STDIN is interactive
```

Collectively these functions are known as the -X or file test operators.

The slightly odd-looking syntax comes from the UNIX file test utility `test` and the built-in equivalents in most UNIX shells. Despite their strange appearance, the file test operators are really functions that behave just like any other built-in unary (single argument) Perl operator, and will happily accept parentheses:

```
print "It's a file!" if -f($filename);
```

If no filename or handle is supplied then the value of $_ is used as a default, which makes for some very terse if somewhat algebraic expressions:

```
foreach (@files) {
    print "$_ is readable textile\n" if -r && -T;    # -T for 'text' file
}
```

Only single letters following a minus sign are interpreted as file tests, so there is never any confusion between file test operators and negated expressions:

```
-o($name)    # test if $name is owned by us
-oct($name)    # return negated value of $name interpreted as octal
```

The full list of file tests is given below, loosely categorized into functional groups. Note that not all of these tests may work, depending on the underlying platform. For instance, operating systems that do not understand ownership in the UNIX model will not make a distinction between -r and -R, since this requires the concept of real and effective user IDs (the Win32 API does support 'impersonation' but this is not the same thing and is not used here). They will also not return anything useful for -o. Similarly, the -b and -c tests are specific to UNIX device files and have no relevance on other platforms.

This tests for the existence of a file:

-e	Return true if file exists. Equivalent to the return value of the `stat` function.

These test for read, write, and execute for effective and real users. On non-UNIX platforms, which don't have the concepts of real and effective users, the capital and lowercase versions are equivalent:

-r	Return true if file is readable by effective user id.
-R	Return true if file is readable by real user id.
-w	Return true if file is writable by effective user id.
-W	Return true if file is writable by real user id.
-x	Return true if file is executable by effective user id.
-X	Return true if file is executable by real user id.

The following test for ownership and permissions (-o returns 1, others ' ' on non-UNIX platforms). Note that these are UNIX based commands. On Windows, files are owned by 'groups' as opposed to 'users':

-o	Return true if file is owned by our real user id.
-u	Return true if file is setuid (chmod u+S, executables only).
-g	Return true if file is setgid (chmod g+S. executables only), this does not exist on Windows.
-k	Return true if file is sticky (chmod +T, executables only), this does not exist on Windows.

These tests for size work on Windows as on UNIX:

-z	Return true if file has zero length (that is, it is empty).
-s	Return true if file has non-zero length (opposite of -z).

The following are file type tests. While -f, -d, -t are generic, the others are platform dependent:

-f	Return true if file is a plain file (that is, not a directory, link, pipe, etc.).
-d	Return true if file is a directory.
-l	Return true if file is a symbolic link.
-p	Return true if file is a named pipe or filehandle is a pipe filehandle.
-S	Return true if file is a UNIX domain socket or filehandle is a socket filehandle.
-b	Return true if file is a block device.
-c	Return true if file is a character device.
-t	Return true if file is interactive (opened to a terminal).

We can use -T and -B to test whether a file is text or binary:

-T	Return true if file is a text file. See below for details.
-B	Return true if file is not a text file. See below details.

The following test for times, and also work on Windows:

-M	Returns the age of the file as a fractional number of days, counting from the time at which the application started (which avoids a system call to find the current time). To test which of two files is more recent we can write: `$file = (-M $file1 > -M $file2)? $file1: $file2;`
-A	Returns last access time.
-C	On UNIX, returns last inode change time (not creation time, as is commonly misconceived; this does return the creation time, but only so long as the inode has not changed since the file was created). On other platforms, it returns the creation time.

Link Transparency and Testing for Links

This section is only relevant if our chosen platform supports the concept of symbolic links, which is to say all UNIX variants, but not most other platforms (in particular, Windows 'shortcuts' are an artifact of the desktop, and nothing to do with the actual filing system).

The stat function, which is the basis of all the file test operators (except -1) automatically follows symbolic links and returns information based on the real file, directory, pipe, etc., that it finds at the end of the link. Consequently, file tests like -f and -d return true if the file at the end of the link is a plain file or directory. We do not therefore have to worry about links when we just want to know if a file is readable:

```
@lines;
if (-e $filename) {
    if (-r $filename) {
        open FILE, $filename;    # open file for reading
        @lines = <FILE>;
    } else {
        die "Cannot open $filename for reading \n";
    }
} else {
    die "Cannot open $filename - file does not exist \n";
}
```

If we want to find out if a file actually is a link, we have to use the -1 test. This gathers information about the link itself and not the file it points to, returning true of the file is in fact a link. A practical upshot of this is that we can test for broken links by testing -1 and -e:

```
if (-l $file and !-e $file) {
    print "'$file' is a broken link! \n";
}
```

This is also useful for testing that a file is not a link when we do not expect it to be. A utility designed to be run under 'root' should check that files it writes to have not been replaced with links to /etc/passwd for example.

Testing Binary and Text Files

-T and -B test files to see if they are text or binary. They do this by examining the start of the file and counting the number of non-text characters present. If this exceeds a third, the file is determined to be binary, otherwise it is determined to be text. If a null (ASCII 0) character is seen anywhere in the examined data then the file is binary.

477

Since -T and -B only make sense in the context of a plain file, they are commonly combined with -f:

```
if (-f $file && -T $file) {
    ...
}
```

-T and -B differ from the other file test operators in that they perform a read of the file in question. When used on a filehandle, both tests read from the current position of the file pointer. An empty file, or a filehandle positioned at the end of the file will return true for both -T and -B since in these cases there is no data to determine which is the correct interpretation.

Reusing the Results of a Prior 'stat' or 'lstat'

The underlying mechanism behind the file test operators is a call to either stat or (in the case of -l, lstat). In order to test the file, each operator will make a call to stat to interrogate the file for information. If we want to make several tests this is inefficient, because a disk access needs to be made in each case.

However, if we have already called stat or lstat for the file we want to test then we can avoid these extra calls by using the special filename _, which will substitute the results of the last call to stat (or lstat) in place of accessing the file. Here is a short example that tests a filename in six different ways based on one call to lstat:

```
#!/usr/bin/perl
# statonce.pl
use warnings;
use strict;

print "Enter filename to test: ";
my $filename = <>;
chomp $filename;

if (lstat $filename) {
    print "$filename is a file \n" if -f _;
    print "$filename is a directory \n" if -d _;
    print "$filename is a link \n" if -l _;

    print "$filename is readable \n" if -r _;
    print "$filename is writable \n" if -w _;
    print "$filename is executable \n" if -x _;
} else {
    print "$filename does not exist \n";
}
```

Note that in this example we have used lstat so the link test -l _ will work correctly. -l requires an lstat and not a stat, and will generate an error if we try to use it with the results of a previous stat:

The stat preceding -l _ wasn't an lstat...

Caching of the results of stat and lstat works for prior file tests too, so we could also write something like this:

```
if (-e $filename) {
    print "$filename exists \n";
    print "$filename is a file \n" if -f _;
}
```

Or:

```perl
if (-f $filename && -T _) {
    print "$filename exists and is a text file \n";
}
```

The only drawback to this is that only -l calls lstat, so we cannot test for a link this way unless the first test is -l.

Using 'stat' Objects

Accessing the values returned by stat can be a little inconvenient, not to mention inelegant. For example, this is how we find the size of a file:

```perl
$size = (stat $filename) [7];
```

Or, printing it out:

```perl
print ((stat $filename)[7]);    # need to use extra parentheses with print
```

Unless we happen to know that the eighth element is the size or we are taking care to write particularly legible code, this leads to unfriendly code. Fortunately we can use the File::stat module instead.

The File::stat module simplifies the use of stat and lstat by overriding them with subroutines that return stat objects instead of a list. These objects can then be queried using one of File::stat's methods, which have the same names as the values that they return.

As an example, this short program uses the size, blksize, and blocks methods to return the size of the file supplied on the command line:

```perl
#!/usr/bin/perl
# filesize.pl
use warnings;
use strict;

use File::stat;

print "Enter filename: ";
my $filename = <>;
chomp $filename;
if (my $stat = stat $filename) {
    print "'$filename' is ", $stat->size,
          " bytes and occupies ", $stat->blksize * $stat->blocks,
          " bytes of disc space \n";
} else {
    print "Cannot stat $filename: $| \n";
}
```

As an alternative to using object methods, we can import thirteen scalar variables containing the results of the last stat or lstat into our program by adding an import list of :FIELDS. Each variable takes the same name as the corresponding method prefixed with the string st_. For example:

```
#!/usr/bin/perl
# filesizefld.pl
use warnings;
use strict;

use File::stat qw(:FIELDS);

print "Enter filename: ";
my $filename = <>;
chomp($filename);
if (stat $filename) {
    print "'$filename' is ", $st_size,
            " bytes and occupies ", $st_blksize * $st_blocks,
            " bytes of disc space \n";
} else {
    print "Cannot stat $filename: $| \n";
}
```

If we want to use the original versions of stat and lstat we can do so by prefixing them with the CORE:: package name:

```
use File::stat;

...

@new_stat = stat $filename;    # use new 'stat'
@old_stat = CORE::stat $filename;    # use original 'stat'
```

Alternatively we can prevent the override from happening by supplying an empty import list:

```
use File::stat qw();    # or '', etc.
```

We can now use the File::stat stat and lstat methods by qualifying them with the full package name:

```
$stat = File::stat::stat $filename;
print "File is ", $stat->size(), " bytes \n";
```

The full list of File::stat object methods and field names is presented in the section 'Interrogating Files' later in the chapter.

Access Control Lists, the Superuser, and the 'filestat' Pragma

The file tests -r, -w, and -x, and their uppercase counterparts determine their return value from the results of the stat function. Unfortunately this does not always produce an accurate result. Some of the reasons that these file tests may produce incorrect or misleading results include:

- ❑ An Access Control List (ACL) is in operation
- ❑ The filesystem is read-only
- ❑ We have superuser privileges

All these cases tend to produce 'false positive' results, implying that the file is accessible when in fact it is not. For example, the file may be writable, but the filesystem is not.

In the case of the superuser, -r, -R, -w, and -W will always return true, even if the file is set as unreadable and unwritable, because the superuser can just disregard the actual file permissions. Similarly, -x and -X will return true if any of the execute permissions (user, group, other) are set. To check if the file is really writable, we must use stat and check the file permissions directly:

```
$mode = ((stat $filename)[2]);
$writable = $mode & 0200;    # test for owner write permission
```

Again, this is a UNIX-specific example. Most other platforms do not support permissions; Windows NT does, but does it a different way.

For the other cases we can try to use the filetest pragma, which alters the operation of the file tests for access by overriding them with more rigorous tests that interrogate the operating system instead. Currently there is only one mode of operation, access, which causes the file test operators to use the underlying access system call, if available:

```
use filetest 'access';
```

This modifies the behavior of the file test operators to use the operating system's access call to check the true permission of a file, as modified by access control lists, or filesystems that are mounted read-only. It also makes an access subroutine, which allows us to make our own direct tests of filenames (note that it does not work on filehandles), available to us. It takes a filename and a numeric flag containing the permissions we want to check for. These are defined as constants in the POSIX module:

R_OK	Test file has read permission.
W_OK	Test file has write permission.
X_OK	Test file has execute permission.
F_OK	Test that file exists. Implied by R_OK, W_OK, or X_OK.

Note that F_OK is implied by the other three, so it need never be specified directly (to test for existence we can as easily use the -e test, or -f if we require a plain file).

While access provides no extra functionality over the standard file tests, it does allow us to make more than one test simultaneously. As an example, to test that a file is both readable and writable we would use:

```
use filetest 'access';
use POSIX;
...
$can_readwrite = access($filename, R_OK|W_OK);
```

The return value from access is undef on failure and '0 but true' (a string that evaluates to zero in a numeric context and true in any other) on success, for instance an if or while condition. On failure $! is set to indicate the reason.

Automating Multiple File Tests

We often want to perform a series of different file tests across a range of different files. Installation scripts, for example, often do this to verify that all the installed files are in the correct place and with the correct permissions.

While it is possible to manually work though a list of files, we can make life a little simpler by using the `File::CheckTree` module instead. This module provides a single subroutine, `validate`, that takes a series of filenames and `-X` style file tests and applies each of them in turn, generating warnings as it does so.

Unusually for a library subroutine, `validate` accepts its input in lines, in order to allow the list of files and tests to be written in the style of a manifest list. As an example, here is `validate` being used to check for the existence of three directories and an executable file installed by a fictional application:

```
$warnings = validate(q{
/home/install/myapp/scripts -d
/home/install/myapp/docs -d
/home/install/myapp/bin -d
/home/install/myapp/bin/myapp -fx
});
```

Using the q or qq quoting operators is traditional for this kind of input. In addition, as we can supply our own possibly interpolated error messages, avoiding enclosing quotes is a good idea.

`validate` returns the number of warnings generated during the test, so we can use it as part of a larger installation script. If we want to disable or redirect the warnings we can do so by defining a signal handler:

```
$SIG{__WARN__} = { };    # do nothing
$SIG{__WARN__} = {print LOGFILE @_};   # redirect to install log
```

In fact this may be necessary in any case, since `validate` (as of Perl 5.6, at least) fails to properly initialize some of its internal variables leading to Use of uninitialized value warnings. We can eliminate these with selective use of `no warnings` or with a signal handler like the ones above.

The same file may be listed any number of times, with different tests applied each time. Alternatively, multiple tests may be bunched together into one file test, so that instead of specifying two tests one after the other they can be done together. Hence, instead of writing two lines:

```
/home/install/myapp/bin/myapp -f
/home/install/myapp/bin/myapp -x
```

We can write both tests as one line:

```
/home/install/myapp/bin/myapp -fx
```

The second test is dependent on the first, so only one warning can be generated from a bunched test. If we want to test for both conditions independently (we want to know if it is not a plain file and we want to know if it is not executable) we need to put the tests on separate lines.

Tests may also be negated by prefixing them with a !, in which case all the individual tests must fail for the line to succeed. For example to test whether a file is neither setuid or setgid:

```
validate(q{
    /home/install/myapp/scripts/myscript.pl    !-ug
})
```

Normal and negated tests cannot be bunched, so if we want to test that a filename corresponds to a plain file that is not executable, we must use separate tests:

```
validate(q{
    /home/install/myapp/scripts/myscript.pl    -f
    /home/install/myapp/scripts/myscript.pl    !-xug
})
```

Rather than a file test operator, the test may also be the command cd. This causes the directory named at the start of the line to be made the current working directory. Any relative paths given after this are taken relative to that directory until the next cd, which may also be relative:

```
validate(q{
    /home/install/myapp cd || die
        scripts           -rd
        cgi               cd
        guestbook.cgi     -xg
        guestbook.cgi     !-u
        ..                cd
        about_us.html     -rf
        text.bin          -f  || warn "Not a plain file"
});
```

validate is entirely insensitive to extra whitespace, so we can use additional spacing to clarify what file is being tested where. In the above example we have indented the files to make it clear which directory they are being tested in.

We can supply our own warnings, and make tests fatal by suffixing the file test with || and either warn or die. These work in exactly the same way as their Perl function counterparts. However, while warn may take an optional descriptive error message die ignores it. In the above example we have terminated immediately if the installation directory does not exist, since the other tests would be pointless. If we do specify our own error messages we can use the variable $file, supplied by the module, to insert the name of the file whose test failed:

```
validate(q{
    /etc         -d  || warn "What, no $file directory? \n"
    /var/spool   -d  || die
})
```

This trick relies on the error messages being interpolated at run time, so using single quotes or the q quoting operator is essential in this case.

Relative pathnames specified to validate before a cd are taken relative to the current directory. Unfortunately validate currently does not take proper account of this when reporting errors and adds a leading / to the pathname, giving the impression that the filename being tested is absolute (this may be fixed in a later release). To work around this, an explicit cd to the current directory suffices:

```
validate(q{
   .    cd
      localfile    -f
})
```

One of the advantages of File::CheckTree is that the file list can be built dynamically, possibly generated from an existing file tree created by File::Find (see later). For example, using File::Find we can determine the type and permissions of each file and directory in a tree, then generate a test list suitable for File::CheckTree to validate new installations of that tree. See 'Finding Files' and the other modules in this section for pointers.

Interrogating Files

While the file test operators are satisfactory for the majority of cases, if we want to interrogate a file in detail then it is sometimes more convenient to use stat or lstat directly and examine the results.

Both functions return details of the filename or filehandle supplied as their argument. lstat is identical to stat except in the case of a symbolic link, where stat will return details of the file pointed to by the link and lstat will return details of the link itself. In either case, a thirteen element list is returned:

```
# stat filehandle into a list
@stat_info = stat FILEHANDLE;

# lstat filename into separate scalars
($dev, $inode, $mode, $nlink, $uid, $gid, $rdev, $size,
    $time, $mtime, $ctime, $blksize, $blocks) = lstat $filename;
```

The thirteen values are always returned, but may not be defined or have meaning in every case, either because they do not apply to the file or filehandle being tested or because they have no meaning on the underlying platform. A full list of File::Stat methods and object names is shown below, including the meanings and index number in the @stat_info array:

Method	Number	Description
dev	0	The device number of the filesystem on which the file resides.
ino	1	The inode of the file.
mode	2	The file mode, combining the file type and the file permissions.
nlink	3	The number of hard (not symbolic) references to the inode underneath the filename.
uid	4	The user id of user that owns the file.
gid	5	The group id of group that owns the file.
rdev	6	The device identifier (block and character special files only).
size	7	The size of the file, in bytes.
atime	8	The last access time, in seconds.
mtime	9	The last modification time, in seconds.
ctime	10	The last inode change time, in seconds.

Method	Number	Description
blksize	11	The preferred block size of the filesystem.
blocks	12	The number of blocks allocated to the file. The product of $stat_info[11] * $stat_info[12] is the size of the file as allocated in the filesystem. However, the actual size of the file in terms of its contents will most likely be less than this as it will only partially fill the last block; use size for that.

Several of the values returned by stat relate to the 'inode' of the file. Under UNIX, the inode of a file is a numeric id, which it is allocated by the filesystem, and which is its 'true' identity, with the filename being just an alias. Since more than one filename may point to the same file, the nlink value may be more than one, though it cannot be less (since then the inode would have no filename and we would not be able to refer to it). The ctime value indicates the last time the node of the file changed. It may often mean the creation time. Conversely, the access and modification times refer to actual file access.

On other platforms, some of these values are either undefined or meaningless. Under Windows, the device number is related to the drive letter, there is no 'inode' and the value of nlink is always '1'. The uid and gid values are always zero, and no value is returned for either blocksize or blocks, either. There is a mode, though only the file type is useful; the permissions are always 777. While Windows NT does have a fairly complex permissions system it is not accessible this way; see below.

Changing File Attributes

UNIX and other platforms that support the concept of file permissions and ownership can make use of the chmod and chgrp functions to modify the permissions of a file from Perl. chmod modifies the file permissions of a file for the three categories user, group, and other. The chown function modifies which user corresponds to the user permissions, and which group corresponds to the group permissions. Every other user and group falls under the other category. Ownership and permissions are therefore inextricably linked.

On UNIX, the file type and the file permissions are combined into the mode value returned by stat. On Windows, the file type is still useful, though the permissions are always set to 777.

File Ownership

File ownership is a highly platform-dependent concept. Perl grew up on UNIX systems, and so attempts to handle ownership in a UNIX-like way. Under UNIX and other platforms that borrowed their semantics from UNIX, files have an owner, represented by the file's user id, and a group owner, represented by the file's group id. Each relates to a different set of file permissions, so the user may have the ability to read and write a file whereas other users in the same group may only get to read it. Others may not have even that, depending on the setting of the file permissions.

File ownership is handled by the chown function, which maps to both the chown and chgrp system calls. It takes at least three parameters; a user id, a group id, and one or more files to change:

```
@successes = chown $uid, $gid, @files;
```

485

The number of files successfully changed is returned. If only one file is given to chown, this allows a simple Boolean test to be used to determine success:

```
unless (chown $uid, $gid, $filename) {
    die "chown failed: $! \n";
}
```

To change only the user or group, supply -1 as the value for the other parameter. For instance, a chgrp function can be simulated with:

```
sub chgrp {
    return chown(shift, -1, @_);
}
```

Note that on most systems (that is, most systems that comprehend file ownership in the first place) usually only the superuser can change the user who owns the file, though the group can be changed to another group that the same user belongs to. It is possible to determine if a change of ownership is permitted by calling the sysconf function:

```
$chown_restricted = sysconf(_PC_CHOWN_RESTRICTED);
```

If this returns a true value then a chown will not be permitted.

chown needs a user or group id to function, it will not accept a user or group name. To deduce a user id from the name, at least on a UNIX-like system, we can use the getpwnam function. Likewise, to deduce a group id from the name we can use the getgrnam function. We can use getpwent and getgrent instead to retrieve one user or group respectively (see earlier in the chapter for more). As a quick example, the following script builds tables of user and group ids, which can be subsequently used in chown:

```
#!/usr/bin/perl
# ids.pl
use warnings;
use strict;

# get user names and primary groups
my (%users, %usergroup);
while (my ($name, $passwd, $uid, $gid) = getpwent) {
    $users{$name} = $uid;
    $usergroup{$name} = $gid;
}

# get group names and gids
my (%groups, @groups);
while (my ($name, $passwd, $gid) = getgrent) {
    $groups{$name} = $gid;
    $groups[$gid] = $name;
}

# print out basic user and group information
foreach my $user (sort {$users{$a} <=> $users{$b}} keys %users) {
    print "$users{$user}: $user, group $usergroup{$user}
($groups[$usergroup{$user}])\n";
}
```

File Permissions

The implementation of file permissions varies widely between different operating systems. Perl supports the UNIX model natively, partly because it grew up on UNIX, but mostly because UNIX file permissions are closely related to the file system. This is academic for many platforms; Windows 9x and MacOS prior to version X do not comprehend permissions at all, and Windows NT has its own security model, which we access with the Win32::FileSecurity and Win32::FilePermissions modules instead.

Perl provides two functions that are specifically related to file permissions, chmod and umask.

The chmod function allows us to set the permissions of a file. Permissions are grouped into three categories: user, which applies to the file's owner, group which applies to the file's group owner, and other, which applies to anyone who is not the file's owner or a member of the file's group owner. Within each category each file may be given read, write, and execute permission.

chmod represents each of the nine values (3 categories x 3 permissions) by a different numeric flag, which are traditionally put together to form a three digit octal number, each digit corresponding to the respective category. The flag values within each digit are 4 for read permission, 2 for write permission, and 1 for execute permission, as demonstrated by the following examples (prefixed by a leading 0 to remind us that these are octal values):

0200	Owner write permission
0040	Group read permission
0001	Other execute permission

The total of the read, write, and execute permissions for a category is 7, which is why octal is so convenient to represent the combined permissions flag. Read, write and execute permission for the owner only would be represented as 0700. Similarly, read, write and execute permission for the owner, read and execute permission for the group and execute only permission for everyone else would be: 0751, which is 0400+0200+0100 + 0040+0010 + 0001.

Having explained the permissions flag, the chmod function itself is comparatively simple, taking a permissions flag, as calculated above, as its first argument and applying it to one or more files given as the second and subsequent arguments. For example:

```
chmod 0751, @files;
```

As with chown, the number of successfully chmodded files is returned, or zero if no files were changed successfully. If only one file is supplied, the return value of chmod can be tested as a Boolean result in an if or unless statement :

```
unless (chmod 0751, $file) {
    die "Unable to chmod: $! \n";
}
```

The umask function, which is the opposite of chmod, allows us to change the default permissions mask used whenever Perl creates a new file. The bits in the umask unset the corresponding bits in the permissions from the permissions used by open or sysopen when the file is created, and the resulting permissions set. Thus the permission bits of the umask mask the permissions that open and sysopen try to set. The following table shows the permission bits that can be used with umask and their meanings:

487

umask number	File Permission
0	Read and write
1	Read and write
2	Read only
3	Read only
4	Write only
5	Write only
6	No read and no write
7	No read and no write

umask only defines the access permissions. Called without an argument, it returns the current value of the umask, which is inherited from the shell, and is typically set to a value of 002 (mask other write permission) or 022 (mask group and other write permissions):

```
$umask = umask;
```

Alternatively, umask may be called with a single numeric parameter, traditionally expressed in octal, or alternatively as a combination of mode flags as described above. For example:

```
umask 022;
```

Overriding the umask explicitly is not usually a good idea, since the user might have it set to a more restrictive value. A better idea is to combine the permissions we want to restrict with the existing umask, using a bitwise OR. For example:

```
umask (022 | umask);
```

The open function always uses permissions of 0666 (read and write for all categories), whereas sysopen allows the permissions to be specified in the call. Since umask controls the permissions of new files by removing unwanted permissions, we do not need to (and generally should not) specify more restrictive permissions to sysopen.

The 'Fcntl' Module

The Fcntl module provides symbolic constants for all of the flags contained in both the permissions and the filetype parts of the mode value. It also provides two functions for extracting each part, as an alternative to computing the values by hand:

```
use Fcntl qw(:mode);    # import file mode constants

$type = IFMT($mode);    # extract file type
$perm = IFMODE($mode);   # extract file permissions

printf "File permissions are: %o \n", $perm;
```

The filetype part of the mode defines the type of the file, and is the basis of the file test operators like -d, -f, and -l that test for the type of a file. The Fcntl module defines symbolic constants for these:

Name	Description	Operator
S_IFREG	Regular file	-f
S_IFDIR	Directory	-d
S_IFLNK	Link	-l
S_IFBLK	Block special file	-b
S_IFCHR	Character special file	-c
S_IFIFO	Pipe or named fifo	-p
S_IFSOCK	Socket	-s
S_IFWHT	Interactive terminal	-t

Note that Fcntl also defines a number of subroutines that test the mode for the desired property. These have very similar names, for example S_IFDIR and S_ISFIFO, and it is easy to get the subroutines and flags confused. Since we have the file test operators, we do not usually need to use these subroutines, so we mention them only to eliminate possibly confusion.

These flags can also be used with sysopen, IO::File's new method and the stat function described previously, where they can be compared against the mode value. As an example of how these flags can be used, here is the equivalent of the -d file test operator written using stat and the Fcntl module:

```
$mode = ((stat $filename)[2]);
$is_directory = $mode & S_IFDIR;
```

Or, to test that a file is neither a socket nor a pipe:

```
$is_not_special = $mode & ^(S_IFBLK | S_IF_CHR);
```

The Fcntl module also defines functions that do this for us. Each function takes the same name as the flag but with S_IF replaced with S_IS. For instance, to test for a directory we can instead use:

```
$is_directory = S_ISDIR($mode);
```

Of course the -d file test operator is somewhat simpler in this case.

The permissions part of the mode defines the read, write, and execute privileges that the file grants to the file's owner, the file's group, and others. It is the basis of the file test operators like -r, -w, -u, and -g that test for the accessibility of a file. The Fcntl module also defines symbolic constants for these:

Name	Description	Number
S_IRUSR	User can read	00400
S_IWUSR	User can write	00200
S_IXUSR	User can execute	00100
S_IRGRP	Group can read	00040
S_IWGRP	Group can write	00020
S_IXGRP	Group can execute	00010
S_IROTH	Others can read	00004
S_IWOTH	Others can write	00002
S_IXOTH	Others can execute	00001
S_IRWXU	User can read, write, execute	00700
S_IRWXG	Group can read, write, execute	00070
S_IRWXO	Others can read, write, execute	00007
S_ISUID	setuid	04000
S_ISGID	setgid	02000
S_ISVTX	sticky (S) bit	01000
S_ISTXT	swap (t) bit	10000

For example, to test a file for user read and write permission, plus execute permission, we could use:

```
$perms_ok = $mode & S_IRUSR | S_IWUSR | S_IRGRP;
```

To test that a file has exactly these permissions and no others we would instead write:

```
$exact_perms = $mode == S_IRUSR | S_IWUSR | S_IRGRP;
```

The file permission flags are useful not only for making sense of the mode value returned by stat but also in the chmod function. Consult the manual page for the chmod system call (on UNIX platforms) for details of the more esoteric bits such as sticky and swap.

Linking, Unlinking, and Renaming Files

The presence of filenames can be manipulated directly with the link and unlink built-in functions. These provide the ability to edit the entries for files in the filesystem, creating new ones or removing existing ones. They are not the same as creating and deleting files, however. On platforms that support the concept, link creates a new link (entry in the filing system) to an existing file, it does not create a copy (except on Windows, where it does exactly this). Likewise, unlink removes a filename from the filing system, but if the file has more than one link, and therefore more than one filename, the file will persist. This is an important point to grasp, because it often leads to confusion.

Linking Files

The `link` function creates a new link (sometimes called a 'hard' link, to differentiate it from a 'soft' or symbolic link) for the named file:

```
if (link $currentname, $newname) {
    print "Linked $currentname to $newname ok \n";
} else {
    warn "Failed to link: $! \n";
}
```

`link` will not create links for directories, though it will create links for all other types of file. For directories we can create symbolic links only. Additionally, we cannot create hard links between different file systems, nor between directories on some file systems (for example, AFS). On UNIX, `link` works by giving two names in the file system the same underlying inode. On Windows and other file systems that do not have this concept, an attempt to link will create a copy of the original file.

On success, `link` returns true and a new filename will exist for the file. The old one continues to exist and can either be used to read, or alter the contents of the file. Both links are therefore exactly equivalent.

Having said that, the file permissions of each link can differ. Immediately after creation, the new link will carry the same permissions and ownership as the original, but this can subsequently be changed with the `chmod` and `chown` built-in functions, to, for example, create a read-only and a read-write entry point to the same data.

Unlinking Files

The opposite of linking is unlinking. Files can be unlinked with the built-in `unlink` function, which takes one or more filenames as a parameter. Alternatively it operates on `$_` if no filename is supplied:

```
unlink $currentname;    # single file

foreach (@files) {
    unlink if /\.bak/;   # unlink $_ if it ends '.bak'
}

unlink <*.bak>;   # the same, via a file glob
```

`unlink` is not necessarily the same as deleting a file, for two reasons. First, if the file has more than one link then it will still be available by other names in the file system. Although we cannot (easily) find out the names of the other links, we can find out how many links a file has through `stat`. We can therefore establish in advance if `unlink` will remove the file from the file system completely, or just one of the links for it by calling `stat`:

```
$links = (stat $filename)[3];
```

Or more legibly with the `File::stat` module:

```
$stat = new File::stat($filename);
$links = $stat->nlink;
```

Second, on platforms that support it (generally UNIX-like ones), if any process has an open filehandle for the file then it will persist for as long as the filehandle persists. This means that even after an `unlink` has completely removed all links to a file it will still exist and can be read, written, and have its contents copied to a new file. Indeed, the `new_tmpfile` method of `IO::File` does exactly this, of which more will be said later in the chapter. Other platforms (such as Windows) will generally reject the attempt to unlink the file so long as a process holds an open filehandle on it.

Note that `unlink` will not unlink directories unless we are on UNIX, Perl was given the `-U` flag, and we have superuser privilege. Even so, it is an inadvisable thing to do, since it will also remove the directory contents including any subdirectories and their contents from the filing system hierarchy, but not recycle the space that they occupy on the disk. Instead they will appear in the `lost+found` directory the next time an `fsck` filing system check is performed, which is unlikely to be what we intended. The `rmdir` built-in command covered later in the chapter is the preferred approach, or the `rmtree` function from `File::Path` for more advanced applications involving multiple directories.

Renaming Files

Given the above, renaming a file is just a case of linking it to a new name, then unlinking it from the old. The following subroutine demonstrates a generic way of doing this:

```
sub rename {
    ($current, $new) = @_;
    unlink $current if link($current, $new);
}
```

The built-in `rename` function is essentially equivalent to the above subroutine:

```
# using the built-in function:
rename($current, $new);
```

This is effective for simple cases but it will fail in a number of situations, most notably if the new filename is on a different filesystem from the old (a floppy disk to a hard drive, or instance). `rename` uses the `rename` system call, if available. However, on many systems it is equivalent to the `link`/`unlink` subroutine above. For a properly portable solution that works across all platforms, consider using the `move` routine from the `File::Copy` module, which has been specifically written to handle most special cases.

Symbolic Links

On platforms that support it, we can also create a `soft` or symbolic link with the built-in `symlink` function. This is syntactically identical to `link` but creates a pointer to the file rather than a direct hard link:

```
if (symlink $currentname, $newname) {
    die "Failed to link: $! \n";
}
```

The return value from `symlink` is 1 on success or 0 on failure. On platforms that do not support symbolic links (a `shortcut` is an invention of the Windows desktop, not the file system), `symlink` produces a fatal error. If we are writing code to be portable then we can protect against this by using `eval`:

```
$linked = eval {symlink($currentname, $newname);};
if (not defined $linked) {
   warn "Symlink not supported \n";
} else {
   warn "Link failed: $! \n";
}
```

To test whether `symlink` is available without actually creating a symbolic link, supply an empty filename for both arguments:

```
$symlinking = eval {symlink('',''); 1};
```

If the `symlink` fails, `eval` will return undef when it tries to execute the `symlink`. If it succeeds, the `1` will be returned. This is a generically useful trick for all kinds of situations of course.

Symbolic links are the links that the `-l` and `lstat` functions check for; hard links are indistinguishable from ordinary filenames because they *are* ordinary filenames. Most operations performed on symbolic links (with the notable exceptions of `-l` and `lstat` of course) are transferred to the linked file, if it exists. In particular, symbolic links have the generic file permissions 777, meaning everyone is permitted to do everything. However, this only means that the permissions of the file that the link points towards take priority. An attempt to open the link for writing will be translated into an attempt to open the linked file, and the permissions of the file checked, rather than those of the symbolic link. Even `chmod` will affect the permissions of the real file, not the link.

Symbolic links may legally point to other symbolic links, in which case the end of the link is the file that the last symbolic link points to. If the file has subsequently been moved or deleted, the symbolic link is said to be 'broken'. We can check for broken links with:

```
if (-l $linkname and !-e $linkname) {
   print "$linkname is a broken link! \n";
}
```

See earlier in the chapter for more on this (and in particular why the special filename _ cannot be used after `-e` in this particular case) and some variations on the same theme.

Copying and Moving Files

One way to copy a file to a new name is to open a filehandle for both the old and the new names, and copy data between them, as this rather simplistic utility attempts to do:

```
#!/usr/bin/perl
# dumbcopy.pl
use warnings;
use strict;

print "Filename: ";
my $infile = <>;
chomp $infile;
print "New name: ";
my $outfile = <>;
chomp $outfile;
```

```
open IN, $infile;
open OUT, "> $outfile";
print OUT <IN>;
close IN;
close OUT;
```

The problem with this approach is that it does not take into account the existing file permissions and ownerships. If we run this on a system with a decent file permissions system (such as UNIX) and the file we are copying happens to executable, the copy will lose the executable permissions. If we run this on a system that cares about the difference between binary and text files we can also corrupt the file unless we also add a call to binmode. In fact this is unnecessary work because Perl provides the File::Copy module to handle these issues for us.

The File::Copy module provides subroutines for moving and copying files without having to directly manipulate them via filehandles. It also correctly preserves the file permissions. To make use of it we just need to use it:

```
use File::Copy;
```

File::Copy contains two primary subroutines, copy and move. copy takes the names of two files or filehandles as its arguments and copies the contents of the first to the second, creating it if necessary. If the first argument is a filehandle it is read from, and if the second is a filehandle it is written to; for example:

```
copy "myfile", "myfile2";   # copy one file to another
copy "myfile", \*STDOUT;   # copy file to standard output
copy LOG, "logfile";   # copy input to filehandle
```

If neither argument is a filehandle, copy does a system copy, in order to preserve file attributes and permissions. This copy is directly available as the syscopy subroutine and is portable across platforms; see later.

copy also takes a third, optional argument, which if specified determines the buffer size to use. For instance, to copy the file in chunks of 16K, we might use:

```
copy "myfile", "myfile2", 16 * 1024;
```

Without a buffer size, copy will default to the size of the file, or 2MB, whichever is smaller. Setting a smaller buffer will cause the copy to take longer, but to use less memory while doing it.

move takes the names of two files (not filehandles) as its arguments, and attempts to move the file named by the first argument to have the name given as the second; for example:

```
move "myfile", "myfile2";   # move file to another name
```

If possible, move will rename the file using the link and unlink functions. If not, it will copy the file using copy and then delete the original. Note however that in this case we cannot set a buffer size as an optional third parameter.

If an error occurs with either copy or move, the filesystem may run out of space. Then the destination file may be incomplete. In the case of a move that tried to copy the file this will lose information. In this case attempting to copy the file and then unlinking the original is safer.

Note also that copy and move (if it has to copy the file) adhere to the setting of binmode for files copied on platforms that care about such things (for example, Windows). To make a copy explicitly binary, use binmode on the filehandles or (if not copying via filehandles) make use of the open pragmatic module described previously in this chapter.

Here is a rewritten version of the file copy utility we started with. Note that it is not only better; it is considerably smaller too:

```perl
#!/usr/bin/perl
# smartcopy.pl
use warnings;
use strict;

use File::Copy;

print "Filename: ";
my $infile = <>;
chomp $infile;
print "New name: ";
my $outfile = <>;
chomp $outfile;

unless (copy $infile, $outfile) {
    print "Failed to copy '$infile' to '$outfile': $! \n";
}
```

As a special case, if the first argument to copy or move is a filename and the second is a directory then the destination file is placed inside the directory with the same name as the source file.

UNIX aficionados will be happy to know that the aliases cp and mv are available for copy and move and can be imported by specifying one or both of them in the import list:

```perl
use File::Copy qw(cp mv);
```

cp and mv are direct aliases for copy and move and work identically to them.

System Level Copies and Platform Portability

As well as the standard copy, which works with either filenames or filehandles, File::Copy defines the syscopy subroutine, which provides direct access to the copy function of the underlying operating system. The copy subroutine calls syscopy if both arguments are filenames and the second is not a directory (see above), otherwise it opens whichever argument is not a filehandle and performs a read-write copy through the filehandles.

The syscopy calls the underlying copy system call supplied by the operating system, and is thus portable across different platforms. Under UNIX, it calls the copy subroutine, as there is no system copy call. Under Windows, it calls the Win32::CopyFile module. Under OS/2 and VMS it calls syscopy and rmscopy respectively. This makes the File::Copy module an effective way to copy files without worrying about platform dependencies.

Comparing Files

The `File::Compare` module is a standard component of the Perl standard library that provides file comparison features for our applications. It provides two main subroutines, `compare` and `compare_text`, both of which are available to us when we use the module:

```
use File::Compare;
```

The `compare` subroutine simply compares two files or filehandles, returning 0 if they are equal, 1 if they are not, and -1 if an error was encountered:

```
SWITCH: foreach (compare $file1, $file2) {
    /^0/ and print("Files are equal"), last;
    /^1/ and print("Files are not equal"), last;
    print "Error comparing files: $! \n";
}
```

`compare` takes a third optional argument, which if specified defines the size of the buffer used to read from the two files or filehandles. This works in an identical manner to the buffer size of `File::Copy`'s `copy` subroutine, defaulting to the size of the file or 2MB, whichever is smaller, if no buffer size is specified. Note that `compare` automatically puts both files into a binary mode for comparison.

The `compare_text` function operates identically to `compare` but takes at its third argument an optional code reference to an anonymous comparison subroutine. Unlike `compare`, `compare_text` compares files in text mode (assuming that the operating system draws a distinction) so without the third parameter `compare_text` simply compares the two files in text mode.

The comparison subroutine, if supplied, should return a Boolean result that returns 0 if the lines should be considered equal and 1 otherwise. The default that operates when no explicit comparison is provided is equivalent to:

```
sub {$_[0] ne $_[1]}
```

We can supply our own comparison subroutines to produce different results. For example, this comparison checks files for case-insensitive equivalence:

```
$result = compare_text ($file1, $file2, sub {lc($_[0]) ne lc($_[1])});
```

Similarly, this comparison uses a named subroutine that strips extra whitespace from the start and end of lines before comparing them:

```
sub stripcmp {
    ($a, $b) = @_;
    $a =~s/^\s*(.*?)\s*$/$1/;
    $b =~s/^\s*(.*?)\s*$/$1/;
    return $a ne $b;
}
$result = compare_text ($file1, $file2, \&stripcmp);
```

For those who prefer more UNIX-like nomenclature, cmp may be used as an alias for compare by importing it specifically:

```
use File::Compare qw(cmp);
```

As a final point, note that compare and compare_text are effectively the same subroutine; supplying a code reference as the third parameter to compare turns it into compare_text, and likewise for cmp if it has been imported.

Finding Files

The File::Find module provides a multipurpose file finding subroutine that we can configure to operate in a number of different ways. It supplies one subroutine find, which takes a first parameter of either a code or hash reference that configures the details of the search, and one or more subsequent parameters defining the starting directory or directories to begin from.

A second, finddepth, finds the same files as find but traverses them in order of depth. This can be handy in cases when we want to modify the filesystem as we go, as we will see later.

If the first parameter to either find or finddepth is a code reference then it is treated as a wanted subroutine that tests for particular properties in the files found. Otherwise it is a reference to a hash containing at least a wanted key and code reference value and optionally more of the following key-value pairs:

Key	Value	Description
wanted	<code reference>	A reference to a subroutine that returns true or false depending on the characteristics of the file.
		Note that passing in a code reference as the first parameter is equivalent to passing:
		{wanted => $coderef}
		Since find does not return any result, a wanted subroutine is required for find to do anything useful.
bydepth	0|1	A Boolean flag that when set causes files to be returned in order of depth. The convenience subroutine finddepth is a shorthand for this flag.
follow	0|1	A Boolean flag that when set causes find to follow symbolic links. When in effect, find records all files scanned in order to prevent files being found more than once (directly and via a link, for example) and to prevent loops (a link linking to it's parent directory). For large directory trees this can be very time consuming. For a faster but less rigorous alternative use follow_fast. This option is disabled by default.
follow_fast	0|1	A Boolean flag that when set causes find to follow symbolic links. Like follow, follow_fast causes find to follow symbolic links. Unlike follow it does not check for duplicate files, and so is faster. It still checks for loops however, by tracking all symbolic links. This option is disabled by default.

Table continued on following page

Key	Value	Description
follow_skip	0|1|2	A three-state flag that determines how find treats symbolic links if either follow or follow_fast is enabled:
		A setting of 0 causes find to die if it encounters a duplicate file, link or directory.
		The default of 1 causes any file that is not a directory or symbolic link to be ignored if it is encountered again. A directory encountered a second time causes find to die.
		A setting of 2 causes find to ignore both duplicate files and directories.
		This flag has no effect if neither of follow or follow_fast is enabled.
no_chdir	0|1	A Boolean flag that when set causes find not to change down into each directory as it scans it. This primarily makes a difference to the wanted subroutine, if any is defined.
untaint	0|1	A Boolean flag that when set causes find to untaint directory names when running in taint (-T) mode. This uses a regular expression to untaint the directory names, which can be overridden with untaint_pattern.
untaint_pattern	<pattern>	The pattern used to untaint directory names if untaint is enabled. The default pattern, which attempts to define all standard legal filename characters is:
		qr/^([-+@\w.\/]+)$/
		If overridden, the replacement regular expression search pattern, compiled with qr. In addition it must contain one set of parentheses to return the untainted name, and should probably be anchored at both ends.
		Note that files with spaces inside the filename will fail this pattern unless the pattern is overridden. If multiple parentheses are used then only the text matched by the first is used as the untainted name.
untaint_skip	0|1	A Boolean flag that when set causes find to skip over directories that fail the test against untaint_pattern. The default is unset, which causes find to die if it encounters an invalid directory name.

For example, this call to find searches for and prints out all files under /home, following symbolic links, untainting as it goes, and skipping over any directory that fails the taint check:

```
@files = find({wanted => sub {print $File::Find::fullname},
    follow => 1, untaint => 1, untaint_skip => 1
}, '/home');
```

The power of find lies in the wanted subroutine. find does not actually return any value, so without this subroutine the search will be performed but will not actually produce any useful result.

To specify a wanted subroutine we can specify a code reference to an anonymous subroutine (possibly derived from a named subroutine) either directly, or as the value of the wanted key in the configuration hash. Each file that is located is passed to this subroutine, which may perform any actions it likes, including removing or renaming the file. For example, here is a simple utility script that renames all files in the target directory or directories into lower case:

```perl
#!/usr/bin/perl
# lcall.pl
use warnings;
use strict;

use File::Find;
use File::Copy;

die "Usage: $0 <dir> [<dir>...] \n" unless @ARGV;
foreach (@ARGV) {
    die "'$_' does not exist \n" unless -e $_;
}

sub lcfile {
    print "$File::Find::dir - $_ \n";
    move ($_, lc $_);
}

finddepth (\&lcfile, @ARGV);
```

In order to handle subdirectories correctly we use finddepth so that files are renamed first, and the directories that contain them second. We also use the move subroutine from File::Copy since this deals with both files and directories without any special effort on our part.

Within the subroutine the variable $_ contains the current filename and the variable $File::Find::dir contains the directory in which the file was found. If follow or follow_fast is in effect then $File::Find::fullname contains the complete absolute path to the file with all symbolic links resolved to their true paths. If no_chdir has been specified then $_ is the absolute pathname of the file, the same as $File::Find::fullname, otherwise it is just the leafname of the file.

Here is an example that searches for files with setuid or setgid bits on UNIX filesystems. Note that it tests -x against $_ first, then reuses the result of that stat in all further tests with the special _ filename:

```perl
#!/usr/bin/perl
# findsuid.pl
use warnings;
use strict;

use File::Find;

my $count = 0;

sub is_suid {
    if (-x && (-u _ || -g _)) {
        $count++;
        print "\t'$File::Find::dir/$_' is ";
```

```
      if (-u _ && -g _) {
          print "setuid and setgid \n";
      } elsif (-u _) {
          print "setuid \n"
      } else {
          print "setgid \n"
      }
   }
}

print "Scanning for files in ", join(', ',@ARGV), ":\n";
find(\&is_suid, @ARGV);
print "$count setuid or setgid executables found \n";
```

When tested against the /bin directory on any reasonably normal UNIX system this should produce output similar to the following:

```
Scanning for files in /bin:
     '/bin/su' is setuid
     '/bin/mount' is setuid
     '/bin/umount' is setuid
     '/bin/ping' is setuid
     '/bin/login' is setuid
5 setuid or setgid executables found
```

If follow or follow_fast is set then the wanted subroutine can make use of the results of the lstat that both these modes use. File tests can then use the special filename _ without any initial file test or explicit lstat. Otherwise no stat or lstat has been done and we need to use an explicit file test on $_. As a final example, here is a utility script that searches for broken links:

```perl
#!/usr/bin/perl
# checklink.pl
use warnings;
use strict;

use File::Find;

my $count = 0;

sub check_link {
    if (-l && !-e) {
        $count++;
        print "\t$File::Find::name is broken \n";
    }
}

print "Scanning for broken links in ", join(', ', @ARGV), ":\n";
find(\&check_link, @ARGV);
print "$count broken links found \n";
```

Note that it has to do both an explicit -l and -e to work, since one requires an lstat and the other a stat, and we do not get a free lstat because in this case as we do not want to follow symbolic links (in follow mode, broken links are discarded before the wanted subroutine is called, which would rather defeat the point).

Another way to create utilities like this is through the `find2perl` script which comes as standard with Perl. This emulates the syntax of the traditional UNIX `find` command, but instead of performing a search, generates a Perl script using `File::Find` that emulates the action of the original command in Perl. Typically, this is faster than using `find`, and it is also an excellent way to create the starting point for utilities like the examples in this section. For example, here is `find2perl` being used to generate a script, called `myfind.pl`, that searches for and prints all files ending in `.bak` that are a week or more old, starting from the current directory:

> **find2perl . -name '*.bak' -type f -mtime +7 -print > myfind.pl**

This is the `myfind.pl` script that it produces:

```
#! /usr/bin/perl -w
    eval 'exec /usr/bin/perl -S $0 ${1+"$@"}'
        if 0; #$running_under_some_shell

use strict;
use File::Find ();

# Set the variable $File::Find::dont_use_nlink if you're using AFS,
# since AFS cheats.

# for the convenience of &wanted calls, including -eval statements:
use vars qw/*name *dir *prune/;
*name    = *File::Find::name;
*dir     = *File::Find::dir;
*prune   = *File::Find::prune;

# Traverse desired filesystems
File::Find::find({wanted => \&wanted}, '.');
exit;

sub wanted {
    my ($dev, $ino, $mode, $nlink, $uid, $gid);

    /^.*\.bak\z/s &&
    (($dev, $ino, $mode, $nlink, $uid, $gid) = lstat($_)) &&
    -f _ &&
    (int(-M _) > 7) &&
    print("$name\n");
}
```

Deciphering File Paths

The `File::Basename` module provides subroutines to analyze and dissect filenames on a variety of different platforms. It contains one principal subroutine, `fileparse`, which attempts to divide a filename into a leading directory path, a basename, and a suffix:

```
use File::Basename;

# 'glob' all files with a three character suffix and parse pathname
foreach (</home/*/*.???>) {
    ($path, $leaf, $suffix) = fileparse($_, '\.\w{3}');
}
```

The path and basename are determined according to the file naming conventions of the underlying filesystem, as determined by the operating system or configured with `fileparse_set_fstype`. The suffix list, if supplied, provides one or more regular expressions, which are anchored at the end of the filename and tested. The first one that matches is used to separate the suffix from the basename. For example, to find any dot + three letter suffix we can use `\.\w\w\w`, or, as in the example above `\.\w{3}`.

To search for a selection of specific suffixes we can either supply a list, or combine all combinations into a single expression. Which we choose depends only on which is more likely to execute faster:

```
fileparse ($filename, '\.txt', '\.doc');   # list of suffixes
fileparse ($filename, '\.(txt|doc));   # combined regular expression

fileparse ($filename, '\.htm', '\.html', \.shtml);   # list of suffixes
fileparse ($filename, '\.s?html?));   # combined regular expression
```

Remember when supplying suffixes that they are regular expressions. Dots in particular must be escaped if they are intended to mean a real dot (however, see the `basename` subroutine detailed next for an alternative approach).

In addition to `fileparse`, `File::Basename` supplies two specialized subroutines, `basename` and `dirname`, which return the leading path and the basename only:

```
$path = dirname($filename);
$leaf = basename($filename, @suffixes);
```

`basename` returns the same result as the first item returned by `fileparse` except that metacharacters in the supplied suffixes (if any) are escaped with `\Q...\E` before being passed to `fileparse`. As a result, suffixes are detected and removed from the basename only if they literally match:

```
# scan for .txt and .doc with 'fileparse'
($path, $leaf, $suffix) = fileparse($filename, '\.(txt|doc)');

# scan for .txt and .doc with 'basename'
$leaf = basename($filename, '.txt', '.doc');
```

`dirname` returns the same result as the second item returned by `fileparse` (the leading directory) on most platforms. For UNIX and MSDOS, however, it will return `'.'` if there is no leading directory or a directory is supplied as the argument. This differs from the behavior produced by `fileparse`:

```
# scan for leading directory with 'fileparse'
print (fileparse('directory/file');   # produce 'file'
print (fileparse('file')[1]);   # produce 'file'
print (fileparse('directory/')[1];   # produce 'directory/'

# scan for leading directory with 'dirname'
print dirname('directory/file');   # produce 'file'
print dirname('file');   # produce '.'
print dirname('directory/');   # produce '.'
```

The filesystem convention for the pathname can be set to one of several different operating systems with the `fileparse_set_fstype` configuration subroutine. This can take one of the following case-insensitive values, corresponding to the appropriate platform:

Value	Platform
AmigaOS	Amiga syntax
MacOS	Macintosh syntax
MSWin32	Microsoft Windows long filenames syntax
MSDOS	Microsoft DOS short filenames (8.3) syntax
OS2	OS/2 syntax
RISCOS	Acorn RiscOS syntax
VMS	VMS syntax

If the syntax is not explicitly set with `fileparse_set_fstype` then a default value is deduced from the special variable `$^O` (see Appendix B for more on `$^O`). If `$^O` is none of the above, filesytem types UNIX style syntax is assumed. Note that if the pathname contains / characters then the format is presumed to be UNIX style whatever the filesystem type specified.

For a more comprehensive approach to portable filename handling, take a look at the `File::Spec` module, covered in Chapter 24.

Filename Globbing

The majority of shells possess a 'wildcard' syntax for specifying multiple files. For instance, `*.doc` means all files ending with `.doc`. Perl provides this same functionality through the file glob operator `glob`, which returns a list of all files that match the glob file pattern that we specify:

```
@files = glob '*.pod';   # return all POD documents
```

The glob pattern (not to be confused with a regular expression search pattern) accepts any pattern that would normally be accepted by a shell, including directories, wildcard metacharacters such as asterisks (zero-or-more), question marks (zero-or-one), and character classes. Here are some more examples demonstrating the different kinds of glob operation that we can perform:

```
# match html files in document roots of all virtual hosts
@html_files = glob '/home/sites/site*/web/*.html';

# match all files in current directory with a three letter extension
@three_letter_extensions = '*.???';

# match all files beginning with a to z
@lcfirst = '[a-z]*';

# match 'file00 to file 49'
@files = glob 'file[0-4][0-9]';

# match any file with a name of three or more characters
@files = glob '???*';
```

Other extended syntaxes can also be used if we use one of the glob operator's optional flags, covered later in the section. See GLOB_BRACE in particular for a useful alternative to character classes.

'glob' Syntax

The glob operator has two different forms. We can call it directly using glob, as we have already seen. More usually, however, we use angle brackets in the style of the readline operator:

```
@files = glob '*.pl'   # explicit glob
@files = <*.pl>   # angle-bracket glob
```

How does Perl tell the difference between a readline and a glob? When Perl encounters an angle bracket construction it examines the contents to determine whether it is a filehandle or not. If so, it is a readline operation. Otherwise, it is a file glob. Which syntax we use is entirely arbitrary; The angle bracket version looks better in loops, but resembles the readline <> operator:

```
foreach (<*.txt>) {
    print "$_ is not a textfile!" if !-T;
}
```

One instance where we might want to use glob is when we want to perform a file glob on a variable. Because a variable between angle brackets looks like a filehandle (or at least, the name of a filehandle), we have to insert braces to force Perl to interpret the expression as a file glob and not a readline operation. In these cases it is usually syntactically simpler to use glob instead:

```
@files = <$filespec>;    # ERROR: attempts to read lines
@files = <${filespec}>;   # ok, but algebraic
@files = glob $filespec;   # better
```

The return value from the globbing operation is a list containing the names of the files that matched. Files are matched according to the current working directory if a relative pattern is supplied, otherwise they are matched relative to the root of the filesystem. The returned filenames reflect this too, incorporating the leading directory path if one was supplied:

```
@files = glob '*.html';    # relative path
@files = glob '/home/httpd/web/*.html';   # absolute path
```

glob combines well with file test operators and array-processing functions like map and grep. For example, to locate all text files in the current directory we can write:

```
@textfiles = grep {-f && -T _} glob('*');
```

The glob function does not recurse, however. To do the same thing over a directory hierarchy we can use the File::Find module with a wanted subroutine containing something similar:

```
sub wanted {
    push @textfiles, $File::Find::name if -f && -T _;
}
```

The `glob` operator was originally a built-in Perl function, but since version 5.6 it is implemented in terms of the `File::Glob` module, which implements UNIX-style file globbing and overrides the built-in core `glob`. An alternative module, `File::DosGlob`, implements Windows/DOS style globbing, with some extensions.

UNIX Style File Globbing

The standard `glob` does file globbing in the style of UNIX. Having said this, it will still work on other platforms. The forward slash is used as a directory separator in patterns, and will match matching files on the filesystem irrespective of the directory separator used naively. In addition, on DOS systems, the backslash is also accepted as a directory separator.

Although we use `File::Glob` by default whenever we make use of the `glob` operator in either of its guises, we can modify and configure the operator more finely by using the module directly. `File::Glob` defines four labels that can be imported to provide different features:

Label	Function
`:glob`	Imports symbols for the flags of `glob`'s optional flag argument. See the flags table later for a list and description of each flag.
`:case`	Treats the file glob pattern as case-sensitive. For example `*.doc` will match `file.doc` but not `file.DOC`.
`:nocase`	Treats the file glob pattern as case-insensitive. For example, `*.doc` will match both `file.doc` and `file.DOC`.
`:globally`	Overrides the core `glob` function. From Perl 5.6 this happens automatically. This will also override a previous override, for example by `File::DosGlob`.
	For example, to import the optional flag symbols and switch the file globbing operator to a case-insensitive mode, we would write:
	`use File::Glob qw(:glob :nocase);`

If not explicitly defined, the case sensitivity of `glob` is determined by the underlying platform (as expressed by the special variable `$^O`). If the value of `$^O` is MSWin32, VMS, os2, dos, riscos, or MacOS then case sensitivity is disabled, otherwise it is enabled. The `:case` and `:nocase` labels override this default if either is present. Temporary case sensitivity can be controlled by passing a flag to the `glob` operator instead, see the section below.

Extended File Globbing

The glob operator accepts a number of optional flags that modify its behavior. These flags are given as a second parameter to `glob` and may be bitwise ORed together to produce multiple effects. To import a set of constants to name the flags use `File::Glob` explicitly specifying the `:glob` label:

```
use File::Glob qw(:glob);
```

The core `glob` function takes only one argument, a prototype, which is still enforced even though it is now based on a two argument subroutine. To supply flags we call the `glob` subroutine in the `File::Glob` package, where the prototype does not apply. For example, to enable brace expansions and match case insensitively we would use:

```
@files = File::Glob::glob $filespec, GLOB_BRACE|GLOB_NOCASE;
```

The full list of flags is:

Flag	Function
GLOB_ERR	Causes glob to return an error if it encounters an error such as a directory that it cannot open. Ordinarily glob will pass over errors. See 'Handling Globbing Errors' below for details.
GLOB_MARK	Return matching directories with a trailing directory separator /.
GLOB_NOCASE	Perform case-insensitive matching. The default is to assume matches are case-sensitive, unless glob detects the underlying platform does not handle case-sensitive filenames, as discussed above. Note that the :case and :nocase import labels override the platform-specific default, and GLOB_NOCASE then applies on a per-glob basis.
GLOB_NOCHECK	Return the glob pattern if no file matches it. If GLOB_QUOTE is also set, the returned pattern is processed according to the rules of that flag. See also GLOB_NOMAGIC.
GLOB_NOSORT	Return files in the order in which they were found. By default files are returned in alphabetical order. In many cases the files will be returned in alphabetical order in any case; specifying this flag speeds up glob.
GLOB_BRACE	Expand curly braces. A list of alternatives separated by commas is placed between curly braces. Each alternative is then expanded and combined with the rest of the pattern. For example, to match any file with an extension of .exe, .bat or .dll we could use: @files = *.{exe, bat, dll} Likewise, to match Perl-like files: @perl_files = *.{pm, pl, ph, pod} See also File::DosGlob below for an alternative approach.
GLOB_NOMAGIC	As GLOB_NOCHECK, but the pattern is returned only if it does not contain any of the wildcard characters *, ?, or [.
GLOB_QUOTE	Treat backslashes \ as escape characters and interpret the following character literally, ignoring any special meaning it might normally have. On DOS/Windows systems, backslash only escapes metacharacters and is treated as a directory separator otherwise. See also File::DosGlob below for an alternative approach.
GLOB_TILDE	Expand the leading tilde ~ of a pattern to the user home directory. For example, ~/.myapp/config might be expanded to /home/gurgeh/.myapp/config.
GLOB_CSH	File globbing in the style of the UNIX C Shell csh. This is a combination of all four of the FreeBSD glob extensions for convenience: GLOB_BRACE|GLOB_NOMAGIC|GLOB_QUOTE|GLOB_TILDE

Handling Globbing Errors

If `glob` encounters an error it puts an error message in `$!` and sets the package variable `File::Glob::GLOB_ERROR` to a non-zero value:

GLOB_NOSPACE	Perl ran out of memory
GLOB_ABEND	Perl aborted due to an error

If the error occurs midway through the scan, and some files have already been found, then the incomplete glob is returned as the result. This means that getting a result from `glob` does not necessarily mean that the file glob completed successfully. In cases where this matters, check `$File::Glob::GLOB_ERROR`:

```
@files = glob $filespec;
if ($File::Glob::GLOB_ERROR) {
    die "Error globbing '$filespec': $! \n";
}
```

DOS-Style File Globbing

DOS-Style File Globbing is provided by the `File::DosGlob` module, an alternative to `File::Glob` that implements file globs in the style of Windows/DOS, with extensions. In order to get DOS-style globbing we must use this module explicitly, to override the UNIX-style globbing that Perl performs automatically (for instance, if we are running on a Windows system we may receive wildcard input from the user that conforms to a DOS rather than UNIX style):

```
use File::DosGlob;    # provide File::DosGlob::glob
use File::DosGlob qw(glob);   # override core/File::Glob's 'glob'
```

Unlike `File::Glob`, `File::DosGlob` does not allow us to configure aspects of its operation by specifying labels to the import list, and it does not even override the core `glob` unless explicitly asked, as in the second example above. If we do not override `glob`, we can call the `File::DosGlob` function by naming it in full:

```
@dosfiles = File::DosGlob::glob ($dosfilespec);
```

Even with `glob` specified in the import list, `File::DosGlob` will only override `glob` in the current package. To override it everywhere we can use GLOBAL_glob:

```
use File::DosGlob qw(GLOBAL_glob);
```

This should be used with extreme caution, however, since it might upset code in other modules that expects `glob` to work in the UNIX style.

Unlike the DOS shell, `File::DosGlob` works with wildcarded directory names, so a file spec of `C:/*/dir*/file*` will work correctly (although it might take some time to complete). It also understands DOS-style backslashes as directory separators, although these may need to be protected:

```
@dosfiles = glob ('my\dos\filepath\*.txt');   # single quoted
@dosfiles = <my\\dos\\filepath\\*.txt>;   # escaped
```

Any mixture of forward and backslashes is acceptable to `File::DosGlob`'s glob; translation into the correct pattern is done transparently and automatically:

```
@dosfiles = <my/dos/filepath\\*.txt>;   # a mixture
```

To search in filenames or directories that include spaces we can either escape them using a backslash (which means that we must interpolate the string and therefore protect literal backslashes):

```
@programfiles = <C:\\Program\ Files\\*.*>;
```

Or, if we use the `glob` literally we can also use double quotes, if the string is enclosed in single quotes (or the q quoting operator):

```
@programfiles = glob 'C:/"Program Files"/*.*';
```

This functionality is actually implemented via the `Text::ParseWords` module, covered in Chapter 18.

Finally, multiple `glob` patterns may be specified in the same pattern if they are separated by spaces. For example, to search for all `.exe` and `.bat` files we could use:

```
@executables = glob('*.exe *.bat');
```

Temporary Files

Temporary files are transient, created by applications for their own internal use, or as temporary status or informational holders. There used to be two basic approaches for creating temporary files in Perl, depending on whether we just want a scratchpad that we can read and write, or want to create a temporary file we can pass around. To do the first, we can create a filehandle with `IO::File` that points to a temporary file that exists only so long as the filehandle is open. To do the second we can deduce the name of a unique temporary filename and then open and close it like an ordinary file, using the POSIX `tmpnam` function (see later in the chapter). However, Perl 5.6.1 now provides us with a third and better approach that involves using `File::Temp`, which returns both a filename and a filehandle.

Creating a Temporary Filehandle

Temporary filehandles can be created with the `new_tmpfile` method of the `IO::File` module. `new_tmpfile` takes no arguments and opens a new temporary file in read-update (and binary, for systems that care) mode, returning the generated filehandle. In the event of an error undef is returned and `$!` is set to indicate the reason. For example:

```
$tmphandle = IO::File->new_tmpfile();
unless ($tmphandle) {
    print "Could not create temporary filehandle: $! \n";
}
```

The `new_tmpfile` method is a Perl interface to the underlying POSIX `tmpfile` library call on systems that provide `tmpfile`. On these (generally UNIX-like) systems, a file exists as long as something is using it, even if it no longer has a filename entered in the filesystem. `new_tmpfile` makes use of this fact to remove the filesystem entry for the file as soon as the filehandle is created, making the temporary file anonymous. This has the additional advantage that when the filehandle is closed the file ceases to exist, since there will no longer be any references to it. This behavior is not supported on platforms that do not support anonymous temporary files.

Temporary Filenames via the POSIX module

While IO::File's new_tmpfile is very convenient for a wide range of temporary file applications, it does not return us a filename that we can use or pass to other programs. To do that, we need to use the POSIX module and the tmpnam routine. Since POSIX is a large module, we can import just tmpnam with:

```
use POSIX qw(tmpnam);
```

The tmpname routine takes no arguments and returns a temporary filename guaranteed to be unique. For example;

```
$tmpname = tmpnam();
print $tmpname;    # produces something like '/tmp/fileV9vJXperl'
```

Filenames are created with a fixed and unchangeable default path, defined by the P_tmpdir value given in the C standard library's stdio.h header file. This path can be changed subsequently, but this does not guarantee that the file does not exist in the new directory. To do that we might resort to a loop like this:

```
do {
    $tmpname = tmpnam();
    $tmpname =~ m|/ ([^/]+) $| && $tmpname = $1;    # strip '/tmp'
    $tmpname = $newpath.$tmpname;    # add new path
} while (-e $tmpname);
```

This rather defeats the point of tmpnam however, which is to create a temporary filename quickly and easily in a place that is suitable for temporary files (/tmp on any vaguely UNIX-like system). It also does not handle the possibility that other processes might be trying to create temporary files in the same place. This is a significant possibility, and a potential source of race conditions. Two processes may call tmpnam at the same time, get the same filename in return, then both open it. To avoid this, we open the temporary file using sysopen and specify the O_EXCL flag, which requires that the file does not yet exist. Here is a short loop that demonstrates a safe way to open the file:

```
# get an open (and unique) temporary file
do {
    $tmpname = tmpnam();
    sysopen TMPFILE, $tmpname, O_RDWR|O_CREAT|O_EXCL;
} until (defined fileno(TMPFILE));
```

If another process creates the same file in between our call to tmpnam and the sysopen, the O_EXCL will cause it to fail and TMPFILE will not be open, and so the loop repeats (see the next section for a better approach). Note that if we only intend to write to the file, O_WRONLY would do just as well, but remember to import the symbols from the POSIX or Fcntl module. Once we have the file open we can use it:

```
# place data into the file
print TMPFILE "This is only temporary \n";
close TMPFILE;

# use the file - read it, write it some more, pass the filename to another
# process, etc.
# ...

# remember to tidy up afterwards!
unlink $tmpname;
```

Since we have an actual tangible filename we can pass it to other processes. This is a common approach when reading the output of another command created with a piped open. For example, here is an anonymous FTP command line client, which we can use to execute commands on a remote FTP server:

```perl
#!/usr/bin/perl
# client.pl
use warnings;
use strict;

use POSIX qw(O_RDWR O_CREAT O_EXCL tmpnam);
use Sys::Hostname;    # for 'hostname'

die "Simple anonymous FTP command line client\n".
    "Usage: $0 <server> <command>\n" unless scalar(@ARGV)>=2;

my ($ftp_server,@ftp_command)=@ARGV;

# get an open and unique temporary file
my $ftp_resultfile;
do {
    # generate a new temporary filename
    $ftp_resultfile = tmpnam();
    # O_EXCL ensures no other process successfully opens the same file
    sysopen FTP_RESULT, $ftp_resultfile, O_RDWR|O_CREAT|O_EXCL;
    # failure means something else opened this filename first, try again
} until (defined fileno(FTP_RESULT));

# run ftp client with autologin disabled (using -n)
if (open (FTP, "|ftp -n > $ftp_resultfile 2>&1")) {
    print "Client running, sending command\n";

    # command: open connection to server
    print FTP "open $ftp_server\n";
    # command: specify anonymous user and email as password
    my $email=getlogin.'@'.hostname;
    print FTP "user anonymous $email\n";
    # command: send command (interpolate list to space arguments)
    print FTP "@ftp_command\n";

    close FTP;
} else {
    die "Failed to run client: $!\n";
}

print "Command sent, waiting for response\n";
my @ftp_results = <FTP_RESULT>;
check_result(@ftp_results);
close FTP_RESULT;
unlink $ftp_resultfile;
print "Done\n";

sub check_result {
    return unless @_;

    print "Response:\n";
    # just print out the response for this example
    print "\t$_" foreach @_;
}
```

Using 'File::Temp'

As of Perl 5.6.1 we have a better approach to creating temporary files, using the `File::Temp` module. This module returns the name and filehandle of a temporary file together, eliminating the possibility of a race condition where the same temporary file is created by another process after we check for its existence but before we open it. Instead of using `sysopen` with the `O_EXCL` flag, as we showed in the previous section, `File::Temp` provides us with the following much simpler syntax using its `tempfile` function:

```
($FILEHANDLE, $filename) = tempfile();
```

However, `tempfile` can take arguments that we can use to gain more control over the created temporary file as shown in the following:

```
($FILEHANDLE, $filename) = tempfile($template, DIR => $dir, SUFFIX = $suffix);
```

The template should contain at least four trailing Xs, which will then be replaced with random letters, so `$template` could be something like `filenameXXXXX`. We can specify explicitly with `DIR` the directory where we would like the temporary file to be created. Otherwise, the file will be created in the directory specified for temporary files by the function `tmpdir` in `File::Spec` (see Chapter 24 for more on `File::Spec`). Finally, at times we might need our temporary file to have a particular suffix, possibly for subsequent processing by other applications. The option `SUFFIX` is there to provide this facility. Note that the chosen suffix would be added after the translation of Xs in the template. So, the following will create a temporary file called `fileXXXX.tmp` (where the four Xs are replaced with four random letters) in the directory `/test/files`:

```
($FILEHANDLE, $filename) = tempfile("fileXXXX", DIR => "/test/files", SUFFIX =
".tmp");
```

However, the recommended interface is to call `tempfile` in scalar instead of list context, returning only the filehandle:

```
$FILEHANDLE = tempfile("fileXXXX", DIR => "/test/files", SUFFIX = ".tmp");
```

The file itself will be automatically deleted when closed. No way to tamper with the filename means no possibility of creating a race condition.

To create temporary directories, `File::Temp` provides us with the `tempdir` function. Using the function without argument creates a temporary directory in the directory set by `tmpdir` in `File::Spec`:

```
$tempdir = tempdir();
```

As with `tempfile`, we can specify a template and explicit directory as arguments to `tempdir`. Here also the template should have at least four trailing Xs that will be translated into four random letters. The `DIR` option overrides the value of `File::Spec`'s `tmpdir`:

```
$tempdir = tempdir("dirXXXX", DIR => "/test/directory");
```

This will create a temporary directory called something like /test/directory/dirdnar, where dnar are four random letters that replaced the four Xs. If the template included parent directory specifications then they are removed before the directory is prepended to the template. In the absence of a template, the directory name is generated from an internal template.

Removing the temporary directory and all its files, whether created by File::Temp or not, can be achieved using the option CLEANUP => 1.

In addition to the functions tempfile and tempdir, File::Temp provides Perl implementations of the mktemp family of temp file generation system calls. These are shown in the following table:

mkstemp	Using the provided template, this function returns the name of the temporary file and a filehandle to it: ($HANDLE, $name) = mkstemp($template); If we are interested only in the filehandle, then we can use mkstemp in scalar context.
mkstemps	This is similar to mkstemp but accepts the additional option of a suffix that is appended to the template: ($HANDLE, $name) = mkstemps($template, $suffix);
mktemp	This function returns a temporary filename but does not ensure that the file will not be opened by a different process: $unopened = mktemp($template);
Mkdtemp	This function uses the given the template to create a temporary directory. The name of the directory is returned upon success and undefined otherwise: $dir = mktemp($template);

Finally, the File::Temp module provides implementations of the POSIX's tmpname and tmpfile functions. As mentioned earlier, POSIX uses the value of P_tmpdir in the C standard library's stdio.h header file as the directory for the temporary file. File::Temp, on the other hand, uses the setting of tmpdir. With a call to mkstemp using an appropriate template, tmpname returns a filehandle to the open file and a filename:

```
($HANDLE, $name) = tmpname();
```

In scalar context, tmpname uses mktemp and returns the full name of the temporary file:

```
$name = tmpname();
```

While this ensures that the file does not already exist, it does not guarantee that this will remain the case. In order to avoid a possible race condition, we should use tmpname in list context.

The File::Temp implementation of the POSIX's tmpfile returns the filehandle of a temporary file. There is no access to the filename, and the file is removed when the filehandle is closed or when the program exits:

```
$HANDLE = tmpfile();
```

For further information on File::Temp consult the documentation.

Manipulating Directories

Directories are similar to files in many ways, they have filenames, permissions and (on platforms that support it) owners, but they are significantly different in others.

At their rawest, files can generally be considered to be character based, with no other internal structure except possibly lines in the case of text files, a fact the readline operator makes use of. Directories on the other hand are record based, each record being the details of a particular entry (be it file, directory, link or special file) in the directory. Accordingly, Perl supports a selection of functions specifically oriented to handling directories in a record-oriented context. These provide an alternative way to scan through and examine files (discussed earlier in the chapter) – which we use depends entirely on our intent, and to a large extent our preferences. Prior to version 5.6, the glob function was implemented by calling a shell, a significant overhead versus the built-in directory functions. From 5.6, glob is based on a module. Though faster than using a shell, and more powerful than the directory functions, using glob is still the heavyweight solution.

As well as reading directories we can also create and destroy them. Perl supports these operations through the functions mkdir and rmdir, which should be synonymously familiar to those with either a MS-Dos or a UNIX background. For more advanced tasks, the File::Path module provides enhanced analogues for these two functions.

Finally, a discussion of directories is not complete without the concept of the current working directory. All of Perl's built-in functions that take a filename as an argument, from open to the unary file test operators, base their arguments relative to the current working directory whenever the given filename is not absolute (that is, does not start with a leading /). We can both find out and change the current working directory, either using Perl's built-in functions or with the more flexible Cwd module.

Reading Directories

Although we cannot open and read directories like ordinary files, we can do the equivalent, using directory handles. For each of the file-based functions open, close, read, seek, tell, and rewind there is an analogue that performs the same function for directories. For example, opendir opens a directory and returns a directory handle:

```
opendir DIRHANDLE, $dirname;
```

Although similar to filehandles in many respects, directory handles are an entirely separate subspecies; they only work with their own set of built-in functions and even occupy their own namespace, so we can quite legally have a filehandle and a directory handle with the same name:

```
open HANDLE, $filename;    # open a filehandle
opendir HANDLE, $dirname;   # open a directory handle

$line = <HANDLE>;   # read a line from $filename
$item = readdir HANDLE;   # read an entry from $dirname

close HANDLE;   # close file $filename
closedir HANDLE;   # close directory $dirname
```

Having said that, just because we can do something does not mean that we should. Giving a filehandle and a directory handle the same name is more than a little confusing.

If opendir fails for any reason (the obvious ones being that the directory does not exist or is in fact a file) it returns undef and sets $! to indicate the reason. Otherwise we can read the items in the directory using readdir:

```
if (opendir DIRHANDLE, $dirname) {
    foreach (readdir DIRHANDLE) {
        print "$dirname contains: $_ \n";
    }
}
```

readdir is similar in spirit to the readline operator, although we cannot use the <...> syntax to read from a directory filehandle. If we do, Perl thinks we are trying to read from a filehandle with the same name. However, like the readline operator, readdir can be called in either a scalar context, where it returns the next item in the directory, or in a list context, where it returns all remaining entries:

```
$diritem = readdir DIRHANDLE;    # read next item
@diritems = readdir DIRHANDLE;   # read all (remaining) items
```

Another example of list context is a foreach loop, as in the example above, of course.

Rather than return a line from a file, readdir returns a filename from the directory. We can then go on to test the filename with file test operators, or stat/lstat to find out more about it. However, if we do this we should take care to append the directory name first or use chdir, otherwise the file test will not take place where we found the file but in the current working directory:

```
opendir DIRHANDLE, '..';   # open parent directory
foreach (readdir DIRHANDLE) {
    print "$_ is a directory  \n" if -d "../$_";
}
closedir DIRHANDLE;
```

Or, using chdir:

```
opendir DIRHANDLE, '..';    # open parent directory
chdir '..';    # change to parent directory
foreach (readdir DIRHANDLE) {
    print "$_ is a directory \n" if -d;    # use $_
}
closedir DIRHANDLE;
```

Note that when we are finished with a directory handle we close it, again using a specialized version of close, closedir. In the event closedir fails, it also returns undef and sets $! to indicate the error. Otherwise it returns true.

Directory Positions

Directory filehandles also have positions, which can be manipulated with the functions seekdir, telldir, and rewinddir, direct directory analogues for the file position functions seek, tell, and rewind. Unlike their plain file counterparts, however, these functions only work on directories (the plain file counterparts also work on directories, but not very usefully), and a directory position set with seekdir must be deduced from telldir; any old arbitrary value is not OK:

```
# find current position of directory handle
$dpos = telldir DIRHANDLE;
# read an item, moving the position forward
$item = readdir DIRHANDLE;

# reset position back to position read earlier
seekdir DIRHANDLE, $dpos;

# reset position back to start of directory

rewinddir DIRHANDLE;
```

Although they are analogous, these functions are not as similar to their file-based counterparts as their names might imply. In particular, seekdir is not nearly as smart as seek; because it does not accept an arbitrary position we cannot seek from the current position, or from the end like we can with seek. seekdir is only good for setting a position previously found with telldir.

Directory Handle Objects

As an alternative to the standard directory handling functions we can instead use the IO::Dir module. This conveniently encapsulates directory filehandles in objects on which we can call methods in exactly the same way that IO::File does for ordinary filehandles:

```
$dirh = new IO::Dir($directory);
```

The main point of IO::Dir is to encapsulate directory handles behind an object-oriented interface, to simplify passing them around and avoid the problems that afflict all handles, file or directory, when we try to manipulate them directly. Each of the standard directory, handling functions is supported by a similarly named method in IO::Dir, minus the trailing dir, so instead of using opendir we can create a new, unassociated IO::Dir object and then use open:

```
$dirh = new IO::Dir;
$dirh->open ($directory);
```

Likewise, we can use read to read from a directory filehandle, seek, tell, and rewind to move around inside the directory and close to close it again:

```
$entry = $dirh->read;    # read an entry
$dpos = $dirh->tell;    # find current position
$dirh->seek($dpos);    # set position
$dirh->rewind;    # rewind to start
@entries = $dirh->read;    # read all entries
```

Directories as Tied Hashes

As an alternative to the object-oriented interface, IO::Dir also supports a tied hash interface, where the directory is represented by a hash and the items in it as the keys of the hash. The values of the hash are lstat objects created via the File::stat package, called on the key in question. These are created at the moment that we ask for it so as not to burden the system with unnecessary lstat calls. If the main purpose of interrogating the directory is to perform stat type operations (including file tests), we can save time by using this interface:

```
# list permissions of all files in current directory
my %directory;
tie %directory, IO::Dir, '.';

foreach (sort keys %directory) {
    printf ("$_ has permissions %o \n", $directory{$_}->mode & 0777);
}
untie %directory;
```

IO::Dir makes use of the tied hash interface to extend its functionality in other ways too. Assigning an integer as the value of an existing key in the hash will cause the access and modification time to be changed to that value. Assigning an array of two integers will cause the access and modification times to be altered to the first and second respectively. If, on the other hand, the entry does not exist then an empty file of the same name is created in the directory, again with the appropriate timestamps:

```
# set all timestamps to the current time:
$now = time;

foreach (keys %directory) {
    $directory{$_} = $now;
}

# create a new file, modified one day ago, accessed now:
$directory{'newfile'} = [$now, $now-24 * 60 * 60];
```

Deleting a key-value pair will also delete a file, but only if the option DIR_UNLINK is passed to the tie as a fourth parameter:

```
# delete backup files ending in .bak or ~
tie %directory, IO::Dir, $dirname, DIR_UNLINK;

foreach (keys %directory) {
    delete $directory{$_} if /(\.bak|~)$/;
}
untie %directory;
```

With DIR_UNLINK specified, deleting an entry from the hash will either call unlink or rmdir on the item in question, depending on whether it is a file or a directory. In the event of failure, the return value is undef and $! is set to indicate the error, as usual.

Finding the Name of a Directory or File from its Handle

As a practical example of using the directory functions, here is a solution to the problem of finding out the name of a directory or file starting from a handle, assuming we know the name of the parent directory (if we do not we just have to search for longer, see File::Find for one simple way to do that):

```
sub find_name {
($handle, $parentdir) = @_;

# find device and inode of directory
($dev, $ino) = lstat $handle;
open PARENT, $parentdir or return undef;
```

```
    foreach (readline PARENT) {
        # find device and node of parent directory entry
        ($pdev, $pino) = lstat '../$_';
        # if it is a match, we have our man
        close PARENT, return $_ if ($pdev == $dev && $pino == $ino);
    }
    close PARENT;
    return undef;    # didn't find it...strange!
    }

    $name = find_name (*HANDLE, "/parent/directory");
    close HANDLE;
```

First, we use lstat to determine the device and inode of the directory (or, possibly, the symbolic link leading to the directory, which is why we use lstat and not stat. Then we open the parent and scan each entry in turn using lstat to retrieve its device and inode. If we find a match, we must be talking about the same entry, so the name of this entry must be the name of the file or directory. (Well, OK, that is not strictly true. On systems that support multiple filenames for the same file we can only say we have found a filename.)

We can adapt this general technique to cover whole filesystems using the File::Find module. See earlier in the chapter for more on this highly useful module that makes extensive use of directory functions to carry out its work.

Creating and Destroying Directories

The simplest way to create and destroy directories is to use the mkdir and rmdir functions. These both create or destroy a single directory, starting at the current working directory if the supplied name is relative. For more advanced applications we can use the File::Path module, which allows us to create and destroy nested chains of directories.

Creating Single Directories

To create a new directory we use the mkdir built-in function. This takes a directory name as an argument and attempts to create a directory with that name. The pathname given to mkdir may contain parent directories, in which case they must exist for the directory named as the last part of the pathname to be created. If the name is absolute, it is created relative to the root of the filing system. If it is relative, it is created relative to the current working directory:

```
# relative - create directory 'scripts' in current working directory
mkdir 'scripts';

# absolute - create 'web' in /home/httpd/sites/$site, which must already exist
mkdir "/home/httpd/sites/$site/web";

# relative - create directory 'scripts' in subdirectory 'lib' in current
# working directory. 'lib' must already exist to succeed.
mkdir 'lib/scripts';
```

mkdir may be given an optional second parameter consisting of a numeric permissions mask, as described earlier in the chapter. This is generally given as an octal number specifying the read, write, and execute permissions for each of the user, group, and other categories. For example, to create a directory with 755 permissions we would use:

```
mkdir $dirname, 0755;
```

We can also use the mode symbols from the `Fcntl` module if we import them first. Here is an example of creating a directory with 0775 permissions, using the appropriate `Fcntl` symbols:

```
use Fcntl qw(:mode);
# $dirname with 0775 permissions
mkdir $dirname, S_RWXU | S_RWXG | S_ROTH | S_XOTH;
```

The second parameter to `mkdir` is a permissions mask, not a generic file mode. It is called a mask because we can remove bits from it to remove those permissions from the created directory. It also applies to permissions only, not the other specialized mode bits such as the `sticky` or `setuid` and `setgid` bits; to set these we must use `chmod` after creating the directory.

The `umask` setting may also remove bits, so the value supplied to `mkdir` does not define the permissions of the directory, only those we are willing to permit. The default mask is `0777`, which permits all access types unless modified by the `umask` setting. A `umask` setting of octal `022` would modify the stated permissions of a created directory from `0777` to `0755`, for example. This is generally better than specifying a more restricted permissions mask directly as it leaves permissions policy to the user.

Creating Multiple Directories

`mkdir` will only create one directory at a time. If we want to create multiple nested directories with `mkdir` we must create each one in turn:

```
# create 'a/b/c':
mkdir 'a';
mkdir 'a/b';
mkdir 'a/b/c';
```

Or alternatively:

```
foreach ('a', 'b', 'c') {
    mkdir $_;
    chdir $_;
}
```

Neither of these solutions is terribly elegant however, and neither takes account of problems like the directory already existing (which will cause `mkdir` to fail but will still produce the right result), the permissions of the parent directory not permitting creating, or a file existing with the same name. Fortunately we can avoid hard-coding a routine that solves all these problems by using the `File::Path` module instead.

`File::Path` provides two routines, `mkpath` and `rmtree`. `mkpath` takes a path specification, containing one or more directory names separated by a forward slash, a Boolean flag to enable or disable a report of created directories, and a permissions mask in the style of `mkdir`. It is essentially an improved `mkdir`, with none of the drawbacks of the simpler function. For example, to create a given directory path:

```
use File::Path;

# create path, reporting all created directories
$verbose = 1;
$mask = 0755;
mkpath ('/home/httpd/sites/mysite/web/data/', $verbose, $mask);
```

One major advantage mkpath has over mkdir is that it takes pre-existing directories in its stride, using them if present and creating new directories otherwise. It also handles directory naming conventions of VMS and OS/2 automatically. In other respects it is like mkdir, using the same permission mask and creating directories from the current working directory if given a relative pathname:

```
# silently create scripts in lib, creating lib first if it does not exist.
mkpath lib/scripts;
```

If mkpath is only given one parameter, as in the above example, the verbose flag defaults to 0, resulting in a silent mkpath, and like mkdir, the permissions mask defaults to 0777.

mkpath can also create multiple chains of directories if its first argument is a list reference rather than a simple scalar. For instance, to create a whole installation tree for a fictional application we could use something like this:

```
mkpath ([
    '/usr/local/apps/myapp/manual',
    '/usr/local/apps/myapp/scripts',
    '/usr/local/apps/myapp/bin',
    '/usr/local/apps/myapp/lib/scripts',
    '/var/log/myapp',
], 1, 0755);
```

In the event of an error, mkpath will croak and return with $! set to the reason of the failed mkdir. To trap a possible croak put the mkpath into an eval:

```
unless (defined eval {mkpath(@paths, 0, 0755)}) {
    print "Error from mkpath: $@ ($!) \n";
}
```

Otherwise, mkpath returns the list of all directories created. Note that if a directory already existed then it is not added to this list. As any return from mkpath indicates that the call was successful overall; an empty list means simply that all the directories requested already existed. Since we often do not care if directories were created or not, just so long as they exist, we usually do not actually check the return value, only trap the error as in the above example.

Destroying Single Directories

To delete a directory we use the rmdir function, which returns 1 on success and 0 otherwise, setting $! to indicate the reason for the error. rmdir takes a single directory name as an argument, or uses the value of $_ if no filename is given:

```
rmdir $dirname;   # remove dirname

rmdir;   # delete directory named by $_
```

rmdir typically fails if the given name is not a valid pathname or does not point to a directory (it might be a file, or a symbolic link to a directory). It will also fail if the directory is not empty.

Deleting nested directories and directories with contents is more problematic. If we happen to be on a UNIX system, logged in as superuser, and if we specified the -U option to Perl when we started our application then we can use unlink to remove the directory regardless of its contents. In general, however, the only recourse we have is to traverse the directory using opendir, removing files and traversing into subdirectories as we go. Fortunately we do not have to code this ourselves, as there are a couple of modules that will greatly simplify the process.

Destroying Multiple Directories

As well as mkpath, the File::Path module provides a second routine rmtree, that performs (loosely speaking) the opposite function. Whereas mkpath creates a series of nested directories, rmtree removes directories, and, by extension, any files in them. rmtree takes three parameters: the first, like mkpath, is a single scalar directory path. It comprises one or more directories separated by forward slashes, or alternatively a reference to an anonymous array of scalar directory paths. If a path starts with a / it is taken to be absolute, otherwise it is assumed to be relative to the current working directory.

The second is, just like mkpath, a Boolean verbosity flag, set to false by default. If enabled, rmtree reports on each file or directory it encounters, indicating whether it used unlink or rmdir to remove it, or whether it skipped over it. Symbolic links are deleted, but not followed.

The third parameter is a safety flag, also Boolean and false by default. If true, rmtree will skip over any file for which the program does not have write permission (or more technically, the program's effective user id does not have write permission), except for VMS, which has the concept of 'delete permission'. Otherwise it will attempt to delete it anyway, which depends not on the file's permissions or owner but on the permissions of the parent directory, like rmdir.

For example:

```
use File::Path;

$verbose = 1;
$safe = 1;
rmtree $path, $verbose, $safe;

# remove three directory trees silently and safely.
rmtree([ $path1, $path2, $path3 ], 0, 1);
```

On success, rmtree returns the number of files deleted. On a fatal error it will croak like mkpath and can be trapped in the same way. Other, non-fatal, errors are carped (via the Carp module) and must be trapped by a warning signal handler:

```
$SIG{__WARN__} = handle_warnings();
```

If the safety flag is not set, rmtree attempts to force the permissions of files directories to make them deletable. In the event of it failing to delete them afterwards it may also be unable to restore the original permissions, leading to potentially insecure permissions. In all such cases the problem will be reported via carp and trapped by the warning signal handler if present.

Moving Around Directories

All of Perl's directory handling functions from opendir to rmdir interpret relative pathnames (that is, pathnames that do not start with a /) as relative to the current working directory. This is generally the directory that the shell was in when it started our applications, otherwise it is simply inherited from the parent process (which technically includes shells too, of course; they are just a special case).

Like a shell, we can change the current working directory too, using the chdir function. chdir takes a directory path as its argument and attempts to change the current working directory accordingly. If the path is absolute it is taken relative to the root directory, otherwise it is taken relative to the current working directory. It returns true on success and false on failure; for example:

```
unless (chdir $newdir) {
   "Failed to change to $newdir: $! \n";
}
```

Note that although Windows preserves a current directory for each drive, the 'current directory' as understood by Perl is a combination of the current drive and the current directory on that drive. If we pass a directory to chdir without a drive letter, we remain on the current drive.

There is no direct way in Perl to determine what the current working directory is, though some shells maintain the current working directory in an environment variable like $ENV{'PWD'}. However, we can use either the POSIX module or the more specialized Cwd module to find out.

Using the POSIX module, we can find the current working directory by calling the getcwd routine, which maps onto the underlying getcwd or getwd (regional variations may apply) routine of the standard C library. This takes no parameters and returns the current working directory as a string:

```
use POSIX qw(getcwd);

$cwd = getcwd;
```

Alternatively, we can use the Cwd module. This is a specialized module dedicated to all issues surrounding the current working directory in a portable and more platform-independent way than the POSIX module allows for (since it will work even if getcwd is not available).

It supplies three different ways to determine the current directory. getcwd and fastcwd are pure Perl implementations that are therefore maximally portable. cwd attempts to use the most natural and safe method to retrieve the current working directory supported by the underlying platform, whether it be UNIX, Windows, VMS, OS/2, etc.

getcwd is an implementation of the real getcwd as provided by POSIX written purely in Perl. It works by opening the parent directory with opendir, then scanning each file in turn using readdir and lstat looking for a match with the current directory using the first two values returned (the dev and lno fields). From this it deduces the name of the current directory, and so on all the way to the top of the filing system.

getcwd avoids using chdir however, because having chdired out of the current directory, permissions may not allow it to chdir back in again. Instead it assembles an increasingly long string of /../../../ to access each directory in turn. This makes it safe, but slow.

fastcwd is also a pure Perl implementation. Instead of accessing each parent directory through an extending string of /.., it uses chdir to jump up to the parent directory and analyze it directly. This makes it a lot faster than getcwd, but may mean that the current working directory changes as a result if fastgetcwd cannot restore the current working directory back to what it was to start with due to the permissions of the directory. fastgetcwd is an alias for fastcwd.

cwd attempts to use the best safe and 'natural' underlying mechanism available for determining the current working directory, for instance calling pwd on a UNIX system. It does not use the POSIX module. If all else fails it uses its own Perl-only getcwd. This makes it the best solution for most applications, since it takes advantage of the underlying support if any is available, but can survive happily (albeit slowly) without.

All three methods will return the true path to the file, resolving and removing any symbolic links (should we be on a platform that supports them) in the pathname. All four functions (including the alias getfastcwd) are automatically imported when we use the module, and are called in the same way, taking no parameters and returning the current working directory:

```
use File::Path;   # import 'getcwd', 'fastcwd', 'fastgetcwd', and 'cwd'

$cwd = getcwd;   # slow, safe Perl
$cwd = fastcwd;   # faster but potentially unsafe Perl
$cwd = getfastcwd;   # alias for 'fastcwd'
$cwd = cwd;   # use native platform support
```

Sometimes we want to find the path to a directory other than the one we are currently in. One way to do that is to chdir to the directory in question; determine the current working directory, and then chdir back. However, we do not need to do this as File::Path allows us to do the same thing with the abs_path (or its alias realpath) and fast_abs_path functions, each of which can be imported into our application by explicitly naming them. Both take a path to a file or directory and return the true absolute path to it, resolving any symbolic links and instances of . or .. as they go:

```
use Cwd qw(abs_path realpath fast_abs_path);

# find the real path of 'filename'
$absdir = abs_path('symboliclink/filename');

# 'realpath' is an alias for 'abs_path'
$absdir = realpath('symboliclink/filename');

# find the real path of our great grand parent directory
$absdir = fast_abs_path('../../..');
```

The equivalent of getcwd is abs_path with an argument of ., and in fact this is exactly what getcwd is, a wrapper to abs_path. Similarly, the fastcwd is a wrapper for fast_abs_path, which has the same potential limitations regarding restoring the original current working directory noted above.

In addition to the various cwd functions and the abs_path routines, File::Path supplies one more routine, chdir, which improves the standard build-in chdir by automatically tracking changes in the environment variable $ENV{'PWD'} in the same manner as some shells do. We can have this chdir override the standard chdir by importing it specifically:

```
# override system 'chdir' with 'chdir' from File::Path
use File::Path qw(chdir);
```

After this, chdir will automatically update $ENV{'PWD'} each time we use it. The original chdir is still available as CORE::chdir, of course.

Summary

In this chapter we covered:

❑ Getting user and group information

❑ Testing files attributes using the unary file test operators and the `stat` and `lstat` functions

❑ Linking, unlinking, renaming, copying, moving, comparing, and finding files

❑ File globbing

❑ Creating temporary files and directories

❑ Reading, creating, destroying, and copying directories

14

Command–Line and Shell Interaction

Mention the word **interaction** and often windows, icons, mice, pointers and so on spring immediately to mind. The truth is that interaction does not have to be that complex a subject to work with. This chapter, and the next in fact, will explore the more simple forms of interacting with Perl through non-graphical means, as a user. This is a broader subject than it might first appear since it covers everything from the command-line processing, through to shells and commands and on to terminal programming.

In this chapter we will examine how to interact with Perl using command-line arguments and shells, and terminal programming will be dealt with in the next chapter. We begin by looking into the special array @ARGV. We then see how Perl processes command-line arguments using the Getopt::Std and Getopt::Long modules. In the section on shells, we see first how to create Perl shells and then how to integrate a shell into Perl.

ParsingCommand-line Arguments

When any Perl program is started, Perl passes any **parameters** (or **arguments**) to the program in the special @ARGV array, which is automatically defined by Perl before the script starts. Perl does not perform any special processing on passed arguments, nor does it look for special arguments – how we deal with passed arguments is entirely up to us. Of course, Perl scripts can still be started with arguments even when they are being run from other programs, so all this still applies even if our script is not being started interactively.

Command-line Conventions

There are several conventions for how command-line arguments are defined, but they all work on the idea of **options** (sometimes called **switches**) and values. In the UNIX world, an option is an argument that is, traditionally, one character long, prefixed with a minus, and optionally followed by a value:

> **program -a 1 -b -2 -c -d**

Options and values can be told apart because options have a minus prefix whereas values do not. If an option is followed by another option, it doesn't have a value. This form of command-line has limitations though. As it happens, the POSIX standard defines a fairly flexible convention for single letter, single minus options that allows bundling of valueless options and also permits values to follow options directly (with no space) or after an equals sign:

> **program -a1 -b=-2 -cd**

The advantage of eliminating a space as the option/value separator is that we can specify otherwise tricky values like negative numbers without ambiguity. The option -cd is a bundle of the options -c and -d. Because options are always single letters, and neither of these example options takes a value, the application can determine that the option is really a bundle of two.

A more recent convention for processing command-line arguments is provided by so-called GNU Long options. Here, a double minus is used as the prefix for long option names that may be descriptive words rather than just single letters.

> **program --option1=1 --option2=-2 --option3 --option4**

Long names break the single letter rule for option names, and so prevent both bundling and appending a value directly to an option. The advantage is that they are easier to remember, and considerably easier to understand. A long option like --verbose is much more comprehensible than -v.

In these examples we used - and --, but strictly speaking these are a UNIX convention. In the Windows world, the original prefix was the forward slash, so we would be typing commands like this:

> **program /a1 /b=-2 /c /d**

More modern Windows command-line applications, particularly those inspired by or ported from UNIX, understand both - and /. However, prefixes aside, the principle is just the same. It is important to realize that unlike wildcards, - and / are not characters interpreted by the shell (be it a DOS or UNIX shell). They are just a convention for the application itself to take note of and handle itself, and as such we are free to handle any kind of prefix or prefixes we like. Adhering to a consistent and recognizable convention is just friendlier for anyone else who wants to use our programs.

Simple option processing is easy to arrange in Perl without additional support, just by inspecting the contents of the @ARGV array. However, once we start adding concepts like options that may take optional values, options that may be defined many times, or options that only accept numeric values, things become more complex and it becomes increasingly hard to define unambiguous command-lines. Fortunately, a lot of the hard work in defining consistent command-line arguments can be done for us by the Getopt::Std and Getopt::Long modules. Both these modules provide extensive support for command-line argument processing, as well as syntax checking.

The '@ARGV' Array

The @ARGV array contains all the arguments that were passed to our program when it was started. The definition of what defines an 'argument' depends not on Perl but on the shell that was used to start our program. However, in most cases spaces separate arguments from one another (UNIX shell programmers may care to look up the IFS environment variable in the shell documentation). For example, if we were to run a Perl program called myscript like this:

> perl myscript -u sventek -p cuckoo

This results in an @ARGV array containing the four values -u, sventek, -p, and cuckoo. Unlike the C language, the first argument is not the program name. Instead, Perl places that information in the special variable $0 (or $PROGRAM_NAME with the English module), in the style of UNIX shells. Unlike shells though, Perl uses $1 and onwards for quite a different purpose, as we saw in Chapter 11 on regular expressions. Perl's reason for assigning the program name to $0 and removing it from the argument list is twofold. In part, it is in deference to shell programming but more significantly it allows us to do clever things with @ARGV that the presence of the program name would make inconvenient. Most notable amongst these is reading input from files passed in @ARGV automatically using the readline operator.

To check the number of arguments we can either use scalar or find the highest element in the array (remember that Perl indexes from zero):

```
scalar(@ARGV);   # number of arguments passed
$#ARGV;    # highest element = no. of arguments -1
```

In this example we are obviously passing arguments that are key-value pairs, so we would probably want to turn them into a hash. This won't work if an odd number of elements were passed, so we need to check for that before blindly turning @ARGV into a hash. We probably ought to check that all the keys start with a minus, since that is the convention we are following. The following code handles all these issues:

```
#!/usr/bin/perl
# turntohash.pl
use warnings;
use strict;

my %args;

if (scalar(@ARGV)%2) {
   die "Odd number of arguments passed to $0";
} else {
   %args = @ARGV;   # convert to hash
   foreach (keys %args) {
      # check each of the keys
      die "Bad argument '$_' does not start with -" unless /^-/;
   }
}
```

This example has its limitations, however. It doesn't handle multiple instances of the same argument. For example, it overrides earlier definitions with later ones. Additionally, we don't make any attempt to check that the arguments have valid names, though we could easily do that within the loop. However, for simple argument parsing, it does the job.

Passing Arguments to Perl Itself

Since Perl passes everything supplied on the command-line to our own programs, we cannot pass arguments to Perl itself when we run a Perl script directly, although the **shebang** line (#!/usr/bin/perl) handles this problem for us elegantly, if we are able to use it. Otherwise, there are two possible solutions to this problem. One is to simply start our script via Perl while supplying any arguments we like to Perl:

> **perl -Mstrict -MMyModule -w myperlscript -u sventek -p cuckoo**

Note that Perl determines the name of the program because it is the first bare argument (that is, not prefixed with a -) to appear on the command-line without an option taking an argument immediately before it. Therefore it must be the program name. All arguments after it are arguments to the program, not to Perl, so this command does not do what we want:

> **perl -w myperlscript -Mstrict -MMyModule**

This actually passes -w to Perl, and -Mstrict and -MMyModule to our script, which is unlikely to be what we intended.

If the name of the program (in this case myperlscript) happens to resemble a command-line option or an optional value for the preceding option, we can make it explicit by using the special - - argument:

> **perl -Mstrict -MMyModule -w -- myperlscript -name sventek -pass cuckoo**

The - - argument is a convention, at least in the UNIX world, which means 'do not process anything past this point'. Perl uses - - to separate its own arguments from the script name and the script's own arguments. If we are using the -s option (see below) to set variables from the command-line, we also need to use - - to stop feeding arguments to -s and to leave them in @ARGV. The program itself is placed after, not before, the - -.

Although this works, it can be rather ugly, not to mention tedious to retype. As an alternative we can also specify arguments to pass to Perl by setting the environment variable PERL5OPT:

```
setenv PERL5OPT "-Mstrict -MPOSIX -w"    # UNIX (csh)
export PERL5OPT="-Mstrict -MPOSIX -w"    # UNIX (ksh/bash)
PERL5OPT="-Mstrict -MPOSIX -w"; export PERL5OPT   # UNIX (older ksh)
set PERL5OPT = -Mstrict -MPOSIX -w    # DOS/Windows
```

Perl sees the value of PERL5OPT when it starts and this is used with every Perl script, removing the need to type it in on a program-by-program basis. See Chapter 1 for more on Perl's environment variables. Having said all this, if we have the ability to set options in the shebang line of a script, this is by far and away the easiest route.

Setting Variables from '@ARGV'

The -s option causes Perl to cease scanning the command-line for options and to treat all options after it as variables set to the value following the option, or 1 if there is no following value. For example:

> **perl -s -debug -- myscript.pl**

This sets the variable $debug inside the script myscript.pl to the value 1. Alternatively, to set a different debug level, we could use:

> **perl -s -debug = 2 -- myscript.pl**

The $debug variable in this example is a global package variable; we can access it from within the script as $main::debug, or declare it with use vars or our (the preferred way from Perl 5.6 onwards). There is no limit to how many variables we may specify in this way.

An interesting, if slightly odd use of -s in the shebang line of a script is shown below. Remember that the use of −w is deprecated in Perl 5.6 and we should use use warnings instead:

```
#!/usr/bin/perl -ws
...
```

This causes Perl to interpret any command-line passed to the script as a series of variables to define. This is possibly useful for debugging applications that otherwise do not take arguments, though probably not a good idea for production code.

Reading Files from '@ARGV'

One of the most common classes of command-line utilities consists of scripts that process one or more files given as arguments. The UNIX commands cat, more, and strings all fall under this banner, as do the DOS utilities type, dir, and del.

Since this is such a common use of command-line arguments, Perl caters for it with a special shortcut when we use the <> operator to read from standard input. Specifically, if we use <>, Perl tries to open each element in @ARGV as a file in turn and returns the lines read. If @ARGV is empty, <> reads from standard input. This allows us to write incredibly terse and to the point scripts because we can eliminate the need to open filehandles or check that the arguments are really files; Perl will handle it for us. For example, here is a simple version of the UNIX cat or DOS type command implemented in Perl:

```
print while <>;
```

Short, isn't it? We can try out this one line program on any text file and it will dutifully print out its contents. It works because <> attempts to read input from the contents of the @ARGV array, taking each entry to be a filename. If nothing is contained in @ARGV then standard input is used instead. Either way, the while loop aliases each line read to $_, which the print prints out:

> **perl -e 'print while <>' file1.txt file2.txt**

Indeed, this is such a common thing to do that Perl lets us place an implicit while (<>) {...} loop around code with the -n or -p options (other options that work in conjunction with -n and -p are -a, -l and -o; see Appendix A for more information on these options). So we could just have said:

> **perl -ne 'print' file1.txt file2.txt**

Be wary however, when using these kinds of example with Windows. The above scripts need to be modified in order for them to work properly. Single quotes do not allow the script within them to be interpolated on Windows so we need to use double quotes to fix the problem. Bear this in mind when executing such scripts and modify them like this:

> **perl -e "print while <>" file1.txt file2.txt**

> **perl -ne "print" file1.txt file2.txt**

Just as with normal file reads, the line count variable $. also works here, so we can print out a file with line numbers by modifying our 'program' to read:

```perl
#!/usr/bin/perl
# cat.pl
use warnings;
use strict;

print "$. : $_" while <>;
```

Or, as a command-line script:

> **perl -ne 'print "$.:$_"' file1.txt file2.txt**

This time in the Windows case we also need to escape some double quotes as well as replace single quotes with doubles. The command-line is then implemented as follows:

> **perl -ne "print \"$.:$_\"" file1.txt file2.txt**

Of course, if we feed this program a binary file it will still work, though the results we see may be less than pretty. The current file being processed is stored in the scalar variable $ARGV, so we can improve our one line program still further by including the filename too:

```perl
print "$ARGV:$.:$_" while <>;
```

Note that if we pass more than one file, the script will happily read each of them in turn under the same filehandle (defined automatically by Perl and made available to us as ARGV). However, Perl does all the opening and closing of files read in this way behind the scenes, so all the files are treated as being part of the same file access. This means that variables like $. will not reset from one file to the next. Depending on what we want to do this can be an advantage or a problem, but if we want to fix this issue we can do so with the eof function:

```perl
#!/usr/bin/perl
# bettercat.pl
use warnings;
use strict;

while (<>) {
    print "$ARGV:$.:$_";
    close (ARGV) if eof;
}
```

This works by closing the current file (via the automatically defined ARGV) if there is no more data to read in it. The eof without a parameter uses the last file read, which happens to be the same file pointed to by ARGV, so we could also have said eof(ARGV) to produce the same effect. Note that eof with empty parentheses will only detect the end of all input (in other words, the end of the last file).

We can manipulate the @ARGV array before using <> to read the filenames in it any way we like, for example to remove non-filename parameters. Here is a simple string-matching program in the style of the UNIX grep command that does just that. The first argument is the pattern to search for. Anything after that is a file to search in, so we just remove the first argument with shift and let <> see the rest:

```
#!/usr/bin/perl
# simplegrep1.pl
use warnings;
use strict;

die "Usage: $0 <pattern> <file> [<file> ...]\n" unless scalar(@ARGV)>1;
my $pattern = shift @ARGV;   # get pattern from first argument
while (<>) {
    print "$ARGV:$. $_" if /$pattern/;
    close (ARGV) if eof;
}
```

Note that when we come to use this program, * will work fine for UNIX shells, since they automatically expand the wildcard and pass an actual list of files to our program. On Windows systems, the standard shell is not so smart and just passes the * as-is. If we want to trap these instances we can check for occurrences of *, ?, and so on and use the glob function in conjunction with the File::DosGlob module to make up for the shell's shortcomings. See Chapter 24 for more information.

'@ARGV' and Standard Input

For good measure we have also checked in the above example that we have been given enough arguments to actually continue. This particular script needs two arguments, so we die with an error, if we get fewer. This forces the user to enter both a pattern and a filename. However, we can force Perl to open standard input by placing the special filename - into @ARGV before we use <>. Here's a modification to the above script that handles this possibility:

```
$pattern = shift @ARGV;
die "Usage: $0 <pattern> [<file> ...]\n" unless @ARGV>1;
@ARGV=('-') unless @ARGV;   # not actually necessary – see below
```

When Perl sees the filename - in @ARGV, it interprets it as a request to read from standard input. We can supply it in the command-line, or as above, place it into @ARGV within the program if circumstances require it. This allows us to use the script in these (admittedly UNIX-like) ways:

> **cat filename | simplegrep pattern -**
> **simplegrep pattern - < filename**

In fact, the line to add - to @ARGV in the example above is not needed. If nothing is present in @ARGV at all, Perl reads from standard input anyway as we already mentioned. When we use <> for the first time, Perl sees that @ARGV is empty and automatically inserts - to cause the read from standard input to take place. If we print $ARGV, we can see that this is the case. This happens when <> is first used, so as long as @ARGV is empty before we use the readline operator, standard input is taken care of for us and all we have to do is change the usage line to allow only one argument:

```
#!/usr/bin/perl
# simplegrep2.pl
use warnings;
use strict;

die "Usage: $0 <pattern> [<file> ...]\n" unless scalar(@ARGV);
my $pattern = shift @ARGV;   #get pattern from first argument
while (<>) {
    print "$ARGV:$.$_" if /$pattern/;
    close (ARGV) if eof;
}
```

Simple Command-line Processing with 'Getopt::Std'

Hand-coded command-line processing is fine when we only have relatively simple command-line arguments to process, but it becomes tricky to handle a larger number of arguments or a more complex syntax. In these cases it is a far better idea to make use of one of the Getopt modules to simplify the task. Fortunately, the standard Perl library comes with two modules specifically designed to simplify the task of reading and parsing command-line arguments: Getopt::Std and Getopt::Long.

The Getopt::Long module is a much more comprehensive and considerably larger module that provides support for long argument names, stricter argument value checking, abbreviations, aliases, and other various features. It supports both POSIX-style arguments and (as its name suggests) GNU Long arguments. We will look first at the simpler Getopt::Std module before we examine in detail Getopt::Long.

The Getopt::Std module is a simple and lightweight module that provides support for single character arguments, with or without values, in compliance with the POSIX standard. That is, any program using it (properly) can be certain that its command-line conforms to the POSIX standard. The module Getopt::Std permits arguments to be clustered together if no values are required and follows the -- convention for ceasing processing of arguments. Parsed arguments are defined as global scalar variables based on the argument name or, if supplied, stored in a hash as key-value pairs.

The use of either module does not preclude the possibility of reading files through <> as described above. After one of the two modules has been used to process command-line options, anything left (or inserted into) @ARGV can then be used with <> as before.

The Getopt::Std module provides command-line processing for traditional minus-prefixed single character options, followed optionally by a value. It provides two functions to define the list of arguments. The first is getopt, which allows us to specify a set of options that take parameters. Any other options (as defined by the fact that they start with -) are considered to be Boolean options that enable something and take no argument. The second is the more versatile getopts, which allows us to explicitly define both Boolean and value options and so can emit a warning about anything that does not appear to be either.

Basic Processing with 'getopt'

The function getopt lets us define a set of arguments that all take an optional value. To use getopt we supply it with a list of letters that correspond to the options that we wish to process. Any option that is not in the list is assumed to be a Boolean flag. For example:

```
use Getopt::Std;
getopt("atef");
```

This defines the options -a, -t, -e, and -f as arguments that take parameters. Then getopt will accept a value immediately after the argument, or separated by either a space or an equals sign. That is, all the following are acceptable:

```
-abc
-a = bc
-a bc
```

When a program containing this code is called, the command-line is parsed and a global scalar variable of the form $opt_X is set, where X is the name of the argument. If we create a script containing the above code and feed it some arguments we can see this in action:

> **perl myscript -a bc –e fg -k 99**

This creates three global scalar variables, assuming that Perl will allow it. If we have use strict or use strict vars in effect then we need to pre-declare these variables with our (or use vars, prior to Perl 5.6) in order to avoid a run-time error. The equivalent direct assignments would have been:

```
$opt_a = "bc";   # option a given value bc
$opt_e = "fg";   # option e given value fg
$opt_k = 1;      # 'k' not in list of arguments, therefore Boolean
```

The moment getopt sees something that is not an option or an option value it terminates and leaves the remainder of @ARGV untouched. In this example @ARGV is left holding 99, because it is neither an option nor a value (since k was not specified in the list of options to getopts and so does not take a value, even if it looks like it from the command-line).

Creating global scalar variables is a little inelegant. As an alternative, we can supply getopt with a reference to a hash as its second argument, say %opt. This causes getopt to populate the hash with the parsed values instead. The processed arguments appear as keys and values in %opts. Again, given the same example arguments as before, $opts{'k'} is defined to be 1 and @ARGV ends up containing 99 as the only unprocessed argument. The following script shows this in action, and also prints out the parsed arguments and whatever is left in @ARGV afterwards, if anything:

```
#!/usr/bin/perl
# getopt.pl
use strict;
use warnings;

use Getopt::Std;

my %opts;
getopt("atef", \%opts);

print "Arguments:\n";
foreach (keys %opts) {
    print "\t$_ => $opts{$_}\n";
}

print "ARGV:\n";
foreach (@ARGV) {
    print "\t$_\n";
}
```

> **perl getopt.pl -a bc –e fg -k 99**
Arguments:
       e => fg
       a => bc
       k => 1
ARGV:
       99

It is worth noting that if we had put **-k 99** as the first argument in the list, the **99** and everything following it, including the **-a** and **-e** options and their arguments, would have remained unprocessed in @ARGV.

If we don't specify a value for an argument that takes one, it defaults to 1, so -a and -a1 are effectively equivalent.

Slightly Smarter Processing with 'getopts'

The more advanced getopts allow us to define both Boolean and value options in its specification. Due to this fact, it can also check for invalid options, which immediately makes it more useful than getopt. Another result of this is that getopts permits us to bundle options together, which we will see in a moment, and thus provides POSIX-compliant command-line processing.

The options are again defined as a list but this time value options are suffixed with a colon, with any letter not suffixed taken to be Boolean. To define three Boolean flags a, e, and t, and a value option f we would use:

```
getopts ("aetf:");   # 'aet' Boolean, 'f' value, defines $opt_X scalars

if ($opt_a) {
...
}
```

Like getopt, getopts takes an optional second parameter of a hash to hold the parsed values; otherwise it defines global scalar variables of the form $opt_X.

```
getopts("aetf:", \%opts);   # ditto, puts values in %opts
```

The order of letters is not important, so the following are all equivalent:

```
getopts("f:ate");
getopts("af:et");
getopts("taf:e");
```

Any option that is not specified in the list will cause getopts to emit the warning Unknown option :X, where X is the option in question. Since this is a warning we can trap it using one of the techniques discussed in Chapter 16, for example by defining and assigning a subroutine to $SIG{__WARN__} if we want to process the unrecognized option ourselves or make the warning fatal by turning it into a die.

We mentioned bundles a moment ago. Bundling is the combination of several single letter arguments into one, and is applicable only if all but the last of the concatenated arguments do not take a value. Unlike getopt, getopts permits bundling (but at the cost of not permitting the value to follow immediately after the option). That is, instead of entering:

> **perl myscript -a -t -e**

We can enter:

> **perl myscript -ate**

A value option can be bundled, but only if it is the last option in the bundle. It follows from this that we can only permit one value option in any given bundle. With the specification **taef** we can legally enter:

> **perl myscript -aetf value**   # ok
> **perl myscript -taef value**   # also ok, different order

But not:

> **perl myscript -fate value**   # value does not follow f argument

The -- argument is recognized and processed by Getopt::Std, causing it to cease processing and to leave all remaining arguments in @ARGV. The -- itself is removed. We can pass on the remaining arguments to another program using system, exec, or open, or read them as files using <> if we wish:

> **perl myscript -aetf value -- these arguments are not processed**

This leaves @ARGV containing these, arguments, are, not, and processed.

More Complex Command-line Processing with 'Getopt::Long'

The Getopt::Long module performs the same role as Getopt::Std but with better parsing, error checking, and richer functionality. It handles single letter options – including bundling – but in addition supports GNU Long options.

The key distinguishing feature between the two modules is that Getopt::Long accepts the double minus prefixed long option naming style. To illustrate what we mean, here are two versions of a putative length argument. Only the first can be handled by Getopt::Std, but both can be parsed by Getopt::Long:

```
-l    # traditional short option
--length = value   # more descriptive long option
```

The Getopt::Long module is very flexible and implements a number of optional features such as abbreviation, case sensitivity, and strict or loose option matching. In order to control the behavior of the module we can make use of the Getopt::Long::Configure subroutine, which allows us to alter the way that command-line arguments are processed. Also Getopt::Long actually provides more features than we may actually want to allow. Accordingly, we can disable these features with Getopt::Long::Configure, or more simply by defining the environment variable POSIXLY_CORRECT. We'll see how to do both of these nearer the end of the section.

Simple Argument Processing

The module Getopt::Long defines one function, GetOptions, to parse the contents of @ARGV. In its simplest form it takes a list of options and scalar references, placing the value of each option into the corresponding reference. Without additional qualification each option is handled as a Boolean flag and the associated scalar is set to 1 if seen. The following code snippet defines two Boolean options; verbose and background:

```perl
#!/usr/bin/perl
# definebool.pl
use warnings;
use strict;

use Getopt::Long;

my ($verbose, $background);    # parse 'verbose' and 'background' flags
GetOptions (verbose => \$verbose, background => \$background);

print "Verbose messages on \n" if $verbose;
```

After this code is executed the variables $verbose and $background are either undefined, or set to the value 1. We can easily use them in conditions, as illustrated above.

If the command-line was processed successfully, GetOptions returns with a True value, otherwise it returns undef. We can therefore use it in conditions and terminate the program if all is not well, for example:

```perl
# print some help and exit if options are not valid
usage(), exit unless GetOptions (verbose => \$verbose, background => \$bg);
```

A warning will be raised by GetOptions for anything that it does not understand, so we are saved from the task of having to describe the problem ourselves.

If we do not supply a reference GetOptions will define a global scalar with the name $opt_<option name> instead, in a similar manner to Getopt::Std. This mode of use is generally deprecated on the basis that defining global variables is not good programming practice, but for completeness, this is how it is done:

```perl
#!/usr/bin/perl
# globvar.pl
use warnings;
use strict;

use Getopt::Long;

our $opt_verbose;    # or 'use vars', before Perl 5.6
GetOptions ('verbose');
```

Note that if we are using strict variables (as we really should) then the our declaration is necessary to prevent Perl producing a run-time error when it tries to set the variable. Note that we need to use our or use vars because the module sets a package variable, and could not see a lexical my variable even if it wanted to.

As an alternative to defining scalar variables using either of the above approaches, GetOptions also accepts a hash reference as its first parameter and will store parsed arguments in it, if present. This is similar to Getopt::Std, but the arguments are inverted compared to getopt or getopts:

```perl
#!/usr/bin/perl
# hashref.pl
use warnings;
use strict;

use Getopt::Long;

my %opts;
GetOptions(\%opts, 'verbose', 'background');
```

One special case bears mentioning here. We might want to handle the case of a single minus (conventionally used to mean 'take input from standard input, not a file'), as used by several UNIX commands and demonstrated earlier with `Getopt::Std`. We can do that using an option name of an empty string:

```
GetOptions('' => \$read_from_stdio);
```

For the time being we have limited our discussion to scalars, but `GetOptions` is also capable of handling multiple values in both list and hash forms. We'll see how to do that a little later, after we have dealt with option prefixes and defining option values.

Option Prefixes

With the exception of the single bare minus, options can be specified with either a single or a double minus, or if we define it first, any prefix we like. The double minus prefix is treated as a special case compared to all other prefixes, however. Firstly, options that have been prefixed with a double minus are treated as case-insensitive by default, whereas all other prefixes are case-sensitive, though we can alter case sensitivity using `Getopts::Long::Config`. This means that `--o` and `--O` both define the option o, whereas `-o` and `-O` define the options o and O. The double minus prefix is also treated differently in option bundling.

The archaic prefix + is also accepted by default, but is now deprecated. We can explicitly disallow it, as well as redefining the prefixes we do allow (for instance the backslash) by specifying our own prefix. There are two ways to do this, the first of which is to specify the new prefix as the first argument to `GetOptions`. However, this is deprecated in modern usage. A better way is to use the `Getopt::Long::Configure` subroutine. To redefine the prefix this way we put something like:

```
# configure a prefix of '/'
Getopt::Long::Configure ("prefix=/");
```

We can also specify a range of prefixes by configuring the `prefix_pattern` option of `Getopt::Long`. This takes a regular expression as an argument, so we just need to express the options we want to allow in terms of a regular expression. To allow single, double, and backslash prefixes, we can use `(-|--|\/)`, as in this example:

```
# configure prefixes of --, - or / (but not +
Getopt::Long::Configure ("prefix_pattern=(--|-|\/)");
```

Note that because `prefix_pattern` is used in a regular expression we must use parentheses to encapsulate the options, and escape any characters that have special significance for regular expressions.

An alternative to simply disabling a prefix is to handle it ourselves before calling `GetOptions`. For example, a few utilities use + to explicitly negate an option. We can handle that by replacing + by `--no` and defining the option to be Boolean:

```
#!/usr/bin/perl
# negate.pl
use warnings;
use strict;

use Getopt::Long;
```

```
# translate + negation to Getopt::Long compatible --no negation
foreach (@ARGV) {
    s/^\+/--no/;   # substitute elements of @ARGV directly
}

my %opts;
GetOptions (\%opts, 'verbose', 'background');
```

This requires defining the options we want to be able to negate as negatable Boolean values. We see how to do that, as well as handle other types of option, next.

Defining Option Values

All the options we have seen so far have been Boolean options. By adding extra information to the option name in the form of attributes we can define (and enforce) different kinds of option, including negatable options, incremental options, and integer value options.

Negatable Boolean Options

A **negatable Boolean option** is one that can be switched off as well as being switched on. The Boolean options we have seen so far are one-way – once we have specified what they are we cannot 'undo' this. That might seem like a strange thing to want to do, but if we are editing a previous command-line or calling an external program from within another, it is often more convenient to disable an option explicitly than check through the arguments to see if it has been set to start with. Some features just make more sense enabled by default too, so we might want to define options for them simply to turn them off.

Negatable Boolean options are defined by suffixing the option name with an exclamation mark. We can use this to create an option that is normally on, but which we can turn off by prefixing the option name with no:

```
$quiet = 1;
GetOptions ("quiet!" => \$quiet);
```

This now allows us to specify -noquiet to switch off quiet mode:

> perl myscript -noquiet

And -quiet to turn it on again:

> perl myscript -noquiet -otheroption -quiet

Sometimes it is useful to know whether an option variable is not set because that is its default value or because it was explicitly cleared by the option. Actually, this is very easy – disabling a negatable option sets the corresponding value to zero, so by setting the original value to the undefined value we can check to see if the value was specified on the command-line or not:

```
#!/usr/bin/perl
# check.pl
use warnings;
use strict;
```

```
use Getopt::Long;

my $option = undef;   # make it undef explicitly, just to make it clear
GetOptions ("option!" => \$option);

if (defined $option) {
    # the option was seen on the command-line
} else {
    # the option was not specified
}
```

Since undef evaluates as zero in a conditional context, we can still carry out simple 'is the option set?' tests in places where we don't care whether the option was specified or not, and still retain that information for use in places where we do. If we are using a hash to define all our options then we don't even need to go this far; we can just test the option name with exists to see if it has been set or not:

```
#!/usr/bin/perl
# exists.pl
use warnings;
use strict;

use Getopt::Long;
my %opts;
GetOptions (\%opts, 'option!');
if (exists $opts{'option'}) {   # the option was seen on the command-line
}
```

Incremental Options

Incremental options increase by one each time they are seen on the command-line, starting from the original value. A classic case of such an option is a **verbose** flag, where the level of information a program returns increases according to the level of verbosity we set, which is equal to the number of verbose options we use.

In order to prevent Perl returning an undefined value error, the starting value of an incremental option variable should be initialized to a defined value, most probably zero. Here is an example of implementing a verbose option as an incremental option:

```
#!/usr/bin/perl
# increment.pl
use warnings;
use strict;

use Getopt::Long;

my $verbose = 0;   # default verbosity = off
GetOptions ("verbose+" => \$verbose);
```

Now, to set different levels of verbosity we just specify the option the required number of times:

> **perl increment.pl -verbose**   # $verbose == 1
> **perl increment.pl --verbose -verbose**   # $verbose == 2
> **perl increment.pl --verbose --verbose -verbose**   # $verbose == 3

In fact we can save a lot of typing and just specify -v several times because GetOptions automatically handles abbreviations for us, as we will see shortly.

Integer, Floating-Point, and String Options

To define an option that takes a value, we modify the option name by suffixing it with either an equals sign for a mandatory value or a colon if the value is optional. Following the equals sign or colon we then specify s, i, or f to acquire a string (that is, anything other than a space), an integer or a floating-point value:

```
GetOptions("mandatorystring=s" => \$option1);
GetOptions("optionalstring:s" => \$option2);
GetOptions("mandatoryinteger=i" => \$option3);
GetOptions("optionalinteger:i" => \$option4);
GetOptions("mandatoryfloat=f" => \$option5);
GetOptions("optionalfloat:f" => \$option6);
```

The Getopt::Long module allows options and values to be separated by either a space or an equals sign. In most cases it does not matter which we use, with the single exception of negative numbers (more about these in a moment):

```
--mandatorystring = text -nextoption ...
--mandatorystring text -nextoption ...
```

The distinction between a mandatory and optional value is, of course, that we can omit the value if it is optional. If we specify an option (say, -mandatorystring) but leave out a mandatory value, GetOptions emits a warning:

Option option requires an argument

The integer and floating-point variations are similar, but also check that the supplied value is an integer or floating-point value. Note that we cannot supply a hexadecimal (or octal or binary) integer. This will cause GetOptions to emit a warning, for example:

Value "0xff" invalid for option integer (number expected)

Options with optional values will parse the following argument only if it does not look like an option itself. This can be important if we want to accept a negative integer as a value. For example, consider the following option and value, as typed on a command-line:

> **perl myscript -absolutezero -273**

If we define absolutezero as a mandatory value (say, an integer), with a name of absolutezero=i then -273 is interpreted as the value of absolutezero by GetOptions. However, if we make the value optional with absolutezero:i then GetOptions will interpret the - of -273 as an option prefix and assume that absolutezero has no value.

We can solve this problem in three ways. The first, as we have just seen, is to make the value mandatory by specifying the name with an equals sign. The second is to use = as a separator between the option name and the value. For example:

> **perl myscript -absolutezero=-273**

The last is to disallow - as an option prefix by redefining the prefix, or prefixes, that GetOptions will recognize, as we discussed earlier.

Abbreviations

GetOptions automatically performs abbreviation matching on its options. That is, if an option can be abbreviated and still be uniquely identified, we can abbreviate it all the way down to a single character, so long as it is still unique. For example, the option verbose, if defined on its own, can be specified as: -verbose, -verbos, -verbo, -verb, -ver, -ve or -v.

If we want to prevent this behavior, we use the Configure subroutine to disable it:

```
Getopt::Long::Configure("no_auto_abbrev");
```

Abbreviation down to single characters is great, but it doesn't work if we have two options that start with the same letter such as:

```
GetOptions(verbose => \$verbose, visible => \$visible);
```

To specify either option we now have to specify at least -ve or -vi respectively. The best way to avoid this problem is simply to give our options more distinct names, but if we can't avoid it we can optionally define an alias.

Aliases

Aliases take the form of a pipe-separated list of names (|). For example, to provide an internationally friendly color option we could use:

```
GetOptions("color|colour" => \$color);
```

The first name in the list is the **true** name – this is the name used to define the $opt_N variable or the key of an options hash if supplied as the first argument, if we use GetOptions in those ways. Aside from this, however, the names are equivalent.

Similarly, we can use an alias to allow one of two options to be recognized by a single letter if neither can be abbreviated:

```
GetOptions("verbose|v" => \$verbose, "visible" => \$visible);
```

Now we can say -v for verbose and -vi for visible. Note that if we want to combine an alias list with an option value specifier, we just put the specifier on the end of the list – we don't need to apply it to every alias. The following short program implements an incremental verbose option that can be incremented and a negatable visible option:

```perl
#!/usr/bin/perl
# visible.pl
use warnings;
use strict;

use Getopt::Long;

my ($verbose, $visible) = (0, -1);

GetOptions(
    "verbose|v+" => \$verbose,
    "visible!" => \$visible,
);

print "Verbose is $verbose\n";
print "Visible is $visible\n";
```

Interestingly, since visible is negatable as novisible and it is the only such option, we can abbreviate it to just -nov or even just -n as there are no other options that begin with n.

Handling Option Values

We have already seen how to read option values into scalar variables and mentioned at the time that GetOptions can also handle multiple values as lists and hashes. It does this in a rather cunning way by checking the type of reference that we supply for each option, and handling it as appropriate.

To recap, this is the preferred way to read in an option that takes a mandatory scalar value (in this case, a string):

```
$filename;
GetOptions("file=s", \$filename);
```

The problem here is that we can only supply one filename. If we supply two by reusing the file option, the second filename simply overwrites the first, since the one scalar variable isn't big enough for both of them. Now, assume we want to allow more than one filename. Since that is equivalent to a list of filenames, we simply supply GetOptions with an array reference instead of a scalar one, as shown in the following short program:

```
#!/usr/bin/perl
# filenames.pl
use strict;
use warnings;

use Getopt::Long;

my @filenames;

GetOptions("file=s" => \@filenames);

print scalar(@filenames)," files entered\n";

foreach (@filenames) {
    print "\t$_\n";
}
```

Now we can reuse the file option as many times as we like, the result of which is a list of filenames held in the array @filenames. We don't even have to be consistent about the prefix:

> perl filename.pl -f foo.txt --f bar.doc -file baz.pl --file clunk.txt

This doesn't allow us to pass several values to a single option however. If we wanted to do that we could do so by using a comma as a separator and then using split ourselves after GetOptions has done its work. If that seems inconvenient, wait a moment until we come to handling values via code references.

In a similar manner to handling a list of values by supplying an array reference, we can also handle a list of key-value pairs by supplying a hash reference. When GetOptions sees a hash reference it automatically looks for an equals sign in the value and tries to split it into a key and value:

```
#!/usr/bin/perl
# config.pl
use warnings;
use strict;

use Getopt::Long;

my %config;

GetOptions("config=s" => \%config);

print scalar(keys %config)," definitions\n";
foreach (sort keys %config) {
    print "\t$_ => $config{$_}\n";
}
```

Now we can use the config option several times to build a hash of configuration variables:

> perl config.pl --config verbose = 3 --config visible = on

GetOptions also allows a code reference in place of a reference to a scalar, array, or hash. This lets us do in-line processing of values as GetOptions processes them. For example, to allow comma separated values to define a list we can define a subroutine to split the supplied value and plug it into the target array:

```
#!/usr/bin/perl
# splitval1.pl
use warnings;
use strict;

use Getopt::Long;

our @file;   # same name as option, 'use vars @file' if Perl < 5.6

sub parsevalue {
    # allow symbolic references within this sub only
    no strict 'refs';

    my ($option, $value) = @_;
    push @$option, split(',', $value);
}

GetOptions("file=s" => \&parsevalue);

print scalar(@file)," files entered\n";
foreach (@file) {
    print "\t$_\n";
}
```

In this example we have defined a subroutine parsevalue and given its reference to GetOptions. When it encounters a file option it passes the name of the option (file), and the value to parsevalue as parameters. In turn, parsevalue splits the value using a comma as the separator and pushes the result onto a variable with the same name as the option. To achieve that we have used a symbolic reference for which we have to (within the subroutine only) disable strict references.

The `parsevalue` subroutine is an example of a generic argument processor. It will work with any option because it uses the name of the option to deduce the array to update. The only catch to this is that we have to define the options as global variables using `our` rather than with `my`, since symbolic references do not resolve to lexically scoped variables. To avoid symbolic references entirely we can put most of the processing work in `parsevalue` but use a temporary anonymous subroutine to assign the result to our variable of choice:

```
#!/usr/bin/perl
# splitval2.pl
use warnings;
use strict;

use Getopt::Long;

my @file;   # lexical, no longer needs to be the same name

sub parsevalue {
    my ($option, $value) = @_;
    return split(',', $value);
}

GetOptions("file=s" => sub {push @file, parsevalue(@_)});
```

Using either version of this program we can now enter filenames either one by one with separate `file` options, or in one big comma separated list:

> **perl splitval2.pl --file first --file second,third,fourth,fifth -f sixth,seventh,eighth**

Documenting Options

In the event of an error occurring when parsing the command-line, it is traditional (and polite) to supply the user with some help about what the problem is, and a brief description of the command-line syntax – the 'usage'. For example, for a script that takes two optional flags and a list of filenames we might write:

```
unless (GetOptions(\%opts, 'verbose', 'visible')) {
    print "Usage $0 [-v|-verbose] [-vi|-visible] filename\n";
}
```

Neither `Getopt::Std` nor `Getopt::Long` support displaying usage information beyond warning of specific problems. Instead we can use the `Pod::Usage` module to place the usage information into the source file itself. See Chapter 18 for more information on pod and the various `Pod` modules, including `Pod::Usage`.

Bundling Options

Bundling, as explained earlier, is the combination of several options into one, a part of the POSIX standard that both `Getopt::Std` and `Getopt::Long` support. For example, we can specify `-a`, `-b`, `-c`, and `-f` options with:

> **perl myscript -abcf filename**

The module `Getopt::Long` supports two kinds of bundling, neither of which is enabled by default. To enable the simplest we call the `Configure` subroutine:

```perl
#!/usr/bin/perl
# bundle1.pl
use warnings;
use strict;

use Getopt::Long;

Getopt::Long::Configure("bundling");

my ($a, $b, $c, $file);
GetOptions(a => \$a, b => \$b, c => \$c, "file=s" => \$file);
```

This enables traditional single-letter bundling with the single minus prefix (in fact, any prefix except the double minus). Any sequence of letters prefixed with a single minus is treated as a collection of single letter options, not a complete option name or abbreviation:

```perl
-abc    # equivalent to -a -b -c, not -abc
```

We can even combine values into the bundle so long as they look like values and not options (this presumes that we defined a, b, and c as value parameters):

```perl
-a1b32c80    # equivalent to -a 1 -b 32 -c 80
```

However, a double minus will never be treated as a bundle, so `--abc` will always set the option abc.

The second kind of bundling causes `GetOptions` to try to match single minus prefixed options to long names first, and only treat them as a bundle if no long option name matches. In this case `-abc` would match the abc option just as `--abc` does. Here is a short example program that uses this form of bundling:

```perl
#!/usr/bin/perl
# bundle2.pl
use warnings;
use strict;

use Getopt::Long;

Getopt::Long::Configure("bundling_override");

my ($a, $b, $c, $abc) = (-1, -1, -1, -1);

GetOptions(a => \$a, b => \$b, c => \$c, "abc:s" => \$abc);

print "a: $a\n";
print "b: $b\n";
print "c: $c\n";
print "abc: $abc\n";
```

If we try out this program with various different arguments we can see how and when the override takes effect:

```
-a -b -c    # sets 'a' 'b' and 'c'
-ab -c      # sets 'a' 'b' and 'c'
-abc        # matches 'abc', sets 'abc'
-acb        # doesn't match 'abc' - sets 'a' 'b' and 'c'
--a         # matches 'a' - sets 'a'
--ab        # abbreviation - sets 'abc'
-A          # doesn't match anything, warns of unknown 'A'
--A         # case insensitive - sets 'a'
--abcd      # doesn't match anything, warns of unknown 'abcd'
-abcd       # sets 'a' 'b' and 'c', warns of unknown option 'd'
```

As this last example illustrates, the long name abc is only matched with a single minus prefix if we specify it completely and exactly, so the letters a to d are interpreted as bundled options instead. Bundles also disable abbreviations, since with bundling in effect abbreviations are no longer uniquely identifiable. For example -ab sets a and b rather than being interpreted as an abbreviation for -abc. However we can still abbreviate --abc as --ab if we use a double minus prefix, since this disables any attempt at bundling.

Case Sensitivity

By default Getopt::Long automatically treats double minus prefixed options as case-insensitive. This is not the case for any other prefix, most notably the single minus prefix, which is considered case-sensitive. However, we can set the sensitivity of double minus prefixed options by configuring ignore_case in our program before we call GetOptions. For example:

```
Getopt::Long::Configure("ignore_case");    # default behavior
Getopt::Long::Configure("no_ignore_case");   # '--Option' case sensitive
```

We can set the sensitivity of all options, including double minus prefixed ones, with ignore_case_always:

```
Getopt::Long::Configure("ignore_case_always");
Getopt::Long::Configure("no_ignore_case_always");
```

Clearing either configuration value with no_ also clears the other, so no_ignore_case and no_ignore_case_always are actually the same. However, no_ignore_case_always sounds better if we then specify ignore_case too. For instance, the default configuration is equivalent to:

```
Getopt::Long::Configure("no_ignore_case_always", "ignore_case");
```

If we wanted to reverse the normal state of affairs and make long options case-sensitive and short options case-insensitive we could do that with the following two configuration changes:

```
#!/usr/bin/perl
# casesens.pl
use warnings;
use strict;

use Getopt::Long;

my %opts;

Getopt::Long::Configure("ignore_case_always", "no_ignore_case");
GetOptions(\%opts, 'verbose', 'visible', 'background');
```

Of course the point of long options is that their name is descriptive and unique, so the case should not matter. Therefore it is doubtful that this configuration is actually all that desirable, even if it is possible.

Handling Unrecognized Option and Value Arguments

When GetOptions encounters an option that it does not recognize, it (usually) issues a warning. However, how it reacts to a value that it does not recognize is another matter. If a value is expected as an optional or mandatory suffix to an option, it is easy to verify that it follows whatever format the option was defined with. But a value that is encountered when no value was expected does not fall under these rules.

In fact, GetOptions has three modes of operation for dealing with unexpected situations such as these.

'permute' Mode

In permute mode (the default unless POSIXLY_CORRECT has been defined in the environment) unexpected value arguments are simply ignored and left in the @ARGV array. Processing continues past the unknown argument while further options and values are parsed as normal. At the exit of the subroutine, @ARGV contains all the arguments that were not used as either options or values. permute mode is set explicitly by calling:

```
Getopt::Long::Configure('permute');
```

The permute mode gets its name because its effect is equivalent to permuting the command-line by moving all the unrecognized value arguments to the end. That is, the following two command-lines are equivalent, assuming that none of the options take a value:

> **perl myscript -a one -b two -c three**
> **perl myscript -a -b -c one two three**

Having GetOptions return unrecognized values (if not options) in @ARGV can be useful, for example in combination with the <> operator as we discussed earlier in the chapter.

However, in permute mode we can handle these unrecognized arguments ourselves by defining a special subroutine and passing a reference to it to GetOptions. This works in a very similar way to the handling of normal options with code references that we looked at earlier. In deference to the fact that this is in the spirit of the <> operator, the name for the option used to trigger this subroutine is <>. The following script simply builds an array called @oob_values containing the unrecognized values; without the subroutine the @ARGV array would contain these values instead:

```perl
#!/usr/bin/perl
# unrecog.pl
use warnings;
use strict;

use Getopt::Long;

my ($verbose, $size, @oob_values);

sub handle_unknown {
    # push  extra values onto out-of-band value list
    push @oob_values, @_;
}

GetOptions(
    "verbose+" => \$verbose,   # verbose option
    "size=i" => \$size,    # size option
    "<>" => \&handle_unknown,  # unknown values
);
```

```
print "Verbose ", $verbose?'on':'off',"\n";
print "Size is ", (defined $size)?$size:'undefined',"\n";
print "Extras: ", join(',', @oob_values),"\n" if @oob_values;
```

Interestingly, handle_unknown is called as each unknown value is encountered, which means that the values of the other option variables may change from one call to the next. It is the current value of these options that we make use of in the processing. For example, the value of $verbose is 0, 1, and then 2 each time handle_unknown is called in the following command-line:

> perl unrecog.pl this -v that -v other

Setting permute mode automatically disables require_order mode. Setting the environment variable POSIXLY_CORRECT to a true value disables permute and enables require_order (see POSIX mode shortly).

'require_order' Mode

In require_order mode, the first encounter with an unknown value argument causes GetOptions to cease processing the rest of @ARGV and return immediately – as if a naked double minus, --, had been encountered. This mode is set explicitly by calling:

```
Getopt::Long::Configure("require_order");
```

Unlike permute mode, it is not possible to define an unknown argument handler in this mode. Setting require_order mode automatically disables permute mode, and is the default if the environment variable POSIXLY_CORRECT is defined.

'pass_through' Mode

In pass_through mode, unrecognized option arguments are passed though untouched in the same way that unrecognized value arguments are passed. This allows unrecognized options and their values to be passed on as arguments to other programs executed from inside Perl. The pass_through mode is not enabled by default, but can be set explicitly by calling:

```
Getopt::Long::Configure("pass_through");
```

The pass_through mode can be combined with either of the require_order and permute modes. In the case of require_order mode, enabling pass_through mode will cause GetOptions to stop processing immediately, but will not cause GetOptions to emit a warning, and will leave the unrecognized option in @ARGV. In the case of permute mode, all unrecognized options and values are collected and left at the end of @ARGV after GetOptions returns. If a <> subroutine has been defined, both unrecognized option and value arguments are passed to it.

Irrespective of which mode is in use, the bare double minus -- always terminates the processing of @ARGV immediately. The -- itself is removed from @ARGV, but the following arguments are left as-is. This applies even if we are using permute mode and have defined a <> subroutine to handle unknown value arguments.

'POSIX' Mode

The Getopt::Long module was written with the POSIX standard for command-line arguments in mind, which is the origin of the double minus prefix for long option names, among other things. This module is more flexible than the POSIX standard strictly allows, however, which can be very convenient or a nuisance, depending on our aims. In order to satisfy both camps, the module can be put into a POSIX-compliant mode, which disables all the non-standard features by defining the environment variable POSIXLY_CORRECT:

```
setenv POSIXLY_CORRECT 1     # UNIX (csh)
export POSIXLY_CORRECT = 1   # UNIX (newer ksh/bash)
POSIXLY_CORRECT = 1; export POSIXLY_CORRECT   # UNIX (older ksh)
set POSIXLY_CORRECT = 1     # Windows
```

We can also set POSIX mode from within Perl by adding POSIXLY_CORRECT to the %ENV hash. In order for this to work properly we have to define the variable in a BEGIN block before the use statement, so that the variable is defined before the module is used:

```
BEGIN {
    $ENV{'POSIXLY_CORRECT'} = 1;
}


use Getopt::Long;
```

Enabling POSIX mode has the following effects:

❑   The archaic + prefix is suppressed. Only - and -- are recognized by default (the configuration option prefix_pattern is set to (--|-)).

❑   Abbreviation matching is disabled (the configuration option auto_abbrev is unset).

❑   Non-option arguments, that is, arguments that do not start with an option prefix and are not values of a preceding option, may not be freely mixed with options and their values. Processing terminates on encountering the first non-option argument. (The configuration option require_order is set.)

As the above shows, the primary effect of POSIXLY_CORRECT is to alter the default values of several of the module's configuration options. We could of course configure them ourselves directly but defining the environment variable is more convenient and will also keep up-to-date should the module change in the future. We can always alter the configuration afterwards, say to re-enable abbreviations, if we choose.

Summary of Configuration Options

We have already mentioned the Configure subroutine in Getopt::Long and described most of its options. Most options are Boolean and can be set by specifying their name to Getopt::Long::Configure, or cleared by prefixing their name with no_. The prefix and prefix_pattern options both take values that are specified with an equals sign. The Configure subroutine will accept any number of options at one time. For example, to enable bundling and to change the allowed prefixes to a single minus or a forward slash we can use:

```
Getopt::Long::Configure("bundling", "prefix_pattern = (-|\/)");
```

Note that it is also perfectly acceptable to call `Configure` more than once if need be.

The following table shows a short summary of each option. Options that have a default value and a POSIX default value alter their default behavior if the environment variable `POSIXLY_CORRECT` is set:

Option Name	Default Values	Action
auto_abbrev	set POSIX: unset	Allows long option names to be abbreviated so long as the abbreviation is unique. Not compatible with single minus options when bundling is in effect.
bundling	unset	Interprets single minus option names as bundles of single character options. Clearing bundling also clears `bundling_override`.
bundling_override	unset	Interprets single minus options as long names if possible, or bundles otherwise. Setting or clearing this option also sets or clears bundling.
default	n/a	Resets all options to their default value, as modified by `POSIXLY_CORRECT`.
getopt_compat	set POSIX: unset	Allows the archaic + as well as - and -- to start options. A shortcut for `prefix_pattern`.
ignore_case	set	Ignores case of long (double minus prefixed) options. Clearing this also clears `ignore_case_always`.
ignore_case_always	unset	Ignores case of all options, however prefixed. Clearing this also clears `ignore_case`, however `ignore_case` may subsequently be set.
pass_through	unset	Allows unknown options to pass through as well as values, rather than raising a warning. Used with `permute` or `require_order`.
permute	set POSIX: unset	Allows unknown values to pass through. Exclusive with `require_order`.
prefix	n/a	Sets the prefix string for options, for example -, or /. Only one prefix can be specified. To set alternative prefixes use `prefix_pattern`.
prefix_pattern	(- | -- | \+) POSIX: (- | --)	Sets the list of prefix strings for options. This is a regular expression pattern therefore special characters like + must be escaped and the whole list enclosed in parentheses.
require_order	unset POSIX: set	Terminates processing on first unrecognized value (or option if `pass_through` set). Exclusive with `permute`.

Shells, Shell Commands, and Perl

Shells are a particular subclass of interactive program that are worth a little special attention. To most people, a shell is what they type commands into. More accurately, a shell is a command interpreter that provides an interface between the user, the operating system, and its services. On a UNIX machine there are many shells to choose from, including the Bourne shell sh, C Shell csh, Korn Shell ksh and the Bourne Again shell bash. Windows has several shells available, the standard one being COMMAND.COM. Windows NT has its own shell, cmd.exe.

Perl was partly created as a better solution to the various different shells and scripts that existed on UNIX systems beforehand. Its major advantage is that, unlike all the shells mentioned above, scripts written in Perl do not depend on any given UNIX or Windows shell being available (though of course Perl itself needs to be available), and have at least a decent chance of working across platforms. Given that, it might be a nice touch if we could actually implement a shell based on Perl itself. Perl does not have a shell mode, as such, but it is very easy to create one, either by running Perl with the right arguments and supplying some code with the -e argument, or more flexibly with a short Perl script.

Perl comes with a couple of modules that close the gap between Perl and the shell it is running in. The module Shell.pm allows unrecognized functions in Perl code to be evaluated by the underlying shell, effectively integrating the shell's own abilities into Perl. This is interesting, although potentially dangerous too, and manifestly non-portable. Conversely, ExtUtils::Command goes the other way, providing emulations of several important UNIX commands that will function on Windows platforms, allowing us to use commands like rm, mv, cp, and chmod on non-UNIX platforms.

If we simply want a shell to try out Perl commands then we can use the Perl debugger as a passable shell by typing:

> **perl -d 1**

This debugs the program 1, but in the process it provides a prompt at which we can define subroutines and evaluate expressions. There is no official Perl shell, but there are several available from CPAN and elsewhere, two of the most popular being perlsh, available from http://www.bgw.org/projects/perlsh/ and psh, available from http://www.focusresearch.com/gregor/psh/ and also from CPAN in the Psh package.

Creating a Simple Perl Shell

Creating a Perl shell is actually remarkably easy. If we don't require any particular degree of sophistication we can generally create a shell script that runs Perl as a shell in one line. Here is an example that uses the -n switch to put an implicit while (<>) {...} around the code we specify with -e:

> **perl -nwe 'eval $_; print "perl>" '**

Or for Windows, which has different quoting rules:

> **perl -nwe "eval $_; print 'perl>' "**

To explain this in more detail, the e switch specifies a line of code for Perl to execute, in this case an eval followed by a prompt. The w enables warnings, which is always a good idea, and the n puts the code specified by e into a permanent loop. When run, this takes Perl code typed in by the user, and evaluates it – a very simple shell. The only catch to this is that it doesn't display the prompt the first time around. Here's a slightly improved shell that fixes that problem, and also adds strict syntax checking for good measure:

> **perl -Mstrict -we "while(1) {print "perl>"; eval <> }"**

This is very similar to the previous example, except that we have used an explicit loop, moving the implicit <> inside the loop as an explicit eval after the prompt. Alternatively, we can use a BEGIN block, as this example shows:

> **perl -nwe 'BEGIN {print "perl> "} eval $_; print "perl> " ';**

Or, for Windows:

> **perl -nwe "BEGIN {print 'perl>'} eval \$_; print 'perl>' ";**

The implementations for UNIX and Windows are slightly different as UNIX systems exchange the single and double quotes and remove the backslash from $_, which is protected only because the outer quotes are doubled.

Writing a More Useful Shell

Executing Perl directly with a short snippet of code to evaluate can give us a usable but primitive shell. We can type this out directly as a command if we haven't previously stored it in a shell script. If we want to spend any time using a Perl shell though, we would be better off writing a short but functional script instead.

Here is a simple Perl script that implements a shell using the ReadLine module (for more on this module see the next chapter). This enables us to take advantage the readline library on our system to provide features such as a history list or in-line editing to make the user's life easier. If the library isn't present, the script will still work, it just won't be as powerful.

```perl
#!/usr/bin/perl
# shell1.pl
use warnings;
use strict;

# create readline object
use Term::ReadLine;
my $term = new Term::ReadLine "Perl Shell";

# switch off any highlighting
$term->ornaments(0);

# enable autoflush (output appears instantly)
$|=1;

# evaluate entered expressions until 'quit'
do {
    my $input = $term->readline("perl> ");
    print("\n"),last if $input eq "quit";
    eval $input;
} while (1);
```

As this script shows, it is possible to create a reasonably able Perl shell with only a few lines of Perl code. The biggest drawback with this shell application is that it evaluates each line as we enter it, so it's no good for multi-line statements like `foreach` loops (or indeed the `do...while` loop above) unless we put them all on one line.

We can fix this in two ways, first by teaching the shell to understand the backslash \ character for line continuation, so it is possible for us to type something like this and get the expected output:

> **perl shell1.pl**
perl> **print "Hello**
perl> **World\n"**

Second, we can look for curly braces on the start and end of lines and keep a count of the number of open braces that haven't been close yet, so we can legitimately type:

> **perl shell1.pl**
perl> **for (1..10) {**
perl> **print "$_";**
perl> **}**

Here is an improved version of our first shell that handles both these cases, and makes a few other improvements on the way:

```perl
#!/usr/bin/perl
# shell2.pl
use warnings;
use strict;

# create readline object
use Term::ReadLine;

my $term = new Term::ReadLine "Perl Shell";

# switch off any highlighting
$term->ornaments(0);

# Enable autoflush (output appears instantly)
$|=1;

# Declare some variables
my $this;     # current line
my $input;    # accumulated input
my $bracing = 0;    # number of unclosed open braces

# Evaluate entered expressions until 'quit'
while (($this = $term->readline("perl> ")) ne "quit") {
    if ($this =~ s/\\$//) {
        # if the line ends with '\', collect more lines
        $input = $this;
        # keep track of the braces even so
        $bracing += ($this =~ /{\s*$/);
        $bracing -= ($this =~ /^\s*}/);
        # get the next line and redo
        $this = $term->readline(" > ");
        redo;
    } else {
        # doesn't end with '\'
        $input .= $this;
```

```
        # keep track of the braces
        $bracing += ($this =~ /{\s*$/);
        $bracing -= ($this =~ /^\s*}/);
        # if braces outstanding, collect more lines
        if ($bracing) {
            $this = $term->readline("{$bracing} > ");
            redo;
        }
    }

    if ($input =~ s/^!\s*//) {
        # input beginning with '!' is a system command
        system $input;
    } elsif ($input =~ s/^\?\s*//) {
        # input beginning with `?` is a 'perldoc' query
        if ($input =~ /^([A-Z]|perl)/) {
            # straight perldoc if it's capitalized or starts 'perl'
            system "perldoc",$input;
        } else {
            # otherwise assume it's a function
            system "perldoc","-f",$input;
        }
    } else {
        # Evaluate it as Perl code
        eval $input;
        warn($@),undef $@ if $@;
    }

    $input="";
}
```

This script contains a few points of interest. First, it uses the redo command to restart the loop without executing the condition in the while loop. This is how the input line is grown without being overridden at the start of the loop. The backslash continuation (the first clause in the upper if statement) is basically similar to the example we saw back when we discussed loops in Chapter 6. The other clause handles lines that don't end with a backslash, and gets another line if there are still braces outstanding. For the sake of simplicity, we don't check for multiple opening or closing braces on the same line, since it is actually quite tricky to handle all possible cases.

Whenever the code cannot immediately be executed, be it because a backslash was used or braces are still outstanding, the shell needs to read another line. It does this by calling readline again, this time with a modified prompt to indicate that the next line is extending previously entered input. In the case of a backslash we change the prompt from perl> to just >. In the case of braces we indicate the level of nesting by putting the value of $bracing into the prompt. In both cases we read another line and concatenate it to the input previously read. We then restart the loop with redo, skipping the readline in the while condition.

If there are no outstanding braces or backlashes we go to the evaluation part of the loop. Here we have embellished things slightly, just to illustrate how features can be added. The second if statement checks the input for a leading ! or ?. Since the conditions are substitution statements that substitute the ! or ? for nothing they are stripped in the process of matching. In the case of !, the shell passes the rest of the input to the real shell to execute – this allows us to 'break out' of our Perl shell if we want to execute a shell command. In the case of ? the shell passes the rest of the input to perldoc and provides us with a basic help system. To keep the command flexible but simple we check the start of the input following the ? and make a guess as to whether it is a manual page (beginning with perl), a module (which almost always begin with a capital letter, with the exception of pragma modules like strict and vars), or a function name (none of the above). This isn't perfect, partly for the reasons just given, but it's not bad for a start.

With this shell we can enter loops, if statements, even define subroutines line by line and still have the shell understand them:

```
perl> sub hello {
{1} > print "Hello World\n"
{1} > }
perl>
perl> hello()
Hello World
perl>
```

We can also read in modules with `use` and then make use of them, for example:

```
perl> use Term::ReadKey
perl> ReadMode 4
perl> use CGI qw(:standard)
perl> use vars '$cgi';
perl> $cgi = new CGI
perl> ...
```

The one thing we have to watch out for is that `my` and `our` variables will not last past the current statement, because they are lexically scoped and exist only inside the scope of the `eval`. To create variables that last from one command to the next we need to declare them with `use vars`. This is probably a candidate for a special command if we decided to extend the shell.

Integrating the Shell into Perl

The standard Perl library comes with a module called `Shell.pm`, which provides the ability for unrecognized function names to be passed to the underlying shell for execution rather than simply raising an error. Whether or not this is a good idea or not is arguable (with most of the argument being on the side of 'not'), but Perl never tries to takes sides, so if we want to do it, we can.

Here is an example script for a shell that integrates the UNIX `ls`, `mv`, and `rm` commands into Perl. It scans the directory supplied as its argument (or the current directory otherwise) and lowercases the filenames of all files and directories it finds, deleting any files that end with a tilde. To find the files it uses `ls` (the argument `-1` makes sure that `ls` return a simple list of files, one per line – usually it will do this anyway when talking to a program but it never hurts to be explicit); to rename them it uses `mv` and to delete them it uses `rm`:

```perl
#!/usr/bin/perl
# xshell1.pl
use warnings;
use strict;

use Shell;

my $dir = (@ARGV)?$ARGV[0]:".";
my @files = split "\n",ls(-1);

foreach (@files) {
    print "File $_ ";
```

```
    if (/~$/) {
        # delete files ending in ~
        rm($_);
        print "deleted";
    } else {
        # rename to lowercase
        my $newname = lc $_;
        if ($newname ne $_) {
            mv($_,lc $_);
            print "renamed $newname";
        } else {
            print "ok";
        }
    }
    print "\n";
}
```

When pointed at a directory containing the files File1, FILE2, File3~, fI1E4, and FIle5~, this script generates the following output:

> **perl xshell1.pl**
File FIle5~ deleted
File File1 mv: 'File1' and 'file1' are the same file
renamed file1
File File3~ deleted
File fIlE4 mv: 'fIlE4' and 'file4' are the same file
renamed file4
File file2 ok
File test.pl ok

The Shell module works regardless of what the underlying shell actually is, though of course the underlying shell may support entirely different commands. Consequently this is a not very portable solution.

Unrestrained access to the underlying shell is also potentially dangerous – we could end up executing all kinds of dangerous commands without meaning to as a result of even a minor bug in our code. A better solution is to restrict the shell commands to those we actually want to allow. We can do that by passing the Shell module a list of the commands we want to access:

```
    use Shell qw(ls mv rm);
```

Now we can make use of the ls, mv, and rm commands, but nothing else will be interpreted as a shell command. As a bonus we can omit the parentheses and use the commands as functions rather than subroutines, because importing their names predeclares them:

```
#!/usr/bin/perl
# xshell2.pl
use warnings;
use strict;

use Shell qw(ls mv rm);

my $dir = (@ARGV)?$ARGV[0]:".";
my @files = split "\n",ls -1;
```

```
foreach (@files) {
    print "File $_ ";
    if (/~$/) {
        # delete files ending in ~
        rm $_;
        print "deleted";
    } else {
        # rename to lowercase
        my $newname = lc $_;
        if ($newname ne $_) {
            mv $_,lc($_);
            print "renamed $newname";
        } else {
            print "ok";
        }
    }
    print "\n";
}
```

If we set the variable $Shell::capture_stderr, we can also capture the standard error of the shell command and retrieve it along with the normal output of the command (if any). This isn't entirely portable however, though it should work in most shells. For example, to list a directory that may not exist:

```
use Shell qw(ls);
$Shell::capture_stderr = 1;
ls $ARGV[0];
```

The catch with this is that should the command generate error output as well as normal output, both will be mixed together. Consequently this approach is better left to situations where the command either generates normal output or an error message, and where the two can be easily distinguished. Of course many people would (correctly) argue that it is better still is to write the thing to use pure Perl to start with.

For the curious who may wonder how this all actually works, the Shell module takes the unusual step of exporting an AUTOLOAD function into our own program, so that unrecognized subroutine calls are passed to it. This is not very usual behavior for a module, but it does demonstrate the flexibility of Perl (as well as how it can get us into trouble if we don't look where we're going).

Emulating UNIX Commands on Windows

Another module related to shell commands that comes as standard with Perl is the ExtUtils::Command module. This provides something of the opposite role to Shell, implementing UNIX commands in Perl such that they can be executed on Windows systems. Here is a list of the implemented commands (the ellipsis(...) indicates that more than one parameter can be passed):

Name	Parameters	Action
cat	file...	Type out the contents of the file(s)
mv	file... newfile|directory	Rename file(s) to newfile or directory

Table continued on following page

Name	Parameters	Action
cp	file... newfile|directory	Copy file(s) to newfile or directory
touch	file...	Update modification time of the file(s)
rm_f	file...	Delete the file(s)
rm_rf	(file|directory)...	Recursively delete files/directories
mkpath	directorypath...	Create each chain of directories passed
eqtime	srcfile dstfile	Give dstfile the same times as srcfile
chmod	mode file...	Change the permissions on the file(s)
test_f	file	Test that file is a file (not a link/directory)

Here's one example of how these commands can be used:

> perl -MExtUtils::Command -e mv filename newfilename

Just because the commands implemented by ExtUtils::Command are designed to work directly from the command-line does not mean that we cannot use them as portable file manipulation tools within our own programs too. However, ExtUtils::Command was not written with programmatic use in mind, so all the subroutines in it use @ARGV as the source for their arguments, requiring us to wrap them with local subroutines that convert arguments passed in @_ to a local copy of the @ARGV array.

As an example, here is the script we introduced earlier using the Shell module, rewritten to be portable by using ExtUtils::Command instead.

```perl
#!/usr/bin/perl
# xshell3.pl
use warnings;
use strict;

use ExtUtils::Command ();    # empty list - no import

# programmatic wrappers for ExtUtils::Command subroutines
sub mv @ARGV = @_;ExtUtils::Command::mv();}
sub cp {@ARGV = @_;ExtUtils::Command::cp();}
sub rm_f {@ARGV = @_;ExtUtils::Command::rm_f();}

my $dir = (@ARGV)?$ARGV[0]:".";
my @files = <$dir/*>;

foreach (@files) {
    print "File $_ ";
    if (/~$/) {
        # delete files ending in ~
        rm_f $_;
        print "deleted";
```

```
    } else {
        # rename to lowercase
        my $newname = lc $_;
        if ($newname ne $_) {
            mv $_,lc($_);
            print "renamed $newname";
        } else {
            print "ok";
        }
    }
  }
  print "\n";
  }
```

A key reason for the existence of this module is to allow Perl modules to compile and build themselves without having to cater for different platforms in their Makefiles. The ExtUtils::Command module makes heavy use of modules in the File:: hierarchy to attempt cross-platform portability.

Summary

In this chapter we have looked at two ways of running Perl interactively: processing command-line arguments and shell programming.

We first looked at the special array @ARGV, how to use it to pass arguments to Perl, how to set variables from it, and how it handles files. We then examined two modules that we can use for processing command-line options. We looked first at the simpler Getopt::Std and its two functions getopt and getopts, before examining in more detail the Getopt::Long module. We saw, among other things, how to define option values, use abbreviations and aliases, document and bundle options, and handle unrecognized options and values.

In the last part of the chapter we examined many aspects of using shells with Perl. We saw how to write Perl shells and integrate the Shell into Perl using the Shell.pm module. Finally, we covered the ExtUtils::Command module, which allows us to implement UNIX commands such that they can be executed on Windows.

15

Terminal Input and Output

We have already seen in Chapter 14 how to use the command-line to interact with Perl. So, amongst other things in this chapter, we will look at how we can communicate with terminals. We then look at a few of the `Term::` family of modules which we can use to manipulate terminal input, and the second part of the chapter concentrates on the other aspect of interacting with terminals: terminal output.

Talking to Terminals

Once upon a time, a **terminal** was a beige colored box with a monochrome screen and a keyboard. In those days computer rooms were populated with mainframes capable of supporting many simultaneous user sessions, and so, in order to allow many simultaneous users, many terminals could be wired up to the computer, each with its own screen and keyboard. In order to save the computer from having to worry about every little detail of user input, such as scrolling the screen or dealing with the effect of a *delete*, terminals became progressively smarter, handling most of the minutiae of user input themselves and only sending the user's input to the computer when they hit *return*. This meant the mainframe itself only had to take note of a user when they actually finished typing a command, rather than for each and every key press.

Terminals quickly became smarter, gaining abilities like being able to reposition the cursor, clear selected parts of the screen, scroll down as well as up, and support colors – modern graphics cards do much the same thing, only in terms of triangles and texture mapping. The object of all this was to relieve the computer of the work of dealing with the screen – instead of moving lines on the display, the computer could just tell the terminal to 'insert a line here' and the terminal would deal with the details of moving text to accommodate the request. Terminal commands took the form of escape sequences (terse sequences of characters precede by an escape (ASCII 27). The first widespread standards were de facto, based around terminals like the VT100, which was subsequently replaced by the ANSI standard that most terminals (real or emulated) comply with to a greater or lesser extent.

In these more enlightened times of windowed desktops and graphical user interfaces, this might all seem entirely historical, but not so. Terminals are inherently bound up with the concept of interactive character input and output. Anywhere that we use a character based interface, from a UNIX X-term to a DOS shell, to the initial dialogue on a serial connection to establish a PPP network connection, we are actually working through a virtual terminal that emulates the features of a real hardware terminal. This is why we can enter text and delete it at a command-line prompt without having to actually program code to handle the delete key – the terminal underlying our shell or application deals with it automatically.

Terminal IO programming is a particular subset of general IO programming that is specifically directed towards the needs and issues of communicating through a terminal – that is, reading input from a **keyboard** and writing output to a **screen**, whatever that keyboard and screen actually turn out to be. The fact that we are almost certainly not using a real terminal does not alter anything – the terminal is just a smart layer of software inserted by the operating system between our program and the user at the keyboard.

Working with terminals can be divided into two main tasks – reading the input, and writing the output. However, before we can look at these two general areas we first need to find out if our program is connected to a terminal in the first place.

A word of warning: one problem with programming terminals is that we can easily put them into a state where they cannot be used afterwards, since terminal settings survive the death of the application that changed them. If the terminal we run a program in is also the terminal that we are using to develop it, this can be more than inconvenient. On UNIX systems the command `stty sane` is invaluable for getting out of this kind of hole – even if we cannot see what we are typing this should reset the terminal back to something usable. Some platforms may also supply a `reset` command that does much the same thing.

Determining if a Script is Interactive

Perl programs (and in fact programs in general) fall into two broad categories – those that interact with an actual user, possibly through a terminal, and those that merely carry on relations with other programs and don't require a terminal. Since we often use programs in both capacities (directly, or via another program) it is useful to be able to tell, from within the program, how it is being used.

Fortunately, Perl has a function designed precisely for this purpose, `-t`. This is one of the `-X` unary operators that test filenames and filehandles for various different kinds of properties such as being a directory, executable, or writable by us, and so on. It tests file handles to see if they are connected to a terminal or not. So by testing `STDIN` with `-t` we can check whether we are getting input from a terminal, and therefore (presumably) a user, or whether our input is coming from a non-terminal device, which most likely means from another program:

```
$interactive = -t STDIN;
```

Of course, just because standard input is coming from a terminal does not necessarily mean that standard output is going to one. So, if we want to prompt the user when our program is being used interactively we ought to check both `STDIN` and `STDOUT`. Here is a short code snippet that prompts the user, if in an interactive session, and reads lines (presumably commands of some kind) from standard input:

```
while (1) {
    print "Cmd> " if -t STDIN && -t STDOUT;
    process_command (<>);
}
```

Reading from the Keyboard

Simple line-based input can be achieved with the <FILEHANDLE> operator, which in the case of standard input is <STDIN> or often simply <> (but only if @ARGV is empty). However, this limits us to complete lines and forces us to wait for the user to type something, since the default behavior of terminals is to wait until return has been pressed before bothering us with whatever was typed. A better solution in this case is to use the Term::ReadKey module, part of the standard Perl library, which handles non-blocking reads and timeouts, allows character to be typed without echoing them back to the screen, and has several other useful features besides.

For simple low-level terminal IO, the third-party Term::ReadKey (available from CPAN) is very useful, and allows us to do quite a few things without having to get our hands dirty with real low-level terminal programming. However, the standard Perl library also provides support for reading complete lines with Term::ReadLine, which attempts to use a built-in readline library if one is present, and which supports the idea of command history. We also have Term::Complete at our disposal, a module that implements word completion. We'll be taking a look at both of these in due course.

Before we embark on a discussion of Term::ReadKey, it is worth mentioning some of the alternatives. On a UNIX system the ever-versatile stty command provides another way to access and program terminals, and if we only wish to deal with UNIX platforms we can often simply call stty. For example, to disable echoing, we can use:

```
system "stty -echo";
```

and to re-enable it:

```
system "stty echo";
```

The advantage of stty is that it deals with local platform issues for us, since it is provided by the operating system. The disadvantage is that it doesn't stand a chance of working on a non-UNIX platform. Another utility that is potentially useful if we happen to know we are running inside an X terminal is xwininfo.

However, for portable applications, using a Perl module with portability in mind is a better idea. Since Term::ReadKey works with most, but not all, platforms, we can compromise and use stty if it is available or a Term::ReadKey subroutine if it isn't available.

Simple Input

The simplest way to read input from the keyboard is the <> readline operator, which reads a single line of text from the current input filehandle. That is usually STDIN, so the following, assuming there is nothing in @ARGV, are equivalent:

```
print <>;
print <STDIN>;
```

Note that if we do have something in @ARGV, the first attempts to open the elements of @ARGV as files, whereas the second reads from standard input, so the distinction can be important. Also note that if STDIN isn't a terminal then either version may block waiting for input if insufficient input has arrived as yet. We cover this in more detail shortly.

Controlling Terminal Input with 'Term::ReadKey'

For situations where simple input techniques like <> will not do on their own, we can use the Term::ReadKey module, available from CPAN. This provides a much greater degree of control over the characteristics of the terminal, and attempts to provide a degree of cross-platform support, so a script written under UNIX still has a chance of working under Windows. As well as providing functionality to read terminal input into our programs, it also provides limited control over the properties of the terminal itself, such as whether or not it should echo typed characters to the screen and what key performs a delete operation.

The Term::ReadKey module tries to implement as many of its features as possible for the platform it finds itself running on. However, not all terminals are created equal, so a DOS shell may not support the same features as a UNIX shell. Since UNIX has always had a fairly detailed idea of what a terminal ought to be, on account of growing up with them (so to speak), most of these features tend to work on UNIX-like systems, but may not work as well, or at all, on other platforms.

Two particular subroutines in the Term::ReadKey package are available for reading input into our program. The ReadKey subroutine reads and returns a single character from the input available, waiting if necessary for it to be typed. In contrast, ReadLine reads entire lines and returns the input as a string. However, the biggest determinant of the behavior of both subroutines is the read mode of the terminal, which Term::ReadKey also allows us to control. Before we can talk about actual input, therefore, we need to look at read modes and find out what they do.

Read Modes

Central to the operation of Term::ReadKey is the concept of **read modes**. The read mode is an aspect of the terminal itself as opposed to the way that we use it, and controls how the terminal receives and processes input characters. There are six modes in total, numbered 0 to 5, with the following meanings:

Mode	Name	Meaning
0	restore	Restore the original Read Mode setting.
1	normal	Set normal cooked mode. Typed characters are echoed to the screen and control characters are interpreted.
2	noecho	Set no-echo cooked mode. Typed characters are not echoed to the screen. Control characters are interpreted.
3	cbreak	Character-break mode. Typed characters are returned immediately to the program, and are not echoed to the screen.
4	raw	Set raw mode. Control characters are read like normal characters, not interpreted.
5	ultra-raw	As with raw, but LF to CR/LF translation is disabled.

Some of these modes are more obvious than others. The normal mode is just what we expect from a normal command-line – characters are echoed as we type them and an action is initiated only when we press return. In addition, control characters are intercepted and handled by the terminal, rather than simply being added to the input.

The noecho mode is the same as normal mode, with the exception that characters are not echoed. This makes it suitable for things like password input. By contrast, cbreak mode causes the terminal to immediately return characters as they are entered, and without echoing them to the screen. This makes it suitable for single key-press applications like menu selections.

The raw and ultra-raw modes both disable the handling of control characters by the terminal. Instead, they are sent back like any other typed character for our program to handle. The ultra-raw mode is identical to raw except that it disables the automatic translation of linefeeds into carriage-return/linefeed pairs on UNIX systems. On Windows systems it has no effect. If the filehandle supplied to ReadKey or ReadLine happens to be a serial connection, parity is also disabled.

The default setting is 0, which is to say, whatever mode the terminal was in when the program was started. To change the read mode we use the ReadMode function from Term::ReadKey. This is automatically imported when we use the module, and takes a single parameter of either a number, or the corresponding named synonyms:

```
use Term::ReadKey;

ReadMode 1;    # set normal cooked mode
ReadMode 2;    # set no-echo mode
ReadMode 'noecho';    # same as above, but more legible
ReadMode 'restore';    # restore the mode to whatever it started as
```

The read mode when we start can be any of these values, though it is most likely to be 1. However, if we have been called from another program then that program may have changed the read mode before calling us. For example, we might be the program another_program being called from this Perl script:

```
use Term::ReadKey;

ReadMode 'noecho';    # suppress output
system("another_program");
ReadMode 'restore';    # restore terminal to original settings
```

If we do change the terminal read mode then it is a good idea to restore it again before we finish, since it is not restored automatically just because we exit. Recall that it is a property of the terminal, not our program or the Term::ReadKey module. If we do not restore the mode we can cause problems for the program that called us, or even the user if we are run directly. For example, if we were to run the above script from a shell and omitted the ReadMode 'restore'; then we would return to the user with echoing disabled, so that any further commands typed would be invisible to them. Obviously this is not a good thing, so to be sure that no unexpected incidents occur we should restore the read mode as a matter of course.

Restoring settings is one good use for an END block. With the following additional definition, we can ensure that our program will restore the terminal before it exits wherever in the program it does so, so long as it exits normally:

```
END {
    ReadMode 'restore';
}
```

To handle abnormal exits we can do the same thing in __DIE__ and signal handlers.

The restore mode has one additional property; when used, it causes the next mode to be set to become the default. In the above case our program exits before this can become relevant, but the following sequence of calls shows it in action:

```
ReadMode 0;    # 'restore' - restores to the default mode
ReadMode 1;    # sets mode 1, changes default mode to 1 as it came after a
               # restore
ReadMode 4;    # sets mode 4 ('raw' mode)
ReadMode 0;    # restores the mode to mode 1
```

It is important to realize that since the read mode is a property of the terminal, it affects all kinds of input, including the <> readline operator, not just the ReadKey and ReadLine subroutines covered below.

Reading a Single Character

Frequently we want to read not a line but a single character from the keyboard, to make a menu selection for example. To do this we can use the ReadKey subroutine in Term::ReadKey:

```
$character = ReadKey 0;
```

The subroutine ReadKey takes two parameters; a mode and an optional file handle. If no filehandle is specified ReadKey defaults to standard input – the above is equivalent to:

```
$character = ReadKey 0, STDIN;
```

The mode of ReadKey can be one of 0, as shown here, -1, or a positive value:

❑   Mode 0 is the blocking mode – ReadKey will wait indefinitely until we enter at least a return, or interrupt the program. Any platform that Perl can run on supports this mode.

❑   A mode of -1 causes ReadKey to enter non-blocking mode. In this case ReadKey does not wait for input but grabs whatever is in the input buffer and returns the first character immediately. If nothing is available, presumably because we have not typed anything, ReadKey returns undef.

❑   A mode with a positive value represents a wait of the given number of seconds, which can be fractional. For example, to wait for half a second we could use:
```
$character = Readkey 0.5;
```

Note, using small delay values in a loop is generally poor programming practice, since it keeps the processor busy unnecessarily.

On exit from ReadKey, $character will contain the first character that we typed, or more correctly, the first character that was available in the keyboard buffer, which may already have characters waiting (and which can be filled by things other than the keyboard, to boot).

Contrary to what we might expect however, ReadKey does not necessarily return immediately after a character is typed, but may not appear to do anything until we also enter *return*. This is not a property of our program but of the terminal itself. In order to persuade the terminal to react instantly we actually need to use the cbreak read mode, which is an entirely different thing. The following short script demonstrates how cbreak mode can be combined with ReadKey to react instantly to a typed character:

```perl
#!/usr/bin/perl
# hitakey.pl
use warnings;
use strict;

use Term::ReadKey;

ReadMode 'cbreak';

print "Hit a key: ";
my $selection = ReadKey 0;

print "You typed $selection\n";
ReadMode 'restore';
```

Since the cbreak mode does not echo the characters we enter, we can use it to create a prompt that checks the entered value before it echoes it or proceeds. For example we could implement a screen-based menu system with selections from 1 to 9 and check the user's input with a script like this (we have omitted the actual menu options for brevity, since they're not the point here):

```perl
#!/usr/bin/perl
# menu.pl
use warnings;
use strict;

use Term::ReadKey;

ReadMode 'cbreak';

print "Enter an option 1 to 9: ";
my $selection = 0;
do {
    $selection = int (ReadKey 0);
} until ($selection > 0 and $selection < 10);

print "You typed $selection\n";
ReadMode 'restore';
```

The cbreak mode can be used with any of the modes of ReadKey to produce interesting effects. For example, this script echoes each character as we type it, but also prints a dot for every half second that we don't type anything:

```perl
#!/usr/bin/perl
# dot.pl
use warnings;
use strict;

use Term::ReadKey;
ReadMode 'cbreak';

# enable autoflush
$| = 1;

my $char;
do {
    $char = ReadKey 0.5;
    print $char?$char:'.';
} until (lc($char) eq 'q');

ReadMode 'restore';
```

Note that to actually get our characters to appear on the screen when we print them we also have to put Perl into `autoflush` mode by setting the `autoflush` variable `$|` to 1. Without this we would see nothing until we entered a *return* (which does not incidentally quit the program), a *q* or *Q* to stop the program running or the amount of output becomes large enough to trigger an automatic write to the screen.

It so happens that the `raw` and `ultra-raw` modes will also work instantly when used with `ReadKey`, but this is not their intended use and they may cause unexpected side effects when used this way. The real point of the `raw` and `ultra-raw` modes is to disable the processing of control characters by the terminal, which will be covered in 'Getting and Setting Control Characters' shortly.

We can also get single characters using the `getch` method from the `Term::Screen` module. This is a third-party module that provides a lot of terminal screen handling features that are otherwise inconvenient to write. We cover it in more detail under 'Writing to the Screen' later in the chapter.

Reading Complete Lines

Whereas `ReadKey` returns single characters to us, complete lines are read by `ReadLine`. However, this subroutine only works completely on UNIX platforms (on others it works in blocking mode but not with non-blocking, instead returning an error warning that non-blocking mode is not supported). For other platforms we can use the `Term::ReadLine` module instead, which we discuss later. Not to be confused with `Term::ReadLine`, `Term::ReadKey`'s `ReadLine` subroutine is very similar to using the `<>` operator, but with the additional flexibility of being able to avoid waiting for input.

Like `ReadKey`, `ReadLine` takes a reading mode as an argument, followed by an optional file handle. To use it in its simplest guise, to read from standard input, we just write:

```
$input = ReadLine 0;   # implicitly read from STDIN
$input = ReadLine 0, *STDIN;  # with an explicit filehandle
```

This is (more or less) identical to writing:

```
$input = <STDIN>;
```

However, like `ReadKey`, `ReadLine` also accepts a mode of `-1` for non-blocking input, and a positive value for a timeout in seconds. Using non-blocking causes `ReadLine` to read whatever is in the input buffer, up to the first return, and to return that. If nothing is in the input buffer or there is an input but not a complete line then `ReadLine` will return the undefined value. Note that this is still true even if we have `cbreak` set as the terminal read mode, since that only causes the terminal to return characters to `ReadLine` immediately – `ReadLine` still wants to see an end-of-line character before it returns anything to us.

A positive value causes `ReadLine` to wait for a set length of time for input and return undef if nothing was entered in the prescribed time limit. For example:

```
print "Give your name - you have 10 seconds to comply: ";
$name = ReadLine 10;
die "Too Slow! Access Denied" unless defined $name;
```

If a non-blocking mode is used, it applies to the first character only – once a character is typed, the call will block until a return is entered. This applies even if we hit *delete*.

For more advanced ways to read lines of input from the user, including history lists and editable command-lines, skip ahead to 'Advanced Line Input with Term::ReadLine'.

Passwords and Invisible Input

If we set the read mode to either cbreak or noecho we can write a script that takes input from the user but does not echo the characters typed back to the terminal. The cbreak mode is more suitable for single character input like the hitakey.pl example we saw earlier. The mode noecho is more suitable for entering complete lines, where we do not want to know what the user is typing until they press return. A good example of this kind of application is a password entry prompt, as in:

```perl
#!/usr/bin/perl
# password.pl
use warnings;
use strict;

use Term::ReadKey;

ReadMode 'noecho';
print "Enter your password: ";
my $password = ReadLine 0;
print "Thanks!\n";
ReadMode 'restore';
```

This makes use of the ReadLine subroutine that comes with Term::ReadKey to read a complete line from the user. Note that we could equally have used cbreak mode here, the only difference being that with cbreak characters would have been sent back to our program as soon as they were typed. Since ReadLine waits for a return to be typed before it returns a value (as we would want for a password prompt), this gains us nothing and just causes extra work for the computer.

Finding and Setting the Screen Size

Sometimes it is useful to know how big the screen actually is, for example when paging output. We can find the screen size with GetTerminalSize, which returns four values for the filehandle passed to it, or standard output otherwise:

```perl
($cwidth, $cheight, $pwidth, $pheight) = GetTerminalSize;
```

Astute readers will have noticed this doesn't have much to do with reading key presses, or any kind of input. Rather, it is supported by Term::ReadKey since it is a useful thing to be able to find out, and it is, without doubt, the kind of thing that programmers of character level IO are often interested in. Since it is an output issue rather than an input one (screens are not generally much use for input), the supplied filehandle ought to be open for output. Under Windows this is actually a requirement:

```perl
# must specify file handle under Windows
($cwidth, $cheight, $pwidth, $pheight) = GetTerminalSize STDOUT;
```

The width and height of the screen in characters is returned in the first two values, with the width and height of the screen in pixels returned in the second two (though this may be zero in many cases). Since we are primarily concerned with character IO here, we can discard the second two values and just write:

```perl
($width, $height) = GetTerminalSize;
```

We can use our knowledge of the screen height to page through output, writing exactly a screenful of output before pausing. The following script does exactly this, and uses ReadKey in cbreak mode to allow the user to scroll another screenful by pressing any key. As a small improvement on this basic design we have prefixed each output line with its line number, and also check the pressed key and exit immediately if it is either *q* or *Q*:

```perl
#!/usr/bin/perl
# page.pl
use warnings;
use strict;

use Term::ReadKey;

my ($width, $height) = GetTerminalSize;

my $count = 0;

ReadMode 'cbreak';

while (<>) {
    print "$.: $_";    # $. added to make example more interesting
    if (++$count == $height) {
        last if lc(ReadKey 0) eq 'q';
        $count = 0;
    }
}

ReadMode 'restore';
```

Having demonstrated how to page text in Perl, it is worth pointing out that all operating systems have a pager program somewhere (more or less on UNIX, for instance), so if all we want to do is page output we can call that program and feed it the output we want to page using a piped open.

On UNIX systems we can also set the screen size using SetTerminalSize, supplying the same four arguments. We may not care about the pixel size (and it frequently doesn't do anything in any case, particularly under Windows), but SetTerminalSize requires we set it anyway, so to preserve the old values we can use:

```perl
# get screen size
($x, $y, $w, $h) = GetTerminalSize;

# set screen size to 80x24
SetTerminalSize (80, 24, $w, $h);
```

This does not, fairly obviously, actually change the size of the screen, but indicates to the terminal what size we would prefer it to be. In some cases, like a UNIX shell window running under the X-Windows system, this might cause the shell window to actually resize itself, but we cannot depend on that behavior. Otherwise the only effect of SetTerminalSize is to cause the operating system to notify any other programs that is reading that terminal through a SIGWINCH signal.

It may happen that another application may try to change the terminal size in a similar manner to the way that SetTerminalSize does. This might happen for example if the user resizes a terminal window on the desktop. In this case we may receive a SIGWINCH signal (assuming that our platform supports it – Windows does not). Ordinarily this would be ignored, but we can respond to it and handle the new screen size with a signal handler:

```
# establish global width/height
($width, $height) = GetTerminalSize;

# set up a signal handler to catch screen size changes
$oldwinch = $SIG{'WINCH'};

sub window_changed {
    ($width, $height) = GetTerminalSize;

    # handle the new size - Text::Wrap might be useful here...
    redraw($width, $height);

    # call the old handler by its code reference, if there was one
    &$oldwinch if $oldwinch;

    # in case the OS clears the handler
    $SIG{'WINCH'} = \&window_changed;
}

$SIG{'WINCH'} = \&window_changed;
```

As an alternative to Term::ReadKey, the Term::Size and Term::Screen packages available from CPAN also provide functionality for getting or setting the terminal size – see later.

Serial Connections and Terminal Speed

It might happen to be that the terminal we are talking to is actually a serial connection connected to a program or user elsewhere. If we expect to be handling potentially slow connections we could then modify the amount of data we actually send, giving slow connections more condensed information. In these cases we can find out the speed of the terminal with GetSpeeds, which takes a filehandle as an argument (or defaults to standard input otherwise) and returns two values, the input speed and the output speed:

```
($baud_in, $baud_out) = GetSpeeds SERIAL_CONNECTION;
```

If the file handle is not a serial connection then this call returns an empty list, which in the above case results in two undefined scalars.

Serial connections are also affected by the raw and ultra-raw read modes, as mentioned earlier. Specifically, the terminal will attempt to override any parity settings if present. This can be slightly surprising if we are reading a serial connection in raw mode, but since setting parity is something of a rarity these days it is unlikely to be that much of a problem in practice.

Line Ending Translation

As we are aware, different operating systems do not use the same line terminator. As a little recap, this is due to historical reasons with Windows systems not using the same line terminator as UNIX. Under UNIX, it is simply a linefeed, or LF for short. Under Windows, it is a return (to be technically accurate **carriage return**) and linefeed, or CR LF for short. The Macintosh and VMS are different again, using LF CR. Needless to say, this can be confusing.

In order to deal with the possibility of seeing CR LF (or LF CR) rather than LF on the end of lines, terminals usually convert CR LF into LF when they see it, returning only the LF to the application (on some systems this is done in cooperation with the underlying C library too).

Most of the time this is just what we need, because it eliminates another source of compatibility issues for us without us having to worry about it. However, if we actually want to turn this feature off we can do so by putting the terminal into ultra-raw mode:

```
ReadMode 'raw';    # regular 'raw' mode
ReadMode 'ultra-raw';    # disables CR/LF->LF translation
```

The catch is that ultra-raw mode is in all other respects like raw mode, which is not necessarily what we wanted to use. On a Windows system this is exactly the same as the regular raw mode, since Windows applications expect to see CR LF and so do not remove the CRs. On a UNIX system this disables the translation so that a CR LF sent to the terminal is passed unchecked as CR LF to the application.

Getting and Setting Control Characters

One of the principle differences between a terminal (whether it be a real screen-and-keyboard terminal or a window on a desktop) and regular IO devices is that terminals can handle a lot of things by themselves without needing the program connected to them to tell them. An obvious example of this is echoing typed characters to the screen; the terminal deals with that automatically without our intervention or involvement.

Less obvious but more interesting are terminal operations like pausing and resuming scrolling, interrupting the running program and deleting characters, words, or lines. Each of these is a different terminal operation, which may (or may not) be associated with a control character, such as *Ctrl-C* to interrupt a program or Ctrl-S to pause scrolling. When a terminal is in a cooked mode, which is to say any read mode other than raw or ultra-raw, each time a character is typed the terminal looks it up in the list of operations to see if it triggers a particular event. (On UNIX, these definitions are kept in the /etc/termcap, /etc/terminfo, and etc/gettydefs files.)

Using the Term::ReadKey subroutine GetControlChars we can, on platforms that support it, access the list of terminal operations and which keys are associated with which functions. Like most of the subroutines in Term::ReadKey an optional filehandle can be supplied, otherwise standard input is used. A list of key-value pairs is returned by GetControlChars, with the key name being the hash key and the key code associated with it being the value. For example, to find out which key code generates an interrupt, we can use:

```
%controlchars = GetControlChars;
print "INTERRUPT is ", ord($controlchars{INTERRUPT});
```

Similarly we can dump out the entire list to the screen with a small program, though since not all platforms support this function we might not actually get any output:

```
#!/usr/bin/perl
# getcontrolchars.pl
use strict;
use warnings;

use Term::ReadKey;

my %controlchars = GetControlChars;

foreach (sort keys %controlchars) {
    print "$_\t=>", ord ($controlchars{$_}), "\n";
}
```

This produces a list resembling (but possibly not exactly the same, depending on where and on what we run the program) the following:

```
> perl getcontrolchars.pl
DISCARD => 15
EOF => 4
EOL => 0
EOL2 => 0
ERASE => 127
ERASEWORD => 23
INTERRUPT => 3
KILL => 21
MIN => 1
QUIT => 28
QUOTENEXT => 22
REPRINT => 18
START => 17
STOP => 19
SUSPEND => 26
SWITCH => 0
TIME => 0
```

This list of operations and characters comes from the terminal, and represents the internal mapping that it is using to process control characters. Many of the operations returned in the list may not be assigned and so have a character value of zero (or 255, depending on the platform) in the returned array – these characters are discarded by the terminal.

Note that if the terminal is not a real terminal, which is usually the case, what it receives may already have been processed by something else first. For instance, the X-Window system defines its own character mapping (the xrdb utility can do this), which takes effect before our terminal even sees the character. Likewise, PC keyboards actually generate 16 bit values, which are translated by the operating system into characters before we see them.

On UNIX platforms only, we can also alter which control characters trigger which operations, using SetControlChars. This takes a list of key-value pairs as arguments and applies them to the terminal's built-in list. Each pair consists of a name, as returned by GetControlChars, followed by the character or character value. A value of zero disables the operation. For example, we can redefine or disable the delete key by setting the ERASE operation:

```
SetControlChars ERASE => 0;    # disables delete
SetControlChars ERASE => 2;    # sets delete to control-B
```

In the following program we extract and print the list of control characters, alter some of them, and then print it out again. Note that the attempted alterations will not produce any effect on Windows systems (and will, in fact, generate an error):

```
#!/usr/bin/perl
# setcontrolchars.pl
use warnings;
use strict;

use Term::ReadKey;
```

```
    my %oldcontrolchars = GetControlChars;

sub dump_list {
    my %controlchars = GetControlChars;
    foreach my $key (sort keys %controlchars) {
        print "$key\t => ",ord($controlchars{$key}),"\n";
        }
    print "\n";
}

dump_list;

# disable interrupt, suspend and erase (delete)
# change eof to whatever suspend is (i.e. ctrl-D to ctrl-Z)
SetControlChars INTERRUPT => 0,
                EOF => $oldcontrolchars{SUSPEND},
                SUSPEND => 0,
                ERASE => 0;

dump_list;

# reset control characters to their old values
SetControlChars %oldcontrolchars;

dump_list;
```

In this program we have disabled the `interrupt` operation, normally bound to *Ctrl-C*, and changed the end-of-file (or more accurately end-of-transmission, EOT) character, *Ctrl-D* under UNIX, to *Ctrl-Z*, which is more like Windows.

Advanced Line Input with 'Term::ReadLine'

Perl provides a module called `Term::ReadLine` as part of the standard library. Although it does little by itself, it provides an interface to a system readline library, if one is installed. Two libraries are currently available (at least on UNIX systems), the standard Perl readline library and the much more capable third party GNU Readline library. GNU Readline is also available under Windows as a Cygwin package.

Whichever library we have installed we can use `Term::ReadLine` to access it – if the GNU library is installed `Term::ReadLine` will automatically use it, so we do not have to cater for different libraries in our own code. The module `Term::ReadLine` will work with no underlying readline library, but few of the advanced features supported by a real readline library, like editable command-lines or command-line history traversal will be available. By writing our programs to use `Term::ReadLine`, however, we can transparently and automatically make use of these features if our program is run on a system where they are installed.

Also supported by `Term::ReadLine` are several standard methods, which we can call on terminal objects created with the module. They are:

Name	Function
ReadLine	Return the name of the underlying library module
new	Create a new terminal object
readline	Read a line. This is the central method of the module
addhistory	Add a new line to the input line history
IN/OUT	Return the input and output file handles of the terminal, respectively. See also findConsole
MinLine	Set a limit on the shortest length of an input line before it is allowed in the input line history
findConsole	Return an array of two strings containing the appropriate filename strings for opening the input and output respectively. See also IN and OUT
Attribs	Return a reference to a hash of internal configuration details
Features	Return a reference to a hash of supported features

In addition Term::ReadLine supplies some **stub methods**. Without an underlying library these have no useful effect, but if one is present they will perform the relevant function. The stubs ensure that we can call these methods even if the library we are using doesn't actually support them. If we want to check if a given method is supported (as we probably should) we can use the Features method to find out.

Name	Function
tkRunning	Enable or disable the tk event loop while waiting for input. Perl-Tk only
ornaments	Enable, disable, or change the decoration of the prompt and input text when using readline
newTTY	Switch the terminal to a new pair of input and output file handles

In addition to the standard methods, the underlying library may define other methods that are unique to it. The GNU library in particular defines a very extensive set of calls, in fact more than we have time to touch on here. For full details, see perldoc Term::ReadLine::Gnu.

Each library adds its own set of features to the list returned by Features so we can also test for them before trying to use the corresponding methods. Before calling any methods, however, we first have to create a terminal object.

Creating a Terminal Object

The Term::ReadLine module is object-oriented, so to use it we first instantiate a terminal object. We give this object a name, presumably a descriptive name for the program, and then optionally typeglobs for the filehandles that we wish to use for input and output:

```
use Term::ReadLine;

# use STDIN and STDOUT by default
$term = new Term::ReadLine "Demo";
```

```
# use file handles IN and OUT explicitly
$term = new Term::ReadLine "Demo", *IN, *OUT;

# use a serial connection (same file handle for both input and output)
$serialterm = new Term::ReadLine "Remote", *SERIAL, *SERIAL;
```

Once we have created a terminal object we can use it to both read and write to the terminal. The following script shows the general idea:

```perl
#!/usr/bin/perl
# termobject.pl
use warnings;
use strict;

use Term::ReadLine;

my $term = new Term::ReadLine "My Demo Application";
print "This program uses ", $term->ReadLine, "\n";

my $input = $term->readline("Enter some text: ");
print "You entered: $input\n";
```

First we load in the Term::ReadLine module. Then, just for curiosity, we use the ReadLine method to find out the name of the underlying package, if any. Then we use the readline method (note the difference in case) to read a line from the terminal, optionally supplying a prompt.

When this program is run it causes Term::ReadLine to look for and load an underlying readline library if it can find one. If it can, it passes control to it for all other functions. The library in turn provides editing functionality for the actual input of text. If we are using the GNU library, we can take advantage of its more advanced features like editable command-lines automatically, since they are provided automatically by the library. In our own code we don't have to raise a finger, which is the point, of course.

If we happen to be using a terminal that isn't connected to standard input and standard output, we need to direct output to the right filehandle, which means passing print the right filehandle. The above happens to work because the terminal is connected to standard out, so a simple print works. We really ought to direct output to the terminal's output, irrespective of whether it is standard output our not. Fortunately we can find both the input and output filehandles from the terminal object using the IN and OUT methods:

```
$input_fh = $term->IN;
$output_fh = $term->OUT;

print $term->OUT "This writes to the terminal";
```

Once created, the filehandles used by the terminal can (usually) be changed with the newTTY method. This takes two typeglobs as arguments and redirects the terminal to them:

```
$term->newTTY *NEWIN *NEWOUT;
```

It is possible, though unlikely, that this will not work if the library does not support the switch. To be sure of success we can interrogate Term::ReadLine to find out whether the newTTY feature (or indeed any feature), is actually supported.

Supported Features

Due to the fact that different readline implementations support different features of Term::ReadLine, we can interrogate the module to find out what features are actually supported using the Features method. This returns a reference to a hash with the keys being the features supported:

```perl
#!/usr/bin/perl
# features.pl
use warnings;
use strict;

use Term::ReadLine;

my $term = new Term::ReadLine "Find Features";
my %features = %{$term->Features};

print "Features supported by ", $term->ReadLine, "\n";
foreach (sort keys %features) {
    print "\t$_ => \t$features{$_}\n";
}
```

When run with Term::ReadLine::Gnu (available from CPAN) installed, this produces the following output:

> **perl features.pl**
Features supported by Term::ReadLine::Gnu
>
> | | |
> |---|---|
> | addHistory => | 1 |
> | appname => | 1 |
> | attribs => | 1 |
> | autohistory => | 1 |
> | getHistory => | 1 |
> | minline => | 1 |
> | newTTY => | 1 |
> | ornaments => | 1 |
> | preput => | 1 |
> | readHistory => | 1 |
> | setHistory => | 1 |
> | stiflehistory => | 1 |
> | tkRunning => | 1 |
> | writeHistory => | 1 |

We should not confuse these features with callable methods. Some, though not all, of these features correspond to methods supported by the underlying library. Unfortunately, the feature names do not always match the names of the methods that implement them. For example the method to add a line of history is addhistory not addHistory.

We can use the feature list to check that a feature exists before trying to use it. For example, to change a terminal to use new filehandles we could check for the newTTY feature, using it if present, and resort to creating a new object otherwise:

```
sub switch_tty {
    ($term, *IN, *OUT) = @_;
    $features = $term->Features;
    if ($features->{newTTY}) {
        $term->newTTY(*IN, *OUT);
    } else {
        $name = $term->appname;
        $term = new Term::ReadLine $name, *IN, *OUT;
    }
    return $term;
}
```

Regardless of which features are actually supported, `Term::ReadLine` defines stub methods for a selected subset so that calling them will not cause an error in our program, even if they don't have any useful effect.

Setting the Prompt Style and Supplying Default Input

The `readline` method takes a prompt string as its argument. This string is printed to the screen using `ornaments` (if any have been defined) that alter the look of the prompt and the entered text. For example, GNU Readline underlines the prompt text by default.

Ornamentation can be enabled, disabled, or redefined with the `ornaments` method. Enabling and disabling the currently defined ornaments is achieved by passing `1` or `0` (a True or False value) to `ornaments`:

```
#!/usr/bin/perl
# ornament.pl
use warnings;
use strict;

use Term::ReadLine;

my $term = new Term::ReadLine "Ornamentation";

# disable ornaments
$term->ornaments(0);
my $plain = $term->readline("A plain prompt: ");
print "You entered: $plain\n";

# enable default ornaments
$term->ornaments(1);
my $fancy = $term->readline("A fancy prompt: ");
print "You entered: $fancy\n";
```

Alternatively the current ornamentation can be redefined by passing four parameters containing terminal capabilities (as deduced by the `Term::Cap` module – see later) as a string. The first two are applied before and after the prompt, and the second two before and after the input text. For example:

```
# define ornaments (md = bold, me = normal)
$term->ornaments('md, me, ,');
$userd = $term->readline("A user-defined prompt: ");
print "You entered: $userd\n";
```

In this example we have used md, which is the terminal capability code for bold, and me, which is the terminal capability code to return to normal. We don't want to change the input line, so we have left those two entries blank.

Note that if we have no termcap library this will fail since Term::Cap is used to determine how to handle ornaments. To enable the ornaments subroutine to work without generating a warning, add:

```
# disable warnings for platforms with no 'termcap' database
$Term::ReadLine::termcap_nowarn = 1;
```

The GNU version of readline supports a second optional parameter that contains the default input text. This is known as the **preput** text and we can test to see if it is supported by checking for the preput feature. Since passing extra parameters is not an error, not checking is fine – we simply won't see the default text. Here is a short example of supplying some default text to the readline method:

```
#!/usr/bin/perl
# defaulttext.pl
use warnings;
use strict;

use Term::ReadLine;

my $term = new Term::ReadLine "Default Input";

my $input = $term->readline("Enter some text: ", "Default Text");
print "You entered: $input\n";
```

If the preput text is supplied and the library supports it, the input line is automatically filled with the default text. The user can then either delete and replace or edit (because GNU Readline supports in-line editing) the default text, or just press *return* to accept it.

Command-Line History

The Term::ReadLine module provides support for command-line history – that is, a record of what has been typed beforehand. This can be used to allow the user to step backward or forward through previous commands, typically using the up and down cursor keys. This functionality is provided automatically (assuming a library is present which supports it) so again we do not have to do anything ourselves to provide it.

We can control the history several ways, however. First, we can lie about previously entered commands by using the addhistory method:

```
$term->addhistory("pretend this was previously entered text");
```

If we have the GNU Readline library we can also remove a line from the history by giving its line number to remove_history:

```
$term->remove_history(1);    # remove line 1 from history, GNU only
```

We can also, using the GNU library, retrieve the whole history as an array with `GetHistory`:

```
@history = $term->GetHistory;
```

We can then step through this array and pass the index numbers to `remove_history` if desired. Of course to prevent the line numbers changing as we proceed, traversing the array in reverse order is recommended. For example, this loop traverses the history array removing all lines that have less than three characters:

```
@history = $term->GetHistory;
# traverse in reverse order, to preserve indices in loop
foreach my $item (reverse 0..$#history) {
    $term->remove_history($item) if length($history[$item])<3);
}
```

We can actually do this automatically with the standard `MinLine` method, which should work regardless of the underlying library. Additionally, we can disable the history entirely by passing an undefined value to it:

```
$term->MinLine(3);    # only record lines of three plus characters
$term->MinLine(undef);   # disable history
```

The GNU Readline library goes far beyond these features however. It also provides support for editing, moving around, saving, loading and searching the history. For a complete, if terse, list of available features see the `Term::ReadLine::Gnu` documentation.

Word Completion

Some shell programs support the concept of 'completion', where the shell attempts to deduce the rest of a partially entered word from the first few letters. We can provide the same feature within our own Perl programs with either the GNU Readline library or the somewhat simpler (but less able) `Term::Complete` module.

This module supplies the `Complete` function, which takes a prompt and a list of words for matching against. This is an example of how we might use it:

```
#!/usr/bin/perl
# complete.pl
use warnings;
use strict;

use Term::Complete;

my @terms = qw(one two three four five six seven eight nine ten);
my $input = Complete("Enter some number words: ",@terms);

print "You entered: $input\n";
```

Completion is triggered if we press the *Tab* key. When this occurs, `Term::Complete` attempts to match the text entered so far against one of the words in the completion list. If there is a unique match, it fills in the rest of the word. For example, if we were to enter e and then press *Tab*, `Term::Complete` would automatically fill in ight for eight, since that is the only word that begins with e.

If there is not a unique match then *Tab* will produce no useful effect. Instead, we can type *Ctrl-D* to have `Term::Complete` return a list of valid matches. If we were to enter t then *Ctrl-D*, the list two, three, ten would be returned, for example.

The `Term::Complete` module supplies several functions that allow various keys to be redefined, with the curious exception of *Tab* for completion. None of these functions are exported by the module so we must access them via their full names. They are as follows:

Function	Keystroke	Action
`Term::Complete::complete`	*Ctrl-D*	List matching completions, if any
`Term::Complete::kill`	*Ctrl-U*	Erase whole line
`Term::Complete::erase1`	*del*	Delete last character
`Term::Complete::erase2`	*backspace*	Delete last character

The `Term::ReadLine::Gnu` package provides a more comprehensive completion mechanism, but depends on the GNU Readline library being installed on the system. This may be more trouble than we want to go to, especially on a non-UNIX or non-Windows system. It is also a much more involved library to program, and is beyond the scope of this book – consult the documentation and the manual page for the `bash` shell (which makes extensive use of GNU Readline) if available.

Writing to the Screen

Perl provides a lot of different approaches to writing to a terminal screen, from simply printing to standard output, through low-level terminal control modules like `Term::Cap` and the `POSIX::Termios` interface through to very high-level modules like the third-party `Curses` module. Somewhere in the middle we can find modules like `Term::ANSIColor` and the third-party `Term::Screen`, which provide a slightly simpler interface to the features of the low-level modules.

The `Term::ANSIColor` module handles the specific problem of using colors and other text attributes like blinking, bold, or underline. Other commands can be sent to the screen by interrogating the terminal capabilities with `Term::Cap`. However, since `Term::Cap` is a rather low-level module, the third-party `Term::Screen` module provides a few of these facilities in a more convenient form. If we plan to do a lot of screen output, however, such as writing a complete text-based GUI application, then we might want to look at the `Curses` module.

Terminal Capabilities

However we want to talk to a terminal, it ultimately boils down to a case of terminal capabilities. There are many different kinds of terminal, both real and simulated, each with its own particular range of features. Even if a terminal supports all the usual features, it may not do it in the same way as another. In order to make sense of the huge range of possible terminals and different terminal features and options UNIX machines make use of a terminal capability or 'termcap' database. A given terminal has a terminal type associated with it. Interested applications can look up in the database to find out how to tell the terminal to do things like move the cursor or change the color of text.

We send commands to terminals in the form of ANSI escape sequences, a series of characters starting with an escape (character 27, or \e). To switch on blue text, for example, we could use:

```
print "\e[34m--this is blue text--\e[0m\n";
```

Of course, this relies on the terminal supporting ANSI escape sequences, which is likely on a UNIX system but is not the case for a DOS shell – if characters like e[32m appear on the screen, it's a safe bet that ANSI isn't supported so the rest of this discussion is likely to be academic.

Remembering that \e[...m is the sequence for change screen colors and that 34 is the number for blue is hardly convenient, however. Worse, while things like the color blue are standard across all terminals (all color terminals, that is), many other terminal capabilities vary widely in the precise escape sequences that control them. For that reason, rather than write escape sequences explicitly we use Term::Cap to find them out for us.

The Term::Cap module is an interface to the terminal capability or 'termcap' database commonly found on UNIX systems that allows us to issue commands to terminals based on what kind of terminal we are using. To use it we create a terminal capability object using Term::Cap, then pass that object information about what we want to do, along with the filehandle of the terminal we want to do it on. In order to use the module therefore, we first have to create a terminal capability object (or **termcap object** for short) that points to the entry in the termcap database that we want to use. We also need a termcap database for Term::Cap to work with, so again, this is academic for platforms that do not possess one.

Creating a Termcap Object

Using the Tgetent method, Term::Cap creates terminal capability objects. In order to use it we must pass it a hash reference, which it blesses, populates with capability strings, and returns to us. In order to work out which entry to look up Tgetent needs to know the terminal name, for example ansi for a standard ANSI terminal, vt100 for a terminal that adheres to the VT100 standard and so on. UNIX shell tools like xterm use their own terminal mode, for example xterm, which is a superset of the ANSI terminal that also knows a few things particular to living inside a window, such as resizing the screen.

In general we want Term::Cap to look up the entry for whatever terminal it is our program happens to be running in, which it can normally deduce from the environment. To tell Tgetent to look at the environment we pass it an anonymous hash containing a key-value pair of TERM and undef:

```
#!/usr/bin/perl
# anonhash.pl
use warnings;
use strict;

use Term::Cap;

# create a terminal capability object - warns of unknown output speed
my $termcap = Term::Cap->Tgetent({ TERM => undef });

print "Capabilities found: ", join(',', sort(keys %{$termcap})), "\n";
```

Just to illustrate what this actually does we have looked at the hash that the termcap object actually is and printed out its keys. That's usually a rather rude way to treat an object, but it serves our purpose for illustrative purposes. Run from a UNIX xterm window, this program produces the following output:

> **perl anonhash.pl**
OSPEED was not set, defaulting to 9600 at ./termcap1.pl line 7
Capabilities found:
OSPEED,PADDING,TERM,TERMCAP,_AL,_DC,_DL,_DO,_IC,_LE,_RI,_UP,_ae,_al,_am,_as,_bc,_b
l,_cd,_ce,_cl,_cm,_co,_cr,_cs,_ct,_dc,_dl,_do,_ei,_ho,_ic,_im,_is,_it,_k1,_k2,_k3,_k4,_k5,_k6,_k7,_k
8,_k9,_kl,_kN,_kP,_kb,_kd,_ke,_kh,_kl,_km,_kr,_ks,_ku,_le,_li,_md,_me,_mi,_mr,_ms,_nd,_pc,_rc,_
sc,_se,_sf,_so,_sr,_ta,_te,_ti,_ue,_up,_us,_xn,_xo

Note that we avoided actually printing out the values of the hash, which contain the ANSI escape
sequences themselves. That is partly because printing them would actually cause the terminal to react to
them, which will likely confuse it considerably and leave it in an unusable state. Escape sequences are
not that interesting to look at in any case; the whole point of the termcap database is that we don't need
to look at them directly.

Disregarding the warning (which we'll come to in a moment) and the upper cased entries, each of the
underscore prefixed entries is a capability of this terminal, and the value of that entry in the hash is the
ANSI escape sequence that creates that effect. By using this object we can generate valid escape
sequences to do the things we want without needing to worry about what the correct sequence is for any
given terminal. In fact, we can disregard the terminal type altogether most of the time, which is the idea,
of course.

If we want to pretend we're an ANSI terminal rather than anything else, or we just happen to know that
the terminal we're using (remembering that we could be in some sort of shell window that doesn't
correspond to any specific terminal) happens to be ANSI compatible, we could write:

```
$termcap = Term::Cap->Tgetent({TERM =>'ansi'});
```

Tgetent also seeks the output speed of the terminal because terminal capabilities may be defined to be
dependent on the speed of the connection. If it isn't told, it will complain with a warning, but retrieve
the terminal capability information anyway based on an assumed speed of 9600bps. In order to silence
this, we can feed it a speed from the POSIX module:

```
#!/usr/bin/perl
# speed.pl
use warnings;
use strict;

use POSIX;
use Term::Cap;

# set the line speed explicitly - but 'POSIX::B9600' may not be defined
my $termcap1 = Term::Cap->Tgetent({
    TERM => undef,
    OSPEED => POSIX::B9600
});
```

Better, we can use the POSIX::Termios package to ask the terminal directly, and then feed that value
to Term::Cap:

```
# interrogate the terminal for the line speed, no need for a constant
my $termios = new POSIX::Termios;
$termios->getattr(fileno(STDOUT));
my $termcap2 = Term::Cap->Tgetent({
    TERM => undef,
    OSPEED => $termios->getospeed
});
```

The `POSIX::Termios` is a very low-level way to control a terminal directly. Modules like `Term::ReadKey` use it, along with `Term::Cap`, behind the scenes to perform many of their functions. We can also use it directly, and we will cover it in more detail later. Of course this might seem a pointless exercise if we know we will be talking to a screen or a shell window that doesn't have a line speed, but `Term::Cap` is not able to assume that, and can't determine it from the terminal type, since that's just an emulation. Additionally, we should not assume that our application won't one day run on a real terminal on the end of a real serial connection.

Clearing the Screen, Moving the Cursor, and Other Tricks

Now we have an object representing the terminal's capabilities we can use it to make the terminal do things. One of the first obvious things to do is clear the screen. The terminal capability code for that is `cl`, so we feed that to the `Tputs` method of `Term::Cap` along with the number 1 to tell `Tputs` to generate a code that does clear the screen (rather than doesn't, strangely – the command needs a parameter), and the filehandle of the terminal:

```
$termcap->Tputs('cl', 1, *STDOUT);
```

Similarly, to move the cursor about we use the `cm` (cursor move) capability with the `Tgoto` method. For instance, to move the cursor to position x = 3 and y = 5 we would use:

```
$termcap->Tgoto('cm', 3, 5, *STDOUT);
```

Then, to write some text in bold we could use:

```
$termcap->Tputs('md', 1, *STDOUT);
print "Bold Text";
```

We can use any capability of the terminal in this way, so long as we have a thorough knowledge of terminal capability codes. Since that is rather a lot of work to go to we might be given to wonder if someone has already done all this work and parceled up the most common features for us. Fortunately, someone has – see `Term::Screen` and the `Curses` module later in the chapter.

Writing in Colors

Most terminal emulations support the ANSI standard for escape sequences that control aspects of the terminal such as cursor position or the appearance of text. Unlike a lot of other escape sequences, the color and text attribute sequences are pretty standard across all terminals, so instead of writing ANSI sequences by hand or resorting to `Term::Cap` we can make use of the `Term::ANSIColor` module from CPAN instead.

This module works by defining an attribute name for each of the escape sequences related to text representation, such as `bold` for bold text and `on_red` for a red background. We can use these attributes to create text in any style we like, with the twin advantages of simplicity and legibility.

There are two basic modes of operation. The first is a functional one, using the subroutines `color` and `colored` to generate strings containing ANSI escape sequences, passing the names of the attributes we want to create as the first argument. The second uses constants to define each code separately, and we will see how to use it shortly. Before we look at a short example of using the `Term::ANSIColor` module, a short word of warning. The effects of using the module will be dependant on the settings of your terminal. For example if your terminal is set to print red on white, the following example will exhibit no noticeable difference. In the meantime, here is a short example of how `color` can be used to generate red text on a white background:

```perl
#!/usr/bin/perl
# text.pl
use warnings;
use strict;

use Term::ANSIColor;

print color('red on_white'), 'This is Red on White';
```

The argument to `color` is a list of attribute names, in this case the attributes `red` and `on_white` to produce red-on-white text. Here we have passed them as space separated terms in a string, but we can also supply the attributes as a list:

```perl
@attributes = 'red';
push @attributes, 'on_white';
print color(@attributes), 'Or supply attributes as a list...';
```

Note that `color` does not print anything by itself. It returns a string to us and leaves it to us to print it or otherwise use it. Similarly, here is how we can produce bold underlined text:

```perl
print color('bold underline'), 'This is bold underlined';
```

We can generate any of the color sequences supported by the ANSI standard using `Term::ANSIColor`, all of which have been given convenient textual names for easy access. The following table lists all the names defined by `Term::ANSIColor`. Note that several attributes have synonyms, and that case is irrelevant – `RED` works as well as `red`:

Name	Action
clear, reset	Reset and clear all active attributes.
bold	Start bolding.
underline, underscore	Start underlining.
blink	Start blinking.
reverse	Reverses both foreground and background colors logically. If no colors are set, inverts white on black to black on white.
concealed	Conceal text.
black, red, green, yellow, blue, magenta	Put text into given color. May be combined with a background color.
on_black, on_red, on_green, on_yellow, on_blue, on_magenta	Put text background into given color. May be combined with a foreground color.

The problem with `color` is that it does not switch off what it switches on. If we run the above programs then whatever escape sequences were in effect at termination continue on after the end of the program. That means that without special care and attention we can end up typing bold underlined green on cyan text at our shell prompt, or even worse. In order to prevent this we need to remember to clear the active attributes before we finish:

```perl
print color('red on_white'), 'This is Red on White', color('reset');
```

This is another case where an END block is potentially useful, of course:

```
# make sure color is switched off before program exits
END {
    print color('reset');
}
```

However, passing reset to the end of all our print statements is clumsy. The colored function solves this problem by automatically adding escape codes to clear the active attributes to the end of the returned string. With colored we don't need to reset the screen ourselves, so the following is exactly equivalent to, but simpler to write than, the previous example:

```
print colored('This is Red on White', 'red on_white');
```

The text to be encapsulated comes first, so we can still pass attributes as a list if we want:

```
my @attributes = ('red', 'on_white');
print colored('Or as a list of attributes...', @attributes);
```

It is important to realize, however, that reset (or the synonymous clear) resets all active ANSI sequences, not just the ones we issued last. This is more obvious with color than colored, which might give the impression that we can switch from green-on-black to red-on-white and back to green-on-black using a reset, which is not the case:

```
print colored('green on black, colored('red on white'), 'and back', 'green');
```

In this example the and back will be white on black, not green, because the reset generated by the internal call to colored overrides the original color setting and then resets it. The reset added by the outer call to colored is therefore redundant.

The function colored has been written with multi-line text in mind. Ordinarily, it places codes at the beginning and end of the string passed as its first argument. If, however, the package variable $Term::ANSIColor::EACHLINE is set to a string of one of more characters then colored splits the line on each occurrence of this separator and inserts codes to clear and then re-establish the passed attributes on either side of it. The most obvious use of this feature is, of course, to set the separator to \n, as in:

```
#!/usr/bin/perl
# multicolor.pl
use warnings;
use strict;

use Term::ANSIColor;

$Term::ANSIColor::EACHLINE = "\n";

my $text = "This is\nan example\nof multiline\ntext coloring\n";

print colored($text, 'bold yellow');
```

There is no reason why we should just apply this to lines. As a slightly different example of what we can do, here is a way to display binary numbers with the 1s emphasized in bold. It works by making the separator 0 and using bold cyan as the attribute:

```
#!/usr/bin/perl
# boldbin.pl
use warnings;
use strict;

use Term::ANSIColor;

my $number = rand 10_000_000;

# my $bintext = sprintf '%b', $number;   # if Perl >=5.6
my $bintext = unpack 'B32', pack('d', $number);

$Term::ANSIColor::EACHLINE ='0';

print colored($bintext, 'bold cyan');
```

The second mode of operation bypasses color and colored entirely by importing symbols for each attribute directly into our own namespace with the :constants label. To use this mode, we need to import the constants from the module by using the :constants tag:

```
use Term::ANSIColor qw(:constants);
```

By doing this, we create a host of constant subroutines, one for each attribute. The constants are all uppercase, so instead of calling color or colored we can now print out attributes directly. Here is red on white text, generated using constants:

```
#!/usr/bin/perl
# constants.pl
use warnings;
use strict;

use Term::ANSIColor qw(:constants);

print RED, ON_WHITE, "This is Red on White", RESET;
```

The values of these constants are strings, so we can also concatenate them with the . operator:

```
$banner = BLUE.ON_RED.UNDERSCORE."Hello World".RESET;
print $banner, "\n";
```

As these examples show, constants suffer from the same problem as color, in that we have to explicitly switch off whatever attributes we switch on. However, if we leave out the commas and set the variable $Term::ANSIColor::AUTORESET then the module will automatically figure things out and add the reset for us:

```
# automatically append reset code
$Term::ANSIColor::AUTORESET = 1;

# look, no commas!
print RED ON_WHITE "This is Red on White";
```

587

This is very clever, but mysterious. We might be given to wonder how this works, since this doesn't look like a legal `print` statement. The answer is that the 'constants' are not strings but subroutines. With the commas, each is called with no arguments. Without the commas, each is called with the rest of the statement as its argument, and returns a string based on its own name prefixed to whatever the rest of the line returns. By working out if they were called with or without arguments each subroutine can work out whether it needs to append a reset or not. Cunning, if a little strange at first glance. Since RED in this example looks exactly like a filehandle, we may prefer to avoid this syntax and live with resets. Notice that we can define the output record separator to produce a similar effect:

```
$/ = RESET;   # automatically suffix all 'print' statements with a reset
print RED, ON_WHITE, "This is Red on White";
```

The advantage of the 'constants' approach is that Perl can check our code at compile time, rather than at run time, since a misspelled constant will cause a syntax error, unlike an attribute string passed to `color` or `colored`, which will only cause a problem when we try to use it. The disadvantage is that we get a lot of attribute constants in the namespace of our code, which isn't always desirable.

Higher-Level Terminal Modules

The `Term::Cap` module gives us the ability to send a range of commands to terminals without having to worry about what kind of terminal we are actually talking to, although it is a little too low-level for convenient use. Fortunately there are several third-party solutions that build on basic terminal capabilities to make our job easier. We're going to mention just two here – `Term::Screen`, which is a friendly wrapper around `Term::Cap` that implements many of the most common functions in an easy to use form, and `Curses`, a terminal programming library vast enough that it has entire books dedicated to it.

'Term::Screen'

The third-party `Term::Screen` module (available at the nearest CPAN mirror) encapsulates a lot of the most common terminal functionality into a simpler and easy to use form, if we want to spend significant time exerting control over the terminal screen and want to avoid writing all our own `Term::Cap` subroutines. Although it is not a standard module it does use `Term::Cap` to do all the actual work, so wherever `Term::Cap` works, `Term::Screen` ought to. It actually uses the UNIX `stty` command to do the dirty work, so it won't work for other platforms. However, it is designed to be subclassed, so an MS-DOS module is a distinct possibility, if not supplied (at least, not yet).

As an example, here is how we can clear the screen and move the cursor with `Term::Screen`. Notice that it is a lot simpler and more legible than the `Term::Cap` version we saw earlier:

```
#!/usr/bin/perl
# movecurs.pl
use warnings;
use strict;

use Term::Screen;

my $terminal = new Term::Screen;
$terminal->clrscr();
$terminal->at(3,4);
$terminal->puts("Here!");
$terminal->at(10,0);
$terminal->puts("Hit a key...");
```

```
my $key = $terminal->getch();
$terminal->at(10,0);
$terminal->puts("You pressed '$key'");
$terminal->at(11,0);
```

This example also demonstrates the getch method, an alternative to using ReadKey from the Term::ReadKey module that we covered earlier. getch is more convenient since it doesn't involve messing about with the terminal read mode, but of course it requires having Term::Screen installed. Of course, Term::ReadKey is not a standard module either.

As an added convenience, Term::Screen's output methods are written so that they return the terminal object created by new Term::Screen. This means they can be used to call other methods, allowing us to chain methods together. For example, we could have concatenated much of the above example script into:

```
$terminal->clrscr->at(3,4)->puts("Here!")->at(10,0)->puts("Hit a key...");
```

The Term::Screen module provides a toolkit of methods for working with terminals. The following table summarizes these, along with the arguments they take:

Name	Action
resize (rows, cols)	Resize the screen, in the same way that Term::ReadKey's SetTerminalSize does.
at (row, col)	Move the cursor to the given row and column of the screen.
normal bold reverse	Set the text style to normal, bold, or reverse respectively. For example $terminal->bold() puts the terminal into bold.
clrscr	Clear the screen and moves the cursor to 0,0.
clreol	Clear from the cursor position to the end of the line.
clreos	Clear from the cursor position to the end of the screen.
il	Insert a blank line before the line the cursor is on.
dl	Delete the line the cursor is on. Lower lines move up.
ic (char) exists_ic	Insert a character at the cursor position. Remainder of line moves right. The method exists_ic returns True if this actually exists as a termcap capability, False otherwise.
dc exists_dc	Delete the character at the cursor position. Remainder of line moves left. The method exists_dc returns True of this actually exists as a termcap capability, False otherwise.
echo noecho	Enable or disable echoing of typed characters to the screen, in the same way that Term::ReadKey's ReadMode does.
puts (text)	Print text to the screen. Identical to print except that it can be chained with at as illustrated above.

Table continued on following page

Name	Action
getch	Return a single character in raw mode.
key_pressed	See if a key has been pressed without actually reading it.
flush_input	Clear any current data in the input buffer.
stuff_input	Insert characters into the input of getch for reading. Note that this only works for getch – it does not put characters into the real input buffer.
def_key (cap, keycode)	Define a function key sequence. char is the character generated by the definition (and read by getch). keycode is what the function key actually generates. The definition causes keycode to be translated into char by the terminal.
get_fn_keys	Define a default set of function key definitions.

All of these methods are fairly explanatory, with the exception of def_key. This programs the function keys (which includes the cursor keys and keys like *insert* and *home*) of a keyboard to return a given character, if the terminal is programmable. The **keycode** is a particular escape sequence such as \e[11~ for function key *F1* or \e[A for the *up* cursor key, and the cap is a terminal capability such as ku for cursor up. That is, to swap the up and down cursor keys we could write:

```
$terminal->def_key('ku', "\e[B~");
$terminal->def_key('kd', "\e[A~");
```

A list of common escape sequences generated by function keys can be found in the Term::Screen module itself, inside the get_fn_keys method. As well as being informative, when called this also resets the definitions to their defaults, handy if we just swapped our cursor keys around:

```
$terminal->get_fn_keys();
```

The is certainly useful, but it does have one liability – with the exception of the ic and dc methods, it assumes that the given capability exists. That is, though it uses Term::Cap to issue escape sequences, it does not actually check that the given capability exists. However, since all the capabilities it supports are fairly standard, it is likely that they will work as advertised.

If even Term::Screen is not up to the task, we might consider turning to the very capable and feature-rich Curses module. However, Curses depends on an implementation of the curses library on our platform – Term::Screen only needs Term::Cap, which is a standard Perl library module.

The Curses Library

The **Curses library** is the granddaddy of all screen manipulation libraries. It supports everything we have discussed so far, including all the tricky details of terminal capabilities, mouse input, and text-based windows as well as many other features. It is quite possible to write entire windowed GUI applications that work entirely in a terminal window using the Curses library. There are many different implementations of Curses, all of which are in the form of C libraries. Most UNIX platforms have a Curses library installed, and several ports exist to other platforms such as Windows, including the free **GNU ncurses** implementation.

Perl supports Curses libraries through the `Curses` module, available from any CPAN mirror. As well as the Curses library, it also supports the extension Panel library, which adds overlapping window support to Curses. Assuming that we have these libraries and the `Curses` module installed, we can write terminal applications using Curses. The actual features of a given Curses library depend on the implementation (early implementations do not support Windows, for example), but all libraries support the same general set of operations.

The C interface to Curses tends to support four different subroutines for each function; the basic feature, the basic feature within a window, the basic feature combined with a cursor movement, and the basic feature combined with a cursor movement within a window. For example, the `addstr` subroutine, which writes text to the screen comes in four different flavors, each with a different set of arguments, as these four different C statements demonstrate:

```
/* write text at cursor */
addstr("Text...");

/* move cursor, write text */
mvaddstr(3, 5, "Text");

/* in window write text at cursor */
waddstr(window, "Text...");

/* in window move cursor, write text */
mvwaddstr(window, 3, 5, "Text");
```

The `Curses` module greatly simplifies this, first by providing an object-oriented interface for programming windows, and secondly by wrapping all of the variants into one Perl subroutine. In order to work out which one we actually want, the `Curses` module merely inspects the number of arguments and their type. This makes the whole business of programming Curses applications much simpler.

Since Curses is a huge library (and not strictly Perl either, for that matter) we cannot hope to document it all here. When perusing the Curses documentation that comes with the library (for example `man curses` or `man ncurses` on a UNIX system) we can make use of the homogenization to mentally · reduce the number of subroutine calls we need to use by stripping off any w or mv prefixes we see.

A Simple Curses Application

A simple Curses program starts with `initscr` that initializes the screen for use by Curses. After this we can configure the terminal in any way we like, for example to switch echoing off. We can send output to the screen with `addstr`, followed by `refresh` to tell Curses to actually draw it. Finally, when we are finished, we call `endwin` to reset the terminal for normal use again. Here is a short example program that lists environment variables one by one and shows the basic structure of a Curses program:

```
#!/usr/bin/perl
# curses1.pl
use warnings;
use strict;

use Curses;

initscr();   # initialize the screen to use curses
cbreak();    # go into 'cbreak' mode
noecho();    # prevent key presses echoing
```

```
# move and addstr as separate actions
attron(A_BOLD|A_UNDERLINE);
move(2, 5);
addstr("Environment Variable Definitions:");
attroff(A_BOLD|A_UNDERLINE);
move(15, 5);
addstr("Hit a key to continue, 'Q' to finish...");

# enable color
start_color();

# define some color pairs
init_pair(1, COLOR_WHITE,COLOR_BLACK);
init_pair(2, COLOR_YELLOW,COLOR_BLACK);
init_pair(3, COLOR_BLACK,COLOR_CYAN);

OUTER: while (1) {
    foreach (sort keys %ENV) {
        attron(COLOR_PAIR(3));   # set black-on-cyan
        addstr(5, 8, " $_ ");   # move and write variable name
        clrtoeol();   # delete anything beyond it
        attron(COLOR_PAIR(2));   # set yellow-on-black
        addstr(6, 8, $ENV{$_});   # move and write variable value
        clrtoeol();   # delete anything beyond it
        move(9, 79);   # move the cursor out of the way
        refresh();   # send output to the screen
        last OUTER if (lc(getch) eq 'q');
    }
}

attron(COLOR_PAIR(1));   # set white-on-black
move(9, 5);
addstr("All Done");
refresh();   # send output to the screen
END {endwin;}   # end Curses properly even on abnormal termination
```

There are a few points to note about this application:

First, all Curses programs that do not use Windows must start with initstr. Similarly, all Curses programs must end with endwin to reset the terminal into a useable state afterwards.

Second, nothing appears on the screen until we call refresh. Up until this point, Curses carries out all the changes in an internal buffer, recording what parts of the screen have been changed. When we call refresh all the changes – and only the changes – made since the last refresh (or initscr) are sent to the terminal in one go. This makes Curses very effective for programming in situations that may involve a slow serial or network connection since it uses only the minimum bandwidth necessary to do the job.

Third, if no coordinates are specified to subroutines that output to the screen then the current cursor position is used instead. This can be seen in the move and addstr pairs, and also in the use of clrtoeol after the addstrs in the loop to clear from the end of the string (which is where the cursor ends up after addstr has finished) to the end of the line.

Fourth, we can enable and disable text attributes like bold or underline by using `attron` and `attroff`. The different attributes can be numerically `or`ed together to switch several attributes on or off at the same time.

Fifth, to use colors in Curses we need to first call `start_color`. Curses handles colors in pairs, setting both foreground and background at once. We therefore define some color pairs using `init_pair`, which takes an arbitrary pair number and a foreground and background color. These pairs can be used with `attron` (and `attroff`) using the `COLOR_PAIR` macro. The whole system is a lot more sophisticated than this of course – this is just a quick example.

Lastly, as we discussed earlier, most Curses features take variable numbers of arguments and determine what to do based on how many there are. To write at a given position of the screen we can therefore use `move` and then `addstr` with one argument, or supply the coordinates and the string as three arguments to `addstr`. The `clrtoeol` subroutine also accepts coordinates, though we haven't used them here.

Curses Windows

The `Curses` module has two modes of operation. The simple mode, which we have just seen, is suitable for full screen programs where we use the entire screen (by which we also mean an entire terminal window on a GUI desktop, of course; Curses has no idea what the terminal 'really is' – that's the point) as a single window. The object-oriented version is useful if we are programming Curses windows, where each window is effectively a small screen in its own right. In this case we do not use `initscr` but create and call methods on window objects. The homogenization of the `Curses` module interface means that we still use the same names for the methods as we did for the functions. Here is how we create a window in Curses:

```
# create a new 20x10 window, top left corner at coordinates 5, 5
$window = new Curses (10, 20, 5, 5);
```

Once we have created a window, we can move the cursor around in it, write to it, refresh it, and set attributes on it, just as we can with the whole screen. Here is a short program to demonstrate the object-oriented Curses window interface. It creates a window, puts something in it, and then moves it across the screen each time we press a key:

```perl
#!/usr/bin/perl
# curses2.pl
use warnings;
use strict;

use Curses;

# create a 3x20 window with top corner at 0, 0
my $window = new Curses(3, 22, 0, 0);

cbreak();   # go into 'cbreak' mode
noecho();   # prevent key presses echoing

# define some colors
start_color();
init_pair(1, COLOR_YELLOW, COLOR_BLUE);
init_pair(2, COLOR_GREEN, COLOR_BLUE);
```

```
# put something in the window
$window->attron(COLOR_PAIR(1));
$window->clear();
$window->box(0, 0);
$window->attron(COLOR_PAIR(2));
$window->addstr(1, 2, "This is a Window");
$window->attroff(COLOR_PAIR(2));

$window->refresh();
getch;

foreach (5..25) {
    $window->mvwin($_, $_);
    $window->refresh();
    last if (lc(getch) eq 'q');
}

END {endwin;}   # end Curses properly even on abnormal termination
```

One irritating aspect of this application is that it leaves a trail of old window borders across the screen as the window moves. This is because windows are not windows in the desktop sense but just predefined boxes of text we can place on the screen at will. To avoid the trailing effect we would need to delete the old window first – fortunately Curses' refresh mechanism means that blanking the whole block and then replacing the window in its new position is as efficient as trying to work out the parts that have changed and only updating them. However, it doesn't take account of the possibility that something else might be underneath the window. To solve that problem we can make use of Panels, an extension to Curses frequently supplied as a secondary library that provides intelligent windows that can stack and overlap. Not all systems support Panels, however, and some provide it as a separate library, so the Curses module may not be able to make use of it directly. We can of course use h2xs to bridge the gap, but we can also make use of a number of third-party modules.

Third-Party Extensions to Curses

Curses is a popular library and has been around for some time now. Consequently, a lot of other libraries and Perl modules have been written that build on Curses to provide everything from simple menus to complete GUI toolkits. Checking CPAN for modules providing more advanced Curses-based features is well worth the time before embarking on a Curses-based project – the Curses::Forms module (for data entry) and Curses::Widgets module (for button bars, dialog boxes and other 'GUI' components) in particular. Other Curses modules include Cdk, which uses a third-party C library built on Curses, and PV.

Programming the Terminal Directly via 'POSIX'

For occasions when modules like Term::ReadKey won't do and we just have to program the terminal directly, we can use the POSIX module. Among many other things, the POSIX module provides a direct low-level interface to the terminal in the POSIX::Termios package, from which we can control any aspect of the terminal we wish. In fact many of the modules we have discussed so far in the chapter make use of this interface, along with modules like Term::Cap, to do most of their work. The drawback is that while many platforms support POSIX compliance, it doesn't necessarily mean that they will be able to handle programming the terminal directly. On UNIX, these techniques will usually work; other platforms may not be so fortunate.

Whereas `Term::Cap` interrogates the termcap database, `POSIX::Termios` is concerned with the terminal itself. That is, `Term::Cap` can tell us what the delete key ought to be; `POSIX::Termios` can tell us what it actually is right now. To use it we first need to create a `termios` object, then associate that object with the file handle of the terminal we want to manipulate:

```
use POSIX;

$termios = new POSIX::Termios;
```

We then tell the object to read the attributes of a terminal by passing a filehandle number to `getattr`. This can be either a simple integer such as 0 for `STDIN`, 1 for `STDOUT`, or 2 for `STDERR`, or a file number extracted from a filehandle with `fileno`:

```
# three different ways to get the attributes of STDIN
$termios->getattr;
$termios->getattr(0);
$termios->getattr(fileno(STDIN));
```

Once we have the attributes in our termios object we can retrieve them with functions like `getospeed` (for the terminal output speed) and `getcc` (for the control characters) and set them with functions like `setospeed` and `setcc`. All this just changes values in a hash, however. Once we have finished modifying the attributes we then set them on a filehandle by using `setattr`. Here is a short program that redefines a few properties of `STDIN` and `STDOUT` by way of an example:

```
#!/usr/bin/perl
# termios.pl
use warnings;
use strict;

use POSIX qw(:termios_h);

my $stdin = fileno(STDIN);
my $stdout = fileno(STDOUT);

print "\nInterrogating STDIN:\n";
my $termios_stdin = new POSIX::Termios;
$termios_stdin->getattr($stdin);

# redefine the erase (delete) key
print "\tErase key is ", $termios_stdin->getcc(VERASE), "\n";
print "Set Erase to Control-D:\n";
$termios_stdin->setcc(VERASE, 4);
print "\tErase key is ", $termios_stdin->getcc(VERASE), "\n";

# set the terminal to no-echo
my $lflag = $termios_stdin->getlflag;
printf "\tLocal flag is %b\n", $lflag;
# Perl<5.6: print "\tLocal flag is ",unpack("B16", pack('n', $lflag)), "\n";
# print "Set Terminal Mode to Noecho\n";
$termios_stdin->setlflag($lflag & ~(ECHO | ECHOK));
printf "\tLocal flag is %b\n", $termios_stdin->getlflag;

# Perl<5.6: print "\tLocal flag is ",
# unpack("B16", pack('n', $termios_stdin->getlflag)), "\n";
```

```
# set changes on STDIN
print "Setting STDIN from termios object\n";
$termios_stdin->setattr($stdin,POSIX::TCSANOW);

# restore original local flag (enable echo)
$termios_stdin->setlflag($lflag | ECHO | ECHOK);
printf "\tLocal flag is %b\n",$termios_stdin->getlflag;
# Perl<5.6: print "\tLocal flag is
# ", unpack("B16", pack('n', $termios_stdin->getlflag)), "\n";
print "Setting STDIN from termios object\n";
$termios_stdin->setattr($stdin, POSIX::TCSANOW);


print "\nInterrogating STDOUT:\n";
my $termios_stdout = new POSIX::Termios;
$termios_stdout->getattr($stdout);
my $old_stdout = new POSIX::Termios;
$old_stdout->getattr($stdout);

# set the output speed
print "\tOutput speed is ",$termios_stdout->getospeed, "\n";
print "Set speed to 9600 bps:\n";
$termios_stdout->setospeed(POSIX::B9600);
print "\tOutput speed is ", $termios_stdout->getospeed, "\n";

# set changes on STDOUT
print "Setting STDOUT from termios object\n";
$termios_stdout->setattr($stdout, POSIX::TCSANOW);
```

When run, this script should produce output similar to the following, if the platform supports termios operations:

> **perl termios.pl**
Interrogating STDIN:
        Erase key is 127
Set Erase to Control-D:
        Erase key is 4
        Local flag is 1000101000111011
Set Terminal Mode to Noecho
        Local flag is 1000101000010011
Setting STDIN from termios object
        Local flag is 1000101000111011
Setting STDIN from termios object

Interrogating STDOUT:
        Output speed is 15
Set speed to 9600 bps:
        Output speed is 13
Setting STDOUT from termios object

For more information on the POSIX module and in particular the subroutines and arguments of the POSIX::Termios module, consult the POSIX manual page and the documentation under:

> **perldoc POSIX**

Summary

In this chapter, we saw how communication with terminals has developed over the years, and how to determine whether a script is interactive. We then covered controlling terminal input using the `Term::ReadKey` module – particularly we looked at read modes and reading single characters.

After this we looked at reading complete lines, and covered the following topics in more depth:

- ❑ Passwords and invisible input
- ❑ Finding and setting the screen size
- ❑ Serial connections and terminal speed
- ❑ Line end translation
- ❑ Getting and setting control characters

We then discussed the creation of terminal objects (their supported features, and the command-line history), following which we discussed terminal capabilities like:

- ❑ Creating a termcap object
- ❑ Clearing the screen
- ❑ Moving the cursor

We briefly looked at the `Term::Screen` module, and then learned about the Curses library, by creating a simple application. Finally, we saw how to program a terminal directly via POSIX.

16

Warnings and Errors

Errors are not something we have a choice about, they are always enabled. Warnings on the other hand we have to enable ourselves. There is usually no good reason for not doing this, but Perl still gives us the choice.

In this chapter we will explore various options that Perl gives us to deal with warnings and errors.

Enabling Warnings

To enable warnings from the command line we can use the -w switch:

> **perl -w myscript.pl**

We can force warnings on, even if the application tries to switch them off by using the -W option instead:

> **perl -W myscript.pl**

Conversely, if we really want to run an application we know works and just have it shut up about warnings, we can use -X:

> **perl -X myscript.pl**

Inside the application, the setting of the -w options is expressed by the special variable $^W. We can switch warnings on and off on a program-wide scale using this variable, or localize it, for example to disable warnings temporarily:

```
sub mywarningpronesub {
    local $^W = 0;
    ...
}
```

This only works for run-time warnings however, since at compile time Perl is clearly not actually assigning variables or running code. From Perl 5.6, use of $^W is deprecated. Instead, we can enable (and disable) warnings from inside the application with the warnings pragma, as we have been doing in our previous examples:

```
use warnings;
```

Unless -W has been specified, we can disable warnings with:

```
sub mywarningpronesub {
    no warnings;
    ...
}
```

But why would it be advantageous to disable warnings? One reason is to suppress warnings from Perl for things that look wrong, but actually are not. For example, only using a variable once is usually an error, but if we are setting a variable for the benefit of other packages, or for reasons not directly connected to the program, we might easily set it once and then never refer to it again. A source control ID string is a good example:

```
#!/usr/bin/perl
$rcsid = '$Id$';
use warnings;
```

Or, better:

```
#!/usr/bin/perl
use warnings;
{
no warnings;    # no warnings inside block
$rcsid = '$id$';
}
```

The warnings pragma is actually a lot more versatile than this and has the potential to allow us to enable or disable warnings selectively. It also works at compile time, unlike $^W. We will cover it in more detail at the end of this section.

Enabling Diagnostics

Occasionally the errors and warnings emitted by Perl are not completely transparent. In these cases we can use the diagnostics pragma to provide a complete (and frequently very long) description of what Perl is trying to tell us. To enable it we just write:

```
use diagnostics;
```

As an example, the following program generates a void context warning:

```
#!/usr/bin/perl
use diagnostics;

2**2;
```

Note that use diagnostics automatically enables warnings if they have not been enabled at this point, but that we can still disable them with no warnings later. This is the warning that Perl produces from the above program when the warnings pragma is enabled:

Useless use of a constant in void context at ./diagnostics.pl line 4 (#1)

And here is what the diagnostics pragma has to say about it:

(W void) You did something without a side effect in a context that does nothing with the return value, such as a statement that doesn't return a value from a block, or the left side of a scalar comma operator. Very often this points not to stupidity on your part, but a failure of Perl to parse your program the way you thought it would. For example, you'd get this if you mixed up your C precedence with Python precedence and said

$one, $two = 1, 2;

when you meant to say

($one, $two) = (1, 2);

Another common error is to use ordinary parentheses to construct a list reference when you should be using square or curly brackets, for example, if you say

$array = (1,2);

when you should have said

$array = [1,2];

The square brackets explicitly turn a list value into a scalar value, while parentheses do not. So when a parenthesized list is evaluated in a scalar context, the comma is treated like C's comma operator, which throws away the left argument, which is not what you want. See perlref for more on this.

This information comes from the perldiag.pod file, which is otherwise available as perldoc perldiag. The (W void) prefix indicates that this is a warning (as opposed to a fatal error, for instance) in the void category.

By default use diagnostics will generate diagnostics for warnings at both the compile and run-time stages. It is not possible to disable diagnostics during the compile stage (no diagnostics does not work), but they can be enabled and disabled at run time with enable diagnostics and disable diagnostics:

```
use diagnostics;
disable diagnostics;

sub diagnose_patient {
    enable diagnostics;
    $undefined_filehandle;
    print $undefined_filehandle "It's worse than that, he's dead Jim";
    disable diagnostics;
}
```

Optionally, -verbose may be specified to have the diagnostics pragma output an introduction explaining the classification of warnings, errors, and other salient information:

```
use diagnostics qw(-verbose);
```

Two variables may also be set to control the output of the diagnostics module prior to using use on it. $diagnostics::PRETTY enhances the text a little for browsing. $diagnostics::DEBUG is for the curious. Both are not set by default but can be enabled with:

```
BEGIN {
        $diagnostics::PRETTY = 1;
        $diagnostics::DEBUG = 1;
}
```

Needless to say, it's not a good idea to enable use diagnostics in programs that generate a lot of warnings, and it should not be present in production code at all. The command line tool splain will generate diagnostic messages from warnings if they have been stored in a file, which is sometimes an acceptable alternative:

> **perl myscript.pl 2>warnings.log**
> **splain -v -p < warnings.log**

The -v (verbose) and -p (pretty) options are optional, they have the same meanings as they do for the diagnostics pragma if specified.

Generating Warnings and Errors

We can generate our own (non-fatal) warnings and (fatal) errors using the warn and die functions. Both functions take a list of arguments, which are passed to print and sent to standard error.

The key distinction between them is of course that die causes the application to exit, whereas warn merely sends a message and allows the application to continue running. The die function returns the value of $! to the caller, which can be retrieved through $? if the caller is also a Perl script. If $! is not set but $? is, then die shifts it right eight places ($? >> 8) and returns that as the exit code, to propagate the exit code from a child process to the parent. The value returned by die (or exit) can also be modified through $? (we will come to this a little later).

If the message passed to either warn or die ends with a newline, then it is printed verbatim, without embellishment. If however no trailing newline is present then Perl will add details of the file and line number to the end of the message (plus a newline). For example:

> **perl -e 'warn "Eek! A Mouse\n"'**   # On Windows: **perl -e "warn \"Eek! A Mouse\n\""**
Eek! A Mouse!

> **perl -e 'warn "Eek! A Mouse"'**   # On Windows: **perl -e "warn \"Eek A Mouse\""**
Eek! A Mouse! at -e line 1.

If no message at all is passed to warn or die then they consult the value of $@ to see if an error has been trapped by an eval statement (see below). In this case they use the message contained in $@ and append "\t...caught" or "\t...propagated" to it, respectively. If even $@ is not defined then they get creative, die simply produces:

> Died at <file> line <line>.

`warn` produces the paranoid:

> Warning: something's wrong at <file> line <line>.

Of course giving either function no arguments is questionable at best, unless we are checking explicitly the result of an `eval`:

```
die if !eval($evalstr) and $@;
```

As a special case for evaluated code, if the `die` function is passed a reference (not a message), then this reference is set into the variable `$@` outside the `eval`. The main point of this is to allow object-oriented programs to raise exceptions as objects rather than messages:

```
eval {
    ...
    die new MyModule::PermissionsException;
}

if ($@) {
if ($@ == MyModule::PermissionsException) {
    ...
} else {
    ...
}
}
```

If `die` is given a reference as an argument and it is not in an `eval` then it simply prints the reference by converting it into a string, as usual.

Intercepting Warnings and Errors

Warnings and errors, whether issued by Perl directly or generated by applications through the `warn` or `die` functions can be trapped within program code using the __WARN__ and __DIE__ pseudo-signal handlers, by defining values for them in the `%SIG` signal handler hash. For example, we can suppress warnings completely by saying:

```
$SIG{__WARN__} = sub{};
```

A more useful warnings handler might embellish the warning before printing it, or redirect it to a file:

```
$SIG{__WARN__} = sub{print WARNLOG, "$0 warning: ", @_, "\n"};
```

We can even call `warn` from inside the handler; the handler itself is disabled for duration of the handler subroutine:

```
$SIG{__WARN__} = sub{warn "$0 warning: ", @_;};
```

603

The `die` handler is defined in much the same way, but unlike a `warn` handler we cannot suppress it completely, only change the message by calling `die` a second time. Any other action will cause Perl to carry on and continue dying with the original arguments. This means that we can use a `die` handler to perform cleanup actions, but we cannot use it to avoid death.

```
$SIG{__DIE__} = sub {
    # send real message to log file
    print LOGFILE "Died: @_";
    # Give the user something flowery
    die "Oh no, not again";
}
```

This approach is useful in things like CGI programs, where we want the user to know something is wrong, but do not want to actually give away potentially embarrassing details.

Deciphering Error Results from System Calls

Many of Perl's functions make calls to the operating system in order to carry out their task; examples of this are the `open` and `close` functions. None of these functions cause fatal errors or even produce warnings if they fail. Instead, they return an undefined value and set the value of the special variable `$!`.

Error Numbers and Names

`$!`, also known as `$ERRNO` if we have used the `English` module, is directly related to the C `errno` value and holds the error status of the last system function called. In a string context it returns a textual description, which we can use in our own messages:

```
warn "Warning - failed: $! \n";
```

In a numeric context it returns the actual value of `errno`, which we can use programmatically. In order to use symbolic names rather than numbers for errors it is convenient to use the `Errno` module:

```
use Errno qw(EAGAIN);

if ($!) {
    # check for EAGAIN in numeric comparison
    sleep(1), redo if $! == EAGAIN;
    # die, using $! in string context
    die "Fatal error: $!\n";
}
```

Alternatively we can avoid importing error symbols and just write them explicitly:

```
sleep(1), redo if $! == Errno::EAGAIN;
```

`Errno` also defines the hash variable `%!`, which looks like a Perl special variable but actually is not. It allows us to check for errors by looking them up as keys in the hash and seeing if they are set to a True value. Because `$!` can only hold one error at a time there can only be one key with a True value, so this is really just an alternative syntax to using `==`:

```
sleep(1), redo if $!{EAGAIN};
```

The `Errno` module is smart in that it understands which errors are actually available on the platform that Perl is running on, so we can check for the existence of a particular symbol with `exists`:

```perl
#!/usr/bin/perl
# errno.pl
use warnings;
use strict;

use Errno;

print "EAGAIN = ", Errno::EAGAIN, "\n" if exists &Errno::EAGAIN;
print "EIO = ", Errno::EIO, "\n" if exists &Errno::EIO;
```

The symbols defined by `Errno` are subroutines, in the style of `use constant`, not scalars. Alternatively, we can use `%!`:

```perl
# continuation of errno.pl
foreach ('EAGAIN','EIO','EVMSERR','EKETHUMP') {
    warn "$_ not supported\n" unless exists $!{$_};
}
```

This will generate the warning **EKETHUMP not supported** on all platforms. `EVMSERR` should only be defined on a VMS system.

Setting the Error Number

In a few cases it can be advantageous to actually set the value of `$!`. Although it can be treated either numerically or as a string, `$!` can only be assigned a numeric value. Despite this, we can still produce a textual message from it:

```perl
$! = 1;
print "$!";   # display 'Operation not permitted'.
```

Setting `$!` should not be done lightly; since we can obscure a previous error that we ought to be handling. A common reason to set it is, as we saw earlier, to handle a child process exit and propagate the child's value of `$!` to the parent.

```perl
if ($?) {
    $! = $? >> 8;
    die "Child exited abnormally: $!";
}
```

Note however that the `die` function automatically performs this job for us if our intent is only to return a child's exit status to a parent process of our own.

Errors from Evaluated Code

Code evaluated inside an `eval` statement, which includes code evaluated indirectly via `do`, `require`, or even `use` (if the module contains a `BEGIN` block) may also set the variable `$!`. However, if the code fails to compile at all (in the event of a syntax error), then the special variable `$@` is set to a textual description of the syntax error. The return value from `eval` is undef in this case, but it may also be undef in many cases that set `$!`, if the return value is determined by a function like `open` that returns undef itself. In order to properly handle an `eval` therefore, we need to check both variables.

```
eval $evalstr;
if ($@) {
    die "Eval error: $@\n";
} elsif ($!) {
    die "Error: $!\n";
}
```

In the event of success, eval returns the value of the last expression that it evaluated, not a Boolean 'success' or 'failure' as we might like. Since this can frequently be 0 or undef, a common trick for checking eval for errors is to explicitly add a final statement of 1 to guarantee that the eval will always return True on success. A syntax error of any kind, on the other hand, will cause eval to return undef since it never gets to the 1.

For example, to find out if the symlink function is supported on our platform we can write:

```
$symlink_ok = eval{symlink("", ""); 1}
```

This works because in the event of the success or failure of the symlink, the eval will always return 1. It will return undef due to a fatal error raised by Perl in the event that the platform does not support symlink. In this case symlink will return 0 but not raise a fatal error if it is supported, since we cannot link an empty filename to itself. The added 1 allows us to ignore the issue of a successful compile but a failed call. Of course if we actually want to return a meaningful value from the eval this is not going to work, but for many cases it's a useful trick.

Extended Error Messages

Some platforms also supply additional error information in the special variable $^E, or $EXTENDED_OS_ERROR with the English module. Currently only OS/2, Windows, and VMS provide additional information here:

OS/2	$^E is set to the last call to the OS/2 API via the underlying C runtime libraries, or directly from Perl. Incidental causes of $! being set are not carried over to $^E.
VMS	$^E may provide more specific information about errors than $!. This is particularly true for the VMS specific EVMSERR, which we mentioned briefly in the example earlier.
Windows	$^E contains the last error returned by the Win32 API, as opposed to $!, which is more generic. It may contain additional information or a better description of the error, but may also be empty even after an error, due to the non-unified nature of the Win32 error reporting system.

For all other platforms, $^E is identical to $!. The best approach for handling $^E therefore is to add it to an error message if it is set and is not equal to the message returned from $!:

```
$message = $!;
$message .= "\n $^E" if $^E ne $!;
warn $message;
```

Finer grained control may be possible by checking $^O ($OSNAME with use English) and dealing with errors in a platform-specific way, but this is overkill for most applications.

'Errno' and The 'POSIX' Module

The POSIX module provides a direct interface from Perl to the underlying C standard library. Many of the functions in this library set errno and therefore the value of $! in Perl, and can be handled in the same way as standard Perl functions like open and close. The POSIX module supplies its own errno function, which is just an explicit numeric evaluation of $! (literally, $!+0), which illustrates how closely $! is linked to the errno value.

The POSIX module also defines constants for the standard system errors like EAGAIN, EINVAL, EPERM and so on, which we can import with the errno_h tag, along with the errno subroutine:

```
use POSIX qw(:errno_h);
```

In general, the Errno module is preferred over this approach since it has better portability across different platforms (it allows us to check for the availability of a given error, for instance). However, for programs that make extensive use of the POSIX module this may be an acceptable alternative.

All (modern) UNIX systems conform closely to the POSIX standard, so the POSIX module works well on these platforms. Windows and other platforms can make some use of the module, but many aspects of it (in particular the API) will not be available. In particular, this module has no direct correspondence to the somewhat approximate POSIX compatibility layer in Windows NT.

Checking the Exit Status of Subprocesses and External Commands

Child processes run by Perl (for example external commands run via system, backticks, and forked processes) return their status in the special variable $? when they exit. This is traditionally a 16-bit value (though it's 32 bit on Windows), containing two eight bit values:

```
my $exitcode = $? >> 8;    # exit code
my $exitsignal = $? & 127;   # signal that caused exit
```

The 'exit code' is the exit value returned by the subprocess. It should be zero for success, and a number corresponding to an error code, such as returning a True value on success or 0 on failure. For example, the UNIX ping command returns 0 if it resolves the IP address, regardless of whether it actually reaches the requested host.

The signal is often 0, but if set indicates that the child died because of a signal which it did not trap or ignore, for example 2 would correspond to a SIGINT and 9 would be a SIGKILL. This is one way we could check for and handle a process terminated by either a signal, or returning with an exit code (the command is in @args):

```
my $result = system(@args);
if (my $signal = $? & 127) {
    warn "External command exited on signal $signal\n";
} elsif (our $! = $? >> 8) {
    # assign $! numerically
    $! = $exitcode;

    # display it textually
    warn "External command existed with error: $!\n";
}
```

We take advantage of the special properties of $!$ to generate a textual message from the returned exit code, but note that this is only appropriate if the exit code corresponds to an `errno` value. The concept of signals is much more concrete on UNIX platforms than others, in particular Windows. For example, when a *CTRL-C* interrupt occurs on Win32, the operating systems generate a new thread to specifically handle that interrupt. This can cause a single-thread application such as UNIX, to become multithreaded, resulting in unexpected behavior.

We can also use $?$ to intercept and change the exit status of an application by redefining it in an END block. For example, to pretend that all is well even if it isn't:

```
END {
    $? = 0 if $? and $ENV{'ALLS_WELL_THAT_ENDS_BADLY'};
}
```

Making Non-Fatal Errors Fatal

The `Fatal` module provides a simple and effective way to promote system-level errors to fatal errors in Perl. Normally when a function like `open` fails, it sets $!$ and returns undef, but does not otherwise flag an error or even a warning. The `Fatal` module allows us to change that. To use it, we simply pass an import list of the functions we want to handle:

```
use Fatal qw(open close);
```

`Fatal` works on the assumption that an undefined or empty value return is a sign of failure, so it will only trap functions like `open` and `close` that adhere to this rule. However, most of Perl's functions that make calls to the operating system, and therefore set $!$ on failure, do exactly this. We can even trap a failed `print` this way, something that we rarely do because of the problems of clarity this would otherwise cause:

```
use Fatal qw(print open close sysopen);
```

The `Fatal` module wraps the named functions in its import list with versions that emit errors, so it can also work on subroutines, so long as they have been previously declared or defined:

```
use Fatal qw(mysubroutine);
```

This works well if we never check for failures ourselves, but otherwise it can be limiting. Rather than simply making failures fatal errors, which we must catch with a signal handler to prevent our application exiting, we can use `Fatal` to supplement our own error checking by producing a fatal error only if the return value is not checked explicitly. To do this we add the special label `:void` (for `void` context) to the import list. Any subroutines or functions listed before this label are treated as before and always issue an error on failure. Any subroutines or functions listed afterward issue an error only if their return value is ignored:

```
use Fatal qw(sysopen :void open close);

open FILE, "> /readonly/area/myfile";   # fails with error

unless (open FILE, "> /readonly/area/myfile") {   # no error issued
    ... handle error explicitly
}

unless (sysopen FILE, "/readonly/area/myfile", O_RDWR|O_CREAT) {
}
```

This works because the wrapper generated by `Fatal` can check for the calling context by examining the value of `wantarray`. If it is defined, the wrapper was called in a scalar or list context and the return value is therefore being used. If it is undefined then the wrapper was called in a void context and the return value is being ignored. In this case the wrapper issues a fatal error.

It is important to realize that the wrappers generated by `Fatal` do not perform compile-time checking, nor does it issue an error if a function or subroutine succeeds in a void context; it will only be triggered in the event of a failure.

Returning Warnings and Errors in Context with 'Carp'

The `Carp` module is one of Perl's most enduringly useful modules. Its primary subroutines `carp` and `croak` work exactly like `warn` and `die` but return details of the calling context rather than the one in which they occurred. They are therefore ideal for library code and module subroutines, since the warning or error will report the line in the code that called them rather than a warning or error in the module source itself.

Both subroutines track back up the stack of subroutine calls looking for a call from a different package. They then use and return the details of that call. The upshot of this is that irrespective of how many subroutine or method calls might have occurred within the package, it is the calling package that resulted in the `carp` or `croak` that is reported:

```
package My::Module;

sub mymodulesub {
    carp "You called me from your own code";
}
```

This generates a message like:

```
You called me from your own code at ./owncode.pl line N.
```

From the point of view of an application developer this gives them a message that originates in their own code, and not in a library module which they have no immediate way of tracing back to the call that caused the warning or error to occur.

The `cluck` and `confess` subroutines are more verbose versions of `carp` and `croak`. They generate messages for the file and line number they were actually called at (unlike `carp` and `croak`, but like `warn` and `die`) but make up for this by generating a full stack trace of subroutine calls in reverse order, from the subroutine they were called from back up to the top of the program.

Here is a short program that demonstrates `carp`, `cluck`, and `confess`. To make things interesting we have used three subroutines each in their own package, to illustrate the effect of calling these subroutines at different points:

```
#!/usr/bin/perl
# carpdemo.pl
use warnings;

&Top::top;
```

```
package Top;
use Carp qw(cluck);
sub top {
    cluck "Called 'top'";
    &Middle::middle;
}

package Middle;
use Carp;
sub middle {
    carp "Are we there yet? Called 'middle'";
    &Bottom::bottom;
}

package Bottom;
use Carp;
sub bottom {
    carp "Here we are. Called 'bottom'";
    confess "I did it!";
}
```

This is the output generated from this program:

```
Called 'top' at ./carpdemo.pl line 8
        Top::top called at ./carpdemo.pl line 3
Are we there yet? Called 'middle' at ./carpdemo.pl line 9
Here we are. Called 'bottom' at ./carpdemo.pl line 16
I did it! at ./carpdemo.pl line 23
        Bottom::bottom called at ./carpdemo.pl line 16
        Middle::middle called at ./carpdemo.pl line 9
        Top::top called at ./carpdemo.pl line 3
```

If the symbol verbose is imported into the application then carp and croak are automatically upgraded into cluck and confess, that is, a stack trace is generated by all four subroutines. We do not typically want to do this within applications, but it is very handy on the command line if we want to get extra detail on a problem:

> **perl -MCarp=verbose myscript.pl**

Since carp and cluck are essentially improved versions of warn they can, like warn be trapped by assigning a handler to $SIG{__WARN__}. Similarly, croak and confess can be caught with $SIG{__DIE__}.

Developers who are engaged in writing server-side applications like CGI scripts should instead make use of the CGI::Carp module. This overrides the default subroutines provided by Carp with versions that are formatted to be compatible with the format of a web server's error log, and is therefore considerably friendlier to log analysis tools, as well as allowing the log to show which script actually generated the message.

Error Logs and System Logs

We frequently want to arrange for errors and logging messages to go to a file rather than directly to the screen. This is simple enough to arrange both within and outside Perl. Outside, we can usually make use of output redirection in the shell to create a log file. Most modern shells (including NT's cmd.exe) allow standard error (filehandle number 2) to be directed with:

> **perl myscript.pl 2>error.log**

From inside Perl we can redirect the STDERR filehandle in a number of ways, which we cover in more detail in Chapter 12. Here is one simple way of doing it, by simply reopening STDERR to a new location:

```
open STDERR, "> /tmp/error.log" or print STDERR "Failed to open error log: $!";
```

> *Note that if this open fails, the original STDERR filehandle remains intact. Since this is likely to be our fallback option, we allow the open to fail but issue a warning about it on the original STDERR.*

On UNIX and UNIX-like platforms we may also make use of the system log, run by the system log daemon syslogd and generally configured by a file called /etc/syslog.conf or similar. Perl provides a standard interface to the UNIX system log through the Sys::Syslog module:

```
use Sys::Syslog;
```

To open a connection to the system log daemon, use openlog. This takes three arguments: a program identifier, so we can be uniquely identified, a string containing optional options and a syslog service, for example user:

```
openlog 'myapp', 0, 'user';
```

Instead of 0 or '', the options can also be a comma separated combination of cons, pid, nowait, and ndelay, which are passed to the underlying socket, for example cons,pid,nowait. Once a connection is established we can log messages with syslog, which takes a priority as its first argument and a printf style format and values as the second and further arguments. The syslog daemon itself takes the priority, for example error, and uses it to determine where the message is sent to, as determined by its own configuration (the file /etc/syslog.conf on most UNIX systems).

```
syslog('debug', 'This is a debug message');
syslog('info', 'Testing, Testing, %d %d %d', 1, 2, 3);
syslog('news|warning', 'News unavailable at %s', scalar(localtime));
syslog('error', "Error! $!");
```

The value of $! is also automatically substituted for the %m format, in syslog only, so the last example above can also be written as:

```
syslog('error', 'Error! %m');
```

The socket type used to the connection may also be set (for openlog) or changed (even in between calls to syslog) with setlogsock, which we could use to switch between local and remote logging services. The default is to use an Internet domain socket. (But note that a UNIX domain socket is often better both from a security and a performance point of view. It is potentially possible to overrun syslog on an Internet domain socket, resulting in lost messages.):

```
setlogsock ('unix');    # use a UNIX domain socket
setlogsock ('inet');    # use an Internet domain socket
```

611

The return value from setlogsock is True if it succeeds, or 0 if it fails. Consult the system documentation for more information on the system log and how to use and configure it.

On Windows NT we can make use of the Win32::Eventlog module, available from CPAN, which provides an interface to the NT system log. For some reason known only to the developers of NT, this log is a binary file and cannot be easily read except with the eventvwr utility. Even then, useful error messages may be hard to find.

Here is a short example of using the Win32::EventLog module:

```perl
#!/perl/bin/perl
# win32.pl
use Win32::EventLog;
use strict;

my $e = new Win32::EventLog($0);
my %hash = (Computer => $ENV{COMPUTERNAME},
    EventType => EVENTLOG_ERROR_TYPE,
    Category => 42,
    Data => "Data about this error",
    Strings => "this is a test error"
);
$e->Report(\%hash);
```

For more information about programming the Event Log on Windows NT, you can use perldoc Win32::Eventlog.

Advanced Warnings

The warnings pragma, introduced in Perl 5.6, allows us to turn warnings on and off within Perl. We saw an example of it in one of its more simple uses earlier. However, it is a lot more powerful than this. The default use of use warnings is actually equivalent to:

```perl
use warnings qw(all);
```

By supplying alternative and more specific category names to the warnings pragma, and especially using no, we can enable or disable warnings selectively. For example, the following disables all void warnings, including the Useless use of .... in void context messages:

```perl
no warnings qw(void);
```

This is a lexically scoped declaration, so we can use it inside (say) a subroutine in the same way we can say things like no strict 'refs', with the effect of the pragma extending only across the body of the subroutine.

Warning pragmas stack up cumulatively, and several categories may also be given at once, so the following are equivalent:

```perl
no warnings 'void';
no warnings 'untie';
no warnings 'uninitialized';
use warnings 'untie';

no warnings qw(void uninitialized);
```

If we want to check whether a warnings group is enabled or not we can do so with
warnings::enabled:

```
$checking_for_void = warnings::enabled('void');
```

We can also manage our own category, if we are programming modules. We can dynamically add a new warnings category under the name of the module with:

```
use warnings::register;
```

To issue warnings in our own category we then simply pass the warning we want to issue to warnings::warn:

```
warnings::warn ('This warning is in our own category');
```

To issue a warning in a specific category, we can pass the category name as the first argument:

```
warnings::warn ('void', 'This warning is in the void category');
```

Code that uses our module may now switch warnings from our module on and off by issuing the appropriate pragmas:

```
no warnings qw(MyModule);
```

Here is a list of all the categories currently supported by the warnings pragma. Note that this is a hierarchical list, so we disable all io warnings except unopened filehandle warnings with no warnings qw(io) followed by use warnings qw(unopened):

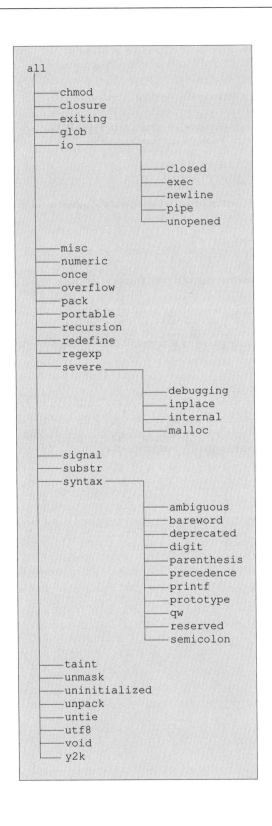

Summary

In the course of this chapter we examined the tools that Perl provides us with for generating warnings and reporting errors. We covered the following:

❑ Obtaining longer descriptions of Perl warnings using the `diagnostics` pragma.

❑ Generating non-fatal and fatal warnings with the warn and die functions, respectively, and trapping them with __WARN__ and __DIE__.

❑ Handling errors that result from system calls.

❑ Making non-fatal errors fatal using the Fatal module.

❑ Determining the context of the resulting warnings and errors using the `Carp` module. We examined the `carp`, `croak`, `cluck`, and `confess` subroutines.

❑ Logging errors.

❑ Using the advanced options of the `warnings` pragma.

17

Debugging

Perl comes with a comprehensive and fully featured debugger. Unlike other languages, however, the debugger is not a separate tool but simply a special mode of the Perl interpreter, which makes use of an external library called `perl5db.pl`. To enable it we simply use the `-d` option, after which we may step through code, set breakpoints, examine, and execute code selectively from inside the debugger.

In addition to the debugger, Perl supplies a number of modules designed for debugging support or simply useful for debugging. In particular the `Safe` module allows us to create a restricted environment for Perl scripts to run in, and the `Test` and `Test::Harness` modules allow us to create automated testing scripts, among other things.

We do not always need to reach for the debugger at the first sign of trouble. With a little thought it is relatively simple to build debugging support into the application itself, which, if done correctly, can greatly help in tracking down problems. It also makes us think about what could go wrong, which itself helps to prevent bugs from occurring.

Irrespective of whether we implement our own debugging framework, it is always a good idea to minimize the amount of trouble we can get into by using the pragmatic modules Perl supplies to aid in developing our code in the first place.

In this chapter we will examine various debugging modules and techniques that Perl makes available to us.

Pragmatic Debugging Support

Before reaching for the debugger it is worth taking some simple and basic precautions that will fix a lot of problems before they start by making use of some of Perl's pragmatic modules. All of these modules are far more effective at preventing problems than curing them (they will do that too, but the process of fixing problems can be painful), so use them to start with rather than adding them later; prevention is better than cure.

The most important Perl module for preventing problems is the `warnings` module, which we examined in Chapter 16.

The second line of defense in good Perl programming is the `use strict` pragma. This tightens up and restricts three areas of Perl's syntax that can otherwise lead to problems:

- ❑ `use strict vars` – variables must be declared with `my` or `our` or written explicitly as package variables.

- ❑ `use strict subs` – barewords are not allowed because of their possible conflict with subroutine names.

- ❑ `use strict refs` – symbolic references are prohibited.

To get all three of these syntax checks at once, simply use:

```
use strict;
```

To get only some of them or disable one temporarily, qualify the pragma:

```
use strict 'vars';    # enable strict variables
no strict 'refs';     # allow symbolic references
```

Any Perl application that is designed to run on a public server or can be accessed by an unqualified user, such as a CGI script, should always have **taint checking** enabled. This is turned on with the `-T` command-line switch, which is commonly combined with `-w`:

> perl -Tw...

If Perl detects that a script is being run under an effective user id, which is different from the real user id (web servers that run on UNIX and UNIX-like platforms commonly do this, see for instance, Apache's `User` and `Group` directives) then `taint` mode is enabled automatically. This security feature only applies when the platform has a meaningful definition of 'effective' and 'real' user ids, which essentially limits it to UNIX platforms. Other platforms must specify `-T` explicitly. There is no way to disable `taint` from within the program once it has been enabled.

Perl's regular expression engine also comes with its own debugging support, which is entirely independent of the Perl debugger. To enable it, we add the following to any Perl script or application:

```
use re qw(debug);
```

Applications that Debug Themselves

It makes a lot of sense to build an application with debugging in mind, since debug support that is tailored to the design of an application is frequently more effective than a generic debugging tool, however powerful it is.

A Simple Debugging System

It pays to add debug support early on when writing code. One typical approach is to write a `debug` subroutine and then call it at appropriate moments:

```
# simple debug
sub debug {
    print STDERR @_,"\n";
}
...
debug "The value of 'scalar' is $scalar";
```

This simple debug routine mimics `print` but sends its output to standard error. But it also cannot be switched off. If we are happy to edit the code to enable or disable debugging we can define two subroutines and keep one of them commented:

```
sub debug {}
# sub debug { print STDERR @_, "\n"; }
```

This will not suffice if we want to be able to enable debugging from outside the program. A better debugging subroutine might use the environment to enable or disable debug messages, as this one does:

```
# a better debug
sub debug {
    print STDERR @_, "\n" if $ENV{'DEBUG'};
}
```

This debug routine only prints out messages if the DEBUG environment variable is set. This is generally better than implementing a `debug` option through a command-line argument, since other people can sometimes switch that on. A CGI debug parameter for example is not a good idea, since it can print out debugging information to an unqualified user if they are able to figure out how to enable it.

A Better Debugging System

Here is a simple script that implements a multi-level debugging scheme, so we can assign different **levels** of `debug` to different messages. Thus, level 2 messages only appear with level 2 `debug` or higher, but level 1 messages appear for any `debug` level. We have also implemented it as a closure, so that the debug level can only be changed through the `debug` subroutine itself or the more specific `debug_level`, which also returns the debug level if we wish to know it programmatically:

```
#!/usr/bin/perl
# debug.pl
use warnings;
use strict;

# define a debugging infrastructure
{
    my $debug_level = $ENV{'DEBUG'};
    $debug_level |= 0;   # set if unset

# return and optionally set debug level
sub debug_level {
    my $old_level = $debug_level;
    $debug_level = $_[0] if @_;
    return $old_level;
}
```

```
# print debug message or set debug level
sub debug {
   # remove first argument, if present
   my $level = shift;

   # @_ will contain more elements if 2+ arguments passed
   if (@_) {
      # 2+ argument calls print debug message if permitted
      print STDERR @_, "\n" if $level <= debug_level();
      } else {
         # one and no-argument calls set level
         debug_level($level?$level:1);
      }
   }
}
```

Having created these debug subroutines and their hidden debug level variable, we can now use them like this:

```
# continuation of debug.pl
# set debugging level explicitly
debug_level(1);

# send some debug messages
debug 1, "This is a level 1 debug message";
debug 2, "This is a level 2 debug message (unseen)";

# change debug level with single argument 'debug'
debug 2;
debug 2, "This is a level 2 debug message (seen)";

# return debugging level programmatically
debug 0, "Debug level is: ", debug_level;

# set debug level to 1 with no argument 'debug'
debug;
debug 0, "Debug level now: ", debug_level;
```

In this scheme we have the choice of letting the environment determine the debugging level, or overriding it with our own value inside the program. This is clearly a lot better than the first attempt, but it is also a lot bigger, which is a waste if we are not actually going to use the debugger. We also waste time passing arguments and processing them. To fix this we can avoid defining the debugging code unless we actually intend to use it. The following example shows one way to do this, by defining the debug subroutine conditionally. To keep the example short we have used a simpler debug routine:

```
#!/usr/bin/perl
# debug2.pl
use warnings;
use strict;

# predeclare 'debug' in the symbol table
use subs 'debug';

if ($ENV{'DEBUG'}) {
    # define a real debug subroutine if debugging is enabled
    *debug = sub {
       print STDERR @_, "\n";
    }
```

```
    } else {
        # otherwise define a useless stub
        *debug = sub {};
    }

    debug "This is a debug message";
```

Now we have a `debug` subroutine that only contains code to perform debugging if we actually have debugging turned on in the environment. Otherwise, a `stub` subroutine is generated so `debug` is still defined but without actually doing anything.

Creating Debug Logs

We might also want to create a **debug log** rather than have debugging messages go to standard error. This is not a problem as we can just redirect standard error to the place we want it to go in the shell. For example, most UNIX shells, and the Windows NT shell `cmd.exe`, will let us do things like the lines that follow. Firstly, on UNIX we can use:

> **DEBUG=1 perl myscript.pl 2> error.log**

And on Windows:

> **set DEBUG=1**
> **perl myscript.pl 2> error.log**

We could also write the application to use another environment variable for a log name:

> **DEBUG=1 DEBUG_LOG="error.log" perl myscript.pl**

Again, on Windows this needs to be changed to:

> **set DEBUG=1**
> **set DEBUG_LOG="error.log"**
> **perl myscript.pl**

All the application needs to do is check for the DEBUG_LOG environment variable and send a logging message to it:

```
    *DEBUG = *STDERR unless defined($ENV{'DEBUG_LOG'}) and
    open DEBUG "> $ENV{DEBUG_LOG}";
```

Here we guarantee the existence of a DEBUG filehandle for `print DEBUG` statements by using STDERR if the debug log is either not defined or cannot be opened.

Adding Calling Context to Debug Messages

A final useful feature that we can add to debugging messages is to include the place that they were issued from. This is invaluable, for finding precisely where a debugging message is coming from. It is particularly useful when locating debugging messages in a large application of many modules and files. We can find this information easily through the `caller` function, covered in some detail back in Chapter 7. With no arguments it returns the details of the current caller, which in the examples above would be the `debug` subroutine itself. To return the details of the subroutine containing the debug message we need to go back up the calling stack one frame by passing 1 to `caller`. The `caller` function returns a list of ten values, of which the first four are the most useful:

```
    ($pkg, $file, $line, $sub) = caller(1);
```

621

Armed with these values we can create a debug message that reports the filename line number, or possibly the subroutine name, as in this case:

```
print STDERR "** $sub | ", @_, "\n";
```

Note that the value of $sub in this case includes the package, so we do not need $pkg in this case. We are assuming here that the subroutine in question is small enough so that we do not need to search it by hand to locate the debug call, and that the package it is defined in is not spread across several files. We are also assuming that only subroutines will be calling it; this will not work if called outside a subroutine. Another more general debug message might use the file and line number instead:

```
print STDERR "** $file:$line | ", @_, "\n";
```

It all depends on what our debugging scheme is designed to handle. The first is more suitable for object programming where the debug calls are coming from object methods, whereas the second is more generic. We can of course construct a more complex conditional message if we like. In any event, we can substitute this code for the print statement in any of the previous debug examples to give us context-specific debug messages with relative ease.

The Perl Debugger

The Perl debugger is a tool for analyzing Perl programs during the course of their execution. It allows us to step line by line through a Perl program, examining the state of variables and calling subroutines interactively. We can set breakpoints in the code and let the program run until it encounters one, passing control back to us in the debugger. We can also execute arbitrary code, define new subroutines, and even use the debugger as a basic Perl shell if we want to.

We can configure the debugger in a number of ways to control its operation and the way in which it reports information to us. Options can be set interactively within the debugger, but we can also set up a configuration file to be read automatically by Perl when we enter debugging mode. I can also set options in the environment variable PERL5DB. The main functionality of the debugger is implemented in the external library perl5db.pl, which makes use of the 'debugging' hooks in the Perl interpreter to provide debugging services. We can therefore customize the debugger through this library. The hooks are a generic interface, so we can also replace the debugger with something else entirely. One example replacement debugger is the Perl profiler, which we will cover later in the chapter.

Starting the Debugger

To start the Perl debugger we use the -d option. For example, to debug a program called mybuggyscript.pl we would use:

> perl -d mybuggyscript.pl

We can combine -d with other flags, for example the taint and warnings flags for really conscientious debugging:

> perl -Twd mybuggyscript.pl

If we combine -d and -e we can debug code supplied directly on the command-line. Since the debugger allows us to type in and execute arbitrary code, this makes for a simple but effective Perl shell. We have to supply a valid program, but it does not have to do anything useful, or indeed anything at all. The value 1 is therefore a legal Perl program:

> **perl -dwe 1;**

The -d flag also accepts an argument that allows us to provide our own alternative debugger. One possible use for this is to use a customized replacement debugger created by modifying the perl5db.pl script that provides the standard debugger. Another is to use an existing alternative like the Perl profiler, which we can do with:

> **perl -d:DProf rapidoffensiveunit.pl**

The profiler collects information about the speed of execution of every part of a Perl program and dumps it to an output file we can analyze later. We will cover it in more detail later in the chapter. Meanwhile, assuming we start the standard debugger, it will load in the Perl script (or code, in the case of -e), execute any BEGIN blocks it finds, and provide us with a prompt ready to execute the first line of code in the program proper. For example:

> **perl -d config.pl**

This is using the config.pl script example from Chapter 6. It produces a standard startup message, the first line of the script (in this case a hash variable declaration) and a prompt:

Default die handler restored.

Loading DB routines from perl5db.pl version 1.07
Editor support available.

Enter h or `h h' for help, or `man perldebug' for more help.

main::(config.pl:3):   my %config=();
    DB<1>

The line my %config=() is the line that is about to be executed. The 3 is the line number in the file at which this statement was found. The DB<1> tells us that the command we are about to execute is the first command, we can go back and re-execute commands later with !<command no>.

The debugger will only start up if the program compiles successfully. If it has errors that prevent this, we will have to fix them before we can use the debugger. Assuming that the program is at least good enough to compile, we can execute debugging commands.

Entering Commands

The debugger supplies a large number of commands to do everything from pulling Perl data apart and scrutinizing it to rewriting the program interactively. It also allows us to execute arbitrary code, which means it can be used as a passable Perl shell (see Chapter 14 for more on the subject of shells).

Simple Debugging Commands – Single Stepping

Debugger commands are single letters followed in some cases by space-separated arguments. One particularly useful command is h, which displays a summary of the currently supported debugger commands (like many things in Perl, the debugger evolves from release to release):

```
DB<1> h
T                Stack trace.
s [expr]  Single step [in expr].
n [expr]  Next, steps over subroutine calls [in expr].
<CR>      Repeat last n or s command.
r                Return from current subroutine.
```

Since the output of h is quite long, we might want to page it by prefixing it with |, so the full command is, |h. (For this to work the platform needs to have a valid pager program configured. UNIX users will be fine, but other platforms may need to configure the pager; consult the configuration section below to see how to configure a pager program.)

Possibly the two most used commands are s, which single-steps through a program one line at a time, and n, which executes the next line. The distinction between these two is that s will step into subroutines and offer them to us to execute line by line, whereas n will call the subroutine and offer the next line in the current context. Here is an example of how we can use s to step through a Perl script, in this case the config.pl script. Note that the bold lines are typed in by us in response to the <> being executed:

```
DB<1> s
main::(config.pl:4):   while (<>) {
DB<1> s
Dante=Too Cool To Kill
main::(config.pl:5):           chomp; #strip linefeed
DB<1>
main::(config.pl:7):           next if /^\s*$/;   # skip to the next iteration on empty lines
DB<1> p $_
Dante=Too Cool To Kill
DB<2> s
main::(config.pl:8):           next if /^\s*#/;   # skip to the next iteration on comments
DB<2> s
main::(config.pl:9):           my ($param, $value) = split("=", $_,2);   # split on first '='
DB<2> s
main::(config.pl:10):          print("No value for parameter '$_'\n"), next unless $value;
DB<2> x $param
0  'Dante'
DB<3> x $value
0  'Too Cool To Kill'
DB<3> s
main::(config.pl:12):          $config{$param} = $value;
DB<3> s
main::(config.pl:4):   while (<>) {
DB<3> s
Joe=I am the Law
main::(config.pl:5):           chomp;  # strip linefeed
DB<3> s
```

```
main::(config.pl:7):         next if /^\s*$/;   # skip to the next iteration on empty lines
  DB<3> s
main::(config.pl:8):         next if /^\s*#/;   # skip to the next iteration on comments
  DB<3> s
main::(config.pl:9):         my ($param, $value)=split("=",$_,2);   # split on first '='
  DB<3> s
main::(config.pl:10):        print("No value for parameter '$_'\n"), next unless $value;
  DB<3> s
main::(config.pl:12):        $config{$param} = $value;
  DB<3> s
main::(config.pl:4):    while (<>) {
  DB<3> x %config
0 'Joe'
1 'I am the Law'
2 'Dante'
3 'Too Cool To Kill'
  DB<4>
```

As it happens (and as the snippet of the help text we showed earlier explains), just entering *return* re-executes the last s or n we used, so we did not need to type s after the first time.

This example output also shows the p command, which prints out values in exactly the same way that Perl's `print` statement does; and the x command, which examines the contents of values, expanding and printing their contents prefixed with an index number if they are arrays or hashes. The x command will descend any number of levels in order to fully display the contents of an array or hash, which makes it very useful.

Running Arbitrary Code

Any line that is not recognized as a debugger command is executed as Perl code (incidentally h does not count as a command proper, so it does not increment the command number in the prompt):

```
DB<1> print "Hello Debugger World\n", 2+2, " is 4\n";
Hello Debugger World
4 is 4
```

In the rare cases where we want to execute code (most probably a subroutine in the script being debugged or defined by ourselves for debugging) that looks like a debugger command, we can resolve it by prefixing the line with anything that is not a valid debugger command, such as ;. For example, the debugger command x examines (dumps out) the contents of variables, so if we want to execute a subroutine called x, we can use:

```
DB<2> ;x 1,2,3
```

This calls x with arguments 1,2,3, rather than triggering the debugger's examine command. Note that having subroutines with the same names as debugger commands is terribly sensible in the first place.

Multiline Commands

Since we can execute arbitrary code, we can do things like write `foreach` loops and define subroutines. We can also, in some cases, come up with very long debugging commands if we need to specify a lot of arguments. If we want to be able to do this without entering the entire command on a single line we can use a backslash at the end of the line to continue the command onto the next line. We can do this as many times as we need to. For example, to define a handy environment dumping command we can define a subroutine:

```
DB<7> sub dumpenv { \
cont:    foreach (sort keys %ENV) { \
cont:       print "$_ => $ENV{$_}\n"; \
cont:    } \
cont: }

DB<8> dumpenv
DISPLAY => :0.0

ENV => /home/gurgeh/.bashrc
HOME => /home/gurgeh
...
```

If we make a mistake and forget a trailing slash at any point the debugger will complain at us and we will have to start again. If we have ReadLine support enabled (automatically provided by the Term::ReadLine module if we have it installed, see Chapter 15) then we can use the up cursor key to re-enter each line again, which is quicker than typing it. If we really like this subroutine we can also define it in an external configuration file so it is automatically available whenever we start the debugger.

Debugging Commands

Having seen how to make use of simple debugging commands like the s, p, and x commands, we can now take a more detailed look at all the commands that are executable from the Perl debugger prompt. In order to make them a little more digestible, we have loosely and informally organized them into the following functional groups:

Help Commands	Action
h	Display a summary of all debugger commands. To display information on a single option, for example, the x command, type h followed by the command letter: h x Rather intelligently, the h command correctly substitutes the current values of recallCommand and shellBang for the commands whose letters are determined by these configuration options, see later.
man [page]	Calls the system manual page viewer for the given page, or perldoc if no such viewer is available. The actual viewer can be configured by setting $DB::doccmd to the viewer command. If no page is supplied, it calls the viewer on itself (for help on using the viewer, fro example, man man or perldoc perldoc). Non-UNIX platforms may experience problems such as leaving the screen in a strange state if they don't support any sensible definition of manual pages. Using a separate window for documentation is a better idea in this case.

Display (Variables)	Action
p [expr]	Print the expression expr to the debugger's output terminal, defined by $DB::OUT, which is independent of wherever STDOUT may have been redirected to (see 'Tracing and Terminals' later). For example: `p $param,'=', $value` p works exactly like the print statement (though it only adheres to the values of $/ and $, if they are set in the same command). References and complex data structures are printed out as-is, in the style of print. For a more intelligent display of complex data, use x.

x [expr]	Evaluate and print out expr as a list, formatting the output prettily. Nested array and hash references are listed recursively. For example:
	
	DB<1> $href={ 'top'=>{ middle=>['left','right', { 'bottom'=>1 }]}}
	DB<2> x $href
	  0 HASH(0x8223380)
	    'top' => HASH(0x822335c)
	    'middle' => ARRAY(0x82232cc)
	      0 'left'
	      1 'right'
	      2 HASH(0x825276c)
	    'bottom' => 1

V [pkg [vars]], X [vars]	These commands list the contents of the named variables from the named package. If vars is omitted, list all variables from the named package. If pkg is also omitted, it lists variables in the current package (frequently main if we are debugging a Perl application and not a module). For example, to display the current value of $DB::doccmd: **DB<1> V DB doccmd** $doccmd = 'man' To list all variables in DB, the debugger's own package: **DB<1> V DB** To list all variables in the current package: **DB<1> V** To list variables selectively in the current package, use the X command instead, which omits the pkg argument: **DB<1> X param value config** Note that the prefix $, @, % etc., should not be supplied to either of X or V, and that all variables with a corresponding name will be displayed, for example, $config, @config and %config, if they exist. If the variable name starts with ~ or !, the name is used as a regular expression and is matched against the names of the variables in the package. Matching (or in the case of !, non-matching) variables are dumped. Remember to use anchors (^ or $) to match variables with prefixes or suffixes.

Table continued on following page

Display (Variables)	Action
T	Display the calling stack, listing the callers of the current subroutine in a similar way to the caller function, if the debugger is halted within a subroutine. If there is no stack to display, it produces nothing. Note that the debugger itself is technically at the top of the stack, but it removes itself when displaying the stack with T.

Display (Source Code)	Action
w	List a window of lines around the current line. The window is chosen to be a sensible range of lines determined by the context around the current line. For example, when debugging a loop or subroutine, w returns the code of the loop or subroutine if it is of a reasonable size.
l	List the next window of lines in the current source file. Again, this is determined by context and will usually follow the window given by w:
	If there is no next window, l will return lines roughly similar to those returned by w. It can be used with the following arguments.
	DB<1> l line
	A single line itself can be displayed by specifying, for example, to list line 7 only:
	DB<1> l 7
	DB<1> l start+lines
	If a start and increment are specified with a +, list lines starting from line number 'start' and listing 'lines' lines in total. For example, to list lines 3 to 7:
	DB<1> l 3+4
	DB<1> l start-end
	If a start and end range are specified with -, list lines starting from line number 'start' and ending at line number 'end'. For example, to list lines 3 to 7:
	DB<1> l 3-7
	DB<1> l sub
	Finally, if a subroutine name is specified, list the first window of lines of the named subroutine. For example:
	DB<1> l mysubroutine
-	Lists the previous window of lines in the current source file. This is the reverse of l and will usually list the previous window before that given by w. If there is no previous window -, like l, will return lines roughly similar to w.
.	List the last line to be executed by the debugger.

Display (Source Code)	Action
f filename	Switch to viewing the named file (or eval expression), which must be loaded (or to be more precise, present as a key in the %INC hash). If the filename does not precisely match an entry in %INC it is used as an unanchored regular expression. For example, to find and view CGI.pm we need only put: DB<1> **f CGI** Normally the debugger will show the appropriate file for the current execution context of the application being debugged, switching between files as necessary. This command is helpful for setting breakpoints in other files. The keys of %INC hold filenames, not package names with colons, so f Term::ReadKey will not work but f Term/ReadKey will. eval statements are remembered and numbered in the order that they are defined, and can be accessed by number. For example, f 3 for the third eval statement.
/pattern	Search forward for the regular expression pattern in the source file. Searches are case-insensitive, and return the next match forward from the position where the last match was found. For example: DB<1> **/$param** A match may be repeated by entering a single / or ?. A second optional / may also be specified, which has no effect (and notably regular expression flags may not be put after it). Without meta characters or other special regular expression terms this is equivalent to a case-insensitive text match.
?pattern	Search backward for the regular expression pattern in the source file. As with /pattern, further matches are carried out from the position of the last successful match, and a single ? or / will rematch with the same pattern.
m expr	Displays the list of methods that may be called on the object (blessed reference) or package name that is the result of expr. Inherited methods are marked with the module from which they are inherited. For example m CGI displays all the methods defined for the CGI module, assuming it is loaded; typing use CGI at the debugger prompt will do that if it isn't.

Commands	Action
! [[-]number]	Repeat or recall a previous command. Without arguments, repeats the last command: DB<1> **!** With a numeric argument, repeats the command with that number. To repeat the 3rd command: DB<1> **!3** With a negative numeric argument, repeats the (n+1)th previous command. To repeat the command before last: DB<1> **!-1** The character used for this command is the same as that used for executing temporary shells from within the debugger, but it can be reconfigured with the recallCommand option.
H [-number]	List previous commands. Without arguments, lists all previous commands: DB<1> **H** An argument of zero or any positive number also lists all previous commands. A negative number lists that many previous commands, including the H command itself. To list the previous command, therefore, use: DB<1> **H -2** To list the six previous commands, excluding the H, use: DB<1> **H -7**
= [alias cmd]	Define command alias. Without arguments, lists currently defined aliases: DB<1> **=** With one argument, gives the command that the alias is an alias to: DB<1> **= next** With arguments, define a command alias. For example, to define aliases for the next, step, and alias commands: DB<10> **= next n** next = n DB<11> **= alias =** alias = = DB<12> **alias step s** step = s Aliases can be made to other aliases. Redefining an alias (by aliasing it to something else) will then alter the effect of all secondary aliases. Note that the alias comes first, the command to be aliased second.

Execution Options	Action
s	Single-step execute the next line, stepping into subroutines if present. Subroutine calls in expressions will also be single-stepped into.
n	Single-step execute the next line, executing and stepping over subroutine calls. If a subroutine call forms part of a larger expression it will still be stopped after, so breaks in mid-expression are possible.
<return>	Repeat the last s or n command, whichever was more recently issued. This allows us to effectively use s and n to set a 'stepping mode' and then use return to execute lines in that mode.
c [line|sub]	Continue executing lines in non-stop mode, optionally setting a once-only breakpoint at the specified line-number or subroutine. Without an argument, it executes the program continuously until it exits or a previously set breakpoint or watch-point is encountered: DB<1> **c** With a line number, enters continuous execution until the given line number is reached: DB<1> **c 12** On return (which will only happen if one of the above criteria is met), c displays a list of the lines that were executed. The subroutine name variant is similar, but stops inside the next call to the named subroutine.
r	Continue executing lines in non-stop mode until the return from the current subroutine. This implicitly sets a once-only breakpoint on the next line after the statement that led to this subroutine call.
q (^D/^C)	Quit the debugger. *Ctrl-D* (or *Ctrl-C* on Windows) is an alias for q.
R	Restart the debugger by causing it to 'exec' itself (this may not work well on some platforms, like Windows). The command history, breakpoints, actions, and debugger options are preserved; other states may be lost.
|	Page output of debugger command or arbitrary code by piping the output DB::OUT to the currently defined pager program, as given by $DB::pager (|more on most UNIX platforms). For example: DB<1> **|V DB** This dumps out all variables in the debugger's own DB package, leading to potentially large output which is paged for easier reading.
||	The same as | above, except that the debugger also uses select to make DB::OUT the currently selected output filehandle for the duration of the command. This is mostly relevant to executing arbitrary code: DB<1> **|| print "This goes to DB::OUT, not STDOUT";**

Table continued on following page

Execution Options	Action
! [shell cmd]	Run a shell command using the shell defined by $ENV{SHELL}, with a command equivalent to $ENV{SHELL} -c 'shell cmd'. Non-UNIX systems may need to reconfigure the shell used first before this will work. Note that this is the same character as the repeat command, but it can be redefined with shellBang.
!! [shell cmd]	Run a shell command in a subprocess, using the shell defined by $ENV{SHELL} and using DB::IN and DB::OUT as standard input and output; this is useful if standard input and output have been redirected. See also the shellBang configuration option, which sets the character used for this command and the one above.

Control	Action
t [expr]	Without arguments, this toggles tracing mode from on to off, and vice-versa: DB<1> **t** With tracing mode enabled, the lines that were executed by the last c or n are listed out when the debugger next returns, giving a complete trace of all code executed. Without this, only the line due to be executed next is listed. If an expression is supplied, trace through that expression. See 'Tracing and Terminals' for more information.

Breakpoints	Action

b [line] [condition]
b sub [condition]
b postpone sub
b compile sub
b load file
	Set a breakpoint to cause the debugger to return to the user from continuous execution, as entered by the c command. The most common form of breakpoints are those set on line numbers. For example, to set a breakpoint at line ten:
	
	   DB<1> **b 10**
	
	Line-number breakpoints may optionally be followed by a condition, which will cause the breakpoint to be triggered only if the condition also holds. The condition is an arbitrary Perl expression of the kind that is used in if or while statements. For example, to break only when the %config hash has at least three key-value pairs defined:
	
	   DB<1> **b 10 keys(%config)>2**
	
	The line number may also be omitted, in which case the breakpoint is set on the next line to be executed. An optional condition may still be set in this case:
	
	   DB<1> **b keys(%config)>2**

Breakpoints	Action
b [line] [condition] b sub [condition] b postpone sub b compile sub b load file	A subroutine breakpoint is set by using b with the name of the subroutine to break in. Execution is halted by the debugger on entry to the subroutine but before the first statement in the subroutine is executed: DB<1> **b mysubroutine** As with line breakpoints, a condition may be specified: DB<1> **b mysubroutine keys(%config)>2** A subroutine reference (supplied in a variable) may also be supplied, however conditions are not supported in this case: DB<1> **b $mysubref** Lesser variants of the b command include b postpone sub, which sets the breakpoint only after the subroutine has been compiled. b compile sub also waits for the subroutine to compile but then sets a breakpoint at the first line of execution. b load file breaks when the named file is loaded by use, require, or do. Note that this is an effective way of breaking inside a BEGIN block if specified prior to starting the debugger in a configuration file or PERL5DB.
L	List all breakpoints and actions currently defined.
S	List all subroutines currently defined, including those defined interactively in the debugger. This is obviously handy for setting breakpoints.
d [line]	Delete the breakpoint at the specified line number, as returned by the L command. If no line number is specified, delete the breakpoint on the next line to be executed, if any is present.
D	Delete all existing breakpoints.

Actions	Action
a [[line] action]	With two arguments, sets an action to be done before the line given by line is executed. The action is any arbitrary Perl code (not, however a debugger command), for example: DB<1> **a 10 print "Got to line 10!\n";** With one or no arguments, deletes the action from the specified line number, or the next line to be executed if the line number is omitted. For example: DB<1> **a 10** Actions are a very effective way of adding temporary code to an application without actually editing it. With actions, we can add additional debug messages and set variables to experimental values, without disturbing the source code.
A	Delete all existing actions.

633

Watchpoints	Action
W [expr]	Without arguments, delete all existing watch expressions (watchpoints). With an argument, sets a watch expression or watchpoint for the debugger to study during execution. If the value of the expression changes, the debugger breaks program execution and returns control to the user. Typically c is used to continue execution until a breakpoint or watchpoint is encountered. If a watchpoint is encountered the debugger will display the old and new values of the expression that triggered the break: DB<1> **W $value** main::(config.pl:5): chomp; # strip linefeed DB<2> **c** nokeyvaluepairhere No value for parameter 'nokeyvaluepairhere' key=value Watchpoint 0: $value changed: old value: undef new value: 'value' main::(config.pl:10): print("No value for parameter '$_'\n"),next unless $value; DB<2> **c** Watchpoint 0: $value changed: old value: 'e' new value: undef main::(config.pl:4): while (<>) { Each watchpoint we set incurs a performance penalty, since the Perl interpreter must track each value watched. Though there is no limit, it makes sense to only watch one or two values at a time. Note that the lowercase w command does not set watchpoints (or indeed have anything to do with them) but prints the source code in the current window.

Prompt	Action
< [action]	Set an action, which can be any arbitrary Perl code, to execute immediately before the debugger prompt is displayed. (We cannot specify debugger commands, however; the { command does that.) For example, to display the current time and date: DB<1> **< print scalar(localtime)** < clears any existing actions set to execute before the prompt. However, see << below. If no action is specified, existing actions are cleared but no new one is set.

Prompt	Action
`<<`	Append an action to execute immediately before the debugger prompt is displayed and after any existing actions. For example, to add the current working directory: **DB<1> use POSIX qw(getcwd);** **DB<2> << print ' ',getcwd**
`< ?`	List the actions currently set to execute before the prompt. For example: Tue Dec 26 15:06:35 2000 /home/gurgeh DB<74> **< ?** Perl commands run before each prompt: < -- print scalar(localtime) < -- print ' ',getcwd
`> [action]`	Set an action to execute immediately after a debugger command to execute program code (that is, s, n, c, r, etc.) has been entered but before any results are displayed. For example: DB<30> **> print "Here we go! \n"** As with < this command clears any and all actions already set to be executed after the prompt. To add to an existing action, use >>. If no action is specified, existing actions are cleared but no new one is set.
`>>`	Append an action to execute immediately after a debugger command to execute program code has been given, and after any already set actions.
`>?`	List the actions currently set to execute after the prompt. For example: DB<1> **>?** Perl commands run after each prompt: > -- print "Here we go!\n"
`{ [cmd]`	Set a debugger command to be executed before each debugger prompt. This works identically to the < command except that it takes a debugger command as an argument instead of arbitrary Perl code. For example, to examine the contents of a variable step-by-step: DB<1> **{ x %config** If no command is specified, all existing commands are removed, the same as < and >. Note that setting commands like s, n, c, and r is perfectly possible, but can potentially have interesting, if not entirely helpful, effects.
`{{ cmd`	Append a new debugger command to be executed before each debugger prompt and after any commands already set .
`{ ?`	List debugger commands set to execute before the prompt. For example: DB<1> **{ ?** Debugger commands run before each prompt: { -- x %config

Configure Options	Action
O	Any number of options may be set with one O command, each option separated from the last by a space. Boolean options may be set on simply by giving their name: DB<1> **O inhibit_exit** inhibit_exit = '1' To clear a Boolean option, or set a non-Boolean option, use an equals sign followed by the new value: DB<1> **O pager=lless inhibit_exit=0** pager = 'lless' inhibit_exit = '0' Alternatively, and at the same time, options may be queried by suffixing them with a ?: DB<1> **O pager? pager='lmore'** pager = 'lless' pager = 'lmore' For more information on configuration options, read on.

Configuring the Debugger

The Perl debugger supports a collection of configuration options that control how it presents output and deals with situations during the course of debugging. These options may be set in a variety of different ways, interactively with the O command, through the environment via the PERLDB_OPTS environment variable, or in a .perldb configuration script.

Interactively

First and most obviously, the O command detailed above can be used to set one or more configuration options interactively from inside the debugger, for example:

DB<101> **O pager=lless recallCommand=[warnlevel=2 dielevel=1 NonStop]**

Through the Environment

Second, options may be specified in the environment variable PERLDB_OPTS, which takes the form of a string with the options to be set in the same format as the O command; for example, on a UNIX shell:

> **PERLDB_OPTS="NonStop warnlevel=2 dielevel=1" perl -d...**

The Windows equivalent is somewhat less terse:

> **set PERLDB_OPTS=NonStop warnlevel=2 dielevel=1**
> **echo %PERLDB_OPTS%**
NonStop warnlevel=2 dielevel=1

The '.perldb' Script

Finally, we can create a configuration file containing arbitrary code, including subroutine definitions useful for debugging and use statements to pull in modules that supply useful debugging features.

This file is called .perldb on UNIX systems, or perldb.ini on Windows and must be placed either in the current directory, or our home directory (as defined by the HOME or LOGDIR environment variables). On UNIX systems it must also be executable and owned by either the superuser or the user running the debugger. Finally, it must not give write permission to 'others'. To arrange that under UNIX, we can use:

> chmod go-w .perldb

On Windows NT, use:

> attrib +r perldb.ini

This makes the file read-only for everyone. Or we can edit perl5db.pl to remove the check in the subroutine is_safe_file (this is potentially a reason for creating a custom debugger).

The reason for these security precautions is that an insecure database configuration file is a large potential security hazard, since the code in it is added to any application if the -d option can be triggered. If Perl detects that our configuration file is insecure on a UNIX platform, it refuses to run it and returns the message:

perldb: Must not source insecure rcfile ././.perldb.
    You or the superuser must be the owner, and it must not
    be writable by anyone but its owner.

The content of the file is actually Perl code run within the DB package, not a configuration file in the traditional sense. To set up aliases we plug in new entries to the %DB::alias hash, and to set options we call the subroutine parse_options (which is supplied by DB).

Aliases take the form of regular expression substitutions, substituting the replacement text for the matching part of the command given in the debugger. We can define more powerful aliases than the = command allows. For example, many debuggers support the stop at and stop in commands to set breakpoints on lines and in subroutines respectively. Since these are two-word commands the = command has trouble defining them, but we can define both in a single alias in a .perldb file:

```
# This is a .perldb configuration file
$DB::alias{'stop'} = 's/stop (at|in)/b/';
```

To set options, use the parse_options subroutine:

```
# set some options
parse_options("pager =|less NonStop AutoTrace");
```

The .perldb file is processed before the contents of PERL_DBOPTS are considered, so PERL_DBOPTS will override options specified in the .perldb file. However, if we define a subroutine called afterinit within the file, it will be called after the PERLDBOPTS options have been processed:

```
# these options will override PERL_DBOPTS
sub afterinit {
   parse_options("AutoTrace");
}
```

637

Since this is a conventional Perl script (if used in an unconventional setting) we can place anything in here:

```
# generally useful stuff

use re 'debug';    # enable regular expression traces

sub dumpenv {
    foreach (sort keys %ENV) {
        print "$_ => $ENV \n";
    }
}
```

Debugger Configuration Options

Configuration options fall into four loose categories: **Debugger**, **Readline**, **Output**, and **Terminal**. Debugger options are related to the operation of the debugger itself. ReadLine Library options control the interface between the debugger and the Term::ReadLine module. Output options are related to the Dumpvalue module, which implements the output display of the x, X, and V commands. Finally, Terminal options control how the debugger connects to terminals for debugging output, this is where the DB::OUT filehandle connects to for debugging output.

The default value returned by O for a number of these values is N/A. This reflects the fact that no explicit value has been set, and that the default is being used, rather than that the value of these options is the string N/A.

Debugger Option	Action
recallCommand	Set the character used for the recall/repeat command Debugger command (by default !). For example: DB<1> **O recallCommand=P**
shellBang	Set the character used for the shell and subprocess commands (by default ! and !!). For example: DB<1> **O shellBang=Z** Note that this is case-sensitive; Z is not the same as z.
pager	Set the command used to run external pagers by the | command (by default |more on UNIX). It should start with a | to pipe output. For example: DB<1> **O pager=|less**
dieLevel warnLevel signalLevel	These three options control how the debugger deals with signals. The dieLevel and warnLevel options deal with the die and warn pseudohandlers. The signalLevel deals with real signals: DB<1> **O dieLevel=1 warnLevel=1** The default of 0 has the debugger leave most signals alone, since many programs install their own handlers to deal with these conditions. Setting 1 will generate a backtrace for dies, warnings, and other signals respectively, and embellish warnings originating from evaled code. Setting 2 will cause the debugger to intercept and rephrase all warnings and errors, irrespective of their origin. In general, don't change these values unless the situation merits it.

Debugger Option	Action
inhibit_exit	If True (default), this prevents stepping from passing over the end of the script (be it the actual end or an exit). If False, the debugger will leave the script and lose context information like global variables.
PrintRet	If True (default), this prints out the return value from subroutines that have just been terminated via the r command. If False, nothing is printed.
frame	Control the printing of messages on entry and exit from subroutines, in addition to the normal trace messages for line numbers. The default is 0, which does nothing. Other values are made up of different bits, which set different display options: bit 1 (1) – not used bit 2 (2) – print messages on entry bit 3 (4) – print function arguments bit 4 (8) – execute tied and overloaded arguments to get their string representations bit 5 (16) – print return value (this affects subroutines returning as a result of any debugger command; the PrintRet configuration option applies only to returning explicitly from a subroutine with r) A frame of 2 (bit 2) or 6 (bits 2 and 3) is the most common. When combined with NonStop it allows us to generate an execution trace of subroutine and function calls within a program: **DB<1> O NonStop frame=6**
maxTraceLen	This is the maximum length to truncate the argument list to, when bit 3 of the frame option is set. The default is 400, which is likely to be long enough for most simple arguments. Set to something shorter to be briefer: **DB<1> O frame=6 maxTraceLen=60**
NonStop	If True, the debugger executes programs continuously (as if c was typed automatically) until interrupted by a breakpoint or watchpoint, or programmatically by $DB::signal or $DB::single. Note that watchpoints and breakpoints can be set prior to entering the debugger via the .perldb script.

Readline Option	Action
tkRunning	If the debugger is running within a tk environment, setting this value to 1 will enable tk events to be processed while the debugger is waiting for input. See the Term::ReadLine section in Chapter 15 for more information.
ornaments	The ANSI escape sequences used to highlight the prompt. See Chapter 15 for details on how to disable or configure these. Note that this can only be done from inside a .perldb script, and may cause strange effects in a non-ANSI shell.
ReadLine	Set to 0 to disable use of the readline library. This is primarily useful for debugging applications, which use readline themselves. Default is 1.

Output Options	Action
arrayDepth	Print only the number of elements specified. If undefined (the default), print all elements.
hashDepth	Print only the number of key-value pairs specified. If undefined (the default), print all pairs.
compactDump	If set to a positive value, and if the length of the line is less than the value, this causes arrays and hashes to be displayed on one line. If set to 1, a suitably large value (400+) is used. Only arrays and hashes that do not contain references will be compacted. The default is off.
veryCompact	If True, this prints arrays and hashes that do not contain references on one line irrespective of how long the resulting line is. The default is off. Setting veryCompact effectively overrides compactDump.
globPrint	If True, print out the contents of globs (treat them as specialized references). Otherwise, do not. The default is off.
DumpDBFiles	If True, print out the arrays holding debugged files. The default is off.
DumpPackages	If True, print out package symbol tables. The default is off.
DumpReused	If True, print out values multiple times if multiple references to them are encountered. Otherwise, REUSED_ADDRESS is inserted instead of repeating the dump. The default is off.
quote	Prints out strings in the configured style. The default is auto, which uses double or single quoted strings, whichever is more appropriate for the string (if it contains a double quote single quotes are used). It can also be set to single or double quotes with quote=" or quote='.
HighBit	If True (default), this prints out characters with their high bit (bit 8) set as-is. Otherwise, it masks out the high bit and prints the result.
undefPrint	If True (default), this represents undefined values with the string undef, otherwise it represents them as empty strings.
UsageOnly	If True, this generates a simple per-package memory usage report. The default is off.

Terminal/Tracing Options	Action
AutoTrace	If True, this enables tracing by default, in the same way that the t command toggles tracing on. The default is 0, off.
LineInfo	A file or pipe to send line number information to (that is the debugger output of actual source code lines). To create a trace file, set to: LineInfo=trace.log.
	To send to an external program (which uses a shorter message), prefix the program name with a pipe. This is how external editors that support Perl debugging interface to the debugger: LineInfo=|debugger.

Terminal/Tracing Options	Action
TTY	This is the name of the terminal to use for debugging output (for example, con on Windows). By default, the output is sent to the current terminal. Note that commands like p and x send their output to this device and not to standard output, so if that is redirected, debugging output still goes to the debugging terminal.
noTTY	If set to a True value, the debugger automatically starts up in NonStop mode. It then connects to the terminal specified by TTY when execution is broken by a breakpoint, watchpoint, or programmatic return like $DB::single. The third party module Term::Rendezvous may also be used to search for a suitable terminal at the point of interrupt.

Tracing and Terminals

The debugger supports two different kinds of tracing. **Line tracing** consists of numbered lines of source code, and is controlled by the AutoTrace option. **Frame tracing** reports the entry and exit details from subroutines and is controlled by the frame configuration option. By default, both go to the same place, the terminal attached to the DB::OUT filehandle. This is usually the same terminal that the program itself is attached to, but importantly is not affected by redirecting standard output or standard error within the program or from the command-line.

Tracing can be used interactively, but is most useful for generating non-interactive traces from running programs. We can stop the debugger from entering an interactive section with the NonStop option; in combination with AutoTrace we can produce a line trace to the screen with:

> **PERLDB_OPTS='NonStop AutoTrace' perl -d myscript.pl**

The frame option is a combined flag that contributes additional information to the trace, depending on which bits are set. If frame is set to 2, the debugger will log all subroutines entered during the course of the program's execution. With NonStop or noTTY also set, this allows us to generate an execution trace of subroutine calls:

> **PERLDB_OPTS='NonStop frame=2' perl -d myscript.pl**

In this example there is no line tracing, so the output we see will contain only subroutine call trace messages. If we wanted line tracing too, we would enable it by adding the AutoTrace option as well. Setting other bits in the frame value produces other values. 22 prints subroutine arguments (4) and return values (16). Here is an example with both AutoTrace and a frame of 22:

> **PERLDB_OPTS='NonStop frame=22 AutoTrace' perl -d myscript.pl**

All of these examples output tracing information to the screen, mixed in with the normal standard output and standard error of the program. Since the debugger uses its own filehandle for output, redirecting standard output and standard error will not redirect the tracing output. To get a trace log we instead use the LineInfo option. This controls where tracing output sent is sent (both line and frame, despite the name). For example, to redirect tracing to a trace log and debug messages (printed out by the program itself) to a debug log, we could use:

> **PERLDB_OPTS='NonStop frame=2 AutoTrace LineInfo=trace.log' perl -d myscript.pl 2> debug.log**

The normal standard output of the program will appear on the screen, while tracing information will go to `trace.log` and error output from the program itself will end up in `debug.log`. If we wanted to capture standard output too, we would do this:

> PERLDB_OPTS='NonStop frame=2 AutoTrace LineInfo=trace.log' perl -d myscript.pl > output.log 2> debug.log

In this instance we have also redirected standard output from the program to a file called `output.log`.

Two other configuration options control how the debugger interacts with terminals: `TTY` and `noTTY`. The `TTY` option determines where non-trace debugger output goes (for example, output from the p and x commands, which could be triggered as actions). The value of the `TTY` option is expected to be interactive, for example another terminal window or a serial port; both `DB::IN` and `DB::OUT` are attached to it. The related `noTTY` option prevents the debugger from attaching to the device named by `TTY` unless and until the debugger is entered interactively; it takes no argument.

Entering the Debugger Programmatically

As well as setting breakpoints and watchpoints from the debugger to break the flow of execution, we can also have the program trigger a break itself. This is especially useful for compile-time statements executed in `BEGIN` blocks, since the debugger will not ordinarily break in these. Instead it executes them and halts on the first line of normal execution. It is also useful if we have specified the `NonStop` or `noTTY` configuration options.

To have a program pass control back to the debugger, set the variable `$DB::single`. This sets the debugger, if running, into single step mode, therefore out of continuous execution mode. For example:

```
#!/usr/bin/perl -T
# an example start to an about-to-be debugged application

# allow debugger to break during compile phase
use warnings;

BEGIN {
    $DB::single = 1;
    ...
}

# now load modules with complex 'BEGIN' blocks so we can debug them
use CGI;
use DBI;
use SomeOtherModule;

...
```

If the debugger is not present, setting this variable has no other effect than to create the variable and give it a value, so it is not detrimental to leave the statement in even if the application is not being debugged.

The debugger enters interactive mode in a slightly different way depending on the value `$DB::single` is set to. Setting `$DB::single=1` gives rise to a debugging prompt as if an s had just been typed, so pressing *return* will cause further s commands to be executed. Setting `$DB::single=2` enters the debugger's interactive mode as if an n has just been typed. Further *return*s will therefore produce n commands.

As an alternative to setting $DB::single to break within a BEGIN block, we can also set one of two more specialized breakpoints. First, the b load file breakpoint can be used to break in a use statement at the point the file is loaded, for example:

DB<1> **b load CGI.pm**

Second, we can use the compile breakpoint to break on the compilation of a subroutine:

DB<1> **b compile mysubroutine**

Both of these work well; which we use depends entirely on what we are trying to achieve at the time.

Another way to trigger a return to the debugger's prompt is to set the value of the variable $DB::signal to a suitable signal number. Both the program and debugger will behave as if the given signal had just been raised, with the debugger's behavior taking precedence, determined by the value of the signalLevel configuration option. For example:

```
# define a signal handler
$SIG{10} = sub {
    print "Hello Debugger \n";
}

# simulate a USR1 signal when debugging
$DB::signal = 10;
```

Note that both the subroutine and the setting of $DB::signal could be defined in the debugger itself. In particular, we could set a debugger action to define $DB::signal at a given line. See Chapter 22 for more on signals.

In addition, and independently of $DB::single, the t command can be simulated by setting the value of $DB::trace to either 0 or 1, enabling or disabling tracing respectively. This allows us to toggle tracing on and off within a program without setting breakpoints. For example, we can define our own tracing environment variable to do the job for us, so we can generate trace output selectively in NonStop mode without any further debugger configuration:

```
...
# trace the next bit
$DB::trace = 1 if $ENV{DO_TRACING};
...
# finished tracing the bit of interest
$DB::trace = 0 if $ENV{DO_TRACING};
...
```

Using Debugger Hooks

Perl grants extra access to the internals of the interpreter to code in the DB package. By placing our own code into this package we can create our own debugger alternatives. We can also extend the capabilities of our own debugging modules.

As a practical example, we can access the list of arguments passed to a subroutine from the DB package, which allows us to determine not only where a subroutine was called, but how. This information is not normally reported by a die or warn, but by placing code into the DB package we can create our own stack trace that reports not just the subroutine stack but the arguments that were passed at each stage too. Here is a module that does just this by registering a handler for the __DIE__ hook.

Note that the subroutine itself is in the package My::StackTrace but the body of the subroutine is placed into the DB package in order to gain access to the subroutine arguments in the @DB::args array, an array not normally available to us:

```perl
# StackTrace.pm
package My::StackTrace;
require 5.000;
use FileHandle;

$SIG{'__DIE__'} = 'My::StackTrace::DumpStack';

sub DumpStack {
    my $msg = shift;
    my ($pack, $file, $line, $subname, $hasargs, $wantarray, $i, @tmp, @args);
    my ($args_safe, $routine);

    # enable argument processing with DB::args;
    package DB;

    # for inclusion in HTML error documents
    print "<PRE><HR>\n" if $ENV{"REMOTE_HOST"};
    print "\n$msg\n";

    $i = 1;
    while (($pack, $file, $line, $subname, $hasargs, $wantarray) = caller($i++)) {
        @args = @DB::args;
        @tmp = caller($i);

        print "$file:$line ";
        print "(in $tmp[3])" if $tmp[3];

        $routine = $pack.'::'. $subname;
        print "\n\t&$routine";
        $args_safe = 1;

        if ($routine =~/SQL_OpenDatabase/o ||
            $routine =~/RPC::PlClient::new/o ||
            $routine =~/DBD::Proxy::dr::connect/o ||
            $routine =~/DBI::connect/o
        ) {
            $args_safe = 0;
        }

        if ($args_safe) {
            if ($hasargs) {
                print "(", join(", ", @args), ")";
            }
        } else {
            if ($hasargs) {
                print "(", scalar(@args), " arguments hidden for security)";
            }
        }
        print "\n";
    }
    print "\n\n";
    print "<HR></PRE>\n" if $ENV{"REMOTE_HOST"};

    exit;    # transmute death into a graceful exit
}

1;
```

This module provides an improved stack trace. Here is a short example program that makes use of it and puts it through its paces:

```
#!/usr/bin/perl
# StackTrace.pl
use warnings;
use strict;

use StackTrace;

sub a {push @_, shift @_; b(@_);}
sub b {push @_, shift @_; c(@_);}
sub c {push @_, shift @_; d(@_);}
sub d {push @_, shift @_; e(@_);}
sub e {
    push @_, shift @_;
    print "@_";
    die "Sudden death";
}

a('Testing', 1, 2, 3);
```

The output from this program is:

```
1 2 3 Testing
Sudden death at ./stacktrace.pl line 12.

./stacktrace.pl:8 (in main::d)
      &main::main::e(1, 2, 3, Testing)
./stacktrace.pl:7 (in main::c)
      &main::main::d(Testing, 1, 2, 3)
./stacktrace.pl:6 (in main::b)
      &main::main::c(3, Testing, 1, 2)
./stacktrace.pl:5 (in main::a)
      &main::main::b(2, 3, Testing, 1)
./stacktrace.pl:15
      &main::main::a(1, 2, 3, Testing)
```

We could make this module a good deal more flexible by adding the ability to trace warnings too, or report only the last subroutine rather than the whole trace, but this simple version illustrates the basic technique. See Chapters 9 and 10 for more on writing modules and the use of packages.

Debugging and Informational Modules

In addition to the Perl debugger, the Perl standard library supplies a number of different modules that are useful for debugging and developing programs in various controlled ways. We will examine here two modules, Dumpvalue and Safe. Other modules, from the B:: family, which have debugging applications will be investigated in Chapter 20.

The 'Dumpvalue' Module

The Dumpvalue module provides the basis for the Perl debugger's configurable output in the x, X, and V commands, and is the source of the 'Output' configuration options such as arrayDepth, compactDump, and globPrint.

However, since the `Dumpvalue` module is an independent part of the Perl library we can make use of it without using the debugger. `Dumpvalue` works through an object-oriented interface, with a dumper object that has configuration options identical to those detailed under 'Output' in the 'Debugger Configuration Options' section.

Basic value output is supported by the `dumpValue` and `dumpValues` methods, which dump out one value and a list of values respectively. For both methods the value or values must be scalars. For example:

```perl
#!/usr/bin/perl
# dumpval.pl
use warnings;
use strict;

use Dumpvalue;

my $dumper = new Dumpvalue(compactDump => 1, globPrint => 1);

my %myhashvariable = (
    'top' => {
        middle => [
            'left', 'right', {
                'bottom' =>
            }
        ]
    }
);

# dump one variable
$dumper->dumpValue(\%myhashvariable)
```

This produces:

```
0  HASH(0x8223380)
  'top' => HASH(0x822335c)
    'middle' => ARRAY(0x82232cc)
      0 'left'
      1 'right'
      2 HASH(0x825276c)
        'bottom' => 1
```

The `dumpValues` method works similarly, but treats its list of arguments as a top- level array:

```perl
# dump several variables
$dumper->dumpValues ($var1, $var2, \@anarray, \%anotherhash);

# dump each element of an array:
$dumper->dumpValues (@myarrayvariable);
```

The `Dumpvalue` module works well with modified tracing arrangements, especially if it is encapsulated in tracing subroutines. For example, the following script illustrates a simple trace subroutine that implements level-based tracing based on the value of the putative environment variable TRACE_ON:

```
#!/usr/bin/perl
# trace.pl
use warnings;
use strict;

{
    use Dumpvalue;

    # private dumper object for 'trace' subroutine
    my $dumper = new Dumpvalue (compactDump => 1);

    my $level = $ENV{'TRACE_ON'};
    $level |= 0;    # default to no tracing

    sub trace {
        $dumper->dumpValues(@_) if $_[0] <= $level;
    }
}

my %hash = (one => 1, two => 2);
my @array = (1..10);

# a level 2 trace statement
trace 2, \%hash, \@array;
```

> TRACE_ON=2 perl trace.pl

```
0 2
1 HASH(0x81269c0)
  'one' => 1
  'two' => 2
2 ARRAY(0x8126ac8)
   0  1
   1  2
   2  3
   3  4
   4  5
   5  6
   6  7
   7  8
   8  9
   9  10
```

The other output method supported by Dumpvalue is dumpvars, which prints out details of package variables. This method is the basis of the X and V debugger commands and takes the form:

```
dumpvars(pkg, var, var...);
```

As with the X command, we can give just a package name to dump all variables, or specify a list of variables (minus data type prefixes) to dump. If the variable name starts with ~ or !, the name is applied as a regular expression and all matching (or in the case of !, non-matching) names are dumped. For example:

```
#!/usr/bin/perl
# dumpvars.pl
use strict;
use warnings;

use Dumpvalue;

my $dumper = new Dumpvalue(compactDump => 1, globPrint => 1);

# dump out '@INC', '%INC', and '%ENV':
$dumper->dumpvars('main', 'INC', 'ENV');

# dump out everything else
$dumper->dumpvars('main', '!(INC|ENV)');

# dump out anything that ends in a digit:
# handy after a regexp!
$dumper->dumpvars('main', '~\d$');
```

The other methods supported by dumper objects all relate to configuration options:

Method	Action
`set_quote('"'|"'"|, 'auto')`	Set options to handle printout with the given quote type. Strings are rendered to use either single quotes, double quotes, or (with `auto`) whichever is most logical. The content of the string is adjusted to fit the quote type.
`set_unctrl('quote'|'unctrl')`	Set the `unctrl` option to vary how non-alphanumeric characters are represented, `quote` when the quote type is a double quote. The `quote` option attempts to escape all characters in a way that allows them to be interpolated back again. The `unctrl` option represents them in a more human readable form, for example `^D` is equivalent to *Ctrl-D*.
`compactDump(0|1|number)`	Set or clear the `compactDump` option
`veryCompact(0|1)`	Set or clear the `veryCompact` option. This also sets the `compactDump` option.
`set (option => value, ...)`	Set or clear general options, for example: `$dumper->set(tick => 'auto');`
`get (option, option, ...)`	Get general options, for example: `@opts = $dumper->get('tick', 'HighBit', 'printUndef');`

Note that a similar kind of functionality is provided by the `Data::Dumper` module, which is also handy for serialization. They both produce legible output for values, so we can use either for this purpose. `Data::Dumper` is covered in Chapter 5 (in the context of printing out values).

The 'Safe' Module

The Safe module creates a protective 'compartment' for the execution of Perl code. Within the compartment, a different namespace prevails, and code within the compartment is not allowed to access variables in other namespaces, even the main namespace. This is somewhat reminiscent of the Java 'Sandbox' concept, code outside the compartment may place variables into the compartment's namespace, but access to anything outside the compartment from within is strictly forbidden.

Additionally, a new operator mask is applied to the compartment, which allows the disabling of operators by removing their opcodes from the mask. The default mask is the :default mask; described in more detail back in Chapter 4, although there is more detail on operator masks later in this chapter.

Creating Compartments

You can use the new method to create the compartment, and then either the reval (restricted eval) method to execute code within the compartment, or the rdo (restricted do) method to execute an external file within the compartment.

```
use Safe;

my $compartment = new Safe;
$compartment->reval($string_to_eval);
$compartment->rdo('myscript.pl');
```

If the code executed in the compartment attempts to reach outside its bounds, or use an operator forbidden by the compartment it fails with an error, at the compile stage in the case of operators, and potentially at either compile or run time in the case of variable access.

Both methods are identical in operation to their functional counterparts eval and do. For example, reval returns the value of the last expression evaluated on success, and sets $@ on an error.

Sharing Variables and Subroutines

Variables may be shared between the outside world and the compartment using the share and share_from methods. The share method takes a list of package variables defined in the current package (global variables) and imports them into the compartment's namespace:

```
# note, variables cannot be lexical - declare with 'our', not 'my'
our $scalar = "This is a scalar";
our (@array, %hash);
sub external {
    # external subroutine...
};
$compartment->share('$scalar', '@array', '%hash', '&external');
```

Alternatively, variables can be imported into the compartment namespace from another named package with share_from. This takes a package name as its first argument and an array reference to a list of variable names similar to that accepted by share:

```
$compartment->share_from('My::Package', ['$scalar', '@array', '%hash',
'&external']);
```

The variables (for example, $My::Package::scalar) must already exist in the named package to be imported into the compartment successfully.

Variables may be retrieved from the compartment in the reverse direction using the `varglob` method. This returns a typeglob of a symbol inside the compartment. For example, to alias a compartment typeglob to an external typeglob:

```
*compartmentvar = $compartment->varglob('varname');
```

Variables with the name varname ($varname, @varname, the subroutine varname, etc.) may now be accessed by the equivalent names $compartmentvar and so on. Alternatively, to set the variable $scalar inside the compartment without aliasing:

```
${$compartment->varglob('scalar')} = "This is a scalar";
```

This allows external code to access variables inside the compartment without needing to know the root namespace of the compartment. If we really want to know the root namespace we can do so with the root method:

```
$cmp_ns = $compartment->root();
```

Using this with symbolic references would allow us to set variables inside the compartment. However this is not encouraged as the point of the compartment is to keep the namespace anonymous to prevent accidental cross talk.

Operator Masks

Other methods of the compartment object relate to the control of the operator mask, and are direct interfaces to the functions of the Opcode module. In brief, they are:

`$c->permit(OP, ...)`	Add the listed operators to those allowed in the compartment.
`$c->permit_only(OP, ...)`	Allow only the listed operators to be executed within the compartment – all others are denied.
`$c->deny(OP, ...)`	Remove the listed operators from those allowed in the compartment.
`$c->deny_only(OP, ...)`	Deny only the listed operators in the compartment, all others are allowed.

As an example, the following method call removes the system and backtick opcodes from the permitted list:

```
$c->deny('system', 'backtick');
```

Similarly, to explicitly enable a more relaxed set of operators, including open, close, and stat:

```
# :browse is a superset of :default plus some others
$c->allow_only(':browse', ':filesys_open');
```

Note that opcodes are not operators; they are the foundations upon which operators are implemented. For a detailed account of operators, opcodes, and means of determining their relationships, see the section on the Opcode module and the use ops pragma in Chapter 4 on 'Operators'. This section also details the opcode categories like :browse and :filesys_open.

The 'Safe' Module in Use

As an example of how we can use the Safe module, here is a short utility that creates and uses a compartment to deny the use of backtick quotes (which includes the qx operator) and to log all uses of system:

```perl
#!/usr/bin/perl
# loggedsystem.pl
use warnings;
use strict;

use Safe;
my $compartment = new Safe;

$compartment->deny('system', 'backtick');

use subs qw(system);

sub system {
    warn "About to execute: @_ \n";
    CORE::system @_;
}

# offer our 'system' to the compartment
$compartment->share('&system');

# test line to prove compartment is working
$compartment->reval('system("ls")');
$compartment->reval('CORE::system("ls")');
warn $@ if $@;

# process command-line
foreach (@ARGV) {
    die "'$_' not found or not executable \n" unless -x;
    $compartment->rdo($_);
    warn $@ if $@;
}
```

Windows users should note that they should exchange the UNIX command ls in this example with the DOS command dir if they want to see an output from this example.

Note that both rdo and reval use eval internally, so to check for errors we need to inspect the value of $@, rather than $!. In both cases the code may not even compile (because it uses a forbidden operator) so checking $@ is vital for using compartments successfully.

If we give this program a name like logsystem we could use it like this:

> **logsystem perl myscript.pl**

The point of this is that not only have we replaced the original system with our own logging version– we have also prevented the script we execute from bypassing us, by disabling the core system function inside the compartment. If the script tries to use CORE::system to get around our logger, it will be denied access by the compartment.

Debugging the Perl Interpreter

It is possible to build Perl with internal debugging support built-in. This has nothing to do with debugging using the -d option, but rather allows us to debug the interpreter itself as it executes code. We can use this to generate various different kinds of information with the -D option, which takes a number of additional parameters. Each parameter enables a different debugging feature and we may enable as many as we see fit. To summarize the perlrun manual page:

1	p	Tokenizing and parsing
2	s	Stack snapshots
4	l	Context (loop) stack processing
8	t	Trace execution
16	o	Method and overloading resolution
32	c	String/numeric conversions
64	P	Print preprocessor command for -P
128	m	Memory allocation
256	f	Format processing
512	r	Regular expression parsing and execution
1024	x	Syntax tree dump
2048	u	Tainting checks
4096	L	Memory leaks (only if Perl was compiled with -DLEAKTEST)
8192	H	Hash dump – usurps values()
16384	X	Scratchpad allocation
32768	D	Cleaning up
65536	S	Thread synchronization

Options have both a numeric and symbolic value, and we may combine either as a value to the -D option. For example, to enable trace execution and stack snapshots we can any of:

> **perl -Dst ...**
> **perl -Dts ...**
> **perl -D10 ...**

If Perl has not been built with internal debugging support, then the -D option will not be available to us. However, we can generate much of the same information, albeit not always in an identical manner, with some of the B modules as described above. Note that unless we are actually interested in debugging Perl itself then we are probably safe not compiling it with the -D option enabled. It is of strictly limited use for debugging applications, for which it was not really designed.

Automated Testing

Perl provides a pair of modules that allow us to easily implement and carry out automated tests. The Test::Harness module provides a mechanism to perform tests mechanically, running through a series of specified tests and checking the results for a satisfactory outcome. The complementary Test module provides a simple toolkit of features to enable us to write scripts that produce output compatible with what the Test::Harness module expects.

The main application of these modules is in creating installable module packages, and the h2xs utility which we cover in Chapter 21 puts together a framework including a Makefile that automatically makes use of Test::Harness. That section is advanced reading for these modules if creating tests for installable module packages is the main goal. However, the modules can be used independently too.

Writing a Test Script

It is not actually necessary to use Test to create tests compatible with Test::Harness, but since the alternative is hard work, it makes sense to use the Test module.

To use the Test module we first need to pass a list of key-value pairs to the plan subroutine. The only required pair key is tests, which defines the number of tests' results that the test script returns. Typically this is placed in a BEGIN block to make sure it initializes before any program code is evaluated:

```
use Test;
BEGIN {plan tests => 8}
```

This specifies that this test script will return eight results, and we will have to ensure that we do indeed return eight results during the course of the script. Normally tests are fatal to Test::Harness if they fail, but we can make tests we expect to fail non-fatal by marking them as todo tests. To do this we add a todo key to the list passed to plan, followed by a reference to an array of test numbers:

```
BEGIN {plan tests => 8, todo => [7, 8]}
```

This marks tests 7 and 8 as non-fatal. The implication is that these tests apply to features that do not yet work; we can write the test for them anyway, and update the code later. If a test starts to work it should be taken off the todo list so that a failure causes Test::Harness to register a fatal problem.

Finally, we can pass a subroutine to be called on failed tests with the onfail key:

```
BEGIN {plan tests => 8, todo => [7, 8], onfail =>
   sub {warn 'Oh no, not again'}
}
```

Test passes a hash containing the keys package, repetition, and result to the subroutine specified by onfail, so we have the option of recording more sophisticated diagnostics if we so choose. Regardless of whether todo or onfail is specified, having given plan a number of tests to expect we now need to perform them. Test provides two subroutines to return test results compatible with Test::Harness, namely ok and skip.

The ok subroutine actually performs tests and takes one or two arguments. The one-argument form simply returns its value, and produces an ok result if that result is True:

```
ok (0);    # an automatic failure
ok (1);    # an automatic success
ok (mysubtotest($testarg1, $testarg2));    # test for true result
```

This is suitable for tests that can be deemed to have succeeded if they return any True result. For other tests, we supply a two-argument form. The first argument is the expected result and must be an expression leading to a result to test against; this value can validly be 0 or even undef. The second argument is the test to perform; again, this can be an expression, for example:

```
# test subroutine call against expected value
use My::Rhyme;
$farming_wife = new My::Rhyme('reason');
ok(3, $farming_wife->count('blind mice'));

# test the results of two calls for equality
ok(search_here('needle', 'haystack'), search_there('needle', 'haystack'));

# test against undef - a function with arguments expected to fail
ok(undef, reassemble_humpty(king => ['horses', 'men']));
```

The second argument may also be a regular expression, in which case it is matched against the expected result:

```
$re_pattern = comple_pattern('test');
$match_text = match_on('default_text');
ok($match_text, qr/$re_pattern/);
```

Other than the regular expression case, the two arguments to ok are equivalent, the ok subroutine simply tests them for equality, so it does not matter which way around we put them. However, the convention is to put the result first, and the test second.

The skip subroutine works exactly as the ok subroutine does but takes a single initial argument that determines whether or not the test should be considered. If it evaluates to a False value the test result is used as normal. If it evaluates to a string value it is used to describe the reason for the test; otherwise skip is automatically used. Either way, the reason is placed after the ok message, prefixed by a #. For example:

```
use Platform::Specific::Package qw(incompatible wise_men);
$message = incompatible($^O);
skip($message, 3, wise_men);
```

In this case the subroutine incompatible should return 0 or undef if the platform is supported, and return a message like Sorry, not supported on this platform if it isn't. Of course the test script itself can define this subroutine itself if the package does not.

Test scripts that wish to check if they are being run through Test::Harness can check for the environment variable HARNESS_ACTIVE, which the Test::Harness module sets when it calls test scripts. If it isn't running then scripts can alter their output or simply refuse to run:

```
die "Not being run by Test::Harness" unless defined $ENV{'HARNESS_ACTIVE'};
```

Note that a test script can execute any code it likes, and define any subroutine it needs to perform the necessary tests. After all, it is an ordinary Perl script, just one that generates a specific output. However, it should avoid printing output to STDOUT explicitly, relying on the ok or skip subroutines instead. It may however print its own messages to STDERR. Doing this selectively is one good use of the HARNESS_ACTIVE environment variable.

Automating Tests

Once we have one or more test scripts we can process them through the Test::Harness module. The module supplies one single subroutine, runtests, which takes one or more script names as arguments. For cross-platform compatibility it is a good idea if the script paths are absolute, but it is not a hard and fast requirement. Here is a script that uses Test::Harness to run though a series of test scripts supplied on the command-line:

```
#!/usr/bin/perl
use warnings;
use Test::Harness;
runtests(@ARGV);
```

As this UNIX-specific example shows, Test::Harness is not a hard module to use. A slightly more complex example might keep all its scripts in a particular subdirectory passed in as an environment variable:

```
#!/usr/bin/perl
use warnings;
use Test::Harness;

die "Path to test scripts not defined" unless $ENV{'TESTSCRIPT_DIR'};

foreach (@ARGV) {
    $_ = $ENV{'TESTSCRIPT_DIR'}."/$_";
}

runtests (@ARGV);
```

In the event that we choose not to use the Test module, runtests expects to get output for each test consisting of a series of lines. The first line should be a test range of the form 1..N. It should then be followed by a series of ok or not ok lines, with # Skip... plus a reason optionally appearing after ok lines, and continue in this manner for as many tests as the range specified. For example:

```
1..8
ok
not ok
ok   # 'Skip': not implemented on this platform
ok
ok
ok
not ok
ok
```

Note that the Test module generates numbered tests, with the number coming after the ok (or not ok) and before the skip comment. This is optional, and we do not need to supply it, but if we do it ought to start at 1 and increment monotonically.

If an entire test script wishes to have itself skipped, it can return a range 1..0, optionally with a reason:

1..0   # Skipped: bottled out at the last moment

runtests will then analyze and produce a statistical analysis of the test results. If all tests were successful, it prints some timing information supplied by the Benchmark module. If any tests failed, it dies with output similar to the following:

FAILED tests 2, 7
Failed 2/8 tests, 75.00% okay

If a test does not return a zero exit code, runtests will also report this. It does not die as a result. The HARNESS_IGNORE_EXITCODE environment variable, if set, suppresses this message.

Test::Harness also makes use of several environment variables, if defined:

HARNESS_FILELEAD_IN_DIR	Specifies the name of a directory in which runtests will check for new files. If a test generates files but does not clean them up afterward, runtests will report them. For example: LEAKED FILES: temp.file
HARNESS_PERL_SWITCHES	Can be used to specify extra options to pass Perl when executing each test. One obvious definition for this variable is -w, to force warnings to be enabled.
HARNESS_IGNORE_EXITCODE	If True, instructs runtests not to check or report on tests that return non-zero exit codes.
HARNESS_COMPILE_TEST	If True, will cause runtests to use the perlcc utility to attempt to compile the test as a stand-alone executable before running it. The object of this is to see whether it works as a stand-alone application, but as perlcc is still relatively new, it might not.
HARNESS_NOTTY	If True, tells runtests to treat its output as a non-terminal device, even if it is a terminal.
runtests	Sets the environment variable HARNESS_ACTIVE. Tests and applications can check for this variable if need be to determine if they are being tested or being run outside of Test::Harness.

Profiling

Profiling is the process of collecting timing statistics for an application. In general this occurs in two steps. First, a raw data file of timing information is generated by running the application in a profiling mode. Second, an analysis tool is then used to read the raw statistics and generate a report.

Perl is no exception in this case, but unlike many other languages it does not use a separate profiling tool. Instead, the Devel::DProf module is provided to alter the behavior of the Perl interpreter itself to generate the raw statistics. Once the file has been generated the dprofpp tool can then be used to analyze the results.

We do not necessarily have to use the profiler to generate timing information, however. Firstly, for very simple cases we can get away with using the times function (covered in Chapter 24), which is the basis of the profiler's statistics and other timing modules as well. Secondly, we can use the Benchmark module to generate timing statistics for repeated execution. As its name suggests, the Benchmark module is not so much aimed at providing detailed timing information as performance statistics; it is handy for testing the speed of a Perl script or application on different platforms.

Profiling Perl Applications

To profile an application we use the Devel::DProf module. This is implemented as an alternative debugger module, which hooks into Perl's debugging interface via the -d option. To specify the profiler rather than the normal debugger we suffix the -d option with :DProf, to specify the profiler module:

> **perl -d:DProf myscript.pl**

This will generate a file of raw profile statistics called tmon.out in the current directory. There are no options that can be supplied to the profiler, not even one to change the name of the output file.

The profiler is essentially a statistics collection package built around the times function, generating a file of raw data as its output. In order to make sense of this file we need to use a profile analyzer such as dprofpp, which is supplied as standard with Perl.

Note that not all modules in the Devel family can be used in this way. Only modules that define a DB subroutine are actually designed to work with Perl's debugging interface. The Devel::DProf module is the only such alternative supplied with Perl as standard, though other third-party modules exist on CPAN.

Generating Profile Reports

On its own the profile information produced by the Devel::DProf module is not of much use to us. Fortunately Perl provides a profile analysis tool called dprofpp that can interpret profile files and generate various kinds of report from them. This tool is written in Perl, so it will work anywhere that Perl does.

By default, dprofpp looks for a file called tmon.out, the name of the profile file generated by Devel::DProf. It then prints out the details of the fifteen most time consuming subroutines. This is a common enough occurrence that we can frequently just type:

> **perl -d:DProf myscript.pl**
> **dprofpp**

We can even have dprofpp run the profiling stage for us, generating and analyzing the tmon.out file in one easy step. The command below is exactly equivalent to the two above:

> **dprofpp -p myscript.pl**

The usual output of dprofpp is a table of subroutines and associated timing statistics (we say *usual* because the -S, -T, and -t options cause dprofpp to generate an execution tree instead). For example, here is a short script that lists installed files using the ExtUtils::Installed module. We use it an example because it is both short and takes a little time to run, and so generates some meaningful statistics (on a UNIX platform):

```perl
#!/usr/bin/perl
# installed.pl
use warnings;
use strict;

use ExtUtils::Installed;

my $inst = ExtUtils::Installed->new();
print join "\n", $inst->modules();
```

> **dprofpp -p installed.pl**

The output reports something similar to the following (the times are of course entirely dependent on the hardware we run the script on):

Total Elapsed Time = 3.638225 Seconds
User+System Time = 1.178225 Seconds

Exclusive Times

%Time	ExclSec	CumulS	#Calls	sec/call	Csec/c	Name
19.5	0.230	0.239	76	0.0030	0.0031	ExtUtils::Packlist::read
12.7	0.150	0.149	1	0.1496	0.1493	SelfLoader::_load_stubs
11.0	0.130	0.269	9	0.0144	0.0299	ExtUtils::Installed::BEGIN
10.3	0.122	0.755	2	0.0608	0.3776	File::Find::_find_dir
9.34	0.1 10	0.138	68	0.0016	0.0020	ExtUtils::MM_UNIX::parse_version
8.49	0.100	0.634	1864	0.0001	0.0003	ExtUtils::Installed::__ANON__
5.94	0.070	0.067	566	0.0001	0.0001	ExtUtils::MM_UNIX::canonpath
5.09	0.060	0.080	4	0.0150	0.0200	ExtUtils::MakeMaker::BEGIN
4.24	0.050	0.076	283	0.0002	0.0003	ExtUtils::MM_UNIX::catdir
3.39	0.040	0.151	283	0.0001	0.0005	ExtUtils::MM_UNIX::catfile
1.70	0.020	0.020	2	0.0100	0.0100	Exporter::export
1.70	0.020	0.020	1	0.0200	0.0200	vars::BEGIN
1.70	0.020	0.030	8	0.0025	0.0037	ExtUtils::MM_UNIX::BEGIN
1.70	0.020	0.289	2	0.0100	0.1445	main::BEGIN
0.85	0.010	0.010	71	0.0001	0.0001	strict::bits

The columns in this report have the following meanings:

Column	Action
%Time	The percentage of time spent in this subroutine as a fraction of the total runtime, not including time spent in subroutines called from this one. The -I option alters this column to include time spent.
ExclSec	The amount of time spent in this subroutine, not including time spent in subroutines called from this one.
CumulS	The amount of time spent in this subroutine, including time spent in subroutines called from this one. This contrasts to ExclSec.
#Calls	The total number of calls made to this subroutine during the course of execution. The sec/call and Csec/c values are computed from this plus ExclSec and CumulS respectively.
sec/call	Time spent on average per call to this subroutine, not including time spent in subroutines called from this one: sec/cal=ExclSec/#Calls. This is in contrast with Csec/c.
Csec/c	Time spent on average per call to this subroutine, including time spent in subroutines called from this one: Csec/c=CumulS/#Calls. Contrast to sec/call.
Name	The name of the subroutine, if available. Anonymous subroutines are still listed under __ANON__ in the package in which they are created. However, see the -A and -R command-line options below.

The dprofpp utility understands a number of command-line options that alter the way that it computes statistics and the way in which it displays them. These can be loosely categorized into five groups: sorting, display, subroutines, timing, and interpretation options:

Sorting Options	Action
-a	Sort subroutines alphabetically (sort on Name column).
-l	Sort by number of subroutine calls (sort on #Calls column).
-U	Do not sort. Subroutines are listed in the order they are found in the profile file. This is more efficient if we want to do our own sorting later, in which case we probably also want to use -q.
-v	Sort by average call time (sort on sec/call column).
-z	The default sort order. Sort by percentage of time used (sort on %Time column).

Display Options	Action
-O number	Limit the number of subroutines displayed to 'number'. The number may be optionally separated from the option by a space. The default is 15, equivalent to -O 15. Setting this value to a negative number will display all subroutines: **> dprofpp -O-1**

Table continued on following page

Display Options	Action
-q	Suppress column headings. This stops dprofpp from generating the column headings line and also the Total and User+System elapsed time lines, making the output easier for machine parsing.
-S	Generate an execution tree showing all subroutine calls instead of a normal profile report, including timing statistics. Multiple calls, even if not consecutive, are listed only once, with a repeat count. Note that this differs from the behavior of -t, and means that the execution tree is not a literal description of the chain of subroutine calls but a hierarchical form of the standard profile report. Contrast to -T and -t.
-T	Generate an execution tree showing all subroutine calls instead of a normal profile report, without statistics. Multiple consecutive calls are listed separately. Contrast to -S and -t.
-t	Generate an execution tree showing all subroutine calls instead of a normal profile report, without statistics. Multiple consecutive calls are listed only once, with a repeat count. This generates a shorter and generally more readable report than -T. Contrast to -S and -T.

Subroutines Options	Action
-A	In older releases of Perl, this causes dprofpp to assign the time spent autoloading a subroutine definition to the subroutine entry *::AUTOLOAD. The default is to include the autoload time in the first call to the subroutine. Newer releases of Perl automatically assign time to AUTOLOAD separately, so this option is redundant.
-g subname	Profile only the named subroutine and the subroutines that it calls. This is handy for profiling a specific part of the application, and isolates calls to subroutines from the named subroutine from calls to them from elsewhere. For example: **> dprofpp -p myscript.pl -g mysubname**

-R	Count calls to anonymous subroutines in the same package separately. The default is to accumulate all anonymous subroutine calls together into an __ANON__ entry. Note that for obvious reasons, dprofpp is not able to give a name for an anonymous subroutine.
	
	At the time of writing there is a bug in the dprofpp, but the original line 556 in the file, shown here:
	
	`if ($opt_R and ($name =~/::(__ANON_|END)$/)) {`
	
	Can be changed to:
	
	`if ($opt_R and ($name =~/(__ANON__|END)$/)) {`
	
	This will allow it to work. In future versions of dprofpp, this bug may well be fixed.

Timing Options	Action
-E	Displays the percentage of time not including time spent in subroutines called from them. This affects only the %Time column and therefore the sort order if sorting by percentage time (-z, the default). This is the default.
-I	Displays the percentage of time including time spent in subroutines called from them. This affects only the %Time column and therefore the sort order if sorting by percentage time (-z, the default).
-s	Display system time only, rather than User+System time, in contrast to -u and -r. See 'Collecting Timing Information Directly' below for an explanation of the distinction between user and system time.
-r	Display elapsed real time, rather than User+System time, in contrast to -s and -u. Note that this value is likely to be fairly meaningless for profiling.
-u	Display user time only, rather than User+System time. Contrast to -s and -r.

Interpretation Options	Action
-F	Generate fake exit timestamps for profiles that are missing them, possibly due to the influence of goto (dprofpp reports that the profile is 'garbled'). Note that the results of using this option are indeterminate.
-p scriptname	Run the profiler on the script to generate a tmon.out file and then generate a report from it. The tmon.out file is left after the command has completed generating a report from it.
-Q	In combination with the -p option, run the profiler to create a tmon.out file, but do not generate a report from the results. For example: **> dprofpp -p myscript.pl -Q**
-V	Print the version number of dprofpp and exit. If a tmon.out file is present then the version number found in the XS_VERSION field inside the file is also reported.

Collecting Timing Information Directly

Perl provides two functions that return information to us about the current time. The time function returns the number of seconds since midnight January 1, 1970 GMT (the notional moment that UNIX was born). Unfortunately, while this is useful for computing real times it is no use for computing execution times because it does not take into account the fact that system time is split between many processes (including operating system calls), and only measures to the nearest second.

> *Before we leave the subject of time, it is worth mentioning the Time::HiRes module, available from CPAN, which replaces both the time and sleep functions with versions that work down to the microsecond. If we want to work with real time at a higher resolution, this is a very useful module to install.*

To examine time from the point of view of the application, we use the `times` function. This function returns not one but four values to us:

```
($user, $system, $cuser, $csystem) = times;
```

The `$user` and `$system` values refer to the user and system time of the current process. The `$cuser` and `$csystem` values refer to the user and system time used by child processes (see Chapter 22), these will have values if we have used `system`, `fork`, the forking version of `open`, and so on and zero otherwise. In and of itself this is not useful, but if we call `times` twice and take the difference between the returned values then we can compute the user and system time taken by the code that was executed between the two calls.

The distinction between `user` and `system` time is simple once the concepts are explained. `user` time is time spent running the application itself, the time is spent in `user` space. `system` time is time spent by the operating system dealing with requests from our application. For example, calls to the `time` function cause the operating system to retrieve the current time, so the time spent doing this is `system` time. By contrast, adding and subtracting numbers does not require operating system services and so this counts as `user` time. The total of `user` and `system` time equates to the total amount of time used.

As an example of the use of both user and system time, consider the following program, which computes the time taken for a loop by calling `times` before and after it:

```perl
#!/usr/bin/perl
# gettime.pl
use warnings;
use strict;

my ($user1, $system1) = times;
my ($a, $t);

# repeat a loop one million times
foreach (1..1000000) {
    # incur some user time
    $a += 2**2000;
    # incur some system time
    $t = time;
}
my ($user2, $system2) = times;

# compute times
my $user = $user2 - $user1;
my $system = $system2 - $system1;
my $total = $user + $system;

print "Time taken: user = $user system = $system total = $total \n";
```

The body of the loop contains two lines. The first line computes 2 to a high power, and consumes a little user time. There are no calls to the operating system involved here, and therefore no system time is taken to do this. The second line uses the Perl `time` function, which makes a call to the operating system and so does consume system time. The assignment also consumes a little user time, but not much in comparison to computing 2 to the power of 2000. If we run this program we get a result similar to the following:

Time taken: user=3.05 system=0.52 total=3.57

If we run this repeatedly we get a slightly different result, simply depending on what else the processor and operating system are involved with at that particular point in time, and how accessible the system clock was. However, the total tends to be almost exactly the same because we are only counting time spent actually running this program, and not other processes that may also be running elsewhere. The wall clock time taken may be quite different to the total, but that is not of any relevance for computing timing information:

```
Time taken: user=3.01 system=0.57 total=3.58
Time taken: user=2.79 system=0.78 total=3.57
Time taken: user=3.06 system=0.52 total=3.58
Time taken: user=3.03 system=0.54 total=3.57
Time taken: user=3.08 system=0.49 total=3.57
```

It is because of these variations that serious testing of application performance is better performed by the Benchmark module.

Testing for Performance

The Benchmark module is a standard part of the Perl library that allows us to write performance tests for our code. It operates on the same basic principles as the profiler, and uses the times function detailed above as the basis for its results. However, it is not aimed at highlighting under-performing code but generating accurate and consistent performance statistics, which it does by repeatedly running code to generate a more representative average time.

Benchmark can be used to run simple time comparisons, shown earlier using times. We do this by creating new raw Benchmark objects with new, which contain absolute times. Then we compare them with timediff to generate a relative Benchmark we can actually use:

```
$start = new Benchmark;
...do time consuming things...
$finish = new Benchmark;

$difference = timediff($start, $finish);

print "Time taken: ", timestr($difference);
```

The real meat of the module is in the timeit, timethis, timethese, and countit subroutines, however.

Benchmark works by generating Benchmark objects that encapsulate times internally. We can generate these objects with subroutines like timethis and timethese, and then print them out in a friendly format using the timestr subroutine. A summary of the methods and subroutines available follows below, and must be given explicitly along with any other subroutines if not qualified by package. For example:

```
# need to import 'timesum' and therefore also 'timediff' and 'timestr'
use Benchmark qw(timesum timediff timestr);
```

Or:

```
# use 'timesum' via package, no need to import 'timediff' or 'timestr'
use Benchmark;
...
print timestr Benchmark::timesum ($difference1, $difference2);
```

663

The Benchmark module provides the following three methods:

Method	Action
new	Class method. Creates a new raw Benchmark object containing absolute times. timediff is needed to convert two of these into a useful result Benchmark object. For example: `$start = new Benchmark;`

debug	Object or class method. Set debugging either globally or per-object:
	
	`# enable debugging on this Benchmark object`
	`$start -> debug(1);`
	
	`# switch off debugging globally`
	`debug Benchmark 0;`

iters	Object method. Returns the number of iterations used to generate this benchmark (for Benchmark objects generated by the timeit, timethis, timethese, and countit subroutines). For example:
	
	`$result = timeit(1000, 'mysubroutine');`
	`$count = $result->iters;`

Basic benchmarking can be done just using the new and timediff functions, as noted above. We can also compute sums of differences with timesum:

Method	Action

timediff	Computes the difference in times between two raw Benchmark objects (as created by new) and returns a new Benchmark object containing the difference. For example:
	
	`$difference = timediff($start, $end);`
	`print timestr $difference;`

*timesum	Computes the sum of times of two relative Benchmark objects (computed themselves with timediff), returning a new Benchmark object. For example:
	
	`$diff1 = timediff ($start1, $end1);`
	`$diff2 = timediff ($start2, $end2);`
	`$total = Benchmark::timesum ($diff1, $diff2);`
	
	Note that this subroutine is not imported by default.

Method	Action

timestr	Generates a friendly string representation of a Benchmark object calculated from timediff (or potentially timesum) above. This is the easy way of turning a Benchmark object into something we can look at. For example:
	
	```print timestr $difference;```
	
	A second optional style argument determines the contents of the returned string, the default is auto:
	
	all Produce all times
	none Produce no times
	noc Produce parent process times only
	nop Produce child process times only
	auto Produce child process times only if they are non-zero (all or noc).
	
	A third parameter may be used to define the format of the output times; it takes the form of a sprintf style format, only without a leading %. The default is 5.2f. For example:
	
	```print timestr ($difference, 'noc', '10.5f');```
	
	See timeit and countit below for some examples of the strings produced by timestr.

Benchmark calculations are performed by the timeit, timethis, timethese, and countit subroutines. Additionally, the cmpthese subroutine generates a table of results from the output of timethese.

'timeit'

Given a number of iterations and some code to test, timeit runs the code for that number of iterations and returns a Benchmark object containing the result. For example:

```
# time one thousand iterations of '2**rand'
$result = timeit(1000, "2**rand");
```

The code may be either given as a string, in which case it is evaled to produce the code to test, or it may be a reference to a subroutine:

```
# time an anonymous subroutine
$result = timeit(1000, sub {2**rand});

# time a named subroutine
$result = timeit(1000, \&mysubroutine);
```

Note that either of these approaches allows compile-time checking of the code, unlike the eval version, but passing arguments is not possible this way. To achieve that, we need to define a new subroutine to pass test arguments for the benchmark:

```
sub testmysubroutine {
    mysubroutine('testing', 1, 2, 3);
}
$result = timeit(1000, \&testmysubroutine);
```

Or use an `eval` string:

```
$result = timeit(1000, "mysubroutine 'test', 1, 2, 3");
```

A test subroutine will incur a slight additional cost, but it should be negligible compared to the actual subroutine unless it is very fast and we are testing it a large number of times.

As a concrete example, this program benchmarks a simple expression by executing it one million times:

```
#!/usr/bin/perl
# timeit.pl
use warnings;
use strict;

use Benchmark;

sub mysubroutine {
    my $timewaster = time**rand;
}

my $result = timeit(1000000, 'mysubroutine');

print "Executed ", $result->iters, " iterations in ", timestr($result),"\n";
```

The output of this program is (but times may vary) something like:

Executed 1000000 iterations in 8 wallclock secs (7.54 usr + 0.46 sys = 8.00 CPU) @ 125000.00/s (n=1000000)

'timethis'

This subroutine combines `timeit` with `timestr` and prints the results to standard output. `timethis` takes four arguments; a count and code string, just as `timeit` does, followed by an optional title and optional style, which has the same meaning and values as the style argument of `timestr` above. For example:

```
# default output
timethis(1000, \&mysub);

# customized output
timethis(1000, \&mysub, "Testing!", 'toc');
```

Alternatively, if the count is negative or zero then `timethis` uses `countit` below instead of `timeit`, with the count interpreted as a minimum number of seconds to run for. Note that time is taken as `User+System` time, not real ('wallclock') time. The actual time taken may therefore be longer. In addition, the last iteration will likely carry the actual time incurred over the limit since the limit will expire while it is in progress.

The return value of `timethis` is a `Benchmark` object, with the same meaning as the result returned from `timeit`. If no title is specified, it defaults to `timethis COUNT`, where `COUNT` is the value of the first argument. Note that the real point of the title is for use by the `timethese` subroutine.

'timethese'

This subroutine carries out bulk benchmark calculations by calling `timethis` multiple times. The arguments of `timethese` are counts. This is applied to every individual benchmark and may be negative to define a minimum time. As with `timethis`, a hash reference with a list of tests to perform is passed to `timestr`. It has the same meaning and values as `timestr`'s style argument.

The hash of tests consists of key value pairs, the keys of which are names for the tests and are used as the titles in `timethis`, and values, which are the actual tests: `evaluable` strings or code references. For example:

```
$resulthashref = timethese (1000, {
    'Test 1' => sub {time()**rand()**rand()},
    'Test 2' => "2 + 2 + 2 + 2 + 2 + 2 + 2 + 2",
    'Test 3' => \&mysub,
}, 'all');
```

The return value from `timethese` is a hash reference containing the same keys as the test hash and with the `Benchmark` result objects as the values. This hash can be passed to `cmpthese` to generate a comparative report.

See the example output of `cmpthese` for an example of the output produced by `timethese` (which is called by `cmpthese`).

'cmpthese'

`cmpthese` carries out bulk benchmark calculations and then generates a comparative report of percentage differences between each pair of tests. This subroutine can either be passed arguments identical to those accepted by `timethese`, in which case it simply calls `timethese` to get a hash of results, or the hash reference containing the results from a previous `timethese`:

```
cmpthese(1000, {
    'Test 1' => sub { time()**rand()**rand() },
    'Test 2' => "2 + 2 + 2 + 2 + 2 + 2 + 2 + 2",
    'Test 3' => \&mysub,
}, 'all');
```

Or:

```
cmpthese($resulthashref);
```

The return result of `cmpthese` is a hash reference of results, the same as that returned by `timethese`, potentially useful if we passed in explicit arguments rather than a result hash reference.

As a practical example, here is a benchmark program that determines whether or not there is any noticeable difference between a named subroutine, an anonymous subroutine, and an evaluated code fragment:

```
#!/usr/bin/perl
# cmpthese.pl
use warnings;
use strict;

use Benchmark qw(cmpthese);
```

```perl
sub mysubroutine {
   my $timewaster = time**rand;
}

cmpthese(1000000, {
'Anon Test' => sub {my $timewaster = time**rand},
   'Eval Test' => 'my $timewaster = time**rand',
   'Ref Test' => \&mysubroutine,
}, 'all');
```

In order to get accurate results we have to push up the number of iterations so that a significant number of seconds elapse, so we give the test one million iterations (for a slower computer we may want to tone this number down a little). The output of this program consists of the output from timethese, followed by a comparative table:

Benchmark: timing 1000000 iterations of Anon Test, Eval Test, Ref Test...
 Anon Test: 6 wallclock secs (5.22 usr 0.74 sys + 0.00 cusr 0.00 csys = 5.96 CPU) @ 167785.23/s (n=1000000)
 Eval Test: 6 wallclock secs (5.27 usr 0.49 sys + 0.00 cusr 0.00 csys = 5.76 CPU) @ 173611.11/s (n=1000000)
  Ref Test: 7 wallclock secs (5.09 usr 0.62 sys + 0.00 cusr 0.00 csys = 5.71 CPU) @ 175131.35/s (n=1000000)

Rate			Eval	Test	Ref Test
Anon	Test	167785/s --	-3%	-4%	
Eval		Test 173611/s 3%	--	-1%	
Ref		Test 175131/s 4%	1%	--	

Apparently an anonymous subroutine is fractionally faster that a named one, with eval bringing up the rear, though there's not much in it.

Conceivably, cmpthese can be used with a self-assembled hash of keys and values. This will work so long as the keys are descriptive labels and the values are Benchmark result objects computed by timethis, timethese, countit, or timediff, and timesum. However, the result is unlikely to be useful unless the same count value is used for each benchmark result in the hash.

Note that there is no way to silence the output of timethese and just display the comparative table.

'countit'

This subroutine computes the number of iterations possible in the given time. It takes two arguments, a time to compute against and the code to compute. It returns the number of iterations that fit into the given time, including the iteration in process when the time expired. For example:

```perl
#!/usr/bin/perl
# countit.pl
use warnings;
use strict;

use Benchmark qw(countit timestr);
sub mysubroutine {
   my $timewaster = time**rand;
}

my $result = countit(10, 'mysubroutine');

print "Executed ", $result->iters, " iterations in ", timestr($result, 'noc'),
"\n";
```

The Benchmark module also contains a caching mechanism for storing the results of null-loops; that is loops containing no body (or at least no body that performs useful work, as determined by Perl's optimization algorithms). This allows the module to subtract its own overheads from the benchmarks it computes.

Mechanism	Action
Enablecache	Enable caching of times for null-loops. Each iteration count used for a null-loop is cached and reused if requested a second time: `Benchmark::enablecache;`
disablecache	Do not cache null-loop times `Benchmark::disablecache;`
clearcache	Clear the cached time for the null-loop for the given number of iterations. For example: `Benchmark::clearcache(1000);`
clearallcache	Clear all cached times for the null-loop: `Benchmark::clearallcache;`

In general we can ignore this caching, it happens automatically and without our intervention. If we want to disable it for any reason we can do so with Benchmark::disablecache.

Summary

We have covered in this chapter various approaches that we can take to debug our programs. We saw first how to write programs that debug themselves, before examining in detail the Perl debugger. We looked at how to start the debugger, the available commands and how to configure the debugger.

We then examined the Dumpvalue and Safe modules and looked briefly at debugging the Perl interpreter before covering automating tests using the Test::Harness module.

Finally, we covered various aspects of profiling.

18

Text Processing and Document Generation

Perl has many strengths and chief among these is its ability to process text in a comprehensive and commanding manner. It is this aspect of Perl that is largely responsible for its success as a CGI scripting language for use on the World Wide Web, which is largely concerned with the receipt, analysis, generation, and dissemination of large quantities of text.

In this chapter we are going to look at Perl's major text-processing features, building on some of the features already seen in Chapter 11 on regular expressions. The text-processing modules that come as part of Perl's standard library can solve many common problems associated with manipulating text, such as tab expansion, determining abbreviations, and the formatting of paragraphs. While these modules are not especially advanced, they eliminate the need for us to code our own solutions, providing a simple way of performing some useful functions.

In the second part of the chapter we look at the other class of text-processing modules, which concern Perl syntax known as **pod**, or **plain old documentation**. Put simply, pod documentation allows us to comment out our code in various forms. The Pod:: family of Perl modules enable us to perform various functions such as creating, transforming, and generally manipulating pod documentation in many different ways.

The final section of this chapter deals with reports, allowing us to format text using layout definitions. Formatting enables us to do many handy things with text, and we will explore, among other things, format structure, page control, and the format datatype. First, we will look at text processing.

Text Processing

Perl provides a flexible text-processing toolkit as part of its core features, of which interpolation and regular expressions are the most powerful features. However, the Perl standard library contains several handy text-processing modules that solve many common problems and can save us a lot of time. These modules are often overlooked when considering Perl's text-processing capabilities simply because the core language already provides such a rich set of functionality.

The main text-processing modules are all members of the `Text::` family of which the following are the most common:

Module	Function
Text::Tabs	Convert tabs to and from spaces
Text::Abbrev	Calculate unique abbreviations from a list of words
Text::ParseWords	Parse text into words and phrases
Text::Wrap	Convert unformatted text into paragraphs
Text::Soundex	Convert similar sounding text into condensed codes

In addition to these modules, many of Perl's other standard modules have more than a little to do with text-processing of one kind or another. We make a brief note of them and where they are covered at the end of this section.

Expanding and Contracting Tabs with 'Text::Tabs'

The `Text::Tabs` module is the simplest of the text-processing modules. It provides two subroutines, `unexpand` for converting sequences of spaces into tab characters, and `expand` for converting tab characters into spaces. Here is how they work:

```
# convert spaces into tabs
$tabbed_text = unexpand($spaced_text);

# convert tabs into spaces
$spaced_text = expand($tabbed_text);
```

Both of these subroutines work on either single strings, as shown above, or lists of strings, as in:

```
@tabbed_lines = unexpand(@spaced_lines);
```

Any spaces or tabs that already exist in the text when it is translated into spaced or tabbed text respectively are not affected, so this is an excellent way to make a document consistently tabbed rather than being tabbed in some places and spaced in others.

Both functions work by calculating the location of the tab positions across the document, and maintaining the correct number of spaces before each stop. The gap between stops (the stop gap, so to speak) is determined by the variable `$tabstop` which is set to the desired tab width, 4 by default. This is actually imported into our own package by default so we can set it with:

```
$tabstop = 8;   # set a tab width of eight characters
```

It is probably better from a namespace-pollution point of view to only import the subroutines and set $tabstop as a package variable, if only to clearly indicate that $tabstop is not a locally defined variable:

```
use Text::Tabs qw(expand unexpand);
```

We can change the spacing of a document using this module, by converting it to tabs and then back to spaces with a different tab width. The following short application uses Text::Tabs to do just this. It takes three or more arguments, an input tab width, an output tab width, and one or more files to process:

```perl
#!/usr/bin/perl
# tabconvert.pl
use warnings;
use strict;

use Text::Tabs qw(expand unexpand);

# insist on at least three arguments
die "Usage: $0 <in width> <out width> <file>...\n" if $#ARGV<2;

# pull in the input and output tab widths
my $width_in = shift @ARGV;
$width_in = 4 unless $width_in;
my $width_out = shift @ARGV;
$width_out = 4 unless $width_out;

# quit if the tab lengths are the same
die "Nothing to do\n" if $width_in eq $width_out;

# die on failure to open @ARGV
$SIG{__WARN__} = sub {die @_};
my @text = <>;

# convert to tabs using input tab width
$Text::Tabs::tabstop = $width_in;
@text = unexpand @text;

# print out text converted to output tab width
$Text::Tabs::tabstop = $width_out;
print expand @text;
```

To use this script to adjust indentation from four to eight characters we would use a command like:

> perl tabconvert.pl 4 8 infile > outfile

Calculating Abbreviations with 'Text::Abbrev'

It is occasionally useful to be able to quickly determine the unique abbreviations for a set of words, for instance when implementing a command-line interface. Assuming we wish to create our own, rather than use an existing solution like Term::Complete or (sometimes) Term::Readline, we can make use of the Text::Abbrev module to precompute a table of abbreviations and their full-name equivalents.

The Text::Abbrev module supplies one function, abbrev, which works by taking a list of words and computing abbreviations for each of them in turn by removing one character at a time from each word and recording the resultant word stalk in a hash table. The Getopt::Long module does something similar for command-line abbreviations, though it doesn't use Text::Abbrev for the job. If the abbreviation has already been seen, it must be because two words share that abbreviation and it is removed from the table. However, if a supplied word is itself an abbreviation of another, it is recorded anyway. Longer abbreviations remain, pointing to the longer word, while shorter abbreviations shared by both words are removed. This short script shows the results of calculating the unique abbreviations for gin, gang, and goolie:

```perl
#!/usr/bin/perl
# goolie.pl
use warnings;
use strict;

use Text::Abbrev;

my $abbreviations;

sub print_hash {
    print "Abbreviations: \n";
    foreach (sort keys %{$abbreviations}) {
        print "\t$_ => $abbreviations->{$_} \n";
    }
}

$abbreviations = abbrev('gin', 'gang', 'goolie');

print_hash($abbreviations);
```

When run, this script produces a hash of unique abbreviations. The single letter g is not present because it does not uniquely identify a single word, but ga, gi, and go are:

> **perl goolie.pl**
Abbreviations:
    ga => gang
    gan => gang
    gang => gang
    gi => gin
    gin => gin
    go => goolie
    goo => goolie
    gool => goolie
    gooli => goolie
    goolie => goolie

Generating an abbreviations table makes it very easy to quickly look up the complete word regardless of how many letters were actually supplied:

```perl
chomp;     # chomps '$_'
SWITCH: foreach ($abbreviations->{$_}) {
    /gin/ and do { print "Gin!"; last; };
    /gang/ and do { print "Gang!"; last; };
    /goolie/ and do { print "Goolie!"; last; };
}
}
```

The `abbrev` function returns either a list suitable for creating a hash or a hash reference, depending on whether it was called in list or scalar context:

```
%abbreviations = abbrev('gin', 'gang', 'goolie');
$abbreviations = abbrev('gin', 'gang', 'goolie');
```

We can also pass in a reference to a hash or a typeglob (deprecated) as the first argument. However, the original contents, if any, are not maintained:

```
# overwrite previous contents of $abbreviations
abbrev($abbreviations, 'ghost', 'ghast', 'ghoul');
```

To add new words to the table we can simply combine two hashes, but if we do so we have to make sure that we remove non-unique abbreviations ourselves:

```
%{$abbreviations} = (%{$abbreviations}, abbrev('giggle'));
delete $abbreviations->{'g'};
```

Since this requires knowing what we placed into the table in the first place, it is less than ideal. The same problem arises if we want to remove a term since new, unique abbreviations may become available. The only way to reliably generate a consistent modified list is to re-execute `abbrev` with the original list plus the additions. A simple way to regenerate the original word list is to check through the existing table looking for keys that match their values – these are the original words:

```
@words = grep {$_ eq $abbreviations->{$_}} keys %{$abbreviations};
abbrev ($abbreviations, @words, 'giggle');
```

Note that the `Term::Complete` module combines abbreviations with a command-line entry mechanism (although it does not use `Text::Abbrev` to determine abbreviations). If we don't need anything more complex, this is a simpler solution than rolling our own with `Text::Abbrev`. See Chapter 15 for more details.

Parsing Words and Phrases with 'Text::ParseWords'

Many applications that accept textual input need to be able to parse the text into distinct words for processing. In most simple cases we can simply get away with using `split`. Since this is such a common requirement, `split` even splits using whitespace as a default. For instance, this rather terse program carves up its input text into a list of words, separated by whitespace and split using `split` with no arguments:

```
#!/usr/bin/perl
# splitwords.pl
use warnings;
use strict;

my @words;
push @words, split foreach(<>);
print scalar(@words), "words: @words \n";
```

While effective, this kind of approach falls short if we want to handle more advanced constructs like quotes. If two or more words are surrounded by quotes we often want to treat them as a single word or phrase, in which case we can't easily use split. Instead we can use the Text::ParseWords module, which handles quotes and produces a list of words and phrases using them.

Parsing Space-Separated Text

The Text::ParseWords module supports the parsing of text into words and phrases, based on the presence of quotes in the input text. It provides four subroutines:

❑ shellwords – processes strings using whitespace as a delimiter, in the same manner as shells

❑ quotewords – handles more general cases where the word separator can be any arbitrary text

❑ nested_quotewords – similar to quotewords, word separator can be any arbitrary text

❑ parse_line – a simpler version of quotewords, which handles a single line of text and which is actually the basis of the other three

The first, shellwords, takes one or more lines of text and returns a list of words and phrases found within them. Since it is set to consider whitespace as the separator between words, it takes no other parameters:

```
@words = shellwords(@input);
```

Here is a short program that shows shellwords in action:

```perl
#!/usr/bin/perl
# shell.pl
use warnings;
use strict;

use Text::ParseWords qw(shellwords);

my @input = (
    'This is "a phrase"',
    'So is\ this',
    q('and this'),
    "But this isn\\'t",
    'And neither \"is this\"',
    );

print "Input: ", join('',@input),"\n";

my @words = shellwords(@input); print scalar(@words), " words:\n";
foreach (@words) {
    print "\t$_\n";
}
```

When run, this program should produce the output:

> **perl shell.pl**
Input: This is "a phrase" So is\ this 'and this' But this isn\'t And neither \"is this\"
13 words:
> This
> is
> a phrase
> So
> is this
> and this
> But
> this
> isn't
> And
> neither
> "is
> this"

This program demonstrates several points about how we use shellwords and its relations. First, we can define phrases with double quotes, or single quotes if we use the q function. We can also define phrases by escaping spaces that we want shellwords to overlook. In order to have shellwords process these backslashes, we have to use single quotes (or q) around the string as a whole to avoid interpolation from evaluating them first. To have shellwords ignore a quote, we can escape it, but to escape a single quote we have to use double quotes around the string and escape it twice (once for interpolation, once for shellwords). Of course a lot of this is simpler if the text is coming from a variable rather than a literal string.

Parsing Arbitrarily Delimited Text

The quotewords subroutine is a more flexible version of shellwords that allows the word separator to be defined. It takes two additional parameters, a regular expression pattern describing the word separator itself, and a keep flag that determines how quotes are handled. This is how we might use it to emulate and modify the result of shellwords. Note the value of the keep flag in each case:

```
# emulate 'shellwords' with 'quotewords'
@words = quotewords('\s+', 0, @lines);

# emulate 'shellwords' but keep quotes and backslashes
@words = quotewords('\s+', 1, @lines);
```

As a more complete example, here is a short program that parses a file of comma-separated lines into a long list of fields:

```
#!/usr/bin/perl
# readpw.pl
use warnings;
use strict;

use Text::ParseWords;

my (@users, @fields);
if (open PASSWD,"/etc/passwd") {
    @users = <PASSWD>;
    chomp @users;    # remove linefeeds
    @fields = quotewords(':', 0, @users);
    close PASSWD;
}
print "@fields";
```

The keep parameter determines whether quotes and backslashes are removed once their work is done, as real shells do, or whether they should be retained in the resulting list of words. If False, quotes are removed as they are parsed. If True, they are retained. The keep flag is almost but not quite Boolean. If set to the special case of delimiters, both quotes and characters that matched the word separator are kept:

```
# emulate 'shellwords' but keep quotes and backlashes and also store the
# matched whitespace as tokens too
@words = quotewords('\s+', 'delimiters', @lines);
```

Batch Parsing Multiple Lines

The /etc/passwd/ example above works, but assembles all the resultant fields of each user into one huge list of words. Far better would be to keep each set of words found on each individual line in a separate list. We can do that with the nested_quotewords subroutine, which returns a list of lists, one list for each line passed in. Here is a short program that uses nested_quotewords to do just that:

```perl
#!/usr/bin/perl
# password.pl
use warnings;
use strict;

use Text::ParseWords;

@ARGV = ('/etc/passwd');
my @users = nested_quotewords(':', 0, <>);

print scalar(@users)," users: \n";
foreach (@users) {
    print "\t${$_}[0] => ${$_}[2] \n";
}
```

This program prints out a list of all users found in /etc/passwd and their user id. When run it should produce something resembling the following:

```
> perl password.pl
16 users:
    root => 0
    bin => 1
    daemon => 2
    adm => 3
    lp => 4
    sync => 5
    shutdown => 6
    halt => 7
    mail => 8
    news => 9
    uucp => 10
    operator => 11
    games => 12
    gopher => 13
    ftp => 14
    nobody => 99
```

As it happens, in this case we could equally well have used `split` with a split pattern of a colon since quotes do not usually appear in a password file. However, the principle still applies.

Parsing a Single Line Only

We mentioned earlier that there were four subroutines supplied by `Text::ParseWords`. The fourth is `parse_line`, and it is the basis of the other three. This subroutine parses a single line only, but is otherwise identical in operation to `quotewords` and takes the same parameters with the exception that the last can only be a scalar string value:

```
@words = parse_line('\s+', 0, $line);
```

The `parse_line` subroutine provides no functional benefit over `quotewords`, but if we only have one line to parse, for example a command-line input, then we can save a subroutine call by calling it directly rather than via `quotewords` or `shellwords`.

Formatting Paragraphs with 'Text::Wrap'

The `Text::Wrap` module provides text-formatting facilities to automate the task of turning irregular blocks of text into neatly formatted paragraphs, organized so that their lines fit within a specified width. Although it is not particularly powerful, it provides a simple and quick solution.

It provides two subroutines; `wrap` handles individual paragraphs and is ideally suited for formatting single lines into a more presentable form and `fill` handles multiple paragraphs and will work on entire documents.

Formatting Single Paragraphs

The `wrap` subroutine formats single paragraphs, transforming one or more lines of text of indeterminate length and converting them into a single paragraph. It takes three parameters; an initial indent string, which is applied to the first line of the resulting paragraph, a following indent string, applied to the second and all subsequent lines, and finally a string or list of strings.

Here is how we could use `wrap` to generate a paragraph with an indent of five spaces on the first line and an indent of two spaces on all subsequent lines:

```
$para = wrap('     ',' ', @lines);
```

Any indentation is permissible. Here is a paragraph formatted (crudely) with HTML tags to force the lines to conform to a given line length instead of following the browser's screen width:

```
$html = wrap("<p>  ", "<br>", $text);
```

If a list is supplied, `wrap` concatenates all the strings into one before proceeding – there is no essential difference between supplying a single string over a list. However, existing indentation, if there is any, is not eliminated so we must take care to deal with this first if we are handling text that has already been formatted to a different set of criteria. For example:

```
map {$_ =~ s/^\s+//} @lines;   # strip leading whitespace from all lines
```

The list can be of any origin, not just an array variable. For example, take this one line reformatting application:

```
print wrap("\t", "", <>);   # reformat standard input/ARGV
```

Tabs are handled by Text::Wrap to expand them into spaces, a function handled by Text::Tabs, previously documented. When formatting is complete, spaces are converted back into tabs, if possible and appropriate. See the section on Text::Tabs for more information.

Customized Wrapping

The Text::Wrap module defines several package variables to control its behavior, including the formatting width, the handling of long words, and the break text.

Formatting Width

This is the most obvious variable to configure. The number of columns to format is held in the package variable Text::Wrap::columns, and has a default value of 76, which is the polite width for things like e-mail messages (to allow a couple of > quoting prefixes to be added in replies before 80 columns is reached). We can change the column width to 39 with:

```
$Text::Wrap::columns = 39;
```

All subsequent calls to wrap will now use this width formatting.

Long Words

Words that are too long to fit the line are left as is (URLs in text documents are a common culprit). This behavior can be altered to a fatal error by setting the variable the following line:

```
$Text::Wrap::huge = 'die';
```

This will cause wrap to die with an error can't wrap '<text>', where <text> is the paragraph text. Unfortunately wrap does not support anything resembling a user-defined subroutine to handle long words, for example by hyphenating them, though since Text::Wrap is not a very complicated module, creating our own customized version to do this would not prove too difficult.

Break Text

Although it is not that likely that we would want to change it, we can also configure the **break text**, that is, the character or characters that separate words. In fact the break text is a regular expression, defined in the package variable $Text::Wrap::break, and its default value is \s for any whitespace character.

As the break text is presumed to lie between words (that is, the actual meaningful content), it is removed from the paragraph before reformatting takes place. That means that while it might seem appealing to specify a break text pattern of \s|- to allow wrap to wrap on hyphenated words, we would lose the hyphen whenever this actually occurred.

Debugging

A limited debugging mode can be enabled by setting the variable $Text::Wrap::debug:

```
$Text::Wrap::debug = 1;
```

The columns, break, and huge variables can all be exported from the Text::Wrap package by specifying them in the import list:

```
use Text::Wrap($columns $huge $break);

$columns = 39;
$huge = 'die';
```

As with any module symbols we import, this is fine for simple scripts but is probably unwarranted for larger applications – use the fully qualified package variables instead.

Formatting Whole Documents

Whole documents can be formatted with the fill subroutine. This will chop the supplied text into paragraphs first by looking for lines that are indented, indicating the start of a new paragraph, and blank lines, indicating the end of one paragraph and the start of another. Having determined where each paragraph starts and ends, it feeds the resulting lines to wrap, before merging the resulting wrapped paragraphs back together.

The arguments passed to fill are the same as those for wrap. Here is how we would use it to reformat paragraphs into unindented and spaced paragraphs:

```
$formatted_document = fill("\n", "", @lines);
```

If the two indents are identical, fill automatically adds a blank line to separate each paragraph from the previous one. Therefore the above could also be achieved with:

```
$formatted_document = fill("", "", @lines);
```

If the indents are not identical then we need to add the blank line ourselves:

```
$formatted_document = fill("\t", "", @lines);
# indent each new paragraph with a tab, paragraphs are continuous

$formatted_document = fill("\n\t", "", @lines);
# indent each new paragraph with a tag, paragraphs are separated
```

All the configurable variables that affect the operation of wrap also apply to fill, of course, since fill uses wrap to do most of the actual work. It is not possible to configure how fill splits text into paragraphs.

Note that if fill is passed lines already indented by a previous wrap operation, then it will incorrectly detect each new line as a new paragraph (because it is indented). Consequently we must remove misleading indentation from the lines we want to reformat before we pass them to fill.

Formatting on the Command Line

Although it is a somewhat simplistic module, Text::Wrap's usage is simple enough for it to be used on the fly on the command-line:

> perl -MText::Wrap -e "fill('','',<>)" -- textfile ...

Here we have used -- to separate Perl's arguments from filenames to be fed to the formatter. We can supply any number of files at once, and redirect the output to a file if we wish.

Matching Similar Sounding Words with 'Text::Soundex'

The Text::Soundex module is different in nature to the other modules in the Text:: family. Whilst modules such as Text::Abbrev and Text::ParseWords are simple solutions to common problems, Text::Soundex tackles a different area entirely. It implements a version of the **Soundex** algorithm developed for the US Census in the latter part of the 19th century, and popularized by Donald Knuth of TeX fame.

The Soundex algorithm takes words and converts them into tokens that approximate the sound of the word. Similar sounding words produce tokens that are either the same or close together. Using this, we can generate soundex tokens for a predetermined list of words, say a dictionary or a list of surnames, and match queries against it. If the query is close to a word in the list, we can return the match even if the query is not exactly right, misspelled7, for example.

Tokenizing Single Words

The Text::Soundex module provides exactly one subroutine, soundex that transforms one word into its soundex token. It can also accept a list of words and will return a list of the tokens, but it will not deal with multiple words in one string:

```
print soundex "hello";    # produces 'H400'
print soundex "goodbye";   # produces 'G310'
print soundex "hilo";   # produces 'H400' - same as 'Hello'
print soundex qw(Hello World);   # produces 'H400W643'
print soundex "Hello World"   # produces 'H464'
```

The following short program shows the Soundex algorithm being used to look up a name from a list given an input from the user. Since we are using Soundex, the input doesn't have to be exact, just similar:

```
#!/usr/bin/perl
# surname.pl
use warnings;
use strict;

use Text::Soundex;

# define an ABC of names (as a hash for 'exists')
my %abc = (
    "Hammerstein" => 1,
    "Pineapples" => 1,
    "Blackblood" => 1,
    "Deadlock" => 1,
    "Mekquake" => 1,
    "Rojaws" => 1,
);

# create a token-to-name table
my %tokens;
foreach (keys %abc) {
    $tokens{soundex $_} = $_;
}
```

```
# test input against known names
print "Name? ";
while (<>) {
    chomp;
    if (exists $abc{$_}) {
        print "Yes, we have a '$_' here. Another? ";
    } else {
        my $token = soundex $_;
        if (exists $tokens{$token}) {
            print "Did you mean $tokens{$token}? ";
        } else {
            print "Sorry, who again? ";
        }
    }
}
```

We can try out this program with various different names, real and imaginary, and produce different answers. The input can be quite different from the name if it sounds approximately right:

> **perl surname.pl**
Name? Hammerstone
Did you mean Hammerstein? Hammerstein
Yes, we have a 'Hammerstein' here. Another? Blockbleed
Did you mean Blackblood? Mechwake
Did you mean Mekquake? Nemesis
Sorry, who again?

Tokenizing Lists of Words and E-Mail Addresses

We can produce a string of tokens from a string of words if we split up the string before feeding it to soundex. Here is a simple query program that takes input from the user and returns a list of tokens:

```
#!/usr/bin/perl
# soundex.pl
use warnings;
use strict;

use Text::Soundex;

while (<>) {
    chomp;    #remove trailing linefeed
    s/\W/ /g;    #zap punctuation, e.g. '.', '@'
    print "'$_' => '@{[soundex(split)]}'\n";
}
```

We can try this program out with phrases to illustrate that accuracy does not have to be all that great, as a guide:

> **perl soundex.pl**
definitively inaccurate
'definitively inaccurate' => 'D153 I526'
devinatovli inekurat
'devinatovli inekurat' => 'D153 I526'

As well as handling spaces we have also added a substitution that converts punctuation into spaces first. This allows us to generate a list of tokens for an e-mail address, for example. By concatenating and storing these with a list of e-mail addresses in the same way as the name example we showed earlier we could easily implement a simple e-mail-matching program. Used correctly we could handle e-mails sent to pestmaster instead of postmaster, for example.

683

The 'Soundex' Algorithm

As the above examples illustrate, Soundex tokens consist of an initial letter, which is the same as that of the original word, followed by three digits that represent the sound of the first, second and third syllable respectively. Since one has one syllable, only the first digit is non-zero. On the other hand, seven has two syllables, so it gets two non-zero digits. Comparing the two results we can notice that both one and seven contain a 5, which corresponds to the syllable containing n in each word.

The Soundex algorithm has some obvious limitations though. In particular, it only resolves words up to the first three syllables. However, this is generally more than enough for simple 'similar sounding' type matches, such as surname matching, for which it was designed.

Handling Untokenizable Words

In some rare cases, the Soundex algorithm cannot find any suitable token for the supplied word. In these cases it usually returns nothing (or to be more accurate, undef). We can change this behavior by setting the variable

```
$Text::Soundex::soundex_nocode:

$Text::Soundex::soundex_nocode = 'Z000';   # a common 'failed' token
print soundex "=>";   # produces 'Z000'
```

If we change the value of this variable we must be sure to set it to something that is not likely to genuinely occur. The value of Z000 is a common choice, but matches many words including Zoo. A better choice in this case might be Q999, but there is no code that is absolutely guaranteed not to occur. If we do not need to conform to the Soundex code system (we might want to pass the results to something else that expects valid Soundex tokens as input) then we can simply define an impossible value like _NOCODE_ or ?000, which soundex cannot generate.

Other Text Processing Modules

As well as the modules in the Text:: family, several other Perl modules outside the Text:: hierarchy involve text-processing or combine text-processing with other functions.

Several of the Term:: modules involve text-processing in relation to terminals. For instance, Term::Cap involves generating ANSI escape sequences from capability codes, while Term::ReadLine provides input line text-processing support. These modules are all covered in Chapter 15.

Documenting Perl

Documentation is always a good idea in any programming language, and Perl is no exception. In fact, because Perl is so good (or, as some might have it, so bad) at allowing us to create particularly indecipherable code, documentation is all the more important. There is also such a thing as too much documentation; the more there is, the more we have to keep up to date with the actual code. If we are documenting every line of code it is probably a sign we need to spend more time making the code easier to understand and less time writing commentary to make up for it.

Like most programming languages, Perl supports simple comments. However, it also attempts to combine the onerous duties of commenting code and documenting software into one slightly less arduous task through the prosaically named **pod** syntax.

Comments

Perl comments are, as we would expect, very simple and traditional. In the style of C++ (but not C) and too many shells to count, they consist of a leading #, plus whatever it is we want to say:

```
# like this
```

Anything after the # is ignored by Perl's interpreter. Comments may be placed on a line of their own, or after existing Perl code. They can even be placed in the middle of statements:

```
print 1 *   # depth
4*   # width
9   # height
;
```

Perl is smart enough not to try to interpret a # inside a string as the start of a comment, but conversely we cannot comment here documents. Also we also cannot comment multiple lines at once, in C-style /*...*/ comments, but we can use pod for that if we want.

plain old documentation

pod is a very simple markup syntax for integrating documentation with the source code that it is documenting. It consists of a series of special one-line tokens that separate pod from anything else in a file (presumably code), and also allows us to define simple structures like headings and lists.

In and of itself, pod does nothing more than regular comments do, except give us the ability to write multi-line comments. However, its simple but flexible syntax also makes it very simple to convert into 'real' documents like text files and HTML documents. Indeed, Perl comes with the pod2text and pod2html tools for this very purpose. The elegance of pod is that if we want to read the documentation for a particular module or library file we can just run pod2text against the module file to generate the documentation. The perldoc utility is just a friendlier interface to the same pod translation process.

Java programmers will be right at home with pod – it is basically a similar (and incidentally, prior) idea to javadoc, which also encourages self-documenting code.

pod Paragraphs

Pod allows us to define documentation paragraphs, which we can insert into other documents – most usually, but by no means exclusively, Perl code. The simplest sequence is =pod ... =cut, which simply states that all the following text is to be taken as pod paragraphs, until the next =cut or the end of the file:

```
...
$scalar = "value";
=pod

This is a paragraph of pod text embedded into some Perl code. It is not indented,
so it will be treated as normal text and word wrapped by pod translators.

=cut
print do_something($scalar);
...
```

Within pod, text is divided into paragraphs, which are simply blocks of continuous text, just as they are anywhere else. A paragraph ends and a new one begins when a completely empty line is encountered. All pod tokens absorb the paragraph after them on the same line or immediately following. Some tokens, such as headings, use this paragraph for display purposes. Others, like =pod and =cut simply ignore it, so we can document the pod itself:

```
=pod this is just a draft document

mysubname - this subroutine doesn't do much of anything
at all and is just serving as an example of how to document it with
a pod paragraph or two

=cut end of draft bit
```

The only partial exception to this is =cut. While translators will absorb text immediately following =cut, Perl itself will not, so we cannot spread a 'cut comment' across more than one line.

Paragraphs and Paragraph Types

If a paragraph is indented then we consider it to be preformatted, much in the same way that the HTML <PRE> tag works. The following example shows three paragraphs two of which are indented:

```
=pod
        This paragraph is indented, so it is taken as
        is and not reformatted by translators like:

        pod2text - the text translator
        pod2html - the HTML translator
        pod2man - the UNIX manual page translator

        Note that 'as is' also means that escaping does not work, and that
        interpolation doesn't happen. What we see is what we get.

This is a second paragraph in the same =pod..=cut section. Since it is
not indented it will be reformatted by translators.

        Again indented
        This is a third paragraph
        Useful for Haikus
=cut
```

Headings

Headings can be added with the =head1 and =head2 tokens, which provide first and second-level headings respectively. The heading text is the paragraph immediately following the token, and may start (and end) on the same line:

```
=head1 This is a level one heading
```

Or:

```
=head2 This is
a level
two heading
```

Or:

```
=head2
As is this
```

Both heading tokens start a pod section in the same way that =pod does if one is not already active. pod sections do not nest, so we only need one =cut to get back to Perl code. In general we tend to use the first form, but it is important to leave an empty line if we do not want our heading to absorb the following paragraph:

```
=head1 This heading has accidentally swallowed up
       this paragraph, because there is no separating line.
=head2 Worse than that, it will absorb this second level heading too
       so this is all one long level one heading, and not the two headings
       and paragraphs as we actually intended.
=cut
```

This is how we should really do it:

```
=head1 This is a level one heading

This is a paragraph following the level one heading.

=head2 This is a level two heading

This a preformatted paragraph following the level 2 heading.

=cut
```

How the headings are actually rendered is entirely up to the translator. By default the text translator pod2text indents paragraphs by four spaces, level-two headings by two, and level-one headings by none – crude, but effective. The HTML translator pod2html uses <Hn> tags, as we might expect.

Lists

Lists can be defined with the =over...=back and =item tokens. The =over token starts a list, and can be given a value such as 4, which many formatters use to determine how much indentation to use. The list is ended by =back, and is optional if the pod paragraph is at the end of the document. =item defines the actual list items of which there should be at least one, and we should not use this token outside an =over...=back section. Here is an example four item list – note again the empty lines that separate the items from the paragraphs between them.

```
=over 4

=item 1

This is item number one on the list

=item 2

This is item number two on the list

=item 3
```

```
This is the third item

=item 4

Guess...

=back
```

Since the =over and =item tokens can take values, and because the only kind of value pod knows is the paragraph, we can also say:

```
=over
4

=item
1

...
```

In practice we probably do not want to do this, but the same caveats about headings and paragraphs also apply here. Note that =over works like =pod, and starts a pod section if one is not active.

The numbers after the =item tokens are purely arbitrary; we can use anything we like for them, including meaningful text. However, to make the job of pod translators easier we should stick to a consistent scheme. For example if we number them, we should do it consistently, and if we want to use bullet points then we should use something like an asterisk. If we want named items, we can do that too. For example, a bullet pointed list with paragraphs:

```
=over 4

=item *
This is a bullet pointed list
=item *
With two items

=back
```

A named items list:

```
=over 4

=item The First Item
This is the description of the first item

=item The Second Item
This is the description of the second item

=back;
```

A named items list without paragraphs:

```
=over 4

=item Stay Alert

=item Trust No one

=item Keep Your Laser Handy

=back
```

pod translators will attempt to do the best they can with pod lists, depending on what it is they think we are trying to do, and the constraints of the document format into which they are converting. The pod2text tool will just use the text after the item name. The pod2html tool is subject to the rules of HTML, which has different tags for ordered, unordered, and descriptive lists (<ol>, <ul>, and <dl>) so it makes a guess based on what the items look like. A consistent item naming style will help it make a correct guess.

If =over is used outside an existing pod section then it starts another one. The =back ends the list but not the pod section, so we also need to add a =cut to return to Perl code:

```
=over 4

=item *
This is item 1

=item *
This is item 2

=back
=cut
```

Translator-Specific Paragraphs

The final kind of pod token are the =for and =begin...=end tokens. The former token takes the name of a specific translator and a paragraph, which is rendered only if that translator is being used. The paragraph should be in the output format of the translator, that is, already formatted for output. Other translators will entirely ignore the paragraph:

```
=for text
This is a paragraph that will appear in documents produced by the pod2text format.

=for html <font color = red>
<p>But this paragraph will appear in <b>HTML</b> documents
</font>
```

Again, like the headings and item tokens, the paragraph can start on the next line as in the first example, or immediately following the format name, as in the second.

Since it is annoying to have to type =for format for every paragraph in a collection of paragraphs we can also use the pair of =begin...=end markers. These operate much like =pod...=cut but mark the enclosed paragraphs as being specific to a particular format:

```
=begin html
<p>Paragraph1
<p><table>......
......</table>
<p>Paragraph2
=end
```

If =begin is used outside an existing pod section then it starts one. The =end ends the format specific section but not the pod section, so we also need to add a =cut to return to Perl code, just as for lists.

```
=begin html
<p>A bit of <b>HTML</b> document
=end
=cut
```

The =begin and =end tokens can also be used to create multi-line comments, simply by providing =begin with a name that does not correspond to any translator. We can even comment out blocks of code this way:

```
=begin disabled_dump_env
foreach (sort keys %ENV) {
    print STDERR, "$_ => $ENV{$_}\n";
}
=end
```

```
=begin comment
This is an example of how we can use pod tokens to create comments.
Since 'comment' is not a pod translator type, this section is never used in
documents created by 'pod2text', 'pod2html', etc.
=end
```

Using pod with 'DATA' or 'END' tokens

If we are using either a __DATA__ or a __END__ token in a Perl script then we need to take special care with pod paragraphs that lie adjacent to them. pod translators require that there must be at least one empty line between the end of the data and a pod directive for the directive to be seen, otherwise it is missed by the translation tools. In other words, write:

```
...
__END__

=head1
...
```

And not:

```
...
__END__
=head1
```

Interior Sequences

We mentioned earlier that pod paragraphs could either be preformatted (indicated by indenting), or normal. Normal paragraphs are reformatted by translators to remove extraneous spaces, newlines, and tabs. Then the resulting paragraph is rendered to the desired width if necessary.

In addition to this basic reformatting, normal paragraphs may also contain interior sequences – specially marked out sections of the text with particular meanings. Each sequence consists of a single capital letter, followed by the text to treat specially within angle brackets. For example:

```
=pod
This is a B<paragraph> that uses I<italic> and B<bold> markup using the
BE<lt>textE<gt> and IE<lt>text<gt> interior sequences. Here is an example code
fragment: C<substr $text,0,1> and here is a filename: F</usr/bin/perl>. All these
things are of course represented in a style entirely up to the translator. See
L<perlpod> for more information.
=cut
```

Note that to specify a real < and > we have to use the E<lt> and E<gt> sequences, reminiscent of the < and &gt HTML entities.

Pod Tools and Utilities

Having documented our code using pod, it is time to generate some documents from it. Perl provides a collection of modules in the Pod:: family that perform various kinds of translations from pod to other formats. Perl also provides utility modules for checking syntax. We can use these modules programmatically in our own documentation utilities, but more commonly we simply use one of the utilities that Perl provides as standard.

All of these tools support both long and short option names, in the manner of the Getopt::Long module (which is what they all use to process the command-line), so we can say -v or --verbose or a number of things in between for the pod2usage tool. We have used the long names below, but all of them can be abbreviated to one extent or another.

Translator Tools

We have already mentioned pod2text and pod2html a few times. Perl also comes with other translators and some utilities based on pod too. All the translators take an input and optional output file as arguments, plus additional options to control their output format. Without either, they take input from standard input and write it to standard output.

The list of pod translators supplied with Perl is as follows:

❑ pod2text – translates pod into plain text. If the -c option is used and Term::ANSIColor is installed (see Chapter 15) colors will also be used.

❑ pod2html – translates pod into HTML, optionally recursing and processing directories and integrating cross-links between pages.

❑ pod2roff, pod2man – both these tools translate pod into UNIX manual pages using the Pod::Man module.

As always, for more details on these translators we consult the relevant perldoc page using the now familiar command-line and substituting our choice of translator:

> **perldoc <translatorname>**

The pod2man translator also supplies font arguments, which only apply to troff, an -official argument for official Perl documentation, and a -lax argument, which is meant to check that all parts of a UNIX manual page are present. Unfortunately at present it does not do this. See:

> **perldoc pod2man**

for details on these.

Note that there are plenty of additional pod translation tools available from CPAN; including translators for RTF/Word, LaTex, Postscript, and plenty of other formats. Chances are that, if it is a halfway popular format, there will be a pod translator for it.

Retrieval Tools

In addition to the translators, Perl provides three tools for extracting information from pods selectively. Of these, perldoc is by far the most accomplished. Although not strictly a translator, perldoc is a utility that makes use of translators to provide a convenient Perl documentation lookup tool. We covered it in detail back in Chapter 1.

To attempt to retrieve usage information about the given Perl script, we can use the pod2usage tool. For example:

> **pod2usage myscript.pl**

The tool searches for a SYNOPSIS heading within the file and prints it out using pod2text. A verbosity flag may be specified to increase the returned information:

-v 1 (default) SYNOPSIS only
-v 2 OPTIONS and ARGUMENTS too
-v 3 All pod documentation

A verbosity of 3 is equivalent to using pod2text directly. If the file is not given with an absolute pathname then -pathlist can be used to provide a list of directory paths to search for the file in.

A simpler and more generic version of pod2usage, is podselect. This tool attempts to locate a level 1 heading with the specified section title and returns it from whichever files it is passed:

> **podselect -s='How to boil an egg' *.pod**

Note that podselect does not do any translation, so it needs to be directed to a translator for rendering into reasonable documentation.

pod Verification

It is easy to make simple mistakes with pod, omitting empty lines or forgetting =cut for example. Fortunately pod is simple enough to be easy to verify as well. The podchecker utility scans a file looking for problems:

> **podchecker poddyscript.pl**

If all is well then it will return:

poddyscript.pl pod syntax OK.

Otherwise it will produce a list of problems, which we can then go and fix, for example:

*** WARNING: file does not start with =head at line N in file poddyscript.pl

This warning indicates that we have started pod documentation with something other than a =head1 or =head2, which the checker considers to be suspect. Likewise:

*** WARNING: No numeric argument for =over at line N in file poddyscript.pl
*** WARNING: No items in =over (at line 17) / =back list at line N in file poddyscript.pl

This indicates that we have an =over...=back pair, which not only does not have a number after the over, but does not even contain any items. The first is probably an omission. The second indicates that we might have bunched up our items so they all run into the =over token, like this:

```
=over
=item item one
=item item two

=back
```

If we had left out the space before the =back we would instead have got:

*** ERROR: =over on line N without closing =back at line EOF in file poddyscript.pl

In short, podchecker is a useful tool and we should use it if we plan to write pod of any size in our Perl scripts.

The module that implements podchecker is called Pod::Checker, and we can use it with either filenames or file handles supplied for the first two arguments:

```
# function syntax
$ok = podchecker($podfile, $checklog, %options);

# object syntax
$checker = new Pod::Checker %options;
$checker->parse_from_file($podpath, $checklog);
```

Both file arguments can be either filenames or filehandles. By default, the pod file defaults to STDIN and the check log to STDERR, so a very simple checker script could be:

```
use Pod::Checker;
print podchecker?"OK":"Fail";
```

The options hash, if supplied, allows one option to be defined: enable or disable the printing of warnings. The default is on, so we can get a verification check without a report using STDIN and STDERR:

```
$ok = podchecker(\*STDIN, \*STDERR,'warnings' => 0);
```

The actual podchecker script is more advanced than this, of course, but not by all that much.

Programming pod

Perl provides a number of modules for processing pod documentation – we mentioned `Pod::Checker` just a moment ago. These modules form the basis for all the pod utilities, some of which are not much more than simple command-line wrappers for the associated module. Most of the time we do not need to process pod programmatically, but in case we do, here is a list of the pod modules supplied by Perl and what each of them does:

Module	Action
`Pod::Checker`	The basis of the podchecker utility. See above.
`Pod::Find`	Search for and return a hash of pod documents. See 'Locating pods' below.
`Pod::Functions`	A categorized summary of Perl's functions, exported as a hash.
`Pod::Html`	The basis for the pod2html utility.
`Pod::Man`	The basis for both the pod2man and the functionally identical pod2roff utilities.
`Pod::Parser`	The pod parser. This is the basis for all the translation modules and most of the others too. New parsers can be implemented by inheriting from this module.
`Pod::ParseUtils`	A module containing utility subroutines for retrieving information about and organizing the structure of a parsed pod document, as created by `Pod::InputObjects`.
`Pod::InputObjects`	The implementation of the pod syntax, describing the nature of paragraphs and so on. In-memory pod documents can be created on the fly using the methods in this module.
`Pod::Plainer`	A compatibility module for converting new style pod into old style pod.
`Pod::Select`	A subclass of `Pod::Parser` and the basis of the podselect utility, `Pod::Select` extracts selected parts of pod documents by searching for their heading titles. Any translator that inherits from `Pod::Select` rather than `Pod::Parser` will be able to support the `Pod::Usage` module automatically.
`Pod::Text`	The basis of the pod2text utility.
`Pod::Text::Color`	Convert pod to text using ANSI color sequences. The basis of the -color option to pod2text. Subclassed from `Pod::Text`. This uses `Term::ANSIColor`, which must be installed; see Chapter 15.
`Pod::Text::Termcap`	Convert pod to text using escape sequences suitable for the current terminal. Subclassed from `Pod::Text`. Requires termcap support, see Chapter 15.
`Pod::Usage`	The basis of the pod2usage utility; this uses `Pod::Select` to extract usage-specific information from pod documentation by searching for specific sections, for example, NAME, SYNOPSIS.

Using Pod Parsers

Translator modules, which is to say any module based directly or indirectly on Pod::Parser, may be used programmatically by creating a parser object and then calling one of the parsing methods:

```
parse_from_filehandle($fh, %options);
```

Or:

```
parse_from_file($infile, $outfile, %options);
```

For example, assuming we have Term::ANSIColor installed, we can create ANSIColor text documents using this short script:

```perl
#!/usr/bin/perl
# parseansi.pl
use warnings;
use strict;

use Pod::Text::Color;

my $parser = new Pod::Text::Color(
    width => 56,
    loose => 1,
    sentence => 1,
);

if (@ARGV) {
    $parser->parse_from_file($_, '-') foreach @ARGV;
} else {
    $parser->parse_from_filehandle(\*STDIN);
}
```

We can generate HTML pages, plain text documents, and manual pages using exactly the same process from their respective modules.

Writing a pod Parser

Writing our own pod parser is surprisingly simple. Most of the hard work is done for us by Pod::Parser, so all we have to do is override the methods we need to replace in order to generate the kind of document we are interested in. Particularly, there are four methods we may want to override:

- ❑ command – Render and output POD commands.
- ❑ verbatim – Render and output verbatim paragraphs.
- ❑ textblock – Render and output regular (non-verbatim) paragraphs.
- ❑ interior_sequence – Return rendered interior sequence.

By overriding these and other methods we can customize the document that the parser produces. Note that the first three methods display their result, whereas interior_sequence returns it. Here is a short example of a pod parser that turns pod documentation into an XML document (albeit without a DTD):

```perl
#!/usr/bin/perl
# parser.pl
use warnings;
use strict;

{
    package My::Pod::Parser;

    use Pod::Parser;

    our @ISA = qw(Pod::Parser);

    sub command {
        my ($parser, $cmd, $para, $line) = @_;
        my $fh = $parser->output_handle;

        $para =~s/[\n]+$//;
        my $output = $parser->interpolate($para, $line);
        print $fh "<pod:$cmd> $output </pod:$cmd> \n";
    }

    sub verbatim {
        my ($parser, $para, $line) = @_;
        my $fh = $parser->output_handle;

        $para =~s/[\n]+$//;
        print $fh "<pod:verbatim> \n $para \n </pod:verbatim> \n";
    }

    sub textblock {
        my ($parser, $para, $line) = @_;
        my $fh = $parser->output_handle;

        print $fh $parser->interpolate($para, $line);
    }

    sub interior_sequence {
        my ($parser, $cmd, $arg) = @_;
        my $fh = $parser->output_handle;

        return "<pod:int cmd=\"$cmd\"> $arg </pod:int>";
    }
}

my $parser = new My::Pod::Parser();

if (@ARGV) {
    $parser->parse_from_file($_) foreach @ARGV;
} else {
    $parser->parse_from_filehandle(\*STDIN);
}
```

To implement this script we need the output filehandle (since the parser may be called with a second argument), which we can get from the output_handle method. We also take advantage of Pod::Parser to do the actual rendering work by using the interpolate method, which in turn calls our interior_sequence method. Pod::Parser provides plenty of other methods too, some of which we can override as well as or instead of the ones we used in this parser, see:

> **perldoc Pod::Parser**

for a complete list of them. The Pod::Parser documentation also covers more methods that we might want to override, such as begin_input, end_input, preprocess_paragraph, and so on. Each of these gives us the ability to customize the parser in increasingly finer-grained ways.

We have placed the Parser package inside the script in this instance, though we could equally have had it in a separate module file. To see the script in action we can feed it with any piece of Perl documentation – the pod documentation itself, for example. On a typical UNIX installation of Perl 5.6, we can do that with:

> perl mypodparser /usr/lib/perl5/5.6.0/pod/perlpod.pod

This generates an XML version of perlpod that starts like this:

```
<pod:head1>NAME</pod:head1>
perlpod - plain old documentation

<pod:head1>DESCRIPTION</pod:head1>
A pod-to-whatever translator reads a pod file paragraph by paragraph,
and translates it to the appropriate output format. There are
three kinds of paragraphs:
<pod:int cmd="L">verbatiml/"Verbatim Paragraph"</pod:int>,
<pod:int cmd="L">commandl/"Command Paragraph"</pod:int>, and
<pod:int cmd="L">ordinary textl/"Ordinary Block of Text"</pod:int>.

<pod:head2>Verbatim Paragraph</pod:head2>
A verbatim paragraph, distinguished by being indented (that is,
it starts with space or tab). It should be reproduced exactly,
with tabs assumed to be on 8-column boundaries. There are no
special formatting escapes, so you can't italicize or anything
like that. A \ means \, and nothing else.

<pod:head2>Command Paragraph</pod:head2>
All command paragraphs start with "=", followed by an
identifier, followed by arbitrary text that the command can
use however it pleases. Currently recognized commands are

<pod:verbatim>
    =head1 heading
    =head2 heading
    =item text
    =over N
    =back
    =cut
    =pod
    =for X
    =begin X
    =end X
</pod:verbatim>
```

By comparing this with the original document we can see how the parser is converting pod tokens into XML tags.

Locating pods

The UNIX-specific Pod::Find module searches for pod documents within a list of supplied files and directories. It provides one subroutine of importance, pod_find, which is not imported by default. This subroutine takes one main argument – a reference to a hash of options including default search locations. Subsequent arguments are additional files and directories to look in. The following script implements a more or less fully-featured pod search based around Pod::Find and Getopt::Long, which we cover in detail in Chapter 14.

```perl
#!/usr/bin/perl
# findpod.pl
use warnings;
use strict;

use Pod::Find qw(pod_find);
use Getopt::Long;

# default options
my $verbose = undef;
my $include = undef;
my $scripts = undef;
my $display = 1;

# allow files/directories and options to mix
Getopt::Long::Configure('permute');

# get options
GetOptions('verbose!' => \$verbose,
    'include!' => \$include,
    'scripts!' => \$scripts,
    'display!' => \$display,
);

# if no directories specified, default to @INC
$include = 1 if !defined($include) and (@ARGV or $scripts);

# perform scan
my %pods = pod_find({
    -verbose => $verbose,
    -inc => $include,
    -script => $scripts,
    -perl => 1
}, @ARGV);

# display results if required
if ($display) {
    if (%pods) {
        foreach(sort keys %pods) {
            print "Found '$pods{$_}' in $_\n";
        }
    } else {
        print "No pods found\n";
    }
}
```

We can invoke this script with no arguments to search @INC, or pass it a list of directories and files to search. It also supports four arguments to enable verbose messages, disable the final report, and enable Pod::Find's two default search locations. Here is one way we can use it, assuming we call it findpod:

> **perl findpod.pl -iv /my/perl/lib 2> dup.log**

This command tells the script to search @INC in addition to /my/perl/lib (-i), produce extra messages during the scan (-v), and to redirect error output to dup.log. This will capture details of any duplicate modules that the module finds during its scan. If we only want to see duplicate modules, we can disable the output and view the error output on screen with:

> **perl findpod.pl -i --nodisplay /my/perl/lib**

The options passed in the hash reference to pod_find are all Boolean and all default to 0 (off). They have the following meanings:

Option	Action
-verbose	Print out progress during scan, reporting all files scanned that did not contain pod information.
-inc	Scan all the paths contained in @INC.
-script	Search the installation directory and subdirectories for pod files. If Perl was installed as /usr/bin/perl then this will be /usr/bin for example.
-perl	Apply Perl naming conventions for finding likely pod files. This strips likely Perl file extensions (.pod, .pm, etc.), skips over numeric directory names that are not the current Perl release, and so on. Both -inc and -script imply -perl.

The hash generated by findpod.pl contains the file in which each pod document was found as the key, and the document title (usually the module package name) as the value. This is the reverse arrangement to the contents of the %INC hash, but contains the same kinds of keys and values.

Reports – The 'r' in Perl

Reports are a potentially useful but often overlooked feature of Perl that date back to the earliest versions of the language. In short, they provide a way to generate structured text such as tables or forms using a special layout description called a format.

Superficially similar in intent to the print and sprintf functions, formats provide a different way to lay out text on a page or screen, with an entirely different syntax geared specifically towards this particular goal. The particular strength of formats comes from the fact that we can describe layouts in physical terms, making it much easier to see how the resulting text will look and making it possible to design page layouts visually rather than resorting to character counting with printf.

Formats and the Format Datatype

Intriguingly, formats are an entirely separate data type, unique from scalars, arrays, hashes, typeglobs, and filehandles. Like filehandles, they have no prefix or other syntax to express themselves and as a consequence often look like filehandles, which can occasionally be confusing.

Formats are essentially the compiled form of a format definition, a series of formatting or picture lines containing literal text and placeholders, interspersed with data lines that describe the information used to fill placeholder and comment lines. As a simple example, here is a format definition that defines a single pattern line consisting mainly of literal text and a single placeholder, followed by a data line that fills that placeholder with some more literal text:

```
# this is the picture line
This is a @<<<<< justified field
# this is the data line
"left"
```

To turn a format definition into a format we need to use the `format` function, which takes a format name and a multi-line format definition, strongly reminiscent of a `here` document, and turns it into a compiled format. A single full stop on its own defines the end of the format. To define the very simple format example above we would write something like this:

```
format MYFORMAT =
This is a @<<<<< justified field
"left"
.
```

Note that the trailing period is very important, as it is the end token that defines the end of the implicit `here` document. A format definition will happily consume the entire contents of a source file if left unchecked.

To use a format we use the `write` function on the filehandle with the same name as the format. For the `MYFORMAT` example above we would write:

```
# print format definition to filehandle 'MYFORMAT'
write MYFORMAT;
```

This requires that we actually have an open filehandle called `MYFORMAT` and want to use the format to print to it. More commonly we want to print to standard output, which we can do by either defining a format called `STDOUT`, or assigning a format name to the special variable `$~` (`$FORMAT_NAME` with the `English` module). In this case we can omit the filehandle and `write` will use the currently selected output filehandle, just like `print`:

```
$~ = 'MYFORMAT';
write;
```

We can also use methods from the `IO::` family of modules, if we are using them. Given an `IO::Handle`-derived filehandle called `$fh`, we can assign and use a format on it like this:

```
$fh->format(MYFORMAT);
$fh->format_write();
```

We'll return to the subject of assigning formats a little later on.

The `write` function (or its `IO::Handle` counterpart `format_write`) generates filled-out formats by combining the picture lines with the current values of the items in the data lines to fill in any placeholder present, in a process reminiscent of, but entirely unconnected to, interpolation. Once it has finished filling out, it sends the results to standard output.

If we do not want to print output we can instead make use of the formline function. This takes a single picture line and generates output from it into the special variable $^A. It is the internal function that format uses to generate its output, and we will see a little more of how to use it later. There is, strangely, no string equivalent of write in the same way that printf has sprintf, but it is possible to create one using formline.

Format picture lines are usually written as static pieces of text, which makes them impossible to adjust to cater for different circumstances like calculated field widths. As an alternative, we can build the format inside a string and then eval it to create the format, which allows us to interpolate variables into the format at the time it is evaluated. Here is an example that creates and uses a dynamically calculated format associated with the STDOUT filehandle:

```perl
#!/usr/bin/perl
# evalformat.pl
use warnings;
use strict;

# list of values for field
my @values=qw(first second third fourth fifth sixth penultimate ultimate);

# determine maximum width of field
my $width=0;
foreach (@values) {
    my $newwidth=length $_;
    $width=$newwidth if $newwidth>$width;
}

# create a format string with calculated width using '$_'
my $definition = "This is the \@".('<'x($width-1))." line\n".
    '$_'."\n.\n";

# define the format through interpolation
eval "format STDOUT = \n$definition";

# print out the field values using the defined format
write foreach @values;
```

The advantage of this approach is it allows us to be more flexible, as well as calculate the size of fields on the fly. The disadvantage is that we must take care to interpolate the \n newlines, but not placeholders and especially not variables in the data lines, which can lead to a confusing combination of interpolated and non-interpolated strings. This can make formats very hard to read if we are not very careful.

Formats and Filehandles

Formats are intimately connected with filehandles, and not just because they often look like them. Formats work by being directly associated with filehandles, so that when we come to use them all we have to do is write to the filehandle and have the associated format automatically triggered.

It might seem strange that we associate a format with a filehandle and then write to the filehandle, rather than specifying which format we want to use when we do the writing, but there is a certain logic behind this mechanism. There are in fact two formats that may be associated with a filehandle; the main one is the one that is used when we write, but we can also have a top-of-page format that is used whenever Perl runs out of room on the current page and is forced to start a new one. Since this is associated with the filehandle, Perl can use it automatically when we use write rather than needing to be told.

701

Defining the Top-of-Page Format

Perl allows two formats to be associated with a filehandle. The main format is used whenever we issue a `write` statement. The top-of-page format, if defined, is issued at the start of the first page and at the top of each new page. This is determined by the special variable `$=` (length of page) and `$-` (the number of lines left). Each time we use `write` the value of `$-` increases. When there is no longer sufficient room to fit the results of the next `write`, a new page is started, a new top-of-page format is written and only then is the result of the last `write` issued.

The main format is automatically associated with the filehandle of the same name, so that the format `MYFORMAT` is automatically used when we use `write` on the filehandle `MYFORMAT`. Giving it the name of the filehandle with the text `_TOP` appended to it can similarly associate the top-of-page format. For instance, to assign a main and top-of-page format to the filehandle `MYFORMAT` we would use something like this:

```
format MYFORMAT =
...main format definition...
.

# define a format that gives the current page number
format MYFORMAT_TOP =
This is page @<<<
$=
-----------------------
.
```

Assigning Formats to Standard Output

Since standard output is the filehandle most usually associated with formats, we can omit the format name when defining formats. Here is a pair of formats defined explicitly for standard output:

```
format STDOUT=
The magic word is "@<<<<<<<<";
$word
.

format STDOUT_TOP=
Page @>
$#
-----------
.
```

We can however omit `STDOUT` for the main format and simply write:

```
format =
The magic word is "@<<<<<<<<";
$word
.
```

This works because standard output is the default output filehandle. If we change the filehandle with `select` then `format` creates a format with the same name as that filehandle instead. The `write` function also allows us to omit the filehandle; to write out the formats assigned to standard output (or whatever filehandle is currently selected) we can simply put:

```
write;
```

Determining and Assigning Formats to Other Filehandles

We are not constrained to defining formats with the same name as a filehandle in order to associate them. We can also find their names and assign new ones using the special variables $~ and $^.

The special variable $~ ($FORMAT_NAME with use English) defines the name of the main format associated with the currently selected filehandle (which will be standard output unless we have issued a select statement). For example, to find out the name of the format associated with standard output we would write:

```
$format = $~;
```

Likewise, to set the current format we can assign to $~:

```
# set standard output format to 'MYFORMAT';
$~ = 'MYFORMAT';

use English;
$FORMAT_NAME = 'MYFORMAT';    # more legibly
```

Note that the variable is set to the name of the format as a string, not to the format itself, hence the quotes.

The special variable $^ ($FORMAT_TOP_NAME with use English) performs the identical role for the top-of-page format:

```
# save name of current top-of-page format
$topform = $^;

# assign new top-of-page format
$^ = 'MYFORMAT_TOP';

# write out main format associated with standard out, using top-of-page format if
necessary
write;

# restore original top-of-page format
$^ = $topform;
```

Setting formats on other filehandles using the variables $~ and $^ requires special maneuvering with select. select makes a different filehandle the default filehandle, and as a by-product causes all the special variables such as $~ to refer to it. The original filehandle is returned, so we can use that to restore the default filehandle once we have finished:

```
# set formats on a different filehandle
$oldfh = select MYHANDLE;
$~ = 'MYFORMAT';
$^ = 'MYFORMAT_TOP';
select $oldfh;
```

A better way to handle this without resorting to `select` is to use the `IO::Handle` module, or `IO::File` if we want to open and close files too. This provides an altogether simpler object-oriented way of setting reports:

```
$fh = new IO::File (">$outputfile");

...

$fh->format_name ('MYFORMAT');
$fh->format_top_name ('MYFORMAT_TOP');

...

write $fh;    # or $fh->format_write ();
```

Format Structure

Having seen how to assign and use formats it's now time to take a look at actually defining them. As we have already explained in brief, formats consist of a collection of picture and data lines, interspersed with optional comments, combined into a `here`-style document that is ended with a single full stop.

Of the three, comments are by far the simplest to explain, but have no effect on the results of the format. They resemble conventional Perl comments and simply start with a # symbol, as this example demonstrates:

```
format FORMNAME =
# this is a comment. The next line is a picture line
This is a pattern line with one @<<<<<<<<<<.
# this is another comment.
# the next line is a data line
"placeholder"
# and don't forget to end the format with a '.':
.
```

Picture and data lines take a little more explaining. Since they are the main point of using formats at all, we will start with picture lines.

Picture Lines and Placeholders

Picture lines consist of literal text intermingled with placeholders, which the `write` function fills in with data at the point of output. If a picture line does not contain any placeholders at all it is treated as literal text, and can simply printed out. Since it does not require any data to fill it out it is not followed by a data line. This means that several picture lines can appear one after the other, as this static top-of-page format illustrates:

```
STATIC_TOP =
This header was generated courtesy of Perl formatting
See Chapter 18 of Professional Perl for details
-----------------------------------------
.
```

Placeholders are defined by either an @ or a ^, followed by a number of <, |, >, or # characters that define the width of the placeholder. Picture lines that contain placeholders must be followed by a data line (possibly with comments in between) that defines the data to be placed into the placeholder when the format is written.

Formats do not support the concept of a variable-width placeholder. The resulting text will always reserve the defined number of characters for the substituted value irrespective of the actual length of the value, even if it is undefined. It is this feature that makes formats so useful for defining structured text output – we can rely on the resulting text exactly conforming to the layout defined by the picture lines. For example, to define a ten-character field that is left justified we would use:

```
This is a ten character placeholder: @<<<<<<<<<
$value_of_placeholder
```

Note that the @ itself counts as one of the characters, so there are nine < characters in the example, not ten. To specify multiple placeholders we just use multiple instances of @, and supply enough values in the data line to fill them. This example has a left, center, and right justified placeholder:

```
This picture line has three placeholders: @<<<@|||@>>>
$first, $second, $third
```

The second example defines three four character wide placeholders. The <, |, and > characters define the justification for fields more than one character wide; we can define different justifications using different characters as we will see in a moment.

Programmers new to formats are sometimes confused by the presence of @ symbols. In this case @ has nothing to do with interpolation, it indicates a placeholder. Because of this, we also cannot define a literal @ symbol by escaping it with a backslash, that is an interpolation feature. In fact the only way to get an actual @ (or indeed ^) into the resulting string is to substitute it from the data line:

```
# this '@' is a placeholder:
This is a literal '@'
# but we can get a literal '@' by substituting one in on the data line:
'@'
```

Simple placeholders are defined with the @ symbol. The caret ^ or 'continuation' placeholder however has special properties that allow it to be used to spread values across multiple output lines. When Perl sees a ^ placeholder it fills out the placeholder with as much text as it reasonably can and then truncates the text it used from the start of the string. It follows from this that the original variable is altered and that to use a caret placeholder we cannot supply literal text. Further uses of the same variable can then fill in further caret placeholders. For example, this format reformats text into thirty-eight columns with a > prefix on each line:

```
format QUOTE_MESSAGE =
>  ^<<<<<<<<<<<<<<<<<<<<<<<<<<<<<<<<<<<<
$message
^<<<<<<<<<<<<<<<<<<<<<<<<<<<<<<<<<<<<<
$message
^<<<<<<<<<<<<<<<<<<<<<<<<<<<<<<<<<<<<<
$message
^<<<<<<<<<<<<<<<<<<<<<<<<<<<<<<<<<<<<<
$message
.
```

This creates a format that processes the text in the variable $message into four lines of forty characters, fitting as many words as possible into each line. When write comes to process this format it uses the special variable $: to determine how and where to truncate the line. By default it is set to ' \n-' to break on spaces, newlines or hyphens, which works fine for most plain text.

There are a number of problems with this format – it only handles four lines, and it always fills them out even if the message is shorter than four lines after reformatting. We will see how to suppress redundant lines and automatically repeat picture lines to generate extra ones with the special ~ and ~~ strings shortly.

Justification

It frequently occurs that the width of a field exceeds that of the data to be placed in it. In these cases, we need to decide how the format will deal with the excess, since a fixed width field cannot shrink (or grow) to fit the size of the data. A structured layout is the entire point of formats. If the data we want to fill the placeholder is only one character wide, we need no other syntax. As an extreme case, to insert six single character items into a format we can use:

```
The code is '@@@@@@'
# use first six elements of digits, assumed to be from 0 to 9.
@digits
```

For longer fields we need to choose how text will be aligned in the field through one of four justification methods, depending on which character we use to define the width of the placeholder:

Placeholder	Alignment	Example
<	Left justified.	@<<<<
>	Right justified.	@>>>>
|	Center justified.	@||||
#	Right justified numeric.	@####

The <, |, and > justification styles are mostly self-explanatory; they align values shorter than the placeholder width to the left, center, or right of the placeholder. They pad the rest of the field with spaces (note that padding with other characters is not supported; if we want to do that we will have to generate the relevant value by hand before it is substituted). If the value is the right length in any case, then no justification occurs. If it is longer, then it is truncated on the right irrespective of the justification direction.

The numeric # justification style is more interesting. With only # characters present it will insert an integer based on the supplied value – for an integer number it substitutes in its actual value, but for a string or the undefined value it substitutes in 0, and for a floating point number it substitutes in the integer part. To produce a percentage placeholder for example we can use:

```
Percentage: @##%
$value * 100
```

If however we use a decimal point character within the placeholder then the placeholder becomes a decimal placeholder, with floating-point values point-justified to align themselves around the position of the point:

```
Result (2 significant places): @####.##
$result
```

This provides a very simple and powerful way to align columns of figures, automatically truncating them to the desired level of accuracy at the same time.

If the supplied result is not a floating-point number then the fractional places are filled in with 0, and for strings and undefined values the ones column is also filled in with 0.

The actual character used by the decimal placeholder to represent the decimal point is defined by the locale, specifically the LC_NUMERIC value of the locale. In Germany for instance, the conventional symbol to separate the integer and fractional parts is a comma, not a point. Formats are in fact the only part of Perl that directly accesses the locale in this way, possibly because of their long history; all other parts of the language adhere to the use locale directive. Although deprecated in modern Perl, we can also use the special variable $# to set the point character.

The final placeholder format is the * placeholder. This creates a raw output placeholder, producing a complete multiple line value in one go and consequently can only be placed after an @ symbol; it makes no sense in the context of a continuation placeholder since there will never be a remainder for a continuation to make use of. For example:

```
> @* <
$multiline_message
```

In this format definition the value of $multiline_message is output in its entirety when the format is written. The first line is prefixed with a > and the last is suffixed with <. No other formatting of any kind is done. Since this placeholder has variable width (and indeed, variable height) it is not often used since it is effectively just a poor version of print that happens to handle line and page numbering correctly.

Data Lines

Whenever a picture line contains one or more placeholders it must be immediately followed by a data line consisting of one or more expressions that supply the information to fill them. Expressions can be literal numeric, string values, variables, or compound expressions:

```
format NUMBER =
Question: What do you get if you multiply @ by @?

6, 9
Answer: @#
6*9
.
```

Multiple values can be given either as an array or a comma separated list:

```
The date is: @###/@#/@#
$year, $month, $day
```

If insufficient values are given to fill all the placeholders in the picture line then the remaining placeholders are undefined and padded out with spaces. Conversely if too many values are supplied then the excess ones are discarded. This behavior changes if the picture line contains ~~ however, as shown below.

If we generate a format using conventional quoted strings rather than the here document syntax we must take special care not to interpolate the data lines. This is made more awkward because in order for the format to compile we need to use \n to create newlines at the end of each line of the format, including the data lines, and these do need to be interpolated. Separating the format out onto separate lines is probably the best approach, though as this example shows even then it can be a little hard to follow:

```
# define page width and output filehandle
$page_width = 80;
$output = "STDOUT_TOP";

# construct a format statement from concatenated strings
$format_st = "format $output = ";
'Page @<<<'. "\n".
'$='. "\n".
('-'x$page_width). "\n".
".\n";   # don't forget the trailing '.'

# define the format - note we do not interploate, to preserve '$='
eval $format_st;
```

Note that continuation placeholders (which are defined by a leading caret) need to be able to modify the original string supplied in order to truncate the start. For this reason an assignable value such as a scalar variable, array element or hash value must be used with these fields.

Suppressing Redundant Lines

format and write support two special picture strings that alter the behavior of the placeholders in the same picture line, both of which are applied if the placeholders are all continuation (caret) placeholders.

The first is a single tilde or ~ character. When this occurs anywhere in a picture line containing caret placeholders the line is suppressed if there is no value to plug into the placeholder. For example, we can modify the quoting format we gave earlier to suppress the extra lines if the message is too short to fill them:

```
format QUOTE_MESSAGE =
> ^<<<<<<<<<<<<<<<<<<<<<<<<<<<<<<<<<
$message
^<<<<<<<<<<<<<<<<<<<<<<<<<<<<<<<<<<~
$message
^<<<<<<<<<<<<<<<<<<<<<<<<<<<<<<<<<<~
$message
^<<<<<<<<<<<<<<<<<<<<<<<<<<<<<<...~
$message
.
```

In this example the bottom three picture lines have a ~ suffix, so they will only be used if $message contains sufficient text to fill them after it has been broken up according to the break characters in $:. When the format is written, the tildes are replaced with spaces. Since they are at the end of the line in this case, we will not see them, which is why conventionally they are placed here. If we have spaces elsewhere in the picture line we can replace one of them with the tilde and avoid the trailing space.

We modify the last picture line to indicate that the message may have been truncated because we know that it will only be used if the message fills out all the previous lines. In this case we have replaced the last three < characters with dots.

The ~ character can be thought of as a zero-or-one modifier for the picture line, in much the same way that ? works in regular expressions. The line will be used if Perl needs it, but it can also be ignored if necessary.

Autorepeating Pattern Lines

If two adjacent tildes appear in a pattern line then `write` will automatically repeat the line while there is still input. If ~ can be likened to the ? zero-or-one metacharacter of regular expressions, ~~ can be likened to *, zero-or-more. For instance, to format text into a paragraph of a set width but an unknown number of lines we can use a format like this:

```
format STDOUT =
^<<<<<<<<<<<<<<<<<<<<<<<<<<~~
$text
.
```

Calling `write` with this format will take the contents of $text and reformat it into a column thirty characters wide, repeating the pattern line as many times as necessary until the contents of $text are exhausted. Anything else in the pattern line is also repeated, so we can create a more flexible version of the quoting pattern we gave earlier that handles a message of any size:

```
format QUOTE =
>~~^<<<<<<<<<<<<<<<<<<<<<<<<<<<<<
$message
.
```

Like ~, the ~~ itself is converted into a space when it is output. It also does not matter where it appears, so in this case we have put it between the > quote mark and the text, to suppress the extra space on the end of the line it would otherwise create.

Note that ~~ only makes sense when used with a continuation placeholder, since it relies on the continuation to truncate the text. Indeed, if we try to use it with a normal @ placeholder Perl will return a syntax error since this would effectively be an infinite loop that repeats the first line. Since `write` cannot generate infinite quantities of text, Perl prevents us from trying.

Page Control

Perl's reporting system uses several special variables to keep track of line and page numbering. We can use these variables in the output to produce things like line and page numbers. We can also set them to control how pages are produced. There are four variables of particular interest:

Variable	Corresponds to:
$=	The page length
$%	The page number
$-	The number of lines remaining
$^L	The formfeed string

$= (or $FORMAT_LINES_PER_PAGE with use English) holds the page length, and by default is set to 60 lines. To change the page length we can assign a new value to $=, for example:

```
$= = 80;    # set page length to 80 lines
```

Or more legibly:

```
use English;
$FORMAT_LINES_PER_PAGE = 80;
```

If we want to generate reports without pages we can set $= to a very large number. Alternatively we can redefine $^L to nothing and avoid (or subsequently redefine to nothing) the 'top-of-page' format.

$% (or $FORMAT_PAGE_NUMBER with use English) holds the number of the current page. It starts at 1 and is incremented by one every time a new page is started, which in turn happens whenever write runs out of room on the current page. We can change the page number explicitly by modifying $%, for example;

```
$% = 1;    # reset page count to 1
```

$- (or $FORMAT_LINES_LEFT with use English) holds the number of lines remaining on the current page. Whenever write generates output it decrements this value by the number of lines in the format. If there are insufficient lines left (the size of the output is greater than the number of lines left) then $- is set to zero, the value of $% is incremented by one and a new page is started, starting with the value of $^L and followed immediately by the top-of-page format, if one is defined. We can force a new page immediately on the next write by setting $- to zero:

```
$- = 0;    # force a new page on the next 'write'
```

Finally, $^L (or $FORMA_FORMFEED with use English) is output by write whenever a new page is started. Unlike the top-of-page format it is not issued before the first page, but it is issued before the top-of-page format for all subsequent pages. By default it is set to a formfeed character, \f, but can be set to nothing or a longer string if required. See 'Creating Footers' below for a creative use of $^L.

As an example of using the page control variables, here is a short program that paginates its input file, adding the name of the file and a page number to the top of each page. It also illustrates creating a format dynamically with eval so we can define not only the height of the resulting pages but their width as well.

```
#!/usr/bin/perl
# paginate.pl
use warnings;
use strict;

no strict 'refs';

use Getopt::Long;

# get parameters from the user
my $height = 60;    # length of page
my $width = 80;     # width of page
my $quote = "";     # optional quote prefix
```

```
GetOptions ('height|size|length:i', \$height,
    'width:i', \$width, 'quote:s', \$quote);

die "Must specify input file" unless @ARGV;

# get the input text into one line, for continuation
undef $/;
my $text = <>;

# set the page length
$= = $height;

# if we're quoting, take that into account
$width -= length($quote);

# define the main page format - a single autorepeating continuation field
my $main_format = "format STDOUT = \n".
                  '^'.$quote.('<' x ($width-1))."~~\n".
                  '$text'. "\n".
                  ".\n";
eval $main_format;

# define the top of page format
my $page_format = "format STDOUT_TOP = \n".
                  '@'.('<' x ($width/2-6)). ' page @<<<'. "\n".
                  '$ARGV,$%'. "\n".
                  '-'x$width. "\n".
                  ".\n";
eval $page_format;

# write out the result
write;
```

To use this program we can feed it an input file and one or more options to control the output, courtesy of the Getopt::Long module, for example:

> **perl paginate.pl input.pl -w 50 -h 80**

Creating Footers

Footers are not supported as a concept by the formatting system, there is no 'bottom-of-page' format. However, with a little effort we can improvise our own footers. The direct and obvious way is to keep an eye on $-, and issue the footer when we get close to the bottom of the page. For instance, if the footer is smaller in lines than the output of the main format we can use something like the following, assuming that we know what the size of output is and that it is consistent.

```
print "\nPage $%\n" if $- < $size_of_format;
```

This is all we need to do, since the next attempt to write will not have sufficient space to fit and will automatically trigger a new page. If we want to make sure that we start a new page on the next write we can set $- to '0' to force it:

```
print ("\nPage $% \n"), $- = 0 if $- < $size_of_format;
```

A more elegant and subtle way of creating a footer is to redefine $^L. This is a lot simpler to arrange, but suffers in terms of flexibility since the footer is fixed once it is defined, so page numbering is not possible unless we redefine the footer on each new page.

For example, if we want to put a two line footer on the bottom of sixty line pages, we can do so by putting the footer into $^L (suffixed with the original formfeed) and then reducing the page length by the size of the footer, in this case to fifty eight lines:

```
# define a footer.
$footer = ('-'x80) . "\nEnd of Page\n";
# redefine the format formfeed to be the footer plus a formfeed
$^L = $footer . "\f";

# reduce page length from default 60 to 58 lines
# if we wanted to be creative we could count the instances of '\n' instead.
$= -= 2;
```

Now every page will automatically get a footer without any tracking or examination of the line count. The only work we have to do now is to add the footer to the last page, since the formatting will not do that for us. That is easily achieved by outputting new line characters up to the page length and then printing the footer ourselves. The number of lines left to fill is already held by $-, so this turns out to be trivial:

```
print ("\n" * $-);   # fill out the rest of the page (to 58 lines)
print $footer;   # print the final footer
```

As we mentioned earlier, arranging for a changing footer such as a page number is slightly trickier, but it can be done by remembering and checking the value of $- after each write:

```
$lines = $-;
write;
redefine_footer() if $- > $lines;
```

This will work for a lot of cases, but will not always work if we are using ~~, since it may cause write to generate more lines than the page has left before we get a chance to check it. Like many things in Perl, which approach is preferable is often down to the particular task at hand.

Combining Reports and Regular Output

It is perfectly possible to print both formatted output, such as that generated by write, and unformatted output, such as that generated by print, on the same filehandle. We have two possible approaches; mixing write and print, or using the formline function to generate formatted text that can then be printed using print at a later date.

Mixing 'write' and 'print'

write and print can be freely mixed together, sending both formatted and unformatted output to the same filehandle. However, print knows nothing about the special formatting variables such as $=, $-, and $% that track pagination and trigger the top-of-page format. Consequently pages will be of uneven length unless we take care of tracking line counts ourselves.

For instance, if we print out a three-line record after each `write`, we can keep `write` up-to-date on what is happening by decrementing `$-`, the number of lines left:

```perl
write;
foreach (@extra_lines) {
    print $_, "\n";
    --$-;    # decrement $-.
}
```

Unfortunately this does not take into account that `$-` might become negative if there is not enough room left on the current page. Due to the complexities of managing mixture of `write` and `print` it is often simpler to either use `formline`, or create a special format that is simply designed to print out the information we were using `print` for. Here's an example that defines several different formats and switches between them to handle different contingencies in outputting records with varying content and structure:

```perl
#!/usr/bin/perl
# multiformat.pl
use warnings;
use strict;

#set the lines remaining on the default page size
$- = 60;
# define some simple records to demonstrate the technique
my @records=(
    {
        main => 'This is the first record, with three extra lines of data',
        extra => ['Extra 1','Extra 2','Extra 3'],
        comment => 'Each part of the record is printed out using a
        different format'
    }, {
        main => 'This is the second record, which has only one extra line',
        extra => ['An extra line']
    }, {
        main => 'The third record has no extra data at all',
        comment => 'So we switch to a different format and print a special
        message instead'
    },{
        main => 'This is the fourth record, with three more extra lines',
        extra => ['Extra 4','Extra 5','Extra 6']
    }
);

# define main format for main body of record
format MAIN =
@#: ^<<<<<<<<<<<<<<<<<<<<<<<<<<<<<<<<<<<<<<<<<
$_+1, $records[$_]{main}
    ^<<<<<<<<<<<<<<<<<<<<<<<<<<<<<<<<<<<<<<<<<~~
$records[$_]{main}
.


# define a format for displaying extra data
format EXTRA =
    [ @<<<<<<<<<<<<<<<<<<<<<<<<< ]
$_
.


# define a format for no extra data
format NO_EXTRA =
    < No extra data for this record >
.
```

```
# define a format for displaying extra data
format COMMENT =
        Comment: ^<<<<<<<<<<<<<<<<<<<<<<<<<<<<<<<<<<
$records[$_]{comment}
        ^<<<<<<<<<<<<<<<<<<<<<<<<<<<<<<<<~~
$records[$_]{comment}
.

# iterate through the list of hashes, using extra format when required
foreach (0..$#records) {
    # write out the main format
    $~ = 'MAIN';
    write;

    if (exists $records[$_]{extra}) {
        # change format
        $~ = 'EXTRA';
        # write out the extra lines
        foreach (@{$records[$_]{extra}}) {
            write;
        }
    } else {
        # change to the no data message format
        $~ = 'NO_EXTRA';
        write;
    }

    $~ = 'COMMENT', write if exists $records[$_]{comment};

}
```

A less flexible but simpler solution to the same problem might use the special @* placeholder to output the extra lines; see earlier for a description of what this placeholder does and its limitations.

Generating Report Text with 'formline'

The formline function is a lower-level interface to the same formatting system that write uses, and is in fact the internal function that write uses to perform its task. formline generates text from a single picture line and a list of values, the result of which is placed into the special variable $^A. For example, this is how we could create a formatted string containing the current time using formline:

```
($sec, $min, $hour) = localtime;
formline '@#/@#/@#', $hour, $min, $sec;
$time = $^A;
print "The time is: $hour:$min.$sec \n";
```

Of course in this case it is probably easier to use sprintf, but we can also use formline to create text from more complex patterns. For instance to format a line of text into an array of text lines we could use formline like this:

```
$text = get_text();   # get a chunk of text from somewhere

@lines;
while ($text) {
    formline '^<<<<<<<<<<<<<<<<<<<', $text;
    push @lines, $^A;
}
```

This code takes the contents of $text and turns it into an array of lines word-wrapped to fit inside a twenty-character column.

formline is only designed to handle single lines, so it ignores newlines in the supplied pattern and treats the whole of the picture text as one line for the purposes of processing. This means that we cannot feed formline a complete format definition and expect it to produce the correct result in $^A.

Strangely, there is no simple way to generate text from write, other than by redirecting filehandles, since write sends its results to a filehandle. However, we can produce a version of write that returns its result instead, in the same way that sprintf returns a string instead of printing it like printf.

```
sub swrite ($@) {
    $picture = shift;
    formline ($picture, @_);
    return $^A;
}
```

This function is a friendly version of formline, but it is not a direct replacement for write, since it only operates on a single picture line and expects a conventional list of values as an argument. However, for generating text for use in print and other code, it is a lot more convenient than either write or formline.

Summary

This chapter dealt with text-processing in some depth. To begin with, we looked at text-processing modules, including Text::Teb and Text::Abbrev. Following this we covered parsing, with particular reference to the following topics:

❑   Parsing space-separated text.
❑   Parsing arbitrarily delimited text.
❑   Batch parsing multiple lines.
❑   Parsing a single line.

A section followed on customized wrapping discussed, among other things, the following topics:

❑   Formatting width.
❑   Long words.
❑   Break text.
❑   Debugging.

Then we looked at tokenizing text, and the Soundex algorithm and module. After this we covered pod, with emphasis on the following topics:

❑   pod paragraphs.
❑   pod tools and utilities.
❑   Programming pod.

The final section in this chapter dealt with reports. We looked at the format datatype, formats and filehandles, format structure (including justification), and page control. To top it all off we briefly talked about combining reports and regular output, and how to generate report text with formline.

19

Object-oriented Perl

Objects are, in a nutshell, a way to hide complexity behind an opaque value which holds not only data, but all the code necessary to access, manipulate, and store it. All objects belong to an object class, and the class defines what kind of object they are. The code that implements the object's features also belongs to the class, and the objects, sometimes called object instances, are simply values that belong to a given class. They 'know' what kind of object they are, and therefore which class the subroutines that can be used through them come from. In Perl, an object class is just a package, and an object instance is just a reference that knows its class and points to the data that defines the state of that particular instance.

Perl was not originally an object-oriented language; only from version 5 did it acquire the necessary features (symbolic references and packages) to implement objects. As a result, Perl's object-oriented features are relatively basic, and not compulsory. Perl takes a belt-and-braces approach to object-oriented programming, espousing no particular object-oriented doctrine (of which there are many), but permitting a broad range of different object-oriented styles.

Many object-oriented languages take a much stricter line. Being strict is the entire point for some languages. Java, for instance, requires that everything be an object, even the main application. Other languages have very precise views about what kind of object model they support, how multiple inheritance works, how public and private variables and methods are defined, how objects are created, initialized, and destroyed, and so on. Perl does not have any particular perspective, which make it both extremely flexible and highly disconcerting to programmers used to a different object-oriented style.

Because Perl does not dictate how object-oriented programming should be done, it can leave programmers who expect a more rigorous framework confused and aimless, which is one reason why Perl sometimes has a bad reputation for object-oriented programming. However, during the course of this chapter we hope to show that by learning the basics of how Perl implements objects, a programmer can wield Perl in a highly effective way to implement object-oriented programs.

In this chapter we introduce object-oriented programming from the Perl perspective. We then go on to using objects (which need not imply an object-oriented program), and then tackle the meat of the chapter – writing object classes, including constructors and destructors, properties and attributes, and single and multiple inheritance. We also take a look at a uniquely Perlish use of objects – mimicking a standard data type by tieing it to an object-oriented class. The DBM modules are a well-known example, but there are many other interesting uses for tied objects too.

Introducing Objects

Object-oriented programming is an entirely different method of implementing libraries and applications from the traditional or functional approach. Object orientation allows us to clearly define the interface to our library, and thereby allows us to abstract the actual implementation so it can be easily reused and adapted through inheritance. Although we can do the same thing in functional implementations, it is a lot harder and more prone to error. Object orientation helps us to rethink the way we design programs so that we gain these advantages more easily. In order to appreciate how Perl implements and provides for object-oriented programming, therefore, a basic grasp of object-oriented concepts is necessary.

Object Concepts

Since this is not a treatise on object orientation, we will not dwell on the fundamentals of object orientation in detail. Indeed, one of the advantages of Perl's approach is that we do not need to pay nearly so much attention to them as we often do in other languages; Perl's hands-on approach means that we can strip away a lot of the jargon that object orientation often brings with it. However, several concepts are key to any kind of object-oriented programming, so here is a short discussion of the most important ones, along with Perl's perspective on them:

Classes

An object class provides the implementation of an object. It consists of **class methods**, which are routines that perform functions for the class as a whole. It also consists of **object methods**, routines that perform functions for individual objects (or object instances). It may also contain package variables, or in object-oriented terminology, class attributes. The details of the class are hidden behind the interface provided by these methods, in the same way that a regular functional module hides its details.

All object classes contain at least one important class method; a constructor that generates new object instances. In addition, they may have a destructor, for tidying up after objects that are destroyed.

Perl implements object classes with packages. In fact, a package is an object class by another name. This basic equivalence is the basis for much of Perl's simple and obvious approach to objects in general. A class method is just a subroutine that takes a package name as its first argument, and an object method is a subroutine that takes an object name as its first argument. Perl automatically handles the passing of this first argument when we use the arrow (->) operator.

Objects

Objects are individual instances of an object class, consisting of an opaque value representing the state of the object but abstracting the details. Because the object implicitly knows what class it belongs to, we can call methods defined in the object class through the object itself, in order to affect the object's state. Objects may contain, within themselves, different individual values called **object attributes** (or occasionally instance attributes).

Perl implements objects through references; the object's state is held by whatever it is that the reference points to, which is up to the object's class. The reference is told what class it belongs to with the `bless` function, which marks the references as belonging to a particular class. Since a class is a package, method calls on the object (using `->`) are translated by Perl into subroutine calls in the package. Perl passes the object as the first argument so the subroutine knows which object to operate on.

An object may have properties and attributes representing its state. The storage of these is up to the actual data type used to store this information; typically it is a hash variable and the attributes are simply keys in the hash. Of course, the point of object orientation is that the user of an object does not need to know anything about this.

Inheritance, Multiple Inheritance, and Abstraction

One important concept of object-oriented programming, and the place where objects score significant gains over functional programming, is **inheritance**. An object's classes may inherit methods and class attributes from parent classes, in order to provide some or all of their functionality; a technique also known as **subclassing**. This allows an object class to implement only those features that differentiate it from a more general parent, without having to worry about implementing the classes contained in its parent. Inheritance encourages code reuse, allowing us to use tried and tested objects to implement our core features rather than reinventing the wheel for each new task. This is an important goal of any programming environment, and one of the principal motivations behind using object-oriented programming.

Multiple inheritance occurs when a subclass inherits from more than one parent class. This is a contentious issue, since it can lead to different results depending on how parent classes are handled when two classes both support a method that a subclass needs. Accordingly, not all object oriented languages allow or support it. **Dynamic inheritance** occurs when an object class is able to change the parent or parents from which it inherits. It also occurs when a new subclass is created on the fly during the course of execution. Again, not all languages allow or support this.

An important element of inheritance is that the subclass does not need to know how the parent class implements its features, only how to use them to implant its own variation – the interface. This gives us abstraction, an important aspect of object-oriented programming that allows for easy reuse of code; the parent class should be able to change its implementation without subclasses noticing.

Inheritance in most object-oriented languages happens through some sort of declaration in the class. In Perl, inheritance is supported through a special array that defines 'is a' relationships between object classes. Logically enough, it is called `@ISA`, and it defines what kind of parent class a given subclass is. If anything is in the `@ISA` array of a package, then the object class defined by that package 'is a' derived class of it.

Perl allows for multiple inheritance by allowing an object class to include more than one parent class name in its `@ISA` array. When a method is not found in the package of an object, its parents are scanned in order of their place in the array until the method is located. If a parent also has an `@ISA` array, it is searched too. Multiple inheritance is not always a good thing, and Perl's approach to it has problems, but it makes up for it by being blindingly simple to understand.

Inheritance in Perl can also be dynamic, since `@ISA` has all the properties of a regular Perl array variable, so it can be modified during the course of a program's execution to add new parent classes, remove existing ones, entirely replace the parent class(es), or reorder them.

Public and Private Methods and Data

Both object classes and object instances may have **public** data, **private** data, and **methods**. Public data and methods make up the defined interface for the object class and the objects it implements that external code may use. Private data and methods are intended for use only by the object class and its objects themselves (such as supporting methods and private state information). Making parts of an object class private is also known as **encapsulation**, though that is not an exclusively object-oriented concept. Good object-oriented design suggests that all data should be encapsulated (accessed by methods, as opposed to being accessed directly). In other words, there should be no such thing as public data in a class or object.

Perl does not have any formal definition of public and private data; it operates an open policy whereby all data and methods are visible to the using package. There is no 'private' declaration, though my can by used to declare file-scoped variables, which are effectively private. The using package is expected to abide by the intended and documented interface and not abuse the fact that it can circumvent it if it chooses.

If we really want to we can enforce various types of privacy (for example with a closure), but only by implementing it by hand in the object class. Strangely, by not having an explicit policy on privacy, Perl is a lot simpler than many object-oriented languages that do, because dubious concepts like friend classes, and selective privacy simply do not exist.

Polymorphism

Another concept that is often associated with objects is **polymorphism**. This is the ability of many different object classes to respond to the same request, but in different ways. In essence, this means that we can call an object method on an object whose class we do not know precisely, and get some form of valid response. The class determines the actual response of the object, but we do not need to know which class the object is contained in, in order to call the method. Inheritance provides a very easy way to create polymorphic classes. By inheriting and overriding methods from a single parent class, many subclasses can behave the same way to the user. Because they inherit a common set of methods, we can know with surety that the parent interface will work for all its subclasses.

In Perl, polymorphism is simply a case of defining two or more methods (subroutines), in different classes (packages), with the same name and handling the same arguments. A method may then be called on an object within any of the classes without knowing in which class the object actually is.

In some cases we might want to use a method which may or may not exist; either we can attempt the call with -> inside an eval, or use the special isa and can methods supported by all objects in order to determine what an object is and isn't capable of. These methods are provided for by the UNIVERSAL object, from which all objects implicitly inherit.

Overloading

Overloading is the ability of an object class to substitute for existing functionality supplied by a parent class or the language itself. There are two types of overloading, **method overloading** and **operator overloading**.

Method overloading is simple in concept. It occurs whenever a subclass implements a method with the same name as a parent's method. An attempt to call that method on the subclass will be satisfied by the subclass, and the parent class will never see it. Its method is said to have been overloaded. In the context of multiple inheritance some languages also support parameter overloading, where the correct method can be selected by examining the arguments passed to the method call, and comparing it to the arguments accepted by the corresponding method in each parent class.

Operator overloading is more interesting. It occurs when an object class implements special methods for the handling of operators defined by the core language. When the language sees that an operator, for which an object class supplies a method, is used adjacent to an object, it replaces the regular use of the operator with the version supplied by the class. For instance, this allows us to 'add' objects together using +, even though objects cannot be added. The object class supplies a meaning for the operator, and returns a new object reflecting the operation.

Perl supports both kinds of overloading. Method overloading is simply a case of defining a subroutine with the same name as the subroutine to be overloaded in the parent. The subclass can still access the parent's method if it wishes, by prefixing the package name with the special SUPER:: prefix. There is no such thing as parameter overloading in Perl, since its parameter passing mechanism (the @_ array) does not lend itself to that kind of examination. However, a method can select a parent class at run-time by analyzing the arguments passed to it.

Operator overloading is also supported through the overload pragmatic module. With this module we can implement an object replacement for any of Perl's built-in operators, including all the arithmetic, logical, assignment, and dereferencing operators.

Adaptabilty (also called Casting or Conversion)

Objects may sometimes be reclassified and assigned to a different class. For instance, a subclass will often use a parent class to create an object, then adjust its properties for its own needs before reclassifying the object as an instance of itself rather than its parent. Objects can also be reclassified en route through a section of code; for example, an object representing an error may be reclassified into a particular kind of error, or reclassified into a new class representing an error that has already been handled.

In Perl, objects can be switched into a new class at any time, even into a class that does not exist. We can bless a reference into any class simply by naming the class. If we also create and fill an @ISA array inside this class, then it can inherit from a parent class too, enabling us to create a functional subclass on the fly.

Programming with Objects

Although Perl supports objects, it does not require that we use them exclusively; it is possible and feasible to use objects from otherwise entirely functional applications. Using objects is therefore not inextricably bound up with writing them. So, before delving into implementation, we will take a brief look at using objects from the outsider's perspective, with a few observations on what Perl does behind the scenes.

Creating Objects

All object classes contain at least one method known in general object-oriented programming circles as a **constructor** – a class method that creates brand new object instances based on the arguments passed to it. In many object-oriented languages (C++ and Java being prime examples) object creation is performed by a keyword called new. Perl allows us to give a constructor any name, since it is just a subroutine. For example:

```
$object = My::Object::Class->new(@args);
```

In deference to other languages that provide a new keyword, Perl also allows us to invert this call and place the new before the package name:

```
$object = new My::Object::Class(@args);
```

This statement is functionally identical to the one above, but bears a stronger resemblance to traditional constructors in other languages. However, since Perl does not give new any special meaning, a constructor method may have any name, and take any arguments to initialize itself. We can therefore give our constructor a more meaningful name. We can have multiple constructors too if we like; it is all the same to Perl:

```
$object = old My::Object::Class(@args);
$object = create_from_file My::Object::Class($filename);
$object = empty My::Object::Class ();
```

Using Objects

The principal mechanism for accessing and manipulating objects is the -> operator. In a non-object-oriented context this is the dereferencing operator, and we use it on an unblessed reference to access the data it points to. For example, to access a hash by reference:

```
$value = $hashref->{'key'};
```

However, in object-oriented use, -> becomes a class access operator, providing the means to call class and object methods (depending on whether the left-hand side is a class name or an object) and access properties on those objects:

```
$object_result = $object->method(@args);

$class_result = Class::Name->classmethod(@args);

$value = $object->{'property_name'};
```

Since an object is at heart a reference, these two uses are not as far apart as they might at first seem; the difference is that a blessed reference allows us to call methods because the reference is associated with a package. A regular reference is not associated with anything, and so cannot have anything called through it.

Accessing Properties

Since an object is just a blessed reference, we can access the underlying properties of the object by dereferencing it just like any other reference. For instance, if the object is implemented in terms of a hash we can access its properties like this:

```
$value = $object->{'property_name'};
```

Similarly, we can set a property or add a new one with:

```
$object->{'property_name'} = $value;
```

We can also undef, delete, push, pop, shift, unshift, and generally manipulate the object's properties using conventional list and hash functions. If the underlying data type is different, say an array, or even a scalar, we can still manipulate it, using whatever processes are legal for that kind of value.

However, this is really nothing to do with object orientation at all, but rather the normal non-object-oriented dereferencing operator. Perl uses it for object orientation so that we can think of dereferencing an object in terms of accessing an object's public data. In other words, it is a syntactic trick to help keep us thinking in object-oriented terms, even though we are not actually performing an object-oriented operation at heart.

One very major disadvantage of accessing an object's data like this, is that we break the interface defined by the object class. The class has no ability to restrain or control how we access the object's data if we access it directly; neither can it spot attempts to access invalid properties. Indeed, even the fact that we know what the underlying data type is breaks the rules of good object-oriented programming. The object should be able to use a hash, array, scalar, or even a typeglob, but we should not have to know. Therefore it is better for us to use methods defined by the class to access and store properties on its objects whenever possible. In an ideal world the class should be even able to change the underlying data representation and still work perfectly in existing code – the object should essentially be an abstract data type.

Calling Class Methods

A class method is a subroutine defined in the class, which operates on a class as a whole, rather than a specific object of that class. To call a class method, we use the -> operator on the package name of the class, which we give as a bare, unquoted term, just as we do for use:

```
$result = My::Object::Class->classmethod(@args);
```

The new class method typically implemented by most classes is one such case of a class method, and the inverted syntax we used before will also work with any other class method, for example:

```
$result = classmethod My::Object::Class(@args);
```

In general this syntax should only be used for constructors, where its ordering makes logical sense.

The subroutine that implements the class method is called with the arguments supplied by us, plus the package name, which is passed first. In other words, this class method call and the following subroutine call are handled similarly for classes that do not inherit:

```
# method call - correct object-oriented syntax
My::Object::Class->method(@args);

# subroutine call - does not handle inheritance
My::Object::Class::method ('My::Object::Class', @args);
```

For classes that do inherit, it uses the @ISA array to search for a matching method if the class in which the method is looked for does not implement it. This is because the -> operator has an additional important property that differentiates method calls from subroutine calls. A subroutine call has no such magic associated with it.

It might seem redundant that we pass the package name to a class method, since the method surely already knows what package it is in, and can find out by using __PACKAGE__ even if it did not know. Again, however, this is only true for classes that do not inherit. If a parent method is called because a subclass did not implement a class method (a result of using the -> operator), then the package name passed will not be that of the parent but that of the subclass.

Calling Object Methods

An object method is a subroutine defined in the class that operates on a particular object instance. To call an object method we use the -> operator on an object of a class that supports that method:

```
$result = $object->method(@args);
```

The subroutine that implements the object method is called with the argument we supply, preceded by the object itself (a blessed reference, and therefore a scalar). Therefore the following calls are again nearly the same:

```
# method call - correct object-oriented syntax
$object->method(@args);

# subroutine call - does not handle inheritance
My::Object::Class::method($object, @args);
```

Just as with class methods, if the package into which the object is blessed does not provide the named method, the -> operator causes Perl to search for it in any and all parent classes, as defined by the @ISA array; the method call will find a method in a parent class (provided it is present), but the subroutine call will not.

Nesting Method Calls

If the return value from a method (class or object) is another object, we can call a second method on it directly, without explicitly using a temporary variable to store the returned object. Such methods usually occur where there is a 'has-a' relationship between two object classes, and objects of the holding class contain instances of the held class as attributes. The result of this is that we can chain several method calls together:

```
print "The top card is ", $deck->card(0)->fullname;
```

This particular chain of method calls is from the Game::Deck example which we provide later in the chapter. It prints out the name of the playing card on the top of the deck of playing cards represented by the $deck object. Game::Deck supplies the card method, which returns a playing card object. In turn, the playing card object (Game::Card, not that we need to know the class) provides the fullname method. We will return to this subject again when we cover 'Has-a' versus 'Is-a' relationships.

Determining what an Object Is

An object is a blessed reference. Calling the ref function on an object returns not the actual data type of the object but the class into which it was blessed:

```
$class = ref $object;
```

If we really need to know the underlying data type (which in a well designed object-oriented application should be never, but it can be handy for debugging) we can use the reftype subroutine supplied by the attributes module, see 'References' in Chapter 5 for details.

However, knowing what class an object belongs to does not always tell us what we want to know; for instance, we cannot easily use it to determine if an object belongs to a subclass of a given parent class, or even find out if it supports a particular method or not.

Determining Inherited Characteristics

The ref function will tell us the class of an object, but it cannot tell us anything more than this. Because determining the nature and abilities of an object is a common requirement, Perl provides the UNIVERSAL object class, which all objects automatically inherit from. UNIVERSAL is a small class, and contains only three methods for identifying the class, capabilities, and version of an object or object class. Because Perl likes to keep things simple, this class is actually implemented as a module in the standard library, and is not a built-in part of the language.

Determining an Object's Ancestry

The isa method, provided by UNIVERSAL to all objects, allows us to determine whether an object belongs to a class or a subclass of that class, either directly or through a long chain of inheritance. For example:

```
if ($object->isa("My::Object::Class")) {
   $class = ref $object;
   if ($class eq "My::Object::Class") {
      print "Object is of class My::Object::Class \n";
   } else {
      print "Object is a subclass of My::Object::Class \n";
   }
}
```

We can also use isa on a class name or string variable containing a class name:

```
$is_child = My::Object::Subclass->isa("MyObjectClass");
$is_child = $packagename->isa($otherpackagename);
```

Before writing class names into our code, however, we should consider the issue of code maintenance. Explicitly hard-coding class names is an obstacle to portability, and can trip up otherwise functional code if used in an unexpected context. If the class name is derived programmatically, it is more acceptable.

Determining an Object's Capabilities

Knowing an object's class and being able to identify its parents does not tell us whether or not it can support a particular method. For polymorphic object classes, where multiple classes provide versions of the same method, it is often more useful to know what an object can do rather than what its ancestry is. The UNIVERSAL class supplies the can method for this purpose:

```
if ($object->can('method')) {
   return $object->method(@args);
}
```

If the method is not found in either the object's class or any of its parents can returns undef. Otherwise, it returns a code reference to the method that was found:

```
if ($methodref = $object->can('method')) {
    $object->$methodref(@args);
}
```

We can also use can on an object class to determine whether it or any of its ancestors provides a given method:

```
foreach (@methods) {
    $can{$_} = My::Object::Class->can('method');
}
```

Again, the package name may also be given in a string variable:

```
$can_do = $package->can($methodname);
```

Alternatively, we can simply try to call the method and see if it works or not, wrapping the call in an eval to prevent it from generating a fatal error:

```
$result = eval {$object->method(@args)};
if ($@) {
    # error - method did not exist
}
```

Determining an Object's Version

The final method provided by the UNIVERSAL object is VERSION, which looks for a package variable called $VERSION in the class on which it is called:

```
# version of a class
$version = $packagename->VERSION;

# version of an object's class
$version = $object->VERSION;

# test version
if ($packagename->VERSION < $required_version) {
    die "$packagename version less than $required_version";
}
```

In practice we usually don't need to call VERSION directly, because the use and require statements do it for us providing we supply a numeric value rather than an import list after a package name:

```
# use class only if it is at least version 1
require My::Object::Class 1.00;
```

Note that use differs from require in that, apart from using an implicit BEGIN block, it imports from the package as well. However, since an object-oriented class should rarely define anything for export, since this breaks the interface and causes problems for inheritance, there is usually no advantage to useing an object class over requireing it.)

However, we can in some cases use version to alter behavior depending on another module's version, using an added method in more recent versions and resorting to a different approach in older versions. For example, here is a hypothetical object having a value assigned to one of its attributes. The old class did not provide a method for this attribute, so we access the attribute directly from the underlying hash. From version 1 onward all attributes are accessed by method:

```
if ($object->VERSION < 1.00) {
    # old version - set attribute directly
    $object->{'attribute'} = $value;
} else {
    # new version - use the provided method instead
    $object->attribute($value);
}
```

Note that we could have done the same thing with can, but this is slower since it tests the entire object hierarchy of parents looking for a method; it's also less clear, since without additional comments it is not obvious why we would be checking for the availability of the method in the first place. In these cases checking the version is the better approach.

Writing Object Classes

Writing an object class is no more difficult than writing a package, it just has slightly different rules. Indeed, an object class is just a package by a different name. Like packages, object classes can spread across more than one file but more often than not are implemented in a single module with the same name (after translation into a pathname) as the package that implements them.

What makes object classes different from packages is that they tend to have specific features within them. The first and most obvious is that they have at least one constructor method. As well as this, all the subroutines take an object or a class name as a first parameter. The package may also optionally define a DESTROY block for destroying objects, analogous to an END block in ordinary packages.

A final difference, and arguably one of the most crucial, is that object classes can inherit methods from one or more parent classes. We are going to leave the bulk of this discussion to later in the chapter, but because inheritance and designing object classes for reuse are so fundamental to object-oriented programming, we will be introducing inheritance examples from time to time before we come to discuss it in full. Fortunately, inheritance in Perl is very easy to understand, at least in the simpler examples given here.

Constructors

The most important part of any object class is its constructor; a class method whose job it is to generate new instances of objects. Typically the main (or only) constructor of an object class is called new, so we can create new objects with any of the following statements:

Using traditional object-oriented syntax:

```
$object = new My::Object::Class;
$object = new My::Object::Class('initial', 'data', 'for', 'object');
```

Or, using class method call syntax:

```
$object = My::Object::Class->new();
$object = My::Object::Class->new('initial', 'data', 'for', 'object');
```

This new method is just a subroutine that accepts a class name as its first parameter (supplied by the ->
operator) and returns an object. At the heart of any constructor is the bless function. When given a
single argument of a reference, bless bestows a new name upon it to mark it as belonging to the
current package. Here is a fully functional (but limited, as we will see in a moment) constructor that
illustrates it in action:

```
#Class.pm
package My::Object::Class;
use strict;

sub new {
    $self = {};     # create a reference to a hash
    bless $self;    # mark reference as object of this class
    return $self;   # return it.
}
```

The problem with this simple constructor is that it does not handle inheritance. With a single argument,
bless puts the reference passed to it into the current package. However, this is a bad idea because the
constructor may have been called by a subclass, in which case the class to be blessed into is the subclass,
and not the class that the constructor is defined in. Consequently, the single argument form of bless is
rarely, if ever used, and we mention it only in passing. Correctly written object classes use the two
argument version of bless to bless the new object into the class passed as the first argument. This
enables inheritance to work correctly, as the object created is now the one asked for, which may be a
subclass inheriting our constructor:

```
sub new {
    $class = shift;
    $self = {};
    bless $self, $class;
    return $self;
}
```

Or, equivalently but much more tersely:

```
sub new {
    return bless {}, shift;
}
```

Typically we want to be able to initialize an object when we create it, which we can do by passing
arguments to the constructor. For example, here is a package that implements the bare essentials of a
playing card class. It takes two additional parameters, a name, and a suit:

```
# card1.pm
package Game::Card1;
use strict;

sub new {
    my ($class, $name, $suit) = @_;
    my $self = bless {}, $class;
```

```
    $self->{'name'} = $name;
    $self->{'suit'} = $suit;
    return $self;
}

1;
```

The underlying representation of the object is a hash, so we can store attributes as hash keys. We could also check that we actually get passed a name and suit, but in this case we are going to handle the possibility that a card has no suit (a joker, for example), or even no name (in which case it is, logically, a blank card). A user of this object could now access the object's properties (in an non-object-oriented way) through the hash reference:

```
#!/usr/bin/perl
# ace.pl
use warnings;
use strict;

use Game::Card1;

my $card = new Game::Card1('Ace', 'Spades');
print $card->{'name'};    # produces 'Ace';
$card->{'suit'} = 'Hearts';    # change card to the Ace of Hearts
```

Just because we can access an object's properties like this does not mean we should. If we change the underlying data type of the object (as we are about to do) this code will break. A better way is to use `accessor` and `mutator` methods, which we cover in the appropriately titled section 'Accessors and Mutators' shortly.

Choosing a Different Underlying Data Type

Objects are implemented in terms of references, therefore we can choose any kind of reference as the basis for our object. The usual choice is a hash, as shown in the previous example, since this provides a simple way to store arbitrary data by key; it also fits well with the 'properties' or 'attributes' of objects, which in general object-oriented parlance are named values that can be set and retrieved on objects.

Using an Array

However, we can also choose other types that might suit our design better. For instance, we can use an array, as this constructor does:

```
# Card.pm
package Game::Card2;
use strict;

use Exporter;

our @ISA = qw(Exporter);
our @EXPORT = qw(NAME SUIT);

use constant NAME => 0;
use constant SUIT => 1;

sub new {
    my ($class, $name, $suit) = @_;
    my $self = bless [], $class;
```

```
    $self->[NAME] = $name;
    $self->[SUIT] = $suit;
    return $self;
}

1;
```

This object is functionally identical to the hash-based one (although, since it is at this point only a constructor, not a terribly useful one), but has a different internal representation. In this simple example, we want to allow users to access properties directly, so we export the constants to them when they use our object with use Exporter. Now the code to use the object looks like this (note that by accessing the object properties directly we are forced to change the code that uses the object. This is why methods are better, as we mentioned earlier):

```
#!/usr/bin/perl
# arrayuse.pl
use warnings;
use strict;

use Game::Card2;    # imports 'NAME' and 'SUIT'

my $card = new Game::Card2('Ace', 'Spades');
print $card->[NAME];    # produces 'Ace'
$card->[SUIT] = 'Hearts';    # change card to the Ace of Hearts
print " of ", $card->[SUIT];    # produces ' of Hearts'
```

The advantage of the array-based object is that arrays are a lot faster to access than hashes are, so performance is improved. The disadvantage is that it is very hard to reliably derive a subclass from an array-based object class because we need to know what indices are taken, and which are safe to use. Though this can be done, it requires extra effort and outweighs the benefits of avoiding a hash. It also makes the implementation uglier, which is usually a sign that we are on the wrong track. For objects that we do not intend to use as parent classes, however, arrays can be an effective choice.

Using a Typeglob

Hashes and arrays are the most logical choice for object implementations because they allow the storage of multiple values within the object. However, we can use a scalar or typeglob reference if we wish. For instance, we can create an object based on a typeglob and use it to provide object-oriented methods for a filehandle. Indeed, this is exactly what the IO::Handle class (which is the basis of the object-oriented filehandle classes IO::File, IO::Dir, and IO::Socket) does.

Here is the actual constructor used by IO::Handle, with additional comments:

```
sub new {
    # determine the passed class, by class method, object method,
    # or preset it to 'IO::Handle' if nothing was passed (subroutine).
    $class = ref($_[0]) || $_[0] || "IO::Handle";
    # complain if additional arguments were passed
    @_ == 1 or croak "usage: new $class";
    # create an anonymous typeglob (from the 'Sybmol' module)
    $io = gensym;
    # bless it into the appropriate subclass of 'IO::Handle'
    bless $io, $class;
}
```

Just as we can dereference a blessed hash or array reference to access and set the underlying values contained within, Perl automatically dereferences the reference to a filehandle contained in a typeglob. So we can pass the objects returned from this handle to Perl's IO functions, and they will use them just as if they were regular filehandles. But because the filehandle is also an object, we can call methods on it as this example of using the IO::File subclass demonstrates:

```perl
#!/usr/bin/perl
# output1.pl
use warnings;
use strict;

use IO::File;

my $object_fh = new IO::File ('> /tmp/io_file_demo');
$object_fh->print ("An OO print statement\n");
print $object_fh "Or we can use the object as a filehandle";

$object_fh->autoflush(1);    # this is much nicer than 'selecting'
close $object_fh;
```

We have already seen the IO:: family of modules in use, most particularly in Chapter 12. Now we can see how and why these modules work as they do.

Using a Scalar

Limited though it might seem, we can also use a scalar to implement an object. For instance, here is a short but functional 'document' object constructor, which takes a filehandle as an optional argument:

```perl
# Document.pm
package Document;
use strict;

# scalar constructor
sub new {
  my $class = shift;

  my $self;
  if (my $fh = shift) {
     local $/ = undef;
     $$self = <$fh>;
  }

  return bless $self, $class;
}
```

We can now go on to implement methods that operate on text, but hide the details behind the object. We can for example create methods to search the document through other methods that hide the details of regular expressions behind a friendlier object-oriented interface.

Using a Subroutine

Finally, we can also use a subroutine as our object implementation, blessing a reference to the subroutine to create an object. In order to do this we have to generate and return an anonymous subroutine on-the-fly in our constructor. This might seem like a lot of work, but it provides us with a way to completely hide the internal details of an object from prying eyes; because all properties are accessed via the subroutine, it can permit or deny whatever kinds of access it likes. We will see an example of this kind of object later in the chapter under 'Keeping Data Private'.

Methods

Methods, as we have already observed, are just subroutines that are designed to be called with the `->` operator. There are two broad types:

❑ Class methods perform tasks related to the class as a whole, and are not tied to any specific object instance.

❑ Object methods perform a task for a particular object instance.

Although in concept these are fundamentally different ideas, Perl treats both types of method as just slightly different subroutines, which differ only in the way that they are called and in the way they process their arguments. With only minor adjustments to our code, we can also create methods that will operate in either capacity, and even as a subroutine too, if the design supports it.

Class Methods

A class method is a method that performs a function for the class as a whole. Constructors, which we have already seen examples of, are a common example, and frequently they are the only class methods an object class provides. Here is another, which sets a pair of global resources that apply to all objects of the class:

```
$MAX_INSTANCES = 100;

sub set_max {
    ($class, $max) = @_;
    $MAX_INSTANCES = $max;
}

sub get_max {
    return $MAX_INSTANCES;
}
```

We would call these class methods from our own code with:

```
My::Object::Class->set_max(1000);
print "Maximum instances: ", My::Object::Class->get_max();
```

Setting and returning class data like this is probably the second most common use for a class method after constructors. Only class-level operations can be performed by a class method, therefore all other functions will be performed by object methods.

A special case of a class method that can set class data is the `import` method, which we dwelt on in Chapter 17. We will take another look at import methods when we come to discuss class data in more detail later on in the chapter.

Object Methods

An object method does work for a particular object, and receives an object as its first argument. Traditionally we give this object a name like `$self` or `$this` within the method, to indicate that this is the object for which the method was called. Like many aspects of object-oriented programming in Perl (and Perl programming in general) it is just a convention, but a good one to follow. Other languages are stricter; we automatically get a variable called `self` or sometimes `this` and so don't have a choice about the name.

Here is a pair of object methods that provide a simple object-oriented way to get and set properties (also known as attributes, but either way they are values) on an object. In this case the object is implemented as a hash, so within the class this translates into setting and getting values from the hash:

```perl
# get a property - read only
sub get {
    ($self, $property) = @_;

    return $self->{$property} if exists $self->{$property};
    return undef;   # no such property!
}

# set a property - return the old value
sub set {
    ($self, $property, $value) = @_;
    $oldvalue = $self->property if exists $self->{$property};
    $self->{$property} = $value;
    return $oldvalue; #may be undef
}
```

In practice the users of our objects could simply dereference them and get to the hash values directly. However, we do not want to encourage this since it bypasses our interface. So instead we provide some methods to do it for them. These methods are still very crude though, since they do not check whether a property is actually valid. We will look at some better ways of handling properties later.

As a more practical example, here are a pair of search methods that belong to the Document object class we created a constructor for earlier, along with the constructor and the rest of the package, to make it a complete example. Note that the wordsearch method itself makes an object-oriented call to the search method to carry out the actual work:

```perl
# Document.pm
package Document;
use strict;

# scalar constructor
sub new {
    my $class = shift;

    my $self;
    if (my $fh = shift) {
        local $/ = undef;
        $$self = <$fh>;
    }

    return bless $self, $class;
}

# search a document object
sub search {
    my ($self, $pattern) = @_;

    my @matches = $$self =~ /$pattern/sg;
    return @matches;
}
```

```
# search and return words
sub wordsearch {
    my ($self, $wordbit) = @_;

    my $pattern = '\b\w*'.$wordbit.'\w*\b';
    return $self->search($pattern);
}

1;
```

We can use this object class to perform simple searches on documents read in by the constructor, in an object-oriented style:

```
#!/usr/bin/perl
# search.pl
use warnings;
use strict;

use IO::File;
use Document;

my $fh = new IO::File('file.txt');
my $document = new Document($fh);

# find words containing e or t
print join(' ', $document->wordsearch('[et]'));
```

If the file file.txt contains this text:

```
This is a file of text to
test the Document object
on.
```

The program produces:

file text to test the Document object

This is not a very well developed object class; it does not allow us to create an object from anything other than a filehandle, and it needs more methods to make it truly useful. However, it is the beginning of a class we could use to abstract simple text operations on documents. Already it has removed a lot of the ugliness of regular expression code and abstracted it behind the class implementation, with relatively little effort.

Multiple Context Methods

Class methods expect a package name as their first argument, whereas object methods expect an object. Other than this, however, they are identical. Since we can determine an object's class by using ref, we can easily write a method that works as both a class and an object method.

The most common kind of method we can develop with this approach is a class method that is adapted to work from objects as well, by extracting the class of the object from it using ref and using that instead. For example:

```
sub classmethod {
    $self = shift;
    $class = (ref $self)?(ref $self):$self;
    ...
}
```

Or, more tersely, using a logical ||:

```
sub classmethod {
   $self = shift;
   $class = ref $self || $self;
   ...
}
```

Or, even more tersely:

```
sub classmethod {
   $class = (ref $_[0]) || $_[0];
   ...
}
```

The methods that use this trick the most are constructors that allow us to create a new object from an old one. This allows users to create new objects without even knowing exactly what they are – abstraction taken to the extreme. Here is a version of the Game::Card constructor that does this:

```
sub new {
   ($class, $name, $suit) = @_;
   $class = (ref $class) || $class;

   $self = bless {}, $class;

   $self->{'name'} = $name;
   $self->{'suit'} = $suit;

   return $self;
}
```

We can also create a subroutine that can be called as a subroutine, in addition to being called as a method. This takes a little more thought, since the first argument is whatever we pass to the subroutine when we use it as such. If the subroutine gets no arguments at all it knows it must have been called as a subroutine and not a method. For example, if a constructor takes no initialization data, we can do this:

```
# a constructor that may be called as a subroutine
sub new {
   $class = (ref $_[0]) || $_[0] || __PACKAGE__;
   return bless {}, $class;
}
```

The first line of this subroutine translates as: 'if we were passed an object, use the class returned as its reference, otherwise if we were passed anything at all use that as the class, otherwise we must have been called as a subroutine so use the name of the package we are in'. We can construct an object from this subroutine using any of the following means:

```
# as class method:
$object = My::Flexible::Constructor::Class->new;
$object = new My::Flexible::Constructor::Class;

# as object method:
$object = $existing_flexible_object->new;

# as subroutine:
$object = My::Flexible::Constructor::Class::new;
```

Here is another version of the Game::Card constructor that also handles being called as a subroutine. Because it takes additional arguments we have to make some assumptions in order to work out what the first argument is. In this case we will assume that the class name, if supplied, will start with Game::. This is a limitation, but one we are willing to accept in this design:

```
sub new {
    ($class, $name, $suit) = @_;
    $class = (ref $class) || $class;

    # check for the first argument and adjust for subroutine call
    unless ($class =~ /Game::/) {
        ($class, $name, $suit) = (__PACKAGE__, $class, $name);
    }

    $self = bless {}, $class;
    $self->{'name'} = $name;
    $self->{'suit'} = $suit;
    return $self;
}
```

Of course, whether or not this is actually worth doing depends on whether we actually expect a method to be called as a subroutine. If this is not part of the design of our object class we should probably avoid implementing it, just to discourage non-object-oriented usage.

Object Data

Object properties, also called object attributes, are values that are stored within the object. We do not necessarily know how they are stored, but we know what they are because the object class documentation will (or at least, should) tell us.

If we know the object's underlying implementation we can access and set these values directly. The attribute becomes just an array element or hash value:

```
print $card->{'suit'};
$card->{'name'} = 'Queen';
```

This is very bad, however, for several reasons. First, since we are bypassing the object class by not calling a method to do this, the object will have no knowledge of what we are doing. Hence it cannot react or correct us if we do something unexpected, like add a season attribute. The design of this class is not supposed to include an attribute for season, but it has no way of knowing what we are doing. Second, if the names of the attributes change, or the implementation alters in any way, we may find that our code breaks. For instance, if we alter the class to use an array rather than a hash as its underlying data type, all our code will instantly break.

Both problems are symptomatic of violating the principle of **encapsulation**, which dictates that the implementation of the object should be hidden behind the interface. They derive from the fact that we, as users of the class, are determining how the object is accessed, when we should really be using an interface provided for us by the class. In other words, we should be using object methods to both get and set the values of the object's attributes.

> *A related concept to both class and object data is the idea of private class and object data. Perl does not provide a strict mechanism for enforcing privacy, preferring that we respect the design of the object class and don't attempt to work around the provided interface. For cases where we do want to keep data private we can resort to several options, which we will cover a little later in the chapter.*

Accessors and Mutators

The methods that are provided to get and set object attributes are known in object-oriented circles as **accessors** and **mutators**. Despite this jargon, they are really just subroutines that set values in a hash, array, or whatever data type we used to implement the object.

Here is an example of accessor and mutator methods for the suit attribute of the Game::Card class (we can just duplicate them for the name attribute), complete with prototypes:

```
# get passed card object and return suit attribute
sub get_suit ($) {
    return shift->{'suit'};
}

# set suit attribute on passed card object
sub set_suit ($$){
    $_[0]->{'suit'} = $_[1];
}
```

Having separate accessor and mutator methods can be a little awkward, however, especially if we have a lot of attributes to deal with. An object with twenty possible attributes needs forty subroutine definitions to handle them. A popular alternative is to combine accessors and mutators into one method, using the number of arguments passed to determine what to do. For example:

```
sub suit ($;$) {
    my ($self, $suit) = @_;

    if ($suit) {
        my $oldsuit = $self->{'suit'};
        $self->{'suit'} = $suit;
        return $oldsuit;
    }

    return $self->{'suit'};
}
```

This accessor/mutator method gets the current value of the suit attribute if no value is passed, or sets it if one is. As a bonus, it also makes a note of and returns the old value of the attribute. We do not need to check whether the attribute exists because we know (because we wrote the class) that the constructor always sets the hash keys up, even if they have undefined values.

This method does not allow us to unset the suit either, in this case intentionally. If we want to permit the suit to be unset we will have to check to see if we were passed a second argument of undef as opposed to no second argument at all. We can do that by replacing the line:

```
if ($suit) {
```

With:

```
if (scalar(@_)>1) {
```

737

Or, more tersely:

```
if ($#_) {
```

Either replacement checks that at least two arguments were passed to the method, without checking what the second argument is, so undef can be passed as the new attribute value, as can an empty string. However, since the fullname method concatenates this attribute into a string, we probably do not want to allow undef, so this is probably the best variation to use:

```
sub suit ($;$){
    ($self, $suit) = @_;

    if (defined $suit) {
        $oldsuit = $self->{'suit'};
        $self->{'suit'} = $suit;
        return $oldsuit;
    }

    return $self->{'suit'};
}
```

This will allow an empty string to set the attribute, but not undef.

Generic Accessors/Mutators

Combining accessors and mutators into one method is an improvement over the case of separate accessors and mutators methods, at least in terms of the number of subroutines we define, but it comes at the cost of increased code complexity.

We do not really want to have to repeat the same subroutine twenty times for each attribute we might want to set or get. However, since all the attributes are essentially just different cases of key-value pairs, we can write one generic accessor/mutator and make all the actual attribute methods wrappers for it, as this example demonstrates:

```
sub _property ($$;$) {
    my ($self, $attr, $value) = @_;

    if (defined $value) {
        my $oldv = $self->{$attr};
        $self->{$attr} = $value;
        return $oldv;
    }

    return $self->{$attr};
}

sub suit ($;$) {return shift->_property('suit', @_);}
sub name ($;$) {return shift->_property('name', @_);}
```

Now each new method we want to add requires just one line of code. Better still, the relationship between the name of the method and the name of the hash key has been reduced to one single instance. The setting and getting of attributes is also fully abstracted now. Subclasses that make use of a parent class containing this method can set and get their own properties without needing to know how or where they are stored. This is a very attractive benefit for a properly written object class.

The underscore at the start of _property is meant to imply that this subroutine is not meant for public consumption, it is a private method for the use of the class only. Perl does not enforce this, but by naming it this way and not including it in the user documentation, we make our intention clear. If a user of the class chooses to ignore the design and use it anyway, they cannot say they have not been warned.

Having a generic accessor/mutator method gives us great power to develop our object class. Anything we implement in this method will apply to all attributes supported by the object. As an example, here is another version that allows new attributes to be created, but only if another force flag is added. We also add a nonfatal flag to determine whether or not an attempt to set a non-existent attribute is fatal or not:

```perl
sub _property ($$;$$$) {
    my ($self, $attr, $value, $force, $nonfatal) = @_;

    if (defined $value) {
        if ($force || exists $self->{$attr}) {
            my $oldv = $self->{$attr};
            $self->{$attr} = $value;
            return $oldv;
        } else {
            croak "Attempt to set non-existent attribute '$attr'"
            unless $nonfatal;
            return undef;
        }
    }

    return (exits $self->{$attr})?$self->{$attr}:undef;
}
```

To handle fatal errors we have made use of croak, from the Carp module; we will need to add a use Carp; line to our object class for it to work. As we covered in Chapter 16, croak reports errors in the context of the caller rather than the place at which the error occurs. This is very useful in packages, and object classes are no exception.

If we are using accessors and mutators for attribute access we should use them everywhere, including inside the object itself. Here is another version of the constructor for the Game::Card class, written to use the methods of the class rather than initializing them directly. We have also added a prototype at the same time:

```perl
sub new ($;$$) {
    my ($class, $name, $suit) = @_;
    $class = (ref $class) || $class;

    my $self = bless {}, $class;
    $self->name($name);
    $self->suit($suit);
    return $self;
}
```

This further protects the object class against alterations, this time of itself. However, it does come at a performance penalty of an additional subroutine call. For the constructor above, this is minor and acceptable, but if we are writing a method that uses a loop to access or modify attributes, we may want to compromise and access the attributes directly (only because we're inside the object class) for speed.

Class Data

Class data is associated with a class as a whole, rather than with an individual object, and is used to define properties that affect the class as a whole. This can include things like global constants that never change, or changing values like serial numbers or a maximum limit on the number of permitted objects.

As an example, here is an object class that generates serial numbers for objects. It keeps a record of the next serial number in the start key of the global variable %conf, and increments it each time a new object is created:

```perl
# extract from Serial.pm
package Serial;
use strict;

use Carp;

our %conf = (
    'start' => 1,
    'increment' => 1,
);

sub new {
    my $class = (ref $_[0]) || $_[0];
    $conf{'start'} = $_[1] if defined $_[1];

    my $self=bless {}, $class;
    $self->{'serial'} = $conf{'start'};
    $conf{'start'} += $conf{'increment'};
    return $self;
}

sub serial {
    return shift->{'serial'};
}

1;
```

Having built this class we can use it to create new Serial objects, as this short script does. If we pass in a serial number, the count is reset to that point:

```perl
#!/usr/bin/perl
# serial1.pl
use warnings;
use strict;

use Serial;

my @serials;
foreach (1..10) {
    push @serials, new Serial;
}

print $serials[4]->serial, "\n";
my $serial = new Serial(2001);
print $serial->serial, "\n";
```

The value of the two serial numbers displayed by this program produces the output:

```
5
2001
```

This shows us that the fifth serial number (index 4, counting from zero) is 5, as we would expect if the loop generated successive serial numbers starting from 1, with an increment of 1. The second serial number has the value 2001 as we specifically requested. If we generated another serial number object it would have a serial number of 2002.

Although it might not seem terribly useful, this is actually a perfectly functional and usable object class because we can inherit from it. Any object can add serial number functionality to itself by inheriting from this object and making sure to call the new method of Serial from its own new method. We will see more about this later.

The class data of the Serial object class is declared with our, which means that it is package data and therefore accessible outside the class. We can configure the object class itself by altering these values. For example, to reset the serial number to 42 and the increment to 7:

```
$Serial::conf{'start'} = 42;
$Serial::conf{'increment'} = 7;
```

Now when we call new we will get serial numbers 42, 49, 56, and so on. However, just as we do not really want to allow users to control object data directly, neither do we want to allow users to set class data without supervision. The better approach is to implement a class method to set, and check, new values for class data. Here is a configure method that we can add to the Serial object class to handle this for us:

```
# extract from Serial.pm
sub configure {
    my $class = shift;
    return unless @_;
    while (my ($key, $value) = (shift, shift)) {
        $key =~ /start/ and $conf{'start'} = int($value), last;
        $key =~ /increment/ and do {
            $value = int($value);
            croak "Invalid value '$_'" unless $value;
            $conf{'increment'} = $value;
            last;
        };
        croak "Invalid name '$key' in import list";
    }
}
```

Better still, we can now change the definition of %conf to make it a lexically scoped variable with my:

```
my %conf = (
    'start' => 1,
    'increment' => 1,
);
```

Defined this way, the configuration hash is inaccessible to external users, and has become private class data – only the `configure` method can alter it, because only it is in the same lexical scope. We can now call this method to configure the class, as shown by this modified version of our script:

```perl
#!/usr/bin/perl
# serial_a.pl
use warnings;
use strict;

use Serial;

Serial->configure(start => 42, increment => 7);

my @serials;
foreach (1..10) {
    push @serials, new Serial;
}

print $serials[4]->serial, "\n";
my $serial = new Serial(2001);
print $serial->serial, "\n";
```

The output from this version of the script is (as a little arithmetic would lead us to expect):

```
70
2001
```

This class method ensures that we only try to set the two configuration values the class actually supports, and also checks that we do not try to set an increment of zero (which would cause all objects to have the same serial number, of course); neither check would be possible if we simply reached in and changed the hash values directly.

Inheriting Class Data

In the class method shown above we ignore the class passed to us because we want to set the class data of this particular class, even if we are being called by a subclass. This means that different objects from different classes, all inheriting from `Serial` will all have different and distinct serial numbers. However, if we wanted to set class data on a per-class basis we would alter the assignments in this method to something like:

```perl
${"$class\:\:conf"}{'start'} = int($value);   # or ${$class.'::conf'}...,
                                              # or ${"${class}::conf"}
```

This sets the value of `$conf{'start'}` as a package variable in whichever package the call to the `configure` method actually originated from; in this version of the class, each class that inherits from `Serial` would have its own configuration and its own sequence of serial numbers.

If we have classes inheriting from each other, each with the same class data values, we need to pay attention to this kind of detail or we can easily end up setting class data in the wrong class. See 'Non-Object Classes' for an example of a class that works this way. An alternative approach that gets around these difficulties is to set class data via objects; we will also look at that in a moment.

Setting Class Data through Import Methods

We mentioned the `import` method briefly earlier in the chapter, and discussed it at some length in Chapter 10. From the point of view of object-oriented programming, the `import` method is just another class method, with the unusual property that the `use` statement calls it. We can easily adapt our earlier example of the `configure` method to work as an `import` method too, simply by renaming it `import`. However, calling `Serial->import` to configure a variable is confusing, so instead we can just create an `import` method that calls the `configure` method, leaving it available under the old name:

```
sub import {
    shift->configure(@_);
}
```

We could also just alias it, if we like typeglobs:

```
*import = &configure;
```

Either way, we can now configure the `Serial` class with:

```
use Serial qw(start => 42, increment => 7);
```

Everything that applies to the import method also applies to the `unimport` method, of course, for when we use `no` rather than `use`. This is a lot less common, but is ideal for controlling Boolean flags, as the next example illustrates.

Non-Object Classes

All the classes we have looked at so far have been object classes, containing at least one constructor. However, we can create classes that work entirely on class data. This might seem like a strange idea, but it makes sense when we also include the possibility of inheritance. Just as inheriting object methods from a parent class allows us to abstract details of an object's workings, we can inherit class methods to abstract class data manipulations.

The following class continues the theme of the previous section by implementing both `import` and `unimport` methods to create a set of Boolean flags stored as class data. It provides methods to get, set, delete, and create new variables, as well as a `list` method to determine which variables exist, or are set or unset. It is also an example of a class-data only package, and contains no constructor at all. Rather than being an object class in its own right, it is designed to be inherited by other object classes to provide them with class data manipulating methods.

```
# Booleans.pm
package Booleans;
use strict;
no strict 'refs';

use Carp;

# establish set boolean vars
sub import {
    my $class = shift;
    map {${"$class\:\:conf"}{$_} = 1} @_;
}

# establish unset boolean vars
sub unimport {
    my $class = shift;
```

743

```perl
    map {${"$class\:\:conf"}{$_} = 0} @_;
}

# private method -- does all the actual work for set, unset, and delete
# only variables already established may be altered here.
sub _set ($$$) {
    my $class = (ref $_[0]) || $_[0];
    unless (exists ${"$class\:\:conf"}{$_[1]}) {
        croak "Boolean $_[1] not imported";
    }

    if (defined $_[2]) {
        ${"$class\:\:conf"}{$_[1]} = $_[2]?1:0;
    } else {
        delete ${"$class\:\:conf"}{$_[1]};
    }
}

# return variable value
sub get ($$) {
    my $class = (ref $_[0]) || $_[0];
    return ${"$class\:\:conf"}{$_[1]};
}
# set a variable
sub set ($$) {
    shift->_set(@_, 1);
}

# clear a variable
sub unset ($$) {
    shift->_set(@_, 0);
}

# delete an existing variable
sub delete ($$) {
    shift->_set(@_, undef);
}

# invent a new variable -- _set doesn't allow this
sub create ($$$) {
    ${"$_[0]\:\:conf"}{$_[1]}=$_[2]?1:0;
}

# return a list of all set, all unset or all variables
sub list ($;$) {
    my ($class,$set)=@_;

    if (defined $set) {
        # return list of set or unset vars
        my @vars;
        foreach (keys %{"$class\:\:conf"}) {
            push @vars,$_ unless ${"$class\:\:conf"}{$_} ^ $set;
        }
        return @vars;
    } else {
        # return list of all vars in set
        return keys %{"$_[0]\:\:conf"};
    }
}

1;
```

This non-object class is designed to be inherited by other classes, which can use the methods it supplies to set their own Boolean flags. This accounts for all the occurrences of things like:

```
%{"$class\:\:conf"}
```

This is a symbolic reference that resolves to the %conf hash in the package that was first accessed through the method call, so every class that makes use of this class gets its own %conf hash, rather than sharing one in Booleans. Indeed, we do not even declare a %conf hash here since it is not necessary, both because we do not expect to use the module directly and because we always refer to the hash by its full package-qualified name, so no our or use vars declaration is necessary. This is an important point, because it means that a subclass can have a conf array just by subclassing from Booleans. It need not declare the hash itself. It is still free to do so, but the point of this class is that all Boolean variable access should be via the methods of this class, so it should never be necessary.

We can test out this class with a short script that does use the module directly, just to prove that it works:

```perl
#!/usr/bin/perl
# booleans.pl
use warnings;
use strict;

use Booleans qw(first second third);
no Booleans qw(fourth fifth);

print "At Start: \n";
foreach (Booleans->list) {
    print "\t$_ is\t:", Booleans->get($_), "\n";
}

Booleans->set('fifth');
Booleans->unset('first');
Booleans->create('ninth', 1);
Booleans->delete('fourth');

print "Now: \n";
foreach (Booleans->list) {
    print "\t$_ is\t:", Booleans->get($_), "\n";
}

print "By state: \n";
print "\tSet variables are: ", join(', ', Booleans->list(1)), "\n";
print "\tUnset variables are: ", join(', ', Booleans->list(0)), "\n";
```

The output of this program is:

```
At Start:
        first is        :1
        fifth is        :0
        fourth is       :0
        third is        :1
        second is       :1
```

Now:

```
first is      :0
fifth is      :1
ninth is      :1
third is      :1
second is     :1
```

By state:

```
Set variables are: fifth, ninth, third, second
Unset variables are: first
```

Clearly the most immediately useful improvement we could make to this class is to have `list` return the flags in the order of creation (if only for cosmetic purposes) but it serves to prove that the class, such as it is, performs as designed.

Accessing Class Data via Objects

We sometimes want to allow users of our object class to find out the contents of our class data, and even in some cases set it. The lazy way to do this is simply to access the data directly, but as we have already noted this is not object-oriented and therefore bad practice. Better is to use a class method, as we did earlier. Both approaches suffer from the fact that we need to use the class name to access either the data or the method to manipulate it, which varies between a class and its subclasses.

An alternative approach, which avoids all this complexity, and also avoids instances of constructing package variable names on the fly with expressions like `$class\:\:variable`, is to store references to the class data in the objects. We can then access and set the class data through the object using an accessor/mutator style method.

In order to use this approach we need to add some private attributes to the object instance that contain references to the class data. The key point of this technique is that we establish a relationship between the object and its class data in the constructor at the moment the object is created. From this point on, so long as we use the object to access the class data, there is no ambiguity as to which class we are referring to, and we do not need to figure out package prefixes or object class names. The object 'knows' which class data applies to it.

Here is a modified version of the constructor for the `Serial` class that provides references for the class data of the class. The key lines are the ones containing the definitions for the _next and _incr attributes:

```perl
# part of serial2/Serial.pm
sub new {
    my $class = (ref $_[0]) || $_[0];
    $conf{'start'} = $_[1] if defined $_[1];

    my $self = bless {}, $class;
    $self->{'serial'} = $conf{'start'};
    $self->{'_next'} = \$conf{'start'};
    $self->{'_incr'} = \$conf{'increment'};
    $conf{'start'} += $conf{'increment'};
    return $self;
}
```

We create the two new attributes by assigning references to the hash values we want to provide access for. We give them underscored names, to indicate that these are intended for private use, not for public access. Finally, we provide object methods that use these new attributes. Here is an accessor/mutator object method that we can append to our `Serial` class that performs this duty for us:

```perl
sub next ($;$) {
    my ($self, $new) = @_;
    ${$self->{'_next'}} = $new if $new;
    return ${$self->{'_next'}};
}
```

Now, if we want to change the serial number for the next object created we can find any existing `Serial` object (or subclass thereof) and use the `next` method, as this short script illustrates:

```perl
#!/usr/bin/perl
# serial2.pl
use warnings;
use strict;

use Serial;

my $serial = new Serial;
print "First serial number is ", $serial->serial, "\n";
$serial->next(10000);
my $serial2 = new Serial;
print "Second serial number is ", $serial2->serial, "\n";
```

When we run this script we get the expected output:

```
First serial number is 1
Second serial number is 10000
```

When we use the `Serial` class directly, the `next` method has exactly the same effect as configuring the increment through the `configure` class method. However, if we create a subclass for this class we can now choose whether to keep the references to `Serial`'s class data, or replace them with references to class data for the subclass. If we change the references to point to class data for the new class, the `next` method will adapt automatically because it works through the reference. When we cover inheritance more fully we'll develop a subclass of `Serial` that makes use of this.

Debugging Object Classes

We frequently want to include some form of debugging support in our code, where messages are conditionally logged depending on the value of a debugging flag set elsewhere. In the case of object classes, we have two different places to put such a flag, as class data in the class itself for overall debugging of all objects in that class, or at a per-object level, using object properties. In the case of class-level debugging, we also have the choice of handling all classes with a single debugging flag, or giving each class its own debugging flag.

This is more than just a debugging design issue; all data must fall into one of these three categories. Debugging support is thus a good general example of how to handle data in an object-oriented context. It pays to consider inheritance here, because it is better to create a generic debugging module and use it in many places, rather than repeat it for each object class we create. So, while we have yet to cover that subject in detail we will introduce some inheritable debugging object classes too. It is never too early to start planning code reuse.

Class-Level Debugging

Class-level debugging revolves around a class data variable, which controls whether debug messages will be printed on a class-wide basis. The debug method itself, which prints out the messages, can work as either a class or object method, but the flag that enables or disables messages applies to all objects.

Here is a simple example that provides two new methods for multi-level debugging support. Any method within the class can use them, and any user of the class can also use them to enable debugging for the class:

```perl
package My::Debuggable::Class;
use switch;

my $debug_level = 0;

# accessor/mutator
sub debug_level {
    my ($self, $level) = @_;
    $debug_level = $level;
}

# debug method
sub debug {
    my ($self, $level) = (shift, shift);
    print STDERR @_, "\n" if $level <= $debug_level;
}
```

We can now write methods that use these debugging methods like so:

```perl
sub a_method {
    my $self = shift;

    $self->debug(1, "This is a level one debug message");
    ...
}
```

Or, from elsewhere:

```perl
My::Debuggable::Class->debug_level(2);
My::Debuggable::Class->debug(1, "A debug message");
$my_debuggable_class_object->debug(2, "Another debug message");
```

We can also inherit the debug methods into a subclass to implement a generic debugging facility for that class:

```perl
package Other::Class;

use Debuggable;
our @ISA = qw(Debuggable);

__PACKAGE__->debug_level(1);
```

Or, from elsewhere:

```
Other::Class->debug_level(1);
$other_class_object->debug(1, "Debug message");
```

In this version, the class provides a global debugging switch; since all objects inherit the same debug flag, all objects would have their debugging messages enabled or disabled according to that debug flag. Alternatively, if we want to enable debugging on a per-class basis, we can do by replacing the private $debug_level with a constructed package variable name, as this adjusted debugging class does:

```
# Debugpack.pm
package Class::Debuggable;
use strict;
no strict 'refs';

# accessor/mutator
sub debug_level {
    my ($self, $level) = @_;
    my $class = (ref $self) || $self;
    ${"$class\:\:debug_level"} = $level;
}

# debug method
sub debug {
    my ($self, $level) = (shift, shift);
    print STDERR @_, "\n" if $level <= ${"$class\:\:debug_level"};
}

1;
```

Note that because we are using symbolic references to compute the name of the class-specific debugging flag we disable strict references for this class only. Now when we enable or disable the debug level for a particular object class, only the objects of that class will notice:

```
# set different debug levels for different classes
Class::One->debug_level(2);
Class::Two->debug_level(1);
Class::Three->debug_level(0);
```

Object-Level Debugging

Debugging at the object level is essentially similar to the class level, but this time we are enabling debugging on particular objects only. To do that, we need to create a debug attribute associated with the object, which we can do in the constructor.

The following debugging class is designed to be inherited, but we could plug its methods into an existing class with only a little modification. It implements an object-level debugging scheme, and is broadly similar to the earlier examples, except that it uses an object attribute instead of class data. The object attribute is stored as a hash key, so any object class that inherits from it must use a hash as its underlying representation, which is an important limitation we need to be aware of when using it (but if we plan to stick to hashes for our objects then we may consider this acceptable).

It also provides a constructor, for classes that want to inherit from it, and a separate initializer to create the debugging flag attribute independently for objects that already exist. This gives us maximum flexibility when using the class in combination with others; we will delve into this in more detail when we come to discuss writing inheritable classes later in the chapter.

```perl
# Object/Debuggable.pm
package Object::Debuggable;
use strict;
no strict 'refs';

# constructor - for new objects
sub new {
    my ($self, $level) = @_;
    my $class = (ref $self) || $self;

    $self = bless {}, $class;
    $self->initialize($level);

    return $self;
}

# initializer - for existing objects
sub initialize {
    my ($self, $level) = @_;
    $self->{'debug_level'} = $level;
}

# accessor/mutator
sub debug_level {
    my ($self, $level) = @_;

    if (defined $level) {
        my $oldlevel = $self->{'debug_level'};
        $self->{'debug_level'} = $level;
        return $oldlevel;
    }

    return $self->{'debug_level'};
}

# debug method
sub debug {
    my ($self, $level) = (shift, shift);
    print STDERR @_, "\n" if $level <= $self->{'debug_level'};
}

1;
```

Implementing a Multiplex Debug Strategy

Having shown three different ways to implement debugging support in our object classes, it would be nice to be able support all of them simultaneously. In fact, with a little thought, we can. Here is a jack-of-all-trades debugging class that implements a single global debugging flag that affects all classes and objects that inherit from it, a per-class debugging flag, and individual debugging flags for each object:

```perl
# Debuggable.pm
package Debuggable;
use strict;
no strict 'refs';
```

```perl
# global debugging flag -- all classes
my $global_level = 0;

# object constructor
sub new {
    my ($self, $level) = @_;
    my $class = (ref $self) || $self;

    $self = bless {}, $class;
    $self->initialize($level);
    return $self;
}

# initializer for existing objects
# (actually just a wrapper for debug_level)
sub initialize {
    my ($self, $level) = @_;
    $self->debug_level($level);
}

# get/set global debug level
sub global_debug_level {
    my ($self, $level) = @_;

    if (defined $level) {
        # set new level, return old one
        my $old = $global_level;
        $global_level = $level;
        return $old;
    }

    # return current global debug level
    return $global_level;
}

# get/set class debug level
sub class_debug_level {
    my ($self, $level) = @_;
    my $class = (ref $self) || $self;

    if (defined $level) {
        # set new level, return old one
        my $old = ${"$class\:\:class_debug"};
        ${"$class\:\:class_debug"} = $level;
        return $old;
    }

    # return current class debug level
    return ${"$class\:\:class_debug"};
}

# get/set object debug level
sub debug_level {
    my ($self, $level) = @_;
    my $class = ref $self;

    # check to see if we were called as class method
    unless (my $class = ref $self) {
        # '$self' is a class name
        return $self->class_debug_level($level);
    }
```

```
        if (defined $level) {
            # set new level, return old one
            my $old = $self->{'debug_level'};
            $self->{'debug_level'} = $level;
            return $old;
        }

        # return current object debug level
        return $self->{'debug_level'};
    }

    sub debug {
        my ($self, $level) = (shift, shift);

        # if no message, set the (class or object) debug level itself
        return $self->debug_level($level) unless @_;

        # write out debug message if criteria allow
        # object debug is allowed if object, class or global flag allows
        # class debug is allowed if class or global flag allows
        my $class = (ref $self) || $self;
        print STDERR @_, "\n" if
        $level <= $global_level ||
        (defined ${"$class\:\:class_debug"} and
        $level <= ${"$class\:\:class_debug"}) ||
        (ref($self) and $level <= $self->{'debug_level'});
    }

    1;
```

This class attempts to handle almost any kind of debugging we might want to perform. We can set debugging globally, at the class level, or on individual objects. If we do not have an object already we can use the constructor, otherwise we can just initialize debugging support with `initialize`, which operates as either a class or object method and sets the class-wide or object-specific flag appropriately. In fact, it just calls `debug_level`, which does exactly the same thing, but `initialize` sounds better in a constructor.

The three accessor/mutator methods all work the same way and perform the same logic, applied to their particular debugging flag, global, class, or object, with the exception of the object-level accessor/mutator, which passes class-level requests to the class method if it is called with a package name rather than an object.

The debug routine itself now checks all three flags to see if it should print a debug message; if any one of the three is higher than the level of the message, it is printed, otherwise it is ignored. Class-level debugging messages ignore the object-level debug flag, since in their case there is no object to consult. As a convenience, if we supply no message at all we can set and get the debug level instead. Since we simply pass the request to `debug_level`, and `debug_level` in turn passes class method calls to `class_debug_level`, we can in fact handle all of the module's functionality except the global flag through `debug`.

To demonstrate all this in action, here is a short script, complete with its own embedded test object class (which does nothing but inherit from `Debuggable`) that tests out the features of the module:

```
#!/usr/bin/perl
# debugged.pl
use warnings;
use strict;
```

```
# a test object class
{
    package Debugged;
    use Debuggable;
    our @ISA = qw(Debuggable);
    sub new {return bless {}, shift;}
}

# create a test object from the test class
my $object = new Debugged;   # defined below so no 'use'

# set debug levels globally, at class level, and on the object
Debugged->global_debug_level(0);
Debugged->class_debug_level(2);
$object->debug_level(1);

# print class and object level debug messages
Debugged->debug(1, "A class debug message");
$object->debug(1, "A debug message");

# find current debug levels with _level methods
print "Class debug level: ", Debugged->class_debug_level, "\n";
print "Object debug level: ", $object->debug_level, "\n";

# find current debug levels with no-argument 'debug'
print "Class debug level: ", Debugged->debug, "\n";
print "Object debug level: ", $object->debug, "\n";

# switch off class and object debug with 1-argument 'debug'
Debugged->debug(0);
$object->debug (0);
```

The output from this program is:

```
A class debug message
A debug message
Class debug level: 2
Object debug level: 1
Class debug level: 2
Object debug level: 1
```

Inheriting from an object class, and then using the subclass as a substitute for the parent class is a good test of inheritance. If the module is written correctly, everything the parent class does should work identically for the subclass. However, to really appreciate this we really need to discuss inheritance properly.

Inheritance and Subclassing

Inheritance is the cornerstone of code reuse in object-oriented programming. By inheriting the properties and methods of one class into another, we can avoid having to reimplement code a second time, while at the same time retaining abstraction in the existing implementation. A well designed object class can allow classes that inherit from it, also known as subclasses, to carry out their own tasks using the parent class as a foundation without knowing more than the bare minimum of how the class is actually implemented. If a subclass can carry out all its work in terms of methods supplied by the parent, it need not know anything at all. Inheritance is thus a powerful tool for abstraction, which in turn allows us to write more robust and more reusable object classes. There is no need to reinvent the wheel, particularly if the wheel is already working and is well tested.

Perl's inheritance mechanism is, yet again, both matter-of-fact and extremely powerful. It consists of two parts, the special package variable @ISA, which defines inheritance simply by naming the class or classes from which an object class inherits methods and/or class data, and the -> operator, which searches the packages named by @ISA whenever the immediate class does not provide a method.

There are many different forms of inheritance in the object-oriented world, but all of them revolve around the basic principles of abstraction and propagation of method calls from subclasses to their parents. Some, but not all, languages permit **multiple inheritance**, where a subclass can inherit from more than one parent. Similarly, some but not all languages permit **dynamic inheritance** (a class's parents can be changed by the class at will). Perl permits both of these mechanisms in the @ISA array; adding more than one package to @ISA is multiple inheritance, and modifying the contents of @ISA programmatically is dynamic inheritance. It is this kind of simple implementation of complex concepts that makes Perl such an endearing language.

One limitation (or strength, depending on how we look at it) of Perl's approach is that subclasses always know who their parents are, but parents have no idea who their children are. There is no way for a parent class to determine what classes may be using it, nor any mechanism, short of returning undef from a constructor, to bar inheritance. Perl's attitude is that classes ought to be inherited, and that knowledge of subclasses is neither necessary nor desirable for good object-oriented programming.

In addition to whatever classes they may explicitly inherit from, all classes inherit automatically from the UNIVERSAL object, which, as we mentioned nearer the start of the chapter, provides the can, isa, and version methods for all objects. We can place our own methods in this special package if we wish, to give all objects new capabilities.

Inheriting from a Parent Class

The basis of all inheritance is the @ISA array, a special package variable, which, if defined, describes the package or packages from which an object class will inherit methods. To inherit from a parent class we need only specify its package name in the @ISA array. For example:

```
package Sub::Class;
use Parent::Class;
our @ISA = qw(Parent::Class);
```

@ISA works hand in glove with the -> operator, which actually enacts the process of searching for inherited methods. Any method call for a method that is not implemented by this class will automatically be forwarded up to the parent class. If it also does not implement the method then its parent class(es) are searched until Perl runs out of ancestors or a matching method is found.

Overriding and Calling Overridden Methods

We frequently want to implement our own version of a method supplied by a parent, but in doing so, we also often want to take advantage of the parent's method, to carry out tasks related to the parent's implementation of our object. We do not necessarily need to know what these are (that is the point of abstraction), but we would still like to have them done for us.

Since by replacing (or in object-oriented terms, overriding) a method in a parent class, we suppress the call to the parent, we need to call it explicitly ourselves in the replacement method if we want to make use of it. For instance, if we are in a package which is a subclass of Parent::Class, we might write:

```
sub a_method {
    $self = shift;
```

```
      $self->Parent::Class::a_method(@_);
      ... do our own thing ...
}
```

The effect of this, is to call the method a_method in the parent class, but with the package or object specified by $self: that of our own class rather than that of our parent's. From the parent's perspective there is not (or should not) be any difference. Our class is a subclass of it and therefore has all the same properties except that which it overrides.

Many objects only have one parent class, but still name the parent class explicitly, as in the example above. This is an irritation – there is only one parent, and so we should not have to mention it. Fortunately, we can make use of the special package prefix SUPER::, which allows us to refer to our parent class without explicitly naming it:

```
sub a_method {
   $self = shift;

   $self->SUPER::a_method(@_);
   ... do our own thing ...
}
```

Note that this is different from writing the incorrect:

```
SUPER->a_method(@_);
```

In this case, the call to a_method gets the package that SUPER resolved to as its first argument – this is not the object making the call.

The SUPER:: package does not actually exist, but evaluates at run time to all of the packages (since we may have more than one) from which this package inherits. Perl carries out another search for the method, starting from each of the packages in @ISA in turn, until it either finds the method, or it runs out of object classes to search. If we only inherit from one parent class then SUPER:: is almost (but not quite) the same as $ISA[0]:::

```
   $self->$ISA[0]::a_method(@_);
```

The difference is subtle, but important. All objects implicitly inherit from the UNIVERSAL object, but only SUPER:: takes this into account when searching for methods. $ISA[0]:: does not.

Overriding and Calling Overridden Constructors

Constructors are an important case of overriding and inheriting from a parent class. Here we frequently want to have a parent class create our object for us, but we want it to create an object of our class, and not its own; to achieve that, we must call the constructor in the parent class with our own class name as the first argument:

```
sub new {
   $self = shift;
   $class = (ref $self) || $self;

   $self = $class->SUPER::new(@_);
   ... do our own thing ...
   return $self;
}
```

If the parent class is well behaved and allows inheritance to take place properly, it should return an object blessed into whatever package we sent it. We do not even know what that package is ourselves, because it was passed to us. It might be our own class, but it might equally be a subclass of ourselves. By avoiding naming a package explicitly, we handle all these possibilities without having to overtly worry about any of them.

Writing Inheritable Classes

In order for an object class to be inheritable, we need to implement it so that it does not contain or refer to any non-inheritable elements. Although this takes a little extra work, it pays dividends because we create object classes that can be reused and customized by implementing subclasses that add to and override the methods of the original.

In addition, the very act of writing an object class with inheritance in mind helps us develop it more robustly, and exposes weaknesses in the design that might otherwise pass unnoticed until much later. The three golden rules for writing inheritable objects are:

❑   Do not refer directly to class data

❑   Always write constructors to use the passed class name

❑   Never, ever, export anything

A fourth less formal but handy rule-of-thumb is:

❑   Work through the passed object

This is a more general form of the second rule, but directed towards object methods rather than constructors. Class methods are off the hook a little here. Since we do not usually expect a class method to be inherited (they work on a class-wide basis), they tend to be more class-specific. Having said that, it is better if we can write our class methods to be inheritable too. Finally, a fifth rule-of-thumb is:

❑   Call parent constructors first

Following this rule ensures that resources are properly allocated by the parent class (or classes) before we do our own initialization. Of course we might need to do some initialization to call a parent constructor, but as a general rule-of-thumb it is a good one to stick to.

More on Class Data through Objects

As we saw earlier, if we do not want to refer to the same class data in every subclass, we need to take special steps involving symbolic references (though we could also use the qualify_to_ref subroutine provided by the Symbol module). The problem with either approach is that we are stuck with it, we cannot choose whether we want to access the original parent's class data or our own version in further subclasses. Grandchildren get the grandparent's data or their own, depending on how the parent decides to implement its class data accessors and mutators.

The solution is to allow the class to be accessed indirectly, through the objects that we build, which we do by building references to the class data as properties of the objects of the class. We have already seen this in action earlier in the chapter when we altered the constructor and accessor/mutator methods of the Serial module to work with the classes' data through object properties. Here is the constructor of the last version of the Serial class again, as a reminder:

```perl
sub new {
    my $class = (ref $_[0]) || $_[0];
    $conf{'start'} = $_[1] if defined $_[1];

    my $self = bless {}, $class;
    $self->{'serial'} = $conf{'start'};
    $self->{'_next'} = \$conf{'start'};
    $self->{'_incr'} = \$conf{'increment'};
    $conf{'start'} += $conf{'increment'};
    return $self;
}
```

The essential point of this design, from an inheritance point of view, is that any object classes that inherit this constructor may override it with their own constructor. This can choose to either leave the references defined in the object alone, or replace them with new references. Here is a complete subclass that does just this, as well as adding a new read-only attribute, at the time of creation:

```perl
# MySerial.pm
package MySerial;
use strict;

use Serial;

our @ISA = qw(Serial);

my $next = 1;
my $plus = 1;

sub new {
    my $class = shift;

    # call Serial::new
    my $self = $class->SUPER::new(@_);

    # override parent serial with our own
    $self->{'serial'} = $next;

    # replace class data references
    $self->{'_next'} = \$next;
    $self->{'_incr'} = \$plus;

    # add a creation time
    $self->{'time'} = time;

    return $self;
}

sub time {
    return shift->{'time'};
}

1;
```

To test out this new subclass we can use a modified version of our last test script:

```
#!/usr/bin/perl
# myserial.pl
use warnings;
use strict;

use MySerial;

my $serial = new MySerial;
print "Serial number ", $serial->serial, " created at ",
scalar(localtime $serial->time), "\n";
$serial->next(10000);
sleep(1);
my $serial2 = new MySerial;
print "Serial number ", $serial2->serial," created at ",
scalar(localtime $serial2->time), "\n";
```

The output of this script should look like (depending on the time we run this script, of course) the following:

```
Serial number 1 created at Mon Jan  1 12:11:17 2001
Serial number 10000 created at Mon Jan  1 12:11:18 2001
```

What makes this subclass interesting is that it can continue to use the methods provided by the parent class, which use the object properties to access the class data. We do not even need to replace the class data with the same kinds of variables – in the original it was a hash of two key-value pairs. In the subclass it is two discrete scalar variables. By altering these properties, the subclass effectively reprograms the parent's methods to work with the class data that the subclass wants to use. We have moved the choice of which class data is accessed from the parent to the subclass.

There is one remaining flaw in the subclass constructor – it sets the attributes of the parent object class directly. In order to enable the subclass to set its class data without referring directly to the hash we should provide a method to set the class data, and a method to set the serial number. Here are two methods that when appended to the Serial class will do the job for us:

```
# private method to set location class data
sub _set_config {
    my ($self, $nextref, $incrref) = @_;

    $self->{'_next'} = $nextref;
    $self->{'_incr'} = $incrref;
}

# private method to set serial number
sub _set _serial {
    $self->{'serial'} = shift;
}
```

We have avoided mentioning a method to set the serial number up to now because it is not a feature we want to allow publicly. Therefore we have given it a leading underscore and called it _set_serial to emphasize that it is for the use of subclasses only. The method to set the class data is similarly only for the use of subclasses, so we have called it _set_config. The subclass constructor can now be modified to use these methods, resulting in this new, correctly object-oriented, constructor:

758

```
# part of MySerial.pm
sub new {
   my $class = shift;

   # call Serial::new
   my $self = $class->SUPER::new(@_);

   # override parent serial with our own
   $self - >_set_serial($next);

   # replace class data references
   $self->set_config(\$next, \$plus);

   # add a creation time
   $self->{'time'} = time;

   return $self;
}
```

Not only is this more correct, it is simpler to understand too. It is not quite perfect though – the time attribute assumes that the Serial class uses a hash as its underlying representation. We may be happy to live with that, but if we wanted to fix that too we could make use of the private _property method we created earlier in 'Generic Accessors/Mutators' for the easy creation of, and access to, attributes. By adding this method to the Serial class we could then replace the line setting the time attribute:

```
$self->{'time'} = time;
```

to:

```
$self->_property('time', time);
```

Exports

Avoiding exports from object classes almost goes without saying. If we export any variable or subroutine from an object class we allow it to be accessed outside the method calling scheme, breaking the design. Avoiding exports is of course very easy; we just do not do it. In particular we do not use the Exporter.

There is one exception to this rule, however, which comes about when we design an object class to be used both with objects, and with a functional interface, as the CGI module does. Here we generally use a default object created inside the package as global data, and use it whenever an explicit object is not passed to us. To do that requires writing the required methods so they can also be called as functions. For example:

```
package My::FunctionalObject;
use strict;
use Exporter;

our @ISA = qw(Exporter);
our @EXPORT_OK = qw(method_or_function);

my $default_object = new My::FunctionalObject;

sub new {
   ...
}
```

```
sub method_or_function {
my $self = (ref $_[0])?shift:$default_object;

return $self->do_something_else (@_);
}
```

This hypothetical method relies on the fact that, if called as a function, its first argument will not be a reference. It uses this fact to test whether it had been called as a function or method, and sets $self to be either the passed object or the default object accordingly. So long as we design all our methods/subroutines so that the first argument passed in the argument list can never be a reference, this technique will work very well.

Private Methods

A private method is one that can only be called from the class in which it is defined, or alternatively, a method that can only be called from a subclass. Both concepts are implemented as specific features in many object-oriented languages. Typically, Perl does not provide any formal mechanism for defining either type of method. However, its pragmatic approach makes both easy to implement, simply by checking the class name within the method. The catch is that although easy to do, this kind of privacy is enforced at run time, rather than at compile time. Pragmatism is good, but it has its drawbacks too.

To make a method private to its own class we can check the package name of the caller and refuse to execute unless it's our own, as returned by the __PACKAGE__ token. Here is the _property method we developed for the Game::Card class from earlier in the chapter, adapted to enforce privacy rather than just implying it with a leading underscore:

```
# _property method private to methods of this class
sub _property ($$;$) {
   my ($self, $attr, $value) = @_;
   my $class = ref $self;
   croak "Attempt to call private method if $class ne __PACKAGE__";

   if ($value) {
      my $oldv = $self->{$attr};
      $self->{$attr} = $value;
      return $oldv;
   }

   return $self->{$attr};
}
```

To restrict access to subclasses and ourselves only, we can make use of the isa method. This returns True if a class is a subclass of the named class, so we can use it to create a subclass-private method like this. This version of _property takes this approach, which makes it much more suitable in an inheritable parent class.

```
# _property method private to methods of this class
sub _property ($$;$) {
   my ($self, $attr, $value) = @_;
   my $class = ref $self;
   croak "Attempt to call private method unless $class->isa(__PACKAGE__)";
```

```
        if ($value) {
            my $oldv = $self->{$attr};
            $self->{$attr} = $value;
            return $oldv;
        }

        return $self->{$attr};
    }
```

Extending and Redefining Objects

Perl's objects are dynamic in more than one way. We can change their ancestry by manipulating the @ISA array, though this is not a common, and arguably not an advisable thing to do. More interestingly and somewhat more usefully, we can call bless on an object a second time to alter the package to which it belongs. We do not need to do this for extending an object class, because we should be able to pass the new class as the first argument to the constructor of a parent class through inheritance, but we can also use bless to create specialized subclasses, to indicate particular situations.

Extending a Parent Class

Properly designed parent classes should be able to create objects in any requested subclass on demand, by virtue of the two-argument form of bless. For example, say we want to extend the DBI module to batch up do requests and then execute them all at once. We could just place our methods directly into the DBI class to ensure that a database handle object (of class DBI) can use them. This is a bad idea, however, because we might break the parent class if it happens to define a method with the same name. This is, again, a case of defining the class interface from outside the class, which is an object-oriented no-no. Instead, the DBI module can bless a returned handle into our own class rather than the DBI class:

```
# Extended/DBI.pm
package Extended::DBI;
use strict;

use DBI;
our @ISA = qw(DBI);

my @cache;

sub do_later {
    my ($dbh, $statement) = @_;

    push @cache, $statement;
    if ($#cache == 3) {
        map {$dbh->do($_)} @cache;
        @cache = ();
    }
}

sub do_now {
    return map {$dbh->do($_)} @cache;
}

1;
```

In our code:

```
use Extended::DBI;

my $dbh = Extended::DBI->connect($dsn, $user, $password);
$dbh->do_later($statement);
$dbh->do_later($another_statement);
...
$dbh->do_now();
```

This works because while we call the DBI class method connect to create the database handle, we pass the name of the class into which we want the returned handle blessed. Inside connect, the new database handle is blessed into the class we asked for, Extended::DBI. The new handle works just like a regular DBI handle, but we can now cache and execute do statements with it too.

Constructing Subclasses On the Fly

Another interesting case of extending a parent object is where the parent object does it itself in order to reflect the circumstances under which it was created. There is no particular reason why a constructor cannot create an object of a different class to the one it is in, or the one passed to it. If we define an @ISA array for the new class (which we can do simply by assigning it with a fully qualified package name), we can also have this new class inherit its methods from ourselves. This gives us the possibility of creating different versions of ourselves for different occasions, an approach that is often referred to as a 'factory object'.

For example, a common approach taken by other object-oriented languages is to represent errors as objects (generically known as **exception** objects) rather than as raw numbers or some other basic data type, so errors can be handled in a more object-oriented style, without relying on an arbitrary system error value. Perl does not support such a concept since error objects are altogether too complicated for a pragmatic language like Perl. However, we can create an error object class that supports various different methods for handling errors, and then subclass this class on the fly when a new type of error occurs. By choosing to do it this way we need not create subclasses for every error type, and we automatically support any new errors that may arise without needing to change the code.

The following example demonstrates an object class that translates system errors, as communicated by the special variable $! (or $ERRNO, if using the English module), into objects whose class is based on the common name for the error, ENOENT for error number 2, for example. Each object class is created on the fly if it does not exist, and an @ISA array is placed into it to subclass it from the parent class passed to the constructor (which is either ourselves or something that inherits from us; either way, the methods of our class can be called from the new subclass). The key parts of the module are the new constructor and the _error_from_errno subroutine:

```
# ErrorClass.pm
package ErrorClass;
use strict;

use Errno;
no strict 'refs';

my %errcache;

sub new {
    my ($class, $error) = @_;
    $class = (ref $class) || $class;
    $error = $error || $!;
```

```
        # construct the subclass name
        my $subclass = $class. '::'. _error_from_errno($error);

        # cause subclass to inherit from us
        unless (@{$subclass. '::ISA'}) {
            @{$subclass. '::ISA'} = qw(ErrorClass);
        }

        # return reference to error, blessed into subclass
        return bless \$error, $subclass;
    }

# return the integer value of the error
sub number {
    my $self = shift;
    return int($$self);
}

# return the message of the error
sub message {
    my $self = shift;
    return ''.$$self;
}

# accessor/mutator
sub error {
    my ($self, $error) = @_;
    if (defined $error) {
        my $old = $$self;
        $$self = $error;
        return $old;
    }
    return $$self;
}

# subroutine to find the name of an error number
sub _error_from_errno {
    my $errno = int(shift);

    # do we already know this one by name?
    if (defined $errcache{$errno}) {
        return $errcache{$errno};
    }

    # otherwise, search for it in the export list
    my ($name, $number);
    foreach $name (@Errno::EXPORT_OK) {
        $number = Errno->$name;
        $errcache{$number} = $name;
        return $name if $errno == $number;
    }

    # unlikely, but just in case...
    return 'UNKNOWN';
}

1;
```

The class works by using the `Errno` package to find names for errors, and then scanning each in turn by calling the constant subroutine defined by `Errno`. When it finds a match, it creates a new subclass comprising the passed class name and the error name, and then blesses the error into that class before returning it. It also caches the error numbers and error names as it searches so it can avoid calling too many subroutines in future.

It is interesting to see just how easily a class can be created in code. The only thing that exists in the subclasses we create is a definition for the @ISA array – everything else is inherited. Despite this, they are still fully functional object classes, with methods that can be called, and, if we wish, they can even be subclassed.

The ErrorClass object class is also an example of an object based on a scalar value, in this case, the value of $!. If no initial value is given, the constructor defaults to using the current value of $! as the basis for the object it is about to return. $! is an interesting value because it has both an integer and a string definition, as we covered in Chapter 16. This object simply blesses that value, which retains its dual nature even when copied to a new variable, and allows the integer and string aspects of it to be retrieved by different accessors. Here is a short script that demonstrates how this class can be used:

```perl
#!/usr/bin/perl
# error.pl
use warnings;
use strict;

use ErrorClass;

# generate an error
unless (open IN, "no.such.file") {
    my $error = new ErrorClass;

    print "Error object ", ref $error, "\n";
    print "\thas number ", $error->number, "\n";
    print "\thas message '", $error->message, "'\n";

    print "It's not there! \n" if $error->isa("ErrorClass::ENOENT");
}
```

Running this script produces the output:

```
Error object ErrorClass::ENOENT
        has number 2
        has message 'No such file or directory'
It's not there!
```

Note that we will also get a warning from Perl because we have only used IN once – we never intended to use it anyway.

The last line of this script demonstrates the real point of the class. Rather than checking numbers or using the Errno module to call a constant subroutine to determine the numeric value of the error, we convert the error into an object. We can now, in a properly object-oriented way, check the type of an error by looking to see what kind of error object it is.

Multiple Inheritance

In object-oriented circles, the whole idea of multiple inheritance is fiercely debated, with many languages banning it outright. The idea of multiple inheritance (inheriting from several parents at once) seems simple enough, but while multiple inheritance is very powerful, it is also a very quick route to object-oriented chaos. Perl abstains from this debate – although it does allow it, it doesn't take great pains to support it either.

To inherit from more than one class is very simple indeed; we just place more than one class into the @ISA array:

```
package My::Subclass;

use Parent::Class::One;
use Parent::Class::Two;

our @ISA = qw(Parent::Class::One Parent::Class::Two);
```

When we come to call a method on My::Subclass, Perl will first check that the package actually implements it. If it does, there is no problem; the method is called and its value returned. If it does not, Perl checks for the method in the parent classes in @ISA, in the order in which they are defined. This means that Parent::Class::One is searched first, including all the classes that it in turn inherits from. If none of them satisfy the method call, Parent::Class::Two is searched. If both packages (or ancestors thereof) define the method then only the one found in Parent::Class::One is called, and the version in Parent::Class::Two is never seen.

The manner of searching is therefore crucially affected by the order in which packages are named in @ISA. The following statement is at first sight the same as the one above, but in actuality differs in the order in which packages are searched, leading to potentially different results:

```
our @ISA = qw(Parent::Class::Two Parent::Class::One);
```

Writing Classes for Multiple Inheritance

Inheriting more than one class into our own is easy; we just add the relevant package names to our @ISA array. Writing a class so that it is suitable for multiple inheritance takes a little more thought. By definition, we can only return one object from a constructor, so having multiple constructors in different parent classes gives the subclass a dilemma; it cannot call a constructor in each parent class, since that will yield it several objects of which it can only return one. It also cannot just call one parent constructor, since that will prevent the other parent classes from doing their part in the construction of the inherited object. The same problem, but to a lesser degree, also affects other methods; do we call all the parent methods that apply, or just one? And in that case, how do we choose which one?

In the case of constructors, the best way to implement the class so that it can easily be a co-parent with other classes is to separate the construction of the object from its initialization. We can then provide a separate method to initialize the object if another constructor has already created it. For example, here is the constructor for the Game::Card class we displayed at the start of the chapter:

```
sub new {
    my ($class, $name, $suit) = @_;
    $class = (ref $class) || $class;

    my $self = bless {}, $class;

    $self->{'name'} = $name;
    $self->{'suit'} = $suit;

    return $self;
}
```

This constructor is fine for single inheritance, but it's no good for multiple inheritance, since the only way a subclass can initialize the name and suit properties is to create an object containing them. If it has already created an object, say with the Serial module, it cannot easily combine the two together. (Well, in fact, it can because both modules produce hash-based objects and combining hashes is easy. But that requires the subclass to mess with the underlying data of the object, which is bad for abstraction.)

Instead, we split the constructor in two, like this:

```
sub new {
    my $class = shift;
    $class = (ref $class) || $class;

    my $self = bless {}, $class;
    $self->initialize(@_);
    return $self;
}

sub initialize {
    my ($self, $name, $suit) = @_;

    $self->{'name'} = $name;
    $self->{'suit'} = $suit;
}
```

With this done, we can now create a subclass that inherits from the Serial, Game::Card, and Debuggable object classes all at the same time, in order to create a serialized debuggable game card class:

```
# Debuggable.pm
package Game::Card::Serial::Debuggable;
use strict;

use Game::Card;
use Serial;
use Debuggable;

our @ISA = qw(Serial Debuggable Game::Card);

sub new {
    my $class = shift;
    $class = (ref $class) || $class;

    my $self = $class->Serial::new;
    $self->Debuggable::initialize();
    $self->Game::Card::initialize(@_);
    return $self;
}
```

We can test that this combined subclass works using the following script:

```
#!/usr/bin/perl
# dsgamecard.pl
use warnings;
use strict;
```

```
use Game::Card::Serial::Debuggable;

my $card = new Game::Card::Serial::Debuggable('Ace', 'Spades');

print $card->fullname, " (", $card->serial, ") \n";
$card->debug(1);
$card->debug(1, "A debug message on object #", $card->serial, "\n");
```

The output from this script should be:

Ace of Spades (1)
A debug message on object #1

Although a simplistic example, classes like this are actually genuinely useful, just for the fact that they combine the features of multiple parent classes. Both the Serial and Debuggable object classes can be added to any other object to add serial numbers and debugging support. This is one of the more common uses of multiple inheritance, and a great example of how object-oriented programming helps encourage code reuse.

In this example we used the Serial module to create the object. In practice, it does not matter which of the three parents actually creates our object (unless of course one of them does not have a separate initializer method). Analyzing the pattern here, we can see that in fact we could call initializer methods on all three parent objects, Serial::initialize, Debuggable::initialize, and Game::Card::Initialize, and create the object ourselves:

```
sub new {
    my $class = shift;
    $class = (ref $class) || $class;

    my $self = bless {}, $class;
    $self->Serial::initialize();
    $self->Debuggable::initialize();
    $self->Game::Card::initialize(@_);
    return $self;
}
```

One problem with this scenario is how to deal with arguments if more than one parent initializer method needs arguments. In this case we did not need to worry about that because only the Game::Card class needs arguments to initialize it. Another is that, implicitly, all the object classes involved have to use a hash as their underlying data representation, since they all presume a hash. However, this is a problem for regular inheritance too, rather than being a specific issue for multiple inheritance. As a rule, alternative object implementations can be good for isolated classes, but they do not work well when inheritance enters the picture.

Drawbacks with Multiple Inheritance

Multiple inheritance can get very messy very quickly, which is one of the reasons why many languages disapprove of it. The normal inheritance hierarchy is rooted at the top and spreads out and down, each subclass adding to and overriding the methods of its parent. Multiple inheritance stands this arrangement on its head, with each subclass inheriting methods from more than one parent, which in turn may inherit methods from more than one grandparent.

This is problematic for two reasons. The first, and nastiest, is that we can end up with a cyclic dependency, where an ancestor inherits from one of its descendants. This is possible to do in single inheritance too, but it is easier to do it accidentally with multiple inheritance. Fortunately Perl can detect this and aborts if we try to create a cyclic dependency.

The second is simply that objects with multiple inheritance can quickly become hard to understand and even harder to debug, because their behavior is no longer predictable, we do not know in advance which parent object will satisfy a given method call without studying all the parent methods and their grandparents and the contents of the @ISA arrays of all the objects concerned.

A particularly nasty but all too common example of object inheritance that is hard to predict is where two parent classes inherit from the same grandparent, or in more general cases, where two ancestors inherit from the same common ancestor. This is programmatic incest, so to speak. We now end up with recombinant branches where a method in the common ancestor can potentially be called by either of two different routes from the original subclass, entirely dependent on the order of parent classes in the @ISA array. There are arguments for designing applications which use object hierarchies like this, but in general recombinant inheritance is a sign that the design of our classes is over complex and that there is probably a different organization of classes that would better suit our purposes.

There is also a rather pragmatic reason why multiple inheritance can cause us problems: it prevents the effective use of prototypes. In many languages, methods can be selected not just by their name but also by the type and number of arguments that they accept. Perl does not support this model, so prototypes of inherited classes are ignored. (Having said this, the Class::Multimethods module on CPAN does provide an argument-list based mechanism for searching for methods in parent classes, if that is what we want to do.)

The bottom line for designing classes with multiple inheritance is therefore to keep them as simple as possible, and avoid complex inverted trees of parent classes if at all possible.

A 'UNIVERSAL' Constructor

As we have already shown, all object classes implicitly inherit from the UNIVERSAL class and therefore can always make use of the can, isa, and VERSION methods that it provides.

With a little thought, we can also add our own methods to UNIVERSAL to make them generic across all the methods in our application. This is not something to be done lightly, because it can cause unexpected problems by inadvertently satisfying a method call that was intended for a different parent class.

Having said this, there are some methods that we can place into UNIVERSAL that are so common among objects that it is worth creating a generic method for them. For instance, we introduced the concept of initializer methods when we talked about multi-classing. The constructor we created as a result of this was totally generic; so we could place it in UNIVERSAL to give all our object classes a new constructor that calls an initializer, then just define an initializer rather than a constructor.

To place anything into UNIVERSAL we only have to specify it as the package name. Here is an example object class that adds a generic new constructor to all objects:

```
# Univeral/Constructor.pm
package UNIVERSAL;
use strict;
```

```
sub new {
    my $class = shift;
    $class = (ref $class) || $class;

    my $self = bless {}, $class;
    $self->initialize(@_);
    return $self;
}

sub initialize { }

1;
```

To use this constructor we now only have to use the module and provide an `initializer` method if we want to actually perform some initialization:

```
package My::Class;
use strict;
use Universal::Constructor;

sub initialize {
    my ($self, $value1, $value2) = @_;

    $self->{'attr1'} = $value1;
    $self->{'attr2'} = $value2;

    return $self;
}

1;
```

Note that we don't need an @ISA definition for this class because it implicitly inherits from UNIVERSAL already. We could similarly, assuming we based all our objects on a hash, create universal accessors, universal mutators, or a universal accessor/mutator of the types we created before. If any object wants to have its own constructor it only has to override the new provided by our universal class, or just not use it at all.

Whether or not putting methods into UNIVERSAL is a good idea or not is debatable. Certainly, over-complex or task-specific methods are a bad idea, as is any kind of class data. If most of our object classes all use the same methods then it can be a workable approach, but in the end it is only one line less than using a different package name and placing it in an @ISA definition.

It is also possible that we want to avoid having another class satisfy a method provided by the UNIVERSAL package. It would be strange, but not impossible, for a parent class to provide a can method (an object that defines an AUTOLOAD method might want to do this to return a True result for methods that it supports but has not yet defined). If we need to avoid calling it, we can explicitly add UNIVERSAL to the start of the @ISA array for our object class (or at the least in front of the class with the troublesome can method). For example:

```
our @ISA = qw(UNIVERSAL Problem::Parent Other::Class);
```

Is-a Versus Has-a

So far we have only talked about one kind of relationship between objects, the is-a relationship. However, not all object relationships can be expressed in terms of is-a. It may be true that a tire is-a wheel, but it does not make sense to say that a deck of playing cards is-a playing card. The other form of relationship is has-a; a deck of cards has-a collection of cards in it.

Perl does not provide support for the has-a relationship inside the language in the same way that the @ISA array supports is-a relationships. However, it does not need to. Since an object is just a scalar value, one object has another just by storing it as an attribute. Using objects to manage groups of other objects is a very effective technique; such objects are sometimes called **containers** or 'container objects'.

Extending our Game::Card example, here is new class Game::Deck, that manages a list of Game::Card objects. This new class allows us to create a new deck of cards of our chosen suits and names, and then deal cards from it. We can also replace them on the top or bottom, peek at any card in the deck, and print out the whole deck:

```perl
# Game/Deck.pm
package Game::Deck;
use strict;

use Game::Card;

### Constructor

sub new {
    my ($class, $suits, $names, $cardclass) = @_;
    my $self = bless {}, $class;

    if ($suits) {
        # create cards according to specified arguments

        # these allow us to specify a single suit or name
        $suits = \$suits unless ref $suits;
        $names = \$names unless ref $names;

        # record the names and suits for later
        $self->{'suits'} = $suits;
        $self->{'names'} = $names;

        # generate a new set cards
        my @cards;
        foreach my $suit (@$suits) {
            foreach my $name (@$names) {
                my $card = new Game::Card($name, $suit);
                bless $card, $cardclass if defined $cardclass;
                push @cards, $card;
            }
        }

        # add generated cards to deck
        $self->{'cards'} = \@cards;
    } else {
        # initialize an empty deck
        $self->{'cards'} = [];
    }

    return $self;
}
```

```perl
### Cards, Suits and Names

# return one or more cards from deck by position
sub card {
   my ($self, @range) = @_;

   return @{$self->{'cards'}} [@range];
}

sub suits {
   return @{shift->{'suits'}};
}

sub names {
   return @{shift->{'names'}};
}

### Deal and Replace

# shuffle cards randomly
sub shuffle {
   my $self = shift;

   # create a hash of card indices and random numbers
   my %order = map {$_ => rand()} (0..$#{$self->{'cards'}});

   # rebuild the deck using indices sorted by random number
   my @newdeck;
   foreach (sort {$order{$a} <=> $order{$b}} keys %order) {
      push @newdeck, $self->{'cards'}[$_];
   }

   # replace the old order with the new one
   $self->{'cards'} = \@newdeck;
}

# deal cards from the top of the deck
sub deal_from_top {
   my ($self, $qty) = @_;

   return splice @{$self->{'cards'}}, 0, $qty;
}

# deal cards from the bottom of the deck
sub deal_from_bottom {
   my ($self, $qty) = @_;

   return reverse splice @{$self->{'cards'}}, -$qty;
}

# replace cards on the top of the deck
sub replace_on_top {
   my ($self, @cards) = @_;

   unshift @{$self->{'cards'}}, @cards;
}

# replace cards on the bottom of the deck
sub replace_on_bottom {
   my ($self, @cards) = @_;
```

```
            push @{$self->{'cards'}}, reverse @cards;
}

### Nomenclature

# return string for specified cards
sub fullnames {
    my ($self, @cards) = @_;

    my $text;
    foreach my $card (@cards) {
        $text .= $card->fullname. "\n";
    }
    return $text;
}

# return string of whole deck ('fullname' for Deck class)
sub fulldeck {
    my $self = shift;

    return $self->fullnames (@{$self->{'cards'}});
}

# print out the whole deck
sub print {
    my ($self, @range) = @_;

    if (@range) {
        print $self->fullnames (@{$self->{'cards'}}[@range]);
    } else {
        print $self->fulldeck;
    }
}

1;
```

To use this class we first call the constructor with a list of suits and card names. We can then manipulate the deck according to our whims. Here is a short script that puts the class through its paces. Note how simple the construction of a standard 52-card deck is:

```
#!/usr/bin/perl
# gamedeck.pl
use warnings;
use strict;

use Game::Deck;

# create a standard deck of playing cards
my $deck = new Game::Deck(
    ['Spades', 'Hearts', 'Diamonds', 'Clubs'],
    ['Ace', 2..10, 'Jack', 'Queen', 'King'],
);

# spread it out, shuffle it, and spread it out again
print "The unshuffled deck looks like this: \n";
$deck->print;
$deck->shuffle;
print "After shuffling it looks like this: \n";
$deck->print;
```

```
# peek at, deal, and replace a card
print "Now for some card cutting... \n";
print "\tTop card is ", $deck->card(0)->fullname, "\n";
my $card = $deck->deal_from_top(1);
print "\tDealt ", $card->fullname, "\n";
print "\tTop card is now ", $deck->card(0)->fullname, "\n";
$deck->replace_on_bottom($card);
print "\tReplaced ", $card->fullname, " on bottom \n";
print "The deck now looks like this: \n";
$deck->print;
```

As we briefly mentioned earlier in the chapter, if the result of calling an object method is another object then we can chain method calls together and avoid storing the intermediate objects in temporary variables. We can see this happening in the above script in the expression:

```
$deck->card(0)->fullname
```

Because the has-a relationship fits this model very well, the meaning of this expression is obvious just by inspection, give me the full name of the first card in the deck.

The concept of the deck implemented by this object class extends readily to other kinds of deck, for example, a hand of cards is really just a small deck; it has an order with a top and bottom card, we can deal from it, and so on. So, to deal a hand of cards we just create a hand deck and then deal cards from the main deck, adding them to the hand. This extension to the test script shows this in action (we have dealt from the bottom just for variety):

```
# gamedeck.pl (continued)
# deal a hand of cards - a hand is just a small deck
my $hand = new Game::Deck;
my @cards = $deck->deal_from_bottom(7);
$hand->replace_on_top(@cards);
print "Dealt seven cards from bottom and added to hand: \n";
$hand->print;
```

This example demonstrates how effective a has-a relationship can be when it fits the requirement for the design of a class.

Autoloading Methods

There is no intrinsic reason why we cannot use the autoloader to load methods on their first use, just as we can load subroutines on their first use in ordinary non-object-oriented packages; both the SelfLoader and AutoLoader modules, which we covered in Chapter 10 will work just as well with methods as they do with subroutines.

We can also generate methods on the fly using the autoloader if we wish. Typically this is useful for accessor or mutator methods when we do not want to define them all at once (or indeed at all, unless we have to). Fortunately, Perl searches for methods in parent classes before it resorts to the autoloader; otherwise this technique would be impractical.

As an example of how we can adapt a class to use autoloading, here is a generic accessor/mutator method and the first two of a long line of specific methods that use it, borrowed from an edition of the Game::Card object class.

```
sub _property ($$;$) {
   my ($self, $attr, $value) = @_;

   if (defined $value) {
       my $oldv = $self->{$attr};
       $self->{$attr} = $value;
       return $oldv;
   }

   return $self->{$attr};
}

sub propone ($;$) {return shift->_property('propone', @_);}
sub proptwo ($;$) {return shift->_property('proptwo', @_);}
...
```

Even though this is an efficient implementation, it becomes less than appealing if we have potentially very many attributes to store. Instead, we can define an AUTOLOAD method to do it for us. Here is a complete and inheritable object class that takes this approach, allowing us to set and get any attribute we please by calling an appropriately named method:

```
# Autoloading.pm
package Autoloading;
use strict;

sub new {return bless {}, shift}

sub _property ($$;$) {
   my ($self, $attr, $value) = @_;

   if ($value) {
       my $oldv = $self->{$attr}{$value};
       $self->{$attr} = $value;
       return $oldv;
   }

   return $self->{$attr};
}

sub AUTOLOAD {
   our $AUTOLOAD;

   my $attr;
   $AUTOLOAD =~ /([^:]+)$/ and $attr = $1;

   # abort if this was a destructor call
   return if $attr eq 'DESTROY';

   # otherwise, invent a method and call it
   eval "sub $attr {return shift->_property('$attr', \@_);}";
   shift->$attr(@_);
}

1;
```

To test out this class we can use the following script:

```perl
#!/usr/bin/perl
# autol.pl
use warnings;
use strict;

use Autoloading;

my $object = new Autoloading;

$object->name('Styglian Enumerator');
$object->number('say 6');

print $object->name, " counts ", $object->number, "\n";
```

The output should be:

Styglian Enumerator counts say 6

This class is, in essence, very similar to examples we covered using the discussion on autoloading in Chapter 10, only now we are in an object-oriented context. Because of that, we have to take an additional step and suppress the call to DESTROY that Perl will make when an object falls out of scope. Otherwise, if this class is inherited by a subclass that defines no DESTROY method of its own, we end up creating an attribute called DESTROY on the object (shortly before it becomes recycled). In this case it would not have done any harm, but it is wasteful.

Another problem with this class is that it is not very selective; it allows any method to be defined, irrespective of whether the class or any subclass actually requires or intends to provide that method. To fix this, we need to add a list of allowed fields to the class and then check them in the autoloader. The following modified example does this, and also creates an object reference to the list of allowed fields (which is created as a hash for easy lookup) to allow the method to be properly inherited:

```perl
package Autoloading2;
use strict;
use Carp;

my %attrs=map {$_ => 1} qw(name number rank);

sub new {
    my $class = shift;

    my $self = bless {},$class;
    $self->{'_attrs'} = \%attrs;

    return $self;
}

sub _property ($$;$) {
    my ($self,$attr,$value) = @_;

    if ($value) {
        my $oldv = $self->{$attr};
        $self->{$attr} = $value;
        return $oldv;
    }
```

```
            return $self->{$attr};
    }

sub AUTOLOAD {
        our $AUTOLOAD;

        my $attr;
        $AUTOLOAD=~/([^:]+)$/ and $attr=$1;

        # abort if this was a destructor call
        return if $attr eq 'DESTROY';

        # otherwise, invent a method and call it
        my $self=shift;
        if ($self->{'_attrs'}{$attr}) {
                eval "sub $attr {return shift->_property('$attr',\@_);}";
                $self->$attr(@_);
        } else {
                my $class=(ref $self) || $self;
                croak "Undefined method $class\:\:$attr called";
        }
    }

sub add_attrs {
        my $self=shift;

        map {$self->{'_attrs'}{$_}=1} @_;
    }

1;
```

This module presets the attributes name, number, and rank as allowed. So any attempt to set a different attribute, for example size, on this class (or a subclass) will be met with an appropriate error, directed to the line and file of the offending method call by the Carp module. Here is a script that tests it out:

```
#!/usr/bin/perl
# auto2.pl
use warnings;
use strict;

use Autoloading;

my $object = new Autoloading;

$object->name('Styglian Enumerator');
$object->number('say 6');
$object->size('little');    # ERROR
print $object->name, " counts ", $object->number, "\n";
print "It's a ", $object->size, " one.\n";
```

When we run this program we get:

> Undefined method Autoloading::size called at auto2.pl line 12

Subclasses can create their own set of attributes simply by defining a new hash and assigning a reference to it to the special _attrs key. However, any subclass that wishes to also allow methods permitted by the parent needs to combine its own attribute list with that defined by the parent. This is done most easily by calling the constructor in the parent, and then appending new fields to the hash attached to the _attrs hash key.

Since this is a generic requirement for all subclasses, the first thing we should do is add a method to the `Autoloading` class that performs this function for subclasses. Here is a method that does what we want, taking a list of attributes and adding them to the hash. Again, we have it working through the object attribute to preserve inheritance:

```
# added to 'Autoloading' class
sub add_attrs {
    my $self = shift;

    map {$self->{'_attrs'}{$_} = 1} @_;
}
```

Having added this method to the parent `Autoloading` class, we can now have subclasses use it to add their own attributes. Here is a subclass that uses it to add two additional attributes to those defined by the parent class:

```
#!/usr/bin/perl
# Autoloading::Subclass
package Autoloading::Subclass;
use warnings;
use strict;

use Autoloading;
our @ISA = qw(Autoloading);

my @attrs = qw(size location);

sub new {
    my $class = shift;

    my $self = $class->SUPER::new();
    $self->add_attrs(@attrs);
    return $self;
}

1;
```

If we adjust our test script to use and create an object of this new class it now works as we intended:

```
Styglian Enumerator counts say 6
It's a little one.
```

Although in this example our main `autoloading` class defines its own attributes, by removing the hard-coded attributes defined in the `Autoloading` module, we could create a generic `autoloading` module suitable for adding to the `@ISA` array of any object wishing to make use of it.

Keeping Data Private

In other (some might say proper) object-oriented languages, methods, class data, and object data may be declared private or public, and in some cases, with varying degrees of privacy (somewhere between absolute privacy and complete public access). Perl does not support any of these concepts directly, but we can provide for all of them with a little thought. We have already seen and covered private methods in the discussion on inheritance. Private class and object data are, however, another matter.

Private Class Data

Keeping class data private is very simple indeed, we just declare our global variables with my to give them a lexical scope of the file that contains them, and prevent them having entries in the symbol table. Since code in the same file can access them, no other object class can touch class data declared this way (not even by declaring the same package name in a different file).

If we want to keep class data private to only a few methods within a file, we can do that too by adding some braces to define a new lexical scope, then defining a lexically scoped variable and methods to use it within them. To emphasize the fact that it is private to the class, we use underscores for the variable name. Here is a simple example:

```
package My::Class;
use strict;

# create private data and methods to handle it

{
   my $_class_private_data;
   sub _set_data {shift; $_class_private_data = shift;}
   sub _get_data {return $_class_private_data;}
}

# methods outside the scope of the private data must use the methods         #
provided to access it

sub store_value {
   my ($self, $value) = @_;
   $self->_set_data($value);
}

sub retrieve_value {
   my $self = shift;
   return $self->_get_data();
}

1;
```

Strictly speaking this is not object-oriented programming at all, but a restriction of scope within a file using a block, a technique we have seen before. However, 'private class data' does not immediately translate into 'lexical variables and block scope' without a little thought.

Private Object Data

Perl's general approach to privacy is that it should be respected, rather than enforced. While it is true that we can access the data underlying any blessed reference, the principles of object-oriented programming request that we do not, and if we do so, it is on our own head if things break later. However, if we really want to enforce the privacy of object data there are a few ways that we can accomplish it. One popular way is to implement the object not in terms of a reference to a basic data type like a hash or array, but as a reference to a subroutine, which alone has the ability to see the object's internal data.

This technique is known as a **closure**, and we introduced it in Chapter 7. Closures in object-oriented programming are no different except that each reference to a newly created closure is turned into an object. The following example demonstrates one way of implementing an object as a closure:

```perl
# Closure.pm
package Closure;
use strict;

use Carp;

my @attrs = qw(size weight shape);

sub new {
    my $class = shift;
    $class = (ref $class) || $class;

    my %attrs = map {$_ => 1} @attrs;

    my $object = sub {
        my ($attr, $value) = @_;

        unless (exists $attrs{$attr}) {
            croak "Attempt to ", (defined $value)?"set":"get",
            " invalid attribute '$attr'";
        }

        if (defined $value) {
            my $oldv = $attrs{$attr};
            $attrs{$attr} = $value;
            return $oldv;
        }

        return $attrs{$attr};
    };
    return bless $object, $class;
}

# generate attribute methods for each valid attribute
foreach my $attr (@attrs) {
    eval "sub $attr {\$_[0]('$attr', \$_[1]);}";
}

1;
```

And here is a short script to show it in action:

```perl
#!/usr/bin/perl
# closure.pl
use warnings;
use strict;

use Closure;

my $object = new Closure;

$object->size(10);
$object->weight(1.4);
$object->shape('pear');
```

```
print "Size:", $object->size,
      " Weight:", $object->weight,
      " Shape:", $object->shape, "\n";

print "Also size:", &$object('size'), "\n";
```

When run, the output of this script should be:

```
Size:10 Weight:1.4 Shape:pear
Also size:10
```

This object class uses a constructor to create and return a blessed code reference to a closure. The closure subroutine itself is just what it seems to be; a subroutine, not a method. However, it is defined inside the scope of the new method, so the lexical variables $class and %attrs created at the start of new are visible to it. At the end of new, both lexical variables fall out of scope, but %attrs is used inside the anonymous subroutine whose reference is held by $object, so it is not recycled by the garbage collector. Instead, the variable becomes persistent, surviving as long as the object created from the closure reference does, and becomes the internal storage for the object's attributes. Each time new is called, a fresh %attrs is created and used by a new closure subroutine, so each object is distinct and independent.

We generate the accessor/mutator methods using an eval, and also demonstrate that, with a little ingenuity, we can avoid naming the attributes in more than one place. This code is evaluated when the module is compiled, so we do not lose any performance as a result of doing it this way.

Another efficiency measure we could use, in order to improve the above example, is to reduce the size of the closure subroutine, since Perl holds a compiled copy of this code for every object we create. With a little inspection, we can see that by passing a reference to the %attrs hash to an external subroutine we can reduce the size of the closure and still retain its persistent data. In fact, we can reduce it to a single line:

```
# Closure2.pm
package Closure;
use strict;

use Carp;

my @attrs = qw(size weight shape);

sub new {
    my $class = shift;
    $class = (ref $class) || $class;

    my %attrs = map {$_ => 1} @attrs;

    my $object = sub {
        return _property_sub(\%attrs, @_);
    };

    return bless $object, $class;
}
```

```
sub _property_sub {
   my ($href, $attr, $value) = @_;

   unless (exists $href->{$attr}) {
      croak "Attempt to ", (defined $value)?"set":"get",
            " invalid attribute '$attr'";
   }

   if (defined $value) {
      my $oldv = $href->{$attr};
      $href->{$attr} = $value;
      return $oldv;
   }

   return $href->{$attr};
}

# generate attribute methods for each valid attribute
foreach my $attr (@attrs) {
   eval "sub $attr {\$_[0]('$attr', \$_[1]);}";
}

1;
```

The _property_sub subroutine in this example bears more than a little resemblance to the _property method we used in earlier examples. Here though, the first argument is an ordinary hash reference, and not the blessed hash reference of an object. We can test this version of the Closure class with the same script as before, and with the same results. However, note the last line of that test script:

```
print "Also size:", &$object('size'), "\n";
```

As this shows, we can call the closure directly rather than via one of its officially defined accessor methods. This does no harm, but if we wanted to put a stop to it we could do so by checking the identity of the caller. There are several ways we can do this, of which the fastest is probably to use the caller function to determine the package of the calling subroutine. If it is the same package as the closure's, then it must be an accessor, otherwise it is an illegal external access. Here is a modified version of the anonymous subroutine from the new constructor that performs this check:

```
my $object = sub {
croak "Attempt to bypass accessor '$_[0]'"
if caller(1) ne __PACKAGE__;
   return _property_sub(\%attrs, @_);
};
```

Now if we try to access the size attribute directly we get:

Attempt to bypass accessor 'size' at closure.pl line 10

Now we have an object class that cannot be used in any way other than the way we intended.

Destroying Objects

Just as we can create objects with a constructor, we can destroy them with a destructor. For many objects this is not a step we need to take, since by eliminating all references to an object, we will cause Perl to perform garbage collection and reclaim the memory it is using. This is also known more generally as **resource deallocation**.

However, for some objects this is not enough; if they contain things like shared memory segments, filehandles, or other resources that are not directly held within the object itself, then these also need to be freed and returned to the system. Fortunately, whenever Perl is given a blessed reference to destroy it checks for a destructor method in the object's class, and if one is defined, calls it.

As an example, here is a destructor for a putative object that contains a local filehandle and a network socket:

```perl
sub DESTROY {
    $self = shift;

    # close a filehandle...
    close $self->{'filehandle'};
    # shutdown a network socket
    shutdown $self->{'socket'};
}
```

Of course, it is not too likely a real object will have both of these at once, but it demonstrates the point. Any system resource held by the object should be destroyed, freed up, or otherwise returned in the destructor.

We can also use destructors for purely informational purposes. Here is a destructor for the `Serial` object class, which takes advantage of the fact that each object has a unique serial number to log a message to the effect that it is being destroyed:

```perl
# destructor for 'Serial' class ...
sub DESTROY {
    my $self = shift;
    print STDERR ref($self), " serial no ", $self->serial, " destroyed\n";
}
```

With this destructor added to the object class, we can now run a program like this to create a collection of serial objects:

```perl
#!/usr/bin/perl
# serialdestroy.pl
use warnings;
use strict;

use Serial;

my @serials;
foreach (1..10) {
    push @serials, new Serial;
}

my $serial = new Serial(2001);
```

When the program ends Perl calls the destructor for each object before discarding the reference, resulting in the following output:

```
Serial serial no 10 destroyed
Serial serial no 9 destroyed
Serial serial no 8 destroyed
Serial serial no 7 destroyed
Serial serial no 6 destroyed
Serial serial no 5 destroyed
Serial serial no 4 destroyed
Serial serial no 3 destroyed
Serial serial no 2 destroyed
Serial serial no 1 destroyed
Serial serial no 2001 destroyed
```

Other than the fact that it is called automatically, a destroy method is no different from any other object method. It can also, from a functional programming point of view, be considered the object-oriented equivalent of an END block.

Destructors and Inheritance

We never normally need to call a destructor directly, since it is called automatically whenever the object passes out of scope and is garbage-collected. However, in the case of inherited classes we have a problem, since destructors are called the same way any other method is called (Perl searches for it and calls the first one it finds in the hierarchy of objects from child to parent). If a subclass does not define a destructor then the destructor in the parent class will be called and all is well. However, if the subclass does, it overrides the parent's destructor.

In order to make sure that all aspects of an object are properly destroyed, we need to take steps to call parent destructors if we don't define a destructor for ourselves. For objects that inherit from only one parent we can do that calling the method SUPER::DESTROY:

```
sub DESTROY {
    $self = shift;

    # destroy our own resources (e.g. a subhash of values for this class):
    undef $self->{'our_own_hash_of_data'};

    # call parent's destructor
    $self->SUPER::DESTROY;
}
```

We should take care to destroy our own resources first. When we are writing constructors it is good practice to call the parent constructor before doing our own initialization. Similarly, when we destroy an object we should destroy our own resources first and then call the parent destructor (reverse order). The logic behind this is simple, we may need to use the parent class to destroy our resources, and destroying the parts of the object it relies on may prevent us from doing that.

Alternatively, and more interestingly, we can re-bless the object into the class of its parent. This is analogous to peeling an onion where each subclass is a layer. Once the subclass has destroyed the object's resources that pertain to it, what is left is, at least for the purposes of destruction, an object of the parent class:

```
sub DESTROY {
    my $self = shift;

    # destroy our own resources
    undef $self->{'our_own_hash_of_data'};

    bless $self, $ISA[0];
}
```

The parent object's class name is defined by the element in the @ISA array – we only have one, so it must be element index zero. What actually happens here is that we catch Perl's garbage collection mechanism with our DESTROY method, remove the resources we are interested in, and then toss the object back to the garbage collector by allowing the reference to go out of scope a second time. But as we re-blessed the object, Perl will now look for the DESTROY method starting at the parent class instead.

Although elegant, this scheme does have one major flaw; it fails if any subclass uses multiple inheritance. In this case, re-blessing the object can cause considerable confusion when the object is passed on to other destructors in different parents of the subclass. Both the examples in the following section would potentially fail if the first parent destructor re-blessed the object before the second sees it.

Destructors and Multiple Inheritance

In objects classes that use multiple inheritance, we have to get more involved, since SUPER:: will only call one parent destructor:

```
sub DESTROY {
    $self = shift;

    ...destroy our own resources...

    $self->First::Parent::Object::DESTROY;
    $self->Second::Parent::Object::DESTROY;
}
```

This is a little ugly, however, since it involves writing the names of the parent packages explicitly. If we change the contents of the @ISA array then this code will break. It also depends on us knowing that the parent object or objects actually have a DESTROY method. A better way to do it is to iterate through the @ISA array and test for parent DESTROY methods:

```
sub DESTROY {
    $self = shift;

    foreach (@ISA) {
        if ($destructor = $_->can('DESTROY')) {
            $self->$destructor;
        }
    }
}
```

Overloading Operators

So far we have looked at objects from the point of view of methods. We can get quite a long way like this, but sometimes it becomes desirable to be able to treat objects as if they were conventional data types. For instance, if we have an object class, which can in some sense be added or concatenated with another object of the same type, we would like to be able to say:

```
$object1 += $object2;
```

Or, rather than presuming we have an add method for the purpose:

```
$object1->add($object2);
```

Unfortunately, we cannot add objects or easily apply any other operator to them, because they are at heart just references, and obey the same rules that normal references do. Instead, what we want to do is redefine the + operator (and by inference, the += operator) so that it works correctly for particular object classes too.

Basic Overloading

This redefinition of standard operators for objects is known as operator overloading, and Perl supports it through the overload module. Presuming that we have an add method for a given object class, we can assign it to the + operator so that when an object of our class is added to anything, it is called to perform the actual 'addition' instead of the default + operator supplied by Perl. Here is an example of an object class that handles addition and addition assignment operations:

```
# addition.pm
package My::Value::Class;
use strict;

use overload '+' => \&add,
'+=' => \&addassign;

sub new {
    my ($class, $value) = @_;
    my $self = bless {}, $class;

    return $self;
}

sub value {
    my ($self, $value) = @_;
    $self->{'value'} = $value if defined $value;
    return $value;
}

sub add {
    my ($operand1, $operand2) = @_;
    my $result=$operand1->new;
    $result->value($operand1->value + $operand2->value);
    return $result;
}
```

```
sub addassign {
    my ($operand1, $operand2) = @_;

    $operand1->value($operand1->value + $operand2 - value);
}

1;
```

The add and addassign methods handle the + and += operators respectively. Unfortunately they only work when both operands are objects of type My::Value::Class. If one operand is not of the right type then we have to be more cautious. Perl automatically flips the operands around so that the first one passed is always of the object type for which the method has been called. Since binary operations take two operands we have broken our usual habit of calling the object $self: $operand1 makes more sense in this case.

Consequently, we only have to worry about the type of the second operand. In this example case we can simply treat it as a numeric value and combine it with the value attribute of our object. To test the operand to see if it is of a type we can add as an object we use ref and isa:

```
sub add {
    my ($operand1, $operand2) = @_;

    my $result = $operand1->new;
    if (ref $operand2 and $operand2->isa(ref $operand1)) {
        $result->value($operand1->value + $operand2->value);
    } else {
        $result->value($operand1->value + $operand2);
    }
    return $result;
}
```

Determining the Operand Order and Operator Name

For some operations the order of the operands can be important, a good example being subtraction, and another being concatenation. In order to deal with this, operator methods are called with a third Boolean flag that indicates whether the operands are given in reverse order, or to put it another way, if the object for which this method is implemented came second rather than first. If set, this flag also tells us by implication that the first operand was not of the correct object class (and possibly not even an object).

As an example, here is a concatenation method that uses this flag. It also checks the type of the other operand passed and returns a different type of result depending on the order; if a plain string was passed as the first argument, a plain string is returned, otherwise a new object is returned. To keep the example simple, we have presumed an object whose textual representation is in the attribute name:

```
sub concatenate {
    my ($operand1, $operand2, $reversed) = @_;

    if ($reversed) {
        # if string came first, return a string
        return $operand2.$operand1->{'name'};
```

```
        } else {
           # if object came first, return an object
           my $result = $operand1->new();
           $result->{'name'} = $operand1->{'name'}.$operand2;
           return $result;
        }
   }
```

Now all we have to do is overload the concatenation operator with this method:

```
   use overload '.' => \&concatenate;
```

Occasionally we might also want to know the name of the operator that triggered the method. This is actually passed in a fourth argument to all operator methods, though we do not usually need it. The obvious and probably most common application is for errors (another is for the nomethod operator method discussed later). For example, to reject operands unless they both belong to the right class (or subclass) we do this:

```
   sub an_operator {
       my ($op1, $op2, $rev, $name)=@_;

       unless (ref $op2 and $op2->isa(__PACKAGE__)) {
           croak "Cannot use '$name' on non-",
           __PACKAGE__, " operands";
       }
   }
```

Overloading Comparisons

An interesting operator to overload is the <=> operator, for comparison. By providing a method for this operator we can allow sort to work with our objects. For example, dealing only with an object to object comparison:

```
   use overload '<=>' => \&compare;

   sub compare {
      ($operand1, $operand2) = @_;
      return $operand1->{'value'} <=> $operand2->{'value'};
   }
```

With this method in place, we can now say (at least for objects of this class):

```
   @result = sort @objects;
```

and get a meaningful result.

This is a more useful operator to overload than it might seem even from the above, because the overload module can deduce the correct results for all the other numeric comparison operations based on it. Likewise, if we define an operator method for cmp, all the string comparison operations can be deduced for it. This deduction is called **autogeneration** by the overload module, and we cover it in more detail in a moment.

Overloading Conversion Operations

The numeric and string conversion of objects are two operators, which we may overload, even though we do not normally think of them as operators. However, objects, being references at heart, do not have useful numeric or string values by default; by overloading these operations, we can create objects that can take part in numeric calculations or be printed out.

Overloading String Conversion

String conversion happens whenever a Perl value is used in a string context, such as concatenation or as an argument to a `print` statement. Since objects ordinarily render themselves as a class name plus a memory address, which is generally less than meaningful, providing a string representation for them can be an extremely useful thing to do.

String conversion is not an operator in the normal sense, so the string conversion operator is represented as a pair of double quotes. Here is how we can assign an operator method for string conversion:

```
use overload '""' => \&render_to_string;
```

We now only have to create an operator method that produces a more sensible representation of the object. For example, this method returns the object name, as defined by a `name` attribute, enclosed within double quotes:

```
sub render_to_string {
    $self = shift;
    return '"'.$self->{'name'}.'"';
}
```

Alternatively, this more debugging-oriented renderer dumps out the contents of the hash being used to implement the object (in the case of other representations we would need to use different methods, of course):

```
sub render_to_string {
    $self = shift;
    $out = "$self:\n";
    map {
        $out .= "\t$_ => $self->{$_} \n"
    } keys %{$self};
    return $out;
}
```

Finally, here an object class that uses a converter to translate date values into different formats, depending on what format we require:

```
# DateString.pm
package DateString;
use strict;

# construct date object and values
sub new {
    my ($class, $time, $format) = @_;
    $class = ref $class || $class;
```

```perl
    $time = time() unless $time;
    my ($d, $m, $y) = (localtime($time))[3, 4, 5];
    my $self = bless {
        day     => $d,
        month   => $m+1,    # months 0-11 to 1-12
        year    => $y+1900,    # years since 1900 to year
        format  => $format || 'Universal'
    }, $class;

    return $self;
}

# only the format can be changed
sub format {
    my ($self, $format) = @_;
    if ($format) {
        $self->{'format'} = $format;
    }
    return $self->{'format'};
}

# the string conversion for this class
sub date_to_string {
    my $self = shift;
    my $format = shift || $self->{'format'};

    my $string;
    SWITCH: foreach ($self->{'format'}) {
        /^US/ and do {
        $string = sprintf "%02d/%02d/%4d", $self->{'month'}, $self->{'day'},
                $self->{'year'};
        last;
    };

    /^GB/ and do {
        $string = sprintf "%02d/%02d/%4d", $self->{'day'}, $self->{'month'},
                $self->{'year'};
        last;
    };

    # universal format
    $string = sprintf "%4d/%02d/%02d",
    $self->{'year'}, $self->{'month'}, $self->{'day'};
}
    $string .= " ($self->{format})";
}

# overload the operator to use convertor
use overload '""' => \&date_to_string;

1;
```

To show how this class operates, here is a short program that prints out the current date in English, US, and Universal format:

```perl
#!/usr/bin/perl
# datestring.pl
use warnings;
use strict;

use DateString;

my $date = new DateString(time);
print "$date \n";
$date->format('GB');
print "$date \n";
$date->format('US');
print "$date \n";
```

Here is what the script produces, assuming we run it on February 14th 2001:

```
2001/02/14 (Universal)
14/02/2001 (GB)
02/14/2001 (US)
```

We wrote these conversion methods in the style of conventional object methods, using `shift` and `$self`. This does not mean they do not receive four arguments like other overloaded operator methods, simply that we do not need or care about them. There is only one operand.

Overloading Numeric Conversion

Just as we can overload string conversion, so we can overload numeric conversion. Numeric conversion takes place whenever a data value is used in a numeric context (such as addition or multiplication), or as an argument to a function that takes a numeric argument.

There are two numeric conversion operators, both of which are specially named since, like string conversion, they do not correspond to any actual operator. The standard numeric conversion is called `0+`, since adding anything to zero is a common trick for forcing a value into a numeric context. Here's how we can assign an operator method for numeric conversions:

```perl
"0+" => \&render_to_number;

sub render_to_number {
    $self = shift;
    return 0+ $self->{'value'};
}
```

Similarly, here is a numeric converter for the date class we converted into a string earlier. The numeric value of a date is not obvious, so we will implement it in terms of a 32-bit integer with two bytes for the year and one byte each for the month and day:

```perl
sub date_as_version {
    $self = shift;
    $year_h = $self->year / 256;
    $year_l = $self->year % 256;
    return pack('C4', $year_h, $year_l, $self->month, $self->day);
}
```

This conversion is not useful for display, but it will work just fine for numeric comparisons, so we can compare date objects using traditional operators like < and == rather than by overloading these operators to have a special meaning for dates:

```
die "Date is in the future" if $day > $today;   # date objects
```

The second numeric conversion handles translation into a Boolean value, which takes place inside the conditions of while and until loops, and also in the ?: operator, unless we overloaded that too. References are always True, since they always have values, so to test objects meaningfully, we need to provide a Boolean conversion. The operator is called bool, and is used like this:

```
"bool" => \&true_or_false;
```

The meaning of truth or falsehood in an object is of course very much up to the object. The return value should be either True or False to Perl; for example 1 for True and the empty string for False:

```
sub true_or_false {
    $self = shift;
    return $self->{'value'}?1:'';
}
```

Note that if we do not provide an overload method for Boolean conversion, the overload module will attempt to infer it from string conversion instead.

Falling Back to Unoverloaded Operations

Earlier in the chapter we introduced the ErrorClass object class, which encapsulated errno values inside an object. While we could compare the object class as a string or convert it into a number, we had to call methods in the object class to do so. It would be much nicer if we could have this dealt with for us.

Here is an extension to the ErrorClass object that does just that. For the sake of this example we will give it the filename ErrorClass/Overload.pm, though it actually adds overloaded methods to the base ErrorClass object class:

```
# ErrorClass/Overload.pm
package ErrorClass;
use strict;

use ErrorClass;

use overload (
    '""'  => \&error_to_string,
    '0+'  => \&error_to_number,
    fallback => 1,
);

sub error_to_string {
    my $class = (ref $_[0]) || $_[0];
    my $package = __PACKAGE__;
    $class =~ /$package\:\:(\w+)/ and return $1;
}

sub error_to_number {
    return shift->number;
}

1;
```

This extension package provides two new methods, error_to_string and error_to_number, which overload the string and numeric conversion operators. Because we do not want to actually change the names of the objects generated by the ErrorClass class, we add the methods directly to the ErrorClass package instead of subclassing as we would ordinarily do.

As well as overloading the operators, we have set the fallback flag. This flag has a very useful function – it permits conversion methods to be called when no overloaded object method is available. Instead of complaining that there is no eq string comparison operation for ErrorClass objects, for example, Perl will 'fall back' to the ordinary string comparison, converting ErrorClass objects into strings in order to carry it out. Without this, we would be able to print out ErrorClass objects and convert them into integers with int, because these are direct uses of the conversion operators, but we would not be able to write a line like this:

```
print "It's not there! \n" if $error eq 'ENOENT';
```

Without fallback, this operation will fail because the eq operator is not overloaded for ErrorClass objects. With fallback, the error will be converted into a string and then eq will compare it to the string ENOENT. In fact, this handles all the string comparison operators, including cmp. Similarly, the numeric conversion operation allows Perl to fall back to all the normal numeric comparison operators.

Here is a modified version of the test script for the ErrorClass module that shows how we can use these new overloaded conversions to simplify our programming with ErrorClass objects:

```
#!/usr/bin/perl
# overload.pl
use warnings;
use strict;

use ErrorClass::Overload;

# generate an error
unless (open STDIN, "no.such.file") {
    my $error = new ErrorClass;

    print "Error object ", ref $error, "\n";
    print "\thas number ", $error->number, "\n";
    print "\thas message '", $error->message, "'\n";
    print "Text represetation '", $error, "'\n";
    print "Numeric representation = ", int($error), "\n";
    print "It's not there! \n" if $error eq 'ENOENT';
}
```

Running this script should produce the output:

```
Error object ErrorClass::ENOENT
        has number 2
        has message 'No such file or directory'
Text representation 'ENOENT'
Numeric representation = 2
It's not there!
```

Overloading and Inheritance

Operators' methods are automatically inherited by child classes, but the hard reference syntax we have used so far does not allow us to specify that an inherited method should be used; it requires us to specify a reference to the actual method (be it in our own class or a parent). However, we can have Perl search our parent classes for the implementation of an overloaded operator by supplying the name of the method rather than a reference to it. Here is how we would overload the <=> operator with an inherited method:

```
use overload '<=>' => "compare";
```

The method name is essentially a symbolic reference, which is looked up using the -> operator internally. This may or may not be a good thing; it allows inheritance, but a hard reference has the advantage of producing a compile-time error if the method does not exist.

Inheriting methods for operators rather than inheriting the overloaded operator assignments can also have a serious effect on performance if we are not careful. If autogeneration (below) is enabled, inheritance can cause Perl a lot of needless extra work as it tries to construct new methods from existing ones. Ordinarily, the search for methods is quick since we only need to see what references exist in the list of overloaded operators. But with inheritance, a search through the hierarchy for each method not implemented in the class is performed – for large inheritance trees that can cause a lot of work.

Autogenerated Operations

When we started out with the overload module we provided methods to handle both the + and += operators. However, we actually only needed the + operation overloaded, because the overload module is smart enough that it can infer operations that have not been overloaded from those that have been.

For instance, the current behavior for the operation += can be inferred from the + operator, since $a += $b is just shorthand for $a = $a + $b, and Perl knows how to do that for our object class. Similarly, if Perl knows how to do subtraction, it also knows how to do a unary minus (since that is just 0-$a) and -=. The ++ and -- operators can likewise be inferred from + and -; they are just $a = $a + 1 and $a = $a - 1. The overload module can even infer abs from '-'. That said, we could often supply more efficient versions of these operators, but autogeneration means that we do not have to.

Unfortunately, just because an operator can be deduced does not mean that it should be. For instance, we may have a date class that allows us to compute differences between dates expressed as strings, as in:

```
'1 Jan 2001' - '30 Dec 2000' = '2 days'
```

A binary subtraction makes sense in this context, but a unary minus does not. There is no such thing as a negative date. In order to distinguish it from the binary subtraction operator, the unary minus is called neg when used in the list supplied to the overload module. So, one way we can implement subtraction but forbid negation is:

```
use overload '-' => \&subtract,
neg => sub {croak "Can't negate that!"};
```

This is awkward if we need to prevent several autogenerated operators, not least because we have to work out what they are to disable them. Instead, to prevent the overload module autogenerating operator methods we can specify the fallback flag. The default value is undefined, which allows autogeneration to take place, but dies if no matching operator method could be found or autogenerated.

The fallback flag is intimately connected to autogeneration; we only saw it in its most basic use before. If set to 1, Perl reverts to the standard operation rather than fail with an error, which is very useful for object classes that define only conversion operations like the ErrorClass::Overload extension we showed earlier.

If fallback is set to 0, however, autogeneration is disabled completely but errors are still enabled (unfortunately there is no way to disable both errors and autogeneration at the same time). A better way to disable negation is like this:

```
use overload '-' => \&subtract,
fallback => 0;
```

We also have the option to supply a default method (for when no other method will suit), by specifying an operator method for the special nomethod keyword. This operates a little like an AUTOLOAD method does for regular methods, and is always called if a method can neither be called nor autogenerated. The fourth argument comes in very handy here, as this nomethod operation method illustrates:

```
sub no_operator_found {
    my $result;

    # deal with some operators here
    SWITCH: foreach ($_[3]) {
        /^ <=> / and do {$result = 0,  last};   # always lexically equal
        /^cmp/ and do {$result = 0, last};   # always numerically equal
        # insert additional operations here

        # croak if the operator is not one we handle
        croak "Cannot $_[3] this";
    }
    return $result;
}

use overload '-' => \&subtract,
'+' => \&add,
nomethod => \&no_operator_found;
```

We can also use this with the fallback flag, in which case autogeneration is disabled. Only explicit addition and subtraction (plus numeric and string comparisons through the nomethod operation) are enabled:

```
use overload '-' => \&subtract,
'+' => \&add,
fallback => 0,
nomethod => \&no_operator_found;
```

Overloadable Operations

Not every operator provided by Perl can be overloaded. Conversely, some of the things we might normally consider functions can be overloaded. The table below summarizes the different categories of operators understood by the 'overload' module and the operators within each category that it handles:

Operator Category	Operators
with_assign	+ - * / % ** << >> x .
assign	+= -= *= /= %= **= <<= >>= x= .=
str_comparison	< <= > >= == !=
3way_comparison	<=> cmp
num_comparison	lt le gt ge eq ne
binary	& | ^
unary	neg ! ~
mutators	++ --
func	atan2 cos sin exp abs log sqrt
conversion	bool "" 0+

For more details on these categories and the overload pragma, see perldoc overload.

Automating Object Class Development

There are several helper modules available for Perl, which automate much of the process of creating new object classes. Two of the more useful third-party modules on CPAN are Class::MethodMaker, which can automatically generate object properties and methods, and Class::Multimethods, which gives Perl the ability to select methods from multiple parent classes based on the type and number of arguments passed (a feature present in several other object-oriented languages but absent from Perl).

Perl does come with the Class::Struct module, however. This provides much more limited but considerably simpler object class generation features than modules like Class::MethodMaker. Several object classes provided by Perl are based on it, including all the hostent, netent, protoent, and servent modules, as well as stat and several others. All of these modules make good working examples of how Class::Struct is used.

The module provides one subroutine, struct. The name is taken from C's struct declaration after which the module is patterned. To use it we supply a list of attributes and their data types, indicated by the appropriate Perl prefix, $ for scalars, @ for arrays, and % for hashes. In return it defines a constructor (new) and a complete set of accessor/mutator methods for each attribute we request. For example, this is how we can create a constructor and six accessor/mutator methods for an address class in one statement:

```
# Address.pm
package Address;
use strict;

use Class::Struct;
```

```
struct (
    name => '$',
    address => '@',
    postcode => '$',
    city => '$',
    state => '$',
    country => '$',
);


1;
```

This object class creates objects with five scalar attributes, and one array attribute whose value is stored as an array reference. When we use this module `struct` is called and the class is fully defined. The constructor new, generated on-the-fly by `struct` accepts initialization of the object with named arguments, so we can create and then print out the fields of an object created by this class using a script like the following:

```
#!/usr/bin/perl
# address.pl
use warnings;
use strict;

use Address;

my $address = new Address(
    name => 'Me Myself',
    address => ['My House', '123 My Street'],
    city => 'My Town',
);

print $address->name," lives at: \n",
    "\t", join("\n\t", @{$address->address}), "\n",
    "in the city of ", $address->city, "\n";
```

This produces the output:

```
Me Myself lives at:
        My House
        123 My Street
in the city of My Town
```

Getting and setting attributes on these automatically generated objects is fairly self-evident. Each accessor/mutator follows the pattern of accessor/mutator methods we have seen before. Scalars are retrieved by passing no arguments, and set by passing one:

```
$name = $address->name;    # get an attribute
$address->name($name);     # set an attribute
```

Array and hash attributes return a reference to the whole array or hash if no arguments are passed, otherwise they return the value specified by the passed index or hash key if one argument is passed, and set the value specified if two arguments are passed:

```
$arrayref = $address->address;
$first_line = $address->address(0);
$address->address(0, $firstline);
```

```
$hashref = $address->hashattr;
$value = $address->hashattr('key');
$address->hashattr('key', $value);
```

The underlying object representation of this class is an array. If we want to be able to inherit the class reliably we are better off using a hash, which we can do by passing `struct` (the name of the class we want to create methods for), followed by the attributes we want to handle in a hash or array reference. If we pass an array reference, the class is based on an array. If we pass a hash reference, it is based on a hash like so:

```
# AddressHash.pm
package Address;
use strict;

use Class::Struct;

struct Address => {
    name => '$',
    address => '@',
    postcode => '$',
    city => '$',
    state => '$',
    country => '$',
};

1;
```

We can create and then print out the fields of the object created by this version of the class using the same script, producing the same output as before.

In fact, we do not even need the `package Address` at the top of this module since `struct` creates subroutines in the package passed to it as the first argument anyway.

We can also use objects as attributes by the simple expedient of naming an object class instead of a Perl data type prefix. Here's a modified `Address` class that replaces the `address` array attribute with a subclass called `Address::Lines` with an explicit `house` and `street` attribute:

```
# AddressNest.pm
package Address;
use strict;

use Class::Struct;

struct 'Address::Lines' => [
    house => '$',
    street => '$',
];

struct (
    name => '$',
    address => 'Address::Lines',
    postcode => '$',
    city => '$',
    state => '$',
    country => '$',
);

1;
```

Since we can chain together object calls if the result of one method is another object, we can modify the test script to be:

```perl
#!/usr/bin/perl
# addressnest.pl
use warnings;
use strict;

use AddressNest;

my $address = new Address(
    name => 'Me Myself',
    city => 'My Town',
);

$address->address->house('My House');
$address->address->street('123 My Street');

print $address->name, " lives at: \n",
    "\t", $address->address->house, "\n",
    "\t", $address->address->street, "\n",
    "in the city of ", $address->city, "\n";
```

We can, if we choose, optionally prefix the attribute type with an asterisk, to make *$, *@, *%, or *Object::Class. When present, this causes the accessor for the attribute to return references rather than values. For example, if we used name => '*$' in the arguments to struct, we could do this:

```perl
$scalar_ref = $address->name;
$$scalar_ref = "My New Name";
$new_scalar = "A Different Name Again";
$address->name(\$newscalar);
```

The same referential treatment is given to array, hash, and object attributes, for example with address => '*@':

```perl
$first_element = $address->address(0);
$$first_element = "My New House";
```

If we want to provide more precise control over attributes we can do so by redefining the accessor/mutator methods with explicit subroutines. Be aware, however, that Perl will warn about redefined subroutines if warnings are enabled. If we need to override a lot of methods, however, the benefits of using Class::Struct begin to weaken and we are probably better off implementing the object class from scratch.

As a final example, if we want to create a class that contains attributes of one type only (most probably scalars), we can create very short class modules, as this rather terse but still fully functional example illustrates:

```perl
# AddressMap.pm
use strict;

use Class::Struct;
struct Address => {map {$_ => '$'} qw(
    name house street city state country postcode)
};

1;
```

For completeness, here is the test script for this last class; note that it is very similar to our first example, which was mostly made up of scalars. Again it produces the same output as all the others:

```perl
#!/usr/bin/perl
# addressmap.pl
use warnings;
use strict;

use AddressMap;

my $address = new Address(
    name => 'Me Myself',
    house => 'My House',
    street => '123 My Street',
    city => 'My Town',
);

print $address->name," lives at:\n",
    "\t", $address->house, "\n",
    "\t", $address->street, "\n",
    "in the city of ", $address->city, "\n";
```

Ties and Tied Objects

One of the more intriguing parts of Perl's support for object-oriented programming is the tied object. Tied objects are somewhat at odds with the normal applications of object orientation. In most object-oriented tasks we take a functional, non object-oriented problem and rephrase it in object-oriented terms. Ties go the other way, taking an object class and hiding it behind a simple non object-oriented variable.

Tied objects allow us to replace the functionality of a standard data type with an object class that secretly handles the actual manipulations, so that access to the variables is automatically and transparently converted into method calls on the underlying object. The object can then deal with the operation as it sees fit. Perl allows us to tie any standard data type, including scalars, arrays, hashes, and filehandles. In each case the operations that the underlying object needs to support vary.

There are many possible uses for tie, from hashes that only allow certain keys to be stored (as used by the fields module), to the DBM family of modules, which use tied hash variables to represent DBM databases. The Perl standard library provides several tied classes, including the fields module and the DBM family of modules, and there are many, many tied class implementations available from CPAN. Before implementing a tied class it is worth checking to see if it has already been done.

Tied object classes are a powerful way to use objects to provide enhanced features in places that are otherwise hard to reach or difficult to implement. The tie makes the object appear as a conventional variable. This allows us to replace ordinary variables with 'smart' ones, so any Perl code that works with the original data type will also work with the tied object, oblivious to the fact that we have replaced it with something else of our own design.

799

Using Tied Objects

Variables are bound to an underlying object with the `tie` function. The first argument to `tie` is the variable to be bound, and the second is the name of the object class, which will provide the functionality of the tied variable. Further arguments are passed to the constructor that is, in turn, used to create the object used to implement this particular variable, which is, of course, determined by the type of variable being tied. For example, to tie a scalar variable to a package called `My::Scalar::Tie` we could put:

```
$scalar;
tie $scalar, 'My::Scalar::Tie', 'initial value';
```

The `initial value` argument is passed to the constructor; in this case it is expected to be used to set up the scalar in some way, but that is up to the constructor. Similarly, to tie a hash variable, this time to a DBM module:

```
tie %dbm, 'GDBM_File', $filename, $flags, $perm;
```

The `GDBM_File` module implements access to DBM files created with the `gdbm` libraries. It needs to know the name of the file to open, plus, optionally, open flags and permissions (in exactly the same way that the `sysopen` function does). Given this, the module creates a new database object that contains an open filehandle for the actual database handle as class data. If we tie a second DBM database to a second variable, a second object instance is created, containing a filehandle for the second database. Of course, we only see the hash variable; all the work of reading and writing the database is handled for us by the DBM module (in this case `GDBM_File`).

The return value from `tie` is an object on success, or undef on failure:

```
$object = tie $scalar, 'My::Scalar::Tie', 'initial value';
```

We can store this object for later use, or alternatively (and more conveniently) we can get it from the tied variable using `tied`:

```
$object = tied $scalar;
```

Handling Errors from 'tie'

Many, though not all, tied object modules produce a fatal error if they cannot successfully carry out the `tie` (the database file does not exist, or we did not have permission to open it, for example). To catch this we therefore need to use `eval`. For example, this subroutine returns a reference to a tied hash on success, or undef on failure:

```
sub open_dbm {
    my $filename = shift;
    my %dbm;

    eval {tie %dbm, 'GDBM_File', $filename};
    if ($@) {
        print STDERR "Dang! Couldn't open $filename: $@";
        return undef;
    }

    return \%dbm;
}
```

This is not a property of `tie`, but rather a general programming point for handling any object constructor that can emit a fatal error, but it's worth mentioning here because it is easy to overlook.

Accessing Nested References

The special properties of a tied variable apply only to that variable; access to the internal values of a tied hash or array is triggered by our use of the tied variable itself. If we extract a reference from a tied hash or array, the returned value is likely to be a simple untied reference, and although attempts to manipulate it will work, we will really be handling a local copy of the data that the tied hash represents and not the data itself.

The upshot of this is that we must always access elements through the tied variable, and not via a reference. In other words, the following is fine:

```
$tied{'key'}{'subkey'}{'subsubkey1'} = "value1";
$tied{'key'}{'subkey'}{'subsubkey2'} = "value2";
$tied{'key'}{'subkey'}{'subsubkey3'} = "value3";
```

But this is probably not:

```
$subhash = $tied{'key'}{'subkey'};
$subhash->{'subsubkey1'} = "value1";
$subhash->{'subsubkey2'} = "value2";
$subhash->{'subsubkey3'} = "value3";
```

Although this appears to work, the extraction of the hash reference $subhash actually caused the tied variable to generate a local copy of the data that the hash represents. Our assignments to it therefore update the local copy, but do not have any effect whatsoever on the actual data that the tied hash controls access to.

Having said that we cannot use internal references, this is not absolutely the case. It is perfectly possible for the tied object class to return a newly tied hash that accesses the nested data we requested, in which case we can use the subreference with impunity, just like the main tied variable. However, this is a lot of effort to go to, and most tied object classes do not go to the lengths necessary to implement it.

Testing a Variable for 'tied'ness

The `tied` function returns the underlying object used to implement the features of the tied variable, or undef otherwise. The most frequent use for this is to test whether a `tie` succeeded. For example, here is another way to trap and test for a failed `tie`:

```
eval {tie %hash, My::Tied::Hash}
handle_error($@) unless tied %hash;
```

We can also call methods on the underlying object class through `tied`. For example, wrapping `tied` and an object method call into one statement:

```
(tied %hash)->object_method(@args);
```

Just because we can call an underlying method does not mean we should, though. If the tied object class documentation provides additional support methods (and most tied classes of any complexity do), calling these is fine. But calling the methods that implement the `tie` functionality itself is a bad idea. The whole point of the `tie` is to abstract these methods behind ordinary accesses to the variable; sidestepping this is therefore breaking the interface design.

'Untie'ing Objects

Tied objects consume system resources just like any other object, or indeed variable. When we are finished with a tied object we should dispose of it so that the object's destructor method, if any, can be called. In the case of the DBM modules this flushes any remaining output and closes the database filehandle.

In many instances, the only reference to the underlying object is the `tie` to the variable, so by undoing the `tie` between the variable and the object we cause Perl to invoke the garbage collector on the now unreferenced object. Appropriately enough, the function to do this is `untie`:

```
untie %hash;
```

`untie` always succeeds, unless the destructor emits a fatal error, in which case we need to trap it with `eval`. The fact it never returns a 'failed' result makes writing a test very easy:

```
handle_error($@) unless eval {untie %hash};
```

If we pass `untie` on a variable that is not tied, nothing happens, but `untie` still succeeds. However, if we want to check explicitly we can do so, for example:

```
untie %hash if tied %hash;
```

Writing Tied Objects

Tied object classes work by providing methods with predefined names for each operation that Perl requires for the data type of the variable being tied. For instance, for tied scalars, an object class needs to define a constructor method called `TIESCALAR`, plus the following additional methods:

Method	Description
FETCH	An accessor method that returns a scalar value.
STORE	A mutator method that stores a passed scalar value.
DESTROY	Optionally, a destructor for the object.

Scalars are the simplest class to tie because we can essentially only do two things to a scalar – read it, which is handled by the FETCH method, and write it, which is handled by the STORE method. We can also tie arrays, hashes, and filehandles if we define the appropriate methods.

Some methods are always mandatory; we always need a constructor for the class, with the correct name for the data type being tied. We also always need a FETCH method, to read from the object. Others are required only in certain circumstances. For instance, we do not need a STORE method if we want to create a read-only variable, but it is better to define one and place a croak in it, rather than have Perl stumble and emit a less helpful warning when an attempt to write to the object is made.

Standard Tie Object Classes

Creating the supporting methods for every required operation can be tedious, particularly for arrays, which require thirteen methods in a fully implemented object class.

Fortunately, Perl removes a lot of the grunt-work of creating tied object classes, by providing template object classes in the standard library that contain default methods which we can inherit from, or override with our own implementations. The default methods mostly just `croak` when they are not implemented, but each module also provides a minimal, but functional, `Std` object class that implements each data type as an object of the same type blessed and returned as a reference.

Module	Data Type
`Tie::Scalar`	Tied scalars.
`Tie::Array`	Tied arrays.
`Tie::Hash`	Tied hashes.
`Tie::Handle`	Tied handles (file, directory, socket, ...).

Module	Data Type
`Tie::StdScalar`	Minimal tied scalar class.
`Tie::StdArray`	Minimal tied array class.
`Tie::StdHash`	Minimal tied hash class.
`Tie::StdHandle`	Minimal tied handle class.

In addition, we can make use of two enhanced tied hash classes:

Module	Description
`Tie::RefHash`	Tied hashes that allow references to be used as the hash keys, overcoming the usual restriction of hash keys to static string values.
`Tie::SubstrHash`	Tied hashes that permit only a fixed maximum length for both keys and values, and, in addition to this, limit the total number of entries allowed in the hash.

Tied Object Methods

The methods we need to define for each data type vary, but loosely fall into the categories of constructor/destructor, accessor/mutator, function implementations, and specialized operations that apply to specific data types. All tied object classes need a constructor, and may implement a destructor. All types except filehandles may also (and usually should) define an accessor and mutator. Arrays, hashes, and filehandles also need to define methods for Perl's built-in functions that operate on those data types, for instance `pop`, `shift`, and `splice` for arrays, `delete`, and `exists` for hashes, and `print`, `readline`, and `close` for filehandles.

We are free to define our own methods in addition to the ones required by the `tie`, and can call them via the underlying object if we desire. We can also create additional class methods; the only one required (for all classes) is the constructor.

The standard library modules define default versions of all these methods, but we may choose to implement a tied object class without them, or even want to override them with our own methods. The following summaries list the methods required by each data type, along with a typical use of the tied variable that will trigger the method, and some brief explanations:

Methods and Uses for Scalars

Here are the creator/destructor methods for scalars:

Method	Use
TIESCALAR class, list	tie $scalar, Class::Name, @args;
DESTROY self	undef $scalar;

The accessor/mutator methods for scalars are as follows:

Method	Use
FETCH self	$value = $scalar;
STORE self, value	$scalar = $value;

Scalars are the simplest tied object class to implement. The constructor may take any arguments it likes, and the only other method that needs to handle an argument is STORE. Note that the constructor is the only method we call directly, so we cannot pass extra arguments to the other methods even if we wanted to, all information required must be conveyed by the object.

Methods and Uses for Arrays

Arrays require the same methods as scalars, but take an additional `index` argument for both FETCH and STORE. These are the creator/destructor methods for arrays:

Method	Use
TIEARRAY class, list	tie @array, Class::Name, @list;
DESTROY self	undef @array;

The accessor/mutator methods for arrays are:

Method	Use
FETCH self, index	$value = $array[$index];
STORE self, index, value	$array[$index] = $value;

We also need implementations for the push, pop, shift, unshift, and splice functions if we want to be able to use these functions on our tied arrays. The function implementation methods are as follows:

Method	Use
PUSH self, list	push @array, @list;
POP self	$value = pop @array;
SHIFT self	$value = shift @array;
UNSHIFT self, list	unshift @array, @list;
SPLICE self, offset, length, list	splice @array, $offset, $length, @list;

Finally, we need methods to handle the extension or truncation of the array. Unique to arrays are the EXTEND, FETCHSIZE, and STORESIZE methods, which implement implicit and explicit alterations the extent of the array; real arrays do this through $#array, as covered in Chapter 5. The extension/truncation methods for arrays are:

Method	Use
CLEAR self	@array = ();
EXTEND self, size	$array[$size] = $value;
FETCHSIZE self	$size = $#array;
STORESIZE self, size	$#array = $size;

Methods and Uses for Hashes

Hashes are more complex than arrays, but ironically are easier to implement. These are the creator/destructor methods for hashes:

Method	Use
TIEHASH class, list	tie %hash, Class::Name, @list;
DESTROY self	undef %hash;

Like arrays, the FETCH and STORE methods take an additional argument, this time of a key name. Here are the accessor/mutator methods for hashes:

Method	Use
FETCH self, key	$value = $hash{$key};
STORE self, key, value	$hash{$key} = $value;

The delete and exists functions are implemented through the DELETE and EXISTS methods. In addition, CLEAR is used for deleting all the elements from a hash. The defined function is implemented in terms of FETCH, so there is no DEFINED method. This is also why there is no EXISTS or DEFINED method for arrays or scalars, since both operations are equivalent to defined for anything except hashes. Here are the function implementation methods for hashes:

Method	Use
CLEAR self	%hash = ();
DELETE self, key	$done = delete $hash{$key};
EXISTS self, key	$exists = exists $hash{$key};

The FIRSTKEY and NEXTKEY methods need a little more explanation. Both methods are needed for the each keyword, which retrieves each key-value pair from a hash in turn. To do this, the class must define some form of iterator that stores the current position, so that the next key produces a meaningful result. This iterator should be reset when FIRSTKEY is called, and incremented when NEXTKEY is called. Both methods should return the appropriate key and value as a list. Finally, when there are no more key-value pairs to return, NEXTKEY should return undef. Here are the each iteration methods:

Method	Use
FIRSTKEY self	($key, $value) = each %hash; # first time
NEXTKEY self, lastkey	($key, $value) = each %hash; # second and subsequent times

Methods and uses for Filehandles

Filehandles are unique among tied variables because they define neither an accessor nor mutator method. Instead, the constructor makes available some kind of resource, typically with open, pipe, socket, or some other method that generates a real filehandle. The creator/destructor methods for filehandles are the following:

Method	Use
TIEHANDLE class, list	tie $fh, Class::Name, @args;
DESTROY self	undef $fh;

Whatever the creator method does, the CLOSE method needs to be defined to undo whatever it creates.

The only other methods required are for the standard filehandle functions: print, printf, and write for output and read, readline, and getc for input. If we are implementing a read-only or write-only filehandle we need only define the appropriate methods, of course.

Function Implementation method	Use
READ self, scalar, length, offset	read $fh, $in, $size, $from
READLINE self	$line = <$fh>
GETC self	$char = getc $fh
WRITE self, scalar, length, offset	write $fh, $out, $size, $from
PRINT self, list	print $fh @args
PRINTF self, format, list	printf $fh $format @values
CLOSE self	close $fh
DESTROY self	undef $fh

An Example Tied Hash Class

The tied hash class below demonstrates a basic use of the tied functionality provided by Perl by creating hashes that can have read, write, or delete access enabled or disabled. It defines methods for all the possible access types for a hash, and so does not need to use Tie::Hash. Despite this, it is very simple to understand.

The design follows a common theme for a lot of tied classes, where the actual data is stored as an element of a hash that represents the object, with other elements holding flags or values that configure how the real data is handled. This is a general template that works well for all manner of 'smart' scalars, arrays, hashes, and filehandles.

```perl
# Permission/Hash.pm
package Permission::Hash;
use strict;

use Carp;

sub TIEHASH {
    my ($class, %cfg) = @_;

    my $self = bless {}, shift;

    $self->{'value'} = ();
    foreach ('read', 'write', 'delete') {
        $self->{$_} = (defined $cfg{$_})?$cfg{$_}:1;
    }

    return $self;
}

sub FETCH {
    my ($self, $key) = @_;
    croak "Cannot read key '$key'" unless $self->{'read'};
    return $self->{'value'}{$key};
}
```

```perl
sub STORE {
    my ($self, $key, $value) = @_;
    croak "Cannot write key '$key'" unless $self->{'write'};
    $self->{'value'}{$key} = $value;
}

sub EXISTS {
    my ($self, $key) = @_;
    croak "Cannot read key '$key'" unless $self->{'read'};
    return exists $self->{'value'}{$key};
}

sub CLEAR {
    my $self = shift;
    croak "Cannot delete hash" unless $self->{'delete'};
    $self->{'value'} = ();
}

sub DELETE {
    my ($self, $key) = @_;
    croak "Cannot delete key '$key'" unless $self->{'delete'};
    return delete $self->{'value'}{$key};
}

sub FIRSTKEY {
    my $self = shift;
    my $dummy = keys %{$self->{'value'}};    #reset iterator
    return $self->NEXTKEY;
}

sub NEXTKEY {
    return each %{shift->{'value'}};
}

1;
```

Because we are creating a tied hash that controls access to a real hash, most of the methods are very simple. We are relaying the operation requested on the tied variable to the real variable inside. This class could be improved a lot, notably by adding proper accessor/mutator methods for the three flags. We could also add other permission types. A more interesting and complex example would be to set the flags on each key, rather than for the hash as a whole. Here is a short script that puts the Permission::Hash class through its paces:

```perl
#!/usr/bin/perl
# permhash.pl
use warnings;
use strict;

use Permission::Hash;

my %hash;
tie %hash, 'Permission::Hash', read => 1, write => 1, delete => 0;

$hash{'one'} = 1;
$hash{'two'} = 2;
$hash{'three'} =3 ;

print "Try to delete a key... \n";
unless (eval {delete $hash{'three'}; 1} ) {
    print $@;
    print "Let's try again... \n";
    (tied %hash)->{'delete'} = 1;
    delete $hash {'three'};
    print "It worked! \n";
```

```
      (tied %hash)->{'delete'} = 0;
   }

   print "Disable writing... \n";
   (tied %hash)->{'write'} = 0;
   unless (eval {$hash{'four'} = 4; 1} ) {
       print $@;
   }
   (tied %hash)->{'write'} = 1;

   print "Disable reading... \n";
   (tied %hash)->{'read'} = 0;
   unless (defined $hash{'one'}) {
       print $@;
   }
   (tied %hash)->{'read'} = 1;
```

When run this script should produce output resembling the following:

```
Try to delete a key...
Cannot delete key 'three' at permhash.pl line 12
Let's try again...
It worked!
Disable writing...
Cannot write key 'four' at permhash.pl line 23
Disable reading...
Cannot read key 'one' at permhash.pl line 30
```

Many other variants on this design can be easily implemented. In the case of hashes alone, we can easily create case-insensitive hashes (apply `lc` to all passed keys), accumulative hashes (make each value an array and append new values to the end in STORE), or restrict the number of keys (count the keys and check whether the key already exists in STORE, before creating a new one), or the names of the keys that can be assigned (pass a list of acceptable keys to the constructor, then check that any key passed to STORE is in that list).

An Example Class Using 'Tie::StdHash'

The standard `Tie` modules provide inheritable methods for all the required actions needed by each type of tied variable, but for the most part, these simply produce more informative error messages for methods we do not implement ourselves. However, each package comes with a `Std` object class that implements a minimal, but functional, tied object of the same class. Here is the implementation of `Tie::StdHash` defined inside the `Tie::Hash` module:

```
package Tie::StdHash;
@ISA = qw(Tie::Hash);

sub TIEHASH  {bless {}, $_[0]}
sub STORE    {$_[0]->{$_[1]} = $_[2]}
sub FETCH    {$_[0]->{$_[1]}}
sub FIRSTKEY {my $a = scalar keys %{$_[0]}; each %{$_[0]}}
sub NEXTKEY  {each %{$_[0]}}
sub EXISTS   {exists $_[0]->{$_[1]}}
sub DELETE   {delete $_[0]->{$_[1]}}
sub CLEAR    {%{$_[0]} = ()}

1;
```

We can use this object class to implement our own tied hash classes, as long as we are willing to accept the implementation of the object as a directly tied hash. As an example, here is a hash class that will limit either the total number of hash keys allowed, or restrict keys to one of a specific list provided when the object is initialized:

```perl
# Limit/Hash.pm
package Limit::Hash;
use strict;

use Carp;
use Tie::Hash;
our @ISA = qw(Tie::StdHash);

sub TIEHASH {
    my ($class, @keys) = @_;

    my $self = $class->SUPER::TIEHASH;
    croak "Must pass either limit or key list" if $#keys == -1;
    if ($#keys) {
        $self->{'_keys'} = {map {$_ => 1} @keys};
    } else {
        croak ",", $keys[0], "' is not a limit" unless int($keys[0]);
        $self->{'_limit'} = $keys[0]+1;    #add one for _limit
    }

    return $self;
}

sub FETCH {
    my ($self, $key) = @_;
    croak "Invalid key '$key'" if defined($self->{'_keys'}) and
    (!$self->{'_keys'}{$key} or $key =~ /^_/);
    return $self->SUPER::FETCH($key);
}

sub STORE {
    my ($self, $key, $value) = @_;
    croak "Invalid key '$key'" if defined($self->{'_keys'}) and
    (!$self->{'_keys'}{$key} or $key =~ /^_/);
    croak "Limit reached" if defined($self->{'_limit'}) and
    (!$self->{'_limit'} or $self->{'limit'} <= scalar(%{$self}));
    $self->SUPER::STORE($key, $value);
}

1;
```

The constructor works by examining the passed arguments and either establishing a limit, or a list of valid keys depending on what it was passed (we assume that establishing a single key is not an unlikely requirement). If a limit was passed, we add one to it to allow for the _limit key itself, which also resides in the hash. If no arguments are passed at all, we complain. Otherwise, we set up two special keys in the hash to hold the configuration.

The only other methods we override are FETCH and STORE. Each method checks that the key is valid, and prevents 'private' underscore prefixed keys from being set. If the key passes the check, we pass the request to the FETCH and STORE methods of Tie::StdHash, our parent.

Technically we do not need to pass the method request up to the parent object from our versions of TIEHASH, FETCH, and STORE since they are obvious implementations. However, it is good practice to use parent methods where possible, so we do it anyway.

```perl
# limithash.pl
#!/usr/bin/perl
use warnings;
use strict;

use Limit::Hash;

tie my %hash, 'Limit::Hash', 'this', 'that', 'other';

$hash{'this'} = 'this is ok';
$hash{'that'} = 'as is this';
print $hash{'this'}, "\n";
$hash{'invalid-key'} = 'but this croaks';
```

When run, this script should produce:

```
this is ok
Invalid key 'invalid-key' at limithash.pl line 13
```

Summary

In this chapter, we were introduced to objects, and concepts relating to objects. We saw how to create objects, and use them by:

- ❑ Accessing properties
- ❑ Calling class methods
- ❑ Calling object methods
- ❑ Nesting method calls

We then learned how to determine what inherited characteristics an object possesses, for example, its ancestry, capabilities, and version. After this, we saw how to write object classes; specifically we looked at constructors and choosing an underlying data type. As well as this, we looked at class, object, and multiple-context methods.

From here we discussed object and class data, which involved learning about accessors and mutators, along with inheriting and setting class data. Then we learned about class and object-level debugging, and implemented a multiplex debug strategy.

A large section was devoted to inheritance and subclassing, and the topics covered included:

- ❑ Inheriting from a parent class
- ❑ Writing inheritable classes
- ❑ Extending and redefining objects
- ❑ Multiple inheritance
- ❑ The UNIVERSAL constructor
- ❑ Autoloading methods

We also saw how to keep class and object data private, and discussed the ins-and-outs of destroying objects. We also saw that it is possible to overload conversion operators as well as normal ones, and that we can 'fall back' to unoverloaded operators if need be.

The final topics involved ties and tied objects, and in this section we saw how to use tied objects, including:

❑   Handling errors from `tie`

❑   Accessing nested references

❑   Testing a variable for `tiedness`

❑   `Untieing` objects

On top of this, we learned, among other things, how to write tied objects, and finished the chapter with an example of a tied hash class, and an example of a class using `Tie::StdHash`.

20

Inside Perl

In this chapter, we will look at how Perl actually works – the internals of the Perl interpreter. First, we will examine what happens when Perl is built, the configuration process and what we can learn about it. Next, we will go through the internal data types that Perl uses. This will help us when we are writing extensions to Perl. From there, we will get an overview of what goes on when Perl compiles and interprets a program. Finally, we will dive into the experimental world of the Perl compiler: what it is, what it does, and how we can write our own compiler tools with it. To get the most out of this chapter, it would be best advised for us to obtain a copy of the source code to Perl. Either of the two versions, stable or development, is fine and they can both be obtained from our local CPAN mirror.

Analyzing the Perl Binary – 'Config.pm'

If Perl has been built on our computer, the configuration stage will have asked us a number of questions about how we wanted to build it. For instance, one question would have been along the lines of building Perl with, or without threading. The configuration process will also have poked around the system, determining its capabilities. This information is stored in a file named `config.sh`, which the installation process encapsulates in the module `Config.pm`.

The idea behind this is that extensions to Perl can use this information when they are being built, but it also means that we as programmers, can examine the capabilities of the current Perl and determine whether or not we could take advantage of features such as threading provided by the Perl binary executing our code.

'perl -V'

The most common use of the Config module is actually made by Perl itself: `perl -V`, which produces a little report on the Perl binary. It is actually implemented as the following program:

```perl
#!/usr/bin/perl
# config.pl
use warnings;
use strict;

use Config qw(myconfig config_vars);

print myconfig();
$"="\n      ";
my @env = map {"$_=\"$ENV{$_}\""} sort grep {/^PERL/} keys %ENV;
print " \%ENV:\n @env\n" if @env;
print " \@INC:\n @INC\n";
```

When this script is run we will get something resembling the following, depending on the specification of the system of course:

> **perl config.pl**
Summary of my perl5 (revision 5.0 version 7 subversion 0) configuration:
  Platform:
    osname=linux, osvers=2.2.16, archname=i686–linux
    uname='linux deep–dark–truthful–mirror 2.4.0–test9 #1 sat oct 7 21:23:59 bst 2000 i686
    unknown '
    config_args='-d –Dusedevel'
    hint=recommended, useposix=true, d_sigaction=define
    usethreads=undef use5005threads=undef useithreads=undef usemultiplicity=undef
    useperlio=undef d_sfio=undef uselargefiles=define usesocks=undef
    use64bitint=undef use64bitall=undef uselongdouble=undef
  Compiler:
    cc='cc', ccflags ='–fno–strict–aliasing –I/usr/local/include –D_LARGEFILE_SOURCE –
D_FILE_OFFSET_BITS=64',
    optimize='-g',
    cppflags='-fno–strict–aliasing –I/usr/local/include'
    ccversion='', gccversion='2.95.2 20000220 (Debian GNU/Linux)', gccosandvers=''
    intsize=4, longsize=4, ptrsize=4, doublesize=8, byteorder=1234
    d_longlong=define, longlongsize=8, d_longdbl=define, longdblsize=12
    ivtype='long', ivsize=4, nvtype='double', nvsize=8, Off_t='off_t', lseeksize=8
    alignbytes=4, usemymalloc=n, prototype=define
  Linker and Libraries:
    ld='cc', ldflags =' –L/usr/local/lib'
    libpth=/usr/local/lib /lib /usr/lib
    libs=–lnsl –ldb –ldl –lm –lc –lcrypt –lutil
    perllibs=–lnsl –ldl –lm –lc –lcrypt –lutil
    libc=/lib/libc–2.1.94.so, so=so, useshrplib=false, libperl=libperl.a
  Dynamic Linking:
    dlsrc=dl_dlopen.xs, dlext=so, d_dlsymun=undef, ccdlflags='-rdynamic'
    cccdlflags='-fpic', lddlflags='-shared –L/usr/local/lib'
    @INC:

```
lib
/usr/local/lib/perl5/5.7.0/i686-linux
/usr/local/lib/perl5/5.7.0
/usr/local/lib/perl5/site_perl/5.7.0/i686-linux
/usr/local/lib/perl5/site_perl/5.7.0
/usr/local/lib/perl5/site_perl
```

How It Works

Most of the output is generated by the `myconfig` function in `Config`. It produces a list of the variables discovered by the `Configure` process when Perl was built. This is split up into four sections: **Platform, Compiler, Linker and Libraries**, and **Dynamic Linking**.

Platform

The first section, platform, tells us a little about the computer Perl was being built on, as well as some of the choices we made at compile time. This particular machine is running Linux 2.4.0-test9, and the arguments −d −Dusedevel were passed to `Configure` during the question and answer section. (We will see what these arguments do when we come to looking at how Perl is built.)

hint=recommended means that the configure program accepted the recommended hints for how a Linux system behaves. We built the `POSIX` module, and we have a `struct sigaction` in our C library.

Next comes a series of choices about the various flavors of Perl we can compile: usethreads is turned off, meaning this version of Perl has no threading support.

Perl has two types of threading support. See Chapters 1 and 22 for information regarding the old Perl 5.005 threads, which allow us to create and destroy threads in our Perl program, inside the Perl interpreter. This enables us to share data between threads, and lock variables and subroutines against being changed or entered by other threads. This is the use5.005threads option above.

The other model, which came with version 5.6.0, is called interpreter threads or **ithreads**. In this model, instead of having two threads sharing an interpreter, the interpreter itself is **cloned**, and each clone runs its own portion of the program. This means that, for instance, we can simulate `fork` on systems such as Windows, by cloning the interpreter and having each interpreter perform separate tasks. Interpreter threads are only really production quality on Win32 – on all other systems they are still experimental. Allowing multiple interpreters inside the same binary is called **multiplicity**.

The next two options refer to the IO subsystem. Perl can use an alternative input/output library called **sfio** (http://www.research.att.com/sw/tools/sfio) instead of the usual **stdio** if it is available. There is also a separate **PerlIO** being developed, which is specific to Perl. Next, there is support for files over 2Gb if our operating system supports them, and support for the `SOCKS` firewall proxy, although the core does not use this yet. Finally, there is a series of 64-bit and long double options.

Compiler

The compiler tells us about the C environment. Looking at the output, we are informed of the compiler we used and the flags we passed to it, the version of GCC used to compile Perl and the sizes of C's types and Perl's internal types. usemymalloc refers to the choice of Perl's supplied memory allocator rather than the default C one.

The next section is not very interesting, but it tells us what libraries we used to link Perl.

Linker and Libraries

The only thing of particular note in this section is useshrplib, which allows us to build Perl as a shared library. This is useful if we have a large number of embedded applications, and it means we get to impress our friends by having a 10K Perl binary. By placing the Perl interpreter code in a separate library, Perl and other programs that embed a Perl interpreter can be made a lot smaller, since they can share the code instead of each having to contain their own copy.

Dynamic Linking

When we use XS modules (for more information on XS see Chapter 21), Perl needs to get at the object code provided by the XS. This object code is placed into a shared library, which Perl dynamically loads at run time when the module is used. The dynamic linking section determines how this is done. There are a number of models that different operating systems have for dynamic linking, and Perl has to select the correct one here. dlsrc is the file that contains the source code to the chosen implementation. dlsymun tells us whether or not we have to add underlines to symbols dynamically loaded. This is because some systems use different naming conventions for functions loaded at run time, and Perl has to cater to each different convention.

The documentation to the Config contains explanations for these and other configure variables accessible from the module. It gets this documentation from **Porting/Glossary** in the Perl source kit.

What use is this? Well, for instance, we can tell if we have a threaded Perl or whether we have to use fork:

```
use Config;

if ($Config{usethreads} eq "define") {
    # we have threads.
    require MyApp::Threaded;
} else {
    # make do with forking
    require MyApp::Fork;
}
```

Note that Config gives us a hash, %Config, which contains all the configuration variables.

Under the Hood

Now it is time to really get to the deep material. Let us first look around the Perl source, before taking an overall look at the structure and workings of the Perl interpreter.

Around the Source Tree

The Perl source is composed of around 2190 files in 186 directories. To be really familiar with the source, we need to know where we can expect a part of it to be found, so it is worth taking some time to look at the important sections of the source tree. There are also several informational files in the root of the tree:

- ❏ Changes* – a very comprehensive list of every change that has been made to the Perl source since Perl 5.000

- ❏ Todo* – lists the changes that haven't been made yet – bugs to be fixed, ideas to try out, and so on

- ❏ MANIFEST – tells us what each file in the source tree does

- ❏ AUTHORS and MAINTAIN – tell us who is 'looking after' various parts of the source

- ❏ Copying and Artistic – the two licenses under which we receive Perl

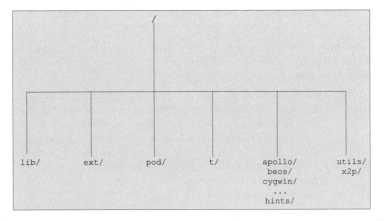

Documentation	The bulk of the Perl documentation lives in the pod/ directory. Platform-specific notes can be found as README.* in the root of the source tree.
Core modules	The standard library of modules shipped with Perl is distributed around two directories: pure-Perl modules that require no additional treatment are placed in lib/, and the XS modules are each given their own subdirectory in the ext/ directory.
Regression tests	When a change to Perl is made, the Perl developers will run a series of tests to ensure that this has not introduced any new bugs or reopened old ones; Perl will also encourage us to run the tests when we build a new Perl on our system. These regression tests are found in the t/ directory.
Platform–specific code	Some platforms require a certain amount of special treatment. They do not provide some system calls that Perl needs, for instance, or there is some difficulty in getting them to use the standard build process. (See Building Perl.) These platforms have their own subdirectories: apollo/, beos/, cygwin/, djgpp/, epoc/, mint/, mpeix/, os2/, plan9/, qnx/, vmesa/, vms/, vos/, and win32/. Additionally, the hints/ subdirectory contains a series of shell scripts, which communicate platform-specific information to the build process.
Utilities	Perl comes with a number of utilities scattered around. perldoc and the pod translators, s2p, find2perl, a2p, and so on. (There is a full list, with descriptions, in the perlutils documentation of Perl 5.7 and above.) These are usually kept in utils/ and x2p/, although the pod translators have escaped to pod/.

Table continued on following page

Helper Files	The root directory of the source tree contains several program files that are used to assist the installation of Perl, (installhtml, installman, installperl) some which help out during the build process (for instance, cflags, makedepend, and writemain) and some which are used to automate generating some of the source files. In this latter category, embed.pl is most notable, as it generates all the function prototypes for the Perl source, and creates the header files necessary for embedding Perl in other applications. It also extracts the API documentation embedded in the source code files.

Eagle-eyed readers may have noticed that we have left something out of that list – the core source to Perl itself! The files *.c and *.h in the root directory of the source tree make up the Perl binary, but we can also group them according to what they do:

Data Structures	A reasonable amount of the Perl source is devoted to managing the various data structures Perl requires, we will examine more about these structures in 'Internal Variable Types' later on. The files that manage these structures – av.c, av.h, cv.h, gv.c, gv.h, hv.c, hv.h, op.c, op.h, sv.c, and sv.h – also contain a wide range of helper functions, which makes it considerably easier to manipulate them. See perlapi for a taste of some of the functions and what they do.
Parsing	The next major functional group in the Perl source code is the part turns our Perl program into a machine-readable data structure. The files that take responsibility for this are toke.c and perly.y, the **lexer** and the **parser**.
PP Code	Once we have told Perl that we want to print 'hello world' and the parser has converted those instructions into a data structure, something actually has to implement the functionality. If we wonder where, for instance, the print statement is, we need to look at what is called the PP code. (PP stands for push-pop, for reasons will become apparent later). The PP code is split across four source files: pp_hot.c contains 'hot' code which is used very frequently, pp_sys.c contains operating-system-specific code, such as network functions or functions which deal with the system databases (getpwent and friends), pp_ctl.c takes care of control structures such as while, eval, and so on. pp.c implements everything else.
Miscellaneous	Finally, the remaining source files contain various utility functions to make the rest of the coding easier: utf8.c contains functions that manipulate data encoded in UTF8; malloc.c contains a memory management system; and util.c and handy.h contain some useful definitions for such things as string manipulation, locales, error messages, environment handling, and the like.

Building Perl

Perl builds on a mind-boggling array of different platforms, and so has to undergo a very rigorous configuration process to determine the characteristics of the system it is being built on.

There are two major systems for doing this kind of probing: the GNU project **autoconf** is used by the vast majority of free software, but Perl uses an earlier and less common system called **metaconfig**.

'metaconfig' Rather than 'autoconf'?

Porting /pumpkin.pod explains that both systems were equally useful, but the major reasons for choosing metaconfig are that it can generate interactive configuration programs. The user can override the defaults easily: autoconf, at the time, affected the licensing of software that used it, and metaconfig builds up its configuration programs using a collection of modular units. We can add our own units, and metaconfig will make sure that they are called in the right order.

The program Configure in the root of the Perl source tree is a UNIX shell script, which probes our system for various capabilities. The configuration in Windows is already done for us, and an NMAKE file can be found in the win32/ directory. On the vast majority of systems, we should be able to type ./Configure -d and then let Configure do its stuff. The -d option chooses sensible defaults instead prompting us for answers. If we're using a development version of the Perl sources, we'll have to say ./Configure -Dusedevel -d to let Configure know that we are serious about it. Configure asks if we are sure we want to use a development version, and the default answer chosen by -d is 'no'.- Dusedevel overrides this answer. We may also want to add the -DDEBUGGING flag to turn on special debugging options, if we are planning on looking seriously at how Perl works.

When we start running Configure, we should see something like this:

> **./Configure -d -Dusedevel**
Sources for perl5 found in "/home/simon/patchbay/perl".
Beginning of configuration questions for perl5.
Checking echo to see how to suppress newlines...
...using −n.
The star should be here—>*

First make sure the kit is complete:

Checking...

And eventually, after a few minutes, we should see this:

Creating config.sh...
If you'd like to make any changes to the config.sh file before I begin
to configure things, do it as a shell escape now (e.g. !vi config.sh).
Press return or use a shell escape to edit config.sh:

After pressing *return*, Configure creates the configuration files, and fixes the dependencies for the source files.

We then type make to begin the build process.

Perl builds itself in various stages. First, a Perl interpreter is built called `miniperl`; this is just like the eventual Perl interpreter, but it does not have any of the XS modules – notably, `DynaLoader` – built in to it. The `DynaLoader` module is special because it is responsible for coordinating the loading of all the other XS modules at run time; this is done through DLLs, shared libraries or the local equivalent on our platform. Since we cannot load modules dynamically without `DynaLoader`, it must be built in statically to Perl – if it was built as a DLL or shared library, what would load it? If there is no such dynamic loading system, all of the XS extensions much be linked statically into Perl.

`miniperl` then generates the `Config` module from the configuration files generated by `Configure`, and processes the XS files for the extensions that we have chosen to build; when this is done, `make` returns to the process of building them. The XS extensions that are being linked in statically, such as `DynaLoader`, are linked to create the final Perl binary.

Then the tools, such as the pod translators, `perldoc`, `perlbug`, `perlcc`, and so on, are generated, these must be created from templates to fill in the eventual path of the Perl binary when installed. The `sed-to-perl` and `awk-to-perl` translators are created, and then the manual pages are processed.

Once this is done, Perl is completely built and ready to be installed; the `installperl` program looks after installing the binary and the library files, and `installman` and `installhtml` install the documentation.

How Perl Works

Perl is a byte-compiled language, and Perl is a byte-compiling interpreter. This means that Perl, unlike the shell, does not execute each line of our program as it reads it. Rather, it reads in the entire file, compiles it into an internal representation, and then executes the instructions.

There are three major phases by which it does this: **parsing**, **compiling**, and **interpreting**.

Parsing

Strictly speaking, parsing is only a small part of what we are talking of here, but it is casually used to mean the process of reading and 'understanding' our program file. First, Perl must process the command-line options and open the program file.

It then shuttles extensively between two routines: `yylex` in `toke.c`, and `yyparse` in `perly.y`. The job of `yylex` is to split up the input into meaningful parts, (tokens) and determine what 'part of speech' each represents. `toke.c` is a notoriously fearsome piece of code, and it can sometimes be difficult to see how Perl is pulling out and identifying tokens; the lexer, `yylex`, is assisted by a **sublexer** (in the functions `S_sublex_start`, `S_sublex_push`, and `S_sublex_done`), which breaks apart double-quoted string constructions, and a number of scanning functions to find, for instance, the end of a string or a number.

Once this is completed, Perl has to try to work out how these 'parts of speech' form valid 'sentences'. It does this by means of grammar, telling it how various tokens can be combined into 'clauses'. This is much the same as it is in English: say we have an adjective and a noun – 'pink giraffes'. We could call that a 'noun phrase'. So, here is one rule in our grammar:

```
adjective + noun => noun phrase
```

We could then say:

```
adjective + noun phrase => noun phrase
```

This means that if we add another adjective – '**violent** pink giraffes' – we have still got a noun phrase. If we now add the rules:

```
noun phrase + verb + noun phrase => sentence
noun => noun phrase
```

We could understand that 'violent pink giraffes eat honey' is a sentence. Here is a diagram of what we have just done:

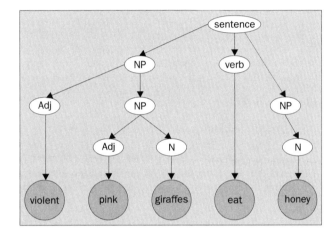

We have completely parsed the sentence, by combining the various components according to our grammar. We will notice that the diagram is in the form of a tree, this is usually called a **parse tree**. This explains how we started with the language we are parsing, and ended up at the highest level of our grammar.

We put the actual English words in filled circles, and we call them **terminal symbols**, because they are at the very bottom of the tree. Everything else is a non-terminal symbol.
We can write our grammar slightly differently:

```
s  : np v np
;
np : adj np
| adj n
| n
;
```

This is called 'Backhaus-Naur Form', or **BNF**; we have a target, a colon, and then several sequences of tokens, delimited by vertical bars, finished off by a semicolon. If we can see one of the sequences of things on the right-hand side of the colon, we can turn it into the thing on the left – this is known as a **reduction**.

The job of a parser is to completely reduce the input; if the input cannot be completely reduced, then a syntax error arises. Perl's parser is generated from BNF grammar in `perly.y`; here is an (abridged) excerpt from it:

```
loop    :   label WHILE '(' expr ')' mblock cont
        |   label UNTIL '(' expr ')' mblock cont
        |   label FOR MY my_scalar '(' expr ')' mblock cont
        |   ...
cont    :
        |   CONTINUE block
        ;
```

We can reduce any of the following into a `loop`:

❑   A label, the token `WHILE`, an open bracket, some expression, a close bracket, a block, and a continue block

❑   A label, the token `UNTIL`, an open bracket, some expression, a close bracket, a block, and a continue block

❑   A label, the tokens `FOR` and `MY`, a scalar, an open bracket, some expression, a close bracket, a block, and a continue block. (Or some other things we will not discuss here.)

And that a continue block can be either:

❑   The token `CONTINUE` and a block

❑   Empty

We will notice that the things that we expect to see in the Perl code – the terminal symbols – are in upper case, whereas the things that are purely constructs of the parser, like the noun phrases of our English example, are in lower case.

Armed with this grammar, and a lexer, which can split the text into tokens and turn them into non-terminals if necessary, Perl can 'understand' our program. We can learn more about parsing and the yacc parser generator in the book *Compilers: Principles, Techniques and Tools, ISBN 0-201100-88-6.*

Compiling

Every time Perl performs a reduction, it generates a line of code; this is as determined by the grammar in `perly.y`. For instance, when Perl sees two terms connected by a plus sign, it performs the following reduction, and generates the following line of code:

```
term | term ADDOP term
        {$$ = newBINOP($2, 0, scalar($1), scalar($3));}
```

Here, as before, we're turning the things on the right into the thing on the left. We take our term, an `ADDOP`, which is the terminal symbol for the addition operator, and another term, and we reduce those all into a term.

Now each term, or indeed, each symbol carries around some information with it. We need to ensure that none of this information is lost when we perform a reduction. In the line of code in braces above, `$1` is shorthand for the information carried around by the first thing on the right – that is, the first term. `$2` is shorthand for the information carried around by the second thing on the right – that is, the `ADDOP` and so on. `$$` is shorthand for the information that will be carried around by the thing on the left, after reduction.

newBINOP is a function that says 'Create a new binary op'. An **op** (short for operation) is a data structure, which represents a fundamental operation internal to Perl. It's the lowest–level thing that Perl can do, and every non–terminal symbol carries around one op. Why? Because every non–terminal symbol represents something that Perl has to do: fetching the value of a variable is an op; adding two things together is an op; performing a regular expression match is an op, and so on. There are some 351 ops in Perl 5.

A binary op is an op with two operands, just like the addition operator in Perl-space – we add the thing on the left to the thing on the right. Hence, along with the op, we have to store a link to our operands; if, for instance, we are trying to compile $a + $b, our data structure must end up looking like this:

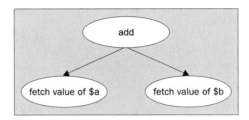

add is the type of binary op that we have created, and we must link this to the ops that fetch the values of $a and $b. So, to look back at our grammar:

```
term | term ADDOP term
        {$$ = newBINOP($2, 0, scalar($1), scalar($3));}
```

We have two 'terms' coming in, both of which will carry around an op with them, and we are producing a term, which needs an op to carry around with it. We create a new binary op to represent the addition, by calling the function newBINOP with the following arguments: $2, as we know, stands for the second thing on the right, ADDOP; newBINOP creates a variety of different ops, so we need to tell it which particular op we want – we need add, rather than subtract or divide or anything else. The next value, zero, is just a flag to say 'nothing special about this op'. Next, we have our two binary operands, which will be the ops carried around by the two terms. We call scalar on them to make them turn on a flag to denote scalar context.

As we reduce more and more, we connect more ops together: if we were to take the term we've just produced by compiling $a + $b and then use it as the left operand to ($a + $b) + $c, we would end up with an op looking like this:

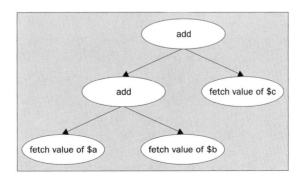

Eventually, the whole program is turned into a data structure made up of ops linking to ops: an op tree. Complex programs can be constructed from hundreds of ops, all connected to a single root; even a program like this:

```
while(<>) {
    next unless /^#/;
    print;
    $oklines++;
} print "TOTAL: $oklines\n";
```

Turns into an op tree like this:

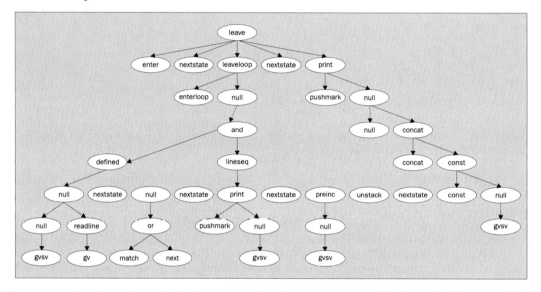

We can examine the op tree of a Perl program using the B::Terse module described later, or with the -Dx option to Perl if we told Configure we wanted to build a debugging Perl.

Interpreting

Once we have an op tree, what do we do with it? Having compiled the program into an op tree, the usual next stage is to do the ops. To make this possible, while creating the op tree, Perl has to keep track of the next op in the sequence to execute. So, running through the tree structure, there is an additional 'thread', like this:

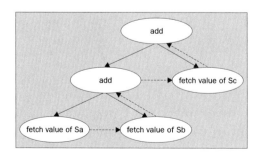

Executing a Perl program is just a matter of following this thread through the op tree, doing whatever instruction necessary at each point. In fact, the main code, which executes a Perl program is deceptively simple: it is the function run_ops_standard in run.c, and if we were to translate it into Perl, it would look a bit like this:

```
PERL_ASYNC_CHECK() while $op = &{$op->pp_function};
```

Each op contains a function reference, which does the work and returns the next op in the thread. Why does the op return the next one? Don't we already know that? Well, we usually do, but for some ops, like the one that implements if, the choice of what to do next has to happen at run time. PERL_ASYNC_CHECK is a function that tests for various things like signals that can occur asynchronously between ops.

The actual operations are implemented in PP code, the files pp*.c; we mentioned earlier that PP stands for push-pop, because the interpreter uses a stack to carry around data, and these functions spend a lot of time popping values off the stack or pushing values on. For instance, to execute $a = $b + $c the sequence of ops must look like this:

❑   Fetch $b and put it on the stack.
❑   Fetch $c and put it on the stack.
❑   Pop two values off the stack and add them, pushing the value.
❑   Fetch $a and put it on the stack.
❑   Pop a value and a variable off the stack and assign the value to the variable.

We can watch the execution of a program with the −Dt flag if we configured Perl with the −DEBUGGING option. We can also use −Ds and watch the contents of the stack.

And that is, very roughly, how Perl works: it first reads in our program and 'understands' it; second, it converts it into a data structure called an **op tree**; and finally, it runs over that op tree executing the fundamental operations.

There's one fly in the ointment: if we do an eval STRING, Perl cannot tell what the code to execute will be until run time. This means that the op that implements eval must call back to the parser to create a new op tree for the string and then execute that.

Internal Variable Types

Internally, Perl has to use its own variable types. Why? Well, consider the scalar variable $a in the following code:

```
$a = "15x";
$a += 1;
$a /= 3;
```

Is it a string, an integer, or a floating-point number? It is obviously all three at different times, depending on what we want to do with it, and Perl has to be able to access all three different representations of it. Worse, there is no 'type' in C that can represent all of the values at once. So, to get around these problems, all of the different representations are lumped into a single structure in the underlying C implementation: a **S**calar **V**ariable, or **SV**.

PVs

The simplest form of SV holds a structure representing a string value. Since we've already used the abbreviation SV, we have to call this a **PV**, a **P**ointer **V**alue. We can use the standard Devel::Peek module to examine a simple SV, (see the section 'Examining Raw Datatypes with Devel::Peek' later in the chapter for more detail on this module):

```
> perl -MDevel::Peek -e '$a = "A Simple Scalar"; Dump($a)'
SV = PV(0x813b564) at 0x8144ee4
  REFCNT = 1
  FLAGS = (POK,pPOK)
  PV = 0x81471a8 "A Simple Scalar"\0
  CUR = 15
  LEN = 16
```

What does this tell us? This SV is stored at memory location C<0x8144ee4>; the location can vary on different computers. The particular type of SV is a PV, which is itself a structure; that structure starts at location C<0x813b564>.

Next comes some housekeeping information about the SV itself: its reference count (the REFCNT field) tells us how many references exist to this SV. As we know from our Perl-level knowledge of references, once this drops to zero, the memory used by the SV is available for reallocation. The flags tell us, in this case, that it's OK to use this SV as a string right now; the POK means that the PV is valid. (In case we are wondering, the pPOK means that Perl itself can use the PV. We shouldn't take advantage of this – the little p stands for 'private'.)

The final three parts come from the PV structure itself: there's the pointer we talked about, which tells us that the string is located at 0x81471a8 in memory. Devel::Peek also prints out the string for us, to be extra helpful. Note that in C, but not in Perl, strings are terminated with \0 – character zero.

Since C thinks that character zero is the end of a string, this causes problems when we want to have character zero in the middle of the string. For this reason, the next field, CUR is the length of the string; this allows us to have a string like a\0b and still 'know' that it's three characters long and doesn't finish after the a.

The last field is LEN, the maximum length of the string that we have allocated memory for. Perl allocates more memory than it needs to, to allow room for expansion. If CUR gets too close to LEN, Perl will automatically reallocate a proportionally larger chunk of memory for us.

IVs

The second-simplest SV structure is one that contains the structures of a PV and an IV: an **Integer Value**. This structure is called a **PVIV**, and we can create one by performing string concatenation on an integer, like this:

```
> perl -MDevel::Peek -e '$a = 1; Dump($a); $a.="2"; Dump($a)'
SV = IV(0x8132fe4) at 0x8132214
  REFCNT = 1
  FLAGS = (IOK,pIOK)
  IV = 1
SV = PVIV(0x8128c30) at 0x8132204
  REFCNT = 1
```

```
FLAGS = (POK,pPOK)
IV = 1
PV = 0x8133e38 "12"\0
CUR = 2
LEN = 3
```

Notice how our SV starts as a simple structure with an IV field, representing the integer value of the variable. This value is 1, and the flags tell us that the IV is fine to use.

However, to use it as a string, we need a PV; rather than change its type to a PV, Perl changes it to a combination of IV and PV. Why? Well, if we had to change the structure of a variable every time we used it as an integer or a string, things would get very slow. Once we have upgraded the SV to a PVIV, we can very easily use it as PV or IV.

Similarly, Perl never downgrades an SV to a less complex structure, nor does it change between equally complex structures.

When Perl performs the string concatenation, it first converts the value to a PV – the C macro **SvPV** retrieves the PV of a SV, converting the current value to a PV and upgrading the SV if necessary. It then adds the 2 onto the end of the PV, automatically extending the memory allocated for it. Since the IV is now out of date, the IOK flag is unset and replaced by POK flags to indicate that the string value is valid.

On some systems, we can use unsigned (positive only) integers to get twice the range of the normal signed integers; these are implemented as a special type known as a UV.

NVs

The third and final (for our purposes) scalar type is an NV (Numeric Value), a floating-point value. The PVNV type includes the structures of a PV, an IV, and an NV, and we can create one just like our previous example:

```
> perl -MDevel::Peek -e '$a = 1; Dump($a); $a.="2"; Dump($a); $a += 0.5; Dump($a)'
SV = IV(0x80fac44) at 0x8104630
  REFCNT = 1
  FLAGS = (IOK,pIOK,IsUV)
  UV = 1
SV = PVIV(0x80f06f8) at 0x8104630
  REFCNT = 1
  FLAGS = (POK,pPOK)
  IV = 1
  PV = 0x80f3e08 "12"\0
  CUR = 2
  LEN = 3
SV = PVNV(0x80f0d68) at 0x8104630
  REFCNT = 1
  FLAGS = (NOK,pNOK)
  IV = 1
  NV = 12.5
  PV = 0x80f3e08 "12"\0
  CUR = 2
  LEN = 3
```

We should be able to see that this is very similar to what happened when we used an IV as a string: Perl had to upgrade to a more complex format, convert the current value to the desired type (an NV in this case), and set the flags appropriately.

Arrays and Hashes

We have seen how scalars are represented internally, but what about aggregates like arrays and hashes? These, too, are stored in special structures, although these are much more complex than the scalars.

Arrays are, as we might be able to guess, a series of scalars stored in a C array; they are called an **AV** internally. Perl takes care of making sure that the array is automatically extended when required so that new elements can be accommodated.

Hashes, or **HV**s, on the other hand, are stored by computing a special value for each key; this key is then used to reference a position in a hash table. For efficiency, the hash table is a combination of an array of linked lists, like this:

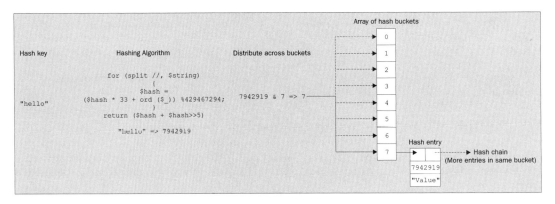

Thankfully, the interfaces to arrays and hashes are sufficiently well-defined by the Perl API that it's perfectly possible to get by without knowing exactly how Perl manipulates these structures.

Examining Raw Datatypes with 'Devel::Peek'

The Devel::Peek module provides us with the ability to examine Perl datatypes at a low level. It is analogous to the Dumpvalue module, but returns the full and gory details of the underlying Perl implementation. This is primarily useful in XS programming, the subject of Chapter 21 where Perl and C are being bound together and we need to examine the arguments passed by Perl code to C library functions.

For example, this is what Devel::Peek has to say about the literal number 6:

```
> perl -MDevel::Peek -e "Dump(6)"
SV = IV(0x80ffb48) at 0x80f6938
REFCNT = 1
FLAGS = (IOK,READONLY,pIOK,IsUV)
UV = 6
```

Other platforms may add some items to FLAGS, but this is nothing to be concerned about. NT may add PADBUSY and PADTMP, for example.

We also get a very similar result (with possibly varying memory address values) if we define a scalar variable and fill it with the value 6:

```
> perl -MDevel::Peek -e '$a=6; Dump($a)'
SV = IV(0x80ffb74) at 0x8109b9c
REFCNT = 1
FLAGS = (IOK,pIOK,IsUV)
UV = 6
```

This is because Devel::Peek is concerned about values, not variables. It makes no difference if the 6 is literal or stored in a variable, except that Perl knows that the literal value cannot be assigned to and so is READONLY.

Reading the output of Devel::Peek takes a little concentration but is not ultimately too hard, once the abbreviations are deciphered:

❑ SV means that this is a scalar value.

❑ IV means that it is an integer.

❑ REFCNT=1 means that there is only one reference to this value (the count is used by Perl's garbage collection to clear away unused data).

❑ IOK and pIOK mean this scalar has a defined integer value (it would be POK for a string value, or ROK if the scalar was a reference).

❑ READONLY means that it may not be assigned to. Literal values have this set whereas variables do not.

❑ IsUV means that it is an unsigned integer and that its value is being stored in the unsigned integer slot UV rather than the IV slot, which indeed it is.

The UV slot is for unsigned integers, which can be twice as big as signed ones for any given size of integer (for example, 32 bit) since they do not use the top bit for a sign. Contrast this to −6, which defines an IV slot and doesn't have the UV flag set:

```
SV = IV(0x80ffb4c) at 0x80f6968
REFCNT = 1
FLAGS = (IOK,READONLY,pIOK)
IV = −6
```

The Dump subroutine handles scalar values only, but if the value supplied to Dump happens to be an array or hash reference, then each element will be dumped out in turn. A second optional count argument may be supplied to limit the number of elements dumped. For list values (that is lists, arrays, or hashes) we need to use DumpArray, which takes a count and a list of values to dump. Each of these values is of course scalar (even if it is a reference), but DumpArray will recurse into array and hash references:

```
> perl -MDevel::Peek -e '@a=(1,[2,sub {3}]); DumpArray(2, @a)'
```

This array has two elements, so we supply 2 as the first argument to DumpArray. We could of course also have supplied a literal list of two scalars, or an array with more elements (in which case only the first two would be dumped).

The example above produces the following output, where the outer array of an IV (index no. 0) and an RV (reference value, index no. 1) can be clearly seen, with an inner array inside the RV of element 1 containing a PV (string value) with the value two and another RV. Since this one is a code reference, DumpArray cannot analyze it any further. At each stage the IOK, POK, or ROK (valid reference) flags are set to indicate that the scalar SV contains a valid value of that type:

```
Elt No. 0  0x811474c
SV = IV(0x80ffb74) at 0x811474c
  REFCNT = 1
  FLAGS = (IOK,pIOK,IsUV)
  UV = 1
Elt No. 1  0x8114758
SV = RV(0x810acbc) at 0x8114758
  REFCNT = 1
  FLAGS = (ROK)
  RV = 0x80f69a4
  SV = PVAV(0x81133b0) at 0x80f69a4
    REFCNT = 1
    FLAGS = ()
    IV = 0
    NV = 0
    ARRAY = 0x81030b0
    FILL - 1
    MAX = 1
    ARYLEN = 0x0
    FLAGS = (REAL)
    Elt No. 0
    SV = PV(0x80f6b74) at 0x80f67b8
      REFCNT = 1
      FLAGS = (POK,pPOK)
      PV = 0x80fa6d0 "two"\0
      CUR = 3
      LEN = 4
    Elt No. 1
    SV = RV(0x810acb4) at 0x80fdd24
      REFCNT = 1
      FLAGS = (ROK)
      RV = 0x81077d8
```

We mentioned earlier in the chapter how Perl can hold both a string and an integer value for the same variable. With Devel::Peek we can see how:

> **perl -MDevel::Peek -e '$a="2701"; $a*1; Dump($a)'**

Or on Windows:

> **perl -mDevel::Peek -e "$a=q(2701); $a*1; Dump($a)"**

This creates a variable containing a string value, then uses it (redundantly, since we do not use the result) in a numeric context and then dumps it. This time the variable has both PV and NV (floating-point) values, and the corresponding POK and NOK flags set:

```
SV = PVNV(0x80f7648) at 0x8109b84
  REFCNT = 1
  FLAGS = (NOK,POK,pNOK,pPOK)
  IV = 0
  NV = 2701
  PV = 0x81022e0 "2701"\0
  CUR = 4
  LEN = 5
```

It is interesting to see that Perl actually produced a floating-point value here and not an integer – a window into Perl's inner processes. As a final example, if we reassign $a in the process of converting it, we can see that we get more than one value stored, but only one is legal:

> **perl -MDevel::Peek -e '$a="2701"; $a=int($a); Dump($a)'**

This produces:

```
SV = PVNV(0x80f7630) at 0x8109b8c
  REFCNT = 1
  FLAGS = (IOK,pIOK)
  IV = 2701
  NV = 2701
  PV = 0x81022e8 "2701"\0
  CUR = 4
  LEN = 5
```

The int subroutine is used to reassign $a an integer value. As we can see from the results of the dump, Perl actually converted the value from a string into a floating point NV value before assigning an integer IV to it. Because the assignment gives the variable a new value (even if it is equal to the string), only the IOK flag is now set.

These are the main features of Devel::Peek from an analysis point of view. Of course in reality we would not be using it from the command line but to analyze values inside Perl code. Here we have just used it to satisfy our curiosity and understand the workings of Perl a little better.

If we have a Perl interpreter combined with DEBUGGING_MSTATS we can also make use of the mstat subroutine to output details of memory usage. Unless we built Perl specially to do this, however, it is unlikelyto be present, and so this feature is not usually available.

Devel::Peek also contains advanced features to edit the reference counts on scalar values. This is not a recommended thing to do even in unusual circumstances, so we will not do more than mention that it is possible here. We can see perldoc Devel::Peek for information if absolutely necessary.

The Perl Compiler

The Perl Compiler suite is an oft-misunderstood piece of software. It allows us to perform various manipulations of the op tree of a Perl program, including converting it to C or bytecode. People expect that if they use it to compile their Perl to stand-alone executables, it will make their code magically run faster, when in fact, usually the opposite occurs. Now we know a little about how Perl works internally, we can determine why this is the case.

In the normal course of events, Perl parses our code, generates an op tree, and then executes it. When the compiler is used, Perl stops before executing the op tree and executes some other code instead, code provided by the compiler. The interface to the compiler is through the O module, which simply stops Perl after it has compiled our code, and then executes one of the 'compiler backend' modules, which manipulate the op tree. There are several different compiler back-ends, all of which live in the 'B::' module hierarchy, and they perform different sorts of manipulations: some perform code analysis, while others convert the op tree to different forms, such as C or Java VM assembler.

The 'O' Module

How does the O module prevent Perl from executing our program? The answer is by using a CHECK block. As we learnt in Chapter 10, Perl has several special blocks that are automatically called at various points in our program's lifetime: BEGIN blocks are called before compilation, END blocks are called when our program finishes, INIT blocks are run just before execution, and CHECK blocks are run after compilation.

```perl
sub import {
    ($class, $backend, @options) = @_;
    eval "use B::$backend ()";
    if ($@) {
        croak "use of backend $backend failed: $@";
    }
    $compilesub = &{"B::${backend}::compile"}(@options);
    if (ref($compilesub) eq "CODE") {
        minus_c;
        save_BEGINs;
        eval 'CHECK {&$compilesub()}';
    } else {
        die $compilesub;
    }
}
```

The 'B' Module

The strength of these compiler back-ends comes from the B module, which allows Perl to get at the C-level data structure which makes up the op tree; now we can explore the tree from Perl code, examining both SV structures, and OP structures.

For instance, the function B::main_start returns an object, which represents the first op in the tree that Perl will execute. We can then call methods on this object to examine its data:

```perl
use B qw(main_start class);

CHECK {
    $x= main_start;
    print "The starting op is in class ", class($x), " and is of type:
        ", $x->ppaddr, "\n";
    $y = $x -> next;
    print "The next op after that is in class ", class($y), " and is of type
        ", $y->ppaddr, "\n";
};
print "This is my program";
```

The class function tells us what type of object we have, and the ppaddr method tells us which part of the PP code this op will execute. Since the PP code is the part that actually implements the op, this method tells us what the op does. For instance:

The starting op is in class OP and is of type: PL_ppaddr[OP_ENTER]
The next op after that is in class COP and is of type: PL_ppaddr[OP_NEXTSTATE]
This is my program

This tells us we have an ENTER op followed by a NEXTSTATE op. We could even set up a little loop to keep looking at the next op in the sequence:

```
use B qw(main_start class);

CHECK {
    $x= main_start;
    print "The starting op is in class ", class($x), " and is of type:
        ", $x->ppaddr, "\n";
    while ($x = $x->next and $x->can("ppaddr")) {
        print "The next op after that is in class ",class($x),
            " and is of type ", $x->ppaddr, "\n";
    }
};
print "This is my program";
```

This will list all the operations involved in the one-line program print This is my program:

The starting op is in class OP and is of type: PL_ppaddr[OP_ENTER]
The next op after that is in class COP and is of type PL_ppaddr[OP_NEXTSTATE]
The next op after that is in class OP and is of type PL_ppaddr[OP_PUSHMARK]
The next op after that is in class SVOP and is of type PL_ppaddr[OP_CONST]
The next op after that is in class LISTOP and is of type PL_ppaddr[OP_PRINT]
The next op after that is in class LISTOP and is of type PL_ppaddr[OP_LEAVE]
This is my program

Since looking at each operation in turn is a particularly common thing to do when building compilers, the B module provides methods to 'walk' the op tree. The walkoptree_slow starts a given op and performs a breadth-first traversal of the op tree, calling a method of our choice on each op. Whereas walkoptree_exec does the same, but works through the tree in execution order, using the next method to move through the tree, similar to our example programs above.

To make these work, we must provide the method in each relevant class by defining the relevant subroutines:

```
use B qw(main_start class walkoptree_exec);
CHECK {
    walkoptree_exec(main_start, "test");
    sub B::OP::test {
        $x = shift;
        print "This op is in class ", class($x), " and is of type:
            ", $x->ppaddr, "\n";
    }
};
print "This is my program";
```

The 'B::' Family of Modules

Now let us see how we can use the O module as a front end to some of the modules, which use the B module.

We have seen some of the modules in this family already, but now we will take a look at all of the B:: modules in the core and on CPAN.

'B::Terse'

The job of B::Terse is to walk the op tree of a program, printing out information about each op. In a sense, this is very similar to the programs we have just built ourselves.

Let us see what happens if we run B::Terse on a very simple program:

```
> perl -MO=Terse -e '$a = $b + $c'
LISTOP (0x8178b90) leave
  OP (0x8178bb8) enter
  COP (0x8178b58) nextstate
  BINOP (0x8178b30) sassign
    BINOP (0x8178b08) add [1]
      UNOP (0x81789e8) null [15]
        SVOP (0x80fbed0) gvsv  GV (0x80fa098) *b
      UNOP (0x8178ae8) null [15]
        SVOP (0x8178a08) gvsv  GV (0x80f0070) *c
    UNOP (0x816b4b0) null [15]
      SVOP (0x816dd40) gvsv  GV (0x80fa02c) *a
-e syntax OK
```

This shows us a tree of the operations, giving the type, memory address and name of each operator. Children of an op are indented from their parent: for instance, in this case, the ops enter, nextstate, and sassign are the children of the list operator leave, and the ops add and the final null are children of sassign.

The information in square brackets is the contents of the targ field of the op; this is used both to show where the result of a calculation should be stored and, in the case of a null op, what the op used to be before it was optimized away: if we look up the 15th op in opcode.h, we can see that these ops used to be rv2sv – turning a reference into an SV.

Again, just like the programs we wrote above, we can also walk over the tree in execution order by passing the exec parameter to the compiler:

```
> perl -MO=Terse,exec -e '$a = $b + $c'
OP (0x80fcf30) enter
COP (0x80fced0) nextstate
SVOP (0x80fc1d0) gvsv  GV (0x80fa094) *b
SVOP (0x80fcda0) gvsv  GV (0x80f0070) *c
BINOP (0x80fce80) add [1]
SVOP (0x816b980) gvsv  GV (0x80fa028) *a
BINOP (0x80fcea8) sassign
LISTOP (0x80fcf08) leave
-e syntax OK
```

Different numbers in the parenthesis or a different order to that shown above may be returned as this is dependent on the version of Perl. This provides us with much the same information, but re-ordered so that we can see how the interpreter will execute the code.

'B::Debug'

B::Terse provides us with minimal information about the ops; basically, just enough for us to understand what's going on. The B::Debug module, on the other hand, tells us everything possible about the ops in the op tree and the variables in the stashes. It is useful for hard-core Perl hackers trying to understand something about the internals, but it can be quite overwhelming at first sight:

```
> perl -MO=Debug -e '$a = $b + $c'
LISTOP (0x8183c30)
    op_next          0x0
    op_sibling       0x0
    op_ppaddr        PL_ppaddr[OP_LEAVE]
    op_targ          0
    op_type          178
    op_seq           6437
    op_flags         13
    op_private       64
    op_first         0x8183c58
    op_last          0x81933c8
    op_children      3
OP (0x8183c58)
    op_next          0x8183bf8
    op_sibling       0x8183bf8
    op_ppaddr        PL_ppaddr[OP_ENTER]
    op_targ          0
    op_type          177
    op_seq           6430
    op_flags         0
    op_private       0
...
-e syntax OK
```

Here's a slightly more involved cross-reference report from the debug closure example debug.pl, which we have already encountered in Chapter 17:

```
#!/usr/bin/perl
# debug.pl
use warnings;
use strict;

# define a debugging infrastructure
{
    my $debug_level = $ENV{'DEBUG'};
    $debug_level| = 0;

    # return and optionally set debug level
    sub debug_level {
        my $old_level = $debug_level;
        $debug_level = $_[0] if @_;
        return $old_level;
    }
}
```

```
    # print debug message or set debug level
    sub debug {
        # remove first argument, if present
        my $level = shift;

        # @_ will contain more elements if 2+ arguments passed
        if (@_) {
            # 2+ argument calls print debug message if permitted
            print STDERR @_, "\n" if $level <= debug_level();
        } else {
            # one and no-argument calls set level
            debug_level($level?$level:1);
        }
    }
}

# set debugging level explicitly
debug_level(1);

# send some debug messages
debug 1, "This is a level 1 debug message";
debug 2, "This is a level 2 debug message (unseen)";

# change debug level with single argument 'debug'
debug 2;
debug 2, "This is a level 2 debug message (seen)";

# return debugging level programmatically
debug 0, "Debug level is: ", debug_level;

# set debug level to 1 with no argument 'debug'
debug;
debug 0, "Debug level now: ", debug_level;
```

Below is the command and the output that is produced:

```
> perl -MO=Xref debug.pl
  File debug.pl
    Subroutine (definitions)
      Package UNIVERSAL
        &VERSION          s0
        &can              s0
        &isa              s0
      Package attributes
        &bootstrap        s0
      Package main
        &debug            s27
        &debug_level      s12
    Subroutine (main)
      Package (lexical)
        $debug_level      i6
      Package main
        %ENV              6
        &debug            &34, &35, &38, &39, &42, &45, &46
        &debug_level      &31, &42, &46
    Subroutine debug
```

```
        Package (lexical)
           $level                i17, 20, 25, 25
        Package main
           &debug_level          &20, &25
           *STDERR               20
           @_                    17, 20, 20
     Subroutine debug_level
        Package (lexical)
           $debug_level          10, 11
        Package main
           @_                    10
     debug.pl syntax OK
```

Subroutine (definitions) details all the subroutines defined in each package found, note the debug and debug_level subroutines in package main. The numbers following indicate that these are subroutine definitions (prefix s) and are defined on lines 12 (debug_level) and 27 (debug), which is indeed where those subroutine definitions end.

Similarly, we can see that in package main the debug_level subroutine is called at lines 31, 42, and 46, and within debug it is called at lines 20 and 25. We can also see that the scalar $debug_level is initialized (prefix i) on line 6, and is used only within the debug_level subroutine, on lines 10 and 11. This is a useful result, because it shows us that the variable is not being accessed from anywhere that it is not supposed to be.

Similar analysis of other variables and subroutines can provide us with similar information, allowing us to track down and eliminate unwanted accesses between packages and subroutines, while highlighting areas where interfaces need to be tightened up, or visibility of variables and values reduced.

'B::Deparse'

As its name implies, the B::Deparse module attempts to 'un-parse' a program. If parsing is going from Perl text to an op tree, deparsing must be going from an op tree back into Perl. This may not look too impressive at first sight:

```
> perl -MO=Deparse -e '$a = $b + $c'
$a = $b + $c;
-e syntax OK
```

It can be extremely useful for telling us how Perl sees certain constructions. For instance, we can show that && and if are almost equivalent internally:

```
> perl -MO=Deparse -e '($a == $b or $c) && print "hi";'
print 'hi' if $a == $b or $c;
-e syntax OK
```

We can also understand the strange magic of while(<>) and the −n and −p flags to Perl:

```
> perl -MO=Deparse -e 'while(<>){print}'
while (defined($_ = <ARGV>)) {
    print $_;
}
-e syntax OK
```

```
> perl -MO=Deparse -pe 1
LINE: while (defined($_ = <ARGV>)) {
  '???';
}
continue {
  print $_;
}
-e syntax OK
```

The '???' represents a useless use of a constant – in our case, 1, which was then optimized away.

The most interesting use of this module is as a 'beautifier' for Perl code. In some cases, it can even help in converting obfuscated Perl to less-obfuscated Perl. Consider this little program, named `strip.pl`, which obviously does not follow good coding style:

```
($text=shift)||die "$0: missing argument!\n";for
(@ARGV){s-$text--g;print;if(length){print "\n"}}
```

`B::Deparse` converts it to this, a much more readable, form:

```
> perl -MO=Deparse strip.pl
  die "$0: missing argument!\n" unless $text = shift @ARGV;
  foreach $_ (@ARGV) {
    s/$text//g;
    print $_;
    if (length $_) {
      print "\n";
    }
  }
```

`B::Deparse` also have several options to control its output. For example, `-p` to add parentheses even where they are optional, or `-l` to include line numbers from the original script. These options are documented in the pod documentation included with the module.

'B::C'

One of the most sought-after Perl compiler backends is something that turns Perl code into C. In a sense, that's what `B::C` does – but only in a sense. There is not currently a translator from Perl to C, but there is a compiler. What this module does is writes a C program that reconstructs the op tree. Why is this useful? If we then embed a Perl interpreter to run that program, we can create a stand-alone binary that can execute our Perl code.

Of course, since we're using a built-in Perl interpreter, this is not necessarily going to be any faster than simply using Perl. In fact, it might well be slower and, because it contains an op tree and a Perl interpreter, we will end up with a large binary that is bigger than our Perl binary itself.

However, it is conceivably useful if we want to distribute programs to people who cannot or do not want to install Perl on their computers. (It is far more useful for everyone to install Perl, of course...)

Instead of using `perl -MO=C`, the `perlcc` program acts as a front-end to both the `B::C` module and our C compiler; it was recently re-written, so there are two possible syntaxes:

If we're using 5.6.0, we can say:

> **perlcc hello.pl**

To create a binary called `hello` with 5.7.0 or 5.6.1 and above, the syntax and behavior is much more like the C compiler:

> **perlcc –o hello hello.pl**

Do not believe that the resulting C code would be readable, by the way; it truly does just create an op tree manually. Here is a fragment of the source generated from the famous 'Hello World' program;

```
static OP op_list[2] = {
  { (OP*)&cop_list[0], (OP*)&cop_list[0], NULL, 0, 177, 65535, 0x0, 0x0 },
  { (OP*)&svop_list[0], (OP*)&svop_list[0], NULL, 0, 3, 65535, 0x2, 0x0 },
};
static LISTOP listop_list[2] = {
  { 0, 0, NULL, 0, 178, 65535, 0xd, 0x40, &op_list[0], (OP*)&listop_list[1], 3 },
  { (OP*)&listop_list[0], 0, NULL, 0, 209, 65535, 0x5, 0x0,&op_list[1], (OP*)&svop_list[0], 1 },
};
```

And there are another 1035 lines of C code just like that. Adding the –S option to `perlcc` will leave the C code available for inspection after the compiler has finished.

'B::CC'

To attempt to bridge the gap between this and 'real' C, there is the highly experimental 'optimized' C compiler backend, B::CC. This does very much the same thing, but instead of creating the op tree, it sets up the environment for the interpreter and manually executes each PP operation in turn, by setting up the arguments on the stack and calling the relevant op.

For instance, the main function from 'Hello, World' will contain some code a little like this:

```
lab_8135840:
  PL_op = &op_list[1];
  DOOP(PL_ppaddr[OP_ENTER]);
  TAINT_NOT;
  sp = PL_stack_base + cxstack[cxstack_ix].blk_oldsp;
  FREETMPS;
lab_82e7ef0:
  PUSHMARK(sp);
  EXTEND(sp, 1);
  PUSHs((SV*)&sv_list[3]);
  PL_op = (OP*)&listop_list[0];
  DOOP(PL_ppaddr[OP_PRINT]);
lab_81bca58:
  PL_op = (OP*)&listop_list[1];
  DOOP(PL_ppaddr[OP_LEAVE]);
  PUTBACK;
  return PL_op;
```

We should be able to see that the code after the first label picks up the first op, puts it into the PL_op variable and calls OP_ENTER. After the next label, the argument stack is extended and an SV is grabbed from the list of pre-constructed SVs. (This will be the PV that says 'Hello, world') This is put on the stack, the first list operator is loaded (that will be print), and OP_PRINT is called. Finally, the next list operator, leave is loaded and OP_LEAVE is called. This is, in a sense, emulating what is going on in the main loop of the Perl interpreter, and so could conceivably be faster than running the program through Perl.

However, the B::C and B::CC modules are still very experimental; the ordinary B::C module is not guaranteed to work but very probably will, whereas the B::CC module is not guaranteed to fail but almost certainly will.

'B::Bytecode'

Our next module, B::Bytecode, turns the op tree into machine code for an imaginary processor. This is not dissimilar to the idea of Java bytecode, where Java code is compiled into machine code for an idealized machine. And, in fact, the B::JVM::Jasmin module discussed below can compile Perl to JVM bytecode. However, unlike Java, there are no software emulations of such a Perl 'virtual machine' (although see http://www.xray.mpe.mpg.de/mailing–lists/perl5–porters/2000–04/msg00436.html for the beginnings of one).

Bytecode is, to put it simply, the binary representation of a program compiled by Perl. Using the B::Bytecode module this binary data is saved to a file. Then, using the ByteLoader module, it is read in memory and executed by Perl.

Getting back to the source code of a byte-compiled script is not simple but not impossible, as in the previous case. There is even a disassembler module, as we'll see below, but it does not produce Perl code. Someone with a very good knowledge of the Perl internals could understand from here what the program does, but not everybody.

The execution speed is just the same as normal Perl, and here too, only the time of reading the script file and parsing it is cut off. In this case, however, there's the additional overhead of reading the bytecode itself, and the ByteLoader module too. So, an overall speed increase can be obtained only on very large programs, whose parsing time would be high enough to justify the effort.

We may ask, how does this magic take place? How does Perl run the binary data as if it was a normal script?

The answer is that the ByteLoader module is pure magic: it installs a 'filter' that lets Perl understand a sequence of bytes in place of Perl code. In Chapter 21 we'll introduce filters and their usage.

Using the bytecode compiler without the perlcc tool (if we're running an older version of Perl, for example) is fairly trivial. The O compiler frontend module can be used for this:

> **perl -MO=Bytecode hello.pl > hello.plc**

To run the bytecode produced, we need to specify the ByteLoader module on the command line, because the file generated this way does not contain the two header lines that perlcc adds for us:

> **perl -MByteLoader hello.plc**

An op tree stored as Perl bytecode can be loaded back into Perl using the `Byteloader` module; `perlcc` can also compile programs to bytecode by saying:

> perlcc -b -o hello.plc hello.pl

The output will be a Perl program, which begins something like:

```
#!/usr/bin/perl
use ByteLoader 0.04;
```

This is then followed by the binary bytecode output.

'B::Disassembler'

The Perl bytecode produced can be 'disassembled' using the `disassemble` tool, placed in the `B` directory under the Perl `lib` path.

The output of this program is a sort of 'Perl Assembler' (thus the name): a set of basic instructions that describe the low level working of the Perl interpreter.

It is very unlikely that someone will find this Assembler-like language comfortable (that's the reason why high-level languages were invented, after all). However, if we already have a good knowledge of the Perl internals, the disassembled code can provide many useful insights about the way Perl works.

The disassemble script is just a front-end for the `B::Disassembler` module, which does all the work. To convert from bytecode to assembler we can use this command line:

> perl disassemble hello.plc

The output, as we can expect if we have some experience with 'regular' Assembler, is very verbose. Our simple 'hello world' script generates 128 lines of output, for a single Perl instruction! Once the bytecode has been disassembled, it can also be regenerated using the opposite `assemble` program:

> perl disassemble hello.plc > hello.S
> perl assemble hello.S > hello.plc

This could be used, for example, to convert bytecode from one Perl version to another. The intermediate assembler should be understood by the two versions, while the binary format can change.

'B::Lint'

Like the `lint` utility for C files, this module acts as a basic 'style checker', looking for various things which may indicate problems. We can select from a variety of checks, by passing a list of the names of the tests to O as follows:

> perl -MO=Lint,context,undefined-subs program.pl

This will turn on the `context` and `undefined-subs` checks. The checks are:

Check Type	Description

context	Warns whenever an array is used in a scalar context, without the explicit scalar operator. For instance:
	
	`$count = @array;`
	
	will give a warning, but:
	
	`$count = scalar @array;`
	
	will not.

implicit-read	Warns whenever a special variable is read from implicitly; for instance: `if(/test/) {...}` is an implicit match against $_.
implicit-write	Warns whenever a special variable will be written to implicitly: `s/one/two/` both reads from and writes to $_, and thus causes an warning in both the above categories.
dollar-underscore	Warns whenever $_ is used explicitly or implicitly.
private-names	Warns when a variable name is invoked which starts with an underscore, such $_self; these variable names are, by convention, private to some module or package.
undefined-subs	Warns when a subroutine is directly invoked but not defined; this will not catch subroutines indirectly invoked, such as through subroutine references which may be empty.
regexp-variables	The regular expression special variables $`, $', and $& slow our program down; once Perl notices one of them in our program, it must keep track of their value at all times. This check will warn if the regular expression special variables are used.
all	Turns on all of the above checks.

For instance, given the following file:

```perl
#!/usr/bin/perl
# B_Lint.pl
use warnings;
use strict;

$count = @file = <>;
for (@file) {
    if (/^\d\d\d/ and $& > 300) {
        print
    } else {
        summarize($_);
    }
}
```

`B::Lint` reports:

> **perl -MO=Lint,all test**
Implicit use of $_ in foreach at test line 4
Implicit match on $_ at test line 5
Use of regexp variable $& at test line 5
Use of $_ at test line 5
Use of $_ at test line 8
Undefined subroutine summarize called at test line 8
test syntax OK

'B::Showlex'

The `B::Showlex` module is used for debugging lexical variables. For instance, when used on the following short file:

```
#!/usr/bin/perl
#B_Showlex.pl
use warnings;
use strict;

my $one = 1;
{
    my $two = "two";
    my $one = "one";
}
```

Again, we can use the O module to drive it:

> **perl -MO=Showlex B_Showlex.pl**

The result shown below may differ slightly depending on the system setup:

Pad of lexical names for comppadlist has 4 entries
0: SPECIAL #1 &PL_sv_undef
1: PVNV (0x80fa0c4) "$one"
2: PVNV (0x816b070) "$two"
3: PVNV (0x8195fa0) "$one"

Pad of lexical values for comppadlist has 4 entries
0: SPECIAL #1 &PL_sv_undef
1: NULL (0x80f0070)
2: NULL (0x80fa130)
3: NULL (0x816b0dc)

This tells us that this program has four lexical key-value pairs; (remember that variables are stored in a hash, effectively) the first is the special variable undef, the undefined value. Then follows our three lexical variables, which have no values before our program is executed.

'B::Xref'

Generating cross-reference tables can be extremely useful to help understand a large program. The `B::Xref` module tells us where subroutines and lexical variables are defined and used. For instance, here is an extract of the output for a program called `Freekai`, (http://simon-cozens.org/software/freekai/) broken down into sections:

> **perl -MO=Xref File**
File freekai
Subroutine (definitions)
  Package UNIVERSAL
     &VERSION   s0
     &can   s0
     &isa   s0
  Package attributes
     &bootstrap   s0
  Package main
     &dotext   s11

First, Xref tells us about the subroutine definitions; the subroutines UNIVERSAL::VERSION, UNIVERSAL::can, UNIVERSAL::isa, and attributes::bootstrap are special subroutines internal to Perl, so they have line number 0. On line 11, Freekai's one subroutine, dotext, is defined.

Subroutine (main)
  Package ?
     ?   &6
     text   &7, &8
  Package Text::ChaSen
     &getopt_argv   &5

This section talks about subroutine calls in the main body of the program; there are some calls that it cannot understand (these are actually handlers to HTML::Parser) and the subroutine Text::ChaSen::getopt_argv is called on line 5.

Package main
  $cset   4
  $p   6, 7, 8, 9
  $res   5
  &dotext   7
  *STDIN   &9, 9

Now we describe the global variables used in the main body of the program: $cset is used on line 4, the subroutine reference &dotext is used on line 7, and so on.

Subroutine dotext
  Package (lexical)
     $deinflected   i19, 21
     $kanji   i19, 20, 21, 21
     $pos   i19, 20, 21
     $yomi   i19, 21

We enter the subroutine dotext and look at the lexical variables used here: i19 says that these variables were all initialized on line 19, and the other numbers tell us which lines the variables were used one.

Package Text::ChaSen
  &sparse_tostr &16

We refer to the subroutine `Text::ChaSen::sparse_tostr` on line 16.

```
Package main
   $_          12, 14, 15, 16, 19
   $cset       21
   @_          12
   @chars         16, 17, 18
```

And, finally, these are the global variables used in this subroutine.

`B::Xref` is an excellent way of getting an overall map of a program, particularly one that spans multiple files and contains several modules.

Here's a slightly more involved cross-reference report from the debug closure example `debug.pl` we have analyzed earlier:

> perl -MO=Xref debug.pl

Below is the output that this command produces:

```
File debug.pl
  Subroutine (definitions)
    Package UNIVERSAL
      &VERSION          s0
      &can                    s0
      &isa                    s0
    Package attributes
      &bootstrap              s0
    Package main
      &debug                  s27
      &debug_level      s12
  Subroutine (main)
    Package (lexical)
      $debug_level      i6
    Package main
      %ENV                    6
      &debug                  &34, &35, &38, &39, &42, &45, &46
      &debug_level      &31, &42, &46
  Subroutine debug
    Package (lexical)
      $level                  i17, 20, 25, 25
    Package main
      &debug_level      &20, &25
      *STDERR               20
      @_                         17, 20, 20
  Subroutine debug_level
    Package (lexical)
      $debug_level      10, 11
    Package main
      @_                         10
debug.pl syntax OK
```

Subroutine (definitions) details all the subroutines defined in each package found; note the debug and debug_level subroutines in package main. The numbers following indicate that these are subroutine definitions (prefix s) and are defined on lines 12 (debug_level) and 27 (debug), which is indeed where those subroutine definitions end.

Similarly, we can see that in package main the debug_level subroutine is called at lines 31, 42, and 46, and within debug it is called at lines 20 and 25. We can also see that the scalar $debug_level is initialized (prefix i) on line 6, and is used only within the debug_level subroutine, on lines 10 and 11. This is a useful result, because it shows us that the variable is not being accessed from anywhere that it is not supposed to be.

Similar analysis of other variables and subroutines can provide us with similar information, allowing us to track down and eliminate unwanted accesses between packages and subroutines, while highlighting areas where interfaces need to be tightened up, or visibility of variables and values reduced.

'B::Fathom'

Turning to the B::* modules on CPAN, rather than in the standard distribution, B::Fathom aims to provide a measure of readability. For instance, running B::Fathom on Rocco Caputo's Crossword server (http://poe.perl.org/poegrams/index.html#xws) produces the following output:

> perl -MO=Fathom xws.perl
237 tokens
78 expressions
28 statements
1 subroutine
readability is 4.69 (easier than the norm)

However, do not take its word as gospel: it judges the following code (due to Damian Conway) as 'very readable'

```
$;=$/;seek+DATA,!++$/,!$s;$_=<DATA>;$s&&print||$g&&do{$y=($x||=20)*($y||8);
sub
i{sleep&f}sub'p{print$;x$=,join$;,$b=~/.{$x}/g}$j=$j;sub'f{pop}sub
n{substr($b,&f%$y,3)=~tr,O,O,}sub'g{$f=&f-1;($w,$w,substr($b,&f,1),O)
[n($f-$x)+
n($x+$f)-(substr($b,&f,1)eq+O)+n$f]||$w}$w="\40";$b=join'',@ARGV?<>:$_,$w
x$y;$b=~s).)$&=~/\w/?O:$w)ge;substr($b,$y)=q++;$g='$i=0;$i?$b:$c=$b;
substr+$c,$i,1,g$i;$g=~s?\d+?($&+1)%$y?e;$i-$y+1?eval$g:do{$i=-1;$b=$c;p;i
1}';sub'e{eval$g;&e}e}||eval||die+No.$;
```

'B::Graph'

The B::Graph module, by Stephen McCamant, is not part of the standard compiler suite, but is available as a separate download from CPAN.

This backend produces a graphical representation of the op tree that the compiler sees. Output is in plain text by default, but this is not very appealing.

With the -vcg and -dot options the module generates vector graphs that can be displayed using, respectively, the VCG (Visualization of Compiler Graphs) program (from http://www.cs.uni-sb.de/RW/users/sander/html/gsvcg1.html) and the GraphViz module with the Graphviz package (available from http://www.graphviz.org/). Both are free software tools, available for UNIX as well as Windows. A VCG graph can be generated with the following command:

> perl -MO=Graph,-vcg -e '$a = $b + $c' > graph.vcg

Here is the graph produced by the module of our old friend, $a = $b + $c.

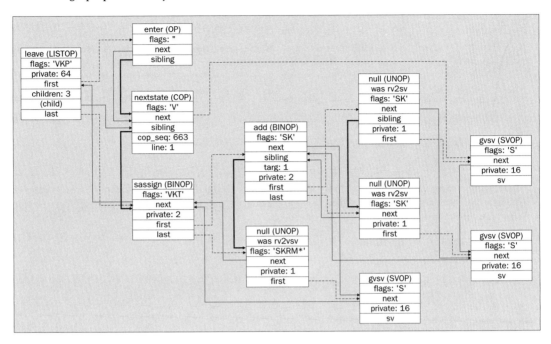

Aside from being nice (plenty of colorful boxes connected by arrows; the colors can't be displayed in the diagram), the output can be very useful if we're going to seriously study the internal working of the Perl compiler. It can be seen as a graphical disassembler, a feature that few programming languages can offer.

'B::JVM::Jasmin'

Finally, one of the most ambitious modules is an attempt to have Perl output Java bytecode; it creates Java assembly code, which is assembled into bytecode with the Jasmin assembler, available from http://mrl.nyu.edu/meyer/jasmin.

It provides a compiler, `perljvm`, which turns a Perl program into a compiled class file. Running:

> perljvm myprog.pl MyProgram

will create `MyProgram.class`.

If this is of interest we should also look in the `jpl/` directory of the Perl source tree; JPL (Java Perl Lingo) is a way of sharing code between Perl and Java, just like XS and embedding shared code between Perl and C. `B::JVM::Jasmin`, on the other hand, makes Perl code run natively on the Java Virtual Machine.

Writing a Perl Compiler Backend

Now that we have looked at the backends that are available to us, let's think about how we can write our own. We'll create something similar to B::Graph, but we will make it a lot more simple – let's call it B::Tree.

We will use the GraphViz module just like B::Graph, because its interface is very simple: to add a node, we say:

```
$g->add_node({name => 'A', label => 'Text to appear on graph'});
```

and to connect two nodes, we say:

```
$g->add_edge({from => 'A', to => 'B'});
```

Let's start off slowly, by just having our backend visit each op and say hello. We need to remember two things: to be a proper backend usable by the O module, we need to define a compile subroutine which returns a subref which does the work; if we are using walkoptree_slow to visit each op, we need to define a method for each class we are interested in.

Here is the skeleton of our module:

```perl
#!/usr/bin/perl
# ourmodule1.pm
package B::Tree;
use strict;

use B qw(main_root walkoptree_slow);

sub compile {
    return sub {walkoptree_slow(main_root, "visit")};
}
sub B::OP::visit {
    print "Hello from this node. \n";
}
1;
```

Now let's change it so that we add a GraphViz node at every op:

```perl
#!/usr/bin/perl
# ourmodule2.pm
package B::Tree;
use strict;

use GraphViz;
use B qw(main_root walkoptree_slow);
sub compile {
    return sub {
        $g = new GraphViz;
        walkoptree_slow(main_root, "visit");
        print $g->as_dot;
    };
}
sub B::OP::visit {
    my $self = shift;
    $g->add_node({name => $$self, label => $self->name});
}
1;
```

This time, we load up the `GraphViz` module and start a new graph. At each op, we add a node to the graph. The node's name will be the address of its reference, because that way we can easily connect parent and child ops; `${$self->first}`, for instance, will give the address of the child. For the label, we use the `name` method to tell us what type of op this is.

Once we have walked the op tree, we print out the graph; at the moment, this will just be a series of non-connected circles, one for each op. Now we need to think about how the ops are connected together, and that's where the difference between the op structures comes into play.

The ops are connected up in four different ways: a `LISTOP` can have many children, a `UNOP` (unary operator) has one child, and a `BINOP` (binary operator) has two children; all other ops have no children.

Let's first deal with the easiest case, the op with no children:

```
sub B::OP::visit {
    my $self = shift;
    $g->add_node({name => $$self, label => $self->name});
}
```

This is exactly what we had before; now, in the case of an `UNOP`, the child is pointed to by the `first` method. This means we can connect an `UNOP` up by adding an edge between `$$unop` and `${$unop->first}`, like so:

```
sub B::UNOP::visit {
    my $self = shift;
    my $first = $self->first;
    $g->add_node({name => $$self, label => $self >name});
    $g->add_edge({from => $$self, to => $$first});
}
```

A `BINOP` is very similar, except that its other child is pointed to by the `last` method:

```
sub B::BINOP::visit {
    my $self = shift;
    my $first = $self->first;
    my $last = $self->last;
    $g->add_node({name => $$self, label => $self->name});
    $g->add_edge({from => $$self, to => $$first});
    $g->add_edge({from => $$self, to => $$last});
}
```

The trickiest one is the `LISTOP`. Here, the first child is pointed to by `first` and the last child by `last`. The other children are connected to each other by the `sibling` method. Hence, if we start at `first`, we can add each `sibling` until we get to `last`:

```
sub B::LISTOP::visit {
    my $self = shift;
    $g->add_node({name => $$self, label => $self->name});
    my $node = $self->first;
    while ($$node != ${$self->last}) {
        $g->add_edge({from => $$self, to => $$node});
        $node = $node->sibling;
    }
    $g->add_edge({from => $$self, to => $$node});    # finally add the last
}
```

And that's it! Putting the whole thing together:

```perl
#!/usr/bin/perl
# ourmodule3.pm
package B::Tree;
use strict;

use GraphViz;
use B qw(main_root walkoptree_slow);
sub compile {
    return sub {
        $g = new GraphViz;
        walkoptree_slow(main_root, "visit");
        print $g->as_dot;
    };
}
sub B::LISTOP::visit {
    my $self = shift;
    $g->add_node({name => $$self, label => $self->name});
    my $node = $self->first;
    while ($$node != ${$self->last}) {
        $g->add_edge({from => $$self, to => $$node});
        $node = $node->sibling;
    }
    $g->add_edge({from => $$self, to => $$node});
}
sub B::BINOP::visit {
    my $self = shift;
    my $first = $self->first;
    my $last = $self->last;
    $g->add_node({name => $$self, label => $self->name});
    $g->add_edge({from => $$self, to => $$first});
    $g->add_edge({from => $$self, to => $$last});
}
sub B::UNOP::visit {
    my $self = shift;
    my $first = $self->first;
    $g->add_node({name => $$self, label => $self->name});
    $g->add_edge({from => $$self, to => $$first});
}
sub B::OP::visit {
    my $self = shift;
    $g->add_node({name => $$self, label => $self->name});
}
1;
```

We can now use this just like B::Graph:

> **perl -I. -MO=Tree -e '$a= $b+$c' | dot –Tps > tree.ps**

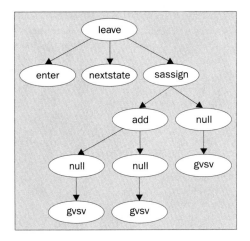

And in fact, this was the module we used to make the tree diagrams earlier on in this chapter!

> *Actually, there was one complication that we did not explore here. Sometimes, unary operators are not really unary; ops that have been simplified to NULLs during the optimization stage will still have siblings which need to be connected to the graph. The full version of* B::Tree *is on CPAN and works around this.*

Summary

In this chapter, we have seen a little bit of how Perl goes about executing a program: the parsing and the execution stages. We have looked at the internal data structures that represent Perl variables, such as SVs, and we have also had a look at the Perl compiler, which transforms the op tree of a program into various different formats: C code, Java assembler, and so on.

For more information on how Perl works internally, look at the `perlguts` and `perlhack` documentation files. `perlguts` is more of a reference on how to use the Perl API as well as how the Perl core works, while `perlhack` is a more general tutorial on how to get to grips with working on the Perl sources.

21

Integrating Perl with Other Programming Languages

In this chapter, we shall explore several ways to integrate Perl with other programming languages. The main theme will be, for reasons that will become evident, integrating with C in both directions.

Using C from Perl will show how to write C code and call it from a Perl program, or how to build a **Perl wrapper** to existing C code, using the **XS** interface (also known as **XSUB**, for e**X**ternal **SUB**routine) to write Perl extensions.

We will also take a look at how to dynamically link to compiled libraries (on systems that support dynamic linking), and perform calls to their exported functions directly from Perl, without the need to compile anything.

Using Perl from C deals with the opposite topic: how to take advantage of Perl's functionalities in C programs. This technique, usually referred to as 'embedding Perl', consists of linking the Perl library with a C project and, using the provided `include` files and definition, implementing a Perl interpreter in the application.

What we discuss here requires some degree of familiarity with the Perl internals, as seen in Chapter 20. Even if there are a number of well established techniques, there are also a lot of pitfalls, undocumented features, and probably even bugs that exist. Last, but not least, the whole knowledge base is subject to change as Perl evolves.

At the end of this chapter, we'll take a quick tour around integration with different languages: from the **JPL** (**J**ava-**P**erl Lingo), to developing with the COM framework on Windows machines, to rather esoteric implementations and possibilities lying around in the labyrinthine world of Perl.

Using C from Perl

Putting some C code at the disposal of Perl is something that one would do for a number of reasons, such as gaining access to otherwise unimplemented low-level system calls and libraries, interfacing with other programs or tools that expose C APIs, or simply speeding up a Perl script by rewriting time-consuming tasks in C.

In fact, a large part of Perl's riches comes from the numerous extensions it has already. Modules are provided to interface the GD (to produce graphic files) and Tk (Tcl's GUI toolkit) libraries, to name a few. Even on specific platforms, there is usually a whole set of modules that puts Perl in a position to interact with every single part of that operating system (for example, on the Windows platform, we have modules to manage the registry, services, event logs, and much more).

All this is made possible by what is called the **XS interface**, a quite complex set of Perl scripts and modules that work together to ease the task of linking C code into Perl. Many major modules, like the ones we just mentioned, make use of this interface to have C code that can be directly seen by Perl as a set of subroutines.

In this chapter, we are going to introduce the use of this interface in its most common form. We will see how to write XS code, and how it interfaces with Perl. For a more complete reference, and some advanced topics not covered here, we can refer to the following manual pages from the standard Perl documentation:

Manual Page	Description
perlxs	The reference manual for the XS format.
perlxstut	An example driven, lightweight tutorial.
perlguts	The official Perl internal's user's guide: explains almost everything anyone needs to know to use Perl and C together.
perlapi	The official Perl internal's API reference (available from version 5.6.0; on earlier versions this was part of perlguts).
perlcall	A lot of information about calling Perl from C, dealing with stack manipulation, creating callback code and other advanced techniques.

We also suggest looking at the *Extension-Building Cookbook* by Dean Roehrich, available on CPAN (search for distributions matching Cookbook on http://search.cpan.org), as well as the *PerlGuts Illustrated* paper by Gisle Aas, available at http://gisle.aas.no/perl/illguts/.

Finally, probably the best and most complete reference material is the source code written by others. The POSIX extension, for example, available in the ext/POSIX directory of the Perl source tree, is a very good example of both basic and advanced techniques. We shouldn't be afraid of learning from existing extensions, as that is one of the benefits of open source after all. We just need to remember to be good citizens, and give the appropriate credits when reusing someone else's work.

An Overview of XS

The 'core' of the XS interface is a Perl script called xsubpp, which is part of the standard ExtUtils distribution. This script translates an XS file, which is basically a C file with some special markers here and there, to a regular C file that is compiled and linked as usual.

The purpose of the XS format is to hide most of the required Perl C API calls from the programmer, so that he or she can concentrate on writing the C code. xsubpp will do its best to automate the interactions between C and Perl, simplifying all the routine jobs of declaring XSUBs and converting data back and forth; as we'll see later.

The process of building a Perl extension is handled by the ExtUtils::MakeMaker module (and the locally installed C compiler and make program, of course) that was introduced in Chapter 10.

The resulting binary will usually be a shared object known as DSO (Dynamic Shared Object), on most UNIX platforms. On 'Windows' it is known as Dynamic Link Library (DLL).

Once we have this library, with all its exported symbols, the job of linking to it and performing calls is done at run-time by the DynaLoader module, which is a special extension often built together with the Perl executable and statically linked to it. There is more detail on this module in Chapter 20.

If our operating system does not support dynamic linking, we can still use the XS interface. Only the build process will differ, because the extension has to be statically linked into the Perl executable (just as DynaLoader is). This means that, by building an extension, a completely new Perl executable will be built. Fortunately, the majority of modern operating systems do support dynamic linking.

The only other bit of glue that needs to be in the process is a Perl module (a regular PM file), which simply inherits from DynaLoader, and is instructed to call the bootstrap function responsible for doing the run-time link to the XS shared object.

'h2xs', or Where to Start

The XS interface was originally developed to provide transparent access to C libraries, which usually come with header files defining the API (function calls, constants, macros, and whatever else). There is in fact, a dedicated Perl script, called h2xs, which handles this task. As the name implies, it is a C header file (.h) to XS translator. It is automatically installed in the bin directory of the Perl's installation, so chances are that if the Perl executable is in the path, it can be called directly in the shell. This command creates stubs in the makefile to handle C integration.

Beyond its original intent, h2xs can, and definitely should, be used as a starting point to create an extension, even if there is no header to translate and we're writing code from scratch. The script has a number of options, which we'll see below, that makes it very flexible. In particular, it can be used to build a skeleton module, with or even without, the XS part (see Chapter 10 for an example of using it on plain Perl modules).

This script, h2xs, will take over all the routine jobs of preparing a module, generating the Makefile.PL, the PM file, a MANIFEST, and everything that should be in every well packaged distribution.

We can suppress the C aspects of the Makefile by adding -X (note the case sensitivity) option. The -n flag specifies the name for the extension. For example:

> **h2xs -X -n Installable::Module**

In addition to these flags, h2xs supports a large number of options to control various aspects of the generated files. For a pure Perl module, the most important of these are:

-h	Print out some usage information about the h2xs utility.
-A	Do not include the AutoLoader module, (see Chapter 10). By default, h2xs generates a module source file including the AutoLoader. If present, the install makefile target automatically calls the AutoSplit module to perform a split on installation. If we do not want to use the AutoLoader, this option will suppress it.
-C	Do not create a Changes file. Instead, h2xs will add a HISTORY section to the pod documentation at the bottom of the module source file.
-P	Suppress generation of the pod documentation in the module source file.
-v	Specify a version number for the module other than the default of 0.01. For example, -v 0.20.
-X	Suppress the XS part of the makefile – pure Perl module distributions should use this. Modules that make use of C code should not.

By default, the created module file incorporates code to use both the Exporter and AutoLoader. As an example, to suppress the lines involving the AutoLoader, we can add the -A option as well:

> **h2xs -XA -n Installable::Module**

Similarly, to create a module with a version of 0.20 and no Changes file, but which does use the AutoLoader:

> **h2xs -C -v 0.20 -n Installable::Module**

Converting C Header Files

To start, let us consider the 'canonical' situation. Suppose we have a C header file, called xs_test.h, with some constants, and a pair of function prototypes, as shown below:

```
#define FIRST 1
#define SECOND 2
#define THIRD 3

int first_function(int number, void *databuffer);
void second_function(char *name, double a, double b);
```

In the simplest case, we can call the h2xs script with the name of the header file as the only argument:

> **h2xs xs_test.h**

This will create a directory called Xs_test (the name is taken from the header file), which contains everything that is needed to build the extension: the PM and XS files (Xs_test.pm and Xs_test.xs), a Makefile.PL, a simple test script, a nicely initialized Changes log, and finally the MANIFEST file:

```
Writing Xs_test/Xs_test.pm
Writing Xs_test/Xs_test.xs
Writing Xs_test/Makefile.PL
Writing Xs_test/test.pl
Writing Xs_test/Changes
Writing Xs_test/MANIFEST
```

Once built with the following command, our extension will simply export all the constants found in the header file.

```
> perl Makefile.Pl
> make
> make test
> su
Password:
# make install
```

This means that we can already write a script with it:

```
#!/usr/bin/perl
# xs_test.pl
use warnings;
use strict;

use Xs_test;

my @names = qw(none foo bar baz);
print $names[SECOND];
```

This will correctly print out bar. Not a big thing yet, but this procedure, applied to more meaningful headers, will provide a good starting point in implementing an existing API.

By default, h2xs can only search the header file for constants (the #define directives above) and make them accessible from the generated extension. The code to access the defined functions must be provided by the programmer. However, if we have installed the C::Scan module, available from CPAN, we can add the -x switch (note the case sensitivity, using a capital X will suppress the XS part of the Makefile) to h2xs and it will recognize function definitions too, and put them in the generated XS file.

For example, by running

```
> h2xs -Ox xs_test.h
```

(we also add the **-O** switch to allow h2xs to overwrite the files we previously generated), some stub code will be added to Xs_test.xs. With this code, we are already able to call Xs_test::first_function from a Perl script, and access the C function defined by this name; as long as we have included the object file that contains the declared function. We will see later how to add external libraries to the build process.

It should be said that this procedure, by itself, is unlikely to be enough for real-world applications: the job done by h2xs and C::Scan can only generate useful interface code for very simple cases. Most of the time, if not always, some coding will be required to successfully implement a C API as a Perl extension.

But the value of these tools should not be underestimated: it's much easier to add the missing pieces on a prepared template, than to start with a blank file and write everything by hand.

Starting from Scratch

The header file name supplied to h2xs is not mandatory: the tool can be used without any existing file to convert. In this case, we must add the −n flag we met earlier, which specifies the name for the extension. Let's see what happens when we call the script like this:

> h2xs -n XS::Test

This time, the directory structure XS/Test is created, and the same set of files seen above is generated:

```
Writing XS/Test/Test.pm
Writing XS/Test/Test.xs
Writing XS/Test/Makefile.PL
Writing XS/Test/test.pl
Writing XS/Test/Changes
Writing XS/Test/MANIFEST
```

The only difference is that our XS::Test extension provides nothing of its own. Still, the generated files are convenient templates with which to start writing our own code, and this is what we will use for the rest of the section as our workbench.

The XS File

Now that we have defined the starting point, let's first see what's in our XS file. We start with what was generated by our last example, a truly bare XS file (Test.xs), and explore its content bit by bit:

```
#include "EXTERN.h"
#include "perl.h"
#include "XSUB.h"
```

The first three lines are standard to every XS file: the included headers contain all the definitions needed to use Perl's internals and write XSUBs Additional #include directives and definitions can be put here, but these three should always be left untouched.

Next, we have two regular C functions.

```
static int
not_here(s)
char *s;
{
    croak("%s not implemented on this architecture", s);
    return -1;
}
```

```
static double
constant (name, arg)
char *name;
int arg;
{
    errno = 0;
    switch (*name) {
    }
    errno = EINVAL;
    return 0;

not_there:
    errno = ENOENT;
    return 0;
}
```

These are put here by default, and work together with the AUTOLOAD function placed in the PM file to give convenient access to C constants. Given the constant name as a string, the constant function returns its corresponding numerical value (or calls not_here to complain with a not implemented error, in case the constant is not defined).

From this point on, we have what is properly called the XS code:

```
MODULE = XS::Test       PACKAGE = XS::Test

double
constant(name, arg)
    char *    name
    int       arg
```

In fact, everything before the MODULE keyword is just plain C, and it will be passed untouched to the compiler. The xsubpp work only begins here, and it concerns the functions defined in this section.

Declaring the 'MODULE' and 'PACKAGE'

The MODULE and PACKAGE directives tell XS, respectively, the name of the module for which the resulting loadable object is being generated, and the namespace, or Perl package, where the functions will be defined (in this case is XS::Test for both). We should never need to change MODULE, but we can, at some point, change to another PACKAGE. This could happen, for example, when we're writing a module that implements different packages or subpackages:

```
# put some functions in XS::Test
MODULE = XS::Test       PACKAGE = XS::Test

# other functions in XS::Test::foo
MODULE = XS::Test       PACKAGE = XS::Test::foo

# in XS::Test::bar
MODULE = XS::Test       PACKAGE = XS::Test::bar
```

Note that PACKAGE can't be changed without declaring (or repeating) MODULE right before it. The first MODULE occurrence, as we've seen, marks the start of the XS section. After this, the file contains function definitions.

XS Functions

In its simplest form, an XS function is just a wrapper for the corresponding C function – that's exactly what the last four lines of our example do:

```
double
constant(name, arg)
    char *   name
    int      arg
```

This snippet defines the XSUB `constant`: to Perl, this means sub `Xs::Test::constant`. That sub, in turn, calls the C function named `constant` (defined before in the same file), passing any input and output parameters, to and from Perl, as required.

The XS definition is very similar to a C function definition, except for the missing semicolons after the parameters type declaration. Note, however, that the return value must be on the line before the function name, so it's not correct to squeeze the lines above to this:

```
/* ERROR: this is wrong */
double constant(name, arg)
    char *   name
    int      arg
```

Types must also be defined after the function name, as in good old pre ANSI C, so this is incorrect:

```
/* ERROR: this is wrong too */
    double
    constant(char *name, int arg)
```

A more elaborate XS function, however, will usually do more than map one-to-one with a C function. This can happen for a number of reasons, including handling complex C data type like structures, providing more 'perlish' syntactic sugar, or grouping a series of calls as one. Last, but not least, if we're writing C code from scratch, we need to provide some code for our functions.

Putting the 'CODE' in

In fact, an XS function can contain code, just like a C function can have a body: but this time, the syntax is more particular. This is the most common form of an XS function:

```
int
first_function(number, databuffer)
    int      number
    void *   databuffer
CODE:
    /* place C code here */
OUTPUT:
    RETVAL
```

The `CODE:` identifier marks the start of the function, while `OUTPUT:` marks its end and returns the indicated value to Perl (`RETVAL` has a special meaning as we will see shortly).

Take care; xsubpp wants functions to be separated by a blank line, so if there is no output to give (for example, if the function is declared to return void), the blank line marks the end of the function.

```
void
first_function()
CODE:
    /* place C code here */

void
second_function()
CODE:
    /* place C code here */
```

There are no brackets to mark the end of the function body, so we have to pay attention to blank lines, which is something that may be confusing at first. Let's see a very simple C function, expressed in XS, which returns the greater one of the two numbers passed:

```
int
maximum(a, b)
    int    a
    int    b
CODE:
    if(a > b) {
        RETVAL = a;
    } else {
        RETVAL = b;
    }
OUTPUT:
    RETVAL
```

As mentione earlier, there is a special variable lying around, which is RETVAL. This variable is automatically defined by xsubpp from the function definition's return type. In this case, RETVAL is declared to be an int. The last two lines are there to return the calculated variable to Perl.

Now that we have added these lines to our Test.xs file, we simply need to rebuild the extension, and our maximum function is already available as a Perl sub:

```
use Xs::Test;
print Xs::Test::maximum(10, 20);
```

This simple script will print out 20, as we would expect.

Complex Output, 'PPCODE' and the Stack

There are times when we want more than one return value (this is Perl, after all, and we shouldn't suffer from the limitations of C). To achieve this result, we should take the following steps:

❑   Use void for the return value. This way, XS will not provide an automatic RETVAL variable.

❑   Use the PPCODE keyword instead of CODE, to let XS know that we're going to handle return values on our own.

863

❑ Allocate the needed number of return values on the stack by calling:

```
EXTEND(SP, number);
```

❑ For each value, use the XST_m* set of macros to actually put the value onto the stack. The macros are XST_mIV, XST_mNV and XST_mPV for the Perl integer, double and string datatypes respectively. The first argument to the macros is the stack position where we want our value to be placed (0 is the first position), and the second argument is the value itself.

❑ Finally, return the desired number of values by ending the function with:

```
XSRETURN(number);
```

There are also different XSRETURN macros to return special values (eg. XSRETURN_UNDEF, XSRETURN_EMPTY, XSRETURN_YES and others).

In the next example, we will make a little example function using this technique: our 'zeroes' function just returns an array composed by the given number of zeroes (equivalent to Perl's (0) x number). We do this by using a variable to loop from 0 to the given number, and for each value of the loop variable, we place the IV 0 at the corresponding stack position.

Here we introduce another keyword, PREINIT, which should be used whenever the function needs to declare local C variables. This is necessary because xsubpp, as we'll see later, actually uses function calls for the XS arguments. If we place our definition of i after the PPCODE keyword, it will result in it being placed after some code has already been evaluated, which will upset the compiler.

```
void
zeroes(number)
    int     number
PREINIT:
    int i;
PPCODE:
    EXTEND(SP, number);
    for(i=0; i<number; i++) {
        XST_mIV(i, 0);
    }
    XSRETURN(number);
```

We can go even further, and inspect the context in which the function was called in Perl, by using the GIMME function (same as Perl's built-in wantarray). Based on this, we may decide to return different results. GIMME returns one of the following values: G_ARRAY when the function is called in list context, and G_SCALAR when it is called in scalar context.

Let's see also how to cope with memory allocation in XS. Perl defines its own API for this, so we have safemalloc and safefree instead of the C's standard malloc and free, as well as Zero instead of memzero. There are additional substitutes like Copy for memcpy, Move for memmove, and so on.

```
void
zeroes(number)
    int     number
PREINIT:
    char *   string;
    int i;
```

```
PPCODE:
    if(number <= 0) {XSRETURN_UNDEF;}
    if(GIMME == G_ARRAY) {
        EXTEND(SP, number);
        for(i=0; i<number; i++) {
            XST_mIV(i, 0);
        }
        XSRETURN(number);
    } else {
        string = (char *) safemalloc(number+1);
        Zero(string, number+1, char);
        for(i=0; i<number; i++) {
            strcat(string, "0");
        }
        EXTEND(SP, 1);
        XST_mPV(0, string);
        safefree(string);
        XSRETURN(1);
    }
```

This version returns an array of zeroes when called in list context, and a string made up of zeroes when called in scalar context.

```
@z = XS::Test::zeroes(3);    # returns (0, 0, 0)
$z = XS::Test::zeroes(3);    # returns "000"
```

As a side note, it should always be kept in mind that we're working at a low level, so we don't have nice Perl error messages when something goes wrong, which is why we added the line:

```
if(number <= 0) {XSRETURN_UNDEF;}
```

This is to avoid allocating a huge amount of memory when the function is called with a negative number, which would make Perl blow up (probably with an Out of memory! error).

Complex Input, Default Values and Variable Input Lists

We have ways to deal with variable input too: again, the power of dealing with Perl's @_ input to a subroutine should not be left without being addressed.

The simplest case is having optional arguments, for which we assume a default value when one is not supplied. To provide default values, we simply assign them to our arguments on the function prototype line.

For example, this function behaves like Perl's built-in rand, which returns a random number between 0 and the given number, or between 0 and 1 when no arguments are given:

```
double
xrand(max=1)
    int max
CODE:
    RETVAL = (double) rand() * max / RAND_MAX;
OUTPUT:
    RETVAL
```

There can be more than one argument for which a default value is defined, but they should always be at the end of the argument list. For example, the following forms are wrong:

```
void
my_function(arg1=NULL, arg2)
    char * arg1
    char * arg2

void
my_function(arg1, arg2=NULL, arg3)
    char * arg1
    char * arg2
    char * arg3
```

While the following are correct:

```
void
my_function(arg1, arg2=NULL)
    char * arg1
    char * arg2

void
my_function(arg1, arg2=NULL, arg3=NULL)
    char * arg1
    char * arg2
    char * arg3
```

A more complex case occurs when the number of arguments is not known in advance. We can use the special identifier '...' (also known as an ellipsis). When it appears in the argument list of the function, any number of arguments can be passed to it. To actually work with the supplied arguments, we can follow this procedure:

❏   Use items to inspect the number of values in the input stack (items is an integer variable automatically defined by xsubpp).

❏   Access a specific value with the ST(n) macro, which returns the element n on the stack.

❏   Since ST returns a pointer to an SV, use the Sv* macros to convert the value to the corresponding C type (as before, we have SvIV, SvNV and SvPV for integers, doubles and strings respectively).

This simple function shows this at work. It accepts a variable list of values (a Perl array, for example) and returns the number of positive integers found in the list:

```
int
find_positive_numbers(...)
PREINIT:
    int i;
CODE:
    RETVAL = 0;
    for(i=0; i<items; i++) {
        if(SvIV(ST(i)) > 0) {
            RETVAL++;
        }
    }
OUTPUT:
    RETVAL
```

The 'TYPEMAP'

So far, we've seen examples with rather plain variables involved, and Perl happily understood C variable types and vice versa. This is true for the most common basic datatypes, but not for the many cases when we will need to define our own mappings. This is done by a special file called typemap, which xsubpp will use when converting from XS to C. In reality, even the work on simple datatypes is done by the default typemap file, which resides in the lib/ExtUtils directory and is always used by xsubpp.

A typemap consists of three parts:

❑ The enumeration of the C types we use (sometimes introduced by an optional TYPEMAP identifier).

❑ An INPUT section, which is used when passing Perl variables to C.

❑ An OUTPUT section, which is used when returning C variables to Perl.

The example below shows the general syntax. We use c_type here as a placeholder for the C datatype, and T_TYPE as our self-defined tag for the datatype:

```
c_type  T_TYPE

INPUT
T_TYPE
    /* code to convert from Perl to C */

OUTPUT
T_TYPE
    /* code to convert from C to Perl */
```

As an example implementation, let's see how the default typemap deals with integers:

```
int T_IV
...
INPUT
T_IV
    $var = ($type)SvIV($arg)
...
OUTPUT
T_IV
    sv_setiv($arg, (IV)$var);
```

The process involves using the SvIV macro to convert from a Perl value (an SV) to a C int, and the sv_setiv function to convert the other way around. There are three special identifiers (which look like Perl variables, but are just patterns for xsubpp to substitute the actual C expressions) that can be used in the typemap code fragments:

$arg	The XS argument, which gets translated into the ST(n) macro.
$var	The corresponding C variable.
$type	The C type, as defined in the XS file.

To see how the mechanism really works, we refer back to the example maximum function from the section entitled 'Putting the 'CODE' in'. The typemap at work produced the following results, which we can see by peeking into the generated Test.c file: our declarations of int a and int b have been translated to:

```
int a = (int)SvIV(ST(0));
int b = (int)SvIV(ST(1));
```

The return value for the function has become:

```
sv_setiv(ST(0), (IV)RETVAL);
```

A custom typemap must be built if we're using C types that are not included in the default one. For example, if our library defines a type, say, little_number, to represent an integer, it must be in the typemap if we want to use input/output values of this type. If we just have a different name for an already defined type, we can use the tags defined in the default typemap:

```
little_number    T_IV
```

This is enough to treat a little_number as if it was an int. A typemap definition can be much more complicated. For example, suppose we have this C structure:

```
typedef struct {
    int red;
    int green;
    int blue;
} my_rgb;
```

we may decide that we want a my_rgb variable passed to our extension as an array reference, holding values for the red, green, and blue components (as in [128, 128, 128]). We implement this in the typemap:

```
my_rgb    T_RGB

INPUT
T_RGB
    if(SvROK($arg) && SvTYPE(SvRV($arg)) == SVt_PVAV) {
        $var.red   =
            (av_fetch((AV*)SvRV($arg), 0, 0) == NULL) ?
                0
            :
                SvIV(*(av_fetch((AV*)SvRV($arg), 0, 0)));
        $var.green =
            (av_fetch((AV*)SvRV($arg), 1, 0) == NULL) ?
                0
            :
                SvIV(*(av_fetch((AV*)SvRV($arg), 1, 0)));
        $var.blue  =
            (av_fetch((AV*)SvRV($arg), 2, 0) == NULL) ?
                0
            :
            SvIV(*(av_fetch((AV*)SvRV($arg), 2, 0)));
    } else
        croak(\"$var is not a reference to an array!\");
```

The above code checks that the argument is a reference, and a reference to an array. If it is, it tries to fetch three values from the referenced array, and assigns them to the red, green, and blue components of the C structure. To be safe in case of failures, we first check the result of `av_fetch` and, in case it is NULL, we use zero for the corresponding component.

Now we can write an XS function that accepts `my_rgb` as input:

```
bool
is_gray(color)
    my_rgb   color
CODE:
    RETVAL = (
        color.red == color.green &&
        color.green == color.blue
    ) ? 1 : 0;
OUTPUT:
    RETVAL
```

and we can use this from Perl as:

```
XS::Test::is_gray([128, 128, 128]);
```

Any other kind of value passed to our function will cause a fatal error (with the message color is not a reference to an array!).

Dealing with the corresponding OUTPUT part requires a different approach. For example, we can use a PPCODE function, as seen above, to return an array of three values for the red, green, and blue components.

A more functional implementation of a C structure can be achieved using the T_PTROBJ tag, defined in the standard typemap. It requires, however, some additional work, which is outlined below:

❑   We add to the typemap a line for a pointer to the structure, specifying the T_PTROBJ tag for it:

```
my_rgb   *   T_PTROBJ
```

❑   When returning a variable, we need to be sure to allocate memory for it. This simple function initializes and returns a `my_rgb` structure:

```
my_rgb *
new_color(r, g, b)
    int r
    int g
    int b
CODE:
    RETVAL = (my_rgb *) safemalloc(sizeof(my_rgb));
    RETVAL->red   = r;
    RETVAL->green = g;
    RETVAL->blue  = b;
OUTPUT:
    RETVAL
```

❑ Now, we add another `PACKAGE` to the XS file, named after the structure, with the addition of a final `Ptr`:

```
MODULE = XS::Test        PACKAGE = my_rgbPtr
```

❑ After this line, we add functions to access the structure members. Here is the one for red, and we can do the same for the green and blue members:

```
int
red(color)
    my_rgb  *   color
CODE:
    RETVAL = color->red;
OUTPUT:
    RETVAL
```

❑ We should also add a `DESTROY` function, to free the allocated memory when the variable we have returned to Perl goes out of scope:

```
void
DESTROY(color)
    my_rgb  *   color
CODE:
    safefree(color);
```

Now that we've done all this, we can use the new_color function, which returns a Perl object blessed into the my_rgbPtr class. To access the underlying C structure, we simply call the methods we've defined on it:

```
my $Black = XS::Test::new_color(0, 0, 0);
print "red component of Black is: ", $Black->red, "\n";
```

Et voila, $Black is now a real C structure implemented in Perl.

The 'Makefile'

The extension we've played with until now, as we have already mentioned, can be built using the standard procedure:

> **perl Makefile.PL**
> **make**
> **make test**
> **su**
Password:
make install

The starting point of the build process is the Makefile.PL, which uses the ExtUtils::MakeMaker module to build a Makefile suitable for make. In most cases, the default file, built for us by h2xs, will do its job. But there are times when something needs to be added to the build process.

The most common case is when the extension is going to use external C libraries, or particular switches need to be passed to the C compiler. If we look at the default Makefile.PL, we will see that it already has pointers for us to fill the missing parts:

```
use ExtUtils::MakeMaker;
# see lib/ExtUtils/MakeMaker.pm for details of how to influence
# the contents of the Makefile that is written
WriteMakefile(
    'NAME' => 'XS::Test',
    'VERSION_FROM' => 'Test.pm',    # finds $VERSION
    'LIBS' => [''],    # e.g., '-lm'
    'DEFINE' => '',    # e.g., '-DHAVE_SOMETHING'
    'INC' => '',    # e.g., '-I/usr/include/other'
);
```

The LIBS, DEFINE and INC parameters to WriteMakefile should satisfy most of our needs; they're even well documented on the right.

There are additional parameters that may sometimes be useful, like CCFLAGS to pass additional switches to the C compiler, or XSOPT to alter the behaviour of xsubpp. The ExtUtils::MakeMaker documentation lists all the options recognized by WriteMakefile. We should note that, normally, most of these should be left to their default, since changing them may result in our extension being unusable.

If we still require more control over the generated Makefile, we can replace (or 'overload') some, or all, of the code that is behind WriteMakefile. To do that, we simply define a sub in a package called MY with the same name of a MakeMaker sub. The output of our sub will override the one produced by the module's sub.

Usually, however, we just need to modify the output of the corresponding MakeMaker function. So, we first call the function from the SUPER package (which is ExtUtils::MakeMaker), then modify its result and return it. This example, which can be added to the Makefile.PL, overrides the constants sub, to move everything that resides in /usr to /tmp/usr:

```
package MY;

sub constants {
    my $inherited = shift->SUPER::constants(@_);
    $inherited =~ s|/usr/|/tmp/usr/|g;
    return $inherited;
}
```

This kind of tweak should be used with caution, and only when it is really needed. If we are having troubles producing a working Makefile, we ought to think about patching MakeMaker.pm, and sharing our work with the perl5-porters mailing list for inclusion in the Perl standard distribution.

Dynamic Linking

If we already have a dynamic library (a shared object on UNIX platforms or a DLL on the Windows platform), we can use a different approach to access the code in there; one which does not require writing extension code and messing with compilers and linkers.

Basically, we make use of the same mechanism Perl makes use of with XS extensions. The library is loaded at runtime, references to its exported symbols are created, and then the library code is executed, as if it was a Perl sub, through this reference.

From the programmer's point of view, this is an all Perl solution and only requires some script coding. Under the hood, however, there's some C code, and really clever code indeed, because we don't know until runtime what the C prototype of the function we're going to call is. So, deep magic (and usually resorting to assembler code) is involved to provide a generic, all-purpose link to anonymous C functions.

There are currently three modules that have been written to address the issue. We'll give them a quick look in descending order of completeness and portability.

Using the 'FFI' Module

The FFI module by, Paul Moore, uses the ffcall library, developed by Bruno Haible for the LISP language; a very powerful set of tools to interface foreign functions (functions defined in external libraries).

The internals of the library are, obviously, quite complex. It uses a lot of assembler code to deal with the way data is passed to and from functions at a very, very, low level.

The Perl module, fortunately, hides all this from our eyes and allows us to link with a shared library in just a few lines of code. We only need to know where (in which library) a function is located, its name, and its C prototype. This prototype then needs to be converted to a 'signature', a short string defining the function's input and output parameter types.

Next we will make a little example program that links to the standard C math library and calls the cos function. First of all, we use the FFI::Library module to link to a shared library. Once we have obtained an FFI::Library object, we can import functions with the function method.

We add some conditions to make our script work on both UNIX and Windows platforms. Firstly, the name of the library, which is different on both platforms (libm.so on UNIX and MSVCRT.DLL on Windows). Secondly, the signature for the function, because we have to use different calling conventions on UNIX and Windows. We'll explain more about signatures and calling conventions below:

```
use FFI;
use FFI::Library;

# dynamically link to the library
$libm = new FFI::Library(
    $^O eq 'MSWin32' ? 'msvcrt' : 'm'
);

# import the cos function
$cos = $libm->function('cos',
    $^O eq 'MSWin32' ? 'sdd' : 'cdd'
);

# $cos is a CODE reference
$result = $cos->(2.0);

print "cos(2.0) = $result\n";
```

The name of the library can be expressed either in an abbreviated form or with a full pathname. In the script above, we have used m for UNIX machines, which is equivalent to the -lm switch to the C compiler: it searches the system library path (for example, /lib, /usr/lib) and adds lib and .so before and after the name, respectively. The library, in fact, resides in /lib/libm.so, so just m is enough. If a library resides in a different location, or uses a different naming scheme, its full path and filename can be specified.

On Windows too, the DLL extension is automatically added, and the library is searched in the default system path. The DLL we specified might reside, for example, in C:\WINNT\SYSTEM32\MSVCRT.DLL, so saying msvcrt is enough. Here too, if a DLL resides in a directory not searched by the system, the full path can be specified.

Signatures for the functions are made up of three distinct parts:

❑   The first letter is the **calling convention**: this is usually c for UNIX (for cdecl) and s for Windows (for stdcall). We should be aware that the s convention requires parameters to be passed in reverse order, so we need to adjust the signature as appropriate.

❑   The second letter is the return value of the function.

❑   From the third letter on, there are the arguments that the function expects (one letter for each argument).

The C prototype for the cos function is double cos (double x), so we have a return value of d (double), and one single parameter d (double too). This makes up our signature as cdd (or sdd for Windows).

Here is another example with this C function:

```
char *strncat(char *dest, const char *src, size_t n);
```

On UNIX machines, this needs to be translated, for use by FFI, into:

```
$strncat = $libc->function('strncat', 'cpppI');
```

The cpppI signature tells us that the function uses c calling convention, returns a pointer (p), and accepts two pointers and an unsigned integer (I).

On Windows, the correct signature is:

```
$strncat = $libc->function('strncat', 'spIpp');
```

The calling convention is s, the return value is a pointer as before, but the parameters are now in reverse order.

The next example shows how to use a callback using FFI, to enumerate the window handles on a Windows machine. A callback is defined using the FFI::callback function, which takes a signature and a code reference, containing the body for the callback. When passing the callback to a C function, we need to get its address using the addr method.

```
use FFI;
use FFI::Library;

my $user32 = new FFI::Library('user32');
```

```
my $enumwindows = $user32->function(
    'EnumWindows', 'siLp'   # note reverse order here!
);

my @windows;

my $cb = FFI::callback('siLL',
    sub {
        my($hwnd, $lparam) = @_;
        push(@windows, $hwnd);
        return 1;
    }
);

$enumwindows->($cb->addr, 100);
print join(', ', @windows), "\n";
```

For more information, and additional tips, tricks, and type definitions, refer to the pod documentation included in the module.

One final note for Windows users. Building the module may require some little hacks to the included ffcall library, but Paul Moore also provides a binary distribution for Perl 5.6.0, which can be installed using ppm:

> **ppm install --location=http://www.perl.com/CPAN/authors/id/P/PM/PMOORE FFI**

Using the 'C::DynaLib' Module

The C::DynaLib module, written by John Tobey, is very similar to FFI. The major differences are that it does not use the ffcall library, and is somewhat more limited – a small number of callbacks can be defined in one go, and it has UNIX support only (it may be possible to build it on a Windows machine with some hacking, but this had not been done at the time of writing).

The usage differs only slightly from what we've seen in the previous paragraph. This is a rewrite of call_cos.pl using C::DynaLib:

```
use C::DynaLib;

# dynamically link to the library
$libm = new C::DynaLib('m');

# import the cos function
$cos = $libm->DeclareSub('cos', 'd', 'd');

# $cos is a CODE reference
$result = $cos->(2.0);

print "cos(2.0) = $result\n";
```

The syntax is different, but the principle is just the same. For more information consult the module's documentation.

Using the 'Win32::API' module

The `Win32::API` module is written by Aldo Calpini. As its name implies, this module works on the Windows platform only. Furthermore, it uses assembler calls that are specific to the Microsoft Visual C++ compiler, so building it with a different environment may be difficult. Also, this module does not support callbacks, so only simple function calls can be made. Here is another rewrite of our `call_cos.pl` sample using `Win32::API`:

```
use Win32::API;

# import the cos function
$cos = new Win32::API('msvcrt', 'cos', 'D', 'D');

# $cos is an object, use the Call() method on it
$result = $cos->Call(2.0);

print "cos(2.0) = $result\n";
```

Again, the principles are just the same, and other information can be found by looking at the module's documentation.

Using Perl from C

Using Perl from C is a technique usually referred to as **embedding Perl**. This means, taking the Perl kernel and embedding it into a C program. There are several different forms of embedding, depending on which functionality of Perl we want to include in our program. We can use, for example, Perl's arrays and hashes as C structures, or we can write Perl code snippets to create them and modify them. We can use external script files that our application will interpret, or we can store the Perl code we want to be evaluated, as strings inside our C program.

In this section, we will see some basic examples of this technique at work. For a more in-depth coverage of the details involved in programming with Perl internals, refer to the same documents that were mentioned in the first section. In most regards, embedding and extending (writing XS extensions) are two sides of the same coin. Knowledge of the Perl's internal structure and its C APIs is required in both tasks.

More specific documentation can be found in the perlembed manual page, and by downloading the `ExtUtils::Embed` module from CPAN. The package contains additional information and examples, which are not included in the standard `ExtUtils` distribution.

First Steps

Writing a C program which makes use of Perl requires, in addition to writing proper C code, a particular build procedure to correctly generate an executable. The compiler must get the same defines, includes, and library paths that were used to build the Perl binary. We must also link the object with the Perl library, which contains the code for the Perl internals we're going to use.

This means, of course, that if we're using this technique, we absolutely need to have a Perl binary that was built on the local machine. It needs to find the required libraries and include files where Perl searches for them. In other words, the configuration saved in `Config.pm` (which was explained in Chapter 20) needs to be the actual configuration of the Perl build in use.

875

If our Perl was built on a different system and installed as a binary, we would probably be unable to write C programs with embedded Perl. So, the first requirement is to download the Perl source tree, and build it on the system we're going to program.

Even when we have successfully built our own Perl, tracing back all the information our compiler needs would not be easy without a little help. Fortunately, we have it – there is a specific module, called ExtUtils::Embed, which deals with all the gory details of finding the correct parameters to satisfy the compiler and linker.

Building a Program (The Hard Way)

Just to better understand what is going on, before taking the easier route, we will take the long, hard one and try to deduce all the needed parameters from Perl itself, using the -V switch;

> *The values shown here are just examples, they are dependent on a system's configuration, (such as OS and C compiler) and may, of course be, different.*

First of all, let's find our compiler and linker:

> **perl -V:cc**
cc='gcc';

> **perl -V:ld**
ld='gcc';

This tells us that we're using the Gnu C compiler, which is what we will use to build our Perl-embedded programs. Now, let's find the path to the include files and libraries:

> **perl -V:archlib**
archlib='/usr/local/perl-5.6/lib/5.6.0/i686-linux';

We'll need to add /CORE to this path, since the standard installation of Perl puts the files there. Now let's find the name of the Perl library which we'll link to, as well as any other library originally used to build Perl:

> **perl -V:libperl**
libperl='libperl.a';

> **perl -V:libs**
libs='-lnsl -lndbm -lgdbm -ldb -ldl -lm -lc -lposix -lcrypt';

Finally, we need the flags that we must pass to the compiler and the linker:

> **perl -V:ccflags**
ccflags='-fno-strict-aliasing -D_LARGEFILE_SOURCE -D_FILE_OFFSET_BITS=64';

> **perl -V:ldflags**
ldflags=' -L/usr/local/lib';

We put all this information together to obtain a command line, which we can use to build our program. Only the name of the source file (we have just called this program.c in the following command) needs to be added to this command, and it will correctly compile with embedded Perl:

```
> gcc program.c -fno-strict-aliasing -D_LARGEFILE_SOURCE -D_FILE_OFFSET_BITS=64
-I/usr/local/perl-5.6/lib/5.6.0/i686-linux/CORE
/usr/local/perl-5.6/lib/5.6.0/i686-linux/CORE/libperl.a
-L/usr/local/lib -lnsl -lndbm -lgdbm -ldb -ldl -lm -lc -lposix -lcrypt
```

Building a Program (The Easy Way)

What we've just seen is quite complex and somewhat boring. We don't want to remember all the four line stuff when compiling a program, which is why we use `ExtUtils::Embed` to reduce everything to this single command:

```
> perl -MExtUtils::Embed -e ccopts -e ldopts
```

With the `ccopts` and `ldopts` functions, the module prints out more or less the same command line we obtained before (with the addition of the `DynaLoader` library, which is needed to use XS extensions from C):

```
> -rdynamic  -L/usr/local/lib
/usr/local/perl-5.6/lib/5.6.0/i686-linux/auto/DynaLoader/DynaLoader.a
-L/usr/local/perl-5.6/lib/5.6.0/i686-linux/CORE
-lperl -lnsl -lndbm -lgdbm -ldb -ldl -lm -lc -lposix -lcrypt
-fno-strict-aliasing -D_LARGEFILE_SOURCE -D_FILE_OFFSET_BITS=64
-I/usr/local/perl-5.6/lib/5.6.0/i686-linux/CORE
```

This one liner is primarily intended to be used (in the UNIX shell) inside backticks, to have the output appended to the compilation command line like this:

```
> gcc -o program program.c 'perl -MExtUtils::Embed -e ccopts -e ldopts'
```

This is the normal procedure used to compile a C program with embedded Perl. But, if even this command line seems too long, or the backticks trick does not work (for example, on Windows machines, where the standard shell has some severe limitations), there is another, possibly simpler, approach provided by `ExtUtils::Embed`. The distribution from CPAN comes with a script called genmake, which produces a Makefile that can be used to build the executable. The procedure is:

```
> perl genmake program.c
Writing Makefile for program
> make
```

genmake uses the `ExtUtils::MakeMaker` module, tweaking it from its original intent to produce Makefiles for Perl modules into producing one for a C program.

Implementing the Perl Interpreter

Now that we've prepared the ground, let's see what is needed to actually write the C program. To start, some header files need to be included:

```
#include <EXTERN.h>
#include <perl.h>
```

We have already seen these two files included in the first section. We can skip the third, XSUB.h, as long as we don't plan to use XS extensions from our code (we'll cover this later).

Then, we need to implement an interpreter, which is an instance of Perl that is kept in a Perl Interpreter structure. We initialize it with the functions:

```
PerlInterpreter *my_perl;
my_perl = perl_alloc();
perl_construct(my_perl);
```

Once the my_perl variable has been allocated and constructed, it can be fed to other functions which actually do the Perl job:

```
perl_parse(my_perl, NULL, argc, argv, env);
perl_run(my_perl);
```

This really explains the double nature of Perl as a compiler and an interpreter. First, the code is parsed and internally compiled by perl_parse. Then, it is run by perl_run.

The parameters to perl_parse are, in order:

❑ The pointer to the Perl interpreter.

❑ A pointer to initialized XSUBs. (See the 'Using Modules' section later in this chapter for this; we'll use NULL for now.)

❑ argc, argv, and env like the ones C's main function gets.

If the env parameter is NULL, the current environment is passed to the interpreter.

After our run, we clean up with the following two functions:

```
perl_destruct(my_perl);
perl_free(my_perl);
```

One thing to note about the perl_parse function, is that it is, by itself, an implementation of the Perl executable that we're familiar with. In fact, it accepts all the switches and options Perl does, in argc and argv. By simply putting it in a main function and passing the relevant arguments, exactly the same functionalities of the Perl binary are implemented.

Of course, we can also provide our own arguments to it. This little program, called pversion.c, prints out the current version of Perl (as **perl –v** does):

```
#include <EXTERN.h>
#include <perl.h>

int main(int argc, char** argv, char** env) {
    PerlInterpreter *my_perl;
    /* we pass a dummy argv[0] */
    char *switches[] = {"", "-v"};
    my_perl = perl_alloc();
    perl_construct(my_perl);
    perl_parse(my_perl, NULL, 2, switches, (char**)NULL);
    perl_run(my_perl);
    perl_destruct(my_perl);
    perl_free(my_perl);
}
```

We can compile our program with one of the two procedures we've seen in the last paragraph;

> gcc –o pversion pversion.c 'perl –MExtUtils::Embed -e ccopts -e ldopts'

or by using the genmake script:

> perl genmake pversion.c
> make

Both procedures (remember, only the second option is available on Windows machines) generate an executable called pversion that will produce, for example, this output:

> pversion
This is perl, v5.6.0 built for i686-linux

Copyright 1987-2000, Larry Wall

Perl may be copied only under the terms of either the Artistic License, or the
GNU General Public License, which may be found in the Perl 5.0 source kit.

Complete documentation for Perl, including FAQ lists, should be found on
this system using 'man perl' or 'perldoc perl'. If you have access to the
Internet, point your browser at http://www.perl.com/, the Perl Home Page.

If a filename is hard coded in the switches, Perl will execute the script by that name, just as the executable does. We can even put a -e switch followed by code there:

```
/* shorter version */
/* note we have to escape quotes and backslashes! */
char *switches[] = {"", "-e", "print \"$]\\n\";"}

/* later, we'll call perl_parse with 3 arguments this time */
perl_parse(my_perl, NULL, 3, switches, (char**)NULL);
```

Note that this calling sequence (perl_alloc, construct, parse, run, destruct, and free) is always needed, even if there is nothing to pass to perl_parse. We can't simply pass a blank argument list, because this corresponds to calling the Perl executable without arguments, so it will read code from standard input, which is probably not what we want. To have the interpreter ready to run code, we usually pass -e 0 on its command line, which results in perl_parse doing nothing. Here, we have a script named do_nothing.c, which shows this:

```
#include <EXTERN.h>
#include <perl.h>

int main(int argc, char** argv, char** env) {
    PerlInterpreter *my_perl;
    /* 'void' command line */
    char *switches[] = {"", "-e", "0"};
    my_perl = perl_alloc();
    perl_construct(my_perl);
    perl_parse(my_perl, NULL, 3, switches, (char**)NULL);
    perl_run(my_perl);
```

879

```
    /* my_perl is now ready to receive orders */

    perl_destruct(my_perl);
    perl_free(my_perl);
}
```

We'll use this skeleton for the next samples, whenever we need a bare implementation of the Perl interpreter.

Embedding Perl Code

We have many ways of embedding Perl code. As said above, the interpreter can execute the script contained in a file. This is a convenient approach, for example, when we want to change some portions of an application without the need to rebuild the executable. This can be seen as having Perl plug-ins added to a C application.

The drawback to this is that the script, or scripts need to be shipped together with the application, which is something we may not want to do. Being normal scripts, anybody can open the scripts and mess with the source code, which could make our application unusable.

We can decide that we want to properly 'embed' Perl code in our application instead of depending on external files. We have already seen that the -e switch can be used to pass code directly to the Perl interpreter, but there is also a more convenient, and efficient, way, which is the eval_pv function, which works like Perl's built-in eval. We take our last sample from the previous section and we make it print Hello, world. This script is called phello.c:

```
#include <EXTERN.h>
#include <perl.h>

int main(int argc, char** argv, char** env) {
    PerlInterpreter *my_perl;
    char *switches[] = {"", "-e", "0"};
    my_perl = perl_alloc();
    perl_construct(my_perl);
    perl_parse(my_perl, NULL, 3, switches, (char**)NULL);
    perl_run(my_perl);

    eval_pv("print \"Hello, world\\n\";", 0);

    perl_destruct(my_perl);
    perl_free(my_perl);
}
```

eval_pv takes a string, containing Perl code, and a flag called croak_on_errors (the zero above). If the flag is set, and the evaluated code produces an error, Perl will die with its own error message (and of course, the C program dies with it). If it is zero, it acts just like eval does, ignoring fatal errors and setting the $@ variable (which can be accessed in C under the name ERRSV). We show how error handling works with this code:

```
/* 'safe' eval */
eval_pv("a deliberate error", 0);
if(SvTRUE(ERRSV)) {
    printf("eval_pv produced an error: %s\n",
        SvPV(ERRSV, PL_na));
}
```

```
/* 'unsafe' eval */
eval_pv("a deliberate error", 1);
/* this is never reached */
printf("too late, we died...\n");
```

In the first part, we use the SvTRUE function to check if the global variable ERRSV is true. If it is, then the evaluated block produced an error (and we report the error message by getting the PV stored in ERRSV). In the second part, the error simply causes the program to end.

Getting Perl Values

The value of defined Perl variables can be obtained using the get_* family of functions. We have get_sv for scalars, get_av for arrays, and get_hv for hashes.

This little program, called dump_inc.c, gets the @INC array using get_av, and dumps its content using av_len to get the array length, and av_fetch to fetch values from it in a loop:

```
#include <EXTERN.h>
#include <perl.h>

int main(int argc, char** argv, char** env) {
    PerlInterpreter *my_perl;
    AV* inc;
    SV** value;
    int i;

    char *switches[] = {"", "-e", "0"};
    my_perl = perl_alloc();
    perl_construct(my_perl);
    perl_parse(my_perl, NULL, 3, switches, (char**)NULL);
    perl_run(my_perl);

    inc = get_av("INC", 0);
    if(NULL != inc) {
        for(i = 0; i <= av_len(inc); i++) {
            value = av_fetch(inc, i, 0);
            if(NULL != value) {
                printf("%s \n", SvPV(*value, PL_na));
            }
        }
    }
    perl_destruct(my_perl);
    perl_free(my_perl);
}
```

The combination of eval and get functions is a powerful means to integrate Perl functionalities into a C program. For example, this function performs a pattern substitution on a string:

```
bool
substitute(char *string[], char *from, char *to, char *flags) {
    char *default_flag = "g";
    SV* instruction;
    SV* result;
```

```
        if(flags == NULL) flags = default_flag;

        /* note we use an SV* to evaluate */
        instruction = newSVpvf(
            "($string = '%s') =~ s/%s/%s/%s",
            *string, from, to, flags
        );

        /* evaluate the code */
        eval_sv(instruction, 0);

        /* oops, something went wrong... */
        if(SvTRUE(ERRSV)) return 0;

        /* $string now contains the new string, let's get it */
        result = get_sv("string", 0);

        /* and give it back to C */
        *string = SvPV(result, PL_na);
        return 1;
}
```

The function can be used comfortably from C as shown in foobar.c below:

```c
#include <EXTERN.h>
#include <perl.h>

int main(int argc, char** argv, char** env) {
    PerlInterpreter *my_perl;
    char *string = "foo is foo";
    char *switches[] = {"", "-e", "0"};

    my_perl = perl_alloc();
    perl_construct(my_perl);
    perl_parse(my_perl, NULL, 3, switches, (char**)NULL);
    perl_run(my_perl);

    printf("string is '%s'\n", string);
    substitute(&string, "foo", "bar", NULL);
    printf("string is now '%s'\n", string);

    perl_destruct(my_perl);
    perl_free(my_perl);
}
```

The program performs the Perl instruction s/foo/bar/g on our string, and correctly outputs:

string is 'foo is foo'
string is now 'bar is bar'

Using Perl Subroutines

Calling a Perl subroutine instead of evaluating pieces of code requires some additional steps. Parameters can't be simply passed from C to a Perl subroutine and vice versa, we have to perform a series of calls to set up the stack, push, and pop parameters to and from it.

This is the usual procedure to call a Perl subroutine from C, supposing our sub is called `foo`:

```
dSP;    /* declare the stack */
int count;

ENTER;    /* prepare the stack */
SAVETMPS;
PUSHMARK(SP);
XPUSHs("bar");    /* push input parameters */
XPUSHi(42);
PUTBACK;    /* finalize the stack */

count = call_pv("foo", 0);    /* call the sub 'foo' */
/* count holds the numbers of return values */

SPAGAIN;    /* query the stack */
for(i=0; i<=count; i++) {
    temp = POPp;    /* pop a string */
}
PUTBACK;    /* clean up */
FREETMPS;
LEAVE;
```

We have used `call_pv` to call a named subroutine, which could have been defined in an external Perl file, or built with an `eval_pv` statement. But if we don't want to pollute Perl's namespace, we can also use a reference to an anonymous subroutine. In the next example, we take the `commify` sub from the Perl FAQ (this sub formats a number with commas to separate thousands, for example 123456 will become 123,456) and store it in a `SV*` in our C program:

```
static SV* commify_sub;

void create_sub() {
    commify_sub = eval_pv(
        "sub {local $_ = shift; \
        1 while s/^(-?\\d+)(\\d{3})/$1,$2/; \
        return $_;}", 0);
}
```

Now that we have obtained `commify_sub`, we can use `call_sv` to actually call the code reference stored in it:

```
int
commify(char *result[], double number) {
    dSP;
    int count;
    int success;

    ENTER;
    SAVETMPS;
    PUSHMARK(SP);
    XPUSHn(number);
    PUTBACK;
    count = call_sv(commify_sub, G_SCALAR);
    SPAGAIN;
```

```
    if(count != 1) {
        success = 0;
    } else {
        *result = POPp;
        success = 1;
    }
    PUTBACK;
    FREETMPS;
    LEAVE;
    return success;
}
```

Our `commify` function, created above, will call our globally stored `commify_sub`. This is now ready to be used from C:

```c
#include <EXTERN.h>
#include <perl.h>

int main(int argc, char** argv, char** env) {
    PerlInterpreter *my_perl;
    char *switches[] = {"", "-e", "0"};
    char *commified;

    my_perl = perl_alloc();
    perl_construct(my_perl);
    perl_parse(my_perl, NULL, 3, switches, (char**)NULL);
    perl_run(my_perl);

    create_sub();

    if(commify(commified, 1675002)) {
        printf("commified: %s\n", commified);
        free(commified);
    }
    if(commify(commified, 39852.12)) {
        printf("commified: %s\n", commified);
        free(commified);
    }

    perl_destruct(my_perl);
    perl_free(my_perl);
}
```

This program will output, as expected, the result from the Perl `commify` sub:

```
commified: 1,675,002
commified: 39,852.12
```

Working with Perl Internals

Some parts of the Perl internals can also be accessed directly from C, without a line of Perl code. For example, Perl variables (scalars, arrays, and hashes) can be created and managed using Perl's C APIs.

This program, hash.c, shows how to build a hash using the newHV function: the hash is stored in a HV structure. We can then store a value in it using hv_store, and query the hash with hv_fetch. Full documentation for the C representation of Perl's variables can be found in the perlguts manual page.

```c
#include <EXTERN.h>
#include <perl.h>

int main(int argc, char** argv, char** env) {
    PerlInterpreter *my_perl;
    char *switches[] = {"", "-e", "0"};
    HV* hash;
    SV** value;

    my_perl = perl_alloc();
    perl_construct(my_perl);
    perl_parse(my_perl, NULL, 3, switches, (char**)NULL);
    perl_run(my_perl);

    /* create the hash */
    hash = newHV();

    /* store the 'test' value... */
    hv_store(hash, "test", 4, newSViv(42), 0);

    /*...and fetch it */
    value = hv_fetch(hash, "test", 4, 0);

    /* first check it is defined */
    if(NULL != value) {
        printf("hash{test}=%d\n", SvIV(*value));
    }

    perl_destruct(my_perl);
    perl_free(my_perl);
}
```

Instead of fetching a single key from the hash, we can iterate through its keys, as per Perl's each function, with this code:

```c
SV* val;
char* key;
I32 keylen;

hv_iterinit(hash);
while ((val = hv_iternextsv(hash, &key, &keylen))) {
    printf("hash{%s}=%s\n", key, SvPV(val, PL_na));
}
```

The next example, do_join.c, goes even further and shows how to call the equivalent of Perl's built-in join directly from C. This is not part of the officially exposed APIs, so this can be considered as a little hack. The prototypes for many of the Perl built-ins are contained in proto.h, which is in the source distribution.

```
#include <EXTERN.h>
#include <perl.h>

int main(int argc, char** argv, char** env) {
    PerlInterpreter *my_perl;
    char *switches[] = {"", "-e", "0"};
    SV* joined;
    SV* stack[4];

    my_perl = perl_alloc();
    perl_construct(my_perl);
    perl_parse(my_perl, NULL, 3, switches, (char**)NULL);
    perl_run(my_perl);

    /* place a dummy SV on top of the stack */
    stack[0] = &PL_sv_undef;

    /* the strings we want to join */
    stack[1] = newSVpv("one", 0);
    stack[2] = newSVpv("two", 0);
    stack[3] = newSVpv("three", 0);

    /* this will hold the result */
    joined = &PL_sv_undef;

    do_join(joined, newSVpv(", ", 0), stack, stack+3);

    printf("and the result is: '%s'\n", SvPV(joined, PL_na));

    perl_destruct(my_perl);
    perl_free(my_perl);
}
```

This program does the equivalent of Perl's join (', ', 'one', 'two', 'three'), producing this output:

and the result is: 'one, two, three'

Using Modules

Using a Perl module is not a problem, as long as the module is pure Perl. For example, to use the Config module, the -MConfig switch can be added to perl_parse, as shown in this code, use_config.c:

```
#include <EXTERN.h>
#include <perl.h>

int main(int argc, char** argv, char** env) {
    static PerlInterpreter *my_perl;
    char *switches[] = {"", "-MConfig", "-e", "0"};
    HV* config;
    SV** osname;
```

```
    my_perl = perl_alloc();
    perl_construct(my_perl);
    perl_parse(my_perl, NULL, 4, switches, (char**)NULL);
    perl_run(my_perl);

    config = get_hv("Config", 0);
    osname = hv_fetch(config, "osname", 6, 0);
    if(NULL != osname) {
        printf("$Config{osname} = '%s'\n", SvPV(*osname, PL_na));
    }

    perl_destruct(my_perl);
    perl_free(my_perl);
}
```

The module could also have been accessed using this code instead:

```
eval_pv("use Config", 0);
```

The program will act just like Perl does: it will search for the Config.pm file in its @INC, read it and evaluate it. This also means that it needs to find the file where it's supposed to be, so the program will not run on a machine without a proper Perl lib directory set up.

As mentioned before, this works only as long as the module is made up of Perl and nothing else. If we try to use a module that uses the XS interface, it will fail miserably. We'll get an error message saying that our Perl can't do dynamic loading.

To use a module that in turn loads a shared library, the DynaLoader module, which takes care of loading the library and providing hooks to its exported symbols, must have been previously initialized.

To do this, we use the second parameter to perl_parse, which we've left to NULL until now. The definition for this parameter in the prototype is void(*xsinit)(void), a function which takes no arguments and returns none.

This function, usually simply defines an XS subroutine to 'bootstrap' DynaLoader: the rest is done by the module itself:

```
void xs_init() {
    char *file = __FILE__;
    newXS("DynaLoader::boot_DynaLoader", boot_DynaLoader, file);
}
```

We also need to provide, before this function, the prototype for the boot_DynaLoader function, defined in the module's library:

```
void boot_DynaLoader (CV* cv);
```

Now xs_init can be passed to perl_parse, and we are able to use XS extensions. This sample program, named use_posix.c, calls a function contained in the POSIX module, which has an XS part:

```
#include "embedded_perl.h"

void boot_DynaLoader (CV* cv);

void xs_init() {
   char *file = __FILE__;
   newXS("DynaLoader::boot_DynaLoader", boot_DynaLoader, file);
}

int main(int argc, char** argv, char** env) {
   dSP;

   perl_prologue();

   printf("using POSIX...\n");
   eval_pv("use POSIX", 0);

   printf("calling POSIX::clock...\n");
   call_pv("POSIX::clock", G_SCALAR|G_NOARGS);

   SPAGAIN;
   printf("POSIX::clock returned %ld\n", POPi);

   perl_epilogue();
}
```

If the genmake script is used to do the build, a file called perlxsi.c is automatically generated and compiled together with the program. This file defines the xs_init function for us, so we only need to include its prototype before the main function:

```
void xs_init();
```

The Java-Perl Lingo

The Java-Perl Lingo (or JPL for short), originally put up by Larry Wall, provides interoperability between Perl and Java. It is composed of two distinct parts: one that allows Java classes and methods to be used from Perl, and another that allows Perl code to be 'embedded' into Java classes. To use this package, a JDK (Java Development Kit) must also be available on our system.

This example shows the first part at work:

```
use JPL::Class 'java::lang::StringBuffer';
$sb = java::lang::StringBuffer->new__s("TEST");
print "Java string: ", $sb->toString___s(), "\n";
```

With the use JPL::Class directive, we import, in Java terms, the desired class. The class becomes a regular Perl package, exposing its methods as Perl methods. We only need to 'decorate' the names with the signature for input and output parameters.

Details for this can be found in the JNI (Java Native Interface) documentation. The JPL delimiter for signatures is a double underscore, so we gather that the new method gets a string (s is a special case for the JNI Ljava/lang/String; signature) as its argument, while the toString method gets no argument and returns a string.

The next example shows how to define a Perl method inside a Java class. We simply define a Java method with the `perl` prefix, and put its body into double brackets:

```
class foo {
    perl int add(int a, int b) {{
        return $a + $b;
    }}
// ...rest of the code here
}
```

The file should be named `foo.jpl`, and it will be compiled by JPL into `foo.class`. The provided JPL tool will perform all the necessary steps for us. The command for this is:

> jpl foo.jpl

In reality, the result will be composed of the Java class, a Perl file, and a dynamic library to provide glue between the two.

Perl and COM

ActiveState's Perl Dev Kit (or PDK for short) contains two tools that allow Perl to be used in a COM environment. The advantages of doing this, in terms of integration, are quite high on the Windows operating systems, where many programming languages and applications make use of the COM architecture.

Take just a quick look at what these tools provide; for further information, refer to the documentation included with the copy of the PDK.

PerlCOM

PerlCOM is, basically, a DLL that exposes a COM interface to a Perl interpreter. Using PerlCOM is very similar to having an embedded Perl. This time, however, it can be embedded in every programming language, or application, which supports COM objects, not only in C as we've seen so far. The next sample shows how to embed PerlCOM, and evaluate a snippet of code inside Visual Basic:

```
Dim my_Perl
Set my_Perl = CreateObject("PerlCOM.Script")

my_Perl.EvalScript("print ""Hello, world!\n"" ")
```

The `my_Perl` object can also be used to access Perl functions and variables directly:

```
my_Perl.EvalScript("$foo = 'bar'")
MsgBox my_Perl.foo

my_Perl.EvalScript( _
    "sub hello {my($name) = @_; return 'Hello '.$name;}" _
)
MsgBox my_Perl.hello("Joe")
```

PerlCOM provides some additional methods for useing Perl modules and datatypes, such as `UsePackage`, and `CreateHash`.

Here we've made some samples using Visual Basic, but PerlCOM objects can be instantiated in a number of other environments, including Microsoft Visual C++ and J++, Delphi, VBA, and even Python.

'PerlCtrl'

`PerlCtrl` is another variation on the COM theme: it is a command line tool that takes a Perl script and turns it into an ActiveX component.

This way, instead of implementing a full-blown Perl interpreter, we can implement a 'control' that exposes only the methods and properties we have defined in the appropriate type library. This requires a bit of coding, in the Perl script itself, to properly define what should and should not be exposed.

In a few words, the script should contain a `%TypeLib` hash (commented out from Perl's view with pod directives, but interpreted by the `PerlCtrl` program) with all the information about the COM interface we are going to expose. Here, we take the code from a sample control implementation, `hello.ctrl`, included with the PDK to illustrate what a `PerlCtrl` program looks like:

```perl
package Hello;
sub Hello {
   return "Hello, world!";
}

=pod

=begin PerlCtrl

%TypeLib = (
   PackageName => 'Hello',

   # DO NOT edit the next 3 lines.
   TypeLibGUID => '{E91B25C6-2B15-11D2-B466-0800365DA902}',
   ControlGUID => '{E91B25C7-2B15-11D2-B466-0800365DA902}',
   DispInterfaceIID=> '{E91B25C8-2B15-11D2-B466-0800365DA902}',

   ControlName => 'Hello World Control',
   ControlVer => 1,
   ProgID => 'Hello.World',

   DefaultMethod => '',

   Methods => {
      'Hello' => {
      RetType => VT_BSTR,
      TotalParams => 0,
      NumOptionalParams => 0,
      ParamList =>[ ]
      },
   },   # end of 'Methods'
```

```
    Properties => {
    } ,
    # end of 'Properties'

);   # end of %TypeLib

=end PerlCtrl

=cut
```

This script is simply passed to the PerlCtrl command line utility that will generate a DLL from our code. This DLL is then registered on our system, and we can instantiate the COM object as we've seen before:

```
Dim my_Hello
Set my_Hello = CreateObject("Hello.World")

MsgBox my_Hello.Hello()
```

The same considerations made about implementing PerlCOM apply, of course, to PerlCtrl objects as well. The resulting object can be instantiated in every language or application that supports COM.

Miscellaneous Languages

So far, we have seen a number of ways to integrate other programming languages with Perl. On CPAN, however, there are also Perl modules that implement different languages, and modules that are designed to implement language parsers. The proverbial flexibility of Perl in text parsing and string handling makes it a perfect candidate for writing language interpreters.

Some of them are purely academic exercises, and far from being fully functional interpreters, but nonetheless they may contain useful bits of code. CPAN offers little gems like Language::Basic by Amir Karger, or Language::Prolog by Jack Shirazi, and the perl-lisp package by Gisle Aas, for example. These are all interesting efforts to implement, at least subsets, of other languages in Perl.

Damian Conway has released a very interesting module called Lingua::Romana::Perligata. This module is an interpreter that uses the ancient latin language as a 'dialect' to write Perl code. Agreed, it is unlikely that someone will actually write programs in this language, but the code that's behind it deserves a mention.

The module has a very complex grammar and uses Latin inflections to distinguish, for example, hashes from scalars. It makes use of the Filter (covered in the next section) and the Parse::Yapp modules (by Francois Desarmenien).

The last of the two modules is a grammar compiler, similar to the UNIX yacc tool. In a few words, it generates a parser based on user-defined rules and syntax. Another similar tool is the Parse::RecDescent module, also written by Damian Conway.

These modules are the building blocks of language design, and if anyone is serious about this topic, they definitely should learn to use them.

The Filter Module

Something that deserves a special mention is the `Filter` module, by Paul Marquess, which gives us the ability to turn Perl into something else. The module makes use of a very powerful feature of the Perl internals, that we saw at work with the `ByteLoader` module in Chapter 20.

The principle is very simple: a hook function is installed, and then it is called when data is read from the program source. This function can modify the data before it is passed to the Perl interpreter. This way, the source code of a program can be modified before it is parsed by Perl. This means, for example, that we can write our code in something that isn't Perl, and using an appropriate filter we can translate it back to Perl before it is interpreted.

The `Filter` distribution, available from CPAN, comes with a module called `Filter::Util::Call`, which hides all the complexities of working with the Perl internals, and allows us to write a Perl filter in a few lines of code.

We'll see how it works with a basic example: this filter reads its input and uses `tr` to shift the letters thirteen places forward in the alphabet. There is a simpleminded 'encoding' algorithm known on the Usenet as `rot13`, and so this script is named `rot13.pm`:

```
package rot13 ;
use Filter::Util::Call ;
sub import {
    filter_add(
        sub {
            my $status;
            tr/n-za-mN-ZA-M/a-zA-Z/
            if ($status = filter_read()) > 0;
            return $status;
        }
    );
}
1;
```

The `import` function, which is called automatically when the module is used, contains a `filter_add` call. It takes a code reference as its argument, which is the hook code for doing the real filtering.

This filter routine takes a line from the file using the `filter_read` function, and uses the $status variable to check for the end of file. The filter works directly on $_, so we use `tr` implicitly on it. The modified $_ is then passed to the Perl interpreter.

We can 'encode' a script with the `rot13` algorithm using the following one liner. The `hello.pl` sample script contains one line (`print "Hello, world\n"`):

> perl -pi.bak -e 'tr/a-zA-Z/n-za-mN-ZA-M/' hello.pl

The script now contains what, at a first glance, looks like funny characters and nothing more (cevag "Uryyb, jbeyq\a"). Of course if we try to execute it, we'll get a syntax error. But it still can be executed using the filter package we've prepared, like this:

> perl -Mrot13 hello.pl
Hello, world!

Although simple, this trick shows a very powerful technique. Of course, much more power can be obtained using an XS extension instead of plain Perl code. The `Filter` distribution contains examples of filters written in C, which may be used as a template for our own filters.

Starting from version 5.6.0, the Perl documentation also includes a `perlfilter` manual page, which explains in more depth the concepts of source filtering and their usage.

Summary

Throughout this chapter, we have seen how Perl can interact with a number of other programming languages, in particular with C. We have looked at this interaction in two different directions; using C from Perl and using Perl from C. This is done by utilizing various tools, interfaces and modules. As a summary we have:

❑   Introduced the XS interface to extend Perl by making use of C.

❑   Seen how Perl can call functions residing in external libraries using dynamic loading.

❑   Seen how to embed the Perl interpreter in a C program.

❑   Reviewed integration with different languages like Java, and (on Windows) Visual Basic, and other COM-aware environments.

❑   Given some pointers to useful tools when implementing language design in Perl.

22

Creating and Managing Processes

When a script is run, regardless of whatever language it has been compiled in, there are certain features common to each execution. In this chapter, we shall be looking at some of these aspects more closely in order to gain a better understanding of processes and how they behave within a program.

First we shall begin by laying a solid foundation on understanding signals. Even simple, single processes will be able to benefit from the proper handling of them. Then we shall move on to the manipulation and behavior of processes before moving on to the subject of how they can be split up and utilized.

Another important aspect of processes, much like the real-life analogy of parents and children, is the communication between them. In the later sections we expand the ideas of using pipes and other objects in handling data between processes. Finally we cover a major new topic, which is experimental in Perl at the present moment – threads. We can still use it at this stage so long as we are careful but threading will be built into future Perl releases, beginning with Perl 6.

Signals

Much like hardware interrupts, **signals** are exception events that happen independently of a process. They are even considered to be 'out of band', since they cannot be deferred for handling. Any signal sent is received by the process instantly, and must be processed immediately. Typically, our operating environment has defined default behaviors for most signals. A UNIX shell, for instance, maps some signals to key sequences, such as KILL to Ctrl-C, and STOP to Ctrl-Z. Other processes, as well as the OS kernel, have the ability to send signals to any designated process.

Every process keeps an index of signals and their defined behaviors. Whenever a process receives a signal, it stops normal execution and executes the behavior defined for that signal. Depending on the signal, that behavior may take some action and return control back to the interrupted routine. Other behaviors may do some cleaning up and exit the program, while others can do nothing, effectively ignoring the signal. Regardless of the signal, Perl allows the programmer to redefine the behaviors of most signals as necessary. The signal index is stored as the hash variable %SIG, with the key value being the signal name, and the value being either a reference to a subroutine to execute, or an appropriate return value. By assigning various values to signals in the hash, we can control how Perl and our process handle different kinds of signals.

To elaborate a little on what kind of signals we have available, we can dump out a list of them by printing out the keys of the %SIG hash:

```perl
#!/usr/bin/perl
# signals.pl
use warnings;
use strict;

foreach (sort keys %SIG) {
    print "$_\n";
}
```

At the system level each signal is denoted as an integer, rather than as the name we know them. As seen from the above, however, Perl does not index the signals in %SIG by their numeric values, but by the name. If we need to cross reference the numeric and names, we can discover them via the kill -1 command (provided we're on a UNIX platform, of course) or through the position of the name in Perl's Config variable sig_name, which is a space-delimited string:

```perl
#!/usr/bin/perl
# siglist.pl
use warnings;
use strict;

use Config;

my @signals = split ' ', $Config{sig_name};
for (0..$#signals) {
    print "$_ $signals[$_] \n" unless $signals[$_] =~ /^NUM/;
}
```

This generates a list of all signals and their associated numbers, skipping over real time signal numbers beginning NUM (in the range between RTMIN and RTMAX):

0 ZERO
1 HUP
2 INT
3 QUIT
4 ILL
5 TRAP
6 ABRT
7 BUS
8 FPE
9 KILL
10 USR1
...

Many of these signals are obscure, unlikely, or only occur if we have certain things enabled. The signal SIGPWR for example, applies to power failure situations and SIGIO occurs only with filehandles set to asynchronous mode using O_ASYNC. The most commonly used signals are as follows (please note that not all of the signals below work on non-UNIX platforms):

Name	Key	Meaning
SIGHUP	HUP	**Hangup** Controlling terminal or process has terminated (for example a modem, hence 'hang up'). Often redefined in daemons to tell them to re-read their configuration files and restart operations.
SIGINT	INT	**Interrupt** Instructs the process to interrupt what it is doing and exit. This signal is trappable (which means we can redefine its handler) so that a process can perform any necessary clean up before doing so. Pressing Ctrl-C on the keyboard is often the manual way to send this signal.
SIGQUIT	QUIT	**Quit** A higher priority signal to shut down and, depending on the system's configuration, may produce a core dump. This signal, too, is trappable.
SIGKILL	KILL	**Kill** An explicit command to tell the process to immediately exit. This signal is not trappable (would we really want to take away the kernel's ability to terminate run-away processes?).
SIGUSR1	USR1	**User-defined signal** While this signal is never used by the kernel, the default behavior for any process receiving the signal is to exit.
SIGUSR2	USR2	**User-defined signal** A second signal for process definition. Like USR1, the default behavior is to exit.
SIGPIPE	PIPE	**Broken pipe** A pipe that a process was either reading from or writing to has been closed by the other end.
SIGALRM	ALRM	**Alarm** An alarm timer for this process has expired. Not supported on Microsoft platforms.
SIGTERM	TERM	**Terminate** Like INT, this instructs the process to exit, and is trappable. This signal has a higher priority than INT, but lower than QUIT and KILL.

Table continued on following page

Name	Key	Meaning
SIGCHLD	CHLD	**Child exit**
		A child process has exited.
SIGFPE	FPE	**Floating point exception**
SIGSEGV	SEGV	**Invalid memory reference**
SIGCONT	CONT	**Continue**
		Resume execution if stopped by a STOP signal.
SIGSTOP	STOP	**Stop**
		The process is halted until it receives a CONT, at which point it resumes operational. This signal is not trappable.
SIGIO	IO	**Asynchronous IO event**
		If a filehandle is set for asynchronous operation (O_ASYNC), this signal is raised whenever an event (for example, more input) occurs on it.
SIGWINCH	WINCH	**Window changed**
		The window or terminal in which the console of a process is running has changed size. Chapter 15 discusses this in more detail.

For a complete list of signals, consult system documentation (> **man 7 signal** on UNIX), but be aware that even on UNIX, some signals are platform dependent. The same documentation should inform us of the default behavior of each signal. Regardless, by manipulating the contents of the %SIG hash we can override these defaults for most signal types, and install our own mechanisms for handling signals.

Signal Handling

A string or subroutine reference may be set as values of the %SIG hash to control what happens when a given signal is received:

Value	Action
DEFAULT or undef	Performs the default behavior as determined by the system.
IGNORE	Instructs the process to take no action in response to the signal. Untrappable signals are unaffected by this setting (such as KILL).
\&subreference	If a subroutine reference is set as the value of a signal then it is called whenever that signal is received. We can then decide how to handle it ourselves, including ignoring it, raising a different signal, dying, and so on.
subroutine	If the name of the subroutine is set as a string, this will be evaluated by &main::subroutine when the signal is received.

For example, to ignore SIGPIPE signals, we would put:

```
$SIG{PIPE} = 'IGNORE';
```

To restore the default handling for SIGINT signals:

```
$SIG{INT} = 'DEFAULT';
```

To find out the current setting of SIGALRM (remembering that undef is equal to DEFAULT):

```
$alarming = $SIG{ALRM};
```

To set a subroutine as a signal handler:

```
$SIG{USR1} = \&usr1handler;
```

The last of these is of course the most interesting. Signal handlers, when called, receive the name of the signal that called them as an argument, so we can assign multiple signals to the same handler, or handle each signal individually.

```
$SIG{HUP}  = \&handler;
$SIG{STOP} = \&handler;
$SIG{USR1} = \&handler;
```

If we set a text string that is not DEFAULT or IGNORE then it is taken as a symbolic reference to a subroutine in the main (not the current) package. So be careful about spelling. Thus:

```
$SIG{INT} = 'DEFLAT';
```

actually means:

```
$SIG{INT} = \&main::DEFLAT;
```

This will silently fail unless we are using the -w flag with Perl, in which case it will merely complain on STDERR that the handler DEFLAT is undefined. Although this is a perfectly legal way to set a signal handler, the fact that it defaults to the main package can cause problems when handling signals inside packages. Note also that though this is a form of symbolic reference, it is not trapped by the use strict refs pragma. Conversely, if we try to set a signal that does not exist, Perl will complain with an error, for example:

No such signal SIGFLARE at...

A practical example for redefining trappable signals would be when our program creates temporary files. A well-behaved program should clean up after itself before exiting, even when unexpectedly interrupted. In the following example we will redefine the INT handler to remove a temporary PID file before exiting. This will keep the program from leaving PID files around when the user interrupts the program with a Ctrl-C:

```
$SIG{INT} = sub {
    warn "received SIGINT, removing PID file and exiting.\n";
    system("rm", "$ENV{HOME}/.program.pid");
    exit 0;
};
```

The 'die' and 'warn' Handlers

In addition to the standard signals, the %SIG hash also allows us to set handlers for Perl's error reporting system, specifically the warn and die functions together with derivatives of them like carp and croak (supplied by the Carp module). These are not true signal handlers but hooks into Perl's internals, which allow us to react to events occurring within Perl. The %SIG hash makes a convenient interface because, aside from some minor differences in behavior, it operates very similarly to signals.

Neither the warn nor die hooks are present as keys in the %SIG hash by default – we have to add them:

```
$SIG{__WARN__} = \&watchout;
$SIG{__DIE__} = \&lastwillandtestament;
```

Both handlers may customize the error or warning before passing it on to a real warn or die (the action of the handler is suppressed within the handler itself, so calling warn or die a second time will do the real thing). A warning handler may choose to suppress the warning entirely; die handlers cannot, however, avert death, but only do a few things on their deathbed, so to speak. See Chapter 16 for more on die, warn, and registering handlers for them.

The hook mechanism is not extensible; the __ prefix and suffix merely distinguish these special handlers from true signal handlers. They do not, however, allow us to create arbitrary signals and handlers.

Writing Signal Handlers

Signal handlers are just subroutines. When they are called, Perl passes them a single parameter: the name of the signal. For example, here is a program containing a very simple signal handler that raises a warning whenever it receives an INT signal, but otherwise does nothing with it:

```perl
#!/usr/bin/perl
# inthandler1.pl
use warnings;
use strict;

sub handler {
    my $sig = shift;
    print "Caught SIG$sig! \n";
}

# register handler for SIGINT
$SIG{INT} = \&handler;

# kill time
while (1) { sleep 1; }
```

Note that since the handler, for all intents and purposes, handled the exception, the program does not exit. If we still want the handler to exit after performing whatever other actions we need done, we must add the exit command to the end of our handler. Here is another handler that implements this scheme, with a private counter. It will catch the first two signals, but defer to the normal behavior on the third reception:

```perl
#!/usr/bin/perl
# inthandler2.pl
use warnings;
use strict;
```

```
{
    # define counter as closure variable
    my $interrupted = 0;

    sub handler {
        foreach ($interrupted) {
            $_ == 0 and warn("Once..."), $interrupted++, last;
            $_ == 1 and warn("Twice..."), $interrupted++, last;
            $_ == 2 and die ("Thrice!");
        }
    }
}

# register handler for SIGINT
$SIG{INT} = \&handler;

# kill time
while (1) { sleep 1; }
```

A few platforms (BSD systems, typically) cancel signal handlers once they have been called. On these systems (and if we want to be maximally portable) we have to reinstall the handler before we exit it, if we wish to call it again:

```
handler {
    $sig = shift;

    # reinstate handler
    $SIG{$sig} = \&handler;

    ... do stuff ...
}
```

To prevent another signal from coming in before we have redefined it, we will do that first in every handler. Since this does no harm even on platforms that do not need it, it is a good piece of defensive programming if we are worried about portability.

Avoid Complex Handlers

The above handlers are good examples of signal handlers in that they do very little. By their nature, signals herald a critical event. In many cases, that condition means that executing complex code, and especially anything that causes Perl to allocate more memory to store a value, is a bad idea. For example, this signal counting handler is not a good idea because it allocates a new key and value for the hash each time a signal it has not previously seen arrives.

```
%sigcount;

sub allocatinghandler {
    $sig = shift;
    $sigcount {$sig}++;
}
```

This is fine though, as we have guaranteed that all the keys of the hash already exist and have defined values:

```
%sigcount = map { $_ => 0 } keys %SIG;

sub nonallocatinghandler {
    $sig = shift;
    $sigcount{$sig}++;
}
```

Regardless, there is one rule of thumb that must be adhered to wherever possible: do the absolute minimum necessary in any signal handler. If we do not, and another signal comes in while we are doing some kind of extensive processing, our program may suffer random core dumps. Perl, like many low-level system calls, is not re-entrant at the lowest levels.

Un-interruptible Signal Handlers

Unlike the warn and die hooks, real signal handlers do not suppress signals while they are running, so if we want to avoid being interrupted a second time while we are still handling a signal, we have to find a way to avoid further signals. One way to do this is simply to disable the handler for the duration of the handler:

```
sub handler {
    $sig = shift;

    $SIG{$sig} = 'IGNORE';
    ... do something ...
    $SIG{$sig} = \&handler;
}
```

A better way is to localize a fresh value for the signal value in $SIG using local. This has the same effect as reassigning it explicitly, but with the advantage that the old value is restored immediately on exiting the handler without our intervention:

```
sub handler {
    local $SIG{shift} = 'IGNORE';

    ... do something...
}
```

We can suppress signals in normal code using the same principles, for instance by temporarily reassigning a signal to a new handler or value. We can do that by either making a record of the old one, or using local to suppress it if we happen to be in a section of code that is scoped appropriately:

```
$oldsig = $SIG{INT};
$SIG{INT} = 'IGNORE';

... code we do not want interrupted ...

$SIG{INT} = $oldsig;
```

As always, these techniques only work on trappable signals.

Aborting System Level Operations

On many versions of UNIX, as well as a few other platforms, signals that occur during some system calls, and in particular during input and output operations, may cause the operation to restart on receiving the return from the signal handler. Frequently we would rather abort the whole operation at this point, since resuming is likely to be either pointless or plain wrong. Unfortunately the only way to abort the interrupted code from inside a signal handler is die or CORE::exit. Moreover, to be able to resume normal execution at a point of our choice rather than jump into a die handler or exit the program, we have to put the die (or rather, the context of the die) inside an eval, since that will exit the eval and resume execution beyond it. So the code we want to abort must all be inside an eval:

```
sub handler {
    $SIG{shift} = 'DEFAULT';
    die;
}

$result = eval {
    $SIG{INT} = \&handler;
    ...read from a network connection...
    $SIG{INT} = 'DEFAULT';
    1;    # return true on completion
}

warn "Operation interrupted! \n" unless $result;
```

If the code in the eval completes successfully it returns 1 (because that is the last expression in the eval). If the handler is called, the die causes the eval to return undef. So we can tell if the handler was called or not by the return value from eval, and therefore we can tell if the code was interrupted. We can vary this theme a little if we want to return an actual result from the eval, so long as we do not need to validly return a false value, we can always use this technique. Note that even though the die itself is not in the eval, the context in which it is called is the eval's context, so it exits the eval, not the program as a whole.

This approach also works for setting and canceling alarms to catch system calls that time out, see 'Alarms' later for more.

Flexibly Installing Signal Handlers

We have already seen how to install a signal handler by hand; simply set the value of the relevant signal in the signal hash:

```
$SIG{INT} = \&handler;
```

While fine for a single signal, this is cumbersome for handling many of them. One way to set up multiple signals is to assign a new hash to %SIG, for example:

```
%SIG = (%SIG, INT => IGNORE, PIPE = \&handler, HUP => \&handler);
```

There is, however, a better way, with the sigtrap pragmatic module. This takes a list of signal actions and signals and assigns each signal the action that immediately preceded it. sigtrap provides two handlers of its own; a stack-trace handler, the default action, and die, which does what it implies. It also provides several keywords for common groups of signals, as well as a keyword for currently unassigned signals.

903

The default action is **stack-trace**, so the following three pragmas all have the same effect; normal-signals is the group comprised of the SIGINT, SIGHUP, SIGPIPE, and SIGTERM signals:

```
use sigtrap qw(INT HUP PIPE TERM);
use sigtrap qw(stack-trace INT HUP PIPE TERM);
use sigtrap qw(stack-trace normal-signals);
```

Alternatively we can choose to set a die handler. Here are two examples of using die with the signals that sigtrap categorizes under error-signals:

```
use sigtrap qw(die ABRT BUS EMT FPE ILL QUIT SEGV SYS TRAP);
use sigtrap qw(die error-signals);
```

We can also supply our own handler, by prefixing it with the keyword handler:

```
use sigtrap qw(handler myhandler ALRM HUP INT);
```

If we want to be sure the handler exists before we install it we can drop the qw and use a sub reference in a regular list:

```
use sigtrap (handler => \&myhandler, ALRM HUP INT);
```

We may assign different handlers to different signals all at the same time; each signal is assigned the handler before it in the list. The signals at the front are assigned stack-trace if the first item in the list is not die or a handler of our own devising:

```
use sigtrap qw(
    stack-trace normal-signals ALRM USR2
    die error-signals
    handler usrhandler USR1 USR2
    die PWR
    handler inthandler INT HUP
);
```

We can specify as many handlers and signals as we like. In addition, later assignments supplant earlier ones, so handler inthandler INT HUP replaces the assignment to stack-trace of these signals in the first line (in the guise of normal-signals). If we want to assign a handler to all signals only if they have not already been assigned or ignored, we can precede the signals we want to trap conditionally with the untrapped keyword. For example, to call the stack-trace handler for normal signals not already trapped:

```
use sigtrap qw(stack-trace untrapped normal-signals);
```

The opposite of untrapped is any; this cancels the conditional assignment of untrapped:

```
use sigtrap qw(stack-trace untrapped normal-signals any ALRM USR1 USR2);
```

If sigtrap is not passed any signal names at all, it defaults to a standard set that is trapped in previous incarnations of the module. This list is also defined as old-interface-signals. The following are therefore equivalent:

```
use sigtrap qw(stack-trace old-interface-signals);
use sigtrap;
```

Sending Signals

The traditional UNIX command (and C system call) for sending signals is `kill`, a curious piece of nomenclature that comes about from the fact that the default signal sent by the `kill` command was 15 - SIGTERM which caused the program to exit. Despite this, we can send any signal using Perl's `kill` function.

The `kill` command takes at least two arguments. The first is a signal number or a signal name given as a string. The second and following arguments are the IDs of processes to kill. The return value from `kill` is the number of processes to which a signal was delivered (which, since they may ignore the signal, is not necessarily the number of processes that acted on it):

```
# tell kids to stop hogging the line
kill 'INT', @mychildren;

# a more pointed syntax
kill INT => @mychildren, $grandpatoo;

# commit suicide (die would be simpler)
kill KILL => $$;    # $$ is our own process ID
kill (9, $$);       # put numerically

# send our parent process a signal
kill USR1 => getppid
```

Sending a signal to a negative process ID will send it to the process group of that process (including any child processes it may have, and possibly the parent process that spawned it too, unless it used `setpgrp`). For example, this instruction will send an HUP signal to every other process in the same process group:

```
kill HUP => -$$;
```

The HUP signal in particular is useful for a parent process to tell all its children to stop what they are doing and re-initialize themselves. The Apache web server does exactly this in forked mode (which is to say, on UNIX but not Windows) if we send the main process an HUP. Of course, the main process does not want to receive its own signal, so we would temporarily disable it:

```
sub huphandler {
   local $SIG{HUP} = 'IGNORE';
   kill HUP => -$$;
}
```

The signal 0 (or ZERO) is special. It does not actually send a signal to the target process or processes at all, but simply checks that those process IDs exist. Since `kill` returns the number of processes to which a signal was successfully sent, for signal 0 it reports the number of processes that exist, which makes it a simple way to test if a process is running:

```
warn "Child $child is dead!" unless kill 0, $child;
```

Alarms

An alarms is a particularly useful kind of signal that is issued whenever an internal timer counts down to zero. We can set an alarm with the `alarm` function, which takes an integer number of seconds as an argument:

```
# set an alarm for sixty seconds from now
alarm 60;
```

If the supplied number is zero, the previous alarm, if any, is cancelled:

```
# cancel alarm
alarm 0;
```

Setting the alarm will cause the process to exit (as per the default behavior of the signal), unless we also set a new handler for the signal:

```
alarmhandler {
    print "Alarm at ", scalar(localtime), "\n";
}

$SIG{ALRM} = \&alarmhandler;
```

Please note that specifying a time interval does not mean that the timer will raise a `SIGALRM` in exactly that interval. What it says is that sometime after that interval, depending on the resolution of the system clock and whether our process is in the current context, a signal will be sent.

A Simple Use of Alarms

We can only ever have `alarm` active at one time, per process, so setting a new alarm value resets the timer on the existing alarm, with zero canceling it as noted above. Here is a program that demonstrates a simple use of alarms, to keep re-prompting the user to input a key:

```
#!/usr/bin/perl
# alarmkey.pl
use strict;
use warnings;

use Term::ReadKey;

# Make read blocking until a key is pressed, and turn on autoflushing (no
# buffered IO)
ReadMode 'cbreak';
$| = 1;

sub alarmhandler {
    print "\nHurry up!: ";
    alarm 5;
}
```

```
$SIG{ALRM} = \&alarmhandler;
alarm 5;

print "Hit a key: ";
my $key = ReadKey 0;
print "\n You typed '$key' \n";

# cancel alarm
alarm 0;

# reset readmode
ReadMode 'restore';
```

We use the Term::ReadKey module to give us instant key-presses without returns, and set $| = 1 to make sure the Hurry up! prompt appears in a timely manner. In this example the alarm 0 is redundant because we are about to exit the program anyway, but in a larger application this would be necessary to stop the rest of the program being interrupted by Hurry up! prompts every five seconds.

Using Alarms to Abort Hung Operations

We can also use alarms to abort an operation that has **hung** or is taking too long to complete. This works very similarly to the eval-and-die example we gave earlier for aborting from a section of code rather than continuing it – this time we use alarms instead to catch an interrupt. Here is a code snippet that aborts from an attempt to gain an exclusive lock over the file associated with the filehandle HANDLE if the lock is not achieved within one minute:

```
sub alarmhandler {
    die "Operation timed out!";
}

sub interrupthandler {
    die "Interrupted!";
}

$SIG{ALRM} = \&alarmhandler;
$SIG{INT} = \&interrupthandler;

$result = eval {
    # set a timer for aborting the lock
    alarm 60;

    # block waiting for lock
    flock HANDLE, LOCK_EX;

    # lock achieved! cancel the alarm
    alarm 0;

    ... read/write to HANDLE ...

    flock HANDLE, LOCK_UN;
    1;   # return true on completion
}

warn @_ unless $result;
```

The alternative approach to this is to turn the lock into a non-blocking lock, then check the return value, sleep for a short while, and then try again. The signal approach is more attractive than this solution in some ways, since it spends less time looping. It is, though, limited by the fact that we can no longer use an alarm for any other purpose until we have stopped using the alarm here for this purpose.

Starting New Processes

Perl supports the creation of new processes through the `fork` function, which is an interface to the operating system's underlying `fork` function, if we have one. Forking is a pre-UNIX concept, and is universal on all UNIX-like operating systems. Other platforms like Windows and Macintosh have chosen the threading model over the forking model, but Perl can still `fork` on these platforms. For those that do not support true forking, Perl emulates it closely. We can also choose to use the native `thread` model instead, should our Perl installation be built to support threads. See below for more information on threads.

The `fork` function spawns a clone of itself, creating a **child** process (the original process is called the **parent** process). The cloning is 'complete' since the child shares the same application code, variables, and filehandles, as the parent. The typical method used to tell the difference between the parent and child is in the return value from `fork`. For the child, it is `zero` and for the parent it is the process ID of the child if successful, `undef` if not. As a result, `fork` is always found in close proximity to an `if` statement, for example:

```
if ($pid = fork) {
   print "Still in the parent process - we started a child with ",
   "process id $pid \n";
} else {
   print "This is the child process\n";

   # terminate child and return success to the parent
   exit 0;
}
```

What the above example does not do, though, is check the return value for a failure of the `fork` operation. If the `fork` failed entirely it would return `undef` and we should always check for this possibility (which might occur if the system has reached a limit on processes or does not have enough memory to create the new process). So, we can check it using `defined`:

```
$pid = fork;
die "Failed to fork: $! \n" unless defined $pid;
if ($pid) {
   # parent
   ...
} else {
   # child
   ...
}
```

Replacing the Current Process with Another

On a related topic, we can replace the current process with a completely different one by using the exec command. This command is a rather dramatic function as it replaces the current process in its entirety with the external command supplied as an argument in the same context. Even the PID is inherited for the calling process:

```
exec 'command', @arguments;
```

In general exec is used with fork to run an external command as a sub-process. We will show some examples of this in action a little later in the chapter. We do not need to check the return value from exec since if it succeeds we will not be there to return to. Consequently the only time that we will continue past an exec is if it fails:

```
# hand over to the next act
exec @command;

# if we get here the exec must have failed
die "Exec failed: $!\n";
```

Several of Perl's built-in functions perform automatic fork-and-execs, including the system and backtick functions, and certain variants of open. We cover all of these later on in this chapter.

Process IDs

The **process ID** of the current process can always be found from the special variable $$ ($PID or $PROCESS_ID with the English module):

```
print "We are process $$\n";
```

A child process can find the process ID of the parent process with the getppid function (not implemented on Win32):

```
$parent = getppid;
print "Our parent is $parent \n";
```

This allows us to use kill to send a signal to the parent process:

```
kill "HUP", $parent;
```

On Win32, there is one caveat to be aware of: **Handles** (the Win32 equivalents of PIDS) are unsigned 32 bit integers, while Perl's 32 bit integers are signed. Due to this fact, PIDS are occasionally interpreted as a negative integer. Any signal sent to a negative integer goes to the entire process group, not just a specific process and these process groups are explained in more detail below.

Process, Groups and Daemons

Whenever a parent process uses fork (either directly or implicitly) to create a child, the child inherits the process group of the parent. **Process groups** become significant when signals are sent to a group rather than a single process. If it is intended to be an independent process then the parent may have its own group ID (which is generally the same as its process ID), otherwise it will have inherited the process group from its own parent.

We can find the process group of a process by using the `getpgrp` function (like `getppid`, this is not implemented on Win32), which takes a process ID as an argument. To find our own process group, we can write:

```
$pgid = getpgrp $$;
```

We can also supply any false value, including `undef`, to get the process group for the current process. This is generally a better idea because not all versions of `getpgrp` are the same, and the only value they have in common is 0. Since Perl maps directly to the underlying function, it means only 0 is truly portable:

```
$pgid = getpgrp 0;
$pgid = getpgrp;
```

In practice we usually do not want to find out the process group, we already know the child will have the same group as the parent. What we often do want to do is change the group, which we can do with `setpgrp`, which takes a process ID and a process group ID as arguments:

```
setpgrp $pid, $pgid;
```

In practice the only process we want to change the group for is our own – if we are a child process and we want to divorce ourselves from the fate of our parent. Likewise, while we can in theory join any group, we generally want to create our own group. Process group IDs are just numbers, and usually have the same value as the process ID that owns the group, that is, there is usually one process whose process ID and process group ID are the same. Children of that process, which didn't change their group have the same process group ID.

To put ourselves in our own group therefore, we simply need to give ourselves a process group ID that is equal to our process ID:

```
setpgrp $$, $$;
```

Again, we can use a false value for both IDs to default to the current process ID, so we can also say:

```
setpgrp 0, 0;
```

Or even just the following (though not quite as portable):

```
setpgrp;
```

Both calls will put the child process into its own group. By doing this we isolate the child from the process group that the parent originally belonged to. Here is a quick example of a **daemon** that performs the role of a back seat driver (that is, it keeps shouting out directions when we're trying to concentrate):

```
#!/usr/bin/perl
# backseat.pl;
# lack of use warnings;
use strict;
```

```
    setpgrp 0, 0;

if (my $pid = fork) {
    # exit if parent
    print "Backseat daemon started with id $pid \n";
    exit 0;
}

# child loops in background
while (1) {
    alarm 60;
    foreach (int rand(3)) {
        $_ == 0 and print ("Go Left! \n"), last;
        $_ == 1 and print ("Go Right! \n"), last;
        $_ == 2 and print ("Wait, go back! \n"), last;
    }
    sleep rand(3)+1;
}
```

Yes, this example did not use warnings. We intentionally left it out this time, since the valid syntax in the foreach loop would otherwise generate spurious warnings to verify our intent. Regardless, note that in this example we changed the process group of the parent, then forked the child before exiting. We could equally fork and then change the process group of the child since it makes little difference. If we do not want to print a friendly message we can also simplify the fork statement to just:

```
fork and exit;    # isn't self documenting code great?
```

Handling Children and Returning Exit Codes

Keeping an eye on children is always a challenging task, and it is just as true for processes as real life. We can get a child to stop if it is running away with itself by killing it (which may involve sending it a friendlier signal like TERM, so it has an opportunity to tidy up and exit, rather than simply killing it outright), but we still have to deal with the remnants regardless of who killed it or why it died.

When a child exits, the operating system keeps a record of its exit value and retains the process in the process table. The process is stored until the exit value is recovered by the parent. We are expected to tidy up after ourselves and recover the return values of child processes when they exit. If we fail to do this, the dead children turn into zombies when the parent exits (no, really – this is all serious UNIX terminology, do not think that it all sounds like a Hammer horror flick) and hang around the process table, dead but not buried. Using the ps command on a system where this is happening reveals entries marked zombie or defunct.

Perl's built-in functions (other than fork) automatically deal with this issue for us, so if we create extra processes with open we do not have to clean up afterwards. For fork and the IPC::Open2 and IPC::Open3 modules (both of which we cover later) we have to do our own housekeeping.

Waiting for an Only Child

If we, as the parent process, want to wait for a child to finish before continuing then there is no problem, we simply use the wait function to cease execution until the child exits:

```
# fork a child and execute an external command in it
exec @command unless fork;

# wait for the child to exit
$child_pid = wait;
```

The process ID of the child is returned by wait, if we need it.

Getting the Exit Status

When wait returns it sets the exit code of the child in the special variable $?. This actually contains two eight-bit values, the exit code and the signal (if any) that caused the child to exit, combined into a sixteen-bit value. To get the actual exit code and signal number we therefore need to use:

```
$exitsig = $? & 0xff;   # signal is lower 8 bits
$exitcode = $? >> 8;    # exit code is upper 8 bits
```

If we import the wait symbols from the POSIX module we can also say things like:

```
use POSIX qw(:sys_wait_h);

$exitsig = WSTOPSIG($?);
$exitcode = WEXITSTATUS($?);
```

> *The POSIX module also contains a few other handy functions in the same vein, we list them all briefly at the end of the section.*

Only one of the exit codes and the signals will be set, so for a successful exit (that is, an exit code of zero), $? will be zero too. This is a convenient Boolean value, of course, so we can test $? for truth to detect a failed process, whether it exited with a non-zero status or aborted by a signal. Of course, since such codes are often left to the discretion of the developer to respect, we cannot always rely on that.

In some cases, particularly if we wrote the external command, the returned code may be an errno value, which we can assign to $! for a textual description of the error.

In the child process/external command:

```
# exit with $! explicitly
exit $! if $!;

# 'die' automatically returns $!
die;
```

In the parent process:

```
wait;
$exitcode = $? >> 8;
if ($exitcode) {
$! = $exitcode;
die "Child aborted with error: $! \n";
}
```

If there are no child processes then `wait` returns immediately with a return value of `-1`. However, this is not generally useful since we should not be in the position of calling `wait` if we did not `fork` first, and if we did attempt to `fork`, we should be testing the return value of that operation. If we are handling more than one process we should use `waitpid` instead.

Handling Multiple Child Processes

If we have more than one child process then `wait` is not always enough, because it will return when any child process exits. If we want to wait for a particular child then we need to use `waitpid`:

```
$pid = fork;
if ($pid) {
   waitpid $pid, 0;
} else {
   ...child...
}
```

Two arguments are taken by `waitpid`. The first is the process ID of the child to wait for. The second argument is a flag that effects the operation of `waitpid`. The most common flag to place here is `WNOHANG`, which tells `waitpid` not to wait if the child is still running but return immediately with `-1`. This argument is one of several constants defined by the `POSIX` module, and we can import it either from the `:sys_wait_h` group or directly:

```
use POSIX qw(:sys_wait_h);
```

Or:

```
use POSIX qw(WNOHANG);
```

We can use this to periodically check for a child's exit without being forced to wait for it:

```
if ($pid = fork) {
   while (1) {
      $waiting = 1;
      if ($waiting and (waitpid $pid, WNOHANG)!= -1) {
         $waiting = 0;
         handle_return_value($? >> 8);
         ...
         last;
      }
      ... check on other children, or do other misc. tasks...
   }
} else {
   ... child ...
}
```

This works for a single child process, but if we have several children to tidy up after we have to collect all their process IDs into a list and check all of them. This is not convenient. Fortunately we can pass -1 to waitpid to make it behave like wait and return with the value of the first available dead child:

```
# wait until any child exits
waitpid -1, 0;

# this is the non-blocking version
waitpid -1, WNOHANG;
```

We do not necessarily want to keep checking for our children exiting, particularly if we do not care about their exit status and simply want to remove them from the process table because we are conscientious and responsible parents. What we need is a way to call waitpid when a child exits without having to check periodically in a loop. Fortunately we can install a signal handler for the SIGCHLD signal that allow us to do exactly this:

```
sub waitforchild {
    waitpid -1, 0;
}

$SIG{CHLD} = \&waitforchild;
```

We do not need to specify WNOHANG here because we know by the fact that the signal handler was called, a child has exited. Unfortunately, if more than one child exits at once, we might only get one signal, so calling waitpid once is not enough. A truly efficient signal handler thus needs to keep calling waitpid until there are no exit codes left to collect, which brings us back to WNOHANG again:

```
sub waitforchildren {
    $pid;
    do {
        $pid = waitpid -1, WNOHANG;
    } until ($pid! == -1);
}

$SIG{CHLD} = \&waitforchildren;
```

This is of course rather tedious, but it is necessary if we are to manage child processes responsibly. On some systems we can get away with simply ignoring SIGCHLD, and have the operating system remove dead children for us:

```
$SIG{CHLD} = 'IGNORE';
```

Or, if we can let the child change its process group, we can let init reap children instead. This is not portable across all systems, though, so in general the above solutions are preferred.

POSIX Flags and Functions

The POSIX module defines several symbols and functions other than WNOHANG for use with the wait and waitpid system calls. We can make all of them available by importing the :sys_wait_h tag:

```
use POSIX qw(:sys_wait_h);
```

There are two flags. One is WNOHANG, which we have already seen. The other, WUNTRACED, also returns process IDs for children that are currently stopped (that is, have been sent a SIGSTOP) and have not been resumed. For example:

```
$possibly_stopped_pid = waitpid -1, WNOHANG | WUNTRACED;
```

In addition, the following convenience functions are defined:

Function	Action
WEXITSTATUS	Extract the exit status, if the process has exited. Equivalent to $? >> 8. For example: `$exitcode = WEXITSTATUS($?);` The exit code is zero if the process was terminated by a signal.
WTERMSIG	Extract the number of the signal that terminated the process, if the process aborted on a signal. For example: `$exitsignal = WTERMSIG($?);` The signal number is zero if the process exited normally (even if with an error).

WIFEXITED	Check that the process exited, as opposed to being aborted by a signal. The opposite of WIFSIGNALED. For example:
	
	 `if (WIFEXITED $?) {`
	 `    return WEXITSTATUS($?)`
	 `} else {return -1};`

WIFSIGNALED	Check that the process terminated on a signal, as opposed to exited. The opposite of WIFEXITED. For example:
	
	 `if (WIFSIGNALED $?) {`
	 `    print "Aborted on signal ",`
	 `    WTERMSIG($?), "\n";`
	 `} elsif (WEXITSTATUS $?) {`
	 `    print "Exited with error ",`
	 `    WEXITSTATUS($?), "\n";`
	 `} else {`
	 `    # exit code was 0`
	 `    print "Success! \n";`
	 `}`

Table continued on following page

915

Function	Action
WSTOPSIG	Extract the number of the signal that stopped the process, if we specified WUNTRACED and the process returned is stopped as opposed to terminated. For example: `$stopsig = WSTOPSIG($?)` This is usually SIGSTOP, but not necessarily.

WIFSTOPPED	If we specified WUNTRACED as a flag, this returns true if the returned process ID was for a stopped process: `if (WIFSTOPPED $?) {`
	`    print "Process stopped by signal ",`
	`    WSTOPSIG($?),"\n";`
	`} elsif (...){`
	`    ...`
	`}`

Communicating Between Processes

Communicating between different processes, or **Inter-Process Communication (IPC)**, is a subject with many facets. Perl provides us with many possible ways to establish communications between processes, from simple unidirectional pipes, through bi-directional socket pairs to fully-fledged control over an externally executed command.

In this section we are going to discuss the various ways in which different processes can communicate with one another, and the drawbacks of each approach whilst paying particular attention to communications with an externally run command. The open function provides a simple and easy way to do this, but unless we trust the user completely it can also be a dangerous one, unless we take the time to do some thorough screening. Instead we can turn to the forking version of open, or use the IPC::Open2 or IPC::Open3 library modules for a safer approach.

Before covering the more advanced ways to establish communications between processes and external programs we will cover the obvious and simple methods like system and do. They may not be sophisticated, but sometimes they are all we need to get the job done.

Very Simple Solutions

If we simply want to run an external program we do not necessarily have to adopt measures like pipes (covered in the next section) or child processes, we can just use the system function:

```
system "command plus @arguments";
```

However, if system is passed a single argument it checks it to see if it contains shell-special characters (like spaces, or quotes), and if present, starts a shell as a sub-process to run the command. This can be dangerous if the details of the command are supplied by the user; we can end up executing arbitrary commands like rmdir.

A better approach is to pass the arguments individually and this causes Perl to execute the command directly, bypassing the shell:

```
system 'command', 'plus', @arguments;
```

However, `system` only returns the exit code of the command, which is great if we want to know if it succeeded or not but fairly useless for reading its output. For that we can use the backtick operator qx, or backtick quotes:

```
# these two statements are identical. Note both interpolate too.
$output = `command plus @arguments`;
$output = qx/command plus @arguments/;
```

Unfortunately, both variants of the backtick operator create a shell, and this time there is no way to avoid it, since there is no way to pass a list of arguments. If we really want to avoid the shell we have to start getting creative using a combination of `open`, `pipe`, and `fork`. Fortunately Perl makes this a little simpler for us, as we will see shortly.

Not to be overlooked, we can also execute external programs with the `do` command if they are written in Perl. This command is essentially an enhanced version of `eval` which reads its input from an external file rather than having it written directly into the code. Its intended purpose is for loading in library files (other than modules, for which `use` or `require` are preferred), which do not generate output. If the script happens to print things to standard output, that will work too, so long as we don't want to control the output.

```
$return_value = do './local_script.pl';
```

The `do` command has a lot of disadvantages, however. Unlike `eval` it does not cache the code executed for later use, and it is strictly limited in what it can do. For more useful and constructive forms of inter-process communication we need to involve pipes.

Pipes

A pipe is, simply put, a pair of file handles joined together. In Perl we can create pipes with the `pipe` function, which takes two filehandle names as arguments. One filehandle is read-only, and the other is write-only. By default, Perl attempts to buffer IO. This is also the case when we want a command to respond to each line without waiting for a series of lines to come through to flush the buffer. So we would write:

```
pipe (READ, WRITE);
select WRITE;
$| = 1;
```

Or, using `IO::Handle`:

```
use IO::Handle;
pipe (READ, WRITE);
WRITE->autoflush(1);
```

We can also create pipes with the `IO::Pipe` module. This creates a 'raw' `IO::Pipe` object that we convert into a read-only or write-only `IO::Handle` by calling either the `reader` or `writer` methods:

```perl
use IO::Pipe;

$pipe = new IO::Pipe;
if (fork) {
    $pipe->reader;
    # $pipe is now a read-only IO::Handle
} else {
    $pipe->writer;
    # $pipe is now a write-only IO::Handle
}
```

The most common use for pipes is for IPC (Inter-Process Communication mentioned earlier), which is why we bring them up here rather than in Chapter 23. As a quick example and also as an illustration of pipes from the filehandle perspective, here is a program that passes a message back and forth between a parent and child process using two pipes and a call to `fork`:

```perl
#!/usr/bin/perl
# message.pl
use warnings;
use strict;

pipe CREAD, PWRITE;    # parent->child
pipe PREAD, CWRITE;    # child->parent

my $message = "S";

if (fork) {
    # parent - close child end of pipes
    close CREAD;
    close CWRITE;

    syswrite PWRITE, "$message \n";
    while (<PREAD>) {
        chomp;
        print "Parent got $_ \n";
        syswrite PWRITE, "P$_ \n";
        sleep 1;
    }
} else {
    # child - close parent end of pipes
    close PREAD;
    close PWRITE;

    while (<CREAD>) {
        chomp;
        print "Child got $_ \n";
        syswrite CWRITE, "C$_ \n";
    }
}
```

As this example shows, both processes have access to the filehandles of the pipes after the `fork`. Each process closes the two filehandles that it does not need and reads and writes from the other two. In order to ensure that buffering does not deadlock the processes waiting for each other's message, we use the system level `syswrite` function to do the actual writing, which also absolves us of the need to set the `autoflush` flag. When run, the output of this program looks like this:

```
Child got : S
Parent got: CS
Child got : PCS
Parent got: CPCS
Child got : PCPCS
Parent got: CPCPCS
Child got : PCPCPCS
Parent got: CPCPCPCS
Child got : PCPCPCPCS
Parent got: CPCPCPCPCS
Child got : PCPCPCPCPCS
Parent got: CPCPCPCPCPCS
Child got : PCPCPCPCPCPCS
Parent got: CPCPCPCPCPCPCS
...
```

Note that this program works because each process reads exactly one line of input and produces exactly one line of output, so they balance each other. A real application where one side or the other needs to read arbitrary quantities of data will have to spend more time worrying about deadlocks; it is all too easy to have each process waiting for input from the other.

Opening and Running External Processes

If the first or last character of a filename passed to open is a **pipe** (|) symbol, the remainder of the filename is taken to be an external command. A unidirectional pipe connects the external process to our program. Input to or output from the external process is connected to our process based on the position of the pipe symbol. If the symbol precedes the command, the program's input (STDIN) is connected to an output statement in our process. If the symbol appends the command, the program's output (STDOUT) is accessed with an input type statement from our process.

If the pipe character occurs at the start of the filename then the input to the external command is connected to the output of the filehandle, so printing to the filehandle will send data to the input of the command. For example, here is a standard way of sending an email on a UNIX system by running the sendmail program and writing the content of the email to it through the pipe:

```
# get email details from somewhere, e.g. HTML form via CGI.pm
($from_addr, $to_addr, $subject, $mail_body, $from_sig) = get_email();

# open connection to 'sendmail' and print email to it
open (MAIL, '|/usr/bin/sendmail -oi -t') || die "Eep! $! \n";
print MAIL <<END_OF_MAIL;
From: $from_addr;
To: $to_addr
Subject: $subject

$mail_body
```

```
    $from_sig
    END_OF_MAIL

    # close connection to sendmail
    close MAIL;
```

If, on the other hand, the pipe character occurs at the end then the output of the external command is connected to the input of the filehandle. Reading from the filehandle we will receive anything that the external command prints. For example, here is another UNIX-based example of using an open to receive the results of a ps (list processes) command:

```
#!/usr/bin/perl
# pid1.pl
use warnings;
use strict;

my $pid = open (PS,"ps aux|") || die "Couldn't execute 'ps': $! \n";
print "Subprocess ID is: $pid \n";
while (<PS>) {
    chomp;
    print "PS: $_ \n";
}
close PS;
```

The return value of open when it is used to start an external process this way, is the process ID of the executed command. We can use this value with functions such as waitpid, which we covered earlier in this chapter.

Note that it is not possible to open an external program for both reading and writing this way, since the pipe is unidirectional. Attempting to pass a pipe in at both ends will only result in the external command's output being chained to nothing, which is unlikely to be what we want. One solution to this is to have the external command write to a temporary file and then read the temporary file to see what happened:

```
if (open SORT, "|sort > /tmp/output$$") {
    ... print results line by line to SORT ...
    close SORT;
    open(RESULT, '/tmp/output$$')
    ... read sorted results ...
    close RESULT;
    unlink '/tmp/output$$';
}
```

Another, better, solution is to use the IPC::Open2 or IPC::Open3 modules, which allow both read and write access to an external program. The IPC:: modules are also covered in this chapter, under 'Bi-directional Pipes to External Processes'.

Bi-directional Pipes

Standard pipes on UNIX are only one-way, but we can create a pair of filehandles that look like just one.

Perl provides a number of functions to create and manage **sockets,** which are bi-directional networking endpoints represented in our applications as filehandles. They can be used to communicate between different processes and different systems across a network.

The `socketpair` function stands from the other socket functions because it does not have any application in networking applications. Instead, it creates two sockets connected back to back, with the output of each connected to the input of the other. The result is something which looks and feels like a bi-directional pipe. This is unsupported on Win32 platforms.

Sockets have domains, types and protocols associated with them. The domain in Perl can be either the Internet or UNIX, the type a streaming socket, datagram socket or raw socket, and the protocol can be something like PF_INET or PF_UNIX (these constants actually stand for **P**rotocol **F**amilies). This is the general form of `socketpair` being used to create a parent and child filehandle:

```
socketpair PARENT, CHILD, $domain, $type, $protocol;
```

However, most of this is fairly irrelevant to `socketpair`; its sockets do not talk to network interfaces or the filesystem, they do not need to listen for connections, they cannot be bound to addresses and finally are not bothered about protocols, since they have no lower level protocol API to satisfy. Consequently, we generally use a UNIX domain socket, since it is more lightweight than an Internet domain socket. We make it streaming so we can use it like an ordinary filehandle, and don't bother with the protocol at all. The actual use of `socketpair` is thus almost always:

```
use Socket;

socketpair PARENT, CHILD, AF_UNIX, SOCK_STREAM, PF_UNSPEC;
```

The symbols AF_UNIX, SOCK_STREAM, and PF_UNSPEC are all defined by the `Socket` module, which provides support for Perl's socket functions. We cover it in a lot more detail in Chapter 23, when we come to real sockets.

Here is a version of the message passing program we showed earlier using a pair of sockets rather than two pairs of pipe handles:

```perl
#!/usr/bin/perl
# socketpair.pl
use warnings;
use strict;

use Socket;

socketpair PARENT, CHILD, AF_UNIX, SOCK_STREAM, PF_UNSPEC;

my $message = "S";

if (fork) {
    syswrite PARENT, "$message \n";
    while (<PARENT>) {
        chomp;
        print "Parent got: $_ \n";
        syswrite PARENT, "P$_ \n";
        sleep 1;
    }
```

```
  } else {
    while (<CHILD>) {
        chomp;
        print "Child got : $_ \n";
        syswrite CHILD, "C$_ \n";
    }
  }
}
```

In fact we could also close the parent and child socket handles in the child and parent processes respectively, since we do not need them – we only need one end of each pipe. We can also use the socket in only one direction by using the shutdown function to close either the input or the output:

```
shutdown CHILD, 1;   # make child read-only
shutdown PARENT, 0;   # make parent write-only
```

The difference between close and shutdown is that close only affects the filehandle itself, the underlying socket is not affected unless the filehandle just closed was the only one pointing to it. In other words, shutdown includes the socket itself, and hence all filehandles associated with it are affected.

This program is a lot more advanced in the way that it manufactures the conduit between the two processes, because it uses Perl's socket support to create the filehandles, but the benefit is that it makes the application simpler to write and generates fewer redundant filehandles.

Avoiding Shells with the Forked 'open'

One problem with using open to start an external process is that if the external command contains spaces or other such characters that are significant to a shell, open will run a shell as a sub-process and pass on the command for it to interpret, so that any special characters can be correctly parsed. The problem with this is that it is potentially insecure if the program is to be run by un-trusted users, as for example is the case with a CGI script. Functions such as exec and system allow us to separate the parameters of a command into separate scalar values and supply them as a list, avoiding the shell.

Unfortunately open does not directly allow us to pass in a command as a list. Instead it allows us to use exec to actually run the command by supplying it with the magic filenames | - or - |. This causes 'open' to create a pipe and then fork to create a child process. The child's standard input or standard output (depending on whether | - or - | was used) is connected to the filehandle opened in the parent. If we then use exec to replace the child process with the external command, the standard input or output is inherited, connecting the external process directly to the filehandle created by open in the parent.

The return value from open in these cases is the process ID of the child process (in the parent) and zero (in the child), the same as the return value from fork, enabling us to tell which process we are now running as.

Of course it is not obligatory to run an external command at this point, but this is by far the most common reason for using a forked open. It is also by far the most common reason for using exec, which replaces the current process by the supplied command. Since exec allows the command to be split up into a list (that is, a list containing the command and arguments as separate elements), we can avoid the shell that open would create if we used it directly (or handed it a scalar string with the complete command and arguments in it). Here's an example of running the UNIX ps command via a forked open:

```perl
#!/usr/bin/perl
# pid2.pl
use warnings;
use strict;

my $pid = open (PS, "-|");
die "Couldn't fork: $! \n" unless defined $pid;
if ($pid) {
    print "Subprocess ID is: $pid \n";
    while (<PS>) {
        chomp;
        print "PS: $_\n";
    }
    close PS;
} else {
    exec 'ps', 'aef';    # no shells here
}
```

Or, more tersely and without recording the process ID:

```perl
#!/usr/bin/perl
# pid3.pl
use warnings;
use strict;

open (PS, "-|") || exec 'ps', 'aux';
while (<PS>) {
    chomp;
    print "PS: $_ \n";
}
close PS;
```

Bi-directional Pipes to External Processes

Perl provides a pair of modules, IPC::Open2 and IPC::Open3, which provide access to bi-directional pipes. These modules have the added advantage that the subroutines they supply, open2 and open3, permit the external commands to be given as a list, again avoiding an external shell.

As we know from Chapter 12, all applications get three filehandles for free when they start which are represented by STDIN, STDOUT, and STDERR. These are the three filehandles all applications use, and they are also the three filehandles with which we can talk and listen to any external process. This is what the piped open does, but only for one of the filehandles. However, due to the facts that STDIN is read-only, and STDOUT and STDERR are write-only, we can in theory create pipes for each of them, since we only need a unidirectional conduit for each handle. This is what the open2 and open3 subroutines provided by IPC::Open2 and IPC::Open3 do. The difference between them is that open2 creates pipes for standard input and output, whereas open3 deals with standard error too.

Using either module is very simple. In the old style of Perl IO programming we supply typeglobs (or typeglob references) for the filehandles to associate with the external command, followed by the command itself:

```perl
use IPC::Open2;

$pid = open2(*RD, *WR, @command_and_arguments);
```

Or:

```
use IPC::Open3;

$pid = open3(*WR, *RD, *ERR, @command_and_arguments);
```

Confusingly, the input and output filehandles of open2 are in a different order in open3. This is a great source for errors, so check carefully, or only use open3 to avoid getting them the wrong way around.

Since typeglobs are considered somewhat quaint these days we can also pass in IO::Handle objects for much the same effect:

```
use IPC::Open2;
use IO::Handle;

$in = new IO::Handle;
$out = new IO::Handle;
$pid = open2($in, $out, 'command', 'arg1', 'arg2');
print $out "Hello there \n";
$reply = <$in>;
```

In a similar vein but without the explicit calls to IO::Handle's new method, we can have open2 or open3 create and return the filehandles for us if we pass in a scalar variable with an undefined value:

```
use IPC::Open3;

$pid = open3($out, $in, $error, 'command', 'arg1', 'arg2');
print $out "Hello there \n";
$reply = <$in>;
```

If we also use IO::Handle in this example the returned filehandles will be easily manipulated with IO::Handle's methods.

Both open2 and open3 perform a fork-and-exec behind the scenes, in the same way that a forked open does. The return value is the process ID of the child that actually executed (with exec) the external command. In the event that establishing the pipes to the external command fails, both subroutines raise a SIGPIPE signal, which we must catch or ignore (this we have covered earlier on in the chapter). Neither subroutine is concerned with the well-being of the actual external command, however, so if the child aborts or exits normally we need to check for ourselves and clean up with waitpid:

```
use POSIX qw(WNOHANG);

$pid = open2($in, $out, 'command', @arguments);
until (waitpid $pid, WNOHANG) {
    # do other stuff, and/or read/writes to $in & $out
}
```

Note that this particular scheme assumes we are using non-blocking reads and writes, otherwise the waitpid may not get called. We can also check for a deceased external process by detecting the EOF condition on the input or error filehandles (or by returning nothing from a sysread), but we still need to use waitpid to clean up the child process.

If we do not want to do anything else in the meantime, perhaps because we have another child process busy doing things elsewhere, we can simply say:

```
# wait for child process to finish
waitpid $pid, 0;
```

If the write filehandle is prefixed with `>&` then the external command is connected directly to the supplied filehandle, so input that arrives on it is sent directly to the external command. The filehandle is also closed in our own process. Similarly, if `<&` is given to the read or error filehandles they are connected directly to the application. Here's a script that illustrates this in action:

```
# Usage: myscript.pl 'somecommand @args'

use IPC::Open3;

print "Now entering $ARGV[0] \n";
$pid = open3('>&STDIN', '<&STDOUT', '<&STDERR', @ARGV);
waitpid $pid, 0;
print "$ARGV[0] finished. \n";
```

Note that we use standard input for the writing handle and standard output for the reading handle. That's because we are in the middle of this transaction; input comes in from standard input but then goes out to the external command, and vice versa for standard output.

Of course this particular script is fairly redundant, but with a little embellishment it could be made useful, for example, logging uses of various commands, checking arguments, and processing tainted data (if we switch on the `-T` option). We also do not have to redirect all three filehandles, only the ones we don't want to deal with:

```
sub open2likeopen3 {
    return open3(shift, shift, '>&STDERR', @_);
}
```

This implements a subroutine functionally identical to `open2` (unless we have redirected standard error already, that is) but with the arguments in the same order as `open3`.

Handling Bi-directional Communications

Some external command will communicate with us on a line-by-line basis. That is, whenever we send them something we can expect at least one line in response. In these cases we can alternate between writing and reading as we did with our `pipe` and `socketpair` examples earlier. Commands like `ftp` are a good example of this kind of application.

However, many commands can accept arbitrary input, and will not send any output until they have received all of the input. The only way to tell such a command that it has all the input it needs is to close the filehandle, so we often need to do something like this:

```
@instructions = <ARGV>;
($in, $out);

# send input and close filehandle
$pid = open2($in, $out, 'command', @arguments);
print $out @instructions;
close $out;
```

```
# receive result
@result = <$in>;
close $in;

# clean up and use the result
waitpid $pid, 0;
print "Got: \n @result";
```

If we want to carry out an ongoing dialogue with an external process then an alternating write-read-write process is not always the best way to approach the problem. In order to avoid deadlocks we have to continually divert attention from one filehandle to the other. Adding standard error just makes things worse.

Fortunately there are two simple solutions, depending on whether we can (or want to) fork or not. First, we can use the select function or the vastly more convenient IO::Select module to poll multiple input filehandles, including both the normal and error output of the external command plus our own standard input. Alternatively, we can fork child processes to handle each filehandle individually. We can even use threads, if we have a version of Perl that is built to use them. We go into more detail on threads later on.

Sharing Data Between Processes

The problem with forked processes, as we have observed before and will observe again when we get to threads, is that they do not share any data between them. Consequently to communicate with each other and share resources, processes need to either establish a channel for communication or find some common point in memory that can be seen by all the processes that need access to it.

In this section we are going to discuss the IPC facilities provided by UNIX systems and their near cousins, generically known as **System V IPC**, after the variant of UNIX on which it first appeared. There are three components to System V IPC: **message queues**, **semaphores** and **shared memory segments**. While the first of these is now rarely used because we can replicate some of its functionality far more easily with pipes, semaphores and shared memory are still very useful, as we will see later in this chapter.

System V IPC is now a fairly venerable part of UNIX, and is not generally portable to non-UNIX platforms that do not comply with POSIX. Some parts of it are also implemented through pipes and socket pairs for ease of implementation. It still has its uses, though, in particular because the objects that we can create and access with it are persistent in memory and can survive the death of the applications that use them. This allows an application to store all its mission-critical data in shared memory, and to pick up exactly where it left off if it is terminated and restarted.

Like most parts of Perl that interface to a lower level library, IPC requires a number of constants that define the various parameters required by its functions. For IPC these constants are defined by the IPC::SysV module, so almost any application using IPC includes the statement:

```
use IPC::SysV;
```

Note that we do not actually have to be on a System V UNIX platform to use IPC, but we do have to be on a platform that has the required IPC support. In general Perl will not even have the modules installed if IPC is not available, and we will have to find alternative means to our goal, some of which are illustrated during the course of the other sections in this chapter. Even on UNIX systems IPC is not always present. If it is, we can usually find out by executing the command:

> **ipcs**

If IPC is available this will produce a report of all currently existing shared memory segments, semaphores, and message queues, usually in that order.

The common theme between IPC message queues, semaphores, and shared memory segments is that they all reside persistently in memory, and can be accessed by any process that knows the resource ID and has access privileges. This differentiates them from most other IPC strategies, which establish private lines of communication between processes that are not so easily accessed by other unrelated processes.

Strictly speaking, Perl's support for IPC is available in the language as the function calls msgctl, msgget, msgrcv, msgsnd, semctl, semget, semop, shmctl, shmget, shmread, and shmwrite. These are merely wrappers for the equivalent C calls, and hence are pretty low-level, though very well documented. However, since these functions are not very easy to use, the IPC:: family of modules includes support for object-oriented IPC access. In the interests of brevity, we will concentrate on these modules only in the following sections.

IPC::SysV

The IPC::SysV module imports all of the specified SysV constants for use in our programs in conjunction with the other IPC modules. The following is a summary of the most widely used constants. To see the full set of what IPC::SysV can export, we can do a perldoc -m on the module, and consult development man pages for further information. Error constants are imported with the core module Errno.

Constant	Purpose
GETALL	Return an array of all the values in the semaphore set.
GETNCNT	Return the number of processes waiting for an increase in value of the specified semaphore in the set.
GETPID	Return the PID of the last process that performed an operation on the specified semaphore in the set.
GETVAL	Return the value of the specified semaphore in the set.
GETZCNT	Return the number of processes waiting for the specified semaphore in the set to become zero.
IPC_ALLOC	Currently allocated.
IPC_CREAT	Create entry if key doesn't exist.
IPC_EXCL	Fail if key exists.

Table continued on following page

Constant	Purpose
IPC_NOERROR	Truncate the message and remove it from the queue if it is longer than the read buffer size (normally keeps the message, and returns an error) when applied to message queues.
IPC_NOWAIT	Error if request must wait.
IPC_PRIVATE	Private key.
IPC_RMID	Remove resource.
IPC_SET	Set resource options.
IPC_STAT	Get resource options.
IPC_W	Write or send permission.
MSG_NOERROR	The same as IPC_NOERROR.
SEM_UNDO	Specifies the operation be rolled when the calling process exits.
SETALL	Set the value of all the semaphores in the set to the specified value.
SETVAL	Set the value of the semaphore in the set to the specified value.
S_IRUSR	00400 – Owner read permission.
S_IWUSR	00200 – Owner write permission.
S_IRWXU	00700 – Owner read/write/execute permission.
S_IRGRP	00040 – Group read permission.
S_IWGRP	00020 – Group write permission.
S_IRWXG	00070 – Group read/write/execute permission.
S_IROTH	00004 – Other read permission.
S_IWOTH	00002 – Other write permission.
S_IRWXO	00007 – Other read/write/execute permission.
ftok	Convert a pathname and a process ID into a key_t type SysV IPC identifier.

Messages Queues

At one time, **message queues** were the only effective way to communicate between processes. They provide a simple queue that processes may write messages into at one end, and read out at the other. We can create two kinds of queue, private and public. Here is an example of creating a private queue:

```
use IPC::SysV qw(IPC_PRIVATE IPC_CREAT S_IRWXU);
use IPC::Msg;

$queue = new IPC::Msg IPC_PRIVATE, S_IRWXU | IPC_CREAT;
```

The new constructor takes two arguments. The first is the queue's identifier, which for a private queue is IPC_PRIVATE. The second is the permissions of the queue, combined with IPC_CREAT if we wish to actually create the queue. Like files, queues have a mask for user, group, and other permissions. This allows us to create a queue that we can write to but applications running under other user IDs can only read, or not read at all.

For a private queue, full user permissions are the most obvious and we specify these with S_IRWXU. This is defined by the Fcntl module, but IPC::SysV imports the symbols for us so we don't have to use Fcntl ourselves. We could also have said 0700 using octal notation. (Permissions are discussed in detail in Chapter 13.)

If the queue is private, only the process that created the queue and any forked children can access it. Alternatively, if it is public, any process that knows the queue's identifier can access it. For a queue to be useful, therefore, it needs to have a known identifier, or key, by which it can be found. The key is simply an integer, so we can create a public queue, which can be written to by processes running under our user ID (that is this application) and only read by others with something like the following:

```
# create a queue for writing
$queue = new IPC::Msg 10023, 0722 | IPC_CREAT;
```

Another process can now access this message queue with:

```
$queue = new IPC::Msg 10023, 0200;
```

On return, $queue will be a valid message object for the queue, or undef if it did not exist. Assuming success, we can now read and write the queue to establish communications between the processes. If we had created a private queue (not specifying the SysV ID key) and we want to send the message queue's key to another process so we can establish communications, we can extract it with id:

```
$queue = new IPC::Msg IPC_PRIVATE, 0722 | IPC_CREAT;
$id = $queue->id;
```

To send a message we use the snd method:

```
$queue->snd($type, $message, $flags);
```

The message is simply the data we want to send. The type is an integer that is a positive long integer, and which can be used by the rcv method to select different messages based on their type. The flags argument is optional, but can be set to IPC_NOWAIT to have the method return if the message could not be sent immediately (in this case $! will be set to EAGAIN). It is possible for error code constants to be imported by the module.

To receive a message we use the rcv method:

```
$message;
$queue->rcv ($message, $length, $type, $flags);
```

The first argument is a scalar variable into which the message is read. The length defines the maximum length of the message to be received. If the message is larger than this length then rcv returns undef and sets $! to E2BIG. The type allows us to control which message we receive, and is an integer with the following possible meanings:

Integer Value	Meaning
0	Read the first message on the queue, regardless of type.
> 0	Read the first message on the queue of the specified type. For example, if the type is 2 then only messages of type 2 will be read. If none are available, this will cause the process to block until one is. However, see IPC_NOWAIT and MSG_EXCEPT below.
< 0	Read the lowest and furthest forward message on the queue with a type equal to or less than the absolute value of the specified type. For example, if the type is -2 then the first message with type 0 will be returned, if no messages of type 0 are present, the first message of type 1 will be returned, or if no messages of type 1 are present, the first message of type 2 will be returned.

The flags may be one or more of:

Flag	Action
MSG_EXCEPT	Invert the sense of the type so that for zero or positive values it retrieves the first message not of the specified type. For instance, a type of 1 causes rcv to return the first message not of type 1.
MSG_NOERRO R	Allow outsize messages to be received by truncating them to the specified length, rather than returning E2BIG as an error.
IPC_NOWAIT	Do not wait for a message of the requested type if none are available but return with $! set to EAGAIN.

Put together, these two functions allow us to set up a multi-level communications queue with differently typed messages for different purposes. The meaning of the type is entirely up to us; we can use it to send different messages to different child processes or threads within our application. Also it can be used as a priority or **Out-Of-Band** channel marker, to name a few examples.

The permissions of a queue can be changed with the set method, which takes a list of key-value pairs as parameters:

```
$queue->set (
    uid => $user_id,    # i.e., like 'chmod' for files
    gid => $group_id,   # i.e., like 'chgrp' for files
    mode => $permissions,   # an octal value or S_ flags
    qbytes => $queue_size   # the queue's capacity
)
```

We can also retrieve an IPC::Msg::stat object, which we can in turn create, modify, and then update the queue properties via the stat method:

```
$stat = $queue->stat;
$stat->mode(0722);
$queue->set($stat);
```

The object that the `stat` method returns is actually an object based on the `Class::Struct` class. It provides the following `get/set` methods (the * designates portions of the `stat` structure that cannot be directly manipulated):

Method	Purpose
uid	The effective UID queue is running with.
gid	The effective GID queue is running with.
cuid*	The UID queue was started with.
cgid*	The GID queue was started with.
mode	Permissions set on the queue.
qnum*	Number of messages currently in the queue.
qbytes	Size of the message queue.
lspid*	PID of the last process that performed a send on the queue.
lrpid*	PID of the last process that performed a receive on the queue.
stime*	Time of the last send call performed on the queue.
rtime*	Time of the last receive call performed on the queue.
ctime*	Time of the last change performed on the stat data structure.

Note that changes made to the object returned by the `stat` method do not directly update the queue's attributes. For that to happen, we need to either pass the updated `stat` object or individual key-value pairs (using the keys listed above as `stat` methods) to the `set` method.

Finally, we can destroy a queue, assuming we have execute permission for it, by calling `remove`:

```
$queue->remove;
```

If we cannot remove the queue, the method returns `undef`, with `$!` set to indicate the reason, most likely `EPERM`. In keeping with good programming practices, it is important that the queue is removed, especially since it persists even after the application exits. However, it is equally important that the correct processes do so, and no process pulls the rug out from under the others.

Semaphores

IPC **Semaphores** are a memory-resident set of one or more numeric flags (also known as semaphore sets) that can be read and written by different processes to indicate different states. Like message queues, they can be private or public having an identifier by which they can be accessed with a **permissions mask** control rolling who can access them.

Semaphores have two uses, firstly, as a set of shared values, which can be read and written by different processes. Secondly, to allow processes to block and wait for semaphores to change value, so that the execution of different processes can be stopped and started according to the value of a semaphore controlled by a different process.

931

The module that implements access to semaphores is IPC::Semaphore, and we can use it like this:

```
use IPC::SysV qw(IPC_CREAT IPC_PRIVATE S_IRWXU);
use IPC::Semaphore;

$size = 4;
$sem = new IPC::Semaphore(IPC_PRIVATE, $size,IPC_CREAT | S_IRWXU);
```

This creates a private semaphore set with four semaphores and owner read, write and execute permissions. To create a public semaphore set we provide a literal key value instead:

```
$sem = new IPC::Semaphore(10023, 4, 0722 | IPC_CREAT);
```

Other processes can now access the semaphore with:

```
$sem = new IPC::Semaphore(10023, 4, 0200);   # or S_IRDONLY
```

As with message queues, we can also retrieve the key of the semaphore set with the id method, should we not know it and have access to the semaphore object that is:

```
$id = $sem->id;
```

Once we have access to the semaphore we can use and manipulate it in various ways, assuming we have permission to do so. A number of methods exist to help us do this:

Name	Action
getall	Return all values as a list. For example:
	`@semvals = $sem->getall;`
getval	Return the value of the specified semaphore. For example:
	`# first semaphore is 0, so 4th is 3`
	`$sem4 = $sem->getval(3);`
setall	Set all semaphore values. For example, to clear all semaphores:
	`$sem->setall( (0) x 4 );`
setval	Set the value of the specified semaphore. For example:
	`# set value of 4th semaphore to 1`
	`$sem->setval(3, 1);`
set	Set the user ID, group ID or permissions of the semaphore. For example:
	`$sem->set(`
	`    uid => $user_id,`
	`    gid => $group_id,`
	`    mode => $permissions,`
	`);`

Alternatively we can get, manipulate, and set a stat object as returned by the stat method in the same manner as IPC::Msg objects.

Name	Action

stat	Generate an IPC::Semaphore::stat object we can manipulate and then use with set. For example:
	
	`$semstat = $sem->stat;`
	
	`$semstat->mode(0722);`
	
	`$sem->set($semstat);`

getpid	Return the process ID of the last process to perform a semop operation on the semaphore set.
getncnt	Return the number of processes that have executed a semop and are blocked waiting for the value of the specified semaphore to increase in value. `$ncnt = $sem->getncnt;`
getzcnt	Return the number of processes that have executed a semop and are blocked waiting for the value of the specified semaphore to become zero.

The real power of semaphores is bound up in the op method, which performs one or more semaphore operations on a semaphore set. This is the mechanism by which processes can block and be unblocked by other processes.

Each operation consists of three values; the semaphore number to operate on, an operation to perform, and a flag value. The operation is actually a value to increment or decrement by, and follows these rules:

- If the value is positive, the semaphore value is incremented by the supplied value. This always succeeds, and never blocks.

- If the supplied value is zero, and the semaphore value is zero, the operation succeeds. If the semaphore value is not zero then the operation blocks until the semaphore value becomes zero. This increases the value returned by getzcnt.

- If the value is negative, then the semaphore value is decremented by this value, unless this would take the value of the semaphore negative. In this case, the operation blocks until the semaphore becomes sufficiently positive enough to allow the decrement to happen. This increases the value returned by getncnt.

We can choose to operate as many semaphores as we like. All operations must be able to complete before the operation as a whole can succeed. For example:

```
$sem->op(
    0, -1, 0,    # decrement semaphore 1
    1, -1, 0,    # decrement semaphore 2
    3, 0 , 0    # semaphore 3 must be zero
);
```

The rules for blocking on semaphores allow us to create applications that can cooperate with each other; one application can control the execution of another by setting semaphore values. Applications can also coordinate over access to shared resources. This a potentially large subject, so we will just give a simple illustrative example of how a semaphore can coordinate access to a common shared resource:

Application 1 creates a semaphore set with one semaphore, value 1, and creates a shared resource, for example a file, or an IPC shared memory segment. However, it decides to do a lot of initialization and so doesn't access the resource immediately.

Application 2 starts up, decrements the semaphore to 0, and accesses the shared resource.

Application 1 now tries to decrement the semaphore and access the resource. The semaphore is zero, so it cannot access, it therefore blocks.

Application 2 finishes with the shared resource and increments the semaphore, an operation that always succeeds.

Application 1 can now decrement the semaphore since it is now 1, and so the operation succeeds and no longer blocks.

Application 2 tries to access the resource a second time. First it tries to decrement the semaphore, but is unable to, and blocks.

Application 1 finishes and increments the semaphore.

Application 2 decrements the semaphore and accesses the resource.

...and so on.

Although this sounds complex, in reality it is very simple. In code, each application simply accesses the semaphore, creating it if isnot present, and then adds two lines around all accesses to the resource to be protected:

```
sub access_resource {
    # decrement semaphore, blocking if it is already zero
    $sem->op(0, -1, 0);
    ... access resource ...
    # increment semaphore, allowing access by other processes
    $sem->op(0, 1, 0);
}
```

If we have more than one resource to control, we just create a semaphore set with more semaphores.

The basis of this approach is that the applications agree to cooperate through the semaphore. Each one has the key for the semaphore (because it is given in a configuration file, for instance), and it becomes the sole basis for contact between them. Even though the resource being controlled has no direct connection to the semaphore, each application always honors it before accessing it. The semaphore becomes a gatekeeper, allowing only one application access at a time.

If we do not want to block while waiting for a semaphore we can specify IPC_NOWAIT for the flag value. We can do this on a 'per semaphore basis' too, if we want, though this could be confusing. For example:

```
sub access_resource {
    return undef unless $sem->op(0, -1, IPC_NOWAIT);
    ... access resource ...
    $sem->op(0, 1, 0);
}
```

We can also set the flag SEM_UNDO (if we import it from IPC::SysV first). This causes a semaphore operation to be automatically undone if the process exits, either deliberately or due to an error. This is helpful in preventing applications that abort while locking a resource and then never releasing it again. For example:

```
$sem->op(0, -1, IPC_NOWAIT | SEM_UNDO);
die unless critical_subroutine();
```

As with message queues, care must be not to leave unused segments around after the last process exits.

We will return to the subject of semaphores when we come to talk about threads, which have their own semaphore mechanism, inspired greatly by the original IPC implementation described above.

Shared Memory Segments

While message queues and semaphores are relatively low level constructs made a little more accessible by the IPC::Msg and IPC::Semaphore modules, shared memory has an altogether more powerful support module in the form of IPC::Shareable. The key reason for this is that IPC::Shareable implements shared memory through a tie mechanism, so rather than reading and writing from a memory block we can simply attach a variable to it and use that.

The tie takes four arguments, a variable (which may be a scalar, an array or a hash), IPC::Shareable for the binding, and then an access key, followed optionally by a hash reference containing one or more key-value pairs. For example, the following code creates and ties a hash variable to a shared memory segment:

```
use IPC::Shareable;

%local_hash;
tie %local_hash, 'IPC::Shareable', 'key', {create => 1};

$local_hash{'hashkey'} = 'value';
```

This creates a persistent shared memory object containing a hash variable which can be accessed by any application or process by tie-ing a hash variable to the access key for the shared memory segment (in this case key):

```
# in a process in an application far, far away...
%other_hash;
tie %other_hash, 'IPC::Shareable', 'key';

$value = $other_hash{'hashkey'};
```

A key feature of shared memory is that, like memory queues and semaphores, the shared memory segment exists independently of the application that created it. Even if all the users of the shared memory exit, it will continue to exist so long as it is not explicitly deleted (we can alter this behavior, though, as we will see in a moment).

Note that the key value is actually implemented as an integer, the same as semaphores and message queues, so the string we pass is converted into an integer value by packing the first four characters into a 32 bit integer value. This means that only the first four characters of the key are used. As a simple example, baby and babyface are the same key to IPC::Shareable.

The tied variable can be of any type, including a scalar containing a reference, in which case whatever the reference points to is converted into a shared form. This includes nested data structures and objects, making shared memory ties potentially very powerful. However, each reference becomes a new shared memory object, so a complex structure can quickly exceed the system limit on shared memory segments. In practice we should only try to tie relatively small nested structures to avoid trouble.

The fourth argument can contain a number of different configuration options that determine how the shared memory segment is accessed:

Option	Function
create	If true, create the key if it does not already exist. If the key does exist, then the tie succeeds and binds to the existing data, unless exclusive is also true. If create is false or not given then the tie will fail if the key is not present.
exclusive	Used in conjunction with create. If true, allows a new key to be created but does not allow an existing key to be tied to successfully.
mode	Determine the access permissions of the shared memory segment. The value is an integer, traditionally an octal number or a combination of flags like S_IRWXU | S_IRGRP.
destroy	If true, cause the shared memory segment to be destroyed automatically when this process exits (but not if it aborts on a signal). In general only the creating application should do this, or be able to do this (by setting the permissions appropriately on creation).
size	Define the size of the shared memory segment, in bytes. In general this defaults to an internally set maximum value, so we rarely need to use it.
key	If the tie is given three arguments, with the reference to the configuration options being the third, this value specifies the name of the shared memory segment: `tie %hash, 'IPC::Shareable' {key => 'key', ...};` For example: `tie @array, 'IPC::Shareable', 'mysharedmem', {` `    create => 1,` `    exclusive => 0,` `    mode => 722,` `    destroy => 1,` `}`

Other than the destroy option, we can remove a shared memory segment by calling one of three methods implemented for the IPC::Shareable object that implements the tie (which may be returned by the tied function):

Option	Function
remove	Remove the shared memory segment, if we have permission to do so.
clean_up	Remove all shared memory segments created by this process.
clean_up_all	Remove all shared memory segments in existence for which this process has permissions to do so.

For example:

```
# grab a handle to the tied object via the 'tied' command
$shmem = tied $shared_scalar;
# use the object handle to call the 'remove' method on it
print "Removed shared scalar" if $shmem->remove;
```

We can also lock variables using the IPC::Shareable object's shlock and shunlock methods. If the variable is already locked, the process attempting the lock will block until it becomes free. For example:

```
$shmem->lock;
$shared_scalar = "new value";
$shmem->unlock;
```

Behind the scenes this lock is implemented with IPC::Semaphore, so for a more flexible mechanism, use IPC::Semaphore objects directly.

As a lightweight alternative to IPC::Shareable, we can make use of the IPC::ShareLite module, naturally available from CPAN. This provides a simple store-fetch mechanism using object methods and does not provide a tied interface. However, it is faster than IPC::Shareable.

Threads

Threads are, very loosely speaking, the low fat and lean version of forked processes. The trouble with fork is that it not only divides the thread of execution into two processes, it divides their code and data too. This means that where we had a group containing the Perl interpreter, %ENV hash, @ARGV array, and the set of loaded modules and subroutines, we now have two groups. In theory, this is wasteful of resources, very inconvenient, and unworkable for large numbers of processes. Additionally, since processes do not share data they must use constructs like pipes, shared memory segments or signals to communicate with each other. In practice, most modern UNIX systems have has become very intelligent in sharing executable segments behind the scenes, reducing the expense of a fork.

Regardless, threads attempt to solve all these problems. Like forked processes, each thread is a separate thread of execution. Also similar to forked processes, newly created threads are owned by the thread that created them, and they have unique identifiers, though these are thread IDs rather than process IDs. We can even wait for a thread to finish and collect its exit result, just like `waitpid` does for child processes. However, threads all run in the same process and share the same interpreter, code, and data, nothing is duplicated except the thread of execution. This makes them much more lightweight, so we can have very many of them, and we don't need to use any of the workarounds that forked processes need.

Thread support in Perl is still experimental. Added in Perl 5.6, work continues into Perl 5.7 and Perl 6. As shipped, most Perl interpreters do not support threads at all, but if we build Perl from scratch, as in Chapter 1, we can enable them. There are actually two types of thread; the current implementation provides for a threaded application but with only one interpreter dividing its attention between them. The newer implementation uses an interpreter that is itself threaded, greatly improving performance. However, this thread support is so new it isn't even available in Perl code yet. The likelihood is that full official thread support will arrive with Perl 6, but that doesn't mean we can't use it now – carefully – for some useful and interesting applications.

Checking for Thread Support

To find out if threads are available programmatically we can check for the `usethreads` key in the `%Config` hash:

```
BEGIN {
    use Config;
    die "Threadbare! \n" unless $Config{'usethreads'};
}
```

From the command line we can check if threads are present by trying to read the documentation, the `Thread` module will only be present if thread support is enabled:

> perldoc Thread

The `Thread` module is the basis of handling threads in Perl. It is an object-oriented module that represents threads as objects, which we can create using new and manipulate with methods. In addition it provides a number of functions that operate on a per-thread basis.

Creating Threads

Threads resemble forked processes in many ways, but in terms of creation they resemble and indeed are subroutines. The standard way of creating a thread, the new method, takes a subroutine reference and a list of arguments to pass to it. The subroutine is then executed by a new thread of execution, while the parent thread receives a thread object as the return value. The following code snippet illustrates how it works:

```
use Thread;

sub threadsub {
    $self = Thread->self;
    ...
}

$thread = new Thread \&threadsub, @args;
```

This creates a new thread, with `threadsub` as its entry point, while the main thread continues on. The alternative way to create a thread is with the `async` function, whose syntax is analogous to an anonymous subroutine. This function is not imported by default so we must name it in the import list to the `Thread` module:

```
use Thread qw(async);

$thread = async {
   $self = Thread->self;
   ...
};
```

Just like an anonymous subroutine, we end the `async` statement with a semicolon; the block may not need it, but the statement does.

The choice of `new` or `async` depends on the nature of the thread we want to start; the two are identical in all respects apart from their syntax. If we only want to start one instance of a thread then `async` should be used whereas `new` is better if we want to use the same subroutine for many different threads:

```
$thread1 = new Thread \&threadsub, $arg1;
$thread2 = new Thread \&threadsub, $arg2;
$thread3 = new Thread \&threadsub, $arg3;
```

Or, with a loop:

```
# start a new thread for each argument passed in @ARGV:
@threads;
foreach (@ARGV) {
   push @threads, new Thread \&threadsub, $_;
}
```

We can do this with a certain level of impunity because threads are so much less resource consumptive than forked processes.

Identifying Threads

Since we can start up many different threads all with the same subroutine as their entry point, it might seem tricky to tell them apart. However, this is not so. First, we can pass in different arguments when we start each thread to set them on different tasks. An example of this would be a filehandle, newly created by a server application, and this is exactly what an example of a threaded server in Chapter 23 does.

Second, a thread can create a thread object to represent itself using the `self` class method:

```
$self = Thread->self;
```

With this thread object the thread can now call methods on itself, for example `tid`, which returns the underlying thread number:

```
$self_id = $self->tid;
```

It is possible to have more than one thread object containing the same thread ID, and this is actually common in some circumstances. We can check for equivalence by comparing the IDs, but we can do better by using the equals method:

```
print "Equal! \n" if $self->equal($thread);
```

Or, equivalently:

```
print "Equal! \n" if $thread->equal($self);
```

Thread identities can be useful for all kinds of things, one of the most useful being thread-specific data.

Thread-specific Data

One of the drawbacks of forked processes is that they do not share any of their data, making communication difficult. Threads have the opposite problem; they all share the same data, so finding privacy is that much harder.

Unlike some other languages, Perl does not have explicit support for thread-specific data, but we can improvise. If our thread all fits into one subroutine we can simply create a lexical variable with my and use that. If we do have subroutines to call and we want them to be able to access variables we create the our can be used. Alternatively we can create a global hash of thread IDs and use the values for thread-specific data:

```
%thread_data;

sub threadsub {
    $id = Thread->self->tid;
    $thread_data{$id}{'Started'} = time;
    ...
    $thread_data{$id}{'Ended'} = time;
}

new Thread \&thread_sub, $arg1;
new Thread \&thread_sub, $arg2;
```

The advantage of using my or our is that the data is truly private, because it is lexically scoped to the enclosing subroutine. The advantage of the global hash is that threads can potentially look at each other's data in certain well-defined circumstances.

Thread Management

Perl keeps a list of every thread that has been created. We can get a copy of this list, as thread objects, with the Thread->list class method:

```
@threads = Thread->list;
```

One of these threads is our own thread. We can find out which by using the `equal` method:

```perl
$self = Thread->self;
foreach (@threads) {
   next if $self->equal($_);
   ...
}
```

Just because a thread is present does not mean that it is running, however. Perl keeps a record of the return value of every thread when it exits, and keeps a record of the thread for as long as that value remains unclaimed. This is similar to child processes that have not had `waitpid` called for them. The threaded equivalent of `waitpid` is the `join` method, which we call on the thread we want to retrieve the exit value for:

```perl
$return_result = $thread->join;
```

The `join` method will block until the thread on which `join` was called exits. If the thread aborts (for example by calling `die`) then the error will be propagated to the thread that called `join`. This means that it will itself die unless the `join` is protected by an `eval`:

```perl
$return_result = eval {$thread->join;}
if ($@) {
   warn "Thread unraveled before completion \n";
}
```

As a convenience for this common construct, the `Thread` module also provides an `eval` method, which wraps `join` inside an `eval` for us:

```perl
$return_result = $thread->eval;
if ($@) {
   warn "Thread unraveled before completion \n";
}
```

It is bad form to ignore the return value of a thread, since it clutters up the thread list with dead threads. If we do not care about the return value then we can tell the thread that we do not want it to linger and preserve its return value by telling it to detach:

```perl
$thread->detach;
```

The catch to this is that if the thread dies, nobody will notice, unless a signal handler for the __DIE__ hook, which checks `Thread->self` for the dying thread, has been registered. To reiterate: if we join a moribund thread from the main thread without precautions we do have to worry about the application dying as a whole.

As a slightly fuller and more complete (although admittedly not particularly useful) example, this short program starts up five threads, then joins each of them in turn before exiting:

```perl
#!/usr/bin/perl
# join.pl
use warnings;
use strict;
```

```
# check we have threads
BEGIN {
    use Config;
    die "Threadbare! \n" unless $Config{'usethreads'};
}
use Thread;

# define a subroutine for threads to execute
sub threadsub {
    my $self = Thread->self;
    print "Thread ", $self->tid, " started \n";
    sleep 10;
    print "Thread ", $self->tid, " ending \n";
}

# start up five threads, one second intervals
my @threads;
foreach (1..5) {
    push @threads, new Thread \&threadsub;
    sleep 1;
}

# wait for the last thread started to end
while (my $thread = shift @threads) {
    print "Waiting for thread ", $thread -> tid, " to end... \n";
    $thread->join;
    print "Ended \n";
}

# exit
print "All threads done \n";
```

Typically, we care about the return value, and hence would always check it. However, in this case we are simply using join to avoid terminating the main thread prematurely.

Variable Locks

When multiple threads are all sharing data together we sometimes have problems stopping them from treading on each other's toes. Using thread-specific data solves part of this problem, but it does not deal with sharing common resources amongst a pool of threads.

The lock subroutine does handle this, however. It takes any variable as an argument and places a lock on it so that no other thread may lock it for as long as the lock persists, which is defined by its lexical scope. The distinction between lock and access is important; any thread can simply access the variable by not bothering to acquire the lock, so the lock is only good if all threads abide by it.

As a short and incomplete example, this subroutine locks a global variable for the duration of its body:

```
$global;

sub varlocksub {
    lock $global;
}
```

It is not necessary to unlock the variable; the end of the subroutine does it for us. Any lexical scope is acceptable, so we can also place locks inside the clauses of if statements, loops, map and grep blocks, and eval statements. We can also choose to lock arrays and hashes in their entirety if we lock the whole variable:

```
lock @global;
lock %global;
lock *global;
```

Alternatively, we can lock just an element, which gives us a form of record-based locking, if we define a record as an array element or hash value:

```
%global;

sub varlocksub {
    $key = shift;
    lock $global{$key};
    ...
}
```

In this version, only one element of the hash is locked, so any other thread can enter the subroutine with a different key and the corresponding value at the same time. If a thread comes in with the same key, however, it will find the value under lock and key (so to speak) and will have to wait.

Condition Variables, Semaphores, and Queues

Locked variables have more applications than simply controlling access. We can also use them as **conditional blocks** by having threads wait on a variable until it is signaled to proceed. In this mode the variable, termed a **condition variable**, takes on the role of a starting line; each thread lines up on the block (so to speak) until the starting pistol is fired by another thread. Depending on the type of signal we send, either a single thread is given the go-ahead to continue, or all threads are signaled.

Condition variables are a powerful tool for organizing threads, allowing us to control the flow of data through a threaded application and preventing threads from accessing shared data in an unsynchronized manner. They are also the basis for other kinds of thread interaction. We can use **thread semaphores**, provided by the Thread::Semaphore module, to signal between threads. We can also implement a **queue** of tasks between threads using the Thread::Queue module. Both these modules build upon the basic features of condition variables to provide their functionality but wrap them in a more convenient form.

To get a feel for how each of these work we will implement a basic but functional threaded application, first using condition variables directly, then using semaphores, and finally using a queue.

Condition Variables

Continuing the analogy of the starting line, to 'line up' threads on a locked variable we use the cond_wait subroutine. This takes a locked variable, unlocks it, and then waits until it receives a signal from another thread. When it receives a signal, the thread resumes execution and relocks the variable. To have several threads all waiting on the same variable we need only have each thread lock and then cond_wait the variable in turn. Since the lock prevents more than one thread executing cond_wait at the same time, the process is automatically handled for us. The following code extract shows the basic technique applied to a pool of threads:

```
$lockvar;    # lock variable - note it is not locked at this point

sub my_waiting_thread {
   # wait for signal
   {
   lock $lockvar;
   cond_wait $lockvar;
   }

   # ...the rest of the thread, where the work is done
}

for (1..10) {
   new Thread \&my_waiting_thread;
}
```

This code snippet shows ten threads, all of which use the same subroutine as their entry point. Each one locks and then waits on the variable $lockvar until it receives a signal. Since we don't want to retain the lock on the variable after we leave cond_wait, we place both lock and cond_wait inside their own block to limit the scope of the lock. This is important since other threads cannot enter the waiting state while we have a lock on the variable; sometimes that is what we want, but more often it isn't.

Having established a pool of waiting threads, we need to send a signal to wake one of them up, which we do with cond_signal:

```
# wake up one thread
cond_signal $lockvar;
```

This will unlock one thread waiting on the condition variable. The thread that is restarted is essentially random; we cannot assume that the first thread to block will be the first to be unlocked again. This is appropriate when we have a pool of threads at our disposal, all of which perform the same basic function. Alternatively, we can unlock all threads at once by calling cond_broadcast thus:

```
# everybody up!
cond_broadcast $lockvar;
```

This sends a message to each thread waiting on that variable, which is appropriate for circumstances where a common resource is conditionally available and we want to stop or start all threads depending on whether the resource is available or not. It is important to realize, however, that if no threads are waiting on the variable, the signal is discarded; it is not kept until a thread is ready to respond to it. It is also important to realize that this has nothing (directly) to do with process signals, as handled by the %SIG array; writing a threaded application to handle process signals is a more complex task; see the Thread::Signal module for details.

Note that the actual value of the lock variable is entirely irrelevant to this process, so we can use it for other things. For instance we can use it to pass a value to the thread at the moment that we signal it. The following short threaded application does just this, using a pool of service threads to handle lines of input passed to them by the main thread. While examining the application, pay close attention to the two condition variables that lay at the heart of the application:

❑ $pool – used by the main thread to signal that a new line is ready. It is waited on by all the service threads. Its value is programmed to hold the number of threads currently waiting, so the main thread knows whether or not it can send a signal or if it must wait for a service thread to become ready.

❑ $line – used by whichever thread is woken by the signal to $pool. Lets the main thread know that the line of input read by the main thread has been copied to the service thread and that a new line may now be read. The value is the text of the line that was read.

The two condition variables allow the main thread and the pool of service threads to cooperate with each other. This ensures that each line read by the main thread is passed to one service thread both quickly and safely:

```perl
#!/usr/bin/perl
# threadpool.pl
use warnings;
use strict;

use Thread qw(cond_signal cond_wait cond_broadcast yield);

my $threads = 3;    # number of service threads to create
my $pool = 0;    # child lock variable and pool counter set to 0 here,
                 # service threads increment it when they are ready for input
my $line="";     # parent lock variable and input line set to "" here, we
                 # assign each new line of input to it, and set it to 'undef'
                 # when we are finished to tell service threads to quit

# a locked print subroutine - stops thread output mingling
sub thr_print : locked {
    print @_;
}

# create a pool of three service threads
foreach (1..$threads) {
    new Thread \&process_thing;
}

# main loop: Read a line, wait for a service thread to become available,
# signal that a new line is ready, then wait for whichever thread picked
# up the line to signal to continue
while ($line = <>) {
    chomp $line;
    thr_print "Main thread got '$line'\n";

    # do not signal until at least one thread is ready
    if ($pool==0) {
        thr_print "Main thread has no service threads available, yielding\n";
        yield until $pool>0;
    }
    thr_print "Main thread has $pool service threads available\n";

    # signal that a new line is ready
    {
        lock $pool;
        cond_signal $pool;
    }
    thr_print "Main thread sent signal, waiting to be signaled\n";
```

```perl
      # wait for whichever thread wakes up to signal us
      {
         lock $line;
         cond_wait $line;
      }
      thr_print "Main thread received signal, reading next line\n";
}

thr_print "All lines processed, sending end signal\n";
# set the line to special value 'undef' to indicate end of input
$line = undef;
{
   lock $pool;
   # tell all threads to pick up this 'line' so they all quit
   cond_broadcast $pool;
}
thr_print "Main thread ended\n";
exit 0;

# the thread subroutine - block on lock variable until work arrives
sub process_thing {
   my $self=Thread->self;
   my $thread_line;

   thr_print "Thread ",$self->tid," started\n";
   while (1) {
      # has the 'quit' signal been sent while we were busy?
      last unless (defined $line);

      # wait to be woken up
      thr_print "Thread ",$self->tid," waiting\n";
      {
         lock $pool;
         $pool++;
         cond_wait $pool; #all threads wait here for signal
         $pool--;
      }

      # retrieve value to process
      thr_print "Thread ",$self->tid," signaled\n";
      $thread_line = $line;

      # was this the 'quit' signal? Check the value sent
      last unless (defined $thread_line);

      # let main thread know we have got the value
      thr_print "Thread ",$self->tid," retrieved data, signaling main\n";
      {
         lock $line;
         cond_signal $line;
      }

      # do private spurious things to it
      chomp ($thread_line=uc($thread_line));
      thr_print "Thread ",$self->tid," got '$thread_line'\n";
   }
   thr_print "Thread ",$self->tid," ended\n";
}
```

Once the basic idea of a condition variable is understood, the way in which this application works becomes clearer. However, a few aspects are still worth pointing out. In particular, the $pool variable is used by the main thread to ensure that it only sends a signal when there is a service thread waiting to receive it. To achieve this, we increment $pool immediately before cond_wait and decrement it immediately afterwards. By doing this we ensure that $pool accurately reflects the number of waiting service threads; if it is zero, the main thread uses yield to pass on execution until a service thread becomes available again.

The means by which the application terminates is also worth noting. Threads do not necessarily terminate just because the main thread does, so in order to exit a threaded application cleanly we need to make sure all the service threads terminate, too. This is especially important if resources needed by some threads are being used by others. Shutting down threads in the wrong order can lead to serious problems. In this application the main thread uses cond_signal to signal the $pool variable and wake up one service thread when a new line is available. Once all input has been read we need to shut down all the service threads, which means getting their entire attention. To do that, we give $line the special value undef and then use cond_broadcast to signal all threads to pick up the new 'line' and exit when they see that it is undef. However, this alone is not enough because a thread might be busy and not waiting. To deal with that possibility, the service thread subroutine also checks the value of $line at the top of the loop, just in case the thread missed the signal.

Finally, this application also illustrates the use of the locked subroutine attribute. The thr_print subroutine is a wrapper for the regular print function that only allows one thread to print at a time. This prevents the output of different threads from getting intermingled. For simple tasks like this one, locked subroutines are an acceptable solution to an otherwise tricky problem that would require at least a lock variable. For longer tasks, locked subroutines can be a serious bottleneck, affecting the performance of a threaded application, so we should use them with care and never for anything likely to take appreciable time.

Semaphores

Although it works perfectly well, the above application is a little more complex than it needs to be. Most forms of threads (whatever language or platform they reside on) support the concept of semaphores and Perl is no different. We covered IPC semaphores earlier, and **thread semaphores** are very similar. They are essentially numeric flags that take a value of zero or any positive number and obey the following simple rules:

- ❏ Only one thread at a time may manipulate the value of a semaphore in either direction.

- ❏ Any thread may increment a semaphore immediately.

- ❏ Any thread may decrement a semaphore immediately if the decrement will not take it below zero.

- ❏ If a thread attempts to decrement a semaphore below zero, it will block until another thread raises the semaphore high enough.

Perl provides thread semaphores through the Thread::Semaphore module, which implements semaphores in terms of condition variables – the code of Thread::Semaphore is actually quite short, as well as instructive. It provides one subroutine and two object methods:

new – create new semaphore, for example:

```
$semaphore = new Thread::Semaphore;    # create semaphore, initial value 1
$semaphore2 = new Thread::Semaphore(0)   # create semaphore, initial value 0
```

up – increment semaphore, for example:

```
$semaphore->up;    # increment semaphore by 1
$semaphore->up(5);    # increment semaphore by 5
```

down – decrement semaphore, blocking if necessary:

```
$semaphore->down;    # decrement semaphore by 1
$semaphore->down(5);    # decrement semaphore by 5
```

Depending on our requirements we can use semaphores as binary stop/go toggles or allow them to range to larger values to indicate the availability of a resource. Here is an adapted form of our earlier threaded application, rewritten to replace the condition variables with semaphores:

```perl
#!/usr/bin/perl
# semaphore.pl
use warnings;
use strict;

use Thread qw(yield);
use Thread::Semaphore;

my $threads = 3;    # number of service threads to create
my $line = "";    # input line

my $main = new Thread::Semaphore;    # proceed semaphore, initial value 1
my $next = new Thread::Semaphore(0);    # new line semaphore, initial value 0

# a locked print subroutine - stops thread output mingling
sub thr_print : locked {
    print @_;
}

# create a pool of three service threads
foreach (1..$threads) {
    new Thread \&process_thing;
}

# main loop: read a line, raise 'next' semaphore to indicate a line is
# available, then wait for whichever thread lowered the 'next' semaphore
# to raise the 'main' semaphore, indicating we can continue.
while ($line = <>) {
    chomp $line;
    thr_print "Main thread got '$line'\n";

    # notify service threads that a new line is ready
    $next->up;
    thr_print "Main thread set new line semaphore, waiting to proceed\n";
```

```
        # do not proceed until value has been retrieved by responding thread
        $main->down;
        thr_print "Main thread received instruction to proceed\n";
    }

    thr_print "All lines processed, sending end signal\n";

    # set the line to special value 'undef' to indicate end of input
    $line = undef;
    # to terminate all threads, raise 'new line' semaphore to >= number of
    # service threads: all service threads will decrement it and read the
    # 'undef'
    $next->up($threads);
    thr_print "Main thread ended\n";
    exit 0;

    # the thread subroutine - block on lock variable until work arrives
    sub process_thing {
        my $self = Thread->self;
        my $thread_line;

        thr_print "Thread ", $self->tid, " started\n";
        while (1) {
            # try to decrement 'next' semaphore - winning thread gets line
            thr_print "Thread ", $self->tid, " waiting\n";
            $next->down;

            # retrieve value to process
            thr_print "Thread ", $self->tid, " signalled\n";
            $thread_line = $line;

            # was this the 'quit' signal? Check the value sent
            last unless (defined $thread_line);

            # let main thread know we have got the value
            thr_print "Thread ", $self->tid, " retrieved data, signaling main\n";
            $main->up;

            # do private spurious things to it
            chomp ($thread_line=uc($thread_line));
            thr_print "Thread ", $self->tid, " got '$thread_line'\n";
        }
        thr_print "Thread ", $self->tid, " ended\n";
    }
```

The semaphore version of the application is simpler than the condition variable implementation, if only because we have hidden the details of all the cond_wait and cond_signal functions inside calls to up and down. Instead of signaling the pool of service threads via a condition variable, the main thread simply raises the **next** semaphore by one, giving it the value 1. Meanwhile, all the service threads are attempting to decrement this semaphore. One will succeed and receive the new line of input, and the others will fail, continuing to block until the semaphore is raised again. When it has copied the line to its own local variable, the thread raises the **main** semaphore to tell the main thread that it can proceed to read another line. The concept is recognizably the same as the previous example, but is easier to follow.

We have also taken advantage of the fact that semaphores can hold any positive value to terminate the application. When the main thread runs out of input it simply raises the 'next' semaphore to be equal to the number of service threads. At this point all the threads can decrement the semaphore, read the value of $line that we again set to undef, and quit. If a thread is still busy the semaphore will remain positive until it finishes and comes back to decrement it – we have no need to put in an extra check in case we missed a signal.

Queues

Many threaded applications, our example a case in point, involve the transport of data between several different threads. In a complex application incoming data might travel through multiple threads, passed from one to the next before being passed out again: a bucket-chain model. We can create pools of threads at each stage along the chain in a similar way to the example application above, but this does not improve upon the mechanism that allows each thread to pass data to the next in line.

The two versions of the application that we have produced so far are limited by the fact that they only handle a single value at a time. Before the main thread can read another line, it has to dispose of the previous one. Even though we can process multiple lines with multiple service threads, the communication between the main thread and the service threads is not very efficient. If we were communicating between different processes we might use a pipe, which buffers output from one process until the other can read it; the same idea works for threads, too, and takes the form of a **queue**.

Perl provides support queues through the Thread::Queue module, which implements simple thread queues in a similar way to the semaphores created by Thread::Semaphore. Rather than a single numeric flag, however, the queue consists of a list to which values may be added to one and removed from the other. At heart this is essentially no more than a shift and pop operation. Using conditional variables and locking the module, however, creates a queue that values may be added to and removed from safely in a threaded environment, following rules similar to those for semaphores:

❏ Only one thread may add or remove values in the queue at a time.

❏ Any thread may add values to a queue immediately.

❏ Any thread may remove values from a queue immediately if there are enough values available in the queue.

❏ If a thread attempts to remove more values than are available, it will block until another thread adds sufficient values to the queue.

The Thread::Queue module provides one subroutine and four methods to create and manage queues:

new – create a new queue, for example:

```
$queue = new Thread::Queue;
```

enqueue – add one or more values to a queue, for example:

```
$queue->enqueue($value);    # add a single value
$queue->enqueue(@values);    # add several values
```

dequeue – remove a single value from a queue, blocking if necessary:

```
$value = $queue->dequeue;    # remove a single value, block
```

dequeue_nb – remove a single value from a queue, without blocking (instead returning undef if nothing is available):

```
$value = $queue->dequeue;    # remove a single value, don't block
if (defined $value) {
    ...
}
```

pending – return the number of values currently in the queue, for example:

```
print "There are ",$queue->pending," items in the queue\n";
```

Using a queue we can rewrite our threaded application again to separate the main thread from the pool of service threads. Since the queue can take multiple values, the main thread no longer has to wait for each value it passes on to be picked up before it can continue. This simplifies both the code and the execution of the program. The queue has no limit, however, so we make sure not to read too much by checking the size of the queue, and yielding if it reaches a limit we choose. Here is a revised version of the same application, using a queue:

```perl
#!/usr/bin/perl
# queue.pl
use warnings;
use strict;

use Thread 'yield';
use Thread::Queue;
use Thread::Semaphore;

my $threads = 3;   # number of service threads to create
my $maxqueuesize = 5;    # maximum size of queue allowed

my $queue = new Thread::Queue;    # the queue
my $ready = new Thread::Semaphore(0);    # a 'start-gun' semaphore
                                         # initialized to 0 each service
                                         # thread raises it by 1

# a locked print subroutine - stops thread output mingling
sub thr_print : locked {
    print @_;
}

# create a pool of service threads
foreach (1..$threads) {
    new Thread \&process_thing, $ready, $queue;
}

# wait for all service threads to increment semaphore
$ready->down($threads);
```

```
# main loop: Read a line, queue it, read another, repeat until done
# yield and wait if the queue gets too large.
while (<>) {
    chomp;
    thr_print "Main thread got '$_'\n";

    # stall if we're getting too far ahead of the service threads
    yield while $queue->pending >= $maxqueuesize;

    # queue the new line
    $queue->enqueue($_);
}

thr_print "All lines processed, queuing end signals\n";

# to terminate all threads, send as many 'undef's as there are service
# threads
$queue->enqueue( (undef)x$threads );
thr_print "Main thread ended\n";
exit 0;

# the thread subroutine - block on lock variable until work arrives
sub process_thing {
    my ($ready,$queue)=@_;

    my $self=Thread->self;
    my $thread_line;

    thr_print "Thread ",$self->tid," started\n";
    $ready->up; #indicate that we're ready to go

    while (1) {
        # wait for queue to deliver an item
        thr_print "Thread ",$self->tid," waiting\n";
        my $thread_line=$queue->dequeue();

        # was this the 'quit' signal? Check the value sent
        last unless (defined $thread_line);

        # do private spurious things to it
        chomp ($thread_line=uc($thread_line));
        thr_print "Thread ",$self->tid," got '$thread_line'\n";
    }
    thr_print "Thread ", $self->tid, " ended\n";
}
```

Since the service threads block if no values are waiting in the queue, this approach effectively handles the job of having service threads wait – we previously dealt with this using condition variables and semaphores. However, we don't need a return semaphore anymore because there is no longer any need for a service thread to signal the main thread that it can continue – the main thread is free to continue as soon as it has copied the new line into the queue.

The means by which we terminate the program has also changed. Originally we set the line variable to undef and broadcast to all the waiting threads. We replaced that with a semaphore, which we raised high enough so that all service threads could decrement it. With a queue we use a variation on the semaphore approach, adding sufficient undef values to the queue so that all service threads can remove one and exit.

We have added one further refinement to this version of the application – a 'start-gun' semaphore. Simply put, this is a special semaphore that is created with a value of zero and increments it by one each service thread as it starts. The main thread attempts to decrement the semaphore by a number equal to the number of service threads, so it will only start to read lines once all service threads are running. Why is this useful? Because threads have no priority of execution. In the previous examples the first service threads will start receiving and processing lines before later threads have even initialized. In a busy threaded application, the activity of these threads may mean that the service threads started last do so very slowly, and may possibly never get the time to initialize themselves properly. In order to make sure we have a full pool of threads at our disposal, we use this semaphore to hold back the main thread until the entire pool is assembled.

There are many other ways that threaded applications can be built and with more depth to the examples than we have shown here. Applications that also need to handle process signals should consider the `Thread::Signal` module, for instance. Perl threads are still experimental, so an in-depth discussion of them is perhaps inappropriate. However, more examples and a more detailed discussion of threaded programming models and how Perl handles threads can be found in the `perlthrtut` manual page by executing:

> **perldoc perlthrtut**

Thread Safety and Locked Code

Due to the fact that threads share data, modules and applications that were not built with them in mind can become confused if two threads try to execute the same code. This generally comes about when a module keeps data in global variables, which is visible to both threads and which is overwritten by each of them in turn. The result is threads that pollute each other's data.

The best solution to avoid this problem is to rewrite the code to allow multiple threads to execute it at once. Code that does this is called **thread safe**. If this is too hard or time consuming we can use the `:locked` subroutine attribute to force a subroutine into a single-threaded mode, only one thread can be inside the subroutine at any one time (other calling threads will block until the current call is completed):

```
singlethreadedsub:locked {
    print "One at a time! Wait your turn! \n";
}
```

This works well for functional applications, but for object-oriented programming locking a method can be overly restrictive; we only need to make sure that two threads handling the same object do not conflict. To do this we can add the `:method` attribute:

```
singlethreadedmethod:locked:method {
    $self = shift;
    ...
}
```

We can also lock a subroutine in code by calling `lock` on it:

```
sub mysub {
    lock \&mysub if $Config{'usethreads'};
    ...
}
```

The main use for this is for applications that we want to work in both threaded and unthreaded environments and which contain subroutines that cannot have two threads executing them at once.

Summary

Over the course of this chapter we have covered the following:

- Signals and how to handle them.
- Using Perl's `fork` function to start new processes.
- Inter-Process Communication and the various ways in which different processes can communicate with one another.
- Sharing of data between processes, using message queues, semaphores, and shared memory segments.
- Thread support in Perl.

Networking with Perl

Network programming is a very large topic. In this chapter, we will attempt to provide a solid foundation in the basic concepts and principles of networking. We will cover the TCP/IP protocol and its close relatives, then move on to developing simple network clients and servers using Perl's standard libraries. We will also look at the functions Perl provides for determining network configurations, and the helper modules that make analyzing this information simpler.

An Introduction to Networks

Most Perl network programming involves establishing connections across, and communicating through, TCP/IP networks. In order to understand how network-programming interfaces work the way that they do, an overview of networking and the TCP/IP protocol in particular can be useful. In pursuit of this, what follows is a somewhat terse but reasonably informative overview of how networks function at a fundamental level, and how TCP/IP bridges the gap between basic network functionality and the application services.

Protocol Layers

For any message to be communicated it must travel through some form of medium. This medium can range from air and space (used for satellite links and packet radio), to copper cabling and fiber optics. The medium of choice for the last twenty years has been copper cabling, due to the ubiquity of cost-effective equipment based on open standards like Ethernet. This supplies the physical part of the network, also known as the physical layer.

On top of this is layered a series of protocols, each providing a specific function – the preceding layer acting as the foundation for the one above. ISO worked on a seven-layer reference model for protocol standardization, to allow multiple vendors to communicate with each other. While it does not define any specific protocol or implementation, many modern protocols were designed against its model. The OSI (Open Systems Interconnection) reference model appears as follows:

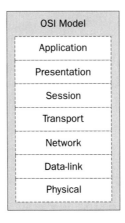

The bottom layer, which we already mentioned, is the communication, or physical, medium. Using Ethernet as an example, this layer includes not only the copper cabling, but also the impedance and voltage levels used on it.

The second layer, known as the data-link layer, defines how that medium is to be used. For instance, our standard telephone systems are analog devices; the voice traffic is carried over analog carrier waves on the wire. Ethernet, like most computer network devices, prefers square waves. Because of this, this layer comprises the circuitry used to encode any transmissions in a form the physical layer can deliver, and decode any incoming traffic. It also has to ensure successful transmission of traffic.

> *If none of this makes any sense, don't despair, as this is typically the domain of electrical and electronic engineers, not programmers.*

The network layer works very closely with the data-link layer. Not only must it ensure that it is providing the data-link layer with information it can encode (handling only digital traffic to digital networks, etc.), but it also provides the addressing scheme to be used on the network.

Transport layers provide handshaking and check to ensure reliability of delivery. Certain protocols demand acknowledgment of every packet of information delivered to the recipient, and if certain portions aren't acknowledged, they are re-sent by this layer.

The session layer is responsible for establishing and maintaining sessions, as its name would suggest. Sessions are typically necessary for larger and multiple exchanges between specific services and/or users, where the order of information transmitted and received is of great importance.

The presentation layer is just that – a layer responsible for presenting a consistent interface or API for anything needing to establish and maintain connections.

Finally, the application layer specifies precisely how each type of service will communicate across these connections. HTTP, NNTP, and SMTP are examples of application protocols.

Frames, Packets, and Encapsulation

In order to put all of this into perspective, let's examine how one of the most prevalent network architectures compares to this reference model. Since we'll be reusing much of this information later in the chapter, we'll look at TCP/IP networks running over Ethernet:

OSI Model	TCP/IP over Ethernet
Application	Application/Terminal
Presentation	
Session	TCP/UDP
Transport	
Network	IP
Data-link	Ethernet Topology
Physical	

As you can see, the Ethernet standard itself (of which, there are several variations and evolutions) encompasses both the physical and data-link layers. At the physical layer, it specifies the electrical signaling, clocking requirements, and connectors.

At the data-link layer, Ethernet transceivers accomplish the encoding and decoding of traffic, and ensure delivery of traffic at both ends of the communication. This last part is actually a bit more involved than one might guess, due to the nature of the physical layer. Since the medium is copper, it should be obvious that only one host (or node) can transmit at a time. If more than one tries to send out a signal simultaneously, all signals are effectively scrambled by the mixed voltage levels. This event is called a collision. The Ethernet specification anticipates that this will happen (especially on extremely busy networks), and so provides a solution. When a collision is detected, each node will wait for a random interval before re-transmitting its data.

In order to prevent particularly long communication sessions between hosts from hogging the line, Ethernet specifies that all communications be of a specific length of data, called a frame. Each frame is delivered only as the wire is sensed as free of traffic. This allows multiple hosts to appear to be communicating simultaneously. In truth, they are cooperatively sending out their frames one at a time, allowing control of the wire to be passed among several hosts before sending out the succeeding frames.

On the receiving end, the specification requires that every node on the network have a unique hardware address (called a MAC address). Every frame is addressed to a specific address, and hence, only the node with that address should actually listen to those frames. Each address is comprised of two 24-bit segments. The first is the manufacturer's ID, assigned by the IEEE body. The last 24 bits are the unique equipment identifiers. The exception, of course, is broadcast traffic, which is not so addressed, since all nodes should be listening for it.

This brings up a couple of caveats that I should mention here; while in theory you should never have to worry about two pieces of off-the-shelf gear having the same MAC address, it can and does happen, especially with those units that allow that address to be reprogrammed. This can cause some quite bizarre network problems that are extremely difficult to isolate if we're not expecting them.

Another caveat is that while each node should only read the frames addressed to it, it doesn't necessarily have to be that way. Low-level network monitoring software ignores this, and reads all traffic. This is called sniffing the wire, and there are legitimate reasons to do this. With the case mentioned above, realizing that two nodes have the same MAC address often requires that you sniff the wire. As you can see, Ethernet is a carefully managed cooperative environment, but it is fallible.

To learn more about Ethernet, or any of the competing standards, we can order publications from the IEEE (Institute of Electrical and Electronics Engineers) web site (http://www.ieee.org/), which governs the standards; or alternatively, from related sites like the Gigabit Ethernet Alliance (http://www.gigabit-ethernet.org/). http://www.ethernet.org/, while offering a few forums discussing Ethernet standards, is not affiliated with any of the official industry bodies. Lastly, we can always search on the Internet for IEEE 802.3, the CSMA/CD specification that defines the operation of Ethernet technologies. For printed references, Macmillan Technical Publishing's *Switched, Fast, and Gigabit Ethernet* ISBN-1578700736, written by Robert Breyer and Sean Riley, is one of the best publications available. It covers the whole gamut of Ethernet networking, including bridging, routing, QOS, and more.

The Internet Protocol

Referring once more to our comparison chart, we now move into the realm of TCP/IP. TCP/IP is actually a bit misleading, since it refers to two separate protocols (and more are used, though not explicitly mentioned). As can be seen, the network layer in the OSI model directly correlates to IP (Internet Protocol), providing an addressing and routing scheme for the networks. Why, if Ethernet provides for addressing via MAC addresses, do we need yet another addressing scheme? The answer is, because of the segmented nature of large networks. The Ethernet MAC system only works if every node addressed is on the same wire (or bridge). If two segments, or even two separate networks, are linked together via a router or host, then a packet addressed from one host on one network to another on the other network would never reach its destination if it could only rely on the MAC address. IP provides the means for that packet to be delivered across the bridging router or host onto the other network, where it can finally be delivered via the MAC address.

We'll illustrate this more clearly in a moment, but first let's get a better understanding of what IP is. IP as we know it today is actually **IPv4**, a protocol that provides a 32 bit segmented addressing system. The protocol specification is detailed in RFC 791 (all RFC documents can be obtained from the RFC Editor's office web site, http://www.rfc-editor.org/, which is responsible for assigning each of them numbers and publishing them).

As an aside, we should notice that we're dealing with more than one governing body just to implement one model. The reason for this is simple; the IEEE, being electrical and electronics engineers, are responsible for the hardware portion of the implementation. Once we move into software, though, most open standards are suggested through RFCs, or 'Request for Comments'. Multiple bodies work closely with the RFC Editor's office, including IANA (Internet Assigned Numbers Authority), IETF (Internet Engineering Task Force), and others.

There is an emerging new standard, called **IPv6**, which offers a larger addressing space and additional features, but we won't be covering them here since IPv6 networks are still fairly rare. You can read more about IPv6 through RFC 2460.

Back to IPv4 and its addressing scheme. Notice that we said that IPv4 provides a segmented 32-bit address space. This address space is similar to MAC addresses, in that we divide the 32 bits into two separate designators. Unlike MAC's manufacturer:unit–# scheme, the first segment refers to the network, and the second the host. Also unlike MAC, the division doesn't have to be equally sized – in fact, it rarely is. While the distinction between the network and host can appear subtle, it's extremely important for routing traffic through disparate networks, as you will see. Regardless of this, an IP address is usually represented as four quads (as in four bits) in decimal form, and incorporates both the network and the host segment: 209.165.161.91.

In RFC 1700, the Assigned Numbers standard, five classes of networks are defined:

Class	Range	Bitmask of first octet
A	0-127	0xxxxxxx
B	128-191	10xxxxxx
C	192-223	110xxxxx
D	224-239	1110xxxx
E	240-255	1111xxxx

The 10.0.0.0 network address, for instance, is a class A network, since the first octet falls in the class A range, and 192.168.1.0 is a class C network. In practice, A-C are reserved for unicast addresses (networks where nodes typically communicate with single end-to-end connections), class D is reserved for multicast (nodes typically talking simultaneously to groups of other nodes), and E is reserved for future use. We need only be concerned with A through C here.

The class of each unicast network determines the maximum size of each network, since each class masks out an additional octet in each IP address, restricting the number of hosts:

Class	Netmask
A	255.0.0.0
B	255.255.0.0
C	255.255.255.0

For instance, a class A network, say 10.0.0.0, has a netmask of 255.0.0.0, which, in binary, would be represented as such:

00001010 00000000 00000000 00000000 Network address
11111111 00000000 00000000 00000000 Netmask

The network administrator knows that the netmask masks (with 1s) all of the bits that he's not allowed to use as valid addresses. Hence, he or she can use any of the last three quads to address a specific host, allowing him or her to potentially address 16,777,216 hosts.

An administrator assigned a class C network, like 198.168.1.0, would only be able to use the last octet, and hence only address 256 hosts (actually, the number of hosts is always 2 less, since 0 is reserved for the network address, and the highest number is usually reserved for network-wide broadcasts, which is 255 in this example):

11000000 10101000 00000001 00000000 Network address
11111111 11111111 11111111 00000000 Netmask

As you might have surmised, an independent authority allocates network addresses, which prevents conflicting addresses. There are also, however, smaller blocks within each class that are set aside for internal use for all organizations (and homes, if need be):

Class	Private IP block
A	10.0.0.0 - 10.255.255.255
B	172.16.0.0 - 172.31.255.255
C	192.168.0.0 - 192.168.255.255

Because these are unregulated addresses, multiple organizations will often use the same blocks internally. This does not cause any conflicts since these blocks are not routable on public networks (like the Internet). Any host on a company network using these blocks needs to either go through a proxy with a public address, or use some sort of network address translation (often referred to as NAT) in order to communicate with other hosts on public networks. Private IP assignments are covered in RFC 1918.

It is important to note that none of this precludes the ability of any network administrator from subdividing internal network blocks in any manner they see fit – dividing the 10.x.x.x class A address space into several class Cs, or even smaller divisions (bit masks can also be applied to the last octet as well). This is performed quite frequently to relieve network congestion and localize traffic onto subnets. This, in essence, creates a classless (or CIDR, Classless InterDomain Routing) network, though it may still appear as one monolithic class network to the outside world.

IP uses these network addresses and masks to determine the proper routing and delivery for each bit of information being sent. Each connection is evaluated as either needing local or remote delivery. Local delivery is the easiest, since IP will actually delegate to the lower layers to deliver the data:

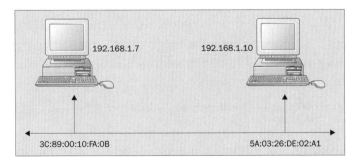

In this example, both hosts are on the same network, so IP requests that Ethernet deliver the data directly. A separate protocol (called ARP – Address Resolution Protocol, which is covered in RFC 826) is used for this. That transaction will go along these lines (imagine that the host above, 192.168.1.7, is sending a message to its neighbor, 192.168.1.10):

- ❑ IP receives a packet (in this case, packet refers to some kind of payload) for delivery.
- ❑ IP determines that local delivery can be done since the destination address appears to be on the same network as its own.
- ❑ An ARP request is broadcasted asking, 'Who has .10?'.
- ❑ 192.168.1.10 replies with its own MAC address.
- ❑ IP hands over the packet to the Ethernet layer for delivery to the MAC in the ARP response.
- ❑ Ethernet delivers the packet directly.

This method will not work, however, when the network is segmented. When this is done, some sort of bridge or router must exist that links the two networks, such as a host with two NICs, or a router. That bridge will have a local address on both networks, and the network will be configured to deliver all traffic that's not for local hosts through the bridge's local address.

Recall that we explained that Ethernet delivers all of its payloads in frames. IP delivers all of its payloads in packets, and both frames and packets have their own addressing schemes. The Ethernet layer is intentionally ignorant of what it is delivering, and who the ultimate recipient is, since its only concern is local delivery. In order to preserve all of that extra addressing information that IP requires, it performs complete encapsulation of the IP packet. That packet, as you may have guessed, has more than just raw data from the upper layers, it begins with a header that includes the IP addressing information, with the remainder taken up by the data itself. Ethernet receives that packet (which must be small enough to fit into an Ethernet frame's data segment), stores the entire packet in its frame's data segment, and delivers it to the local recipient's MAC address.

Accordingly, remote traffic is processed at two layers. Once IP determines that it is delivering to a remote host, it requests the local address of the router or **gateway**, and has Ethernet deliver the packet to the gateway, and the gateway forwards to the other network for local delivery:

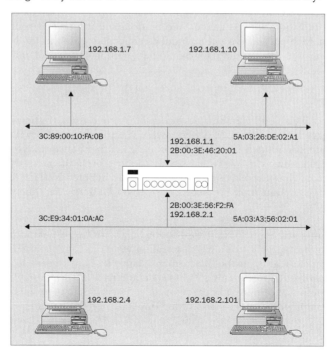

So, if 192.168.1.7 wanted to send a message to 192.168.2.4, the transaction would look like:

❏ IP receives a packet for delivery.

❏ IP determines that local delivery cannot be done since the destination address appears to be on a different network from its own, and so needs to deliver it through the local gateway (referred to as the default route in networking terms), which it has previously been informed is 192.168.1.1.

❏ An ARP request is broadcasted asking, 'Who has .1?'

❏ 192.168.1.1 replies with its own MAC address.

❏ IP hands over the packet to the Ethernet layer for delivery to the MAC in the ARP response.

❏ Ethernet delivers the packet to the gateway.

❏ The gateway examines the packet, and notices the IP address is meant for its other local network.

❏ The IP layer on the gateway's other local port receives the packet.

❏ IP determines that it can deliver the packet locally.

❏ An ARP request is broadcasted asking, "Who has .4?"

❏ 192.168.2.4 replies with its own MAC address.

❏ IP hands over the packet to the Ethernet layer for delivery to the MAC in the ARP response.

❏ Ethernet delivers the packet.

IP is also responsible for another very important task: if the upper layers hand it large bundles of data (each individual bundle would be considered an IP datagram), it must break them apart into something small enough for it to handle with its header information, and still be encapsulated into a single frame. When this happens, each packet sent out includes a sequence number in the header, allowing the receiving end's IP layer to reconstruct the original datagram from the individual packets.

UDP & TCP

By now, we should have a good idea how networks deliver and route traffic as needed, and we've covered the first three layers of the OSI Model with illustrations from TCP/IP over Ethernet. We can also see that IP could also route traffic from Ethernet to another network layer, such as token ring, or PPP over a MODEM connection. We're now ready to move on to the next two layers in the OSI model, Transport and Session. These two layers are combined and handled by TCP (Transmission Control Protocol) and UDP (User Datagram Protocol). We'll cover UDP since it's the simpler of the two protocols.

UDP provides a simple transport for any applications that don't need guarantees for delivery or data integrity. It may not be apparent from that description what the benefits of UDP are, but it does have a few. For one, UDP gains a great deal of performance since less work needs to be done. There's a great deal of overhead involved in maintaining TCP's state and data integrity. UDP applications can send and forget. Another benefit is the ability to broadcast (or multicast) data to groups of machines. TCP is a tightly controlled end-to-end protocol, permitting only one node to be addressed.

NTP (Network Time Protocol) is one application protocol that derives some great advantages from using UDP over TCP. Using TCP, a time server would have to wait and allow individual machines to connect and poll the time, meaning that redundant traffic is generated for every additional machine on the network. This would mean a second or more could elapse between the time being sent and the time being received, meaning an incorrect time being recorded. Using UDP allows it to multicast its time synchronization traffic in one burst and have all machines receive and respond accordingly, relieving a significant amount of traffic, which can be better used for other services. In this scenario, it's not critical that each machine be guaranteed delivery of that synchronization data since it's not likely that a machine will drift much, if at all, between the multicast broadcasts. As long as it receives some of the broadcasts occasionally, it will stay in sync, and bandwidth is preserved.

TCP, on the other hand, is much more expensive to maintain, but if you need to ensure that all the data arrives intact, there's no other alternative. TCP also allows state-full connections, with each exchange between nodes acknowledged and verified. If any portion of the data fails to come in, TCP will automatically request a retransmission, and the same would occur for any data arriving that fails to generate the same checksum.

Another important feature is TCP's use of internal addressing. Every application using a TCP connection is assigned a unique port number. Server applications typically will use the same port to listen on, to ensure that all clients know what IP port they need to connect to for reaching that service. TCP connections take this one step farther, by maintaining each completed circuit by independent local and remote IP:port pairs. This allows the same server to serve multiple clients simultaneously since the traffic is segregated according to the combined local and remote addresses and ports. It's important to note that while UDP has a concept of ports as well, being a connectionless protocol, no virtual circuits are built, it simply sends and receives on the port the application has registered with the UDP layer, and hence, the same capabilities do not exist. Also note that port addressing for UDP and TCP exist independently, allowing you to run a UDP and a TCP application on the same port number simultaneously.

The port portion of the IP:port pair is only 16 bits, though that rarely presents a problem. Traditionally, ports 1-1023 are reserved as privileged ports, which means that no service should be running on these ports that hasn't been configured by the system administrator. Web servers, as an example, run on port 80, and mail services run on port 25. When a user application connects to such a service, it is assigned a random high number port that is currently unused. Therefore, the connection to a web server will typically look like `209.165.161.91:80 <-> 12.18.192.3:4616`.

These features make TCP the most widely used protocol on the Internet. Applications like web services (HTTP protocol) would certainly not be as enjoyable if the content came in out of order and occasionally corrupted. The same goes for other application protocols like mail (SMTP), and news (NNTP).

Both protocols are covered by their own RFCs: 768 for UDP, and 793 for TCP.

ICMP

ICMP (Internet Control Message Protocol) is another protocol that should be mentioned for completeness. It's not a transport protocol in its own right, but a signaling protocol used by the other protocols. For instance, should a problem arise that appears to blocking all datagrams from reaching the recipient, IP would use ICMP to report the problem to the sender. The popular **ping** command generates ICMP messages ('Echo Request' message, in this case) too, to verify that the desired hosts are on the network, and 'alive'.

ICMP can deliver a range of messages including Destination Unreachable, Time Exceeded, Redirect Error, Source Quench, Parameter Problem, and a wide variety of sub-messages. It can also provide some network probing with Echo/Timestamp/Address Mask Request and Replies.

ICMP is more fully documented in RFC 792.

Other Protocols

It is important to realize that other protocols exist at various levels of the OSI reference model, such as IPX, Appletalk, NetBEUI, and DecNET. Perl can even work with some of these protocols. We won't be covering them here, though, since a clear majority of Perl applications reside in the TCP/IP domain. Furthermore, the principles illustrated here will apply in part to the operation of other types of networks.

Presentation/Application Layers

The last part of our OSI model comparison to examine is the presentation and application layers. TCP/IP doesn't actually have any formal presentation services, but there are many that can be optionally used as needed. Terminal applications, for instance, use a character-based service called the Network Virtual Terminal. Many applications, however, simply send their data and commands directly through the transport layer for direct handling by the application.

As mentioned earlier, SMTP, HTTP, and NNTP are examples of application protocols that work directly with the transport protocol. The only thing that these types of protocols specify is how they are to use the connection presented by the lower layers. For HTTP, as an example, the protocol specifies that each connection will consist of simple query and response pairs, and what the syntax and commands allowed in the queries are.

Anonymous, Broadcast, and Loopback Addresses

Any address within a network with a host segment (the host segment, remember, is the unmasked portion of any network address) that consists entirely of ones or zeros is not normally treated as a specific network interface. By default, a host with segments containing all zeros is an 'anonymous' address (since it is, in actuality, the network's address) that can be set as the sender in a TCP/IP packet. For example: 192.168.0.0.

Of course, a receiving system is entirely within its rights to ignore anonymous transmissions sent to it. This is not a valid address for the recipient however. Conversely, setting the host segment to all ones is a broadcast to all of the systems that have IP addresses in that range, for example: 192.168.255.255.

Pinging this address would result in every host on that subnet returning that echo request (at least, it does with UNIX systems, Windows NT appears to ignore it).

In addition, most hosts define the special address 127.0.0.1 as a self-referential address, also known as the loopback address. The loopback address allows hosts to open network connections to themselves, which is actually more useful than it might seem; we can for example run a web browser on the same machine as a web server without sending packets onto the network. This address, which is usually assigned to the special host name **localhost**, is also useful for testing networking applications when no actual network is available.

Networking with Perl

Sockets are Perl's interface into the networking layer, mapping the details of a network connection into something that looks and feels exactly like a filehandle. This analogy didn't start with Perl, of course, but came into popular usage with BSD UNIX. Perl merely continues that tradition, just as it is with other languages.

Sockets

There are two basic kinds of sockets: Internet Domain and UNIX domain sockets. Internet Domain sockets (hereafter referred to as INET sockets) are associated with an IP address, a port number, and a protocol, allowing you to establish network connections. UNIX domain sockets, on the other hand, appear as files in the local filing system, but act as a FIFO stack and are used for communication between processes on the same machine.

Sockets have a type associated with them, which often determines the default protocol to be used. INET stream sockets use the TCP protocol, since TCP provides flow control, state, and session management. INET datagram sockets, on the other hand, would naturally use UDP. Information flows in the same way that it does with a regular filehandle, with data read and written in bytes and characters.

Some socket implementations already provide support for the IPv6 protocol or handle other protocols such as IPX, X25, or AppleTalk. Depending on the protocol used, various different socket types may or may not be allowed. Other than stream and datagram sockets, a 'raw' socket type exists, which gives a direct interface to the IP protocol. Other socket types supported will be documented in the socket(2) man page on a UNIX-like system.

'Socket.pm'

Since Perl's socket support is a wrapper for the native C libraries (on UNIX, anyway), it can support any type your system can. Non-UNIX platforms may have varying or incomplete support for sockets (like Windows), so check your Perl documentation to determine the extent of your support. At the very least, standard INET sockets should be supported on most platforms.

The socket functions are a very direct interface. One consequence of this is that the idiosyncrasies of the original C API poke through in a number of places, notably the large number of numeric values for the various arguments of the socket functions. In addition, the address information arguments required by functions like bind, connect, and send need to be in a packed **sockaddr** format that is acceptable to the underlying C library function. Fortunately, the Socket module provides constants for all of the socket arguments, so we won't have to memorize those numeric values. It also provides conversion utilities like inet_aton and inet_ntoa that convert string addresses into the packed form desired and returned by the C functions.

A summary of Perl's socket functions is given overleaf, some directly supported by Perl, the rest provided by Socket.pm. Each of them is explained in more detail later in the chapter.

General:

Function	Description
socket	Create a new socket filehandle in the specified domain (Internet or UNIX) of the specified type (streaming, datagram, raw, etc.) and protocol (TCP, UDP, etc.). For example: `socket(ISOCK, PF_INET, SOCK_STREAM, $proto);`
shutdown	Close a socket and all filehandles that are associated with it. This differs from a simple `close`, which only closes the current process's given filehandle, not any copies held by child processes. In addition, a socket may be closed completely or converted to a read-only or write-only socket by shutting down one half of the connection. For example: `shutdown(ISOCK, 2);`
socketpair	Generate a pair of UNIX domain sockets linked back-to-back. This is a quick and easy way to create a full-duplex pipe (unlike the `pipe` function) and is covered in more detail in Chapter 22. For example: `socketpair(RSOCK, WSOCK, SOCK_STREAM, PF_UNSPEC);`

Servers:

Function	Description
bind	Bind a newly created socket to a specified port and address. For example: `bind ISOCK, $packed_addr;`
listen	(*Stream sockets only*) Set up a queue for receiving incoming network connection requests on a bound socket. For example: `listen ISOCK, $qsize;`
accept	(*Stream sockets only*) Accept and create a new communications socket on a bound and listened to server socket. For example: `accept CNNCT, ISOCK;`

Clients:

Function	Description
connect	Connect a socket to a remote server at a given port and IP address, which must be bound and listening to the specified port and address. Note: while datagram sockets can't really connect, this is supported. This sets the default destination for that type. For example: `connect ISOCK, $packed_addr;`

Options:

Function	Description
getsockopt	Retrieve a configuration option from a socket. For example: `$opt = getsockopt ISOCK, SOL_SOCKET, SO_DONTROUTE;`
setsockopt	Set a configuration option on a socket. For example: `setsockopt ISOCK, SOL_SOCKET, SO_REUSEADDR, 1;`

IO:

Function	Description
send	Send a message. For UDP sockets this is the only way to send data, and an addressee must be supplied, unless a default destination has already been set by using the connect function. For TCP sockets no addressee is needed. For example: `send ISOCK, $message, 0;`
recv	Receive a message. For a UDP socket, this is the only way to receive data, and returns the addressee (as a `sockaddr` structure) on success. TCP sockets may also use `recv`. For example: `$message = recv ISOCK, $message, 1024, 0;`

Conversion Functions:

Function	Description
inet_aton	*aton = ASCII to Network byte order.* Convert a hostname (for example, www.myserver.com) or textual representation of an IP address (for example, `209.165.161.91`) into a four byte packed value for use with INET sockets. If a host name is supplied, a name lookup, possibly involving a network request, is performed to find its IP address (this is a Perl extra, and not part of the C call). Used in conjunction with `pack_sockaddr_in`. For example: `my $ip = inet_aton($hostname);`
inet_ntoa	*ntoa = Network byte order to ASCII* Convert a four byte packed value into a textual representation of an IP address, for example, `209.165.161.91`. Used in conjunction with `unpack_sockaddr_in`.

Table continued on following page

Function	Description
pack_sockaddr_in	Generate a sockaddr_in structure suitable for use with the bind, connect, and send functions from a port number and a packed four-byte IP address. For example: my $addr = pack_sockaddr_in($port, $ip); The IP address can be generated with inet_aton.
unpack_sockaddr_in	Extract the port number and packed four-byte IP address from the supplied sockaddr_in structure: my ($port, $ip) = unpack_sockaddr_in($addr);

sockaddr_in	Call either unpack_sockaddr_in or pack_sockaddr_in depending on whether it is called in a list (unpack) or scalar (pack) context:
	
	my $addr = sockaddr_in($port, $ip);
	
	my ($port, $ip) = sockaddr_in($addr);
	
	The dual nature of this function can lead to considerable confusion, so using it in only one direction or using the pack and unpack versions explicitly is recommended.

pack_sockaddr_un	Convert a pathname into a sockaddr_un structure for use with UNIX domain sockets: my $addr = pack_sockaddr_un($path);
unpack_sockaddr_un	Convert a sockaddr_un structure into a pathname: my $path = unpack_sockaddr_un($addr);

sockaddr_un	Call either unpack_sockaddr_un or pack_sockaddr_un depending on whether it is called in a list (unpack) or scalar (pack) context:
	
	my $addr = sockaddr_in($path);
	
	my ($path) = sockaddr_in($addr);
	
	This function is even more confusing than sockaddr_in, since it only returns one value in either case. Using it for packing only, or using the pack and unpack versions explicitly is definitely recommended.

In addition to the utility functions, Socket supplies four symbols for special IP addresses in a pre-packed format suitable for passing to pack_sockaddr_in:

Symbol	Description
INADDR_ANY	Tells the socket that no specific address is requested for use, we just want to be able to talk directly to all local networks.
INADDR_BROADCAST	Uses the generic broadcast address of 255.255.255.255, which transmits a broadcast on all local networks.
INADDR_LOOPBACK	The loopback address for the local host, generally 127.0.0.1.
INADDR_NONE	An address meaning 'invalid IP address' in certain operations. Usually 255.255.255.255. This is invalid for TCP for example, since TCP does not permit broadcasts.

Opening Sockets

The procedure for opening sockets is the same for both UNIX and INET sockets; it only differs depending on whether you're opening a client or server connection. Server sockets typically follow three steps: creating the socket, initializing a socket data structure, and binding the socket and the structure together:

```
socket(USOCK, PF_UNIX, SOCK_STREAM, 0) || die "socket error: $!\n";
$sock_struct = sockaddr_un('/tmp/server.sock');
bind(USOCK, $sock_struct) || die "bind error: $!\n";
```

Of course, you may also need to insert a setsockopt call to fully configure the socket appropriately, but the above three steps are needed as a minimum. Opening client connections is similar: create socket, create the packed remote address, and connect to the server:

```
socket(ISOCK, PF_INET, SOCK_STREAM, getprotobyname('tcp')) || die "socket error:
$!\n";
$paddr = sockaddr_in($port, inet_aton($ip));
connect(ISOCK, $paddr) || die "connect error: $!\n";
```

Configuring Socket Options

The socket specification defines a number of options that may be set for sockets to alter their behavior. For direct manipulation of socket options, we can make use of Perl's built-in getsockopt and setsockopt functions, which provide low-level socket option handling capabilities. For the most part we rarely want to set socket options; however, there are a few socket options that are worth dealing with from time to time. These options apply almost exclusively to INET sockets.

The getsockopt function takes three arguments: a socket filehandle, a protocol level, and the option to set. Protocol level refers to the level the desired level operates at in the network stack. TCP, for instance, is a higher-level protocol than IP, and so has a higher value. We needn't bother with the particular values, though, since constants are available. setsockopt takes the same three arguments, but it can also include a value to set the option to. Leaving that argument out effectively unsets that option.

Options include:

Option	Description
SO_ACCEPTCONN	The socket is listening for connections.
SO_BROADCAST	The socket is enabled for broadcasts (used with UDP).
SO_DEBUG	Debugging mode enabled.
SO_LINGER	Sockets with data remaining to send continue to exist after the process that created them exits, until all data has been sent.
SO_DONTROUTE	The socket will not route. See also MSG_DONTROUTE in 'Reading from and Writing to Sockets' below.
SO_ERROR	(Read-only) The socket is in an error condition.
SO_KEEPALIVE	Prevent TCP/IP closing the connection due to inactivity by maintaining a periodic exchange of low-level messages between the local and remote sockets.
SO_DONTLINGER	Sockets disappear immediately, instead of continuing to exist until all data has been sent.
SO_OOBINLINE	Allow 'out of band' data to be read with a regular recv – see 'Reading fromand Writing to Sockets' below.
SO_RCVBUF	The size of the receive buffer.
SO_RCVTIMEO	The timeout value for receive operations.
SO_REUSEADDR	Allow bound addresses to be reused immediately.
SO_SNDBUF	The size of the send buffer.
SO_SNDTIMEO	The timeout period for send operations.
SO_TYPE	The socket type (stream, datagram, etc.).

Of these, the most useful is SO_REUSEADDR, which allows a given port to be reused, even if another socket exists that's in a TIME_WAIT status. The common use for this is to allow an immediate server restart, even if the kernel hasn't finished it's garbage collection and removed the last socket:

```
setsockopt SERVER, SOL_SOCKET, SO_REUSEADDR, 1;
```

We can be a little more creative with the commas to provide an arguably more legible statement:

```
setsockopt SERVER => SOL_SOCKET, SO_REUSEADDR => 1;
```

The SO_LINGER option is also useful, as is its opposite, SO_DONTLINGER. Usually the default, SO_DONTLINGER causes sockets close immediately when a process exits, even if data remains in the buffer to be sent. Alternatively, you can specify SO_LINGER, which causes sockets to remain open as long as they have data still to send to a remote client.

```
setsockopt SERVER, SOL_SOCKET, SO_DONTLINGER, 1;
```

SO_KEEPALIVE informs the kernel that TCP messages should be periodically sent to verify that a connection still exists on both ends. This feature can be handy for connections going through a NAT firewall, since that firewall has to maintain a table of connection translations, which are expired automatically after an interval with no activity. It also provides a periodic link test for those applications that keep predominantly idle connections, but need to be assured that a valid connection is maintained.

```
setsockopt SERVER, SOL_SOCKET, SO_KEEPALIVE, 1;
```

SO_BROADCAST sets or tests a socket for the ability to broadcast, an option which is only applicable to UDP sockets. SO_TYPE is a read-only option that returns the socket type. SO_ERROR indicates that the socket is in an error condition, though $!$ is an alternative.

The getsockopt function simply retrieves the current value of a socket option:

```
my $reusable = getsockopt SERVER, SOL_SOCKET, SO_REUSEADDR;
```

For experienced developers, there are also some lower-level options The expert network programmer can use getsockopt and setsockopt at lower levels in the protocol stack by supplying a different level as the protocol level argument. The Socket module does not define symbols for these levels since they are nothing directly to do with sockets, so to get useful names we must include the sys/socket.ph definition file:

```
require 'sys/socket.ph'.
```

This file defines symbols for all the system constants related to networking on the platform in question, including SOL_ symbols for lower-level protocols. The most interesting for us are:

Symbol	Description
SOL_IP	IP version 4 protocol
SOL_TCP	TCP protocol
SOL_UDP	UDP protocol
SOL_IPV6	IP version 6 protocol
SOL_RAW	'raw' protocol (SOCK_RAW)
SOL_IPX	IPX protocol
SOL_ATALK	Appletalk protocol
SOL_PACKET	'packet' protocol (SOCK_SEQPACKET)

Each protocol defines its own set of options. The only one of immediate interest to us here is TCP_NODELAY, which disables buffering at the TCP protocol level, essential for sending things like typed characters in real time across network connections:

```
setsockopt CONNECTION, SOL_TCP, TCP_NODELAY, 1;
```

Reading from and Writing to Sockets

Reading from and writing to sockets is handled by the `recv` and `send` functions, respectively. This is used with datagram sockets more often than with other types, but it's a valid call for all of them. As was mentioned above, Perl merely wraps the C function, so the syntax and behaviors are the same. While we'll be covering them in some detail here, you can get more information directly from the development manual pages (see `recv(2)` and `send(2)`).

The `send` function takes four arguments; a socket filehandle, a message, a numeric flag (which in most cases can be '0'), and an addressee, in the form of a `sockaddr_in` or `sockaddr_un` structure:

```
send SOCKET, $message, $flags, $addressee;
```

Since stream sockets are connected, we can omit the last argument for that type. For other types, the addressee is a `sockaddr` structure built from either a host and port number, or a local pathname, depending on the socket domain:

```
my $inetaddr = sockaddr_in($port, inet_aton($hostorip));
my $unixaddr = sockaddr_un($pathname);
```

The `flags` argument is a little more interesting, and is combined from a number of flags with symbols (defined by the `Socket` module) that alter the form or way in which the message is sent:

Send Flag	Description
MSG_OOB	Send an Out-Of-Band (that is, high priority) message.
MSG_DONTROUTE	Ignore the local network gateway configuration and attempt to send the message directly to the destination.
MSG_DONTWAIT	Do not wait for the message to be sent before returning. If the message would have blocked, the error EAGAIN (see the Errno module in Chapter 16) is returned, indicating that we must try again later.
MSG_NOSIGNAL	TCP sockets only. Do not raise a SIGPIPE signal when the other end breaks the connection. The error EPIPE is still returned.

For example:

```
use Errno qw(EAGAIN EPIPE);

$result = send SOCKET, $message, MSG_DONTWAIT|MSG_NOSIGNAL, $addressee;
if ($result == EAGAIN) {
...
}
```

The `recv` function also takes four arguments, but instead of an addressee, it specifies a length for the data to be received. It resembles the `read` function in several ways; the arguments are a socket filehandle, as before, then a scalar variable into which the message is placed and an expected length, followed up by a flags argument as before. The return value on success is the `sockaddr` structure for the client:

```
my $message;    # scalar to store message in
my $length = 1024;    # expected maximum length
my $sender = recv SOCKET, $message, $length, $flags;
```

The length argument is in fact somewhat arbitrary, since the size of the message is determined when it is read and adjusted accordingly. However, the supplied length is used to pre-allocate storage for the received message, so a size that is equal to or larger than the message will allow Perl to perform slightly quicker. Conversely, configuring a too large message will waste time to start with. A `reasonable` value is therefore the best idea.

The `flags` argument allows us to modify the way in which we receive messages:

Receive Flag	Description
MSG_OOB	Receive an Out-Of-Band message rather than a message from the normal message queue, unless OOB messages are being put at the head of the queue of normal messages by setting the SO_OOBINLINE socket option (see 'Configuring Socket Options').
MSG_PEEK	Examine and return the data of the next message on the socket without removing it.
MSG_WAITALL	Wait until a message has been completely received before attempting to retrieve it.
MSG_ERRQUEUE	Retrieve a message from the error queue rather than the normal message queue.
MSG_NOSIGNAL	TCP sockets only. Do not raise a SIGPIPE signal when the other end breaks the connection. The error 'EPIPE' is still returned.

For example:

```
my $message;
my $sender = recv SOCKET, $message, 1024,MSG_PEEK|MSG_WAITALL;
```

Note that depending on the socket implementation, the `send` and `recv` methods may accept more or different flags from those listed above. However, these are reasonably typical for most platforms, and certainly most UNIX platforms.

Closing Sockets

Like all other in-memory variables, Perl performs reference counting on sockets, and will close them automatically, should all the existing references go out of scope. In keeping with good programming practice, we should explicitly release unneeded resources, and Perl provides a way to do so. In fact, since sockets are in most ways filehandles, you can use the same function you would on a filehandle, like this:

```
close ISOCK;
```

There is a caveat to this rule, however. If a child has been forked that has a handle to the same socket, `close` only affects the process that called it. All other children with a handle to the socket will still have access to it, and the socket remains in use. A workaround for this situation exists in the `shutdown` function:

```
shutdown(ISOCK, 2);
```

This function closes the socket completely, even for any child processes with handles to it. The second argument to this function is what instructs shutdown to do this, and changing that value illuminates further capabilities of shutdown. Sockets can provide bi-directional communication, and shutdown will allow you to shut down either of the two channels independently. If we wish the socket to become a read-only socket, we can call shutdown with a second argument of 1. To make it write-only, we call it with a second argument of 0. The Socket module also defines constants for these values, which make them slightly friendlier:

```
shutdown SOCKET, SHUT_RD;     # shutdown read
shutdown SOCKET, SHUT_WR;     # shutdown write
shutdown SOCKET, SHUT_RDWR;    # shutdown completely
```

'IO::Socket.pm'

Although the Socket module makes using the socket functions possible, it still leaves a lot to be desired. To make life simper all round, the IO::Socket module and its children, IO::Socket::INET and IO::Socket::UNIX, provide a friendlier and simpler interface that automatically handles the intricacies of translating host names into IP addresses and thence into the sockaddr structure as well as translating protocol names into numbers and even services into ports.

All the socket functions are represented as methods; new sockets are created, bound, listened to, or connected with the new method, and all other functions become methods of the resulting filehandle object:

```
$socket->accept;
$udpsocket->send("Message in a Datagram", 0, $addressee);
$tcpsocket->print("Hello Network World!\n");
$socket->close;
```

The main distinctions from the native Perl functions are in the way they are created and configured.

Configuring Socket Options

Options can be set on sockets at creation time using the new method, but the IO::Socket modules also support getsockopt and setsocketopt methods. These are direct interfaces to the functions of the same name and behave identically to them, though usage syntax differs:

```
$connection->setsockopt(SOL_SOCKET, SO_KEEPALIVE => 1);
```

The IO::Socket modules also allow us to configure aspects of the socket when we create it, though not with the same flexibility as getsockopt and setsockopt. The arguments differ for Internet and UNIX domain sockets, in accordance with their different behaviors.

The full range of options accepted by the new method of `IO::Socket::INET` can be seen below:

INET Options	Description
LocalAddr LocalHost	(*Server only*) The local address or hostname to serve optionally followed by the port number or service name (which may additionally be followed by a default in parentheses) prefixed by a colon. For example: `127.0.0.1` `127.0.0.1:4444` `127.0.0.1:myservice(4444)` `www.myserver.com` `www.myserver.com:80` `www.myserver.com:http`
LocalPort	(*Server only*) The local port number or service name, if not given in `LocalAddr/LocalHost`. For example: `80` `http`
Listen	(*Server only*) The size of the queue to establish on the bound server socket. The maximum possible size is defined on a platform basis by the constant `SOMAXCONN`. Default: 5
Multihomed	(*Server only*) Boolean value. Listen for connections on all locally available network interfaces. Default: 0
Reuse	(*Server only*) Boolean value. Set the `SO_REUSEADDR` option to free up the socket for immediate reuse. Default: 0
PeerHost	(*Client only*) The remote address or hostname to connect to optionally followed by a port number or service name (which may additionally be followed by a default in parentheses) prefixed by a colon. For example: `127.0.0.1` `127.0.0.1:4444` `127.0.0.1:myservice(4444)` `www.myserver.com` `www.myserver.com:80` `www.myserver.com:http`
PeerPort	(*Client only*) The remote port number or service name, if not given in `PeerAddr/PeerHost`. For example: `80` `http`

Table continued on following page

INET Options	Description
Proto	The protocol number, or more sensibly, name. For example:
	`tcp`
	`udp`
	`icmp`
	The type is set implicitly from the socket type if it is SOCK_STREAM, SOCK_DGRAM, or SOCK_RAW.
	Default: `tcp`
Timeout	Timeout value for socket operations, in seconds. Default: 0 (no timeout).
Type	The socket type. For example:
	`SOCK_STREAM (for TCP)`
	`SOCK_DGRAM (for UDP)`
	`SOCK_RAW (for ICMP)`
	`SOCK_SEQPACKET`
	The socket type is set implicitly from the protocol if it is `tcp`, `udp`, or `icmp`.
	Default: SOCK_STREAM

If only one argument is passed to the new method of IO::Socket::INET, it is assumed to be a client's peer address, including the port number or service name.

```
my $server = new IO::Socket::INET($server_address_and_port);
```

The new method of IO::Socket does not have this shorthand: defining the socket domain is mandatory.

The new method of the IO::Socket::UNIX module is considerably simpler. It takes only four arguments, three of which we have already seen:

UNIX Option	Description
Local	(*Server only*) The pathname of the socket connection in the filesystem, for example:
	`/tmp/myapp_socket`
	The pathname should be somewhere that the server has the ability to create a file. A previous file should be checked for and removed first if present.
Listen	(*Server only*) Specify that this is a server socket, and set the size of the queue to establish on the bound server socket. The maximum possible size is defined on a platform basis by the constant SOMAXCONN.
	Note that unlike INET sockets, it is the setting of this parameter, not Local or Peer, that causes the module to bind and listen to the socket. It is not implied by Local.
	Default: 5

UNIX Option	Description
Peer	(*Client only*) The pathname of the socket connection in the filesystem, for example: `/tmp/myapp_socket`

Type	The socket type, for example:
	
	`SOCK_STREAM`
	
	`SOCK_DGRAM`
	
	`SOCK_RAW`
	
	`SOCK_SEQPACKET`
	
	Default: `SOCK_STREAM`

If using new via the parent `IO::Socket` module we must also supply a domain for the socket:

```
my $socket = new IO::Socket(Domain => PF_INET, ...);
```

This may be from the `PF_` family of constants, for example `PF_INET` or `PF_UNIX` (or indeed `PF_APPLETALK`, etc.). These are not to be confused with the `AF_` constants (as supplied to `gethostbyaddr`, or `getnetbyaddr`, which are from the address family of symbols).

Now that we've covered all of the basics of using both `Socket` and `IO::Socket` methodologies, we'll illustrate them will sample applications. We'll cover both client and server implementations, using both methodologies, and using both TCP and UDP protocols.

TCP INET Examples

A server is simply an application that listens for and accepts incoming connections from client applications. Once the connection is established, the two ends may then carry out whatever service the server is there to perform – receive a file, send a web page, relay mail, and so on.

In general, a server creates a TCP socket to listen for incoming connections, by first creating the socket with `socket`, and then assigning it to server duty with the `bind` function. The resulting socket is not connected, nor can it be used for communications, but it will receive notification of clients that connect to the address and port number otof which it is bound. To prepare to receive connections, we use the `listen` function, which creates an internal queue for incoming connections to collect. We then use the `accept` function to pull a connection request from the queue and create a socket filehandle for it. With it, we can communicate with the remote system. Behind the scenes, TCP sends an acknowledgment to the client, which creates a similar socket to communicate with our application.

A Simple TCP Socket Server

The following simple application demonstrates one way to create a very simple TCP server operating over an INET socket, using Perl's built-in socket functions:

```perl
#!/usr/bin/perl
# tcpinetserv.pl
use strict;
use warnings;
use Socket;
```

```perl
my $proto = getprotobyname('tcp');
my $port = 4444;

# Create 'sockaddr_in' structure to listen to the given port
# on any locally available IP address
my $servaddr = sockaddr_in($port, INADDR_ANY);

# Create a socket for listening on
socket SERVER, PF_INET, SOCK_STREAM, $proto
    or die "Unable to create socket: $!";

# bind the socket to the local port and address
bind SERVER, $servaddr or die "Unable to bind: $!";

# listen to the socket to allow it to receive connection requests
# allow up to 10 requests to queue up at once.
listen SERVER, 10;

# now accept connections
print "Server running on port $port...\n";
while (accept CONNECTION, SERVER) {
    select CONNECTION; $| = 1; select STDOUT;
    print "Client connected at ", scalar(localtime), "\n";
    print CONNECTION "You're connected to the server!\n";
    while (<CONNECTION>) {
        print "Client says: $_\n";
    }
    close CONNECTION;
    print "Client disconnected\n";
}
```

We use the Socket module to define the constants for the various socket functions – PF_INET means create an INET socket (we could also have said PF_UNIX for a UNIX domain socket or even PF_APPLTALK for a Macintosh Appletalk socket). SOCK_STREAM means create a streaming socket, as opposed to SOCK_DGRAM, which would create a datagram socket. We also need to specify a protocol. In this case we want TCP, so we use the getprotobyname function to return the appropriate protocol number – we explore this and similar functions at the end of the chapter.

Once the constants imported from Socket are understood, the socket function becomes more comprehensible; it essentially creates a filehandle that is associated with a raw, unassigned socket. To actually use it for something, we need to program it. First, we bind it to listen to port 4444 on any locally available IP address using the bind function. The bind function is one of the esoteric socket functions that requires a packet C-style data structure, so we use the sockaddr_in function to create something that is acceptable to bind from ordinary Perl values. The special INADDR_ANY symbol tells bind to listen to all local network interfaces; we could also specify an explicit IP address with inet_aton:

```perl
# bind to the loopback address
# (will only respond to local clients, not remote)
bind SERVER, inet_aton('127.0.0.1');
```

The `listen` function enables the socket's queue to receive incoming network connections, and sets the queue size. It takes the socket as a first argument and a queue size as the second. In this case, we said `10` to allow up to ten connections to queue; after that, the socket will start rejecting connections. We could also use the special symbol (again defined by `Socket`) of `SOMAXCONN` to create a queue of the maximum size supported by the operating system:

```
# create a queue of the maximum size allowed
listen SERVER, SOMAXCONN;
```

Having gone through all this setup work, the actual server is almost prosaic – we simply use `accept` to generate sockets from the server socket. Each new socket represents an active connection to a client. In this simple example we simply print a hello message and then print out whatever the client sends until it disconnects. In order to make sure that anything we send to the client is written out in a timely manner we set autoflush on the socket filehandle. This is an important step since our response to the client may never reach them since our socket is waiting for enough data to fill the buffer before flushing it to the client. IO buffering is enabled in Perl by default. Alternatively, we could have used the `syswrite` function, which explicitly bypasses any buffering.

A Simple TCP 'IO::Socket' Server

The `IO::Socket` module simplifies all this somewhat by relieving us from having to do all of the low level `sockaddr_in` manipulation socket function calls. Here is the same server written using `IO::Socket`:

```perl
#!/usr/bin/perl
# tcpioinetserv.pl
use warnings;
use strict;

use IO::Socket;

my $port = 4444;

my $server = IO::Socket->new(
    Domain    => AF_INET,
    Proto     => 'tcp',
    LocalPort => $port,
    Listen    => SOMAXCONN,
);

print "Server running on port $port...\n";
while (my $connection = $server->accept) {
    print "Client connected at ", scalar(localtime), "\n";
    print $connection "You're connected to the server!\n";
    while (<$connection>) {
        print "Client says: $_";
    }
    close $connection;
    print "Client disconnected\n";
}
```

This is altogether simpler, as well as being easier to read. Note that we didn't need to specify a socket type, since the `IO::Socket` module can work it out from the protocol – TCP means it must be a `SOCK_STREAM`. It also has the advantage that autoflushing is enabled by default on the newly created sockets, so we don't have to do it ourselves.

As a slightly simplified case for when we know we want an INET socket we can use the IO::Socket::INET module directly, obviating the need for the Domain argument:

```
my $server = new IO::Socket::INET(
    Proto     => 'tcp',
    LocalPort => $port,
    Listen    => SOMAXCONN,
);
```

The filehandles returned by either approach work almost identically to 'ordinary' filehandles for files and pipes, but we can distinguish them from other filehandles with the -S file test:

```
print "It's a socket!" if -S CONNECTION;
```

Filehandles returned by the IO::Socket modules also support all the methods supported by the IO::Handle class, from which they inherit, so we can for example say:

```
$socket->autoflush(0);
$socket->printf("%04d %04f", $int1, $int2);
$socket->close;
```

See Chapter 12 for more on the IO::Handle module and the other modules in the 'IO' family.

Our example above lacks one primary attribute necessary for a true multi-user server – it can only handle one connection at a time. A true server would either fork or use threads to handle each connection, freeing up the main process to continue to accept concurrent connections. For more information on that aspect, please consult Chapter 22.

A Simple TCP Socket Client

While servers listen for and accept network connections, clients originate them. Implementing a client is similar to creating a server, although simpler. We start out by creating an unconnected stream socket of the correct domain and protocol with socket. We then connect the socket to the remote server with the connect function. If the result of the connect is not a failure, then this is all we have to do, apart from use the socket. Once we're done, we need to close the socket, in order to maintain our status as good denizens on the host.

The following simple application demonstrates a very simple INET TCP client, using Perl's built-in socket functions:

```
#!/usr/bin/perl
# tcpinetclient.pl
use warnings;
use strict;

use Socket;

my $proto = getprotobyname('tcp');
my $host = inet_aton('localhost');
my $port = 4444;
```

```
# Create 'sockaddr_in' structure to connect to the given
# port on the IP address for the remote host
my $servaddr = sockaddr_in($port, $host);

# Create a socket for connecting on
socket SERVER, PF_INET, SOCK_STREAM, $proto
    or die "Unable to create socket: $!";

# bind the socket to the local port and address
connect SERVER, $servaddr or die "Unable to connect: $!";

# enable autoflush
select SERVER; $| = 1; select STDOUT;

# communicate with the server
print "Client connected.\n";
print "Server says: ", scalar(<SERVER>);
print SERVER "Hello from the client!\n";
print SERVER "And goodbye!\n";
close SERVER;
```

The initial steps for creating the client are identical to those for the server. First, we create a socket of the right type and protocol. We then connect it to the server by feeding `connect` the socket filehandle and a `sockaddr_in` structure. However, in this case the address and port are those of the server, not the client (which doesn't have a port until the connection succeeds). The result of the `connect` is either an error, which returns undef and we catch with a `die`, or a connected socket. If the latter, we enable autoflush on the server connection to ensure data is written out in a timely manner, read a message from the server, send it a couple of messages, and close the connection.

Clients may bind to a specific port and address if they wish to, just like servers, but may not listen on them. It is not common that we would want to create a bound client, but one possible use is to prevent two clients on the same machine from talking to the server at the same time. This would only be useful if SO_REUSEADDR is not set for the socket.

A Simple TCP 'IO::Socket' Client

Again, we can use the `IO::Socket` module to create the same client in a simpler fashion, avoiding the need to convert the hostname to a packed internet address with `inet_aton` and setting autoflush:

```
#!/usr/bin/perl
# tcpioinetclient.pl
use warnings;
use strict;

use IO::Socket;

my $host = 'localhost';
my $port = 4444;

my $server = IO::Socket->new(
    Domain   => PF_INET,
    Proto    => 'tcp',
    PeerAddr => $host,
    PeerPort => $port,
);
```

```
die "Connect failed: $!\n" unless $server;

# communicate with the server
print "Client connected.\n";
print "Server says: ", scalar(<$server>);
print $server "Hello from the client!\n";
print $server "And goodbye!\n";
close $server;
```

As with the server, we can also eliminate the `Domain` argument by using the `IO::Socket::INET` module directly:

```
my $server = new IO::Socket::INET(
    Proto    => 'tcp',
    PeerAddr => $host,
    PeerPort => $port,
);
```

In fact, if we use `IO::Socket::INET` we can omit the protocol too, and combine the address and port together. This gives us a single argument, which we can pass without a leading name:

```
my $server = new IO::Socket::INET("$host:$port");
```

This one argument version only works for creating INET TCP clients, since all other uses of the `IO::Socket` modules require at least one other argument. Fortunately, creating an INET TCP client is a common enough requirement that it's still a useful shortcut.

Reading from and Writing to TCP Sockets

Socket filehandles that represent the ends of a TCP connection are trivial to use for input and output. Since TCP streams data, we can read and write it in bytes and characters, just as we do with any normal filehandle:

```
# send something to the remote socket
print SOCKET "Send something to the other end\n";

# get something back
my $message = <SOCKET>;
```

As we mentioned in the previous examples, Perl buffers IO by default, since the message will only reach the client as we fill the buffer and force a flush. For that reason, we need to either use the `syswrite` function, or set `autoflushing` to 1 after selecting our handle:

```
select SOCKET; $| = 1; select STDOUT;
```

The `IO::Socket` modules sets `autoflush` automatically on the socket filehandles it creates, so we don't have to worry when using it. If we wanted to send individual key presses in real time, we might also want to set the `TCP_NODELAY` option as an additional measure.

We can also use send and recv to send messages on TCP connections, but in general we don't usually want to – the whole point of a streaming socket is that it is not tied to discrete messages. These functions are more useful (indeed, necessary) on UDP sockets. On a TCP connection, their use is identical – except that we do not need to specify a destination or source address since TCP connections, being connection-oriented, supply this information implicitly.

Determining Local and Remote Addresses

We occasionally might care about the details of either the local or the remote address of a connection. To find our own address we can use the Sys::Hostname module, which we cover at the end of the chapter. To find the remote address we can use the getpeername function. This function returns a packed address sockaddr structure, which we will need to unpack with unpack_sockaddr_in:

```
my ($port, $ip) = unpack_sockaddr_in(getpeername CONNECTION);
print "Connected to: ", inet_ntoa($ip), ", port $port\n";
```

We can use this information for a number of purposes, for example keeping a connection log, or rejecting network connections based on their IP address:

```
# reject connections outside the local network
inet_ntoa($ip) !~ /^192\.168\.1\./ and close CONNECTION;
```

A quirk of the socket API is that there is no actual 'reject' capability – the only way to reject a connection is to accept it and then close it, which is not elegant but gets the job done. This does open the possibilities of Denial of Service (DoS) attacks, though, and care needs to be taken to protect against such.

The IO::Socket::INET module also provides methods to return the local and remote address of the socket:

```
# find local connection details
my $localaddr = $connection->sockaddr;
my $localhost = $connection->sockhost;
my $localport = $connection->sockport;

# find remote connection details
my $remoteaddr = $connection->peeraddr;
my $remotehost = $connection->peerhost;
my $remoteport = $connection->peerport;
```

As with other methods of the IO::Socket::INET module, unpacking the port number and IP address is done for us, as is automatic translation back into an IP address, so we can do IP-based connection management without the use of unpack_sockaddr_in or inet_ntoa:

```
# reject connections outside the local network
$remoteaddr =~ /^192.168.1/ and close CONNECTION;
```

We can also reject by host name, which can be more convenient but which can also be unreliable because it may require DNS lookups on which we cannot necessarily rely. The only way to verify that a host name is valid is to use gethostbyname on the value returned by peerhost and then check the returned IP address (or possibly addresses) to see if one matches the IP address returned by peeraddr. Comparing both forward and reverse name resolutions is a good security practice to employ. See the end of the chapter and the discussion on the host functions for more details.

UDP INET Examples

UDP servers and clients have many uses. The NTP protocol, for instance, relies on it to conserve bandwidth by broadcasting time synchronization information to multiple clients simultaneously. Obviously, clients missing the occasional broadcast aren't a critical issue. If it is imperative that your clients receive all of your broadcasts, then you should be using TCP.

A Simple UDP Socket Server

Here is an example of a simple INET UDP server, written using Perl's built-in socket functions. It is similar to the TCP server, creating a server socket and binding it, but differs in that you don't listen to it (that call is restricted to stream and sequential packet sockets):

```perl
#!/usr/bin/perl
# udpinetserv.pl
use warnings;
use strict;

use Socket;

my $proto = getprotobyname('udp');
my $port = 4444;

# Create 'sockaddr_in' structure to listen to the given port
# on any locally available IP address
my $servaddr = sockaddr_in($port, INADDR_ANY);

# Create a socket for listening on
socket SERVER, PF_INET, SOCK_DGRAM, $proto
    or die "Unable to create socket: $!";

# bind the socket to the local port and address
bind SERVER, $servaddr or die "Unable to bind: $!";

# now receive and answer messages
print "Server running on port $port...\n";
my $message;
while (my $client = recv SERVER, $message, 1024, 0) {
    my ($port, $ip) = unpack_sockaddr_in($client);
    my $host = gethostbyaddr($ip, AF_INET);
    print "Client $host:$port sent '$message' at ", scalar(localtime), "\n";
    send SERVER, "Message '$message' received", 0, $client;
}
```

The key difference with this server is that because UDP is connectionless we do not generate new filehandles with accept and then communicate over them. Instead, we read and write messages directly using the send and recv functions. Each of those functions takes optional flags (which we did not use, hence the argument of 0 on both calls), and they are documented in your development man pages:

> **man 2 recv**
> **man 2 send**

Every message we receive comes with the sender's address attached. When we retrieve a message with recv we get the remote address of the client (as a sockaddr_in structure for INET servers or a sockaddr_un structure for UNIX domain ones), which we can feed directly to the send function to return a response.

A Simple UDP' IO::Socket' Server

Again we can use the IO::Socket modules to do the same thing in a clearer way:

```perl
#!/usr/bin/perl
# udpioinetserv.pl
use warnings;
use strict;

use IO::Socket;

my $port = 4444;

my $server = new IO::Socket(
    Domain    => PF_INET,
    LocalPort => $port,
    Proto     => 'udp',
);

die "Bind failed: $!\n" unless $server;

print "Server running on port $port...\n";
my $message;
while (my $client = $server->recv($message, 1024, 0)) {
    my ($port, $ip) = unpack_sockaddr_in($client);
    my $host = gethostbyaddr($ip, AF_INET);
    print "Client $host:$port sent '$message' at ", scalar(localtime), "\n";
    $server->send("Message '$message' received", 0, $client);
}
```

The send and recv methods of IO::Socket are simply direct interfaces to the functions of the same name, so the client address passed to the send method is a sockaddr_in (or sockaddr_un, in the UNIX domain) structure. We'll cover both send and recv in more depth shortly.

A Simple UDP Socket Client

Whereas TCP clients create a dedicated connection to a single host with each socket, a UDP client can broadcast packets to any host it wishes to with the same socket. Consequently, we do not use connect but use send and recv immediately on the created socket:

```perl
#!/usr/bin/perl
#udpinetclient.pl
use warnings;
use strict;

use Socket;

my $proto = getprotobyname('udp');
my $host = inet_aton('localhost');
my $port = 4444;
```

```
# Create a socket for sending & receiving on
socket CLIENT, PF_INET, SOCK_DGRAM, $proto
    or die "Unable to create socket: $!";

# Create 'sockaddr_in' structure to connect to the given
# port on the IP address for the remote host
my $servaddr = sockaddr_in($port, $host);

# communicate with the server
send CLIENT, "Hello from client", 0, $servaddr or die "Send: $!\n";
my $message;
recv CLIENT, $message, 1024, 0;
print "Response was: $message\n";
```

The UDP socket is free to communicate with any other UDP client or server on the same network. In fact, we can bind and listen to a UDP socket and use it as a client to send a message to another server as well.

A Simple UDP IO::Socket Client

The IO::Socket version of this client is:

```
#!/usr/bin/perl
# udpioinetclient.pl
use warnings;
use strict;

use IO::Socket;

my $host = 'localhost';
my $port = 4444;

my $client = new IO::Socket(
    Domain   => PF_INET,
    Proto    => 'udp',
);

die "Unable to create socket: $!\n" unless $client;

my $servaddr = sockaddr_in($port, inet_aton($host));
$client->send("Hello from client", 0, $servaddr) or die "Send: $!\n";
my $message;
$client->recv($message, 1024, 0);
print "Response was: $message\n";
```

We can also use IO::Socket::INET directly and omit the Domain argument:

```
my $client = new IO::Socket::INET(Proto => 'udp');
```

Unfortunately, because the send and recv methods are direct interfaces to the send and recv functions, the recipient address is still a sockaddr_in structure and we have to do the same contortions to provide send with a suitable addressee that we do for the built-in function version. This aside, IO::Socket still makes writing UDP clients simpler, if not quite as simple as TCP clients.

Broadcasting

One of the key benefits of UDP is that we can broadcast with it. In fact, broadcasting is trivially easy to do once we realize that it simply involves sending messages to the broadcast address of the network we want to communicate with. For the `192.168` network, the broadcast address is `192.168.255.255`:

```perl
my $port = 444;
my $broadcast = '192.168.255.255';
my $broadcastaddr = ($port, inet_aton($broadcast));
```

The special address `255.255.255.255` may therefore be used to broadcast to any local network. The pre-packed version of this address is given the symbolic name `INADDR_BROADCAST` by the `Socket` and `IO::Socket` modules:

```perl
$udpsocket->send("Hello Everybody", 0, INADDR_BROADCAST);
```

Standard UDP makes no provision for narrowing the hosts to which a broadcast is sent – everything covered by the broadcast address will get the message. An enhancement to UDP called Multicast UDP provides for selected broadcasting, subscribers, and other enhancements to the standard UDP protocol. However, it is more complex to configure and requires multicast-aware routers and gateways if broadcasts are to travel beyond hosts on the immediate local network. The `IO::Socket::Multicast` module found on CPAN provides a programming interface to this capability.

UNIX Sockets

UNIX domain sockets are the second type of socket that we can create. Whereas INET sockets allow remote communications via the networking infrastructure of the operating system, UNIX domain sockets work through the filing system, restricting communications to local processes. They behave (and are used) in the same manner as INET sockets, and are preferred for inter-process communication where no networking support is needed. The absence of network support makes this a lighter-weight implementation with higher performance.

As the name implies, UNIX domain sockets may not be supported on non-UNIX systems.

A Simple UNIX Socket Server

Writing an application to a UNIX domain socket is almost identical to writing it to use an INET socket:

```perl
#!/usr/bin/perl
# unixserv.pl
use warnings;
use strict;

use Socket;

my $file = '/tmp/unixserv_socket';

# Create 'sockaddr_un' structure to listen the local socket
my $servaddr = sockaddr_un($file);

# remove an existing socket file if present
unlink $file;
```

```
# Create a socket for listening on
socket SERVER, PF_UNIX, SOCK_STREAM, 0
    or die "Unable to create socket: $!";
# bind the socket to the local socket
bind SERVER, $servaddr or die "Unable to bind: $!";

# listen to the socket to allow it to receive connection requests
# allow up to 10 requests to queue up at once.
listen SERVER, 10;

# now accept connections
print "Server running on file $file...\n";
while (accept CONNECTION, SERVER) {
    select CONNECTION; $| = 1; select STDOUT;
    print "Client connected at", scalar(localtime), "\n";
    print CONNECTION "You're connected to the server!\n";
    while (<CONNECTION>) {
        print "Client says: $_";
    }
    close CONNECTION;
    print "Client disconnected\n";
}
```

First, we create a socket, but now we make it a UNIX domain socket by specifying PF_UNIX for the socket domain. We also do not specify a protocol – unlike INET sockets, UNIX domain sockets do not care about the protocol ahead of time – so instead we give it a value of 0 for the protocol.

Before we create the socket we clear away the filename created, if any, by the previous incarnation of the server, otherwise we may not be able to create the new socket. The address for bind still needs to be converted into a form it will accept, but since we are converting a UNIX domain address (a filename), we use sockaddr_un rather than sockaddr_in. Other than these changes, the server is identical.

A Simple UNIX 'IO::Socket' Server

The IO::Socket implementation of this server is similarly changed in only the barest details from the INET version. One important, but perhaps not obvious, difference is that an explicit Listen argument must be given to the new method for the socket to be bound and listened to. Without this, the server will generate an 'invalid argument' error from accept. This is not the case with INET sockets, though we can specify a Listen argument if we want.

```
#!/usr/bin/perl
# iounixserv.pl
use warnings;
use strict;

use IO::Socket;

my $file = '/tmp/unixserv_socket';

# remove previous socket file, if present
unlink $file;
```

```perl
my $server = IO::Socket->new(
    Domain    => PF_UNIX,
    Type      => SOCK_STREAM,
    Local     => $file,
    Listen    => 5,
);

die "Could not bind: $!\n" unless $server;

print "Server running on file $file...\n";
while (my $connection = $server->accept) {
    print $connection "You're connected to the server!\n";
    while (<$connection>) {
        print "Client says: $_\n";
    }
    close $connection;
}
```

A Simple UNIX Socket Client

The UNIX domain version of the client is also almost identical to its INET counterpart:

```perl
#!/usr/bin/perl
# unixclient.pl
use warnings;
use strict;

use Socket;

my $file = '/tmp/unixserv_socket';

# Create 'sockaddr_un' structure to connect to the given
# port on the IP address for the remote host
my $servaddr = sockaddr_un($file);

# Create a socket for connecting on
socket SERVER, PF_UNIX, SOCK_STREAM, 0
    or die "Unable to create socket: $!";

# bind the socket to the local socket
connect SERVER, $servaddr or die "Unable to connect: $!";

# enable autoflush
select SERVER; $| = 1; select STDOUT;

# communicate with the server
print "Client connected.\n";
print "Server says: ", scalar(<SERVER>);
print SERVER "Hello from the client!\n";
print SERVER "And goodbye!\n";
close SERVER;
```

Again, we create a socket in the UNIX domain and specify a protocol of '0'. We provide connect with a UNIX domain address compiled by sockaddr_un and connect as before. Together, this server and client operate identically to their INET counterparts – only they do it without consuming network resources. The only drawback is that a remote client cannot connect to our UNIX domain-based server. Of course, in some cases, we might actually want that, for security purposes for example.

A Simple UNIX 'IO::Socket' Client

The IO::Socket version of this client is:

```perl
#!/usr/bin/perl
# iounixclnt.pl
use warnings;
use strict;

use IO::Socket;

my $file = '/tmp/unixserv_socket';

my $server = IO::Socket->new(
    Domain   => PF_UNIX,
    Type     => SOCK_STREAM,
    Peer     => $file,
);

die "Connect failed: $!\n" unless $server;

# communicate with the server
print "Client connected.\n";
print "Server says: ", scalar(<$server>);
print $server "Hello from the client!\n";
print $server "And goodbye!\n";
close $server;
```

Determining Local and Remote Pathnames

When called on a UNIX domain socket, getpeername should return the name of the file being accessed by the other end of the connection. This would normally be the same as the file used for this end, but the presence of symbolic or hard links might give the client a different pathname for its connection than that of the server.

```perl
# get remote path
my $remotepath = unpack_socket_un(getpeername);
```

The IO::Socket::UNIX module provides the peerpath and hostpath to return the name of the file used by the local and remote sockets respectively:

```perl
my $localpath = $server->hostpath;
my $remotepath = $server->peerpath;
```

Multiplexed Servers

So far in this chapter, we have covered networking fundamentals implementing simple single-client TCP/IP servers that are capable of handling only one connection at a time.

For UDP this isn't too much of a limitation, since UDP works on a message-by-message basis. For TCP it is severely limiting, however, because while one client has the server's attention, connection requests from other clients must wait in the queue until the current client disconnects. If the number of requests exceeds the size of the queue specified by listen, connection requests will begin to bounce.

In order to solve this problem we need to find a way to multiplex the server's attention, so that it can handle multiple clients at once. Depending on our requirements, we have three options:

❑ Give the server the ability to monitor all client connections at once. This involves using the select function to provide one loop with the ability to respond to any one of several connections whenever any one of them becomes active. This kind of server is called a 'non-forking' or 'polling' server. Although it is not as elegant or efficient as a forking or threading server (code-wise), a polling server does have the advantage that it will work on any platform.

❑ Dedicate a separate process to each connection. This involves the fork function, and consists of forking a new child process to manage each connection. This kind of server is called a 'forking' server. However, fork may not be available on all platforms.

❑ Spawn a new thread to handle each connection. This is a similar idea to the forking server but is much more resource-efficient since threads are much more lightweight than separate processes. This kind of server is called a threaded server. However, like the fork function, threads are not always available to us, though this situation is improving and threads are available on more platforms than fork. Perl has two different thread models, as we discussed in Chapter 22, and we may or may not have access to either of them.

We'll consider and give an example of each kind of server in the following section, illustrating the basic similarities and differences between them.

Polling Servers

If we want to write a single process server that can handle multiple connections we need to use the select function, or more conveniently, the IO::Select module. Both the function and the module allow us to monitor, or poll, a collection of filehandles for events, in particular readability. Using this information we can build a list of filehandles and watch for activity on all of them. One of the filehandles is the server socket, and if input arrives on it, we accept the new connection. Otherwise, we read from an existing client's filehandle, and do whatever processing we need to, based on what it sends. Developing a selecting server is actually simple, once the basics of the select function are understood.

The 'select' Function

The select function has two completely different uses in Perl. The standard use takes one argument that changes the default output filehandle (STDOUT is the unstated default filehandle for functions like print, but we can change that). The select function also has a four-argument version, which takes three bitmasks (read, write, and exceptions) and an optional timeout value. We can use this version of select to continuously scan multiple filehandles simultaneously for a change in their condition, and react whenever one of them becomes available for reading or writing, or enters an error condition.

The bitmasks represent the file numbers, also called file descriptors, of filehandles that we are interested in communicating with; the first bit refers to filehandle number 0 (usually STDIN), the second to 1 (STDOUT) and the third to 2 (STDERR). Every new filehandle that we create contains inside it a low-level file descriptor, which we can extract with fileno.

Using select effectively requires first extracting the file numbers from the filehandles we want to monitor, which we can do with fileno, then building bitmasks from them, which we can do with vec. The following code snippet creates a mask with bits set for standard input and a handle created with one of the IO:: modules, for example IO::Socket:

```
my @handles;
$mask = 0;

push @handles, \*STDIN;
vec($mask, fileno(STDIN), 1);
push @handles, $handle;
vec($mask, fileno($handle), 1);
```

We can now feed this mask to `select`. The `@handles` array is going to be useful later, but we will disregard it for now.

The `select` function works by writing new bitmasks indicating the filehandles that are actually in the requested state into the passed arguments; each bit initially set to '1', will be turned off if the handle is not either readable or writable, and does not have an exception (meaning an unusual condition, such Out-Of-Band data), and left at '1' otherwise. To preserve our mask for a later date, we have to assign it to new scalars that `select` will assign its result to. If we don't want to know about writable file descriptors, which is likely, we can pass undef for that bitmask:

```
my ($read, $except) = ($mask, $mask);
while (my $got = select $read, undef, $except) {
    $except?handle_exception:handle_read;
    my ($read, $except) = ($mask, $mask);
}
```

Here `handle_read` and `handle_exception` are subroutines, which we have yet to write. We can also write, more efficiently but marginally less legibly:

```
while (my $got = select $read = $mask, undef, $except = $mask) {
    $except?handle_exception:handle_read;
}
```

If `select` is not given a fourth argument for a timeout, it will wait forever for something to happen, at which point the number of interesting file descriptors is returned. If a fourth parameter of a timeout in seconds is specified `$got` will contain '0':

```
my ($read, $except);
while ('forever') {
    while (my $got = select $read = $mask, undef, $except = $mask, 60) {
        $except?handle_exception:handle_read;
    }
    print "Nothing happened for an entire minute!\n";
}
```

The only remaining aspect to deal with is how to handle the result returned by `select`. We can again use `vec` for this, as well as the `@handles` array we created earlier but have not until now used. In essence, we scan through the array of filehandles, checking for the bit that represents its file descriptor in the mask. If it is set, that file descriptor is up to something and we react to it:

```
handle_read {
    foreach (@handles) {
        vec($read, fileno $_) and read_from_client($_);
    }
}
```

Both select and the IO::Select module are unbuffered operations. That is, they operate directly on file descriptors. This means that buffers are ignored and buffered IO functions such as print and read may produce inconsistent results; for example, there may be input in the filehandle buffer but not at the system level, so the file descriptor shows no activity when there is in fact data to be read.

Therefore, rather than using print, read, and other buffered IO functions, we must use system level IO functions like sysread and syswrite, which write directly to the file descriptor and avoid the buffers. Note that simply setting '$| = 1' is not adequate – see Chapter 12 for more details. Also note that one advantage of forked and threaded servers is that they do not have this requirement to use system IO, though we may choose to do so anyway.

The' IO::Select' Module

Having described how the select function works, we don't actually need to use it because the IO::Select module provides a far friendlier interface to the select function. Instead of building bitmasks, we just create an object and add filehandles to it:

```
new IO::Select;

my $selector = new IO::Select(\*STDIN, $handle);
```

To scan for active filehandles we then use the can_read method. The return value from both functions is an array of the filehandles (not file descriptors) that are currently in the requested state:

```
my @handles = $selector->can_read;
```

We can now iterate commands for each handle:

```
foreach (@handles) {
    read_from_client $_;
}
```

The counterpart to can_read, can_write, scans for writable filehandles. The has_exception method checks for filehandles that are in an exception state. To add a new handle, for example from an accept, we use add:

```
$selector->add($server->accept);
```

Finally, to remove a handle, we use remove:

```
$selector->remove($handle);
```

These are the primary methods supplied by IO::Select. There are other, less commonly used methods. For completeness, we will mention each of them briefly:

Method	Description
exists	Called with a filehandle, returns the filehandle if it is present in the select object, and undef if not. For example: `$selector->add($fh) unless $selector->exists($fh);`
handles	Returns an array of all the filehandles present in the select object: `my @handles = $selector->handles;`
count	Returns the number of filehandles present in the select object: `my $handles = $selector->count;`
bits	Returns a bitmask representing the file numbers of the registered filehandles, suitable for passing to the select function: `my $bitmask = $selector->bits;`

select	Class method. Performs a select in the style of the function but using select objects rather than bitmasks. Three array references are returned, each holding the handles that were readable, writable, and exceptional (so to speak) respectively. An optional fourth argument containing a timeout in seconds may also be supplied. For example:
	
	 `my ($readers, $writers, $excepts) = select IO::Select(`
	 `    $read_selector, $write_selector,`
	 `    $except_selector, 60    # timeout`
	 `);`
	
	 `foreach (@{$readers}) {`
	 `    ...`
	 `}`
	
	 This function is essentially similar to calling can_read, can_write and has_exception on three different select objects simultaneously. It mimics the simultaneous polling of these three conditions with three different bitmasks that the select function performs. Note that the same select object can be passed for all three select object arguments.

Armed with this interface, we can now build a simple multiplexing server based on the select function.

A Simple Polling Server

Here is an example of a simple INET polling TCP server. It uses IO::Select to monitor a collection of filehandles, and reacts whenever one of them becomes active. The first handle to be monitored is the server socket, and we check for it especially when an input event occurs. If the server socket is active, it means a new connection request has arrived, so we accept it. Otherwise, it means a client has sent us something, so we respond:

```perl
#!/usr/bin/perl
# ioselectserv.pl
use warnings;
use strict;

use IO::Socket;
use IO::Select;

my $serverport = 4444;

# create a socket to listen on
my $server = new IO::Socket(
    Domain    => PF_INET,
    Proto     => 'tcp',
    LocalPort => $serverport,
    Listen    => SOMAXCONN,
);

die "Cannot bind: $!\n" unless $server;

# create a 'select' object and add server fh to it
my $selector = new IO::Select($server);

# stop closing connections from aborting the server
$SIG{PIPE} = 'IGNORE';

# loop and handle connections
print "Multiplex server started on port $serverport...\n";
while (my @clients = $selector->can_read) {
    # input has arrived, find out which handles(s)
    foreach my $client (@clients) {
        if ($client == $server) {
            # it's a new connection, accept it
            my $newclient = $server->accept;
            syswrite $newclient, "You've reached the server\n";

            my $port = $newclient->peerport;
            my $name = $newclient->peerhost;
            print "New client $port:$name\n";
            $selector->add($newclient);
        } else {
            # it's a message from an existing client
            my $port = $client->peerport;
            my $name = $client->peerhost;
            my $message;
            if (sysread $client, $message, 1024) {
                print "Client $name:$port sent: $message";
                syswrite $client, "Message received OK\n";
            } else {
                $selector->remove($client);
                $client->shutdown(SHUT_RDWR);
                print "Client disconnected\n";   # port, name not defined
            }
        }
    }
}
```

This passable server handles new connections, carries out a simple exchange of messages with a client, and drops them when they disconnect. The `select` call causes Perl to raise `SIGPIPE` signals that will cause our application to abort if not trapped. In this case, we choose to ignore them and detect the closing of the connection by getting a read event on a filehandle with no data – sysread returns 0 bytes read. As we discussed in Chapter 12, this is the only reliable way to check for closed connections at the system level, as `eof` does not work on unbuffered connections.

A Simple Forking Server

The alternative to using a single process to read from multiple connections is to use multiple processes to read from a single connection. The following server uses `fork` to generate an individual child process for each child connection:

```perl
#!/usr/bin/perl
# ioforkserv.pl
use warnings;
use strict;

use IO::Socket;

# Turn on autoflushing
$| = 1;

my $port = 4444;

my $server = IO::Socket->new(
    Domain    => PF_INET,
    Proto     => 'tcp',
    LocalPort => $port,
    Listen    => SOMAXCONN,
    Reuse     => 1,
);

die "Bind failed: $!\n" unless $server;

# tell OS to clean up dead children
$SIG{CHLD} = 'IGNORE';

print "Multiplex server running on port $port...\n";
while (my $connection = $server->accept) {
    my $name = $connection->peerhost;
    my $port = $connection->peerport;
    if (my $pid = fork) {
        close $connection;
        print "Forked child $pid for new client $name:$port\n";
        next;    # on to the next connection
    } else {
        # child process - handle connection
        print $connection "You're connected to the server!\n";
        while (<$connection>) {
            print "Client $name:$port says: $_";
            print $connection "Message received OK\n";
        }
        print "Client $name:$port disconnected\n";
        $connection->shutdown(SHUT_RDWR);
    }
}
```

When the server receives a connection, it accepts it and then forks a child process. It then closes its copy of the connection since it has no further use for it – the child contains its own copy, and can use that. Having no further interest in the connection, the main process returns to the `accept` call and waits for another connection.

Meanwhile, the child communicates with the remote system over the newly connected socket. When the `readline` operator returns a false value, an indication of the end-of-file condition, the child determines that the remote end has been closed, and shuts down the socket.

Because each connection communicates with a separate child process, each connection can coexist with all the others. The main process, freed from the responsibility of handling all the communication duty, is free to accept more connections, allowing multiple clients to communicate with the server simultaneously.

A Simple Threaded Server

The alternative to forking processes is to use threads. Like forking, threads may or may not be available on our platform, so which we use may be as much a matter of circumstance as choice. Instructions on how to build a thread-capable Perl are included in Chapter 1.

Assuming we do have threads, we can write a multiplexed server along very similar lines to the forking server. The threaded version is however simpler, as well as considerably less resource hungry. Below is a threaded version (designed for Perl's older threaded model) of the forking server we showed above:

```perl
#!/usr/bin/perl
# iothreadserv.pl
use warnings;
use strict;

BEGIN {
    use Config;
    die "No thread support!\n" unless $Config{'usethreads'};
}
use Thread;
use IO::Socket;

# Autoflushing on
$| = 1;

my $port = 4444;

my $server = IO::Socket->new(
    Domain    => PF_INET,
    Proto     => 'tcp',
    LocalPort => $port,
    Listen    => SOMAXCONN,
    Reuse     => 1,
);

die "Bind failed: $!\n" unless $server;

print "Multiplex server running on port $port...\n";
while (my $connection = $server->accept) {
    my $name = $connection->peerhost;
    my $port = $connection->peerport;

    my $thread = new Thread(\&connection, $connection, $name, $port);
    print "Created thread ",$thread->tid," for new client $name:$port\n";
    $thread->detach;
}
```

```
# child thread - handle connection
sub connection {
    my ($connection, $name, $port) = @_;
    $connection->autoflush(1);
    print $connection "You're connected to the server!\n";
    while (<$connection>) {
        print "Client $name:$port says: $_";
        print $connection "Message received OK\n";
    }
    $connection->shutdown(SHUT_RDWR);
}
```

When the server receives a connection, it accepts it and spawns a new thread to handle it. We pass the connection filehandle to the new thread on start up. We don't need to worry about locking variables either, since each thread cares only about its own connection. Of course, in a real server environment, when performing more complex tasks such as database queries, we would probably need to worry about this, but this simple example can get away without them. We also pass in the name of the host and the port number, though we could have easily passed these inside the thread as well.

The main thread is only concerned with accepting new connections and spawning child threads to deal with them. It doesn't care about what happens to them after that (though again a more complex server probably would), so it uses the detach method to renounce all further interest in the child.

Threads all run in the same process, so there are no process IDs to manage, no child processes to ignore, and no duplicate filehandles to close. In fact, all the threads have access to all the same filehandles, but since each thread only cares about its own particular filehandle, none of them treads on etheach others' toes. It's a very simple design and it works remarkably well. More information about threaded processes in Perl can be found in Chapter 22.

Getting Network Information

All systems have network information configured locally (unless of course they are diskless workstations, in which case their configuration was loaded from the network and stored in memory). This information includes things like host names and IP addresses, network services and so on.

General information about addresses (both hostnames and resolved IPs), networks, services, and protocols can usually be accessed through a standard suite of operating system functions to which Perl provides a direct mapping. Alternatively, for the specific and common purpose of finding the name of our own system (which is more complex than it might at first appear), we can use the Sys::Hostname module.

Hostname queries in particular will also make use of any name resolution services available on the system, including DNS, NIS/NIS+, and files, if configured. This is because they use the underlying operating system calls to do the actual work rather than attempting to parse local configuration files. Not only does this make them more portable, it also makes them able to work on both local and remote hostnames.

A lot of the functions detailed here, particularly for hosts and networks, are wrapped and made easier to use by the utility functions inet_aton and inet_ntoa, covered under Sockets earlier in the chapter. The IO::Socket module further abstracts the details of service, protocol, and network configuration from the user; in these cases we may be able to avoid actually calling any of these functions directly.

System Network Files

All networked systems hold information about hosts, services, networks, and protocols. UNIX systems keep this information in a set of specially formatted files in the /etc directory, while Windows NT stores them under \WinNT\system32\drivers\etc:

Hosts:	/etc/hosts
Networks:	/etc/networks
Services:	/etc/services
Protcols:	/etc/protocols

To extract information from these files, UNIX defines a standard set of C library functions, analogues of which are available within Perl as built-in functions. Because Perl tries to be a platform-independent language, many of these functions also work on other systems such as Windows or VMS, though they don't always read the same files or formats as the UNIX equivalents.

Perl provides no fewer than twenty built-in functions for making inquiries of the system network configuration. They are divided into four groups of five, for hosts, networks, services, and protocols respectively. Each group contains three functions for getting, resetting, and closing the related network information file, plus two functions for translating the name of the host, network, service, or protocol to and from its native value. The table below summarizes all twenty (functions marked with an * are not supported on Win32 platforms, and many applications will not run because of their use):

	Read	Reset	Close	From Name	To Name
Hosts	gethostent	sethostent	endhostent*	gethostbyname	gethostaddr
Networks	getnetent	setnetent	endnetent*	getnetbyname	getnetbyaddr
Services	getservent	setservent	endservent*	getservbyname	getservbyport
Protocols	getprotoent	setprotoent	endprotoent*	getprotobyname	getprotobynumber*

Perl's versions of these functions are smart and pay attention to the contexts in which they are called. If called in a scalar context, they return the name of the host, network, service or protocol. For example:

```
# find the service assigned to port 80 (it should be 'http')
my $protocol = getprotobyname('tcp');
my $servicename = getservbyport(80, $protocol);
```

The only exception to this is the -name functions, which return the other logical value for the network information being queried – the IP address for hosts and networks, the port number for services, and the protocol number for protocols:

```
# find out what port this system has 'http' assigned to
my $httpd_port = getservbyname('http', $protocol);
```

Called in a list context, each function returns a list of values that varies according to the type of information requested. We can process this list directly, for example:

```perl
#!/usr/bin/perl
# listserv.pl
use warnings;
use strict;

while (my ($name, $aliases, $port, $proto) = getservent) {
    print "$name\t$port/$proto\t$aliases\n";
}
```

Alternatively we can use one of the four Net:: family modules written for the purpose of making these values easier to handle. Each module overrides the original Perl built-in function with a new object-oriented version that returns an object, with methods for each value:

```perl
#!/usr/bin/perl
# listobjserv.pl
use warnings;
use strict;

use Net::servent;

while (my $service = getservent) {
    print 'Name    : ', $service->name, "\n";
    print 'Port No: ', $service->port, "\n";
    print 'Protocol: ', $service->proto, "\n";
    print 'Aliases: ', join(', ', @{$service->aliases}), "\n\n";
}
```

These four modules all accept an optional `fields` argument that imports a variable for each part of the returned list. For the Net::servent module, the variables are the subroutines prefixed with s_, so the alternative way of writing the above is:

```perl
#!/usr/bin/perl
# listfldserv.pl
use warnings;
use strict;

use Net::servent qw(:FIELDS);

while (my $service = getservent) {
    print 'Name    : ', $s_name, "\n";
    print 'Port No: ', $s_port, "\n";
    print 'Protocol: ', $s_proto, "\n";
    print 'Aliases: ', join(', ', @s_aliases), "\n\n";
}
```

Importing the variables still overrides the core functions however. We can get them back by prefixing them with CORE::, as in:

```perl
($name, $aliases, $proto) = CORE::getprotobyname($name_in);
```

Alternatively, we can gain access to the object methods without the overrides by passing an empty import list:

```perl
#!/usr/bin/perl
# listcorserv.pl
use warnings;
use strict;

use Net::servent ();

while (my $service = Net::servent::getservent) {
    print 'Name    : ', $service->name, "\n";
    print 'Port No: ', $service->port, "\n";
    print 'Protocol: ', $service->proto, "\n";
    print 'Aliases: ', join(', ', @{$service->aliases}), "\n\n";
}
```

We will cover each of the four kinds of network information in a little more detail below.

Hosts

Host information consists of an IP address followed by a primary name and possibly one or more aliases. On a UNIX server, this is defined in the /etc/hosts file, of which a semi-typical example might be:

```
127.0.0.1       localhost    localhost.localdomain    myself
192.168.1.10    borahorzagobachul.culture.gal        horza
192.168.1.102   sleepersevice.culture.gal            sleeper
192.168.1.103   littlerascal.culture.gal             rascal
192.168.1.1     hub.chiark.culture.gal        hub    chiark
```

Host information is also available via DNS, NIS, NIS+, files, and a number of other name resolution protocols; the gethostent, gethostbyname, and gethostbyaddr will all use these automatically if they are configured on the system. Whatever the eventual origin of the information, each definition (or 'entry', hence gethostent) comprises an IP address, a primary name, and a list of aliases. The gethostent function retrieves one of these in turn from the local host configuration, starting from the first:

```perl
#!/usr/bin/perl
# listhost.pl
use warnings;
use strict;

while (my ($name, $aliases, $type, $length, @addrs) = gethostent) {
    print "$name\t[$type]\t$length\t$aliases\n";
}
```

Here the name and aliases are as listed above in the example hosts file. The type and length are the address type (2, or AF_INET for Internet addresses, which is in fact the only supported type) and length (4 for IPv4 and 16 for IPv6). The list of addresses comprises all the IP addresses to which this entry applies. In a local host configuration file this should only be one element in length, so we could also get away with saying:

```perl
my ($name, $aliases, $type, $length, @addrs) = gethostent;
```

The format of the address or addresses is a packed string of four bytes (or octets) describing the IP address. To get a string representation we need to process it with unpack or use the Socket module's inet_ntoa subroutine, which we'll come back to in a moment or two.

Since gethostent only operates on the local host configuration, this is okay. For network lookups as performed by gethostbyname or gethostbyaddr we may get more than one address. Alternatively, if gethostent is called in a scalar context, it just returns the name:

```
#!/usr/bin/perl
# listhostnames.pl
use warnings;
use strict;

my @hosts;
while (my $name = gethostent) {
    push @hosts, $name;
}
print "Hosts: @hosts\n";
```

gethostent resembles the opendir and readdir directory functions, except that the open happens automatically and there is no filehandle that we get to see. However, Perl does keeps a filehandle open internally, so if we only want to pass partway through the defined hosts we should close that filehandle with:

```
endhostent;
```

If the resolution of the request involves a network lookup to a remote DNS or NIS server, endhostent will also close down the resulting network connection.

We can also carry out the equivalent of rewinddir with the sethostent function:

```
sethostent 1;
```

If we are querying the local host file, this rewinds to the start of the file again. If we are making network queries, this tells the operating system to reuse an existing connection if one is already established. More specifically, it tells the operating system to open and maintain a TCP connection for queries rather than use a one-off UDP datagram for the query. In this case, we can shutdown the TCP connection with:

```
sethostent 0;
```

Rather than scanning host names one by one, we can do direct translations between name and IP address with the gethostbyname and gethostbyaddr functions. Both these functions will cause the operating system to make queries of any local and remote name resolution services configured.

In list context, both functions return a list of values like gethostent. In scalar context, they return the name (for gethostbyaddr) or address (for gethostbyname):

```
($name, $aliases, $type, $length, @addrs) = gethostbyname($name);
$name = gethostbyaddr($addr, $addrtype);
$addr = gethostbyname($name);
```

In the event that the host could not be found, both functions return undef (or an empty list, in list context) and set $? (not, incidentally, $!) to indicate the reason. We can use $? >> 8 to obtain a real exit code that we can assign to $!, however (see Chapter 16 for more on this and the Errno module too).

The addrtype parameter of gethostbyaddr specifies the address format for the address supplied. There are two formats we are likely to meet, both of which are defined as symbolic constants by the Socket module:

AF_INET	Internet address
AF_INET6	IPv6 Internet address

In all cases, the addresses returned (and in the case of gethostbyaddr, the address we supply) are in packed form. This isn't (except by sheer chance) printable, and it isn't very convenient to pass as a parameter either. We can use pack and unpack to convert between 'proper' integers and addresses (the following example is for IPv4, or AF_INET addresses, on a little-endian machine):

```perl
$addr = pack('C4', @octets);
@octets = unpack('C4', $addr);
```

More conveniently, we can make use of the inet_aton and inet_ntoa functions from the Socket module to convert between both addresses and hostnames and IP strings of the form n1.n2.n3.n4. For example, this short script looks up and prints out the IP addresses for the hostnames given on the command line:

```perl
#!/usr/bin/perl
# hostlookup.pl
use warnings;
use strict;

use Socket qw(/inet/);

die "Give me a hostname!\n" unless @ARGV;

while (my $lookup = shift @ARGV) {
    my ($name, $aliases, $type, $length, @addrs) = gethostbyname($lookup);
    if ($name) {
        foreach (@addrs) {
            $_ = inet_ntoa($_);
        }
        if ($name eq $lookup) {
            print "$lookup has IP address: @addrs\n";
        } else {
            print "$lookup (real name $name) has IP address: @addrs\n";
        }
    } else {
        print "$lookup not found\n";
    }
}
```

We could use this script like this:

> **perl hostlookup.pl localhost rascal hub chiark**

And we would get (assuming the host file example above and no network lookups):

localhost has IP address: 127.0.0.1
rascal (real name rascal.culture.gal) has IP address: 192.168.1.103
hub (real name hub.chiark.culture.gal) has IP address: 192.168.1.1
chiark (real name hub.chiark.culture.gal) has IP address: 192.168.1.1

Likewise, to look up a host by address:

```
$localhostname = gethostbyaddr(inet_aton('127.0.0.1'));
```

Or to find the true name, using a hostname lookup:

```
$localhostname = gethostbyaddr(inet_aton('localhost'));
```

While we're examining this particular example, it is worth noting that for finding the hostname of our own system we are better off using the Sys::Hostname module, described later in the chapter.

One word of warning – be aware that both gethostbyname and gethostbyaddr reset the pointer used by gethostent in the same way that sethostent does, so they cannot be used in a loop of gethostent calls.

The object-oriented override module for the host query functions is Net::hostent. It provides both an object-oriented alternative and on request, a collection of imported scalar variables that are set by each request. Strangely, however, it only provides an object-oriented interface for gethostbyname and gethostbyaddr, not gethostent, so to avoid resetting the pointer of gethostent we have to take a two-stage approach. Here is a short program to list all hosts in the object-oriented style:

```perl
#!/usr/bin/perl
# listobjhost.pl
use warnings;
use strict;

use Net::hostent;
use Socket qw(inet_ntoa);

my @hosts;
while (my $host = gethostent) {
    push @hosts, $host;
}

while (my $host = shift @hosts) {
    $host = gethostbyname($host);
    print 'Name      : ', $host->name, "\n";
    print 'Type      : ', $host->addrtype, "\n";
    print 'Length    : ', $host->length, " bytes\n";
    print 'Aliases   : ', join(', ', @{$host->aliases}), "\n";
    print 'Addresses: ', join(', ', map {inet_ntoa($_)}
        @{$host->addr_list}), "\n\n";
}
```

And again using variables:

```perl
#!/usr/bin/perl
# listfldhost.pl
use warnings;
use strict;

use Net::hostent qw(:FIELDS);
use Socket qw(inet_ntoa);

my @hosts;
while (my $host = CORE::gethostent) {
    push @hosts, $host;
}

while (my $host = shift @hosts) {
    $host = gethostbyname($host);
    print 'Name      : ', $h_name, "\n";
    print 'Type      : ', $h_addrtype, "\n";
    print 'Length    : ', $h_length, " bytes\n";
    print 'Aliases   : ', join(', ', @h_aliases), "\n";
    print 'Addresses: ', join(', ', map{inet_ntoa($_)} @h_addr_list), "\n\n";
}
```

If we only want to import some variables, we can pass them directly in the import list, but we must also import the overrides we want to use if so:

```perl
use Net::hostent qw($h_name @h_aliases @h_addr_list gethostent);
```

We use the CORE:: prefix here partly to remind ourselves that gethostent is not being overridden, and partly to protect ourselves in case a future version of the Net::hostent module extends to cover it.

gethostbyname and gethostbyaddr also return objects. gethostbyaddr automatically makes use of the Socket module to handle conversions so we can supply an IP address like 127.0.0.1 without needing to worry about whether it will be understood or not. In addition, the Net::hostent module supplies a shorthand subroutine, gethost, which calls either gethostbyname or gethostbyaddress, depending on whether its argument looks like an IP address or a hostname.

Networks

Networks are simply groups of IP addresses that have been assigned a network name. For example, for the host file example given earlier, 127 and 192.168.1 are potential groupings that may be given a network:

```
loopback    127.0.0.0
localnet    192.168.1.0
```

Networks are therefore essentially very much like hosts; see below:

```perl
($name, $aliases, $type, $netaddr) = getnetent;
```

Or, in scalar context:

```
$netname = getnetent;
```

All these values have the same meanings as the same values returned by gethostent etc., only of course for networks. The $netaddr is now an IP address for the network and unlike hosts, where there is only one, this refers to many.

```
use Socket qw(/inet/);

$netip = inet_ntoa($netaddr);
$netaddr = inet_aton('192.168');
```

The setnetent function resets the pointer in the network information file to the start or (in the case of NIS+ lookups) preserves an existing network connection if one happens to be active. Like sethostent it takes a Boolean flag as a parameter, and switches between TCP and UDP connections for network requests. For file-based access, using getnetbyname or getnetbyaddr also resets the pointer of getnetent in the local network file. The endnetent function closes the network information file or network connection.

getnetbyname and getnetbyaddr work similarly to their 'host' counterparts, except for network addresses. Like gethostbyname, getnetbyname will do a remote lookup if the host network configuration is set to do that, although this is considerably more rare.

```
$netaddr = getnetbyname('mynetwork');
$netname = getnetbyaddr('192.168.1', AF_INET);   # from 'Socket'
```

The object-oriented override module for the network query functions is Net::netent. Like Net::hostent, it does not override getnetent, only getnetbyaddr and getnetbyname. Since both these functions reset the pointer of getnetent we have to collect names (or addresses) first, then subsequently run through each one with getnetbyname or getnetbyaddr. Here's a script that dumps out network information in the same vein as the object-oriented host script earlier:

```
#!/usr/bin/perl
# getobjnet.pl
use warnings;
use strict;

use Net::netent;
use Socket qw(inet_ntoa);

my @nets;
while (my $net = CORE::getnetent) {
    push @nets, $net;
}
while (my $net = shift @nets) {
    $net = getnetbyname($net);
    print 'Name     : ', $net->name, "\n";
    print 'Type     : ', $net->addrtype, "\n";
    print 'Aliases  : ', join(', ', @{$net->aliases}), "\n";
    print 'Addresses: ', $net->addr_list, "\n\n";
}
```

Note that this script will happily return nothing at all if we don't have any configured networks, which is quite possible. The field-based version of this script is:

```
#!/usr/bin/perl
# getfldnet.pl
use warnings;
use strict;

use Net::netent qw(:FIELDS);
use Socket qw(inet_ntoa);

my @nets;
while (my $net = CORE::getnetent) {
    push @nets, $net;
}

while (my $net = shift @nets) {
    $net = getnetbyname($net);
    print 'Name      : ', $n_name, "\n";
    print 'Type      : ', $n_addrtype, "\n";
    print 'Aliases   : ', join(', ', @n_aliases), "\n";
    print 'Addresses: ', $n_net, "\n\n";
}
```

In addition, Net::netent defines the getnet subroutine. This attempts to produce the correct response from whatever is passed to it by calling either getnetbyname or getnetbyaddr depending on the argument. Like gethost, it automatically handles strings that look like IP addresses so we can say:

```
$net = gethost('192.168.1');
print $net->name;    # or $n_name;
```

Network Services

All networked hosts have the ability to service network connections from other hosts in order to satisfy various kinds of request; anything from a web page to an email transfer. These services are distinguished by the port number that they respond to; web service (HTTP) is on port 80, FTP is on port 21, SMTP (for email) on port 25, and so on.

Rather than hard-code a port number into applications that listen for network connections, we can instead configure a service, assign it to a port number, and then have the application listen for connections on the service port number. On UNIX systems, this association of service to port number is done in the /etc/services file, a typical sample of which looks like this:

```
tcpmux      1/tcp    # TCP port service multiplexer
ftp-data    20/tcp
ftp         21/tcp
telnet      23/tcp
smtp        25/tcp   mail
time        37/tcp   timserver
time        37/udp   timserver
nameserver  42/tcp   name   # IEN 116
whois       43/tcp   nicname
domain      53/tcp   nameserver   # name-domain server
domain      53/udp   nameserver
finger      79/tcp
www         80/tcp   http   # World Wide Web HTTP
www         80/udp   # Hypertext Transfer Protocol
```

A real services file contains a lot more than this, but this is an indicative sample. We can also define our own services, though on a UNIX system they should be on at least port 1024 or higher, since many ports lower than this are allocated as standard ports for standard services. Furthermore, only the administrator has the privileges to bind to ports under 1024. For example:

```
myapp      4444/tcp  myserver   # My server's service port
```

Each entry consists of a primary service name, a port number and a network protocol, and an optional list of aliases. The getservent function retrieves one of these in turn from the local host configuration, starting from the first. For example, as we showed earlier in the general discussion:

```perl
#!/usr/bin/perl
# listserv.pl
use warnings;
use strict;

while (my ($name, $aliases, $port, $proto) = getservent) {
    print "$name\t$port/$proto\t$aliases\n";
}
```

Here name, aliases, and port are reasonably self-evident. The protocol is a numeric value describing the protocol number – 6 for TCP, 7 for UDP, for example. We can handle this number and convert it to and from a name with the protocol functions such as getprotoent and getprotobynumber, which we will come to in a moment.

setservent resets the pointer for the next getservent to the start of the services file, if given a true value. endservent closes the internal filehandle. These are similar to their network and host counterparts, but are far less likely to open network connections for queries (DNS and NIS do not do this, but NIS+ conceivably might).

Services are related to ports, not addresses, so the function getservbyport returns a list of parameters for the service defined for the named port, or an empty list otherwise. Since ports may be assigned to different services using different network protocols, we also need to supply the protocol we are interested in:

```perl
$protocol = getprotobyname('tcp');

($name, $aliases, $port, $proto) = getservbyport(80, $protocol);
($name, $aliases, $port, $proto) = getservbyname('http', $protocol);
```

Or, in scalar context, for our user-defined service:

```perl
$name = getservbyport(4444, $protocol);
$port = getservbyname('myserver', $protocol);
```

The object-oriented override module for service queries is Net::servent, and we saw examples of using it in both the object-oriented style and with imported variables earlier. Unlike the host and network modules, Net::servent does override getservent, so we can iterate through services without having to collect names or port numbers into a list first and then running through the result with 'getservbyname or getservbyport.

In addition, Net::servent defines the getserv as a convenience subroutine that maps a passed argument onto either getservbyproto or getservbyname depending on whether the passed argument looks numeric or not.

Network Protocols

Protocols are defined in terms of numbers at the network level – 0 for IP, 6 for TCP, 17 for UDP and so on. These are designated standards defined in RFCs. Locally, these numbers are associated with a user-friendly name, so instead of referring to 'protocol number 6' we can say 'tcp' instead. For example, here are a few entries from a typical /etc/protocols file on a UNIX server:

```
ip         0     IP   # internet pseudo protocol number
icmp       1     ICMP   # internet control message protocol
igmp       2     IGMP   # Internet Group Management
ipencap    4     IP-ENCAP   # IP encapsulated in IP (officially `IP')
tcp        6     TCP   # transmission control protocol
udp        17    UDP   # user datagram protocol
```

This file is not one we are expected ever to add to; although we can create a protocol if we want. We can, however, interrogate it.

We can list the protocol definitions defined for the local system with the getprotoent, which works in the familiar way, reading the first entry in the list and then each subsequent entry every time it is called. In scalar context, it returns the protocol name:

```
$firstprotoname = getprotoent;
```

In list context it returns a list of values consisting of the primary name for the protocol, the port number, and any aliases defined for it. This short script illustrates how we can use it to dump out all the protocol details defined on the system:

```
#!/usr/bin/perl
# listprot.pl
use warnings;
use strict;

while (my ($name, $aliases, $proto) = getprotoent) {
    print "$proto $name ($aliases)\n";
}
```

endprotoent closes the internal filehandle, and setprotoent resets the pointer for the next entry to be returned by getprotoent to the start of the file if given a true value, as usual. Also as usual, calling getprotobyname and getprotobynumber also resets the pointer. As with their similarly named brethren, getprotobyname and getprotobynumber return the port number and port name respectively in a scalar context:

```
$proto_name = getprotobynumber($proto_number);
$proto_number = getprotobyname($proto_name);
```

In list context, they return the same values as getprotoent.

The object-oriented override module for protocols is `Net::protoent`, which overrides the `getprotoent`, `getprotobyname`, and `getprotobynumber` functions with equivalents that return objects. Here is the object-oriented way of listing protocol information using `Net::protoent`:

```perl
#!/usr/bin/perl
# listobjproto.pl
use warnings;
use strict;

use Net::protoent;

while (my $protocol = getprotoent) {
    print "Protocol: ", $protocol->proto, "\n";
    print "Name    : ", $protocol->name, "\n";
    print "Aliases : ", join(', ', @{$protocol->aliases}), "\n\n";
}
```

As with the other `Net::` modules that provide object-oriented wrappers for Perl's network information functions, we can also import variables that automatically take on the values of the last call. The equivalent field-based script is:

```perl
#!/usr/bin/perl
# listfldproto.pl
use warnings;
use strict;

use Net::protoent qw(:FIELDS);

while (my $protocol = getprotoent) {
    print "Protocol: ", $p_proto, "\n";
    print "Name    : ", $p_name, "\n";
    print "Aliases : ", join(', ', @p_aliases), "\n\n";
}
```

In addition, `Net::protoent` defines the `getproto` subroutine as a convenient way to produce a valid response from almost any passed value. Numeric values are passed to `getprotobynumber`; anything else is presumed to be a name and passed to `getprotobyname`.

Determining the Local Hostname

Determining the local hostname for the system can sometimes be a tricky thing. Firstly, a system can happily have more than one network interface and therefore more than one name. Secondly, the means by which the hostname is defined varies wildly from one operating system to another.

If we just want to open a network connection to a service or application (such as a web server) running on the local machine, we can often get away with simply connecting to the local loopback IP address. However, this is not enough if we need to identify ourselves to the application at the other end.

On most UNIX platforms, we can execute the **hostname** command to find the name of the host, or failing that name, uname -n, or alternatively we can use the `gethostbyname` function to try to identify the true name of the local host from one of its aliases. The `localhost` alias approach should work on any system that has it defined as the hostname for the loopback address in either DNS or the hosts file. Be aware, though, that it may not always return a fully qualified name (hostname.domain).

Because of this confusing mess of alternative approaches Perl comes with the `Sys::Hostname` module which attempts all of these methods and more in turn, with different tests depending on the underlying platform. It provides a single subroutine, `hostname`, which hides all of these mechanics from us and allows us simply to say:

```perl
#!/usr/bin/perl
# hostname.pl
use warnings;
use strict;

use Sys::Hostname;

print "We are: ", hostname, "\n";
```

This will try to produce the correct result on almost any platform (even, interestingly, Symbian's EPOC) and is probably the best solution for both simplicity and portability.

Summary

In this chapter, we covered networking with Perl in some detail. We started by explaining how the Internet protocols work, and how packets are routed from network to network. We then moved on to explaining how to use the `Socket` and `IO::Socket` modules to create network clients and servers. Specifically, we covered:

❑ Using `Socket.pm`; we covered how to create simple servers and clients that connect and listen to specified sockets. We showed how to do this using TCP, UDP, and UNIX domain sockets.

❑ Using `IO::Socket` we repeated every example used above in the simpler format used with the `IO::Socket` module.

❑ Broadcasting with UDP, and how to send packets to multiple destinations simultaneously.

Later, we covered how to use forking, threading, and polling to create network servers that can deal with multiple requests from clients. We had examples of each type of server included in the text, which can be adapted to any other projects.

In the last section of this chapter, we looked at retrieving different kinds of network information, and discussed the following topics:

❑ Getting host information, including a portable way to discover the local hostname, and how to discover the IP address of a specified hostname, and to acquire any aliases it might have.

❑ Getting network information and discovering what host or IP address is part of what network, and whether network names have been defined.

❑ We described how to discover what network services are available on our system.

❑ Finally, we saw how to examine the network protocols available to our system, even though it is very rare to ever update this information

The examples throughout this chapter performed similar tasks in different ways (including writing the applications in an object-oriented style).

24

Writing Portable Perl

Perl runs on every major operating system, and most of the minor ones, from VOS and Cray to Mac OS and Windows, and, of course, UNIX. Most of the time, Perl code will work the same on any of these platforms, because Perl is one of the most portable programming languages around.

It may be difficult to see how a language, or any program written in that language, could work the same across all of these disparate platforms. They are often significantly different in, amongst other things, memory management, file systems, and networking. The developers of Perl have done their best to hide these differences, but it is still possible to write Perl code that runs properly on only one platform.

A portable Perl program may be portable only on all UNIX platforms (sometimes, depending on the task, that in itself is difficult or impossible). Most often though, 'portable Perl' is code that will work on all the platforms Perl runs on. Calling fork on Mac OS or symlink on MS Windows are two examples of non-portable code, since the functionality for those functions does not exist on those platforms. However, the great thing about Perl is that the overwhelming majority of Perl code is portable.

Remember, no code is universal – no matter what it is, it will always fail on some platform, somewhere. However, where Perl does exist, most Perl code will run; or it can be made to run, if the author of the code keeps some portability guidelines in mind.

Maybe We Shouldn't Bother?

Before we start with any programming task, we should give at least a moment of thought to the scope of the project. Think about where the program will be used, who will use it, and what its lifetime might be. If we are writing a ten line script for the cron daemon to export our CVS tree to our home directory on our Linux box every night, it is probably a waste of time bothering to make sure the program will run on Windows and Mac OS. It is probably even a waste of time to concentrate on making it portable to multiple UNIX platforms, with multiple versions of cvs, and with other CVS repositories and users. It is enough to know how to talk to our CVS server, get our CVS repository, and find our home directory.

However, a module placed on CPAN for parsing XML should run anywhere Perl runs, if possible. That's a general task, not specific to any platform, because it may be used by any number of users in any number of ways. It will save ourselves and our users time and headaches if portability is taken care of at the beginning.

There are many choices between these extremes – it might be tempting to use Mac-specific file specifications in a module for sending and receiving Apple events in Mac OS, but what happens when someone wants to use the module on Perl under Mac OS X, which uses UNIX-style file specifications? Sometimes it is best to write portably, even if we think it might not be necessary, if there's a chance that someone might be using our code on a different platform.

Newlines

Perhaps the most common portability problem is improper use of the newline character. In most operating systems, lines in files are terminated by a specific character sequence. This logical end of line is called the newline, and is represented in Perl, and many other languages, by the symbolic representation \n.

Many portability problems are rooted in the incorrect assumption that a newline is the same thing as a line feed (octal 012, the LF in CRLF), which it isn't. The newline has no absolute, portable value; it is a logical concept. Unfortunately, there are plenty of historical reasons why we have a line feed, a carriage return (CR), and a newline. It is reasonable to suspect that if time travel were possible, going back to standardize a single newline character would be a worthwhile goal, but alas, we are stuck with the problem and need to deal with it.

UNIX defines newline as the octal number 012. Mac OS uses 015 (carriage return / CR). On Windows, it is represented by two bytes together, 015 and 012 (CRLF). On Windows (and other DOS-like platforms), those bytes are automatically translated to the single newline character when reading and writing a file; this is done by Perl to aid portability. We can get the exact data in the file without translation by calling the binmode operator on the file handle:

```
open $file, "< $binaryfile" or die "Can't open file: $!";
binmode($file);
```

Since binmode has no effect on other systems, it should be used for cross platform code that deals with binary data (assuming it is known that the data will be binary). Note that because DOS-like platforms will convert two characters into one, using binmode can break the use of seek and tell. We will however, be safe using seek if we stick to seeking to locations we obtained from tell and no others.

Some of this may be confusing. Here's a handy reference for the ASCII CR and LF characters.

	Octal	Hex	Decimal	Ctrl
LF (line feed)	012	x0A	10	\cJ
CR (carriage return)	015	x0D	13	\cM

	UNIX	DOS/Windows	Mac
\n	LF	CRLF	CR
\r	CR	CR	LF

Often, a file we want to read will be taken from another platform. If the file we are reading is native – that is, uses the same newline as our operating system, then, we can use the common idiom:

```
while (<$file>) {
    chomp;
    # ... do something with the data in $_
}
```

However, that won't work if the file is not native. chomp, <>, and other operators assume that the file is terminated with the native newline, so reading a DOS text file in UNIX will not work properly without some extra work.

There are several ways to deal with this. We can preprocess the file before reading it, either by sucking in all the data and doing a global fix, or by changing it on disk before reading it in. A simpler method however, is to change the input record separator variable $/, which determines the definition for newline, and defaults to the native newline. So, to read a DOS file on a UNIX system, we would code something like this:

```
{
    local $/ = "\015\012";    # temporary change
    while (<$file>) {
        # read file with \015\012
        chomp;    # chomp \015\012
        ...
    }
}
# $/ reverts to previous value automatically
```

We may need to use something like this, if we are reading a file from a network file system, or portable media (like CD-ROM), where the file is not native, or if we have a file transferred over the network from one system to another without text translation.

A similar problem occurs when reading and writing sockets. Sockets are doubly troublesome because different protocols use different newlines, and some will even allow for more than one. For example, the HTTP protocol requires CRLF in headers, but the content itself may be terminated with any of CR, LF, or CRLF, or may be binary data without newlines at all. Even though the HTTP specification requires CRLF in the headers, an HTTP server might not be compliant, perhaps sending plain LF instead.

While Perl will automatically use the proper newline for the native platform when handling files, it will, by default, use the UNIX values for sockets and most other forms of I/O. With sockets, it is best to be specific, and use the absolute value instead of the symbolic representation.

```
print $socket "Hi there client!\015\012";   # right
print $socket "Hi there client!\r\n";   # wrong
```

To write to a socket, we need to know what newline is expected by the protocol. Reading from the socket is, however, a little bit more flexible. Most protocols will use either LF or CRLF, so we can adjust on the fly, converting either one to whatever our local newline happens to be. Since both end in LF, we can set $/ to LF. Bear in mind, however, that the Mac uses CR as its newline character so a Mac-based protocol may require that character. If we don't want to remember the absolute values, we can import $CR, $LF, and $CRLF variables from the Socket module.

```
#!/usr/bin/perl
# importabs.pl
use warnings;
use strict;

use Socket qw(:DEFAULT :crlf);

{
    local $/ = $LF;
    while (<$socket>) {
        s/$CR?$LF/\n/;    # not sure if CRLF or LF
        ...
    }
}
```

Similarly, functions that return text data (like a function that fetches a web page), may translate newlines before returning the data, so the caller doesn't have to worry about it.

```
sub fetch_page {
    ...
    $html =~ s/$CR?$LF/\n/g;
    return $html;
}
```

Files and File Systems

Most platforms structure files in a hierarchical fashion, and support the notion of a unique path to a file. How that path is represented may differ significantly between operating systems. For example, UNIX is one of the few operating systems with the concept of a single root directory. UNIX uses / as, path separator, while DOS-like systems use \. Mac OS uses :. VOS uses the native pathname characters >, <, and %. RISC OS Perl uses . for path separator and : for file systems and disk names. RISC OS, VOS, and DOS-like Perl interpreters, can all emulate the use of /.

Thankfully, Perl ships with the `File::Spec` module, which provides simple functions to create file specifications for the current platform:

```
use File::Spec::Functions;   # export functions
chdir(updir());   # change dir, up one dir
$file = catfile(curdir(), 'temp', 'file.txt');
open $fh, "< $file" or die $!;
```

On UNIX and DOS-like platforms, `$file` would be `./temp/file.txt`. On Mac OS, it would be `:temp:file.txt`. On VMS, it would be `[.temp]file.txt`. This is one of those cases where using the module is often much better than trying to figure out all of the options for ourselves.

For writing file specifications portably, use `File::Spec` (see below for more on `File::Spec`). For parsing file specs portably, use `File::Basename`:

```
use File::Basename;
($file, $dir) = fileparse($file);
```

If newlines are the most common portability problem, then non-portable file specifications are not far behind. We should use these modules when we want to be portable and not hardcode paths if possible. This is especially a problem in scripts like `Makefile.PL`s and test suites, which often assume / as a path separator for subdirectories.

Even when on a single platform (if we can call UNIX a single platform), we must remember not to count on the existence or the contents of particular system specific files or directories like `/etc/passwd`, `/etc/sendmail.cf`, `/etc/resolv.conf`, or even `/tmp/`. For example, `/etc/passwd` may exist but may not contain the encrypted passwords, because the system is using some form of enhanced security; or it may not contain all the accounts, because the system is using NIS. Instead it is better to use `getpwnam` and its relatives, to get information about a user. If code does need to rely on such a file, we should include a description of the file and its format in the code's documentation, then we make it easy for the user to override the default location of the file.

We must not have two files of the same name within different cases, like `test.pl` and `Test.pl`, as many file systems are case insensitive. Whitespace in filenames is tolerated on most systems, but not all, and many systems (DOS, and VMS for example.) cannot have more than one `.` in their filenames. Others only allow a limited subset of characters in names. If filenames are limited to word characters (a-z, A-Z, 0-9, _), plus `.` for the extension, this should be sufficient on most systems. We should also keep them to the 8.3 convention for maximum portability, since some older platforms and file systems cannot use files that do not fit the convention.

Likewise, when using the `AutoSplit` module, we should try to keep our functions to 8.3 naming and case-insensitive conventions; or, at the least, make it so that the resulting files have a unique, case insensitive, first eight characters. When a function is autosplit, it is saved to disk using the name of the function, and if we have functions called `getSomething` and `getSomethingElse`, then the subroutine names will be truncated and will therefore become indistinguishable.

If it is possible that a filename contains strange characters, it is safest to open it with `sysopen` instead of open. The `open` function can translate characters like >, <, and |, which may be the wrong thing to do (of course, it may also be the right thing). If we do use `open`, and the filename in a variable is unknown, don't assume > won't be the first character of the filename. We must always use < explicitly to open a file for reading, unless we want the user to be able to specify a pipe open.

```
open(FILE, $file) or die $!;      # wrong
open(FILE, "< $file") or die $!;   # right
```

Beyond path differences, there are many other fundamental differences between file systems. Some don't support hard links (link) and symbolic links (symlink, readlink, lstat, -l). Some don't support the access to, creation of, or changing of timestamps for files. Modifying timestamps is usually supported, but may have a granularity of something other than one second (FAT uses two seconds).

Portable File Handling with 'File::Spec'

File::Spec provides a standard toolkit of filename conversion methods that work across all the common platforms that support Perl. The actual implementation is provided by a submodule that implements the details of file naming on the platform in question, as determined by the value of the special variable $^O. On a UNIX system for example, File::Spec automatically uses the File::Spec::UNIX module. The platforms supported by File::Spec are:

'$^O'	'File::Spec' module
MacOS	File::Spec::Mac
os2	File::Spec::OS2
MSWin32	File::Spec::Win32
VMS	File::Spec::VMS
All others	File::Spec::UNIX

File::Spec provides two interfaces. The standard object interface imports no functions but provides class methods, which we can call in the usual manner, for example:

```
use File::Spec;
...
$newpath = File::Spec->canonpath($path);
```

For translations, we can also make use of two File::Spec submodules at the same time. For example, the following subroutine converts an arbitrary Macintosh pathname into a Windows one (see the table below for an explanation of the methods used in this example):

```
use File::Spec::Win32;
use File::Spec::Mac;

sub mac2win {
    $mac_path = shift;
    @ary = File::Spec::Mac->splitpath $mac_path;
    $ary[1] = File::Spec::Win32->catdir(File::Spec::Mac->splitdir $ary[1]);
    return File::Spec::Win32->catpath @ary;
}
```

Alternatively, we can use `File::Spec`'s methods as functions if we use the `File::Spec::Functions` module instead:

```
use File::Spec::Functions;
...
$newpath = canonpath($path);
```

Not all of `File::Spec`'s methods are exported automatically by `File::Spec::Functions`. By default, the functions that are exported are: canonpath, catdir, catfile, curdir, file_name_is_absolute, no_upwards, path, rootdir, and updir. The functions that are exported only if we ask for them are: abs2rel, catpath, devnull, rel2abs, splitpath, splitdir, tmpdir.

For example, to get the `devnull` and `tmpdir` functions we would use:

```
use File::Spec::Functions qw(devnull tmpdir);
```

`File::Spec` provides eighteen routines for the conversion and manipulation of filenames:

Subroutine	Action
canonpath($path)	Returns the filename cleaned up to remove redundant elements such as multiple directory separators or instances of the current directory (as returned by curdir), and any trailing directory separator if present. It does not resolve parent directory elements; we use no_upwards for that. For example: `$canonical = canonpath($path);`
catdir(@dirs)	Concatenates a list of directory names to form a directory path, using the directory separator of the platform. For example: `$path = catdir(@directories);`
catfile/join(@dirs, $file)	Concatenates a list of directory names followed by a filename to form a file path, using the directory separator of the platform. On platforms where files and directories are syntactically identical, (DOS/Windows and UNIX both fall into this category), this produces exactly the same result as catdir. join is an alias for catfile. For example: `$filepath = join(@dirs, $filename);`
curdir	Returns the filename of the current directory, . on DOS/Windows and UNIX systems.
devnull	Returns the filename of the null device, which reads but ignores any output sent to it. This is /dev/null under UNIX.

Table continued on following page

Subroutine	Action
rootdir	Returns the filename of the root of the filesystem and the prefix to filenames that makes them absolute rather than relative. This is / on UNIX and \ on DOS/Windows. This is also frequently the name of the directory separator.
tmpdir	Returns the first writable directory found in the two-element list $ENV{TMPDIR} and /tmp. Returns ' ' if neither directory is writable.
updir	Returns the filename for the parent directory, . . on many platforms including DOS/Windows and UNIX.
no_upwards($path)	Resolves the supplied filename to remove any parent directory elements, as returned by updir, and returns it. It does not resolve symbolic links. However, we can use abs_path or realpath from the File::Path module for that. It can be used in combination with canonpath above. For example: `$path = no_upwards($path);` `$path = canonpath($path);`
case_tolerant	Returns true if the case of filenames is not significant, or false if it is.
file_name_is_absolute ($path)	Returns true if the filename is absolute, that is it starts with an anchor to the root of the filesystem, as returned by rootdir. For example: `$path = rel2abs($path) unless` `file_name_is_absolute($path);`
path	Returns the value of the environment variable PATH – identical to $ENV{'PATH'}.
splitpath($path, 0|1)	Returns a three element list consisting of the volume, directory path, and filename. On systems that do not support the concept of a 'volume', such as UNIX, the first element is always undef. For platforms like DOS/Windows, it may be something like C: if the supplied pathname is prefixed with that volume identifier. On platforms that do not distinguish file names from directory names, the third element is simply the last element of the pathname, unless the second Boolean argument is true, or the path ends in a trailing directory separator (e.g /), a current directory name (e.g. .), or a parent directory name (e.g. ..). `($vol, $dirs, $file) = splitpath($path, 1);` The directory path can be further split into individual directories using splitdir.

Subroutine	Action
`splitdir($dirs)`	Returns a list of directories split out from the supplied directory path, as returned in the second element of the list produced by `splitpath`. It uses the directory separator of the platform. Note that `splitdir` requires directories only, so we use `splitpath` to remove the volume and file elements on platforms that support those concepts. For example:
	`@dirs = splitdir($dirs);`
	Leading, trailing, and multiple directory separators will create empty strings in the resulting list. Using `canonpath` first will prevent all but the leading empty string.
`catpath($vol, $dirs, $file)`	Combines a three element list containing a volume, directory path, and filename, and returns a complete path. On platforms that do not support the concept of volumes, the first element is ignored. For example:
	`$path = catpath($vol, $dirs, $file);`
	The directory path can be generated by `catdir` or alternatively determined from another pathname via `splitpath`.
`abs2rel($relativepath, $base)`	Takes an absolute pathname and generates a relative pathname, relative to the base path supplied. If the base path is not specified, it generates a pathname relative to the current working directory as determined by `cwd` from the `File::Path` module. The volume and filename of the basepath are ignored. For example:
	`$relpath = abs2rel($abspath);`
`rel2abs($relativepath, $base)`	Combines a relative pathname and a base path and returns an absolute pathname based on the combination of the two. If the base path is not specified, the current working directory, as determined by `cwd` from the `File::Path` module, is used as the base path. The volume and filename of the basepath are ignored. For example:
	`$abspath = rel2abs($relname);`

Endianness and Number Width

Different types of CPUs store integers and floating-point numbers in different orders (called **endianness**) and widths (32-bit and 64-bit being the most common today). Any time that binary data is read or written with different architectures involved, these differences can become an issue. Most of the time this occurs when writing files with `pack`. For instance, we can write four bytes representing the hex number 0x12345678 (305419896 in decimal) to a file in this way:

```
print $file pack 'l', 0x12345678;
```

We can later read it back in like this:

```
$line = <$file>;
print unpack 'l', $line;
```

This prints the decimal value 305419896. However, if this is done on an Intel x86 computer and the file is transferred over to a Motorola 68K computer, and we then read it in with the same program, we would get 2018915346, because the order of the bytes is reversed; instead of 0x12345678 we get 0x78563412.

To avoid this problem in network connections, the pack and unpack functions have the n (16-bit) and N (32-bit) formats for network order. These are guaranteed to be portable, as they are defined as big-endian, regardless of hardware platform.

Differing widths can cause truncation, even between platforms of equal endianness. The platform of shorter width loses the upper parts of the number. Most platforms can only count up to $2^{(32-1)}$. If we have a 64-bit platform and store 2^{42} with pack (using the q and Q formats), we will lose badly if we try to unpack it on a 32-bit platform. Even seemingly innocuous pack formats like I, can be dependent on the local C compiler's definitions, and may be nonportable. It's best to stick with n and N when porting between platforms.

One can circumnavigate the problems of width and endianness by representing the data unambiguously, like writing numbers out in plain text. Using a module like Data::Dumper or Storable, can also ensure the correct values are maintained.

System Interaction

Perl provides a nice environment to program in, but also relies on the system, and is limited by it. There are certain things we just shouldn't do in order to be portable:

- ❑ Don't delete or re-name open files. Some platforms won't allow it. untie or close the file before doing anything to it

- ❑ Don't open the same file more than once at the same time for writing. Some platforms place a mandatory lock on files opened for writing

- ❑ Don't count on filename globbing. Use opendir, readdir, and closedir instead. As of Perl 5.6, the default glob is implemented with the portable File::Glob module by default; however, some people might not be using Perl 5.6, or might be using Perl built to use the old style csh glob instead of File::Glob. It may be best to use the built-in directory functions

- ❑ Don't count on per-program environment variables or current directories, such as $TEMP or $HOME

- ❑ Don't count on a specific environment variable existing in %ENV. Don't count on %ENV entries being case sensitive, or even case preserving

- ❑ Don't count on user accounts, whether it is specific information about a user, or the existence of users at all

- ❑ Don't count on signals or %SIG for anything

- ❑ Don't count on specific values of $!

Platforms that rely primarily on a Graphical User Interface (GUI) for user interaction do not all provide a command line. A program requiring a command line interface might not work everywhere. In most cases this is probably for the user of the program to deal with, so don't stay up late worrying about it too much. If a Mac developer wants to use our command line tool, they'll convert it to a droplet or rewrite it, so it will be usable. Even platforms that do have a command line might not be able to execute programs in the same way UNIX does, by putting the path to `perl` after `#!` on the first line and making the file executable.

Inter-Process Communication (IPC)

Whereas system interaction involves a big list of things not to do to retain maximum portability, in general, inter-process communication is something we just don't do at all. Don't directly access the system in code, which is meant to be portable. That means, no `system`, `exec`, `fork`, `pipe`, `` `` ``, `qx//`, open with a pipe, or any of the other things that makes being a Perl and UNIX hacker really fun (for more on IPC see Chapter 22).

Commands that launch external processes are generally supported on most platforms (though many of them do not support any type of forking). The problem with using them arises from where we invoke them. External tools are often named differently on different platforms, they may not be available in the same location, might accept different arguments, can behave differently, and often present their results in a platform dependent way. Consequently, we should seldom depend on them to produce consistent results. Then again, if we are calling `netstat -a`, we probably don't expect it to run on both UNIX and CP/M.

Opening a pipe to `sendmail` is one especially common bit of Perl code:

```
open(my $mail, '|/usr/sbin/sendmail -t') or die "cannot fork sendmail: $!";
```

This is fine for systems programming when `sendmail` is known to be available, but it is not fine for many non UNIX systems, and even some UNIX systems that may not have `sendmail` installed, or may have it installed elsewhere. If a portable solution is needed, see the various distributions on CPAN that deal with it. `Mail::Mailer` and `Mail::Send` in the `MailTools` distribution are commonly used and provide several mailing methods including `mail`, `sendmail`, and direct SMTP (via `Net::SMTP`) if a mail transfer agent is not available. `Mail::Sendmail` is a stand-alone module that provides simple, platform independent mailing.

> *Note that the UNIX System V IPC (`msg*`, `sem*`, `shm*`) is not available even on all UNIX platforms, so we should also try to avoid using those.*

Instead of directly accessing the system, use a module if one is available, that may internally implement the functionality with platform-specific code, but expose a common interface.

External Subroutines (XS)

XS, explored in Chapter 21, is a language used to create an extension interface between Perl and some C library that we may wish to use with Perl. While XS code can usually be made to work with any platform; dependent libraries, header files, etc., might not be readily available or portable, or the XS code itself might be platform-specific, just as Perl code might be. If the libraries and headers are portable, then it is normally reasonable to make sure the XS code is portable, too.

A different type of portability issue arises when writing XS code – availability of a C compiler on the end user's system. Many Mac OS or Windows users might not have compilers, and those compilers will sometimes be expensive, hard to obtain, hard to use, or all of the above; and the initial setup to get the source working for the build may be prohibitive to many users. Furthermore, C brings with it its own portability issues, and writing XS code will expose us to some of those. Writing purely in Perl is an easier way to achieve portability.

Modules

In general, the standard modules, those included with the standard Perl distribution, work across platforms. Notable exceptions are the platform specific modules (like ExtUtils::MM_VMS) and DBM modules.

There is no one DBM module available on all platforms. SDBM_File and the others are generally available on all UNIX and DOS like ports, but not in MacPerl, where only NBDM_File and DB_File are available.

The good news is, that at least some DBM modules should be available, and AnyDBM_File will use whichever module it can find. Of course, then the code needs to be fairly strict, dropping to the lowest common denominator (for example, not exceeding 1K for each record, and not using exists on a hash key) so that it will work with any DBM module.

One very useful module for achieving portability in programs is the POSIX module. It provides nearly all the functions and identifiers found in the POSIX 1003.1 specification. Now, there is no guarantee that all of the functions will work on a given platform. It depends on how well the platform has implemented POSIX 1003.1. Most of it will work, however, and can provide a good way to achieve portability.

Many of the modules on the CPAN are portable. However, many are not. Many of them could be portable, but are not, simply because the author only had access to one platform. Sometimes the module will have noted in its documentation what platforms it will work on, but one of the best places to look is the CPAN Testers web site (http://testers.cpan.org/). CPAN Testers is a group of volunteers that tests modules on CPAN and reports (usually PASS or FAIL) for the given module with a given distribution of Perl on a given platform. This is useful for module authors, not just so that they can get help in making the module as portable as possible, but also as a sanity check to make sure their module works even on the platforms they intended it to work on.

The CPAN Testers results are cross-referenced on the CPAN Search site (http://search.cpan.org/), so when we find a module on that site, we are told which platforms it has been tested on, and what the results were. CPAN Search is a great tool in its own right, providing a central location for information about the various module distributions on CPAN.

Time and Date

The system's notion of time of day and calendar date is controlled in widely different ways. We can't assume the time zone is stored in $ENV{TZ}, and even if it is, we can't assume that we can control the time zone through that variable.

We shouldn't assume that the epoch starts at 00:00:00, January 1, 1970, because that is OS- and implementation specific. It is better to store a date in an unambiguous representation. The ISO-8601 standard defines YYYY-MM-DD as the date format. A text representation (like 1979-07-12) can be easily converted into an OS specific value using a module like Date::Parse. An array of values, such as those returned by localtime, can be converted to an OS specific representation using Time::Local. Be careful, however: converting between unambiguous representations of times and dates can be very slow, so, if the calculations are internal to the program, then it is usually better to use the native values.

When calculating specific times, such as for tests in time or date modules, it may be appropriate to calculate an offset for the epoch.

```
require Time::Local;
$offset = Time::Local::timegm(0, 0, 0, 1, 0, 70);
```

The value for $offset in UNIX will be 0, but in Mac OS it will be some large number. $offset can then be added to a UNIX time value to get what should be the proper value on any system:

```
$nativetime = $unixtime + $offset;
```

Character Sets and Character Encoding

We should assume little about character sets. We must assume nothing about numerical values (ord, chr) of characters: the decimal value of a may be 97 in ASCII, but may be something entirely different in another character set, like EBCDIC. We shouldn't assume that the alphabetic characters are encoded contiguously (in the numeric sense). We shouldn't assume anything about the ordering of the characters. The lowercase letters may come before or after the uppercase letters; the lowercase and uppercase may be interlaced so that both a and A come before b; the accented and other international characters may be interlaced so that ä comes before b.

Furthermore, it may be unreasonable to assume that a single character is one byte. In various character sets, a character may constitute more than one byte. Unicode is becoming more prevalent, and its characters also often occupy more than one byte, too. If Unicode text will be used, then we use the UTF8 directive in Perl 5.6. With use utf8, regular expressions and many string functions will treat the characters in Unicode text as characters instead of individual bytes.

```
@bytes = split //, "\x{263A}";    # 3 elements in @bytes
{
    use utf8;
    @chars = split //, "\x{263A}";    # 1 element in @char
}
```

Unicode handling in Perl 5.6 is still incomplete and subject to change in future revisions. See Chapter 25 for more on Unicode.

Internationalization

If we may assume POSIX (a rather large assumption), we may read more about the POSIX locale system from the `perllocale` and `POSIX.pm` documentation. The locale system at least attempts to make things a little bit more portable, or at least more convenient and native-friendly for non english users. The system affects character sets and encoding, regular expressions, sort order, date and time formatting, and more. Simply adding `use locale` to the top of our program will make it respect the behavior of the current locale, if set.

While the `locale` directive will do most of the work for us, one thing to keep especially in mind is that when using regular expressions, we don't use `[a-zA-Z]` to match letters and `[0-9]` to match numerals; instead, we use meta characters like `\w` and `\d`, or the POSIX character classes like `[:alpha:]` and `[:digit:]`. Exactly what constitutes an alpha or a numeric changes depending on the locale, so we let Perl do the work for us.

Internationalization is examined in Chapter 26.

System Resources

If our code is destined for systems with severely constrained (or missing) virtual memory systems, then we want to be especially mindful of avoiding wasteful constructs such as:

```
@lines = <VERY_LARGE_FILE>;   # bad

while (<FILE>) {$file .= $_}   # sometimes bad
$file = join('', <FILE>);   # better
```

The difference between the last two constructs may appear unintuitive to some people. The first repeatedly grows a string, whereas the second allocates a large chunk of memory in one go. On some systems, the second is more efficient that the first.

Security

Most multiuser platforms provide basic levels of security, usually implemented at the filesystem level. Some, however, do not. Thus the notion of user ID, or home directory, or even the state of being logged-in, may be unrecognizable on many platforms. If we write programs that are security-conscious, it is usually best to know what type of system we will be running under so that we can write code explicitly for that platform (or class of platforms).

Style

For those times when it is necessary to have platform specific code, consider keeping the platform specific code in one place; this will make porting to other platforms easier. We might keep the platform-specific code in its own module, or have a separate module for each platform, or in the base code, with just different subroutines or code blocks for each case.

We use the `Config` module and the special variable `$^O` to differentiate between platforms (as described in 'Platforms' below), if necessary. However, we should probably only separate code based on platform, if we know for sure that the different platforms have different requirements. For instance, the `File::Spec` module loads another platform specific module depending on what platform is running, to construct proper file specifications for that platform. Its code looks something like this:

```
%module =
(
    MacOS => 'Mac',
    MSWin32 => 'Win32',
    os2 => 'OS2',
    VMS => 'VMS'
);

$module = 'File::Spec::' . ($module{$^O} || 'Unix');
eval "require $module" or die $@;
@ISA = ($module);
```

In the above case, and in others, the choice is clear-cut: we know exactly what behavior a specific platform will require, and select the code based on which platform is in use. However, sometimes we don't know, or would be better off not guessing, which platforms support a given block of code. For example, the MS Windows operating system does not support `fork`. However, Perl on Windows, as of Perl 5.6, can emulate `fork`. So, if we had code like this:

```
die "Sorry, no fork! \n" if $^O eq 'MSWin32';
```

we would be excluding users of Perl 5.6 unnecessarily, while catching users of older versions of Perl. If a specific function is required, we can check for the existence of that function by trying to execute it with `eval`:

```
eval {fork()};
die $@ if $@ && $@ =~ /(?:not |un)implemented/;
```

There are problems with this method. The text returned by `$@` may differ from platform to platform, or even function to function on one platform. Furthermore, a function may not return `unimplemented` until after it is processed, so if we don't give it the correct number of arguments, we can get a prototype error. In addition, of course, we may not want to actually use the function to make sure it is there. Therefore, we would need to pass it arguments that are acceptable to the prototype of the function, and it will either do nothing, or execute in the way we want. So, if we want to use `getpwuid` to get a user name from a user ID, and `die` if the function is unimplemented, we can try:

```
eval {getpwuid(0)};   # 'getpwuid' with argument triggers prototype error
die $@ if $@ && $@ =~ /(?:not |un)implemented/;
my $user = getpwuid($uid);
```

Or:

```
$user = eval {getpwuid($uid)};
die $@ if $@ && $@ =~ /(?:not |un)implemented/;
```

We might, of course, not wish to die if it is unimplemented, but we may wish to just ask for a user name if $user is false. Of course, there are many reasons why it could be false. It could be that there is no user for that user id, or that getpwuid is not implemented, or that there is some bug in the OS, or a broken /etc/passwd file. We might not care why $user is false, we may only care about getting a name, so if it is false, we just prompt for a user name:

```
$user = eval {getpwuid($uid)};
unless ($user) {
    print 'What is the user name?';
    chomp($user = <STDIN>);
}
```

We could extend this a bit further. Even though this code already works on UNIX, MS Windows, Mac OS, and just about any other Perl platform, we might want to bring up a dialog box in Mac OS.

```
$user = eval {getpwuid($uid)} || query('What is the user name?');

sub query
{
    $question = @_;
    $answer;

    if ($^O eq 'MacOS')
    {
        $answer = MacPerl::Ask($question);
    }
    else
    {
        print $question, ' ';
        chomp($answer = <STDIN>);
    }

    return $answer;
}
```

To add code for a Windows dialog box, we just add another test, this time for $^O eq 'MSWin32', and bring up a Windows dialog if it is true. Until then, Windows will just use the default. This is nice because it is not only very portable, but it is easy to make future changes, because the code is well encapsulated.

We must be careful not to depend on a specific output style for errors, such as when checking $! after a system call or $@ after an eval. Some platforms expect a certain output format, and Perl on those platforms may have been adjusted accordingly. Most specifically, we don't anchor a regular expression when testing an error value, because the error might be wrapped by the system in some other text. For example:

```
print $@ =~ /^Expected text/ ? 'OK' : 'Not OK';    # wrong
print $@ =~ /Expected text/ ? 'OK' : 'Not OK';    # right
```

We should be especially mindful to keep all of these issues in mind in the tests we supply with our module or program. Module code may be fully portable, but its tests might not be. This often happens when tests spawn off other processes or call external programs to aid in the testing, or when (as noted above) the tests assume certain things about the file system and paths.

Platforms

As of version 5.002, Perl is built with a $^O variable that indicates the operating system for which it was built. This was implemented to help speed up code that would otherwise have to use the Config module and get the value of $Config{osname}. Of course, to get more detailed information about the system, looking into %Config is certainly recommended.

It might be useful for us to look at a platform's $^O or $Config{archname} value. This is often useful for setting platform specific values. Below is an incomplete table of some of the more (or less) popular platforms. Note that how $^O and $Config{archname} are determined is platform dependent, and in some cases just hard-coded by the person who builds for that platform.

Operating System	'$^O'	'$Config{archname}'
AIX	Aix	aix
Amiga DOS	amigaos	m68k-amigos
BSD/OS	bsdos	i386-bsdos
Darwin	darwin	darwin
dgux		dgux
AViiON-dgux		
DYNIX/ptx	dynixptx	i386-dynixptx
FreeBSD	freebsd	freebsd-i386
HP-UX	Hpux	PA-RISC1.1
IRIX	Irix	irix
Linux	Linux	arm-linux
Linux	linux	i386-linux, i586-linux, i686-linux
Linux	linux	ppc-linux
Mac OS	MacOS	
MachTen PPC	machten	Powerpc-machten
MPE/iX	mpeix	PA-RISC1.1
MS-DOS	dos	
NeXT 3	next	next-fat
NeXT 4	next	OPENSTEP-Mach
openbsd	openbsd	i386-openbsd
OS/2	os2	

Table continued on following page

Operating System	'$^O'	'$Config{archname}'
OS/390	os390	os390
OS400	os400	os400
OSF1	dec_osf	alpha-dec_osf
PC-DOS	dos	
POSIX-BC	posix-bc	BS2000-posix-bc
reliantunix-n	svr4	RM400-svr4
RISC OS	riscos	
SCO_SV	sco_sv	i386-sco_sv
SINIX-N	svr4	RM400-svr4
sn4609	unicos	CRAY_C90-unicos
sn6521	unicosmk	t3e-unicosmk
sn9617	unicos	
CRAY_J90-unicos		
SunOS	solaris	i86pc-solaris
SunOS	solaris	sun4-solaris
SunOS4	sunos	sun4-sunos
VM/ESA	vmesa	Vmesa
VMS	VMS	
VOS	VOS	
Windows 95	MSWin32	MSWin32-x86
Windows 98	MSWin32	MSWin32-x86
Windows NT	MSWin32	MSWin32-x86, MSWin32-ALPHA, MSWin32-ppc

UNIX

Perl works on a bewildering variety of UNIX and UNIX-like platforms (for example, most of the files in the hints directory in the source code kit). On most of these systems, the value of $^O is determined either by lowercasing and stripping punctuation from the first field of the string returned by typing uname -a (or a similar command) at the shell prompt, or by testing the file system for the presence of uniquely named files such as a kernel or header file. Since the value of $Config{archname} may depend on the hardware architecture, it can vary more than the value of $^O.

DOS and Derivatives

Perl has long been ported to Intel-style microcomputers running under systems like PC-DOS, MS-DOS, OS/2, and most Windows platforms. Users familiar with COMMAND.COM or CMD.EXE style shells should be aware that there may be subtle differences in using \ or / as a path separator. System calls accept either / or \ as the path separator; however, many command line utilities of DOS vintage treat / as the option prefix, so may get confused by filenames containing /. Aside from calling any external programs, / will work just fine, and probably better, as it is more consistent with popular usage, and avoids the problem of remembering what characters to escape in our filename strings, and what not to. So we should stick with / unless we know that we need to use \.

The DOS FAT file system can only accommodate 8.3 filenames. FAT32, HPFS (OS/2), and NTFS (NT) file systems can have longer filenames, and are case insensitive but case preserving. DOS also treats several filenames as special, such as AUX, PRN, NUL, CON, COM1, LPT1, LPT2, etc. Unfortunately, these filenames won't even work if we include an explicit directory prefix. It is best to avoid such filenames, if we want our code to be portable to DOS and its derivatives. Unfortunately, it's hard to know what these all are.

Users of these operating systems may also wish to make use of scripts such as pl2bat.bat, pl2cmd, or the commercial Perl2Exe to put wrappers around scripts. ActiveState, the company that releases ActivePerl, also wrote the Perl Package Manager, the system used primarily by Windows systems to get Perl modules that we mentioned in Chapter 1 of this book. This includes prebuilt binaries of modules that need a C compiler. See the documentation for PPM in ActivePerl, and download packages from http://www.activestate.com/packages/.

Mac OS

Mac OS is in some ways the most problematic platform, since there is no native, built-in command line. MacPerl, the version of Perl for Mac OS, does have several facilities for working around this limitation, such as droplets and run-times.

> For more information on how to do really cool stuff in MacPerl, check out the various MacPerl mailing lists on http://www.macperl.org/, or the authoritative reference on MacPerl, MacPerl: Power and Ease, from Prime Time Freeware.

In the MacPerl application, we can't run a program from the command line; programs that expect @ARGV to be populated can be edited with something like the following, which brings up a dialog box asking for the command line arguments.

```
if (!@ARGV)
{
    @ARGV = split /\s+/, MacPerl::Ask('Arguments?');
}
```

A MacPerl script saved as a droplet will populate @ARGV with the full pathnames of the files dropped onto the script, just as a Perl script in UNIX called with filenames passed to it will have those names passed into @ARGV.

A command line interface does exist for Mac OS. Macintosh Programmer's Workshop (MPW) is currently a free development environment from Apple. MacPerl was first introduced as an MPW tool, and MPW can be used like a shell:

perl myscript.plx some arguments

MPW is dissimilar to a UNIX shell, having its own conventions, commands, and behaviors, but the basic concepts are the same. ToolServer is another free application from Apple that provides access to MPW tools from MPW and the MacPerl application, which allows MacPerl programs to use `system`, backticks, and even `piped open`.

Any module requiring XS compilation is right out for most Mac users, because compilers on Mac OS are not very common (and often expensive). Some XS modules that can work with MacPerl are built and distributed in binary form on the CPAN, and are available from MacPerl Module Porters at http://pudge.net/mmp/.

MacPerl is currently at version 5.004. MacPerl 5.6 is currently in development, but any features of Perl from 5.004_01 and later, such as the new `open my $file` idiom, will not work under the current version of MacPerl.

Directories in Mac OS are specified with any path including the volume, such as `volume:folder:file` being absolute, and any others, including `:file`, being relative. Files are stored in the directory in alphabetical order. Filenames are limited to 31 characters, and may include any character except for `Null` and `:`, which is reserved as the path separator.

Mac OS has no concept of the UNIX `flock`, so `flock` is not implemented. Mac OS will put a mandatory lock on any file opened for writing (in most cases), and we can do a Mac OS lock on a file with the functions `FSpSetFLock` and `FSpRstFLock` in the `Mac::Files` module. Also, `chmod(0444, $file)` and `chmod(0666, $file)` (implementations of the UNIX `chmod` command using octal switches to specify the permissions) are mapped to `FSpSetFLock` and `FSpRstFLock`.

Mac OS is the proper name for the operating system, but the value in `$^O` is Mac OS. To determine architecture, version, or whether Perl is running as the MacPerl application or the MPW tool, check:

```
($version) = $MacPerl::Version =~ /^(\S+)/;
$is_app = $MacPerl::Version =~ /App/;
$is_tool = $MacPerl::Version =~ /MPW/;
$is_ppc = $MacPerl::Architecture eq 'MacPPC';
$is_68k = $MacPerl::Architecture eq 'Mac68K';
```

Mac OS X, based on NeXT's OpenStep OS, can run MacPerl natively, under the **Classic** environment. The new Carbon API, which provides much of the Classic API under the new environment, may be able to run a slightly modified version of MacPerl in the new environment, if someone wants it in the future. Mac OS X and its Open Source brother, Darwin, both run UNIX Perl natively. It is unclear what the `$^O` value will be for Mac OS X, since it is not yet released, but only available as a beta, but in the betas, it too, was `darwin`. The MacPerl toolbox modules (`Mac::Files`, `Mac::Speech`, etc.) may be ported to Mac OS X at some point, so many Mac-specific scripts will work under either Mac OS or Mac OS X.

Other Perls

Perl has been ported to many platforms that do not fit into any of the categories listed above. Some, such as AmigaOS, Atari MiNT, BeOS, HP MPE/iX, QNX, Plan 9, VOS, and VMS, have been well integrated into the standard Perl source code kit. We may need to see the ports directory on CPAN for information, and possibly binaries, for the likes of aos, Atari ST, LynxOS, RISCOS, Novell Netware, Tandem Guardian, etc. Some of these OSes may fall under the UNIX category.

Function Implementations

Listed below are functions that are either completely unimplemented, or else have been implemented differently on various platforms. Following each description will be, in parentheses, a list of platforms to which the description applies. Larry Wall once noted that, 'Perl is, in intent, a cleaned up and summarized version of that wonderful seminatural language known as UNIX.' Almost everything in core Perl will work in UNIX, so we note only those places where some platform might differ from the expected behavior for UNIX.

When in doubt, we can consult the platform-specific README files in the Perl source distribution, and any other documentation resources accompanying a given port. We should be aware, moreover, that even among UNIX-like systems there are variations.

Function	Platform Variations
binmode(FILEHANDLE)	**Win32**: The value returned by tell may be affected after the call, and the file handle may be flushed.
	Mac OS, RISC OS: Meaningless.
	VMS: Reopens the file and restores the pointer; if function fails, the underlying file handle may be closed, or the pointer may be in a different position.
chmod(LIST)	**Win32**: Only good for changing 'owner' read write access. 'Group', and 'other' bits are meaningless, as is setting the executable bit.
	Mac OS: Only limited meaning. Disabling/enabling write permission is mapped to locking/unlocking the file.
	RISC OS: Only good for changing 'owner' and 'other' read/write access.
	VOS: Access permissions are mapped onto VOS access control list changes.
chown(LIST)	**Win32**: Does nothing, but won't fail.
	Mac OS, Plan9, RISC OS, VOS: Not implemented.

Table continued on following page

Function	Platform Variations
chroot(FILENAME) chroot(FILENAME)	**Win32, Mac OS, VMS, Plan9, RISC OS, VOS, VM/ESA**: Not implemented.
crypt(PLAINTEXT, SALT)	**Win32**: In rare cases, may not be available if library or source was not provided when building Perl. **VOS**: Not implemented.
dbmclose(HASH)	**VMS, Plan9, VOS**: Not implemented.
dbmopen(HASH, DBNAME, MODE)	**VMS, Plan9, VOS**: Not implemented.
dump(LABEL)	**Win32**: Not implemented. **Mac OS, RISC OS**: Not useful. **VMS**: Invokes VMS debugger.
endpwent	**Win32, Mac OS, MPE/iX, VM/ESA**: Not implemented.
exec(LIST)	**Mac OS**: Not implemented. **VM/ESA**: Implemented via Spawn.
Fcntl(FILEHANDLE, FUNCTION, SCALAR)	**Win32, VMS**: Not implemented.
flock(FILEHANDLE, OPERATION)	**Win32**: Available only on Windows NT (not on Windows 95). **Mac OS, VMS, RISC OS, VOS**: Not implemented.
fork	**Win32, Mac OS, AmigaOS, RISC OS, VOS, VM/ESA**: Not implemented. As of Perl 5.6, however, the Win32 port does have support for fork.
getlogin	**Mac OS, RISC OS**: Not implemented.
getpgrp(PID)	**Win32, Mac OS, VMS, RISC OS, VOS**: Not implemented.
getppid	**Win32, Mac OS, VMS, RISC OS**: Not implemented.
getpriority(WHICH, WHO)	**Mac OS, Win32, VMS, RISC OS, VOS, VM/ESA**: Not implemented.
getpwnam(NAME)	**Win32, Mac OS**: Not implemented. **RISC OS**: Not useful.
getgrnam(NAME)	**Win32, Mac OS, VMS, RISC OS**: Not implemented.
getnetbyname(NAME)	**Win32, Mac OS, Plan9**: Not implemented.
getpwuid(UID)	**Win32, Mac OS**: Not implemented. **RISC OS**: Not useful.

Function	Platform Variations
`getgrgid(GID)`	**Win32, Mac OS, VMS, RISC OS**: Not implemented.
`getnetbyaddr(ADDR, ADDRTYPE)`	**Win32, Mac OS, Plan9**: Not implemented.
`getprotobynumber(NUMBER)`	**Mac OS**: Not implemented.
`getservbyport(PORT, PROTO)`	**Mac OS**: Not implemented.
`getpwent`	**Win32, Mac OS, VM/ESA**: Not implemented.
`getgrent`	**Win32, Mac OS, VMS, VM/ESA**: Not implemented.
`gethostent`	**Win32, Mac OS**: Not implemented.
`getnetent`	**Win32, Mac OS, Plan9**: Not implemented.
`getprotoent`	**Win32, Mac OS, Plan9**: Not implemented.
`getservent`	**Win32, Plan9**: Not implemented.
`setpwent`	**Win32, Mac OS, RISC OS, MPE/iX**: Not implemented.
`setgrent`	**Win32, Mac OS, VMS, MPE/iX, RISC OS**: Not implemented.
`sethostent(STAYOPEN)`	**Win32, Mac OS, Plan9, RISC OS**: Not implemented.
`setnetent(STAYOPEN)`	**Win32, Mac OS, Plan9, RISC OS**: Not implemented.
`setprotoent(STAYOPEN)`	**Win32, Mac OS, Plan9, RISC OS**: Not implemented.
`setpgrp(PID, PGRP)`	**Win32, Mac OS, VMS, RISC OS, VOS**: Not implemented.
`setpriority(WHICH, WHO, PRIORITY)`	
`setservent(STAYOPEN)`	**Win32, Plan9, RISC OS**: Not implemented.
`setsockopt(SOCKET, LEVEL, OPTNAME, OPTVAL)`	**Mac OS, Plan9**: Not implemented.
`endpwent`	**Win32, Mac OS, MPE/iX, VM/ESA**: Not implemented.
`endgrent`	**Win32, Mac OS, MPE/iX, RISC OS, VM/ESA, VMS**: Not implemented.
`endhostent`	**Win32, Mac OS**: Not implemented.
`endnetent`	**Win32, Mac OS, Plan9**: Not implemented.
`endprotoent`	**Win32, Mac OS, Plan9**: Not implemented.
`endservent`	**Win32, Plan9**: Not implemented.

Table continued on following page

Function	Platform Variations
`getsockopt(SOCKET, LEVEL, OPTNAME)`	**Mac OS, Plan9**: Not implemented.
`glob(EXPR)` `glob`	**Win32**: Features depend on external `perlglob.exe` or `perlglob.bat`. May be overridden with something like `File::DosGlob`, which is recommended.
	Mac OS: Globbing built-in, but only * and ? meta characters are supported.
	RISC OS: Globbing built-in, but only * and ? meta characters are supported. Globbing relies on operating system calls, which may return filenames in any order. As most file systems are case insensitive, even 'sorted' filenames will not be in case sensitive order.
`ioctl(FILEHANDLE, FUNCTION, SCALAR)`	**Win32**: Available only for socket handles, and it does what the `ioctlsocket` call in the Winsock API does.
	VMS: Not implemented.
	RISC OS: Available only for socket handles.
`kill(SIGNAL, LIST)`	**Win32**: Unlike UNIX platforms, `kill(0, $pid)` will actually terminate the process.
	Mac OS, RISC OS: Not implemented, hence not useful for taint checking.
`link(OLDFILE, NEWFILE)`	**Win32**: Hard links are implemented on Win32 (Windows NT and Windows 2000) under NTFS only.
	Mac OS, MPE/iX, VMS, RISC OS: Not implemented.
	AmigaOS: Link count not updated because hard links are not quite that hard (They are sort of halfway between hard and soft links).
`lstat(FILEHANDLE)` `lstat(EXPR)` `lstat`	**Win32**: Return values may be bogus. **VMS, RISC OS**: Not implemented.
`msgctl(ID, CMD, ARG)` `msgget(KEY, FLAGS)` `msgsnd(ID, MSG, FLAGS)` `msgrcv(ID, VAR, SIZE, TYPE, FLAGS)`	**Win32, Mac OS, VMS, Plan9, RISC OS, VOS**: Not implemented.
`open(FILEHANDLE, EXPR)` `open(FILEHANDLE)`	**Win32, Mac OS, RISC OS**: open to `|-` and `-|` are unsupported.
	Mac OS: The | variants are supported only if `ToolServer` is installed.

Function	Platform Variations
`pipe(READHANDLE, WRITEHANDLE)`	**Mac OS**: Not implemented. **MiNT**: Very limited functionality.
`readlink(EXPR)` `readlink`	**Win32**, **VMS**, **RISC OS**: Not implemented.

`semctl(ID, SEMNUM, CMD, ARG)`
`semget(KEY, NSEMS, FLAGS)`
`semop(KEY, OPSTRING)`
	Win32, **Mac OS**, **VMS**, **RISC OS**, **VOS**: Not implemented.

`shmctl(ID, CMD, ARG)`
`shmget(KEY, SIZE, FLAGS)`
`shmread(ID, VAR, POS, SIZE)`
`shmwrite(ID, STRING, POS, SIZE)`
	Win32, **Mac OS**, **VMS**, **RISC OS**, **VOS**: Not implemented.

`socketpair(SOCKET1, SOCKET2, DOMAIN, TYPE, PROTOCOL)`	**Mac OS**, **Win32**, **VMS**, **RISC OS**, **VOS**, **VM/ESA**: Not implemented.

`stat(FILEHANDLE)`
`stat(EXPR)`
`stat`
	Win32: device and inode are not meaningful.
	
	MacOS: mtime and atime are the same, and ctime is creation time instead of inode change time.
	
	VMS: device and inode are not necessarily reliable.
	
	RISC OS: mtime, atime and ctime all return the last modification time. Device and inode are not necessarily reliable.

`symlink(OLDFILE, NEWFILE)`	**Win32**, **VMS**, **RISC OS**: Not implemented.
`syscall(LIST)`	**Win32**, **Mac OS**, **VMS**, **RISC OS**, **VOS**, **VM/ESA**: Not implemented.
`sysopen(FILEHANDLE, FILENAME, MODE, PERMS)`	**Mac OS**, **OS/390**, **VM/ESA**: The traditional 0, 1, and 2 modes are implemented with different numeric values on some systems. Though the flags exported by Fcntl (O_RDONLY, O_WRONLY, O_RDWR) should work everywhere.

Table continued on following page

Function	Platform Variations
system(LIST)	**Win32**: As an optimization, may not call the command shell specified in $ENV{PERL5SHELL}. system(1, @args) spawns an external process and immediately returns its process designator, without waiting for it to terminate. Return value may be used subsequently in wait or waitpid.
	Mac OS: Only implemented if ToolServer is installed.
	RISC OS: There is no shell to process meta characters, and the native standard is to pass a command line terminated by \n, \r or \0 to the spawned program. Redirection, such as > foo, is performed (if at all) by the runtime library of the spawned program. system LIST will call the UNIX emulation library's exec emulation, which attempts to provide emulation of the stdin, stdout, stderr in force in the parent, providing the child program uses a compatible version of the emulation library. scalar will call the native command line direct and no such emulation of a child UNIX program exists. Mileage will vary.
	MiNT: Far from being POSIX compliant. Because there may be no underlying /bin/sh, system trying to work around the problem by forking and execing the first token in its argument string. Handles basic redirection (< or >) on its own behalf.
times	**Win32**: 'cumulative' times will be bogus. On anything other than Windows NT, 'system' time will be bogus, and 'user' time is actually the time returned by the clock function in the C runtime library.
	Mac OS: Only the first entry returned is non zero.
	RISC OS: Not useful.
truncate(FILEHANDLE, LENGTH)	**Win32**: If a FILEHANDLE is supplied, it must be writable and opened in append mode (use open(FH, '>filename')> or
truncate(EXPR, LENGTH)	sysopen(FH,...,O_APPEND|O_RDWR). If a filename is supplied, it should not be held open elsewhere.
	VMS: Not implemented.
	VOS: Truncation to zero length only.
umask(EXPR)	Returns undef where unavailable, as of version 5.005.
umask	**AmigaOS**: umask works, but the correct permissions are set only when the file is finally closed.

Function	Platform Variations
utime(LIST)	**Win32**: May not behave as expected. Behavior depends on the C runtime library's implementation of utime, and the file system being used. The FAT file system typically does not support an access time field, and it may limit timestamps to a granularity of two seconds.
	Mac OS, VMS, RISC OS: Only the modification time is updated.
wait waitpid(PID, FLAGS)	**Win32**: Can only be applied to process handles returned for processes spawned using system(1, ...). Unless we are using Perl 5.6 where there's support for fork.
	Mac OS, VOS: Not implemented.
	RISC OS: Not useful.

Summary

In this chapter, we looked at many portability issues that we should be aware of if we want to write cross-platform programs. We have covered differences between various platforms in the way they handle newlines, filenames and using the File::Spec module, endianness, system interaction, IPC, XS, modules, time and date, character sets and character encoding, internationalization, system resources, security, and style.

We have also explored Perl's support for particular platforms, namely UNIX, DOS, MS Windows, and Mac. Finally, we looked at a number of Perl functions with peculiar implementations, which are not implemented, or which are meaningless on non-UNIX platforms.

25

Unicode

Symbols are used to convey and to record meaning. We have been using them since time immemorial – they have been the building blocks of communication, from the earliest inscriptions on cave walls to the multitude of scripts that are used today. The language that the modern PC can deal with at the lowest level has only two symbols, traditionally represented by us as zeros and ones. People in every culture have programmed the computer to interact with them using their own set of symbols. Certain combination of zeros and ones were invented to stand for letters of the alphabet, monetary units, arithmetic symbols – things that made sense to humans.

Just as most microprocessors would like to see a language of fixed high and low voltages being spoken on their data buses instead of some fancy noise, humans would like to see the computer respond to them in their own native language. Things were fine until recently, when most of the people using computers belonged to the English-speaking world, or had previously taught themselves English.

The Internet brought about a paradigm shift, with people and machines across cultures interacting with each other. Half a decade ago, a company could not have had its web pages in multiple languages rendered correctly on browsers all over the world. Due to the variety of ways in which information in various languages could be stored, it was also difficult for a program to deal with multiple language input. It used to be impossible to have an online document containing multiple scripts, for example, an English newspaper containing a Japanese haiku or a quote from a speech in Russian. We are looking at two problems here:

- ❑ We have many different ways of representing our symbols (character codes and encoding).
- ❑ We have many different sets of symbols (languages).

Whom Does It Affect?

This affects almost everyone involved with creating software to be used across language boundaries. The world is a big place and most of it is still untouched by information technology. In addition, people will prefer software that uses their native symbols and language – not someone else's! Even today, the reaches of the Internet and the World Wide Web are not really utilized if the audience is limited only to people who share a particular language – it does not make economic sense to people doing business using various mechanisms running on computers and over networks. Therefore, by extension, it affects the creators of those mechanisms.

What Are the Solutions?

These problems were recognized quite some time ago and now we have many solutions that have been implemented and are evolving, most of them working together to make sure that data is usable by everyone. We have technologies such as **XML**, **locales** and **Unicode** to help us internationalize our applications and web pages. We don't have any magic fixes yet, but we are moving towards the solution. What we are going to look at in this chapter is a solution to the first problem mentioned above, and how Perl can help. We also take a look at a small example of how Perl can also help solve the second problem using Unicode.

Characters and Unicode 101

There is a lot of confusion in this field since the terminology varies and definitions are not universally accepted. Let us take a look at some of these. A set or a collection of distinct characters is called a **character repertoire**. It is defined by giving a name for each character and a visible presentation as an example. A sample of a character repertoire may look like:

Character	Value
The English lowercase alphabet a.	a
The English lowercase alphabet b.	b
:	:
The English upper case alphabet Z.	z

A table that establishes one-to-one correspondence between characters from a repertoire and a table of non-negative integers is called a **character code** or a **character set**. The integer corresponding to a character is also called its **code position** since it also serves as an index in the character set.

A sample character set may look like this (using decimal values):

The English lowercase alphabet y	121
The English lowercase alphabet z	122
The character {	123
The character |	124

The most well known character set so far has been the one defined by the **ASCII standard**. Many character sets were developed later to cater for a growing variety of character repertoires with a growing number of characters.

The character sets specified by the ISO 8859 family of standards extend the ASCII character set in different ways for different cultures and their character repertoires. However, all of them are supersets of ASCII in the sense that code positions 0-127 contain the same characters as in ASCII. Furthermore, positions 128-159 are unused (reserved for control characters) and positions 160-255 are used differently in different members of the ISO 8859 family. For example the ISO 8859-1 character set extends ASCII to cover West European characters – a repertoire identified as 'Latin alphabet No. 1.' ISO 8859-2 does the same for Central and East European characters – 'Latin alphabet No. 2,' and so on to ISO 8859-15.

Standard	Name of alphabet	Characterization
ISO 8859-1	Latin alphabet No. 1	'Western,' 'West European'
ISO 8859-2	Latin alphabet No. 2	'Central European,' 'East European'
ISO 8859-3	Latin alphabet No. 3	'South European;' 'Maltese and Esperanto"
ISO 8859-4	Latin alphabet No. 4	'North European'
ISO 8859-5	Latin/Cyrillic alphabet	(for Slavic languages)
ISO 8859-6	Latin/Arabic alphabet	(for the Arabic language)
ISO 8859-7	Latin/Greek alphabet	(for modern Greek)
ISO 8859-8	Latin/Hebrew alphabet	(for Hebrew and Yiddish)
ISO 8859-9	Latin alphabet No. 5	'Turkish'
ISO 8859-10	Latin alphabet No. 6	'Nordic' (Sámi, Inuit, Icelandic)
ISO 8859-11	Latin/Thai alphabet	(for the Thai language)
(Part 12 has not been defined)		
ISO 8859-13	Latin alphabet No. 7	'Baltic Rim'
ISO 8859-14	Latin alphabet No. 8	'Celtic'
ISO 8859-15	Latin alphabet No. 9	An update to Latin1 with a few modifications and the addition of the Euro currency symbol. Nicknamed Latin0

The Windows character set, more properly called Windows code page 1252, is similar to ISO 8859-1, but uses positions 128-159 (reserved for control characters in ISO 8859-1) for printable characters. MS-DOS had its own character sets called code pages. CP 437, the original American code page, and CP 850, extended for the West European languages, have largely the same repertoire as ISO 8859-1 but with characters in different code positions.

Various character sets may be found all over the world, such as ISCII in India, Big5 in Taiwan, and JIS X 0208:1997 in Japan. Now back to our two problems. The first step towards solving the first problem would be to have a single character set or a table that served all of the character repertoires in the world. There have been two major efforts towards solving this problem.

The **ISO 10646 project** of the International **O**rganization for **S**tandardization (ISO, counter-intuitively) defines the mother of all character sets – the **Universal Character Set** (**UCS**). The ISO 10646 standard defines a 32-bit character set, with only the first 65534 positions assigned as of now. This subset of the UCS is also known as the **Basic Multilingual Plane**, or **Plane 0**. It has enough character space to encompass practically all known languages. This not only includes Latin, Greek, Arabic, Hebrew, Armenian, Georgian, but also encompasses scripts such as Devanagari, Bengali, Gurumukhi, Gujarati, Oriya, Tamil, Telugu, Kannada, Malayalam, Thai, Khmer, Lao, Runic, Cherokee, Sinhala, Katakana, Hiragana, Hangul and Chinese, Japanese and Korean ideographs. The UCS also has a lot of space outside the Basic Multilingual Plane for hieroglyphics and some selected artistic scripts such as Klingon, Cirth, and Tengwar, which may be implemented in the future. This space in the UCS was reserved for other 'planes' that could be switched by using escape sequences.

The other effort was the **Unicode Project** organized by a consortium of multilingual software development houses. The **Unicode Standard**, published by the **Unicode Consortium** also has information other than just the character sets, for example algorithms for handling bi-directional texts, say, a mixture of Latin and Hebrew (Hebrew is written right to left). Around 1991, the ISO and the Unicode Consortium agreed that it would make more sense to have one universal standard instead of two different ones, and so now, the Unicode Standard defines a character repertoire and character set corresponding to Plane 0 of the UCS, or the Basic Multilingual Plane. Unicode characters are represented as U+xxxx where xxxx is the code position in hexadecimal. For example, the code for a white smiley face is written as U+263A. That solved half of the first problem.

The other half is to do with the representation of those non-negative integers for storage and transmission encoding. Data is usually composed of **octets** or **bytes** of **8 bits**. For ASCII, 7 bits were enough to represent a code position, for other larger character sets like those for the Chinese, Japanese and Korean languages, or for the UCS, this is grossly insufficient. Therefore, we have many encoding schemes using more than a byte to represent a character. Now, for Universal Character Set, the two most obvious choices would be to use a fixed size of two or four bytes since any one of the 2^{32} characters can be accommodated in 4 bytes, or 32 bits. These encoding schemes are known as **UCS-2** and **UCS-4** respectively. However there are problems associated with them. Most importantly, programs expecting ASCII as input would fail even for plain (ASCII repertoire) text, since they have not been designed to handle multi-byte encoding. Plain ASCII repertoire text would unnecessarily take up twice or four times the space required. Furthermore, strings encoded in UCS-2 or UCS-4 may contain characters like \, 0 or / having special significance in filenames in various operating systems. Therefore, UCS-2 or UCS-4 would not work well as a universal encoding scheme.

Annex R of the ISO 10646-1 standard and RFC 2279 define a variable length encoding scheme called **UTF-8**. In this scheme, a character from the ASCII repertoire (U+0000 to U+007F) looks like an ASCII character encoded in a single byte (such as 0x00 to 0x7F). Any higher character is encoded as a sequence of 2 to 6 bytes, according to a scheme where the first byte has the highest bit set and gives the count for the number of bytes to follow for that character. More information about UTF-8 can be acquired from http://www.ietf.org/rfc/rfc2279.txt.

Data in Perl

From Perl 5.6 onwards, strings are not treated as sequences of bytes but instead as sequences of numbers in the range 0 to (2^{32})-1, using an encoding scheme based on UTF-8. Perl may store a string containing characters between 0x00 to 0x7F with fixed 8-bit encoding, but will promote it to UTF-8 if it is involved in an operation with another UTF-8 encoded string. Therefore, it converts between UTF-8 and fixed 8 bit encoding wherever necessary. As a result, we should not rely upon the encoding used by Perl internally. The whole idea of Unicode support in Perl is to spare us the burden of such details.

Unless told otherwise, a typical operator will deal with characters, or sequences of characters. We can explicitly tell Perl to treat strings like byte sequences by surrounding the concerned operator with the scope of a use bytes directive. We have to explicitly tell Perl to allow UTF-8 encoded characters within literals and identifier strings by the use utf8 directive. Variable names could thus be in Hindi, Thai, Japanese, one's own native language, or any of the many supported symbols. For example:

```
$♔♕♖♗♘♙ = "Hello Unicode Chess Pieces";
```

If UTF-8 is in use, string literals in Unicode can be specified using the \x{} notation:

```
$string = "\x{48}\x{49}\x{263A}";
```

Note: use utf8 *is a temporary device. Eventually it will be implicit when Unicode support is completely transparent to the user.*

However, even if we do not explicitly tell Perl anything about our strings, the operators will still treat them correctly. That is, all operands with single byte encoded characters will remain so, until they get involved in expressions or operations with anything having a wider encoding. Then, all programs that expected 8 bit encoded ASCII and gave out 8 bit encoded ASCII, should still work as they did before. If an ASCII encoded operand is involved in an operation with an UTF-8 encoded operand, the 8-bit encoded operand is promoted to UTF-8.

Unicode and Regular Expressions

Perl 5.6 has Unicode support for regular expressions. So, how does one specify Unicode characters in a regular expression? Unicode characters may be represented as \x{hex number here} so that matching data with /\x{05D0}/ is the same as matching it with Hebrew letter א. In order to do this, we need to use the use utf8 directive to tell Perl that it may encounter Unicode characters in a literal. Also, even if the Unicode character lies between 0x80 and 0xFF, it must be enclosed in braces in order to be recognized as Unicode; \x80 is not the same as the Unicode character \x{80}. However, unless one writes poetry in hexadecimal, seeing many of those sprinkled throughout regular expressions will not be a pretty sight. This is where the use charnames directive comes in handy. The name specified for the character by the Unicode standard, enclosed within braces in a named character escape sequence \N{}, may be used instead of the code itself. For example, if we wanted to match the character for a white chess king \x{2654} we would use the following:

```
use utf8;
use charnames ":full";   # use Unicode with full names
$chess_piece = "Opponents move \N{WHITE CHESS KING}";
$chess_piece =~ /\N{WHITE CHESS KING}/;   # this will match
```

Short names can also be used instead of full names:

```
use utf8;
use charnames ":full";   # use Unicode with full names
print " \N{CYRILLIC CAPITAL LETTER PSI} is a psi in Cyrillic \n";
use charnames ":short";   # use Unicode with short names
print " \N{Cyrillic:Psi} is also a capital psi in Cyrillic \n";
```

We can also restrict the language:

```
use utf8;
use charnames qw(cyrillic);   # restricts charnames to the cyrillic script
print " \N{Psi} is also a capital psi in Cyrillic";
```

We can match characters based on **Unicode character properties**. A property is used as a shortcut for character classes in regular expressions. The properties are usually of the form \p{IsPROPERTY} and its complement \P{IsPROPERTY}. For example, we can use \p{IsCntrl} to match any character belonging to the set of control characters, whereas \P{IsCntrl} matches any character belonging to its complement set – any character that is **not** a control character is matched:

```
if ($var =~ /\p{IsCntrl}/) {print "control character found";}
```

The Unicode Consortium publishes data associated with these properties in machine-readable format. This data is used to create the tables and files Perl uses in order to have properties that can be used as character classes. There are certain standard Unicode properties where no character can belong to more than one category.

A few examples of standard Unicode properties are:

❑ IsLu – An uppercase letter.

❑ IsNd – A decimal digit number.

❑ IsPd – A dash (punctuation character).

Perl also has certain **composite properties** implemented as combinations of basic standard Unicode properties, other composite properties and other basic pattern elements.

For example:

❑ IsASCII – Equivalent to the character class [\x00-\x7f].

❑ IsSpace – Equivalent to the character class [\t\n\f\r\p{IsZ}] where \p{IsZ} is given below.

❑ IsZ – Same as the set consisting of IsZl (line separator), IsZp (paragraph separator) and IsZs (space separator).

Unicode **block properties** can be used to determine if a certain character belongs to a certain script, or to test the range of a script. The block properties are of the form \p{InSCRIPTNAME}, its complement being \P{InSCRIPTNAME}, where SCRIPTNAME may be replaced by Arabic, Armenian, Bopomofo and so on. So we could write:

```
if ($var =~ /\P{InHebrew}) {warn "I only understand the Hebrew script!";}
```

A complete list of the properties available on our system can be found by exploring the contents of the Unicode subdirectory, where the Perl library files are stored. To find out where these libraries are stored we can issue this command at the prompt:

> **perl -V**

All the files corresponding to the InSCRIPTNAME properties can be found in OUR_PERL_LIBPATH\unicode\In\.

We can have a look at the files that actually implement these properties. For example, let us look at one such file, Devanagari.pl residing in this subdirectory:

```
# !!!!!!!   DO NOT EDIT THIS FILE   !!!!!!!
# This file is built by mktables.PL from e.g. Unicode.300.
# Any changes made here will be lost!
return <<'END';
0900 097F
END
```

The second last line is important in the implementation. This file simply says return the range delimiters (in hex) for the block that constitutes the Devanagari script.

Writing Our Own Character Property

If for some reason we need a character property that we cannot locate, it is possible for us to write our own. We do this by writing a subroutine using the name of the property desired. In a manner similar to that we saw in the file Devanagari.pl, we return a list of characters, or character ranges (in hexadecimal), we want the property to match, one per line. Existing property names may also be used instead of returning the ranges in hexadecimal. For example:

```
+utf8::InBasicLatin
```

would be the same as:

```
0000    007F
```

Now, if we want a property called InBasicLatinOrGreek (Greek and Latin, except that here we are talking about the BasicLatin script and not the language) this is what must be done:

```
sub IsBasicLatinOrGreek {
    return <<'END';
    +utf8::InGreek
    +utf8::InBasicLatin
    END
}
```

For specifying a character that should not match a certain property, we prefix the property with a bang (!) to signify negation, or use the - sign. So if we want a property to match a character that is not Greek, say, we should create a subroutine called IsUnderstandable (assuming that we understand all other scripts) as follows:

```
sub IsUnderstandable {
    return <<'END';
    !utf8::InGreek
    END
}
```

Or using the alternative method:

```
sub IsUnderstandable {
    return <<'END';
    -utf8::InGreek
    END
}
```

These scripts create a character property that matches any character that is not Greek to us (or anyone who agrees to the Greek script as defined by the Unicode standard).

The `tr` operator now supports the conversion of Latin-1 to UTF-8 and vice versa:

```
tr/\x00-\xff//CU;   # convert $_ from Latin-1 into Unicode
tr/\x00-\x{ff}//UC;  # convert $_ from Unicode into Latin-1
```

Another question that could arise is how Perl decides whether to match data as bytes or as characters. Well the answer is that if a regexp contains Unicode characters, then the string to be matched is treated like a sequence of characters, otherwise it is treated as a sequence of bytes. This is done when the pattern is compiled.

The `use utf8` pragma may be used to tell the engine to match a Unicode character for a period (.) in an expression. The `\X` metasymbol tells the engine to match a **combining character sequence**, consisting of a base character followed by one or more **mark** characters (diacritical marks like the umlaut or a cedilla).

We can force the engine to match a byte even in the middle of a UTF-8 string by using the `\C` escape sequence, which matches any byte from values 0 to 255. Postponing the decision until runtime when the matching happens is something that is in the 'to do' list for Perl as of 5.6. We are still waiting for support for matching characters, if we get some in the string to be matched.

Bi-directional Scripts

Languages such as Arabic, Hebrew, Farsi, Urdu, and Yiddish are written from **right to left**. However, embedded segments of text in other languages or numeric data, such as phone numbers, are written from **left to right**.

Since it is possible to have segments of data written in different directions, the scripts of these languages are called bi-directional (or **bidi**) scripts. For example:

```
HHHHHHHH HHHH HHHH    phone 12345    HHHHHHHHHHHHHHHHH
<------- <--- <---     ----> ---->    <---------------
```

Here we have the Hebrew characters, H, written right to left and Latin characters and numerals written left to right. The --> and <-- represent the directions of the text.

In these scripts, the data may be stored in two ways, either with characters in **visual** or **physical** order. This means having the characters ordered as they are presented on the screen or with characters stored in the logical order, in other words the order in which they are read and spoken.

Since it would be much easier to process data stored in the way it is read and spoken, the logical or physical order is preferred. This would be clear after looking at the following, interesting exercise:

Try searching for a word in a string if it were stored in the order opposite to the order in which it is spoken!

Now try the same thing with the following sentence:

!nekops si ti hcihw ni redro eht ot etisoppo redro eht ni derots erew ti fi gnirts a ni drow a rof gnihcraes yrT

The Unicode standard specifies an algorithm called the **bidi algorithm**, according to which the **rendering process** is responsible for switching from the logical order of the characters, to the visual order for displaying the glyphs.

Perl provides character properties that classify characters based on their bidi properties. A complete list of bidi properties on our system can be determined by looking at the files in OUR_PERL_LIBPATH\unicode\Is\ and so the property names corresponding to them are IsBidiAN, IsBidiB, IsBidiCS, and so on. People who perform bi-directional rendering can use these character properties for things such as determining whether a character is to be rendered left to right or right to left.

Rendering bidi

There are a few other things that need to be known in order to understand how rendering of the bidi scripts is handled. A detailed description of the bidi algorithm is available in an annex to the Unicode standard, called **Technical Report #9** (available from http://www.unicode.org/).

This report defines a few special codes, called **Directional Formatting Codes**, to associate segments of text with the directions in which they should be rendered. These codes affect only the directional properties of characters, and, thus, should be ignored for all other processing or analysis of the text except rendering for display.

Some of the basic codes and what they mean are as follows:

❑ LRE (left to right embedding) – The following text is embedded left to right.

❑ RLE (right to left embedding) – The following text is embedded right to left.

❑ RLO (right to left override) – Force following characters to be right to left.

❑ LRO (left to right override) – Force following characters to be left to right.

❑ PDF (pop directional format) – Restore the direction to what it was before the last LRE, RLE, RLO, LRO. The word pop is used since the bidi algorithm requires the usage of a stack where Directional Formatting Codes are pushed as they are encountered.

An easy way to embed right to left text within, say, English text, is to enclose the text between an RLE code and a PDF code:

```
eeeee eeeee eeeee RLE RIGHT-TO-LEFT-TEXT PDF eeeee eeeeee eee eee
```

1051

There are some other **implicit** formatting codes – implicit in the sense that they do not result in the creation of a directional boundary. This will be clear with the help of a simple example.

For the purposes of this example, assume that all characters shown in UPPER CASE are in the Arabic script.

Suppose that a word processor stores a sentence in the logical order, typed in as follows:

```
"WELCOME TO THE DESERT!", said the camel, in Arabic, to the world.
```

In the absence of any formatting codes, implicit bidi re-ordering would render it thus:

"TRESED EHT OT EMOCLEW!", said the camel, in Arabic, to the world.

Note that the exclamation mark was not treated as a part of the Arabic sentence. To rectify this, the word processor could have stored it within an explicitly created directional boundary as follows:

```
"<RLE>WELCOME TO THE DESERT!<PDF>", said the camel, in Arabic, to the world.
```

This would have been rendered as we wanted it:

"!TRESED EHT OT EMOCLEW", said the camel, in Arabic, to the world.

Now, the creation of an explicit directional boundary (and the stack pushing and popping that goes with it) could have been avoided by adding an implicit formatting code (RLM – right to left directional mark) after the exclamation mark. Then the sentence is stored as follows:

```
"WELCOME TO THE DESERT!<RLM>", said the camel, in Arabic, to the world.
```

This would also have been rendered as desired:

"!TRESED EHT OT EMOCLEW", said the camel, in Arabic, to the world.

Every Unicode character has been assigned a **Bi-directional Character Type** that determines one or more of the following:

❑ How it is to be rendered (directly important in the absence of any explicit directional formatting codes).

❑ If its directional properties are affected by that of the adjacent characters (in other words if they belong to the weaker bidi character types). Examples include plus sign, minus sign, degree, currency symbols, colon, comma, full stop, numerals, and so on.

❑ Whether it has anything to do with direction or not – if it is a **neutral character**. Examples include paragraph separator, tab, line separator, form feed, general punctuation, space, and so on.

There are various **embedding levels** that specify how deeply the associated text has been embedded. For example, consider the following sentence:

```
This sentence in Latin script has a "QUOTE IN ARABIC SCRIPT" embedded within it.
```

The text outside the quotes has an embedding level of 0, whereas the text within the quotes (shown in ALL CAPITALS and assumed to be in the Arabic script) has an embedding level of 1.

Each level has a default direction called the **embedding direction**. This direction is L (left to right) if the level number is even and R (right to left) if the level number is odd.

Every paragraph has a default embedding level, and thus a default direction associated with it. This is also called the **base direction** of the paragraph. For example:

```
A paragraph with a beginning like this in the Latin script would have a default
embedding level as Level 0, and hence its base direction would be left to right.
```

What the bidi Algorithm Does

The bidi algorithm uses all these formatting codes and embedding levels for analyzing text to decide how it should be rendered. Here is briefly how it goes about doing it:

- ❏ It breaks up the text into paragraphs by locating the paragraph separators. This is necessary because all the directional formatting codes are only effective within a paragraph. Furthermore this is where the base direction is set. The rest of the algorithm treats the text on a paragraph-by-paragraph basis.

- ❏ The directional character types and the explicit formatting codes are used to resolve all the levels of embedding in the text.

- ❏ The text is then broken up into lines, and the characters are re-ordered on a line-by-line basis for rendering on the screen.

Perl and bidi

Since Perl is a language frequently used for text processing, it is natural that Perl should have bidi capabilities. We have an implementation of the bidi algorithm on Linux that can be used by Perl.

We require a C library named **FriBidi**, which is basically a free implementation of the bidi algorithm, written by Dov Grobgeld. A Perl module has also been written by the same author, acting as an interface to the C library and is available as FriBidi-0.03.tar.gz from http://imagic.weizmann.ac.il/~dov/freesw/FriBidi.

The FriBidi module enables us to do the following:

- ❏ Convert an ISO 8859-8 string to a FriBidi Unicode string:

    ```
    iso8859_8_to_unicode($string);
    ```

- ❏ Perform a logical to visual transformation. In other words, run the string obtained above through the bidi algorithm:

    ```
    log2vis($UniString, $optionalBaseDirection);
    ```

    This calculates the base direction if not passed as the second argument, returns the re-ordered string in scalar context, and additionally returns the base direction as the second element of the list in an array context.

❑ Convert the string obtained above to an ISO 8859-8 character set:

```
unicode_to_iso8859_8($toDisplay);
```

This makes sure that it is in a 'ready-to-display' format, assuming the terminal can display ISO 8859-8 characters (such as xterm).

❑ Translate a string from a FriBidi Unicode string to capRTL and vice versa:

```
caprtl_to_unicode($capRTLString);
```

```
unicode_to_caprtl($fribidiString);
```

The capRTL format is where the CAPITAL LETTERS are mapped as having a strong **right to** left character property (**RTL**). This format is frequently used for illustrating bidi properties on displays with limited ability, such as ASCII-only displays.

The following is a small example to demonstrate FriBidi's capabilities.

First, we create a small file with the following text, named bidisample:

THUS, SAID THE CAMEL TO THE MEN, "...there is more than one way to do it."
AND THE MEN REPLIED "...now we see what you mean by bidi",
RISING WITH CONTENTMENT WRIT ON THEIR FACES.

This is the code to render the above file in bidi fashion:

```perl
#!/usr/bin/perl
# bidirender.pl
use warnings;
use strict;

use FriBidi;

my ($uniStr, $visStr, $outStr);

open (BIDISAMPLE,"bidisample");
while(<BIDISAMPLE>){
    chop;   # remove line separator
    $uniStr = caprtl_to_unicode ( $_ );   # convert line to FriBidi string
    $visStr = log2vis ( $uniStr );   # run it through the bidi algorithm
    $outStr = unicode_to_caprtl ( $visStr );   # convert it back to format
                                               # that can be displayed on
                                               # usual ASCII terminal
print $outStr,"\n";
}
```

> **perl bidirender.pl**
"theres more than one way to do it..." ,NEM EHT OT LEMAC EHT DIAS SUHT
,"now we see what you mean by bidi..." DEILPER NEM EHT DNA
.SECAF RIEHT NO TIRW TNEMTNETNOC HTIW GNISIR

Perl, I18n and Unicode

Now let us take a brief look at a solution to the problem of language barriers. A more extensive view of internationalization can be found in Chapter 26. Unicode helps us out in this matter, by providing a uniform way of representing all possible characters of all the living languages in this world.

We are about to see how easy it is to enable people all over the world to understand what we are saying in their own language. This example may be tried out by anyone with a day or two of Perl experience. Although it is in no way complete, with no error checking and pretense of handling any real-world complexity, it demonstrates the ease with which Perl handles Unicode. Let us imagine the following scenario:

An airport wants to have information kiosks at various locations outside the arrival lounge for foreign tourists. They need the information to be displayed in Arabic, Japanese, Russian, Greek, English, Spanish, Portuguese, and a whole host of other languages. They would like the kiosks to enable the user to view information about the city, events, weather, flight schedule, sight-seeing tours, and also be able to make and confirm reservations in affiliated hotels.

Our task here is obviously to create a Perl program that is able to handle Unicode and, therefore, to an extent, solve this problem. The first thing we need to do is create a template HTML file containing a few HTML tags, but with the text replaced by text 'markers' – M1, M2, M3, and so on. We one file for each language, in the following format (obviously, all the files should contain Unicode text encoded in UTF-8):

```
M1:charset "string corresponding to charset"
M2:title "string corresponding to title"
M3:heading "string corresponding to heading"
M4:text "text string"
```

To put the task in another way, we need to write a program that takes in the language name as the input and accordingly generates a file called `outfile.html` by filling in the template file with the strings in the language requested. The outputted file should be UTF-8 encoded Unicode.

This involves a few things such as installing Unicode fonts, installing a Unicode editor, creating template HTML files, writing scripts, and so on. Let us look at these step-by-step.

Installing Unicode Fonts

For UNIX with the X Window System and Netscape Navigator, information regarding Unicode fonts for X11 in general can be found on http://www.cl.cam.ac.uk/~mgk25/ucs-fonts.html. The latest version of the UCS fonts package is available from http://www.cl.cam.ac.uk/~mgk25/download/ucs-fonts.tar.gz.

For Windows with IE 5.5, Unicode fonts can be selected during installation or can be downloaded from http://www.microsoft.com/typography/multilang/default.htm. Another good place for links to fonts is http://www.ccss.de/slovo/unifonts.htm.

Installing a Unicode Editor

For UNIX with the X Window System **Yudit** is a good choice of an editor that supports UTF-8. Available from http://www.yudit.org/.

For Windows 95 and 98 Sharmahd Computing's **UniPad** is a good editor, available from http://www.sharmahd.com/unipad/. For Windows NT and 2000, **Notepad** is able to handle Unicode.

Creating the HTML Template

Now we can go about creating the template HTML files and the string resource files. The next script is simply an HTML template, called `templateLeft.html` that we will use with our program:

```
<html>
<head>
<meta http-equiv="Content-Type" Content="text/html" Charset=M1:charset>
<title>M2:title</title>
</head>
<body>
<h1>M3:heading</h1><hr>
<p>M4:text</p>
</body>
</html>
```

Note that this is intuitively correct for languages written from left to right but for languages written the other way, we need a modified template to follow suit. So for languages such as Arabic, we can simply right-justify the displayed text using the ALIGN attribute and setting its value to RIGHT. This should be done for all text in the body of the document to be displayed in the correct direction, that is from right to left. This is the template `templateRight.html` that we will use with right-to-left languages:

```
<html>
<head>
<meta http-equiv="Content-Type" Content="text/html" Charset=M1:charset>
<title>M2:title</title>
</head>
<body>
<h1 ALIGN=RIGHT>M3:heading</h1><hr>
<p ALIGN=RIGHT>M4:text</p>
</body>
</html>
```

This next image is the sample string resource file for the English language using UniPad:

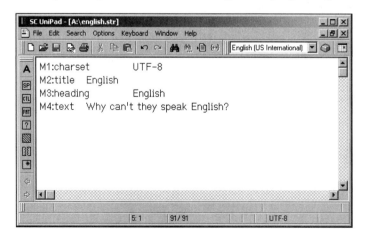

The following image is a screenshot of a sample string file for the Arabic language. Note the rendering of Arabic text from left to right:

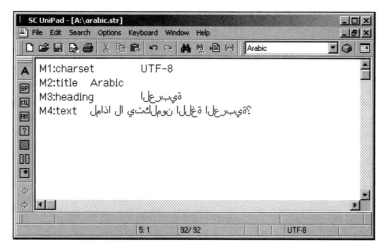

Processing the Resource Files

The fourth stage in our solution to the problem is creating the Perl script. This script will process the resource files it is given and generate the localized pages:

```perl
#!/usr/bin/perl
# Xlate.pl
use warnings;
use strict;

my ($langname,$filename, $marker, $mark, $value, $wholefile, $thisval, $template,
%valueof);

print "Enter the language for the output html file: \n";
$langname = lc<>;    # get language name and turn it into lowecase
chomp $langname;

$filename = $langname . ".str";    # generate filename from language name
open(LANGFILE, "$filename");

#read in the markers & values in a hash
while(<LANGFILE>) {
    chomp($_);
    ($marker, $value) = split("\t", $_);
    $valueof{$marker} = $value;
}
close(LANGFILE);
# use the correct template
if ($langname =~ /arabic|hebrew/) {
$template = 'templateRight.html';
} else {$template = 'templateLeft.html'}

open(TMPLT,$template);
open(OUTFILE, ">$langname.html");

$wholefile=join('', <TMPLT>);    # slurp entire file into a string
```

```
close TMPLT;

foreach $mark (keys %valueof) {
    $thisval = $valueof{$mark};    # get the value related to the marker
    $wholefile =~ s/$mark/$thisval/g;    # do the replacement
}

print OUTFILE $wholefile;    # write out complete langname.html file
print "output written to $langname.html \n";
close OUTFILE;
```

This is the big surprise – the script looks too simple. In fact, no extra processing is required to handle Unicode.

Running the Script

Now we can execute the code in the usual way and provide the language required:

> **perl Xlate.pl**
Enter the language for the output html file:
english
output written to english.html
> **perl Xlate.pl**
Enter the language for the output html file:
arabic
output written to arabic.html

The Output Files

After running the script and having it produce the *.html files, we can open them in a browser and see what has been written.

The following is a screenshot of the english.html file generated by the script:

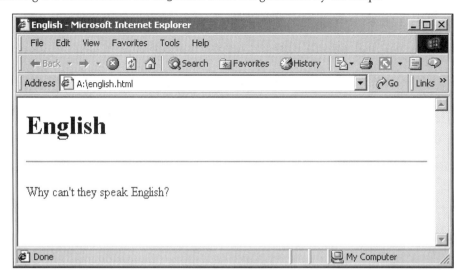

Next, is the `arabic.html` file generated by the script. Note the direction of Arabic script as rendered by the browser:

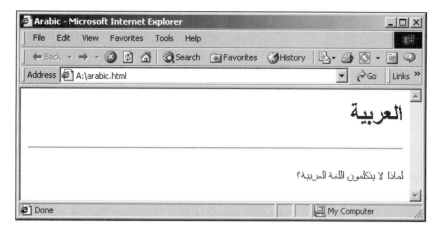

There are more examples of the same phrase written in different languages at http://www.trigeminal.com/samples/provincial.html, thanks to Michael Kaplan. A few more such sites are http://www.columbia.edu/kermit/utf8.html (hosted by the Kermit Project), http://www.unicode.org/unicode/standard/WhatIsUnicode.html (hosted by the Unicode Consortium) and http://hcs.harvard.edu/~igp/glass.html (hosted by the IGP).

This simple method of replacing text markers is still widely used. However, localizing a large web site takes much more than just being able to handle Unicode strings. Things such as cultural preferences, date format, currency (which are covered in Chapter 26) need to be taken into consideration. This means we should probably turn to using methods such as HTML::Template, HTML::Mason, HTML::Embperl or maybe something like XML::Parser in order to create an industrial strength multilingual site.

Work in Progress

There are still a few things about Unicode support in Perl that are under development. For instance, it is not possible right now to determine if an arbitrary piece of data is UTF-8 encoded or not. We cannot force the encoding to be used when performing I/O to anything other than UTF-8, and will have a problem if the pattern during a match does not contain Unicode, but the string to be matched at runtime does. Also the use utf8 pragma is on its way out. In order to follow the current state of Unicode support in Perl, one can join the Perl-unicode mailing list by sending a blank message to majordomo@perl.org with a subject line saying subscribe perl-unicode.

Summary

All said and done, we should not need to worry ourselves about the support of Unicode within Perl unless we really have to. All code we create will work just as well as it did before Unicode support came on the scene. So we only need to use it when dealing with foreign scripts for example, but more on using Perl around the world in Chapter 26.

In this chapter we have looked at the details concerning the use of Perl with non-standard characters such as symbols or some foreign writings. We began with the problems we face as Perl is used across the globe and then we looked at what can be done to provide solutions. As a summary, we have:

❑   Seen how people have tackled the issue of providing an international coding system.

❑   Looked at how Unicode can be used in regular expressions and tried our hand at writing our own character property.

❑   Demonstrated how Perl can be used to deal with texts in languages that are written from right to left as opposed to left to right such as English.

❑   Provided a real world example of how we can deal with language barriers across the world.

26

Locale and Internationalization

Not everybody understands English, and not everybody expresses dates in the standard US format for example, 2/20/01. Instead, people worldwide speak hundreds of different languages and express themselves in almost as many alphabets. Furthermore, even if they do speak the same language, they may have different ways of expressing dates, times, and so on. This chapter aims to provide us with the tools to write Perl programs in many different languages, and to see the kinds of problems we may encounter along the way.

We will take a look at the kinds of ways we can develop a multilingual application in Perl, be it for a web site or for something entirely different. Going multilingual does not only mean expressing messages in different languages, but also adapting the minor details of our site, for instance, to obey the conventions of other cultures. To use the example mentioned above, it means that we must change the presentation of a date or time. Catering for other languages will always be a good thing to do, attracting more visitors to our website.

As an example, we may be surprised with the results if we translated a personal home page from Spanish into German. Its popularity and number of hits would rise rapidly, and visitors will be especially surprised at how the page may be instantly translated into German – if someone in Germany accessed it. The same goes for all multilingual websites: the site does its best to guess the country of origin of the user, and show messages accordingly. For instance, if we connect to Google from a Spanish domain (.es), for example melmac.ugr.es we will immediately get the URL http://www.google.com/intl/es/, which is in Spanish. This is a neat trick that deduces the location from the **T**op-**L**evel **D**omain (**TLD**) of our machine, and it will score points with the Spanish-speaking population.

However, **localization** is not as easy as showing two different pages depending on where the client comes from. It is also a matter of knowing the language that the user, or more correctly, the user's application's client, is immersed in. The site will then show information in such a way that the client, and therefore the user, can understand it. For example, a quantity such as 3'5 will not mean much to an English person, but it means 3.5 to a Spaniard. The application must be aware of its cultural 'location', and act accordingly.

If we live in a country whose native language is not English, undergoing this process is a must. We will need to use it for undertaking tasks as simple as alphabetical sorting, showing quantities, or matching regular expressions. Our program will not work correctly, at least from the point of view of the user, if we do not use the right **locale** settings.

The good news is that many people have already thought about this problem in depth. There are several frameworks that make writing multilingual and localized applications easier. It will come as even better news to readers of this book, that Perl has excellent support for this, as we shall soon see.

In this chapter, we will see several ways of creating Perl applications for a multilingual environment, from simple tricks such as storing messages in different languages, and sorting according to local uses, to recognizing a foreign language or conjugating foreign verbs. At this early stage it is important to note that most of the programs presented in this chapter will not work in non-POSIX machines, including Win9x, and Macs.

Why Go Locale?

Suppose we want to create a Spanish web site to show the number of firms investing in a particular venture. Users should be able to access the site and find out the names of the primary investors, and the site should be designed accordingly. One basic hurdle to overcome would be the need to show a list of those firms in alphabetical order.

First, we need to create a plain text file in which we can list the firms. Note that these are in no alphabetical order. We call this file `firms.txt`:

```
Chilindrina
Ántico
Cflab.org
Cantamornings
Cántaliping
Andalia
Zinzun.com
```

We can use a simple Perl command line that prints a sorted list on the screen (note that on Windows the special characters are not displayed properly):

> **perl -e 'print sort <>;' firms.txt**
Andalia
Cantamornings
Cflab.org
Chilindrina
Cántaliping
Zinzun.com
Ántico

This is not ideal though. In Spanish, 'Ch' is used as a stand-alone letter, coming after 'C' in the alphabet (although admittedly, this is slowly being phased out). The letters 'A' and 'Á' are in fact the same, the only difference being that the latter has an acute accent, so they should go together. To help solve this problem, we can find a useful tutorial included with Perl itself, by typing:

> **perldoc perllocale**

This should tell us most of what we need to know about `locale`, a method that most versions of UNIX use for taking alphabets and time/date expressions into account .

Once we are happy with the basic principles and concepts, we can leave the reading for later on, and just add a simple part to our command line. When applied to the same file, and when issued from a computer with the Spanish locale installed, we can expect something like the following output:

> perl -e 'use locale; print sort <>;' firms.txt
```
Andalia
Ántico
Cántaliping
Cantamornings
Cflab.org
Chilindrina
Zinzun.com
```

There is a great likelihood that something slightly different will be displayed on our computer (if it uses Linux or another strain of UNIX), but this will allow us to gauge differences between English, Spanish, and whatever locale sorting we have. In any case, this is not completely correct even for the Spanish traditional sorting, although it is an improvement on the last attempt. The 'ch' was still not considered to be a different letter, but at least accented vowels were not alphabetized as different characters from their unaccented counterparts. The bad ordering of the 'ch' could be a bug in the locale implementation of our system (or maybe a bug in our understanding of the local alphabetization rules, as we will see later on). It could be improved for other Spanish locale implementations, so in order to fix it, we have to delve a little deeper into what locale actually means.

The locale framework is concurrent with the phrase 'When in Rome, do as the Romans do' – computers have to use the local alphabet and local numbers. This is the reason why localization was included into the POSIX standard, (that is, the set of functions and files that should be understood by all UNIX platforms). There are some non-UNIX platforms, such as Windows NT (which has a slightly flawed implementation of the POSIX standard) which can use the locale set of functions, also known as NLS (for **N**ational **L**anguage **S**upport). If one arrives at Perl from the C field, all functions, constants etc. related to locale are in the `locale.h` header file.

This header distributes localization elements into several categories:

LC_COLLATE	Collation or sorting.
LC_CTYPES	Character types, distinguishing whether a character is alphanumeric or not.
LC_MONETARY	Handling monetary amounts.
LC_TIME	Displaying time.
LC_MESSAGES	Messages, not used in Perl by default.

There are a few more categories that are not so widely used, whose names should give away their meanings: LC_PAPER, LC_NAME, LC_ADDRESS, and LC_MEASUREMENT, LC_IDENTIFICATION.

These constants can be used as environment variables, or else using the POSIX setlocale function. This means we have to use POSIX to have them available in our program. Going back to our problem regarding the alphabet of the Spanish language, we can locate a locale definition on the Internet, which effectively includes the traditional sorting, that is, 'ch' after 'c'. One place in which such a locale definition can be found, amongst many others, is under the name locales-es-2.1-1mdk.noarch.rpm, at http://www.ping.be/linux/locales/.

We can install it by issuing the following command:

> **rpm -Uvhf locales-es-2.1-1mdk.noarch.rpm**

The **f** option is needed since one of the files, LC_COLLATE, conflicts with the existing settings; the file was renamed and then moved back to its original value, (we need to do this, or the locale settings will not work properly in Spanish). One of the locales included in that package is es@tradicional. This should sort the 'ch' in the traditional way. However, this implementation does not work very well, as we will see.

There is a more complete list of locales for Linux available from IBM DeveloperWorks, at http://oss.software.ibm.com/developerworks/opensource/locale/download.html.

This includes locales such as **Maltese**, which will be required later. These locales are still in beta stages, and thus look set to change considerably in the future.

After installing the package, we can create the following short script:

```
#!/usr/bin/perl
# sort.pl
use warnings;
use strict;

use POSIX qw(LC_COLLATE setlocale strcoll);

setlocale(LC_COLLATE, 'es_US');
print sort {strcoll($a, $b);} <>;
```

When we run this program we will obtain the following output:

> **perl sort.pl firms.txt**
Andalia
Ántico
Cántaliping
Cantamornings
Cflab.org
Chilindrina
Zinzun.com

Before we continue, this program probably needs a bit of explanation. Instead of using the use locale pragma, it relies on POSIX calls to do sorting correctly. By default, locale uses the locale settings contained in the LC_* UNIX environment variables. However, in this case we want to be able to change locale in runtime. The POSIX setlocale function allows us to do this; we take the locale category we want to change as the first argument. We then take the locale we want to change it to as the second argument. It must be a valid locale, that is, it must correspond to a file already installed on our system. If it works correctly, it returns the name of the locale it has been set to; in this case, es_US. The reason for using this locale is that, for some strange reason, it seems to be the only one to use the 'traditional' Spanish ordering.

The problem with setting locales using this function (instead of the pragma), is that despite what is said in the `perllocale` documentation, the Perl functions `cmp` and `sort` do not use it by default. For this reason we need to use an alternative form of `sort`, `sort {expr}`, and the `POSIX` function `strcoll`, which compares (or collates, hence the name) using the setting specified in the `setlocale` call.

Delving Deeper into Local Culture

Now, suppose we have a scenario where a user views the site and wants to add another firm to the list of investors. Using the current code, they would have to undertake this process in Spanish, therefore eliminating the likelihood of nonSpanish speaking firms investing through the site. At first this may seem a difficult task because it is impossible to find out where the user is from, since Spanish autonomous regions do not have their own top level domains. It would however, be possible if there was only one user in each region responsible for liaising through our web site.

So, how can we use those different locales? To start with, we need to find the way locales are called. Locales usually have three, sometimes four parts, written in the following way: `xx_YY.charset@dialect`. Breaking this down would perhaps make it easier to understand.

- ❏   xx represents the language.
- ❏   YY represents the country.
- ❏   `charset` is the character set, such as `ISO8859-15` (for Latin languages) or `KOI8` (for Russian).
- ❏   `@dialect` is a particular modality, for instance, a dialectal variety, such as `no@nynorsk` in Norwegian. It also represents special symbols such as `ca_ES@euro` (which is a variant of the `ca_ES` locale including the euro symbol).

Following this form, a typical Spanish locale would be `es_ES.iso885915`, or `es_ES@euro`, which can be found in any of the above-mentioned web sites if they are not already installed in the system. On the same page we can find locales for Basque, Catalan and Galician – the three other official languages in Spain.

Getting back to the example, we decide to greet the visitors to our site in their own language and show them the local time (of our site) using the format favored by them. The site will then show them how much money each company has invested. In order to do this, we start by creating a new plain text file called `firms_money.txt`:

```
Ántico 1000000
Chilindrina 2000.35
Cflab.org 123456.7
Cantamornings 6669876
Cántaliping 46168.5
Andalia 4567987
Zinzun.com 33445
```

We also need to remember that a Spanish language web site can be accessed from all over the world, and that there are large Spanish-speaking populations in South America, Central America, and North America. This adds an extra issue; different countries will more than likely have different currencies. Not everyone would understand the value of a given number of Pesetas offhand, and users may want to use the site to find out the amount of money invested in their own currency. A more general solution would be considering the names of the people connecting to our site from different parts of the world.

```perl
#!/usr/bin/perl
# invest.pl
use warnings;
use strict;

use Finance::Quote;
use POSIX qw (localeconv setlocale LC_ALL LC_CTYPE strftime strcoll);

my %clientMap = (
    'Jordi' => ['ca_ES', 'Hola', "aquí está el teu inform per"],
    'Patxi' => ['eu_ES', 'Kaixo', "egunkaria hemen hire"],
    'Miguelanxo' => ['gl_ES', 'Olá', "aquí está o seu relatório pra"],
    'Orlando' => ['es_AR', 'Holá', "aquí está tu informe para"],
    'Arnaldo' => ['es_CO', 'Holá', "aquí está tu informe para"],
    'Joe', ['en_US', 'Hi', "here's your report for"]
);
```

This script takes as its arguments the name of the client, and the name of the file that contains the firm and amount of money invested. In our case, our file is firms_money.txt.

```perl
# Firm Quantity
die "Usage: $0 <clientName> <fileName>\n" if $#ARGV <1;
my ($clientName,$fileName) = @ARGV;
# default
my ($locale, $hello, $notice) = ('es_ES', 'Hola',
'aquí está tu informe para');


if ($clientMap{$clientName}) {
    ($locale, $hello, $notice) = @{$clientMap{$clientName}};
}

setlocale(LC_ALL, $locale);   # use settings
```

Arguments are read in the lines above, and locales assigned. The default value in Spain is (somewhat unsurprisingly) Spanish. If the name of the client given as the first argument in the command line is a key in clientMap, the values are assigned to the three variables that represent the locale name, the hello message, and the message to be given as an introduction. The locale name is then used in the setlocale function to assign that value to all categories.

```perl
my %investments;
open(F, "<$fileName");   # open file and process it
while (<F>) {
    chop;
    my ($firm, $invest) = split;
    $investments{$firm} = $invest;
}
close F;
```

The file has been read, and entered into the %investments hash, keyed by the name of the firm.

```perl
# obtain time info
my ($sec, $min, $hour, $mday, $mon, $year, $wday) = localtime (time);
print "$hello $clientName, $notice ",
strftime("%c", $sec, $min, $hour, $mday, $mon, $year, $wday), "\n";
```

Currency conversion is used in the lines below. The objective of these lines is to show how information about the local international currency name and symbol is also contained in the `locale` settings; they are retrieved using the `localeconv` POSIX function. This function returns a hash reference, but we only use the keys `int_curr_symbol`, which references the three letter international name of the currency, such as USD (for US dollars) and ESP (Spanish pesetas), and `currency_symbol`. The `currency_symbol` references the symbol of such currency, such as $ for the US dollar (amongst others), and £ for the British pound.

```
#Set up currency conversion
my $q = Finance::Quote->new;

$q->timeout(60);
my $lconv = localeconv(); chop($lconv->{int_curr_symbol});
my $conversion_rate=$q->currency("ESP",$lconv->{int_curr_symbol}) || 1.0;

for (sort {strcoll($a,$b);} keys %investments) {
    printf
    ("%s %.2f ESP %.2f %s %s \n",
    $_, $investments{$_},
    $investments{$_}*$conversion_rate,
    $lconv->{int_curr_symbol},
    $lconv->{currency_symbol}
    );
}
```

Now, we can use the script and obtain output such as the following. Of course the exact output will depend on the country we are in, the date, time, currency rates, etc.

> **perl invest.pl Arnaldo firms_money.txt**
Holá Arnaldo, aquí está tu informe para 13 dic 2000 14:56:22 CET
Andalia 4567987.00 ESP 52530160.34 USD $
Ántico 1000000.00 ESP 11499630.00 USD $
Cántaliping 46168.50 ESP 530920.67 USD $
Cantamornings 6669876.00 ESP 76701106.15 USD $
Chilindrina 2000.35 ESP 23003.28 USD $
Cflab.org 123456.70 ESP 1419706.37 USD $
Zinzun.com 33445.00 ESP 384605.13 USD $

> **perl invest.pl Patxi firms_money.txt**
Kaixo Patxi, egunkaria hemen hire 00-12-13 14:57:38 CET
Andalia 4567987.00 ESP 4567987.00 ESP Pts
Ántico 1000000.00 ESP 1000000.00 ESP Pts
Cántaliping 46168.50 ESP 46168.50 ESP Pts
Cantamornings 6669876.00 ESP 6669876.00 ESP Pts
Chilindrina 2000.35 ESP 2000.35 ESP Pts
Cflab.org 123456.70 ESP 123456.70 ESP Pts
Zinzun.com 33445.00 ESP 33445.00 ESP Pts

> **perl invest.pl Orlando firms_money.txt**
Holá Orlando, aquí está tu informe para 13 dic 2000 14:57:59 CET
Andalia 4567987.00 ESP 23995.27 USD $
Ántico 1000000.00 ESP 5252.92 USD $
Cántaliping 46168.50 ESP 242.52 USD $
Cantamornings 6669876.00 ESP 35036.33 USD $
Chilindrina 2000.35 ESP 10.51 USD $
Cflab.org 123456.70 ESP 648.51 USD $
Zinzun.com 33445.00 ESP 175.68 USD $

> **perl invest.pl Joe firms_money.txt**
Hi Joe, here's your report for Wed 13 Dec 2000 02:59:49 PM CET
Andalia 4567987.00 ESP 24019.30 USD $
Cantamornings 6669876.00 ESP 35071.41 USD $
Chilindrina 2000.35 ESP 10.52 USD $
Cflab.org 123456.70 ESP 649.16 USD $
Cántaliping 46168.50 ESP 242.76 USD $
Zinzun.com 33445.00 ESP 175.86 USD $
Ántico 1000000.00 ESP 5258.18 USD $

Barring bugs such as the alphabetic ordering in Basque (whose alphabet does not include the letter 'c', and thus, no word starting with 'c' can possibly go before 'd') and the dancing of the 'ch' from one place to another, this should look like something native speakers would feel comfortable with.

First thing we put into this program is the Finance::Quote module (available from CPAN). The main use of this module is for stock quotes, but it is basically a front end for doing searches over the Yahoo Finance servers. This also means that we must be on-line to take advantage of it. Each time we try to get a currency conversion rate, it is forwarded to a UserAgent. This requests the rate from Yahoo, manipulates it, and gives it back to us. It might also take a while, depending on the speed of the connection, and it could result in some additional errors, depending on the state of the Yahoo site. The program would work perfectly without this currency conversion, but the point of including it here is to show another aspect of localization: local currencies.

The subsequent lines create a hash of arrays with the (theoretically unique) names of the customers, and set a different locale, currency, and greeting, with respect to the local language. If the name given is none of the above, it defaults to the es_ES locale and greetings. From that line on, the following action takes place: locale is set, file is read, and system time is read and converted to local time. The strftime function is used; this function formats time into a string using different options; in this case, %c instructs it to use the preferred date format for the local settings. This format will even translate weekday names, in addition to putting date and time in the local favorite arrangement. For instance, Americans prefer 12-hour clocks plus AM/PM, while many Europeans opt for 24 hour clocks.

A Finance::Quote object is then created, setting the timeout, so that it will only wait 60 seconds for the answer. The object is used in the next line, where it is asked for the conversion rate between the Spanish peseta (ESP) and local currency. If the quantities in the file were in euros, we could have used the es_ES@euro locale instead, and conversions would have been made from euros instead of from pesetas.

Finally, the hash containing the firm names and investment is printed in three columns: name, investment in pesetas, and investment translated into the local currency. It should be noted, however, that the period (.) is used as separator for decimals in English speaking countries, whilst the comma is used in Latin countries.

We could even mix and match several settings; for instance, in the case of our friend, Alberto, who lives in Miami, we would have used en_US, for currency and numbers, and es_MX (for México), or es_CU (Cuba) for sorting:

```
setlocale(LC_COLLATE, 'es_MX');
setlocale(LC_NUMERIC, 'en_US');
setlocale(LC_MONETARY, 'en_US');
setlocale(LC_TIME, 'en_US');
```

We will probably be better off using the es_US locale, which can be downloaded from one of the above mentioned pages, if not already on the system.

However, there are several things that may cause problems. Every time a new language shows up, we will have to go back to the original code, grok what was there, and modify it a little. What would happen, if all of a sudden the user needed another phrase? would they have to modify the whole hash table they had created from scratch? This is why we start to look for something better: a whole framework for internationalization of programs. The idea would be to have a way to store program messages in several languages, and retrieve them using a key, preferably the short version of the message. In reality there are two of them:

❑ gettext – a GNU standard tool for internationalization. It is widely used by many GNU applications. The current version at the time of writing is 0.10.35. It is directly available from http://www.gnu.org/software/gettext/gettext.html and is supported by several tools, and an EMACS mode. For more information regarding this subject, refer to a book such as **Professional Linux Programming** from Wrox Press, *ISBN 1861003013*.

❑ Locale::Maketext – a complete and purely Perl based solution. At the time of writing the latest version is 0.18. The documentation (available by typing **> Perldoc Locale::Maketext**, after installation) includes a synopsis. It is important to note that at present, Locale::Maketext is still in its early stages.

For the purposes of our site, we have decided upon gettext, since it has very good support in Perl. The first thing we have to do is to create a so-called **Portable Object** (PO) file, which contains the necessary information to translate messages. The main elements of PO files are the keywords msgid and msgstr, which contain the plain (in this case, Spanish) and translated string, respectively. A file can just be created using a text editor (or EMACS + PO mode) in this form:

```
msgid "Hola"
msgstr "Olá"
```

A set of these messages in a file, along with other information such as comments, and context, is called a **catalogue**, and corresponds to a **domain**, which is usually a language. For instance, the file above could be saved as CA.po, for the Catalan language.

There are also a couple of editors we can use to edit PO files. **POedit**, which is available from http://www.volny.cz/v.slavik/poedit/, has a simple to use interface based on the GTK library. As an alternative, if we favor the desktop environment, **KBabel** is available as a part of the KDE software development kit, which can be obtained from http://www.kde.org. For the time being, we opt for the Perl way, and choose to use Locale::PO, an object oriented class for creating PO files. The following program is written using this module:

```
#!/usr/bin/perl
# pocreate.pl
use warnings;
use strict;

use Locale::PO;

my $i;
```

```
my %hash = (
    "EN" => ['Hello', "here's your report for"],
    "EU" => ['Kaixo', "egunkaria hemen hire"],
    "CA" => ['Hola', "aquí está el teu inform per"],
    "GA" => ['Olá', "aquí está o seu relatório pra"],
    "FR" => ['Salut', "voici votre raport pour"],
    "DE" => ['Hallo', "ist hier ihr Report für"],
    "IT" => ['Ciao', "qui è il vostro rapporto per"]
);

my @orig = ("Hola", "aquí está tu informe para");
```

For each element in this hash, a PO file is created. This file receives a reference to an array of Locale::PO objects, which features as main elements' a msgid, containing the key to the message, and a msgstr, the translation of the message to the language represented in the file.

After saving the file using the Locale::PO->save_file_fromarray function, it is converted to an internal format using the MsgFormat command. We are using the Spanish equivalent as keys, but any other language, such as English, can be used. Theoretically, these are the files that should be handled by the team of translators in charge of localizing a program.

```
for (keys %hash) {
    my @po;
    for ($i = 0; $i <= $#orig; $i++) {
        $po[$i] = new Locale::PO();
        $po[$i]->msgid($orig[$i]);
        $po[$i]->msgstr($hash{$_}->[$i]);
    }
    Locale::PO->save_file_fromarray("$_.po",\@po);
    `MsgFormat . $_ < $_.po`;
}
```

Running this program produces files similar to the following CA.po (for the Catalan language):

```
msgid "Hola"
msgstr "Hola"


msgid "aquí está tu informe para"
msgstr "aquí está el teu inform per"
```

These files can be used by any program compliant with gettext (that is, any program that uses the libgettext library). In the case of Perl, there are two modules that use them: Locale::PGetText and Locale::gettext. The main difference between them is that the first is a pure Perl implementation of gettext, using its own machine readable file formats, while the second needs to have gettext installed. In both cases, .po files have to be compiled to a machine readable file. We will opt for the first, but both are perfectly valid. Indeed, a program that belongs to the Locale::PGetText module is called in the following line of the above code:

```
MsgFormat . $_ < $_.po;
```

The following program produces a database file, which can then be read by Locale::PGetText. The implementation of this module is reduced to a few lines; it merely reads the DB file and ties it to a hash. The hash is accessed using a couple of functions, shown in the following example, which is an elaboration of the previous invest.pl program:

```perl
#!/usr/bin/perl
# pouse.pl
use warnings;
use strict;

use Finance::Quote;
use POSIX qw(localeconv setlocale LC_ALL LC_CTYPE strftime strcoll);
use Locale::PGetText;    # this is new

# in this case only the locale is needed, the rest is stored in PO files
my %clientMap = (
    'Jordi' => 'ca_ES',
    'Patxi' => 'eu_ES',
    'Miguelanxo' => 'gl_ES',
    'Orlando' => 'es_AR',
    'Arnaldo' => 'es_CO',
    'Joe' => 'en_US'
);

die "Usage: $0 <clientName> <fileName> \n" if $#ARGV <1;
my ($clientName,$fileName) = @ARGV;
my $locale = $clientMap{$clientName} || 'es_ES';
setlocale(LC_ALL, $locale);    # use settings

my %investments;
open(F,"<$fileName");    # open file and process it
while (<F>) {
    chop;
    my ($firm, $invest) = split;
    $investments{$firm} = $invest;
}
close F;
```

Local messages are retrieved from the PO files using functions from the Locale::PGetText module. The directory where the files are located, is first set with setLocaleDir and then the corresponding file is loaded.

```perl
my ($lang) = ($locale =~ /^(\w{2})/);

Locale::PGetText::setLocaleDir('/root/txt/properl');
# change to our own dir here

Locale::PGetText::setLanguage(uc($lang));
#Spanish for 'hello'
my $hello = gettext("Hola");

#Spanish for 'Here is your report for'
my $notice = gettext("Aquí está tu informe para");
```

```
#The rest is the same as invest.pl

#Set up currency conversion
my $q = Finance::Quote->new;

$q->timeout(60);
my $lconv = localeconv(); chop($lconv->{int_curr_symbol});
my $conversion_rate=$q->currency("ESP", $lconv->{int_curr_symbol}) || 1.0;
```

This will output exactly the same as the last but one example, invest.pl, with the only difference being, that in this case, we did not need to code the translated languages explicitly within the program. Adding new languages and messages is just a matter of adding the name of a person, and the locale, and the currency they use. The program will select the relevant file itself, extracting the language code from the two first letters of the locale name. In this case, the directory /root/txt/properl should be substituted for the directory in which our own .po files reside. The main change from the previous version is around the lines where Locale::PGetText functions are used: the two letter code for the language is extracted from the locale name and translated to all capitals; this code is used to set the language, using the function setLanguage. This in turn loads the corresponding database file; messages are then obtained from the DB, and used as they were in the previous example. This is not a huge improvement, but at least we can now build, bit by bit, a multilingual dictionary of words and phrases that can be used and reused in all of our applications, with a common (and simple) interface.

We soon realize that looking for an archetypal name in each place and deducing their mother tongue (and everything else) is not very efficient. Besides, it is not very efficient to have to translate every single message by hand. What is needed is a way of automating the process. For example, using the Internet to do the job.

Suppose now, that we want to go one step further and design a web site (which we will call El Escalón), enabling users all over the world to log in using their own specific username, and then to type a short report. The following program implements these ideas (note that it will not work on Windows as it uses the WWW::Babelfish module, which is only available on UNIX systems):

```perl
#!/usr/bin/perl -T
# babelfish.pl
use warnings;
use strict;

use CGI qw(:standard *table);
use Locale::Language;
use WWW::Babelfish;

print header, start_html(-bgcolor => 'white', -title => "El Escalón");
```

We find out the language from the TLD, or by using any of the other tricks contained in the grokLanguage subroutine. If nothing works, we can always query the user.

```perl
my ($TLD) = (remote_host() =~ /\.(\D+)$/);
print start_form;
my $language = grokLanguage($TLD) || print "Your language",
                textfield('language');    # English name of the language
```

We now ask the user to type in their name and report; messages are translated using the `translate` subroutine.

```
if ($language) {    # language has been set
    print start_table({bgcolor => 'lightblue', cellspacing => 0,
                      cellpadding => 5}),
        Tr(td([translate("What is your code name?", $language),
                      textfield('codename')])), "\n",
        Tr(td([translate('Type in your report', $language),
                      textfield('report')])), "\n",
        Tr(td([translate('What is your assessment of the situation', $language),
        popup_menu('situation',
            [translate('Could not be worse', $language),
             translate('Pretty good', $language),
             translate('Could be worse', $language)])])), "\n",
        end_table;
}

print p({align => 'center'}, submit()), end_form, end_html;
```

For a more fuller description of the methods supported by the `WWW::Babelfish` module, we can do the usual command:

> perldoc WWW::Babelfish

In this next subroutine, we use one of these methods to hide the call to the `WWW::Babelfish` module. The arguments it takes are the message in English, and the name of the language to which the message is going to be translated.

```
sub translate {
    my ($toTranslate, $language) = @_;
    my $tr;
    eval {
        $tr = new WWW::Babelfish();
    };

    if (!$tr) {
        print("Error connecting to babelfish: $@");
        return $toTranslate;
    }

    my $translated = $tr->translate('source' => 'English',
                                    'destination' => $language,
                                    'text' => $toTranslate );

    print $language, " ", $tr->error if $tr->error;
    $translated = $toTranslate unless defined ($translated);
    return $translated;
}
```

This subroutine tries to find out the language of the client using several tricks, which will be explained later.

```
sub grokLanguage {
    # Returns the name of the language, in English, if possible
    my $TLD = shift;
    return param('language') if (param('language'));   # try predefined
    my ($ua) = user_agent() =~ /\[(\w+)\]/ ;   # and now from the user agent
    return code2language($ua) if ($ua);
    return code2language($TLD) if (defined ($TLD));
    # Or from the top-level domain
    return;
}
```

This file is rather long, but it performs many functions. First, using the subroutine grokLanguage it tries to find out what language we speak, deducing it via the following channels (in order of precedence):

❑   The declaration of the user; for example, by calling it using something like: http://myhost/cgi-bin/babelfish.pl?language=German or http://myhost/cgi-bin/babelfish.pl?language=Spanish.

❑   The user_agent string, sent from the browser (at least, from Netscape Navigator and MS Internet Explorer) to the server, which in some cases takes this form: Mozilla/4.75 [es] (X11; U; Linux 2.2.16-22smp i686).

The [es] means it is a client compiled for the Spanish language. Not all languages are represented, and this might not be valid for browsers outside the Mozilla realm, but if this information is there, we can take advantage of it. This code is translated to a language name using code2language, which is part of the Locale::Language module.

Then it tries to deduce our language from the top-level domain of our computer. Our server receives, along with the name of the file the client requires, a wealth of information from the client. For example, it receives the host name of the computer of the client. In some cases, the host name will not be resolved, that is, converted from its numerical address, and it will only get an address of the form 154.67.33.3. From this address it would be difficult to ascertain the native language of the client in the area of the calling computor; in many other cases, generic TLDs such as .com or .net are used.

Finally, the computer is revealed as something like somecomputer.somedomain.it, which means that this calling computer is most probably in Italy. In this case we use the Perl module Locale::Language, which comes along with Locale::Country, to deduce the language from the two-letter TLD code. This is a good hunch at best, since in most countries more than one language is spoken, but at least we can use it as a fallback method if the other two fail. The code2language function in this module understands most codes, and translates them to the English name of the language that is spoken. However, there is a small caveat here: the language code need not be the same as the TLD code; for instance, UK is the top level domain for the United Kingdom, but it is the code for the Ukrainian language. However, we can expect that most English clients will be caught by one of the other methods. The right way to proceed, would be to convert TLD to country name, and then to one or several language codes or names. This is not practical, however, so we have to make do with the above method, which will work in at least some cases.

Once the language is known (or guessed), it is used to translate messages from English to several other languages (the `translate` subroutine performs this task). It uses the `WWW::Babelfish` module (available on CPAN), which is a front end to the translating site at: http://babelfish.altavista.com/. This site then takes phrases in several languages, translates them to English, and back again. All this implies two requirements:

❑   The user must be on-line; each call to translate means a call to Babelfish.

❑   The language requiring translation must be included in this list.

In summary, the program could determine which language the user is accustomed to speaking. Of course, this is not the best solution in terms of speed or completeness for a multilingual web site. If we receive more than a couple of requests an hour, we will be placing a heavy load on Babelfish, and we will have access cut down. A solution based on `gettext` can suffice for a few languages and a few messages, but it will not scale up particularly well. The best solution is to keep messages in a relational database, indexed by message key and language, and have a certified translator to do all the translation. Another possible solution in Windows (and other operating systems with shared libraries) is to use one file for each language, and load the file which best suits the language of the user during run-time.

It's About Time: Time Zones

It goes without saying that different areas of the globe fall into different time zones, and users from different countries will log in at different local times. To take this into account, we can create a Perl program to remind us of the local time. Just by inputting the name of the city and general zone we are in, our computer returns local time:

```perl
#!/usr/bin/perl
# zones.pl
use warnings;
use strict;

use Time::Zone;
use POSIX;

die "Usage = $0 City Zone \n" if $#ARGV < 1;
my ($city, $zone) = @ARGV;
$ENV{TZ} = "$zone/$city";
tzset();
```

The following `POSIX` call returns the time zone, and DST (**D**aylight **S**aving **T**ime) zone, the computer is set to:

```perl
my ($thisTZ, $thisDST) = tzname();
my $offset = tz_offset($thisTZ);
my ($sec, $min, $hour) = localtime(time + $offset);
print qq(You are in zone $thisTZ
Difference with respect to GMT is ),$offset/3600, qq( hours
And local time is $hour hours $min minutes $sec seconds
);
```

When issued with the following example commands, the program outputs something similar to:

> **perl zones.pl Cocos Indian**
You are in zone CCT
Difference with respect to GMT is 8 hours
And local time is 14 hours 34 minutes 38 seconds

> **perl zones.pl Tokyo Asia**
You are in zone JST
Difference with respect to GMT is 9 hours
And local time is 18 hours 4 minutes 42 seconds

> **perl zones.pl Tegucigalpa America**
You are in zone CST
Difference with respect to GMT is -6 hours
And local time is 12 hours 4 minutes 48 seconds

Time zone notation is hairy stuff. There are at least three ways of denoting it:

❑ Using a (normally) 3 letter code, such as GMT (Greenwich Mean Time), CET (Central European Time), or JST (Japan Standard time). A whole list can be found in the file `/usr/lib/share/zoneinfo/zone.tab` (in a RedHat >=6.x system; we might have to look for it in a different place, or not find it at all, in a different system). The `Locale::Zonetab` module also provides a list, and comes with examples. Here is a list of the codes for all time-lines. These are not exactly the same as time zones, as a country might choose to follow the time-line it falls into:

Change with respect to GMT	Time zone denomination
-11	NT
-10	HST
-9	YST
-8	PST
-7	MST
-6	CST
-5	EST
-4	EWT
-3	ADT
-2	AT
-1	WAT
0	GMT
1	CET
2	EET

Change with respect to GMT	Time zone denomination
3	BT
4	ZP4
5	ZP5
6	ZP6
7	(No denomination)
8	WST
9	JST
10	EAST
11	EADT
12	NZT

❑ Using delta with respect to GMT; GMT+1 for instance, or GMT-12.

❑ Using the name of a principal city and zone; but zones are not exactly continents. There are ten zones: Europe, Asia, America, Antarctica, Australia, Pacific, Indian, Atlantic, Africa and Arctic. For instance, the time zone a Spaniard is in would be Madrid/Europe. This denomination has the advantage of also including Daylight Saving Time information (more on this later).

❑ there are several other notations: A to Z (used by US Military), national notations (for instance, in the US)... well, a whole lot of them. There is a lot of information in the Date::Manip pod page.

The whole time zone aspect is a bit more complicated, since local time changes according to **Daylight Saving Time**, a French invention to make people go to work by night and come back in broad daylight. We therefore have two options: go back to old times, when people worked to the sun, or use local rules by asking the users, which is the approach most operating systems take. Most operating systems include information for all possible time zones; for instance, Linux includes local time and time zone information in the /usr/lib/share/zoneinfo directory, which has been compiled using the zic compiler from time zone rule files. The baseline is that we really have to go out of our way, and ask a lot of local information to find out what the local time zone is. Most people just ask, or take time from the local computer. Ideally, a GPS-equipped computer would have a lookup table allowing it to know the local time for every co-ordinates in the world.

In our case, we solve the problem the fast way. In most cases, knowing the name of the most populous city in the surroundings, and the general zone out of the ten mentioned above is all we need. From this information, the three letter code of the time zone, along with DST information, is obtained using POSIX functions tzset and tzname. The first sets the time zone to the one contained in the TZ environment variable, and the second deduces the time zone and DST information from it. This information is later used to compute the offset in seconds with respect to local time, which is used to compute the new time by adding that offset, in seconds, to actual time. Finally, all the above information is printed out. We will skip formatting it in the way required by locale, since we have seen that already in a previous section. Besides, city and general zone might not be enough information to find out which locale the user prefers.

Looks Like a Foreign Language

Continuing with our scenario, we were not too convinced by the setup of our reporting web site. There were many reports, coming in from many well-known (and not so well-known) domains, and we could not find out which language they were written in. Even though we can not translate between these languages, we would like at least to know which language was being used. The following script goes some way to remedying this situation:

```perl
#!/usr/bin/perl -T
# langident.pl
use warnings;
# lack of use strict;

use CGI qw(:standard);
use Locale::Language;
use Lingua::Ident;
print header, start_html;

if (!param('phrase')) {
   print start_form,
   "->", textfield('phrase'), "<-", end_form;
} else {
   my @dataFiles = qw(data.de data.eu data.en data.fr data.it data.mt
                      data.nl data.ko);
   for (@dataFiles) {
     if ( ! -e $_ ) {
        print "Will not work: File $_ does not exist";
        exit;
      }
   }
   print em(param('phrase')), br,
   "Looks ";
   my $i = new Lingua::Ident( @dataFiles );
   my $lang = $i->identify(param('phrase'));
   my ($langCode) =  $lang =~ /^(\w{2})/;
   print code2language($langCode), " to me!";
}

print end_html;
```

This program prints a text field, which invites the user to key in a phrase, in a language-independent way. It then takes its input and tries to find out what language it is written in using the Lingua::Ident module. To do that, a previous step is needed:

> **trainlid xx < sample.xx > data.xx**

This has to be done for each sample.* we have. There are some samples supplied with the Lingua::Ident module, but we also look at three samples extracted from appropriate web pages say, namely Maltese, Basque, and Dutch (sample.mt, sample.eu and sample.nl). The trainlid program, which comes with the module, creates a data.* file with letter combination frequencies. As an argument, it takes the name of the locale the language refers to, and as input, a file with a sample of a language, and then it outputs the frequency file.

The `data.*` files are then used to initialize the `Lingua::Ident` module. This will enable it to identify as many languages as it is given. Unfortunately, this is done statistically, and it is not guaranteed to identify the correct language; Dutch and German are often mistaken for each other, but it will work for most languages, as can be seen in the following figures:

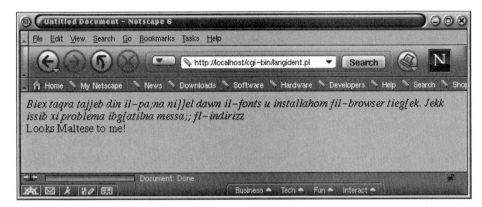

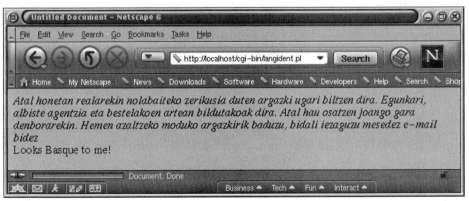

Conjugating in Portuguese

A rather striking way of learning a foreign language would be to use Perl. Surprisingly, a very useful module called `Lingua::PT::Conjugate` has been written, for the purpose of conjugating Portuguese verbs. It includes two utilities, conjug, and treinar, the first for conjugating, and the second for interactive training with Portuguese verbs. For instance, we could type:

> **conjug i ficar pres**
ficar :
pres   fico ficas fica ficamos ficais ficam

This is the equivalent of the verb 'to do' in English, conjugated in present tense, from the first person in the singular to the third person in the plural. It does not use ISO-8859-1 encoding (due to the **i** in **conjug i**). The following script utilizes this module, although it should be noted that this is not Windows compliant because the `WWW::Babelfish` module cannot be installed on Windows systems:

```perl
#!/usr/bin/perl -T
# conjug.pl
use warnings;
# lack of use strict here

use CGI qw(:standard *table);
use WWW::Babelfish;
use Lingua::PT::Conjugate;

print header, start_html(-bgcolor => 'white', -title => "Conjugando");
if (!param(verb)) {
    my %tenses =
        (pres  => Present,
         perf  => Perfect,
         imp   => Imperfect,
         fut   => Future,
         mdp   => Pluscuamperfect,
         cpres => 'Subjunctive Present',
         cimp  => 'Subjunctive Imperfect',
         cfut  => 'Subjunctive Future',
         ivo   => Imperative,
         pp    => 'Past Participle',
         grd   => Gerund);
    my @labels = keys %tenses;
    my %persons =
        (1 => I,
         2 => You,
         3 => 'He/She/It',
         4 => We,
         5 => You,
         6 => They);
    my @labelsP = keys %persons;
```

After setting up data for the combo boxes (popup_menu), here comes the program itself:

```
print start_table({bgcolor => 'lightblue', cellspacing => 0,
                   cellpadding => 5}),
start_form,
Tr(td(["English Verb",
    textfield('verb')])), "\n",
Tr(td(['Tense',,
    popup_menu('tense' , \@labels, 'pres', \%tenses)])), "\n",
Tr(td(['Person',
    popup_menu('person', \@labelsP, 1, \%persons)])),
Tr(td({colspan => 2, align => 'center'}, submit())),
end_form, end_table;
```

This is the part of the script that processes the form, translates the verb, and conjugates it:

```
} else {
   print h1("Translating ", param('verb'), " to ", param('tense'),
           " in person ", param('person')),
       p(em (conjug(translate(param('verb')), param('tense'), param('person')))
       );
}

print end_html;

sub translate {
   my ($toTranslate) - @_;
   my $tr = new WWW::Babelfish() || return $toTranslate;
   my $translated = $tr->translate('source' => 'English',
                                   'destination' => 'Portuguese',
                                   'text' => "$toTranslate");
   print $language, " ", $tr->error if $tr->error;
   $translated = $toTranslate unless defined ($translated);
   return $translated;
}
```

In this script, our knowledge of the WWW::Babelfish module is used to translate the gerund (that is, the English form of the verb ending in '-ing') of the verb from English to Portuguese, and then conjugate the verb in Portuguese. Verbs in Portuguese are pretty much the same as many other Latin languages: they have to be conjugated, and have different forms for different tenses and different persons, not just a couple of forms as in English. Thus, we have to state the person (first, second, or third, singular or plural) and the tense.

The script follows two paths, depending on whether it is called for the first time or called with a verb. If it is called directly, it prints a form that queries for the verb, which should be entered in gerund form, since this seems to be the way of getting infinitives in Babelfish. The tense is then requested, and this takes the English form as a parameter, and the script outputs the Portuguese form (for instance, ivo as in imperativo, which means, obviously enough, imperative).

Once the verb has been set, the script, using a version of the translate subroutine locked for Portuguese, translates the verb into Portuguese, then conjugates it by calling the Lingua::PT::Conjugate::conjug method. This method takes the verb, tense, and person as arguments, and returns the verb form. For instance, typing in driving and selecting the first person plural in the future tense (we will drive) will be processed by the program as:

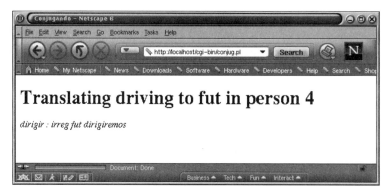

The only problem is that there is no such module for other languages as well, though if we want to work with other languages, CPAN includes several 'national' modules that take into account national peculiarities. The two main groups are the No::* set, and the Cz::* set.

The Cz:: set includes Cz::Cstocs, Cz::Sort, and Cz::Time. The reasoning for the presence of these modules is basically due to the fact that locale settings for the Czech and Slovak languages seem to be broken, so these modules include their own sorting and time display routines. Cz::Cstocs encodes from il2 to ASCII and back. These modules will probably be made obsolete with better locale modules, and Unicode/UTF8 encoding.

The No:: set also includes modules for date and sorting in Norway, No::Dato and No::Sort respectively. In addition, several modules that might be useful for e-commerce applications are available:

❑   No::KontoNr – checks social security numbers.

❑   No::PersonNr – checks account numbers.

❑   No::Telenor – computes, phone call prices for different telephone companies, times, and days of the week.

The 'Lingua::*' Modules

We can extend our login/report based web site so that users can be known by a pseudonym or nickname (this may not seem very useful, but it is not an uncommon feature on many sites these days). The major new feature though, is that users should now be able to type their report into the site, and the site can give them feedback on their report, judging it on its readability rating. The following code implements these new ideas (note that the Lingua::EN::Fathom module cannot be installed on a Windows machine as yet):

```
#!/usr/bin/perl -T
# report.pl
use warnings;
# lack of use strict

use CGI qw( :standard *table *ul);
use Lingua::EN::Syllable;
use Lingua::EN::Nickname;
use Lingua::EN::Fathom;
```

```
    print header, start_html(-bgcolor => white, -title => "Reporting");

if (!param(report)) {
    print start_table({bgcolor => lightblue,
                        cellspacing => 0, cellpadding => 5}), start_form,
    Tr(td(["Name" , textfield('name')])), "\n",
    Tr(td(["Report" , textarea('report')])), "\n",
    Tr(td({colspan => 2, align => center}, submit())),
    end_form, end_table;

} else {
    my $text = new Lingua::EN::Fathom;
    $text->analyse_block(param(report));
    my $numSyll = syllable(param(report));
    print h1("Received report by ", nickroot(param(name)), ":"),
    p(em(param(report))),
    p("Which has received the following ratings"),
    start_ul, li("Fog = ", $text->fog),
    li("Kincaid = ", $text->kincaid),
    li("Flesch = ", $text->flesch),
    end_ul,
    p("And you will be paid ", $numSyll*0.25,
      "\$ for $numSyll syllables"),
}
print end_html;
```

This script manages to use all three Lingua modules mentioned above (we may have some problems building the Lingua::En::Fathom module in English, but we can try and build it in Linux and then copy the resulting files to Windows). The main topic of the Lingua modules is (the English) language; and there are modules for syntactic parsing, recognizing gender, and so forth. There are also a few modules that deal with Russian (Lingua::RU::Charset), and the Portuguese module mentioned above. Hopefully, this will be extended in the future, but for the moment, we have to make do with the many modules that deal with the English language. In this case, we are using modules that count syllables (Lingua::EN::Syllable), and find the real name that corresponds to a nickname such as 'Joe' or 'Jimmy' (Lingua::EN::Nickname). Most curious of all, Lingua::EN::Fathom analyzes text for readability, assigning it three standard indices called **Kincaid**, **Flesch**, and **Fog**. Kincaid returns the Flesch-Kincaid grade level for the text. Flesch grades the text from 0 to 100 according to its readability; a score between 60 and 70 being ideal. Fog returns the (theoretical) mental age needed to understand the text.

The structure of the script is very similar to the others in this chapter. It checks if the CGI parameter report is present. If it is not present, it prints the form, requesting the nickname and the report. If it is present, it is processed, creating a Fathom object, which analyzes text, counts syllables, and computes the name corresponding to the nickname, using nickroot from the following lines (taken from the above code):

```
    $text->analye_block(param(report));
    my $numSyll = syllable(param(report));
    print h1("Received report by ", nickroot(param(name)), ":"),
    p(em( param(report) )),
```

1085

The rest is printing, and calling the `fog`, `kincaid`, and `flesch` functions to get the respective indices. The expected style of result is shown in the following figure:

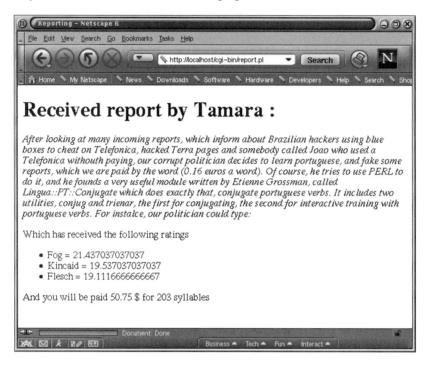

This does not say much about the linguistic reporting skills of 'Tamara'. A fog index of 21 is way out (18 would already be pretty difficult to understand), and the Kincaid index is also quite far from the optimal (between 7 and 8).

A small piece of advice here: `nickroot` *does not appear in the Nickname POD;* `rootname` *is mentioned instead. The documentation, (version 1.1) is badly out of sync with the current release.*

Spelling and Stemming

A simple way to improve the readability ratings of the reports submitted by users would be to check the spelling for errors. The previous program has therefore been modified to check English spelling and correct it, if possible:

This code is not Windows compliant. Although the `Lingua::Ispell` *module can be installed on Windows, the code will not work, because the Windows spellchecker does not work in the same way as the* `ispell` *program on UNIX*

```
#!/usr/bin/perl -T
# spell.pl
use warnings;
# lack of use strict
```

```
use CGI qw(:standard *table *ul);
use Lingua::EN::Syllable;
use Lingua::EN::Nickname;
use Lingua::EN::Fathom;
use Lingua::Ispell qw(spellcheck);

print header, start_html(-bgcolor => white,
                             -title => "Reporting");
if (!param(report)) {
    print start_table({bgcolor => 'lightblue', cellspacing => 0,
                       cellpadding => 5}), start_form,
    Tr(td(["Name" , textfield('name')])), "\n",
    Tr(td(["Report" , textarea('report')])), "\n",
    Tr(td({colspan => 2, align => 'center'}, submit())), end_form, end_table;
} else {
    my $text = new Lingua::EN::Fathom;
    my $report = param('report');
    $text->analyse_block($report);
    my $numSyll = syllable($report);
    $report =~ s/\n//g;    # needed by spellcheck
```

Most of the new code is below. The correct path to ispell is set, and then the text is spell checked:

```
$Lingua::Ispell::path = '/usr/bin/ispell';
my @checks = spellcheck($report);
my %errors;
for (@checks) {
    $errors{$_->{term}} = $_->{misses} if ( $_->{type} = 'miss');
}
print h1("Received report by ", nickroot(param(name)), ":"),
p(em(param(report))),
p("Which has received the following ratings"),
start_ul, li("Fog = ", $text->fog ),
li("Kincaid = ", $text->kincaid),
li("Flesch = ", $text->flesch),
end_ul,
p("And had the following misspellings "), start_ul;
for (keys %errors) {
    print li($_, " Suggestions :", join(" ", @{$errors{$_}}));
}
print end_ul, p("And you will be paid ", $numSyll*0.25, "\$ for
                 $numSyll syllables ");
}
print end_html;
```

As we can see, this program is quite similar to the previous example. In the highlighted lines, the path to the ispell program is set in the following line:

```
$Lingua::Ispell::path = '/usr/bin/ispell';
```

and spellcheck is called in the following line:

```
my @checks = spellcheck($report);
```

This function returns an array of references to hashes, which has several keys for each word in the input string; `term` contains the original word, `type` is the flag set by `ispell`. We should pay attention if `type` is none or `miss`. In this last case, a new key, `misses`, can be used. This contains an array of possible correct spellings of the word. We only flag near misses and place them in the `%errors` hash, and print them afterwards.

Take into account that the `ispell` utility seems to be a bit obsolete, and may not be widely available. Indeed, it has been replaced with `aspell` in the current RedHat Linux distributions, but there is no difference in results, since `aspell` includes an `ispell` wrapper in the package. If we type in an English name and a report composed of the following phrases, the program will return something like this:

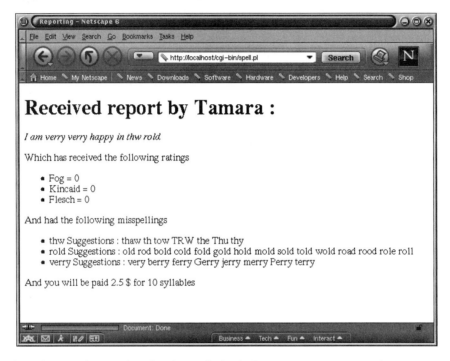

Perl can play other word games besides the spell check. For instance, in many information retrieval applications, it is sometimes useful to know the root of a word. Take the case where somebody is searching for the word 'birds'. They may also be looking for 'birdies', 'bird' or 'bird's nest'. The operation that extracts the root of a word is called **stemming**, and it is a language dependent operation. Incidentally, this operation is very easy in English, with conjugations that have only a few forms, no declinations, and no male/female variation in adjectives. Difficulties may arise in other languages such as Basque, which has 14 different declinations or cases, and 3 different numbers: singular, plural and *mugagabe*, indefinite or collective. There is, however, a `Lingua::Stem` module that can help (in the English case at least):

```perl
#!/usr/bin/perl
# stem.pl
use warnings;
use strict;
```

```
use Lingua::Stem qw(stem);
my @words = qw(birds birdie flying flown worked working);
my $stemmer = Lingua::Stem->new(-locale => 'EN-US');
my $stems   = $stemmer->stem(@words);
print "Word \tStem \n";
while (@$stems) {
    print pop @words, "\t", pop @$stems, "\n";
}
```

This returns something like this:

> **perl stem.pl**

Word	Stem
working	work
worked	work
flown	flown
flying	fly
birdie	birdi
birds	bird

Well, it is not perfect. It cannot spot irregular verbs, or familiar diminutives such as 'birdie'. However, it would be useful in a search engine looking for all strings in a text containing the stem, so that more matches would be returned. Of course, this is not the ultimate information retrieval pre-processing system; synonyms, numbers, and names will have to be taken into account, as well as the weight of words within the text, but in any case, stemming is the first step in many information retrieval applications.

Writing Multilingual Web Pages

In order to give an example of a multilingual web page, we are going to create two forms. The first allows users to input their name, and the language they understand. User information will be stored in cookies by the first script for use in the second script. The second script will then display, amongst other things, a greeting in the users' chosen language, and will also allow users to type in text and have it translated into Spanish.

```
#!/usr/bin/perl -T
# form.pl
use warnings;
# lack of use strict;

use CGI qw(:standard *table);
use Locale::Language;
use Locale::Country;

if (!param('name')) {
    print header, start_html(-bgcolor => 'white', -title => "ID card"),
    start_table({bgcolor => 'lightblue', cellspacing => 0, cellpadding => 5}
    ), start_form,

    Tr(td("Name" ),td({colspan => 3},textfield('name'))), "\n",
```

```
      Tr(td(["Language you understand",
      radio_group('lang', [English, French, Spanish])])), "\n",
      Tr(td({colspan => 4, align => 'center'}, submit())), end_form, end_table;

   } else {    #Process form and set cookie
      my @cookies;
      push(@cookies,
      cookie(-name => 'name', -value => param('name'),
            -expires => '+3M', -path => '/cgi-bin'));
      push(@cookies, cookie (-name => 'lang', -value =>
                              language2code(param('lang')),
                              -expires => '+3M', -path => '/cgi-bin'));

      print header(-cookie => \@cookies),
      start_html(-bgcolor => 'white', -title => "ID card accepted"),
            "Application accepted \n";
   }
   print end_html;
```

This example is pretty straightforward: by default, it prints a form, and if the name field is already filled, it is processed. The language is also processed to a language code: en, fr, or es. The path in the cookie function will have to be changed to whatever path our script resides in. The expiry date can also be changed to suit any other needs; in our case it was set to 3 months.

Next, we will use a comma separated flatfile called messages.txt to store our multilingual messages. Our application will then search through it, displaying the correct language on our report form. Of course, this depends on the language that the user has indicated that they understand.

All messages are normalized, with no capitals, so that capitalization can be established by the application:

```
hello, hola, salut
please, por favor, s'il vous plait
here is, aquí está, voici
welcome, bienvenido, bienvenu
today's date is, la fecha del día es, aujourd'hui est le
your name, su nombre, votre nom
report, informe, rapport
send, enviar, envoyer
received, recibido, reçu
by, por, par
```

Since languages are taken from cookies, and we set the cookies ourselves, we would not expect this to give an error (but there will always be nonvalid input when one expects valid input). Again note that the script will not work on Windows, since the WWW::Babelfish module cannot be installed:

```
#!/usr/bin/perl -T
# babel.pl
use warnings;
# lack of strict
```

```
use CGI qw(:standard *table);
use locale;
use IO::File;
use POSIX;
use WWW::Babelfish;
use Locale::Language;

if (cookie('name')) {
    my $name = cookie('name');
    my $language = cookie('lang');

    print header, start_html(-bgcolor => 'white', -title => "Reporting");
    setlocale(LC_TIME, cookie('locale'));
    # If it does not exist, defaults to local
```

So far, common processing is used for both showing and processing the form. Now, if the report CGI parameter is not present, it will show the form. If it is present, it will process it.

```
if (!param('report')) {    #Show form
    my ($sec, $min, $hour, $mday, $mon, $year, $wday) = localtime (time);
    print h2(ucfirst(getMessage('hello', $language)),
    " $name,", getMessage("today's date is", $language),
    strftime("%c", $sec, $min, $hour, $mday, $mon, $year, $wday), "\n");

    print start_table({bgcolor => 'lightblue', cellspacing => 0,
                        cellpadding => 5}),
    start_form,
    Tr(td([ucfirst(getMessage('report', $language)) ,
    textarea(-rows => 10,
            -columns => 50,
            -name => 'report')])), "\n",
    Tr(td({colspan => 2, align => 'center'},
          submit(ucfirst(getMessage('send', $language))))),
    end_form, end_table;
```

If the form has been completed, we have the parameter report. We then have to process it:

```
} else {   # process it and show it in English
    print h2(ucfirst(getMessage('received', $language)),
    getMessage('report', $language),
    getMessage('by', $language), " $name"),
    p(b("Original"), param('report')),
    p(em (translate(param('report'), code2language($language))));
}
} else {   # ask login
    print redirect(-uri => '/cgi-bin/form.pl');
}
print end_html;
```

The getMessage subroutine (below) opens up a filehandle to the flatfile database, taking the key and the language code as parameters. It then places each phrase into an array, and then searches it, returning the desired element. The other subroutine, translate, does exactly as expected – it translates our report into Spanish. Beware, however, that Babelfish cannot translate every language into any other language. In our case, users selecting French as the language they understand, will not have their report translated into Spanish. For a full listing of languages Babelfish can translate to and from, visit http://www.infotektur.com/demos/babelfish/en.html.

This is the getMessage subroutine used in the babel.pl script:

```perl
sub getMessage {
    my ($key,$language) = @_;
    chomp ($key,$language);
    my $filename = 'messages.txt';
    my $counter = -1;

    my $fh = new IO::File;
    $fh->open("< $filename") or die "Can't open '$filename': $!\n";

    my (@messages,@final);
    while (<$fh>) {
        @messages = (split ', ');
        push @final, @messages;
    }

    chomp @final;

    foreach (@final){
        my $msg;
        $counter++;

        if($_ =~ /$key/ and $language =~ /es/){
            $msg = $final[$counter+1];
            return $msg;
        }
        elsif ($_ =~ /$key/ and $language =~ /fr/) {
            $msg = $final[$counter+2];
            return $msg;
        }
        elsif ($_ =~ /$key/ and $language =~ /en/) {
            $msg = $final[$counter];
            return $msg;
        }
        else {
            next;
        }
    }
}
```

and here is the translate subroutine:

```perl
sub translate {
    my ($toTranslate, $language) = @_;
    my $tr = new WWW::Babelfish() || return $toTranslate;
    my $translated = $tr->translate('source' => $language,
                                    'destination' => 'Spanish',
                                    'text' => $toTranslate);
    print $language, " ", $tr->error if $tr->error;
    $translated = $toTranslate unless defined ($translated);
    return $translated;
}
```

This script is basically a form processing CGI; the only difference being that we make use of the locale to show the date, and the selected language for the messages. Recall that the user selected the locale, in their choice of country and language, in the sign in script. Cookies are retrieved using standard `CGI.pm` instructions. If the cookie name is not present, we redirect the script to `form.pl`. If it is present, there are two different paths it could take, depending on whether the parameter `report` has been set, or not.

We have taken the 'atomic' approach to messages, putting words or short phrases into the database and building up phrases little by little. We could also insert whole phrases, but in that case we would have to include every possible message. For instance, in this script, the phrase Received report by is made up of three different atoms, `Received`, `report`, and `by`.

We now briefly show how these scripts are implemented in, say, a simple multilingual web site. First we run the `form.pl` script and the user will input their name and the language they understood:

After submitting the form, a screen showing acceptance is displayed. Now we move to using the second script, `babel.pl`, to perform our translation from the selected language to Spanish, as hard-coded in the script:

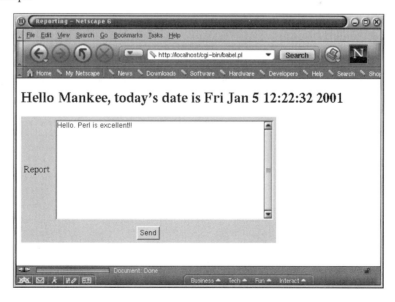

And the result of the call to Babelfish is as below:

Creating our own Local Perl module

Despite all the precautions we have taken thus far to make our site multilingual, some countries still have peculiarities that we have not catered for. This can be important when writing a program or representing any user interface. For instance, local geographical divisions are often quite specific to a place: there are states in the US, provinces in Canada, etc. Along similar lines, postal or ZIP codes are also specific to a place – routines for converting from postal code to geographical place (and back) could be quite useful when processing, for example, a mail order. Some other modules could serve as a front-end to national news services, stock tickers, search engines, etc.

At the time of writing, only two countries have been fortunate enough to have some of these modules written for them: the Czech Republic and Norway (as we have seen in previous sections). We will try to take the first steps towards the creation of other object sets; in this case, the Es::* set. The first problem to arise is how we should name the module. We could use the continent::country convention, (especially in Europe, where everybody is part of one big family), or just go for the national two-letter code; but in this case, should the language code or the national ISO code be used? Our suggestion is that it will depend upon the topic of the module. Matters relative to the whole Spanish state should be called Es::*, while matters peculiar to an autonomous region should follow the locale convention: languagecode_COUNTRYCODE. For instance, national Catalan modules could be named Ca_ES::*. This is only a suggestion, and the right way to baptize a module is to issue a request for comments in the news:comp.lang.Perl.modules and/or other national discussion groups, such as Perl-es@egroups.com. More details can also be found in the Modules FAQ, available by entering

> **perldoc perlmodlib**.

One of the varying aspects between countries is the id card number. In Spain, it is the same number as the national revenue service code and includes a letter, which acts as a checksum. The following Es::Nif package can be used to check an **NIF** (**N**úmero de **I**dentificación **F**iscal, or fiscal identification number).

```perl
#!/usr/bin/perl
# ES/Nif.pm
use strict;

package ES::Nif;
# Check that the letter of the Spanish NIF is correct. A Spanish personal
# NIF is a set of numbers followed by a letter. It can be expressed in upper
# or lower case, separated by a dash or not.
```

```
use Carp qw(carp);

sub check {
   my $nif = shift;
   carp "Incorrect NIF format: $nif \n" if $nif !~ /^(\d+)\-?(\w)$/;
   my ($number, $letter) = ($1, $2);
   return letter($number) eq uc($letter);
}

sub letter {
   my $number = shift;
   my $mod = $number % 23;
   my ($digit1, $digit2) = split(//, $mod);
   my $letterComputed = $::lookup[$digit1][$digit2];
   return $letterComputed;
}
```

This routine is called when the package is declared in a program. It reads the letter codes and builds up the lookup table:

```
INIT {
   my $i = 0;
   while (<DATA>) {
       my @data = split;
       push(@{$::lookup[$i++]}, @data);
   }
}
"No te lo digo";   # this is a true value
# taken from http://www.terra.es/personal2/bomb009/telefonos.htm

__DATA__
T R W A G M Y F P D
X B N J Z S Q V H L
C K E T
```

The letter in the fiscal number is found using the remainder of dividing the id number by 23, that is, DNI % 23. The result is then looked up in a double entry table; the first digit corresponds to the row, the second digit to the column, remembering that we start counting from zero. For instance, if DNI % 23 = 12, we would look up second row and third column, that is, N.

There are only two routines, one computes the letter from the number, and the other checks it against the letter that comes with the NIF. They can be used like this:

```
#!/usr/bin/perl
# ES/Nif.pl
use warnings;
use strict;

use ES::Nif;

print "Checking $ARGV[0] ";
if (ES::Nif::check($ARGV[0])) {
   print "Correct";
} else {
   chop($ARGV[0]);   # This chops off letter
   print "Incorrect. Letter should be ", ES::Nif::letter($ARGV[0]);
}
print "\n";
```

This would produce an output similar to:

```
> perl ES/Nif.pl 2345678U
Checking 2345678U Incorrect. Letter should be T
> perl ES/Nif.pl 3332210Q
Checking 3332210Q Correct
```

Summary

Over the course of this chapter, we have taken a look at Perl internationalization and localization from different angles. As an overview we have:

❏ Seen how to use the locale framework in order to present information according to local conventions.

❏ Covered modules and tools available that deal with languages, alphabets, time zones, etc.

❏ Looked at how we can use Perl to help us identify and manipulate unknown languages when we come across them.

❏ Created a basic translation page using flatfiles incorporating three common languages.

❏ Illustrated guidelines and possible topics for module creation, as well as writing our own simple module.

Command Line Options

The following is a list of the available switches, which can be appended to the calling of Perl from the command line. The exact syntax for calling Perl from the command line is as follows:

> perl (switches) (--) (programfile) (arguments)

Switch	Function
-0 (octal)	This sets the record separator $/ by specifying the character's number in the ASCII table in octal. For example, if we wanted to set our separator to the character e we would say perl -0101. The default is the null character, and $/ is set to this if no argument is given.
-a	-a can be used in conjunction with -n or -p. It enables autosplit, and uses whitespace as the default delimiter. Using -p will print out the results, which are always stored in the array @F.
-C	Enables native wide character system interfaces.
-c	This is a syntactic test only. It stops Perl executing, but reports on any compilation errors that a program has before it exits. Any other switches that have a runtime effect on your program will be ignored when -c is enabled.
-d filename	This switch invokes the Perl debugger. The Perl debugger will only run once you have gotten your program to compile. Enabling -d allows you to prompt debugging commands such as install breakpoints, and many others.

Table continued on following page

Switch	Function
-D(number) -D(list)	-D will set debugging flags, but only if you have debugging compiled into your program. The following table shows you the arguments that you may use for -D, and the resulting meaning of the switch.

Argument (number)	Argument (character)	Operation
1	p	Tokenizing and parsing
2	s	Stack snapshots
4	l	Label stack Processing
8	t	Trace execution
16	o	Object method lookup
32	c	String/numeric conversions
64	p	Print preprocessor command for -p
128	m	Memory allocation
256	f	Format processing
512	r	Regular expression processing
1024	x	Syntax tree dump
2048	u	Tainting checks
4096	L	Memory leaks
8192	H	Hash dump
16384	X	Scratchpad allocations
32768	D	Cleaning up
65536	S	Thread synchronization

Switch	Function
-e	This allows you to write one line of script, by instructing Perl to execute text following the switch on the command line, without loading and running a program file. Multiple calls may be made to -e in order to build up scripts of more than one line.
-F/pattern/	Causes -a to split using the pattern specified between the delimiters. The delimiters may be / /, " ", or ' '.
-h	Prints out a list of all the command line switches.
-i(extension)	Modifies the <> operator. Makes a backup file if an argument is given. The argument is treated as the extension that the saved file is to be given.
-I (directory)	Causes a directory to be added to the search path when looking for files to include. This path will be searched before the default paths, one of which is the current directory, the other is generally /usr/local/lib/Perl on UNIX and C:\perl\bin on Windows.

Switch	Function
-l(octal)	-l adds line endings, and defines the line terminator by specifying the character's number in the ASCII table in octal. If it is used with -n or -p, it will chomp the line terminator. If the argument is omitted, then $\ is given the current value of $/. The default value of the special variable $/ is newline.
-(mM)(-)module	Causes the import of the given module for use by your script, before executing the program.
-n	Causes Perl to assume a while (<>) {My Script} loop around your script. Basically it will iterate over the filename arguments. It does no printing of lines.
-p	This is the same as -n, except that it will print lines.
-P	-P causes your program to be run through the C preprocessor before it is compiled. Bear in mind that the preprocessor directives begin with #, the same as comments, so preferably use ;# to comment your script when you use the -P switch.
-s	This defines variables with the same name as the switches that follow on the command line. The other switches are also removed from @ARGV. The newly-defined variables are set to 1 by default. Some parsing of the other switches is also enabled.
-S	Causes Perl to look for a given program file using the PATH environment variable. In other words, it acts much like #!
-T	Stops data entering a program from performing unsafe operations. It is a good idea to use this when there is a lot of information exchange occurring, like in CGI programming.
-u	This will perform a core dump after compiling the program.
-U	This forces Perl to allow unsafe operations.
-v	Prints the version of Perl that is currently being used (includes VERY IMPORTANT Perl info).
-V(:variable)	Prints out a summary of the main configuration values used by Perl during compiling. It will also print out the value of the @INC array.
-w	Invokes the raising of many useful warnings based on the (poor or bad) syntax of the program being run.
	This switch has been deprecated in Perl 5.6, in favor of the use warnings pragma.
-W	Enables **all** warnings.
-X	This will disable **all** warnings. We already know that we always use use warnings when writing our programs. So you will not need this.
-x(directory)	Tells Perl to get rid of extraneous text that precedes the shebang line. All switches on the shebang line will still be enabled.

Special Variables

This is a categorized listing of the predefined variables provided by Perl. The longer and more descriptive 'English' names become available when using the English module with use English.

Default Variables and Parameters

Variable	English Name	Description
$_	$ARG	This global scalar acts as a default variable for function arguments and pattern-searching space – with many common functions, if an argument is left unspecified, $_ will be automatically assigned. For example, the following statements are equivalent: chop($_) and chop $_ =~ m/*expr*/ and m/*expr*/
@_	n/a	The elements of this array are used to store function arguments, which can be accessed (from within a function definition) as $_[*num*]. The array is automatically local to each function.
@ARGV	n/a	The elements of this array contain the command line arguments intended for use by the script.
$ARGV	n/a	This contains the name of the current file when reading from the null filehandle <>. <> is a literal, and defaults to standard input, <STDIN>, if no arguments are supplied from elements in @ARGV.

Regular Expression Variables (all read-only)

Variable	English Name	Description
$(num)	n/a	The scalar $n contains the substring matched to the n'th grouped subpattern in the last pattern match, and remains in scope until the next pattern match with subexpressions. It ignores matched patterns occurring in nested blocks that are already exited. If there are no corresponding groups, then the undefined value is returned.
$&	$MATCH	This scalar contains the string matched by the last successful pattern match. Once again, this will not include any strings matched in nested blocks. For example: `'UnicornNovember' =~ /Nov/;` `print $&;` will print Nov. For versions of Perl since 5.005, this is not an expensive variable to use.
$'	$POSTMATCH	This scalar holds the substring following whatever was matched by the last successful pattern match. For example, if we say: `'UnicornNovember' =~ /Nov/;` $' will return ember.
$`	$PREMATCH	This scalar holds the substring preceding whatever was matched by the last successful pattern match. For example, if we say: `'UnicornNovember' =~ /Nov/;` $` will return Unicorn.
$+	$LAST_PAREN_MATCH	This scalar holds the last substring matched to a grouped subpattern in the last search. It comes in handy if you're not sure which of a set of alternative subpatterns matched. For example, if you successfully match on `/(ab)*|(bc*)/`, then $+ stores either $1 or $2, depending on whether it was the first or second grouped subpattern that matched. For example, following: `'UnicornNovember' =~ /(Nov)|(Dec)/;` $+ will return Nov.

Variable	English Name	Description
$*	$MULTILINE_MATCHING	This sets to 1 to do multi-line matching within a string, or 0 to tell Perl that it can assume that strings contain a single line, for the purpose of optimizing pattern matches. Pattern matches on strings containing multiple newlines can produce confusing results when $* is 0. Default is 0. (Mnemonic: * matches multiple things.) This variable influences the interpretation of only ^ and $. A literal newline can be searched for even when $* == 0. Use of $* is deprecated in modern Perl, supplanted by the /s and /m modifiers on pattern matching.

@+	@LAST_MATCH_END	This array lists the back pointer positions (in the referenced string) of the last successful match. The first element @+[0] contains the pointer's starting position following that match, each subsequent value corresponds to its position just after having matched the corresponding grouped subpattern. For example, following:
		
		`'UnicornNovember' =~ /(U)\w?(N)/;`
		
		@+ will return: (8,1,8), while following:
		
		`'UnicornNovember' =~ /(Uni)\w?(Nov)/;`
		
		@+ will return: (10,3,10).

@-	@LAST_MATCH_START	This array lists the front pointer positions (in the referenced string) of the last successful match. The first element @-[0] contains the pointer's starting position prior to that match, each subsequent value corresponds to its position just before having matched the corresponding grouped subpattern. For example following:
		
		`'UnicornNovember' =~ /(Uni)\w?(Nov)/;`
		
		@- will return: (0,0,7), while following:
		
		`'UnicornNovember' =~ /(Uni)(\w?)(Nov)/;`
		
		@- will return: (0,0,3,7).

Input/Output Variables

Variable	English Name	Description
$.	$INPUT_LINE_NUMBER	This scalar holds the **current line number** of the last filehandle on which you performed either a read, seek, or tell. It is reset when the filehandle is closed.
		NB: <> never does an explicit close, so line numbers increase across ARGV files. Also, localizing $. has the effect of localizing Perl's notion of 'the last read filehandle'.
$/	$INPUT_RECORD_SEPARATOR	This scalar stores the **input record separator**, which by default is the newline \n. If it's set to " ", input will be read one paragraph at a time.
$\	$OUTPUT_RECORD_SEPARATOR	This scalar stores the **output record separator** for print – normally this will just output consecutive records without any separation (unless explicitly included). This variable allows you to set it for yourself. For example:

		`$\ = "-";`
		`print "one";`
		`print "two";`

		will print: one-two-.
$|	$OUTPUT_AUTOFLUSH	This corresponds to an internal flag used by Perl to determine whether buffering should be used on a program's write/read operations to/from files. If the value is TRUE ($| is greater than 0), buffering is disabled.
$,	$OUTPUT_FIELD_SEPARATOR	This is the **output field separator** for print. Normally this will just output consecutive fields without any separation (unless explicitly included). This variable allows you to set it for yourself. For example:
		`$, = "-";` `print "one", "two";`
		will print: one-two.
$"	$LIST_SEPARATOR	This is the **output field separator** for array values interpolated into a double-quoted string (or similar interpreted string), the default is a space. For example:

		`$" = "-";`
		`@ar = ("one", "two", "three");`
		`print "@ar";`

		will print: one-two-three.

Variable	English Name	Description

`$;`	`$SUBSCRIPT_SEPARATOR`	This is the **subscript separator** for multidimensional array emulation. If you refer to a hash element as:
		
		`$foo{$a, $b, $c}`
		
		it really means
		
		`$foo{join($;, $a, $b, $c)}`

Filehandle/format Variables

Variable	English Name	Description
`$#`	`$OFMT`	This holds the **output format** for printed numbers. **NB: The use of this variable has been deprecated.**
`$|`	`$OUTPUT_AUTOFLUSH`	This corresponds to an internal flag used by Perl to determine whether **buffering** should be used on a program's write/read operations to/from files, if its value is TRUE (`$|` is greater than 0), then buffering is disabled.
`$%`	`$FORMAT_PAGE_NUMBER`	The current page number of the selected output channel.
`$=`	`$FORMAT_LINES_PER_PAGE`	The current **page length**, measured in printable lines, the default is 60. This only becomes important when a top-of-page format is invoked, if a `write` command does not fit into a given number of lines, then the top-of-page format is used, before any printing past the page length continues.
`$-`	`$FORMAT_LINES_LEFT`	The number of lines left on a page, when a page is finished, it's given the value of `$=`, and is then decremented for each line outputted.
`$~`	`$FORMAT_NAME`	The currently selected **format name**, the default is the name of the filehandle.
`$^`	`$FORMAT_TOP_NAME`	The name of the **top-of-page format**.
`$:`	`$FORMAT_LINE_BREAK_CHARACTERS`	The set of characters after which a string may be broken to fill continuation fields (starting with `^`) in a format – default is `' \n-'` to break on whitespace or hyphens.
`$^L`	`$FORMAT_FORMFEED`	This holds a character that is used by a format's output to request a form feed, default is `\f`.
`$^A`	`$ACCUMULATOR`	This is the current value of the `write()` accumulator for `format()` lines. A format contains `formline()` calls that put their result into `$^A`. After calling its format, `write()` prints out the contents of `$^A` and empties. We never really see the contents of `$^A` unless we call `formline()` ourselves and then look at it.

Error Variables

Variable	English Name	Description
$?	$CHILD_ERROR	This holds the status value returned by the last pipe close, backtick (``` `` ```) command, or `system()` operator.
$@	$EVAL_ERROR	This holds the **syntax error message** from the last `eval()` command, it evaluates to null if the last `eval()` parsed and executed correctly (although the operations you invoked may have failed in the normal fashion).
$!	$ERRNO	If used in a numeric context, this returns the current value of *errno*, with all the usual caveats (so you shouldn't depend on $! to have any particular value unless you've got a specific error return indicating a system error).
		If used in a string context, it returns the corresponding system error string. We can assign a set *errno* value to $! if, for instance, we want it to return the string for that error number, or we want to set the exit value for the `die()` operator.
$^E	$EXTENDED_OS_ERROR	This returns an **extended error message**, with information specific to the current operating system. At the moment, this only differs from $! under **VMS**, OS/2, and Win32 (and for MacPerl). On all other platforms, $^E is always the same as $!.

System Variables

Variable	English Name	Description
$$	$PROCESS_ID	The **process ID** (pid) of the Perl process running the current script.
$<	$REAL_USER_ID	The **real user ID** (uid) of the current process.
$>	$EFFECTIVE_USER_ID	The **effective uid** of the current process.
		NB: $< and $> can only be swapped on machines supporting `setreuid()`.
$(	$REAL_GROUP_ID	The **real group ID** (gid) of the current process.
$)	$EFFECTIVE_GROUP_ID	The **effective group ID** (gid) of the current process.
$0	$PROGRAM_NAME	The name of the file containing the Perl script being executed.
$^X	$EXECUTABLE_NAME	The name that the Perl binary was executed as.

Variable	English Name	Description
$]	n/a	The version number of the Perl interpreter, including patchlevel / 1000, can be used to determine whether the interpreter executing a script is within the right range of versions.
		See also use VERSION and require VERSION for a way to fail if the interpreter is too old.
$[	n/a	The index of the first element in an array, and of the first character in a substring. Default is 0.
		As of release 5 of Perl, assignment to $[is treated as a compiler directive, and cannot influence the behavior of any other file. Its use is highly discouraged.
$^O	$OSNAME	The name of the operating system under which this copy of Perl was built, as determined during the configuration process, identical to $Config{'osname'}.
$^T	$BASETIME	The time at which the current script began running, in seconds since the beginning of 1970. Values returned by -M, -A, and -C filetests are based on this value.
$^W	$WARNING	The current value of the warning switch, either TRUE or FALSE
%ENV	n/a	Your current environment, altering its value changes the environment for child processes.
%SIG	n/a	Used to set handlers for various signals.
$^C	$COMPILING	The current value of the flag associated with the -c switch. Mainly of use with -MO=... to allow code to alter its behavior when being compiled, such as to AUTOLOAD at compile time rather than normal, deferred loading. See perlcc. Setting $^C = 1 is similar to calling B::minus_c.
$^D	$DEBUGGING	The current value of the debugging flags.
$^F	$SYSTEM_FD_MAX	The maximum system file descriptor, ordinarily 2.
$^I	$INPLACE_EDIT	The current value of the inplace-edit extension. Use undef to disable inplace editing.
$^M	n/a	Perl can use the contents of $^M as an emergency memory pool after die()ing. Suppose that your Perl was compiled with DPERL_EMERGENCY_SBRK and used Perl's malloc. Then
		$^M = 'a' x (1 << 16);
		would allocate a 64K buffer for use when in emergency.
$^P	$PERLDB	The internal variable for debugging support.
$^R	$LAST_REGEXP_ CODE_RESULT	The result of evaluation of the last successful regular expression assertion.

Table continued on following page

Variable	English Name	Description
$^S	$EXCEPTIONS_ BEING_CAUGHT	Current state of the interpreter. Undefined if parsing of the current module/eval is not finished (may happen in $SIG{__DIE__} and $SIG{__WARN__} handlers). True if inside an eval(), otherwise false.
$^V	$PERL_VERSION	The revision, version, and subversion of the Perl interpreter, represented as a string composed of characters with those ordinals. This can be used to determine whether the Perl interpreter executing a script is in the right range of versions.

Others

Variable	English Name	Description
@INC	n/a	A list of places to look for Perl scripts for evaluation by the do EXPR, require, or use constructs.
%INC	n/a	Contains entries for each filename that has been included via do or require. The key is the specified filename, and the value the location of the file actually found. The require command uses this array to determine whether a given file has already been included.

C

Function Reference

The first table in this appendix lists the file test operators. The syntax of these tests can take one of the following forms:

```
-X filehandle
-X expression
-X
```

X here is one of the following letters: ABCMORSTWX bcdefgkloprstuwxz. If the filehandle or expression argument is omitted, the file test is performed against $_, with the exception of -t, which tests STDIN.

Here is a complete rundown of what each file test checks for:

Test	Meaning
-A	How long in days between the last access to the file and latest startup.
-B	True if the file is a binary file (Compare with -T).
-C	How long in days between the last inode change and latest startup.
-M	How long in days between the last modification to the file and latest startup.
-O	True if the file is owned by a real uid/gid.
-R	True if the file is readable by a real uid/gid.

Table continued on following page

Test	Meaning
-S	True if the file is a socket.
-T	True if the file is a text file (compare with -B).
-W	True if the file is writable by a real uid/gid.
-X	True if the file is executable by a real uid/gid.
-b	True if the file is a block special file.
-c	True if the file is a character special file.
-d	True if the file is a directory.
-e	True if the file exists.
-f	True if the file is a plain file, not a directory.
-g	True if the file has the setgid bit set.
-k	True if the file has the sticky bit set.
-l	True if the file is a symbolic link.
-o	True if the file is owned by an effective uid/gid.
-p	True if the file is a named pipe or if the filehandle is a named pipe.
-r	True if the file is readable by an effective uid/gid.
-s	True if the file has non-zero size, returns size of file in bytes.
-t	True if the filehandle is opened to a tty.
-u	True if the file has the setuid bit set.
-w	True if the file is writable by an effective uid/gid.
-x	True if the file is executable by an effective uid/gid.
-z	True if the file has zero size.

The following table includes an alphabetical list of every function in Perl 5.6. Marked against its name will be the syntax for the function, a brief description of what it does and any directly related functions:

Function	Syntax	Description
abs	abs *value* abs	Returns the absolute (non-negative) value of an integer. For example abs(-1) and abs(1) both return 1 as a result. If no *value* argument is given, abs returns the absolute value of $_.
accept	accept *newsocket, genericsocket*	Accepts an incoming socket connect with sessions enabled if applicable.

Function	Syntax	Description
alarm	alarm *num_seconds* alarm	Starts a timer with *num_seconds* seconds on the clock before it trips a SIGALRM signal. Before the timer runs out, another call to alarm cancels it and starts a new one with *num_seconds* on the clock. If *num_seconds* equals zero, the previous timer is cancelled without starting a new one.
atan2	atan2 *x, y*	Returns the arctangent of x/y within the range $-\pi$ to π.
bind	bind *socket, name*	Binds a network address (TCP/IP, UDP, etc) to a *socket*, where *name* should be the packed address for the socket.
binmode	Binmode *filehandle*	Sets the specified *filehandle* to be read in binary mode explicitly for those systems, that cannot do this automatically. UNIX and MacOS can and thus binmode has no effect under these OS's.
bless	bless *ref, classname* bless *ref*	Takes the variable referenced by *ref* and makes it an object of class *classname*.
caller	caller *expression* caller	Called within a subroutine, caller returns a list of information outlining what called it, that is the sub's context. This actually returns the caller's package name, its filename, and the line number of the call. Returns the undefined value if not in a subroutine. If *expression* is used, also returns some extra debugging information to make a stack trace.
chdir	chdir *new_directory* chdir	Changes your current working directory to *new_directory*. If *new_directory* is omitted, the working directory is changed to that one specified in $ENV(HOME).
chmod	chmod *list*	Changes the permissions on a list of files. The first element of list must be the octal representation of the permissions to be given to it.
chomp	chomp *variable* chomp *list* chomp	Usually removes \n from a string. Actually removes the trailing record separator as set in $/ from a string or from each string in a list and then returns the number of characters deleted. If no argument is given, chomp acts on $_.
chop	chop *variable* chop *list* chop	Remove the last character from a string, or from each string in a list, returning the (last) character chopped. If no argument is given, chop acts on $_.

Table continued on following page

Function	Syntax	Description
chown	chown *list*	Changes the ownership on a list of files. Within *list*, the first two elements must be the user ID and group ID of that user and group to get ownership, followed by any number of filenames. Setting -1 for either ID means, 'Leave this value unchanged.'
chr	chr number chr	Returns ASCII character number *number*. If *number* is omitted, $_ is used.
chroot	chroot *directory* chroot	Changes the root directory for all further path lookups to *directory*. If *directory* is not given, $_ is used as the new root directory.
close	close *filehandle* close	Closes the file, pipe or socket associated with the nominated *filehandle*, resetting the line counter $. as well. If *filehandle* is not given, closes the currently selected filehandle. Returns true on success.
closedir	closedir *dirhandle*	Closes the directory opened by opendir() given by *dirhandle*.
connect	connect *socket*, *address*	Tries to connect to a *socket* at the given *address*.
continue	continue *block*	A flow control statement rather than a function. If there is a continue attached to a block (typically in a while or foreach), it is always executed just before the conditional is about to be evaluated again.
cos	cos *num_in_radians*	Calculates and returns the cosine of a number given in radians. If *num_in_radians* is not given, calculates the cosine of $_.
crypt	crypt *plaintext*, *key*	A one-way encryption function (there is no decrypt function) that takes some *plaintext* (a password usually) and encrypts it with a two character *key*.
dbmclose	dbmclose *hash*	Deprecated in favor of untie(). Breaks the binding between a dbm file and the given *hash*.
dbmopen	dbmopen *hash*, *dbname*, *mode*	Deprecated in favor of tie(). Binds the specified *hash* to the database *dbname*. If the database does not exist, it is created with the specified read\write *mode*, given as an octal number.
defined	defined *expression* defined	Checks whether the value, variable, or function in *expression* is defined. If *expression* is omitted, $_ is checked.

Function	Syntax	Description
delete	delete $hash{key} delete @hash{keys %hash}	Deletes one or more specified *keys* and their corresponding values from the *hash*. Returns the associated values.
die	die *message*	Writes *message* to the standard error output and then exits the currently running program with $! as its return value.
do	do *filename*	Executes the contents of *filename* as a Perl script. Returns undef if it cannot read the file.
dump	dump *label* dump	Initiates a core dump to be undumped into a new binary executable file, which when run will start at *label*. If *label* is left out, the executable will start from the top of the file.
each	each *hash*	Returns the next key/value pair from a *hash* as a two-element list. When *hash* is fully read, returns null.
endgrent	engrent	Frees the resources used to scan the /etc/group file or system equivalent.
endhostent	endhostent	Frees the resources used to scan the /etc/hosts file or system equivalent.
endnetent	endnetent	Frees the resources used to scan the /etc/networks file or system equivalent.
endprotoent	endprotoent	Frees the resources used to scan the /etc/protocols file or system equivalent.
endpwent	endpwent	Frees the resources used to scan the /etc/passwd file or system equivalent.
endservent	endservent	Frees the resources used to scan the /etc/services file or system equivalent.
eof	eof *filehandle* eof() eof	Returns 1 if *filehandle* is either not open or will return the end of file on the next read. eof() checks for the end of the pseudo file containing the files listed on the command line as the program was run. If eof does not have an argument, it will check the last file to be read.
eval	eval *string* eval *block* eval	Parses and executes *string* as if it were a mini-program and returns its result. If no argument is given, it evaluates $_. If an error occurs or die() is called eval returns undef. Works similarly with *block* except eval *block* is parsed only once. eval *string* is re-parsed each time eval executes.

Table continued on following page

Function	Syntax	Description
exec	exec *command*	Abandons the current program to run the specified system *command*.
exists	exists *$hash{$key}*	Returns true if the specified *key* exists within the specified *hash*.
exit	exit *status*	Terminates current program immediately with return value *status*. N.B. The only universally recognized return values are 1 for failure and 0 for success.
exp	exp *number*	Returns the value of e to the power of *number* (or $_ if number is omitted).
fcntl	fcntl *filehandle, function, args*	Calls the fcntl function, to use on the file or device opened with *filehandle*.
fileno	fileno *filehandle*	Returns the file descriptor for *filehandle*.
flock	flock *filehandle, locktype*	Tries to lock or unlock a write-enabled file for use by the program. Note that this lock is only advisory and that other systems not supporting flock will be able to write to the file. *locktype* can take one of four values; LOCK_SH (new shared lock), LOCK_EX (new exclusive lock), LOCK_UN (unlock file) and LOCK_NB (do not block access to the file for a new lock if file not instantly available). Returns true for success, false for failure.
for	for *loop iterator block*	Perl's C-style for loop works exactly like the corresponding while loop. There is one minor difference: The first form implies a lexical scope for variables declared with my in the initialization expression.
foreach	foreach *loop iterator statement*	The foreach loop iterates over a normal list value and sets the variable VAR to be each element of the list in turn. The foreach keyword is actually a synonym for the for keyword, so you can use foreach for readability, or for for brevity.
fork	fork	System call that creates a new system process also running this program from the same point the fork was called. Returns the new process's ID to the original program, 0 to the new process, or undef if the fork did not succeed.
format	format	Declares an output template for use with write().

Function	Syntax	Description
formline	formline *template*, *list*	An internal function used for formats. Applies *template* to the *list* of values and stores the result in $^A. Always returns true.
getc	getc *filehandle* getc	Waits for the user to press Return and then retrieves the next character from *filehandle*'s file. Returns undef if at the end of a file. If *filehandle* is omitted, uses STDIN instead.
getgrent	getgrent	Gets the next group record from /etc/group or the system equivalent, returning an empty record when the end of the file is reached.
getgrgid	getgrgid *gid*	Gets the group record from /etc/group or the system equivalent whose ID field matches the given group number *gid*. Returns an empty record if no match occurs.
getgrnam	getgrnam *name*	Gets the group record from /etc/group or the system equivalent whose name field matches the given group *name*. Returns an empty record if no match occurs.
gethostbyaddr	gethostbyaddr *address*, *addrtype* gethostbyaddr *address*	Returns the hostname for a packed binary network *address* of a certain address type. By default, addrtype is assumed to be IP.
gethostbyname	gethostbyname *hostname*	Returns the network address given its corresponding *hostname*.
gethostent	gethostent	Gets the next network host record from /etc/hosts or the system equivalent, returning an empty record when the end of the file is reached.
getlogin	getlogin	Returns the user ID for the currently logged in user.
getnetbyaddr	getnetbyaddr *address*, *addrtype* getnetbyaddr *address*	Returns the net name for a given network *address* of a certain address type. By default, *addrtype* is assumed to be IP.

Table continued on following page

Function	Syntax	Description
getnetbyname	getnetbyname *name*	Returns the net address given its corresponding net *name*.
getnetent	getnetent	Gets the next entry from /etc/networks or the system equivalent, returning an empty record when the end of the file is reached.
getpeername	getpeername *socket*	Returns the address for the other end of the connection to this *socket*.
getpgrp	getpgrp *process_id* getpgrp	Returns the process group in which the specified process is running. Assumes current process if *process_id* is not given.
getppid	getppid	Returns the process ID of the current process's parent process.
getpriority	getpriority *type*, *id*	Returns current priority for a process, process group, or user as determined by *type*.
getprotobyname	getprotobyname *name*	Returns the number for the protocol given as *name*.
getprotobynumber	getprotobynumber *number*	Returns the name of the protocol given its *number*.
getprotoent	getprotoent	Gets the next entry from /etc/protocols or the system equivalent, returning an empty record when the end of the file is reached.
getpwent	getpwent	Gets the next entry from /etc/passwd or the system equivalent, returning an empty record when the end of the file is reached.
getpwnam	getpwnam *name*	Gets the password record whose login name field matches the given *name*. Returns an empty record if no match occurs.
getpwuid	getpwuid *uid*	Gets the password record whose user ID field matches the given *uid*. Returns an empty record if no match occurs.
getservbyname	getservbyname *name*, *protocol*	Returns the port number for the *named* service on the given *protocol*.
getservbyport	getservbyport *port*, *protocol*	Returns the port name for the service *port* on the given *protocol*.

Function	Syntax	Description
getservent	getservent	Gets the next entry from /etc/services or the system equivalent, returning an empty record when the end of the file is reached.
getsockname	getsockname *socket*	Returns the address for this end of the connection to this socket.
getsockopt	getsockopt *socket, level, optname*	Returns the specified socket option or undef if an error occurs.
glob	glob *expression* glob	Returns a list of filenames matching the regular *expression* in the current directory. If *expression* is omitted, the comparison is made with $_.
gmtime	gmtime *time*	Returns a nine-element integer array representing the given *time* (or *time*() if not given) converted to GMT. By index order, the nine elements (all zero-based) represent: 0 Number of seconds in the current minute 1 Number of minutes in the current hour 2 Current hour 3 Current day of month 4 Current month 5 Number of years since 1900 6 Weekday (Sunday = 0) 7 Number of days since January 1 8 Whether daylight savings time is in effect
goto	goto *tag* goto *expression* goto *&subroutine*	Looks for *tag* either given literally of dynamically derived by resolving expression and resumes execution of the program there on the provision that it is not inside a construct which requires initializing. For example, a for loop. Alternatively, goto *&subroutine* switches a call to *subroutine* for the currently running subroutine.

Table continued on following page

Function	Syntax	Description
grep	grep *expression, list* grep *{block} list*	Evaluates a given *expression* or *block* of code against each element in *list* and returns a list of those elements for which the evaluation returned true.
hex	hex *string* hex	Reads in *string* as a hexadecimal number and returns the corresponding decimal equivalent. Uses $_ if string is omitted.
if	if *expression block*	Executes *block* if *expression* is true.
if..else	if *expression block1* else *block2*	Executes *block1* if *expression* is true, otherwise executes *block2*.
if..elsif	if *expression1 block1* elsif *expression2 block2* else *block3*	If *expression1* is true, *block1*, otherwise, if *expression2* is true then *block2* is executed. If both *expression1* and *expression2* are false then *block3* is executed.
import	import *module list* import *module*	Patches a module's namespace into your own, incorporating the listed subroutines and variables into your own package (or all of them if *list* is not given).
index	index *string, substring, position* index *string, substring*	Returns the zero-based position of *substring* in *string* first occurring after character number *position*. Assumes *position* equals zero if not given. Returns -1 if match not found.
int	int *number* int	Returns the integer section of *number*, or $_ if *number* is omitted.
ioctl	ioctl *filehandle, function, argument*	Calls the ioctl function, to use on the file or device opened with *filehandle*.
join	join *character, list*	Returns a single string comprising the elements of *list*, separated from each other by *character*.
keys	keys *hash*	Returns a non-ordered list of the keys contained in *hash*.
kill	kill *signal, process_list*	Sends a *signal* to the processes and/or process groups in *process_list*. Returns number of signals successfully sent.

Function	Syntax	Description
last	last *label* last	Causes the program to break out of the *labeled* loop (or the innermost loop, if *label* is not given) surrounding the command and to continue with the statement immediately following the loop.
lc	lc *string*	Returns *string* in lower case, or $_ in lower case if *string* is omitted.
lcfirst	lcfirst *string*	Returns *string* with the first character in lower case. Works on $_ if *string* is omitted.
length	Length *expression*	Evaluates *expression* and returns the number of characters in that value. Returns length $_ if *expression* is omitted.
link	link *thisfile*, *thatfile*	Creates a hard link in the filesystem, from *thatfile* to *thisfile*. Returns true on success, false on failure.
listen	listen *socket*, *max_connectons*	Listens for connections to a particular *socket* on a server and reports when the number of connections exceeds *max_connections*.
local	local *var*	Declares a 'private' variable, which is available to the subroutine in which it is declared and any other subroutines, which may be called by this subroutine. Actually creates a temporary value for a global variable for the duration of the subroutine's execution.
localtime	localtime *time*	Returns a nine-element array representing the given *time* (or *time()* if not given) converted to system local time. See *gmtime()* for description of elements.
log	log *number*	Returns the natural logarithm for a *number*. That is, returns x where $e^x = number$.
lstat	lstat *filehandle* lstat *expression* lstat	Returns a thirteen-element status array for the symbolic link to a file and not the file itself. See stat() for further details.

Table continued on following page

Function	Syntax	Description
m//	m//	Tries to match a regular expression pattern against a string.
map	map *expression*, *list* map *{block}* *list*	Evaluates a given *expression* or *block* of code against each element in *list* and returns a list of the results of each evaluation.
mkdir	mkdir *dirname*, *mode*	Creates a directory called *dirname* and gives it the read\write permissions as specified in *mode* (an octal number).
msgctl	msgctl *id*, *cmd*, *arg*	Calls the System V IPC msgctl function.
msgget	msgget *key*, *flags*	Calls the System V IPC msgget function.
msgrcv	msgrcv *id*, *var*, *size*, *type*, *flags*	Calls the System V IPC msgrcv function.
msgsnd	msgsnd *id*, *msg*, *flags*	Calls the System V IPC msgsnd function.
my	my *variable_list*	Declares the variables in variable_list to be lexically local to the block or file it has been declared in.
next	next *label* next	Causes the program to start the next iteration of the *labeled* loop (or the innermost loop, if *label* is not given) surrounding the command.
no	no *module_name*	Removes the functionality and semantics of the named module from the current package. Compare with use() which does the opposite.
oct	oct *string* oct	Reads in *string* as an octal number and returns the corresponding decimal equivalent. Uses $_ if string is omitted.
open	open *filehandle*, *filename* open *filehandle*	Opens the file called *filename* and associates it with *filehandle*. If *filename* is omitted, *open* assumes that the file has the same name as *filehandle*.
opendir	opendir *dirhandle*, *dirname*	Opens the directory called *dirname* and associates it with *dirhandle*.
ord	ord *expression*	Returns the numerical ASCII value of the first character in *expression*.

Function	Syntax	Description
pack	pack *template*, *list*	Takes a *list* of values and puts them into a binary structure using *template* (a sequence of characters as shown below) to give the structure an ordered composition. The possible characters for *template* are: a Null-padded ASCII string A Space-padded ASCII string b A bit string (low-to-high) B A bit string (high-to-low) c A signed char value C An unsigned char value d A double-precision float in the native format f A single-precision float in the native format h A hexadecimal string, low to high H A hexadecimal string, high to low

Table continued on following page

Function	Syntax	Description
pack (continued)	pack *template*, *list*	i A signed integer
		I An unsigned integer
		l A signed long value
		L An unsigned long value
		n A big-endian short (16-bit) value
		N A big-endian long (32-bit) value
		p A pointer to a null-terminated string
		P A pointer to a fixed-length string
		q A signed quad (64-bit) value
		Q An unsigned quad (64-bit) value
		s A signed short (16-bit) value
		S An unsigned short (16-bit) value

Function	Syntax	Description
pack (continued)	pack *template*, *list*	v A little-endian short (16-bit) value
		V A big-endian long (32-bit) value
		u An uuencoded string
		w A BER compressed integer - an unsigned integer in base 128, high-bit first.
		x A null byte
		X Back up a byte
		Z A null-padded, Null-terminated string
		@ Null-fill to absolute position
package	package *namespace*	Declares that the following block of code is to be defined within the specified *namespace*.
pipe	pipe *readhandle*, *writehandle*	Opens and connects two filehandles, such that the pipe reads content from *readhandle* and passes it to *writehandle*.
pop	pop *array* pop	Removes and returns the last element (at largest index position) from *array*. Pops @ARGV if *array* is not specified.
pos	pos *scalar*	Returns the position in *scalar* of the character following the last m//g match. Uses $_ for *scalar* if omitted.

Table continued on following page

Function	Syntax	Description
print	print *filehandle list* print *list* print	Prints a *list* of comma-separated strings to the file associated with *filehandle* or STDOUT if not specified. If both arguments are omitted, prints $_ to the currently selected output channel.
printf	printf *filehandle format*, *list* printf *format*, *list*	As print() but prints to the output channel using a specified *format*.
prototype	prototype *function*	Returns the prototype of a *function* as a string or undef if the prototype does not exist.
push	push *array*, *list*	Adds the elements of *list* to the *array* at position max_index.
q/ /	q/*string*/	Alternative method of putting single quotes around a string.
qq/ /	qq/*string*/	Alternative method of putting double quotes around a string.
quotemeta	quotemeta *expression*	Scans through *expression* and returns it having prefixed all the metacharacters with a backslash.
qr/ /	qr/*strings*/	Method used for quoting and compiling its *string* element as a regular expression.
qw/ /	qw/*strings*/	Returns a list of strings, the elements of which are created by splitting a *string* by whitespace, or the *strings* sent to qw//.
qx/ /	qx/*string*/	Alternative method of backtick-quoting a *string* (which now acts as a command-line command).
rand	rand *expression*	Evaluates expression and then returns a random value x where $0 <= x <$ the value of *expression*.

read	read *filehandle*, *scalar*,
	    length, *offset*
	read *filehandle*, *scalar*,
	    length
		Reads *length* number of bytes in from *filehandle*, placing them in *scalar*. Starts by default from the start of the file, but you can specify *offset*, the position in the file you wish to start reading from. Returns the number of bytes read, zero if at the end of the file or undef if file does not exist.

Function	Syntax	Description
readdir	readdir *dirhandle*	Returns the next entry in the directory specified by *dirhandle*, or if being used in list context, the entire contents of the directory.
readline	readline *filehandle*	Returns a line from *filehandle*'s file if in scalar context, else returns a list containing all the lines of the file as its elements.
readlink	readlink *linkname*	Returns the name of the file at the end of symbolic link *linkname*.
readpipe	readpipe *command*	Executes *command* on the command line and then returns the standard output generated by it as a string. Returns a list of lines from the standard output if in list context.
recv	recv *socket, scalar,* *length, flags*	Receives a *length* byte message over the named *socket* and reads it into a *scalar* string.
redo	redo *label* redo	Causes the program to restart the current iteration of the *labeled* loop (or the innermost loop, if *label* is not given) surrounding the command without checking the while condition.
ref	ref *reference* ref	Returns the type of object being referenced by *reference*, or a package name if the object has been blessed into a package.
rename	rename *oldname, newname*	Renames file *oldname* as *newname*. Returns 1 for success, 0 otherwise.
require	require *file* require *package* require *num* require	Ensures that the named *package* or *file* is included at runtime. If *num* is argument, ensures that version of Perl currently running is greater than or equal to *num* (or $_ if omitted).
reset	reset *expression*	Resets all variables in current package beginning with one of the characters in *expression* and all ?? searches to their original state.
return	return *expression*	Returns the value of *expression* from a subroutine or eval().
reverse	reverse *list*	Returns either *list* with its elements in reverse order if in list context or a string consisting of the elements of *list* concatenated together and then written backwards.

Table continued on following page

Function	Syntax	Description
rewinddir	rewinddir *dirhandle*	Resets the point of access for readdir() to the top of directory *dirhandle*.
rindex	rindex *string*, *substring*, *position* rindex *string*, *substring*	Returns the zero-based position of the last occurrence of *substring* in *string* at or before character number *position*. Returns -1 if match not found.
rmdir	rmdir *dirname*	If directory *dirname* (or that given in $_ if omitted) is empty, it is removed. Returns true on success, false otherwise.
s///	s/*matchstring*/*replacestring*/	Searches for *matchstring* in $_ and replaces it with *replacestring* if found.
scalar	scalar *expression*	Evaluates *expression* in scalar context and returns the resultant value.
seek	seek *filehandle*, *position*, *flag*	Sets the *position* (character number) in a file denoted by *filehandle* from which the file will be read/written. *flag* tells seek whether to goto character number *position* (*flag* = 0), number current position + *position* (*flag* = 1), or number EOF + *position* (*flag*=2). Returns 1 on success, 0 otherwise.
seekdir	seekdir *dirhandle*, *position*	Sets the *position* (entry number) in a directory denoted by *dirhandle* from which directory entries will be read.
select	select *filehandle* select	Changes the current default filehandle (starts as STDOUT) to *filehandle*. Returns the current default filehandle if *filehandle* is omitted.
select	select *rbits*, *wbits*, *ebits*, *timeout*	Calls the system select command to wait for *timeout* seconds until one (if any) of your filehandles become available for reading or writing and returns either success or failure.
semctl	semctl *id*, *sem_num*, *command*, *argument*	Calls the System V IPC semctl function.
semget	semget *id*, *semnum*, *command*, *argument*	Calls the System V IPC semget function.
semop	semop *key*, *opstring*	Calls the System V IPC semop function.
send	send *socket*, *message*, *flags*, *destination* send *socket*, *message*, *flags*	Sends a *message* from a *socket* to the connected socket, or, if *socket* is disconnected, to *destination*. Takes account of any system *flags* given to it.

Function	Syntax	Description
setgrent	setgrent (*void*)	The setgrent function rewinds the file pointer to the beginning of the /etc/group file.
sethostent	sethostent *stayopen*	The sethostent function specifies, if stayopen is true (1), that a connected TCP socket should be used for the name server queries and that the connection should remain open during successive queries. Otherwise, name server queries will use UDP datagrams.
setnetent	setnetent *stayopen*	The setnetent function opens and rewinds the database. If the stayopen argument is non-zero, the connection to the net database will not be closed after each call to getnetent (either directly, or indirectly through one of the other *getnet** functions).
setpgrp	setpgrp *process_id*, *process_group*	Sets the *process_group* in which the process with the given *process_id* should run. The arguments default to 0 if not given.
setpriority	setpriority *which*, *id*, *priority*	Adds to or diminishes the priority of either a process, process group, or user, as determined by *which* and specifically identified by its *id*.
setprotoent	setprotoent *stayopen*	The setprotoent function opens and rewinds the /etc/protocols file. If stayopen is true (1), then the file will not be closed between calls to getprotobyname or getprotobynumber.
setpwent	setpwent (*void*)	The setpwent function rewinds the file pointer to the beginning of the /etc/passwd file.
setservent	setservent *stayopen*	The setservent function opens and rewinds the /etc/services file. If stayopen is true (1), then the file will not be closed between calls to getservbyname and getservbyport.
setsockopt	setsockopt *socket*, *level*, *option*, *optional_value*	Sets the *option* for the given *socket*. Returns undef if an error occurs.

Table continued on following page

1131

Function	Syntax	Description
shift	shift *array* shift	Returns the element at position 0 in array and then removes it from array. Returns undef if there are no elements in the array. Shifts @_ within subroutines and formats and @ARGV otherwise if *array* is omitted.
shmctl	shmctl *id, command, argument*	Calls the System V IPC shmctl function.
shmget	shmget *key, size, flags*	Calls the System V IPC shmget function.
shmread	shmread *id, variable, position, size*	Calls the System V IPC shmread function.
shmwrite	shmwrite *id, string, position, size*	Calls the System V IPC shmwrite function.
shutdown	shutdown *socket, manner*	Shuts down the *socket* specified in the following *manner*. 0 Stop reading data 1 Stop writing data 2 Stop using this socket altogether
sin	sin *expression* sin	Evaluates *expression* as a value in radians and then returns the sine of that value. Returns the sine of $_ if expression is omitted.
sleep	sleep *n* sleep	Causes the running script to 'sleep' for *n* seconds or forever if *n* is not given.
socket	socket *filehandle, domain, type, protocol*	Opens a socket and associates it to the given *filehandle*. This socket exists within the given *domain* of communication, is of the given *type* and uses the given *protocol* to communicate.
socketpair	socketpair *sock1, sock2, domain, type, protocol*	Creates a pair of sockets named *sock1* and *sock2*. These sockets exist within the given *domain* of communication, are of the given *type* and use the given *protocol* to communicate.

Function	Syntax	Description
sort	sort *subroutine list* sort *block list* sort *list*	Takes a *list* of values and returns it with the elements having been sorted into an order. If *subroutine* is given, uses that to sort *list*. If *block* is given, this is used as an anonymous subroutine to sort *list*. If neither is given, *list* is sorted by simple string comparisons.

splice	splice *array, offset,*
	    length, list
	splice *array, offset,*
	    length
	splice *array, offset*
		Takes *array* elements from index *offset* to (*offset*+*length*) and replaces them with the elements of *list*, if any. If *length* is removed, removes all the elements of array from index *offset* onwards. If negative, leaves that many elements at the end of the array. If offset is negative, splice starts from index number (maxindex-*offset*). Returns the last element removed if in scalar context or undef if nothing was removed.

split	split /*pattern*/, *string,* *limit* split /*pattern*/, *string* split /*pattern*/ split	Takes the given *string*, and returns it as an array of smaller strings where any instances in the string matching *pattern* have been used as the delimiter for the array elements. If given, *limit* denotes the number of times the pattern will be searched for in the string. If *string* is omitted, $_ is split. If *pattern* is omitted, $_ is split by whitespace.
sprintf	sprintf *format, list*	As printf() but prints *list* to a string using a specified *format*.
sqrt	sqrt *expression* sqrt	Evaluates *expression* and then returns the square root of either it or $_ if it was left out of the call.
srand	srand *expression* srand	Seeds the random number generator.
stat	stat *filehandle* stat *expression* stat	Returns a thirteen element array comprising the following information about a file named by *expression*, represented by *filehandle* or contained in $_. (by index number) 0 $dev Device number of filesystem 1 $ino Inode number

Table continued on following page

Function	Syntax	Description
stat (continued)	stat *filehandle* stat *expression* stat	2 $mode File mode 3 $nlink Number of links to the file 4 $uid User ID of file's owner 5 $gid Group ID of file's owner 6 $rdev Device identifier 7 $size Total size of file 8 $atime Last time file was accessed 9 $mtime Last time file was modified 10 $ctime Last time inode was changed 11 $blksize Preferred block size for file I/O 12 $blocks Number of blocks allocated to file

Function	Syntax	Description
study	study *string* study	Tells Perl to optimize itself for repeated searches on *string* or on $_ if *string* is omitted.
sub	sub *subname* *block* sub *subname* sub *block*	Declares a *block* of code to be a subroutine with the name *subname*. If *block* is omitted, this is just a forward reference to a later declaration. If *subname* is omitted, this is an anonymous function declaration.
substr	substr *string*, *position*, *length*, *replacement* substr *string*, *position*, *length* substr *string*, *position*	Returns a substring of *string* that is *length* characters long starting with the character at index number *position*. If given, that substring is then silently replaced with *replacement*. If *length* is not given, substr assumes the entire string from *position* onwards.
symlink	symlink *oldfile*, *newfile*	Creates *newfile* as a symbolic link to *oldfile*. Returns 1 on success, 0 on failure.
syscall	syscall *list*	Assumes the first element in the *list* is the name of a system call and calls it, taking the other elements of the *list* to be arguments to that call.
sysopen	sysopen *filehandle*, *filename*, *mode*, *permissions* sysopen *filehandle*, *filename*, *mode*	Opens file *filename* under the specified *mode* and associates it with the given *filehandle*. *permissions* is the octal value representing the permissions that you want to assign to the file. If not given, the default is 0666.
sysread	sysread *filehandle*, *scalar*, *length*, *offset* sysread *filehandle*, *scalar*, *length*	Reads *length* number of bytes in from *filehandle*, placing them in *scalar* using the system call read. Starts by default from the start of the file, but you can specify *offset*, the position in the file you wish to start reading from. Returns the number of bytes read, zero if at the end of the file or undef if file does not exist.
sysseek	sysseek *filehandle*, *pos*, *flag*	Sets the system position for the file denoted by *filehandle*. *Flag* tells sysseek whether to goto position number *pos* (*flag* = 0), number current position + *pos* (*flag* = 1), or number EOF + pios (*flag* = 2). Returns 1 on success, 0 otherwise.

Function	Syntax	Description
system	system *list*	Forks the process that the current program is running on, lets it complete and then abandons the current program to run the specified system command in *list*. This will be the first element of *list* and any arguments to it are stored in subsequent list elements.
syswrite	syswrite *filehandle, scalar, length, offset* syswrite *filehandle, scalar, length* syswrite *filehandle, scalar*	Writes *length* number of bytes from the *scalar* to the file denoted by *filehandle*, starting at character number *offset* if specified. If *length* is not given, writes the entire scalar to the file.
tell	tell *filehandle* tell	Returns the current read\write position for the file marked by *filehandle*. If filehandle is not given, the info is given for the last accessed file.
telldir	telldir *dirhandle*	Returns the current readdir position for the directory marked by *dirhandle*.
tie	tie *variable, classname, list*	Binds the named *variable* to package class *classname*, which works on a variable of that type. Passes any arguments (in *list*) to the new function of the class (TIESCALAR, TIEHASH, or TIEARRAY).
tied	tied *variable*	Returns a reference to the object tied to the given *variable*.
time	time	Returns the number of non-leap seconds elapsed since Jan 1, 1970. Can be translated into recognizable time values with gmtime() and localtime().
times	times	Returns a four-element list holding the user and system CPU times (in seconds) for both the current process and its child processes. The list is comprised as follows: $user Current process user time $system Current process system CPU time

Function	Syntax	Description
times (continued)	times	$cuser Child process user time $csystem Child process system time
tr///	tr/string1/string2/	Transliterates a string (also known as y///).
truncate	truncate filehandle, length truncate expression, length	Truncates the file given by filehandle or named literally by expression to length characters. Returns true on success, false otherwise.
uc	uc string uc	Returns string in upper case, or $_ in upper case if string is omitted.
ucfirst	ucfirst string ucfirst	Returns string with the first character in upper case. Works on $_ if string is omitted.
umask	umask expression umask	Returns the current umask and then sets it to expression if this is given. The umask is a group of three octal numbers representing the access permissions for a file or directory of its owner, a group and other users, where execute = 1, write = 2, and read = 4. So a umask of 0777 would give all permissions to all three levels of user. 0744 would restrict all except the owner to read access only.
undef	undef expression undef	Removes the value of expression, leaving it undefined, else just returns the undefined value.
unless	unless condition block	Similar to the simple if statement, the statement runs along the lines of 'unless this exists, then {...}'.
unlink	unlink list	Deletes the files specified in list (or $_ if not given), returning the number of files deleted. NB: For UNIX users, unlink() removes a link to each file but not the fields themselves if other links to them still exist.

Table continued on following page

1137

Function	Syntax	Description
unpack	unpack *template*, *string*	The reverse of pack(). Takes a packed *string* and then uses *template* to read through it and return an array of the values stored within it. See pack() for how *template* is constructed.
unshift	unshift *array*, *list*	Adds the elements of *list* in the same order to the front (index 0) of *array*, returning the number of elements now in *array*.
untie	untie *variable*	Unbinds the *variable* from the package class it had previously been tied to.
until	until *expression block*	Executes *block* until *expression* becomes true.
use	use *module version list* use *module list* use *module* use *version*	Requires and imports the (*listed* elements of the) named *module* at compile time. Checks module being used is the specified *version* if combined with *module* and *list*. use *version* meanwhile makes sure that the Perl interpreter being used is no older than the stated *version*.
utime	utime *atime*, *mtime*, *filelist*	Sets the access (*atime*) and modification (*mtime*) times on files listed in *filelist*, returning the number of successful changes that were made.
values	values *hash*	Takes the named *hash* and returns a list containing copies of each of the values in it.
vec	vec *string*, *offset*, *bits*	Takes *string* and regards it as a vector of unsigned integers. Then returns the value of the element at position *offset* given that each element has 2 to the power of *bits* in it.
wait	wait	Waits for a child process to die and then returns the process ID of the child process that did or -1 if there are no child processes.
waitpid	waitpid *pid*, *flags*	Waits for the child process with process ID *pid* to die.
wantarray	wantarray	Returns true if the subroutine currently running is running in list context. Returns false if not. Returns undef if the subroutine's return value is not going to be used.

Function	Syntax	Description
warn	warn *message*	Prints *message* to STDERR, but does not throw an error or exception.
while	while *expression* *block*	Executes *block* as long as *expression* is true.
write	write *filehandle* write *expression* write	Writes a formatted record to *filehandle*, the file named after evaluating *expression*, or the current default output channel if neither are given.
y///	y/*string1*/*string2*/	Transliterates a string (also known as tr///).

Regular Expressions

Pattern Matching Operators

Match – 'm//'

Syntax: m/pattern/

If a match is found for the pattern within a referenced string (default $_), the expression returns true. Note that if the delimiters // are used, the preceding m is not required.

Modifiers: g, i, m, o, s, x

Substitution – 's///'

Syntax: s/pattern1/pattern2/

If a match is found for pattern1 within a referenced string (default $_), the relevant substring is replaced by the contents of pattern2, and the expression returns true.

Modifiers: e, g, i, m, o, s, x

Quoting - 'qr//'

Syntax: qr/string/imosx

This operator quotes and compiles its string as a regular expression. string is interpolated the same way as pattern in m/pattern/. It returns a Perl value which may be used instead of the corresponding /string/imosx expression.

Since Perl may compile the pattern at the moment of execution of qr() operator, using qr() may have speed advantages in some situations, notably if the result of qr() is used standalone.

Modifiers: i, m, o, s, x

Transliteration –' tr///' or 'y///'

Syntax: tr/pattern1/pattern2/
       y/pattern1/pattern2/

If any characters in pattern1 match those within a referenced string (default $_), instances of each are replaced by the corresponding character in pattern2, and the expression returns the number of characters replaced.

Note that if one character occurs several times within pattern1, only the first will be used. For example, tr/abbc/xyz/ is equivalent to tr/abc/xyz/.

Modifiers: c, d, s

Delimiters

Patterns may be delimited by character pairs <>, (), [], {} or any other non-word character. For example, s<pattern1><pattern2> and s#pattern1#pattern2# are both equivalent to s/pattern1/pattern2/.

Binding Operators

Binding Operator - '=~'

Syntax: $refstring =~ m/pattern/

Binds a match operator to a variable other than $_. Returns true if a match is found.

Negation Operator - '!~'

Syntax: $refstring !~ m/pattern/

Binds a match operator to a variable other than $_. Returns true if a match is not found.

Modifiers

Match and Substitution

The following can be used to modify the behavior of match and substitution operators:

Cancel Position Reset - '/c'

Used only with global matches, that is as m//gc, to prevent the search cursor returning to the start of the string if a match cannot be found. Instead, it remains at the end of the last match found.

1142

Evaluate Replacement – '/e'

Evaluate the second argument of the substitution operator as an expression.

Global Match – '/g'

Finds all the instances in which the pattern matches the string rather than stopping at the first match. Multiple matches will be numbered in the operator's return value.

Case-insensitive – '/i'

Matches pattern against string whilst ignoring the case of the characters in either pattern or string.

Multi-line Mode – '/m'

The string to be matched against is to be regarded as a collection of separate lines, with the result that the metacharacters ^ and $ which would otherwise just match the beginning and end of the entire text now also match the beginning and end of each line.

One-time Pattern Compilation - '/o'

If a pattern to match against a string contains variables, these are interpolated to form part of the pattern. Later these variables may change and the pattern will change with it when next matched against. By adding /o the pattern will be formed once and will not be recompiled even if the variables within have changed value.

Single-line Mode – '/s'

The string to be matched against will be regarded as a single line of text, with the result that the metacharacter '.' will match against the newline character, which it would not do otherwise.

Free-form – '/x'

Allow the use of whitespace and comments inside a match to expand and explain the expression.

Transliteration

The following can be used to modify the behavior of the transliteration operator:

Complement - '/c'

Use complement of `pattern1`, substitutes all characters *except* those specified in `pattern1`.

delete - '/d'

Deletes all the characters found but not replaced.

squash - '/s'

Multiple replaced characters squashed – only returned once to transliterated string.

Localized modifiers

Syntax:

```
/CaseSensitiveTxt((?i)CaseInsensitiveTxt)CaseSensitiveText/

/CaseInsensitiveTxt((?-i)CaseSensitiveTxt)CaseInsensitiveText/i
```

The following inline modifiers can be placed within a regular expression to enforce or negate relevant matching behavior on limited portions of the expression:

Modifier	Description	Inline enforce	Inline negate
/i	case insensitive	(?i)	(?-i)
/s	single-line mode	(?s)	(?-s)
/m	multi-line mode	(?m)	(?-m)
/x	free-form	(?x)	(?-x)

Metacharacters

Metacharacter	Meaning
[abc]	Any one of a, b, or c.
[^abc]	Anything other than a, b, and c.
\d \D	A digit; a non-digit.
\w \W	A 'word' character; a non-'word' character.
\s \S	A whitespace character; a non-whitespace character.
\b	The boundary between a \w character and a \W character.
.	Any single character (apart from a new line).
(abc)	The phrase 'abc' as a group.
?	Preceding character or group may be present 0 or 1 times.
+	Preceding character or group is present 1 or more times.
*	Preceding character or group may be present 0 or more times.
{x,y}	Preceding character or group is present between x and y times.
{,y}	Preceding character or group is present at most y times.
{x,}	Preceding character or group is present at least x times.
{x}	Preceding character or group is present x times.

Non-greediness for Quantifiers

Syntax: (pattern)+?
         (pattern)*?

The metacharacters + and * are greedy by default, and will try to match as much as possible of the referenced string (while still achieving a full pattern match). This 'greedy' behavior can be turned off by placing a ? immediately after the respective metacharacter. A non-greedy match finds the minimum number of characters matching the pattern.

Grouping and Alternation

'|' For Alternation

Syntax: `pattern1|pattern2`

By separating two patterns with | we can specify that a match on one *or* the other should be attempted.

'()' For Grouping and Backreferences ('capturing')

Syntax: `(pattern)`

This will group elements in `pattern` – if those elements are matched, a backreference is made to one of the numeric special variables ($1, $2, $3 etc.)

'(?:)' For Non-backreferenced Grouping ('clustering')

Syntax: `(?:pattern)`

This will group elements in *pattern* without making backreferences.

Lookahead/behind assertions

'(?=)' for positive lookahead

Syntax: `pattern1(?=pattern2)`

This lets us look for a match on 'pattern1 followed by `pattern2`', without back-referencing `pattern2`.

'(?!)' for negative lookahead

Syntax: `pattern1(?!pattern2)`

This lets us look for a match on 'pattern1 **not** followed by `pattern2`', without back-referencing `pattern2`.

'(?<=)' for positive lookbehind

Syntax: `pattern1(?<=pattern2)`

This lets us look for a match on 'pattern1 preceded by `pattern2`', without back-referencing `pattern2`. This only works if `pattern2` is of fixed width.

'(?<!)' for negative lookbehind

Syntax: `pattern1(?<!pattern2)`

This lets us look for a match on 'pattern1 **not** preceded by `pattern2`', without back-referencing `pattern2`. This only works if `pattern2` is of fixed width.

Backreference Variables

Variable	Description
\num (num = 1, 2, 3...)	Within a regular expression, \num returns the substring that was matched with the numth grouped pattern in that regexp.
$num (num = 1, 2, 3...)	Outside a regular expression, $num returns the substring that was matched with the numth grouped pattern in that regexp.
$+	This returns the substring matched with the last grouped pattern in a regexp.
$&	This returns the string that matched the whole regexp, this will include portions of the string that matched (?:) groups, which are otherwise not backreferenced.
$`	This returns everything preceding the matched string in $&.
$'	This returns everything following the matched string in $&.

Other

'(?#)' for comments

Syntax: (?#comment_text)

This lets us place comments within the body of a regular expression, an alternative to the /x modifier.

Standard Pragmatic Modules

The following is a list of the pragmatic modules, which are installed with Perl 5.6. They have been ordered alphabetically. Note that these module names are case sensitive and are given as they should be written in a use statement.

Using pragmatic modules affects the compilation of Perl programs. These modules are lexically scoped and so to use, or to uninclude, them with no like this:

```
use attrs;
use warnings;
no integer;
no diagnostics;
```

is effective only for the duration of the block in which the declaration was made. Furthermore, these declarations may be reversed within any inner blocks in the program.

Module	Function
attributes	Gets or sets the attribute values for a subroutine or variable.
attrs	Gets or sets the attribute values for a subroutine. **Deprecated in Perl 5.6** in favor of attributes.
autouse	Moves the inclusion of modules into a program from compile time to runtime. Specifically, it postpones the module's loading until one of its functions is called.
base	Takes a list of modules, requires them and then pushes them onto @ISA. Essentially, it will establish an 'IS-A' relationship with these classes at compile time.
blib	Used on the command line as -Mblib switch to test your scripts against an uninstalled version of the package named after the switch.
caller	Causes program to inherit the pragmatic attributes of the program, which has called it.
charnames	Allows you to specify a long name for a given string literal escape.
constant	Allows you to define constants as a name=>value pair.
diagnostics	Returns verbose output when errors occur at runtime. This verbose output consists of the message that Perl would normally give plus any accompanying text that that error contained in the perldiag manpage.
fields	Takes a list of valid class fields for the package and enables the class fields at compile time.
filetest	Changes the operation of the -r, -w, -x, -R, -W, and -X file test operators.
integer	Changes the mathematical operators in a program to work with integers only and not floating point numbers.
less	Currently not implemented.
lib	Adds the listed directories to @INC.
locale	Enables\disables POSIX locales for built-in operations.
open	Sets default disciplines for input and output.
ops	Restricts potentially harmful operations occurring during compile time.
overload	Allows you to overload built-in Perl operations with your own subroutines.
re	Allows you to alter the way regular expressions behave.
sigtrap	Enables some simple signal handlers.
strict	Enforces the declaration of variables before their use.
subs	Allows you to predeclare subroutine names.
utf8	Enables\disables Unicode support. Note that at the time of writing, Unicode support in Perl was incomplete.
vars	Allows you to predeclare global variable names.
warnings	Switches on the extra syntactic error warning messages.

Standard Functional Modules

The standard modules are those that are installed with our distribution of Perl. They are listed here alphabetically.

Module	Function
AnyDBM_File	Acts as a universal virtual base class for those wanting to access any of the five types of DBM file.
AutoLoader	Works with Autosplit to delay the loading of subroutines into the program until they are called. These subroutines are defined following the __END__ token in a package file.
AutoSplit	Splits a program into files suitable for autoloading or selfloading.
B	The Perl compiler module.
B::Asmdata	Contains autogenerated data about Perl ops used in the generation of bytecode.
B::Assembler	Assembles Perl bytecode for use elsewhere.
B::Bblock	Used by B::CC to walk through 'basic blocks' of code.
B::Bytecode	Compiler backend for generating Perl bytecode.
B::C	Compiler backend for generating C source code.
B::CC	Compiler backend for generating optimized C source code.

Table continued on following page

Module	Function
B::Debug	Walks the Perl syntax tree, printing debug info about ops.
B::Deparse	Compiler backend for generating Perl source code from compiled Perl.
B::Disassembler	Disassembles Perl bytecode back to Perl source.
B::Graph	Compiler backend for generating graph-description documents that show the program's structure.
B::Lint	Module to catch dubious constructs.
B::Showlex	Shows the file-scope variables for a file or the lexical variables for a subroutine if one is specified.
B::Stackobj	Helper module for CC backend.
B::Stash	Shows what stashes are loaded.
B::Terse	Walks the Perl syntax tree, printing terse info about ops.
B::Xref	Compiler backend for generating cross-reference reports.
Benchmark	Contains a suite of routines that let you benchmark your code.
ByteLoader	Used to load byte-compiled Perl code.
bytes	Perl pragma to force byte semantics rather than character semantics.
CGI	The base class that provides the basic functionality for generating web content and CGI scripting.
CGI::Apache	Backward compatibility module. **Deprecated in Perl 5.6.**
CGI::Carp	Holds the equivalent of the Carp module's error logging functions CGI routines for writing time-stamped entries to the HTTPD (or other) error log.
CGI::Cookie	Allows access and interaction with Netscape cookies.
CGI::Fast	Allows CGI access and interaction to a FastCGI web server.
CGI::Pretty	Generates 'pretty' HTML code on server in place of slightly less pretty HTML written in the CGI script file.
CGI::Push	Provides a CGI interface to server-side push functionality. For example, as used with channels.
CGI::Switch	Backward compatibility module. **Deprecated in Perl 5.6.**
CPAN	Provides you with the functionality to query, download, and build Perl modules from any of the CPAN mirrors.

Module	Function
CPAN::FirstTime	Utility for CPAN::Config to ask a few questions about the system and then write a config file.
CPAN::Nox	As CPAN module, but does not use any compiled extensions during its own execution.
Carp	Provides warn() and die() functionality with the added ability to say in which module something failed and what it was.
Carp::Heavy	Carp guts. For internal use only.
Class::Struct	Lets you declare C-style struct-like complex datatypes and manipulate them accordingly.
Config	Allows access to the options and settings used by Configure to build this installation of Perl.
Cwd	Gets the pathname of the current working directory.
DB	Programmatic interface to the Perl debugger's API (Application Programming Interface). NB: This may change.
DB_File	Provides an interface for access to Berkeley DB version 1.x. Note that you can access versions 2.x and 3.x of Berkeley DB with this module but will have only the version 1.x functionality.
Data::Dumper	Returns a stringified version of the contents of an object, given a reference to it.
Devel::DProf	A Perl code profiler. Generates information on the frequency of calls to subroutines and on the speediness of the subroutines themselves.
Devel::Peek	A debugging tool for those trying to write C programs interconnecting with Perl programs.
Devel::SelfStubber	Stub generator for a SelfLoading module.
DirHandle	Provides an alternative set of functions to opendir(), closedir(), readdir() and rewinddir().
Dumpvalue	Dumps info about Perl data to the screen.
DynaLoader	Dynamically loads C libraries when required into your Perl code.
English	Allows you to call Perl's special variables by their 'English' names.
Env	Allows you to access the key\value pairs in the environment hash %ENV as arrays or scalar values.
Errno	Exports (to your code) the contents of the errno.h include file. This contains all the defined error constants on your system.
Exporter	Implements the default import method for modules.

Table continued on following page

Module	Function
Exporter::Heavy	The internals of the Exporter module.
ExtUtils::Command	Contains equivalents of the common UNIX system commands for Windows users.
ExtUtils::Embed	Contains utilities for embedding a Perl interpreter into our C/C++ programs.
ExtUtils::Install	Contains three functions for installing, uninstalling, and installing-as-autosplit/autoload programs.
ExtUtils::Installed	Keeps track of what modules are and are not installed.
ExtUtils::Liblist	Determines which libraries should be used in an install and how to use them and sends its finding for inclusion in a Makefile.
ExtUtils::MakeMaker	Used to create makefiles for an extension module.
ExtUtils::Manifest	Utilities to write and check a MANIFEST file.
ExtUtils::Miniperl	Contains one function to write perlmain.c, a bootstrapper between Perl and C libraries.
ExtUtils::Mkbootstrap	Contains one function to write a bootstrap file for use by DynaLoader.
ExtUtils::Mksymlists	Contains one function to write linker options files for dynamic extension.
ExtUtils::MM_Cygwin	Contains methods to override those in ExtUtils::MM_Unix when ExtUtils::MakeMaker is used on a Cygwin system.
ExtUtils::MM_OS2	Contains methods to override those in ExtUtils::MM_Unix when ExtUtils::MakeMaker is used on an OS\2 system.
ExtUtils::MM_Unix	Contains the methods used by ExtUtils::MakeMaker to work.
ExtUtils::MM_VMS	Contains methods to override those in ExtUtils::MM_Unix when ExtUtils::MakeMaker is used on a VMS system.
ExtUtils::MM_Win32	Contains methods to override those in ExtUtils::MM_Unix when ExtUtils::MakeMaker is used on a Windows system.
ExtUtils::Packlist	Contains a standard .packlist file manager.
ExtUtils::testlib	Adds blib/* directories to @INC.
Fatal	Provides a way to replace functions, which return false with functions that raise an exception if not successful.
Fcntl	Loads the libc fcntl.h defines.
File::Basename	Provides functions that work on a file's full path name.
File::CheckTree	Allows you to specify file tests to be made on directories and files within a directory all at once.

Module	Function
File::Compare	Compares the contents of two files.
File::Copy	Copies files or directories.
File::DosGlob	Implements DOS-like globbing but also accepts wildcards in directory components.
File::Find	Searches/traverses a file tree for requested file.
File::Glob	Implements the FreeBSD glob routine.
File::Path	Creates or deletes a series of directories.
File::Spec	Group of functions to work on file properties and paths.
File::Spec::Functions	Support module for File::Spec.
File::Spec::Mac	Contains methods to override those in File::Spec::Unix when File::Spec is used on a MacOS system.
File::Spec::OS2	Contains methods to override those in File::Spec::Unix when File::Spec is used on an OS/2 system.
File::Spec::Unix	Methods used by File::Spec.
File::Spec::VMS	Contains methods to override those in File::Spec::Unix when File::Spec is used on a VMS system.
File::Spec::Win32	Contains methods to override those in File::Spec::Unix when File::Spec is used on a Win32 system.
File::stat	A by-name interface to Perl's built-in stat() functions.
FileCache	Allows you to keep more files open than the system allows.
FileHandle	Provides an OO-style implementation of filehandles.
FindBin	Locates the directory holding the currently running Perl program.
GDBM_File	Provides an interface for access and makes use of the GNU Gdbm library.
Getopt::Long	Enables the parsing of long switch names on the command line.
Getopt::Std	Enables the parsing of single-character switches and clustered switches on the command line.
I18N::Collate	Compares 8-bit scalar data according to the current locale. **Deprecated in Perl 5.004.**
IO	Front-end to load the IO modules listed below.
IO::Dir	Provides an OO-style implementation for directory handles.

Table continued on following page

1157

Module	Function
IO::File	Based on FileHandle, it provides an OO-style implementation of filehandles.
IO::Handle	Provides an OO-style implementation for I/O handles.
IO::Pipe	Provides an OO-style implementation for pipes.
IO::Poll	Provides an OO-style implementation to system poll calls.
IO::Seekable	Provides seek(), sysseek() and tell() methods for I/O objects.
IO::Select	Provides an OO-style implementation for the select system call.
IO::Socket	Provides an OO-style implementation for socket communications.
IO::Socket::INET	Provides an OO-style implementation for AF_INET domain sockets.
IO::Socket::UNIX	Provides an OO-style implementation for AF_UNIX domain sockets.
IPC::Msg	Implements a System V Messaging IPC object class.
IPC::Open2	Opens a process for both reading and writing.
IPC::Open3	Opens a process for reading, writing, and error handling.
IPC::Semaphore	Implements a System V Semaphore IPC object class.
IPC::SysV	Exports all the constants needed by System V IPC calls as defined in your system's libraries.
Math::BigFloat	Enables the storage of arbitrarily long floating-point numbers.
Math::BigInt	Enables the storage of arbitrarily long integers.
Math::Complex	Enables work with complex numbers and associated mathematical functions.
Math::Trig	Provides all the trigonometric functions not defined in the core of Perl.
NDBM_File	Provides access to 'new' DBM files via tied hashes.
Net::Ping	Provides the ability to ping a remote machine via TCP, UDP and ICMP protocols.
Net::hostent	Replaces the core gethost*() functions with those that return Net::hostent objects.
Net::netent	Replaces the core getnet*() functions with those that return Net::netent objects.
Net::protoent	Replaces the core getproto*() functions with those that return Net::protoent objects.
Net::servent	Replaces the core getserv*() functions with those that return Net::servent objects.

Module	Function
O	This is the generic front-end for the Perl compiler. The back-ends in the B module group are all addressed with this.
Opcode	Allows you to disable named opcodes when compiling Perl code.
open	Sets Perl pragma to default disciplines for input and output.
Pod::Checker	Provides a syntax error checker for pod documents.
	Note that this was still in beta at the time of publication.
Pod::Html	pod to HTML converter.
Pod::InputObjects	A set of objects that can be used to represent pod files.
Pod::Man	pod to *roff converter.
Pod::Parser	Base class for creating pod filters and translators.
Pod::Select	Used to extract selected sections of pod from input.
Pod::Text	pod to formatted ASCII text converter.
Pod::Text::Color	pod to formatted, colored ASCII text converter.
Pod::Text::Termcap	Converts pod data to ASCII text with format escapes.
Pod::Usage	Print a usage message from embedded pod documentation.
POSIX	Provides access to (nearly) all the functions and identifiers named in the POSIX international standard 1003.1.
Safe	Creates a number of 'safe' compartments in memory in which Perl code can be tested and the functions for this testing.
SDBM_File	Provides access to sdbm files via tied hashes.
Search::Dict	Provides function to look for a key in a dictionary file.
SelectSaver	Selects a filehandle on creation, saves it and restores it on destruction.
SelfLoader	As Autoloader, works with Autosplit to delay the loading of subroutines into the program until they are called. These subroutines are defined following the __DATA__ token in a package file.
Shell	Allows shell commands to be run transparently within Perl programs.
Socket	Imports the definitions from libc's socket.h header file and makes available some network manipulation functions.
Symbol	Qualifies variable names and creates anonymous globs.
Sys::Hostname	Makes several attempts to get the system hostname and then caches the result.
Sys::Syslog	Perl's interface to the libc syslog(3) calls.

Table continued on following page

Module	Function
Term::Cap	Provides the interface to a terminal capability database.
Term::Complete	Provides word completion on the word list in an array.
Term::ReadLine	Provides access to various 'readline' packages.
Test	Provides a simple framework for writing test scripts.
Test::Harness	Implements a test harness to run a series of test scripts and returns the results.
Text::Abbrev	Takes a list and returns a hash containing the elements of the list as the values and unambiguous abbreviations of each element as their respective keys.
Text::ParseWords	Provides functions for parsing a text file into an array of tokens or an array of arrays.
Text::Soundex	Implementation of the Soundex Algorithm.
Text::Tabs	Works through lines of text replacing tabs with spaces, or if space-saving, replacing spaces with tabs if there are none in the text.
Text::Wrap	Simple paragraph formatter. Takes text, wraps lines around text boundaries, and controls the indenting of the text.
Tie::Array	Base class for tied arrays.
Tie::Handle	Base class definitions for tied handles.
Tie::Hash	Base class definitions for tied hashes.
Tie::RefHash	Allows you to use references as the keys in a hash if it is tied to this module.
Tie::Scalar	Base class definitions for tied scalars.
Tie::SubstrHash	Allows you to rigidly define key and value lengths within the hash for the entire time it is tied to this module.
Time::gmtime	Object-based interface to Perl's built-in gmtime() function.
Time::Local	Provides efficient conversion functions between GMT and local time.
Time::localtime	Object-based interface to Perl's built-in localtime() function.
Time::tm	Internal object used by Time::gmtime and Time::localtime.
UNIVERSAL	The base class for ALL classes (blessed references).
User::grent	Object-based interface to Perl's built-in getgr*() functions.
User::pwent	Object-based interface to Perl's built-in getpw*() functions.
Win32::ChangeNotify	Monitors events related to files and directories.
Win32::Console	Use the Win32 console and character mode functions.

Module	Function
Win32::Event	Use Win32 event objects from Perl.
Win32::EventLog	Process Win32 event logs from Perl.
Win32::File	Manage file attributes in Perl.
Win32::FileSecurity	Manage FileSecurity discretionary access control lists in Perl.
Win32::IPC	The base class for Win32 synchronization objects.
Win32::Internet	Access to WININET.DLL functions.
Win32::Mutex	Use Win32 mutex objects from Perl.
Win32::NetAdmin	Manage network groups and users in Perl.
Win32::NetResource	Manage network resources in Perl.
Win32::ODBC	Use the ODBC extension for Win32.
Win32::OLE	Use the OLE Automation extensions.
Win32::OLE::Const	Extract the constant definitions from TypeLib.
Win32::OLE::NLS	Use the OLE national language support.
Win32::OLE::Variant	Create and modify OLE VARIANT variables.
Win32::PerfLib	Access the Windows NT performance counter.
Win32::Process	Create and manipulate processes.
Win32::Semaphore	Use Win32 semaphore objects from Perl.
Win32::Service	Manage system services in Perl.
Win32::Sound	Plays with Windows sounds.
Win32::TieRegistry	Manipulate a registry.
Win32API::File	Low-level access to Win32 system API calls for files/dirs.
Win32API::Net	Manage Windows NT LanManager API accounts.
Win32API::Registry	Low-level access to Win32 system API calls from WINREG.H.
XSLoader	Dynamically loads C or C++ libraries as Perl extensions.

Perl Resources

Books

This is a list of books that the reader may find interesting.

Perl Programming

Beginning Perl, Simon Cozens, Wrox Press (*ISBN 1861003439*).

CGI Programming with Perl (Second Edition), Scott Guelich, Shashir Gundavaram, and Gunther Birznieks, O'Reilly and Associates (*ISBN 1565924193*).

Learning Perl, Randal L. Schwartz and Tom Christiansen, O'Reilly and Associates (*ISBN 1565922840*).

Learning Perl/Tk, Nancy Walsh, O'Reilly and Associates (*ISBN 1565923146*).

Mastering Algorithms with Perl, Jon Orwant, Jarkko Hietaniemi, and John Macdonald, O'Reilly and Associates (*ISBN 1565923987*).

Mastering Regular Expressions, Jeffrey E. F. Friedl, O'Reilly and Associates (ISBN 1565922573).

Object Oriented Perl, Damien Conway, Manning (*ISBN 1884777791*).

Perl Cookbook, Tom Christiansen and Nathan Torkington, O'Reilly and Associates (*ISBN 1565922433*).

Programming Perl (Third Edition), Larry Wall, Tom Christiansen, and Jon Orwant, O'Reilly and Associates (*ISBN 0596000278*).

Programming the Perl DBI, Alligator Descartes and Tim Bruce, O'Reilly and Associates (*ISBN 1565926994*).

Linux Based Books

Beginning Linux Programming, Neil Matthew and Richard Stones, Wrox Press (*ISBN 1861002971*)

Professional Apache, Peter Wainwright, Wrox Press (*ISBN 1861003021*)

Professional Linux Programming, Neil Matthew and Richard Stones, Wrox Press (*ISBN 1861003013*)

Web Sites

There are a great many resources on the Internet for Perl, here are just a few places we might want to start looking up.

ActiveState
http://www.activestate.com/

CPAN, the Comprehensive Perl Archive Network
http://www.cpan.org/

MacPerl
http://www.macperl.org/

Perl Documentation
http://www.perldoc.com/

The Perl Journal
http://www.itknowledge.com/tpj/

Perl Mongers
http://www.pm.org/

Perl Month
http://www.perlmonth.com/

Perl News
http://www.news.perl.org/

Perl O'Reilly
http://perl.oreilly.com/

Use Perl
http://use.perl.org/

Support, Errata, and p2p.wrox.com

One of the most irritating things about any programming book is when you find that bit of code you've just spent an hour typing simply doesn't work. You check it a hundred times to see if you've set it up correctly and then you notice the spelling mistake in the variable name on the book page. Of course, you can blame the authors for not taking enough care and testing the code, the editors for not doing their job properly, or the proofreaders for not being eagle-eyed enough, but this doesn't get around the fact that mistakes do happen.

We try hard to ensure no mistakes sneak out into the real world, but we can't promise that this book is 100% error free. What we can do is offer the next best thing by providing you with immediate support and feedback from experts who have worked on the book and try to ensure that future editions eliminate these gremlins. We also now commit to supporting you not just while you read the book, but once you start developing applications as well through our online forums where you can put your questions to the authors, reviewers, and fellow industry professionals.

In this appendix we'll look at how to:

❑   Enroll in the **Programmer To Programmer**™ forums at http://p2p.wrox.com.

❑   Post and check for errata on our main site, http://www.wrox.com.

❑   E-mail technical support queries or feedback on our books in general.

Between all three of these support procedures, you should get an answer to your problem in no time at all.

The Online Forums at p2p.wrox.com

Join the Professional Perl Programming mailing list for author and peer support. Our system provides **Programmer To Programmer™** support on mailing lists, forums, and newsgroups all in addition to our one-to-one e-mail system, which we'll look at in a minute. Be confident that your query is not just being examined by a support professional, but by the many Wrox authors and other industry experts present on our mailing lists.

How to Enroll for Support

Just follow these simple instructions:

1. Go to http://p2p.wrox.com in your favorite browser.
Here you'll find any current announcements concerning P2P – new lists created, any removed and so on:

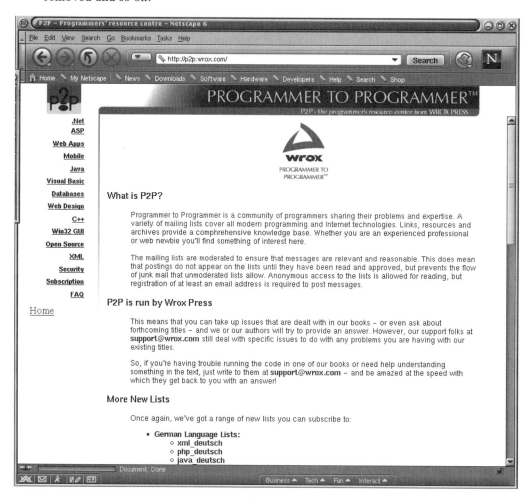

2. Click on the Open Source button in the left hand column.

3. Choose to access the Pro Perl list.

4. If you are not a member of the list, you can choose to either view the list without joining it or create an account in the list, by hitting the respective buttons.

5. If you wish to join, you'll be presented with a form in which you'll need to fill in your e mail address, name, and a password (of at least 4 alphanumeric characters). Choose how you would like to receive the messages from the list and then hit Save.

6. Congratulations. You're now a member of the Professional Perl Programming mailing list.

Why this System Offers the Best Support

You can choose to join the mailing lists to receive mails as they are contributed, or a daily digest, or you can receive them as a weekly digest. If you don't have the time or facility to receive the mailing list, then you can search our online archives. You'll find the ability to search on specific subject areas or keywords. As these lists are moderated, you can be confident of finding good, accurate information quickly. Mails can be edited or moved by the moderator into the correct place, making this a most efficient resource. Junk and spam mail are deleted, and your own email address is protected by the unique Lyris system from web-bots that can automatically hoover up newsgroup mailing list addresses. Any queries about joining, or leaving lists, or any query about the list should be sent to: support@wrox.com.

Checking the Errata Online at www.wrox.com

The following section will take you step by step through the process of posting errata to our web site to get that help. The sections that follow, therefore, are:

❑ Finding a list of existing errata on the web site.

❑ Adding your own erratum to the existing list.

There is also a section covering how to e-mail a question for technical support. This comprises:

❑ What your e-mail should include.

❑ What happens to your e-mail once it has been received by us.

Finding an Erratum on the Web Site

Before you send in a query, you might be able to save time by finding the answer to your problem on our web site – http://www.wrox.com.

Each book we publish has its own page and its own errata sheet. You can get to any book's page by clicking on Books on the left hand navigation bar. To view the errata for that book, click on the Book errata link on the right hand side of the book information pane, underneath the book information.

We update these pages regularly to ensure that you have the latest information on bugs and errors.

Add an Erratum

If you wish to point out an erratum to put up on the web site or directly query a problem in the book page with an expert who knows the book in detail then e-mail support@wrox.com, with the title of the book and the last four numbers of the ISBN in the subject field of the e-mail. Clicking on the submit errata link on the web site's errata page will send an e-mail using your e-mail client. A typical email should include the following things:

❑ The **name, last four digits of the ISBN**, and **page number** of the problem in the Subject field.

❑ Your **name, contact info**, and the **problem** in the body of the message.

We won't send you junk mail. We need the details to save both your time and ours. If we need to replace a disk or CD we'll be able to get it to you straight away. When you send an e-mail it will go through the following chain of support:

Customer Support

Your message is delivered to one of our customer support staff who will be the first people to read it. They have files on most frequently asked questions and will answer anything general immediately. They answer general questions about the book and the web site.

Editorial

Deeper queries are forwarded to the technical editor responsible for that book. They have experience with the programming language or particular product and are able to answer detailed technical questions on the subject. Once an issue has been resolved, the editor can post the erratum to the web site.

The Authors

Finally, in the unlikely event that the editor can't answer your problem, they will forward the request to the author. We try to protect the author from any distractions from writing. However, we are quite happy to forward specific requests to them. All Wrox authors help with the support on their books. They'll mail the customer and the editor with their response, and again all readers should benefit.

What We Can't Answer

Obviously with an ever-growing range of books and an ever-changing technology base, there is an increasing volume of data requiring support. While we endeavor to answer all questions about the book, we can't answer bugs in your own programs that you've adapted from our code. So, while you might have loved the chapters on file handling, don't expect too much sympathy if you cripple your company with a routine that deletes the contents of your hard drive. But do tell us if you're especially pleased with the routine you developed with our help.

How to Tell Us Exactly What You Think

We understand that errors can destroy the enjoyment of a book and can cause many wasted and frustrated hours, so we seek to minimize the distress that they can cause.

You might just wish to tell us how much you liked or loathed the book in question. Or you might have ideas about how this whole process could be improved. If this is the case, you should e-mail feedback@wrox.com. You'll always find a sympathetic ear, no matter what the problem is. Above all you should remember that we do care about what you have to say and we will do our utmost to act upon it.

Index

A Guide to the Index

This index covers numbered chapters but not the Appendices. It is arranged alphabetically, word-by-word, with Symbols and numerals preceding the letter A in the order:

- ! # $ % & (" * , . / : ; ? @ [\ ^ _ ` { | ~ + < = > 0 1 2 3 4 5 6 7 8 9

(although a hyphen immediately followed by another character is ignored so that –a option appears under a).

Where a main heading has both page references and subheadings, the unmodified page references will include any major treatment of the topic, while the sub headings identify passages dealing with specific aspects only.

Acronyms, rather than their expansions, have been selected as main entries on the grounds that unfamiliar acronyms are easier to construct than to expand.

Symbols

- (minus sign)
  named parameters, 233
  prefix identifying an option, 526
  special filename for standard input, 531, 537
– (unary minus) operator, 42, 91, 98, 793, 795
  as argument separator, 528
  precedence and assignment, 107
– prefix
  bare double minus aborts processing of @ARGV, 548
  case insensitivity in Getopt::Long, 546
  for GNU Long options, 526
! (unary not) operator, 87, 93
! debugger command, 630, 632
! suffix for negatable Boolean options, 538
!! debugger command, 632
!~ (regexp binding) operator, 101
(hash symbol)
  how to escape it, 390
  indicating comments, 36, 685
#! see shebang lines.
$ (dollar)
  interpolation, 337
$ scalar variable prefix, 35
  filehandles, reading from, 427
$- special variable, 702, 710-711
$! special variable, 604, 762
  example of a scalar on which a class is based, 764
  errno value, 607
  setting value of, 605
$# special variable, 707

$#array, 122
  assigning to, changes array size in memory, 123
$$ scalar derefencing prefix, 102, 145
$% special variable, 710
$. special variable, 104, 530
$: special variable, 706
$? special variable, 607
$@ special variable, 605, 651, 880
$[special variable, 127
$^ special variable, 703
$^A special variable, 714
$^E special variable, 606
$^F special variable, 446
$^H special variable, 280
$^L special variable, 710, 712
$^O special variable, 1031
$^V special variable, 68
$^W special variable, 280, 599
$_ special variable, 39, 44
$| special variable, 981, 983
  autoflush mode, 432, 568
  print output buffering, 71, 432
  TCP server example, 981
$~ special variable, 700, 703
$= special variable, 702, 710
$0 special variable, 527
$a and $b variables
  package variables used in sorting, 126
$DB::single variable, 642
$DB::trace variable, 643
$diagnostics::DEBUG variable, 602
$diagnostics::PRETTY variable, 602

$ERRNO, 604
$EXTENDED_OS_ERROR
   extended error messages, 606
$ISA[0]::
   differences from SUPER::, 755
$line variable
   condition variables, 945
$opt_X global variables
   getopt function, 533
   GetOptions function, 536
   getopts function, 534
$pool variable
   condition variables, 945
$PROGRAM_NAME special variable, 527
% (percent sign)
   hash declaration, 37, 129
   prototyped suroutine definitions, 238
   modulus operator, behavior with negative numbers, 90
%! hash variable, 604
%$ hash derefencing prefix, 145
%..d and %..0d placeholders, 55
%b, %o, %x and %X placeholders, 56
%Config hash
   usethreads key, 938
%e, %f and %g placeholders, 59
%ENV special variable, 39, 138
   configuring programs using, 140
   includes environment variables, 32
   setting POSIX mode by adding, 549
   taint checking and use of, 140
%EXPORT TAGS hash variable, 326
%INC special hash
   checking the availability of modules, 286
   records code loaded into memory, 277, 282
%SIG hash
   controlling received signals, 898
   handlers for error reporting system, setting, 900
   signals, 896
%TypeLib hash, PerlCtrl, 890
& (ampersand) code prefix
   anonymous subroutines, 217
   code references, 239
   disabling prototype definitions, 242
   subroutines, 216
& mode, 464
   &= mode and, 465
& operator (bitwise AND), 94
&& operator, 93
&= mode, 464
   & mode and, 465
(?:...) syntax
   extended patterns, 372
"" (string conversion operator), 788
* (asterisk)
   as repetition modifier, 354
   as zero-or-more quantifier, 358
* placeholder format see @*
* typeglob prefix, 161
   introduced, 38
* wildcard character
   searching for, with pattern-matching program, 531
*$ typeglob derefencing prefix, 145
*xsinit parameter, perl_parse, 887
, (comma) operator, 101, 119, 185

. (period) concatenation operator, 91
   combination assignment example, 98
   introduced, 43
   meaning lost inside character classes, 353
   matching arbitrary characters, 352
   overloading, 787
. debugger command, 628
. format end token, 700
.. (range) operator, 103
... (ellipsis)
   passing a varying number of arguments, 866
.al files, 311
.perldb configuration file, 637
/ (forward slash) debugger command, 629
/ee modifier, 409
/etc directory, UNIX, 1001, 1003, 1009, 1011
/g global pattern match modifier, 373
   matching several times, 378
   not used with qr operator, 398
   when numbered variables are overridden, 380
/m modifier, 384
/o flag
   interpolation, 342
   once-only pattern match modifier, 394
/s modifier, 384
/x pattern match modifier, 389
: (colon)
   identifying an optional value, 540
   separator, 141
:: (double colon) separator
   use statement translates to directory separator, 277
   package declaration namespace separator, 258, 269
:constants label, 587
:default tag, 110
:filesys_open tag, 110
:locked subroutine
   single-threaded mode, enforcing, 953
:subprocess tag, 110
; (semi-colon) statement terminator, 35
? (question mark)
   as delimiter, 350
   as repetition modifier, 354
   non-greedy matches, 359
   perldoc call, 554
? debugger command, 629
?: (ternary) operator, 105, 189
   nesting, 190
?: numeric conversion operator, 791
???, 840
@ (at sign)
   array variable prefix, 37, 117
   interpolation, 337
   placeholder definition, 700, 705
   prototype definitions, 238
@# numeric justification style, 706
@$ array derefencing prefix, 145
@* multiline placeholder, 707, 714
@_ array
   behavior when called by subroutines, 262
   passing arguments using ExtUtils::Command, 558
@_ special variable
   passing directly into subroutines, 232
   subroutines, 228

@ARGV special variable, 39
converting into a hash, 527
passing arguments using ExtUtils::Command, 558
pattern matching from standard input, 531
reading files from, 529
readline operator and, 428
use for passing parameters, 525
@EXPORT package variable
adding tags to with Exporter module, 326
defines symbols for Exporter module, 323
selecting symbols to be exported, 324
@EXPORT_FAIL array, 328
@EXPORT_OK array
adding tags to with Exporter module, 326
defining conditional exports with, 324
@INC special variable, 39
example program to dump contents, 881
example script to search for POD modules, 699
modifying directly, 283
modifying with the lib pragma, 284
stores paths to search for requested code, 276, 283
@ISA package variable
basis of object inheritance mechanism, 322, 719, 754
behavior with multiple inheritance, 765
support for has-a relationship different, 770
[...] anonymous array constructor, 127, 151
compared to backslash operator, 143, 156
\ (backslash)
anonymous subroutines, 217
creating a reference to a variable, 38
interpolation, 337
multiline commands, 553, 625
\ unary operator, 102
compared to [...] and {...} constructors, 143, 156
creating a reference to a variable with, 143
\b metacharacter, 351
\G metacharacter, 383
\Q metacharacter, 345
^ (caret) symbol
character classes, 353
placeholder definition, 705
suppressing redundant lines, 708
^ operator (bitwise Exclusive OR), 94
_ (underscore)
character case conversion using, 96
identifying a private method, 739, 778
__ (double underscore)
JPL delimiter for signatures, 888
__DATA__ token, 314, 690
__DIE__ hook
registering a handler for, 643
__DIE__ pseudo-signal handler, 603
__DIE__ signal handler
example using, 296
__END__ token, 690
use with AutoLoader module, 311
__PACKAGE__ token, 304
checking when enforcing privacy, 760
example using, 299
__WARN__ pseudo-signal handler, 603
_Property method
Game::Card class, enforcing privacy, 760
` (backtick)
accessing with MacPerl programs, 1034
archaic module separator, 277
backtick opcode, 110, 650

backtick operator qx, 917
compiling C with embedded Perl on UNIX, 877
quoting strings with, 63
{ } (braces)
as delimiter, 350, 553
{ command, Perl debugger, 635
{...} hash reference constructor, 138
compared to backslash operator, 143, 156
{? command, Perl debugger, 635
{{ (double braces)
JPL delimiter for Perl method body in Java, 889
{{ command, Perl debugger, 635
| (pipe symbol), 919
matching alternative terms, 355
| command, Perl debugger, 631
| operator (bitwise OR), 94
|| command, Perl debugger, 631
|| operator, 93
~ (tilde) picture string suffix
suppressing redundant lines, 708
~ operator (bitwise NOT), 94
~~ autorepeating line formats, 709, 712
+ (plus sign)
as repetition modifier, 354
prefix, 537, 549
+ operator
overloading with the add method, 786
++ (unary plus) operator, 42, 91, 98, 793, 795
precedence and assignment, 107
+= operator
overloading with the addassign method, 786
< (less than / open angle bracket)
pod interior sequences and, 691
< command, Perl debugger, 634
<? command, Perl debugger, 635
<< introducing a here document, 65, 67
<< (shift) operator, 91
<< command, Perl debugger, 635
<=> operator, 100
overloading, 787
use in numeric sorting operations, 126
<> (diamond or readline) operator
detecting EOF condition, 999
example script for shell mode, 552
filehandles, reading from 426--428
Getopt:: modules and, 532
introduced, 43
reads files from @ARGV, then standard input, 529
<> option
working like <> operator, 547
<FILEHANDLE> operator, 563
= (equals sign) assignment operator, 36
= command, Perl debugger, 630
= identifying a mandatory value, 540
=~operator, 101
== (equality) operator, 99
=> (digraph) operator
compared to the comma, 37, 102
=> operator
barewords allowed to left of, 68
hash key-value separator, 129
=begin...=end token sequence, pod, 689
=cut token, pod, 685, 687
=for token, pod
pod2html tool obeys rules of, 689
=item token, pod, 687, 688

=over...=back token sequence, pod, 687
=pod...=cut token sequence, 685
-> (arrow) operator, 102
  basis of object inheritance mechanism, 754
  differentiates methods calls from subroutine calls, 723
  dual use, for dereferencing and class accesss, 722
> (greater than / close angle bracket)
  pod interior sequences and, 691
> command, Perl debugger, 635
>&, prefixing filehandles with, 925
>? command, Perl debugger, 635
>> (shift) operator, 91
>> command, Perl debugger, 635
0+ numeric conversion operator, 790
1, as module return statement, 276
8-bit encoding, Perl 5.6+, 1046

A

a command, Perl debugger, 633
A command, Perl debugger, 633
-a option
  command-line scripts, 31
-A option, h2xs scripts, 858
a2p utility, 819
abbreviations, 541-542, 546, 549
  precomputing in text and command lines, 673
  stemming, 1088
abs function, 61
abs2rel function, File::Spec module, 1023
abstraction
  inheritance as a tool for, 753
  object oriented concept aiding code reuse, 719
accept socket function, 968
accessing dynamic libraries, 871
accountable packages
  building Perl from source as, 14
ACLs (Access Control Lists)
  superuser, filestat pragma and, file test operators, 480
ActiveState
  ActivePerl 5.6, problems listing installed modules, 287
  availability of ActivePerl, 13
  PDK tools for COM environments, 889
  PPM utility, 25
  Registers .pl file extension on Windows, 28
ActiveX components
  PerlCtrl converts scripts into, 890
adaptability
  modifying inherited object properties, 721
add method
  overloading the + operator, 786
addassign method
  overloading the += operator, 786
addhistory method,
  Term::ReadLine module, 575, 579
addition operator
  terminal symbol for, 824
addstr subroutine, Curses module, 591
AF_INET address format, 1003, 1005
airport information kiosks example, 1055
  processing the resource files, 1057
alarm function, 906

alarm signal, 897, 906
  hung operations, aborting, 907
  using, 906
Alias module
  attr subroutine, 235
  const subroutine, 236
  CPAN, 234
  deficiencies of, 235
alias subroutine, 234
aliases
  creating for filehandles and subroutines, 270
  creating a typeglob alias, 162, 309, 316
  default argument variable in, 134
  defining in Perl debugger, 630
  editing from the symbol table, 318
  for variables and subroutines, 316
  Getopt::Long module, 541
  grep function, 211, 212
  import mechanism uses, 268
  map function, 211
  setting when configuring the Perl debugger, 637
  subroutines, 229
  using to alter a global variable locally, 270
  variable aliasing, 162
  with foreach loops, 199
  with while loops, 201
alignment, numeric values, 707
all check, B::Lint module, 844
alphabets, non-Latin, 1045, 1049
  conventions determine sorting, 1064
AmigaOS, 1035
ampersand
  see & (under Symbols)
anchors
  efficiency, 392
  moving start anchor to current position, 383
  regular expressions, 351
  repetition and, 360
angle brackets
  see < and > (under Symbols)
anonymous addresses, 966
anonymous array constructor, 127
anonymous subroutines, 215, 217
  calling, 217
  closures, 249
  code references, 239
  eval statements, 396
  parameters, 249
  sort function, 218
anonymous typeglobs, 301, 309
ANSI terminals, 583
any keyword, 904
application protocols, 966
applications
  exiting with die function, 602
arbitrary code
  execution by the Perl debugger, 625
arguments
  see also **parameters.**
  differentiating methods by checking number, 735, 737, 738
  generic argument processor, 544
  passing to Perl from scripts, 528
  passing to Perl scripts, 30, 525
  subroutines, 228
arithmetical operators, 89
ARP (Address Resolution Protocol), 962-964

array elements
changing the starting index, 127
indexing and identifying, 118
Array Variables (AVs) internal variable type, 830
arrayDepth debugger option, 640, 645
arrays, 117
see also **lists.**
accessing references within, 146
adding elements, 122
array manipulation functions apply to @INC, 284
associative see **hashes.**
constructor methods based on, 729
converting into hashes, 133
converting into scalars, 127
counting elements, 121
destroying using the undef function, 125, 168
direct references and references to copies, 127
distinction from lists, 117
environment variables as, 141
evaluation in scalar context, 41
flattening, avoiding, 240
GetOptions multiple values as, 542
indexing by element number, 198
internal representation of, 830
interpolating, 340
introduced as being ordered lists, 37
locking, 943
looping over using while, 201
looping over using foreach, 122
modifying the contents of an array, 119
object representation of classes built with struct, 797
passing into subroutines, 147, 229, 231
range operator, 198
removing elements and their values, 121, 124, 168
resizing and truncating, 123
self-modifying, looping on, 202
splice function, 120
tied object class methods, 804
truncating by assigning a new list, 125
undefined values, 245
arrays of hashes
indexed set of key-value pairs, 138
arrow operator
see -> (under Symbols)
Artistic file, 819
ASCII (Americal Standard Code for Information Interchange), 1045
assignable subroutines, 250
Assigned Numbers, IP, 961
assignment operator, 89
dangerous assignments, 268
precedence, 106
associative arrays see **hashes.**
associativity, 106
arithmetical operators, 90
asterisk
see * (under Symbols)
async function
threads, 939
asynchronous IO event signal, 898
at method, Term::Screen module, 589
atan2 function, 61
Atari MiNT, 1035
attr subroutine, Alias module, 234, 235
Attribs method, Term::ReadLine module, 575

attribute lists
accessing, 252
defining as subroutines, 251
special attributes, 252
subroutines, 251
attributes
creating for an object class, 739
stored as hash keys, inheritance, 749
using objects as in Class::Struct module, 797
attributes module, 252
package attributes, 253
attributes, files
changing file ownership, 485
changing file permissions, 487
setting at system level IO, using fcntl, 459
AUTHORS file, 819
auto_abbrev option, 541, 550
autoconf
metaconfig compared, 821
autoflush variable, 981, 983
autoflush mode, 568
print output buffering, 71, 432
TCP server example, 981
autogeneration, 787
infering operator behavior, 793
AutoLoad function
C content of XS files used by, 861
used by Shell.pm, 557
autoload method example, 774
modified to use list of allowed fields, 775
autoload subroutines, 226, 304
defining subroutines on the fly using, 308
goto statement, 227
use as substitute for a collection of subroutines, 305
AutoLoader module, 304, 310
calling subroutines, 312
creating installable packages, 311
h2xs script flag to suppress use, 858
installing modules on, manually, 26
use to load methods, 773
visibility of subroutines to, 314
autoloading class
modified to allow new subclass attributes, 777
automated testing, 653, 655
automatically localized variables, 262
autorepeating pattern lines, 709
AutoSplit module, 304, 311, 1019
installing modules on, manually, 26
Autosplit subroutine
optional Boolean arguments, 313
AutoTrace debugger option, 640, 641
autouse pragma, 290
limit use to production versions, 291
simpler alternative to autoloading modules, 310
AVs (array variables) internal variable type, 830
awk utility, 345
awk-to-perl translator, 822

B

b command, Perl debugger, 632, 643
B module, 834
class function, 835
ppaddr method, 835
walkoptree_exec method, 835
walkoptree_slow method, 835

B::Bytecode module, 842
B::C module, 840
B::CC module, 841
B::Debug module, 837
    debug and debug_level subroutines, 839
B::Deparse module, 839
B::Disassembler module, 843
B::Fathom module, 848
B::Graph module, 848
B::JVM::Jasmin module, 849
B::Lint module, 843
B::Showlex module, 845
B::Terse module, 836
    compiler back-end example, 850
    op trees, examining, 826
B::Xref module, 845
babel.pl multilingual web page example, 1090, 1093
    getMessage subroutine, 1092
    translate subroutine, 1092
background color, 584
Backhaus-Naur Form, 823
backreferences, 374
    syntax confusion problems, 375
backslash
    see \ (under Symbols)
backtick
    see ` (under symbols)
bareword strings, 67
Basic language, 891
Basic Multilingual Plane, 1046
Basque language, 1067, 1070, 1080, 1088
BEGIN blocks, 182, 297
    example illustrating use, 296, 298
    example script for shell mode, 552
    executed before main compilation phase, 296
    modifying %INC to take effect at compile-time, 286
    modifying @INC to take effect at compile-time, 284
Benchmark module, 657, 663
    caching, 669
    methods tabluated, 664
    subroutines decribed, 665
BeOS, 1035
bidi (bi-directional) scripts, 1050
    justification of HTML templates, 1056
    operation of the Linux bidi algorithm, 1053
    operation of the Unicode bidi algorithm, 1053
bi-directional character types, Unicode, 1052
bi-directional communication, 925
bi-directional pipes, 921
    external processes, 923
big integers, 54
binary & text files, handling, 433
    file test operators, 476-477
    open pragma, 434
binary data
    running with Perl, 842
binary distributions
    availability for various operating systems, 9
    compared to compiling from source, 12
binary integers, 53, 55
binary operations, 87, 825, 851
bind socket function, 968, 980
binding operators
    regular expressions, 346

binmode function, 433, 1016
    portability onto different platforms, 1035
BINOPs, 851
bitmasks
    $^H and $^W, 280
    network addresses, 961
    select function, 993
bitwise operations
    distinction from Boolean operations, 94
    effect of << and >> shift operators, 91
    interpretation, effects of use integer pragma, 61
bless function
    see also object orientation.
    assigning a package name to a hard reference, 149
    calling a second time, 761, 783
    part of all constructor methods, 728
    objects as blessed references, 719, 722
    two argument version
        creates subclasses on demand, 761
        preserves inheritance, 728
blinking text, 585
block properties, Unicode, 1048
blocking processes, 933
blocks, 175, 177
    allowing to return values, 181
    as loops, 180
    BEGIN, 182
    CHECK, 183
    define the scope of lexical variables, 48, 778
    definition of, 177
    do, 181
    END, 182
    in Perl statements, 178
    INIT, 183
    introduced, 43
    main program, defining as, 179
    naked, 178
    nesting, 181
    switches, 192
BNF (Backhaus-Naur Form), 823
bold method, Term::Screen module, 589
bold text, 585
bold, terminal capability code for, 579
Boolean conversion operator, 791
Boolean flags
    setting as class data, 743
Boolean operators
    bitwise operators distinguished from, 94
    evaluation as true or false, 93
Boolean options, 538
braces see { (under Symbols)
branching see control constructs.
break text, 680
breakpoints, 632
broadcast addresses, 966, 971, 989
    see also multicasting.
broken pipe signal, 897
browser user_agent, 1076
buffering
    block-/line-buffering, writing to filehandles, 432
    problems from unbuffered select operations, 995, 997
    TCP server example, 981
    unbuffered filehandles, manipulating at system level IO, 452

building Perl from source, **14**
  autoconf, 821
  compared to binary distributions, 12
  Configure program, 821
  differences for Windows and Macintosh, 17
  list of other supported platforms, 17
  metaconfig, 821
  operating systems capable of, 9
built-in functions
  system network configuration enquiries, 1001
bundles
  CPAN archive categorized by, 21
bundling arguments, 534
bundling options, 526, 535, 544, 550
bundling_override option, 545, 550
bytecode, 842
  disassembling, 843
  Perl interpreter uses, 27
ByteLoader module, 842

C

C code
  access to external libraries with Makefile.pl, 870
  calling from a Perl program, 856
  compiling with embedded Perl, 877
  embedding Perl in, 875
  example building a hash variable, 885
  example linking to C math library, 872, 874, 875
  limits module installation with CPAN module, 18
  limits module installation with cpan-mac, 26
  limits module installation with make tools, 26
  script to access header files, 859
  socket functions connect to C libraries, 967
  translating Perl into, 840
  using Perl modules, 886
  XS functions as wrappers for C functions, 862
c command, Perl debugger, 631
-C option, h2xs scripts, 858
C::Dynalib module, 874
C::Scan module, 859
cacheout method, FileCache module, 446
caching
  converted scalar values, 52
  filehandles, caching many, 446
  mechanism in Benchmark module, 669
calculating adjusted formats example script, 701
calculation errors
  caused by floating-point base changes, 57
  caused by rounding, 58
  caused by use integer pragma, 60
call_pv and call_sv functions, 883
caller function, 221
  checking calling subroutine and package, 319, 621, 781
calling context, subroutines, 246
calling conventions, FFI, 873
can method
  determining an object's capabilities, 725
  UNIVERSAL object, 226
can_read method, IO::Select, 995
can_write method, IO::Select, 995
canonpath function, File::Spec module, 1021
Caputo, Rocco, 848
Carbon API, 1034

caret symbol see ^ (under Symbols)
carp function, 609, 900
Carp module, 609
  carp, cluck, confess and croak subroutines, 609
  using CGI::Carp module instead of, 610
  croak method, 609, 739, 900
carriage returns, 1017
  translating, 571
case
  manipulating upper and lower case characters, 75, 96, 339
  option prefixes and case sensitivity, 537, 546
case_tolerant function, File::Spec module, 1022
casting, 721
catalogues
  storage of PO file messages, 1071
catdir function, File::Spec module, 1021
catfile function, File::Spec module, 1021
catpath function, File::Spec module, 1023
cbreak mode, Term::ReadKey module, 564
  invisible input and passwords, 569
  making terminals react immediately, 566
CGI module
  exception to rule discouraging exports, 759
CGI scripts
  disabling functions and operators, 110
  translate subroutine in multilingual web page, 1092
CGI::Carp module, 610
Changes file
  h2xs script flag to suppress creation, 858
Changes* file, 819
character classes
  character class metacharacters, 365
  regular expressions, 352
  repetition modifiers, 355
  syntax, 354
character codes, 73
  interpolating, 338
character sets
  see also **locale; Unicode character set.**
  character repertoires and, 1044
  conversion with the tr operator, 1050
  differing, as internet problem, 1043
  effects of string operators depend on, 97, 100
  ISO (8859-1), 1045
  MS-DOS, 1045
  non-Latin alphabets, 1045, 1049, 1064
  order in bidirectional scripts, 1051
  portability, 1027
  Windows (code page 1252), 1045
characters
  echoing, 567
  reading singly, 566
chdir function
  moving around directories, 514, 520
CHECK blocks, 183, 299
  called after main compilation and BEGIN blocks, 300
  example illustrating use, 296
  O module, 834
child exit signal, 898
child processes
  closing sockets after forking, 975
  effects of changing %ENV special variable, 140
  handling, 911
  multiple child processes, 913
  server multiplexing solution, 993, 998
  waiting for, 912

chmod function
file permissions, setting, 487
flag values, 487
portability onto different platforms, 1035
chomp and chop functions, 72
chown function
file ownership, changing, 485
portability onto different platforms, 1035
user/group id, needing, 486
chr function, 73
operation of vec function compared to, 79
unpack 'c' function compared to, 77
chroot function
portability onto different platforms, 1036
CIDR (Classless InterDomain Routing), 962
cl terminal capability code, 584
class data, 740
accessing via objects, 746, 756
setting Boolean flags as, 743
setting through import methods, 743
class function, B module, 835
class level debugging, 748
class methods defined, 732
Class::MethodMaker module, 795
Class::Multimethods module, 768, 795
Class::Struct module, 795
classes
creating programmatically, 764
example based on a scalar, 764
helper methods for creating, 795
implemented in Perl with packages, 718
no-object classes, 743
writing an object class, 727
writing for multiple inheritance, 765
writing with inheritance in mind, 756
clean command, 21
clearing terminal screens, 584
clients
example application creating TCP, 982-983
example application creating UDP, 987-988
example application creating UNIX, 991-992
opening sockets, 971
close function, 975
compared to shutdown, 922
closedir function
closing directory handles, 514
closures, 248, 779, 780
anonymous subroutines, 249
clreol method, Term::Screen module
clreos and clrscr methods and, 589
clrtoeol, Curses module, 592
cluck subroutine, Carp module, 609
clustering modifier
extended patterns, 352
cm terminal capability code, 584
cmp operator, 100
overloading, 787
use in string sorting operations, 126
cmpthese subroutine, Benchmark module, 667
code
interpolating, 341
thread safe, 953
code positions, characters, 1044
code references
GetOptions multiple values as, 543
prototype definitions, 239

CODE: identifier, XS functions, 862
code2language function
Locale::Language module, 1076
collisions see **namespaces,** collisions; **network collisions.**
colon see **:** (under Symbols)
colored subroutine, Term::ANSIColor module, 486
color subroutine and, 584
colors
IO programming, 581
writing in, 584
COM (Component Object Model), 889
combination assignment operators, 97
comma operator, 101, 119, 185
command line history
retrieving, 580
Term::ReadLine module, 579
command line interfaces
see also **shells.**
portability of programs with, 1025
command line programming, 525
command-line options
Perl as generic command-line utility, 31
Perl interpreter, alternatives, 27
shebang line support and, 29
syntax, 30
using Configure --help to investigate, 16
command-line utilities
needed for starting and configuring CPAN, 19
comma-separated text
parsing example script, 677
comments, 36, 685
multiline comments using =begin...=end, 690
while loop for skipping past, 347
commify subroutine
example of using from C code, 883, 884
compactDump debugger option, 640, 645
compactDump method, dumper object, 648
company networks
private IP address blocks for, 962
comparison operators, 99
compartment object
methods tabulated, 650
compartments, Safe module, 649
compilation, 824
data structures, 826
identifying compilers with the -V option, 876
reduction, 824
subroutines, delaying using stubs, 309
compilation dialog, re module, 403
compile subroutine, 850
Compiler see **Perl Compiler**
compiler backend modules, 834, 850
compiler variable
configuration process, 817
compile-time
lexical variable scope determined at, 257, 259
our keyword operates at, 261
compiling from source
see **building Perl from source.**
Complete function, Term::Complete module, 580
complex data structures, 135, 151
adding to or modifying, 154
creating programmatically, 155
hard references as basis for, 142
traversing, 158

compliment modifier, 411
composite properties, Unicode, 1048
compound statements, 175, 177
  goto statement, 209
concatenation operator, 91
  combination assignment example, 98
  introduced, 43
  meaning lost inside character classes, 353
  matching arbitrary characters, 352
  overloading, 787
concealed text, 585
cond_broadcast subroutine, 944
cond_signal subroutine, 944
cond_wait subroutine, 943
condition variables, 943
  $line and $pool variables, 945
conditional blocks, 943
conditional loops, 195, 200
conditional statements, 183
  declaring variables in inverted conditional
    statements, 185
  else statements, 185
  elseif statements, 185
  if statements, 185
  inverted, 185
  logical operators, writing conditions with, 188
  multi-branched conditions, 192
    returning values from, 194
  switch statements, 192
  ternary operator, 189
  unless keyword, 187
confess subroutine, Carp module, 609
Config module, 815, 1029
  myconfig function, 817
  perl –V, 816
  platforms, 1031
config.sh file, 815
configuration
  checking details using myconfig or -V option, 16
  programs using %ENV special variable, 140
configure method
  Serial object class, 741
Configure program, 821
configuring Perl for UNIX, 15
configuring a threaded Perl, 17
connect socket function, 968, 982
const subroutine, Alias module, 236
constant pragma, 169
constant references, 171
constants, 169
  checking for and listing, 172
  constant::declared hash, 172
  declaring list and hash constants, 171
  defining by assigning a reference to a typeglob, 169
constructors, 727
  see also [...] and {...} (under Symbols).
  based on subroutines, 731
  common errors in using, 144
  flexible syntax, 721, 723
  fully object-oriented example, 758
  overriding and calling overridden, 755
  overriding inherited, 757
  using data types other than hashes, 729
container objects, 770

context
  expressions used to define constants, 170
  scalar, list and void introduced, 40
  void, handling, 247
context check, B::Lint module, 844
continue clause, 206
  for loops, 207
continue signal, 898
control characters, 339, 1048
  terminals, 572
control constructs, 175
  blocks, 177
  conditional statements, 183
  goto statement, 209
  if ... else statements, 185
  introduced, 43
  loops, 195
  multi-branched conditions, 192
  switches, 192
  ternary operator, 189
conversion of integers, 54
conversion of objects, 721
  overloading conversion operations, 788
cooked mode
  terminals, 572
cookies
  multilingual web page example, 1089
Copying file, 819
core modules, 819
CORE::exit
  aborting system level operations with, 903
CORE:: prefix, 220
  calling getpw* functions, 472
  calling stat and lstat functions, 480
  CORE:: functions used by POSIX, 463
  preventing Net::modules from overriding variables,
    1007,1010
CORE::system, 652
cos function, 61
  example program calling from C math, 872, 874, 875
counting array elements, 121
countit subroutine, Benchmark module, 668
CPAN (Comprehensive Perl Archive Network)
  Alias module, 234
  building and installing module packages, 18
  configuring options, 24
  CPAN Testers, 1026
  ExtUtils::Embed module from, 875
  Filter module from, 892
  Finance::Quote module, 1070
  main website, URL for, 9
  modules implementing other languages, 891
  national modules for Norwegian and Czech, 1084
  pod translators from, 692
  portability, 1026
  pre-built distributions available from, 12
  reloading a module and its index, 23
  requirements of modules destined for, 330
  source distributions from, 14
  starting and configuring, 19
  uploading modules to, 334
  using module to update packages, 18
  WWW::Babelfish module, 1074, 1077
CR/LF to LF translation, 571
create option
  shared memory segments, 936

croak function, 609, 739, 900
cross-platform capabilities, 1015
  see also **portability of programs.**
  binmode() operator, 1016
  feature of the Perl language, 8
  functions, 1035
  importing unrecognized symbols, 328
  modules, 1026
  sockets, 1017
  system interaction, 1024
  XS, 1025
cross-reference tables, 845
Crossword Server, 848
crypt function, 76
  portability onto different platforms, 1036
culture and locale, 1067
curdir function, File::Spec module, 1021
currency conversion
  Spanish website example, 1069
Curses library, 590
  third-party extensions to, 594
Curses module, 581, 591
  addstr subroutine, 591
  clrtoeol, 592
  Panels, 594
  refresh mechanism, 594
  simple application, 591
Curses windows, 593
Curses::Forms module, 594
cursor, moving, 584
customized text wrapping, 680
cwd function, Cwd module
  finding current directory, 521
Cwd module
  finding current directory, 521
  getcwd, fastcwd, cwd & getfastcwd functions, 521
cyclic dependencies, 768
Cygwin Windows port, 13
Czech language
  CPAN national module for, 1084

D

d command, Perl debugger, 633
D command, Perl debugger, 633
-D flag
  setting configuration options with, 15
-D option
  debugging the perl interpreter, 652
daemons, 910
data integrity
  requirements favor use of TCP over UDP, 965
data lines, formats
  picture lines and, 707
DATA pseudo-filehandle
  filehandles, creating, 422
data structures, 820
  compiling, 826
data types, 36
  see also **scalars, arrays, hashes, references,**
    typeglobs.
  dereferencing different, 145
  determining object, with ref and reftype, 725
  examining, 830

filehandles, 416
  formats as a distinct datatype for reporting, 699
  internal, 827
  raw, 830
  tied object methods for different, 804
  type mapping in XS functions, 867
  variables, indicated by prefixes not declaration, 35
Data::Dumper module, 160, 1024
database handle object
  DBI class, 761
datagrams
  datagram sockets, 921
  manipulation by Internet Protocol, 964
date, portability, 1026
date formats, 1070
  date format converter, 788, 790
  internationalization and, 1063
Date::Parse module, 1027
daylight saving time, 1079
DB package
  coding alternative debugger in, 643
DBI class
  database handle object, 761
DBM modules
  not available on all platforms, 1026
  use tied objects, 799
dbmclose function
  portability onto different platforms, 1036
dc method, Term::Screen module, 589
debug method, Benchmark module, 664
debug subroutine
  B::Debug module, 839
debug_level subroutine, B::Debug module, 839
debugging, 617
  $Text::Wrap::debug, 681
  adding calling context to debug messages, 621
  applications that debug themselves, 618
  conditional debugging script example, 621
  debugger hooks, 643
  debugging and informational modules, 645
  debugging the perl interpreter, 652
  Exporter module verbose mode, 329
  interactively, entering, 642
  lexical variables, 845
  multilevel debugging script example, 619
  multiplex debugging strategy, 750
  object classes, generic module, 747
  output configuration depends on Dumpvalue, 645
  output options tabulated, 640
  Perl profiler introduced, 623
  pragmatic debugging support, 617
  re module, 402
  readline options tabulated, 639
  regular expressions, 401
  running arbitrary code, 625
  terminal/tracing options tabulated, 640, 641
  traversing complex data structures for, 159
debugging, Perl debugger, 622
  action commands tabulated, 633
  breakpoint commands tabulated, 632, 633
  commands tabulated, 626, 630
  complex data structures with, 159
  configuration options, 636, 638, 639
  controls tabulated, 632
  entering programmatically, 642
  execution options tabulated, 631, 632

debugging, Perl debugger (*continued***)**
  prompts tabulated, 634, 635
  single stepping, 624
  source display commands tabulated, 628, 629
  variables display commands tabulated, 627, 628
  watchpoint commands tabulated, 634
decimals
  representation in Germany, 707
  representation in Latin countries, 1063, 1070
declarations
  see also **package declarations; variable declarations**.
  modules and subroutines, 176
decrementing scalar variables, 98
def_key method, Term::Screen module, 590
default input
  terminal IO programming, 578
default option, Getopt::Long module, 550
default values
  assigning in XS functions, 866
defined function, 164
delete command, 302
  removes array values but not elements, 124
  removes hash keys and values, 132
delete modifier, 411
delete_package subroutine, 303, 318
delimiters
  arbitrary, handling with quotewords, 677
  characters that can be used as, 349
  question marks (?) as, 350
  regular expressions, 349
  strings, types available, 62
  suppressing within the split function, 69
deny method, compartment object, 650
deparsing, 839
dequeue method, Thread::Queue module, 951
dequeue_nb method, Thread::Queue module, 951
dereferencing, 145
  accessing object properties by, 722
  code interpolation, 341
  multidimensional arrays, 152
design
  tied object classes, example template, 807
destroy methods, tied objects, 802
destroy option
  shared memory segments, 936
destructors, 782
  inheritance and, 783
  multiple inheritance and, 784
  should dispose of tied objects, 802
Devel::DProf module, 656, 657
Devel::Peek module, 830
  abbreviations used in, 831
  Dump and DumpArray subroutines, 831
  int and mstat subroutines, 833
  SVs, examining, 828
devnull function, File::Spec module, 1021
diacritical marks, 1050
diagnostics pragma, 600
  controlling output, 602
  enabling and disabling, 601
  splain tool, 602
  -verbose switch, 602

dialog boxes
  portability onto different platforms, 1030
diamond operator *see* **<>** *(under Symbols).*
die function, 602
  exceptions, 603
  intercepting warnings, 603
die handlers, 603, 900
  using with error-signals, 904
dieLevel debugger option, 638
digraph operator
  compared to the comma, 102
directional formatting codes, 1051
directories, 513
  as tied hashes, 515
  creating, 517
    multiple directories, using mkpath function, 518
    single directories, using mkdir function, 517
  destroying, 519
    multiple directories, using rmtree function, 520
    single directories, using rmdir function, 519
  directory handles, 513
    encapsulating in objects, using IO::Dir module, 515
  finding directory/file name from its handle, 516
  manipulating, overview, 513
  moving around, 520
    changing current directory, using chdir function, 520
    finding current directory, using Cwd module, 521
    finding current directory, using POSIX's getcwd routine, 521
  positions, manipulating, 514
    seekdir, telldir & rewinddir functions, 514
  reading, 513
    opendir, readdir, chdir & closedir functions, 513
  temporary directories, creating using tempdir() function, File::Temp module, 511
directories method, ExtUtils::Installed module, 288
directory_tree method
  ExtUtils::Installed module, 288
disable diagnostics, 601
disablecache mechanism, Benchmark module, 669
disabling functions and operators, 110
disabling warnings
  while using undefined value, 167
disambiguation
  debugger commands, 625
  parentheses, use in functions and subroutines, 109
disassemble tool, 843
disassembler module, 842
display options, dprofpp utility, 659, 660
dl method, Term::Screen module, 589
DLL (Dynamic Link Libraries), 857, 871, 891
dlsrc, 818
dlsymun, 818
do ... until and do ... while loops, 203
  loop control statements not used in, 208
do blocks, 181
  avoiding precedence related problems with, 189
  multi-branched conditions, 193
    returning values from, 194
do loops, 200
do statement, 917
  compared to require and use, 277
do_join.c program, 885
document definition mode, 65

document formatting
  see also **page control and numbering; paragraph formatting.**
  alignment of numeric values, 707
  customized text wrapping, 680
  interconverting tabs and spaces, 673
  multiformat reports, 713
  width setting with ~~, 709
document search example, 734
documentation
  see also **POD.**
  CPAN manual pages, 11
  options, with usage information, 544
  Perl, 819
  perldoc introduced, 10
  programs, using comments and POD, 684
  requirements, modules destined for CPAN, 331
  XS interface, 856
dollar–underscore check, B::Lint module, 844
domains
  storage of PO file messages, 1071
DOS (Disk Operating System)
  character sets, 1045
  running Perl on, 1033
double brackets
  JPL delimiter for Perl method body in Java, 889
double colon see :: *(under Symbols).*
double minus see – *(under Symbols).*
double quotes
  variable interpolation and, 39, 342
double underscore see __ *(under Symbols).*
down method, Thread::Semaphore module, 948
dprofpp profile analysis tool, 657
  command line options, 659-661
  meanings of report columns, 659
DSO (Dynamic Shared Objects), 857, 871
dump function
  listing Opcodes and descriptions, 112
  portability onto different platforms, 1036
Dump subroutine, Devel::Peek module, 831
DumpArray subroutine, Devel::Peek module, 831
dumpDBFiles debugger option, 640
dumper objects
  table of supported methods, 648
dumpPackages debugger option, 640
dumpReused debugger option, 640
Dumpvalue module, 645
  accessing the symbol table using, 272
  debugger Output options, 638
dumpvars method, 647
–Dusedevel
  Configure program, 821
DynaLoader module, 822, 857, 877, 887
dynamic inheritance, 754
dynamic linking, 818
dynamic scope, 257

E

-e option
  command-line scripts, 31
  example program using Perl interpreter, 879
each function, 135
EACHLINE variable, Term::ANSIColor module, 586
EAGAIN constant, POSIX module, 607

echo method, Term::Screen module, 589
echoing characters, 567
editors, 1055, 1071
efficient coding
  left side of Boolean operators, 94
EINVAL constant, POSIX module, 607
ellipsis (...)
  passing a varying number of arguments, 866
else and elseif statements, 183, 185
  unless keyword, 187
email
  tokenizing addresses, 683
embed.pl installation file, 820
embedding
  code into strings, 341
  embedding levels, 1052
  Perl in COM-supporting applications, 889
  Perl in C, requires Perl built on local machine, 875
empty patterns
  regular expressions, 394
emulating UNIX commands
  Windows, using ExtUtils Command, 557
enable diagnostics, 601
encapsulation, 720, 736
  IP packets within Ethernet frames, 963
encoding
  character sets, 1045
  Filter module, 892
encryption
  passwords, using the crypt function, 76
END blocks, 182, 299
  called as program exits, 296
  example illustrating use, 296
  restoring original settings, 565
end tokens, 65
endgrent function
  closing file, 474
  portability onto different platforms, 1037
endhostent function, 1004
  portability onto different platforms, 1037
endianness, 1023
endnetent function, 1008
  portability onto different platforms, 1037
endprotoent function, 1011
  portability onto different platforms, 1037
endpwent function
  closing internal file pointer, 470
  portability onto different platforms, 1036, 1037
endservent function
  portability onto different platforms, 1037
English module
  $ERRNO, 604
  $EXTENDED_OS_ERROR, 606
enqueue method, Thread::Queue module, 950
Env.pm module, 141
environment variables, 32
  see also **%ENV special variable.**
  changing separators, 141
  debugging error log, 621
  general environment variables, 32
  importing with Env.pm module, 141
  localization constants as, 1066
  PERL5DB, 33
  PERL5LIB, 32
  PERL5OPT, 29
  specific environment variables, 32
  used by Test::Harness module, 656
  Windows specific, 33

eof (End Of File) function, 429, 530
  detecting eof condition, reading from filehandles, 429
  seek function, clearing eof condition, 435
EPERM constant, POSIX module, 607
equal method, threads, 941
equals sign *see* = *(under Symbols).*
erase1 and erase2 functions
  Term::Complete module, 581
errno function, POSIX module, 607
Errno module, 604
  %! hash variable, 604
  exists function, 605
Errno package
  constant subroutine, 763
errno_h tag, 607
error handling
  eval_pv function, 880
  fatal errors from failed tie function, 800
  using an error object class, 762
error logs, 611
error messages
  examples of ICMP, 966
  extended, 606
  quoting the main package, 268
error numbers, 604
  errno function, POSIX, 607
  setting, 605
error_to_string and error_to_number methods, 792
ErrorClass object, 763
  overloading, 791
errors, 599
  see also **calculation errors.**
  $!, error status, 604
  Carp module, 609
  diagnostics pragma, 600
  fatal, 608
  from evaluated code, 605
  from functions that make system calls, 604
  generating, 602
  intercepting, 603
  promoting system errors to fatal, 608
  warnings, 599
error-signals, 904
Es::Nif package, 1094
escaping
  colors, 584
  quotes and spaces in text, 677
  Unicode named characters, 1047
Ethernet
  frames, 959
  IP packets and Ethernet frames, 963
  TCP/IP running over, as network example, 959
eval function, 726, 780, 800
eval statements
  anonymous subroutines, 396
  errors from evaluated code, 605
  interpolation of quotes, 342
  interpolation of text inside string variables, 343
  regular expressions, generating, 395
  system level operations, aborting, 903
  threads, 941
eval_pv function, 880
  alternative way to call modules, 887
eval_sv function
  example program using for pattern substitution, 881
evaluation modifier, 408
eventvwr utility, 612

exceptions
  see also **errors.**
  die function, 603
exclamation mark *see* ! *(under Symbols).*
exclusive option
  shared memory segments, 936
exec command, 909
  portability onto different platforms, 1036
execution order, special blocks, 296, 297
exists function, 166
  Errno module, 605
exists_dc method, Term::Screen module, 589
exists_ic method, Term::Screen module, 589
exit codes, 911
  external commands, 607
  getting, 912
  subprocesses, 607
exiting applications
  die function, 602
exp function, 61
expand and unexpand subroutines, 672
export lists
  adding tags with Exporter module, 326
export_fail method, Exporter module, 328
export_to_level method, Exporter module, 329
Exporter module
  debugging in verbose mode, 329
  explicitly listing symbols for export, 324
  export_to_level method, 329
  handling failed exports, 328
  importing symbols with common prefixes, 323
  introduced, 296
  provides generic import subroutine, 322
  require_version method, 328
exporting
  see also **import methods.**
  alternatives to the Exporter module, 319
  avoiding, from object classes, 759
  inadvisable for object oriented modules, 322
  symbols from a module, 316
  variables and subroutines
    BEGIN blocks allow before compilation, 298
expressions, 175
  difference from statements, 176
extended error messages, 606
extended patterns, 389
  (?:...) syntax, 372
  regular expressions, 351, 352
extending a parent class, 761
extending an array, 122
Extensible Markup Language *see* **XML.**
extensions
  impementing C APIs as, 856
external processes, 919
  bi-directional communication, 925
  bi-directional pipes, 923
external programs, running, 916
external subroutines *see* **XS**
ExtUtils::Command module, 557
  introduced, 551
ExtUtils::Embed module, 875
  genmake script, 877, 879, 888
  simplifies Perl embedding, 877
ExtUtils::Installed module, 286
  example script illustrating use of, 289
  methods tabulated, 287

ExtUtils::MakeMaker module, 332
 role in interactions with C code, 857, 870-871, 877

F

f command, Perl debugger, 629
-F option
 command-line scripts, 31
factorials
 example of subroutine for calculating, 46
factory objects, 762
fallback flags, 792
 suppressing unwanted autogeneration, 794
false values, 184
fastcwd function, Cwd module
 finding current directory, 521
Fatal module, 608
fcntl function, 459
 actions supported, table of, 459-461
 ioctl function and, 459
 setting filehandle attributes, 459
Fcntl module, 929
 portability onto different platforms, 1036
 symbolic constants for flags, providing, 488
  filetype and permissions constants, 489
Features method, Term::ReadLine module, 575, 577
fetch methods, tied objects, 802
FETCH_X_ATTRIBUTES subroutines, 253
FFI module, 872
 example enumerating window handles, 873
fields module
 uses tied objects, 799
file extensions
 .pl and .pm distinguished, 275
file systems, 1018
file test operators, 475
 ACLs, superuser & filestat pragma, 480
 binary and text files, testing, 477
 functional classification, 475-477
  binary & text, 433
 link transparency & testing, 477
 multiple file tests, automating, 482
 overview, 475
 reusing results of prior stat/lstat, 478
 stat objects, using with File::stat module, 479
 unary operators, 513m 562
File::Basename module, 1019
 basename & dirname subroutines, 502
 fileparse routine, analyzing file paths, 501
 values for different operating platforms, 502
File::CheckTree module
 validate subroutine, automating multiple file tests, 482
File::Compare module
 compare & compare_text subroutines, 496
File::Copy module
 copy & move.copy subroutines, copying & moving files, 494
 syscopy subroutine, making system-level copies, 495
File::DosGlob module
 DOS-style file globbing functionality, 507
File::Find module
 find & finddepth subroutines, finding files, 497
 find2perl script, 501
 finding directory/file name from its handle, 516

 follow & follow_fast subroutines, 499
 key-value pairs, optional, 497
 wanted subroutine, 499
File::Glob module, 1024
 UNIX-style file globbing, 505
  error-handling, 507
  extended globbing and labels, 505
File::Path module
 mkpath function, creating multiple directories, 518
 rmtree function, destroying multiple directories, 520
File::Spec module, 1019
 abs2rel function, 1023
 canonpath function, 1021
 case_tolerant function, 1022
 catdir function, 1021
 catfile function, 1021
 catpath function, 1023
 curdir function, 1021
 devnull function, 1021
 file_name_is_absolute function, 1022
 join function, 1021
 no_upwards function, 1022
 path function, 1022
 platforms supported by, 1020
 portable file handling, 1020
 rel2abs function, 1023
 rootdir function, 1022
 splitdir function, 1023
 splitpath function, 1022
 tmpdir function, 1022
 updir function, 1022
File::Spec::Functions module, 1021
File::stat module
 methods & object names, list of, 484
 stat objects, using, 479
File::Temp module
 mktemp system calls, implementing, 512
 POSIX's tmpname & tmpfile functions, implementing, 512
 tempdir() function, creating temporary directories, 511
 tempfile() function, creating temporary files, 511
file_name_is_absolute function
 File::Spec module, 1022
FileCache module, 446
 cacheout method, caching many filehandles, 446
<FILEHANDLE> operator, 563
filehandles, 416, 917
 as datatypes, 416
 as IO fundamentals, definition, 416
 binary & text files, handling, 433
 caching many using FileCache module, 446
 creating, 417
  arbitrary filenames, opening, 419
  DATA pseudo-filehandle, using, 422
  IO::File module, using, 420
  open function, using, 417
  pipe, socket & socketpair functions, using, 423
  reading/writing/updating, opening files for, 418
  STDIN & STDOUT standard filehandles, opening, 419
  sysopen mode flags, using, 421
 creating a local version, 264
 creating an alias to, 270
 default STDOUT, changing, 442
 distinguishing those returned by IO::Socket module, 982
 duplicating & aliasing, 444
 eof function, detecting end-of-file condition, 429

filehandles (*continued*)
format datatypes can resemble, 699
formats associated with, 701, 703
introduced, 38
locking files, using flock function, 436, 439
passing using typeglobs, 161
polling for activity, server multiplexing, 993, 995, 996
prefixing with >&, 925
random access, seek function, 434-435
  object-oriented with IO::Seekable module, 437
  tell function, finding current position, 437
  writing at end of file, 436
reading and writing to socket, 984
reading from, with read function, 428
reading from, with readline (<>) operator, 426
reading single characters, with getc function, 428
redirecting, 445, 611
referring to, using typeglobs, 424
referring to, using IO::File & IO::Handle modules, 426
STDIN, STDOUT & STDERR standard filehandles, 416, 446
system level IO handling, 452-465
temporary filehandles, creating using new_tmpfile method, IO::File module, 508
threaded server access to, 1000
tied object class methods, 806
treated as objects, 731
truncating & resizing files, 437
typeglobs and, 425
writing to, using print function, 430
  block-/line-buffering and autoflush mode, 432
  printf function as alternative to print, 432
fileno function, 465
extracting file descriptor from filehandle, 465
files
attributes, changing, 485
comparing, using File::Compare module, 496
copying & moving, with File::Copy module, 494
copying & moving, 493
distinguishing file types, 289
DOS, 1033
file test operators, 475
filenames and, 467
finding directory/file name from its handle, 516
finding, using File::Find module, 497
globbing filenames, 503
  DOS-style, using File::DosGlob module, 507
  not to be relied upon, 1024
  UNIX-style, using File::Glob module, 505
  using glob operator, 503
group info, retrieving, 468, 473
interrogating, using stat/lstat functions, 484
linking, unlinking & renaming, 490-492
  symlink function, creating symbolic links, 492
newlines in files from other platforms, 1017
overview, 467
pack() function, 1023
parsing specifications, 1019
path names, 1018
paths, analyzing using File::Basename, 501
portability, 1018
portability of specifications, 1019
symbolic constants for flags, Fcntl module, 488
system interaction, 1024
system level copies & platform portability, 495

temporary files, 508
  creating using tempfile() function, File::Temp module, 511
  filehandles, creating using new_tmpfile method, IO::File module, 508
  filenames, creating using tmpname function, POSIX module, 509
user info, retrieving, 468-470
  User::pwent module, 470
files method, ExtUtils::Installed, 288
filestat pragma
ACLs, superuser and, file test operators, 480
fill subroutine, Text::Wrap module, 681
Filter module, 892
Finance::Quote module, 1070
find2perl utility, 819
FindBin module, 285
findConsole method, Term::ReadLine module, 575
FINISH literal marker, 376
firewalls
use of SO_KEEPALIVE option, 973
firstkey method
tied hash functions, 806
flags, recv function, 975
flags, send function, 974
flatfiles
multilingal message storage, 1090
flattening
lists, avoiding, 240
nested lists, 151
  source of unexpected results, 155
floating-point numbers, 56
accuracy compared to integers, 57
converting into integers, 58
converting into strings, 58
floating point exception signal, 898
flock function, locking files, 436, 439
establishing file locks, 440
fcntl function and, file locking support, 460
flags, 440
limitations, 442
not implemented in Mac OS, 1034
portability onto different platforms, 1036
flow control statements *see* **control constructs.**
flush_input method, Term::Screen module, 590
fonts, Unicode, 1055
foobar.c example program, 882
footers, 711
for loops, 195
continue clause, 207
forcing installation, 21
foreach loops, 195
indexing arrays by element number, 198
nested regular expression oops, 380
range operator, 198
redo statements, 205
regular expressions, handling results from, 379
variable aliasing, 199
with multi-branched conditions, 198
writing better loops with, 197
foreach statement
introduced, 44
iterating over hashes using, 134
looping over arrays using, 122
traversing complex data structures, 158

fork function, 908
  inefficiency of, 937
  portability onto different platforms, 1036
  simulating on Windows, 817
  when to avoid, 1025
forked open, 922
forking
  closing sockets after, 975
  effects of changing %ENV special variable, 140
forking servers, 993, 998
form.pl script
  multilingual web page example, 1089, 1093
formats
  assigning to standard output, 702
  distinct reporting datatype, 699
  dynamically calculated, 701
  filehandles and, 701
  structure of, and defining, 704
  suppressing redundant lines, 708
formats, integer, 53, 55
formats, string, 80, 679
  see also **document formatting; padding; paragraph
    formatting.**
formfeed character, 710
formline function, 701, 713, 714
forward recursion, 224
frame debugger option, 639
frame tracing, Perl debugger, 641
frames, Ethernet
  communication length limit, 959
  distinguished from IP packets, 963
Freekai, 845
fribidi library and FriBidi module, 1053
FSpRstFLock() and FSpSetFLock() functions, 1034
ftok constant, IPC::SysV module, 928
fully qualified definitions
  alternative to package declarations, 300
functional modules
  compared to pragmatic modules, 275
functional programming
  using objects in, 721
functions
  see also **undef function**
  built-in functions, network configuration enquiries,
    1001
  comparing undef, exists and delete, 166
  disabling using the ops and no ops pragmas, 110
  distinguishing from operators, 87
  introduced, 47
  parentheses change behavior of, 108, 109
  portable onto different platforms, 1035

G

Game::Card class, 728
  _Property method, enforcing privacy, 760
  accessors and mutators, 737
  autoloading example, 773
Game::Card constructor, 728
  modified to allow calling as a subroutine, 736
  modified to allow new object creation, 735
  modified to use methods of the class, 739
  splitting to provide for multiple inheritance, 765
Game::Deck class, 728, 770

gateways
  IP processing of remote traffic, 963
GDBM_File module
  tie function, binding a hash vairable to, 800
generic methods
  adding to the Universal class, 768
genmake script, ExtUtils::Embed, 877, 888
  example program mimicking perl -v, 879
gensymb subroutine, 301
get (option) method, dumper object, 648
get_* functions
  Perl embedded in C code, 881
get_fn_keys method, Term::Screen module, 590
get_results subroutine, 165
GETALL constant, IPC::SysV module, 927
getall method
  semaphores, 932
getattr function
  termios object, 595
getc function, 430
  reading single characters, filehandles, 430
getch method, Term::Screen module, 568, 589, 590
GetControlChars subroutine
  Term::ReadKey module, 572
getcwd function, 285
getcwd routine, POSIX module
  finding current directory, 521
getfastcwd function, Cwd module
  finding current directory, 522
getgrent function
  group information, retrieving, 473
  portability onto different platforms, 1037
getgrgid function
  portability onto different platforms, 1037
getgrnam function
  portability onto different platforms, 1036
GetHistory function, 580
gethost subroutine, Net::hostent, 1007
gethost* functions
  warning about using within loops, 1006
gethostbyaddr function, 1003-1004
gethostbyname function, 985, 1003-1004, 1012
gethostent function, 1003-1004
  portability onto different platforms, 1037
getlogin function
  portability onto different platforms, 1036
getMessage subroutine
  babel.pl multilingual web page example, 1092
GETNCNT constant, IPC::SysV module, 927
getnet subroutine, 1009
getnet* functions, 1008
getnetbyaddr function
  portability onto different platforms, 1037
getnetbyname function
  portability onto different platforms, 1036
getnetent function, 1008
  portability onto different platforms, 1037
getopt function, 532
Getopt::Long module, 526, 532, 535
  aliases, 541
  basis of Pod command line tools, 691
  configuration options tabulated, 550
  example script for POD searching, 698
  POSIX compliance and, 549
  separators and negative integers, 540

Getopt::Long::Configure subroutine, 537, 541, 545
  introduced, 535
Getopt::Std module, 526, 532
  recognizes --, 535
getopt_compat option, 550
GetOptions function, 535
  abbreviations, 541
  handling multiple values, 542
  unrecognized options and values, 547
getopts function
  compared with getopt, 534
  specifying Boolean and value options, 534
getospeed function
  termios object, 595
getpeername function, 985, 992
getpgrp function, 910
  portability onto different platforms, 1036
GETPID constant, IPC::SysV module, 927
getppid function, 909
  portability onto different platforms, 1036
getpriority function
  portability onto different platforms, 1036
getproto subroutine, 1012
getprotobyname function, 980
getprotobynumber function
  portability onto different platforms, 1037
getprotoent function, 1011
  portability onto different platforms, 1037
getpwent function
  fields returned, list of, 468
  portability onto different platforms, 1037
  user, retrieving, 468
getpwnam() function, 1019
  portability onto different platforms, 1036
  user id, deducing from name, 470
getpwuid function
  portability onto different platforms, 1036
  user name, deducing from user id, 470
getservbyname function, 1001
getservbyport function, 1010
  portability onto different platforms, 1037
getservent function, 1010
  portability onto different platforms, 1037
getsockopt function, 969, 971, 973, 976
  portability onto different platforms, 1038
GetSpeeds function, 571
GetTerminalSize function, 569
gettext tool, 1071, 1072
GETVAL constant, IPC::SysV module, 927
getval method
  semaphores, 932
GETZCNT constant, IPC::SysV module, 927
GIMME function, 864
glob function
  portability onto different platforms, 1038
glob operator, 503
  DOS-style globbing, File::DosGlob module, 507
  filename globbing, 503, 1024
  syntax, 504
  UNIX-style globbing, File::Glob module, 505
    error-handling, 507
    extended globbing, 505
global package variables
  declaring lexically using our keyword, 261
  declaring using strict, 260
  declaring with use vars, 260

global variables
  see also **our keyword.**
  altering locally through an alias, 270
  introduced, 47
  package variables as, 259
  package-global and file-global variables, 260
globPrint debugger option, 640, 645
GMT (Greenwich Mean Time) differences, 1078
GNU gettext tool, 1071
GNU long options, 526
GNU readline, 574
goto statement, 209
  autoload subroutines, 227
  subroutines, 225
graphical output
  checking availability of the GD module, 286
GraphViz module, 848
GraphViz nodes, adding at each op, 850
greedy matches, 392
grep function, 210, 211
  loops, 195
  using regular expressions within, 347
grokLanguage subroutine, 1074
groups, process, 909
guaranteed delivery
  requirement favors TCP over UDP, 965
gzipped tarballs, 24

H

H command, Perl debugger, 626, 630
-h option, h2xs scripts, 858
h command, Perl debugger, 626
h2xs script, 653
  automates installable package processes, 330, 331, 332
  calling C code from Perl, 857
  use for pure Perl extension modules, 858
handlers
  see also **error handling.**
  avoiding complex, 901
  die, 900
  flexibly installing, 903
  handling children, 911
  pipes, 917
  signals, 898
  specifiying several, 904
  un-interruptible, 902
  warn, 900
  writing, 900
handy.h file, 820
hangup signal, 897
hard references, 142
HARNESS_ environment variables, 655, 656
has_exception method, IO::Select, 995
hash reference constructor, 138
hash symbol *see # (under Symbols)*
hash variable indicator *see % (under Symbols)*
Hash Variables (HVs) internal variable type, 830
hashDepth debugger option, 640
hashes, 129
  accessing and iterating over, 134
  adding and modifying hash values, 131
  classes built with struct subroutine, 797

hashes (*continued*)
  converting
    hash reference values into arrays, 146
    hashes into arrays of arrays or hashes, 138
    hashes into lists and arrays, 138
    hashes into scalars, 137
    lists and arrays into, 133
  counting elements, 137
  evaluation in scalar context, 41
  flipping, 241
  GetOptions multiple values as, 542
  internal representation of, 830
  introduced as lists of key-value pairs, 37
  listing and sorting keys in, 130
  locking, 943
  looping over with while loops, 203
  named parameters, 233
  passing into subroutines, 147, 229, 231
  passing named arguments with, 136
  populated by getopt function, 533
  populated by GetOptions function, 536
  removing keys and values, 132
  reversing, 133
  sorting and indexing, 135
  tied object class example, 807, 810
  tied object class methods, 805
hashes of hashes, 103, 153
  see also **lists of lists.**
hashes of typeglobs
  symbol table as example, 267
head1 and head2 tokens, POD, 686
header files, C
  example script to access, 859
help commands
  Perl debugger, tabulated, 626
helper files, 820
helper modules, 795
here documents, 65
  format definitions resemble, 700
hexadecimal integers, 53, 55
  see also **Unicode character set.**
HighBit debugger option, 640
history, command line, 579
  retrieving, 580
HOME environment variable, 32
hook function, 892
hostname queries, 1000
  determining the local hostname, 1012
  script to return IP addresses from, 1005
hostpath method, IO::Socket::UNIX, 992
hosts
  system network configuration enquiries, 1001, 1003
HP MPE/iX platform, 1035
HTML (Hypertext Markup Language)
  generating tags with an import subroutine, 321
  generating with CGI by suppressing imports, 319
  paragraph formatting using Text::Wrap, 679
  pod2html tool obeys rules of, 689
  returning using an autoloader instead of CGI, 308
  tag generator, AUTOLOAD subroutine, 226
  templates for airport kiosk example, 1056
  text markers for foreign languages, 1055
hung operations, aborting, 907
HUP signal, 905
HVs (Hash Variables) internal variable type, 830

I

-i option
  command-line scripts, 31
-I option, 283
ic method, Term::Screen module, 589
ICMP (Internet Control Message Protocol)
  use by IP to report problems, 965
ID card numbers, 1094
IEEE (Institute of Electrical and Electronics Engineers)
  assignment body for MAC addresses, 959
if ... else statements, 183, 185
  see also **ternary operator.**
  introduced, 44
  inverting syntax of, 185
  unless keyword, 187
ignore_case options, 550
  enabling with Getopt::Long::Configure, 546
il method, Term::Screen module, 589
implicit formatting codes, 1052
implicit–read check, B::Lint module, 844
implicit–write check, B::Lint module, 844
import lists
  additional uses, 321
  methods of defining, 278, 324
import methods
  see also **exporting.**
  defining local methods for Exporter module, 329
  setting class data, 743
import subroutines, 316
  autouse only works with modules using default, 290
  can be ignored for simple requirements, 316
  essential feature of the use statement, 278
  example inventing HTML tag generators, 321
  examples of increasing versatility, 319, 320
  suppressing with empty parameter lists, 319
importing Java classes and methods, 888
importing symbols
  from another package, 316
  warnings about advisability, 321
IN method, Term::ReadLine module, 575-576
INADDR_ socket symbols, 971, 980
INADDR_BROADCAST socket symbol, 989
include files
  identifying with the -V option, 876
incremental options, 539
incrementing scalar variables, 98
incrementing undefined values, 168
indenting
  adjusting browser text display, 679
  paragraph formatting with Text::Wrap, 681
index function, 73
index numbers
  identifying array elements, 118
indexed hashes, 135
INET sockets, 967
inet_ conversion utilities, 967
inet_aton socket function, 969, 980, 1005
inet_ntoa socket function, 969, 1004, 1005
information retrieval *see* **searching**
informational modules, 645
inheritance, 719, 753
  attributes stored as hash keys, 749
  classes built with Class::Struct, 797

inheritance (*continued*)
destructors and, 783
inheriting class data, 742
needs two-argument bless function, 728
overloading operators and, 793
rules for writing inheritable classes, 756
inhibit_exit debugger option, 639
INIT blocks, 183, 299
example illustrating use, 296
execute after main compilation, 300
initializer methods
multiple inheritance example, 767
initscr
Curses module, 591
not used with Curses windows, 593
in-line modifiers, 363
input/output *see* **IO (Input & Output).**
install command
get, make and test for stepwise install, 20
installable packages
adding test scripts, 334
creating from a module source, 332
working directory tree for, 331
installing modules
CPAN commands for, 20
Macintosh systems, 26
manually, 24, 25
on other platforms, 27
installing Perl
binary distributions on UNIX, 13
binary distributions on Windows, 13
helper files, 820
installperl program, 822
MacPerl, 14
pre-built distributions, 12
int subroutine, Devel::Peek module, 833
integer pragma, 60
bitwise NOT operator effects, 95
forcing signed integer arithmetic, 91
modulus operator on negative numbers, 90
Integer Values (IVs) internal variable type, 828
integers
accuracy compared to floating-point numbers, 57
available representations, 53
conversion into floating point numbers, 54
conversion into strings, 54
converting floating-point numbers into, 58
formatting as strings, 55
out-of-range results converted to floating point, 54
shift operator manipulates as binary, 91
shortcomings of int function, 58
use integer pragma, 60
interactive programs
determining if script is, 562
interfaces
see also **encapsulation.**
arguments against circumventing, 720
interior sequences, pod, 691
internal addressing, TCP, 965
internal variable types, 827
NVs, 829
PVs, 828
internationalization, 1028, 1043, 1063
see also **locale; languages other than English.**
airport information kiosks example, 1055
aspects other than language translation, 1063
categories of localization under POSIX, 1065

framework for programs in general, 1071
multilingual web page example, 1089
retrieving local messages from PO files, 1073
time zones and, 1077
Unicode and, 1055
website designed using WWW::Babelfish, 1074
Windows National Language Support, 1065
internet domain sockets *see* **INET sockets.**
interoperability with Java, 888
interpolation
/o flag, 342
arrays, 340
body of a here document, 65
character codes, 338
code, 341
context, 342
HTML tag names into a subroutine, 309
metacharacters, 338
problem when using formats, 701, 708
problem when using shellwords subroutine, 677
protecting strings against, 344
quotemeta function, 75, 344
regular expressions, 342
string, 337
syntax, 337
text inside string variables, 343
variables, 39, 340
interpretation options, dprofpp utility, 661
interpreter threads, 817
interpreting, 826
Inter-Process Communication *see* **IPC**
interrupt signal, 897
invalid IP address, 971
invalid memory reference signal, 898
invest.pl example program, 1067, 1073, 1074
invisible input, reading, 569
IO (Input & Output) using filehandles, 415
directories, 513
filehandles, 416
files & filenames, 467
system level IO, 452
attribute setting, using fcntl function, 459
controlling devices, using ioctl function, 462
opening filehandles, using sysopen function, 453
positioning filehandles, using sysseek function, 458
POSIX & standard IO, moving between, 464
POSIX module IO, 462
reading unbuffered filehandles, using sysread function, 456
writing unbuffered filehandles, using syswrite function, 457
IO (Input & Output) using terminals, 561
advanced line input, 574
colors, 581, 584
command line history, 579
complete lines, reading, 568
Curses library, 590
cursor, moving, 584
default input, 578
high level modules, 588
invisible input and passwords, 569
keyboards, reading from, 563
line based input, 563
line ending translation, 571
paging ouput, 570
preput text, 579
programming terminals directly via POSIX, 594
prompt style, 578

IO (Input & Output) using terminals (continued)
reading single character, 566
screen size, finding and resetting, 569
screens, clearing, 584
screens, writing to, 581
simple input, 563
terminal input, controlling, 564
terminal objects, creating, 575
terminal speed, 571
terminals, 562
word completion, 580
IO:: modules
compared with typeglobs for passing filehandles, 161
IO::Dir module
encapsulating directory handles in objects, 515
tied hash interface support, 515
IO::File module
filehandles, creating, 420
sysopen mode flags, using, 421
filehandles, referring to, 426
filehandles, writing to, 431
new method, using sysopen function via, 456
new_tmpfile method, creating temporary filehandles, 508
IO::Handle class, 730
IO::Handle module, 448, 700, 704
built-in function methods, 448
configuration methods
global and per-filehandle, 449
creation methods, 448
default variables vs. IO::Handle methods, changing default STDOUT filehandle, 444
filehandles, referring to, 426
utility methods, 450
IO::Handle objects, 924
IO::Pipe module, 918
IO::Seekable module, 437
object-oriented random access, filehandles, 437
IO::Select module, 926
methods tabulated, 996
polling servers using, 993, 995, 996
IO::Socket module, 976
using instead of Socket, 981, 983, 987, 988, 990, 992
IO::Socket::INET module, 977, 982, 984, 985, 988
IO::Socket::Multicast module, 989
IO::Socket::UNIX module, 978, 992
ioctl function, 462
controlling devices at system level IO, 462
fcntl function and, 459
portability onto different platforms, 1038
IOK flag, 831
IP (Internet Protocol)
components of 32-bit address space, 961
datagram manipuatlion by, 965
invalid addresses, 971
IPv4 and IPv6 versions, 960
network layer of TCP/IP, 960
payload delivered in packets, 963
processing of local and remote traffic, 963
script to return IP addresses from hostname, 1005
IP:port pairs, 965
IPC (Inter Process Communication), 916
mesage queues, 928
pipes, 918
portability of code, 1025
semaphores, 931

shared memory segments, 935
System V IPC, 926
IPC::Msg::stat object
retrieving, 930
IPC::Open2 and IPC::Open 3 modules, 911
bi-directional pipes, 923
communicating between processes, 916
open2 subroutine, 923
read and write access external programs, 920
IPC::Semaphore module, 932
IPC::Shareable module, 935
shlock method, 937
shunlock method, 937
IPC::ShareLite module, 937
IPC::SysV module, 926, 927
message queues, 928
IPC_ALLOC constant, IPC::SysV module, 927
IPC_CREAT constant, IPC::SysV module, 927
IPC_EXCL constant, IPC::SysV module, 927
IPC_NOERROR constant, IPC::SysV module, 928
IPC_NOWAIT constant, IPC::SysV module, 928
IPC_NOWAIT flag, 930
IPC_PRIVATE constant, IPC::SysV module, 928
IPC_RMID constant, IPC::SysV module, 928
IPC_SET constant, IPC::SysV module, 928
IPC_STAT constant, IPC::SysV module, 928
IPC_W constant, IPC::SysV module, 928
ipcs command, 927
ISA method
determining an object's ancestry, 725
enforcing privacy, 760
ISO (International Organization for Standardization)
ISO 8859 standards, ASCII and UCS, 1045
networking reference model, 958
IsUV flag, 831
iterating loops, 195
iters method, Benchmark module, 664
ithreads, 817
IVs (Integer Values) internal variable type, 828

J

Jasmin assembler, 849
Java bytecode
outputting from Perl, 849
Java language
importing classes and methods of, 888
join function, 127, 348
C code example as equivalent, 885
File::Spec module, 1021
join method, threads, 941
JPL (Java-Perl Lingo), 888
JPL::Class module, 888
justification
data in fixed width fields, 706
placeholders in formats, 705
sprintf placeholder width and, 83

K

KBabel editor, 1071
keep parameter, quotewords subroutine, 677

key option
  shared memory segments, 936
key_pressed method, Term::Screen module, 590
keyboards
  reading from, 563
keys function, 134
  listing keys in a hash, 130
key-value pairs
  defining hashes, 129
  unordered within hashes, 37
kill
  kill function, Term::Complete module, 581
  kill function, portability onto different platforms, 1038
  kill signals, 897
  UNIX command for sending signals, 905

L

l command, Perl debugger, 628
L command, Perl debugger, 633
-l option
  command-line scripts, 31
labels
  nested loops, 208
languages
  see also **markup languages; programming languages.**
languages other than English, 891, 1043, 1063
  see also **alphabets, non-Latin; Basque; Czech; Latin;**
    Norwegian; Portugese; Spanish.
  bidirectional scripts, 1050
  establishing the client language, 1076
  identifying by statistical methods, 1081
  justification of HTML templates, 1056
  multilingual web page example, 1089
  reporting website script, 1080
  sites offering example phrases in, 1059
  sorting and alphabetization rules, 1064
  translation capabilities of WWW::Babelfish, 1091
  using locale names to set messages, 1074
  using Perl to learn, 1082
last statements
  do not work in if blocks, 180
  introduced, 45
  loops, 195, 204
  multi-branched conditions, 193
  nested loops, 207
  not used in do ... while loops, 208
Latin language, 891
layout *see* **document formatting.**
lean matches, 359
leaning-toothpick-syndrome, 349
left associativity, arithmetical operators, 90
length function, 73
letter counting program, 168
lexer, 820
lexical scope
  defining, to keep class data private, 778
lexical variables, 264
  see also **my keyword.**
  debugging, 845
  introduced, 47
  preferred over package variables, 303
  preserving, outside their scope, 266
  scope determined at compile-time, 257, 259
  symbolic references can't be used with, 150

lib pragma
  modifying @INC with, 284
libraries
  calculating relative locations, 285
  identifying with the -V option, 876
  modules and, 275
libraries variable
  configuration process, 818
library package management, 287
line based input, 563
  advanced, 574
line ending translation, 571
line separator
  redefining, reading from filehandles, 426
line terminators
  removing with chop and chomp, 72
line tracing, Perl debugger, 641
linefeeds, 1016, 1017
  translating CR/LF into, 571
LineInfo debugger option, 640, 641
Lingua::* modules, 1084
Lingua::Ident module, 1080
Lingua::Ispell module, 1086
Lingua::stem module, 1088
link function
  linking files, 491
  portability onto different platforms, 1038
linker variable
  configuration process, 818
Linux
  packages for standard installation, 13
list context, 41
list operators
  precedence and evaluation, 108
list processors
  converting scalar subroutines into, 231
Listen argument, 990
listen socket function, 968, 981
listing and searching
  CPAN archive, with a, b, d, i, and m commands, 22
LISTOPs, 851
lists
  see also **arrays.**
  assigning to scalars, 119
  converting into hashes, 133
  converting into scalars, 127
  converting strings into, 69
  defining in POD, 687
  distinction from arrays, 117
  evaluation in scalar context, 41
  flattening 151, 155, 240
  looping over, 201
  passing by references, 231
  passing to subroutines, 229
  undefined values, 245
lists of lists
  see also **hashes of hashes.**
  using references and [...] notation, 151
loading code, 277
loading modules
  postponing until functions are called, 290
local function
  localizing fresh signal values, 902
local import methods, 329

local keyword, 262
    creating filehandle and subroutine aliases, 271
    distinction from my, our and use vars, 263
    manipulating the symbol table using, 270
locale, 1063
    see also **alphabets, non-Latin; character sets.**
    categories of localization under POSIX, 1065
    installing from the internet, 1066
    LC_COLLATE variable used in sorts, 101
    locale settings introduced, 1064
    perllocale documentation, 1067
    perllocale tutorial, 1065
    representation of decimals defined by, 707
    structure explained, 1067
    technology for internationalization, 1044
    using locales to set message languages, 1074
locale pragma, 1028, 1065, 1066
Locale::gettext and Locale::PGetText, 1072
Locale::Language module
    code2language function, 1076
Locale::Maketext and Locale::PO modules, 1071
Locale::Zonetab module, 1078
localhost, 966
localization *see* **internationalization.**
localtime() function, 1027
lock subroutine, 942
locked attribute, 251
    threaded programming, 252
locking files, *see* **flock function.**
locks, 942
    conditional blocks, 943
    implementation in Mac OS, 1034
    non-blocking, 908
    record-based locking, 943
    unlocking threads, 944
log function, 61
LOGDIR environment variable, 32
logging errors, 611
    Sys::Syslog module, 611
    Win32::Eventlog module, 612
logical operators, 93
    conditional statements, 183
    precedence, 188
    writing conditions with, 188
long and extra long numbers
    sprintf placeholders for 16, 32 and 64-bit, 81
look command, 21
loop variables
    automatically localized, 262
loopback address, 966, 971, 1012
looping performance test program, 662
looping tools, 44
loops, 195
    see also **control constructs.**
    blocks as, 180
    conditional, 195
    continue clause, 206
    control statements not used in do ... while, 208
    controlling execution, 204
    do, 200
    do ... until loops, 203
    do ... while loops, 203
    for, 195
    foreach, 195, 197
        with multi-branched conditions, 198
    grep function, 195
    hashes, looping over, 203
    incrementing loop variable, 206
    indexing arrays by element number, 198
    iterating, 195
    last statements, 204
    lists and arrays, looping over, 201
    loop modifiers introduced, 45
    map function, 195
    nested, 207
    next statements, 204
    number of matches, counting, 386
    redo statements, 204
    regular expressions, 378
    self-modifying arrays, looping on, 202
    until, 195, 200
    variable aliasing with foreach, 199
    variable aliasing with while, 201
    variables, 196
    while, 195, 200
lstat function
    interrogating files, 484
    portability onto different platforms, 1038
    reusing results of prior stat/lstat, file test operators, 478
lvalue attribute, 251
    assignable subroutines, 250
    assignable values, 252
    introduced, 89
    reference type returned by ref function, 148
    ternary operators with functions that return, 191

M

m command, Perl debugger, 629
MAC addresses, 959, 963, 964
Mac OS
    running Perl on, 1033
Mac OS X, 1034
Mac::Files module, 1034
machine code, turning op tree into, 842
Macintosh
    building Perl from source, 17
    installing modules, 26
    installing Perl binary distributions on, 14
    MPW Programmers Workbench, 14, 17, 26, 1034
    POSIX localization won't work on, 1064
MacPerl, 14, 26, 29, 1033
Mail::Mailer and Mail::Send modules, 1025
main package
    status as root namespace, 259, 267
main program
    defining as a block, 179
main_start function, B module, 834
MAINTAIN file, 819
Makefile.pl, 331-332, 334, 870
    h2xs script generates, 857, 859
malloc.c file, 820
man command, Perl debugger, 626
MANIFEST file, 819
    h2xs script generates, 857, 859
map function, 210
    converting scalar subroutines into list processors, 232
    example illustrating use of, 211
    loops, 195
    using regular expressions within, 347

markup languages *see* **HTML; XML**
masking
  bitmask manipulations on 64-bit systems, 95
match dialog, re module, 403
match operator
  delimiters, 349
  non-matches, checking for, 347
  regular expressions, 346
matching *see* **patterm matching.**
Math::BigInt package
  introduced, 54
Math::Trig module
  introduced, 62
mathematical functions, 61
mathematical operators *see* **numerical operators**
maxTraceLen debugger option, 639
McCamant, Stephen, 848
md and me terminal capability codes, 579
memory
  memory allocation functions, 864
  subroutines, closures as form of, 248
message queues, 926, 928
  access by processes, 929
  destroying, 931
  permissions, changing, 930
metacharacters
  character class, 365
  escaping non-alphanumeric characters, 340
  interpolating, 338
  POSIX character classes, 366
  property, 366
  regular expressions, 351
  special characters, 339
  whitespace, 348
  zero-width, 365, 368
metaconfig
  autoconf compared, 821
method attribute, 251
  locking on per-object basis, 253
method overloading, 720
methods
  accessors and mutators, 737
    autoloading example, 773
    for class data, 746
    generic accessors/mutators, 738, 759
  adding generic methods to the universal class, 768
  callable as subroutines, 735
  calling class methods, 723
  calling object methods, 724
  class and object methods distinguished, 732
  functions, writing methods callable as, 759
  listing using the debugger m command, 629
  multiple context methods, 734
  nesting method calls, 724
miniperl, 822
MinLine method, Term::ReadLine module, 575, 580
mkdir built-in function
  mkpath function and, 519
  single directories, creating, 517
mkpath function, File::Path module
  mkdir function and, 519
  multiple directories, creating, 518
mktemp temporary file generation system calls
  File::Temp module, implementing, 512
mode option
  shared memory segments, 936

modifiers
  width and precision, for sprintf placeholders, 82
MODIFY_X_ATTRIBUTES subroutines, 253
modules, 275
  1, as return statement for, 276
  checking installation and availability, 286
  core, 819
  CPAN, building and installing, 18
  custom, creating for Spanish language, example, 1094
  declaring in XS files, 861
  distinguished from packages, 276
  example script listing, 289
  functional and object orientated, 278
  functional and pragmatic distinguished, 275, 280
  libraries and, 275
  out-of-date modules, 23
  portability of programs and, 1026
  postponing loading until use, 290, 291
  preconfiguring using BEGIN blocks, 299
  successful loading requires return statements, 276
  using from within C code, 886
  well-behaved, 295
modules method, ExtUtils::Installed, 287
modulus operator
  negative numbers, behavior depends on use integer, 90
MPW (Macintosh Programmers Workbench), 14, 17, 26, 1034
MSG_ flags, Socket module, 974, 975
MSG_EXCEPT and MSG_NOERROR flags, 930
MSG_NOERROR constant, IPC::SysV module, 928
msgctl, msgget, msgrcv and msgsnd functions
  portability onto different platforms, 1038
mstat subroutine, Devel::Peek module, 833
multi-branched conditions, 192
  last statements, 193
  returning values from, 194
  using foreach loops with, 198
multicasting
  see also **broadcast addresses.**
  Multicast UDP, 989
  network addresses for unicasting and, 961
  using UDP rather than TCP, 964
multidimensional arrays, 103, 119
  can't be declared explicitly, 151
  dereferencing, 147
  using references to create, 151
multiline commands
  backslash used for continuing, 553, 625
multilingual sites *see* **internationalization.**
multiple child processes, 913
multiple context methods, 734
multiple file tests
  automating, file test operators, 482
multiple inheritance, 754, 764
  destructors and, 784
  drawbacks, 767
multiplexed servers, 992
multiplicity
  multiple interpreters in the same binary, 817
my function
  thread-specific data, 940
my keyword, 48, 265
  see also **lexical variables.**
myconfig function, Config module, 817

N

n command, Perl debugger, **631**
-n option
    command-line scripts, 31
    h2xs scripts, 858, 860
    implicit while loop, 529, 551
naked blocks, **178**
name resolution services, **1000, 1003**
named characters, Unicode, **1047**
named parameters
    distinguishing from unnamed, 233
    passing to subroutines with hashes, 136
named subroutines, **215**
named unary operators, **88, 107**
namespaces
    avoiding collisions with package declarations, 276
    restrictions placed by Safe module, 649
    risk of collisions from exporting definitions, 295
naming conventions
    functional and pragmatic distinguished, 280
    Spanish language module, 1094
    variables, 36
negatable Boolean options, **538**
nested hashes, **153**
    modifying the contents of, 154
nested lists, **739**
    modifying the contents of, 154
    unexpected results from flattening, 151
nested loops, **207**
    labels, 208
    regular expressions, 380
nested references, **801**
nested_quotewords subroutine
    Text::ParseWords module, 678
nesting method calls, **724**
Net:: modules
    processing results of network configuration queries, 1002
Net::hostent module, **1006**
Net::netent module, **1008**
Net::protoent module, **1012**
Net::servent module, **1002, 1010**
netmasks, network addresses, **961**
network addresses
    determining local and remote, 985
    Internet Protocol, 961
network collisions, **959**
network information, accessing, **1000**
network programming, **957**
network protocols see protocols.
networks, **957**
    built-in system configuration functions, 1001
    diagrams comparing local and remote delivery, 963
    network services, 1009
    script to return configured networks, 1008
    system network configuration enquiries, 1001, 1007
new keyword, **721**
new lines, **339**
    definition of on various platforms, 1016
    matching to dots, 384
    portability, 1016
    sockets, 1018
new method
    Benchmark module, 664

IO::File module, 456
    sysopen function, using via new method, 456
IO::Socket::INET module, options, 977
IO::Socket::UNIX module, options, 978
Term::ReadLine module, 575
threads, 938
new processes, **908**
new subroutine
    Thread::Queue module, 950
    Thread::Semaphore module, 948
new_tmpfile method, IO::File module
    creating temporary filehandles, 508
newBINOP function, **825**
newTTY method, Term::ReadLine module, **575-576**
next statements
    do not work in if blocks, 180
    introduced, 45
    loops, 195, 204
    nested loops, 207
    next LINE, 207
    not used in do ... while loops, 208
nextkey method
    tied hash functions, 806
nicknames for users, **1084**
NLS (National Language Support)
    Windows NT localization implementation, 1065
NMAKE file, **821**
no statement
    calling require and unimport, 317
    disabling module features with, 279
    modifying @INC with no lib, 284
no_ see under the rest of the word.
noecho method, Term::Screen module, **589**
noecho mode, Term::ReadKey module, **564**
    invisible input and passwords, 569
nomethod keyword, **794**
non-blocking input, **568**
non-blocking locks, **908**
non-greedy matches, **358, 359, 392**
non-matches
    checking for, within regexp, 347
non-option arguments, **549**
NonStop debugger option, **639, 641, 642**
non-word boundaries, matching, **368**
no-object classes, **743**
normal method, Term::Screen module, **589**
normal mode, Term::ReadKey module, **564**
Norwegian language
    CPAN national module for, 1084
Notepad editor
    Unicode and, 1055
NoTTY debugger option, **641, 642**
NTP (Network Time Protocol)
    example of protocol using UDP over TCP, 965
numbered variables, **357**
    regular expressions, 371
    when overridden, 380
numbers
    see also **integers; floating point numbers.**
    available representations, 52
    converting strings into, 68
    formatting print output with $#, 71
    page numbering, 710
    sprintf placeholders for 16, 32 and 64-bit, 81
    strings and, not distinguished strongly, 51
    width of stored, and portability, 1023

numeric comparison, 194
numeric conversion
    commify subroutine inserts commas, 883
    overloading, 790
numeric justifcation, 706
Numeric Values (NVs) internal variable type, 829
numerical operators, 42
    arithmetic, 89
NVs (Numeric Values) internal variable type, 829

O

O command, Perl debugger, 636
O module, 834
    compile subroutine, 850
object classes see classes.
object level debugging, 749
object methods, 732
object orientation, 717
    see also bless function.
    autouse and object oriented modules, 290
    basic concepts reviewed, 718
    flexibility of Perl approach, 717
    function of the arrow operator, 103
    overloading operators with the overload pragma, 113
    simplicity of Perl approach, 9
object programming
    debug messages with added context, 622
objects
    adaptability, 721
    as blessed references, 719, 722
    creating with constructor methods, 721
    determining ancestry using the ISA method, 725
    determining capabilities with the can method, 725
    determining class and data type, 725
    determining version, 726
    introduced, 38
    properties, defining to be inaccessible outside
        object's methods, 250
    properties, modifying inherited, 721
    using as attributes in Class::Struct module, 797
octal notation, 53, 55, 339
ok test subroutine, 654
old-interface-signals, 904
once-only pattern match modifier, 394
    qr operator as replacement for, 398
onfail key, 653
op see operations (ops).
op method
    semaphores, 933
op trees, 826
    connecting ops, 851
    first op, returning object that represents, 834
    graphical representation of, 848
    GraphViz nodes, adding at each op, 850
    machine code, turning into, 842
    manipulating, 833
    un-parsing, 839
    walking, 835
Opcode module, 110
    compartment object methods refer to, 650
    complete list of tags, 111
    listing Opcodes and descriptions, 112

open function, 38, 417
    arbitrary filenames, opening, 419
    communicating between processes, 916
    filehandles, creating, 417
    forked open, 922
    modes, 418
    opening files for reading/writing/updating, 418
    opening STDIN & STDOUT, 419
    portability onto different platforms, 1038
    security issues, 922
open pragma, 434
    handling binary & text files, 434
open2 and open3 subroutines, 923
opendir function
    opening directories, 513
openlog function, Sys::Syslog module, 611
operands
    determining order and names of, 786
operating systems
    contents of %ENV special variable, 139
    list of, offering Perl support, 9
operations (ops), 825
    see also op trees.
    checking for asynchrous signals, 827
    connecting, 851
    returning object that represents first op, 834
operator masks, Safe module, 650
operator methods
    investigating third and fourth arguments, 787
operators, 87
    disabling using the ops and no ops pragmas, 110
    distinguishing from functions, 87
    infering behavior by autogeneration, 793
    introduced, 42
    overall categorization, 88
    overloading and inheritance, 793
    overloading core, by object class methods, 721
    overloading to have objects treated as scalars, 38
    overloading to work with objects, 785
    overriding with the overload pragma, 113
    precedence and associativity tabulated, 106
    table of overloadable operations, 795
ops and no ops pragmas, 110
optional parameters, subroutines, 241
options
    checking whether set, 538
    compared to values, 526
    defining as integer, string or floating-point, 540
    mandatory or optional values, 540
    prefixes and case sensitivity, 537
ord function, 73
    pack 'c' function compared to, 77
ornaments debugger option, 639
ornaments method
    Term::ReadLine module, 575, 578
OS/2
    extended error messages, 606
OSI (Open Systems Interconnection)
    protocol reference model, 958
our function
    thread-specific data, 940
our keyword, 48, 261
    see also global variables.
    distinction from use vars, my and local, 261, 263
OUT method, Term::ReadLine module, 575-576

Out-Of-Band channel markers, 930
out-of-date modules, 23
output redirection, 611
overlapping matches, 386
overload pragma, 113, 721, 795
overloading
method and operator overloading, 720
overloading operators, 785
inheritance and, 793
objects to be treated as scalars, 38
overload pragma supports, 721
overriding with the overload pragma, 113
table of overloadable operations, 795
overridden methods, 754
constructors, 755
overriding operators, 113
overwriting typeglobs, 162
ownership, files
changing using chown function, 485

P

p command, Perl debugger, 627
-p option
command-line scripts, 31
-P option, h2xs scripts, 858
pack function, 127, 970, 1005, 1023
compared to sprintf, 76
template characters supported, list of, 77
pack_sockaddr_in function, 970
pack_sockaddr_un function, 970
package declarations, 258, 300, 861
package variables, 257
forbidding, 303
listing contents with the Perl debugger, 627
localizing inside blocks and subroutines, 262
scope determined at run-time, 257, 259
Packagename::$AUTOLOAD special variable, 305
packages
access through the symbol table hierarchy, 267
attributes, 253
declarations, 258, 300
declaring in XS files, 861
differences between object classes and, 727
distinguished from modules, 258, 276
essential to object-oriented Perl, 717
finding a package name programmatically, 303
import mechanisms as package interfaces, 316
must be named when calling class methods, 724
naming, only in package declaration, 304
package keyword, 330
package scope, needless use, 257
removing with the delete command, 302
packets
IP payload unit, compared to frames, 963
packlist method, ExtUtils::Installed, 288
padding
formatted text with the repetition operator, 92
sprintf placeholder width and, 83
page control and numbering, 709, 712
pagination example script, 710
paging debugger output, 631
pager option, 638
Panels, 594

paragraph formatting, 681, 686
parameters
see also arguments.
anonymous subroutines, 249
named, 233
number of, defining, 237
optional, 241
overridding, 234
passing to subroutines, 228
scope, 237
variables, requiring rather than values, 240
parent classes
array-based constructors unsuitable, 730
parentheses
changing behavior of functions and subroutines, 108
changing interpretation with unary plus, 91
distinguishing functions from operators, 88
overriding precedence with, 107
regular expressions, 371
parse_line subroutine
Text::ParseWords module, 679
parse_options subroutine, 637
parsevalue subroutine, 544
parsing, 822
Backhaus-Naur Form, 823
command line arguments, 525
parse trees, 823
parser, in Perl source code, 820
Perl interpreter uses perl_parse, 878
POD documents, 695
example parser generating XML, 695
un–parsing, 839
words and phrases
using split and Text::ParseWords, 675
pass_through mode, GetOptions, 548
pass_through option, 550
passwords, reading, 569
PATH environment variable, 32
path function, File::Spec module, 1022
pathnames
converting Macintosh into Windows, 1020
portability, 1018
UNIX, determining local and remote, 992
pattern match modifiers, 351, 362
/g, 373
in-line modifiers, 363
matching several times, 378
once-only, 394
qr operator, 398
regular expressions, 351
pattern matching, 347
see also anchors; regular expressions.
/ee modifier, 409
/m modifier, 384
/s modifier, 384
arbitrary characters, 352
backreferences, 374
character classes, 352
extracting matched text, 369
grouping alternatives, 355
in-line modifiers, 363
introduced, 75
lean matches, 359
metacharacters, 351
multiple lines, 384
non-greedy matches, 358

pattern matching, (*continued***)**
    non-word boundaries, 368
    number of matches, counting, 386
    overlapping matches, 386
    pattern match modifiers, 351, 362
    performance, 391
    position, 382
    regexp engine, 346, 357
    repetitions
        repetition modifiers, 354
        sequences of characters, repeating, 355
        specifying number of, 356
    sequential terms, 361
    several times, 378
    special variables, 369
    study function, 393
    substitution, 407
    substitution operator, 346, 362, 407
    transliteration operator, 409
    word boundaries, 368
    word characters, 392
    zero-width patterns, 386
PAUSE (Perl Authors Upload Server), 335
PDF (Pop Directional Format) code, 1051
PDK (Perl Development Kit), 889
peeraddr method, IO::Socket::INET, 985
peerpath method, IO::Socket::UNIX, 992
pending method, Thread::Queue module, 951
performance issues
    inheriting methods for operators, 793
    regular expressions, 391
    statistics from the Perl profiler, 657
    using UDP or TCP, 964
performance testing, 663
    example script listing installed files, 658
    example benchmarking program, 666
Perl
    advantages listed, 8
    building, 821
    C, translating into, 840
    compiling, 824
    configuration, 815
    documentation, 819
    flavors, 817
    helper files, 820
    interpreting, 826
    Java bytecode, outputting, 849
    portability onto different platforms, 1015
    release history, 10
    source tree, 818
    stable and development versions, 10, 12
    testing for module and Perl versions, 279
    versatility as both strength and weakness, 8
    workings, as byte-compiled language, 822
Perl 5.6
    CHECK blocks introduced with, 297
    string encoding based on UTF-8, 1046
    used for examples throughout this book, 10
Perl 6, 10
Perl Compiler, 833
    B module, 834
    O module, 834
    writing, 850
Perl debugger *see* **debugging, Perl debugger.**
Perl internals
    direct access from C code, 884

Perl interpreter, 826
    debugging, 652
    example scripts for, 878, 879
    implementing in C with embedded Perl, 878
    uses bytecode intermediate, 27
Perl Mongers
    main website URL, 9
Perl Package Manager, 1033
perl –V, 816
PERL_ASYNC_CHECK function, 827
PERL_DEBUG_MSTATS variable, 33
PERL_DESTRUCT_LEVEL variable, 33
perl_parse function, 878, 887
PERL5DB environment variable
    debugger configuration and, 33, 622
PERL5LIB environment variable, 32
PERL5OPT environment variable, 29
    passing arguments to Perl, 528
PerlCOM
    environments supporting, 889
PerlCtrl command-line tool, 890
perldb.ini configuration file, 637
PERLDB_OPTS environment varaible, 636
    overriding when setting options, 637
perldiag.pod file, 601
perldoc command, 10
    location of perldoc utility, 819
    perldiag, 601
    perldoc as POD interface, 685
    perllocale tutorial, 1065
perljvm compiler, 849
PERLLIB *see* **PERL5LIB.**
perly.y file, 820
Permission::Hash class, 808
permissions mask, 931
permissions, files
    changing using chmod & umask functions, 487
    symbolic constants for flags, provided by Fcntl
        module, 489
permit method, compartment object, 650
permute mode, GetOpt::Long module, 547, 550
personal names, 683
PF_ constants, socket module, 979, 980
PF_INET and PF_UNIX protocols, 921
pi
    example of a constant and its calcluation, 170
picture lines, formats, 704
    data lines and, 707
pIOK flag, 831
pipe symbol *see* **|** *(under Symbols)*
pipe function, 917
    filehandles, creating, 423
    portability onto different platforms, 1039
    when to avoid, 1025
pipes, 917
    broken pipe signal, 897
    bi-directional, 920
placeholders, 700
    format picture lines, 704
    justification and, 706
    placeholder modifiers, 82
    raw output placeholder, 707
    sprintf function, 54, 56
Plain Old Documentation *see* **POD**
Plan 9, 1035

platform variable
 Configure process, 817
platforms, 1031
 functions portable on different, 1035
 platform-independence *see* **cross-platform
  capabilities; portability of programs.**
 platform specific code, 819
playing card example *see* **Game::Card class;
  Game::Deck class.**
PO (Portable Object) files, 1071
POD (Plain Old Documentation), 685
 see also **documentation.**
 defining lists in, 688
 example parser generating XML, 695
 h2xs script flag to suppress creation, 858
 list of translators, 691
 locating using Pod::Find, 698
 processing programmatically, 694
Pod:: modules, 691, 694
Pod::Checker module, 693
Pod::Find module
 example script for searching, 698
Pod::Parser module, 694
 methods to override in writing parsers, 695
pod2 documentation tools, 11
pod2html tool, 685, 687, 689
pod2roff and pod2man tools, 691
pod2text tool, 685
pod2usage tool, 692
podchecker tool, 693
podselect tool, 692
POedit, 1071
Pointer Values (PVs) internal variable type, 828
POK flag, 832, 828
polling servers, 993
polymorphism, 720
pop function, 123
 in bidi algorithm PDF code, 1051
port addressing, TCP, 965
portability of programs, 8, 1015
 see also **cross-platform capabilities.**
 binmode() operator, 1016
 character sets, 1027
 command line interfaces, 1025
 CPAN modules, 1026
 date, 1026
 dialog boxes, 1030
 disadvantage of source distributions, 12
 DOS, 1033
 endianness, 1023
 file systems, 1018
 functions, 1035
 globbing filenames and, 1024
 internationalization, 1028
 IPC, 1025
 Mac OS, 1033
 modules, 1026
 new lines, 1016
 number width, 1023
 pack() function, 1024
 platform specific code, keeping in one place, 1028
 platforms, 1031
 POSIX module, 1026
 problems with using Shell.pm, 556, 557
 security, 1028

 sockets, 1017
 system interaction, 1024
 system resources, 1028
 time, 1026
 UNIX, 1032
 unpack() function, 1024
 using ExtUtils::Command, 558
 when to make portable, 1016
 XS, 1025
ports, network services, 1009
Portugese language example, 1082
position
 regular expressions, 382
 retaining between regular expressions, 383
positive numbers
 example XS function to count, 866
POSIX character classes, 366
POSIX module, 914
 errno function, 607
 getcwd routine, finding current directory, 521
 portability, 1026
 system errors, 607
 system level IO, 462
  file descriptor routines, 463
  filehandle routines, 463
  standard IO & POSIX, moving between, 464
 terminal IO programming, 594
 tmpfile & tmpname functions, implementing by
  File::Temp module, 512
 tmpname function, creating temporary filenames, 509
 wait symbols, 912
POSIX standard
 Getopt::Long module compliance, 549
 localization, 1064, 1065
 options, 526, 544
POSIX::Termios interface, 581
 terminal IO programming, 594
 terminal speed, 583
POSIXLY_CORRECT mode, 547, 549
postal codes
 clue to locale, 1094
PostScript, 692
PP code, 820
 interpreting programs, 827
pp*.c file, 827
ppaddr method, B module, 835
PPCODE keyword, XS functions, 863, 869
PPM utility
 installing CPAN modules on Windows, 25
pPOK
 PVs, 828
Practical Extraction and Reporting Language, 10
 otherwise see **Perl**
pragmatic modules
 compared to functional modules, 275, 280
 lexical scope, 281
precedence, 106
 arithmetical operators, 90
 assignment operators, 89
 combination assignment operators, 98
 in nested ternary operators, 191
 overriding with parentheses, 107
 symbolic and named logical operators, 93
pre-compiled regular expressions, 348
prefix option, 550
prefix_pattern option, 537, 550

prefixes
double prefix dereferencing syntax, 147
option prefixes, configuring, 537
variables use instead of declaration, 35
preformatting paragraphs, 686
PREINIT keyword, 864
preput text, 579
presentation layer
OSI network protocol model, 966
print function
filehandles, referring to, 425
filehandles, writing to, 430
mixing write and print, 712
printf function
compared to sprintf, 80
filehandles, writing to, 432
PrintRet debugger option, 639
priority channel markers, 930
private class data, 742, 777
private IP address blocks
availability for company networks, 962
private methods, 760
private data and, compared to public, 720
private object data, 777-778
private queues, 928
private–names check, B::Lint module, 844
processes
bi-directional communication, 925
bi-directional pipes, 923
blocking, 933
communicating between, 916
daemons, 910
external, 919, 923
message queues, 928
multiple child processes, 913
process groups, 909
process IDs, 909
replacing, 909
semaphores, 931
shared memory segments, 935
sharing data between, 926
signals, 896
starting new, 908
threads, 937
processing order
precedence and associativity determine, 106
profiling, 656
programming languages
BASIC, 891
CPAN modules implementing other, 891
integrating Perl with other, 855
Java, 888
Prolog, 891
programming with Perl
language does not impose good practices, 8
programs
executing, 826
exiting with die function, 602
getting overall maps of, 847
running external, 916
when to make portable, 1016
Prolog language, 891
prompt style
terminal IO programming, 578
properties
see also **Unicode character properties.**
accessing object, by dereferencing, 722

object methods to get and set, 733
property metacharacter, 366
protocols
see also **ARP; IP; TCP; UDP.**
ISO 7-layer reference model, 958
numeric values identifying, 1010, 1011
other than IP, TCP and UDP, 966
PF_INET and PF_UNIX, 921
script to return protocol details on a system, 1011
supported by various socket implementations, 967
system network configuration enquiries, 1001
prototype definitions
code references, 239
disabling, 242
optional parameters, 241
scalar operators, converting subroutines to, 239
scope and number of parameters, defining, 237
subroutines, 236
variables, requiring rather than values, 240
prototypes
inheritance and, 768
sorting with named subroutines, 126
source for, of Perl built-in functions, 885
supplying for autouse subroutine declaration, 290
ps command, 911
running via forked open, 922
pseudonyms for users, 1084
pseudo-signal handler
intercepting warnings and errors, 603
public methods and data
compared to private, 720
public queues, 928
push function, 122, 240
complex data structures, 154
push-pop, 820, 827
puts method, Term::Screen module, 589
PVIVs (Pointer Value-Integer Value), 828
PVs (Pointer Values) internal variable type, 828

Q

q command, Perl debugger, 631
q operator, 62
see also **quoting operators.**
QNX platforms, 1035
qq operator, 62, 342
qr operator, 62
/g modifier not used with, 398
pattern match modifiers, 398
predefining search patterns, 397
replacement for 'once-only' modifier, 398
qualify subroutine, 301
qualify-to-ref subroutine
alternative when use strict applies, 302
Symbol module, 756
Queen's Dilemma, 224
question mark see **?** (under Symbols).
queues, 928
access by processes, 929
destroying, 931
permissions, changing, 930
Thread::Queue module, 950
threads, 943, 950
quit signal, 897
quote debugger option, 640

quotemeta function, 75, 344
metacharacter equivalent, 340
quotes
available quoting styles for delimiting strings, 62
reading files from @ARGV in Windows, 529
requirement for, in hashes, 129
single quotes as delimiters, 349
Text::ParseWords preserves phrases, 675
variable interpolation and, 40
quotewords subroutine, Text::ParseWords module
keep parameter, 677
quoting operators, 62, 342
pattern match modifiers with qr, 398
predefining search patterns, 397
qr operator in combination with reqexp, 348
qw operator, 62, 119
qx operator, 62, 917, 342
Safe module script to deny use, 651
when to avoid, 1025

R

r and R commands, Perl debugger, 631
random numbers
XS example program to generate, 865
range operator, 103
arrays, 198
example, 376
extracting lines with, 376
extracting text between two regexps, 369
use with regular expressions, 105
ranges
character classes, 353
raw datatypes, 830
raw mode, Term::ReadKey module, 564
raw sockets, 921
rcv method, 929
rdo method, 649
re module
debugging mode, 402
taint mode, 401
read function
reading from filehandles, 428
read modes, Term::ReadKey module, 564
readability of code, 36
readability ratings script, 1084
readdir function
reading directory items, 514
ReadKey subroutine
echoing characters, 567
modes, 566
parameters, 566
reading single character, 566
Term::ReadKey module, 564
Readline debugger option, 639
readline libraries, 574
preput text, 579
readline and ReadLine methods
Term::ReadLine module, 575
Readline module
example script for shell mode, 552
readline operator, (<>)
$ scalar variable, using, 427
@ARGV array and readline, 428
detecting EOF condition, 999

example script for shell mode, 552
filehandles, reading from, 426
Getopt:: modules and, 532
introduced, 43
line numbers, counting, 427
line separator, redefining, 426
reads files from @ARGV, then standard input, 529
'while' loops, aliasing readline in, 427
ReadLine subroutine, Term::ReadKey module, 564
readline terminal object, 575
readlink function
portability onto different platforms, 1039
ReadMode function, Term::ReadKey module, 565
READONLY flag, 831
recallCommand debugger option, 638
recompilation of regular expressions, avoiding, 394
record-based locking, 943
recursion, subroutines, 223
recv function, 969, 974, 986
redefining objects, 761
redirection
STDERR filehandle, 611
trace and debugging information, 642
redo statements
do not work in if blocks, 180
in foreach and while loops, 205
introduced, 46
loops, 195, 204
nested loops, 207
not used in do ... while loops, 208
reduction, 823
compiling, 824
redundant lines, 708
ref function, 148
determining object class, 725
traversing complex data structures, 159
reference and dereference operators, 102
reference count
editing, 833
scalar variables, 828
references
accessing nested references, 801
assignment of, preserves lexical variables, 266
blessed references, 149
checking reference types, 148
comparing, 144
creating complex data structures with, 151
defining constants by assigning to a typeglob, 169
hard and symbolic types, 142
hard, and object orientation, 10
objects as blessed references, 719, 722
passing arguments to subroutines, 161
passing arrays and hashes into subroutines as, 147
scalar pointers to existing variables, 38
soft, now deprecated, 10
taking references to arrays, 127
typeglobs, 163
types, returned by the ref function, tabulated, 148
using to create complex data structures, 156
using to create multidimensional arrays, 151
refs component
strict pragma, 219
reftype function, 149
determining object data types, 725
regexps see **regular expressions**
regexp–variables check, B::Lint module, 844
regression tests, 819

regular expression engine, 346, 357
  debugging support, 618
  key featue of text manipulation, 8
regular expressions, 337, 345
  see also anchors, pattern matching.
  advanced patterns, 352
  character class metacharacters, 365
  clustering modifier, 352
  compared with wildcards, 363
  converting strings into lists, 69
  debugging, 401
    re module, 402
  delimiters, 349
  documenting, 389
  empty patterns, 394
  eval function, generating with, 395
  evaluation modifier, 408
  extended patterns, 352, 389
  interpolation, 342
  list contexts, 379
  loops, 378
  making more specific, 391
  matched text and interpolation, substituting, 407
  matching, 194
  nested loops, 380
  once-only pattern match modifier, 394
  parantheses and numbered variables, 371
  pre-compiled, 348
  prefix_pattern option, 537
  preparing with the qr operator, 63
  qr operator, 348
  quotemeta function, 344
  range operator, 376
  recompilation, avoiding, 394
  regular expression binding operators, 101
  scalar contexts, 378
  sequences of characters, repeating, 355
  split function, 347
  strings, protecting against interpolation, 344
  strings, treatment of, 1050
  subpatterns
    eliminating vague, 391
    types of, 365
  syntax, 350
  taintedness, 401
  Unicode support for, in Perl 5.6+, 1047
  use in searching CPAN, 22
  use of range operator with, 105
  uses within Perl, 346
  validity of, checking, 399
  writing efficient, 391
  zero-width lookahead assertion, 352
  zero-width metacharacters, 368
rel2abs function, File::Spec module, 1023
relative library locations, 285
reloading CPAN and its index, 23
remove_history method
  addhistory method and, 579
removing a package, 302
rename function
  renaming files, 492
repeating matches
  regular expressions, 354
repetition modifiers, 354
  anchors and, 360
  regexp engine, 357
repetition operator, 91

reporting, 699
  combining reports and regular output, 712
  page control and numbering, 709, 712
require statement
  compared to do and use, 277
  determining an object's version, 726
  execution order of special blocks, 297
require_order mode, GetOptions, 548
require_order option, 550
require_version method, Exporter module, 328
reset command, 562
resize method, Term::Screen module, 589
resource deallocation, 782
resource files
  processing for airport kiosk example, 1057
restore mode, Term::ReadKey module, 564
return statements
  required for successful loading of modules, 276
  returning values from subroutines, 243
RETVAL special variable, 863
reusable code see modules.
reval method, 649
reverse function, 125
  transposing hash keys and values using, 133
reverse method, Term::Screen module, 589
reverse recursion, 224
rewinddir function
  directory positions, manipulating, 514
RGB (Red-Green-Blue) color model
  passing RGB values to XS as an array, 868
RLE codes
  embedding right-to-left text, 1051
rmdir function
  single directories, destroying, 519
rmtree function, File::Path module
  multiple directories, destroying, 520
Rocco Caputo's Crossword server, 848
ROK flag, 832
rootdir function, File::Spec module, 1022
rot13.pm example script, 892
rounding errors, 58
RTL (Right To Left) character property, 1054
running Perl
  depends on platform, 27
  directly, 27
  MacPerl, 29
runtests subroutine, 655
run-time
  package variable scope determined at, 257, 259

S

s command, Perl debugger, 631
S command, Perl debugger, 633
-s option
  setting variables from the command line, 528
S_I* family of constants, IPC::SysV module, 928
s2p utility
  location, 819
Safe module, 649
  introduced, 617
  script to deny use of backtick quotes, 651
safemalloc and safefree functions, 864

save_file_fromarray function
Locale::PO class, 1072
scalar context, 41
counting array elements in, 121
errors from assigning a list in, 155
scalar function, 121
scalar operators
subroutines as, 239
scalar subroutines
converting into list processors, 231
Scalar Variables internal variable type *see* **SVs.**
scalars, 51
basing an object class on, 764
constructor methods based on, 731
converting hashes into, 137
identified by $ prefix, 35
introduced, 37
outputting using Dumpvalue, 646
tied object class methods, 804
value conversion and caching, 52
scope, 257
global and lexical variables distinguished, 47
lexical variables defined by blocks, 48, 778
package scope, examption from rules of, 259
pragmatic modules have lexical scope, 281
preserving lexical variables outside, 266
subroutine parameters, 237
variables in shell script example, 555
screens
clearing, 584
Curses library, 590
initializing for use by Curses, 591
size, finding and setting, 569
writing to, 581
scripts
see also **bidi scripts; CGI scripts; h2sx scripts.**
block properties, Unicode, 1040
calculating relative library locations, 285
determining if interactive, 562
diacritical marks, 1050
searching
CPAN archive, with a, b, d, i, and m commands, 22
search patterns, predefining, 397
search patterns, regular expressions, 345
source files with the Perl debugger, 629
stemming as pre-processing operation, 1089
security issues
configuring the Perl debugger, 637
portability of programs, 1028
problems from quoting strings using backticks, 64
socket API can't reject connections, 985
sed tool, UNIX, 408
sed–to–perl translator, 822
seek function, 434, 1016
end-of-file condition, clearing, 435
random access, filehandles, 434
sysseek function and, 458
whence flag values and, 434
seekdir function
directory positions, manipulating, 514
select function, 926, 993
changing filehandles with, 702, 703
special variables, using to configure other
filehandles, 443
STDOUT standard filehandle, changing default, 442
two versions distinguished, 993

SelectSaver module
default STDOUT, changing
default variables vs. IO::Handle methods, using, 444
STDOUT standard filehandle, restoring default
automatically, 443
self class, 939
self-defining subroutines, 309
SelfLoader module, 304, 310, 314
use to load methods, 773
self-modifying arrays, 202
SEM_UNDO constant, IPC::SysV module, 928
semaphores, 926, 931
blocking processes, 933
op method, 933
start-gun, 953
threads, 943, 947
undoing the operation of, 935
using as binary stop/go toggles, 948
semctl and semget functions
portability onto different platforms, 1039
semi-colon (;) statement terminator, 35
semop function
portability onto different platforms, 1039
send function, 969, 974, 986
sendmail
opening pipe to, 1025
separators
environment variables use colon, 141
module, translated by use statement, 277
namespace double-colon, 258
word, configuring with breaktext, 680
word, parsing with Text::Parseword, 676
sequence number
use of range operator with, 104
sequences of characters, matching repeating, 355
sequential terms, matching, 361
serial connections, terminals, 571
serial numbering example, 740
Serial object class
configure method, 741
constructor providing references to class data, 746
illustrating informational use of destructors, 782
servers
example application creating polling TCP, 996
example application creating TCP, 979, 981
example application creating UDP, 986, 987
example application creating UNIX, 989, 990
multiplexing options, 993, 999
opening server sockets, 971
session layer, OSI network model, 964
set (option) method, dumper object, 648
set method
message queues, 930
semaphores, 932
set_quote and set_unctrl methods
dumper object, 648
SETALL constant, IPC::SysV module, 928
setall method, semaphores, 932
SetControlChars function, 573
setgrent function
resetting pointer to start, 474
sethostent function, 1004
portability onto different platforms, 1037
setlocale function
localization constants and, 1066
use instead of use locale pragma, 1066

setlogsock function, Sys::Syslog module, **611**
setnetent function, **1008**
    portability onto different platforms, 1037
setpgrp function, **910**
    portability onto different platforms, 1037
setpriority function
    portability onto different platforms, 1037
setprotoent function, **1011**
    portability onto different platforms, 1037
setpwent function
    portability onto different platforms, 1037
    resetting pointer for next record, 469
setservent function, **1010**
    portability onto different platforms, 1037
setsockopt function, **969, 971, 973, 976**
    portability onto different platforms, 1037
SetTerminalSize function, **570**
SETVAL constant, IPC::SysV module, **928**
setval method, semaphores, **932**
sfio library, **817**
share and share_from methods, Safe module, **649**
shared memory segments, **926, 935**
    removing, 937
shebang lines
    command-line options and, 29
    MacPerl, 14
    passing arguments to Perl, 528
    standard on UNIX platforms, 28
shells, **551**
    see also **command line interfaces.**
    avoiding, 922
    creating a shell mode for Perl, 551, 558
    examples from UNIX and Windows, 551
    Perl debugger as effective shell, 551, 623
Shell.pm module, **551, 555**
    restricting commands, to minimize dangers, 556
shellBang debugger option, **638**
shellwords subroutine
    Text::ParseWords module, 676
shift function, **123**
shift operators
    forcing signed integer arithmetic, 91
shlock method, IPC::Shareable module, **937**
shmctl, shmget, shmread and shmwrite functions
    portability onto different platforms, 1039
shunlock method, IPC::Shareable module, **937**
shutdown function, **922**
shutdown socket function, **968, 975**
SIGALRM signal, **897**
SIGCHLD signal, **898**
    multiple child processes, 914
SIGCONT, SIGFPE and SIGIO signals, **898**
SIGHUP, SIGINT and SIGKILL signals, **897**
signalLevel debugger option, **638, 643**
signals, **895**
    %SIG hash, 896
    alarms, 906
    any keyword, 904
    default handling of, restoring, 899
    die handlers, 900
    error-signals, 904
    generating list of, 896
    handlers, 898
        avoiding complexity, 901
        flexibly installing, 903
        un-interruptible, 902

    setting subroutines as, 899
    writing, 900
    hung operations, aborting, 907
    HUP, 905
    ignoring, 898
    localizing fresh values for, 902
    multiple, 903
    negative process IDs, sending to, 905
    sending, 905
    specifiying several, 904
    subroutines, setting as signal handlers, 899
    suppressing, 902
    system level operations, aborting, 903
    Thread::Signal module, 953
    trapping conditionally, 904
    untrapped keyword, 904
    warn handlers, 900
    ZERO, 905
signatures
    access to shared libraries with FFI, 872
    JPL delimiter is double underscore, 888
SIGPIPE, SIGQUIT and SIGTERM signals, **897**
SIGSEGV and SIGSTOP signals, **898**
sigtrap pragmatic module, **903**
SIGUSR1 and SIGUSR2 signals, **897**
SIGWINCH signal, **898**
    terminal window size, 570
simple input, **563**
sin function, **61**
single stepping, **624, 631, 642**
single-threaded mode, **953**
size option
    shared memory segments, 936
skip test subroutine, **654**
slices, array, **118**
    using reverse on a range, 125
snd method, **929**
sniffing the wire, **960**
SO_ socket options, **972**
sockaddr format, **967**
sockaddr method, IO::Socket::INET, **985**
sockaddr_in function, **970, 974, 980, 983, 987**
sockaddr_un function, **970, 974, 987, 990**
socket function, **968, 980**
    filehandles, creating, 424
socket.pm
    flags tabulated, 974, 975
    tabular summary of functions, 967
socketpair function, **921, 968**
    filehandles, creating, 424
    portability onto different platforms, 1039
sockets, **921**
    closing, 975
    configuring options, 971
    configuring with IO::Socket module, 976
    example client application using UNIX sockets, 991,
        992
    example server application using UNIX sockets, 989,
        990
    example TCP client application using INET, 982, 983
    example TCP polling server application, 996
    example TCP server application using INET, 979, 981
    example UDP client application using INET, 987, 988
    example UDP server application using INET, 986, 987
    internet domain and UNIX domain, 967
    networking interface similar to filehandles, 967, 975

sockets (*continued*)
new lines, 1018
opening server sockets, 971
portability, 1017
reading from and writing to, 974, 984
read-only and write-only, 976
table of socket options, 972
using in only one direction, 922
SOL_ symbols, 973
sort function, 125, 135
anonymous subroutines, 218
depends on alphabetization rules, 1064
perllocale documentation misleading, 1067
sorting lists and arrays, 125
sorting options, dprofpp utility, 659
soundex subroutine, Text::Soundex module, 682
sounds of words, matching, 682
source filtering, 893
source tree, 818
space characters
see also whitespace.
character case conversion using, 96
converting into tabs with unexpand, 672
Spanish language
CPAN custom module, 1094
Spanish website example, 1063, 1064
currency conversion, 1069
multilingual web page, 1089
special blocks
listed in execution order, 296, 297
special characters
Perl supports C conventions, 40
special variables
see also $... ; @...; %ENV.
affecting print statement output, 71
creating a local version of, 264
exempt from package scope rules, 259
introduced, 39
Packagename::$AUTOLOAD, 305
RETVAL defining XS code output, 863
using $_ as an iterator, 44
spelling checker example script, 1086
splain tool, diagnostics, 602
splice function, 120
relationship to pop and shift functions, 124
relationship to push and unshift functions, 123
split function, 675
converting strings into lists, 69
empty patterns, 394
interpolation, 342
parsing words and phrases, 675
regexp as first argument, 347
whitespace, 348
splitdir function, File::Spec module, 1023
splitpath function, File::Spec module, 1022
sprintf function, 80
%e, %f and %g placeholders, 59
converting lists to formatted strings, 128
introduced as string formatter, 54
pack function compared to, 76
placeholders listed, 80
sqrt function, 61
squash modifier, 411
stack trace
creating via a DB package subroutine, 644, 645
handler, sigtrap pragmatic module, 903

stacking XS return values, 864
standard error *see* STDERR.
standard input *see* STDIN.
standard output *see* STDOUT.
START literal marker, 376
start-gun semaphore, 953
stat function
File::stat module, using stat objects, 479
interrogating files, 484
message queues, 931
portability onto different platforms, 1039
reusing results of prior stat/lstat & testing, 478
semaphores, 933
statements, 175
as expressions, 177
blocks, 177
difference from expressions, 176
statistical operations
example using autoload, 306
language identification using, 1081
STDERR filehandle, 417
redirecting, 611
redirecting output away from, 621
STDIN standard filehandle, 416
filehandles, creating, 419
pattern matching from, using @ARGV, 531
standard input and output, 925
STDIN, STDOUT and STDERR filehandles
determining if a script is interactive, 562
exempt from package scope rules, 259
getting attributes of, 595
redefining properties of, 595
STDOUT standard filehandle, 416
assigning formats to, 702
filehandles, creating, 419
select function, changing default filehandle, 442
SelectSaver module, restoring default filehandle
automatically, 443
standard input and output, 925
stemming, 1088
stop signal, 898
Storable module, 1024
storage
increasing efficiency with vector strings, 79
numeric lists as strings, 128
store methods, tied objects, 802
streaming sockets, 921
strict module, 48, 259, 280
declaring global package variables, 260
subroutines, 219
strict pragma
pragmatic debugging aid, 618
suspending for symbolic references, 150
strict subroutines, 219
string formats, 80, 679
see also document formatting; padding; paragraph
formatting.
string interpolation, 337
context, 342
embedding code into strings, 341
metacharacters, 338
variables, 340
string operators
comparison operators, 100
concatenation and repetition, 91, 98
incrementing, 99

strings
    bitwise operations on, 95
    converting floating-point numbers into, 58
    converting into lists and hashes, 69
    converting into numbers, 68
    hash keys must be, 129
    interpolation, protecting against, 344
    low-level string conversions, 76
    numbers and, not distinguished strongly, 51
    overloading string conversions, 788
    padding formatted text, 92
    returning lengths of strings and substrings, 73
    searching for with pattern-matching program, 530
    separators and whitespace, 64
    string equality tests, 194
    string formatting, 80
    string functions, 71
    support for is comprehensive, 62
    symbolic references as, 150
    treated as binary values, 79
    variables, interpolation of text contained in, 343
struct subroutine, 795
stty command, 563
stty sane command, 562
stub methods, Term::ReadLine module, 575
stubs
    defining subroutines as, to delay compilation, 309
study function, 393
stuff_input method, Term::Screen module, 590
style checker, 843
sub keyword, 46, 216
subclasses, 719
    building example with multiple inheritance, 766
    constructing on the fly, 762
    subclassing, inheritance and abstraction, 719
sublexer, 822
subpatterns
    eliminating vague, 391
    extracting with loops, 379
    types of, 365
subprocesses
    exit status, 607
subroutine options, dprofpp utility, 660
subroutines, 215
    & code prefix, 216
    @_ special variable, 228
        passing directly into subroutines, 232
    Alias module, subroutines of, 234
    aliasing, 229, 270
    anonymous, 215, 217
    as scalar operators, 239
    assignable, 250
    attribute lists, available from Perl 5.6, 251
    autoloading, 226
    automatic generation with import lists, 321
    behavior of @_ array when called by, 262
    Benchmark module, 665
    benchmarking example program, 667
    built-in functions, overridding, 220
    caller function, 221
    calling, 216
    calling context, 246
    checking for on-the-fly, 226
    closures, 248
    constructor methods based on, 731, 735
    CORE:: prefix, 220
    declaring, 216

goto statement, switching between, 210, 225
intercepting calls to non-existent, 305
introduced and described, 46
listing defined, using the Perl debugger, 633
memory, closures as form of, 248
named and anonymous, 215
named parameters, 233
optional parameters and variables, 241-242
overridding parameters, 234
package attributes, 253
parameters, defining number of, 237
predeclaring, 219
recursion, 223
return statements, 243
scalar, converting into list processors, 231
scope of parameters, 237
scoping variables to be invisible to, 180
setting as signal handlers, 899
simple debugging system, 619
single-threaded mode, enforcing, 953
sorting with named subroutines, 126
stack, details held on an internal, 221
strict, and the strict pragma, 219
tau-recursion, 210
timing statistics from dprofpp, 658
using in C programs, 882
using to keep data private, 778
requiring variables, rather than values, 240
visibility of localized variables to, 263
void context, 247
subroutines, defining
    defining as a stub, 309
    defining attributes as, 251
    defining on the fly using autoloaders, 308
    defining on-the-fly, 226
    prototype definitions, 236
        disabling, 242
    previously defined, calling, 216
    replacing multiple definitions using autoload, 305
subroutines, passing data
    arrays, passing, 229
    defining arguments, 228
    hashes, passing, 229
    lists, passing, 229
    lists, passing several, 230
    parameters, passing, 228
    parentheses change behavior of, 108, 109
    passing arrays or hashes in as references, 147
    passing named arguments with hashes, 136
    passing values into, 216
    references, passing lists and hashes by, 231
    undefined values, returning, 244
    using references not typeglobs to pass arguments, 161
    values, returning, 243
subs component, strict pragma, 219
subs pragma, 215
    built-in functions, overridding, 220
substitution function, 75
substitution operator
    matched text and interpolation, substituting, 407
    regular expressions, 346, 362, 407
subtr function, 74
    vec function compared to, 79
SUPER:: prefix, 755
    differences from $ISA[0]::, 755
SUPER::DESTROY method, 783

superusers
ACLs, filestat pragma and, file test operators, 480
supported platforms, 9
sustitute subroutines
example using autoloaders, 306
Sv* macros, XS functions, 866, 867
SvPV macro, 829
SVs (Scalar Variables) internal variable type, 827
Devel::Peek module, examining with, 828
IVs, 828
NVs, 829
reference counts on, editing, 833
switch statements, 192
foreach loops, 198
labels, 208
last statements, 193
switches see **options.**
Symbol module
delete_package function, 303
qualify_to_ref subroutine, 756
used to manipulate variable names, 301
symbol tables, 267
accessing as hashes, 271
editing the symbol table directly, 270
example script to print the hierarchy, 272
hierarchies of tables, 269
introduced, 258
symbolic references, 149
symbols
importing and exporting, 316
importing by modules, 278
symlink function
portability onto different platforms, 1039
symbolic & hard links, comparing, 493
symbolic links, creating, 492
sys/socket.ph definition file, 973
Sys::Hostname module, 1000, 1013
Sys::Syslog module, 611
openlog and setlogsock functions, 611
syscall method
portability onto different platforms, 1039
syslog daemon, 611
sysopen function, 453
bitwise operations on flags and masks, 95
mode flags, creating filehandles, 421
open function, reasons for prefering sysopen, 453
open function, when to use instead of, 1019
opening filehandles at system level IO, 453
IO::File's new method, using sysopen via, 456
non-blocking IO, 454
open mode flags, 453
permissions mask, specifying, 455
portability onto different platforms, 1039
sysread function and, 457
sysread function, 456
reading unbuffered filehandles at system level IO, 456
sysopen function and, 457
sysseek function, 458
positioning filehandles at system level IO, 458
seek & tell functions and, 458
whence flag, using, 458
system calls
deciphering error results from, 604
system constants, socket.ph, 973
system errors
POSIX module constants for, 607
promoting to fatal errors, 608

system function, 916
accessing with MacPerl programs, 1034
portability onto different platforms, 1040
when to avoid, 1025
system interaction, 1024
system level IO see **IO (Input & Output) using filehandles.**
system level operations, aborting, 903
system logs, 611
opening connections to, 611
socket type, setting, 611
system network files
Windows and UNIX, 1001
system opcode, 650
system resources, 1028
system time, 666
distinguished from user time, 662
System V IPC, 926
syswrite function, 457, 919
writing unbuffered filehandles at system level IO, 457

T

t command, Perl debugger, 632
T command, Perl debugger, 628
-t function, 562
T_PTROBJ tag
typemap files, xsubpp, 869
tab characters
converting into spaces with expand, 672
Tab key, word completion, 580
tail recursion, 225
taint checking
pragmatic debugging aid, 618
using %ENV special variable and, 140
tainted variables, 401
tau-recursion, 210, 225
TCP (Transmission Control Protocol)
example INET client application, 982, 983
example INET server application, 979, 981
example polling INET server application, 996
INET stream sockets use, 967
NTP uses UDP over, 965
suitability compared with UDP, 965
TCP/IP
archtecture of, running over Ethernet, 959
TCP_NODELAY option, 973, 984
tell function, 437, 1016
finding current position, filehandles' random access, 437
sysseek function and, 458
telldir function
directory positions, manipulating, 514
tempdir() function, File::Temp module
creating temporary directories, 511
tempfile() function, File::Temp module
creating temporary files, 511
templates
h2xs tools viewed as, 860
HTML, for airport kiosk example, 1056
using interpolated here documents, 66
Term:: modules
text processing capabilities, 684

Term::ANSIColor module, 581
  color subroutine, 584
  colored subroutine, 584, 586
  colors, 584
  EACHLINE variable, 586
Term::Cap module, 579
  termcap database, 582
  Tgetent method, 582
  Tgoto method, 584
  Tputs method, 584
Term::Complete module, 563, 580, 675
  Complete function, 580
  erase1 and erase2 functions, 581
  kill function, 581
Term::ReadKey module, 907
  GetControlChars subroutine, 572
  keyboards, reading from, 563
  read modes, 564
  reading single character, 566
  ReadKey subroutine, 564
  ReadLine subroutine, 564
  ReadMode function, 565
  terminal input, controlling, 564
Term::ReadLine module
  addhistory method, 575, 579
  advanced line input, 574
  Attribs method, 575
  command line history, 579
  configuring CPAN, 19
  debugger interface and Readline options, 638
  default input, 578
  Features method, 575, 577
  findConsole method, 575
  IN method, 575, 576
  keyboards, reading from, 563
  MinLine method, 575, 580
  modes, 568
  new method, 575
  newTTY method, 576
  non-blocking input, 568
  ornaments method, 578
  OUT method, 575, 576
  prompt style, 578
  reading complete lines, 568
  readline method, 575
  ReadLine method, 575
  stub methods, 575
Term::ReadTerm module
  configuring CPAN, 19
Term::Screen module, 581, 588
  at method, 589
  bold method, 589
  clreol method, 589
  clreos method, 589
  clrscr method, 589
  dc method, 589
  def_key method, 590
  designed for UNIX, 588
  dl method, 589
  echo method, 589
  exists_dc method, 589
  exists_ic method, 589
  flush_input method, 590
  get_fn_keys method, 590
  getch method, 568, 589, 590
  ic method, 589
  il method, 589

  key_pressed method, 590
  noecho method, 589
  normal method, 589
  puts method, 589
  resize method, 589
  reverse method, 589
  stuff_input method, 590
termcap object and databases, 581-582
terminal IO programming, 562
  advanced line input, 574
  colors, 581, 584
  command line history, 579
  complete lines, reading, 568
  Curses library, 590
  cursor, moving, 584
  default input, 578
  high level modules, 588
  invisible input and passwords, 569
  keyboards, reading from, 563
  line ending translation, 571
  paging ouput, 570
  preput text, 579
  programming terminals directly via POSIX, 594
  prompt style, 578
  reading single character, 566
  screen size, finding and resetting, 569
  screens, clearing, 584
  screens, writing to, 581
  stty command, 563
  terminal input, controlling, 564
  terminal objects, 575
    creating, 575
  terminal speed, 571
  word completion, 580
terminal objects, creating, 575
terminal options, Perl debugger, 640, 641
terminal symbols, 823
terminals
  capabilities, 578, 581
  clearing screen, 584
  colors, 584
  control characters, 572
  cooked mode, 572
  Curses library, 590
  cursor, moving, 584
  high level modules, 588
  immediate reaction to character input, 566
  paging ouput, 570
  programming directly via POSIX, 594
  read modes, 564
  restoring original settings, 565
  screen size, finding and resetting, 569
  screens, writing to, 581
  serial connections, 571
  speed, 583
  talking to, 561
  terminal types, 582
terminate signal, 897
termios object, 595
  getattr and getospeed functions, 595
ternary operators, 87, 105, 189, 851
  nesting, 190
  using with expressions that return lvalues, 191
Test module, 653
test scripts
  adding to an installable package, 334

Test::Harness module, 653, 655
  environment variables, 656
TestExport demonstration module, 324, 326
tests of existence, 166
text attributes
  bold, 579
  colors, 584
  enabling or disabling with Curses module, 593
  underline, 585
text processing, 672
  key to Perl's success, 671
  modules other than Text::, 684
text readability, 1085
  spelling checker, 1086
Text:: standard modules, 672
Text::Abbrev module, 673
Text::ParseWords module, 675
  nested_quotewords subroutine, 678
  parse_line subroutine, 679
  quotewords subroutine, 677
  shellwords subroutine, 676
Text::Soundex module, 682
Text::Tabs module, 672
Text::Wrap module
  customized wrapping, 680
  fill subroutine, 681
  wrap subroutine, 679
Tgetent method, Term::Cap module, 582
Tgoto method, Term::Cap module, 584
thr_print subroutine, 947
Thread module, 938
thread safe code, 953
Thread::Queue module, 943, 950
  dequeue method, 951
  dequeue_nb method, 951
  enqueue method, 950
  new subroutine, 950
  pending method, 951
Thread::Semaphore module, 943, 947
  down method, 948
  new subroutine, 948
  up method, 948
Thread::Signal module, 953
threaded servers, 993, 999
threading
  requires building Perl from source, 17
threads, 937
  cond_wait subroutine, 943
  creating, 938
  eval method, 941
  identifying, 939
  ithreads, 817
  join method, 941
  list of created threads, 940
  locked attribute, 252
  locked code, 953
  management, 940
  queue of tasks, 943
  queues, 950
  safety, 953
  semaphores, 943, 947
    using as binary stop/go toggles, 948
  shutting down, 947
  single-threaded mode, 953
  start-gun semaphore, 953
  support, checking, 938
  threading models, 817

  thread-specific data, 940
  unlocking, 944
  variable locks, 942
tie function, 799
  accessing elements should avoid references, 801
  design example template, 807
  Perl objects as scalars, 38
  standard template object classes, 803
  tied hash class example, 807
  tied hash class example using Tie::StdHash, 810
  writing tied objects, 802
tie mechanisms
  shared memory segments, 935
Tie::StdHash class, 809
tied function
  Env.pm module as a tied object class, 142
  methods for each data type tabulated, 803
  testing for a tied variable, 801
tied hashes
  directories as, 515
tilde see ~ (under Symbols).
time
  portability of system time, 1026
  time formats, 1070
  time function, 661
  time synchronization, 965
  time zones, 1077
Time::Local module, 1027
timediff method, Benchmark module, 664
timeit subroutine, Benchmark module, 665
timers, 906
times function, 662
  Perl profiler and, 657
  portability onto different platforms, 1040
timestr method, Benchmark module, 665
timesum method, Benchmark module, 664
timethese subroutine, Benchmark module, 667
timethis subroutine, Benchmark module, 666
timing options, dprofpp utility, 661
tkRunning debugger option, 639
tkRunning method, Term::ReadLine module, 575
TLD (Top Level Domain)
  deducing user locations from, 1063, 1074, 1076
tmpdir function, File::Spec module, 1022
tmpfile function, POSIX module
  File::Temp module, implementing, 512
tmpnam function, POSIX module
  File::Temp module, implementing, 512
  temporary filenames, creating, 509
todo key, 653
Todo* file, 819
toke.c file, 820
  yylex and yyparse routines, 822
tokens
  parsing Perl inupt, 822
  tokenizing sounds, 682
  using instead of pod2text and pod2html, 690
ToolServer, 1034
top-of-page formats, 702, 703
Tputs method, Term::Cap module, 584
tr operator, 892
  character set conversion, 1050
tracing
  Perl debugger line and frame tracing, 641
  subroutine example using Dumpvalue, 646
trainlid program, Lingua::Ident module, 1080

translate subroutine
  babel.pl multilingual web page example, 1092
translating messages, 1071
translating Perl into C, 840
translation using WWW::Babelfish routine, 1075
transliteration modifiers, 411
transliteration operator, 75, 409
transport layer, OSI network model, 964
true values, 184
truncate function, 438
  portability onto different platforms, 1040
  truncating files, 438
TTY debugger option, 641, 642
typeglobs, 161, 424
  accessing, 163
  aliasing, 301
  assignments and aliasing, 270
  assignments and overwriting, 162
  compared to references and IO:: modules, 161
  constructor methods based on, 730
  defining constants by assigning references to, 169
  defining with asterisk prefix, 161
  filehandles, referring to, 424
  introduced, 38
  making assignments to, 269
  relationship with the symbol table, 267
typemap files, xsubpp script, 867
  defining custom typemaps, 868
  T_PTROBJ tag, 869

U

UCS (Universal Character Set), 1046
UCS Transformation Format 8 (UTF-8), 1046, 1055, 1059
UDP (User Datagram Protocol), 964
  example INET client application, 987, 988
  example INET server application, 986, 987
  INET datagram sockets use, 967
  suitability compared with TCP, 965
ultra-raw mode
  disabling CR/LF to LF translation, 572
  Term::ReadKey module, 564
umask function
  file permissions, changing, 487
  permission bits, 487
  portability onto different platforms, 1040
unary minus, 42, 91, 98, 793, 795
  precedence and assignment, 107
unary operators, 42, 851
  compared to binary and ternary, 87, 851
  unary file test operators, 475, 513, 562
  here document << as, 67
  named unary operators, 88, 107
unary plus, 42, 91, 98, 109
  precedence and assignment, 107
unary NOT operator, 87, 95
unbuffered operations see **buffering.**
undef function, 164, 168
  removes array values but not elements, 124
  removes hash values but not keys, 132
undefined value, 38, 164, 184
  disabling warnings while using, 167
  returning from subroutines, 244
  use to indicate failure in a process, 165
  wantarray function, 246

undefined–subs check, B::Lint module, 844
undefPrint debugger option, 640
underlined text, 585
underscore
  see also _ (under Symbols)
  character case conversion using, 96
  identifying a private method, 739, 778
underscore annotated integers, 53
ungetc function, 430
unicast and multicast networks, 961
Unicode character properties, 1048
  writing, 1049
Unicode character set, 1043, 1046
  see also **character sets.**
  availablity of fonts, 1055
  bidirectional character types, 1052
  bidirectional scripts algorithm, 1051, 1053
  regular expressions and, 1047
  suitable editors, 1055
  supported from Perl 5.6, 10, 1046
un-interruptible signal handlers, 902
UniPad editor, 1055
Universal object, 720, 725
  adding generic methods to, 768
  automatic inheritance from, 754
  SUPER:: searches but $ISA[0]:: won't, 755
UNIVERSAL::can subroutine, 226, 846
UNIVERSAL::isa subroutine, 846
UNIVERSAL::VERSION subroutine, 846
UNIX
  commands implementable with ExtUtils::Command, 557
  commands to find local hostname, 1012
  configuring Perl for, 15
  example UNIX client application, 991, 992
  example UNIX server application, 989, 990
  installing modules on, manually, 24
  installing Perl binary distributions on, 13
  integrating commands into Perl shell, 555
  pathnames, determining local and remote, 992
  Running Perl on, 28, 1032
  system network files, 1001
  UNIX domain sockets, 921, 967
  Windows, emulating commands on, 557
unless keyword, 187
unlink function, 491
unlocking threads, 944
UNOPs see **Unary Operators.**
unpack function, 77, 970, 1004-1005
  portability, 1024
unpack_sockaddr_in function, 970, 985
unpack_sockaddr_un function, 970
unrecognized values, example script, 547
unshift function, 123
unsigned integers, 831
untainting data, 401
  environment variables, 140
untie function, 802
until loops, 195, 200
  redo statements, 205
untrapped keyword, 904
up method, Thread::Semaphore module, 948
updir function, File::Spec module, 1022
  no_upwards function, 1022
use (pragma) see **(pragma name).**
use bytes directive, 1047

use function
  can cause inheritance problems, 726
use statement
  calling require and import, 317
  compared to do and require, 277
  execution order of special blocks, 297
UsegeOnly debugger option, 640
usemymalloc, 817
user support
  see also **documentation.**
  CPAN and Perl Mongers, 9
user time, 666
  distinguished from system time, 662
User::grent module
  group info, retrieving, 474
User::pwent module
  :DEFAULT & :FIELDS tags, using, 471
  user info, retrieving, 470
user_agent information
  establishing the client language, 1076
user-defined signals, 897
users
  example script to print list of, 678
useshrplib, 818
usethreads key
  %Config hash, 938
usethreads option, 17
**UTF-8 (UCS Transformation Format 8), 1046, 1055,
  1059**
utf8 pragma, 1050, 1059
  use utf8 directive, 1047
utf8.c file, 820
util.c file, 820
utilities, 819
utime function
  portability onto different platforms, 1041
UV slot, 831

V

v command, Perl debugger, 647
V command, Perl debugger, 627
-V option
  checking configuration details, 16
  use in embedded perl example, 876
-v option, h2xs scripts, 858
validate method, ExtUtils::Installed, 289
validate subroutine, File::CheckTree module
  automating multiple file tests, file test operators,
    482
value conversion
  carried out automatically for scalars, 51
value function, 134
values
  compared to options, 526
  examining with debugger x command, 625
  returning from subroutines, 243
  undefined, 244
varglob method, Safe module, 650
variables
  see also **global variables; lexical variables; , loop
    variables; package variables.**
  aliasing, 162
    with foreach loops, 199
    with while loops, 201

  binding to objects with the tie function, 800
  C representation, 885
  combination assignment operators, 97
  condition, 943
  declaration
    example, 302
    inverted conditional statements, 185
    lexical variables, 265
    local C variables in XS, 864
    package variables, 260
  defining using BEGIN blocks, 299
  dumping using dumpvars, 647
  examining with debugger x command, 625
  GetOptions function, 536
  getting values using get_*, 881
  in loops, 196
  interpolation, 39, 340
  interpolation of text contained in, 343
  introduced and their prefixes explained, 35
  lexical and package scope, 257
  locking variables shared by a thread pool, 942
  numbered, 371
  optional variables in subroutines, 242
  scope in shell script example, 555
  scoping so invisible from subroutines, 180
  setting from the command line using -s, 528
  sharing across compartment boundaries, 649
  special, in regular expressions, 369
  subroutines, 240
  tainted, 401
  type mapping in XS functions, 867
  variable types, internal, 827
vars component
  strict pragma, 219
vars pragma
  our keyword as replacement for, 261
  use vars declaration, 260
VCG (Visualization of Compiler Graphs), 848
vec function, 993, 994
  compared to chr and substr functions, 79
vector strings, 79
  bitwise operations on, 97
verbose option, 539, 692
  diagnostics, 602
verbs
  conjugation using WWW::Babelfish, 1083
verification, pod, 693
VERSION method
  determining an object's version, 726
version method, ExtUtils::Installed, 289
version numbering
  example program mimicking perl -v, 878
  Perl release history, 10
    see also Perl 5.6
  stable and development versions, 10, 12
  testing for module and Perl versions, 279
version strings, 68
  sprintf placeholders, 84
veryCompact debugger option, 640
veryCompact method, dumper object, 648
visibility
  see also **scope.**
  lexical variables, 265
  localized variables inside subroutine calls, 263
Visual Basic, 889
Visualization of Compiler Graphs (VCG), 848
VMS platforms, 1035
  extended error messages, 606

void context, 42
    provided by do blocks, 181
    subroutines, 247
VOS platforms, 1035
vt100, 582

W

w command, Perl debugger, 628
W command, Perl debugger, 634
-w switch, 599
W void prefix, 601
WAIS (Wide Area Information Server)
    searches using CPAN::WAIT module, 18
wait function, 912
    portability onto different platforms, 1041
waitpid function, 913
    portability onto different platforms, 1041
walkoptree_exec method, B module, 835
walkoptree_slow method, B module, 835
Wall, Larry, 888, 1035
wantarray function, 42
    see also GIMME function.
    calling context, 246
    void context, 247
warn function, 602
    intercepting warnings, 603
warn handlers, 603, 900
warnings pragma, 599
    $^W special variable, 599
    advanced warnings, 612
    Carp module, 609
    categories, 613
    enabling, 599
    generating, 602
    intercepting, 603
    introduced, 41
    recommendation to use always, 48
    selective enabling and disabling, 612
    suppressing, reasons for, 600
    turning off, 599
warnLevel debugger option, 638
watchpoints, 634
WEXITSTATUS function, 915
whence flag, 434
    seek function and, 434
    sysseek function, using by, 458
while loops, 195, 200
    hashes, looping over, 203
    introduced, 47
    looping over lists and arrays, 201
    nested regular expression oops, 380
    redo statements, 205
    regular expressions, handling results from, 379
    self-modifying arrays, looping on, 202
    variable aliasing, 201
whitespace
    see also document formatting; space character.
    /x pattern match modifier, 389
    absorbing with the split function, 69
    delimiter used by Text::ParseWords, 676
    improving code readability, 36
    metacharacter, 348
WIFEXITED, WIFSIGNALED and WIFSTOPPED
    functions, 915-916

wildcards
    compared with regular expressions, 363
Win32::API module, 875
Win32::Eventlog module, 612
window changed signal, 898
windows, Curses, 593
Windows, Microsoft
    ActiveState and Cygwin ports, 13
    building Perl from source, 17
    C::Dynalib module can't be used under, 874
    character set compared to ISO 8859-1, 1045
    converting Perl scripts to batch files, 29
    emulating UNIX commands on, 557
    envirXonment variables specific to, 33
    example website using WWW::Babelfish won't work
        on, 1074
    extended error messages, 606
    FFI calling convention parameters reversed, 873
    fork function, simulating on, 817
    incomplete support for sockets, 967
    installing modules on, manually, 25
    installing modules on, using ActiveState ppm, 25
    installing Perl binary distributions on, 13
    internationalization via shared libraries, 1077
    POSIX localization implemented on NT, 1065
    POSIX localization won't work on Win9x, 1064
    problems with quotes in reading scripts, 529
    Registering .pl file extension, 28
    spell checker example won't work on, 1086
    system network files, 1001
    UNIX option conventions understood by, 526
    Win32::API use restricted to, 875
WNOHANG flag, 913
word boundaries, matching, 368
word characters, matching, 392
word completion
    IO programming, 580
wrap subroutine, Text::Wrap module, 679
write function, 701, 702
    mixing write and print, 712
    returning text from, 715
    suppressing redundant lines, 708
WriteMakefile subroutine, 871
WSTOPSIG function, 916
WTERMSIG function, 915
WUNTRACED flag, 915
WWW::Babelfish module, 1074
    multilingual web page example, 1090
    supported languages, 1091
    using to learn foreign languages, 1082

X

x (repetition operator), 91
x command, Perl debugger, 627, 647
X command, Perl debugger, 627
-X files, see file test operators.
-x and -X options, h2xs scripts, 858-859
-X switch, 599
XML (Extensible Markup Language)
    example pod parser generating, 695
    technology for internationalization, 1044
xor operator, 93
xrdb utility, 573

XS (External Subroutine) interface, 856, 1025
  C code using Perl modules and, 887
  content of XS files, 860
  dynamic linking, 818
  functions as wrappers for C functions, 862
  putting code in XS functions, 862
xshell example scripts, 555, 556, 558
XSRETURN macros, 864
XST_m* macros, 864
xsubpp script, 857
  conversions use typemap lookups, 867
  requirements of XS code, 863, 864
xwininfo utility, 563

Y

Yudit editor, 1055
yylex and yyparse routines, toke.c file, 822

Z

ZERO signal, 905
zero-or-more quantifier
  unexpected results with, 358
zeros
  example program to create an array of, 865
zero-width lookahead assertion
  extended patterns, 352
zero-width metacharacters, 365, 368
zero-width patterns, 386
zombies, 911